OpenGL®

SUPERBIBLE

Fifth Edition

OpenGL®

SUPERBIBLE

Fifth Edition

Comprehensive Tutorial and Reference

Richard S. Wright, Jr.
Nicholas Haemel
Graham Sellers
Benjamin Lipchak

▲▼Addison-Wesley

Upper Saddle River, NJ • Boston • Indianapolis • San Francisco
New York • Toronto • Montreal • London • Munich • Paris • Madrid
Cape Town • Sydney • Tokyo • Singapore • Mexico City

The publisher offers excellent discounts on this book when ordered in quantity for bulk purchases or special sales, which may include electronic versions and/or custom covers and content particular to your business, training goals, marketing focus, and branding interests. For more information, please contact:

> U.S. Corporate and Government Sales
> (800) 382-3419
> corpsales@pearsontechgroup.com

For sales outside the United States please contact:

> International Sales
> international@pearson.com

Visit us on the Web: informit.com/aw

Library of Congress Cataloging-in-Publication Data:

OpenGL super bible : comprehensive tutorial and reference / Richard S. Wright Jr. ...
[et al.]. — 5th ed.
    p. cm.
  ISBN 978-0-321-71261-5 (pbk. : alk. paper) 1. Computer graphics. 2. OpenGL. I. Wright, Richard S., 1965- II. Wright, Richard S., 1965-
OpenGL super bible.
  T385.W728 2010
  006.6'6—dc22

                          2010014489

ISBN-13: 978-0-32-171261-5
ISBN-10: 0-32-171261-7
Text printed in the United States on recycled paper at Edwards Brothers in Ann Arbor, Michigan.
Second Printing November 2010

Editor-in-Chief:
Mark Taub

Acquisitions Editor:
Debra Williams Cauley

Development Editor:
Songlin Qiu

Managing Editor:
Kristy Hart

Project Editor:
Anne Goebel

Copy Editor:
Geneil Breeze

Indexer:
Brad Herriman

Proofreader:
Language Logistics, LLC

Technical Reviewers:
Brian Collins
Chris "Xenon" Hanson

Publishing Coordinator:
Kim Boedigheimer

Cover Designer:
Alan Clements

Senior Compositor:
Gloria Schurick

For my wife, LeeAnne,
For not killing me in my sleep
(when I deserved it).

To the memory of Richard S. Wright, Sr.
Thanks, Dad, for just letting me be a nerd.

—Richard S. Wright, Jr.

To my wife, Anna,
Who has put up with all my engineering nonsense and
given me undying love and support.

And to my parents for providing me with encouragement and more
LEGOs than I could get both arms around.

—Nicholas Haemel

For my wife, Chris, and my son, Jeremy.
I have everything I need in you.

—Graham Sellers

Contents at a Glance

Table of Contents

Preface to the Fifth Edition

In nature, occasionally a forest becomes overgrown, and the forest ecosystem begins to collapse a bit under its own weight. Lightning sometimes strikes and burns down the forest, enabling a fresh new start, and a new blueprint from what was before emerges. The fifth edition of this book has undergone just such a radical transformation. We have burnt the fourth edition to the ground, and save for a few isolated patches, this entire book represents new growth.

The same can be said for OpenGL. With OpenGL 3.0, the word *deprecated* was introduced to the specification for the first time. Features and functionality were marked for removal, and developers were urged to move forward. A leaner, meaner OpenGL was envisioned as the baggage of the fixed pipeline was jettisoned. Things don't always go as planned, however. During the late 1990s OpenGL was besieged in what is sometimes now called the *API Wars*, by Microsoft's Direct 3D API. Ultimately developers, however, are in charge of dominant APIs, and OpenGL refused to die. Instead it flourished and has become the world standard for real-time 3D graphics rendering. Again developers seem to have spoken, and despite the efforts of OpenGL's own greatest champions on the ARB, the fixed pipeline simply refuses to die off. Today, we have two flavors of OpenGL, the *compatibility profile* and the *core profile*.

For this reason, it is entirely likely that the fourth edition of this book, which covers what could now simply be called the classic OpenGL 2.1 fixed function profile, will remain in demand for years to come. The fixed function pipeline has a tremendous amount of legacy behind it, is very easy to program for, and is today fully hardware accelerated on a modern graphics card. Many nonperformance minded and nongraphics specialists may well prefer this programming model for some time to come. Only time will tell.

Meanwhile, we were faced with what to do for the fifth edition of this book. OpenGL is being updated every 6 months or so, and we had two updates during the writing of this book! Trying to cover the compatibility and the core profile simultaneously leads to a lot of confusion. In addition, many of the newer more modern effects are only possible with shaders. The fixed pipeline mode of graphics programming, while still useful to many, seems more and more rudimentary with each passing year. So, moving forward, we thought it best to focus this edition solely on the core profile. As far as I know, this will be the first book on the market to do so. In teaching OpenGL at Full Sail University, I faced a huge challenge trying to figure out how to teach OpenGL without the fixed pipeline. I, as well as many others that I have observed, taught shader programming as an extension of the fixed pipeline. How do you *start* to use OpenGL without several initially boring chapters on shader programming? A number of tools allow you to write shaders in an IDE type environment, and some have taken this as the initial approach. This has its uses, and I have no criticism of this approach. My preference, however, is to have an actual *program* that I can run that does something interesting. This is how I learned to program...then I can send the program to my mom, girlfriend, buddy, boss, and so on, and show them how clever I am. This is a powerful feedback mechanism when it comes to mastering new technologies. It's how I learned, and it was the pattern of the first four (and best-selling) editions of this book. It's an approach I did not want to abandon for this edition either. I hope you like the results of our efforts.

—**Richard S. Wright, Jr.**

Preface to the Fourth Edition

My career has been built on a long history of making "stupid" choices and accidentally being right. First, I went to Microsoft's DOS, instead of the wildly popular CP/M. Later, I recall, friends counseled me that Windows was dead, and too hard to program for, and that OS/2 was the future (you couldn't lose by sticking with IBM, they'd say).

Just got lucky, I guess.

There were a few other minor wrong turns that just happened to fortunately have me pointed away from some other collapsing industry segment, but my next really big stupid decision was writing the first edition of this book. I had already built a nice comfortable career out of fixing SQL database problems and was making the transition to large-scale enterprise IT solutions in the healthcare industry. A book on OpenGL? I had no idea what I was doing. The first time I read the official OpenGL specification, I had to all but breathe in a paper bag, my first co-author quit in disgust, and the whole project was very nearly canceled before the book was half-finished.

As soon as the book came out, I had some meager credibility outside my normal field of expertise. I was offered a job at Lockheed-Martin/Real3D doing "real" OpenGL work. My then-current boss (God bless you, David, wherever you are!) tried really hard to talk me out of throwing my career away. Everybody knows, he insisted, that whatever Microsoft does is going to be the way the industry goes, and Microsoft's Talisman graphics platform was going to bury OpenGL into obscurity. Besides, there was only one other book on OpenGL in existence; how big a thing could it possibly be?

Eleven years have passed, and as I finish yet the fourth edition of this book (and look at a shelf full of OpenGL books), the number of people reading this who remember the short-lived hype of Talisman would probably fit in the back of my minivan. An OpenGL engineer I used to know at IBM had in her e-mail signature: "OpenGL. It's everywhere. Do the math." This has never been truer than it is today.

OpenGL today is the industry-leading standard graphics API on nearly every conceivable platform. This includes not only desktop Windows PCs and Macs, but also UNIX workstations, location-based entertainment systems, major game consoles (all but one), handheld gaming devices, cell phones, and a myriad of other embedded systems such as avionic and vehicle instrumentation.

Across platforms, OpenGL is the undisputed champion of 3D content creation applications, 3D games, visualization, simulation, scientific modeling, and even 2D image and video editing. OpenGL's widespread success can be attributed to its elegance and ease of use, its power and flexibility, and the overwhelming support it has received from the developer and IHV communities. OpenGL can be extended as well, providing all the bene-fits of an open standard, as well as giving vendors the ability to add their own proprietary added value to implementations.

You have probably heard that programmable hardware is the future of 3D graphics programming, and of graphics APIs. This is no longer true. Programmable hardware is no longer in the future; it is here now, today, even on the lowest cost motherboard embedded 3D chipsets. It is not a fluke that this edition follows the last at the closest interval of the series. The pace of evolving graphics technology is simply staggering, and this edition brings you up-to-date on the now-latest OpenGL version 2.1.

We have reinforced the chapters on fixed-pipeline programming, which is not going away anytime soon, and have affectionately deemed them "The Old Testament;" still relevant, illustrative, and the foundation on which the "New Testament" of programmable hard-ware is based. I find the analogy quite appropriate, and I would refute anyone who thinks the fixed pipeline is completely dead and irrelevant. The rank and file of application devel-opers (not necessarily cutting-edge game developers) would, I'm sure, agree.

That said, we have still trimmed some dead weight. Color Index mode is ignored as much as possible, some old paletted rendering material from the Windows chapter has been pruned, and we have eliminated all the old low-level assembly-style shader material to make room for updated and expanded coverage of the high-level shading language (GLSL). You'll also find a whole new chapter on OpenGL on handheld systems, totally rewritten Mac OS X and Linux chapters, and a really great new chapter on advanced buffer tech-niques such as off-screen rendering and floating-point textures.

Another big change some readers will notice is that the *OpenGL SuperBible* has been acquired and adopted into the Addison-Wesley Professional OpenGL series. I can't begin to express how grateful I am and how humbled I feel by this honor. I myself have worn out the covers on at least one edition of every volume in this series.

One of the reasons, I think, for the longevity of this book has been the unique approach it takes among OpenGL books. As much as possible, we look at things through the eyes of someone who is excited by 3D graphics but knows very little about the topic. The purpose of a tutorial is to get you started, not teach you everything you will ever need to know. Every professional knows that you never reach this place. I do occasionally get some criti-cism for glossing over things too much, or not explaining things according to the strictest engineering accuracy. These almost never come from those for whom this book was intended. We hope for a great many of you that this will be your first book on OpenGL and 3D graphics. We hope for none of you that it will be your last.

Well, I did make one really "smart" decision about my career once. Once upon a time in the early 1980s, I was a student looking at a computer in an electronics store. The sales-man approached and began making his pitch. I told him I was just learning to program and was considering an Amiga over his model. I was briskly informed that I needed to get serious with a computer that the rest of the world was using. An Amiga, he told me, was not good for anything but "making pretty pictures." No one, he assured me, could make a living making pretty pictures on his computer. Unfortunately, I listened to this "smart" advice and regretted it for more than ten years. Thank God I finally got stupid.

As for making a living "making pretty pictures?" Do the math.

Oh, and my latest stupid decision? I've left Windows and switched to the Mac. Time will tell if my luck holds out.

—Richard S. Wright, Jr.

Preface to the Third Edition

I have a confession to make. The first time I ever heard of OpenGL was at the 1992 Win32 Developers Conference in San Francisco. Windows NT 3.1 was in early beta (or late alpha), and many vendors were present, pledging their future support for this exciting new graphics technology. Among them was a company called Silicon Graphics, Inc. (SGI). The SGI representatives were showing off their graphics workstations and playing video demos of special effects from some popular movies. Their primary purpose in this booth, however, was to promote a new 3D graphics standard called OpenGL. It was based on SGI's proprietary IRIS GL and was fresh out of the box as a graphics standard. Significantly, Microsoft was pledging future support for OpenGL in Windows NT.

I had to wait until the beta release of NT 3.5 before I got my first personal taste of OpenGL. Those first OpenGL-based screensavers only scratched the surface of what was possible with this graphics API. Like many other people, I struggled through the Microsoft help files and bought a copy of the *OpenGL Programming Guide* (now called simply "The Red Book" by most). The Red Book was not a primer, however, and it assumed a lot of knowledge that I just didn't have.

Now for that confession I promised. How did I learn OpenGL? I learned it by writing a book about it. That's right, the first edition of the *OpenGL SuperBible* was me learning how to do 3D graphics myself...with a deadline! Somehow I pulled it off, and in 1996 the first edition of the book you are holding was born. Teaching myself OpenGL from scratch enabled me somehow to better explain the API to others in a manner that a lot of people seemed to like. The whole project was nearly canceled when Waite Group Press was acquired by another publisher halfway through the publishing process. Mitchell Waite stuck to his guns and insisted that OpenGL was going to be "the next big thing" in computer graphics. Vindication arrived when an emergency reprint was required because the first run of the book sold out before ever making it to the warehouse.

That was a long time ago, and in what seems like a galaxy far, far away....

Only three years later 3D accelerated graphics were a staple for even the most stripped-down PCs. The "API Wars," a political battle between Microsoft and SGI, had come and gone; OpenGL was firmly established in the PC world; and 3D hardware acceleration was as common as CD-ROMs and sound cards. I had even managed to turn my career more toward an OpenGL orientation and had the privilege of contributing in some small ways to the OpenGL specification for version 1.2 while working at Lockheed-Martin/Real3D. The second edition of this book, released at the end of 1999, was significantly expanded and corrected. We even made some modest initial attempts to ensure that all the sample programs were more friendly in non-Windows platforms by using the GLUT framework.

Now, nearly five years later (eight since the first edition!), we bring you yet again another edition, the third, of this book. OpenGL is now without question the premier cross-platform real-time 3D graphics API. Excellent OpenGL stability and performance are available on even the most stripped-down bargain PC today. OpenGL is also the standard for UNIX and Linux operating systems, and Apple has made OpenGL a core fundamental technology for the new Mac OS X operating system. OpenGL is even making inroads via a new specification, OpenGL ES, into embedded and mobile spaces. Who would have thought five years ago that we would see Quake running on a cell phone?

It is exciting that, today, even laptops have 3D acceleration, and OpenGL is truly everywhere and on every mainstream computing platform. Even more exciting, however, is the continuing evolution of computer graphics hardware. Today, most graphics hardware is programmable, and OpenGL even has its own shading language, which can produce stunningly realistic graphics that were undreamed of on commodity hardware back in the last century (I just had to squeeze that in someplace!).

With this third edition, I am pleased that we have added Benjamin Lipchak as a co-author. Benj is primarily responsible for the chapters that deal with OpenGL shader programs; and coming from the ARB groups responsible for this aspect of OpenGL, he is one of the most qualified authors on this topic in the world.

We have also fully left behind the "Microsoft Specific" characteristics of the first edition and have embraced a more multiplatform approach. All the programming examples in this book have been tested on Windows, Mac OS X, and at least one version of Linux. There is even one chapter apiece on these operating systems, with information about using OpenGL with native applications.

—Richard S. Wright, Jr.

Acknowledgments

Thanks to Nick and Graham for picking up so much weight of the book for this edition. Thanks for debugging my code, finding stupid mistakes before the readers did, and generally for being smarter than me most of the time, but letting me take most of the credit anyway. Thank you Debra Williams Cauley for believing in yet another edition of this book, holding my hand, and not sending the enforcer to my house when I was late...continually. Songlin, someday I will learn the difference between "your" and "you're" and "it's" and "its." Thank you for making it look like I did get past the eighth grade and not making me feel like a fool along the way. Brian Collins and Chris "Xenon" Hanson did a terrific job of looking over the early material too and caught more than a few potentially embarrassing snafus. I am forever grateful. I owe you both a beer anytime you're in town.

Thanks to Full Sail University for letting me teach OpenGL for more than ten years now, while still continuing my "day job"—especially Rob Catto for looking the other way more than once and running interference when things get in my way on a regular basis. To my very good friends and associates in the graphics department there, Wendy "Kitty" Jones, Kent Ward, and Nick Bullock, thanks for all the support, emotional and physical, the occasional Thai food, and sometimes just doing my job for me.

Special thanks to Software Bisque (Steve, Tom, Daniel, and Matt) for giving me something "real" to do with OpenGL every day and providing me with possibly the coolest day (and night) job anybody could ever ask for. I also have to thank my family, LeeAnne, Sara, Stephen, and Alex. You've all put up with a lot of mood swings, rapidly changing priorities, and an unpredictable work schedule, not to mention a good measure of motivation when I really needed it.

Finally, thank you Apple for not making me wait to "install important updates, do not shut off your computer" every single time I needed to reboot to change operating systems. AMD/ATI thanks for the cool new toys you sent my way to help out too. I'm so glad to see you guys doing all you can to support the OpenGL standard.

—Richard S. Wright, Jr.

First, thanks, Richard, for including me on another great adventure in creating an OpenGL publishing milestone. Without your dedication and commitment, computer graphics students would not have the necessary tools to learn 3D graphics. It has been a pleasure working with you over the years to help support 3D graphics and OpenGL specifically. Thanks to Graham for helping me bring this edition into the OpenGL 3.3 stratosphere. Your watchful eye has saved me much trouble and helped to keep this book true to its theme. Thank you, Debra Williams Cauley, for easing us back into the publishing process and guiding my unfamiliar hands through the finish line. Your patience is unequaled and undeserved. And, Songlin, thanks for your watchful eye and for polishing my raw text.

This work could not be successful without all of the great feedback provided by so many. A special thanks goes to Mark Young of AMD for meticulously reviewing all of my work and providing excellent feedback without having any responsibility to do so. Brian Collins and Chris Hanson, you both have been critical to making sure the material is top quality and bug-free. Thanks for your timely feedback.

I also want to thank AMD and all of the great developers in the OpenGL group. You have been incredibly supportive and helpful in making OpenGL 3.3 available on real hardware, getting samples working, and making my job possible. Thanks to Mark Young, Mais Alnasser, Ken Wang, Jaakko Konttinen, Murat Balci, Bird Zhang, Zhihong Wang, Frank Li, Erick Zolnowski, Qun Lin, Jesse Zhou, Ethan Wei, Zhaohua Dong, and many others. You all have done a tremendous job. A special thanks goes to the Khronos standards body group and all participating companies who have worked hard to keep OpenGL current, relevant, and competitive as the only true cross-platform 3D API.

And of course I couldn't have completed this project without the support of my family and friends. To my wife, Anna: You have put up with all of my techno-mumble-jumble all these years while at the same time saving lives and making a difference in medicine in your own right. Thanks for your patience and support; I could never be successful without you.

—**Nicholas Haemel**

Thanks so much to my co-authors, Richard and Nick, and to our publishers for putting faith in me to cut my authoring teeth on a chunk of a publication like this one. It has been a privilege working with you on this project, and I hope that this is the first of many. Thanks to Dave for saying "Sure, I like Graham." Thanks, Debra, for pushing and prodding me as needed (and it was often needed) to get me to deliver. Thanks to Songlin for teaching me how to properly format a document. The feedback I received from our tech reviewers Brian Collins and Chris "Xenon" Hanson was most helpful...and reassuring that I hadn't said anything silly.

I'd like to extend a warm thanks to my colleagues at AMD. In particular I'd like to thank Mark Young, who read what I had written when it was in a very unrefined state, even before it had gotten to the tech reviewers. Mark also put a massive amount of effort into updating the OpenGL reference in the appendix of this book. That really goes above and beyond—thanks! Cheers to Jaakko, Murat, and everyone else who offered suggestions and help while I was concocting the examples for this book. I've really enjoyed our brainstorms. Your input was extremely valuable and half of what I do just wouldn't work if it weren't for you guys. Thanks to Bill and Nick (again) for helping me get involved in Khronos and the ARB. Pierre, you've been a great mentor. Thanks to Suki for letting me step well outside my job description and get my hands on pretty much anything I want. You've provided an incredible opportunity for me, and I appreciate it.

Everyone who's helped me along the way deserves thanks: My old colleagues at Epson; the folks on the ARB—thanks for being so accepting of this guy who just showed up one day. Many of these guys are my competitors, and I appreciate that we've been able to work together on so many things.

Finally, I owe a huge thanks to my family. Chris, you're amazing. You've given me so much, and I love you. Jeremy, you're awesome. Mum, Dad, thanks for making me! Barry and Phyllis, thanks for making Chris!

—Graham Sellers

About the Authors

Richard S. Wright Jr. has been using OpenGL for more than 15 years and has taught OpenGL programming in the game design degree program at Full Sail University near Orlando, Florida, for more than 10. Currently, Richard is a Senior Engineer at Software Bisque, where he is the technical lead for Seeker, a 3D solar system simulator, and the product manager for their full dome theater planetarium products.

Previously with Real 3D/Lockheed Martin, Richard was a regular OpenGL ARB attendee and contributed to the OpenGL 1.2 specification and conformance tests back when mammoths still walked the earth. Since then, Richard has worked in multidimensional database visualization, game development, medical diagnostic visualization, and astronomical space simulation on Windows, Linux, Mac OS X, and various handheld platforms.

Richard first learned to program in the eighth grade in 1978 on a paper terminal. At age 16, his parents let him buy a computer with his grass-cutting money instead of a car, and he sold his first computer program less than a year later (and it was a graphics program!). When he graduated from high school, his first job was teaching programming and computer literacy for a local consumer education company. He studied electrical engineering and computer science at the University of Louisville's Speed Scientific School and made it halfway through his senior year before his career got the best of him and took him to Florida. A native of Louisville, Kentucky, he now lives in Lake Mary, Florida. When not programming or dodging hurricanes, Richard is an avid amateur astronomer and photography buff. Richard is also, proudly, a Mac.

Nicholas Haemel has been involved with OpenGL for more than 12 years, soon after its wide acceptance. He graduated from the Milwaukee School of Engineering with a degree in Computer Engineering and a love for embedded systems, computer hardware, and making things work. Soon after graduation he put these skills to work for the 3D drivers group at ATI, developing graphics drivers and working on new GPUs.

Nick is now a Member of the Technical Staff at Advanced Micro Devices (AMD) in the OpenGL group and has been a key contributor to driver architecture, design, and development. He has also led all key initiatives and projects for the Workstation OpenGL market. Nick has contributed to the OpenGL Architecture Review Board, now part of The Khronos Group, for the past four years and has participated in defining the OpenGL 3.0, 3.1, 3.2, 3.3, and 4.0 specifications as well as related extensions and GL Shading Language versions. In addition to OpenGL, he has contributed to OpenGL ES, WebGL, and EGL working groups.

Nick's graphics career began at age 9 when he first learned to program 2D graphics using Logo Writer. After convincing his parents to purchase a state-of-the-art 286 IBM compatible PC, it immediately became the central control unit for robotic arms and other remotely programmable devices. Fast-forward 20 years, and the devices being controlled are GPUs the size of a fingernail but with more than 2 billion transistors. Nick's interests also extend to business leadership and management, strengthened by a recent MBA from the University of Wisconsin-Madison, where he now resides. When not working on accelerating the future of graphics hardware, Nick enjoys the outdoors as a competitive sailor, mountaineer, ex-downhill ski racer, road biker, and photographer.

Graham Sellers is a classic geek. His family got their first computer (a BBC Model B) right before his sixth birthday. After his mum and dad stayed up all night programming it to play "Happy Birthday," he was hooked and determined to figure out how it worked. Next came basic programming and then assembly language. His first real exposure to graphics was via "demos" in the early nineties, and then through Glide, and finally OpenGL in the late nineties. He holds a master's degree in Engineering from the University of Southampton, England.

Currently, Graham is a manager on the OpenGL driver team at AMD. He represents AMD at the ARB and has contributed to many extensions and to the core OpenGL Specification. Prior to that, he was a team lead at Epson, implementing OpenGL-ES and OpenVG drivers for embedded products. Graham holds several patents in the fields of computer graphics and image processing. When he's not working on OpenGL, he likes to disassemble and reverse engineer old video game consoles (just to see how they work and what he can make them do). Originally from England, Graham now lives in Orlando, Florida, with his wife and son.

Introduction

Welcome to the fifth edition of the *OpenGL SuperBible*. For over a decade, we have striven to provide the world's best introduction to not only OpenGL, but 3D graphics programming in general. This book is both a comprehensive reference and a tutorial that teaches you how to use this powerful API to create stunning 3D visualizations, games, and other graphics of all kinds. Starting with basic 3D terminology and concepts, we take you through basic primitive assembly, transformations, lighting, and texturing, and eventually bring you into the full power of the programmable graphics pipeline with the OpenGL Shading Language.

Regardless of whether you are programming on Windows, Mac OS X, Linux, or a handheld gaming device, this book is a great place to start learning OpenGL and how to make the most of it on your specific platform. The majority of the book is highly portable C++ code hosted by the GLUT or FreeGLUT toolkit. You also find OS-specific chapters that show how to wire OpenGL into your native window systems. Throughout the book, we try to make few assumptions about how much previous knowledge the reader has of 3D graphics programming topics. This yields a tutorial that is accessible by both the beginning programmer and the experienced programmer beginning OpenGL.

What's New in This Edition

Readers of the previous editions will notice right away that this book is smaller. What happened? In OpenGL 3.0, certain features were marked as *deprecated*, that is, they were flagged as candidates for removal from future versions of OpenGL. Thus far, largely due to developer pressure, nothing has been officially removed from OpenGL. Instead, currently we have two flavors of OpenGL, the compatibility profile that contains all the latest functionality plus the deprecated features, and the core profile, which contains none of the deprecated functionality. Because the point of marking features as deprecated is to move the standard forward, this edition does not cover any of the deprecated functionality, but instead focuses only on the core profile. The core profile as of OpenGL 3.3 to be specific.

We kept the very popular reference material found at the end of the book; however, it has been pruned also of any deprecated functions. This is a great place to start if you want to make the most modern and forward-looking OpenGL programs possible. The chapters that make up the tutorial section of the book are 95% or more all brand new material. We did not want to take the approach of building on the deprecated OpenGL functionality, and thus brand new material with a brand new approach was called for. This includes all of the operating system specific chapters for this edition, which have been mostly totally rewritten from the ground up as well.

The OpenGL ES chapter now specifically covers using OpenGL ES on the iPhone. This includes the iPod Touch and the iPad, and some of the samples from earlier in the book have been ported to these devices as well. This is a welcome addition as when the last edition was written, there was no comparable mainstream OpenGL ES device that any reader (with a Mac) could make use of so easily.

The GLTools library has been significantly enhanced with this edition. A collection of stock shaders enables you to get started right away learning how to use shaders before actually delving into writing shaders of your own. In addition, a collection of lightweight C++ classes allows for management of your geometry batches and supports creating and manipulating your own matrix stacks. Like the old GLU library, this library should be thought of as a set of helper routines only, not a complete programming framework for using OpenGL.

How This Book Is Organized

The OpenGL SuperBible is divided into three parts. Part I is the basic OpenGL/3D graphics tutorial. Part II covers more advanced OpenGL programming topics, and Part III covers some OS specific features that help you make the most of OpenGL on your chosen platform. These three parts are followed by three appendices, which include pointers to other good OpenGL references and tutorials, a short glossary, and a complete reference section of the core profile.

Part I: Basic Concepts

You learn how to construct a program that uses OpenGL, how to set up your 3D-rendering environment, and how to create basic objects and light and shade them. Then we delve deeper into using OpenGL and introduce you to GLSL and how to create your own shaders. These chapters are a good way to introduce yourself to 3D graphics programming with OpenGL and provide the conceptual foundation on which the more advanced capabilities later in the book are based.

Chapter 1—Introduction to 3D Graphics and OpenGL. This introductory chapter is for newcomers to 3D graphics. It introduces fundamental concepts and some common vocabulary.

Chapter 2—Getting Started. In this chapter, we provide you with a working knowledge of what OpenGL is, where it came from, and where it is going. You write your first program using OpenGL, find out what headers and libraries you need to use, learn how to set up your environment, and discover how some common conventions can help you remember OpenGL function calls. We also introduce the OpenGL state machine and error-handling mechanism.

Chapter 3—Basic Rendering. Here, we present the building blocks of 3D graphics programming. You basically find out how to tell a computer to create a three-dimensional object with OpenGL using geometric primitives, use a shader, and set uniforms and attributes. You also learn the basics of hidden surface removal, blending and antialiasing, and different ways to query the OpenGL driver for implementation specifics.

Chapter 4—Basic Transformations: A Vector/Matrix Primer. Now that you're creating three-dimensional shapes in a virtual world, how do you move them around? How do you move yourself around? These are the things you learn here. There is remarkably little actual OpenGL in this chapter, but we cover concepts you really need to know before you can move forward.

Chapter 5—Basic Texturing. Texture mapping is one of the most useful features of any 3D graphics toolkit. You learn how to wrap images onto polygons and how to load and manage multiple textures at once.

Chapter 6—Thinking Outside the Box: Nonstock Shaders. Now that we have the basics of the client side of OpenGL programming down, it's time to devote some time to the server side, how to write shaders with GLSL. This chapter provides a gentle introduction with some useful examples that build on what you've learned using the stock shaders.

Chapter 7—More Advanced Texture Topics. Beyond basic texturing, in this chapter we cover Cube Maps, 3D textures, and just using textures for data storage. We also cover point sprites here and some other kinds of nonvisual texture applications.

Part II: Intermediate to Advanced Ideas

In the second part of the book, we go a bit more in-depth. This is where the really cool stuff starts happening with OpenGL, and knowing how to make use of these more advanced topics is what will separate you from the more casual 3D dabblers. Not only will more visual effects be within your grasp, but many of these topics are performance-oriented as well.

Chapter 8—Buffer Objects: Storage Is Now in Your Hands. OpenGL no longer supports client-side storage of data. In this chapter, you learn the in and outs of the different kinds of storage buffers used in OpenGL, including how to render into your own off-screen frame buffers.

Chapter 9—Advanced Buffers: Beyond the Basics. Taking buffers up a notch, this chapter shows you how to go the extra mile and some very useful, but not always typical, buffer formats.

Chapter 10—Fragment Operations: The End of the Pipeline. There is still quite a bit of processing that goes on once the fragment shader has turned loose of color, depth, and other data. This chapter talks about some per-fragment operations, including the very useful stencil test.

Chapter 11—Advanced Shader Usage. This chapter extends your shader programming to include the optional middle stage of shader programming, the Geometry Shader. In addition, more advanced shader management and usage patterns such as uniform blocks are covered.

Chapter 12—Advanced Geometry Management. The final chapter covers advanced methods and tricks for managing your geometry and rendering operations. Some useful features of OpenGL are available to optimize processing of large amounts of geometry and eliminating geometry that cannot be seen ahead of time. Finally, there are actually some useful timing features that are now built-in to OpenGL.

Part III: Platform-Specific Notes

The third and last part of the book is less about OpenGL than about how different operating systems interface with and make use of OpenGL. Here we wander outside the "official" OpenGL specification to see how OpenGL is supported and interfaced with on Windows, Mac OS X, Linux, and handheld devices such as the iPhone using OpenGL ES 2.0.

Chapter 13—OpenGL on Windows. Here, you learn how to write real Windows programs that use OpenGL. You learn about Microsoft's "wiggle" functions that glue OpenGL rendering code to Windows device contexts.

Chapter 14—OpenGL on OS X. In this chapter, you learn how to use OpenGL in native Mac OS X applications. Sample programs show you how to start working, primarily with Cocoa, using the Xcode development environment.

Chapter 15—OpenGL on Linux. This chapter discusses GLX, the OpenGL extension used to support OpenGL applications through the X Window System on UNIX and Linux. You learn how to create and manage OpenGL contexts as well as how to create OpenGL drawing areas.

Chapter 16—OpenGL ES on Mobile Devices. This chapter is all about how OpenGL is pared down to fit on handheld and embedded devices. We cover what's gone, what's new, and how to get going even with an emulated environment. We even port one of our desktop example programs to the iPhone.

Conventions Used in This Book

The following typographic conventions are used in this book:

- Code lines, commands, statements, variables, and any text you type or see on-screen appear in a `computer` typeface.

- *Italics* highlight technical terms when they first appear in the text and are being defined.

About the Companion Web Site

This is the second time this book has shipped without a CD-ROM. Welcome to the age of the Internet! Instead, all our source code is available online at our support Web site:

www.starstonesoftware.com/OpenGL

Here you find the source code to all the sample programs in the book, as well as prebuilt projects for Developers Studio (Windows) and Xcode (Mac OS X). For Linux users we have makefiles for command-line building of the projects as well. We even plan to post a few tutorials and some code updates, so check back from time to time, even after you've downloaded all the source code.

PART I

Basic Concepts

Contrary to what you may have heard, 3D graphics programming with OpenGL (or any other 3D API for that matter), is not *all* about the shaders. Quite a bit of work must be done on the client side, be it with C, C++, C#, JavaScript, and so on, to manage those shaders and to feed them geometry, transformation matrices, and other miscellaneous goodies.

Part I of this book is really a tutorial—a 3D graphics programming tutorial, from almost first principles, and of course built on OpenGL, the industry standard for real-time 3D graphics rendering.

Shader programming is *very* exciting, but this book is not intended to be a shader programming book. In fact, knowing how to write great shaders gets you nowhere without the knowledge of how to manage your scene; set up your viewing, modeling, and projection matrices; load textures...I think you get my point.

To get you going, we provide a small inventory of "stock shaders" that perform the most common rendering tasks. You might even find that for simple 3D rendering, these shaders provide everything you need. It is unlikely, though, that you'll be satisfied with stopping there once you've mastered the higher level ropes. We also provide you a GLSL "QuickStart" before launching into Part II, "Intermediate to Advanced Ideas," so you won't have to wait to start getting creative on your own as you master the rest of the OpenGL API.

You will find that the online world (as well as some other fine books) is a rich repository of advanced, as well as simple and clever shader code for a great many purposes. Once you have a good working knowledge of how to make best use of all those great shaders, you are going to want to write some of your own. For that, we point you to some excellent resources in Appendix A, "Further Reading."

CHAPTER 1

Introduction to 3D Graphics and OpenGL

by Richard S. Wright, Jr.

WHAT YOU'LL LEARN IN THIS CHAPTER:

- A brief overview of the history of computer graphics
- How we make 3D graphics on a 2D screen
- About the basic 3D effects and terminology
- How a 3D coordinate system and the viewport works
- What vertices are and how we use them
- About the different kinds of 3D projections

This book is about OpenGL, a programming interface for creating real-time 3D graphics. Before we begin talking about what OpenGL is and how it works, you should have at least a high-level understanding of real-time 3D graphics in general. Perhaps you picked up this book because you want to learn to use OpenGL, but you already have a good grasp of real-time 3D principles. If so, great: Skip directly to Chapter 2, "Getting Started." If you bought this book because the pictures look cool and you want to learn how to do this on your computer...you should probably start here.

A Brief History of Computer Graphics

The first computers consisted of rows and rows of switches and lights. Technicians and engineers worked for hours, days, or even weeks to program these machines and read the results of their calculations. Patterns of illuminated bulbs conveyed useful information to the computer users, or some crude printout was provided. You might say that the first form of computer graphics was a panel of blinking lights. (This idea is supported by stories of early programmers writing programs that served no useful purpose other than creating patterns of blinking and chasing lights!)

Times have changed. From those first "thinking machines," as some called them, sprang fully programmable devices that printed on rolls of paper using a mechanism similar to a teletype machine. Data could be stored efficiently on magnetic tape, on disk, or even on rows of hole-punched paper or stacks of paper-punch cards. The "hobby" of computer graphics was born the day computers first started printing. Because each character in the alphabet had a fixed size and shape, creative programmers in the 1970s took delight in creating artistic patterns and images made up of nothing more than asterisks (*).

Going Electric

Paper as an output medium for computers is useful and persists today. Laser printers and color inkjet printers have replaced crude ASCII art with crisp presentation quality and photographic reproductions of artwork. Paper and ink, however, can be expensive to replace on a regular basis, and using them consistently is wasteful of our natural resources, especially because most of the time we don't really need hard-copy output of calculations or database queries.

The cathode ray tube (CRT) was a tremendously useful addition to the computer. The original computer monitors, CRTs were initially just video terminals that displayed ASCII text just like the first paper terminals—but CRTs were perfectly capable of drawing points and lines as well as alphabetic characters. Soon, other symbols and graphics began to supplement the character terminal. Programmers used computers and their monitors to create graphics that supplemented textual or tabular output. The first algorithms for creating lines and curves were developed and published; computer graphics became a science rather than a pastime.

The first computer graphics displayed on these terminals were *two-dimensional*, or *2D*. These flat lines, circles, and polygons were used to create graphics for a variety of purposes. Graphs and plots could display scientific or statistical data in a way that tables and figures could not. More adventurous programmers even created simple arcade games such as *Lunar Lander* and *Pong* using simple graphics consisting of little more than line drawings that were refreshed (redrawn) several times a second.

The term *real-time* was first applied to computer graphics that were animated. A broader use of the word in computer science simply means that the computer can process input as fast as or faster than the input is being supplied. For example, talking on the phone is a real-time activity in which humans participate. You speak, and the listener hears your communication immediately and responds, allowing you to hear immediately and respond again, and so on. In reality, there is some delay involved due to the electronics, but the delay is usually imperceptible to those having the conversation. In contrast, writing a letter or an e-mail is not a real-time activity.

Applying the term *real-time* to computer graphics means that the computer is producing an animation or a sequence of images directly in response to some input, such as joystick movement or keyboard strokes. Real-time computer graphics can display a wave form being measured by electronic equipment, numerical readouts, or interactive games and visual simulations.

Going 3D

The term three-dimensional, or 3D, means that an object being described or displayed has three dimensions of measurement: width, height, and depth. An example of a two-dimensional object is a piece of paper on your desk with a drawing or writing on it, having no perceptible depth. A three-dimensional object is the can of soda next to it. The soft drink can is round (width and depth) and tall (height). Depending on your perspective, you can alter which side of the can is the width or height, but the fact remains that the can has three dimensions. Figure 1.1 shows how we might measure the dimensions of the can and piece of paper.

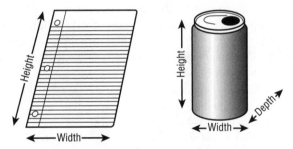

FIGURE 1.1   Measuring two- and three-dimensional objects.

For centuries, artists have known how to make a painting appear to have real depth. A painting is inherently a two-dimensional object because it is nothing more than canvas with paint applied. Similarly, 3D computer graphics are actually two-dimensional images on a flat computer screen that provide an illusion of depth, or a third dimension.

The first computer graphics no doubt appeared similar to what's shown in Figure 1.2, where you can see a simple three-dimensional cube drawn with 12 line segments. What makes the cube look three-dimensional is *perspective*, or the angles between the lines that lend the illusion of depth.

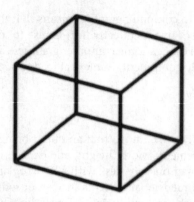

FIGURE 1.2   A simple wireframe 3D cube.

To truly see in 3D, you need to actually view an object with both eyes or supply each eye with separate and unique images of the object. Look at Figure 1.3. Each eye receives a two-dimensional image that is much like a temporary photograph displayed on each retina (the back part of your eye). These two images are slightly different because they are received at two different angles. (Your eyes are spaced apart on purpose!) The brain then combines these slightly different images to produce a single, composite 3D picture in your head.

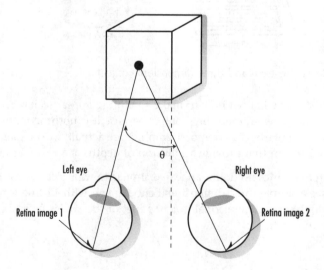

FIGURE 1.3   How you see three dimensions.

In Figure 1.3, the angle between the images becomes smaller as the object goes farther away. You can amplify this 3D effect by increasing the angle between the two images. View-Master (those hand-held stereoscopic viewers you probably had as a kid) and 3D movies capitalize on this effect by placing each of your eyes on a separate lens or by providing color-filtered glasses that separate two superimposed images. These images are usually overenhanced for dramatic or cinematic purposes. Of late this effect has become more popular on the personal computer as well. Shutter glasses that work with your graphics card and software switch between one eye and the other, with a changing perspective displayed on-screen to each eye, thus giving a "true" stereo 3D experience. Unfortunately, many people complain that this effect gives them headaches or makes them dizzy!

A computer screen is one flat image on a flat surface, not two images from different perspectives falling on each eye. As it turns out, most of what is considered to be 3D computer graphics is actually an approximation of true 3D. This approximation is achieved in the same way that artists have rendered drawings with apparent depth for years, using the same tricks that nature provides for people with one eye.

You might have noticed at some time in your life that if you cover one eye, the world does not suddenly fall flat. What happens when you cover one eye? You might think you are still seeing in 3D, but try this experiment: Place a glass or some other object just out of arm's reach, off to your left side. (If it is close, this trick won't work.) Cover your right eye with your right hand and reach for the glass. (Maybe you should use an empty plastic one!) Most people have a more difficult time estimating how much farther they need to reach (if at all) before touching the glass. Now, uncover your right eye and reach for the glass, and you can easily discern how far you need to lean to reach the glass. You now know why people with one eye often have difficulty with distance perception.

Perspective alone is enough to create the appearance of three dimensions. Note the cube shown previously in Figure 1.2. Even without coloring or shading, the cube still has the appearance of a three-dimensional object. Stare at the cube for long enough, however, and the front and back of the cube switch places. Your brain is confused by the lack of any surface coloration in the drawing. There just isn't enough information in this image for your brain to be certain of what it perceives. The reason the world doesn't suddenly look flat when you cover one eye is that many of the 3D world's effects are still present when viewed two-dimensionally. The effects are just enough to trigger your brain's ability to discern depth. One clue is surface shading due to lighting, another is that nearby objects appear larger than distant objects. This perspective effect is called *foreshortening*. This effect and color changes, textures, shading, and variations of color intensities together add up to our perception of a three-dimensional image.

3D Graphics Techniques and Terminology

With each chapter of this book there is one or more example programs that demonstrate the programming techniques discussed. Although this chapter intentionally avoids programming specific topics, it too has an example program intended to demonstrate the techniques and the terminology that you need to be familiar with at a minimum to get the most from this book. This chapter's single example program is called BLOCK and you can find it in the Chapter 1 folder of the example programs that accompany this book.

The process by which mathematical and image data is transformed into a 3D dimensional image is called *rendering*. When used as a verb, it is the process that your computer goes through to create the three dimensional image. Rendering is also used as a noun, simply to refer to the final image produced. The word "rendering" is used a lot in this book. Now let's take a look at some of the other terms and processes that take place during rendering.

Transformations and Projections

Figure 1.4 shows the initial output of the BLOCK example program, which shows a line drawing of a cube on a table or platform. By *transforming*, or moving the points around, and drawing lines between them we can produce the illusion of a 3D world on a flat 2D screen. The earliest flight simulators employed technology no more sophisticated than this.

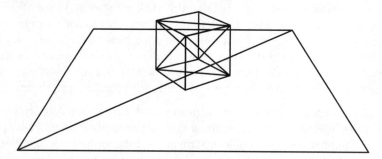

FIGURE 1.4   A simple wireframe cube and table.

The points themselves are called *vertices* (or vertex in the singular), and they are moved around in space with a convenient mathematical construct called a *transformation matrix* (we cover this in some detail in Chapter 4, "Basic Transformations: A Vector/Matrix Primer"). Another matrix, a *projection matrix* takes care of the mathematics necessary to turn our 3D coordinates into two-dimensional screen coordinates, where the final line drawing actually takes place.

Rasterization

The actual drawing, or filling in of the pixels between each vertex to make the lines is called *rasterization*. We can further clarify our 3D intent with transformed and rasterized lines by employing *hidden surface removal*. Figure 1.5 shows the output of our BLOCK program when you press the space for the first time. Although still using just points and lines, the illusion of a block on a table becomes quite a bit more convincing.

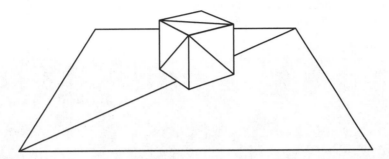

FIGURE 1.5   Hiding the back sides of solid geometry enhances the 3D illusion.

Although drawing with lines, or *wireframe rendering* as it is often called, has its uses, most of the time we render not with lines, but with solid triangles. Triangles and polygons are also rasterized, or filled in just like lines are. The earliest graphics hardware could fill in triangles using a solid color, but as shown in Figure 1.6, this does not enhance the 3D illusion. Early games and simulation technology would make adjoining polygons different solid colors, which would help, but fell short of a convincing simulation of reality.

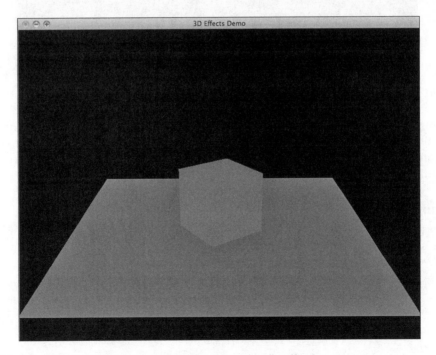

FIGURE 1.6   Filling in geometry with solid colors is hardly effective.

Shading

In Figure 1.7 (press the space bar again if you are running the BLOCK sample program) we show the effects of *shading*. By varying the color values across the surface (between vertices), we can easily create the effect of a light shining on a red cube.

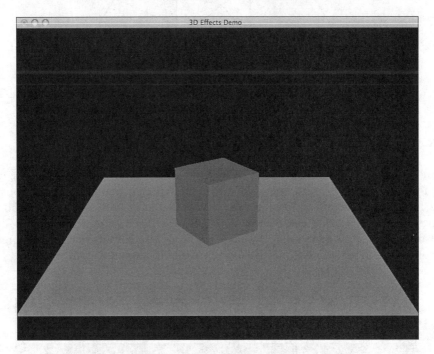

FIGURE 1.7   Shading the surface creates the illusion of light.

Lighting and shading are very large areas of specialty in the field of 3D graphics, and there are entire books written on this subject alone! *Shaders* (sounds very similar!) on the other hand are individual programs that execute on the graphics hardware to process vertices and perform rasterization tasks.

Texture Mapping

The next hardware advance was *texture mapping*. A texture is simply a picture that we map to the surface of a triangle or polygon. As you can see in Figure 1.8, textures add a whole new level of realism to our rendering.

FIGURE 1.8   A single texture is worth a thousand triangles!

Textures are fast and efficient on modern hardware, and a single texture can reproduce a surface that might take thousands or even millions of triangles to represent otherwise.

Blending

Finally, in Figure 1.9 we show the effects of *blending*. Blending allows us to mix different colors together. This reflection effect is done simply by drawing the cube upside down first. Then we draw the floor blended over the top of it, followed by the right side up cube. You really are seeing "through" the floor to the inverted cube below. Your brain just says, "Oh... a reflection." Blending is also how we make things look transparent. In fact, what you are really seeing in Figure 1.9 is *through* the wooden floor.

FIGURE 1.9   Using blending to create a reflection effect.

Connecting the Dots

That is pretty much computer graphics in a nut shell. Solid 3D geometry is nothing more than connecting the dots between vertices and then rasterizing the triangles to make objects solid. Transformations, shading, texture, and blending: Any computer rendered scene you see in a movie, video game, or scientific simulation is made up of nothing more than various applications of these four things.

Common Uses for 3D Graphics

Three-dimensional graphics have many uses in modern computer applications. Applications for real-time 3D graphics range from interactive games and simulations to data visualization for scientific, medical, or business uses. Higher-end 3D graphics find their way into movies and technical and educational publications as well.

Real-Time 3D

As defined earlier, real-time 3D graphics are animated and interactive with the user. One of the earliest uses for real-time 3D graphics was in military flight simulators. Even today, flight simulators are a popular diversion for the home enthusiast. Figure 1.10 shows a screenshot from a popular flight simulator that uses OpenGL for 3D rendering (www.x-plane.com).

FIGURE 1.10   An OpenGL-based flight simulator, courtesy of x-plane.com.

The applications for 3D graphics on the personal computer are almost limitless. Perhaps the most common use today is for computer gaming. Hardly a title ships today that does not require a 3D graphics card to play. Although 3D has always been popular for scientific visualization and engineering applications, the explosion of cheap 3D hardware has empowered these applications like never before. Business applications are also taking advantage of the new availability of hardware to incorporate more and more complex business graphics and database mining visualization techniques. Even the modern GUI is being affected and has evolved to take advantage of 3D hardware capabilities. The Macintosh OS X, for example, uses OpenGL to render all its windows and controls for a powerful and eye-popping visual interface.

Figures 1.11 through 1.15 show some of the myriad applications of real-time 3D graphics on the modern personal computer. All but one of these images were rendered real-time using OpenGL.

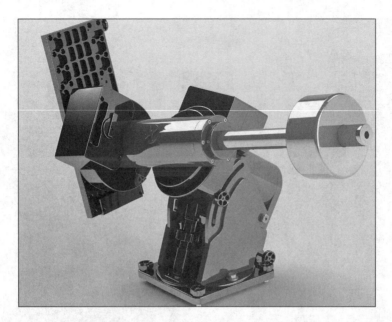

FIGURE 1.11 3D graphics used for computer-aided design (CAD) (image courtesy of Software Bisque).

FIGURE 1.12 3D graphics used for architectural or civil planning (image courtesy of Real 3D, Inc.).

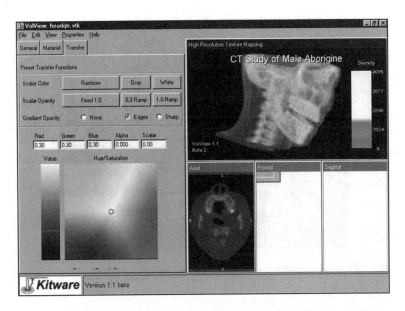

FIGURE 1.13   3D graphics used for medical imaging applications (VolView by Kitware).

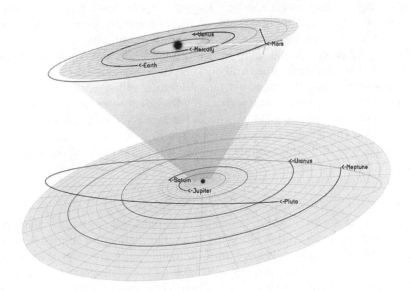

FIGURE 1.14   3D graphics used for scientific visualization (image courtesy of Software Bisque, Inc.).

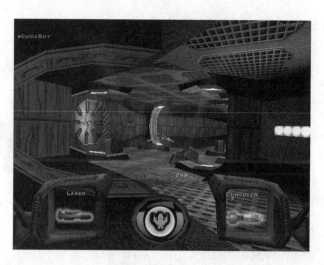

FIGURE 1.15   3D graphics used for entertainment (Descent 3 from Outrage Entertainment, Inc.).

Non-Real-Time 3D

Some compromise is required for real-time 3D applications. Given more processing time, you can generate higher quality 3D graphics. Typically, you design models and scenes, and a ray tracer or scan-line renderer processes the definition to produce a high-quality 3D image. The typical process is that some modeling application uses real-time 3D graphics to interact with the artist to create the content. Then the frames are sent to another application (the ray tracer or an offline renderer) or subroutine, which renders the image. Rendering a single frame for a movie such as *Toy Story* or *Shrek* could take hours on a very fast computer, for example. The process of rendering and saving many thousands of frames generates an animated sequence for playback. Although the playback might appear real-time, the content is not interactive, so it is not considered real-time, but rather pre-rendered.

Shaders

The current state of the art in real-time computer graphics is *programmable shading*. Today's graphics cards are no longer dumb rendering chips, but highly programmable rendering computers in their own right. Like the term *CPU* (*central processing unit*), the term *GPU* has been coined, meaning *graphics processing unit*, referring to the programmable chips on today's graphics cards. These are highly parallelized and very, very fast. Just as important, the programmer can reconfigure how the card works to achieve virtually any special effect imaginable.

Every year, shader-based graphics hardware gains ground on tasks traditionally done by the high-end ray tracing and software rendering tools mentioned previously. Figure 1.16

shows an image of the earth in Software Bisque's *Seeker* solar system simulator. This application uses a custom OpenGL shader to generate a realistic and animated view of the earth more than 60 times a second. This includes atmospheric effects, the sun's reflection in the water, and even the stars in the background. A color version of this figure is shown in Color Plate 1 in the Color insert.

FIGURE 1.16   Shaders allow for unprecedented real-time realism (image courtesy of Software Bisque, Inc.).

Basic 3D Programming Principles

Now, you have a pretty good idea of the basics of real-time 3D. We've covered some terminology and some sample applications on the personal computer. How do you actually create these images on your computer? Well, that's what the rest of this book is about! You still need a little more introduction to the basics, which we present here.

Not a Toolbox

OpenGL is basically a low-level rendering API. You do not tell OpenGL to "Draw this model over there"—you have to put together a model yourself by loading the triangles and applying the necessary transformations as well as the proper textures, shaders, and if necessary blending modes. This gives you a great deal of low-level control. The beauty of using a low-level API such as OpenGL instead of a higher level toolkit is that you cannot only reimplement many standard 3D rendering algorithms, you can invent your own and even make new discoveries for shortcuts, performance tricks, and artistic visualization techniques.

Coordinate Systems

Let's consider now how we describe objects in three dimensions. Before you can specify an object's location and size, you need a frame of reference to measure and locate against. When you draw lines or plot points on a simple flat computer screen, you specify a position in terms of a row and column. For example, a standard VGA screen has 640 pixels from left to right and 480 pixels from top to bottom. To specify a point in the middle of the screen, you specify that a point should be plotted at (320,240)—that is, 320 pixels from the left of the screen and 240 pixels down from the top of the screen.

In OpenGL, or almost any 3D API, when you create a window to draw in, you must also specify the *coordinate system* you want to use and how to map the specified coordinates into physical screen pixels. Let's first see how this applies to two-dimensional drawing and then extend the principle to three dimensions.

2D Cartesian Coordinates

The most common coordinate system for two-dimensional plotting is the Cartesian coordinate system. Cartesian coordinates are specified by an x coordinate and a y coordinate. The x coordinate is a measure of position in the horizontal direction, and y is a measure of position in the vertical direction.

The *origin* of the Cartesian system is at x=0, y=0. Cartesian coordinates are written as coordinate pairs in parentheses, with the x coordinate first and the y coordinate second, separated by a comma. For example, the origin is written as (0,0). Figure 1.17 depicts the Cartesian coordinate system in two dimensions. The x and y lines with tick marks are called the *axes* and can extend from negative to positive infinity. This figure represents the true Cartesian coordinate system pretty much as you used it in grade school. Today, differing window mapping modes can cause the coordinates you specify when drawing to be interpreted differently. Later in the book, you'll see how to map this true coordinate space to window coordinates in different ways.

The x-axis and y-axis are perpendicular (intersecting at a right angle) and together define the xy plane. A *plane* is, most simply put, a flat surface. In any coordinate system, two axes (or two lines) that intersect at right angles define a plane. In a system with only two axes, there is naturally only one plane to draw on.

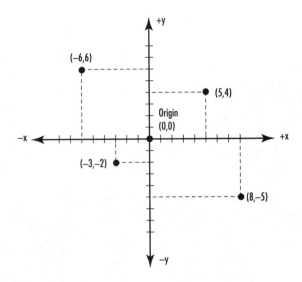

FIGURE 1.17   The Cartesian plane.

Coordinate Clipping

A window is measured physically in terms of pixels. Before you can start plotting points, lines, and shapes in a window, you must tell OpenGL how to translate specified coordinate pairs into screen coordinates. You do this by specifying the region of Cartesian space that occupies the window; this region is known as the clipping region. In two-dimensional space, the clipping region is the minimum and maximum x and y values that are inside the window. Another way of looking at this is specifying the origin's location in relation to the window. Figure 1.18 shows two common clipping regions.

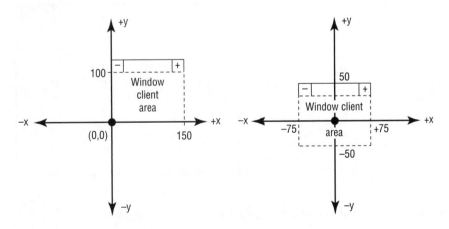

FIGURE 1.18   Two clipping regions.

In the first example, on the left of Figure 1.18, x coordinates in the window range left to right from 0 to +150, and the y coordinates range bottom to top from 0 to +100. A point in the middle of the screen would be represented as (75,50). The second example shows a clipping area with x coordinates ranging left to right from –75 to +75 and y coordinates ranging bottom to top from –50 to +50. In this example, a point in the middle of the screen would be at the origin (0,0). It is also possible using OpenGL functions (or ordinary Windows functions for GDI drawing) to turn the coordinate system upside down or flip it right to left. In fact, the default mapping for Windows windows is for positive y to move down from the top to bottom of the window. Although useful when drawing text from top to bottom, this default mapping is not as convenient for drawing graphics.

Viewports: Mapping Drawing Coordinates to Window Coordinates

Rarely will your clipping area width and height exactly match the width and height of the window in pixels. The coordinate system must therefore be mapped from logical Cartesian coordinates to physical screen pixel coordinates. This mapping is specified by a setting known as the *viewport*. The viewport is the region within the window's client area that is used for drawing the clipping area. The viewport simply maps the clipping area to a region of the window. Usually, the viewport is defined as the entire window, but this is not strictly necessary; for instance, you might want to draw only in the lower half of the window.

Figure 1.19 shows a large window measuring 300x200 pixels with the viewport defined as the entire client area. If the clipping area for this window were set to 0 to 150 along the x-axis and 0 to 100 along the y-axis, the logical coordinates would be mapped to a larger screen coordinate system in the viewing window. Each increment in the logical coordinate system would be matched by two increments in the physical coordinate system (pixels) of the window.

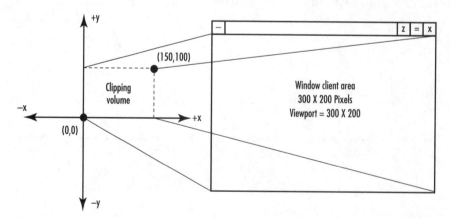

FIGURE 1.19   A viewport defined as twice the size of the clipping area.

In contrast, Figure 1.20 shows a viewport that matches the clipping area. The viewing window is still 300x200 pixels, however, and this causes the viewing area to occupy the lower-left side of the window.

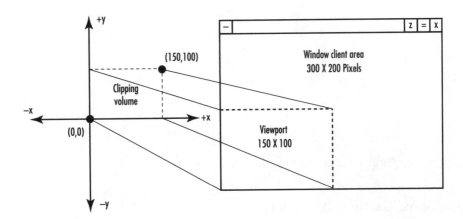

FIGURE 1.20   A viewport defined as the same dimensions as the clipping area.

You can use viewports to shrink or enlarge the image inside the window and to display only a portion of the clipping area by setting the viewport to be larger than the window's client area.

The Vertex—A Position in Space

In both 2D and 3D, when you draw an object, you actually compose it with several smaller shapes called *primitives*. Primitives are one- or two-dimensional entities or surfaces such as points, lines, and triangles that are assembled in 3D space to create 3D objects. For example, a three-dimensional cube consists of six two-dimensional squares made of two triangles each, each placed on a separate face. Each corner of the square (or of any primitive) is called a *vertex*. These vertices are then specified to occupy a particular coordinate in 3D space. A vertex is nothing more than a coordinate in 2D or 3D space. Creating solid 3D geometry is little more than a game of *connect-the-dots*! You learn about all the OpenGL primitives and how to use them in Chapter 3, "Basic Rendering."

3D Cartesian Coordinates

Now, we extend our two-dimensional coordinate system into the third dimension and add a depth component. Figure 1.21 shows the Cartesian coordinate system with a new axis, z. The z-axis is perpendicular to both the x- and y-axes. It represents a line drawn perpendicularly from the center of the screen heading toward the viewer. (We have rotated our view of the coordinate system from Figure 1.17 to the left with respect to the y-axis and down and back with respect to the x-axis. If we hadn't, the z-axis would come straight out at you, and you wouldn't see it.) Now, we specify a position in three-dimensional space with three coordinates: x, y, and z. Figure 1.21 shows the point (–4,4,4) for clarification.

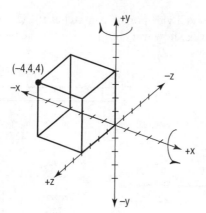

FIGURE 1.21   Cartesian coordinates in three dimensions.

Projections: Getting 3D to 2D

You've seen how to specify a position in 3D space using Cartesian coordinates. No matter how we might convince your eye, however, pixels on a screen have only two dimensions. How does OpenGL translate these Cartesian coordinates into two-dimensional coordinates that can be plotted on a screen? The short answer is "trigonometry and simple matrix manipulation." Simple? Well, not really; we could actually go on for many pages explaining this "simple" technique and lose most of our readers who didn't take or don't remember their linear algebra from college. You learn more about it in Chapter 4, and for a deeper discussion, you can check out the references in Appendix A, "Further Reading." Fortunately, you don't need a deep understanding of the math to use OpenGL to create graphics. You might, however, discover that the deeper your understanding goes, the more powerful a tool OpenGL becomes!

The first concept you really need to understand is called *projection*. The 3D coordinates you use to create geometry are flattened or *projected* onto a 2D surface (the window background). It's like tracing the outlines of some object behind a piece of glass with a black marker. When the object is gone or you move the glass, you can still see the outline of the object with its angular edges. In Figure 1.22, a house in the background is traced onto a flat piece of glass. By specifying the projection, you specify the *viewing volume* that you want displayed in your window and how it should be transformed.

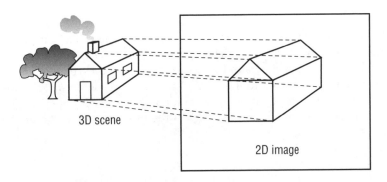

FIGURE 1.22   A 3D image projected onto a 2D surface.

Orthographic Projections

You are mostly concerned with two main types of projections in OpenGL. The first is called an *orthographic*, or parallel, projection. You use this projection by specifying a square or rectangular viewing volume. Anything outside this volume is not drawn. Furthermore, all objects that have the same dimensions appear the same size, regardless of whether they are far away or nearby. This type of projection (shown in Figure 1.23) is most often used in architectural design, computer-aided design (CAD), or 2D graphs. Frequently, you also use an orthographic projection to add text or 2D overlays on top of your 3D graphic scenes.

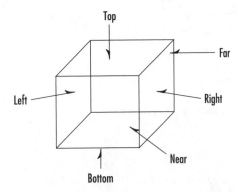

FIGURE 1.23   The clipping volume for an orthographic projection.

You specify the viewing volume in an orthographic projection by specifying the far, near, left, right, top, and bottom clipping planes. Objects and figures that you place within this viewing volume are then projected (taking into account their orientation) to a 2D image that appears on your screen.

Perspective Projections

The second and more common projection is the *perspective projection.* This projection adds the effect that distant objects appear smaller than nearby objects. The viewing volume (see Figure 1.24) is something like a pyramid with the top shaved off. The remaining shape is called the *frustum.* Objects nearer to the front of the viewing volume appear close to their original size, but objects near the back of the volume shrink as they are projected to the front of the volume. This type of projection gives the most realism for simulation and 3D animation.

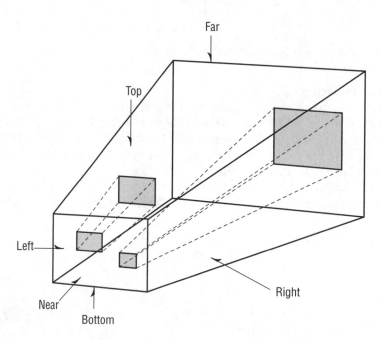

FIGURE 1.24   The clipping volume (frustum) for a perspective projection.

Summary

In this chapter, we introduced the basics of 3D graphics. You saw why you actually need two images of an object from different angles to be able to perceive true three-dimensional space. You also saw the illusion of depth created in a 2D drawing by means of perspective, hidden line removal, coloring, shading, and other techniques. The Cartesian coordinate system was introduced for 2D and 3D drawing, and you learned about two methods used by OpenGL to project three-dimensional drawings onto a two-dimensional screen.

We purposely left out the details of how these effects are actually created by OpenGL. In the chapters that follow, you find out how to employ these techniques and take maximum advantage of OpenGL's power. In the sample code distribution, you'll find one program for this chapter that demonstrates some of the 3D effects covered here. In this program, Block, pressing the spacebar advances you from a wireframe cube to a fully lit and textured block reflected in a glossy surface. You won't understand the code at this point, but it makes a powerful demonstration of what is to come. By the time you finish this book, you will be able to revisit this example and improve on it yourself, or even be able to write it from scratch.

CHAPTER 2

Getting Started

by Richard S. Wright, Jr.

WHAT YOU'LL LEARN IN THIS CHAPTER:

- Where OpenGL came from and where it's going

- How the extension mechanism works and why it's important

- About the core profile and deprecated functionality

- How to detect OpenGL programming errors

- How to pass performance hints to OpenGL

- How to get a basic project up and going in Visual C++ or Xcode

- How to use GLUT for a basic program framework

Now that you have had an introduction to the basic terminology and the ideas behind 3D graphics, it's time to get down to business. Before using OpenGL, we need to talk about what OpenGL is and what it is not so that you have an understanding of both the power and the limits of this Application Programming Interface (API). This chapter is about the "Big Picture" of how OpenGL operates and how to set up the rendering framework for your 3D masterpieces.

What Is OpenGL?

OpenGL is strictly defined as "a software interface to graphics hardware." In essence, it is a 3D graphics and modeling library that is highly portable and very fast. Using OpenGL, you can create elegant and beautiful 3D graphics with exceptional visual quality. The greatest advantage to using OpenGL is that it is orders of magnitude faster than a ray tracer or software rendering engine. Initially, it used algorithms carefully developed and optimized by Silicon Graphics, Inc. (SGI), an acknowledged world leader in computer graphics and animation. Over time, OpenGL has evolved as other vendors have contributed their expertise and intellectual property to develop high-performance implementations of their own.

The OpenGL API itself is not a programming language like C or C++. It is more like the C runtime library, which provides some prepackaged functionality. On the other hand, the OpenGL specification includes GLSL, the OpenGL Shading Language, which actually is a very C-like programming language. GLSL, however, does not control your application's flow and logic, but rather it is intended for rendering operations. At a high level, application programs are not *written in* OpenGL, as much as they *use* OpenGL. There really is no such thing as an "OpenGL program" (with the aforementioned exception of shader programs) but rather a program the developer wrote that "happens" to use OpenGL as one of its Application Programming Interfaces (APIs). You might use the C runtime library to access a file or the Internet, and you might use OpenGL to create real-time 3D graphics.

OpenGL is intended for use with computer hardware that is designed and optimized for the display and manipulation of 3D graphics. Software-only implementations of OpenGL are also possible, and the older Microsoft implementations, and Mesa3D (www.mesa3d.org) fall into this category. Apple also makes a software implementation available on OS X as a fallback mechanism. With these software-only implementations, rendering may not be performed as quickly, and some advanced special effects may not be available at all. However, using a software implementation means that your program can potentially run on a wider variety of computer systems that may not have a full-featured 3D accelerated graphics processor available.

OpenGL is used for various purposes, from CAD engineering and architectural applications to modeling programs used to create computer-generated monsters and machines in blockbuster movies. The introduction of an industry-standard 3D API to mass-market operating systems such as Microsoft Windows and the Macintosh OS X has some exciting repercussions. With hardware acceleration and fast PC microprocessors now common-place, 3D graphics have become standard components of consumer and business applications, not only of games and scientific applications.

Evolution of a Standard

The forerunner of OpenGL was IRIS GL from Silicon Graphics. Originally a 2D graphics library, it evolved into the 3D programming API for that company's high-end IRIS graphics workstations. These computers were more than just general-purpose computers; they had specialized hardware optimized for the display of sophisticated graphics. The hardware provided ultra-fast matrix transformations (a prerequisite for 3D graphics), hardware support for depth buffering, and other features.

Sometimes, however, the evolution of technology is hampered by the need to support legacy systems. IRIS GL had not been designed from the onset to have a vertex-style geometry processing interface, and it became apparent that to move forward SGI needed to make a clean break.

OpenGL is the result of SGI's efforts to evolve and improve IRIS GL's portability. The new graphics API would offer the power of GL but would be an "open" standard, with input from other graphics hardware vendors, and would allow for easier adaptability to other hardware platforms and operating systems. OpenGL would be designed from the ground up for 3D geometry processing.

The OpenGL ARB

An open standard is not really open if only one vendor controls it. SGI's business at the time was high-end computer graphics. Once you're at the top, you find that the opportunities for growth are somewhat limited. SGI realized that it would also be good for the company to do something good for the industry to help grow the market for high-end computer graphics hardware. A truly open standard embraced by a number of vendors would make it easier for programmers to create applications and content that is available for a wider variety of platforms. Software is what really sells computers, and if SGI wanted to sell more computers, it needed more software that would run on its computers. Other vendors realized this, too, and the OpenGL Architecture Review Board (ARB) was born.

Although SGI originally controlled licensing of the OpenGL API, the founding members of the OpenGL ARB were SGI, Digital Equipment Corporation, IBM, Intel, and Microsoft. On July 1, 1992, version 1.0 of the OpenGL specification was introduced. Over time, the ARB grew to consist of many more members, many from the PC hardware community, and it met four times a year to maintain and enhance the specification and to make plans to promote the OpenGL standard.

Over time, SGI's business fortunes declined for reasons well beyond the scope of this book. In 2006, an essentially bankrupt SGI transferred control of the OpenGL standard from the ARB to a new working group at The Khronos Group (www.khronos.org). The Khronos Group is a member-funded industry consortium focused on the creation and maintenance of open media standards. Most ARB members were already members of Khronos, and the transition was essentially painless. Today, the Khronos Group continues to evolve and promote OpenGL and its sibling API, OpenGL ES, which is covered in Chapter 16, "OpenGL ES on Mobile Devices."

OpenGL exists in two forms. The industry standard is codified in the *OpenGL Specification.* The specification describes OpenGL in very complete and specific (the similarity in words here is not an accident!) terms. The API is completely defined, as is the entire state machine and how various features work and operate together. Hardware vendors such as AMD, NVIDIA, Intel, or Apple then take this specification and implement it. This *implementation,* then, is the embodiment of OpenGL in a form that software developers and customers can use to generate real-time graphics. For example, a software driver and a graphics card in your PC together make up an OpenGL implementation.

The OpenGL Extension Mechanism

With OpenGL being a "standard" API, you might think that hardware vendors are able to compete only on the basis of performance and perhaps visual quality. However, the field of 3D graphics is very competitive, and hardware vendors are constantly innovating, not just in the areas of performance and quality, but in graphics methodologies and special effects. OpenGL allows vendor innovation through its extension mechanism. This mechanism works in two ways. First, vendors can add new functions to the OpenGL API that developers can use. Second, new tokens or enumerants can be added that will be recognized by existing OpenGL functions.

Making use of new enumerants or tokens is simply a matter of adding a vendor-supplied header file to your project. Vendors must register their extensions with the OpenGL Working Group (a subset of the Khronos Group), thus keeping one vendor from using a value used by someone else. Conveniently, there is a standard header file glext.h that includes these extensions.

Gone are the days when games would be recompiled for a specific graphics card. You have already seen that you can check for a string identifying the vendor and version of the OpenGL driver. Determining whether an extension is supported is a two-step process. First, you ask OpenGL how many extensions are supported by the current implementation.

```
GLint nNumExtensions;
glGetIntegerv(GL_NUM_EXTENSIONS, &nNumExtensions);
```

Then you can get the name of a specific extension by calling glGetStringi, which returns the name of an individual extension. For example, to check for the swap control extension on Windows, you could loop through all the extensions, looking for the one you want. Once found, you would get the function pointer for that function and call it appropriately.

```
GLint nNum;
glGetIntegerv(GL_NUM_EXTENSIONS, &nNum);

for(GLint i = 0; i< nNum; i++)
  if(strcmp("WGL_EXT_swap_control", (const char *)glGetStringi(GL_EXTENSIONS, i)) ==
0)
  {
  wglSwapIntervalEXT =
      (PFNWGLSWAPINTERVALEXTPROC)wglGetProcAddress("wglSwapIntervalEXT");

  if(wglSwapIntervalEXT != NULL)
    wglSwapIntervalEXT(1);
  }
```

A shortcut toolkit function is included in the GLTools library, which is discussed shortly:

```
int gltIsExtSupported(const char *extension);
```

This function returns 1 if the named extension is supported or 0 if it is not. The GLTools library contains a whole set of helper and utility functions for use with OpenGL, and many are used throughout this book. All the functions are prototyped in the file gltools.h.

This example also shows how to get a pointer to a new OpenGL function under Windows. The windows function wglGetProcAddress returns a pointer to an OpenGL function (extension) name. Getting a pointer to an extension varies from OS to OS; this topic is dealt with in more detail in Part III of this book. Fortunately, 99% of the time you can just use a shortcut library called GLEW as we have and you "auto-magically" get extension function pointers for whatever functionality is supported by the driver.

Whose Extension Is This?

Using OpenGL extensions, you can provide code paths in your code to improve rendering performance and visual quality or even add special effects that are supported only by a particular vendor's hardware. But who owns an extension? That is, which vendor created and supports a given extension? You can usually tell just by looking at the extension name. Each extension has a three-letter prefix that identifies the source of the extension. Table 2.1 provides a sampling of extension identifiers.

TABLE 2.1   A Sampling of OpenGL Extension Prefixes

Prefix	Vendor
SGI_	Silicon Graphics
ATI_	ATI Technologies
AMD_	Advanced Micro Devices
NV_	NVIDIA
IBM_	IBM
WGL_	Microsoft
EXT_	Cross-Vendor
ARB_	ARB Approved

It is not uncommon for one vendor to support another vendor's extension. For example, some NVIDIA extensions are widely popular and supported on ATI hardware. When this happens, the competing vendor must follow the original vendor's specification (details on how the extension is supposed to work). Frequently, everyone agrees that the extension is a good thing to have, and the extension has an EXT_ prefix to show that it is (supposed) to be vendor-neutral and widely supported across implementations.

Finally, we also have ARB-approved extensions. The specification for these extensions has been reviewed (and argued about) by the OpenGL ARB. These extensions usually signal the final step before some new technique or function finds its way into the core OpenGL specification.

Licensing and Conformance

An implementation of OpenGL is either a software library that creates three-dimensional images in response to the OpenGL function calls or a driver for a hardware device (usually a display card) that does the same. Hardware implementations are many times faster than software implementations and are now standard even on the most inexpensive PCs.

A vendor who wants to create and market an OpenGL implementation must first license OpenGL from The Khronos Group. They provide the licensee with a sample implementation (entirely in software) and a device driver kit if the licensee is a PC hardware vendor. The vendor then uses this to create its own optimized implementation and can add value with its own extensions. Competition among vendors typically is based on performance, image quality, and driver stability.

In addition, the vendor's implementation must pass the OpenGL conformance tests. These tests are designed to ensure that an implementation is complete (it contains all the necessary function calls) and produces 3D rendered output that is reasonably acceptable for a given set of functions.

Software developers do not need to license OpenGL or pay any fees to make use of OpenGL drivers. OpenGL is natively supported by most operating systems, and licensed drivers are provided by the hardware vendors themselves.

The Future of OpenGL

Most companies recognize that competition is good for everyone in the long run and will endorse, support, and even contribute to industry standards. The Architecture Review Board under the Khronos Group today is strong, vibrant, and active. Lately, revisions to the OpenGL specification have been rolling out at a rate greater than one per year, and as of this writing, the latest version was OpenGL 3.3 & 4.0, both released at the 2010 Game Developers Conference. For more than 15 years, literally millions of man years have been invested in OpenGL technology, books, tutorials, sample code, and application programs across every category. This momentum will carry OpenGL into the foreseeable future as the API of choice for a wide range of applications and hardware platforms. All this also makes OpenGL well positioned to take advantage of future 3D graphics innovations. With the addition of the OpenGL shading language in version 2.0, OpenGL has shown its continuing adaptability to meet the challenge of an evolving 3D graphics programming pipeline. Finally, OpenGL is a specification that has shown that it can be applied to a wide variety of programming paradigms. From C/C++ to Java and Visual Basic, even newer languages such as C# are now being used to create PC games and applications using OpenGL. OpenGL is here to stay.

OpenGL Versus Direct3D

Like political or religious affiliations, the choice of programming language or API is often based somewhat on reason and somewhat on emotional considerations—"this is how I was raised" or equivalently "this is the API I learned first and I'm most comfortable with it." This is of course the only logical reason anyone would choose Direct3D over OpenGL...ahem.

If you are brand new to the world of 3D graphics programming, you may not be aware that there is a perceived war between OpenGL and Direct3D, two competing standards. This is unfortunate because they are both viable alternatives for anyone doing real-time 3D work, and they both do have their advantages. Unfairly, OpenGL is often compared to DirectX. DirectX is a family of game technology APIs from Microsoft that includes Direct3D, the 3D rendering API that Microsoft promotes for game programming. You might like your hamburger better than my steak, but it is not fair to compare my steak to an entire restaurant! In fact, most Windows games that use OpenGL also make use of the other non-rendering components of DirectX to facilitate sound playback, joystick controls, network play, and so on.

Direct3D is a proprietary standard owned by Microsoft and is used extensively on the Windows platform for games, and variants of Direct3D are used on their XBox gaming console platform and some Windows mobile devices. In the early days of Direct3D, the API was very difficult to use, substantially lacking in features compared to OpenGL, and suffered from some inherent software inefficiencies. Microsoft employed some questionable tactics to help Direct3D become the "standard" for Windows game programming for a few years that are somewhat unaffectionately called "The API Wars." In the minds of many, this war continues. To be fair to Microsoft, they have worked with hardware vendors and software vendors for more than ten years now, and currently Direct3D is a usable and well-documented API that is quite popular among game programmers interested solely in Microsoft platforms.

OpenGL, however, is still quite popular among Windows game developers and is the overwhelming choice for software developers making nongame 3D applications such as the vis-sim industry, content creation tools, scientific visualization, business graphics, and so on. The "emotional" choice between OpenGL and Direct3D usually boils down to liking or disliking Direct3D's object-oriented COM (Component Object Model) methodology, versus OpenGL's state machine abstraction or just an inherent love or hate for Microsoft. On the non-Microsoft platforms, such as the Mac OSX or iPhone, Linux (not just desktop, the majority of handheld smart phone devices use a UNIX variant), or Sony and Nintendo gaming devices, OpenGL or an OpenGL-like API is the de facto standard. When you look at the entire 3D graphics industry as a whole, OpenGL has substantially more presence than does Direct3D.

There are also a few of those "reasons" why you might choose OpenGL over Direct3D as well. For one, OpenGL is cross-platform and portable, and OpenGL drivers exist for nearly every 3D hardware device in existence. If you are interested in games, you should do some market research; the Windows desktop is not the lion's share of the gaming industry. The second reason is that OpenGL is an open standard and benefits from the knowledge and experience of all the leading 3D hardware vendors. These vendors must cooperate on OpenGL to make it attractive and powerful for developers to use. Developers after all make the software that people buy their hardware for. Because OpenGL is a "software interface to graphics hardware," having the hardware vendors involved in the evolution of the spec is essential. This brings us to the last and possibly the "best" reason anyone might choose OpenGL over Direct3D, the extension mechanism.

The extension mechanism allows hardware vendors to compete not just on performance and image quality, but also on true technological innovation. Hardware vendors can add features to their hardware and expose them via OpenGL anytime they want. They do not have to have the ARB's approval, they do not need Microsoft's approval, and they do not have to wait for the next version of OpenGL (or Direct3D) to be released. There is simply no corollary in the Direct3D world. Microsoft decides what goes into the API and to some extent (some would say unfairly) influences the hardware architecture by proxy. The latest, greatest hardware features are always readily available via a vendor's OpenGL driver and the associated extensions. For example, when DirectX 10-capable hardware shipped, Windows users had to use Windows Vista to gain access to games that made use of new DirectX 10 features. However, all of that new functionality was also exposed in OpenGL via the extension mechanism and was available for Windows XP users immediately if their games used OpenGL and of course had the latest hardware and drivers. For many years vendors such as NVIDIA or ATI (now AMD) would showcase their latest hardware innovations with demos written in OpenGL; they simply had too. This alone perpetually keeps OpenGL slightly ahead of Direct3D when it comes to access to the latest and greatest 3D hardware innovations.

Deprecated Functionality

For more than a decade, the OpenGL standard evolved by adding new functionality to each release. New functionality was typically vetted by the extension process whereby features would be added as vendor-specific or joint-vendor extensions, they would be refined and become ARB extensions, and finally they would be included in the core API specification. No functionality was ever removed from OpenGL during this process. This ensured 100% backward compatibility with older code, and as newer hardware became available, existing applications would simply run faster. Developers could also easily gradually update their code to take advantage of newer rendering techniques or new performance enhancing functionality as it was introduced without having to rewrite existing and working code.

Realistically though, this process can only go on for so long. Over time GPU and computer architectures have evolved significantly. Performance trade-offs and engineering compromises that were made 15 years ago no longer apply today. As a result some of the OpenGL API has become somewhat antiquated. Many vendors sought to reduce the size of the OpenGL API for the first time ever by removing features and functionality that were seldom used in modern code, or that performed significantly worse than newer techniques. The ARB decided that OpenGL 3.0 would be the breaking point and for the first time in OpenGL's history some of the "dead weight" of the legacy OpenGL API would be jettisoned from the API. Vendors could continue to support OpenGL 2.1 drivers for legacy code, but newer applications targeted for OpenGL 3.0 or later would have to abandon older API functions and conventions. It seemed like a good idea at the time....

OpenGL 3.0

There is an old saying about the best laid plans of mice and men: They don't always go as planed. The ARB is made up of graphics hardware vendors, and vendors have customers, and customers must be kept happy. Many customers (software developers) saw the model of relegating OpenGL 2.1 drivers to legacy status to mean one thing in reality. That was that those drivers would quickly become a low priority for vendors and would not be as well-maintained or updated for new hardware, and they would be forced to abandon millions of dollars worth of investment in OpenGL. A compromise of sorts was reached, and in OpenGL 3.0, no functionality was actually removed, but rather marked as *deprecated*. Deprecated functionality would still be in the driver, but it served as a notice to software vendors that they should stop using some OpenGL features and migrate to newer and more modern ways of doing things. OpenGL 3.1 we were told would see these features removed... or so we thought.

OpenGL 3.x

OpenGL 3.1 saw a most spectacular feat of hair splitting. One that any oily politician would recognize as truly masterful. Indeed, all deprecated OpenGL functionality was removed from the core OpenGL specification. However, a new OpenGL extension `GL_ARB_compatibility` was introduced. Many software developers who where looking forward to a more streamlined API saw this extension simply as, "plus all the deprecated OpenGL features we promised to remove but didn't." This meant that a hardware vendor could produce an OpenGL 3.1 driver and at least optionally not include any deprecated functionality. This, however, simply did not happen. One of the ARB members, NVIDIA, has publicly stated that it will never remove any old functionality. While developers in some application categories (notably games) have decried this move, objectively what else was NVIDIA, or indeed any other hardware vendor, to do? Should a hardware company ignore its customers and enforce a standard because the company thinks it is in its best interests? We have seen this happen before. It rarely turns out well, and no one wants this sort of ugliness in the OpenGL community.

OpenGL 3.2 refined this business slightly, doing away with the extension and instead dividing OpenGL into a core profile and a compatibility profile. Core profile implementations would be smaller and contain none of the older deprecated functionality. Conformance with the specification required the core functionality but left the compatibility profile as optional.

The reality is that deprecated OpenGL features are far too well understood by the vast majority of developers using OpenGL today. Many may be slower than the newer methods, but they are easier to use and very convenient. Any engineer knows that trade-offs are often made between ease of use and implementation, maintainability, developer proficiency, and of course performance. Performance is not always the overriding concern in every application category. The compatibility profile is likely to be around for a long time.

Nothing But the Core

So, where does that leave us? The previous edition of this book covered OpenGL 2.1, which is the classic OpenGL implementation with the fixed functionality pipeline that allowed the optional use of shaders. The core profile is in its simplest abbreviated form, "just shaders." You must write a shader to do anything. There is no built-in lighting model, no convenient matrix stacks, no simple texture application, and no easy-to-code immediate mode for sending down vertex data. In fact, some of the geometric primitives have even been eliminated. It is no wonder that developers in many quarters are in no hurry to "modernize" their code. To make matters worse, most of the available tutorials and books to date have focused on showing how to move from the fixed pipeline to the shader only way of doing things. This of course means that the easiest path to mastery for a new OpenGL programmer is to start with the fixed functionality and then transition to shaders. This is simply not a productive way to promote the use of the new core profile of OpenGL, and it is not an approach that we use in this book.

Using OpenGL

OpenGL is a procedural rather than a descriptive graphics API. Instead of describing the scene and how it should appear, the programmer actually prescribes the steps necessary to achieve a certain appearance or effect. These "steps" involve calls to the many OpenGL commands. These commands are used to draw graphics primitives such as points, lines, and triangles in three dimensions. In addition, OpenGL supports texture mapping, blending, transparency, animation, and many other special effects and capabilities. Exactly how all of this takes place is covered in more detail in Chapter 3, "Basic Rendering." This chapter's primary concern is how to get your OpenGL projects up and going.

OpenGL does not include any functions for window management, user interaction, or file I/O. Each host environment (such as Mac OS X or Microsoft Windows) has its own functions for this purpose and is responsible for implementing some means of handing over to OpenGL the drawing control of a window. In addition there is no "OpenGL file format" for models or virtual environments. Programmers construct these environments to suit their own high-level needs and then carefully program them using the lower-level OpenGL commands.

Our Supporting Cast

To be useful any computer program must consist of something other than rendering operations. There needs to be a means by which a user can interact with the program either via keyboard, mouse, joystick, or some other input mechanism. In addition, windows must be opened and maintained (on most, but not all operating systems), files found and loaded, and so on. C and C++ are nice portable programming languages available on most platforms today. Programming languages, however, make use of APIs to do a great deal of work in the typical program. OpenGL is one example of an API and is a portable API that is also available on most modern computer platforms. Interfacing with the operating system's means of interacting with the user or managing windows on-screen unfortunately is most often done with nonportable OS-specific APIs.

GLUT

In the beginning, there was AUX, the OpenGL auxiliary library. The AUX library was created to facilitate the learning and writing of OpenGL programs without the programmer being distracted by the minutiae of any particular environment, be it UNIX, Windows, or whatever. You wouldn't write "final" code when using AUX; it was more of a preliminary staging ground for testing your ideas. A lack of basic GUI features limited the library's use for building useful applications.

AUX has since been replaced by the GLUT library for cross-platform programming examples and demonstrations. GLUT stands for *OpenGL utility toolkit* (not to be confused with the standard GLU—OpenGL utility library). Mark Kilgard, while at SGI, wrote GLUT as a more capable replacement for the AUX library and included some GUI features to at least make sample programs more usable under X Windows. This replacement includes using pop-up menus, managing other windows, and even providing joystick support. GLUT is not public domain, but it is free and free to redistribute. GLUT is widely available on most UNIX distributions (including Linux) and is natively supported by Mac OS X, where Apple maintains and extends the library. On Windows, GLUT development has been discontinued. Because GLUT was originally not licensed as open source, a new GLUT implementation, *freeglut,* has sprung up to take its place. All the Windows GLUT-based samples in this book make use of the freeglut library, which is also available on the book's official Web site.

For most of this book, we use GLUT as our program framework. This decision serves two purposes. The first is that it makes most of the book accessible to a wider audience. With a little effort, experienced Windows, Linux, or Mac programmers should be able to set up GLUT for their programming environments and follow most of the examples in this book.

The second point is that using GLUT eliminates the need to know and understand basic GUI programming on any specific platform. Although we explain the general concepts, we do not claim to write a book about GUI programming, but rather about OpenGL. Using GLUT for the basic coverage of the API, we make life a bit easier for Windows/Mac/Linux novices as well.

It's unlikely that all the functionality of a commercial application will be embodied entirely in the code used to draw in 3D. Although GLUT does have some limited GUI functionality, it is very simple and abbreviated as far as GUI toolkits go. Thus you can't rely entirely on the GLUT library for everything. Nevertheless, the GLUT library excels in its role for learning and demonstration exercises and hiding all the platform-specific details of window creation and OpenGL context initialization. Even for an experienced programmer, it is still easier to employ the GLUT library to iron out 3D graphics code before integrating it into a complete application.

GLEW

As mentioned previously, the OpenGL API has grown primarily via the extension mechanism. The extension mechanism can be used to obtain function pointers to any OpenGL function that has been added to the core since OpenGL 1.0. An easy way to obtain full access to the OpenGL 3.3 API is to make use of an extension loading library that automatically initializes all of these new function pointers and includes the needed typedefs, constants, and enumerated values for you. There are more than one of these extension loading libraries to choose from, and one of the most well maintained open source libraries is GLEW, or the OpenGL extension wrangler library. The use of this library to initialize the full OpenGL functionality available via the driver couldn't be much easier. A single C source file and header file need to be added to your project, and a single initialization function is called on program startup. The details of this are covered when we walk through writing our first OpenGL program in just a few pages. To make things even simpler, the GLEW library is prepackaged in the GLTools library. In fact, the GLTools library actually depends on the GLEW library.

GLTools

Every craftsman has a toolbox full of his favorite tools. Programmers are no different. There are useful and reusable functions that all 3D programmers need for just about any OpenGL program they are going to write. GLTools began life in the third edition of this book. Over time it has grown and provides a lot of shortcuts and handy tools, much like the OpenGL utility library (GLU) used to. GLTools includes a 3D math library to manipulate matrices and vectors and relies on GLEW for full OpenGL 3.3 support of functions that generate and render some simple 3D objects and manage your view frustum, camera, and transformation matrices.

OpenGL API Specifics

OpenGL was designed by some clever people who had a lot of experience designing graphics programming APIs. They applied some standard rules to the way functions were named and variables were declared. The API is simple and clean, easy for vendors to extend, and easy for programmers to remember. OpenGL tries to avoid as much *policy* as possible. Policy refers to assumptions that the designers make about how programmers will use the API. This keeps OpenGL flexible, powerful, and expressive. You can literally invent an entirely new method of rendering a special effect or scene just by being clever with the API and shading language.

This philosophy has contributed to the longevity and evolution of OpenGL. Still, as time marches on, unanticipated advances in hardware capabilities and the creativity of developers and hardware vendors have taken their toll on OpenGL as it has progressed through the years. Despite this, OpenGL's basic API has shown surprising resilience to new unanticipated features. The ability to compile ten-year-old source code with little to no changes is a substantial advantage to many application developers, and OpenGL has managed for years to add new features with as little impact on old code as possible. Now, with the core profile, we have a new leaner and more modern OpenGL, and this process can start afresh.

Data Types

To make it easier to port OpenGL code from one platform to another, OpenGL defines its own data types. These data types map to a specific minimal format on all platforms. The various compilers and environments have their own rules for the size and memory layout of various variable types, so by using the OpenGL defined variable types, you can insulate your code from these types of changes in how variables will be represented. Table 2.2 lists the OpenGL data types and their minimum sizes.

TABLE 2.2   OpenGL Variable Types' Corresponding C Data Types

OpenGL Data Type	Minimum Bit Width	Description
GLboolean	1	True or false boolean value
GLbyte	8	Signed 8-bit integer
GLubyte	8	Unsigned 8-bit integer
GLchar	8	String character
GLshort	16	Signed 16-bit integer
GLushort	16	Unsigned 16-bit integer
GLhalf	16	Half precision floating-point value
GLint	32	Signed 32-bit integer
GLuint	32	Unsigned 32-bit integer
GLsizei	32	Unsigned 32-bit integer
GLenum	32	Unsigned 32-bit integer
GLfloat	32	32-bit floating-point number
GLclampf	32	32-bit floating-point number in range [0, 1]
GLbitfield	32	32-bits
GLdouble	64	64-bit double precision number
GLclampd	64	64-bit double precision number in range [0, 1]
GLint64	64	Signed 64-bit integer
GLuint64	64	Unsigned 64-bit integer
GLsizeiptr	native pointer size	Unsigned integer
GLintptr	native pointer	Signed integer
GLsync	native pointer	Sync object handle

All data types start with a GL to denote OpenGL. Most are followed by a familiar sounding C data type (byte, short, int, float, and so on), but you should note that these do not necessarily correspond directly to C data types. The OpenGL specification requires that these data types at a minimum have the storage listed in Table 2.2; however, although values outside some of these ranges are possible, only values within the specified ranges have valid meaning to the OpenGL implementation. Notice that some have a u first to denote an unsigned data type, such as ubyte to denote an unsigned byte. For some uses, a more descriptive name is given, such as size to denote a value of length or depth. For example, GLsizei is an OpenGL variable denoting a size parameter that is represented by an integer. The clamp designation is a hint that the value is expected to be "clamped" to the range 0.0–1.0. The GLboolean variables are used to indicate true and false conditions; GLenum, for enumerated variables; and GLbitfield, for variables that contain binary bit fields, and so on.

Pointers and arrays are not given any special consideration. An array of ten GLshort variables is simply declared as

```
GLshort shorts[10];
```

and an array of ten pointers to GLdouble variables is declared with

```
GLdouble *doubles[10];
```

OpenGL Errors

In any project, you want to write robust and well-behaved programs that respond politely to their users and have some amount of flexibility. Graphical programs that use OpenGL are no exception, and if you want your programs to run smoothly, you need to account for errors and unexpected circumstances. OpenGL provides a useful mechanism for you to perform an occasional sanity check in your code. This capability can be important because, from the code's standpoint, it's not really possible to tell whether the output was the Space Station Freedom or the Space Station Melted Crayons!

Internally, OpenGL maintains a set of four error flags. Each flag represents a different type of error. Whenever one of these errors occurs, the corresponding flag is set. To see whether any of these flags is set, call glGetError:

```
GLenum glGetError(void);
```

The glGetError function returns one of the values listed in Table 2.3. If more than one of these flags is set, glGetError still returns only one distinct value. This value is then cleared, and when glGetError is called again it returns either another error flag or GL_NO_ERROR. Usually, you want to call glGetError in a loop that continues checking for error flags until the return value is GL_NO_ERROR.

TABLE 2.3   OpenGL Error Codes

Error Code	Description
GL_INVALID_ENUM	The enum argument is out of range.
GL_INVALID_VALUE	The numeric argument is out of range.
GL_INVALID_OPERATION	The operation is illegal in its current state.
GL_OUT_OF_MEMORY	Not enough memory is left to execute the command.
GL_NO_ERROR	No error has occurred.

You can take some peace of mind from the assurance that if an error is caused by an invalid call to OpenGL, the command or function call is ignored. The only exceptions to this are any OpenGL functions that take pointers to memory (that may cause a program to crash if the pointer is invalid).

Identifying the Version

As mentioned previously, sometimes you want to take advantage of a known behavior in a particular implementation. If you know for a fact that you are running on a particular vendor's graphics card, you may rely on some known performance characteristics to enhance your program. You may also want to enforce some minimum version number for a particular vendor's drivers. What you need is a way to query OpenGL for the vendor and version number of the rendering engine (the OpenGL driver). The GL library can return version- and vendor-specific information about itself by calling glGetString:

```
const GLubyte *glGetString(GLenum name);
```

This function returns a static string describing the requested aspect of the GL library. The valid parameter values are listed under glGetString in Appendix C, "OpenGL Man Pages for (Core) OpenGL 3.3," along with the aspect of the GL library they represent.

Getting a Clue with glHint

There is more than one way to skin a cat; so goes the old saying. The same is true with 3D graphics algorithms. Often a trade-off must be made for the sake of performance, or perhaps if visual fidelity is the most important issue, performance is less of a considera-tion. Often an OpenGL implementation may contain two ways of performing a given task—a fast way that compromises quality slightly and a slower way that improves visual quality. The function glHint allows you to specify certain preferences of quality or speed for different types of operations. The function is defined as follows:

```
void glHint(GLenum target, GLenum mode);
```

The `target` parameter allows you to specify types of behavior you want to modify. These values, listed under `glHint` in Appendix C, include hints for texture compression quality, antialiasing accuracy, and so on. The `mode` parameter tells OpenGL what you care most about—faster render time and nicest output, for instance—or that you don't care (the only way to get back to the default behavior). Be warned, however, that implementations are not required to honor calls into `glHint`; it's the only function in OpenGL whose behavior is intended to be entirely vendor-specific.

The OpenGL State Machine

Drawing 3D graphics is a complicated affair. In the chapters ahead, we cover many OpenGL functions. For a given piece of geometry, many things can affect how it is drawn. Is the object blended with the background? Are we performing front or back face culling? What, if any, texture is currently bound? The list could go on and on.

We call this collection of variables the *state* of the pipeline. A state machine is an abstract model of a collection of state variables, all of which can have various values or just be turned on or off and so on. It simply is not practical to specify all the state variables whenever we try to draw something in OpenGL. Instead, OpenGL employs a state model or state machine to keep track of all these OpenGL state variables. When a state value is set, it remains set until some other function changes it. Many states are simply on or off. Depth testing for example (see Chapter 3) is either turned on or turned off. Geometry drawn with depth testing turned on is checked to make sure it is in front of any objects behind it before being rendered. Any geometry drawn *after* depth testing is turned back off (a 2D overlay for example) is then drawn without the depth comparison.

To turn these types of state variables on and off, you use the following OpenGL function:

```
void glEnable(GLenum capability);
```

You turn the variable back off with the corresponding opposite function:

```
void glDisable(GLenum capability);
```

For the case of depth testing, for instance, you can turn it on by using the following:

```
glEnable(GL_DEPTH_TEST);
```

And you turn it back off with this function:

```
glDisable(GL_DEPTH_TEST);
```

If you want to test a state variable to see whether it is enabled, OpenGL again has a convenient mechanism:

```
GLboolean glIsEnabled(GLenum capability);
```

Not all state variables, however, are simply on or off. Many of the OpenGL functions yet to come set up values that "stick" until changed. You can query what these values are at any time as well. A set of query functions allows you to query the values of Booleans, integers, floats, and double variables. These four functions are prototyped thus:

```
void glGetBooleanv(GLenum pname, GLboolean *params);
void glGetDoublev(GLenum pname, GLdouble *params);
void glGetFloatv(GLenum pname, GLfloat *params);
void glGetIntegerv(GLenum pname, GLint *params);
```

Each function returns a single value or a whole array of values, storing the results at the address you supply. The various parameters are documented in the reference section in Appendix C (there are a lot of them!). Most may not make much sense to you right away, but as you progress through the book, you will begin to appreciate the power and simplicity of the OpenGL state machine.

Setting Up Windows Projects

There are many options for building programs on Microsoft Windows. For this book, we use Visual C++ 2008, Express Edition. This compiler is available from Microsoft for free and can be downloaded from http://www.microsoft.com/exPress/. The projects created with this edition of Visual Studio should also work with later versions of this development environment.

As mentioned previously, all our projects in this book depend on GLEW, GLTools, and, on Windows, the freeglut utility libraries. GLEW is "built-in" to GLTools because GLTools requires GLEW in order to get to OpenGL 3.0 or later features. freeglut, however, is a stand-alone library and may be used in conjunction with other OpenGL libraries or not at all if you want to use the native system services (see Chapters 13 through 16). The first order of business before starting your first new project, or rebuilding any of the projects included with this book, is to add these libraries' include folders to Visual Studio's include search path. You need to do this anytime you add a new SDK or library to your programming repertoire. If you've never done this before, relax; it's a piece of cake, and you only have to do this once, not each time you set up a new project.

Including Paths

Open Visual C++ and from the main menu select Tools and then Options from the bottom of the drop-down menu. The Options dialog is shown in Figure 2.1. Expand the Projects and Solutions tree item and select VC++ Directories; then make sure Show Directories For is set to Include Files.

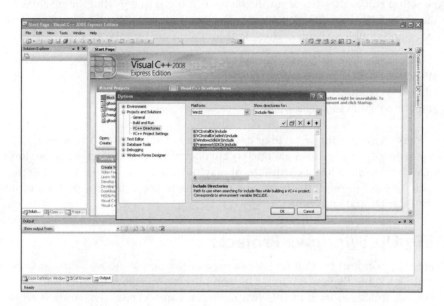

FIGURE 2.1   Adding a path to be searched for include files.

The list below this combo box shows all the folders that will be searched when you include a header file in your source code. You need to add the include path for GLTools and for freeglut. Do this by selecting the last empty line in the list. Click this line twice, and it becomes an edit field with a browse button to the right as shown in Figure 2.2.

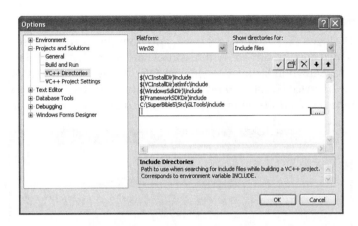

FIGURE 2.2   Type or browse for the search path to be added.

Click the Browse button, and a file browser dialog is displayed. Navigate to the GLTools include folder and select it as shown in Figure 2.3. Make sure you select the /include folder and not the GL folder beneath it. Do the same for the freeglut library. Now, Visual C++ is configured for finding the GLTools and the freeglut libraries. Time to build our first project!

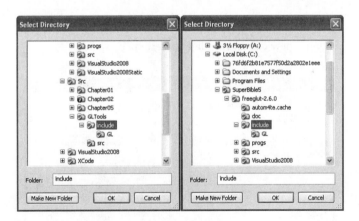

FIGURE 2.3   Selecting the include directories.

Creating the Project

Open Visual C++ if you don't still have it open, and from the main menu select File, New Project. GLUT-based applications are Win32 console mode applications, so make the appropriate selections as shown in Figure 2.4, and click OK. On the following dialog prompt shown in Figure 2.5, select Empty Project. This prevents Visual C++ from creating what it considers a standard console-based project and allows us to create our own from scratch.

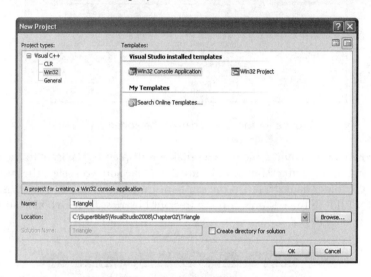

FIGURE 2.4   Creating a new console mode application.

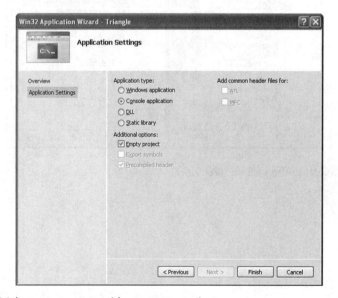

FIGURE 2.5   Make sure you start with an empty project.

Adding Our Files

Now it's time to create our main source file. For this project, we create a C++ file called triangle.cpp. Do this by selecting File, New, and select File again from the main menu. Select a new C++ file as shown in Figure 2.6.

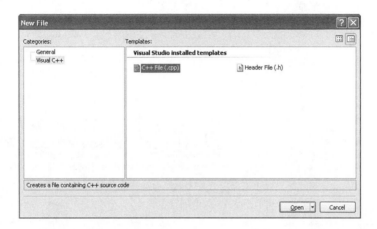

FIGURE 2.6   Adding a new C++ source file.

As you can see in Figure 2.7 the source file is unnamed (the comments were added manually). Save the file as Triangle.cpp. This still does not add the file to our project, however. To do this, right-click the Source Files folder in the Solution Explorer window. Select Add, Existing Item, and then navigate the file system until you've located the Triangle.cpp source file.

We are almost there now. Finally, we need to add the GLTools and freeglut libraries to our project. There is more than one way to add a library to our project, and we use the simplest and easiest to verify visually. Right-click the project name and select Add, Existing Item just like you did for the Triangle.cpp file. This time, however, navigate to the /Freeglut-2.6.0/VisualStudio2008Static/Release folder and select freeglut_static.lib as shown in Figure 2.8.

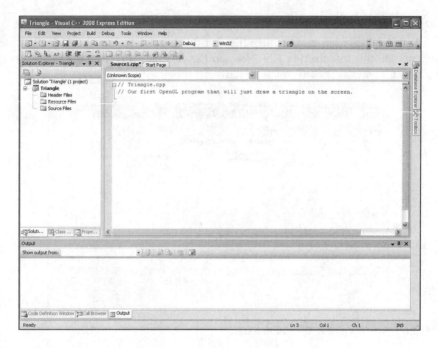

FIGURE 2.7 Our empty unnamed source file.

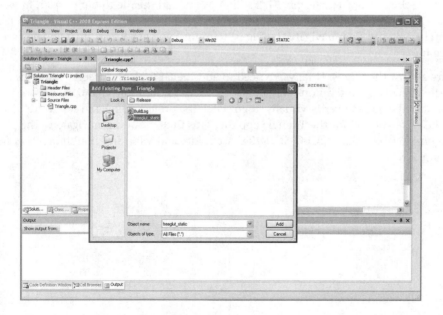

FIGURE 2.8 Select the freeglut_static library and add it to the project.

Do the same for the GLTools library, which is located in the /VisualStudio2008/GLTools/Release folder. Figure 2.9 shows our completed project all ready for us to start our first OpenGL program!

FIGURE 2.9   Our completed Visual C++ project.

Setting Up Mac OS X Projects

Xcode is the Integrated Development Environment (IDE) provided by Apple for developing Mac OS X applications. Xcode is free and can be found on your OS X installation DVD or from the http://developer.apple.com Web site. Xcode projects have been set up for all the example programs in this book. As mentioned previously, all the OpenGL examples in this book use two utility libraries, GLUT and GLTools. The GLUT library ships as a standard framework on OS X, and Xcode knows how to use GLUT without any special settings other than adding the framework to your project. GLTools, however, is a third-party library (included with this book), and you need to configure Xcode to use this library for the projects in this book or for your own fresh projects that you want to create based on this library.

Custom Build Settings

At a minimum, you must tell Xcode where the GLTools headers are located for the projects included with this book to compile (note, prebuilt 32/64-bit binaries for Snow Leopard are also included in the Mac OS X source distribution). We do this by adding a custom setting to the Xcode Source Trees preference setting. This dialog can be accessed from the Xcode/Preferences menu and is shown in Figure 2.10. The setting that must be added is GLTOOLS_INCLUDE, which is the path to the GLTools include files. Note that if you are using a version of OS X earlier than 10.6, you will also have to rebuild this library yourself or include the GLTools source files in all your projects. Settings can be added by clicking the + button and typing directly into the table shown on the dialog. You can also drag a folder from finder and drop it on this edit control. In this case, the SuperBible files are located on the Desktop, but you may want to put them somewhere else as suits your own organizational style. If you move these files, though, you need to update this path variable.

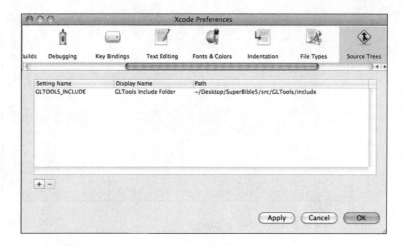

FIGURE 2.10   Adding a custom setting to Xcode.

Creating a New Project

This should be sufficient to get the included Xcode project files to work should you want to build the samples yourself or make changes to them as part of your experimentation while you learn. Let's walk though creating a brand new project. The first step is to select File, New Project from the main Xcode menu. This displays the dialog shown in Figure 2.11. On the right you see any recent projects you may have been working on, and in Figure 2.11 you can see some things the author has worked on recently at the time of this writing. On the left you see Create a New Xcode Project. Click that button to create your first project.

FIGURE 2.11   Starting a new project with Xcode.

Next click the Cocoa Application icon from the list of Mac OS X project templates as shown in Figure 2.12. Although we will be using C++, GLUT, the basic program framework, is actually implemented using Cocoa, and this is the simplest way to start.

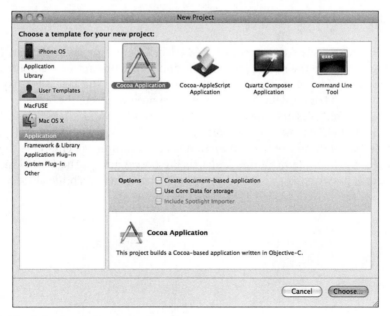

FIGURE 2.12   Selecting a Cocoa Application.

In our example, we called our project "Triangle." This is going to be our first example program. On the left-hand side of our Xcode project window you see the Overview pane, and we expanded some of the groups so that you can see the project's structure. This is shown in Figure 2.13.

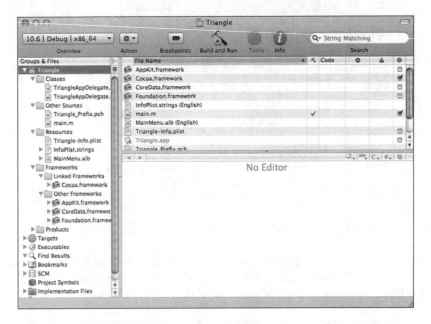

FIGURE 2.13   Our fresh Cocoa application.

The Xcode project template is not ready for GLUT or OpenGL programming at this time. We are going to remove the starter project code and start with our own simplified GLUT-based program. For a more in-depth look at using OpenGL on the Mac, see Chapter 14, "OpenGL on OS X." For our GLUT-based project we need to delete the TriangleAppDelegate.* files and the main.m file. You can highlight these files in Xcode by clicking once on the filename and then pressing the Delete key. Go ahead and click the Also Move to Trash button in the confirmation sheet to completely eliminate the files. You can also delete the MainMenu.xib file under the Resources group. The final cleaned up Xcode project is shown in Figure 2.14. Leave the Triangle_Prefix.pch file alone.

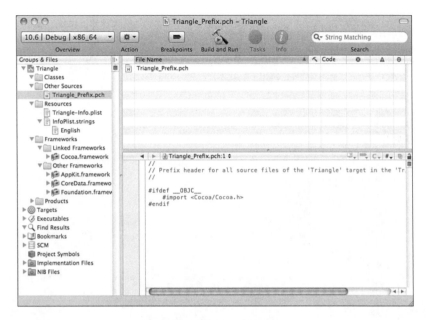

FIGURE 2.14   Our project with the default code removed.

Frameworks, Headers, and Libraries

Next we need to add the GLUT and OpenGL frameworks to our project. Right-click the Frameworks folder group and select Add, Existing Framework. Select the GLUT and OpenGL frameworks in the next dialog. The appearance of this dialog changes from time to time, but regardless you should see a list of available frameworks. Click one to highlight it and hold the command key down to click and select multiple frameworks. For our project, we only need GLUT and OpenGL.

Finally, we need to add the GLTools library. GLTools is a static library instead of a framework, and we need to add this in a different manner. There is more than one way to do this, and I am quite sure some people are going to write in to tell me their way is better. If you don't know how to do this yet, then you will probably like my way better than yours!

First we must add the GLTools header path to our header search paths setting. Do this by right-clicking the project name under Groups & Files and select Get Info. Make sure the Configuration setting is set to All Configurations as shown in Figure 2.15. Scroll down to the Search Paths grouping and click in the Header Search Paths field. Type in $(GLTOOLS_INCLUDE). When you press Enter or change fields, it automatically expands to the value we set for this variable previously.

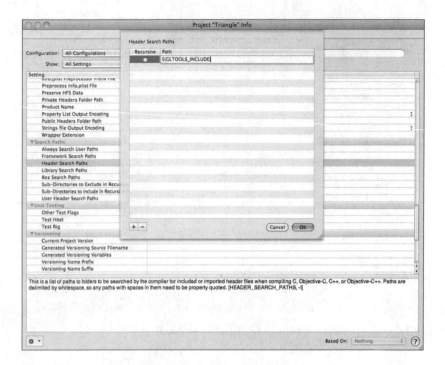

FIGURE 2.15   Adding the GLTools include path to the project.

Finally, we need to add the GLTools.a library file to the project. You can do this by drag-ging the GLTools.a file (located in /XCode/GLTools folder in the book source code files) and dropping it on the Frameworks folder in Xcode. You can also right-click Frameworks and select Add, Existing Files and then navigate to and select the GLTools.a file manually. Drag and drop is typically so much easier!

That's all there is to getting your Xcode project ready to go. All we need to do now is add a C++ source file and start coding! Right-click the Other Sources folder and select Add, New File. This presents the dialog shown in Figure 2.16.

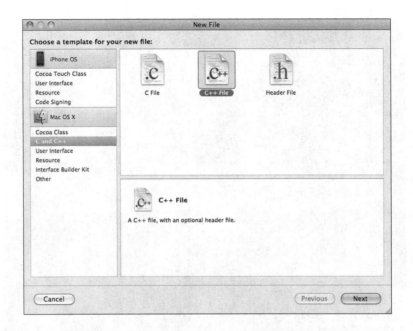

FIGURE 2.16   Adding a new C++ source file to our project.

Select C++ File as shown, and in the following dialog name and save your program file as
Triangle.cpp. Go ahead and uncheck the Also Create Triangle.h as we don't need a header
for our main program file as we aren't really creating a C++ class. To build a project in
Xcode press command-B, and to build and run your project press command-R. Of course,
so far we have no source code at all. Let's get started with our first OpenGL program!

Your First Triangle

Now that we have laid the groundwork, it is finally time to start coding! Our first example
program simply draws a red triangle on a blue background. This may not seem very ambi-
tious at first, but it covers all the necessary steps and creates a complete demonstration
framework that we can use for the rest of the book. You get a tour of GLUT and use your
first GLTools helper functions and classes along the way. Figure 2.17 shows the output of
our Triangle program, and Listing 2.1 lists our first program in its entirety. We then dissect
it line by line.

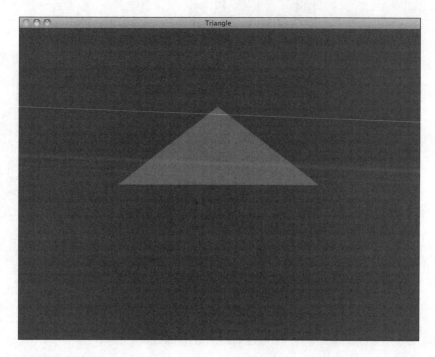

FIGURE 2.17   The output of our first OpenGL program.

LISTING 2.1   Simply Draw a Triangle

```
// Triangle.cpp
// Our first OpenGL program that will just draw a triangle on the screen.

#include <GLTools.h>        // OpenGL toolkit
#include <GLShaderManager.h>  // Shader Manager Class

#ifdef __APPLE__
#include <glut/glut.h>       // OS X version of GLUT
#else
#define FREEGLUT_STATIC
#include <GL/glut.h>         // Windows FreeGlut equivalent
#endif

GLBatch        triangleBatch;
GLShaderManager  shaderManager;


///////////////////////////////////////////////////////////////////////////////
```

```
// Window has changed size, or has just been created. In either case, we need
// to use the window dimensions to set the viewport and the projection matrix.
void ChangeSize(int w, int h)
  {
  glViewport(0, 0, w, h);
  }


/////////////////////////////////////////////////////////////////////////////
// This function does any needed initialization on the rendering context.
// This is the first opportunity to do any OpenGL related tasks.
void SetupRC()
  {
  // Blue background
  glClearColor(0.0f, 0.0f, 1.0f, 1.0f );

  shaderManager.InitializeStockShaders();

  // Load up a triangle
  GLfloat vVerts[] = { -0.5f, 0.0f, 0.0f,
            0.5f, 0.0f, 0.0f,
            0.0f, 0.5f, 0.0f };

  triangleBatch.Begin(GL_TRIANGLES, 3);
  triangleBatch.CopyVertexData3f(vVerts);
  triangleBatch.End();
  }


/////////////////////////////////////////////////////////////////////////////
// Called to draw scene
void RenderScene(void)
  {
  // Clear the window with current clearing color
  glClear(GL_COLOR_BUFFER_BIT | GL_DEPTH_BUFFER_BIT | GL_STENCIL_BUFFER_BIT);

  GLfloat vRed[] = { 1.0f, 0.0f, 0.0f, 1.0f };
  shaderManager.UseStockShader(GLT_SHADER_IDENTITY, vRed);
  triangleBatch.Draw();

  // Perform the buffer swap to display the back buffer
  glutSwapBuffers();
  }
```

```
/////////////////////////////////////////////////////////////////////////////
// Main entry point for GLUT based programs
int main(int argc, char* argv[])
  {
  gltSetWorkingDirectory(argv[0]);

  glutInit(&argc, argv);
  glutInitDisplayMode(GLUT_DOUBLE | GLUT_RGBA | GLUT_DEPTH | GLUT_STENCIL);
  glutInitWindowSize(800, 600);
  glutCreateWindow("Triangle");
  glutReshapeFunc(ChangeSize);
  glutDisplayFunc(RenderScene);

  GLenum err = glewInit();
  if (GLEW_OK != err) {
    fprintf(stderr, "GLEW Error: %s\n", glewGetErrorString(err));
    return 1;
    }

  SetupRC();

  glutMainLoop();
  return 0;
  }
```

What to "Include"

To begin any C++ (or even just C) program, we need to include the headers that contain the function and class definitions that we will use in our program. For our purposes, the bare minimum will be the following headers.

```
#include <GLTools.h>         // OpenGL toolkit
#include <GLShaderManager.h>    // Shader Manager Class

#ifdef __APPLE__
#include <glut/glut.h>       // OS X version of GLUT
#else
#define FREEGLUT_STATIC
#include <GL/glut.h>         // Windows/Linux FreeGlut equivalent
#endif
```

The GLTools.h header contains the bulk of the GLTools C-like stand-alone functions, while the GLTools C++ classes each have their own header file. GLShaderManager.h brings in the GLTools shader manager class. You cannot render in OpenGL (core profile) without a shader. The shader manager not only allows you to build and manage your own shaders, it comes with a set of "stock shaders" that perform a few rudimentary and basic rendering operations. We go into more detail about this in Chapter 3.

GLUT gets a different treatment depending on whether you are building on a Mac. On Windows and Linux, we use the static library version of freeglut and thus need the FREEGLUT_STATIC preprocessor macro defined ahead of it.

Starting GLUT

Next, we skip down to the last function in the listing, the entry point of all C programs, which is where program execution actually starts:

```
/////////////////////////////////////////////////////////////////
// Main entry point for GLUT based programs
int main(int argc, char* argv[])
    {
    gltSetWorkingDirectory(argv[0]);
```

Console-mode C and C++ programs always start execution with the function main. If you're an experienced Windows nerd, you might wonder where WinMain is in this example. It's not there because we start with a console-mode application, so we don't have to start with window creation and a message loop. With Win32, you can create graphical windows from console applications, just as you can create console windows from GUI applications. These details are buried within the GLUT library. (Remember, the GLUT library is designed to hide just these kinds of platform details.)

The GLTools function gltSetWorkingDirectory sets the current working directory. This is actually not necessary on Windows, as the working directory is by default the same directory as the program executable. On Mac OS X, however, this function changes the current working folder to be the /Resources folder inside the application bundle. A GLUT preferences setting does this automatically, but this method is safer and always works, even if that setting is changed by another program. This comes in handy later when we want to load texture files or model data.

Next, we do some standard GLUT-based setup. The first order of business is a call to glutInit, which simply passes along the command-line parameters and initializes the GLUT library.

```
glutInit(&argc, argv);
```

Next, we must tell the GLUT library what type of display mode to use when creating the window:

```
glutInitDisplayMode(GLUT_DOUBLE | GLUT_RGBA | GLUT_DEPTH | GLUT_STENCIL);
```

The flags here tell it to use a double-buffered window (`GLUT_DOUBLE`) and to use RGBA color mode (`GLUT_RGBA`). A double-buffered window means the drawing commands are actually executed on an off-screen buffer and then quickly swapped into view on the window later. This method is often used to produce animation effects and is demonstrated later in this chapter. The `GLUT_DEPTH` bit flag allocates a depth buffer as part of our display so we can perform depth testing, and likewise `GLUT_STENCIL` makes sure we also have a stencil buffer available. Both the depth and stencil tests are covered later.

Next, we tell GLUT how big to make the window and to go ahead and create the window, with a caption that reads, "Triangle":

```
glutInitWindowSize(800, 600);
glutCreateWindow("Triangle");
```

Internally GLUT runs a system native message loop, intercepts the appropriate messages, and then calls callback functions you register for different events. This is somewhat limited compared to using a real system-specific framework, but it greatly simplifies getting a program up and running, and the minimal events are supported for a demo framework. Here, we must set a callback function for when the window changes size so that we can set up the viewport, and we register a function that will contain our OpenGL rendering code.

```
glutReshapeFunc(ChangeSize);
glutDisplayFunc(RenderScene);
```

The `ChangeSize` and `RenderScene` functions are described in just a bit, but before we start the main message loop running, there are still two things we need to take care of. The first is to initialize the GLEW library. Recall the GLEW library initializes all the missing entry points in our OpenGL driver to make sure we have the full OpenGL API available to us. A call to `glewInit` does the trick, and we check to make sure nothing goes wrong with the driver initialization before we try and do any rendering.

```
GLenum err = glewInit();
if (GLEW_OK != err) {
  fprintf(stderr, "GLEW Error: %s\n", glewGetErrorString(err));
  return 1;
  }
```

The final piece of preparation is the call `SetupRC`.

```
SetupRC();
```

This function has nothing to do with GLUT actually but is a convenient place to do any OpenGL initialization we need performed before the actual rendering begins. The RC stands for rendering context, which is the logical handle to a running OpenGL state machine. A rendering context must be created before any OpenGL function will work, and GLUT sets this up for us when we first create the window. The OS-specific chapters (Chapters 13 through 16) delve into more detail about this. Throughout the book, this is where we preload textures, set up geometry, shaders, and so on.

Finally, it's time to start the main program loop and end the main function.

```
glutMainLoop();
return 0;
}
```

The `glutMainLoop` function never returns after it is called until the main window is closed and needs to be called only once from an application. This function processes all the operating system-specific messages, keystrokes, and so on until you terminate the program. It also makes sure those callback functions we registered earlier are called appropriately.

Coordinate System Basics

In nearly all windowing environments, the user can at any time change the size and dimensions of the window. Even if you are writing a game that always runs in full-screen mode, the window is still considered to change size at least once—when it is created. When this happens, the window usually responds by redrawing its contents, taking into consideration the window's new dimensions. Sometimes, you might want to simply clip the drawing for smaller windows or display the entire drawing at its original size in a larger window. For our purposes, we usually want to scale the drawing to fit within the window, regardless of the size of the drawing or window. Thus, a very small window would have a complete but very small drawing, and a larger window would have a similar but larger drawing.

In Chapter 1, "Introduction to 3D Graphics and OpenGL," we discussed how the viewport and viewing volume affect the coordinate range and scaling of 2D and 3D drawings in a 2D window on the computer screen. Now, we examine the setting of viewport and clipping volume coordinates in OpenGL. Setting up your coordinate system is a bit of a prerequisite to drawing objects and getting them on-screen where you want them!

Although our drawing is a 2D flat triangle, we are actually drawing in a 3D coordinate space. For this chapter, we are going to use the default Cartesian coordinate system, which stretches from -1 to +1 in the X, Y, and Z directions. X is the horizontal axis, Y is the vertical axis, and positive Z comes out of the screen toward you. The coordinate (0, 0, 0) then is in the center of the screen. In Chapter 4, "Basic Transformations: A Vector/Matrix Primer," we go into more detail about setting up alternative coordinate systems. For our purposes, we draw the triangle in the xy plane at z = 0. Your perspective is along the positive z-axis to see the triangle at z = 0. If you're feeling lost here, review this material in Chapter 1.

Figure 2.18 shows how this basic Cartesian coordinate system looks. Many drawing and graphics libraries use window coordinates (pixels) for drawing commands. Using a real floating-point (and seemingly arbitrary) coordinate system for rendering is one of the hardest things for many beginners to get used to. After you work through a few programs, though, it quickly becomes second nature.

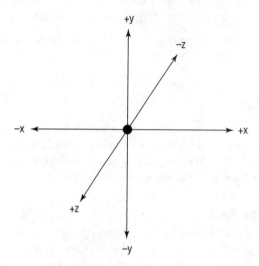

FIGURE 2.18   Cartesian space.

Defining the Viewport

Because window size changes are detected and handled differently under various environments, the GLUT library provides the function glutReshapeFunc, which registers a callback that the GLUT library calls whenever the window dimensions change. The function you pass to glutReshapeFunc is prototyped like this:

```
void ChangeSize(GLsizei w, GLsizei h);
```

We chose ChangeSize as a descriptive name for this function, and we will use that name for our future examples.

```
void ChangeSize(int w, int h)
  {
  glViewport(0, 0, w, h);
  }
```

The ChangeSize function receives the new width and height whenever the window size changes. We can use this information to modify the mapping of our desired coordinate system to real screen coordinates, with the help of the OpenGL function glViewport. To understand how the viewport definition is achieved, let's look more carefully at the `ChangeSize` function where it calls `glViewport` with the new width and height of the window. The `glViewport` function is defined as

```
void glViewport(GLint x, GLint y, GLsizei width, GLsizei height);
```

The x and y parameters specify the lower-left corner of the viewport within the window, and the width and height parameters specify these dimensions in pixels. Usually, x and y are both 0, but you can use viewports to render more than one drawing in different areas of a window. The viewport defines the area within the window in actual screen coordinates that OpenGL can use to draw in (see Figure 2.19). The current clipping volume/coordinate system is then mapped to the new viewport. If you specify a viewport that is smaller than the window coordinates, the rendering is scaled smaller, as you see in Figure 2.19.

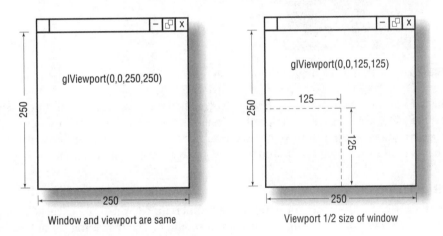

FIGURE 2.19   Viewport-to-window mapping.

Cartesian Coordinates to Pixels

OpenGL takes care of the mapping between Cartesian coordinates and window pixels when it comes time to rasterize (actually draw) your geometry on-screen. One thing you need to keep in mind is that changing the viewport does not change the underlying coordinate system. Because we are using the default -1 to +1 mapping, changing the window size for our triangle has some interesting results, which you can see in Figure 2.20.

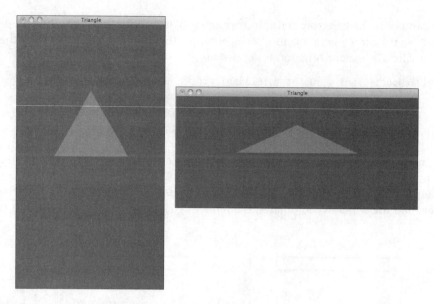

FIGURE 2.20   Clipping volume (coordinate system) and viewport independence.

On the left you can see how the +/- 1 range is stretched more vertically than horizontally, and on the right, you can see the opposite effect. We need to cover some more ground before getting tangled up in how to change your coordinate system in response to window size changes, and we do so very thoroughly in Chapter 4 as promised earlier.

Setting Things Up

Before starting the GLUT main loop in the main function, we called the SetupRC function. This is where we do some one-time setup for our program. The first thing we did was set the background color with this call:

```
glClearColor(0.0f, 0.0f, 1.0f, 1.0f );
```

This function sets the color used for clearing the window. The prototype for this function is

```
void glClearColor(GLclampf red, GLclampf green, GLclampf blue, GLclampf alpha);
```

GLclampf is defined as a float under most implementations of OpenGL. Each parameter contains the weight of that color component in the final color desired. This function does not clear the background right away, but rather sets the color that will be used when the color buffer is cleared (possibly repeatedly) later.

RGB Color Space

In OpenGL, a single color is represented as a mixture of red, green, blue, and alpha (used for transparency) components. The range for each component can vary from 0.0 to 1.0. This is similar to the Windows specification of colors using the RGB macro to create a COLORREF value. The difference is that in Windows each color component in a COLORREF can range from 0 to 255, giving a total of 256x256x256—or more than 16 million colors. With OpenGL, the values for each component can be any valid floating-point value between 0 and 1, thus yielding a virtually infinite number of potential colors. Practically speaking, color output is limited on most devices to 24 bits (16 million colors) total.

Naturally, OpenGL takes this color value and converts it internally to the nearest possible exact match with the available video hardware. Table 2.4 lists some example colors and their component values.

TABLE 2.4   Some Common Composite Colors

Composite Color	Red Component	Green Component	Blue Component
Black	0.0	0.0	0.0
Red	1.0	0.0	0.0
Green	0.0	1.0	0.0
Yellow	1.0	1.0	0.0
Blue	0.0	0.0	1.0
Magenta	1.0	0.0	1.0
Cyan	0.0	1.0	1.0
Dark gray	0.25	0.25	0.25
Light gray	0.75	0.75	0.75
Brown	0.60	0.40	0.12
Pumpkin orange	0.98	0.625	0.12
Pastel pink	0.98	0.04	0.7
Barney purple	0.60	0.40	0.70
White	1.0	1.0	1.0

The last argument to glClearColor is the alpha component, which is used for blending and special effects such as transparency. Transparency refers to an object's capability to allow light to pass through it. Suppose you want to create a piece of red stained glass, and a blue light happens to be shining behind it. The blue light affects the appearance of the red in the glass (blue + red = purple). You can use the alpha component value to generate a red color that is semitransparent so that it works like a sheet of glass—an object behind it shows through. There is more to this type of effect than just using the alpha value, and we demonstrate how this works in Chapter 3. Until then, you should leave the alpha value as 1.

Stock Shaders

Nothing can be rendered in the OpenGL core profile without a shader. In Chapter 6, "Thinking Outside the Box: Nonstock Shaders," we talk about how to write your own shaders, as well as how to compile and link them for use. Until then, we make use of a number of simple stock shaders that are managed by the shader manager. We declared an instance of the shader manager at the top of the source file like this:

```
GLShaderManager   shaderManager;
```

We also go over these stock shaders and how to use them in Chapter 3. The shader manager needs to compile and link its own shaders, though, so we must call the InitializeStockShaders method as part of our OpenGL initialization.

```
shaderManager.InitializeStockShaders();
```

Specifying Vertices

The next thing we do is set up our triangle. In OpenGL a triangle is a type of "primitive," a basic 3D drawing element. We go into great detail about all seven of the different primitives you can use in OpenGL in Chapter 3. For now, just know that a triangle primitive is a list of vertices or points in space that make up a triangle. We specify the vertices by putting them in a single floating-point array. This array, named vVerts, contains the x, y, and z pair of all three vertices in Cartesian coordinates. Note how we made the z coordinate zero for all three points.

```
// Load up a triangle
GLfloat vVerts[] = { -0.5f, 0.0f, 0.0f,
           0.5f, 0.0f, 0.0f,
           0.0f, 0.5f, 0.0f };
```

Submitting a batch of vertices for rending is covered in not one, but two chapters: Chapter 3, "Basic Rendering," and in more lower level detail again in Chapter 12, "Advanced Geometry Management." A simple GLTool wrapper class encapsulates our batch of triangles, and we declared an instance of this GLBatch class near the top of the source file.

```
GLBatch   triangleBatch;
```

In our setup function, the following code builds a batch of triangles containing just three vertices. We talk more about how this works in Chapter 3.

```
triangleBatch.Begin(GL_TRIANGLES, 3);
triangleBatch.CopyVertexData3f(vVerts);
triangleBatch.End();
```

2

Getting Down to Business

Finally, it's time to actually do the rendering! Previously we set the clear color to blue; now we need to execute a function to do the actual clearing:

```
glClear(GL_COLOR_BUFFER_BIT | GL_DEPTH_BUFFER_BIT | GL_STENCIL_BUFFER_BIT);
```

The glClear function clears a particular buffer or combination of buffers. A buffer is a storage area for image information. The red, green, blue, and alpha components of a drawing are usually collectively referred to as the *color buffer* or *pixel buffer*.

More than one kind of buffer (color, depth, and stencil) is available in OpenGL, and these buffers are covered in more detail later in the book. In the preceding example, we use the bitwise OR operator to simultaneously clear all three of these buffers. For the next few chapters, all you really need to understand is that the color buffer is the place where the displayed image is stored internally and that clearing the buffer with glClear removes the last drawing from the window. You will also see the term *framebuffer*, which refers to all these buffers collectively given that they work in tandem.

The next three lines of code are where the real action takes place and are the subject of most of the entire next chapter! We set up an array of floating-point numbers to represent the color red (with an alpha of 1.0), and pass this to a stock shader, the GLT_SHADER_IDENTITY shader. This shader does nothing but render geometry on-screen in the default Cartesian coordinate system, using the color specified.

```
GLfloat vRed[] = { 1.0f, 0.0f, 0.0f, 1.0f };
shaderManager.UseStockShader(GLT_SHADER_IDENTITY, vRed);
triangleBatch.Draw();
```

The GLBatch method Draw simply submits the geometry to the shader and ta-da!—red triangle...well, almost. There is one last detail. When we set up our OpenGL window, we specified that we wanted a double buffered rendering context. This means rendering occurs on a back buffer and then is swapped to the front when we are done. This prevents the viewer from seeing the scene being rendered, along with a likely flickering between animation frames. Buffer swaps are done in a platform-specific manner, but GLUT has a single function call that does this for you:

```
glutSwapBuffers();
```

Now, you may take a bow. You have rendered your first triangle with OpenGL.

Putting a Little Life into It!

We have now seen how to put GLUT to work doing the most important thing a graphical demo framework can do, which is to render something on the screen. For a little extra utility, we also want to have a way for the user to interact with a rendering, perhaps by pressing the arrow keys. A little animation can liven up just about any graphics demo. The example program Move does just this. It draws a square in the middle of the window (actually, we use another one of those primitives, this time a `GL_TRIANGLE_FAN`), and in response to the arrow keys it moves the square up and down or side to side. We leave it to you to figure out which of those two types of movement the up and down arrow keys achieve.

Special Keys

GLUT supports another callback function, called `glutSpecialFunc`. This function registers a function that is called whenever a special key is pressed. In GLUT parlance, this is one of the function keys or one of the directional keys (arrow keys, page up/down, and so on). The following line is added to our main function to register the `SpecialKeys` callback function for this purpose.

```
glutSpecialFunc(SpecialKeys);
```

The `SpecialKeys` function is defined like this:

```
void SpecialKeys(int key, int x, int y)
```

It receives a keycode for the key being pressed, and also the x and y location (in pixels) of the mouse cursor in case that is also useful.

For the Move example program, we store the vertices in an array that is global to the scope of the module so that we can modify the blocks position when the keys are pressed. Listing 2.2 shows the complete code for the `SpecialKeys` function, where we also do collision detection with the edge of the window so that the block cannot be moved outside the window. Notice we can easily update our batch positions by copying in the new vertex data.

```
squareBatch.CopyVertexData3f(vVerts);
```

LISTING 2.2   Handling the Arrow Keys to Move Our Block Around on the Screen

```
// Respond to arrow keys by moving the camera frame of reference
void SpecialKeys(int key, int x, int y)
  {
  GLfloat stepSize = 0.025f;

  GLfloat blockX = vVerts[0];   // Upper left X
  GLfloat blockY = vVerts[7];   // Upper left Y

  if(key == GLUT_KEY_UP)
    blockY += stepSize;
```

```
    if(key == GLUT_KEY_DOWN)
        blockY -= stepSize;

    if(key == GLUT_KEY_LEFT)
        blockX -= stepSize;

    if(key == GLUT_KEY_RIGHT)
        blockX += stepSize;

    // Collision detection
    if(blockX < -1.0f) blockX = -1.0f;
    if(blockX > (1.0f - blockSize * 2)) blockX = 1.0f - blockSize * 2;;
    if(blockY < -1.0f + blockSize * 2) blockY = -1.0f + blockSize * 2;
    if(blockY > 1.0f) blockY = 1.0f;

    // Recalculate vertex positions
    vVerts[0] = blockX;
    vVerts[1] = blockY - blockSize*2;

    vVerts[3] = blockX + blockSize*2;
    vVerts[4] = blockY - blockSize*2;

    vVerts[6] = blockX + blockSize*2;
    vVerts[7] = blockY;

    vVerts[9] = blockX;
    vVerts[10] = blockY;

    squareBatch.CopyVertexData3f(vVerts);

    glutPostRedisplay();
    }
```

Refreshing the Display

The last line of the SpecialKeys function tells GLUT that it needs to update the window contents.

```
glutPostRedisplay();
```

GLUT by default updates the window by calling the RenderScene function when the window is created and when the window either changes size or is in need of being repainted. This happens anytime the window is minimized and restored, maximized, covered and redisplayed, and so on. Calling `glutPostRedisplay` yourself is a way in which you can let GLUT know that something has changed and it's time to rerender the scene. This comes in especially handy in the next section.

Simple Automated Animation

In the Move example program, when we pressed an arrow key, we updated the geometry position and then called the `glutPostRedisplay` function to trigger a screen refresh. What would happen if we put a `glutPostRedisplay` call at the end of the `RenderScene` function? If you are thinking you'd get a program that continually repainted itself, you'd be right. Don't worry, this isn't an infinite loop, though. The repaint message is actually a message posted to an internal message loop, and other window events are also serviced between screen refreshes. This means you can still look for keystrokes, mouse movement, window size changes, and program termination.

Listing 2.3 shows a modified `RenderScene` function that builds on what we did in the Move example program. Instead of using keystrokes to move the square, we made a function called `BounceFunction` that we call every time we render to update the square position. It collides with the edges of the window and bounces around inside the window frame. Note at the end, there is a call to `glutPostRedisplay` so that the window continually repaints itself.

LISTING 2.3   The Rendering Function for the Animated Bounce Example Program

```
///////////////////////////////////////////////////////////////////////////
// Called to draw scene
void RenderScene(void)
    {
    // Clear the window with current clearing color
    glClear(GL_COLOR_BUFFER_BIT | GL_DEPTH_BUFFER_BIT | GL_STENCIL_BUFFER_BIT);

    GLfloat vRed[] = { 1.0f, 0.0f, 0.0f, 1.0f };
    shaderManager.UseStockShader(GLT_SHADER_IDENTITY, vRed);
    squareBatch.Draw();

    // Flush drawing commands
    glutSwapBuffers();

    BounceFunction();
    glutPostRedisplay(); // Redraw
    }
```

Summary

We covered a lot of ground in this chapter. We introduced you to OpenGL, told you a little bit about its history, introduced the OpenGL utility toolkit (GLUT), GLEW and GLTools, and presented the fundamentals of writing a program that uses OpenGL. Using GLUT, we showed you the easiest possible way to create a window and draw in it using OpenGL commands. You learned to use the GLUT library to create windows that can be resized, as well as create a simple animation. You were also introduced to the process of using OpenGL for drawing—composing and selecting colors, clearing the screen, drawing both a triangle and a rectangle, and setting the viewport within the window frame. We discussed the various OpenGL data types and the headers required to build programs that use OpenGL and walked you through setting up a project in either Visual Studio (Windows) or Xcode (Mac OS X).

The OpenGL state machine underlies almost everything you do from here on out, and the extension mechanism makes sure you can access all the OpenGL features supported by your hardware driver, regardless of your development tool. You also learned how to check for OpenGL errors along the way to make sure you aren't making any illegal state changes or rendering commands. With a little coding finally under your belt, you are ready to dive into some other ideas you need to be familiar with before you move forward.

CHAPTER 3

Basic Rendering

by Richard S. Wright, Jr.

WHAT YOU'LL LEARN IN THIS CHAPTER:

- About the basic OpenGL rendering architecture
- How to use the seven OpenGL geometric primitives
- How to use stock shaders
- How to use uniforms and attributes
- How to submit geometry with the GLBatch helper class
- How to perform depth testing and back face culling
- How to draw transparent or blended geometry
- How to draw antialiased points, lines, and polygons

If you've ever had a chemistry class (and probably even if you haven't), you know that all matter consists of atoms and all atoms consist of only three things: protons, neutrons, and electrons. All the materials and substances you have ever come into contact with—from the petals of a rose to the sand on the beach—are just different arrangements of these three fundamental building blocks. Although this explanation is a little oversimplified for almost anyone beyond the third or fourth grade, it demonstrates a powerful principle: With just a few simple building blocks, you can create highly complex and beautiful structures.

The connection is fairly obvious. Objects and scenes that you create with OpenGL also consist of smaller, simpler shapes, arranged and combined in various and unique ways. This chapter explores these building blocks of 3D objects, called *primitives*, and the various ways you can combine them on-screen. All primitives in OpenGL are one-, two-, or three-dimensional objects, ranging from single points to lines and groups of triangles. In this chapter, you learn everything you need to know to draw objects in three dimensions from these simpler shapes.

The Basic Graphics Pipeline

A primitive in OpenGL is simply a collection of vertices, hooked together in a predefined way. A single point for example is a primitive that requires exactly one vertex. Another example is a triangle, a primitive made up of three vertices. Before we talk about the different kinds of primitives, let's take a look first at how a primitive is assembled out of individual vertices. The basic rendering pipeline takes three vertices and turns them into a triangle. It may also apply color, one or more textures, and move them about. This pipeline is also programmable; you actually write two programs that are executed by the graphics hardware to process the vertex data and fill in the pixels (we call them fragments because actually there can be more than one fragment per pixel, but more on that later) on-screen. To understand how this basic process works in OpenGL, let's take a look at a simplified version of the OpenGL rendering pipeline, shown here in Figure 3.1.

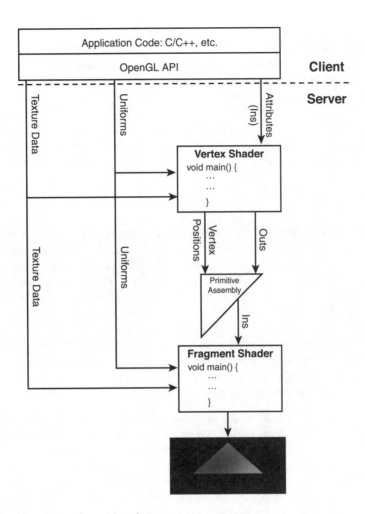

FIGURE 3.1   How to render a triangle.

Client-Server

First notice that we have divided the pipeline in half. On the top is the *client* side, and on the bottom is the *server*. Basic client-server design is applied when the client side of the pipeline is separated from the server side functionally. In OpenGL's case, the client side is code that lives in the main CPU's memory and is executed within the application program, or within the driver in main system memory. The driver assembles rendering commands and data and sends to the server for execution. On a typical desktop computer, the server is across some system bus and is in fact the hardware and memory on the graphics card.

Client and server also function asynchronously, meaning they are both independent pieces of software or hardware, or both. To achieve maximum performance, you want both sides to be busy as much as possible. The client is continually assembling blocks of data and commands into buffers that are then sent to the server for execution. The server then executes those buffers, while at the same time the client is getting ready to send the next bit of data or information for rendering. If the server ever runs out of work while waiting on the client, or if the client has to stop and wait for the server to become ready for more commands or data, we call this a pipeline stall. Pipeline stalls are the bane of performance programmers, and we really don't want CPUs or GPUs standing around idle waiting for work to do.

Shaders

The two biggest boxes in Figure 3.1 are for the vertex shader and the fragment shader. A shader is a program written in GLSL (we get into GLSL programming in Chapter 6, "Thinking Outside the Box: Nonstock Shaders"). GLSL looks a whole lot like C; in fact these programs even start with the familiar main function. These shaders must be compiled and linked together (again much like a C or C++ program) from source code before they can be used. The final ready-to-use shader program is then made up of the vertex shader as the first stage of processing and the fragment shader as the second stage of processing. Note that we are taking a simplified approach here. There is actually something called a geometry shader that can (optionally) fit between here, as well as all sorts of feedback mechanisms for moving data back and forth. There are also some post fragment processing features such as blending, stencil, and depth testing, which we also cover later.

The vertex shader processes incoming data from the client, applying transformations, or doing other types of math to calculate lighting effects, displacement, color values, and so on. To render a triangle with three vertices, the vertex shader is executed three times, once for each vertex. On today's hardware, there are multiple execution units running simultaneously, which means all three vertices are processed simultaneously. Graphics processors today are massively parallel computers. Don't be fooled by clock speed when comparing them to CPUs. They are orders of magnitude faster at graphics operations.

Three vertices are now ready to be rasterized. The primitive assembly box in Figure 3.1 is meant to show that the three vertices are then put together and the triangle is rasterized, fragment by fragment. Each fragment is filled in by executing the fragment shader, which outputs the final color value you will see on-screen. Again, today's hardware is massively parallel, and it is quite possible a hundred or more of these fragment programs could be executing simultaneously.

Of course to get anything to happen, you must feed these shaders some data. There are three ways in which you the programmer pass data to OpenGL shaders for rendering: attributes, uniforms, and textures.

Attributes

An attribute is a data element that changes per vertex. In fact, the vertex position itself is actually an attribute. Attributes can be floating-point, integer, or boolean data, and attributes are always stored internally as a four component vector, even if you don't use all four components. For example, a vertex position might be stored as an x, a y, and a z value. That would be three out of the four components. Internally, OpenGL makes the fourth component (W if you just have to know) a one. In fact, if you are drawing just in the xy plane (and ignoring z), then the third component will be automatically made a zero, and again the fourth will be made a one. To complete the pattern, if you send down only a single floating-point value as an attribute, the second and third components are zero, while the fourth is still made a one. This default behavior applies to any attribute you set up, not just vertex positions, so be careful when you don't use all four components available to you. Other things you might change per vertex besides the position in space are texture coordinates, color values, and surface normals used for lighting calculations. Attributes, however, can have any meaning you want in the vertex program; you are in control.

Attributes are copied from a pointer to local client memory to a buffer that is stored (most likely) on the graphics hardware. Attributes are only processed by the vertex shader and have no meaning to the fragment shader. Also, to clarify that attributes change per vertex, this does not mean they cannot have duplicate values, only that there is actually one stored value per vertex. Usually, they are different of course, but it is possible you could have a whole array of the same values. This would be very wasteful, however, and if you needed a data element that was the same for all the attributes in a single batch, there is a better way.

Uniforms

A uniform is a single value that is, well, uniform for the entire batch of attributes; that is, it doesn't change. You set the values of uniform variables usually just before you send the command to render a primitive batch. Uniforms can be used for virtually an unlimited number of uses. You could set a single color value that is applied to an entire surface. You could set a time value that you change every time you render to do some type of vertex animation (note the uniform changes once per batch, not once per vertex here). One of the most common uses of uniforms is to set transformation matrices in the vertex shader (this is almost the entire purpose of Chapter 4, "Basic Transformations: A Vector/Matrix Primer").

Like attributes, uniform values can be floating-point, integer, or boolean in nature, but unlike attributes, you can have uniform variables in both the vertex and the fragment shader. Uniforms can be scalar or vector types, and you can have matrix uniforms. Technically, you can also have matrix attributes, where each column of the matrix takes up one of those four component vector slots, but this is not often done. There are even some special uniform setting functions we discuss in Chapter 5, "Basic Texturing," that deal with this.

Texture

A third type of data that you can pass to a shader is texture data. It is a bit early to try and go into much detail about how textures are handled and passed to a shader, but you know from Chapter 1, "Introduction to 3D Graphics and OpenGL," basically what a texture is. Texture values can be sampled and filtered from both the vertex and the fragment shader. Fragment shaders typically sample a texture to apply image data across the surface of a triangle. Texture data, however, is more useful than just to represent images. Most image file formats store color components in unsigned byte values (8 bits per color channel), but you can also have floating-point textures. This means potentially any large block of floating-point data, such as a large lookup table of an expensive function, could be passed to a shader in this way.

Outs

The fourth type of data shown in the diagram in Figure 3.1 are outs. An out variable is declared as an output from one shader stage and declared as an in in the subsequent shader stage. Outs can be passed simply from one stage to the next, or they may be interpolated in various ways. Client code has no access to these internal variables, but rather they are declared in both the vertex and the fragment shader (and possibly the optional geometry shader). The vertex shader assigns a value to the out variable, and the value is constant, or can be interpolated between vertexes as the primitive is rasterized. The fragment shader's corresponding in variable of the same name receives this constant or interpolated value. In Chapter 6, we see how this works in more detail.

Setting Up Your Coordinate System

In Chapter 1, we introduced the two kinds of projections that we most often use in 3D graphics (orthographic and perspective). These projections, or types of coordinate systems, are really just a specially formed 4 x 4 transformation matrix. These and other types of matrices are the topic of the next chapter, so we don't want to get lost in the details too soon here. Suffice it to say, you need a projection matrix of one of these types to render geometry in the appropriate coordinate system. If you do not use one of these matrices, you get a default orthographic projection where the axes range only from -1.0 to 1.0. Our example programs in Chapter 2, "Getting Started," made use of this coordinate system, and this was useful given that all three of the sample programs were essentially 2D. For this chapter, however, we want to begin to move on a bit.

The Math3d library that is part of GLTools contains functions that construct different kinds of matrices for you, and you learn to use and apply them in Chapter 4. For this chapter, we use the GLFrustum class as a container for our projection matrix.

Orthographic Projections

Typically, we use orthographic projections for 2D drawings, and we keep the z coordinate at 0.0 for our geometry. The z-axis, however, can extend to any length we want. Figure 3.2 shows an example orthographic projection that stretches -100 to +100 in all three directions. This viewing volume as it is sometimes called will contain all of your geometry. If you specify geometry outside the viewing volume, it is clipped, meaning it is literally cut along the boundary of the viewing volume. In an orthographic projection everything that falls within this space is displayed on-screen, and there is really no concept of a camera or eye coordinate system. To set this up, we call the GLFrustum method, SetOrthographic.

```
GLFrustum::SetOrthographic(GLfloat xMin, GLfloat xMax, GLfloat yMin,
                     GLfloat yMax, GLfloat zMin, GLfloat zMax);
```

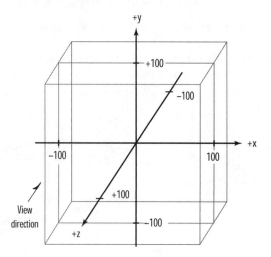

FIGURE 3.2   A Cartesian viewing volume measuring 200 x 200 x 200.

Perspective Projections

A perspective projection performs perspective division to shorten and shrink objects that are farther away from the viewer. The width of the back of the viewing volume does not have the same measurements as the front of the viewing volume after being projected to the screen. Thus, an object of the same logical dimensions appears larger at the front of the viewing volume than if it were drawn at the back of the viewing volume. Figure 3.3 shows an example of a geometric shape called a *frustum*. A frustum is a truncated section of a pyramid viewed from the narrow end to the broad end, with the viewer back some distance from the narrow end.

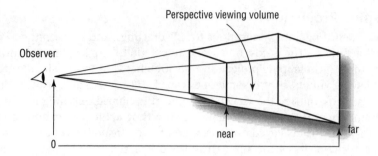

FIGURE 3.3   A perspective projection defined by a frustum.

The GLFrustum class constructs a frustum for you with the function SetPerspective.

GLFrustum::SetPerspective(float fFov, float fAspect, float fNear, float fFar);

The parameters are the field-of-view angle in the vertical direction, the aspect ratio of the width to the height of your window, and the distances to the near and far clipping planes (see Figure 3.4). You find the aspect ratio by dividing the width (w) by the height (h) of the window or viewport.

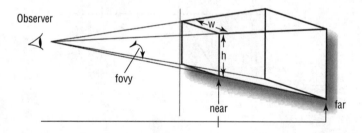

FIGURE 3.4   The frustum as defined by the GLFrustum class's SetPerspective method.

Using the Stock Shaders

In the OpenGL Core Profile, there is no built-in rendering pipeline; you must specify a shader before you can submit geometry for rendering. This presents a bit of a chicken and egg scenario (which came first, the chicken or the egg) when learning graphics programming. The approach we think works best is to supply a set of *stock shaders* that you can use for the first part of this book. These stock shaders are managed by the GLTools C++ class GLShaderManager and provide a simple baseline of common rendering needs. Programmers with simple needs may even find the stock shaders sufficient for all their anticipated tasks. With time, however, it is unlikely that all but the most casual 3D programmer will be happy being kept in this box, and thus near the end of the introductory section of this book is Chapter 6.

The GLShaderManager must be initialized before use, and in all the sample programs you find an instance of GLShaderManager near the top of the source file and a call to InitializeStockShaders in SetupRC.

```
shaderManager.InitializeStockShaders();
```

Attributes

OpenGL supports up to 16 different generic attributes that can be set per vertex. These are numbered 0 through 15 and can be associated with any specific variable in your vertex shader (how to do this is covered in Chapter 6). The stock shaders all use a consistent variable naming convention internally and the same attribute slot for each variable. These attributes are listed in Table 3.1 and represent the most common basic attributes needed for simple rendering needs. The attribute mechanism is quite flexible and can be used in ways far beyond these few predefined values. You learn more about this in Chapter 6 and Chapter 11, "Advanced Shader Usage."

TABLE 3.1   GLShaderManager Predefined Attribute Identifiers

Identifier	Description
GLT_ATTRIBUTE_VERTEX	Three component (x, y, z) vertex position
GLT_ATTRIBUTE_COLOR	Four component (r, g, b, a) color value
GLT_ATTRIBUTE_NORMAL	Three components (x, y, z) surface normal
GLT_ATTRIBUTE_TEXTURE0	Primary two component (s, t) texture coordinate
GLT_ATTRIBUTE_TEXTURE1	Secondary two component (s, t) texture coordinate

Uniforms

To render geometry, you need to submit the attribute arrays for your object, but first you must bind to the shader program you want to use and supply the program's uniforms. The GLShaderManager class takes care of this for you (for now). The function UseStockShader selects one of the stock shaders and supplies the uniforms for that shader, all in one function call.

```
GLShaderManager::UseStockShader(GLenum shader, …);
```

The … signifies in C (or C++) that the function takes a variable number of parameters. In the function itself, it pulls the appropriate arguments off the stack based on which shader you selected, which are the uniforms that the particular shader requires. Each of the stock shaders is discussed next. Although all of the uniforms may not make sense to you at this point, they should by the time you finish the introductory section of this book. This is a section you may want to bookmark, as you may find yourself referring back to this reference periodically.

The Identity Shader

The identity shader simply draws geometry using the default Cartesian coordinate system (-1.0 to 1.0 on all axes). A single color is applied to all fragments, and the geometry is solid and unshaded. The only attribute used is GLT_ATTRIBUTE_VERTEX. The vColor parameter contains the desired color.

```
GLShaderManager::UseStockShader(GLT_SHADER_IDENTITY, GLfloat vColor[4]);
```

The Flat Shader

This shader extends the identity shader by allowing a 4 x 4 transformation matrix to be specified for geometry transformations. This is typically the premultiplied modelview matrix and the projection matrix, often called the modelview projection matrix (this is explained further in Chapter 4). The only attribute used is GLT_ATTRIBUTE_VERTEX.

```
GLShaderManager::UseStockShader(GLT_SHADER_FLAT, GLfloat mvp[16], GLfloat
vColor[4]);
```

The Shaded Shader

This shader's only uniform is the transformation matrix that is to be applied to the geometry. Both the GLT_ATTRIBUTE_VERTEX and the GLT_ATTRIBUTE_COLOR are used by the shader. Color values are interpolated smoothly between vertices (smooth shading this is called).

```
GLShaderManager::UseStockShader(GLT_SHADER_SHADED, GLfloat mvp[16]);
```

The Default Light Shader

This shader creates the illusion of a single diffuse light source located at the eye position. Essentially, it makes things look shaded and lit. Uniforms needed are the modelview matrix, the projection matrix, and the color value to use as the base color. Required attributes are GLT_ATTRIBUTE_VERTEX and GLT_ATTRIBUTE_NORMAL. Most lighting shaders require the normal matrix as a uniform. This shader derives the normal matrix from the modelview matrix—convenient, but not terribly efficient. Bear that in mind for performance-sensitive applications.

```
GLShaderManager::UseStockShader(GLT_SHADER_DEFAULT_LIGHT, GLfloat mvMatrix[16],
GLfloat pMatrix[16], GLfloat vColor[4]);
```

Point Light Shader

The point light shader is similar to the default light shader, but the light position may be specified. This shader takes four uniforms, the modelview matrix, the projection matrix, the light position in eye coordinates, and the base diffuse color of the object. Attributes used are GLT_ATTRIBUTE_VERTEX and GLT_ATTRIBUTE_NORMAL.

```
GLShaderManager::UseStockShader(GLT_SHADER_POINT_LIGHT_DIFF, GLfloat mvMatrix[16],
GLfloat pMatrix[16], GLfloat vLightPos[3], GLfloat vColor[4]);
```

Texture Replace Shader
This shader transforms geometry by the given modelview projection matrix and uses the
texture bound to the texture unit specified in nTextureUnit. Fragment colors are taken
directly from the texture sample. Attributes used are GLT_ATTRIBUTE_VERTEX and
GLT_ATTRIBUTE_TEXTURE0.

```
GLShaderManager::UseStockShader(GLT_SHADER_TEXTURE_REPLACE,
              GLfloat mvpMatrix[16], GLint nTextureUnit);
```

Texture Modulate Shader
This shader multiplies a base color by a texture from texture unit nTextureUnit. Attributes
used are GLT_ATTRIBUTE_VERTEX and GLT_ATTRIBUTE_TEXTURE0.

```
GLShaderManager::UseStockShader(GLT_SHADER_TEXTURE_MODULATE, GLfloat mvpMatrix[16],
GLfloat vColor, GLint nTextureUnit);
```

Textured Point Light Shader
This shader modulates (multiplies) a texture by a diffuse lighting calculation, given a
light's position in eye space. Uniforms are the modelview matrix, projection matrix, the
light position in eye space, the base color of the geometry, and the texture unit to use.
Attributes used are GLT_ATTRIBUTE_VERTEX, GLT_ATTRIBUTE_NORMAL, and
GLT_ATTRIBUTE_TEXTURE0.

```
GLShaderManager::UseStockShader(GLT_SHADER_TEXTURE_POINT_LIGHT_DIFF,
GLfloat mvMatrix, GLfloat pMatrix[16], GLfloat vLightPos[3],
GLfloat vBaseColor[4], GLint nTextureUnit);
```

Connecting The Dots

When (and if) you first learned to draw any kind of 2D graphics on any computer system,
you probably started with pixels. A pixel is the smallest element on your computer
monitor, and on color systems that pixel can be any one of many available colors. This is
computer graphics at its simplest: Draw a point somewhere on the screen and make it a
specific color. Then build on this simple concept, using your favorite computer language
to produce lines, polygons, circles, and other shapes and graphics—perhaps even a GUI.

With OpenGL, however, drawing on the computer screen is fundamentally different.
You're not concerned with physical screen coordinates and pixels, but rather positional
coordinates in your viewing volume. It is the job of your shader program and rasterization
hardware to get your points, lines, and triangles projected from your established 3D space
to the 2D image seen on your computer screen.

Points and Lines

To start drawing solid geometry, we use seven geometric primitives defined by OpenGL. Primitives are rendered in a single batch that contain all the vertices and associated attributes for a given primitive. Essentially, all the vertices in a given batch are assembled into one of these primitives. Table 3.2 lists these seven primitives and briefly describes their purpose.

TABLE 3.2   OpenGL Geometric Primitives

Primitive	Description
GL_POINTS	Each vertex is a single point on the screen.
GL_LINES	Each pair of vertices defines a line segment.
GL_LINE_STRIP	A line segment is drawn from the first vertex to each successive vertex.
GL_LINE_LOOP	Same as GL_LINE_STRIP, but the last and first vertex are connected.
GL_TRIANGLES	Every three vertices define a new triangle.
GL_TRIANGLE_STRIP	Triangles share vertices along a strip.
GL_TRIANGLE_FAN	Triangles fan out from an origin, sharing adjacent vertices.

The example program Primitives demonstrates rendering each one of these. Start the program and press the space bar to progress from GL_POINTS to GL_TRIANGLE_STRIP. You can also use the arrow keys to rotate the rendering on the x and y axes.

Points

Points are the simplest primitive. Each vertex specified is simply a single point on the screen. By default, points are one pixel in size. You can change the default point size by calling glPointSize.

```
void glPointSize(GLfloat size);
```

The glPointSize function takes a single parameter that specifies the approximate diameter in pixels of the point drawn. Not all point sizes are supported, however, and you should make sure the point size you specify is available. Use the following code to get the range of point sizes and the smallest interval between them:

```
GLfloat sizes[2];      // Store supported point size range
GLfloat step;          // Store supported point size increments

// Get supported point size range and step size
glGetFloatv(GL_POINT_SIZE_RANGE,sizes);
glGetFloatv(GL_POINT_SIZE_GRANULARITY,&step);
```

Here, the sizes array contains two elements that contain the smallest and largest valid value for glPointsize. In addition, the variable step holds the smallest step size allowable between the point sizes. The OpenGL specification requires only that one point size, 1.0, be supported, but most implementations support a wide range of point sizes. For example, you may find a range for point sizes from 0.5 to 256.0, with 0.125 the smallest step size. Specifying a size out of range is not interpreted as an error. Instead, the largest or smallest supported size is used, whichever is closest to the value specified.

By default, point size, unlike other geometry, is not affected by the perspective division. That is, they do not become smaller when they are further from the viewpoint, and they do not become larger as they move closer. Points are also always square pixels, even if you use glPointSize to increase the size of the points. You just get bigger squares! To get round points, you must draw them antialiased (coming up later in this chapter).

Another way to set the point size is to enable program point size mode.

```
glEnable(GL_PROGRAM_POINT_SIZE);
```

This mode allows you to set the point size programmatically in the vertex shader or the geometry shader, both of which are beyond the scope of this chapter. For completeness, the shader built-in variable is gl_PointSize, and in your shader source code, you'd simply set it like this:

```
gl_PointSize = 5.0;
```

Figure 3.5 shows the initial output from the Primitives example program. The point size was set to 4.0, and an array of vertices is used that is shaped roughly like the state of Florida.

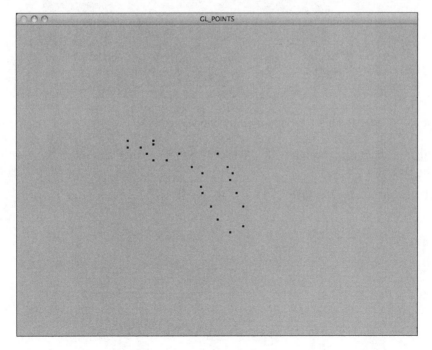

FIGURE 3.5 A set of points along the coastline of Florida.

Lines

Next up the ladder from points are individual line segments. A line segment is drawn between two vertices, so a batch of lines should consist of an even number of vertices, one for each end of the line segment. If we use the same set of points used in the previous figure to draw a series of lines, every two points along the Florida coast will form a new line segment. This of course would leave gaps between each separated line segment as shown in Figure 3.6.

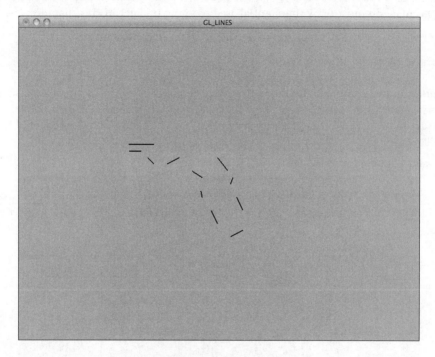

FIGURE 3.6   Separated lines, each formed by two vertices.

Lines are by default one pixel in width. The only way to change a line's width is with the function glLineWidth.

```
void glLineWidth(GLfloat width);
```

Line Strips

For a true connect-the-dots parallel, line strips draw line segments from one vertex to the next continually. To make a continuous line around the state of Florida with separated lines, each of the connecting vertices would have to be specified twice. Once as the end of one line segment, and then sent down again as the beginning of the next line segment. Moving all this extra data and transforming the same point twice is waste of bandwidth and clock cycles on the GPU. Figure 3.7 shows the same set of points again, this time drawn as a GL_LINE_STRIP.

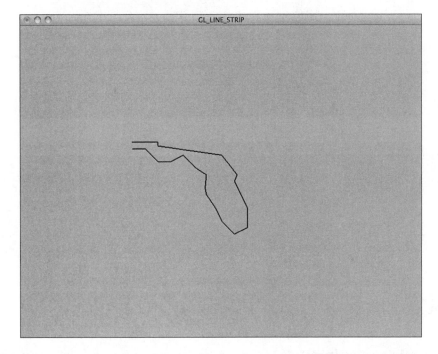

FIGURE 3.7   A line strip simply connects the dots from start to finish.

Line Loops

A simple extension to line strips, a line loop draws an extra line segment from the end of the batch back to the beginning. This provides a net savings of only one vertex but is convenient when you are trying to close a loop or line-based figure. Figure 3.8 shows the inevitable conclusion of our rendering of the outline of the state of Florida in the Primitives example program.

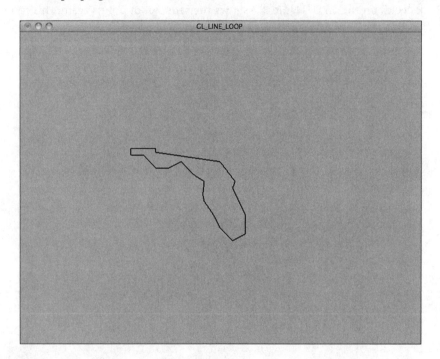

FIGURE 3.8   Closing the final gap with a line loop.

Drawing Triangles in 3D

You've seen how to draw points and lines and even how to draw some enclosed polygons with GL_LINE_LOOP. With just these primitives, you could easily draw any shape possible in three dimensions. You could, for example, draw six squares and arrange them so they form the sides of a cube.

You might have noticed, however, that any shapes you create with these primitives are not filled with any color; after all, you are drawing only lines. In fact, arranging six squares produces just a wireframe cube, not a solid cube. To draw a solid surface, you need more than just points and lines; you need polygons. A polygon is a closed shape that may or may not be filled with colors or texture data, and it is the basis for all solid-object composition in OpenGL.

Individual Triangles

The simplest solid polygon possible is the triangle, with only three sides. Rasterization hardware just loves triangles, and so this is now the only type of polygon that OpenGL supports. Every three vertices simply form a new triangle. Figure 3.9 shows two triangles drawn with six vertices numbered V0 through V5.

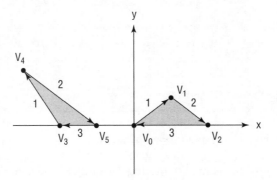

FIGURE 3.9   Two triangles drawn using GL_TRIANGLES.

Figure 3.10 shows the next step of the Primitives example program. Here, we don't draw one triangle, but four triangles in the shape of a pyramid. The arrow keys allow you to rotate the pyramid and look at it from different angles. There is no bottom on the pyramid, so you can also look up inside it.

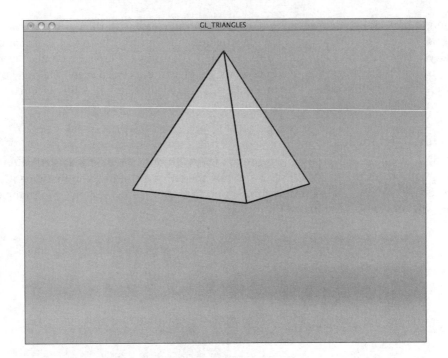

FIGURE 3.10   Triangles forming a four-sided pyramid.

Note that in our example here (and continuing forward), we have outlined the green triangles with black lines. Because there is no shading or texture across the triangles, this helps the individual triangles stand out. This black outline is not a natural behavior of primitives. This was achieved by drawing the geometry solid and then drawing a black wireframe version of the geometry right over the top of the solid. We show you how this is done in more detail in the upcoming section on glPolygonOffset.

Winding

An important characteristic of any triangle is illustrated in Figure 3.9. Notice the arrows on the lines that connect the vertices. When the first triangle is drawn, the lines are drawn from V0 to V1, and then to V2, and finally back to V0 to close the triangle. This path is in the order in which the vertices are specified, and for this example, that order is clockwise from your point of view. The same directional characteristic is present for the second triangle as well.

The combination of order and direction in which the vertices are specified is called *winding*. The triangles in Figure 3.9 are said to have clockwise winding because they are literally wound in the clockwise direction. If we reverse the positions of V4 and V5 on the triangle on the left, we get counterclockwise winding. Figure 3.11 shows two triangles, each with opposite windings.

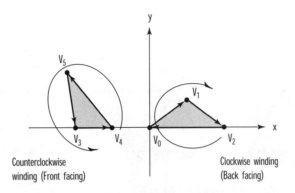

FIGURE 3.11   Two triangles with different windings.

OpenGL, by default, considers polygons that have counterclockwise winding to be front facing. This means that the triangle on the left in Figure 3.11 shows the front of the triangle, and the one on the right shows the back of the triangle.

Why is this issue important? As you will soon see, you will often want to give the front and back of a polygon different physical characteristics. You can hide the back of a triangle altogether or give it a different color and reflective property. Texture images are also reversed on the back sides of triangles. It's important to keep the winding of all polygons in a scene consistent, using front-facing polygons to draw the outside surface of any solid objects. If you need to reverse the default behavior of OpenGL, you can do so by calling the following function:

```
glFrontFace(GL_CW);
```

The GL_CW parameter tells OpenGL that clockwise-wound polygons are to be considered front-facing. To change back to counterclockwise winding for the front face (this is the default anyway), use GL_CCW.

Triangle Strips
For many surfaces and shapes, you need to draw several connected triangles. You can save a lot of time by drawing a strip of connected triangles with the GL_TRIANGLE_STRIP primitive. Figure 3.12 shows the progression of a strip of three triangles specified by a set of five vertices numbered V0 through V4. Here, you see that the vertices are not necessarily traversed in the same order in which they were specified. The reason for this is to preserve the winding (counterclockwise) of each triangle. The pattern is V0, V1, V2; then V2, V1, V3; then V2, V3, V4; and so on.

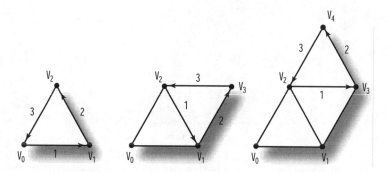

FIGURE 3.12   The progression of a `GL_TRIANGLE_STRIP`.

There are two advantages to using a strip of triangles instead of specifying each triangle separately. First, after specifying the first three vertices for the initial triangle, you need to specify only a single point for each additional triangle. This saves a lot of program or data storage space when you have many triangles to draw. The second advantage is mathematical performance and bandwidth savings. Fewer vertices means a faster transfer from your computer's memory to your graphics card and fewer times your vertex shader must be executed. Figure 3.13 shows the next step in the Primitives example program. Here, a triangle strip is drawn to create a circular band.

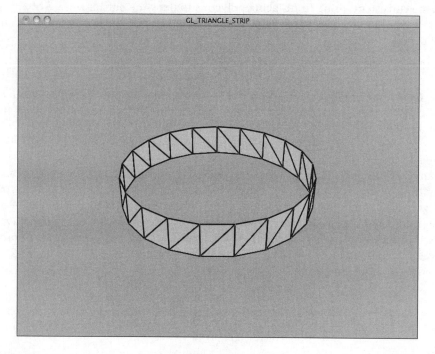

FIGURE 3.13   A circular band made of a triangle strip.

Triangle Fans

In addition to triangle strips, you can use GL_TRIANGLE_FAN to produce a group of connected triangles that fan around a central point. Figure 3.14 shows a fan of three triangles produced by specifying four vertices. The first vertex, V0, forms the origin of the fan. After the first three vertices are used to draw the initial triangle, all subsequent vertices are used with the origin (V0) and the vertex immediately preceding it (Vn–1) to form the next triangle.

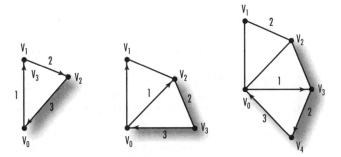

FIGURE 3.14   The progression of GL_TRIANGLE_FAN.

Figure 3.15 shows the final step of the Primitives example program. We've drawn six triangles around the origin of the triangle fan, which we raised ever so slightly to give it a little depth. Don't forget you can use the arrow keys to rotate the figures around.

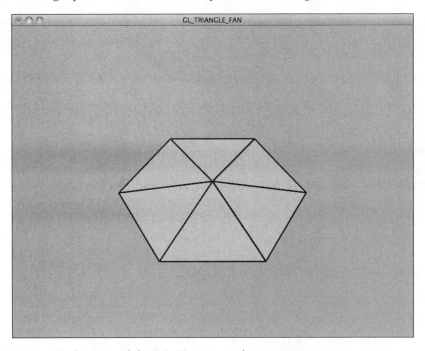

FIGURE 3.15   Final output of the Primitives example, GL_TRIANGLE_FAN.

A Simple Batch Container

The GLTools library contains a simple container class called GBatch. This class can contain a single batch of any of the seven primitives listed in Table 3.2, and it knows how to render the primitives when using any of the stock shaders supported by the GLShaderManager. Using the GLBatch class is simple. First initialize the batch, telling the class the type of primitive it represents, the number of vertices it will contain, and optionally, one or two sets of texture coordinates:

```
void GLBatch::Begin(GLenum primitive, GLuint nVerts, GLuint nTextureUnits = 0);
```

Then, at a minimum, copy in an array of three component (x, y, z) vertices.

```
void GLBatch::CopyVertexData3f(GLfloat *vVerts);
```

Optionally, you can also copy in surface normals, colors, and texture coordinates as well:

```
void GLBatch::CopyNormalDataf(GLfloat *vNorms);
void GLBatch::CopyColorData4f(GLfloat *vColors);
void GLBatch::CopyTexCoordData2f(GLfloat *vTexCoords, GLuint uiTextureLayer);
```

When you are finished, you can call End to signify you are done copying in data, and the internal flags will be set so the class knows which attributes it contains.

```
void GLBatch::End(void);
```

You can actually copy new data in anytime you like, as long as you do not change the size of the class, and once you call the End function, you cannot add new attributes (that is you can't decide *now* I also want surface normals too).

The actual underlying OpenGL mechanism for submitting attributes is actually far more flexible than this. The GLBatch class, however, is simply a convenience class, much like using GLUT is convenient so you don't have to worry about OS specifics until you are ready.

Let's take a quick look at using the class to render a single triangle. In the Triangle example from Chapter 2 (the simplest example we have), we declared an instance of the GLBatch class near the top of the source file:

```
GLBatch triangleBatch;
```

Then in the SetupRC function, we set up the triangle with three vertices.

```
// Load up a triangle
GLfloat vVerts[] = { -0.5f, 0.0f, 0.0f,
                      0.5f, 0.0f, 0.0f,
                      0.0f, 0.5f, 0.0f };

triangleBatch.Begin(GL_TRIANGLES, 3);
triangleBatch.CopyVertexData3f(vVerts);
triangleBatch.End();
```

Finally, in the RenderScene function, we select the appropriate stock shader and call the Draw function.

```
GLfloat vRed[] = { 1.0f, 0.0f, 0.0f, 1.0f };
shaderManager.UseStockShader(GLT_SHADER_IDENTITY, vRed);
triangleBatch.Draw();
```

While the GLBatch class provides a convenient mechanism for containing and submitting geometry, it is not fully representative of the full breadth and power of OpenGL for geometry management. Chapter 12, "Advanced Geometry Management," goes into far more detail on this topic. The reason we don't cover this material earlier in the book is simply because we want you to be able to start rendering as soon as possible. One of the best ways to learn is by doing, and too much explanation before seeing anything on-screen can be very frustrating, much less error prone.

Unwanted Geometry

By default, every point, line, or triangle you render is rasterized on-screen and in the order in which you specify when you assemble the primitive batch. This can sometimes be problematic. One problem that can occur is if you draw a solid object made up of many triangles, the triangles drawn first can be drawn over by triangles drawn afterward. For example, let's say you have an object such as a torus (donut shaped object) made up of many triangles. Some of those triangles are on the back side of the torus, and some on the front sides. You can't see the back sides—at least you aren't *supposed* to see the backsides (omitting for the moment the special case of transparent geometry). Depending on your orientation, the order in which the triangles are drawn may simply make a mess of things. Figure 3.16 shows the output of the sample program GeoTest (short for Geometry Test Program) with the torus rotated slightly (use the arrow keys to see this yourself).

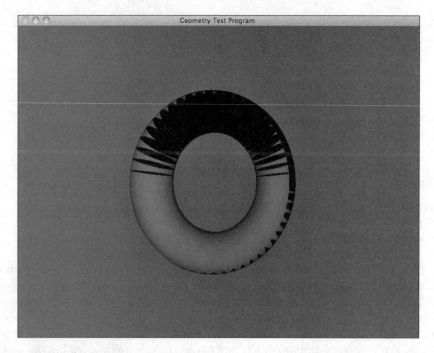

FIGURE 3.16   An object with some of the far-side triangles drawn on top of near-side triangles.

One potential solution to this problem would be to sort the triangles and render the ones farther away first and then render the nearer triangles on top of them. This is called the *painters algorithm* and is very inefficient in computer graphics for two reasons. One is that you must write to every pixel twice wherever any geometry overlaps, and writing to memory slows things down. The second is that sorting individual triangles would be prohibitively expensive. There is a better way.

Front and Back Face Culling

One of the reasons OpenGL makes a distinction between the front and back sides of triangles is for culling. Back face culling can significantly improve performance and corrects problems like those shown in Figure 3.16. Right-click the GeoTest example program and select the Toggle Cull Backface menu option. Figure 3.17 shows the output.

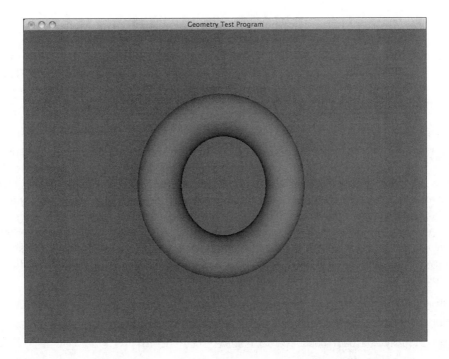

FIGURE 3.17   Correctly rendered object with the back sides of triangles eliminated.

This is very efficient, as a whole triangle is thrown away in the primitive assembly stage of rendering, and no wasteful or inappropriate rasterization is performed. General face culling is turned on like this:

```
glEnable(GL_CULL_FACE);
```

and turned back off with the counterpart:

```
glDisable(GL_CULL_FACE);
```

Note, we did not say whether to cull the front or back of anything. That is controlled by another function, glCullFace.

```
void glCullFace(GLenum mode);
```

Valid values for the mode parameter are GL_FRONT, GL_BACK, or GL_FRONT_AND_BACK. To throw away the insides of opaque (nontransparent) geometry takes two lines of code then.

```
glCullFace(GL_BACK);
glEnable(GL_CULL_FACE);
```

Culling away the front of solid geometry is also useful in some circumstances, for example, showing a rendering of the insides of some figure. When rendering transparent objects (blending is coming up soon), we often render an object twice, once with transparency on, culling the front sides, and then again with the back sides turned off. This layers the object with the back side rendered before the front side, a requirement for rendering things transparently.

Depth Testing

Depth testing is another effective technique for hidden surface removal. The concept is simple: When a pixel is drawn, it is assigned a value (called the z value) that denotes its distance from the viewer's perspective. Later, when another pixel needs to be drawn to that screen location, the new pixel's z value is compared to that of the pixel that is already stored there. If the new pixel's z value is higher, it is closer to the viewer and thus in front of the previous pixel, so the previous pixel is obscured by the new pixel. If the new pixel's z value is lower, it must be behind the existing pixel and thus is not obscured. This maneuver is accomplished internally by a depth buffer with storage for a depth value for every pixel on the screen. Almost all the samples in this book use depth testing.

You should request a depth buffer when you set up your OpenGL window with GLUT. For example, you can request a color and a depth buffer like this:

```
glutInitDisplayMode(GLUT_DOUBLE | GLUT_RGBA | GLUT_DEPTH);
```

To enable depth testing, simply call

```
glEnable(GL_DEPTH_TEST);
```

If you do not have a depth buffer, then enabling depth testing will just be ignored.

Depth testing further solves a performance issue when drawing multiple objects. Even though back face culling can eliminate triangles on the back sides of an object, what about having to separate overlapping objects? The painters algorithm, which we mentioned previously, is so named after a technique used by painters. Simply paint the background objects first and then paint the near objects over the top of them. This may use a trivial amount of paint on the canvas (much less be useful for manual painting), but for graphics hardware, this results in repeated writes to the same fragment location, each of which has a performance overhead. Too much overwrite slows down the rasterization process, and we call such renderings *fill limited*. The reverse of the painters algorithm actually speeds up fill performance. Draw the objects nearest you first, and then the objects farther away. The depth test eliminates pixel writes that would fall under existing pixels, saving a considerable amount of memory bandwidth.

Sorting objects relative to the viewer's position is not difficult, but what about an object that overlaps itself? Back to our DepthTest sample program; we can orient the torus (again, use the arrow keys for this) such that part of the torus overlaps a nearer portion that happened to be rendered first. Figure 3.18 shows what this looks like.

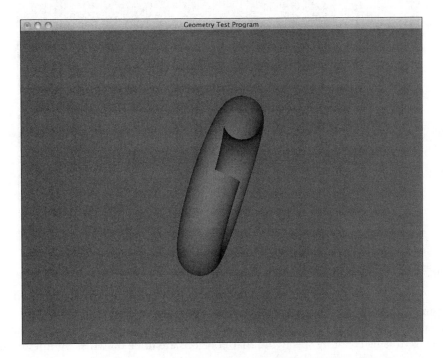

FIGURE 3.18   Self-overlapping objects without depth testing can be problematic.

Right-click the window and select Toggle Depth Test from the pop-up menu. This simply calls `glEnable` to turn on depth testing, and Figure 3.19 shows the correctly rendered object.

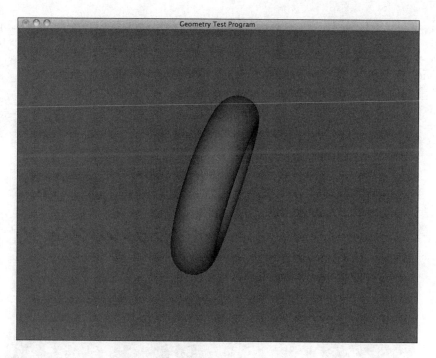

FIGURE 3.19   Correct depth testing on the torus.

Polygon Modes

Polygons (triangles) don't have to be solid. By default, polygons are drawn solid, but you can change this behavior by specifying that polygons are to be drawn as outlines or just points (only the vertices are plotted). The function glPolygonMode allows polygons to be rendered as filled solids, as outlines, or as points only. In addition, you can apply this rendering mode to both sides of the polygons or only to the front or back.

```
void glPolygonMode(GLenum face, GLenum mode);
```

Like in face culling, the face parameter can be GL_FRONT, GL_BACK, or GL_FRONT_AND_BACK. The mode parameter can be GL_FILL (the default), GL_LINE, or GL_POINT. Figure 3.20 shows the output from GeoTest when you select Set Line Mode.

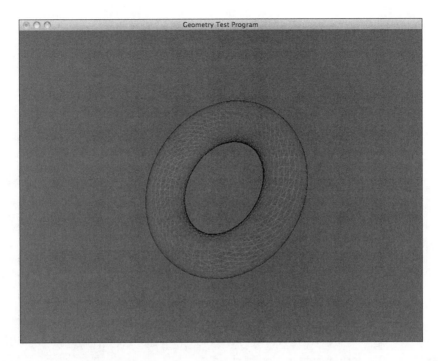

FIGURE 3.20   The torus in wireframe mode.

This wireframe rendering is accomplished simply by calling `glPolygonMode` to set the fronts and backs of polygons to outline mode.

```
glPolygonMode(GL_FRONT_AND_BACK, GL_LINE);
```

Drawing the torus as a point cloud is also easily accomplished. Selecting Set Point Mode from the context menu in GeoTest causes the polygon mode to be set as follows:

```
glPolygonMode(GL_FRONT_AND_BACK, GL_POINT);
```

Figure 3.21 shows the torus with only the vertices drawn as points. In this case, we did make the points a bit larger by calling `glPointSize` with an argument of 5.0.

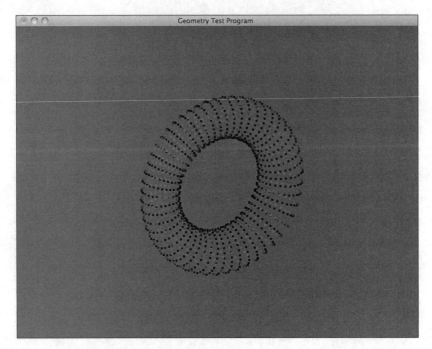

FIGURE 3.21   The torus drawn as a point cloud.

Polygon Offset

While the depth buffer can have positive visual and performance effects, sometimes it just gets a little in the way, and you might need to fib to it just a little bit. This happens whenever you intentionally want to draw two pieces of geometry in the same place. This might sound odd, but consider two cases. At times, you may want to draw a large plane and then draw a smaller shape over the plane but in the same physical location. This is called *decaling*, and you might for example draw a star shape over a flat surface to make a design. In this case, the depth values of the star will be the same or nearly the same as the values in the depth buffer from drawing the original plane. This causes fragments to pass or fail the depth test unpredictably and can leave nasty visual artifacts from what is commonly called *z-fighting*.

Another case (and easier to demonstrate with our current examples), is when you want to draw solid geometry but want to highlight the edges. In the example program Primitives, presented earlier, triangles, triangle fans, and triangle strips were all drawn in green but with black lines showing the individual triangles. This is not the default behavior, and we had to take special care to make this happen. By default, simply drawing a triangle strip would leave the ring looking like that shown in Figure 3.22.

To see the triangle edges, we would need to draw the strip using `glPolygonMode` as shown in the previous section. The results of drawing thick black lines in wireframe mode just creates the wireframe only as shown in Figure 3.23.

FIGURE 3.22   A triangle strip with no edges highlighted.

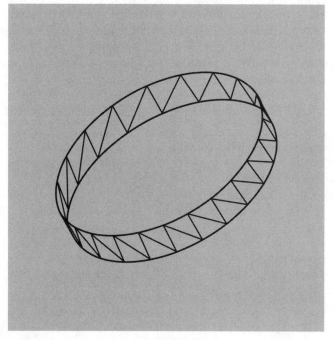

FIGURE 3.23   A triangle strip but just the edges.

The problem is that if you draw the wireframe in the same location as the solid strips, you get the aforementioned z-fighting problem. The solution you might think is to offset the second draw in the z direction ever so slightly. This would do the trick, but you'd have to be careful to make sure you moved in the z toward the camera only and enough to offset the depth test but no so much that you'd see a gap between the geometry layers. There is a better way.

The `glPolygonOffset` function shown here allows you to tweak the depth values of fragments, thus offsetting the depth values but not the actual physical location in 3D space.

```
void glPolygonOffset(GLfloat factor, GLfloat units);
```

The total offset applied to fragments is given by this equation:

$$\text{Depth Offset} = (DZ \times \text{factor}) + (r \times \text{units})$$

`DZ` is the change in depth values (the z) relative to the screen area of the polygon, and `r` is the smallest value that produces a change in depth buffer values. There are no hard and fast rules for foolproof values, and some experimentation may be required on your part. Negative values bring the z closer to you, and positive values move them farther away. For the Primitives example program, we used the value of -1.0 for both the `factor` and `units` parameters.

In addition to using `glPolygonOffset` to set up your offset values, you must enable polygon offset separately for filled geometry (`GL_POLYGON_OFFSET_FILL`), lines (`GL_POLYGON_OFFSET_LINE`), and points (`GL_POLYGON_OFFSET_POINT`). Listing 3.1 shows a function from the Primitives example program that renders a green batch of primitives and then draws a black wireframe version over it. Note that we used thicker, antialiased lines for the outlines for a better appearance. We talk more about antialiasing in the upcoming section on blending.

LISTING 3.1   Function to Draw a Primitive Batch in Green, Followed by Black Wireframe Version

```
void DrawWireFramedBatch(GLBatch* pBatch)
    {
    // Draw the batch solid green
    shaderManager.UseStockShader(GLT_SHADER_FLAT,
                transformPipeline.GetModelViewProjectionMatrix(), vGreen);
    pBatch->Draw();

    // Draw black outline
    glPolygonOffset(-1.0f, -1.0f);        // Shift depth values
    glEnable(GL_POLYGON_OFFSET_LINE);
```

```
// Draw lines antialiased
glEnable(GL_LINE_SMOOTH);
glEnable(GL_BLEND);
glBlendFunc(GL_SRC_ALPHA, GL_ONE_MINUS_SRC_ALPHA);

// Draw black wireframe version of geometry
glPolygonMode(GL_FRONT_AND_BACK, GL_LINE);
glLineWidth(2.5f);
shaderManager.UseStockShader(GLT_SHADER_FLAT,
            transformPipeline.GetModelViewProjectionMatrix(), vBlack);
pBatch->Draw();

// Put everything back the way we found it
glPolygonMode(GL_FRONT_AND_BACK, GL_FILL);
glDisable(GL_POLYGON_OFFSET_LINE);
glLineWidth(1.0f);
glDisable(GL_BLEND);
glDisable(GL_LINE_SMOOTH);
}
```

Figure 3.24 shows how the two passes are finally superimposed.

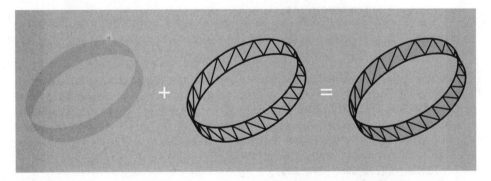

FIGURE 3.24   Our "assembled" rendering with both solid and wireframe drawings.

Cutting It Out with Scissors

Another way to improve rendering performance is to update only the portion of the screen that has changed. You may also need to restrict OpenGL rendering to a smaller rectangular region inside the window. OpenGL allows you to specify a scissor rectangle within your window where rendering can take place. By default, the scissor rectangle is the size of the window, and no scissor test takes place. You turn on the scissor test with the ubiquitous glEnable function:

glEnable(GL_SCISSOR_TEST);

You can, of course, turn off the scissor test again with the corresponding glDisable function call. The rectangle within the window where rendering is performed, called the scissor box, is specified in window coordinates (pixels) with the following function:

void glScissor(GLint x, GLint y, GLsizei width, GLsizei height);

The x and y parameters specify the lower-left corner of the scissor box, with width and height being the corresponding dimensions of the scissor box. Listing 3.2 shows the rendering code for the sample program Scissor. This program clears the color buffer three times, each time with a smaller scissor box specified before the clear. The result is a set of overlapping colored rectangles, as shown in Figure 3.25.

LISTING 3.2   Using the Scissor Box to Render a Series of Rectangles

```
void RenderScene(void)
    {
    // Clear blue window
    glClearColor(0.0f, 0.0f, 1.0f, 0.0f);
    glClear(GL_COLOR_BUFFER_BIT);

    // Now set scissor to smaller red sub region
    glClearColor(1.0f, 0.0f, 0.0f, 0.0f);
    glScissor(100, 100, 600, 400);
    glEnable(GL_SCISSOR_TEST);
    glClear(GL_COLOR_BUFFER_BIT);

    // Finally, an even smaller green rectangle
    glClearColor(0.0f, 1.0f, 0.0f, 0.0f);
    glScissor(200, 200, 400, 200);
    glClear(GL_COLOR_BUFFER_BIT);

    // Turn scissor back off for next render
    glDisable(GL_SCISSOR_TEST);

    glutSwapBuffers();
    }
```

FIGURE 3.25   Shrinking scissor boxes.

Blending

You already learned that OpenGL rendering places color values in the color buffer under normal circumstances. You also learned that depth values for each fragment are also placed in the depth buffer. When depth testing is turned off (disabled), new color values simply overwrite any other values already present in the color buffer. When depth testing is turned on (enabled), new color fragments replace an existing fragment only if they are deemed closer to the near clipping plane than the values already there. Under normal circumstances then, any drawing operation is either discarded entirely, or just completely overwrites any old color values, depending on the result of the depth test. This obliteration of the underlying color values no longer happens the moment you turn on OpenGL blending:

```
glEnable(GL_BLEND);
```

When blending is enabled, the incoming color is combined with the color value already present in the color buffer. How these colors are combined leads to a great many and varied special effects.

Combining Colors

First, we must introduce a more official terminology for the color values coming in and already in the color buffer. The color value already stored in the color buffer is called the destination color, and this color value contains the three individual red, green, and blue components, and optionally a stored alpha value as well. A color value that is coming in as a result of more rendering commands that may or may not interact with the destination color is called the source color. The source color also contains either three or four color components (red, green, blue, and optionally alpha). Note that anytime you omit an alpha value, OpenGL assumes it is 1.0.

How the source and destination colors are combined when blending is enabled is controlled by the blending equation. By default, the blending equation looks like this:

$$Cf = (Cs * S) + (Cd * D)$$

Here, `Cf` is the final computed color, `Cs` is the source color, `Cd` is the destination color, and `S` and `D` are the source and destination blending factors. These blending factors are set with the following function:

```
glBlendFunc(GLenum S, GLenum D);
```

As you can see, `S` and `D` are enumerants and not physical values that you specify directly. Table 3.3 lists the possible values for the blending function. The subscripts stand for source, destination, and color (for blend color, to be discussed shortly). `R`, `G`, `B`, and `A` stand for Red, Green, Blue, and Alpha, respectively.

TABLE 3.3   OpenGL Blending Factors

Function	RGB Blend Factors	Alpha Blend Factor
GL_ZERO	(0,0,0)	0
GL_ONE	(1,1,1)	1
GL_SRC_COLOR	(Rs,Gs,Bs)	As
GL_ONE_MINUS_SRC_COLOR	(1,1,1) – (Rs,Gs,Bs)	1 – As
GL_DST_COLOR	(Rd,Gd,Bd)	Ad
GL_ONE_MINUS_DST_COLOR	(1,1,1) – (Rd,Gd,Bd)	1 – Ad
GL_SRC_ALPHA	(As,As,As)	As
GL_ONE_MINUS_SRC_ALPHA	(1,1,1) – (As,As,As)	1 – As
GL_DST_ALPHA	(Ad,Ad,Ad)	Ad
GL_ONE_MINUS_DST_ALPHA	(1,1,1) – (Ad,Ad,Ad)	1 – Ad
GL_CONSTANT_COLOR	(Rc,Gc,Bc)	Ac
GL_ONE_MINUS_CONSTANT_COLOR	(1,1,1) – (Rc,Gc,Bc)	1 – Ac
GL_CONSTANT_ALPHA	(Ac,Ac,Ac)	Ac
GL_ONE_MINUS_CONSTANT_ALPHA	(1,1,1) – (Ac,Ac,Ac)	1 – Ac
GL_SRC_ALPHA_SATURATE	(f,f,f)*	1

Where f = min(As, 1 – Ad).

Remember that colors are represented by floating-point numbers, so adding them, subtracting them, and even multiplying them are all perfectly valid operations. Table 3.3 may seem a bit bewildering, so let's look at a common blending function combination:

```
glBlendFunc(GL_SRC_ALPHA, GL_ONE_MINUS_SRC_ALPHA);
```

This function tells OpenGL to take the source (incoming) color and multiply the color (the RGB values) by the alpha value. Add this to the result of multiplying the destination color by one minus the alpha value from the source. Say, for example, that you have the color Red (1.0f, 0.0f, 0.0f, 0.0f) already in the color buffer. This is the destination color, or Cd. If something is drawn over this with the color blue and an alpha of 0.6 (0.0f, 0.0f, 1.0f, 0.6f), you would compute the final color as shown here:

Cd = destination color = (1.0f, 0.0f, 0.0f, 0.0f)

Cs = source color = (0.0f, 0.0f, 1.0f, 0.6f)

S = source alpha = 0.6

D = one minus source alpha = 1.0 – 0.6 = 0.4

Now, the equation

$$Cf = (Cs * S) + (Cd * D)$$

evaluates to

$$Cf = (Blue * 0.6) + (Red * 0.4)$$

The final color is a scaled combination of the original red value and the incoming blue value. The higher the incoming alpha value, the more of the incoming color is added and the less of the original color is retained.

This blending function is often used to achieve the effect of drawing a transparent object in front of some other opaque object. This particular technique does require, however, that you draw the background object or objects first and then draw the transparent object blended over the top.

For example, in the Blending sample program, we use transparency to achieve the illusion of a partially transparent red rectangle that we can move about on a white background. Also in the window are a red, blue, green, and black rectangle. Using the cursor keys, you can move the transparent rectangle around and over the other colors. The output of this program is shown in Figure 2.26.

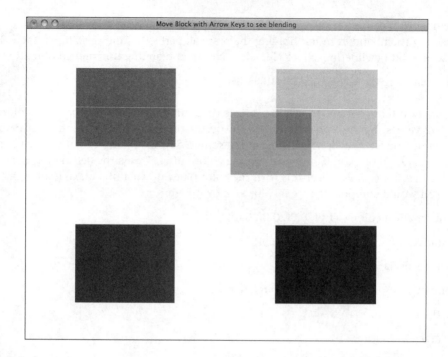

FIGURE 3.26   The movable red rectangle blending with the background colors.

This example is based on the Move example program from Chapter 2. In this case, however, the background is white, and we also draw the four other colored blocks in fixed locations. The red transparent block is drawn with blending turned on, and a red color that has an alpha set to 0.5.

```
GLfloat vRed[] = { 1.0f, 0.0f, 0.0f, 0.5f };
glEnable(GL_BLEND);
glBlendFunc(GL_SRC_ALPHA, GL_ONE_MINUS_SRC_ALPHA);
shaderManager.UseStockShader(GLT_SHADER_IDENTITY, vRed);
squareBatch.Draw();
glDisable(GL_BLEND);
```

It is interesting to note that the white simply dilutes the red color, the black darkens it, and blending red with red is simply...just still red.

Changing the Blending Equation

The blending equation we showed you earlier,

$$Cf = (Cs * S) + (Cd * D)$$

is the default blending equation. You can actually choose from five different blending equations, each given in Table 3.4 and selected with the following function:

```
void glBlendEquation(GLenum mode);
```

TABLE 3.4 Available Blend Equation Modes

Mode	Function
GL_FUNC_ADD (default)	$Cf = (Cs * S) + (Cd * D)$
GL_FUNC_SUBTRACT	$Cf = (Cs * S) - (Cd * D)$
GL_FUNC_REVERSE_SUBTRACT	$Cf = (Cd * D) - (Cs * S)$
GL_MIN	$Cf = min(Cs, Cd)$
GL_MAX	$Cf = max(Cs, Cd)$

In addition to glBlendFunc, you have even more flexibility with this function:

```
void glBlendFuncSeparate(GLenum srcRGB, GLenum dstRGB, GLenum srcAlpha, GLenum dstAlpha);
```

Whereas glBlendFunc specifies the blend functions for source and destination RGBA values, glBlendFuncSeparate allows you to specify blending functions for the RGB and alpha components separately.

Finally, as shown in Table 3.4, the GL_CONSTANT_COLOR, GL_ONE_MINUS_CONSTANT_COLOR, GL_CONSTANT_ALPHA, and GL_ONE_MINUS_CONSTANT_ALPHA values all allow a constant blending color to be introduced to the blending equation. This constant blending color is initially black (0.0f, 0.0f, 0.0f, 0.0f), but it can be changed with this function:

```
void glBlendColor(GLclampf red, GLclampf green, Glclampf blue, GLclampf alpha);
```

Antialiasing

Another use for OpenGL's blending capabilities is antialiasing. Under most circumstances, individual rendered fragments are mapped to individual pixels on a computer screen. These pixels are square (or squarish), and usually you can spot the division between two colors quite clearly. These jaggies, as they are often called, catch the eye's attention and can destroy the illusion that the image is natural. These jaggies are a dead giveaway that the image is computer generated! For many rendering tasks, it is desirable to achieve as much realism as possible, particularly in games, simulations, or artistic endeavors. Figure 3.27 shows the output for the sample program Smoother. In Figure 3.28, we zoomed in on a line segment and some points to show the jagged edges.

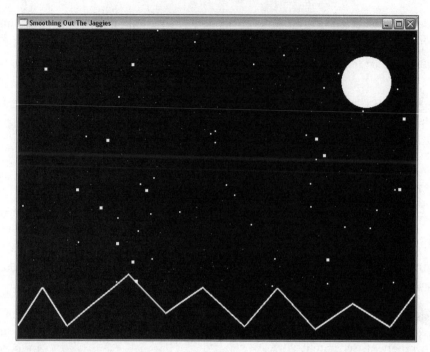

FIGURE 3.27   Output from the program Smoother.

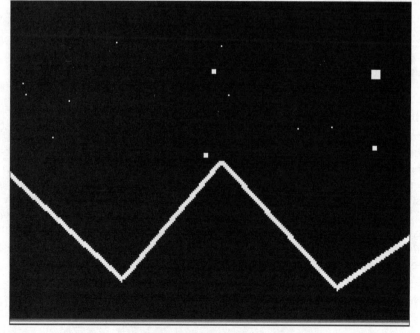

FIGURE 3.28   A closer look at some jaggies.

To get rid of the jagged edges between primitives, OpenGL uses blending to blend the color of the fragment with the destination color of the pixel and its surrounding pixels. In essence, pixel colors are smeared slightly to neighboring pixels along the edges of any primitives.

Turning on antialiasing is simple. First, you must enable blending and set the blending function to be the same as you used in the preceding section for transparency:

```
glEnable(GL_BLEND);
glBlendFunc(GL_SRC_ALPHA, GL_ONE_MINUS_SRC_ALPHA);
```

You also need to make sure the blend equation is set to GL_ADD, but because this is the default and most common blending equation, we don't show it here. After blending is enabled and the proper blending function and equation are selected, you can choose to antialias points, lines, and/or polygons (any solid primitive) by calling glEnable:

```
glEnable(GL_POINT_SMOOTH);    // Smooth out points
glEnable(GL_LINE_SMOOTH);     // Smooth out lines
glEnable(GL_POLYGON_SMOOTH);  // Smooth out polygon edges
```

You should use GL_POLYGON_SMOOTH with care. You might expect to smooth out edges on solid geometry, but there are other tedious rules to making this work. For example, geometry that overlaps requires a different blending mode, and you may need to sort your scene from front to back. We won't go into the details because this method of solid object antialiasing has fallen out of common use and has largely been replaced by a superior route to smoothing edges on 3D geometry called multisampling. This feature is discussed in the next section. Without multisampling, you can still get this overlapping geometry problem with antialiased lines that overlap. For wireframe rendering, for example, you can usually get away with just disabling depth testing to avoid the depth artifacts at the line intersections.

Listing 3.3 shows the code from the Smoother program that responds to a pop-up menu that allows the user to switch between antialiased and nonantialiased rendering modes. When this program is run with antialiasing enabled, the points and lines appear smoother (fuzzier). In Figure 3.29, a zoomed-in section shows the same area as Figure 3.27, but now with the jagged edges smoothed out.

LISTING 3.3 Switching Between Antialiased and Normal Rendering

```
///////////////////////////////////////////////////////////////////////
// Reset flags as appropriate in response to menu selections
void ProcessMenu(int value)
    {
    switch(value)
        {
        case 1:
            // Turn on antialiasing, and give hint to do the best
            // job possible.
            glBlendFunc(GL_SRC_ALPHA, GL_ONE_MINUS_SRC_ALPHA);
            glEnable(GL_BLEND);
            glEnable(GL_POINT_SMOOTH);
            glHint(GL_POINT_SMOOTH_HINT, GL_NICEST);
            glEnable(GL_LINE_SMOOTH);
            glHint(GL_LINE_SMOOTH_HINT, GL_NICEST);
            glEnable(GL_POLYGON_SMOOTH);
            glHint(GL_POLYGON_SMOOTH_HINT, GL_NICEST);
            break;

        case 2:
            // Turn off blending and all smoothing
            glDisable(GL_BLEND);
            glDisable(GL_LINE_SMOOTH);
            glDisable(GL_POINT_SMOOTH);
            glDisable(GL_POLYGON_SMOOTH);
            break;

        default:
            break;
        }

    // Trigger a redraw
    glutPostRedisplay();
    }
```

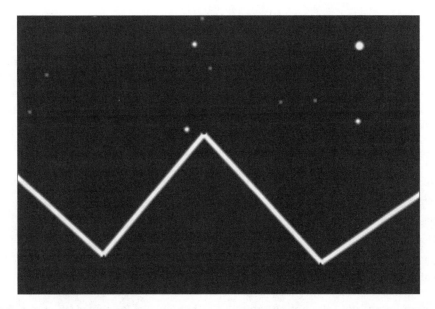

FIGURE 3.29   No more jaggies!

Note especially here the calls to the `glHint` function discussed in Chapter 2. There are many algorithms and approaches to achieve antialiased primitives. Any specific OpenGL implementation may choose any one of those approaches, and perhaps even support two! You can ask OpenGL, if it does support multiple antialiasing algorithms, to choose one that is very fast (`GL_FASTEST`) or the one with the most accuracy in appearance (`GL_NICEST`).

Multisampling

One of the biggest advantages to antialiasing is that it smoothes out the edges of primitives and can lend a more natural and realistic appearance to renderings. Point and line smoothing is widely supported, but unfortunately polygon smoothing is not available on all platforms. Even when `GL_POLYGON_SMOOTH` is available, it is not as convenient a means of having your whole scene antialiased as you might think. Because it is based on the blending operation, you would need to sort all your primitives from front to back! Yuck.

A more modern addition to OpenGL to address this shortcoming is multisampling. When this feature is supported (it is an OpenGL 1.3 or later feature), an additional buffer is added to the framebuffer that includes the color, depth, and stencil values. All primitives are sampled multiple times per pixel, and the results are stored in this buffer. These samples are resolved to a single value each time the pixel is updated, so from the programmer's standpoint, it appears automatic and happens "behind the scenes." Naturally, this extra memory and processing that must take place are not without their performance penalties, and some implementations may not support multisampling for multiple rendering contexts.

To get multisampling, you must first obtain a rendering context that has support for a multisampled framebuffer. This varies from platform to platform, but GLUT exposes a bitfield (`GLUT_MULTISAMPLE`) that allows you to request this until you reach the operating system-specific chapters in Part III. For example, to request a multisampled, full-color, double-buffered framebuffer with depth, you would call

```
glutInitDisplayMode(GLUT_DOUBLE | GLUT_RGB | GLUT_DEPTH | GLUT_MULTISAMPLE);
```

You can turn multisampling on and off using the `glEnable`/`glDisable` combination and the `GL_MULTISAMPLE` token:

```
glEnable(GL_MULTISAMPLE);
```

or

```
glDisable(GL_MULTISAMPLE);
```

Another important note about multisampling is that when it is enabled, the point, line, and polygon smoothing features via antialiasing are ignored if enabled. This means you cannot use point and line smoothing at the same time as multisampling. On a given OpenGL implementation, points and lines may look better with smoothing turned on instead of multisampling. To accommodate this, you might turn off multisampling before drawing points and lines and then turn on multisampling for other solid geometry. The following pseudocode shows a rough outline of how to do this:

```
glDisable(GL_MULTISAMPLE);
glEnable(GL_POINT_SMOOTH);

// Draw some smooth points
// ...
glDisable(GL_POINT_SMOOTH);
glEnable(GL_MULTISAMPLE);
```

Of course if you do not have a multisampled buffer to begin with, OpenGL behaves as if `GL_MULTISAMPLE` were disabled.

STATE SORTING

Turning different OpenGL features on and off changes the internal state of the driver. These state changes can be costly in terms of rendering performance. Frequently, performance-sensitive programmers go to great lengths to sort all the drawing commands so that geometry needing the same state is drawn together. This state sorting is one of the more common techniques to improve rendering speed in games.

The multisample buffers use the RGB values of fragments by default and do not include the alpha component of the colors. You can change this by calling `glEnable` with one of the following three values:

- `GL_SAMPLE_ALPHA_TO_COVERAGE`—Use the alpha value.

- `GL_SAMPLE_ALPHA_TO_ONE`—Set alpha to 1 and use it.

- `GL_SAMPLE_COVERAGE`—Use the value set with `glSampleCoverage`.

When `GL_SAMPLE_COVERAGE` is enabled, the `glSampleCoverage` function allows you to specify a value that is ANDed (bitwise) with the fragment coverage value:

```
void glSampleCoverage(GLclampf value, GLboolean invert);
```

This fine-tuning of how the multisample operation works is not strictly specified by the specification, and the exact results may vary from implementation to implementation.

Summary

We covered a lot of ground in this chapter. In fact if you are brand new to OpenGL or 3D graphics programming in general, this may well be the most important foundational chapter in the book. Beginning with an explanation of how today's programmable hardware renders with shaders, we covered how to set up your 3D coordinate space, organize your vertices and other attributes into primitive batches, and render them with the appropriate shader and uniform values.

Front and back face winding and face culling are an important part of a great many graphics rendering algorithms, as well as an important part of your performance tuning efforts. You saw how depth testing is almost a prerequisite for most 3D scenes, and even how to use it to speed up fill performance, or fib to it by adding a small offset to fragments you need to be coincident with other geometry. A huge number of special effects and techniques make use of blending, and this topic is revisited again in the next chapter where we show a more dramatic use of blending to create a simple reflection effect. Finally, you saw how antialiasing and multisampling can add a significant quality improvement to computer-generated images.

We encourage you to experiment with what you have learned in this chapter. Use your imagination and create some of your own 3D objects before moving on to the rest of the book. You'll then have some personal samples to work with and enhance as you learn and explore new techniques throughout the book. In the next chapter, we are really going to bring your objects to life!

CHAPTER 4

Basic Transformations: A Vector/Matrix Primer

by Richard S. Wright, Jr.

WHAT YOU'LL LEARN IN THIS CHAPTER:

- What a vector is, and why you should care

- What a matrix is, and why you should care more

- How we use matrices and vectors to move geometry around

- The OpenGL conventions of the modelview and projection matrices

- What a camera is, and how to apply its transformation

- How to transform a point lights position into eye coordinates

In Chapter 3, "Basic Rendering," you learned how to draw points, lines, and triangles in 3D. To turn a collection of shapes into a coherent scene, you must arrange them in relation to one another and to the viewer. In this chapter, you start moving shapes and objects around in your coordinate system. The ability to place and orient your objects in a scene is a crucial tool for any 3D graphics programmer. As you will see, it is actually convenient to describe your objects' dimensions around the origin and then transform the objects into the desired positions.

Is This the Dreaded Math Chapter?

In most books on 3D graphics programming, yes, this would be the dreaded math chapter. However, you can relax; we take a more moderate approach to these principles than some texts.

The keys to object and coordinate transformations are two matrix conventions used by OpenGL programmers. To familiarize you with these matrices, this chapter strikes a compromise between two extremes in computer graphics philosophy. On the one hand, we could warn you, "Please review a textbook on linear algebra before reading this chapter." On the other hand, we could perpetuate the deceptive reassurance that you can "learn to do 3D graphics without all those complex mathematical formulas." But we don't agree with either camp.

In reality, you can get along just fine without understanding the finer mathematics of 3D graphics, just as you can drive your car every day without having to know anything at all about automotive mechanics and the internal combustion engine. But you had better know enough about your car to realize that you need an oil change every so often, that you have to fill the tank with gas regularly, and that you must change the tires when they get bald. This knowledge makes you a responsible (and safe!) automobile owner. If you want to be a responsible and capable OpenGL programmer, the same standards apply. You need to understand at least the basics so you know what can be done and what tools best suit the job. If you are a beginner, you will find that, with some practice, matrix math and vectors will gradually make more and more sense, and you will develop a more intuitive (and powerful) ability to make full use of the concepts we introduce in this chapter.

So even if you don't already have the ability to multiply two matrices in your head, you need to know what matrices are and that they are the means to OpenGL's 3D magic. But before you go dusting off that old linear algebra textbook (doesn't everyone have one?), have no fear: The GLTools library has a component called Math3d that contains a number of useful 3D math routines and data types that are compatible with OpenGL. Although you don't have to do all your matrix and vector manipulation yourself, you still know what they are and how to apply them. See—you can eat your cake and have it too!

A Crash Course in 3D Graphics Math

There are a good many books on the math behind 3D graphics, and a few of the better ones that we have found are listed in Appendix A, "Further Reading." We do not pretend here that we are going to cover everything that is *important* for you to know. We are not even going to try and cover everything you *should* know. In this chapter, we are just going to cover what you really *need* to know. If you're already a math wiz, you should skip immediately to the section ahead on the modelview matrix. Not only do you already know what we are about to cover, but most math fans will be somewhat offended that we did not give sufficient space to their favorite feature of homogeneous coordinate spaces.

Imagine one of those reality TV shows where you must escape a virtual swamp filled with crocodiles. How much 3D math do you really need to know to *survive*? That's what the next two sections are going to be about, 3D math survival skills. The crocodiles do not care if you really know what a homogeneous coordinate space is or not.

Vectors, or Which Way Is Which?

We already covered the concept of a vertex and 3D Cartesian coordinates in Chapters 1, "Introduction to 3D Graphics and OpenGL," and Chapter 2, "Getting Started." Basically, a vertex is a position in XYZ coordinate space, and a given position in space is defined by exactly one and only one unique XYZ triplet. An XYZ value, however, can also represent a *vector* (in fact, for the mathematically pure in heart, a vertex is actually a vector too...there, we threw you a bone). A vector is perhaps the single most important foundational concept to understand when it comes to manipulating 3D geometry. Those three values (X, Y, and Z) combined represent two important values: a direction and a magnitude.

Figure 4.1 shows a point in space (picked arbitrarily) and an arrow drawn from the origin of the coordinate system to that point in space. The point can be thought of as a vertex when you are stitching together triangles, but the arrow can be thought of as a vector. A vector is first, simply a direction from the origin toward the point in space. We use vectors all the time in OpenGL to represent directional quantities. For example, the x-axis is the vector (1, 0, 0). Go positive one unit in the X direction, and zero in the Y and Z direction. A vector is also how we point where we are going, for example, which way is the camera pointing, or in which direction do we want to move to get away from that crocodile!

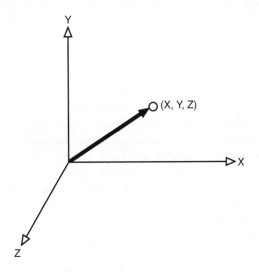

FIGURE 4.1   A point in space is both a vertex and a vector.

The second quantity a vector can represent is the magnitude. The magnitude of a vector is the length of the vector. For our X-axis vector (1, 0, 0), the length of the vector is one. A vector with a length of one, we call a *unit vector*. If a vector is not a unit vector and we want to scale it to make it one, we call that *normalization*. Normalizing a vector scales it such that its length is one. Unit vectors are important when we only want to represent a direction and not a magnitude. A magnitude can be important as well; for example, it can tell us how far we need to move in a given direction—how far away I need to get from that crocodile.

The math3d library has two data types that can represent a three- or four-component vector: `M3DVector3f` can represent a three-component vector (X, Y, Z), and `M3DVector4f` can represent a four component vector (X, Y, Z, W). The W coordinate is typically set to 1.0. The X, Y, and Z values are scaled by dividing by W, and dividing by 1.0 essentially leaves the XYZ values alone. They are defined as arrays simply as follows:

```
typedef float M3DVector3f[3];
typedef float M3DVector4f[4];
```

Declaring a three-component vector is as simple as

```
M3DVector3f vVector;
```

Likewise you can declare and initialize a four-component vertex.

```
M3DVector4f vVertex = { 0.0f, 0.0f, 1.0f, 1.0f };
```

Now, an array of three-component vertices, such as for a triangle:

```
M3DVector3f vVerts[] = { -0.5f, 0.0f, 0.0f,
                          0.5f, 0.0f, 0.0f,
                          0.0f, 0.5f, 0.0f };
```

We need to be careful here not to gloss over that fourth W component too much. Most of the time when you specify geometry with vertex positions, a three component vertex is all you want to store and send to OpenGL. For many directional vectors, such as a surface normal (used for lighting calculations), again, a three-component vector suffices. However, we soon delve into the world of matrices, and to transform a 3D vertex, you must multiply it by a 4 x 4 transformation matrix. The rules are you must multiply a four-component vector by a 4 x 4 matrix; if you try and use a three-component vector with a 4 x 4 matrix...the crocodiles will eat you! More on what all this means soon. Essentially, if you are going to do your own matrix operations on vectors, then you will probably want four-component vectors in many cases.

Dot Product

Vectors can be added, subtracted, and scaled by simply adding, subtracting, or scaling their individual XYZ components. An interesting and useful operation, however, that can be applied only to two vectors is called the *dot product*.

The dot product between two (three-component) unit vectors returns a scalar (just one value) that represents the angle between the two vectors. For this to work, the two vectors must be unit length, and the value returned falls between -1.0 and +1.0. The number is actually the cosine of the angle between the vectors. This operation is done extensively between a surface normal vector and a vector pointing toward a light source in diffuse lighting calculations. We even do this ourselves in shader code in Chapter 6, "Thinking Outside the Box: Nonstock Shaders." Figure 4.2 shows two vectors, V1 and V2, and how the angle between them is represented.

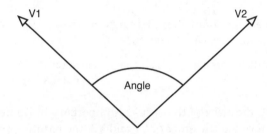

FIGURE 4.2   The dot product returns the angle between two vectors.

The math3d library again has some useful functions that use the dot product operation. For starters, you can actually get the dot product itself between two vectors with the function m3dDotProduct3.

```
float m3dDotProduct3(const M3DVector3f u, const M3DVector3f v);
```

The actual dot product is a value between -1 and +1 that represents the cosine of the angle between the two unit vectors. A slightly higher level function, m3dGetAngleBetweenVectors3, actually returns this angle in radians.

```
float m3dGetAngleBetweenVectors3(const M3DVector3f u, const M3DVector3f v);
```

Cross Product

Another useful mathematical operation between two vectors is the *cross product*. The cross product between two vectors is a third vector perpendicular to the plane defined by the first two vectors. For the cross product to work, the two vectors don't have to be unit length either. Figure 4.3 shows two vectors, V1 and V2, and their cross product V3.

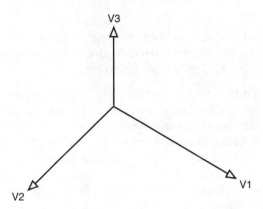

FIGURE 4.3   The cross product returns a third vector perpendicular to the other two.

Again, the math3d library has a function that takes the cross product of two vectors and returns the resulting vector, m3dCrossProduct3.

```
void m3dCrossProduct3(M3DVector3f result, const M3DVector3f u,
                                          const M3DVector3f v);
```

Unlike the dot product, the order of the vectors is important. In Figure 4.3, V3 is the result of V2 cross V1. If you reversed the order of V1 and V2, the resulting vector V3 would point in the opposite direction. Applications of the cross product are numerous, from finding surface normals of triangles, to constructing transformation matrices.

The Matrix

The matrix is not just a Hollywood movie trilogy, but an exceptionally powerful mathematical tool that greatly simplifies the process of solving one or more equations with variables that have complex relationships to each other. One common example of this, near and dear to the hearts of graphics programmers, is coordinate transformations. For example, if you have a point in space represented by x, y, and z coordinates, and you need to know where that point is if you rotate it some number of degrees around some arbitrary point and orientation, you would use a matrix. Why? Because the new x coordinate depends not only on the old x coordinate and the other rotation parameters, but also on what the y and z coordinates were as well. This kind of dependency between the variables and solution is just the sort of problem that matrices excel at. For fans of the *Matrix* movies who have a mathematical inclination, the term *matrix* is indeed an appropriate title.

Mathematically, a matrix is nothing more than a set of numbers arranged in uniform rows and columns—in programming terms, a two-dimensional array. A matrix doesn't have to be square, but each row or column must have the same number of elements as every other row or column in the matrix. Figure 4.4 presents some examples of matrices. They don't represent anything in particular but serve only to demonstrate matrix structure. Note that it is also valid for a matrix to have a single column or row. A single row or column of numbers would more simply be called a vector, as discussed previously. In fact, as you will soon see, we can think of some matrices as a table of column vectors.

$$\begin{bmatrix} 1 & 4 & 7 \\ 2 & 5 & 8 \\ 3 & 6 & 9 \end{bmatrix} \begin{bmatrix} 0 & 42 \\ 1.5 & 0.877 \\ 2 & 14 \end{bmatrix} \begin{bmatrix} 1 \\ 2 \\ 3 \\ 4 \end{bmatrix}$$

FIGURE 4.4   Three examples of matrices.

Matrix and vector are two important terms that you see often in 3D graphics programming literature. When dealing with these quantities, you also see the term *scalar*. A scalar is just an ordinary single number used to represent magnitude or a specific quantity (you know—a regular old, plain, simple number...like before you cared or had all this jargon added to your vocabulary).

Matrices can be multiplied and added together, but they can also be multiplied by vectors and scalar values. Multiplying a point (a vector) by a matrix (a transformation) yields a new transformed point (a vector). Matrix transformations are actually not too difficult to understand but can be intimidating at first. Because an understanding of matrix transformations is fundamental to many 3D tasks, you should still make an attempt to become familiar with them. Fortunately, only a little understanding is enough to get you going and doing some pretty incredible things with OpenGL. Over time, and with a little more practice and study (see Appendix A), you will master this mathematical tool yourself.

In the meantime, like previously for vectors, you will find a number of useful matrix functions and features available in the math3d library. The source code to this library is also available in the files math3d.h and math3d.cpp in the GLTools source code folder. This 3D math library greatly simplifies many tasks in this chapter and the ones to come. One "useful" feature of this library is that it lacks incredibly clever and highly optimized code! This makes the library highly portable and easy to understand. You'll also find it has a very OpenGL-like API.

In your 3D programming tasks with OpenGL, you will use two dimensions of matrix almost exclusively; 3 x 3 and 4 x 4. The math3d library has matrix data types for these dimensions as well:

```
typedef float M3DMatrix33f[9];
typedef float M3DMatrix44f[16];
```

Many matrix libraries define a two-dimensional matrix as a two-dimensional array in C. The OpenGL convention bucks this trend and uses a one-dimensional array. The reason is that OpenGL uses a matrix convention called *Column-Major* matrix ordering. We talk more about this soon, however, talking about all the things you can do with a matrix mathematically is just a bit too abstract for our tastes. Let's explain first what we are trying to accomplish and then show how the matrix makes it possible.

Understanding Transformations

If you think about it, most 3D graphics aren't really 3D. We use 3D concepts and terminology to describe what something looks like; then this 3D data is "squished" onto a 2D computer screen. We call the process of squishing 3D data down into 2D data *projection*, and we introduced both orthographic and perspective projections back in Chapter 1. We refer to the projection whenever we want to describe the type of transformation (orthographic or perspective) that occurs during projection, but projection is only one of the types of transformations that occur in OpenGL. Transformations also allow you to rotate objects around; move them about; and even stretch, shrink, and warp them.

Three types of geometric transformations can occur between the time you specify your vertices and the time they appear on the screen: viewing, modeling, and projection. In this section, we examine the principles of each type of transformation, summarized in Table 4.1.

TABLE 4.1   Summary of the OpenGL Transformation Terminology

Transformation	Use
Viewing	Specifies the location of the viewer or camera
Modeling	Moves objects around the scene
Modelview	Describes the duality of viewing and modeling transformations
Projection	Sizes and reshapes the viewing volume
Viewport	A pseudo-transformation that scales the final output to the window

Eye Coordinates

An important concept throughout this chapter is that of eye coordinates. Eye coordinates are from the viewpoint of the observer, regardless of any transformations that may occur; you can think of them as "absolute" screen coordinates. Thus, eye coordinates represent a virtual fixed coordinate system that is used as a common frame of reference. All the transformations discussed in this chapter are described in terms of their effects relative to the eye coordinate system.

Figure 4.5 shows the eye coordinate system from two viewpoints. On the left (a), the eye coordinates are represented as seen by the observer of the scene (that is, perpendicular to the monitor). On the right (b), the eye coordinate system is rotated slightly so you can better see the relation of the z-axis. Positive x and y are pointed right and up, respectively, from the viewer's perspective. Positive z travels away from the origin toward the user, and negative z values travel farther away from the viewpoint into the screen.

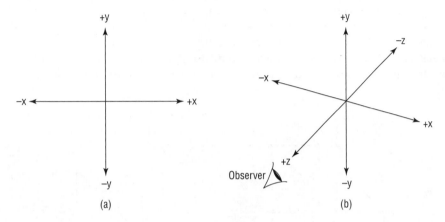

FIGURE 4.5   Two perspectives of eye coordinates.

When you draw in 3D with OpenGL, you use the Cartesian coordinate system. In the absence of any transformations, the system in use is identical to the eye coordinate system just described.

Viewing Transformations

The viewing transformation is the first to be applied to your scene. It is used to determine the vantage point of the scene. By default, the point of observation in a perspective projection is at the origin (0,0,0) looking down the negative z-axis ("into" the monitor screen). This point of observation is moved relative to the eye coordinate system to provide a specific vantage point. When the point of observation is located at the origin, as in a perspective projection, objects drawn with positive z values are behind the observer. In an orthographic projection, however, the viewer is assumed to be infinitely far away on the positive z-axis and can see everything within the viewing volume.

The viewing transformation allows you to place the point of observation anywhere you want and look in any direction. Determining the viewing transformation is like placing and pointing a camera at the scene.

In the grand scheme of things, you must apply the viewing transformation before any other modeling transformations. The reason is that it appears to move the current working coordinate system in respect to the eye coordinate system. All subsequent transformations then occur based on the newly modified coordinate system. Later, you see more easily how this works, when we actually start looking at how to make these transformations.

Modeling Transformations

Modeling transformations are used to manipulate your model and the particular objects within it. These transformations move objects into place, rotate them, and scale them. Figure 4.6 illustrates three of the most common modeling transformations that you will apply to your objects. Figure 4.6a shows translation, in which an object is moved along a given axis. Figure 4.6b shows a rotation, in which an object is rotated about one of the axes. Finally, Figure 4.6c shows the effects of scaling, where the dimensions of the object are increased or decreased by a specified amount. Scaling can occur nonuniformly (the various dimensions can be scaled by different amounts), so you can use scaling to stretch and shrink objects.

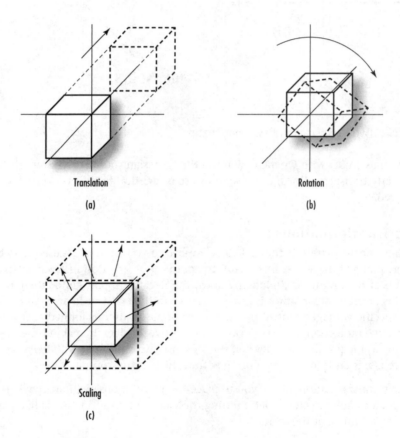

Translation

(a)

Rotation

(b)

Scaling

(c)

FIGURE 4.6   The modeling transformations.

The final appearance of your scene or object can depend greatly on the order in which the modeling transformations are applied. This is particularly true of translation and rotation. Figure 4.7a shows the progression of a square rotated first about the z-axis and then translated down the newly transformed x-axis. In Figure 4.7b, the same square is first translated

down the x-axis and then rotated around the z-axis. The difference in the final disposi-
tions of the square occurs because each transformation is performed with respect to the
last transformation performed. In Figure 4.7a, the square is rotated with respect to the
origin first. In 4.7b, after the square is translated, the rotation is performed around the
newly translated origin.

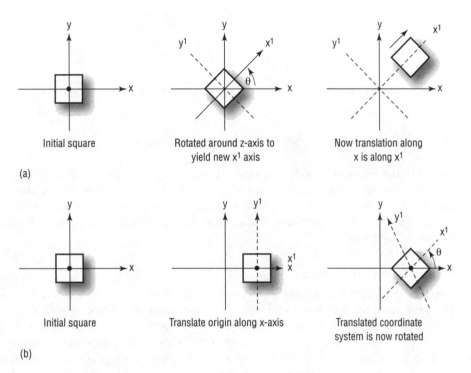

FIGURE 4.7   Modeling transformations: rotation/translation and translation/rotation.

The Modelview Duality

The viewing and modeling transformations are, in fact, the same in terms of their internal
effects as well as their effects on the final appearance of the scene. The distinction between
the two is made purely as a convenience for the programmer. There is no real difference
visually between moving an object backward and moving the reference system forward; as
shown in Figure 4.8, the net effect is the same. (You experience this effect firsthand when
you're sitting in your car at an intersection and you see the car next to you roll forward; it
might seem to you that your own car is rolling backward.) The viewing transformation is
simply a modeling-like transformation that is applied to the entire scene, where objects in
your scene often each have their own individual model transformation, applied after the
viewing transformation. The term *modelview* indicates that these two transformations are
combined in the transformation pipeline into a single matrix—the modelview matrix.

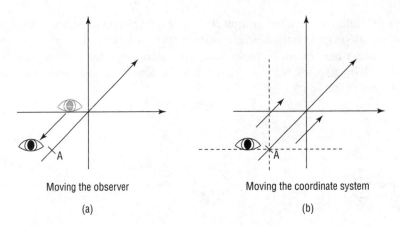

Moving the observer

(a)

Moving the coordinate system

(b)

FIGURE 4.8   Two ways of looking at the viewing transformation.

The viewing transformation, therefore, is essentially nothing but a modeling transformation that you apply to a virtual object (the viewer) before drawing objects. As you will soon see, new transformations are repeatedly specified as you place more objects in the scene. By convention, the initial transformation provides a reference from which all other transformations are based.

Projection Transformations

The projection transformation is applied to your vertices after the modelview transformation. This projection actually defines the viewing volume and establishes *clipping planes*. The clipping planes are plane equations in 3D space that OpenGL uses to determine whether geometry can be seen by the viewer. More specifically, the projection transformation specifies how a finished scene (after all the modeling is done) is projected to the final image on the screen. You learn more about two types of projections—orthographic and perspective—later in this chapter.

In an orthographic, or parallel, projection, all the polygons are drawn on-screen with exactly the relative dimensions specified. Lines and polygons are mapped directly to the 2D screen using parallel lines, which means no matter how far away something is, it is still drawn the same size, just flattened against the screen. This type of projection is typically used for rendering two-dimensional images such as blueprints or two-dimensional graphics such as text or on-screen menus.

A perspective projection shows scenes more as they appear in real life instead of as a blueprint. The hallmark of perspective projections is foreshortening, which makes distant objects appear smaller than nearby objects of the same size. Lines in 3D space that might be parallel do not always appear parallel to the viewer. With a railroad track, for instance, the rails are parallel, but using perspective projection, they appear to converge at some distant point.

The benefit of perspective projection is that you don't have to figure out where lines converge or how much smaller distant objects are. All you need to do is specify the scene using the modelview transformations and then apply the perspective projection matrix. Linear algebra works all the magic for you. Figure 4.9 compares orthographic and perspective projections on two different scenes.

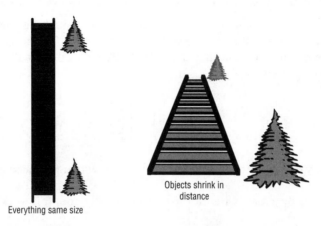

Everything same size

Objects shrink in distance

FIGURE 4.9 A side-by-side example of an orthographic versus perspective projection.

Orthographic projections are used most often for 2D drawing purposes where you want an exact correspondence between pixels and drawing units. You might use them for a schematic layout, text, or perhaps a 2D graphing application. You also can use an orthographic projection for 3D renderings when the depth of the rendering has a very small depth in comparison to the distance from the viewpoint. Perspective projections are used for rendering scenes that contain wide-open spaces or objects that need to have the foreshortening applied. For the most part, perspective projections are typical for 3D graphics. In fact, looking at a 3D object with an orthographic projection can be somewhat unsettling.

Viewport Transformations

When all is said and done, you end up with a two-dimensional projection of your scene that will be mapped to a window somewhere on your screen. This mapping to physical window coordinates is the last transformation that is done, and it is called the viewport transformation. Usually, a one-to-one correspondence exists between the color buffer and window pixels, but this is not always strictly the case. In some circumstances, the viewport transformation remaps what are called "normalized" device coordinates to window coordinates. Fortunately, this is something you don't need to worry about, and the graphics hardware does this for you.

The Modelview Matrix

The modelview matrix is a 4 x 4 matrix that represents the transformed coordinate system you are using to place and orient your objects. The vertices you provide for your primitives are used as a single-column matrix (a vector) and multiplied by the modelview matrix to yield new transformed coordinates in relation to the eye coordinate system.

In Figure 4.10, a matrix containing data for a single vertex is multiplied by the modelview matrix to yield new eye coordinates. The vertex data is actually four elements with an extra value, w, that represents a scaling factor. This value is set by default to 1.0, and rarely will you change it yourself.

$$
\begin{bmatrix} X \\ Y \\ Z \\ W \end{bmatrix} \begin{bmatrix} 4 \times 4 \\ M \end{bmatrix} = \begin{bmatrix} X_e \\ Y_e \\ Z_e \\ W_e \end{bmatrix}
$$

FIGURE 4.10   A matrix equation that applies the modelview transformation to a single vertex.

Multiplying a vertex by a matrix transforms it. How exactly does this work?

Matrix Construction

As mentioned previously, OpenGL represents a 4 x 4 matrix not as a two-dimensional array of floating values, but as a single array of 16 floating-point values. This approach is different from many math libraries, which do take the two-dimensional array approach. For example, OpenGL prefers the first of these two examples:

```
GLfloat matrix[16];       // Nice OpenGL friendly matrix
GLfloat matrix[4][4];     // Popular, but not as efficient for OpenGL
```

OpenGL can use the second variation, but the first is a more efficient representation. The reason for this becomes clear in a moment. These 16 elements represent the 4 x 4 matrix, as shown in Figure 4.11. When the array elements traverse down the matrix columns one by one, we call this column-major matrix ordering. In memory, the 4 x 4 approach of the two-dimensional array (the second option in the preceding code) is laid out in a row-major order. In math terms, the two orientations are the transpose of one another.

$$
\begin{bmatrix}
a_0 & a_4 & a_8 & a_{12} \\
a_1 & a_5 & a_9 & a_{13} \\
a_2 & a_6 & a_{10} & a_{14} \\
a_3 & a_7 & a_{11} & a_{15}
\end{bmatrix}
$$

FIGURE 4.11   Column-major matrix ordering.

The real magic lies in the fact that these 16 values represent a particular position in space and an orientation of the three axes with respect to the eye coordinate system (remember that fixed, unchanging coordinate system we talked about earlier). Interpreting these numbers is not hard at all. The four columns each represent a four-element vector. To keep things simple for this book, we focus our attention on just the first three elements of the vectors in the first three columns. The fourth column vector contains the x, y, and z values of the transformed coordinate system's origin.

The first three elements of the first three columns are just directional vectors that represent the orientation (vectors here are used to represent a direction) of the x-, y-, and z-axes in space. For most purposes, these three vectors are always at 90° angles from each other and are usually each of unit length (unless you are also applying a scale or shear). The mathematical term for this (in case you want to impress your friends) is orthonormal when the vectors are unit length, and orthogonal when they are not. Figure 4.12 shows the 4 x 4 transformation matrix with the column vectors highlighted. Notice that the last row of the matrix is all 0s with the exception of the very last element, which is 1.

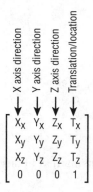

FIGURE 4.12   How a 4 x 4 matrix represents a position and orientation in 3D space.

The most amazing thing is that if you have a 4 x 4 matrix that contains the position and orientation of a nonidentity coordinate system, and you multiply a vertex expressed in the identity coordinate system (expressed as a column matrix or vector) by this matrix, the result is a new vertex that has been transformed to the new coordinate system. This means that any position in space and any desired orientation can be uniquely defined by a 4 x 4 matrix, and if you multiply all of an object's vertices by this matrix, you transform the entire object to the given location and orientation in space!

The Identity Matrix

There are a number of important types of transformation matrices you need to be familiar with before we start trying to use them. The first is the identity matrix. Multiplying a vertex by the identity matrix is equivalent to multiplying it by one; it does nothing to it. As shown in Figure 4.13, the identity matrix contains all zeros except a series of ones that traverse the matrix diagonally.

$$\begin{bmatrix} 8.0 \\ 4.5 \\ -2.0 \\ 1.0 \end{bmatrix} \begin{bmatrix} 1.0 & 0 & 0 & 0 \\ 0 & 1.0 & 0 & 0 \\ 0 & 0 & 1.0 & 0 \\ 0 & 0 & 0 & 1.0 \end{bmatrix} = \begin{bmatrix} 8.0 \\ 4.5 \\ -2.0 \\ 1.0 \end{bmatrix}$$

FIGURE 4.13   Multiplying a vertex by the identity matrix yields the same vertex matrix.

Objects drawn using the identity matrix are untransformed; they are at the origin (last column), and the x, y, and z axes are defined to be the same as those in eye coordinates. You can make an identity matrix in OpenGL like this:

```
GLfloat m[] = { 1.0f, 0.0f, 0.0f, 0.0f,      // X Column
                0.0f, 1.0f, 0.0f, 0.0f,      // Y Column
                0.0f, 0.0f, 1.0f, 0.0f,      // Z Column
                0.0f, 0.0f, 0.0f, 1.0f };    // Translation
```

or using the math3d type `M3DMatrix44f`:

```
M3DMatrix44f m = { 1.0f, 0.0f, 0.0f, 0.0f,      // X Column
                   0.0f, 1.0f, 0.0f, 0.0f,      // Y Column
                   0.0f, 0.0f, 1.0f, 0.0f,      // Z Column
                   0.0f, 0.0f, 0.0f, 1.0f };    // Translation
```

There is also a shortcut function in the math3d library, `m3dLoadIdentity44`, that initializes an empty matrix with identity.

```
void m3dLoadIdentity44(M3DMatrix44f m);
```

If you recall, the very first stock (vertex) shader we used in the book was called the identity shader. It did not transform your vertices at all, but drew them in the default coordinate system with no matrix applied to the vertices at all. We could have multiplied them all by the identity matrix, but that would have been a wasteful and pointless operation.

Translations

A translation matrix simply translates your vertices along one or more of the three axes. Figure 4.14 shows, for example, translating a cube up the y-axis ten units.

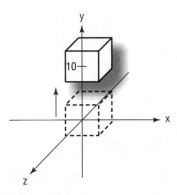

FIGURE 4.14 A cube translated ten units in the positive y direction.

The math3d library makes a translation matrix for you using the function m3dTranslationMatrix44.

```
void m3dTranslationMatrix44(M3DMatrix44f m, float x, float y, float z);
```

Rotations

To rotate an object about one of the three coordinate axes, or indeed any arbitrary vector, you have to devise a rotation matrix. Again, a math3d function comes to the rescue:

```
m3dRotationMatrix44(M3DMatrix44f m, float angle, float x, float y, float z);
```

Here, we perform a rotation around the vector specified by the x, y, and z arguments. The angle of rotation is in the counterclockwise direction measured in radians and specified by the argument angle. In the simplest of cases, the rotation is around only one of the coordinate systems' cardinal axes (x, y, or z).

You can also perform a rotation around an arbitrary axis by specifying x, y, and z values for that vector. To see the axis of rotation, you can just draw a line from the origin to the point represented by (x,y,z). The following code for example creates a rotation matrix that rotates vertices 45 degrees around an arbitrary axis specified by (1,1,1), as illustrated in Figure 4.15.

```
M3DMatrix44f m;
m3dRotationMatrix(m3dDegToRad(45.0), 1.0f, 1.0f, 1.0f);
```

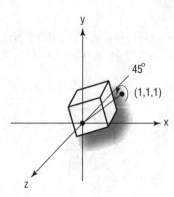

FIGURE 4.15   A cube rotated about an arbitrary axis.

Notice in this example the use of the math3d macro m3dDegToRad. This macro converts degrees to radians because unlike computers, most programmers prefer to think in terms of degrees. The advantage to using the macro instead of an inline function (for you C++ purists we are sure to hear from) is that if the value is a hard-coded literal, the conversion occurs at compile time, and there is no runtime penalty for converting between degrees and radians.

Scaling

Our final transformation matrix is a scaling matrix. A scaling transform changes the size of your object by expanding or contracting all the vertices along the three axes by the factors specified. Creating a scaling matrix with the math3d library is similar to the method for creating a translation or rotation matrix.

```
M3DMatrix44f m;
void m3dScaleMatrix44(M3DMatrix44f m, float xScale, float yScale, float zScale);
```

Scaling does not have to be uniform, and you can use it to both stretch and squeeze objects along different directions. For example, a 10 x 10 x 10 cube could be scaled by two in the x and z directions as shown in Figure 4.16.

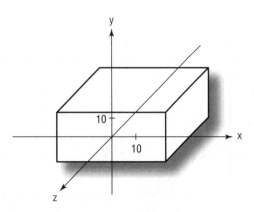

FIGURE 4.16   A nonuniform scaling of a cube.

Adding Transformations Together

Rarely will we want to perform just one of these types of transformations. Rather, we will want to add them together. To place an object where we want it, we may need to translate it to a given location and then rotate it to its desired orientation. Because a 4 x 4 transformation matrix contains both a position and an orientation, you might think one matrix could contain both of these transformations. You'd be right!

Adding two transformations together is as simple as multiplying the two matrices together. The resulting matrix contains the combined transformations, all in one neat little package. The term *add* of course mathematically means addition, but we do not actually "add" the two matrices together; they are multiplied. To deal with this terminology conflict, we usually use the term *concatenate* to mean when two transformations are combined in this way. There is a trick to matrix multiplication that you need to be aware of, though; the order of the operations matters. For example, multiplying a rotation matrix by a translation matrix is not the same as multiplying a translation matrix by a rotation matrix. This was discussed and demonstrated back in Figure 4.7.

The math3d library function `m3dMatrixMultiply44` multiplies two matrices together for you and returns the result:

```
void m3dMatrixMultiply44(M3DMatrix44f product,
                         const M3DMatrix44f a, const M3DMatrix44f b);
```

Let's look at a concrete example of adding these transformations together now.

Applying a Modelview Matrix

In the Move example program in Chapter 2, we moved a red square around the window in response to the arrow keys being pressed. We did this by brute force, updating the coordinates of the triangle fan and then re-creating the primitive batch. The better way to do this is to create the batch one time, usually centered around the origin, and then apply a matrix, the modelview matrix in fact, to the vertices when we render the batch. In the original program, we used the identity shader, which performed no transformations on the vertices; it just passed them through and rendered them in the default Cartesian coordinate system. Another stock shader, the flat shader, accepts a 4 x 4 transformation matrix as one of its parameters.

```
GLShaderManager::UseStockShader(GLT_SHADER_FLAT, M3DMatrix44f m, GLfloat vColor[4]);
```

This shader multiples each vertex by the matrix m before rendering the primitive. In our modified Move example program for this chapter, we keep track of the squares position with two variables yPos and xPos. We can easily create a translation matrix now.

```
m3dTranslationMatrix44(mTranslationMatrix, xPos, yPos, 0.0f);
```

The translation matrix could then be sent to the shader before drawing the object like thus:

```
shaderManager.UseStockShader(GLT_SHADER_FLAT, mTranslationMatrix, vRed);
squareBatch.Draw();
```

To make things more interesting (as well as demonstrate an important point), we also make the square spin as we move it about. Spinning the square in the xy plane involves rotating it around the z-axis. Listing 4.1 shows the entire RenderScene function from our modified Move program.

LISTING 4.1   Code to Translate Then Rotate the Square On the Screen

```
void RenderScene(void)
    {
    // Clear the window with current clearing color
    glClear(GL_COLOR_BUFFER_BIT | GL_DEPTH_BUFFER_BIT | GL_STENCIL_BUFFER_BIT);

    GLfloat vRed[] = { 1.0f, 0.0f, 0.0f, 1.0f };

    M3DMatrix44f mFinalTransform, mTranslationMatrix, mRotationMatrix;

    // Just Translate
    m3dTranslationMatrix44(mTranslationMatrix, xPos, yPos, 0.0f);
```

```
// Rotate 5 degrees every time we redraw
static float yRot = 0.0f;
yRot += 5.0f;
m3dRotationMatrix44(mRotationMatrix, m3dDegToRad(yRot), 0.0f, 0.0f, 1.0f);

m3dMatrixMultiply44(mFinalTransform, mTranslationMatrix, mRotationMatrix);

shaderManager.UseStockShader(GLT_SHADER_FLAT, mFinalTransform, vRed);
squareBatch.Draw();

// Perform the buffer swap
glutSwapBuffers();
}
```

Note how we created the translation matrix mTranslationMatrix and the rotation matrix mRotationMatrix separately. Then we multiplied them together to create the final transformation matrix:

```
m3dMatrixMultiply44(mFinalTransform, mTranslationMatrix, mRotationMatrix);
```

The flat shader takes just one matrix argument, and it multiplies the vertices by that matrix. This "modelview" matrix moves our square around on the screen by translating the vertices within the default coordinate system, which if you recall goes from -1 to +1 on all three axes. This simple coordinate system, however, does not always meet our needs, and it would be convenient to think of our objects in a much bigger coordinate space. Perhaps then another matrix will allow us to scale any coordinate space we like down to this -1 to +1 range. Indeed, this second type of matrix transformation is called projection, and we talk about this shortly.

More Objects

Squares and triangles are going to be just a bit tedious very soon for the purposes of demonstrations. Before going any further, let's introduce some stock objects that are built into the GLTools library. Recall the GLBatch class that serves the purpose of containing a list of vertices and renders them as a specific type of primitive batch. A new class we introduce here is the GLTriangleBatch class. This class is specifically intended to be just a container of triangles. Each vertex can have a surface normal for lighting computations and a texture coordinate. The exact internal implementation of the GLTriangleBatch class uses techniques that aren't discussed until Chapter 12, "Advanced Geometry Management." For now, suffice it to say they organize triangles in the most efficient means available (indexed vertex arrays) and actually store the geometry on the graphics card (using vertex buffer objects).

Using the Triangle Batch Class

Building your own triangle batch object is a simple matter. The recipe is fairly simple. First, you need to make an instance of the object.

```
GLTriangleBatch    myCoolObject;
```

Then begin the mesh by telling the container the maximum number of vertices you plan to use.

```
myCoolObject.BeginMesh(200);              // 200 verts in my cool object.
```

Now add triangles to taste. The AddTriangle member function takes an array of three vertices, an array of three normals, and an array of three texture coordinates.

```
void GLTriangleBatch::AddTriangle(M3DVector3f verts[3], M3DVector3f vNorms[3],
                                                M3DVector2f vTexCoords[3])
```

Don't worry about duplicate vertex data (you might be thinking strips or fans would be more efficient). The GLTriangleBatch class searches for duplicates and optimizes your batch every time you add a vertex. In fact, for very large batches, you may find this executes increasingly slowly every time you add a new triangle.

When you are done adding triangles, call End.

```
myCoolObject.End();
```

Now, simply select your favorite stock shader and call the Draw function.

```
myCoolObject.Draw();
```

You can of course use these objects with your own shaders too, and we talk about the convention you need to follow for this and the GLBatch class in Chapter 6.

The GLTools library contains a number of utility functions that fill a GLTriangleBatch class with an object for you. The example program Objects cycles through these with a press of the spacebar and renders them using the same wireframe technique we used in Chapter 3's Primitives example program. You can also use the arrow keys to rotate each object around to examine them in more detail. Let's take a look at each one in turn.

Making a Sphere

A fundamental shape used for many "handmade" objects is the simple sphere. The gltMakeSphere function takes a reference to a triangle batch, the radius of the sphere, and the number of slices and stacks of which to compose the sphere.

```
void gltMakeSphere(GLTriangleBatch& sphereBatch, GLfloat fRadius,
                        GLint iSlices, GLint iStacks);
```

Figure 4.17 shows the output from the Objects example program for the sphere. While the radius of the sphere should be fairly obvious, the `iSlices` and `iStacks` parameters warrant a little explanation. You can think of the sphere as a series of bands of triangles that go around the sphere. The `iStacks` parameter is the number of these bands stacked from the bottom of the sphere to the top. The `iSlices` parameter is the number of triangle pairs that stretch around the sphere. Typically the number of slices is twice the number of stacks for a nice symmetric sphere. Think about why—there are 360 degrees around a sphere, but only 180 (half that) from the top to the bottom. Another thing to note is these spheres are wrapped around the z-axis, thus +Z is at the top of the sphere, and –Z is at the bottom.

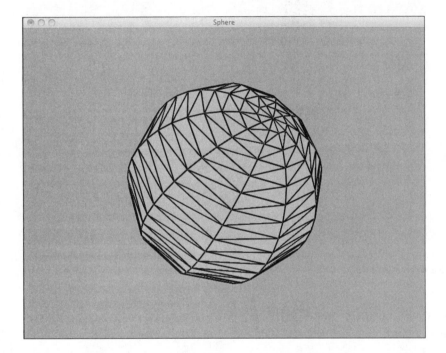

FIGURE 4.17   A sphere.

Making a Torus

Another interesting and useful object is the torus. A torus is a ring-shaped doughnut and is shown in Figure 4.18. The GLTools function to create a torus is `gltMakeTorus`.

```
void gltMakeTorus(GLTriangleBatch& torusBatch, GLfloat majorRadius, GLfloat
minorRadius, GLint numMajor, GLint numMinor);
```

The majorRadius is the radius from the center to the outer edge of the torus, while the minorRadius is the radius to the inner edge. The numMajor and numMinor parameters serve a similar purpose to the iSlices and iStacks parameters for spheres; they are the numbers of subdivisions along the major radius, and again along the inner minor radius.

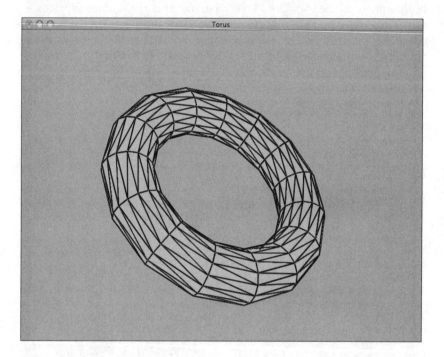

FIGURE 4.18   A torus.

Making a Cylinder or a Cone

A hollow cylinder is made with the function gltMakeCylinder.

```
void gltMakeCylinder(GLTriangleBatch& cylinderBatch, GLfloat baseRadius, GLfloat
topRadius, GLfloat fLength, GLint numSlices, GLint numStacks);
```

Cylinders grow up the positive z-axis from zero, and you can specify both the base and top radius. Figure 4.19 shows a cylinder with two equal radii, and Figure 4.20 shows one with one end set to zero. This essentially makes a cone, but you could just as easily make a funnel shape as well. The numSlices parameter is the number of triangle pairs that circle the z-axis, and the numStacks parameter is the number of rings stacked from the bottom to the top of the cylinder.

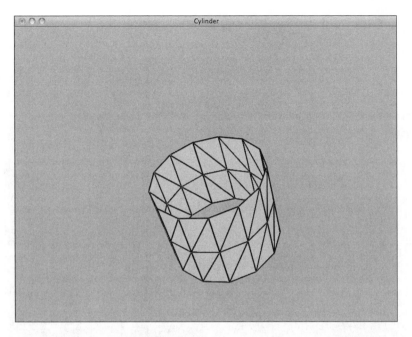

FIGURE 4.19   A cylinder with two equal radii.

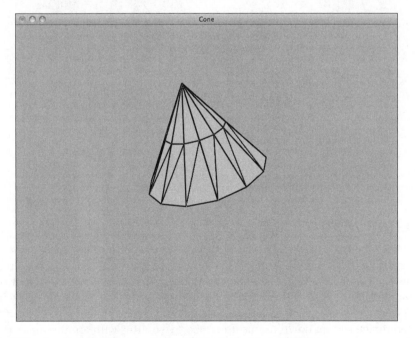

FIGURE 4.20   A cylinder with one end's radius set to zero…a cone.

Making a Disk

Our final surface is the disk. Disks are drawn with loops of triangle bands divided into some number of slices. You can specify an inner radius for a washer type shape or leave it zero to make the disk solid. The gltMakeDisk function, with a by now familiar looking API does the work of filling a GLTriangleBatch with the disk shape, shown in Figure 4.21.

```
void gltMakeDisk(GLTriangleBatch& diskBatch, GLfloat innerRadius, GLfloat
outerRadius, GLint nSlices, GLint nStacks);
```

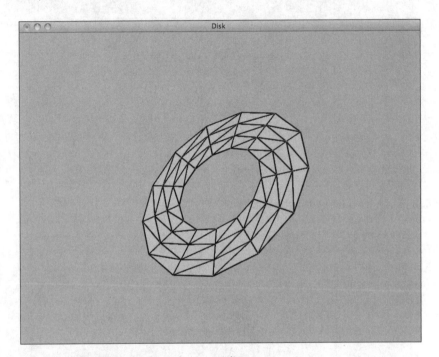

FIGURE 4.21   A disk with an inner and outer radius.

Now that we have some more interesting objects to draw, let's get back to our discussion of creating alternate coordinate systems, or projections for our 3D scenes.

Projection Matrix

The modelview matrix essentially moves your geometry around in eye coordinates. So far, we've been using that default coordinate system that ranges from -1 to +1 on your screen or window (and actually +/-1 in the Z direction, too). What if we want a different coordinate system? Well, the truth is this small coordinate range is really the only one your hardware works with. The trick to using a different coordinate system is to convert your desired coordinate system down to this unit cube. We do this with another matrix: the projection matrix.

The next two example programs Orthographic and Perspective, are not going to be covered in detail from the standpoint of their source code. These examples help to highlight the difference between an orthographic and a perspective projection. These interactive samples make it much easier for you to see firsthand how the projection can distort the appearance of an object. If possible, you should run these examples while reading the next two sections.

Orthographic Projections

The orthographic projection that we have used for most of this book so far is square on all sides. The logical width is equal at the front, back, top, bottom, left, and right sides. This produces a parallel projection, which is useful for drawings of specific objects that do not have any foreshortening when viewed from a distance. This is good for 2D graphics such as text or architectural drawings for which you want to represent the exact dimensions and measurements on-screen.

Figure 4.22 shows the output from the sample program Orthographic in this chapter's subdirectory in the source distribution. To produce this hollow, tubelike box, we used an orthographic projection just as we did for all our previous examples. Figure 4.23 shows the same box rotated more to the side so you can see how long it actually is.

FIGURE 4.22   A hollow square tube shown with an orthographic projection.

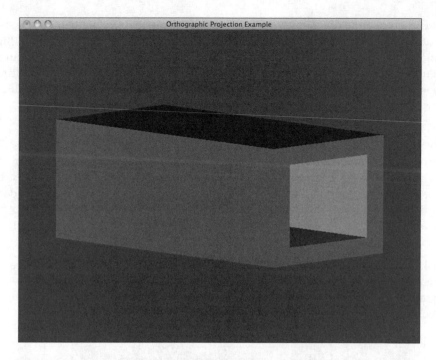

FIGURE 4.23   A side view showing the length of the square tube.

In Figure 4.24, you're looking directly down the barrel of the tube. Because the tube does not converge in the distance, this is not an entirely accurate view of how such a tube appears in real life. To add some perspective, we must use a perspective projection.

Recall from Chapter 3 that we can create an orthographic projection matrix with the math3d library or by using the GLFrustum class as shown here.

```
GLFrustum::SetOrthographic(GLfloat xMin, GLfloat xMax, GLfloat yMin, GLfloat yMax,
GLfloat zMin, GLfloat zMax);
```

FIGURE 4.24 Looking down the barrel of the tube.

Perspective Projection

If you recall, we already discussed the perspective projection back in Chapter 3. Figures 3.3 and 3.4 in that chapter show the geometry of our geometric shape called a frustum. A frustum is a truncated section of a pyramid viewed from the narrow end to the broad end. As a reminder from Chapter 3, we set up perspective projections using the GLFrustum class.

```
GLFrustum::SetPerspective(float fFov, float fAspect, float fNear, float fFar);
```

The parameters for the SetPerspective function are a field-of-view angle in the vertical direction (in degrees), the aspect ratio of the width to height, and the distances to the near and far clipping planes (refer to Figure 3.4). You find the aspect ratio by dividing the width (w) by the height (h) of the window or viewport. The GLFrustum class constructs the appropriate 4 x 4 projection matrix based on these parameters, which then becomes part of our overall transformation pipeline.

Foreshortening adds realism to our earlier orthographic projections of the square tube (see Figures 4.25, 4.26, and 4.27). The only substantial change we made was the switch to a perspective projection.

FIGURE 4.25   The square tube with a perspective projection.

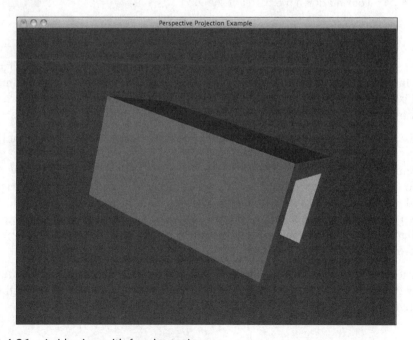

FIGURE 4.26   A side view with foreshortening.

FIGURE 4.27   Looking down the barrel of the tube with perspective added.

The ModelviewProjection Matrix

Let's take a look at how we might put all this together. The ModelviewProjection example program draws a wireframe torus rotating in the middle of the screen. Figure 4.28 shows one frame of the output of this program. We use an instance of the GLFrustum class called viewFrustum to set up a perspective projection matrix for our rendering. The ChangeSize function in Listing 4.2 shows how we set up our viewport and set our perspective matrix.

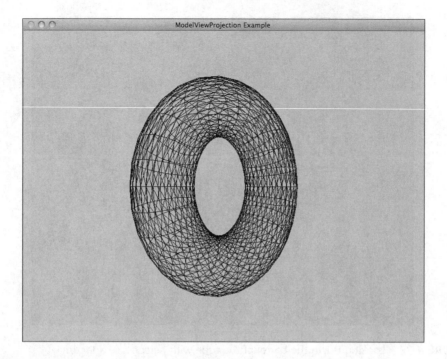

FIGURE 4.28   A spinning torus, transformed by the ModelviewProjection matrix.

LISTING 4.2   Matrix Operations for the ModelviewProjection Example Program

```
// Global view frustum class
GLFrustum           viewFrustum;

. . .

// Set up the viewport and the projection matrix
void ChangeSize(int w, int h)
    {
    // Prevent a divide by zero
    if(h == 0)
        h = 1;

    // Set Viewport to window dimensions
    glViewport(0, 0, w, h);

    viewFrustum.SetPerspective(35.0f, float(w)/float(h), 1.0f, 1000.0f);
    }
```

```
// Called to draw scene
void RenderScene(void)
    {
    // Set up time based animation
    static CStopWatch rotTimer;
    float yRot = rotTimer.GetElapsedSeconds() * 60.0f;

    // Clear the window and the depth buffer
    glClear(GL_COLOR_BUFFER_BIT | GL_DEPTH_BUFFER_BIT);

    // Matrix Variables
    M3DMatrix44f mTranslate, mRotate, mModelview, mModelViewProjection;

    // Create a translation matrix to move the torus back and into sight
    m3dTranslationMatrix44(mTranslate, 0.0f, 0.0f, -2.5f);

    // Create a rotation matrix based on the current value of yRot
    m3dRotationMatrix44(mRotate, m3dDegToRad(yRot), 0.0f, 1.0f, 0.0f);

    // Add the rotation to the translation, store the result in mModelView
    m3dMatrixMultiply44(mModelview, mTranslate, mRotate);

    // Add the modelview matrix to the projection matrix,
    // the final matrix is the ModelViewProjection matrix.
    m3dMatrixMultiply44(mModelViewProjection,
    viewFrustum.GetProjectionMatrix(),mModelview);

    // Pass this completed matrix to the shader, and render the torus
    GLfloat vBlack[] = { 0.0f, 0.0f, 0.0f, 1.0f };
    shaderManager.UseStockShader(GLT_SHADER_FLAT, mModelViewProjection, vBlack);
    torusBatch.Draw();


    // Swap buffers, and immediately refresh
    glutSwapBuffers();
    glutPostRedisplay();
    }
```

In the RenderScene function, we create four 4 x 4 matrix variables. The mTranslate variable holds the initial translation, where we move the torus back -2.5 units on the z-axis.

```
m3dTranslationMatrix44(mTranslate, 0.0f, 0.0f, -2.5f);
```

Then we create a rotation matrix and store it in mRotate.

```
m3dRotationMatrix44(mRotate, m3dDegToRad(yRot), 0.0f, 1.0f, 0.0f);
```

Note how we made use of the CStopWatch class (a part of the GLTools library) to make our rotation rate based on the amount of time that has passed. Essentially we are rotating at a rate of 60 degrees per second. You should always base your animation rates on the passage of time, rather than a purely frame-based approach. For example, it is tempting to make animation code like this:

```
static GLfloat yRot = 0;
yRot += 1.0f;
m3dRotationMatrix44(mRotate, m3dDegToRad(yRot), 0.0f, 1.0f, 0.0f);
```

Code like this rotates your object very slowly when the frame rate is low and very quickly when the frame rate is high, so the programmer tends to tweak the number added to yRot until the animation looks just right (Goldilocks programming!). However, the frame rate varies on different machines, different driver revisions, and so on, yielding unpredictable animation speeds on different machines. Time, however, flows constant, regardless of frame rate. A higher frame rate should yield a smoother animation, not a faster animation.

Back to our task of transforming our torus—our next step is to add the translation and the rotation together by performing a matrix multiply. Remember, the order of operations is important, and here we first translate and then rotate the torus.

```
m3dMatrixMultiply44(mModelview, mTranslate, mRotate);
```

It should now be out in front of us and spinning in place, at least as far as the modelview matrix is concerned. Remember though that we set up a perspective projection matrix for our desired coordinate system. Now we need to reduce that coordinate system to the unit cube range, which we do by multiplying the projection matrix by the modelview matrix. Again, the order of operations is very important!

```
m3dMatrixMultiply44(mModelViewProjection, viewFrustum.GetProjectionMatrix(),
mModelview);
```

The resulting matrix mModelViewProjection contains the concatenated form of all of our transformations and the projection to the screen. This is just simply magic! Don't you just want to crack one of those linear algebra books in Appendix A now?

The last step is to send our matrix to the flat shader and submit the torus attributes. The flat shader does nothing more than just transform the vertices by the provided matrix (by doing a vector to matrix multiply) and color the geometry solid using the color specified, in this case black.

```
shaderManager.UseStockShader(GLT_SHADER_FLAT, mModelViewProjection, vBlack);
torusBatch.Draw();
```

The Transformation Pipeline

Now that you have an understanding of how the modelview matrix and the projection matrix are used to get things where you want them on-screen, let's take a look at the transformation pipeline in its entirety. Figure 4.29 provides a flowchart of the process. First, your vertex is treated as a 1 x 4 matrix in which the first three values are the x, y, and z coordinates. The fourth number is a scaling factor that you can apply manually if desired. This is the w coordinate, usually 1.0 by default, and you will seldom really modify this value directly.

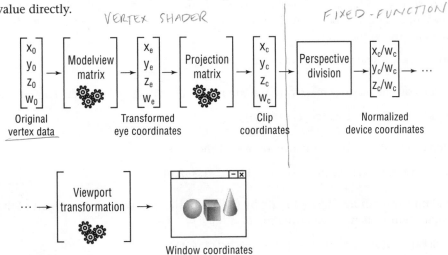

FIGURE 4.29   The vertex transformation pipeline.

The vertex is then multiplied by the modelview matrix, which yields the transformed eye coordinates. The eye coordinates are then multiplied by the projection matrix to yield clip coordinates. Clip coordinates fit in that small unit +/-1.0 coordinate system we mentioned previously. OpenGL effectively eliminates all data outside this clipping space. The clip coordinates are then divided by the w coordinate to yield normalized device coordinates. The w value may have been modified by the projection matrix or the modelview matrix, depending on the transformations that occurred. The perspective divide happens for you as a part of the primitive assembly process.

Finally, your coordinate triplet is mapped to a 2D plane by the viewport transformation. This is also represented by a matrix, but not one that you specify or modify directly. OpenGL sets it up internally depending on the values you specified to glViewport.

Using a Matrix Stack

Because matrix manipulation is such an important part of 3D graphics, almost every programmer's toolbox contains a set of functions or classes for creating and manipulating them. In fact the math3d library contains a rich assortment of functions for this purpose.

Transformations are often applied in a hierarchical manner, with one or more objects being drawn relative to one another. This would require a great deal of matrix construction and management by your client code to traverse a complex scene in 3D space. Traditionally, a matrix stack has been employed to facilitate this, and the GLTools library builds such as utility class on top of the math3d matrix functions. This class is called GLMatrixStack. Readers familiar with the now deprecated OpenGL matrix stacks in the compatibility profile will find this class familiar.

The constructor of the class allows you to specify the maximum depth of the stack, with the default stack depth being 64. This matrix stack is also initialized to have the identity matrix already on the stack.

```
GLMatrixStack::GLMatrixStack(int iStackDepth = 64);
```

You can load the identity matrix on the top matrix by calling LoadIdentity.

```
void GLMatrixStack::LoadIdentity(void);
```

Or you can load an arbitrary matrix on top of the stack.

```
void GLMatrixStack::LoadMatrix(const M3DMatrix44f m);
```

In addition you can multiply a matrix by the top of the matrix stack. The result of the multiplication is then stored at the top of the stack.

```
void GLMatrixStack::MultMatrix(const M3DMatrix44f);
```

Finally, getting the top value off the matrix stack is simply done with GetMatrix, which comes with two overloads suitable for use with the GLShaderManager or just getting a copy of top matrix.

```
const M3DMatrix44f& GLMatrixStack::GetMatrix(void);
void GLMatrixStack::GetMatrix(M3DMatrix44f mMatrix);
```

Push and Pop

The real value of a matrix class is the ability to save the state by pushing it and then restoring the state later by popping it. With the GLMatrixStack class, you can save the current matrix value by pushing the matrix on the stack with the PushMatrix function. This actually copies the current matrix value and places the new value at the top of the stack. Likewise, PopMatrix removes the top matrix and restores the value underneath. There are several overloads for each of these:

```
void GLMatrixStack::PushMatrix(void);
void PushMatrix(const M3DMatrix44f mMatrix);
void PushMatrix(GLFrame& frame);

void GLMatrixStack::PopMatrix(void);
```

In addition to pushing the current matrix on the stack, you can also push an arbitrary matrix on the top of the stack via the M3DMatrix44f data type or the GLFrame class (more on GLFrame soon).

Affine Transformations

The GLMatrixStack class also has built-in support for creating rotations, translating, and scaling matrices. The appropriate functions are listed here.

```
void MatrixStack::Rotate(GLfloat angle, GLfloat x, GLfloat y, GLfloat z);
void MatrixStack::Translate(GLfloat x, GLfloat y, GLfloat z);
void MatrixStack::Scale(GLfloat x, GLfloat y, GLfloat z);
```

These functions work similarly to their lower level math3d counterparts, with one exception. The Rotate function takes degrees instead of radians to more closely mimic the now deprecated OpenGL function glRotate. All three of these functions create the appropriate transformation matrix and then multiply it by the top of the matrix stack, essentially adding the transformation to the current matrix (remember you add transformations by multiplying the matrices).

Managing Your Pipeline

You can probably guess that having a matrix stack for both the modelview matrix and the projection matrix carries a lot of advantages. Very often you will also need to retrieve both of these matrices and multiply them to get the modelview projection matrix. Another useful matrix is the normal matrix, which is used for lighting computations and is derived from the modelview matrix. Another utility class, GLGeometryTransform keeps track of these two matrix stacks for you and quickly retrieves the top of either matrix stack, the modelview projection matrix, or the normal matrix.

Let's take a look at how we use all these classes together in the example program SphereWorld. SphereWorld will see several revisions in this chapter, and initially it just displays a rotating torus in wireframe mode over a green gridded ground, as shown in Figure 4.30.

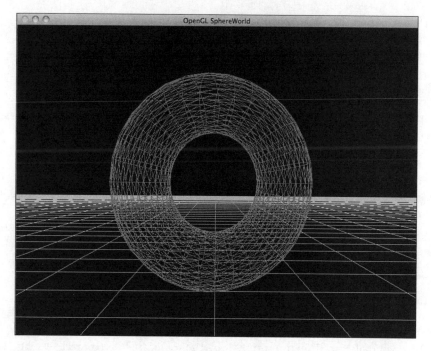

FIGURE 4.30   The beginnings of SphereWorld.

At the top of the SphereWorld source file, we declare an instance of `GLMatrixStack` for the modelview matrix and the projection matrix. We use the `GLFrustum` class to construct our projection matrix, and finally an instance of the `GLGeometryTransform` class to manage our matrix stacks.

```
GLMatrixStack        modelViewMatrix;      // Modelview Matrix
GLMatrixStack        projectionMatrix;     // Projection Matrix
GLFrustum            viewFrustum;          // View Frustum
GLGeometryTransform  transformPipeline;    // Geometry Transform Pipeline
```

Listing 4.3 shows the `ChangeSize` and `RenderScene` functions from our initial SphereWorld.

LISTING 4.3   Initial SphereWorld Transformations

```
/////////////////////////////////////////////////////
// Screen changes size or is initialized
void ChangeSize(int nWidth, int nHeight)
    {
    glViewport(0, 0, nWidth, nHeight);
```

```
        // Create the projection matrix, and load it on the projection matrix stack
        viewFrustum.SetPerspective(35.0f, float(nWidth)/float(nHeight), 1.0f, 100.0f);
        projectionMatrix.LoadMatrix(viewFrustum.GetProjectionMatrix());

        // Set the transformation pipeline to use the two matrix stacks
        transformPipeline.SetMatrixStacks(modelViewMatrix, projectionMatrix);
        }


// Called to draw scene
void RenderScene(void)
    {
    // Color values
    static GLfloat vFloorColor[] = { 0.0f, 1.0f, 0.0f, 1.0f};
    static GLfloat vTorusColor[] = { 1.0f, 0.0f, 0.0f, 1.0f };

    // Time Based animation
    static CstopWatch    rotTimer;
    float yRot = rotTimer.GetElapsedSeconds() * 60.0f;

    // Clear the color and depth buffers
    glClear(GL_COLOR_BUFFER_BIT | GL_DEPTH_BUFFER_BIT);


    // Save the current modelview matrix (the identity matrix)
    modelViewMatrix.PushMatrix();

    // Draw the ground
    shaderManager.UseStockShader(GLT_SHADER_FLAT,
                                 transformPipeline.GetModelViewProjectionMatrix(),
                                 vFloorColor);
    floorBatch.Draw();

    // Draw the spinning Torus
    modelViewMatrix.Translate(0.0f, 0.0f, -2.5f);
    modelViewMatrix.Rotate(yRot, 0.0f, 1.0f, 0.0f);
    shaderManager.UseStockShader(GLT_SHADER_FLAT,
                transformPipeline.GetModelViewProjectionMatrix(),
                                                vTorusColor);
    torusBatch.Draw();

    // Restore the previous modleview matrix (the identity matrix)
    modelViewMatrix.PopMatrix();
```

4

```
// Do the buffer Swap
glutSwapBuffers();

// Tell GLUT to do it again
glutPostRedisplay();
}
```

In the `ChangeSize` function, we set up our perspective projection. Because this is where we get notified of the window's dimensions (or if they change), this is a reasonable place to put this code. The `viewFrustum` instance of the `GLFrustum` class sets up the projection matrix for us, and then we load that into our projection matrix object `projectionMatrix`.

```
// Create the projection matrix, and load it on the projection matrix stack
    viewFrustum.SetPerspective(35.0f, float(nWidth)/float(nHeight), 1.0f, 100.0f);
    projectionMatrix.LoadMatrix(viewFrustum.GetProjectionMatrix());
```

The last thing we do here is initialize the `GLGeometryTransform` instance `transformPipeline` by setting its internal pointers to our instances of the modelview matrix stack and projection matrix stacks.

```
transformPipeline.SetMatrixStacks(modelViewMatrix, projectionMatrix);
```

We really could have done this in the `SetupRC` function as well, but resetting them when the window changes size does no harm, and it keeps our matrix and pipeline setup all in one place.

Next, in the `RenderScene` function, we begin rendering our geometry by first saving the modelview matrix, which has been set to the identity matrix by default.

```
// Save the current modelview matrix (the identity matrix)
    modelViewMatrix.PushMatrix();
```

This may seem pointless given that the next thing we do is draw the ground, which doesn't get transformed at all. It is good practice to save your matrix state at the beginning of your rendering pass and then restore it at the end with a corresponding `PopMatrix`. This way you do not have to reload the identity matrix every time you render, plus for organizational purposes it's going to come in handy very soon when we add the camera.

Now, finally the code to move our torus into place. We begin by calling `Translate` to apply a translation matrix to the top of the matrix stack. This moves the torus back away from the origin (where we are) so that we can see it. This is followed by a rotation with `Rotate`. The parameters to `Rotate` rotate the torus around the y-axis, and `yRot` is derived from the amount of time that has passed since the last frame.

```
// Draw the spinning Torus
    modelViewMatrix.Translate(0.0f, 0.0f, -2.5f);
    modelViewMatrix.Rotate(yRot, 0.0f, 1.0f, 0.0f);
    shaderManager.UseStockShader(GLT_SHADER_FLAT,
                    transformPipeline.GetModelViewProjectionMatrix(),
                                            vTorusColor);

    torusBatch.Draw();
```

The final matrix is then passed to the shader as a uniform, and the torus batch is submitted to render the object. Rather than getting the current modelview matrix and the projection matrix and then multiplying them, we can now simply ask the `transformPipeline` for the concatenated matrix. This makes our code much cleaner, less cluttered, and easier to read. This transformation matrix is still at the top of our stack, so we remove it, restoring identity by calling `PopMatrix`.

```
modelViewMatrix.PopMatrix();
```

Spicing It Up!

SphereWorld is pretty simple—one piece of fixed geometry (the floor) and a single object being transformed (rotating). So far it looks like we've put in a lot of plumbing for very little net benefit. Let's add something else to SphereWorld and see how it fits into our new transformation pipeline.

Figure 4.31 shows the output from SphereWorld2. In SphereWorld2, we add a blue sphere, this time revolving around the torus. Let's take a look at our changes, shown in Listing 4.4. For this listing we added line numbers to make it easier to discuss the flow of what's going on.

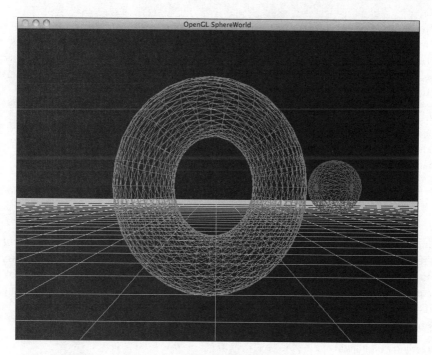

FIGURE 4.31   Finally a sphere in SphereWorld2.

LISTING 4.4   Adding a Sphere to SphereWorld2

```
1   // Save the current modelview matrix (the identity matrix)
2   modelViewMatrix.PushMatrix();
3
4   // Draw the ground
5   shaderManager.UseStockShader(GLT_SHADER_FLAT,
6           transformPipeline.GetModelViewProjectionMatrix(),
7                                           vFloorColor);
8   floorBatch.Draw();
9
10  // Draw the spinning Torus
11  modelViewMatrix.Translate(0.0f, 0.0f, -2.5f);
12
13  // Save the Translation
14  modelViewMatrix.PushMatrix();
15
16  // Apply a rotation and draw the torus
17  modelViewMatrix.Rotate(yRot, 0.0f, 1.0f, 0.0f);
18  shaderManager.UseStockShader(GLT_SHADER_FLAT,
```

```
19              transformPipeline.GetModelViewProjectionMatrix(),
20                                          vTorusColor);
21  torusBatch.Draw();
22 modelViewMatrix.PopMatrix(); // "Erase" the Rotation from before
23
24 // Apply another rotation, followed by a translation, then draw the sphere
25 modelViewMatrix.Rotate(yRot * -2.0f, 0.0f, 1.0f, 0.0f);
26 modelViewMatrix.Translate(0.8f, 0.0f, 0.0f);
27 shaderManager.UseStockShader(GLT_SHADER_FLAT,
28            transformPipeline.GetModelViewProjectionMatrix(),
29                                          vSphereColor);
30 sphereBatch.Draw();
31
32 // Restore the previous modleview matrix (the identity matrix)
33 modelViewMatrix.PopMatrix();
```

For this example, we added a new `PushMatrix` at line 14, just after we perform the translation to move our scene back and away from us. We then continue as with the first program by performing a rotation in line 17 and then finally rendering the torus. On line 22, we called `PopMatrix`. This restores the matrix that we saved on line 14; essentially as far as the matrix stack is concerned, the rotate never took place now. If we were to render the sphere using this matrix, it would be stationary in the middle of the spinning torus because it would simply be translated back -2.5 on the z-axis. Try it!

For our purposes though, we applied our own different rotation, in the opposite direction around the y-axis, and just for dramatic purposes, we doubled the speed. The rotation is followed by a translation in line 26, which moves the sphere out on the x-axis. The net effect is that the sphere is revolving around the torus. The last thing we do is restore identity to the top of the matrix stack with our last call to `PopMatrix` on line 33. Hopefully, now you can begin to see how saving and restoring the transformation matrix can be very useful. But wait...it gets better!

Moving Around Using Cameras and Actors

To represent a location and orientation of any object in your 3D scene, you can use a single 4 x 4 matrix that represents its transform. Working with matrices directly, however, can still be somewhat awkward, so programmers have always sought ways to represent a position and orientation in space more succinctly. Fixed objects such as terrain (or the floor in SphereWorld) are often untransformed, and their vertices usually specify exactly where the geometry should be drawn in space. Objects that move about in the scene are often called actors, paralleling the idea of actors on a stage.

Actors have their own transformations, and often other actors are transformed not only with respect to the world coordinate system (eye coordinates), but also with respect to other actors. Each actor with its own transformation is said to have its own frame of reference, or local object coordinate system. It is often useful to translate between local and world coordinate systems and back again for many nonrendering-related geometric tests.

An Actor Frame

A simple and flexible way to represent a frame of reference is to use a data structure (or class in C++) that contains a position in space, a vector that points forward, and a vector that points upward. Using these quantities, you can uniquely identify a given position and orientation in space. The following class from the GLTools library, GLFrame, makes use of the math3d library and stores this information all in one place:

```
class GLFrame
    {
    protected:
        M3DVector3f vLocation;
        M3DVector3f vUp;
        M3DVector3f vForward;

    public:
    . . .
    };
```

Using a frame of reference such as this to represent an object's position and orientation is a powerful mechanism. To begin with, you can use this data directly to create a 4 x 4 transformation matrix. Referring back to Figure 4.12, the up vector becomes the y column of the matrix, whereas the forward-looking vector becomes the z column vector, and the position is the translation column vector. This leaves only the x column vector, and because we know that all three axes are unit length and perpendicular to one another (orthonormal), we can calculate the x column vector by performing the cross product of the y and z vectors. Listing 4.5 shows the GLFrame method GetMatrix, which does exactly that.

LISTING 4.5   Code to Derive a 4 x 4 Matrix from a Frame

```
/////////////////////////////////////////////////////////////////////
// Derives a 4x4 transformation matrix from a frame of reference
void GLFrame::GetMatrix(M3DTMatrix44f mMatrix, bool bRotationOnly = false)
    {
    // Calculate the right side (x) vector, drop it right into the matrix
    M3DVector3f vXAxis;
    m3dCrossProduct(vXAxis, vUp, vForward);

    // Set matrix column does not fill in the fourth value...
    m3dSetMatrixColumn44(matrix, vXAxis, 0);
```

```
    matrix[3] = 0.0f;

    // Y Column
    m3dSetMatrixColumn44(matrix, vUp, 1);
    matrix[7] = 0.0f;

    // Z Column
    m3dSetMatrixColumn44(matrix, vForward, 2);
    matrix[11] = 0.0f;

    // Translation (already done)
    if(bRotationOnly == true)
        {
        matrix[12] = 0.0f;
        matrix[13] = 0.0f;
        matrix[14] = 0.0f;
        }
    else
        m3dSetMatrixColumn44(matrix, vOrigin, 3);

    matrix[15] = 1.0f;
    }
```

The `GLMatrixStack` class contains three overrides that even allow you to use the `GLFrame`
class instead of a full matrix.

```
void GLMatrixStack::LoadMatrix(GLFrame& frame);
void GLMatrixStack::MultMatrix(GLFrame& frame);
void GLMatrixStack::PushMatrix(GLFrame& frame);
```

Euler Angles: "Use the Frame, Luke!"

Some graphics programming books recommend an even simpler mechanism for storing an
object's position and orientation: *Euler angles*. Euler angles require less space because you
essentially store an object's position and then just three angles—representing a rotation
around the x-, y-, and z-axes—sometimes called yaw, pitch, and roll. A structure like this
might represent an airplane's location and orientation:

```
struct EULER {
    M3DVector3f  vPosition;
    GLfloat      fRoll;
    GLfloat      fPitch;
    GLfloat      fYaw;
    };
```

Euler angles are a bit slippery and are sometimes called "oily angles" by some in the industry. The first problem is that a given position and orientation can be represented by more than one set of Euler angles. Having multiple sets of angles can lead to problems as you try to figure out how to smoothly move from one orientation to another. Occasionally, a second problem called "gimbal lock" comes up; this problem makes it impossible to achieve a rotation around one of the axes. Lastly, Euler angles make it more tedious to calculate new coordinates for simply moving forward along your line of sight or trying to figure out new Euler angles if you want to rotate around one of your own local axes.

Some literature today tries to solve the problems of Euler angles by using a mathematical tool called *quaternions*. Quaternions, which can be difficult to understand, really don't solve any problems with Euler angles that you can't solve on your own by just using the frame of reference method covered previously. To be sure, quaternions are vastly superior to Euler angles, but the argument of quaternions over frames is a bit less conclusive. We already promised that this book would not get too heavy on the math, so we will not debate the merits of each system here. But we should say that the Quaternion versus linear algebra (matrix) debate is more than 100 years old and by far predates their application to computer graphics!

Camera Management

There is really no such thing as a camera transformation in OpenGL. We use the camera as a useful metaphor to help us manage our point of view in some sort of immersive 3D environment. If we envision a camera as an object that has some position in space and some given orientation, we find that our current frame of reference system can represent both actors and our camera in a 3D environment.

To apply a camera transformation, we take the camera's actor transform and flip it so that moving the camera backward is equivalent to moving the whole world forward. Similarly, turning to the left is equivalent to rotating the whole world to the right. To render a given scene, we usually take the approach outlined in Figure 4.32.

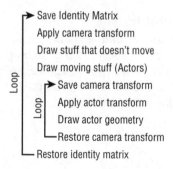

FIGURE 4.32   Typical rendering loop for a 3D environment.

The GLFrame class contains a function that retrieves an appropriately conditioned camera matrix:

```
void GetCameraMatrix(M3DMatrix44f m, bool bRotationOnly = false);
```

Here we added the flexibility that you can get the camera's rotation transform only. The C++ default parameter here allows you to ignore this unless you have some special need for this feature. For example, a frequently employed technique for immersive environments is the sky box. A sky box is simply a big box with a picture of the sky on it. You and your immediate surroundings are rendered inside this box. As you move around, the sky and background should move (rotate only) as well, but you do not want to be able to walk up to the edge of the sky. You would simply apply only the rotation component of the camera transform to your sky box, while everything else in the world would be transformed by the full camera transform.

Let's add a camera to SphereWorld so you can get a better idea of how this works in general. Listing 4.6 shows the important parts of SphereWorld2, which contains the ability to move around via the arrow keys.

LISTING 4.6   Adding a Camera to SphereWorld2

```
GLFrame                    cameraFrame;  // Global camera instance



// Respond to arrow keys by moving the camera frame of reference
void SpecialKeys(int key, int x, int y)
    {
    float linear = 0.1f;
    float angular = float(m3dDegToRad(5.0f));

    if(key == GLUT_KEY_UP)
        cameraFrame.MoveForward(linear);

    if(key == GLUT_KEY_DOWN)
        cameraFrame.MoveForward(-linear);

    if(key == GLUT_KEY_LEFT)
        cameraFrame.RotateWorld(angular, 0.0f, 1.0f, 0.0f);

    if(key == GLUT_KEY_RIGHT)
        cameraFrame.RotateWorld(-angular, 0.0f, 1.0f, 0.0f);
    }

// Called to draw scene
void RenderScene(void)
```

```
{
// Color values
static GLfloat vFloorColor[] = { 0.0f, 1.0f, 0.0f, 1.0f};
static GLfloat vTorusColor[] = { 1.0f, 0.0f, 0.0f, 1.0f };
static GLfloat vSphereColor[] = { 0.0f, 0.0f, 1.0f, 1.0f };

// Time Based animation
static CStopWatch   rotTimer;
float yRot = rotTimer.GetElapsedSeconds() * 60.0f;

// Clear the color and depth buffers
glClear(GL_COLOR_BUFFER_BIT | GL_DEPTH_BUFFER_BIT);

// Save the current modelview matrix (the identity matrix)
modelViewMatrix.PushMatrix();

M3DMatrix44f mCamera;
cameraFrame.GetCameraMatrix(mCamera);
modelViewMatrix.PushMatrix(mCamera);

// Draw the ground
shaderManager.UseStockShader(GLT_SHADER_FLAT,
        transformPipeline.GetModelViewProjectionMatrix(),
                                        vFloorColor);
floorBatch.Draw();

// Draw the spinning Torus
modelViewMatrix.Translate(0.0f, 0.0f, -2.5f);

// Save the Translation
modelViewMatrix.PushMatrix();

    // Apply a rotation and draw the torus
    modelViewMatrix.Rotate(yRot, 0.0f, 1.0f, 0.0f);
    shaderManager.UseStockShader(GLT_SHADER_FLAT,
            transformPipeline.GetModelViewProjectionMatrix(),
                                            vTorusColor);
    torusBatch.Draw();
modelViewMatrix.PopMatrix(); // "Erase" the Rotation from before

// Apply another rotation, followed by a translation, then draw the sphere
modelViewMatrix.Rotate(yRot * -2.0f, 0.0f, 1.0f, 0.0f);
modelViewMatrix.Translate(0.8f, 0.0f, 0.0f);
```

```
shaderManager.UseStockShader(GLT_SHADER_FLAT,
        transformPipeline.GetModelViewProjectionMatrix(),
                                    vSphereColor);

sphereBatch.Draw();

// Restore the previous modleview matrix (the identity matrix)
modelViewMatrix.PopMatrix();
modelViewMatrix.PopMatrix();

// Do the buffer Swap
glutSwapBuffers();

// Tell GLUT to do it again
glutPostRedisplay();
    }
```

The SpecialKeys function is called whenever one of the arrow keys is pressed. Member functions of the GLFrame class are called on the camera object cameraFrame in response to the up and down arrows (moving forward and backward) and the left and right arrows (rotating side to side).

Adding More Actors

The GLFrame class makes a good camera class, but it's also useful for actors. Often you have a number of objects scattered around, and you manage each object's position and orientation in space individually. The GLFrame class makes a fine container for these locations/orientations. Let's say for SphereWorld3, we want to add 50 random spheres floating about. At last, it really will be "SphereWorld."

Instead of one big listing, we walk you though the changes to add these spheres to our world. For starters, we need a list of sphere positions.

```
#define NUM_SPHERES 50
GLFrame spheres[NUM_SPHERES];
```

Note, we don't need 50 actual spheres. We just draw one sphere 50 times, each time at a different location. In SetupRC, we initialize our spheres to have random locations in our world.

```
// Randomly place the spheres
for(int i = 0; i < NUM_SPHERES; i++) {
    GLfloat x = ((GLfloat)((rand() % 400) - 200) * 0.1f);
    GLfloat z = ((GLfloat)((rand() % 400) - 200) * 0.1f);
    spheres[i].SetOrigin(x, 0.0f, z);
    }
```

For the y position, we set the spheres to be at 0.0. This makes them appear to float at eye level. Finally, in the RenderScene function, this simple code renders all of the spheres in their correct location.

```
floorBatch.Draw();

for(int i = 0; i < NUM_SPHERES; i++) {
    modelViewMatrix.PushMatrix();
    modelViewMatrix.MultMatrix(spheres[i]);
    shaderManager.UseStockShader(GLT_SHADER_FLAT,
            transformPipeline.GetModelViewProjectionMatrix(),
                                                vSphereColor);
    sphereBatch.Draw();
    modelViewMatrix.PopMatrix();
    }
```

We place this code after we draw the floor (shown previously), but it really could have been anywhere, as long as it was *after* the camera transform was applied to the top of the modelview matrix stack. Figure 4.33 shows the output of SphereWorld3.

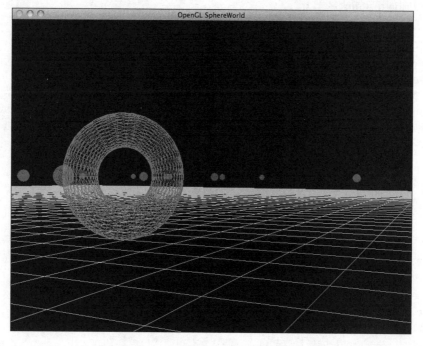

FIGURE 4.33   SphereWorld with a camera and sphere inhabitants.

What About Lights?

Transforming geometry is all well and good, but the last thing we should talk about before finishing this chapter is transforming lights. For geometry transformations, we typically set up our transformation matrices, pass them into the shaders, and let the hardware transform all the vertices for us. For light sources, we typically do things a bit differently. A light position needs to be converted to eye coordinates too, but the matrix passed in to the shader transforms our geometry, not the light. A fixed light such as a point light does not move—or does it? Remember with our camera analogy, the whole world actually moves relative to the camera, and this includes our light sources.

Let's make one more addition to SphereWorld. In SphereWorld4 we add a single point light. So far, we have been rendering SphereWorld in wireframe mode. Figure 4.34 shows what SphereWorld looks like when we take out the call to `glPolygonMode` in the `SetupRC` function.

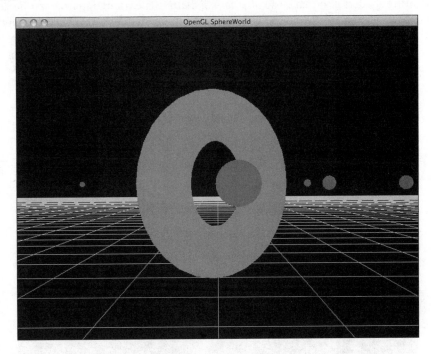

FIGURE 4.34   SphereWorld with no shading.

Transforming a fixed light position into eye coordinates is relatively simple, and you only have to do it once per frame. Here's how we do it in SphereWorld4.

```
// Transform the light position into eye coordinates
M3DVector4f vLightPos = { 0.0f, 10.0f, 5.0f, 1.0f };
M3DVector4f vLightEyePos;
m3dTransformVector4(vLightEyePos, vLightPos, mCamera);
```

The light position in world coordinates is stored in the vLightPos variable, which contains the x, y, z, and w coordinate of the light position. You must have a w coordinate (and it must be 1.0) because you cannot multiply only a three component vector by a 4 x 4 matrix. Using our previously acquired camera matrix mCamera, we transform the light position using our math3d function m3dTransformVector4. We introduced the stock shaders back in Chapter 3; now is your first chance to see the point light stock shader in action. For example, to render one of the blue spheres, we use the appropriate shader and pass in the uniforms like this:

```
shaderManager.UseStockShader(GLT_SHADER_POINT_LIGHT_DIFF,
                    transformPipeline.GetModelViewMatrix(),
                    transformPipeline.GetProjectionMatrix(),
                        vLightEyePos, vSphereColor);
```

Many lighting shaders also make use of a *normal matrix*. The normal matrix can be derived from the modelview matrix with some effort, and this shader does so. This is not optimal however, and when we get into writing our own shaders in Chapter 6, we talk more about this. For now, this simple point shader does the trick, and you can see the output of our final version of SphereWorld for this chapter in Figure 4.35.

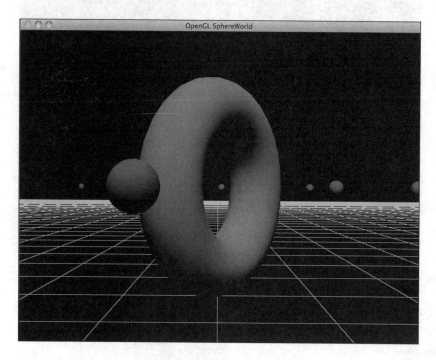

FIGURE 4.35   SphereWorld with a point light source.

Summary

In this chapter, you learned concepts crucial to using OpenGL for the creation of 3D scenes. Even if you can't juggle matrices in your head, you now know what matrices are and how they are used to perform the various transformations. You also learned how to manipulate the modelview and projection matrix stacks to place your objects in the scene and determine how they are viewed on-screen. This chapter also introduced the powerful concept of a frame of reference, and you saw how easy it is to manipulate frames and convert them into transformations.

Finally, we began to make more use of the GLTools and math3d libraries that accompany this book. These libraries are written entirely in portable C++ and provide you with a handy toolkit of miscellaneous math and helper routines that can be used along with OpenGL.

Surprisingly, we did not cover a single new OpenGL function call in this entire chapter. Yes, this *was* the math chapter, and you might not have even noticed if you think math is just about formulas and calculations. Vectors, matrices, and the application thereof are absolutely crucial to being able to use OpenGL to render 3D objects and worlds. Even if you use a different 3D math library, or even roll your own, you will still find yourself following the patterns laid out in this chapter for manipulating your geometry and 3D worlds. Now, go ahead and start making some!

CHAPTER 5

Basic Texturing

by Richard S. Wright, Jr.

WHAT YOU'LL LEARN IN THIS CHAPTER:

How To	Functions You'll Use
Load texture images	`glTexImage/glTexSubImage`
Set texture mapping parameters	`glTexParameter`
Manage multiple textures	`glGenTextures/glDeleteTextures/glBindTexture`
Generate mipmaps	`glGenerateMipmap`
Use anisotropic filtering	`glGetFloatv/glTexParameter`
Load compressed textures	`glCompressedTexImage/glCompressedTexSubImage`

Up until now, you have been rendering with points, lines, and triangles, and you've seen how you can shade their surfaces by calculating color values and interpolating between them to simulate lighting effects. This is all well and good, and there are a substantial number of 3D application market segments where this is all that is required. A tremendous shortcut to greater realism, however, is *texture mapping*. A texture is simply image data that can be applied to a triangle in your scene, filling in the solid areas with filtered *texels* (the texture-based equivalent of pixels). Figure 5.1 shows the dramatic effect a few texture files can add to your 3D renderings.

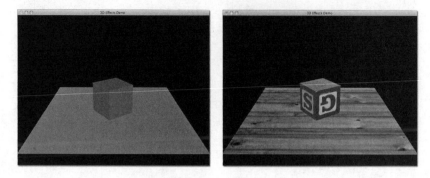

FIGURE 5.1   The stark contrast between textured and untextured geometry.

As you will come to see, however, in Chapter 7, "More Advanced Texture Topics," textures have come to mean a great deal more than just image data and are a key ingredient to most modern 3D rendering algorithms.

Raw Image Data

In the beginning, there were bitmaps. And they were…good enough. The original electronic computer displays were monochrome (one color), typically green or amber, and every pixel on the screen had one of two states: on or off. Computer graphics were simple in the early days, and image data was represented by bitmaps—a series of ones and zeros representing on and off pixel values. In a bitmap, each bit in a block of memory corresponds to exactly one pixel's state on the screen. Figure 5.2 shows an image of a horse represented as a bitmap. Even though only two colors are used (black and white dots), the representation of a horse is still apparent. Compare this image with the one in Figure 5.3, which shows a grayscale image of the same horse. In this pixel rectangle (sometimes still called pixmaps by the old timers), each pixel has one of 256 different intensities of gray. The term bitmap is often applied to images that contain grayscale or full-color data. This description is especially common on the Windows platform in relation to the poorly named .BMP (bitmap) file extension. Many would argue that, strictly speaking, this is a gross misapplication of the term. In this book, we never refer to pixel data as bitmaps. Color Plate 2 shows these two images again, but along side a full color RGB version.

FIGURE 5.2   A real bitmapped image of a horse.

FIGURE 5.3   A pixmap (pixel rectangle) of a horse.

Pixel Packing

Image data is rarely packed tightly into memory. On many hardware platforms, each row of an image should begin on some particular byte-aligned address for performance reasons. Most compilers automatically put variables and buffers at an address alignment optimal for that architecture. OpenGL, by default, assumes a 4-byte alignment, which is appropriate for many systems in use today. Many programmers misjudge the amount of memory required to store an image if they simply multiply the width by the height by the number of bytes per pixel. For example, if you have an RGB image with three components (a red, a green, and a blue), each of which is stored in one byte (8 bits per color channel, this is actually quite typical), how much memory would you need for each row of the image if the image was say 199 pixels wide?

You might think, well, simply 199 x 3 (one for each of the three color channels), which would be 597 bytes per row of image data. You *might* be right. If you're a good programmer, though, you really, really hate that word *might*! If your hardware's native architecture is for 4-byte alignment (which most are), then the image will have an extra *three bytes* added to the end of each row of empty padding (making each row 600 bytes), just to make the memory address of each row start on an address that is evenly divisible by 4. Many times, however, this works out by itself, especially if you stick to power of two textures (more on this later), but you should keep an eye on it because missing little things like this has a tendency to catch you with a strange hard-to-find memory-related bug somewhere down the road. Although this may seem like a waste of memory, this arrangement allows most CPUs to more efficiently grab blocks of data.

Many uncompressed image file formats also follow this convention. The previously mentioned Windows .BMP file format uses 4-byte alignment for its pixel data; however, the Targa (.TGA) file format is 1-byte aligned...no wasted space. Why other than for memory allocation purposes is this important to OpenGL? Because when you hand image data to OpenGL or ask OpenGL for image data, it needs to know how you want your data packed or unpacked in memory.

You can change how pixel data is stored and retrieved by using the following functions:

```
void glPixelStorei(GLenum pname, GLint param);
void glPixelStoref(GLenum pname, GLfloat param);
```

If you want to change to tightly packed pixel data, for example, you make the following function call:

```
glPixelStorei(GL_UNPACK_ALIGNMENT, 1);
```

GL_UNPACK_ALIGNMENT specifies how OpenGL unpacks image data from data buffers. Likewise, you can use GL_PACK_ALIGNMENT to tell OpenGL how to pack data being read from pixel buffers and placed in a user-specified memory buffer. The complete list of pixel storage modes available through this function is given in Table 5.1 and explained in more detail in Appendix C, "OpenGL Man Pages for (Core) OpenGL 3.3."

TABLE 5.1 `glPixelStore` Parameters

Parameter Name	Type	Initial Value
GL_PACK_SWAP_BYTES	GLboolean	GL_FALSE
GL_UNPACK_SWAP_BYTES	GLboolean	GL_FALSE
GL_PACK_LSB_FIRST	GLboolean	GL_FALSE
GL_UNPACK_LSB_FIRST	GLboolean	GL_FALSE
GL_PACK_ROW_LENGTH	GLint	0
GL_UNPACK_ROW_LENGTH	GLint	0
GL_PACK_SKIP_ROWS	GLint	0
GL_UNPACK_SKIP_ROWS	GLint	0
GL_PACK_SKIP_PIXELS	GLint	0
GL_UNPACK_SKIP_PIXELS	GLint	0
GL_PACK_ALIGNMENT	GLint	4
GL_UNPACK_ALIGNMENT	GLint	4
GL_PACK_IMAGE_HEIGHT	GLint	0
GL_UNPACK_IMAGE_HEIGHT	GLint	0
GL_PACK_SKIP_IMAGES	GLint	0
GL_UNPACK_SKIP_IMAGES	GLint	0

Pixmaps

Of more interest and somewhat greater utility on today's full-color computer systems are pixmaps. A pixmap is similar in memory layout to a bitmap; however, each pixel may be represented by more than one bit of storage. Extra bits of storage for each pixel allow either intensity (sometimes referred to as *luminance* values) or color component values to be stored. You cannot draw a pixmap directly into the color buffer with the OpenGL core profile, but you can read the contents of the color buffer directly as a pixmap using this function:

```
void glReadPixels(GLint x, GLint y, GLSizei width, GLSizei height,
                  GLenum format, GLenum type, const void *pixels);
```

You specify the x and y in window coordinates of the lower-left corner of the rectangle to read followed by width and height of the rectangle in pixels. If the color buffer stores data differently than what you have requested, OpenGL takes care of the necessary conversions. This capability can be very useful. The pointer to the image data, *pixels, must be valid and must contain enough storage to contain the image data after conversion, or you will likely get a nasty memory exception at runtime. Also be aware that if you specify window coordinates that are out of bounds, you will get data only for the pixels within the actual OpenGL frame buffer.

The fourth argument to glReadPixels is the format, which specifies the color layout of the data elements pointed to by pixels and can be one of the constants listed in Table 5.2.

TABLE 5.2   OpenGL Pixel Formats

Constant	Description
GL_RGB	Colors are in red, green, blue order.
GL_RGBA	Colors are in red, green, blue, alpha order.
GL_BGR	Colors are in blue, green, red order.
GL_BGRA	Colors are in blue, green, red, alpha order.
GL_RED	Each pixel contains a single red component.
GL_GREEN	Each pixel contains a single green component.
GL_BLUE	Each pixel contains a single blue component.
GL_RG	Each pixel contains a red followed by a blue component.
GL_RED_INTEGER	Each pixel contains a red integer component.
GL_GREEN_INTEGER	Each pixel contains a green integer component.
GL_BLUE_INTETER	Each pixel contains a blue integer component.
GL_RG_INTEGER	Each pixel contains a red followed by a green integer component.
GL_RGB_INTEGER	Each pixel contains a red, green, and blue integer component, in that order.
GL_RGBA_INTEGER	Each pixel contains a red, green, blue, and alpha integer component, in that order.
GL_BGR_INTEGER	Each pixel contains a blue, green, and red integer component, in that order.
GL_BGRA_INTEGER	Each pixel contains a blue, green, red, and alpha integer component, in that order.
GL_STENCIL_INDEX	Each pixel contains a single stencil value.
GL_DEPTH_COMPONENT	Each pixel contains a single depth value.
GL_DEPTH_STENCIL	Each pixel contains a depth and a stencil value.

The last three formats, GL_STENCIL_INDEX, GL_DEPTH_COMPONENT, and GL_DEPTH_STENCIL, are used for reading and writing directly to the stencil and depth buffers. The type parameter interprets the data pointed to by the *pixels parameter. It tells OpenGL what data type within the buffer is used to store the color components. The recognized values are specified in Table 5.3.

TABLE 5.3   Data Types for Pixel Data

Constant	Description
GL_UNSIGNED_BYTE	Each color component is an 8-bit unsigned integer.
GL_BYTE	Signed 8-bit integer.
GL_UNSIGNED_SHORT	Unsigned 16-bit integer.
GL_SHORT	Signed 16-bit integer.
GL_UNSIGNED_INT	Unsigned 32-bit integer.
GL_INT	Signed 32-bit integer.
GL_FLOAT	Single-precision float.

Constant	Description
GL_HALF_FLOAT	Half-precision float.
GL_UNSIGNED_BYTE_3_2_2	Packed RGB values.
GL_UNSIGNED_BYTE_2_3_3_REV	Packed RGB values.
GL_UNSIGNED_SHORT_5_6_5	Packed RGB values.
GL_UNSIGNED_SHORT_5_6_5_REV	Packed RGB values.
GL_UNSIGNED_SHORT_4_4_4_4	Packed RGBA values.
GL_UNSIGNED_SHORT_4_4_4_4_REV	Packed RGBA values.
GL_UNSIGNED_SHORT_5_5_5_1	Packed RGBA values.
GL_UNSIGNED_SHORT_1_5_5_5_REV	Packed RGBA values.
GL_UNSIGNED_INT_8_8_8_8	Packed RGBA values.
GL_UNSIGNED_INT_8_8_8_8_REV	Packed RGBA values.
GL_UNSIGNED_INT_10_10_10_2	Packed RGBA values.
GL_UNSIGNED_INT_2_10_10_10_REV	Packed RGBA values.
GL_UNSIGNED_INT_24_8	Packed RGBA values.
GL_UNSIGNED_INT_10F_11F_11F_REV	Packed RGBA values.
GL_FLOAT_32_UNSIGNED_INT_24_8_REV	Packed RGBA values.

It is worth pointing out the glReadPixels copies data from your graphics hardware, usually across the bus to system memory. When this is the case, your application will block until the memory transfer has completed. In addition, if you specify a pixel layout different from the native arrangement of your graphics hardware, there will be an additional performance penalty as the data is reformatted.

Packed Pixel Formats

The packed formats listed in Table 5.3 were introduced in OpenGL 1.2 (and later) as a means of allowing image data to be stored in a more compressed form that matched a range of color graphics hardware. Display hardware designs could save memory or operate faster on a smaller set of packed pixel data. These packed pixel formats are still found on some PC hardware and may continue to be useful for future hardware platforms.

The packed pixel formats compress color data into as few bits as possible, with the number of bits per color channel shown in the constant. For example, the GL_UNSIGNED_BYTE_3_3_2 format stores 3 bits of the first component, 3 bits of the second component, and 2 bits of the third component. Remember, the specific components (red, green, blue, and alpha) are still ordered according to the format parameter. The components are ordered from the highest bits (most significant bit, or MSB) to the lowest (least significant bit, or LSB). GL_UNSIGNED_BYTE_2_3_3_REV reverses this order and places the last component in the top 2 bits, and so on. Figure 5.4 shows graphically the bitwise layout for these two arrangements. All the other packed formats are interpreted in the same manner.

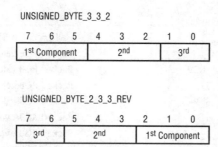

FIGURE 5.4   Sample layout for two packed pixel formats.

These format and data type parameters are used for a number of other image- and texture-related functions, and we will make reference to these tables again later. For our glReadPixels function, by default, the read operation is performed on the back buffer for double-buffered rendering contexts, and the front buffer for single-buffered rendering contexts. You can change the source of these pixel operations by using this function:

```
void glReadBuffer(GLenum mode);
```

The mode parameter can be any one of GL_FRONT, GL_BACK, GL_LEFT, GL_RIGHT, GL_FRONT_LEFT, GL_FRONT_RIGHT, GL_BACK_LEFT, GL_BACK_RIGHT, or even GL_NONE.

Saving Pixels

We have covered enough now to do something useful with pixel data. The gltWriteTGA function in the GLTools library reads color data from the front color buffer and saves it to an image file in the Targa file format. Being able to save your current OpenGL rendering to a standard image file format can come in handy. The complete listing for the gltWriteTGA function is shown in Listing 5.1.

LISTING 5.1   The gltWriteTGA Function to Save the Screen as a Targa File

```
/////////////////////////////////////////////////////////////////
// Capture the current viewport and save it as a targa file.
// Be sure to call SwapBuffers for double buffered contexts or
// glFinish for single buffered contexts before calling this function.
// Returns 0 if an error occurs, or 1 on success.
GLint gltWriteTGA(const char *szFileName)
    {
    FILE *pFile;                    // File pointer
    TGAHEADER tgaHeader;            // TGA file header
    unsigned long lImageSize;       // Size in bytes of image
    GLbyte     *pBits = NULL;       // Pointer to bits
    GLint iViewport[4];             // Viewport in pixels
    GLenum lastBuffer;              // Storage for the current read buffer
```

```
                              // setting
    // Get the viewport dimensions
    glGetIntegerv(GL_VIEWPORT, iViewport);

    // How big is the image going to be (targas are tightly packed)
    lImageSize = iViewport[2] * 3 * iViewport[3];

    // Allocate block. If this doesn't work, go home
    pBits = (GLbyte *)malloc(lImageSize);
    if(pBits == NULL)
        return 0;

    // Read bits from color buffer
    glPixelStorei(GL_PACK_ALIGNMENT, 1);
    glPixelStorei(GL_PACK_ROW_LENGTH, 0);
    glPixelStorei(GL_PACK_SKIP_ROWS, 0);
    glPixelStorei(GL_PACK_SKIP_PIXELS, 0);

    // Get the current read buffer setting and save it. Switch to
    // the front buffer and do the read operation. Finally, restore
    // the read buffer state
    glGetIntegerv(GL_READ_BUFFER, &lastBuffer);
    glReadBuffer(GL_FRONT);
    glReadPixels(0, 0, iViewport[2], iViewport[3], GL_BGR,
                GL_UNSIGNED_BYTE, pBits);
    glReadBuffer(lastBuffer);

    // Initialize the Targa header
    tgaHeader.identsize = 0;
    tgaHeader.colorMapType = 0;
    tgaHeader.imageType = 2;
    tgaHeader.colorMapStart = 0;
    tgaHeader.colorMapLength = 0;
    tgaHeader.colorMapBits = 0;
    tgaHeader.xstart = 0;
    tgaHeader.ystart = 0;
    tgaHeader.width = iViewport[2];
    tgaHeader.height = iViewport[3];
    tgaHeader.bits = 24;
    tgaHeader.descriptor = 0;

    // Do byte swap for big vs little endian
#ifdef __APPLE__
```

5

```
    LITTLE_ENDIAN_WORD(&tgaHeader.colorMapStart);
    LITTLE_ENDIAN_WORD(&tgaHeader.colorMapLength);
    LITTLE_ENDIAN_WORD(&tgaHeader.xstart);
    LITTLE_ENDIAN_WORD(&tgaHeader.ystart);
    LITTLE_ENDIAN_WORD(&tgaHeader.width);
    LITTLE_ENDIAN_WORD(&tgaHeader.height);
#endif

    // Attempt to open the file
    pFile = fopen(szFileName, "wb");
    if(pFile == NULL)
        {
        free(pBits);     // Free buffer and return error
        return 0;
        }

    // Write the header
    fwrite(&tgaHeader, sizeof(TGAHEADER), 1, pFile);

    // Write the image data
    fwrite(pBits, lImageSize, 1, pFile);

    // Free temporary buffer and close the file
    free(pBits);
    fclose(pFile);

    // Success!
    return 1;
    }
```

Reading Pixels

The Targa image format is a convenient and easy to use image format, and it supports both simple color images and images with alpha. We will continue to use this format for our texture work in this book, and now present the opposite function, which is to load a Targa file from disk.

```
GLbyte *gltReadTGABits(const char *szFileName, GLint *iWidth, GLint *iHeight,
                                 GLint *iComponents, GLenum *eFormat);
```

The first argument is the filename (with the path if necessary) of the Targa file to load. The Targa image format is a well-supported and common image file format. Unlike JPEG files, Targa files (usually) store an image in its uncompressed form. The gltReadTGABits function opens the file and then reads in and parses the header to determine the width, height, and data format of the file. The number of components can be one, three, or four for luminance, RGB, or RGBA images, respectively. The final parameter is a pointer to a GLenum that receives the corresponding OpenGL image format for the file. If the function call is successful, it returns a newly allocated pointer (using malloc) to the image data read directly from the file. If the file is not found, or some other error occurs, the function returns NULL. The complete listing for the gltReadTGABits function is given in Listing 5.2.

LISTING 5.2   The Function to Load Targa Files for Use in OpenGL

```
///////////////////////////////////////////////////////////////////////
// Allocate memory and load targa bits. Returns pointer to new buffer,
// height, and width of texture, and the OpenGL format of data.
// Call free() on buffer when finished!
// This only works on pretty vanilla targas... 8, 24, or 32 bit color
// only, no palettes, no RLE encoding.
GLbyte *gltReadTGABits(const char *szFileName, GLint *iWidth, GLint *iHeight,
                                GLint *iComponents, GLenum *eFormat)
    {
    FILE            *pFile;         // File pointer
    TGAHEADER       tgaHeader;      // TGA file header
    unsigned long   lImageSize;     // Size in bytes of image
    short           sDepth;         // Pixel depth;
    GLbyte          *pBits = NULL;  // Pointer to bits

    // Default/Failed values
    *iWidth = 0;
    *iHeight = 0;
    *eFormat = GL_RGB;
    *iComponents = GL_RGB;

    // Attempt to open the file
    pFile = fopen(szFileName, "rb");
    if(pFile == NULL)
        return NULL;

    // Read in header (binary)
    fread(&tgaHeader, 18/* sizeof(TGAHEADER)*/, 1, pFile);

    // Do byte swap for big vs little endian
#ifdef __APPLE__
    LITTLE_ENDIAN_WORD(&tgaHeader.colorMapStart);
    LITTLE_ENDIAN_WORD(&tgaHeader.colorMapLength);
```

```
        LITTLE_ENDIAN_WORD(&tgaHeader.xstart);
        LITTLE_ENDIAN_WORD(&tgaHeader.ystart);
        LITTLE_ENDIAN_WORD(&tgaHeader.width);
        LITTLE_ENDIAN_WORD(&tgaHeader.height);
#endif

        // Get width, height, and depth of texture
        *iWidth = tgaHeader.width;
        *iHeight = tgaHeader.height;
        sDepth = tgaHeader.bits / 8;

        // Put some validity checks here. Very simply, I only understand
        // or care about 8, 24, or 32 bit targa's.
        if(tgaHeader.bits != 8 && tgaHeader.bits != 24 && tgaHeader.bits != 32)
            return NULL;

        // Calculate size of image buffer
        lImageSize = tgaHeader.width * tgaHeader.height * sDepth;

        // Allocate memory and check for success
        pBits = (GLbyte*)malloc(lImageSize * sizeof(GLbyte));
        if(pBits == NULL)
            return NULL;

        // Read in the bits
        // Check for read error. This should catch RLE or other
        // weird formats that I don't want to recognize
        if(fread(pBits, lImageSize, 1, pFile) != 1)
        {
        free(pBits);
        return NULL;
        }

        // Set OpenGL format expected
        switch(sDepth)
            {
#ifndef OPENGL_ES
            case 3:     // Most likely case
                *eFormat = GL_BGR;
                *iComponents = GL_RGB;
                break;
#endif
```

```
#ifdef WIN32
      case 3:     // Most likely case
         *eFormat = GL_BGR;
         *iComponents = GL_RGB;
         break;
#endif
#ifdef linux
      case 3:     // Most likely case
         *eFormat = GL_BGR;
         *iComponents = GL_RGB;
         break;
#endif
      case 4:
         *eFormat = GL_BGRA;
         *iComponents = GL_RGBA;
         break;
      case 1:
         *eFormat = GL_LUMINANCE;
         *iComponents = GL_LUMINANCE;
         break;
       default:     // RGB
      // If on the iPhone, TGA's are BGR, and the iPhone does not
      // support BGR without alpha, but it does support RGB,
      // so a simple swizzle of the red and blue bytes will suffice.
      // For faster iPhone loads however, save your TGA's with an Alpha!
#ifdef OPENGL_ES
        for(int i = 0; i < lImageSize; i+=3)
           {
           GLbyte temp = pBits[i];
           pBits[i] = pBits[i+2];
         pBits[i+2] = temp;
           }
#endif
         break;
      }

   // Done with File
   fclose(pFile);

   // Return pointer to image data
   return pBits;
   }
```

You may notice that the number of components is not set to the integers 1, 3, or 4, but GL_LUMINANCE8, GL_RGB8, and GL_RGBA8. OpenGL recognizes these special constants as a request to maintain full image precision internally when it manipulates the image data. For example, for performance reasons, some OpenGL implementations may down-sample a 24-bit color image to 16 bits internally. This is especially common for texture loads on some implementations in which the display output color resolution is only 16 bits, but a higher bit depth image is loaded. These constants are requests to the implementation to store and use the image data as supplied at their full 8-bit-per-channel color depth.

Loading Textures

The first necessary step in applying a texture map to geometry is to load the texture into memory. Once loaded, the texture becomes part of the current texture state (more on this later). Three OpenGL functions are most often used to load texture data from a memory buffer (which is, for example, read from a disk file):

```
void glTexImage1D(GLenum target, GLint level, GLint internalformat,
          GLsizei width, GLint border,
          GLenum format, GLenum type, void *data);

void glTexImage2D(GLenum target, GLint level, GLint internalformat,
          GLsizei width, GLsizei height, GLint border,
          GLenum format, GLenum type, void *data);

void glTexImage3D(GLenum target, GLint level, GLint internalformat,
          GLsizei width, GLsizei height, GLsizei depth, GLint border,
          GLenum format, GLenum type, void *data);
```

These three rather lengthy functions tell OpenGL everything it needs to know about how to interpret the texture data pointed to by the data parameter.

The first thing you should notice about these functions is that they are essentially three flavors of the same root function, glTexImage. OpenGL supports one-, two-, and three-dimensional texture maps and uses the corresponding function to load that texture and make it current. OpenGL also supports cube map textures, but we are going to save those for Chapter 7. You should also be aware that OpenGL copies the texture information from data when you call one of these functions. This data copy can be quite expensive, and in the section "Texture Objects," coming up soon, we discuss some ways to help mitigate this problem.

The target argument for these functions should be GL_TEXTURE_1D, GL_TEXTURE_2D, or GL_TEXTURE_3D, respectively. You may also specify proxy textures by specifying GL_PROXY_TEXTURE_1D, GL_PROXY_TEXTURE_2D, or GL_PROXY_TEXTURE_3D and using the function glGetTexParameter to retrieve the results of the proxy query. Proxy textures as well as some other interesting texture targets are covered in Chapter 7.

The level parameter specifies the mipmap level being loaded. Mipmaps are covered in an upcoming section called "Mipmapping," so for nonmipmapped textures (just your plain old ordinary texture mapping), always set this to 0 (zero) for the moment.

Next, you have to specify the internalformat parameter of the texture data. This information tells OpenGL how many color components you want stored per texel and possibly the storage size of the components and/or whether you want the texture compressed. Table 5.4 lists the most common values for this function. A complete listing is given in Appendix C.

TABLE 5.4   Most Common Texture Internal Formats

Constant	Meaning
GL_ALPHA	Store the texels as alpha values
GL_LUMINANCE	Store the texels as luminance values
GL_LUMINANCE_ALPHA	Store the texels with both luminance and alpha values
GL_RGB	Store the texels as red, green, and blue components
GL_RGBA	Store the texels as red, green, blue, and alpha components

The width, height, and depth parameters (where appropriate) specify the dimensions of the texture being loaded. It is important to note that prior to OpenGL 2.0, these dimensions must be integer powers of 2 (1, 2, 4, 8, 16, 32, 64, and so on). There is no requirement that texture maps be square (all dimensions equal), but a texture loaded with non-power of 2 dimensions on older OpenGL implementations will cause texturing to be implicitly disabled. Even though OpenGL 2.0 (and later) allows non-power of 2 textures, this is no guarantee that they will necessarily be fast on the underlying hardware. Many performance-minded developers still avoid non-power of two textures for this reason.

The border parameter allows you to specify a border width for texture maps. Texture borders allow you to extend the width, height, or depth of a texture map by an extra set of texels along the borders. Texture borders play an important role in the discussion of texture filtering to come. For the time being, always set this value to 0 (zero).

The last three parameters—format, type, and data—are identical to the corresponding arguments when you used glReadPixels in the previous section. Valid values for format are listed in Table 5.2, and valid values for type are listed in Table 5.3.

Using the Color Buffer

One- and two-dimensional textures may also be loaded using data from the color buffer. You can read an image from the color buffer and use it as a new texture by using the following two functions:

```
void glCopyTexImage1D(GLenum target, GLint level, GLenum internalformat,
                      GLint x, GLint y,
                      GLsizei width, GLint border);
```

```
void glCopyTexImage2D(GLenum target, GLint level, GLenum internalformat,
                      GLint x, GLint y,
                      GLsizei width, GLsizei height, GLint border);
```

These functions operate similarly to glTexImage, but in this case, x and y specify the location in the color buffer to begin reading the texture data. The source buffer is set using glReadBuffer. Note that there is no glCopyTexImage3D; you can't load volumetric data from a 2D color buffer!

Updating Textures

Repeatedly loading new textures can become a performance bottleneck in time-sensitive applications such as games or simulation applications. If a loaded texture map is no longer needed, it may be replaced entirely or in part. Replacing a texture map can often be done much more quickly than reloading a new texture directly with glTexImage. The function you use to accomplish this is glTexSubImage, again in three variations:

```
void glTexSubImage1D(GLenum target, GLint level,
                     GLint xOffset,
                     GLsizei width,
                     GLenum format, GLenum type, const GLvoid *data);

void glTexSubImage2D(GLenum target, GLint level,
                     GLint xOffset, GLint yOffset,
                     GLsizei width, GLsizei height,
                     GLenum format, GLenum type, const GLvoid *data);

void glTexSubImage3D(GLenum target, GLint level,
                     GLint xOffset, GLint yOffset, GLint zOffset,
                     GLsizei width, GLsizei height, GLsizei depth,
                     GLenum format, GLenum type, const GLvoid *data);
```

Most of the arguments correspond exactly to the parameters used in glTexImage. The xOffset, yOffset, and zOffset parameters specify the offsets into the existing texture map to begin replacing texture data. The width, height, and depth values specify the dimensions of the texture being "inserted" into the existing texture.

A final set of functions allows you to combine reading from the color buffer and inserting or replacing part of a texture. These glCopyTexSubImage variations do just that:

```
void glCopyTexSubImage1D(GLenum target, GLint level,
                         GLint xoffset,
                         GLint x, GLint y,
                         GLsizei width);
```

```
void glCopyTexSubImage2D(GLenum target, GLint level,
                         GLint xoffset, GLint yoffset,
                         GLint x, GLint y,
                         GLsizei width, GLsizei height);

void glCopyTexSubImage3D(GLenum target, GLint level,
                         GLint xoffset, GLint yoffset, Glint zoffset,
                         GLint x, GLint y,
                         GLsizei width, GLsizei height);
```

You may have noticed that no glCopyTexImage3D function is listed here. The reason is that the color buffer is 2D, and there simply is no corresponding way to use a 2D color image as a source for a 3D texture. However, you can use glCopyTexSubImage3D to use the color buffer data to set a plane of texels in a three-dimensional texture.

Texture Objects

So far, you have seen a couple of ways to load a texture and some methods of replacing a texture. It has been many years since we've seen hardware that could only support a single texture, and thus OpenGL has along the way evolved a means of managing multiple textures and switching between them. The texture image itself is a part of what is called the *texture state*. The texture state comprises the texture image itself and a set of texture parameters that control how filtering and texture coordinates behave. The use of the glTexParameter function to set these texture state parameters is covered shortly. First, though, let's take a look at how we would load up and manage several different textures.

Function calls such as glTexImage and glTexSubImage move a large amount of memory around and possibly need to reformat the data to match some internal representation. Switching between textures or reloading a different texture image could potentially be a costly operation. Texture objects allow you to load up more than one texture state at a time, including texture images, and switch between them very quickly. The texture state is maintained by the currently bound texture object, which is identified by an unsigned integer. You allocate a number of texture objects with the following function:

```
void glGenTextures(GLsizei n, GLuint *textures);
```

With this function, you specify the number of texture objects and a pointer to an array of unsigned integers that will be populated with the texture object identifiers. You can think of them as handles to different available texture states. To "bind" to one of these states, you call this function:

```
void glBindTexture(GLenum target, GLuint texture);
```

The `target` parameter needs to specify `GL_TEXTURE_1D`, `GL_TEXTURE_2D`, or `GL_TEXTURE_3D`, and `texture` is the specific texture object to bind to. Hereafter, all texture loads and texture parameter settings affect only the currently bound texture object. To delete texture objects, you call the following function:

```
void glDeleteTextures(GLsizei n, GLuint *textures);
```

The arguments here have the same meaning as for `glGenTextures`. You do not need to generate and delete all your texture objects at the same time. Multiple calls to `glGenTextures` have very little overhead. Calling `glDeleteTextures` multiple times may incur some delay, but only because you are deallocating possibly large amounts of texture memory.

You can test texture object names (or handles) to see whether they are valid by using the following function:

```
GLboolean glIsTexture(GLuint texture);
```

This function returns `GL_TRUE` if the integer is a previously allocated texture object name or `GL_FALSE` if not.

Texture Application

Loading a texture is only the first step toward getting a texture applied to geometry. At a minimum we must also supply texture coordinates and set up the texture coordinate wrap modes and texture filter. Finally, we may choose to mipmap our textures to improve texturing performance and/or visual quality. Of course in all of this, we are assuming our shaders are doing the "right thing." For this chapter, we stick to 2D texture examples and use the stock shaders. In the next chapter, when we begin writing our own shaders, we see how to apply textures from the level of the shaders. For now, we restrict ourselves to the client side of texture mapping technique.

Texture Coordinates

In general, textures are mapped to geometry directly by specifying a *texture coordinate* for each vertex. Texture coordinates are either specified as an attribute to the shader or calculated algorithmically. Texels in a texture map are addressed not as a memory location (as you would for pixmaps), but as a more abstract (usually floating-point values) texture coordinate. Typically, texture coordinates are specified as floating-point values that are in the range 0.0 to 1.0. Texture coordinates are named s, t, r, and q (similar to vertex coordinates x, y, z, and w), supporting from one- to three-dimensional texture coordinates, and optionally a way to scale the coordinates.

Figure 5.5 shows one-, two-, and three-dimensional textures and the way the texture coordinates are laid out with respect to their texels.

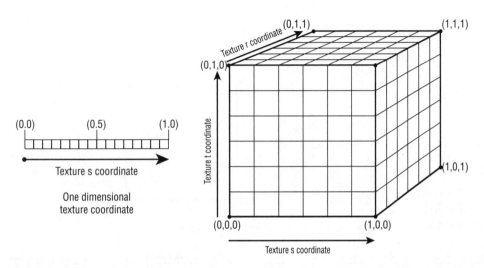

FIGURE 5.5   How texture coordinates address texels.

Because there are no four-dimensional textures, you might ask what the q coordinate is for. The q coordinate corresponds to the w geometric coordinate. This is a scaling factor applied to the other texture coordinates; that is, the actual values used for the texture coordinates are s/q, t/q, and r/q. By default, q is set to 1.0. While this may seem rather arbitrary, it does come in handy for some advanced texture coordinate generation algorithms, such as shadow mapping.

One texture coordinate is applied per texture (yes, there is a way to apply more than one texture at a time!) for each vertex. OpenGL then stretches or shrinks the texture as necessary to apply the texture to the geometry as mapped. (This stretching or shrinking is applied using the current texture filter; we discuss this issue shortly as well.) Figure 5.6 shows an example of a two-dimensional texture being mapped to a square (perhaps a triangle fan) piece of geometry. Note that the corners of the texture correspond to the corners of the geometry.

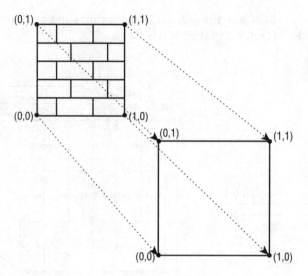

FIGURE 5.6   Applying a two-dimensional texture to a quad.

Rarely, however, do you have such a nice fit of a square texture mapped to a square piece of geometry. To help you better understand texture coordinates, we provide another example in Figure 5.7. This figure also shows a square texture map, but the geometry is a triangle. Superimposed on the texture map are the texture coordinates of the locations in the map being extended to the vertices of the triangle.

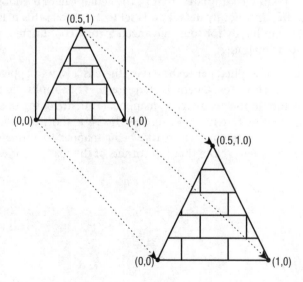

FIGURE 5.7   Applying a portion of a texture map to a triangle.

Texture Parameters

More effort is involved in texture mapping than slapping an image on the side of a triangle. Many parameters affect the rendering rules and behaviors of texture maps as they are applied. These texture parameters are all set via variations on the function `glTexParameter`:

```
void glTexParameterf(GLenum target, GLenum pname, GLfloat param);
void glTexParameteri(GLenum target, GLenum pname, GLint param);
void glTexParameterfv(GLenum target, GLenum pname, GLfloat *params);
void glTexParameteriv(GLenum target, GLenum pname, GLint *params);
```

The first argument, `target`, specifies which texture mode the parameter is to be applied to and may be GL_TEXTURE_1D, GL_TEXTURE_2D, GL_TEXTURE_3D, GL_TEXTURE_CUBE_MAP, or GL_TEXTURE_RECT (more on these last two in Chapter 7). The second argument, `pname`, specifies which texture parameter is being set, and finally, the `param` or `params` argument sets the value of the particular texture parameter.

Basic Filtering

There is almost never a one-to-one correspondence between texels in the texture map and pixels on the screen. A careful programmer could achieve this result, but only by texturing geometry that was carefully planned to appear on-screen such that the texels and pixels lined up. (This is actually often done when OpenGL is used for image processing applications.) Consequently, texture images are always either stretched or shrunk as they are applied to geometric surfaces. Because of the orientation of the geometry, a given texture could even be stretched and shrunk at the same time across the surface of some object.

The process of calculating color fragments from a stretched or shrunken texture map is called texture *filtering*. Using the texture parameter function, OpenGL allows you to set both magnification and minification filters. The parameter names for these two filters are GL_TEXTURE_MAG_FILTER and GL_TEXTURE_MIN_FILTER. For now, you can select from two basic texture filters for them, GL_NEAREST and GL_LINEAR, which correspond to nearest neighbor and linear filtering. Make sure you always choose one of these two filters for the GL_TEXTURE_MIN_FILTER—the default filter setting does not work without mipmaps (see the later section "Mipmapping").

Nearest neighbor filtering is the simplest and fastest filtering method you can choose. Texture coordinates are evaluated and plotted against a texture's texels, and whichever texel the coordinate falls in, that color is used for the fragment texture color. Nearest neighbor filtering is characterized by large blocky pixels when the texture is stretched especially large. An example is shown in Figure 5.8. You can set the texture filter (for GL_TEXTURE_2D) for both the minification and the magnification filter by using these two function calls:

```
glTexParameteri(GL_TEXTURE_2D, GL_TEXTURE_MAG_FILTER, GL_NEAREST);
glTexParameteri(GL_TEXTURE_2D, GL_TEXTURE_MIN_FILTER, GL_NEAREST);
```

FIGURE 5.8   Nearest neighbor filtering up close.

Linear filtering requires more work than nearest neighbor but often is worth the extra overhead. On today's commodity hardware, the extra cost of linear filtering is negligible. Linear filtering works by not taking the nearest texel to the texture coordinate, but by applying the weighted average of the texels surrounding the texture coordinate (a linear interpolation). For this interpolated fragment to match the texel color exactly, the texture coordinate needs to fall directly in the center of the texel. Linear filtering is characterized by "fuzzy" graphics when a texture is stretched. This fuzziness, however, often lends a more realistic and less artificial look than the jagged blocks of the nearest neighbor filtering mode. A contrasting example to Figure 5.8 is shown in Figure 5.9. You can set linear filtering (for GL_TEXTURE_2D) simply enough by using the following lines:

```
glTexParameteri(GL_TEXTURE_2D, GL_TEXTURE_MAG_FILTER, GL_LINEAR);
glTexParameteri(GL_TEXTURE_2D, GL_TEXTURE_MIN_FILTER, GL_LINEAR);
```

FIGURE 5.9   Linear filtering up close. (Color Plate 3 in the Color insert shows nearest neighbor and linear filtering side-by-side.)

Texture Wrap

Normally, you specify texture coordinates between 0.0 and 1.0 to map out the texels in a texture map. If texture coordinates fall outside this range, OpenGL handles them according to the current texture wrapping mode. You can set the wrap mode for each coordinate individually by calling `glTexParameteri` with `GL_TEXTURE_WRAP_S`, `GL_TEXTURE_WRAP_T`, or `GL_TEXTURE_WRAP_R` as the parameter name. The wrap mode can then be set to one of the following values: `GL_REPEAT`, `GL_CLAMP`, `GL_CLAMP_TO_EDGE`, or `GL_CLAMP_TO_BORDER`.

The `GL_REPEAT` wrap mode simply causes the texture to repeat in the direction in which the texture coordinate has exceeded 1.0. The texture repeats again for every integer texture coordinate. This mode is useful for applying a small tiled texture to large geometric surfaces. Well-done seamless textures can lend the appearance of a seemingly much larger texture, but at the cost of a much smaller texture image. The other modes do not repeat, but are "clamped"—thus their name.

If the only implication of the wrap mode is whether the texture repeats, you would need only two wrap modes: repeat and clamp. However, the texture wrap mode also has a great deal of influence on how texture filtering is done at the edges of the texture maps. For GL_NEAREST filtering, there are no consequences to the wrap mode because the texture coordinates are always snapped to some particular texel within the texture map. However, the GL_LINEAR filter takes an average of the pixels surrounding the evaluated texture coordinate, and this creates a problem for texels that lie along the edges of the texture map.

This problem is resolved quite neatly when the wrap mode is GL_REPEAT. The texel samples are simply taken from the next row or column, which in repeat mode wraps back around to the other side of the texture. This mode works perfectly for textures that wrap around an object and meet on the other side (such as spheres).

The clamped texture wrap modes offer a number of options for the way texture edges are handled. For GL_CLAMP, the needed texels are taken from the texture border or the TEXTURE_BORDER_COLOR (set with glTexParameterfv). The GL_CLAMP_TO_EDGE wrap mode forces texture coordinates out of range to be sampled along the last row or column of valid texels. Finally, GL_CLAMP_TO_BORDER uses only border texels whenever the texture coordinates fall outside the range 0.0 to 1.0. Border texels are loaded as an extra row and column surrounding the base image, loaded along with the base texture map.

A typical application of the clamped modes occurs when you must texture a large area that would require a single texture too large to fit into memory, or that may be loaded into a single texture map. In this case, the area is chopped up into smaller "tiles" that are then placed side-by-side. In such a case, not using a wrap mode such as GL_CLAMP_TO_EDGE can sometimes cause visible filtering artifacts along the seams between tiles. Rarely, even this is not sufficient, and you will have to resort to texture border texels.

Putting It All Together

We have gone over a lot of the features and requirements for texture mapping, but we've yet to go over a concrete example program. Let's take a look now at a complete example program, Pyramid, that draws a pyramid and applies the texture, much like as shown in Figures 5.6 and 5.7. Figure 5.10 shows the output of our first example program this chapter.

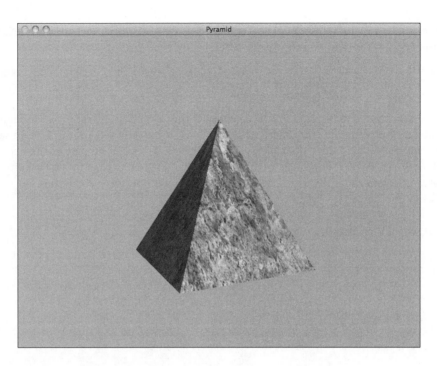

FIGURE 5.10 Our textured pyramid.

Loading the Texture

Our first step is to load the texture stone.tga. We do this in the SetupRC function as shown here:

```
glGenTextures(1, &textureID);
glBindTexture(GL_TEXTURE_2D, textureID);
LoadTGATexture("stone.tga", GL_LINEAR, GL_LINEAR, GL_CLAMP_TO_EDGE);
```

The variable textureID was declared at the top of the source file (pyramid.cpp) like this:

```
GLuint textureID;
```

The glGenTextures function allocates a single texture object and places it in this variable. We use the textureID value to identify our single texture, and the call to glBindTexture does our initial bind to this texture state. The glGenTextures function only reserves a texture object ID; it is a lightweight function really. The new texture state is not actually created and initialized until you call glBindTexture for the first time. Correspondingly, we have used a ShutdownRC function that is called when the program is terminated that deletes the texture object.

```
glDeleteTextures(1, &textureID);
```

The actual loading of the texture image and the setting of the texture state is done by the function LoadTGATexture, which is prototyped as follows:

```
bool LoadTGATexture(const char *szFileName, GLenum minFilter, GLenum magFilter,
                                                  GLenum wrapMode);
```

This function takes the filename of the image file, the desired minification and magnification filter, and the texture coordinate wrap mode. It completely sets up the texture state, and because it is placed after the call to glBindTexture, it becomes a part of the texture object identified by textureID. Listing 5.3 shows the LoadTGATexture function in its entirety. Although not a part of GLTools, we use this function for several example programs.

LISTING 5.3   Complete Texture Loading Function

```
// Load a TGA as a 2D Texture. Completely initialize the state
bool LoadTGATexture(const char *szFileName, GLenum minFilter,
                                    GLenum magFilter, GLenum wrapMode)
    {
    GLbyte *pBits;
    int nWidth, nHeight, nComponents;
    GLenum eFormat;

    // Read the texture bits
    pBits = gltReadTGABits(szFileName, &nWidth, &nHeight, &nComponents, &eFormat);
    if(pBits == NULL)
        return false;

    glTexParameteri(GL_TEXTURE_2D, GL_TEXTURE_WRAP_S, wrapMode);
    glTexParameteri(GL_TEXTURE_2D, GL_TEXTURE_WRAP_T, wrapMode);

    glTexParameteri(GL_TEXTURE_2D, GL_TEXTURE_MIN_FILTER, minFilter);
    glTexParameteri(GL_TEXTURE_2D, GL_TEXTURE_MAG_FILTER, magFilter);

    glPixelStorei(GL_UNPACK_ALIGNMENT, 1);
    glTexImage2D(GL_TEXTURE_2D, 0, nComponents, nWidth, nHeight, 0,
                                    eFormat, GL_UNSIGNED_BYTE, pBits);

    free(pBits);

    if(minFilter == GL_LINEAR_MIPMAP_LINEAR ||
        minFilter == GL_LINEAR_MIPMAP_NEAREST ||
        minFilter == GL_NEAREST_MIPMAP_LINEAR ||
        minFilter == GL_NEAREST_MIPMAP_NEAREST)
```

```
    glGenerateMipmap(GL_TEXTURE_2D);

    return true;
    }
```

The one thing we haven't discussed is the call to glGenerateMipmap and the mipmap based filters. Mipmaps are coming up in a couple of sections, and we hold off on this until we actually use this feature.

Specifying Texture Coordinates

After loading the texture in SetupRC, we call the function MakePyramid and pass an instance of GLBatch called pyramidBatch.

```
MakePyramid(pyramidBatch);
```

This function manually constructs a pyramid out of individual triangles and places them in the pyramidBatch container class. We are not going to list the entire function here, but there is something interesting going on there that we need to talk about. Previously when we used the GLBatch class, we used the CopyVertexData function to copy an entire array of data into the batch at once. The GLBatch class also contains functions that allow you to build a batch one vertex at a time. This looks suspiciously like the old and now deprecated *immediate mode* of the OpenGL compatibility profile and is sure to raise some heckles. True immediate mode is without a doubt the slowest means possible to assemble a vertex batch, but it can be convenient and can simplify manual geometry construction. This feature of the GLBatch class is not a true immediate mode emulation either, so if you are familiar with immediate mode already, forget most of what you know; our implementation is simplified.

Let's take a look at how we begin constructing the triangle batch.

```
pyramidBatch.Begin(GL_TRIANGLES, 18, 1);
```

This starts the batch, pretty much like we've started any GLBatch. Notice the last parameter now is a 1. This means there is going to be one texture applied to this batch. We used the C++ feature of default parameters, and if you leave this parameter off, it is automatically set to zero. You can actually apply more than one texture at a time, and we cover how this works in Chapter 7.

Now, see how we add the first two vertices of the triangles on the bottom of the pyramid.

```
// Bottom of pyramid
pyramidBatch.Normal3f(0.0f, -1.0f, 0.0f);
pyramidBatch.MultiTexCoord2f(0, 0.0f, 0.0f);
pyramidBatch.Vertex3f(-1.0f, -1.0f, -1.0f);
```

```
pyramidBatch.Normal3f(0.0f, -1.0f, 0.0f);
pyramidBatch.MultiTexCoord2f(0, 1.0f, 0.0f);
pyramidBatch.Vertex3f(1.0f, -1.0f, -1.0f);
```

The `Normal3f` method adds a surface normal to the batch. The `MultiTexCoord2f` adds a texture coordinate, and finally, `Vertex3f` adds the vertex position. An important rule for the `GLBatch` that does not apply to the old-style immediate mode is that if you specify normals or texture coordinates for any vertex, you must do so for every vertex. This removes some of the flexibility of the old style, but does make it run a bit faster. The `Normal3f` and `Vertex3f` functions are pretty self-explanatory, but `MultiTexCord2f` has three parameters, and the first is an integer:

```
void GLBatch::MultiTexCoord2f(GLuint texture, GLclampf s, GLclamp t);
```

There, aside from the texture coordinates, you specify the texture layer with `texture`. Until we get to multitexture in Chapter 7, always set this to zero for the stock shaders.

For mathematically derived, or hand modeled geometry, this means of setting vertex data can be convenient and can streamline code. Here, we show how we calculate the surface normal for one of the sides of the pyramid, and then use it for all three vertices.

```
// Front of Pyramid
m3dFindNormal(n, vApex, vFrontLeft, vFrontRight);
pyramidBatch.Normal3fv(n);
pyramidBatch.MultiTexCoord2f(0, 0.5f, 1.0f);
pyramidBatch.Vertex3fv(vApex);             // Apex

pyramidBatch.Normal3fv(n);
pyramidBatch.MultiTexCoord2f(0, 0.0f, 0.0f);
pyramidBatch.Vertex3fv(vFrontLeft);        // Front left corner

pyramidBatch.Normal3fv(n);
pyramidBatch.MultiTexCoord2f(0, 1.0f, 0.0f);
pyramidBatch.Vertex3fv(vFrontRight);       // Front right corner
```

Surface normals are directional vectors that say which way the face (or vertex) is facing. This is a requirement of most lighting models. We go over this as an example shader in the next chapter.

Remember, copying a large amount of data one element at a time is something akin to filling a swimming pool one tea cup at a time. You should not do this in a performance-sensitive situation. Often the startup costs are negligible, and this works out. If, however, your geometry is dynamic and you are changing it frequently, this is probably the worst way to move a large amount of geometry data around.

Finally, let's see how we actually render the pyramid in our example program. Note how we must again bind to our texture object `textureID`.

```
glBindTexture(GL_TEXTURE_2D, textureID);
shaderManager.UseStockShader(GLT_SHADER_TEXTURE_POINT_LIGHT_DIFF,
                        transformPipeline.GetModelViewMatrix(),
                        transformPipeline.GetProjectionMatrix(),
                        vLightPos, vWhite, 0);


pyramidBatch.Draw();
```

Strictly speaking, binding to the texture was not necessary because we only have one texture in our project, and we had already bound to it when we loaded the texture. Rarely will this be the case, however, so you are hereby reminded that you need to be bound to the texture you want to use when you submit a geometry batch. The bind could have actually also been placed after the shader. As long as it's bound before the geometry is submitted, that texture will be the one used.

For this example, we used a new stock shader too, `GLT_SHADER_TEXTURE_POINT_LIGHT_DIFF`. This shader sets a point light in our scene, shades the geometry using the specified color, in this case `vWhite`, and then multiples this by the texture color. The result is our shaded, texture pyramid shown previously in Figure 5.10.

Mipmapping

Mipmapping is a powerful texturing technique that can improve both the rendering performance and the visual quality of a scene. It does this by addressing two common problems with standard texture mapping. The first is an effect called *scintillation* (aliasing artifacts) that appears on the surface of objects rendered very small on-screen compared to the relative size of the texture applied. Scintillation can be seen as a sort of sparkling that occurs as the sampling area on a texture map moves disproportionately to its size on the screen. The negative effects of scintillation are most noticeable when the camera or the objects are in motion.

The second issue is more performance-related but is due to the same scenario that leads to scintillation. That is, a large amount of texture memory must be loaded and processed through filtering to display a small number of fragments on-screen. This causes texturing performance to suffer greatly as the size of the texture increases.

The solution to both of these problems is to simply use a smaller texture map. However, this solution then creates a new problem: When near the same object, it must be rendered larger, and a small texture map will then be stretched to the point of creating a hopelessly blurry or blocky textured object.

The solution to both of these issues is *mipmapping*. Mipmapping gets its name from the Latin phrase *multum in parvo*, which means "many things in a small place." In essence, you load not a single image into the texture state, but a whole series of images from largest to smallest into a single "mipmapped" texture state. OpenGL then uses a new set of filter modes to choose the best-fitting texture or textures for the given geometry. At the cost of some extra memory (and possibly considerably more processing work), you can eliminate scintillation and the texture memory processing overhead for distant objects simultaneously, while maintaining higher resolution versions of the texture available when needed.

A mipmapped texture consists of a series of texture images, each one half the size on each axis or one-fourth the total number of pixels of the previous image. This scenario is shown in Figure 5.11. Mipmap levels do not have to be square, but the halving of the dimensions continues until the last image is 1 x 1 texel. When one of the dimensions reaches 1, further divisions occur on the other dimension only. Using a square set of mipmaps requires about one-third more memory than not using mipmaps.

 ....

FIGURE 5.11   A series of mipmapped images.

Mipmap levels are loaded with `glTexImage`. Now the level parameter comes into play because it specifies which mip level the image data is for. The first level is 0, then 1, 2, and so on. If mipmapping is not being used, only level 0 is ever loaded. By default, to use mipmaps, all mip levels must be populated. You can, however, specifically set the base and maximum levels to be used with the `GL_TEXTURE_BASE_LEVEL` and `GL_TEXTURE_MAX_LEVEL` texture parameters. For example, if you want to specify that only mip levels 0 through 4 need to be loaded, you call `glTexParameteri` twice as shown here:

```
glTexParameteri(GL_TEXTURE_2D, GL_TEXTURE_BASE_LEVEL, 0);
glTexParameteri(GL_TEXTURE_2D, GL_TEXTURE_MAX_LEVEL, 4);
```

Although `GL_TEXTURE_BASE_LEVEL` and `GL_TEXTURE_MAX_LEVEL` control which mip levels are loaded (potentially saving some memory), you can also specifically limit the range of loaded mip levels to be used by using the parameters `GL_TEXTURE_MIN_LOD` and `GL_TEXTURE_MAX_LOD` instead.

Mipmap Filtering

Mipmapping adds a new twist to the two basic texture filtering modes GL_NEAREST and GL_LINEAR by giving four permutations for mipmapped filtering modes. They are listed in Table 5.5.

TABLE 5.5   Texture Filters, Including Mipmapped Filters

Constant	Description
GL_NEAREST	Perform nearest neighbor filtering on the base mip level
GL_LINEAR	Perform linear filtering on the base mip level
GL_NEAREST_MIPMAP_NEAREST	Select the nearest mip level and perform nearest neighbor filtering
GL_NEAREST_MIPMAP_LINEAR	Perform a linear interpolation between mip levels and perform nearest neighbor filtering
GL_LINEAR_MIPMAP_NEAREST	Select the nearest mip level and perform linear filtering
GL_LINEAR_MIPMAP_LINEAR	Perform a linear interpolation between mip levels and perform linear filtering; also called trilinear mipmapping

Just loading the mip levels with glTexImage does not by itself enable mipmapping. If the texture filter is set to GL_LINEAR or GL_NEAREST, only the base texture level is used, and any mip levels loaded are ignored. You must specify one of the mipmapped filters listed for the loaded mip levels to be used. The constants have the form GL_FILTER_MIPMAP_SELECTOR, where FILTER specifies the texture filter to be used on the mip level selected. The SELECTOR specifies how the mip level is selected; for example, GL_NEAREST selects the nearest matching mip level. Using GL_LINEAR for the selector creates a linear interpolation between the two nearest mip levels, which is again filtered by the chosen texture filter. Selecting one of the mipmapped filtering modes without loading the mip levels results in an invalid texture state. Don't do this.

Which filter you select varies depending on the application and the performance requirements at hand. GL_NEAREST_MIPMAP_NEAREST, for example, gives very good performance and low aliasing (scintillation) artifacts, but nearest neighbor filtering is often not visually pleasing. GL_LINEAR_MIPMAP_NEAREST is often used to speed up games because a higher quality linear filter is used, but a fast selection (nearest) is made between the different-sized mip levels available.

Using nearest as the mipmap selector (as in both examples in the preceding paragraph), however, can also leave an undesirable visual artifact. For oblique views, you can often see the transition from one mip level to another across a surface. It can be seen as a distortion line or a sharp transition from one level of detail to another. The GL_LINEAR_MIPMAP_LINEAR and GL_NEAREST_MIPMAP_LINEAR filters perform an additional interpolation between mip levels to eliminate this transition zone, but at the extra cost of substantially more processing overhead. The `GL_LINEAR_MIPMAP_LINEAR` filter is often referred to as trilinear mipmapping and until recently was the gold standard (highest fidelity) of texture filtering. More recently, anisotropic texture filtering (covered in the upcoming section, "Anisotropic Filtering") has become widely available on OpenGL hardware but even further increases the cost (performance-wise) of texture mapping.

Generating Mip Levels

As mentioned previously, mipmapping requires approximately one-third more texture memory than just loading the base texture image. It also requires that all the smaller versions of the base texture image be available for loading. Sometimes this can be inconvenient because the lower resolution images may not necessarily be available to either the programmer or the end user of your software. While having precomputed mip levels for your textures yields the very best results, it is convenient and somewhat common to have OpenGL generate the textures for you. You can generate all the mip levels for a texture once you loaded level zero with the function `glGenerateMipmap`.

```
void glGenerateMipmap(GLenum target);
```

The target parameter can be `GL_TEXTURE_1D`, `GL_TEXTURE_2D`, `GL_TEXTURE_3D`, `GL_TEXTURE_CUBE_MAP`, `GL_TEXTURE_1D_ARRAY`, or `GL_TEXTURE_2D_ARRAY` (more on these last three in Chapter 7). The quality of the filter used to create the smaller textures may vary widely from implementation to implementation. In addition, generating mipmaps on the fly is usually slower than actually loading prebuilt mipmaps, something to think about in performance critical applications. For the very best visual quality (as well as for consistency), you should load your own pregenerated mipmaps.

Mipmaps in Action

The example program Tunnel shows off all the topics discussed so far in this chapter and demonstrates visually the different filtering and mipmap modes. This sample program loads three textures at startup and then switches between them to render a tunnel. The tunnel has a brick wall pattern with different materials on the floor and ceiling. The output from Tunnel is shown in Figure 5.12.

FIGURE 5.12   A tunnel rendered with three textures and mipmapping. (Also shown in Color Plate 4.)

The Tunnel program shows off mipmapping and the different mipmapped texture filtering modes as well. Pressing the up- and down-arrow keys moves the point of view back and forth in the tunnel, and the context menu (right-click menu) allows you to switch between six different filtering modes to see how they affect the rendered image. The complete source code is provided in Listing 5.4.

LISTING 5.4   Source Code for the Tunnel Sample Program

```
// Tunnel.cpp
// Demonstrates mipmapping and using texture objects
// OpenGL SuperBible
// Richard S. Wright Jr.
#include <GLTools.h>
#include <GLShaderManager.h>
#include <GLFrustum.h>
#include <GLBatch.h>
#include <GLFrame.h>
#include <GLMatrixStack.h>
#include <GLGeometryTransform.h>
```

```
#ifdef __APPLE__
#include <glut/glut.h>
#else
#define FREEGLUT_STATIC
#include <gl/glut.h>
#endif


GLShaderManager        shaderManager;        // Shader Manager
GLMatrixStack           modelViewMatrix;       // Modelview Matrix
GLMatrixStack           projectionMatrix;      // Projection Matrix
GLFrustum              viewFrustum;         // View Frustum
GLGeometryTransform    transformPipeline;    // Geometry Transform Pipeline

GLBatch            floorBatch;
GLBatch            ceilingBatch;
GLBatch            leftWallBatch;
GLBatch            rightWallBatch;

GLfloat            viewZ = -65.0f;

// Texture objects
#define TEXTURE_BRICK    0
#define TEXTURE_FLOOR    1
#define TEXTURE_CEILING 2
#define TEXTURE_COUNT    3
GLuint  textures[TEXTURE_COUNT];
const char *szTextureFiles[TEXTURE_COUNT] = { "brick.tga",
                            "floor.tga", "ceiling.tga" };



///////////////////////////////////////////////////////////////////////////
// Change texture filter for each texture object
void ProcessMenu(int value)
    {
    GLint iLoop;

    for(iLoop = 0; iLoop < TEXTURE_COUNT; iLoop++)
        {
        glBindTexture(GL_TEXTURE_2D, textures[iLoop]);

        switch(value)
```

```
        {
        case 0:
            glTexParameteri(GL_TEXTURE_2D,
                    GL_TEXTURE_MIN_FILTER, GL_NEAREST);
            break;

        case 1:
            glTexParameteri(GL_TEXTURE_2D, GL_TEXTURE_MIN_FILTER, GL_LINEAR);

            break;

        case 2:
            glTexParameteri(GL_TEXTURE_2D,
         GL_TEXTURE_MIN_FILTER, GL_NEAREST_MIPMAP_NEAREST);
            break;

        case 3:
            glTexParameteri(GL_TEXTURE_2D,
          GL_TEXTURE_MIN_FILTER, GL_NEAREST_MIPMAP_LINEAR);
            break;

        case 4:
            glTexParameteri(GL_TEXTURE_2D,
          GL_TEXTURE_MIN_FILTER, GL_LINEAR_MIPMAP_NEAREST);
            break;

        case 5:
            glTexParameteri(GL_TEXTURE_2D,
            GL_TEXTURE_MIN_FILTER, GL_LINEAR_MIPMAP_LINEAR);
            break;
        }
    }

    // Trigger Redraw
    glutPostRedisplay();
    }


/////////////////////////////////////////////////////////////////
// This function does any needed initialization on the rendering
// context.  Here it sets up and initializes the texture objects.
void SetupRC()
    {
```

```
GLbyte *pBytes;
GLint iWidth, iHeight, iComponents;
GLenum eFormat;
GLint iLoop;

// Black background
glClearColor(0.0f, 0.0f, 0.0f,1.0f);

shaderManager.InitializeStockShaders();

// Load textures
glGenTextures(TEXTURE_COUNT, textures);
for(iLoop = 0; iLoop < TEXTURE_COUNT; iLoop++)
    {
    // Bind to next texture object
    glBindTexture(GL_TEXTURE_2D, textures[iLoop]);

    // Load texture, set filter and wrap modes
    pBytes = gltReadTGABits(szTextureFiles[iLoop],&iWidth, &iHeight,
                       &iComponents, &eFormat);

    // Load texture, set filter and wrap modes
    glTexParameteri(GL_TEXTURE_2D, GL_TEXTURE_MAG_FILTER, GL_NEAREST);
    glTexParameteri(GL_TEXTURE_2D, GL_TEXTURE_MIN_FILTER, GL_NEAREST);
    glTexParameteri(GL_TEXTURE_2D, GL_TEXTURE_WRAP_S, GL_CLAMP_TO_EDGE);
    glTexParameteri(GL_TEXTURE_2D, GL_TEXTURE_WRAP_T, GL_CLAMP_TO_EDGE);
    glTexImage2D(GL_TEXTURE_2D, 0, iComponents, iWidth, iHeight,
                            0, eFormat, GL_UNSIGNED_BYTE, pBytes);
    glGenerateMipmap(GL_TEXTURE_2D);
    // Don't need original texture data any more
    free(pBytes);
    }

// Build Geometry
GLfloat z;
floorBatch.Begin(GL_TRIANGLE_STRIP, 28, 1);
for(z = 60.0f; z >= 0.0f; z -=10.0f)
    {
    floorBatch.MultiTexCoord2f(0, 0.0f, 0.0f);
    floorBatch.Vertex3f(-10.0f, -10.0f, z);

    floorBatch.MultiTexCoord2f(0, 1.0f, 0.0f);
    floorBatch.Vertex3f(10.0f, -10.0f, z);
```

```
    floorBatch.MultiTexCoord2f(0, 0.0f, 1.0f);
    floorBatch.Vertex3f(-10.0f, -10.0f, z - 10.0f);

    floorBatch.MultiTexCoord2f(0, 1.0f, 1.0f);
    floorBatch.Vertex3f(10.0f, -10.0f, z - 10.0f);
    }
floorBatch.End();

ceilingBatch.Begin(GL_TRIANGLE_STRIP, 28, 1);
for(z = 60.0f; z >= 0.0f; z -=10.0f)
    {
    ceilingBatch.MultiTexCoord2f(0, 0.0f, 1.0f);
    ceilingBatch.Vertex3f(-10.0f, 10.0f, z - 10.0f);

    ceilingBatch.MultiTexCoord2f(0, 1.0f, 1.0f);
    ceilingBatch.Vertex3f(10.0f, 10.0f, z - 10.0f);

    ceilingBatch.MultiTexCoord2f(0, 0.0f, 0.0f);
    ceilingBatch.Vertex3f(-10.0f, 10.0f, z);

    ceilingBatch.MultiTexCoord2f(0, 1.0f, 0.0f);
    ceilingBatch.Vertex3f(10.0f, 10.0f, z);
    }
ceilingBatch.End();

leftWallBatch.Begin(GL_TRIANGLE_STRIP, 28, 1);
for(z = 60.0f; z >= 0.0f; z -=10.0f)
    {
    leftWallBatch.MultiTexCoord2f(0, 0.0f, 0.0f);
    leftWallBatch.Vertex3f(-10.0f, -10.0f, z);

    leftWallBatch.MultiTexCoord2f(0, 0.0f, 1.0f);
    leftWallBatch.Vertex3f(-10.0f, 10.0f, z);

    leftWallBatch.MultiTexCoord2f(0, 1.0f, 0.0f);
    leftWallBatch.Vertex3f(-10.0f, -10.0f, z - 10.0f);

    leftWallBatch.MultiTexCoord2f(0, 1.0f, 1.0f);
    leftWallBatch.Vertex3f(-10.0f, 10.0f, z - 10.0f);
    }
leftWallBatch.End();
```

5

```
    rightWallBatch.Begin(GL_TRIANGLE_STRIP, 28, 1);
    for(z = 60.0f; z >= 0.0f; z -=10.0f)
        {
        rightWallBatch.MultiTexCoord2f(0, 0.0f, 0.0f);
        rightWallBatch.Vertex3f(10.0f, -10.0f, z);

        rightWallBatch.MultiTexCoord2f(0, 0.0f, 1.0f);
        rightWallBatch.Vertex3f(10.0f, 10.0f, z);

        rightWallBatch.MultiTexCoord2f(0, 1.0f, 0.0f);
        rightWallBatch.Vertex3f(10.0f, -10.0f, z - 10.0f);

        rightWallBatch.MultiTexCoord2f(0, 1.0f, 1.0f);
        rightWallBatch.Vertex3f(10.0f, 10.0f, z - 10.0f);
        }
    rightWallBatch.End();
    }


///////////////////////////////////////////////////
// Shutdown the rendering context. Just deletes the
// texture objects
void ShutdownRC(void)
    {
    glDeleteTextures(TEXTURE_COUNT, textures);
    }



///////////////////////////////////////////////////
// Respond to arrow keys, move the viewpoint back
// and forth
void SpecialKeys(int key, int x, int y)
    {
    if(key == GLUT_KEY_UP)
        viewZ += 0.5f;

    if(key == GLUT_KEY_DOWN)
        viewZ -= 0.5f;

    // Refresh the Window
    glutPostRedisplay();
    }


/////////////////////////////////////////////////////////////////////
```

```
// Change viewing volume and viewport.  Called when window is resized
void ChangeSize(int w, int h)
    {
    GLfloat fAspect;

    // Prevent a divide by zero
    if(h == 0)
        h = 1;

    // Set Viewport to window dimensions
    glViewport(0, 0, w, h);

    fAspect = (GLfloat)w/(GLfloat)h;

    // Produce the perspective projection
    viewFrustum.SetPerspective(80.0f,fAspect,1.0,120.0);
    projectionMatrix.LoadMatrix(viewFrustum.GetProjectionMatrix());
    transformPipeline.SetMatrixStacks(modelViewMatrix, projectionMatrix);

    }

/////////////////////////////////////////////////////////
// Called to draw scene
void RenderScene(void)
    {
    // Clear the window with current clearing color
    glClear(GL_COLOR_BUFFER_BIT);

    modelViewMatrix.PushMatrix();
        modelViewMatrix.Translate(0.0f, 0.0f, viewZ);

        shaderManager.UseStockShader(GLT_SHADER_TEXTURE_REPLACE,
                        transformPipeline.GetModelViewProjectionMatrix(),
                                                                0);

        glBindTexture(GL_TEXTURE_2D, textures[TEXTURE_FLOOR]);
        floorBatch.Draw();

        glBindTexture(GL_TEXTURE_2D, textures[TEXTURE_CEILING]);
        ceilingBatch.Draw();

        glBindTexture(GL_TEXTURE_2D, textures[TEXTURE_BRICK]);
        leftWallBatch.Draw();
```

```
            rightWallBatch.Draw();

    modelViewMatrix.PopMatrix();

    // Buffer swap
    glutSwapBuffers();
    }


/////////////////////////////////////////////////////
// Program entry point
int main(int argc, char *argv[])
    {
    gltSetWorkingDirectory(argv[0]);

    // Standard initialization stuff
    glutInit(&argc, argv);
    glutInitDisplayMode(GLUT_DOUBLE | GLUT_RGB);
    glutInitWindowSize(800, 600);
    glutCreateWindow("Tunnel");
    glutReshapeFunc(ChangeSize);
    glutSpecialFunc(SpecialKeys);
    glutDisplayFunc(RenderScene);

    // Add menu entries to change filter
    glutCreateMenu(ProcessMenu);
    glutAddMenuEntry("GL_NEAREST",0);
    glutAddMenuEntry("GL_LINEAR",1);
    glutAddMenuEntry("GL_NEAREST_MIPMAP_NEAREST",2);
    glutAddMenuEntry("GL_NEAREST_MIPMAP_LINEAR", 3);
    glutAddMenuEntry("GL_LINEAR_MIPMAP_NEAREST", 4);
    glutAddMenuEntry("GL_LINEAR_MIPMAP_LINEAR", 5);

    glutAttachMenu(GLUT_RIGHT_BUTTON);

    GLenum err = glewInit();
    if (GLEW_OK != err) {
        fprintf(stderr, "GLEW Error: %s\n", glewGetErrorString(err));
        return 1;
        }


    // Startup, loop, shutdown
```

```
    SetupRC();
    glutMainLoop();
    ShutdownRC();

    return 0;
    }
```

In this example, you first create identifiers for the three texture objects. The array textures will contain three integers, which will be addressed by using the macros TEXTURE_BRICK, TEXTURE_FLOOR, and TEXTURE_CEILING. For added flexibility, you also create a macro that defines the maximum number of textures that will be loaded and an array of character strings containing the names of the texture map files:

```
// Texture objects
#define TEXTURE_BRICK   0
#define TEXTURE_FLOOR   1
#define TEXTURE_CEILING 2
#define TEXTURE_COUNT   3
GLuint  textures[TEXTURE_COUNT];
const char *szTextureFiles[TEXTURE_COUNT] =
                               { "brick.tga", "floor.tga", "ceiling.tga" };
```

The texture objects are allocated in the SetupRC function:

```
glGenTextures(TEXTURE_COUNT, textures);
```

Then a simple loop binds to each texture object in turn and loads its texture state with the texture image and texturing parameters:

```
for(iLoop = 0; iLoop < TEXTURE_COUNT; iLoop++)
    {
    // Bind to next texture object
    glBindTexture(GL_TEXTURE_2D, textures[iLoop]);

    // Load texture, set filter and wrap modes
    // Load texture, set filter and wrap modes
    pBytes = gltReadTGABits(szTextureFiles[iLoop],&iWidth, &iHeight,
                                        &iComponents, &eFormat);

    // Load texture, set filter and wrap modes
    glTexParameteri(GL_TEXTURE_2D, GL_TEXTURE_MAG_FILTER, GL_NEAREST);
    glTexParameteri(GL_TEXTURE_2D, GL_TEXTURE_MIN_FILTER, GL_NEAREST);
    glTexParameteri(GL_TEXTURE_2D, GL_TEXTURE_WRAP_S, GL_CLAMP_TO_EDGE);
    glTexParameteri(GL_TEXTURE_2D, GL_TEXTURE_WRAP_T, GL_CLAMP_TO_EDGE);
```

```
    glTexImage2D(GL_TEXTURE_2D, 0, iComponents, iWidth, iHeight,
                              0, eFormat, GL_UNSIGNED_BYTE, pBytes);
    glGenerateMipmap(GL_TEXTURE_2D);

    // Don't need original texture data any more
    free(pBytes);
    }
```

With each of the three texture objects initialized, you can easily switch among them during rendering to change textures:

```
glBindTexture(GL_TEXTURE_2D, textures[TEXTURE_FLOOR]);
floorBatch.Draw();

glBindTexture(GL_TEXTURE_2D, textures[TEXTURE_CEILING]);
ceilingBatch.Draw();
...
...
```

Finally, when the program is terminated, you only need to delete the texture objects for the final cleanup:

```
///////////////////////////////////////////////////
// Shut down the rendering context. Just deletes the
// texture objects
void ShutdownRC(void)
    {
    glDeleteTextures(TEXTURE_COUNT, textures);
    }
```

Also note that when the mipmapped texture filter is set in the Tunnel sample program, it is selected only for the minification filter:

```
glTexParameteri(GL_TEXTURE_2D, GL_TEXTURE_MAG_FILTER, GL_LINEAR);
glTexParameteri(GL_TEXTURE_2D, GL_TEXTURE_MIN_FILTER, GL_LINEAR_MIPMAP_LINEAR);
```

This is typically the case because after OpenGL selects the largest available mip level, no larger levels are available to select from. Essentially, this is to say that after a certain threshold is passed, the largest available texture image is used, and there are no additional mipmap levels to choose from.

Anisotropic Filtering

Anisotropic texture filtering is not a part of the core OpenGL specification, but it is a widely supported extension that can dramatically improve the quality of texture filtering operations. Earlier in this chapter, you learned about the two basic texture filters: nearest neighbor (GL_NEAREST) and linear (GL_LINEAR). When a texture map is filtered, OpenGL uses the texture coordinates to figure out where in the texture map a particular fragment of geometry falls. The texels immediately around that position are then sampled using either the GL_NEAREST or the GL_LINEAR filtering operations.

This process works perfectly when the geometry being textured is viewed directly perpendicular to the viewpoint, as shown on the left in Figure 5.13. However, when the geometry is viewed from an angle more oblique to the point of view, a regular sampling of the surrounding texels results in the loss of some information in the texture (it looks blurry!). A more realistic and accurate sample would be elongated along the direction of the plane containing the texture. This result is shown on the right in Figure 5.13. Taking this viewing angle into account for texture filtering is called anisotropic filtering.

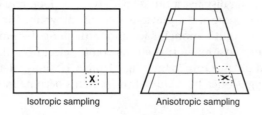

Isotropic sampling   Anisotropic sampling

FIGURE 5.13 Normal texture sampling versus anisotropic sampling.

You can apply anisotropic filtering to any of the basic or mipmapped texture filtering modes; applying it requires three steps. First, you must determine whether the extension is supported. You can do this by querying for the extension string GL_EXT_texture_filter_anisotropic. You can use the GLTools function named gltIsExtSupported for this task:

```
if(gltIsExtSupported("GL_EXT_texture_filter_anisotropic"))
    // Set Flag that extension is supported
```

After you determine that this extension is supported, you can find the maximum amount of anisotropy supported. You can query for it using glGetFloatv and the parameter GL_MAX_TEXTURE_MAX_ANISOTROPY_EXT:

```
GLfloat fLargest;
. . .
. . .
glGetFloatv(GL_MAX_TEXTURE_MAX_ANISOTROPY_EXT, &fLargest);
```

The larger the amount of anisotropy applied, the more texels are sampled along the direction of greatest change (along the strongest point of view). A value of 1.0 represents normal texture filtering (called isotropic filtering). Bear in mind that anisotropic filtering is not free. The extra amount of work, including other texels, can sometimes result in substantial performance penalties. On modern hardware, this feature is getting quite fast and is becoming a standard feature of popular games, animation, and simulation programs.

Finally, you set the amount of anisotropy you want applied using glTexParameter and the constant GL_TEXTURE_MAX_ANISOTROPY_EXT. For example, using the preceding code, if you want the maximum amount of anisotropy applied, you would call glTexParameterf as shown here:

```
glTexParameterf(GL_TEXTURE_2D, GL_TEXTURE_MAX_ANISOTROPY_EXT, fLargest);
```

This modifier is applied per texture object just like the standard filtering parameters.

The sample program Anisotropic provides a striking example of anisotropic texture filtering in action. This program displays a tunnel with walls, a floor, and ceiling geometry; it is essentially a revved up version of the previous example program, Tunnel. The arrow keys move your point of view (or the tunnel) back and forth along the tunnel interior. A right-click of the mouse brings up a menu that allows you to select from the various texture filters and turn on and off anisotropic filtering. Figure 5.12 shows the tunnel using trilinear filtered mipmapping. Notice how blurred the patterns become in the distance, particularly with the bricks.

Now compare Figure 5.12 with Figure 5.14, in which anisotropic filtering has been enabled (Color Plate 4 in the color insert shows these figures side by side). The mortar between the bricks is now clearly visible all the way to the end of the tunnel. In fact, anisotropic filtering can also greatly reduce the visible mipmap transition patterns for the GL_LINEAR_MIPMAP_NEAREST and GL_NEAREST_MIPMAP_NEAREST mipmapped filters.

FIGURE 5.14 Anisotropic tunnel sample with anisotropic filtering. (Also shown in Color Plate 4.)

Texture Compression

Texture mapping can add incredible realism to any 3D rendered scene, with a minimal cost in vertex processing. One drawback to using textures, however, is that they require a lot of memory to store and process. Early attempts at texture compression were crudely storing textures as JPG files and decompressing the textures when loaded before calling `glTexImage`. These attempts saved disk space or reduced the amount of time required to transmit the image over the network (such as the Internet) but did nothing to alleviate the storage requirements of texture images loaded into graphics hardware memory.

Native support for texture compression was added to OpenGL with version 1.3. Earlier versions of OpenGL may also support texture compression via extension functions of the same name. You can test for this extension by using the `GL_ARB_texture_compression` string.

Texture compression support in OpenGL hardware can go beyond simply allowing you to load a compressed texture; in most implementations, the texture data stays compressed even in the graphics hardware memory. This allows you to load more texture into less memory and can significantly improve texturing performance due to fewer texture swaps (moving textures around) and fewer memory accesses during texture filtering.

Compressing Textures

Texture data does not have to be initially compressed to take advantage of OpenGL support for compressed textures. You can request that OpenGL compress a texture image when loaded by using one of the generic compression values in Table 5.6 for the `internalFormat` parameter of any of the `glTexImage` functions.

TABLE 5.6   Generic Compressed Texture Formats

Compressed Format	Base Internal Format
GL_COMPRESSED_RGB	GL_RGB
GL_COMPRESSED_RGBA	GL_RGBA
GL_COMPRESSED_SRGB	GL_RGB
GL_COMPRESSED_SRGB_ALPHA	GL_RGBA
GL_COMPRESSED_RED	GL_RED
GL_COMPRESSED_RG	GL_RG (Red Green)

In addition to these generic compression formats, a number of specific compression formats were added to OpenGL 3.2—GL_COMPRESSED_SIGNED_RED_RGTC1, GL_COMPRESSED_RG_RGTC2, and GL_COMPRESSED_SIGNED_RG-RGTC2. These are used for various single and dual color channel compressed textures. Essentially, they replace the functionality of GL_LUMINANCE and GL_LUMINANCE_ALPHA from the compatibility profile.

Compressing images this way adds a bit of overhead to texture loads but can increase texture performance due to the more efficient usage of texture memory. If, for some reason, the texture cannot be compressed, OpenGL uses the base internal format listed instead and loads the texture uncompressed.

When you attempt to load and compress a texture in this way, you can find out whether the texture was successfully compressed by using `glGetTexLevelParameteriv` with `GL_TEXTURE_COMPRESSED` as the parameter name:

```
GLint compFlag;
. . .
glGetTexLevelParameteriv(GL_TEXTURE_2D, 0, GL_TEXTURE_COMPRESSED, &compFlag);
```

The `glGetTexLevelParameteriv` function accepts a number of new parameter names pertaining to compressed textures. These parameters are listed in Table 5.7.

TABLE 5.7   Compressed Texture Parameters Retrieved with `glGetTexLevelParameter`

Parameter	Returns
GL_TEXTURE_COMPRESSED	The value 1 if the texture is compressed, 0 if not
GL_TEXTURE_COMPRESSED_IMAGE_SIZE	The size in bytes of the compressed texture
GL_TEXTURE_INTERNAL_FORMAT	The compression format used

Parameter	Returns
GL_NUM_COMPRESSED_TEXTURE_FORMATS	The number of supported compressed texture formats
GL_COMPRESSED_TEXTURE_FORMATS	An array of constant values corresponding to each supported compressed texture format
GL_TEXTURE_COMPRESSION_HINT	The value of the texture compression hint (GL_NICEST/GL_FASTEST)

When textures are compressed using the values listed in Table 5.6, OpenGL chooses the most appropriate texture compression format. You can use glHint to specify whether you want OpenGL to choose based on the fastest or highest quality algorithm:

```
glHint(GL_TEXTURE_COMPRESSION_HINT, GL_FASTEST);
glHint(GL_TEXTURE_COMPRESSION_HINT, GL_NICEST);
glHint(GL_TEXTURE_COMPRESSION_HINT, GL_DONT_CARE);
```

The exact compression format varies from implementation to implementation. You can obtain a count of compression formats and a list of the values by using GL_NUM_COMPRESSED_TEXTURE_FORMATS and GL_COMPRESSED_TEXTURE_FORMATS. To check for support for a specific set of compressed texture formats, you need to check for a specific extension for those formats. For example, nearly all desktop implementations support the GL_EXT_texture_compression_s3tc texture compression format. If this extension is supported, the compressed texture formats listed in Table 5.8 are all supported, but only for two-dimensional textures.

TABLE 5.8   Compression Formats for GL_EXT_texture_compression_s3tc

Format	Description
GL_COMPRESSED_RGB_S3TC_DXT1	RGB data is compressed; alpha is always 1.0.
GL_COMPRESSED_RGBA_S3TC_DXT1	RGB data is compressed; alpha is either 1.0 or 0.0.
GL_COMPRESSED_RGBA_S3TC_DXT3	RGB data is compressed; alpha is stored as 4 bits.
GL_COMPRESSED_RGBA_S3TC_DXT5	RGB data is compressed; alpha is a weighted average of 8-bit values.

Loading Compressed Textures

Using the functions in the preceding section, you can have OpenGL compress textures in a natively supported format, retrieve the compressed data with the glGetCompressedTexImage function (identical to the glGetTexImage function for uncompressed textures), and save it to disk. On subsequent loads, the raw compressed data can be used, resulting in substantially faster texture loads. Be advised, however, that some vendors may cheat a little when it comes to texture loading to optimize texture storage or filtering operations. This technique works only on fully conformant hardware implementations.

To load precompressed texture data, use one of the following functions:

```
void glCompressedTexImage1D(GLenum target, GLint level,
                            GLenum internalFormat,
                            GLsizei width,
                            GLint border, GLsizei imageSize, void *data);

void glCompressedTexImage2D(GLenum target, GLint level, GLenum internalFormat,
                            GLsizei width, GLsizei height,
                            GLint border, GLsizei imageSize, void *data);

void glCompressedTexImage3D(GLenum target, GLint level,
                            GLenum internalFormat,
                            GLsizei width, GLsizei height, GLsizei depth,
                            GLint border, Glsizei imageSize, GLvoid *data);
```

These functions are virtually identical to `glTexImage`. The only difference is that the `internalFormat` parameter must specify a supported compressed texture image. If the implementation supports the `GL_EXT_texture_compression_s3tc` extension, this would be one of the values from Table 5.8. There is also a corresponding set of `glCompressedTexSubImage` functions for updating a portion or all of an already-loaded texture that mirrors the `glTexSubImage` functionality.

Texture compression is a popular texture feature. Smaller textures take up less storage, transmit faster over networks, load faster off disk, copy faster to graphics memory, allow for substantially more texture to be loaded onto hardware, and generally texture slightly faster to boot! Don't forget, though, as with so many things in life, there is no such thing as a free lunch. Something may be lost in the compression. The `GL_EXT_texture_compression_s3tc` method, for example, works by stripping color data out of each texel. For some textures, this results in substantial image quality loss (particularly for textures that contain smooth color gradients). Other times, textures with a great deal of detail and variation are visually nearly identical to the original uncompressed version, with the color shift almost unnoticed. The choice of texture compression method (or indeed no compression) can vary greatly depending on the nature of the underlying image.

A Final Example

Our final example program for this chapter is SphereWorld, a tour de force in the OpenGL techniques we have covered so far. Shown in Figure 5.15, SphereWorld is populated by floating spheres hovering over a reflective marble floor. The reflection effect is a simple smoke and mirrors trick—render the world inverted first, then render the marble floor over it, and blend with the background using a small alpha value. Then render the world right side up, and presto—a simple reflection effect. You can also move around with the arrow keys. The only real new thing in this example program is a small change to the

LoadTGA function, where we change the internal format parameter to be the generic compressed texture format GL_COMPRESSED_RGB.

```
glTexImage2D(GL_TEXTURE_2D, 0, GL_COMPRESSED_RGB, nWidth, nHeight, 0,
                                    eFormat, GL_UNSIGNED_BYTE, pBits);
```

FIGURE 5.15   SphereWorld, complete with reflective marble floor.

Summary

This chapter was essentially texture mapping 101—the first course and the fundamentals you need to master before going on to the more intermediate and advanced techniques. You are at this point equipped to start building interesting 3D scenes and applying texture to your surfaces. We covered how to load a texture from image data, pass it to OpenGL, and apply it to geometry with texture coordinates. You saw how to set the different image filters and what they do, as well as how to use the hardware to generate mipmaps, and use them to improve both the performance of your rendering and the visual quality. We also covered a more advanced filter option, anisotropic filtering, and you saw via the tunnel and anisotropic example programs the dramatic difference these settings make visually. Finally, we covered texture compression, both how to compress a texture on the fly, as well as how to load a precompressed texture directly.

Essentially, at this point we have covered everything that 3D graphics really *is*. We simply transform points around, connect the dots with primitives, and fill in their interiors with either computed color values, or texels sampled and filtered from an image file. Sometimes we also blend the results together. Really, this is pretty much "it" when it comes to how to compose and render just about any 3D scene you can imagine. For the rest of this book, we are going to essentially take these same topics of the first few chapters and start digging deeper and deeper. Get your shovel and proceed to Chapter 6, "Thinking Outside the Box: Nonstock Shaders!"

CHAPTER 6

Thinking Outside the Box:
Nonstock Shaders

by Richard S. Wright, Jr.

WHAT YOU'LL LEARN IN THIS CHAPTER:

- How to write your own shaders that work with GLBatch

- About the different GLSL variable types

- About GLSL's built-in functions

- How to roll your own lighting shaders

- How to use one- and two-dimensional textures in GLSL

- How to chisel out individual fragments

In Chapter 3, "Basic Rendering," you were first introduced to shaders and how to use them. If you skipped it to get right into shader programming, you really need to review that chapter first and make sure you understand how we use attributes and uniforms, and how we pass them into a shader from our client-side code. In that chapter we focused our attention entirely on the client side of things, and we used some prebuilt stock shaders that performed some routine and typical rendering operations. In this chapter, we go a bit deeper into the client side of things, but we are finally going to see how to write our own shaders, the server side of using shaders: shader programming and the shading language.

GLSL 101

The OpenGL Shading Language (GLSL) is a C-like high-level language that is compiled and linked by your OpenGL implementation and (usually) runs entirely on the graphics hardware. Shader programs look a lot like C, they start with the main function as their entry point, and you can write functions in GLSL that accept parameters and return values. Figure 3.1 from Chapter 3 is repeated here as Figure 6.1 and shows our basic shader architecture.

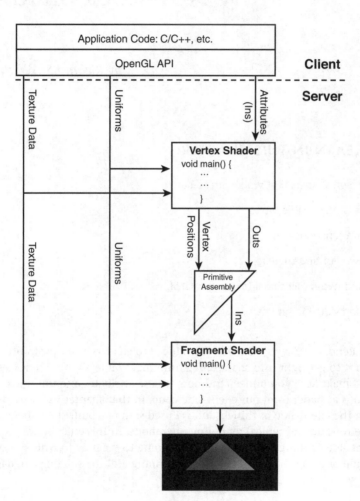

FIGURE 6.1   Our basic shader architecture.

As shown here, we need at a minimum two shaders: a vertex shader and a fragment shader. An optional third shader stage called a geometry shader is covered in more detail in Chapter 11, "Advanced Shader Usage." You submit data to the vertex shader in one of three different ways: attributes, which is a per vertex data item; uniforms, which are constant (thus *uniform*) for the entire batch of vertex data; and finally in Chapter 5, "Basic Texturing," you learned to load and use texture data as well. You can also set uniforms and texture data for your fragment shader. It doesn't make any sense to send vertex attributes to the fragment shader, because the fragment shader is only concerned with filling in the fragments (pixels basically) as the primitive is rasterized. Per vertex data, however, can be passed on to the fragment shader by the vertex program. In this case, however, the data may be constant (every fragment sees the same value), or the values may be interpolated in different ways across the surface of the primitive.

Shader programs look a lot like C programs; they start with the function `main` and use the same character set and commenting conventions and many of the same preprocessor directives. A complete language specification can be found in the OpenGL Shading Language Specification. Appendix A, "Further Reading," has some Web pointers to help you find this document as well as other good references and supplemental tutorials. For our purposes, we are going to make what should be a safe assumption, which is that you already are familiar with C/C++, and thus we focus on GLSL from a C/C++ programmer's perspective.

Variables and Data Types

A good place to start for learning GLSL is to discuss the data types available to you. There are only four: integers (both signed and unsigned), floats (single precision only as of OpenGL 3.3), and Booleans (bool). There are no pointers in GLSL, and there are no strings or characters of any kind. Functions can return any of these data types but can also be declared as void, but again, no void pointers allowed. The use of these data types in GLSL mirrors their usage in C/C++.

```
bool bDone = false;       // Boolean true or false
int iValue = 42;          // Signed integer
uint uiValue = 3929u;     // unsigned integer
float fValue = 42.0f;     // Floating point value
```

Vector Types

An exciting and unique feature of GLSL (as compared to C/C++) is the availability of vector data types. All four of the basic data types can be stored in two-, three-, or four-dimensional vectors. The complete list of vector data types is listed in Table 6.1.

TABLE 6.1   GLSL Vector Data Types

Types	Description
vec2, vec3, vec4	2, 3, and 4 component floating-point vectors
ivec2, ivec3, ivec4	2, 3, and 4 component integer vectors
uvec2, uvec3, uvec4	2, 3, and 4 component unsigned integer vectors
bvec2, bvec3, bvec4	2, 3, and 4 component Boolean vectors

A vector data type can be declared just like any other kind of variable; for example, you would declare a vertex position as a four-component floating-point vector like this:

```
vec4 vVertexPos;
```

You can also initialize a vector with a constructor:

```
vec4 vVertexPos = vec4(39.0f, 10.0f, 0.0f, 1.0f);
```

This should not be confused with C++ class constructors. GLSL vector data types are not classes; they are their own built-in data type. Vectors can be assigned to one another, added together, scaled by a scalar (nonvector type), and so on.

```
vVertexPos = vOldPos + vOffset;
vVertexPos = vNewPos;
vVertexPos += vec4(1.0f, 1.0f, 0.0f, 0.0f);
vVertexPos *= 5.0f;
```

Another unique feature to GLSL is how we can address individual elements of a vector. If you are familiar with the union construct from C/C++, vectors are like unions on steroids. We use the dot notation to address up to four vector elements, but we can use any of the following three sets of identifiers: xyzw, rgba, or stpq. Typically we would use the xyzw set of identifiers when referring to vertex type data.

```
vVertexPos.x = 3.0f;
vVertexPos.xy = vec2(3.0f, 5.0f);
vVertexPos.xyz = vNewPos.xyz;
```

Then rgba when doing color work.

```
vOutputColor.r = 1.0f;
vOutputColor.rgba = vec4(1.0f, 1.0f, 0.5f, 1.0f);
```

And finally, when working with texture coordinates, stpq.

```
vTexCoord.st = vec2(1.0f, 0.0f);
```

The choice of which set of identifiers you use is completely arbitrary as far as GLSL is concerned; for example, you could easily do something like this:

```
vTexCoord.st = vVertex.st;
```

However, what you cannot do is mix the different groups within a single vector access, such as this:

```
vTexCoord.st = vVertex.xt;    // mixing of x and t is not allowed!
```

Vector data types also support *swizzling*. A swizzle is when you swap two or more vector elements. For example, if you were converting color data from RGB ordering to BGR ordering, the following line of code would do the trick:

```
vNewColor.bgra = vOldColor.rgba;
```

Vector data types are not only native to GLSL, they are native to the hardware. They are fast, and operations are performed on all the components at once. For example, the following operation

```
vVertex.x = vOtherVertex.x + 5.0f;
vVertex.y = vOtherVertex.y + 4.0f;
vVertex.z = vOtherVertex.z + 1.0f;
```

would execute much faster if you instead use the native vector notation:

```
vVertex.xyz = vOtherVertex.xyz + vec3(5.0f, 4.0f, 1.0f);
```

Matrix Types
In addition to the vector data types, GLSL supports a number of matrix types. Unlike the vector types, however, the matrix types are all floating-point only—sorry, no integer or Boolean matrices, as these are not practically useful. Table 6.2 lists the supported matrix types.

TABLE 6.2   GLSL Matrix Types

Type	Description
mat2, mat2x2	2 columns and 2 rows
mat3, mat3x3	3 columns and 3 rows
mat4, mat4x4	4 columns and 4 rows
mat2x3	2 columns and 3 rows
mat2x4	2 columns and 4 rows
mat3x2	3 columns and 2 rows
mat3x4	3 columns and 4 rows
mat4x2	4 columns and 2 rows
mat4x3	4 columns and 3 rows

A matrix is essentially an array of vectors in GLSL—column vectors, in fact (a review of column major vector ordering from Chapter 4, "Basic Transformations: A Vector/Matrix Primer," may be in order here). For example, to set the last column of a 4 x 4 matrix, you would write code similar to this:

```
mModelView[3] = vec4(0.0f, 0.0f, 0.0f, 1.0f);
```

Conversely, to retrieve the last column of a matrix:

```
vec4 vTranslation = mModelView[3];
```

Or even a finer grained query:

```
vec3 vTranslation = mModelView[3].xyz;
```

Matrices can be multiplied by vectors too; a common use of this is to transform a vertex by the ModelViewProjection matrix, such as:

```
vec4 vVertex;
mat4 mvpMatrix;
...
...
vOutPos = mvpMatrix * vVertex;
```

Also, just like vectors, the matrix data types have their own constructors too. For example, to hard code an inline 4 x 4 matrix, you can write code like this:

```
mat4 vTransform = mat4(1.0f, 0.0f, 0.0f, 0.0f,
                       0.0f, 1.0f, 0.0f, 0.0f,
                       0.0f, 0.0f, 1.0f, 0.0f,
                       0.0f, 0.0f, 0.0f, 1.0f);
```

In this case we made the transformation matrix the identity matrix. A quicker constructor for matrices that fills in just the diagonal with a single value can also be used.

```
mat4 vTransform = mat4(1.0f);
```

Storage Qualifiers

Shader variable declarations may optionally have a storage qualifier specified. Qualifiers are used to flag variables as input variables (`in` or `uniform`), output variables (`out`), or constants (`const`). Input variables receive data either from the OpenGL client (attributes submitted via C/C++) or from the previous shader stage (for example, variables passed from the vertex shader to the fragment shader). Output variables are variables you write to in any of the shader stages that you want to be seen by the subsequent shader stages, for example, passing data from the vertex shader to the fragment shader or writing the final fragment color by the fragment shader. Table 6.3 lists the primary variable qualifiers.

TABLE 6.3 Variable Storage Qualifiers

Qualifier	Description
<none>	Just a normal local variable, no outside visibility or access.
const	A compile-time constant, or a read-only parameter to a function.
in	A variable passed in from a previous stage.
in centroid	Passed in from a previous state, uses centroid interpolation.
out	Passed out to the next processing stage or assigned a return value in a function.
out centroid	Passed out to the next processing stage, uses centroid interpolation.
inout	A read/write variable. Only valid for local function parameters.
uniform	Value is passed in from client code and does not change across vertices.

One variable qualifier inout can only be used when declaring a parameter to a function. Because GLSL does not support pointers (or references), this is the only way to pass a value to a function and allow the function to modify and return the value of the same variable. For example, this function declaration

```
int CalculateSometing(float fTime, float fStepSize, inout float fVariance);
```

would return an integer (perhaps a pass/fail flag), but also could modify the value of the fVariance variable, and the calling code could read the new value back from the variable as well. In C/C++, to allow modification of a parameter, you might well declare the function this way using a pointer:

```
int CalculateSomething(float fTime, float fStepSize, float* fVariance);
```

The centroid qualifier has no effect unless rendering is being done to a multisampled buffer. In a single sampled buffer, interpolation is always performed from the center of a pixel. With multisampling, when the centroid qualifier is used, the interpolated value is selected so that it falls within the primitive *and* the pixel. See Chapter 9, "Advanced Buffers: Beyond the Basics," for more details about how multisampling works.

By default parameters are interpolated between shader stages in a perspective correct manner. You can specify nonperspective interpolation with the noperspective keyword or even no interpolation at all with the flat keyword. You can also optionally use the smooth keyword to explicitly state the variable is smoothly interpolated in a perspective correct manner, but that is already the default. Here are a few example declarations.

```
smooth out vec3 vSmoothValue;
flat out vec3 vFlatColor;
noperspective float vLinearlySmoothed;
```

A Real Shader

Finally, let's take a look at a real shader pair that does something useful. The
`GLShaderManager` class has a stock shader called the identity shader. This shader does not
transform geometry and draws a primitive with a single color. Perhaps that's just a little
too simple. Let's take it up a notch and show how we might also shade a primitive such as
a triangle by using different color values for each vertex. Listing 6.1 shows our vertex
shader, and Listing 6.2 shows our fragment shader.

LISTING 6.1   The ShadedIdentity Shader Vertex Program

```
// The ShadedIdentity Shader
// Vertex Shader
// Richard S. Wright Jr.
// OpenGL SuperBible
#version 330

in vec4 vVertex;          // Vertex position attribute
in vec4 vColor;           // Vertex color attribute

out vec4 vVaryingColor;   // Color value passed to fragment shader

void main(void)
    {
    vVaryingColor = vColor;// Simply copy the color value
    gl_Position = vVertex; // Simply pass along the vertex position
    }
```

LISTING 6.2   The ShadedIdentity Shader Fragment Program

```
// The ShadedIdentity Shader
// Fragment Shader
// Richard S. Wright Jr.
// OpenGL SuperBible
#version 330

out vec4 vFragColor;      // Fragment color to rasterize
in vec4 vVaryingColor;    // Incoming color from vertex stage

void main(void)
    {
    vFragColor = vVaryingColor;   // Interpolated color to fragment
    }
```

GLSL Versions

The first uncommented line in each shader is the version specifier:

```
#version 330
```

This specifies that the minimum version of GLSL that this shader requires is 3.3. If the OpenGL driver does not support at least GLSL version 3.3, then the shader will not compile. OpenGL 3.2 introduced GLSL version 1.5, OpenGL 3.1 introduced version GLSL 1.4, and OpenGL 3.0 introduced GLSL version 1.3. Sound confusing? Right...you're not the only one, and with OpenGL 3.3, the ARB decided to keep the GLSL version number in sync with the main OpenGL version for all future versions beginning with 3.3. In fact the OpenGL 4.0 specification was released at the same time as version 3.3, and the shading language for OpenGL 4.0 is also 4.0. Requiring 4.0 in a shader would look like this:

```
#version 400
```

If you examine the stock shaders in the GLTools source code, you find no such version information. GLTools is intended to run with the compatibility profile and uses the older shader conventions from GLSL 1.1. In fact GLTools runs fine with OpenGL drivers as old as version 2.1. Remember GLTools is only meant to be a "helper" and as a starting place for using OpenGL.

Attribute Declarations

Attributes are specified per vertex by your C/C++ client-side OpenGL code. In the vertex shader, these are declared simply as in.

```
in vec4 vVertex;
in vec4 vColor;
```

Here we declared two inbound attributes, a four-component vertex position, and a four-component vertex color value. The example program ShadedTriangle uses this shader specifically, and we make use of the GLBatch class to set up three vertex positions and three color values. How the GLBatch class communicates these values to the shader is coming up in the section "Compiling, Binding, and Linking." Remember as we discussed in Chapter 3, with GLSL you can have a maximum of 16 attributes per vertex program. *Also, each attribute is always a four-component vector, even if you don't use all four components.* For example, if you specified just a single float as an attribute, internally, it would still take up the space of four floating-point values.

Something else to remember is that variables marked as in are read-only. It might seem clever to reuse a variable name for some intermediate computations in a shader, but the GLSL compiler in your driver will generate an error if you attempt this.

Declaring the Output

Next we declared one output variable for our vertex program, again a four-component floating-point vector.

```
out vec4 vVaryingColor;
```

This variable will be the color value specified for this vertex that is to be passed on to the fragment shader. In fact, this variable must be declared as an `in` variable for the fragment shader, or you receive a linker error when you attempt to compile and link the shaders together.

When you declare a value as `out` in a vertex shader and as an `in` in the fragment shader, the value of the variable that the fragment shader receives is an interpolated value. By default, this is done in a perspective correct manner, and an additional qualifier, `smooth`, may be specified before the variable to ensure this is done. You can also specify `flat` to state that no interpolation should be done, or `noperspective` for a straight linear interpolation between values. Some additional considerations are warranted when you use `flat` that we discuss in the "Provoking Vertex" section later in this chapter.

Vertex Action

Finally, we get to the main body of our vertex program, which is executed once for each vertex in our batch.

```
void main(void)
    {
    vVaryingColor = vColor;
    gl_Position = vVertex;
    }
```

This is pretty simple really. We assign the incoming color attribute to the outgoing interpolated value and assign the incoming vertex value directly to `gl_Position` with no transformations. The variable `gl_Position` is a predefined built-in four-component vector that contains the one required output of the vertex shader. The values going into `gl_Position` are used by the geometry stage to assemble your primitive. Remember, since we are doing no additional transformations, our vertex will map only to the Cartesian coordinate range +/- 1.0 on all three axes.

Fragging the Triangle

Now we turn our attention to the fragment program. When rendering a primitive, such as a triangle, once the three vertices have been processed by the vertex program, they are assembled into triangle, and the triangle is rasterized by the hardware. The graphics hardware figures out where the individual fragments belong on your screen (or, more accurately in your color buffer) and executes an instance of your fragment program for each and every fragment (just a pixel if you are not doing any multisampling) in the triangle. The final output color for our fragment program is a four-component floating-point vector that we declare like this:

```
out vec4 vFragColor;
```

If we have only one output from our fragment program, it is internally assigned as "output zero." This is the first output of the fragment shader, and it goes to the buffer destination set by glDrawBuffers, which is by default GL_BACK, the back color buffer (for double buffered contexts, that is!). Often the actual color buffer does not really contain four floating-point components, and so the output values are mapped to the range of the destination buffer. Most of the time, this may just be four unsigned byte components, for example (0 through 255 for each component). We also could have output integer values using ivec4, and they too would be mapped to the range of the color buffer. Outputting more than just a color value is possible, as well as writing to multiple buffers at once, but these topics are well beyond the scope of this introductory chapter.

Coming into our fragment shader is the smoothly interpolated color value, passed in by the vertex program upstream. This is declared simply as an in variable:

```
in vec4 vVaryingColor;
```

Finally, the main body of the fragment shader is even more trivial than the vertex shader. It simply assigns the smoothly interpolated color value directly to the fragment color.

```
void main(void)
   {
   vFragColor = vVaryingColor;
   }
```

The final output showing this shader in action can be seen in Figure 6.2.

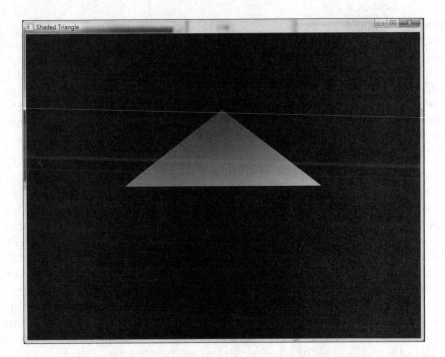

FIGURE 6.2   Output from the ShadedTriangle program.

Compiling, Binding, and Linking

Now that we have seen a simple shader in action, we need to discuss how a shader is actually compiled and linked for use in OpenGL. Shader source code is handed off to the driver, compiled, and finally linked much like you would any C/C++ program. In addition, attribute names in your shader need to be *bound* to one of the 16 preallocated attribute slots made available by GLSL. Along the way, we can check for errors and even receive diagnostic information back from the driver about why our attempt to build the shader failed.

The OpenGL API does not support any kind of file I/O operations. It is up to you the programmer to obtain the source code for your shaders in whatever method works best for you and your application. One of the simplest is to store the shaders in plain ASCII text files. It is then a simple matter to load the text files from disk using typical file system functions. In our examples we use this approach, and we adopt the convention that vertex shaders have a file extension of .vp, and fragment shaders have a file extension of .fp. An alternative is to store the text as character arrays hard coded in your C/C++ source code. This is a bit tedious to edit, however, and while it makes your programs more self-contained, it is cumbersome to modify the shaders or experiment with the source code. You can of course also generate the shader source code algorithmically, or perhaps retrieve it from a database, or an encrypted data file of some kind. These alternatives might appeal to you for shipping an application, but for learning and just for development and debugging purposes, nothing beats a plain old text file.

The GLTools function `gltLoadShaderPairWithAttributes` is a real heavy lifter for loading and initializing shaders. The complete listing is shown in Listing 6.3, and going through this function we cover all the necessary elements of loading a shader.

LISTING 6.3   The `gltLoadShaderPairWithAttributes` Function

```
/////////////////////////////////////////////////////////////////
// Load a pair of shaders, compile, and link together.
// Specify the complete source text for each shader. After
// the shader names, specify the number of attributes,
// followed by the index and attribute name of each attribute
GLuint gltLoadShaderPairWithAttributes(const char *szVertexProg,
                                const char *szFragmentProg, ...)
    {
    // Temporary Shader objects
    GLuint hVertexShader;
    GLuint hFragmentShader;
    GLuint hReturn = 0;
    GLint testVal;

    // Create shader objects
    hVertexShader = glCreateShader(GL_VERTEX_SHADER);
    hFragmentShader = glCreateShader(GL_FRAGMENT_SHADER);

    // Load them. If fail clean up and return null
    // Vertex Program
    if(gltLoadShaderFile(szVertexProg, hVertexShader) == false)
        {
        glDeleteShader(hVertexShader);
        glDeleteShader(hFragmentShader);
        cout << "The shader at " << szVertexProg
                            << " could not be found.\n";
        return (GLuint)NULL;
        }

    // Fragment Program
    if(gltLoadShaderFile(szFragmentProg, hFragmentShader) == false)
        {
        glDeleteShader(hVertexShader);
        glDeleteShader(hFragmentShader);
```

```cpp
        cout << "The shader at " << szFragmentProg
                                 << " could not be found.\n";
        return (GLuint)NULL;
        }

    // Compile them both
    glCompileShader(hVertexShader);
    glCompileShader(hFragmentShader);

    // Check for errors in vertex shader
    glGetShaderiv(hVertexShader, GL_COMPILE_STATUS, &testVal);
    if(testVal == GL_FALSE)
        {
        char infoLog[1024];
        glGetShaderInfoLog(hVertexShader, 1024, NULL, infoLog);
        cout << "The shader at " << szVertexProg
            << " failed to compile with the following error:\n"
            << infoLog << "\n";
        glDeleteShader(hVertexShader);
        glDeleteShader(hFragmentShader);
        return (GLuint)NULL;
        }

    // Check for errors in fragment shader
    glGetShaderiv(hFragmentShader, GL_COMPILE_STATUS, &testVal);
    if(testVal == GL_FALSE)
        {
        char infoLog[1024];
        glGetShaderInfoLog(hFragmentShader, 1024, NULL, infoLog);
        cout << "The shader at " << hFragmentShader
            << " failed to compile with the following error:\n"
            << infoLog << "\n";
        glDeleteShader(hVertexShader);
        glDeleteShader(hFragmentShader);
        return (GLuint)NULL;
        }

    // Create the final program object, and attach the shaders
    hReturn = glCreateProgram();
    glAttachShader(hReturn, hVertexShader);
    glAttachShader(hReturn, hFragmentShader);
```

```
// Now, we need to bind the attribute names to their specific locations
// List of attributes
va_list attributeList;
va_start(attributeList, szFragmentProg);

// Iterate over this argument list
char *szNextArg;
int iArgCount = va_arg(attributeList, int);     // Number of attributes
for(int i = 0; i < iArgCount; i++)
    {
    int index = va_arg(attributeList, int);
    szNextArg = va_arg(attributeList, char*);
    glBindAttribLocation(hReturn, index, szNextArg);
    }
va_end(attributeList);

// Attempt to link
glLinkProgram(hReturn);

// These are no longer needed
glDeleteShader(hVertexShader);
glDeleteShader(hFragmentShader);

// Make sure link worked too
glGetProgramiv(hReturn, GL_LINK_STATUS, &testVal);
if(testVal == GL_FALSE)
    {
    char infoLog[1024];
    glGetProgramInfoLog(hReturn, 1024, NULL, infoLog);
    cout << "The program " << hReturn
        << " failed to link with the following error:\n"
        << infoLog << "\n";
    glDeleteProgram(hReturn);
    return (GLuint)NULL;
    }

// All done, return our ready to use shader program
return hReturn;
}
```

Specifying the Attributes

The function prototype takes the name of the vertex program file, the name of the fragment program file, and then a variable number of parameters that specify the attributes.

```
GLuint gltLoadShaderPairWithAttributes(const char *szVertexProg,
                              const char *szFragmentProg, ...);
```

If you've never seen a function declaration that takes a variable argument list before, the ... at the end of the argument list may look like a typo. Other C examples that take a variable argument list are functions such as `printf` or `sprintf`. For this function, however, the first extra parameter is the number of attributes that your vertex program contains. This is followed by a zero-based index for the first attribute, and the attribute name as a character array. The attribute slot number and name are then repeated for as many times as necessary. For example, to load a shader that has a vertex position and surface normal attributes, the call to `gltLoadShaderPairWithAttributes` might look something like this:

```
hShader = gltLoadShaderPairWithAttributes("vertexProg.vp",
                "fragmentProg.fp", 2, 0, "vVertexPos", 1, "vNormal");
```

The choice of 0 and 1 for the two attribute locations is arbitrary, as long as the values are in the range 0 – 15. We might just as well have picked 7 and 13. The GLTools classes `GLBatch` and `GLTriangleBatch`, however, use a consistent set of attribute locations, specified by the following `typedef`:

```
typedef enum GLT_SHADER_ATTRIBUTE { GLT_ATTRIBUTE_VERTEX = 0,
              GLT_ATTRIBUTE_COLOR, GLT_ATTRIBUTE_NORMAL,
              GLT_ATTRIBUTE_TEXTURE0, GLT_ATTRIBUTE_TEXTURE1,
              GLT_ATTRIBUTE_TEXTURE2, GLT_ATTRIBUTE_TEXTURE3,
              GLT_ATTRIBUTE_LAST};
```

As long as you use these attribute location identifiers, you can start using your own shaders that work alongside the stock shaders supplied in the `GLShaderManager` class. It also means we can continue using the `GLBatch` and `GLTriangleBatch` classes to submit geometry until Chapter 12, "Advanced Geometry Management," when we cover the submission of vertex attributes in greater detail.

Setting the Source Code

The first order of business is to create two shader objects, one each for the vertex and fragment shaders.

```
hVertexShader = glCreateShader(GL_VERTEX_SHADER);
hFragmentShader = glCreateShader(GL_FRAGMENT_SHADER);
```

We can then use these two shader IDs for loading the shader source code. We skip the frivolous details of the `gltLoadShaderFile` function, as most of what it does is simply load the text of the shader from disk using the filename specified. Once this is accomplished, however, the following code feeds the shader source code to the shader object. Note too that we have to do this twice—once for the vertex shader and again for the fragment shader.

```
GLchar *fsStringPtr[1];

fsStringPtr[0] = (GLchar *)szShaderSrc;
glShaderSource(shader, 1, (const GLchar **)fsStringPtr, NULL);
```

The szShaderSrc variable is a simple character pointer that points to the entire text of the shader, and shader is the object ID of the shader object we are loading.

Compiling the Shaders

Compiling the shaders is a simple one-shot deal.

```
glCompileShader(hVertexShader);
glCompileShader(hFragmentShader);
```

Each OpenGL implementation has a built-in GLSL compiler that is provided by the hardware vendor. The idea is that any given vendor would be most qualified to build compilers for their own hardware. Of course just like with C/C++ code any number of things, such as syntax errors, implementation bugs, and so on, can prevent your GLSL shader from compiling. To check for failure, we use the glGetShader function with the GL_COMPILE_STATUS token.

```
glGetShaderiv(hVertexShader, GL_COMPILE_STATUS, &testVal);
```

If the value of testVal on return is GL_FALSE, then the source code failed to compile. It would be difficult indeed to write shaders if the only thing we could find out from our implementation was a simple pass or fail for our efforts. On a compile fail, we can check the shader info log with the glGetShaderInfoLog function to see what went wrong. In our current example, we display the error message to the console, clean up our shader objects, and return NULL.

```
if(testVal == GL_FALSE)
    {
    char infoLog[1024];
    glGetShaderInfoLog(hVertexShader, 1024, NULL, infoLog);
    cout << "The shader at " << szVertexProg
        << " failed to compile with the following error:\n"
        << infoLog << "\n";
    glDeleteShader(hVertexShader);
    glDeleteShader(hFragmentShader);
    return (GLuint)NULL;
    }
```

Getting Attached and Binding

Getting our GLSL source code to compile is half the battle, but before we can link them, we must make a small detour. First, we have to create our final shader program object and attach the vertex and fragment shaders to it.

```
hReturn = glCreateProgram();
glAttachShader(hReturn, hVertexShader);
glAttachShader(hReturn, hFragmentShader);
```

Now, our shader is ready to be linked. However, there is something important we must do before linking the shader programs, and that is bind our attribute variable names to specific numeric attribute locations. The function glBindAttribLocation performs this task; its prototype is as follows:

```
void glBindAttribLocation(GLuint shaderProg, GLuint attribLocation,
                          const GLchar *szAttributeName);
```

It takes the identifier of the shader in question, the attribute location to be bound, and the name of the attribute variable. For example, in the GLTools stock shaders, we adopted the convention of always using the variable name vVertex for the vertex position attribute and the value GLT_ATTRIBUTE_VERTEX (the value 0) for the attribute location. You can duplicate this yourself easily enough.

```
glBindAttribLocation(hShader, GLT_ATTRIBUTE_VERTEX, "vVertex");
```

The binding of attribute locations in this way must be done before linking. In our code here, we iterate through the variable argument list and simply call this function repeatedly for each attribute we need bound.

```
// Iterate over this argument list
char *szNextArg;
int iArgCount = va_arg(attributeList, int);     // Number of attributes
for(int i = 0; i < iArgCount; i++)
    {
    int index = va_arg(attributeList, int);
    szNextArg = va_arg(attributeList, char*);
    glBindAttribLocation(hReturn, index, szNextArg);
    }
va_end(attributeList);
```

Linking the Shaders

Finally, it's time to link our shaders, after which we can also dispose of our vertex and fragment shader objects.

```
glLinkProgram(hReturn);

// These are no longer needed
glDeleteShader(hVertexShader);
glDeleteShader(hFragmentShader);
```

Just as with compiling, there are number of reasons linking could fail. For example, it will fail if you declare an out variable in the vertex program but do not declare it in the fragment program; or perhaps you do, but the two declarations are of different types. Thus before returning we check for an error and display any diagnostic message just as we did for the compilation step.

You now have an OpenGL GLSL shader that is 100% ready to go. We should also mention now that you've created a shader program, that when you are done with it (perhaps on program termination), you should delete it with the following function.

```
void glDeleteProgram(GLuint program);
```

Using the Shader

To use our GLSL shader, we must select it with the glUseProgram function as shown here:

```
glUseProgram(myShaderProgram);
```

This sets our shader as active, and all submitted geometry is now processed by our vertex and fragment shader programs. Uniforms and textures should be set up before submitting vertex attributes, and we show how this is done very soon. Submitting vertex attributes, however, is a big topic—big enough to warrant its own chapter in fact—and this topic is discussed in more detail in Chapter 12. For now, we allow the GLBatch and GLTriangleBatch classes to manage our geometry for us.

In our first example program for this chapter, ShadedTriangle, we loaded our Triangle into an instance of GLBatch called triangleBatch using the simplest (what we called the "identity") coordinate system:

```
// Load up a triangle
GLfloat vVerts[] = { -0.5f, 0.0f, 0.0f,
                      0.5f, 0.0f, 0.0f,
                      0.0f, 0.5f, 0.0f };

GLfloat vColors [] = { 1.0f, 0.0f, 0.0f, 1.0f,
                       0.0f, 1.0f, 0.0f, 1.0f,
                       0.0f, 0.0f, 1.0f, 1.0f };
```

```
triangleBatch.Begin(GL_TRIANGLES, 3);
triangleBatch.CopyVertexData3f(vVerts);
triangleBatch.CopyColorData4f(vColors);
triangleBatch.End();

myIdentityShader = gltLoadShaderPairWithAttributes("ShadedIdentity.vp",
                    "ShadedIdentity.fp", 2, GLT_ATTRIBUTE_VERTEX, "vVertex",
                    GLT_ATTRIBUTE_COLOR, "vColor");
```

We also set different colors for each vertex, red, green, and blue, respectively. Finally we loaded our shader pair using the gltLoadShaderPairWithAttributes function that we have previously gone over. Note how we have two sets of attributes, vertex and color values, matching the sets of data supplied to the GLBatch class.

Submitting the batch for rendering is now simply a matter of selecting our shader and letting the GLBatch class submit our vertex attributes:

```
glUseProgram(myIdentityShader);
triangleBatch.Draw();
```

The final shaded triangle, the result of all this effort so far was shown in Figure 6.2.

Provoking Vertex

The ShadedTriangle example is a great demonstration of how smooth interpolation between vertices takes place. With each vertex having a different color value, what you see in the triangle shown in Figure 6.2 is essentially the color values for the plane in color space represented by these three color coordinates. Cool, huh? We can, however, also set variables passed from one shader stage to the next as flat. If you have a single value that must be constant for an entire batch, it would be best to use a uniform as we discussed in Chapter 3. Sometimes, however, it is useful to have a value that is unique over the entire surface of a primitive such as our triangle but needs to change per triangle. Sending down a large number of triangles, one triangle per batch for example when using uniforms, would be very inefficient. This is where the flat storage qualifier comes in. In our ShadedTriangle.vp shader, we declare our outgoing smoothly shaded color value in this way:

```
out vec4 vVaryingColor;
```

If, however, we declared it to be flat (and don't forget the corresponding in variable in the fragment shader must be declared as flat too), such as shown next, the resulting triangle is solid blue.

```
flat out vec4 vFlatColor;
```

When each vertex of a primitive has a different value for a flat shaded variable, only one of the variables can be applied "flatly." The default convention is to use the value specified for the last vertex of the primitive, which in our case, blue was the color used for the last of the three vertices in our triangle. This convention is called the *provoking vertex*, and it can be changed from the last vertex to the first vertex with the following function:

```
void glProvokingVertex(GLenum provokeMode);
```

Valid values for provokeMode are GL_FIRST_VERTEX_CONVENTION and GL_LAST_VERTEX_CONVENTIONS (the default).

The example program ProvokingVertex shows this in action. It is a slight modification of the ShadedTriangle program in fact. Pressing the space bar switches the convention, and the triangle switches back and forth from solid blue to solid red.

Shader Uniforms

While attributes are needed for per-vertex positions, surface normals, texture coordinates, and so on, a uniform is how we pass data into a shader that stays the same—is *uniform*—for the entire primitive batch. Probably the single most common uniform for a vertex shader is the transformation matrix. Previously, we allowed the GLShaderManager class to do this for us, with built-in support for the stock shaders and their needed uniforms. Now that we are writing our own shaders, we need to be able to set our own uniforms, and not just for matrix values; any shader variable can be specified as a uniform, and uniforms can be in any of the three shader stages (even though we only talk about vertex and fragment shaders in this chapter). Making a uniform is as simple as placing the keyword uniform at the beginning of the variable declaration:

```
uniform float fTime;
uniform int iIndex;
uniform vec4 vColorValue;
uniform mat4 mvpMatrix;
```

Uniforms cannot be marked as in or out, they cannot be interpolated (although you can copy them into interpolated variables) between shader stages, and they are always read-only.

Finding Your Uniforms

After a shader has been compiled and linked, you must "find" the uniform location in the shader. This is done with the function glGetUniformLocation.

```
GLint glGetUniformLocation(GLuint shaderID, const GLchar* varName);
```

This function returns a signed integer that represents the location of the variable named by varName in the shader specified by shaderID. For example, to get the location of a uniform variable named "vColorValue", we would do something like this:

```
GLint iLocation = glGetUniformLocation(myShader, "vColorValue");
```

Shader variable names are case-sensitive, and if the return value of glGetUniformLocation is -1, it means the uniform name could not be located in the shader. You should bear in mind that even if a shader compiles correctly, a uniform name may still "disappear" from the shader if it is not used directly in the shader. You do not need to worry about uniform variables being optimized away, but if you declare a uniform and then do not use it, the compiler will toss it out.

Setting Scalars and Vector Uniforms

A single scalar or vector data type can be set with any of the following variations on the glUniform function:

```
void glUniform1f(GLint location, GLfloat v0);
void glUniform2f(GLint location, Glfloat v0, GLfloat v1);
void glUniform3f(GLint location, GLfloat v0, GLfloat v1, GLfloat v2);
void glUniform4f(GLint location, GLfloat v0, GLfloat v1, GLfloat v2,
                                                        GLfloat v3);

void glUniform1i(GLint location, GLint v0);
void glUniform2i(GLint location, GLint v0, GLint v1);
void glUniform3i(GLint location, GLint v0, GLint v1, GLint v2);
void glUniform4i(GLint location, GLint v0, GLint v1, GLint v2, GLint v3);
```

For example, consider the following four variables declared in a shader.

```
uniform float fTime;
uniform int iIndex;
uniform vec4 vColorValue;
uniform bool bSomeFlag;
```

To find and set these values in the shader, your C/C++ code might look something like this.

```
GLint locTime, locIndex, locColor, locFlag;
locTime = glGetUniformLocation(myShader, "fTime");
locIndex = glGetUniformLocation(myShader, "iIndex");
locColor = glGetUniformLocation(myShader, "vColorValue");
locFlag = glGetUniformLocation(myShader, "bSomeFlag");
...
...
```

```
glUseProgram(myShader);
glUniform1f(locTime, 45.2f);
glUniform1i(locIndex, 42);
glUniform4f(locColor, 1.0f, 0.0f, 0.0f, 1.0f);
glUniform1i(locFlag, GL_FALSE);
```

Note that we used an integer version of glUniform to pass in a bool value. Booleans can also be passed in as floats, with 0.0 representing false, and 1.0 representing true.

Setting Uniform Arrays

The glUniform function also comes in flavors that take a pointer, potentially to an array of values.

```
void glUniform1fv(GLint location, GLuint count, GLfloat* v);
void glUniform2fv(GLint location, GLuint count, Glfloat* v);
void glUniform3fv(GLint location, GLuint count, GLfloat* v);
void glUniform4fv(GLint location, GLuint count, GLfloat* v);

void glUniform1iv(GLint location, GLuint count, GLint* v);
void glUniform2iv(GLint location, GLuint count, GLint* v);
void glUniform3iv(GLint location, GLuint count, GLint* v);
void glUniform4iv(GLint location, GLuint count, GLint* v);
```

Here, the count value represents how many elements are in each array of x number of components, where x is the number at the end of the function name. For example, if you had a uniform with four components, such as one shown here:

```
uniform vec4 vColor;
```

In C/C++, you could represent this as an array of floats:

```
GLfloat vColor[4] = { 1.0f, 1.0f, 1.0f, 1.0f };
```

But this is a single array of four values, so passing it into the shader would look like this:

```
glUniform4fv(iColorLocation, 1, vColor);
```

On the other hand, if you had an array of color values in your shader,

```
uniform vec4 vColors[2];
```

Then in C++, you could represent the data and pass it in like this:

```
GLfloat vColors[2][4] = {{ 1.0f, 1.0f, 1.0f, 1.0f },
                         { 1.0f, 0.0f, 0.0f, 1.0f }};
...
glUniform4fv(iColorLocation, 2, vColors);
```

At its simplest, you can set a single floating-point uniform like this:

```
GLfloat fValue = 45.2f;
glUniform1fv(iLocation, 1, &fValue);
```

Setting Uniform Matrices

Finally, we see how to set a matrix uniform. Shader matrix data types only come in the floating-point variety, and thus we have far less variation. The following functions load a 2 x 2, 3 x 3, and 4 x 4 matrix, respectively.

```
glUniformMatrix2fv(GLint location, GLuint count, GLboolean transpose,
                                                  const GLfloat *m);
glUniformMatrix3fv(GLint location, GLuint count, GLboolean transpose,
                                                  const GLfloat *m);
glUniformMatrix4fv(GLint location, GLuint count, GLboolean transpose,
                                                  const GLfloat *m);
```

The variable count represents the number of matrices stored at the pointer parameter m (yes, you can have arrays of matrices!). The Boolean flag transpose is set to GL_TRUE if the matrix is already stored in column major ordering (the way OpenGL prefers). Setting this value to GL_FALSE causes the matrix to be transposed when it is copied into the shader. This might be useful if you are using a matrix library that uses a row major matrix layout instead (for example, Direct3D uses row major ordering).

The Flat Shader

Let's look at an example shader now that makes use of some uniforms. In our stock shader collection, we had a flat shader that did nothing but transform our geometry and set it to a single color. The only vertex attributes used were the vertex positions, and it required the use of two uniforms, a single transformation matrix, and a color value.

The example program FlatShader simply loads a spinning torus and sets the color to blue. We render it in wireframe mode via the glPolygonMode function so we can see we really do have 3D geometry. The majority of the OpenGL client code is fairly trivial by now, so we do not list the entire program. The complete shaders, however, are shown in Listings 6.4 and 6.5.

LISTING 6.4   The Flat Shader Vertex Program

```
// Flat Shader
// Vertex Shader
// Richard S. Wright Jr.
// OpenGL SuperBible
#version 330
```

```
// Transformation Matrix
uniform mat4  mvpMatrix;

// Incoming per vertex
in vec4 vVertex;

void main(void)
    {
    // This is pretty much it, transform the geometry
    gl_Position = mvpMatrix * vVertex;
    }
```

LISTING 6.5   The Flat Shader Fragment Program

```
// Flat Shader
// Fragment Shader
// Richard S. Wright Jr.
// OpenGL SuperBible
#version 130

// Make geometry solid
uniform vec4 vColorValue;

// Output fragment color
out vec4 vFragColor;

void main(void)
   {
   gl_FragColor = vColorValue;
   }
```

In the vertex program shown in Listing 6.4 we have a single uniform, our concatenated transformation matrix.

```
uniform mat4    mvpMatrix;
```

The sole geometry processing performed by this shader is to transform the vertex by the ModelviewProjection matrix. As you can see, multiplying a matrix data type by a vector data type in GLSL is quite natural.

```
gl_Position = mvpMatrix * vVertex;
```

In the fragment shader shown in Listing 6.5, we have again only a single uniform, a four-component color value that will be applied to the rasterized fragments.

```
uniform vec4 vColorValue;
```

On the client side, the FlatShader example program loads these two shader files and obtains indices to the two uniforms in the SetupRC function.

```
GLuint flatShader;
GLint locMP;
GLint locColor;
...

...
flatShader = gltLoadShaderPairWithAttributes("FlatShader.vp", "FlatShader.fp",
                                1, GLT_ATTRIBUTE_VERTEX, "vVertex");


locMVP = glGetUniformLocation(flatShader, "mvpMatrix");
locColor = glGetUniformLocation(flatShader, "vColorValue");
```

The RenderScene function is shown in Listing 6.6 in its entirety. It simply renders a rotating torus in place (remember we also set the polygon mode to GL_LINE). After selecting the flat shader, the uniforms for the geometry color and transformation matrix are set before calling the Draw function on the torus object. The final output is shown in Figure 6.3.

LISTING 6.6   Making Use of the New Flat Shader

```
// Called to draw scene
void RenderScene(void)
    {
    static CStopWatch rotTimer;

    // Clear the window and the depth buffer
    glClear(GL_COLOR_BUFFER_BIT | GL_DEPTH_BUFFER_BIT);

    modelViewMatrix.PushMatrix(viewFrame);
    modelViewMatrix.Rotate(rotTimer.GetElapsedSeconds() * 10.0f,
                                    0.0f, 1.0f, 0.0f);


    GLfloat vColor[] = { 0.1f, 0.1f, 1.f, 1.0f };

    glUseProgram(flatShader);
    glUniform4fv(locColor, 1, vColor);
    glUniformMatrix4fv(locMVP, 1, GL_FALSE,
            transformPipeline.GetModelViewProjectionMatrix());
```

```
torusBatch.Draw();

modelViewMatrix.PopMatrix();


glutSwapBuffers();
glutPostRedisplay();
}
```

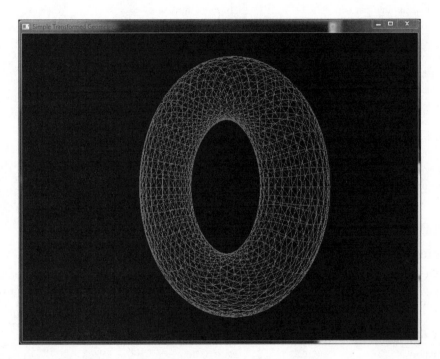

FIGURE 6.3   Output from the FlatShader program.

Built-In Functions

Nearly all high-level programming languages have a selection of standard functions that come along for the ride. In C/C++, we have the standard C Runtime library, standard I/O functions, and so on. GLSL also contains a number of useful built-in functions, mostly that perform mathematical operations on either a single scalar value or on an entire vector at once. Some of these are very general in nature, and some are selected because of their applicability to typical graphics rendering algorithms. The functions listed in the following tables are taken almost verbatim from the GLSL language specification.

Trigonometry Functions

Table 6.4 lists the trigonometry functions that are supported by GLSL. These functions are defined for `float`, `vec2`, `vec3`, and `vec4` data types. Here we denote the data type by anyFloat, meaning any of these four floating-point data types.

TABLE 6.4   Trigonometric Functions

Function	Description
anyFloat radians(anyFloat `degrees`)	Converts degrees to radians
anyFloat degrees(anyFloat `radians`)	Converts radians to degrees
anyFloat sin(anyFloat `angle`)	Trigonometric sine
anyFloat cos(anyFloat `angle`)	Trigonometric cosine
anyFloat tan(anyFloat `angle`)	Trigonometric tangent
anyFloat asin(anyFloat x)	Arc sine
anyFloat acos(anyFloat x)	Arc cosine
anyFloat atan(anyFloat y, anyFloat x)	Arc tangent of y / x
anyFloat atan(anyFloat y_over_x)	Arc tangent of y_over_x
anyFloat sinh(anyFloat x)	Hyperbolic sine
anyFloat cosh(anyFloat x)	Hyperbolic cosine
anyFloat tanh(anyFloat x)	Hyperbolic tangent
anyFloat asinh(anyFloat x)	Arc hyperbolic sine
anyFloat acosh(anyFloat x)	Arc hyperbolic cosine
anyFloat atanh(anyFloat x)	Arc hyperbolic tangent

Exponential Functions

Like the trigonometric functions, the exponential functions work on the floating-point data types (floats and floating-point vectors). The complete list of exponential functions is given in Table 6.5.

TABLE 6.5   Exponential Functions

Function	Description
anyFloat pow(anyFloat x, anyFloat y)	x raised to the y power
anyFloat exp(anyFloat x)	Natural exponent of x
anyFloat log(anyFloat x)	The natural logarithm of x
anyFloat exp2(anyFloat x)	2 raised to the power of x
anyFloat log2(anyFloat `angle`)	Base 2 logarithm of x
anyFloat sqrt(anyFloat x)	Square root of x
anyFloat inversesqrt(anyFloat x)	Inverse square root of x

Geometric Functions

A number of general purpose geometric functions are also included in GLSL. Some of these functions have specific argument types (cross product for example); others accept any of the floating-point vector types (vec2, vec3, and vec4), which we refer to here only as vec. These functions are listed in Table 6.6.

TABLE 6.6   Geometric Functions

Function	Description
float length(vec2/vec3/vec4 x)	Returns the length of the vector x
float distance(vec p0, vec p1)	Returns the distance between p0 and p1
float dot(vec x, vec y)	Returns the dot product of x and y
vec3 cross(vec3 x, vec3 y)	Returns the cross product of x and y
vec normalize(vec x)	Returns a unit length vector in the same direction as x
vec faceforward(vec N, vec I, vec nRef)	if dot(Nref, I) < 0 return N, else return –N
vec reflect(vec I, vec N)	Returns reflection direction for incident vector I and surface orientation N
vec refract(vec I, vec N, float eta)	Returns refraction vector for incident vector I, surface orientation N, and ratio of indices of refraction eta

Matrix Functions

Many matrix operations are done using the regular mathematical operators. Some useful matrix functions, however, are listed in Table 6.7. Each of these functions is specific and takes a specific argument data type, which is shown in the table.

TABLE 6.7   Matrix Functions

Function	Description
mat matrixCompMult(mat x, mat y)	Multiplies two matrices together component by component. This is not the same as the linear algebraic matrix multiply.
mat2 outerProduct(vec2 c, vec2 r)	Returns a matrix that is the outer product of the two vectors specified.
mat3 outerProduct(vec3 c, vec3 r)	
mat4 outerProduct(vec4 c, vec4 r)	
mat2x3 outerProduct(vec3 c, vec2 r)	
mat3x2 outerProduct(vec2 c, vec3 r)	
mat2x4 outerProduct(vec4 c, vec2 r)	
mat4x2 outerProduct(vec2 c, vec4 r)	
mat3x4 outerProduct(vec4 c, vec3 r)	
mat4x3 outerProduct(vec3 c, vec4 r)	

TABLE 6.7   Matrix Functions   continued

Function	Description
mat2 transpose(mat2 m)	Returns a matrix that is the transpose of the matrix specified.
mat3 transpose(mat3 m)	
mat4 transpose(mat4 m)	
mat2x3 transpose(mat3x2 m)	
mat3x2 transpose(mat2x3 m)	
mat2x4 transpose(mat4x2 m)	
mat4x2 transpose(mat2x4 m)	
mat3x4 transpose(mat4x3 m)	
mat4x3 transpose(mat3x4 m)	
float determinant(mat2 m)	Returns the determinant of the matrix specified.
float determinant(mat3 m)	
float determinant(mat4 m)	
mat2 inverse(mat2 m)	Returns a matrix that is the inverse of the matrix specified.
mat3 inverse(mat3 m)	
mat4 inverse(mat4 m)	

Vector Relational Functions

Scalar values can be compared using the standard equality operators (<, <=, >, >=, ++, !=). For vector comparisons, the functions listed in Table 6.8 are provided. All of these functions return a Boolean vector of the same number of dimensions as the arguments.

TABLE 6.8   Vector Relational Functions

Function	Description
bvec lessThan(vec x, vec y)	Returns component by component the result of x < y.
bvec lessThan(ivec x, ivec y)	
bvec lessThan(uvec x, uvec y)	
bvec lessThanEqual(vec x, vec y)	Returns component by component the result of x <= y.
bvec lessThanEqual(ivec x, ivec y)	
bvec lessThanEqual(uvec x, uvec y)	
bvec greaterThan(vec x, vec y)	Returns component by component the result of x > y.
bvec greaterThan(ivec x, ivec y)	
bvec greaterThan(uvec x, uvec y)	

Function	Description
bvec greaterThanEqual(vec x, vec y) bvec greaterThanEqual(ivec x, ivec y) bvec greaterThanEqual(uvec x, uvec y)	Returns component by component the result of x >= y.
bvec equal(vec x, vec y) bvec equal(ivec x, ivec y) bvec equal(uvec x, uvec y) bvec equal(bvec x, bvec y)	Returns component by component the result of x == y.
bvec notEqual(vec x, vec y) bvec notEqual(ivec x, ivec y) bvec notEqual(uvec x, uvec y) bvec notEqual(bvec x, bvec y)	Returns component by component the result of x != y.
bool any(bvec x)	Returns true if any component of x is true.
bool all(bvec x)	Returns true if all components of x are true.
bvec not(bvec x)	Returns component wise complement of x.

Common Functions

Finally we present the list of general purpose functions. All of these functions work on and return both scalar and vector data types (see Table 6.9).

TABLE 6.9   Common Functions

Function	Description
anyFloat abs(anyFloat x) anyInt abs(anyInt x)	Returns the absolute value of x.
anyFloat sign(anyFloat x) anyInt sign(anyInt x)	Returns 1.0 or -1.0 depending on the sign of x.
anyFloat floor(anyFloat x)	Returns the lowest whole number not larger than x.
anyFloat trunc(anyFloat x)	Returns the nearest whole number not larger than the absolute value of x.
anyFloat round(anyFloat x)	Returns the value of the nearest integer to x. The fraction 0.5 may round in either direction. (This is implementation-dependent.)
anyFloat roundEven(anyFloat x)	Returns the value of the nearest integer to x. The fraction 0.5 rounds to the nearest even integer.
anyFloat ceil(anyFloat x)	Returns the value of the nearest integer greater than x.
anyFloat fract(anyFloat x)	Returns the fractional part of x.

TABLE 6.9 Common Functions   continued

Function	Description
anyFloat mod(anyFloat x, float y) anyFloat mod(anyFloat x, anyFloat y)	Returns the modulus of x mod y.
anyFloat modf(anyFloat x, out anyFloat i)	Returns the fractional part of x and sets i to be the integer remainder.
anyFloat min(anyFloat x, anyFloat y) anyFloat min(anyFloat x, float y) anyInt min(anyInt x, anyInt y) anyInt min(anyInt x, int y) anyUInt min(anyUInt x, anyUInt y) anyUint min(anyUInt x, uint y)	Returns the smaller of x and y.
anyFloat max(anyFloat x, anyFloat y) anyFloat max(anyFloat x, float y) anyInt max(anyInt x, anyInt y) anyInt max(anyInt x, int y) anyUInt max(anyUInt x, anyUInt y) anyUint max(anyUInt x, uint y)	Returns the larger of x and y.

anyFloat clamp(anyFloat x,
        anyFloat minVal,
        anyFloat maxVal)
anyFloat clamp(anyFloat x,
        float minVal,
        float maxVal);
anyInt clamp(anyInt x,
        anyInt minVal,
        anyInt maxVal)
anyInt clamp(anyInt x,
        int minVal,
        int maxVal)
anyUint clamp(anyUint x,
        anyUint minVal,
        anyUint maxVal);
anyUint clamp(anyUint x,
        uint minVal,
        uint maxVal)
	Returns x clamped to the range minVal to maxVal.

Function	Description

anyFloat mix(anyFloat x,
          anyFloat y,
          anyFloat a)
anyFloat mix(anyFloat x,
          anyFloat y,
          float a)
	Returns the linear blend of x and y, as a varies from 0 to 1

anyFloat mix(anyFloat x,
          anyFloat y,
          anyBool a)
	Returns the components of x where a is false and the components of y where a is true.

anyFloat step(anyFloat edge, anyFloat x) anyFloat step(float edge, anyFloat x)	Returns 0.0 if x is less than edge, or 1.0 otherwise.

anyFloat smoothstep(anyFloat edge0,
anyFloat edge1,
          anyFloat x)
anyFloat smoothStep(float edge0,
          float edge1,
          anyFloat x)
	Returns 0.0 if x <= edge0, and 1.0 if x >= edge1, and a smooth Hermite interpolation between 0.0 and 1.0 in between.

anyBool isnan(anyFloat x) anyBool isinf(anyFloat x)	Returns true if x is Nan. Returns true if x is positive or negative infinity.
anyInt floatBitsToInt(anyFloat x) anyUint floatBitsToUint(anyFloat x)	Converts floating-point values to integer values.
anyFloat intBitsToFloat(anyInt x) anyFloat uintBitsToFloat(anyUint x)	Converts integers to floating-point values.

Simulating Light

We now have a pretty good foundation for using GLSL, and it's time to start writing some more sophisticated shaders. Simulating light is a foundational technique for computer graphics and is not overly complex, so it makes for a great demonstration of shader programming techniques. Simulating light, illumination, and material properties is itself a topic worthy of an entire book, and in fact many such books do exist! Here we go over the basics of computer lighting and use GLSL to implement them. It is on these following simple methods that the more advanced techniques are based.

Simple Diffuse Lighting

The most common type of light applied to surfaces in 3D graphics is *diffuse* light. Diffuse light is a directional light that is reflected off a surface with an intensity proportional to the angle at which the light rays strike the surface. Thus, the object surface is brighter if the light is pointed directly at the surface than if the light grazes the surface from a greater angle. Essentially it is the diffuse lighting component of many lighting models that produces the shading (or change in color) across a lit object's surface.

To determine the intensity of the light at a given vertex, we need two vectors. The first is the direction to the light source. Some lighting techniques supply only the vector pointing to the light source; we call this *directional* light because all the vertices see the same vector to the light source. This works well if the light source is very far (or infinitely far) away from the objects being illuminated. Think sunlight falling on all the players on a football field. The angle of the sunlight does not change significantly from one side of the field to the other. On the other hand if the game is being played at night, then the effects of a single overhead light might well be seen as the player or other objects move about on the field. If the lighting code is supplied instead with the position of the light source, then we must in our shader subtract the transformed (eye coordinates) position of the vertex from the position of the light source to determine the vector to the light source.

Surface Normals

The second vector we need for diffuse lighting (and indeed as you will see, more than just this) is the surface normal. A line from the vertex in the upward direction starts in some imaginary plane (or your triangle) at a right angle. This line is called a normal vector. The term *normal vector* might sound like something the *Star Trek* crew members toss around, but it just means a line perpendicular to a real or imaginary surface. A vector is a line pointed in some direction, and the word *normal* is just another way for eggheads to say perpendicular (intersecting at a 90 degree angle). As if the word *perpendicular* weren't bad enough! Therefore, a normal vector is a line pointed in a direction that is at a 90 degree angle to the front surface of your polygon. Figure 6.4 presents examples of 2D and 3D normal vectors.

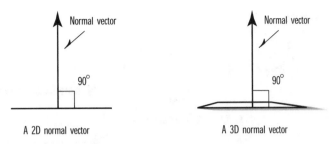

A 2D normal vector   A 3D normal vector

FIGURE 6.4   A 2D and a 3D normal vector.

You might already be asking why we must specify a normal vector for each vertex. Why can't we just specify a single normal for a polygon and use it for each vertex? We can; however, sometimes you don't want each normal to be exactly perpendicular to the surface of the polygon. You may have noticed that many surfaces are not flat! You can approximate these surfaces with flat, polygonal sections, but you end up with a jagged or multifaceted surface. You can create the illusion of smooth surfaces with flat polygons by "tweaking" the surface normals such that they smooth out the surface. On a sphere for example, each vertex's surface normal is exactly perpendicular to the actual surface of the sphere, not the individual triangles that are being used to render the sphere.

Vertex Lighting

Figure 6.5 shows these two vectors that we need for diffuse lighting. The intensity of the light at the vertex is calculated by taking the vector dot product of the vector to the light source and the surface normal. These two vectors need to be unit length as well, as the dot product will return a value from +1.0 to -1.0. A dot product of 1.0 occurs when the surface normal and the lighting vector are pointing the same direction, and a value of -1.0 is returned when the two vectors are pointing in opposite directions. A dot product of 0.0 is when the two vectors are at a 90 degree angle to one another. This value from +1.0 to -1.0 is actually the cosine of the angle between these two vectors. You can probably guess that positive values mean the light is falling on the vertex, with the larger the value (closer to 1) the more intense the lighting effect, and the closer to zero (or less than zero) the weaker the lighting effect.

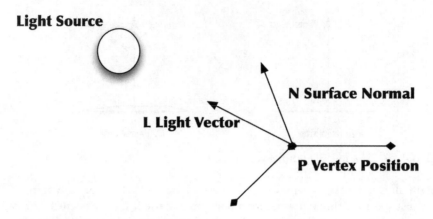

FIGURE 6.5   Basic vectors for diffuse lighting.

We can multiply the dot product value by a color value for the vertex and obtain a lit color value based on the intensity of the light at that vertex. Smoothly shading these color values between vertices is sometimes called *vertex lighting*, or *Gouraud shading*. In GLSL, the dot product part is pretty easy, usually just something like this:

```
float intensity = dot(vSurfaceNormal, vLightDirection);
```

The Point Light Diffuse Shader

Let's take a look at our next example program, DiffuseLight. This program demonstrates a simple diffuse lighting shader on a blue sphere. It uses a point light source so you can also see how we determine this in a shader. Of course using a directional light source would be simpler since we'd already supply this vector, but we, as they say, leave that as an exercise for the reader. Listing 6.7 shows the complete DiffuseLight.vp vertex shader.

LISTING 6.7   The Diffuse Light Vertex Shader

```
// Simple Diffuse lighting Shader
// Vertex Shader
// Richard S. Wright Jr.
// OpenGL SuperBible
#version 330

// Incoming per vertex... position and normal
in vec4 vVertex;
in vec3 vNormal;

// Set per batch
uniform vec4    diffuseColor;
```

```
uniform vec3    vLightPosition;
uniform mat4    mvpMatrix;
uniform mat4    mvMatrix;
uniform mat3    normalMatrix;


// Color to fragment program
smooth out vec4 vVaryingColor;

void main(void)
    {
    // Get surface normal in eye coordinates
    vec3 vEyeNormal = normalMatrix * vNormal;

    // Get vertex position in eye coordinates
    vec4 vPosition4 = mvMatrix * vVertex;
    vec3 vPosition3 = vPosition4.xyz / vPosition4.w;

    // Get vector to light source
    vec3 vLightDir = normalize(vLightPosition - vPosition3);

    // Dot product gives us diffuse intensity
    float diff = max(0.0, dot(vEyeNormal, vLightDir));

    // Multiply intensity by diffuse color, force alpha to 1.0
    vVaryingColor.xyz = diff * diffuseColor.xyz;
    vVaryingColor.a = 1.0;

    // Let's not forget to transform the geometry
    gl_Position = mvpMatrix * vVertex;
    }
```

Only two attributes are specified for our shader: the vertex position, vVertex, and the surface normal, vNormal. In contrast, we need five uniforms for this shader:

```
uniform vec4    diffuseColor;
uniform vec3    vLightPosition;
uniform mat4    mvpMatrix;
uniform mat4    mvMatrix;
uniform mat3    normalMatrix;
```

The diffuseColor contains the color of our sphere, vLightPosition is the light position in eye coordinates, mpvMatrix is the ModelviewProjection matrix, and mvMatrix is the Modelview matrix. You've seen these before when using the stock shaders (albeit on the client side). What's new is this 3 x 3 normalMatrix.

The surface normal is typically submitted as one of the vertex attributes. However, the surface normal must be rotated so that its direction is in eye space. You can't multiply it by the Modelview matrix to do this either, as the Modelview matrix also contains a translation that when you do the math affects the direction of the vector too. Instead, we usually pass in a *normal matrix* as a uniform, which consists of just the rotational component of the Modelview matrix. Fortunately for us, the GLTransformationPipeline class that we've already been using has a function, GetNormalMatrix, that returns this for us. Getting the normal direction in eye coordinates is then a simple matrix multiply:

```
vec3 vEyeNormal = normalMatrix * vNormal;
```

Outside of the main function, we also declare a smoothly shaded color value, vVaryingColor.

```
smooth out vec4 vVaryingColor;
```

Other than transforming the geometry, this is the only output of the vertex shader. The fragment program is trivial and simply assigns this incoming value to the output fragment color.

```
vFragColor = vVaryingColor;
```

Because we are passing in the light position instead of the vector to the light source, we must transform the vertex position into eye coordinates and subtract it from the light position.

```
vec4 vPosition4 = mvMatrix * vVertex;
vec3 vPosition3 = vPosition4.xyz / vPosition4.w;

// Get vector to light source
vec3 vLightDir = normalize(vLightPosition - vPosition3);
```

The eye coordinates of the vertex cannot be multiplied by a matrix that contains the projection, thus the reason we must have the Modelview matrix separately for this shader. It is here that that w coordinate rears its head. It is important that you perform this division in case the transformation matrix contains any scaling quantities (refer back to Chapter 4 to see why this is or isn't important to you).

Vectors are just beautiful aren't they? To get the vector to the light, we simply subtract these two vectors and normalize the result. Now we can use the dot product to determine the intensity of the light on this vertex. Note too how we used the GLSL function max to restrict our intensity to a positive value between zero and one.

```
float diff = max(0.0, dot(vEyeNormal, vLightDir));
```

The final part of our lighting computation is to multiply the surface color by the light intensity. In this case, only the rgb components as we let the alpha go unmodified by lighting.

```
vVaryingColor.rgb = diff * diffuseColor.rgb;
vVaryingColor.a = diffuseColor.a;
```

Listing 6.8 shows just the SetupRC and RenderScene functions from the DiffuseLight example program.

LISTING 6.8   Setup and Rendering Code from the DiffuseLight Example

```
// This function does any needed initialization on the rendering
// context.
void SetupRC(void)
    {
    // Background
    glClearColor(0.3f, 0.3f, 0.3f, 1.0f );

    glEnable(GL_DEPTH_TEST);
    glEnable(GL_CULL_FACE);

    shaderManager.InitializeStockShaders();
    viewFrame.MoveForward(4.0f);

    // Make the sphere
    gltMakeSphere(sphereBatch, 1.0f, 26, 13);

    diffuseLightShader = gltLoadShaderPairWithAttributes(
                "DiffuseLight.vp", "DiffuseLight.fp", 2,
                GLT_ATTRIBUTE_VERTEX, "vVertex",
                GLT_ATTRIBUTE_NORMAL, "vNormal");

    locColor = glGetUniformLocation(diffuseLightShader, "diffuseColor");
    locLight = glGetUniformLocation(diffuseLightShader, "vLightPosition");
    locMVP = glGetUniformLocation(diffuseLightShader, "mvpMatrix");
    locMV  = glGetUniformLocation(diffuseLightShader, "mvMatrix");
    locNM  = glGetUniformLocation(diffuseLightShader, "normalMatrix");
    }

// Called to draw scene
void RenderScene(void)
```

```
{
static CStopWatch rotTimer;

// Clear the window and the depth buffer
glClear(GL_COLOR_BUFFER_BIT | GL_DEPTH_BUFFER_BIT);

modelViewMatrix.PushMatrix(viewFrame);
modelViewMatrix.Rotate(rotTimer.GetElapsedSeconds() * 10.0f,
                                         0.0f, 1.0f, 0.0f);

GLfloat vEyeLight[] = { -100.0f, 100.0f, 100.0f };
GLfloat vDiffuseColor[] = { 0.0f, 0.0f, 1.0f, 1.0f };

glUseProgram(diffuseLightShader);
glUniform4fv(locColor, 1, vDiffuseColor);
glUniform3fv(locLight, 1, vEyeLight);
glUniformMatrix4fv(locMVP, 1, GL_FALSE,
            transformPipeline.GetModelViewProjectionMatrix());
glUniformMatrix4fv(locMV, 1, GL_FALSE,
                        transformPipeline.GetModelViewMatrix());
glUniformMatrix3fv(locNM, 1, GL_FALSE,
                            transformPipeline.GetNormalMatrix());
sphereBatch.Draw();

modelViewMatrix.PopMatrix();

glutSwapBuffers();
glutPostRedisplay();
}
```

This is your first substantial use of a nonstock shader, and you can see that five separate calls to the glUniform functions are required to set up this shader in the rendering function. A common mistake, especially among programmers used to the old fixed pipeline, is to make further changes to one of the matrix stacks after setting the shader uniform but before rendering the geometry. Remember, the glUniform functions do not copy a reference to the data into the shaders; they copy the actual data into the shaders. This also presents an opportunity for eliminating a few function calls for uniform values that do not change frequently. The final output of our diffusely shaded sphere is shown in Figure 6.6.

FIGURE 6.6   The DiffuseLight example program.

The ADS Light Model

One of the most common lighting models, especially to those familiar with the now deprecated fixed function pipeline, is the ADS lighting model. ADS stands for Ambient, Diffuse, and Specular. It works on a simple principle, which is that objects have three material properties, which are the Ambient, Diffuse, and Specular reflectivity. These properties are assigned color values, with brighter colors representing a higher amount of reflectivity. Light sources have these same three properties and are again assigned color values that represent the brightness of the light. The final color value of a vertex is then the sum of the lighting and material interactions of these three properties.

Ambient Light

Ambient light doesn't come from any particular direction. It has an original source somewhere, but the rays of light have bounced around the room or scene and become directionless. Objects illuminated by ambient light are evenly lit on all surfaces in all directions. You can think of ambient light as a global "brightening" factor applied per light source. This lighting component really approximates scattered light in the environment that originates from the light source.

To calculate the contribution an ambient light source makes to the final vertex color, the ambient material property is scaled by the ambient light values (the two color values are just multiplied), which yields the ambient color contribution. In GLSL shader speak, we would write this like so:

```
uniform vec3 vAmbientMaterial;
uniform vec3 vAmbientLight;
vec3 vAmbientColor = vAmbientMaterial * vAmbientLight;
```

Diffuse Light

Diffuse light is the directional component of a light source and was the subject of our previous example lighting shader. In the ADS lighting model, the diffuse material and lighting values are multiplied together, as is done with the ambient components. However, this value is then scaled by the dot product of the surface normal and lighting vector (the diffuse intensity). Again, in shader speak, this might look something like this:

```
uniform vec3 vDiffuseMaterial;
uniform vec3 vDiffuseLight;
float fDotProduct = max(0.0, dot(vNormal, vLightDir));
vec3 vDiffuseColor = vDiffuseMaterial * vDiffuseLight * fDotProduct;
```

Note that we did not simply take the dot product of the two vectors, but also employed the GLSL function max. The dot product can also be a negative number, and we really can't have negative lighting or color values. Anything less than zero needs to just be zero.

Specular Light

Like diffuse light, specular light is a highly directional property, but it interacts more sharply with the surface and in a particular direction. A highly specular light (really a material property in the real world) tends to cause a bright spot on the surface it shines on, which is called the specular highlight. Because of its highly directional nature, it is even possible that depending on a viewer's position, the specular highlight may not even be visible. A spotlight and the sun are good examples of sources that produce strong specular highlights, but of course they must be shining on an object that is "shiny."

The color contribution to the specular material and lighting colors is scaled by a value that requires a bit more computation than we've done so far. First we must find the vector that is reflected by the surface normal and the inverted light vector. The dot product between these two vectors is then raised to a "shininess" power. The higher the shininess number, the smaller the resulting specular highlight turns out to be. Some shader skeleton code that does this is shown here.

```
uniform vec3 vSpecularMaterial;
uniform vec3 vSpecularLight;
float shininess = 128.0;
```

```
vec3 vReflection = reflect(-vLightDir, vEyeNormal);
float EyeReflectionAngle = max(0.0, dot(vEyeNormal, vReflection);
fSpec = pow(EyeReflectionAngle, shininess);
vec3 vSpecularColor = vSpecularLight * vSpecularMaterial * fSpec;
```

The shininess parameter could easily like anything else be a uniform. Traditionally (from the fixed pipeline days), the highest specular power is set to 128. Numbers greater than this tend to have a diminishingly small effect.

The ADS Shader
The final color of the vertex, given our last three examples, then could be computed as follows:

```
vVertexColor = vAmbientColor + vDiffuseColor + vSpecularColor;
```

The sample program ADSGouraud implements just such a shader. We have, however, made a simplification. Instead of passing in separate material and lighting colors/intensities, we just pass in a single color value for each of the ambient, diffuse, and specular materials. You could think of this as premultiplying the material property by the lighting colors. Unless you are going to vary the material properties per vertex, this makes for an easy optimization. The Gouraud part of the sample name is because we compute the lighting values per vertex and then use color space interpolation between vertices for the shading. The complete listing of the vertex shader is given in Listing 6.9.

LISTING 6.9 The ADSGouraud Shader Vertex Program

```
// ADS Point lighting Shader
// Vertex Shader
// Richard S. Wright Jr.
// OpenGL SuperBible
#version 330

// Incoming per vertex... position and normal
in vec4 vVertex;
in vec3 vNormal;

// Set per batch
uniform vec4    ambientColor;
uniform vec4    diffuseColor;
uniform vec4    specularColor;

uniform vec3    vLightPosition;
uniform mat4    mvpMatrix;
uniform mat4    mvMatrix;
```

```
uniform mat3    normalMatrix;

// Color to fragment program
smooth out vec4 vVaryingColor;

void main(void)
    {
    // Get surface normal in eye coordinates
    vec3 vEyeNormal = normalMatrix * vNormal;

    // Get vertex position in eye coordinates
    vec4 vPosition4 = mvMatrix * vVertex;
    vec3 vPosition3 = vPosition4.xyz / vPosition4.w;

    // Get vector to light source
    vec3 vLightDir = normalize(vLightPosition - vPosition3);

    // Dot product gives us diffuse intensity
    float diff = max(0.0, dot(vEyeNormal, vLightDir));

    // Multiply intensity by diffuse color, force alpha to 1.0
    vVaryingColor = diff * diffuseColor;

    // Add in ambient light
    vVaryingColor += ambientColor;

    // Specular Light
    vec3 vReflection = normalize(reflect(-vLightDir, vEyeNormal));
    float spec = max(0.0, dot(vEyeNormal, vReflection));
    if(diff != 0) {
        float fSpec = pow(spec, 128.0);
        vVaryingColor.rgb += vec3(fSpec, fSpec, fSpec);
    }

    // Don't forget to transform the geometry!
    gl_Position = mvpMatrix * vVertex;
    }
```

We won't list the entire fragment shader, as all it does is assign the incoming vVaryingColor to the fragment color.

```
vFragColor = vVaryingColor;
```

For a given triangle, there are only three vertices and many more fragments that fill out the triangle. This makes vertex lighting and Gouraud shading very efficient, as all the computations are done only once per vertex. Figure 6.7 shows the output of the ADSGouraud example program.

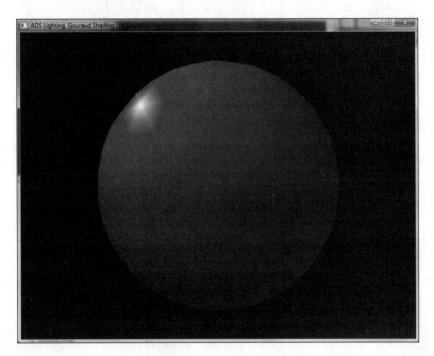

FIGURE 6.7   Per-vertex-based lighting (Gouraud shading).

Phong Shading

One of the drawbacks to Gouraud shading is clearly apparent in Figure 6.7. Note the star-burst pattern of the specular highlight. On a still image, this might almost pass as an intentional artistic effect. The running sample program, however, rotates the sphere and shows a characteristic flashing that is a bit distracting and generally undesirable. This is caused by the discontinuity between triangles because the color values are being interpo-lated linearly through color space. The bright lines are actually the seams between individ-ual triangles. One way to reduce this effect is to use more and more vertices in your geometry. Another, and higher quality, method is called *Phong shading*. With Phong shading, instead of interpolating the color values between vertices, we interpolate the surface normals between vertices. Figure 6.8 shows the output from the ADSPhong sample program (Figures 6.7 and 6.8 are shown side-by-side in Color Plate 5).

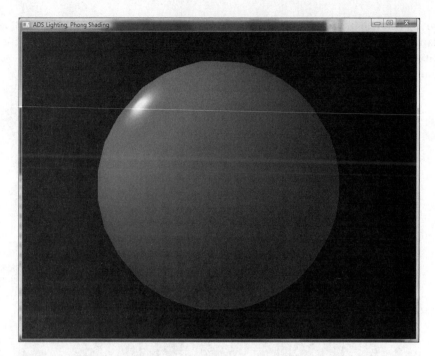

FIGURE 6.8   Per-pixel-based lighting (Phong shading).

The trade-off is of course we are now doing significantly more work in the fragment program, which is going to be executed significantly more times than the vertex program. The basic code is the same as for the ADSGouraud example program, but this time there is some significant rearranging of the shader code. Listing 6.10 shows the new vertex program.

LISTING 6.10   ADSPhong Vertex Shader

```
// ADS Point lighting Shader
// Vertex Shader
// Richard S. Wright Jr.
// OpenGL SuperBible
#version 330

// Incoming per vertex... position and normal
in vec4 vVertex;
in vec3 vNormal;

uniform mat4   mvpMatrix;
uniform mat4   mvMatrix;
```

```
uniform mat3    normalMatrix;
uniform vec3    vLightPosition;

// Color to fragment program
smooth out vec3 vVaryingNormal;
smooth out vec3 vVaryingLightDir;

void main(void)
    {
    // Get surface normal in eye coordinates
    vVaryingNormal = normalMatrix * vNormal;

    // Get vertex position in eye coordinates
    vec4 vPosition4 = mvMatrix * vVertex;
    vec3 vPosition3 = vPosition4.xyz / vPosition4.w;

    // Get vector to light source
    vVaryingLightDir = normalize(vLightPosition - vPosition3);

    // Don't forget to transform the geometry!
    gl_Position = mvpMatrix * vVertex;
    }
```

All the lighting computations depend on the surface normal and light direction vector.
Instead of passing a computed color value one from each vertex, we pass these two
vectors:

```
smooth out vec3 vVaryingNormal;
smooth out vec3 vVaryingLightDir;
```

Now the fragment shader has significantly more work to do than before, and it is shown
in Listing 6.11.

LISTING 6.11   ADSPhone Fragment Shader

```
// ADS Point lighting Shader
// Fragment Shader
// Richard S. Wright Jr.
// OpenGL SuperBible
#version 330

out vec4 vFragColor;
```

```
uniform vec4      ambientColor;
uniform vec4      diffuseColor;
uniform vec4      specularColor;

in vec3 vVaryingNormal;
in vec3 vVaryingLightDir;

void main(void)
    {
    // Dot product gives us diffuse intensity
    float diff = max(0.0, dot(normalize(vVaryingNormal),
                              normalize(vVaryingLightDir)));

    // Multiply intensity by diffuse color, force alpha to 1.0
    vFragColor = diff * diffuseColor;

    // Add in ambient light
    vFragColor += ambientColor;

    // Specular Light
    vec3 vReflection = normalize(reflect(-normalize(vVaryingLightDir),
                                 normalize(vVaryingNormal)));
    float spec = max(0.0, dot(normalize(vVaryingNormal), vReflection));

    // If the diffuse light is zero, don't even bother with the pow function
    if(diff != 0) {
        float fSpec = pow(spec, 128.0);
        vFragColor.rgb += vec3(fSpec, fSpec, fSpec);
        }
    }
```

On today's hardware higher quality rendering choices such as Phong shading are often practical. The visual quality is dramatic, and performance is often only marginally compromised. Still, on lower powered hardware (such as an embedded device) or in a scene where many other already expensive choices have been made, Gouraud shading may be the best choice. A general shader performance optimization rule is to move as much processing out of the fragment shaders and into the vertex shader as possible. With this example, you can see why.

Accessing Textures

Accessing a texture map from a shader is very simple. Texture coordinates are passed to your vertex shader as attributes. These attributes are usually smoothly interpolated between vertices in the fragment shader. The fragment shader uses these interpolated texture coordinates to *sample* the texture. The currently bound texture object is already set up for mipmapping/nonmipmapping, the filtering mode, wrap mode, and so on. The sampled filtered texture color comes back as an RGBA color value that you can write directly to the fragment or combine with other color calculations. We get more in depth with using textures in and out of GLSL in the next chapter. With this section we at least get you going with the basics.

Just the Texels Please

The TexturedTriangle example program represents the simplest possible shader that uses texture. Its goal is simple, draw a single triangle and put a texture on it. You can see where we are going with this in Figure 6.9.

FIGURE 6.9   The Textured Triangle program.

On the client side, the C/C++ code to render the triangle is pretty trivial, and setting up a triangle with texture coordinates is nothing we haven't already done with the stock shaders. The vertex program that receives our vertex attributes is shown in Listing 6.12.

LISTING 6.12   The TexturedTriangle Vertex Program

```
// The TexturedIdentity Shader
// Vertex Shader
// Richard S. Wright Jr.
// OpenGL SuperBible
#version 330

in vec4 vVertex;
in vec2 vTexCoords;

smooth out vec2 vVaryingTexCoords;

void main(void)
    {
    vVaryingTexCoords = vTexCoords;
    gl_Position = vVertex;
    }
```

The key part of this short vertex program is the incoming vertex attribute vTexCoords that contains the s and t texture coordinates for this vertex and the outgoing variable vVaryingTexCoords. This is all that is required to get the texture coordinates to interpolate across the surface of our triangle.

The fragment program, shown in Listing 6.13, is also short and contains something we haven't talked about yet.

LISTING 6.13   The TexturedTriangle Fragment Program

```
// The TexturedIdentity Shader
// Fragment Shader
// Richard S. Wright Jr.
// OpenGL SuperBible
#version 330

uniform sampler2D colorMap;

out vec4 vFragColor;
in vec4 vVaryingTexCoords;

void main(void)
    {
    vFragColor = texture(colorMap, vVaryingTexCoords.st);
    }
```

Up near the top, there is a new variable type, a `sampler2D`:

```
uniform sampler2D colorMap;
```

A sampler is actually just an integer (you use `glUniform1i` to set its value), and it represents the texture unit where the texture you will be sampling is bound. The 2D part of `sampler2D` indicates that it is a 2D texture, and you can also have 1D, 3D, and other types of samplers (which are all covered in the next chapter). For now, we always set this value to zero to indicate texture unit 0. In Chapter 5 we covered texture objects as a means to manage any number of different texture states, and we used the function `glBindTexture` to select between the different texture objects. All these texture binds were actually binding to the default texture unit, texture unit 0. There are actually many texture units, and each can have its own texture object bound to it. Using more than one texture at a time allows for a lot of very cool effects and is a powerful technique, and we jump into that in the next chapter.

Setting the sampler uniform and rendering the triangle in the client code are pretty straightforward.

```
glUseProgram(myTexturedIdentityShader);
glBindTexture(GL_TEXTURE_2D, textureID);
GLint iTextureUniform = glGetUniformLocation(myTexturedIdentityShader,
                                                      "colorMap");
glUniform1i(iTextureUniform, 0);

triangleBatch.Draw();
```

In the shader, we call the texture mapping built-in function `texture` to sample our texture using the interpolated texture coordinates and assign the color value directly to the fragment color.

```
vFragColor = texture(colorMap, vVaryingTexCoords.st);
```

Light the Texels

Now that you know how to sample a texture, let's do something a little more interesting with those filtered texel values—for example, adding a texture to the ADSPhong shader. With all of our lighting shaders, we essentially multiplied our base color values by the intensity of the light, either per vertex, or per pixel. The modified ADSPhong shader, which we call ADSTexture, samples the texture and then multiplies the texture color values by the light intensity. The output of the example program LitTexture is shown in Figure 6.10. Take careful note of the nice white specular highlight in the upper left-hand corner of the sphere.

FIGURE 6.10   Combining light and texture in LitTexture.

This white specular highlight presents the one special consideration we must make when lighting a textured surface. The sum of the ambient and diffuse light could potentially be as bright as solid white, which in color space is all 1s. Multiplying a texture color by white simply results in the original undimmed texel color values. This means there is no way to multiply a texture color by a valid lighting value and get a white specular highlight to show up...well, at least that's the way it's *supposed* to work.

The reality is that often the results of our lighting calculations, including the specular highlight, spill a bit over 1.0 for each color channel. This means it is *possible* at least to oversaturate the colors and get a white specular highlight. The correct approach, however, is to multiply the sum of the ambient and diffuse light intensity by the texture color and then add the specular light contribution afterward. Listing 6.14 shows how we modified our ADSPhong fragment shader to do just this.

LISTING 6.14   The ADSTexture Fragment Program

```
// ADS Point lighting Shader
// Fragment Shader
// Richard S. Wright Jr.
// OpenGL SuperBible
#version 330
```

```
out vec4 vFragColor;

uniform vec4      ambientColor;
uniform vec4      diffuseColor;
uniform vec4      specularColor;
uniform sampler2D colorMap;

smooth in vec3 vVaryingNormal;
smooth in vec3 vVaryingLightDir;
smooth in vec2 vTexCoords;

void main(void)
    {
    // Dot product gives us diffuse intensity
    float diff = max(0.0, dot(normalize(vVaryingNormal),
                              normalize(vVaryingLightDir)));

    // Multiply intensity by diffuse color, force alpha to 1.0
    vFragColor = diff * diffuseColor;

    // Add in ambient light
    vFragColor += ambientColor;

    // Modulate in the texture
    vFragColor *= texture(colorMap, vTexCoords);

    // Specular Light
    vec3 vReflection = normalize(reflect(-normalize(vVaryingLightDir),
                                         normalize(vVaryingNormal)));
    float spec = max(0.0, dot(normalize(vVaryingNormal), vReflection));
    if(diff != 0) {
        float fSpec = pow(spec, 128.0);
        vFragColor.rgb += vec3(fSpec, fSpec, fSpec);
        }
    }
```

Discarding Fragments

Fragment shaders have the option of aborting processing and simply not writing any fragment color (or depth, or stencil for that matter) values. The statement discard simply stops the fragment program in its tracks. A common use for this statement is to perform an *alpha test*. Normal blending operations require a read from the color buffer, two multiplies (at least), a sum of colors, and then writing the value back to the color buffer. If the alpha is zero, or very near zero, the fragments are essentially invisible. It's a poor performance choice to draw things that are invisible! Much less, this creates an invisible pattern in the depth buffer, which can cause depth testing anomalies. An alpha test simply checks for some threshold value and completely discards the fragment when the alpha falls below that value. For example, to test for an alpha less than say 0.1, you might do something like this:

```
if(vColorValue.a < 0.1f)
    discard;
```

A cool and animated effect that makes use of this feature is an erosion shader. An erosion shader makes geometry look like it is eroding away over time. With the discard statement, you have per-pixel control over which fragments are drawn and which are not. The example program Dissolve performs just such an effect. We start with a texture that has an appropriate noise or cloud pattern. These are easy enough to make with most photo editing software packages. For our example here, we used the one shown in Figure 6.11.

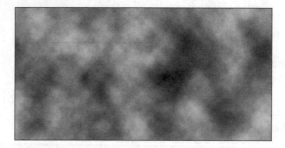

FIGURE 6.11   A cloud texture we use for our erosion effect.

We set up a time-based uniform in our client code that cycles from 1.0 to 0.0 over a period of 10 seconds. Our goal is to make our object (a green torus) "melt" over that 10 second period. We do this by sampling the cloud texture and comparing one of the color components to our countdown variable, discarding the fragment completely when the color value is greater than the threshold. Listing 6.15 shows the complete source for this fragment shader.

LISTING 6.15   The Dissolve Fragment Shader

```
// ADS Point lighting Shader with dissolve effect
// Fragment Shader
// Richard S. Wright Jr.
// OpenGL SuperBible
#version 330

out vec4 vFragColor;
```

```
uniform vec4        ambientColor;
uniform vec4        diffuseColor;
uniform vec4        specularColor;
uniform sampler2D   cloudTexture;
uniform float         dissolveFactor;

smooth in vec3 vVaryingNormal;
smooth in vec3 vVaryingLightDir;
smooth in vec2 vVaryingTexCoord;

void main(void)
    {
    vec4 vCloudSample = texture2D(cloudTexture, vVaryingTexCoord);

    if(vCloudSample.r < dissolveFactor)
        discard;

    // Dot product gives us diffuse intensity
    float diff = max(0.0, dot(normalize(vVaryingNormal),
                            normalize(vVaryingLightDir)));

    // Multiply intensity by diffuse color, force alpha to 1.0
    vFragColor = diff * diffuseColor;

    // Add in ambient light
    vFragColor += ambientColor;

    // Specular Light
    vec3 vReflection = normalize(reflect(-normalize(vVaryingLightDir),
                                    normalize(vVaryingNormal)));
    float spec = max(0.0, dot(normalize(vVaryingNormal), vReflection));
    if(diff != 0) {
        float fSpec = pow(spec, 128.0);
        vFragColor.rgb += vec3(fSpec, fSpec, fSpec);
        }
    }
```

This is essentially again a modification of the ADSPhong light fragment program. The dissolve effect is simply woven into this shader. First we need the uniforms for the texture sampler and our countdown timer.

```
uniform sampler2D    cloudTexture;
uniform float          dissolveFactor;
```

Then we sample our texture and determine whether the red color value (chosen arbitrarily, considering it's a grayscale image) is below the countdown value; we discard the fragment completely.

```
vec4 vCloudSample = texture(cloudTexture, vVaryingTexCoord);

if(vCloudSample.r < dissolveFactor)
    discard;
```

Also note that we do this early in the fragment shader. There is no point in performing the expensive per-pixel lighting computations if the fragment is not going to be drawn anyway. The output (at least a single frame of the animation) of the sample program Dissolve is shown in Figure 6.12.

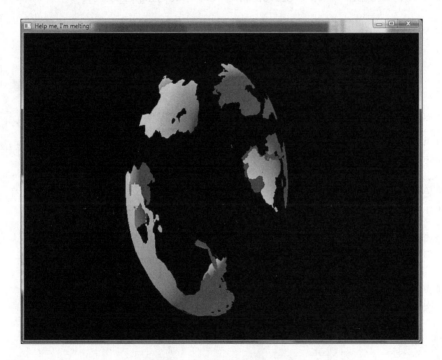

FIGURE 6.12   The output of the sample Dissolve program.

Cell Shading—Texels as Light

All of our examples of texture mapping, in this chapter and the last, have used 2D textures. Two-dimensional textures are typically the simplest and easiest to understand. Most people can quickly get the intuitive feel for putting a 2D picture on the side of a piece of 2D or 3D geometry. Let's take a look now at a one-dimensional texture mapping example that is commonly used in computer games to render geometry that appears on-screen like a cartoon. *Toon shading*, which is often referred to as *cell shading*, uses a one-dimensional texture map as a lookup table to fill geometry with a solid color (using `GL_NEAREST`) from the texture map.

The basic idea is to use the diffuse lighting intensity (the dot product between the eye space surface normal and light directional vector) as the texture coordinate into a one-dimensional texture that contains a gradually brightening color table. Figure 6.13 shows one such texture, with four increasingly bright red texels (defined as RGB `unsigned byte` color components).

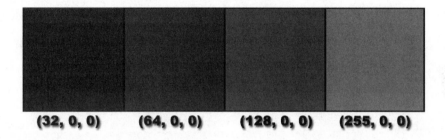

FIGURE 6.13   A one-dimensional color lookup table.

Recall that the diffuse lighting dot product varies from 0.0 at no intensity to 1.0 at full intensity. Conveniently, this maps nicely to a one-dimensional texture coordinate range. Loading this one-dimensional texture is pretty straightforward as shown here:

```
glGenTextures(1, &texture);
glBindTexture(GL_TEXTURE_1D, texture);
GLubyte textureData[4][3] = { 32,  0, 0,
                              64,  0, 0,
                             128,  0,  0,
                             255,  0,  0};

glTexImage1D(GL_TEXTURE_1D, 0, GL_RGB, 4, 0, GL_RGB,
                                GL_UNSIGNED_BYTE, textureData);
glTexParameteri(GL_TEXTURE_1D, GL_TEXTURE_MIN_FILTER, GL_NEAREST);
glTexParameteri(GL_TEXTURE_1D, GL_TEXTURE_MAG_FILTER, GL_NEAREST);
glTexParameteri(GL_TEXTURE_1D, GL_TEXTURE_WRAP_S, GL_CLAMP_TO_EDGE);
```

This code is from the example program ToonShader, which renders a spinning torus with the toon shading effect applied. Although the `GLTriangleBatch`, which we use to create the torus, supplies a set of two-dimensional texture coordinates, we ignore them in our vertex program, which is shown in Listing 6.16.

LISTING 6.16   The Toon Vertex Shader

```
// Cell lighting Shader
// Vertex Shader
// Richard S. Wright Jr.
// OpenGL SuperBible
#version 330

// Incoming per vertex... position and normal
in vec4 vVertex;
in vec3 vNormal;

smooth out float textureCoordinate;

uniform vec3     vLightPosition;
uniform mat4     mvpMatrix;
uniform mat4     mvMatrix;
uniform mat3     normalMatrix;

void main(void)
    {
    // Get surface normal in eye coordinates
    vec3 vEyeNormal = normalMatrix * vNormal;

    // Get vertex position in eye coordinates
    vec4 vPosition4 = mvMatrix * vVertex;
    vec3 vPosition3 = vPosition4.xyz / vPosition4.w;

    // Get vector to light source
    vec3 vLightDir = normalize(vLightPosition - vPosition3);

    // Dot product gives us diffuse intensity
    textureCoordinate = max(0.0, dot(vEyeNormal, vLightDir));

    // Don't forget to transform the geometry!
    gl_Position = mvpMatrix * vVertex;
    }
```

Other than the transformed geometry position, the only output of this shader is an interpolated texture coordinate textureCoordinate, which is represented as a single float. The
computation of the diffuse lighting component is virtually identical to the DiffuseLight
example.

The fragment program for our Toon shader simply samples our one-dimensional texture and writes its value to the framebuffer fragment.

```
vFragColor = texture(colorTable, textureCoordinate);
```

The resulting output is shown in Figure 6.14. Both the red color ramp texture and the toon shaded torus are also shown together in Color Plate 6.

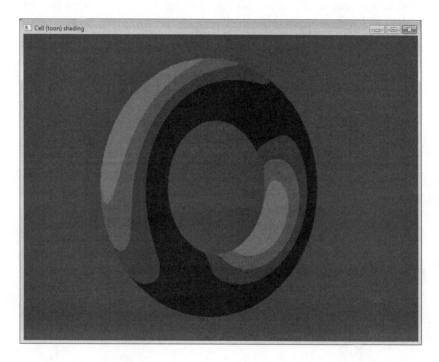

FIGURE 6.14   Our toon shaded torus.

Summary

In this chapter, we broke free of the canned stock shaders that we used throughout the first five chapters. For now, the GLBatch type classes in GLTools provide an easy way to send down the most typical vertex attributes, and you saw how easy it is to hook your own shader attributes up to those classes. We covered how similar GLSL is to C/C++ and the catalog of built-in functions that can be used, as well as how to write your own. We have gone over two lighting models and implemented them with a shader, discussed the pros and cons of doing your expensive computations in the vertex or fragment shader, and just touched on how to access texture data in your shaders.

Not only did we map 2D textures to geometry surfaces, but you saw how you can use textures as "data," by using it as a lookup value for eliminating geometry via the discard statement, and as a one dimensional color table to implement cell shading.

We have only just scratched the surface of what can be done with GLSL in this chapter. In the chapters that lie ahead, you learn more about GLSL and learn even more exciting rendering techniques as we cover more of the OpenGL API and shading language. Why wait though? You already know more than enough to start experimenting yourself, either by modifying the shaders covered so far or dreaming up your own!

CHAPTER 7

More Advanced Texture Topics

by Richard S. Wright, Jr. and Graham Sellers

WHAT YOU'LL LEARN IN THIS CHAPTER:

• How to use rectangle textures

• How to use a six-sided texture called a cube map

• How to apply more than one texture simultaneously

• How to create point sprites

• How to make more texture accessible to your shaders with texture arrays

• How to query the driver about texture support with proxies

In Chapter 5, "Basic Texturing," you first learned the ropes of texture mapping with OpenGL. Primarily we were concerned with the basics: loading a 2D image file, using texture coordinates, the different wrap modes, and so on. Now it's time to dig a little deeper and expand on that knowledge base. You soon see that texture data can take on the form of far more than just a 2D image file loaded from disk, and sometimes textures don't even contain visual data or a picture of any kind at all! Finally, you see how sometimes textures don't even really *exist*, but are literally made up on the fly by the fragment program.

Rectangle Textures

First, we continue to build upon our experience with using image files for texture, images that we actually want to display in some way. Chapter 5 was mostly about 2D images using the texture target GL_TEXTURE_2D, and we also showed how to use GL_TEXTURE_1D in the previous chapter as a color lookup table for cell shading. For one-, two-, and three-dimensional textures (remember GL_TEXTURE_3D, too), we typically mapped textures to geometry with normalized texture coordinates that ranged from 0.0 to 1.0. We could stray outside that range and use the various texture coordinate wrapping modes to determine whether the texture would repeat in different ways or be clamped down to the edges of the texture image.

Another useful alternative to two-dimensional texture images is the texture target GL_TEXTURE_RECTANGLE. This texture target mode works mostly like GL_TEXTURE_2D, with a couple of exceptions. First, they cannot be mipmapped, which means you can only load level zero with glTexImage2D. Second, the texture coordinates are not normalized, which simply means rather than range from 0.0 to 1.0 across the image, the texture coordinates actually address pixels. Texture coordinate (5, 19) is actually six pixels from the left, and 20 pixels up (remember, we programmers start counting at zero!) into the image. Furthermore, texture coordinates cannot repeat, and they do not support texture compression.

This is convenient for many applications where OpenGL is used to process and present image data rather than using textures for surface features of 3D models. Hardware support for texture rectangles is also simpler than normal 2D texture mapping, making them fast and efficient as well.

Loading a Rectangle Texture

Listing 7.1 shows the function to load a Targa file as a texture rectangle. This is similar to the LoadTGATexture that we used previously for GL_TEXTURE_2D textures. The most notable change is of course that all the texture functions now are using GL_TEXTURE_RECTANGLE as their first parameter instead of GL_TEXTURE_2D. This change applies to any texture function that works with rectangle textures. We also removed the code that checked for mipmapped texture filters as they are no longer allowed; you must use either GL_NEAREST or GL_LINEAR filter modes. We left the wrapMode parameter in place, but the GL_REPEAT and GL_REPEAT_MIRRORED wrap modes are not supported with rectangle textures either.

LISTING 7.1   Loading a Rectangle Texture

```
bool LoadTGATextureRect(const char *szFileName, GLenum minFilter,
                                     GLenum magFilter, GLenum wrapMode)
    {
    GLbyte *pBits;
    int nWidth, nHeight, nComponents;
    GLenum eFormat;

    // Read the texture bits
    pBits = gltReadTGABits(szFileName, &nWidth, &nHeight,
                                 &nComponents, &eFormat);
    if(pBits == NULL)
        return false;
```

```
glTexParameteri(GL_TEXTURE_RECTANGLE, GL_TEXTURE_WRAP_S, wrapMode);
glTexParameteri(GL_TEXTURE_RECTANGLE, GL_TEXTURE_WRAP_T, wrapMode);

glTexParameteri(GL_TEXTURE_RECTANGLE, GL_TEXTURE_MIN_FILTER, minFilter);
glTexParameteri(GL_TEXTURE_RECTANGLE, GL_TEXTURE_MAG_FILTER, magFilter);

glPixelStorei(GL_UNPACK_ALIGNMENT, 1);
glTexImage2D(GL_TEXTURE_RECTANGLE, 0, nComponents, nWidth, nHeight, 0,
                                  eFormat, GL_UNSIGNED_BYTE, pBits);
free(pBits);

return true;
}
```

Using a Rectangle Texture

Figure 7.1 shows an image of the OpenGL logo that we use for our first example program. This is a Targa file with an alpha channel, and we are going to put it up on the screen in front of our running example SphereWorld. This image is 300 pixels wide by 155 pixels high.

FIGURE 7.1   The OpenGL logo texture.

Loading this file as a rectangle texture looks much like loading our previous 2D texture files. Note also the change to GL_TEXTURE_RECTANGLE in the glBindTexture function call.

```
glBindTexture(GL_TEXTURE_RECTANGLE, uiTextures[3]);
LoadTGATextureRect("OpenGL-Logo.tga", GL_NEAREST, GL_NEAREST,
                                     GL_CLAMP_TO_EDGE);
```

Our goal for the example program TextureRect is to display the OpenGL logo on the screen in the lower right-hand corner of the display. When drawing 2D in screen space, it is common to create an orthographic projection matrix that matches the screen size. We choose to make the coordinate system match the pixels on the screen, but put the origin (0, 0) in the lower left-hand corner of the screen instead of the upper left-hand corner. This keeps all our drawing coordinates in a nice neat first quadrant Cartesian system. Setting up this projection matrix is shown in the following code:

```
M3DMatrix44f mScreenSpace;
m3dMakeOrthographicMatrix(mScreenSpace, 0.0f, 800.0f, 0.0f, 600.0f,
                                                -1.0f, 1.0f);
```

We create the rectangle where we will display the OpenGL logo using the GLBatch class and a triangle fan. Note how the texture coordinates specified range from 0.0 to the width or height of the logo.

```
int x = 500;
int y = 155;
int width = 300;
int height = 155;
logoBatch.Begin(GL_TRIANGLE_FAN, 4, 1);

// Upper left hand corner
logoBatch.MultiTexCoord2f(0, 0.0f, height);
logoBatch.Vertex3f(x, y, 0.0);

// Lower left hand corner
logoBatch.MultiTexCoord2f(0, 0.0f, 0.0f);
logoBatch.Vertex3f(x, y - height, 0.0f);

// Lower right hand corner
logoBatch.MultiTexCoord2f(0, width, 0.0f);
logoBatch.Vertex3f(x + width, y - height, 0.0f);

// Upper right hand corner
logoBatch.MultiTexCoord2f(0, width, height);
logoBatch.Vertex3f(x + width, y, 0.0f);

logoBatch.End();
```

Now that we have a batch with vertices and texture coordinates, it's time to render. First we need a texture mapping shader that can use a rectangle texture. This again is a trivial modification of just about any 2D texture shader, and we only need to change the sampler from a sampler2D type to a samplerRect type. Listing 7.2 shows just the fragment shader from this sample program.

LISTING 7.2   Fragment Shader for the TextureRect Example Program

```
// Rectangle Texture (replace) Shader
// Fragment Shader
// Richard S. Wright Jr.
// OpenGL SuperBible
#version 330

out vec4 vFragColor;

uniform samplerRect  rectangleImage;

smooth in vec2 vVaryingTexCoord;

void main(void)
    {
    vFragColor = texture(rectangleImage, vVaryingTexCoord);
    }
```

Finally, we render the logo over the top of the normal SphereWorld output screen. To accomplish this, we enable blending again and turn off depth testing. Otherwise, since we are changing our coordinate system, we could easily end up with depth values from the underlying 3D scene, preventing our 2D images from being rendered correctly.

```
// Turn blending on, and depth testing off
glEnable(GL_BLEND);
glDisable(GL_DEPTH_TEST);

glUseProgram(rectReplaceShader);
glUniform1i(locRectTexture, 0);
glUniformMatrix4fv(locRectMVP, 1, GL_FALSE, mScreenSpace);
glBindTexture(GL_TEXTURE_RECTANGLE, uiTextures[3]);
logoBatch.Draw();

// Restore no blending and depth test
glDisable(GL_BLEND);
glEnable(GL_DEPTH_TEST);
```

The final output of our work is shown in Figure 7.2 and is also shown in Color Plate 7.

FIGURE 7.2   Our final texture rectangle displayed over our 3D scene.

Cube Maps

A cube map is treated as a single texture object but it is made up of six square (yes, they must be square!) 2D images that make up the six sides of a cube. Applications of cube maps range from 3D light maps, reflections, and highly accurate environment maps. Figure 7.3 shows the layout of six square images composing a cube map that we use for the Cubemap sample program.

FIGURE 7.3   The layout of six cube faces in the Cubemap sample program.

These six 2D tiles represent the view of the world from six different directions (negative and positive X, Y, and Z). Essentially, a cube map is projected onto an object as if the cube map were surrounding the object itself.

Loading Cube Maps

Cube maps add six new values that can be passed into glTexImage2D:

GL_TEXTURE_CUBE_MAP_POSITIVE_X, GL_TEXTURE_CUBE_MAP_NEGATIVE_X,
GL_TEXTURE_CUBE_MAP_POSITIVE_Y, GL_TEXTURE_CUBE_MAP_NEGATIVE_Y,
GL_TEXTURE_CUBE_MAP_POSITIVE_Z, and GL_TEXTURE_CUBE_MAP_NEGATIVE_Z.

These constants represent the direction in world coordinates of the cube face surrounding the object being mapped. For example, to load the map for the positive X direction, you might use a function that looks like this:

```
glTexImage2D(GL_TEXTURE_CUBE_MAP_POSITIVE_X, 0, GL_RGBA, iWidth, iHeight,
                         0, GL_RGBA, GL_UNSIGNED_BYTE,
                                             pImage);
```

To take this example further, look at the following code segment from the Cubemap sample program. Here, we store the name and identifiers of the six cube map faces in an array and then use a loop to load all six images into a single texture object:

```
const char *szCubeFaces[6] = { "pos_x.tga", "neg_x.tga", "pos_y.tga",
                    "neg_y.tga","pos_z.tga", "neg_z.tga" };

GLenum  cube[6] = {  GL_TEXTURE_CUBE_MAP_POSITIVE_X,
                     GL_TEXTURE_CUBE_MAP_NEGATIVE_X,
                     GL_TEXTURE_CUBE_MAP_POSITIVE_Y,
                     GL_TEXTURE_CUBE_MAP_NEGATIVE_Y,
                     GL_TEXTURE_CUBE_MAP_POSITIVE_Z,
                     GL_TEXTURE_CUBE_MAP_NEGATIVE_Z };

. . .
. . .

    glTexParameteri(GL_TEXTURE_CUBE_MAP, GL_TEXTURE_MAG_FILTER, GL_LINEAR);
    glTexParameteri(GL_TEXTURE_CUBE_MAP, GL_TEXTURE_MIN_FILTER,
                                            GL_LINEAR_MIPMAP_LINEAR);
    glTexParameteri(GL_TEXTURE_CUBE_MAP, GL_TEXTURE_WRAP_S,
                                    GL_CLAMP_TO_EDGE);
    glTexParameteri(GL_TEXTURE_CUBE_MAP, GL_TEXTURE_WRAP_T,
                                    GL_CLAMP_TO_EDGE);
    glTexParameteri(GL_TEXTURE_CUBE_MAP, GL_TEXTURE_WRAP_R,
                                    GL_CLAMP_TO_EDGE);

    GLbyte *pBytes;
    GLint iWidth, iHeight, iComponents;
    GLenum eFormat;

    // Load Cube Map images
    for(i = 0; i < 6; i++)
        {
        // Load this texture map
        (GL_TEXTURE_CUBE_MAP, GL_GENERATE_MIPMAP, GL_TRUE);
        pBytes = gltLoadTGABits(szCubeFaces[i], &iWidth, &iHeight,
                                    &iComponents, &eFormat);
        glTexImage2D(cube[i], 0, iComponents, iWidth, iHeight, 0, eFormat,
                                    GL_UNSIGNED_BYTE, pBytes);
        free(pBytes);
        }
        glGenerateMipmap(GL_TEXTURE_CUBE_MAP);
```

Texture coordinates for cube maps seem a little odd at first glance. Unlike a true 3D texture, the S, T, and R texture coordinates represent a signed vector from the center of the texture map. This vector intersects one of the six sides of the cube map. The texels around this intersection point are then sampled to create the filtered color value from the texture.

Making a Skybox

The most common use of cube maps is to create an object that reflects its surroundings. The six images used for the Cubemap sample program were provided courtesy of The Game Creators, Ltd. (www.thegamecreators.com). This cube map is applied to a sphere, creating the appearance of a mirrored surface. This same cube map is also applied to the skybox, which creates the background being reflected.

A skybox is nothing more than a big box with a picture of the sky on it. Another way of looking at it is as a picture of the sky on a big box! Simple enough. An effective skybox contains six images that contain views from the center of your scene along the six directional axes. If this sounds just like a cube map, congratulations, you're paying attention! For our Cubemap sample program a large box is drawn around the scene, and the cube map texture is applied to the six faces of the cube. The skybox is drawn using the GLTools function gltMakeCube, which simply fills a GLBatch container with triangles that make up a cube with the specified radius. In our case, we chose a cube that was 20 units in each direction from the origin.

```
gltMakeCube(cubeBatch, 20.0f);
```

This function assigns 2D texture coordinates to the GLT_ATTRIBUTE_TEXTURE0 attribute slot such that a 2D image is applied to each face of the cube. However, this does not suit our needs for a cube map as we need 3D texture coordinates that represent a vector to where on the cube map to sample texels. The GLBatch class only supports 2D texturing, so this simply isn't going to work out of the box. The solution is to write a custom vertex shader that calculates the texture coordinates for us. In fact, this is simple given that each corner of the cube in vertex space is also a vector to that location from the center of the cube. All we have to do is normalize this vector, and we have a ready-made cube map texture coordinate. The source code to the skybox shader vertex program is provided in Listing 7.3. Its sole purpose is to transform the vertex positions by the modelviewprojection matrix, and to derive a texture coordinate from the original vertex position.

LISTING 7.3   The Cube Mapped Vertex Shader

```
// Skybox Shader
// Vertex Shader
// Richard S. Wright Jr.
// OpenGL SuperBible
#version 330

// Incoming per vertex... just the position
in vec4 vVertex;

uniform mat4   mvpMatrix; // Transormation matrix
```

```
// Texture Coordinate to fragment program
varying vec3 vVaryingTexCoord;

void main(void)
    {
    // Pass on the texture coordinates
    vVaryingTexCoord = normalize(vVertex.xyz);

    // Don't forget to transform the geometry!
    gl_Position = mvpMatrix * vVertex;
    }
```

The fragment program, which is provided in Listing 7.4, receives the three-component texture coordinate and samples the cube map at that location. Note that for a cube map, the sampler type is samplerCube.

LISTING 7.4   The Cube Mapped Fragment Shader

```
// Skybox Shader
// Fragment Shader
// Richard S. Wright Jr.
// OpenGL SuperBible
#version 330

out vec4 vFragColor;

uniform samplerCube   cubeMap;

varying vec3 vVaryingTexCoord;

void main(void)
    {
    vFragColor = texture(cubeMap, vVaryingTexCoord);
    }
```

One final note about skyboxes is that when you use mipmapping with a cube map, you can often get seams along the edges where two sides join. (This really also applies to any application of cube maps.) OpenGL internally adjusts its own filtering rules to help eliminate these seams when you enable GL_TEXTURE_CUBE_MAP_SEAMLESS, like so:

```
glEnable(GL_TEXTURE_CUBE_MAP_SEAMLESS);
```

Making a Reflection

Texturing the skybox is straightforward. Creating the reflection is just a bit more involved. To begin with we must create in our shader a reflection vector using the surface normal and the vector to the vertex in eye coordinates. In addition, to provide a true reflection, we also take the orientation of the camera into account. The camera's rotation matrix is extracted from the GLFrame class and inverted. This is then supplied to the shader as a uniform along with the other transformation matrices where it is used to rotate the aforementioned reflection vector, which is actually our cube mapped texture coordinates. Without this rotation of the texture coordinates, the cube map will not correctly reflect the surrounding skybox as the camera moves around in the scene.

Listing 7.5 provides the source for the Reflection.vp vertex shader. The corresponding fragment shader is essentially the same code as for the skybox shader; it simply uses the interpolated cube mapped texture coordinates to sample the cube map and apply it to the fragment.

LISTING 7.5   The Reflection Vertex Shader

```
// Reflection Shader
// Vertex Shader
// Richard S. Wright Jr.
// OpenGL SuperBible
#version 330

// Incoming per vertex... position and normal
in vec4 vVertex;
in vec3 vNormal;

uniform mat4    mvpMatrix;
uniform mat4    mvMatrix;
uniform mat3    normalMatrix;
uniform mat4    mInverseCamera;

// Texture coordinate to fragment program
smooth out vec3 vVaryingTexCoord;

void main(void)
    {
    // Normal in Eye Space
    vec3 vEyeNormal = normalMatrix * vNormal;

    // Vertex position in Eye Space
    vec4 vVert4 = mvMatrix * vVertex;
    vec3 vEyeVertex = normalize(vVert4.xyz / vVert4.w);
```

```
// Get reflected vector
vec4 vCoords = vec4(reflect(vEyeVertex, vEyeNormal), 1.0);

// Rotate by flipped camera
vCoords = mInverseCamera * vCoords;
vVaryingTexCoord.xyz = normalize(vCoords.xyz);

// Don't forget to transform the geometry!
gl_Position = mvpMatrix * vVertex;
}
```

Figure 7.4 shows the output of the Cubemap sample program. Notice how the sky and surrounding terrain are reflected correctly off the surface of the sphere. Moving the camera around the sphere (by using the arrow keys) reveals the correct background and sky view reflected accurately off the sphere as well.

FIGURE 7.4   Output from the Cubemap sample program. (This figure also appears as Color Plate 8.)

Multitexture

Your previous exposure to texture mapping was to load a single texture into a texture object. When you wanted to use that texture, you bound to the texture object of the texture you wanted, and then set the single uniform sampler in the fragment program...to zero. Why zero? Because zero was the index of the texture unit to which your texture was bound. Modern OpenGL implementations support the capability to apply two or more textures to geometry simultaneously by allowing you to bind separate texture objects to each of some number of available texture units. You can query the implementation to see how many texture units are available like this:

```
GLint iUnits;
glGetIntegerv(GL_MAX_TEXTURE_UNITS, &iUnits);
```

By default, the first texture unit is the active texture unit. All texture binding operations affect the currently active texture unit. You can change the current texture unit by calling glActiveTexture with the texture unit identifier as the argument. For example, to switch to the second texture unit and bind to a specific texture, you would do something like the following:

```
glActiveTexture(GL_TEXTURE1);
glBindTexture(GL_TEXTURE_2D, textureID);
```

It is important to keep track of which texture unit is currently active when using multiple textures in your rendering. These texture units are agnostic as to the dimensionality of the textures as well; they could be 1-, 2-, or 3-dimensional textures or cube maps or texture rectangles.

Multiple Texture Coordinates

Textures are applied to geometry by the interpolation of texture coordinates. There is nothing preventing you from using one set of texture coordinates for any number of texture units, or layers as they are sometimes called. You might also compute texture coordinates like we did for the skybox in the previous example, or you might have separate sets of texture coordinates for each texture; they are after all nothing more than one more set of attributes for your batch. None of these scenarios are uncommon.

The GLBatch class by default does not provide any texture coordinates as an attribute array. You can, however, specify up to four sets of texture coordinates when you call the Begin function with the nTextureUnits parameter.

```
void GLBatch::Begin(GLenum primitive, GLuint nVerts,
                              GLuint nTextureUnits = 0);
```

Two functions are provided for supplying texture coordinates. The first is CopyTexCoordData2f and is the fastest as it copies an entire set of texture coordinates all at once.

```
void GLBatch::CopyTexCoordData2f(M3DVector2f *vTexCoords,
                                 GLuint uiTextureLayer);
```

The second is when using the slower one-vertex-at-a-time immediate modelike interface. Two options allow you to specify a two-dimensional texture coordinate, one at a time.

```
void GLBatch::MultiTexCoord2f(GLuint texture, GLclampf s, GLclampf t);
void GLBatch::MultiTexCoord2fv(GLuint texture, M3DVector2f vTexCoord);
```

A Multitextured Example

Multiple kinds of textures can be combined in an almost infinite variety of ways. A huge number of techniques rely on using two or more textures at once in a shader. Again, we refer you to Appendix A, "Further Reading," for some resources on additional 3D techniques. To demonstrate how easy it is to combine multiple textures, we build on our last cube mapped example by adding a bit of tarnish to the mirrored ball in the center of the scene. The tarnish texture, tarnish.tga, is shown in Figure 7.5.

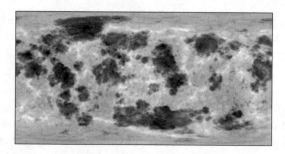

FIGURE 7.5   The tarnish texture map.

We bind this two-dimensional texture to texture unit GL_TEXTURE1 and then multiply the texture color from the tarnish texture by the color of the cube map texture. Where the tarnish texture is dark, it darkens the reflection, and where it is light or nearly white, it has little to no effect on the reflected texture. The resulting output of this effect is shown in Figure 7.6.

FIGURE 7.6 Output from the Multitexture sample program. (This figure also appears as Color Plate 9.)

The client side of this operation is fairly simple. Given that `tarnishTexture` is the texture object containing the tarnish texture, and `cubeTexture` is the texture object name containing the cube map, the following binds these two textures, each to their own texture unit.

```
// Set textures to their texture units
glActiveTexture(GL_TEXTURE1);
glBindTexture(GL_TEXTURE_2D, tarnishTexture);
glActiveTexture(GL_TEXTURE0);
glBindTexture(GL_TEXTURE_CUBE_MAP, cubeTexture);
```

Recall previously that the sphere batch contained a set of two-dimensional texture coordinates that went unused in the cube map example program. Now we modify our shader code so that these texture coordinates are used for the tarnish texture, while we continue to compute the cube map texture coordinates. Rather than relist the entire vertex program, we just talk about the three lines of shader code added. First, we added the attribute for the two-dimensional texture coordinates used by the tarnish texture.

```
in vec2 vTexCoords;
```

Then of course, we need these interpolated, so we set up a set of coordinates that can be smoothly interpolated between vertices.

```
smooth out vec2 vTarnishCoords;
```

Finally, we simply assign the attributes to the interpolated variable.

```
vTarnishCoords = vTexCoords.st;
```

This is really nothing that you wouldn't ordinarily do for normal texture mapping. The bigger changes come in the fragment program, which is shown in its entirety in Listing 7.6.

LISTING 7.6   The Reflection Shader with Multitexture Support

```
// Reflection Shader with multitexture
// Fragment Shader
// Richard S. Wright Jr.
// OpenGL SuperBible
#version 330

out vec4 vFragColor;

uniform samplerCube   cubeMap;
uniform sampler2D     tarnishMap;

smooth in vec3 vVaryingTexCoord;
smooth in vec2 vTarnishCoords;

void main(void)
    {
    vFragColor = texture(cubeMap, vVaryingTexCoord.stp);
    vFragColor *= texture(tarnishMap, vTarnishCoords);
    }
```

Note that we now have two samplers, `cubeMap`, which is of type `samplerCube`, and `tarnishMap`, which is of the type `sampler2D`. These two textures are sampled with their respective texture coordinates, and the resulting filtered color values are simply multiplied together, yielding the final fragment color.

Point Sprites

Point sprites are an exciting feature supported by OpenGL version 1.5 and later. Although OpenGL has always supported texture mapped points, prior to version 1.5 this meant a single texture coordinate applied to an entire point. Large textured points were simply large versions of a single filtered texel. With point sprites (which are now the default point rendering mode in OpenGL 3.0 and later), you can place a 2D textured image anywhere on-screen by drawing a single 3D point.

Probably the most common application of point sprites is for particle systems. A large number of particles moving on-screen can be represented as points to produce a number of visual effects. However, representing these points as small overlapped 2D images can produce dramatic streaming animated filaments. For example, Figure 7.7 shows a well-known screen saver on the Macintosh powered by just such a particle effect.

FIGURE 7.7   A particle effect in the flurry screen saver.

Before point sprites, achieving this type of effect was a matter of drawing a large number of textured quads (or triangle fans) on-screen. This could be accomplished either by performing a costly rotation to each individual face to make sure that it faced the camera, or by drawing all particles in a 2D orthographic projection. Point sprites allow you to render a perfectly aligned textured 2D square by sending down a single 3D vertex. At one-quarter the bandwidth of sending down four vertices for a quad and no client-side matrix monkey business to keep the 3D quad aligned with the camera, point sprites are a potent and efficient feature of OpenGL.

Texturing Points

Point sprites are easy to use. On the client side, the only thing you have to do is simply bind to a 2D texture (and don't forget to set the appropriate uniform for the texture unit!), as point sprites are now the default point rasterization mode, with the only exception being when point smoothing is enabled. You cannot use point sprites and antialiased points at the same time. In the fragment program, there is a built-in variable gl_PointCoord, which is a two-component vector that interpolates the texture coordinates across the point. Listing 7.7 shows the fragment shader for the PointSprites example program.

LISTING 7.7   Texturing a Point Sprite in the Fragment Shader

```
// SpaceFlight Shader
// Fragment Shader
// Richard S. Wright Jr.
// OpenGL SuperBible
#version 330

out vec4 vFragColor;

in vec4 vStarColor;

uniform sampler2D  starImage;

void main(void)
    {
    vFragColor = texture(starImage, gl_PointCoord) * vStarColor;
    }
```

So for a point sprite, you do not need to send down texture coordinates as an attribute. Since a point is a single vertex, you wouldn't have the ability to interpolate across the points surface any other way. Of course there is nothing preventing you from providing a texture coordinate anyway or deriving your own customized interpolation scheme.

Point Sizes

There are two ways to set a point size; the first is the glPointSize function.

```
void glPointSize(GLfloat size);
```

This function sets the diameter of the point in pixels for both aliased and antialiased points. This function and how to determine the available point size ranges was covered in Chapter 3, "Basic Rendering." You can also set the point size programmatically in the vertex shader. First you have to enable point size mode:

```
glEnable(GL_PROGRAM_POINT_SIZE);
```

Then in your vertex program, a built-in variable `gl_PointSize` can be set, which determines the final rasterized size of the point. A common use for this is to determine the size of a point based on its distance. When you use the `glPointSize` function to set the size of points, they are unaffected by the perspective divide, making all the points the same size no matter how far away they are.

The following formula is often used to implement distance-based point size attenuation:

$$size = \sqrt{\left(\frac{1}{a + b * d + c * d^2}\right)}$$

where d is the distance of the point from the eye and a, b, and c are configurable parameters of a quadratic equation. You can store those in uniforms and update them with your application, or if you have a particular set of parameters in mind, you might want to make them constants in your vertex shader. For example, if you want a constant size, set a to a nonzero value and b and c to zero. If a and c are zero and b is nonzero, then point size will fall off linearly with distance. Likewise, if a and b are zero but c is nonzero, then point size will fall off quadratically with distance.

Putting This All Together

Let's now take a look at an example program that makes use of the point sprite features discussed so far. The PointSprite example program creates an animated star field that appears as if you were flying forward through it. This is accomplished by placing random points out in front of your field of view and then passing a time value into the vertex shader as a uniform. This time value is used to move the point positions so that over time they move closer to you and then recycle when they get to the near clipping plane to the back of the frustum. In addition, we scale the size of the stars so that they start off very small but get larger as they get closer to your point of view. The result is a nice realistic effect...all we need is some planetarium or space movie music!

Figure 7.8 shows our star texture map that is applied to the points. It is simply a Targa file that we load in the same manner we loaded any other 2D texture so far. Points can also be mipmapped, and because they can range from very small to very large, it's probably a good idea to do so.

FIGURE 7.8   The star texture map. (Also shown in Color Plate 10.)

We are not going to cover all of the details of setting up the star field effect, as it's pretty routine and you can check the source yourself if you want to see how we pick random numbers. Of more importance is the actual rendering of code in the RenderScene function:

```
glClear(GL_COLOR_BUFFER_BIT);

// Turn on additive blending
glEnable(GL_BLEND);
glBlendFunc(GL_ONE, GL_ONE);

// Let the vertex program determine the point size
glEnable(GL_PROGRAM_POINT_SIZE);

// Bind to our shader, set uniforms
glUseProgram(starFieldShader);
glUniformMatrix4fv(locMVP, 1, GL_FALSE, viewFrustum.GetProjectionMatrix());
glUniform1i(locTexture, 0);

// fTime goes from 0.0 to 999.0 and recycles
float fTime = timer.GetElapsedSeconds() * 10.0f;
fTime = fmod(fTime, 999.0f);
glUniform1f(locTimeStamp, fTime);

// Draw the stars
starsBatch.Draw();
```

First you might notice we do not clear the depth buffer. That's because we are going to use additive blending to blend our stars with the background. Because the dark area of our texture is black (zero in color space), we can get away with just adding the colors together as we draw. Transparency with alpha would require that we depth sort our stars, and that is an expense we certainly can do without. After turning on point size program mode, we bind to our shader and set up the uniforms. Of interest here is that we have a timer, which drives what will end up being the z position of our stars that recycles so that it just counts 0 to 999. Listing 7.8 provides the source code to the vertex shader, which also has some interesting features.

LISTING 7.8   Vertex Shader for the Star Field Effect

```
// SpaceFlight Shader
// Vertex Shader
// Richard S. Wright Jr.
// OpenGL SuperBible
#version 330

// Incoming per vertex... position and normal
in vec4 vVertex;
in vec4 vColor;
```

```
uniform mat4    mvpMatrix;
uniform float   timeStamp;

out vec4 vStarColor;

void main(void)
    {
    vec4 vNewVertex = vVertex;
    vStarColor = vColor;

    // Offset by running time, makes it move closer
    vNewVertex.z += timeStamp;

    // If out of range, adjust
    if(vNewVertex.z > -1.0)
        vNewVertex.z -= 999.0;

    // Custom size adjustment
    gl_PointSize = 30.0 + (vNewVertex.z / sqrt(-vNewVertex.z));

    // If they are very small, fade them up
    if(gl_PointSize < 4.0)
        vStarColor = smoothstep(0.0, 4.0, gl_PointSize) * vStarColor;


    // Don't forget to transform the geometry!
    gl_Position = mvpMatrix * vNewVertex;
    }
```

The vertex z position is offset by the timestamp uniform. This is what causes the animation where the stars move closer to you. We need to check the position, and when they get to the near clipping plane, we simply recycle their position back to the far clipping plane. We used an inverse square root function to make the stars grow ever larger as they get nearer and set the final size in the gl_PointSize variable. If the star sizes are too small, you will get flickering sometimes, so we do one final check, and when a point size is less than 4.0, we dim the color progressively so that it fades into view instead of just popping up near the far clipping plane. The final output is shown in Figure 7.9.

FIGURE 7.9   Flying through space with point sprites. (Also shown in Color Plate 10.)

Point Parameters

A couple of features of point sprites (and points in general actually) can be fine-tuned with the function glPointParameter. Figure 7.10 shows the two possible locations of the origin (0,0) of the texture applied to a point sprite.

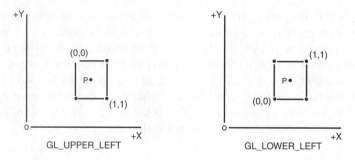

FIGURE 7.10   Two potential orientations of textures on a point sprite.

Setting the GL_POINT_SPRITE_COORD_ORIGIN parameter to GL_LOWER_LEFT places the origin of the texture coordinate system at the lower-left corner of the point:

```
glPointParameteri(GL_POINT_SPRITE_COORD_ORIGIN, GL_LOWER_LEFT);
```

The default orientation for point sprites is GL_UPPER_LEFT.

Other nontexture-related point parameters can also be used to set the alpha such that points can fade with alpha blending with distance from the eye point. See the glPointParameter function entry in Appendix C, "OpenGL Man Pages for (Core) OpenGL 3.3," for details of these other parameters.

Shaped Points

There is more you can do with point sprites besides apply a texture using gl_PointCoord for texture coordinates. Another built-in variable is gl_FragCoord. As is true when any other primitive is being rendered, gl_FragCoord contains the screen space coordinate of the current fragment. The x and y components of this coordinate, therefore, vary across the area of the point. However, the z and w components are constant because the point is rendered as a flat plane, parallel to the near and far planes.

You can use gl_PointCoord to implement a number of things other than just texture coordinates. For example, you can make nonsquare points by using the discard keyword in your fragment shader to throw away fragments that lie outside your desired point shape. The following fragment shader code produces round points:

```
vec2 p = gl_PointCoord * 2.0 - vec2(1.0);
if (dot(p, p) > 1.0)
    discard;
```

Or perhaps an interesting flower shape:

```
vec2 temp = gl_PointCoord * 2.0 - vec2(1.0);
if (dot(temp, temp) > sin(atan(temp.y, temp.x) * 5.0))
    discard;
```

These are simple code snippets that allow arbitrary shaped points to be rendered. Figure 7.11 shows a few more examples of interesting shapes that can be generated this way.

FIGURE 7.11   Interesting point shapes generated analytically from `gl_PointCoord`.

Rotating Points

Because points in OpenGL are rendered as axis-aligned squares, rotating the point sprite must be done by modifying the texture coordinates used to read the sprite's texture. To do this, simply create a 2D rotation matrix in the fragment shader and multiply it by `gl_PointCoord` to rotate it around the z-axis. The angle of rotation could be passed from the vertex or geometry shader to the fragment shader as an interpolated variable. The value of the variable can, in turn, be calculated in the vertex or geometry shader or can be supplied through a vertex attribute. Listing 7.9 shows a slightly more complex point sprite fragment shader that allows the point to be rotated around its center.

LISTING 7.9   Naïve Rotated Point Sprite Fragment Shader

```
#version 330

uniform sampler2D sprite_texture;
```

```
in float angle;

out vec4 color;

void main(void)
{
    const float sin_theta = sin(angle);
    const float cos_theta = cos(angle);
    const mat2 rotation_matrix = mat2(cos_theta, sin_theta,
                                      -sin_theta, cos_theta);
    const vec2 pt = gl_PointCoord - vec2(0.5);
    color = texture(sprite_texture, rotation_matrix * pt + vec2(0.5));
}
```

This example allows you to generate rotated point sprites. However, of course, the value of angle will not change from one fragment to another within the point sprite. That means that the rotation matrix will also be constant for every fragment in the point. It is therefore much more efficient to calculate the rotation matrix in the vertex shader and pass it as a mat2 varying to the fragment shader rather than calculating it at every fragment. Here's an updated vertex and fragment shader pair that allows you to draw rotated point sprites. First, the vertex shader is shown in Listing 7.10.

LISTING 7.10   Rotated Point Sprite Vertex Shader

```
#version 330

uniform matrix mvp;

in vec4 position;
in float angle;

out mat2 rotation_matrix;

void main(void)
{
    const float sin_theta = sin(angle);
    const float cos_theta = cos(angle);

    rotation_matrix = mat2(cos_theta, sin_theta,
                           -sin_theta, cos_theta);
    gl_Position = mvp * position;
}
```

And second, the fragment shader is shown in Listing 7.11.

LISTING 7.11   Rotated Point Sprite Fragment Shader

```
#version 330

uniform sampler2D sprite_texture;

in mat2 rotation_matrix;

out vec4 color;

void main(void)
{
    const vec2 pt = gl_PointCoord - vec2(0.5);
    color = texture(sprite_texture, rotation_matrix * pt + vec2(0.5));
}
```

As you can see, the potentially expensive sin and cos functions have been moved out of the fragment shader and into the vertex shader. If the point size is large, this pair of shaders performs much better than the earlier, brute force approach of calculating the rotation matrix in the fragment shader.

Texture Arrays

Previously in this chapter we discussed the fact that several textures could be accessed at once via the different texture units. This is extremely powerful and useful as your shader can have access to several texture objects at once. We can actually take this a bit further using a feature called texture arrays. With a texture array, you can load up several 2D images into a single texture object. The concept of having more than one image in a single texture is not new. This happens with mipmapping, as each mip level is a distinct image, and with cube mapping, where each face of the cube map has its own image and even its own set of mip levels. With texture arrays, however, you can have a whole array of texture images bound to a single texture object and then index through them in the shader, thus greatly increasing the amount of texture data available to your shaders.

Loading a 2D Texture Array

To demonstrate texture arrays, we revisit the Smoother sample program from Chapter 3. In this program we drew a stylized 2D mountain range with lines, stars of various sizes, and a white circle representing the moon. For the TextureArray sample program, we use our new point sprite capabilities to spruce up the stars a bit and display an animated series of moon images using a 2D texture array (there are actually 1D texture arrays too!). Twenty-nine separate images of the moon are provided, numbered moon00.tga through moon28.tga, which we load into a single texture object. We set a uniform that represents the time passed, and every second we switch to the next moon image in our array. Over 30 seconds, you see an animation showing the moon's monthly cycle.

Texture arrays add two new texture targets as valid parameters to most texture management functions, GL_TEXTURE_1D_ARRAY and GL_TEXTURE_2D_ARRAY. For our array of two-dimensional moon images, we create and bind to our texture object just like any other texture, except we change the target parameter.

```
GLuint moonTexture;
. . .
. . .
glGenTextures(1, &moonTexture);
glBindTexture(GL_TEXTURE_2D_ARRAY, moonTexture);
```

The same goes for setting the texture parameters, the wrap modes and filters.

```
glTexParameteri(GL_TEXTURE_2D_ARRAY, GL_TEXTURE_WRAP_S, GL_CLAMP_TO_EDGE);
glTexParameteri(GL_TEXTURE_2D_ARRAY, GL_TEXTURE_WRAP_T, GL_CLAMP_TO_EDGE);
glTexParameteri(GL_TEXTURE_2D_ARRAY, GL_TEXTURE_MIN_FILTER, GL_LINEAR);
glTexParameteri(GL_TEXTURE_2D_ARRAY, GL_TEXTURE_MAG_FILTER, GL_LINEAR);
```

So far just changing the texture target parameter is pretty intuitive. Actually loading the texture data now takes a bit of a leap; for 2D texture arrays, we use the glTexImage3D function.

```
void glTexImage3D(GLenum target, GLint level, GLint internalformat,
                  GLsizei width, GLsizei height, GLsizei depth, GLint border,
                  GLenum format, GLenum type, void *data);
```

For the target parameter, we again use GL_TEXTURE_2D_ARRAY, and the depth parameter represents the "slice" or array index of our 2D image. One of the nice things about using this function is you can load an entire array of 2D images all in one shot. One of the drawbacks about using this function is that it requires you to load an array of 2D images all in one shot—this is not always that convenient, especially if you have, say, 29 separate images of the moon to load.

There is a simple workaround for this, and it's a feature of all the glTexImageXD functions that we haven't mentioned yet. If you put NULL in for the last parameter (thus there is no texture data to copy), OpenGL reserves the texture memory for you but leaves it uninitialized. Then you can use the glTexSubImageXD family of functions to update the texture later (all of these functions were covered in Chapter 5). For our purposes, we need to reserve twenty-nine 64 x 64 RGBA images, so our code looks like this:

```
glTexImage3D(GL_TEXTURE_2D_ARRAY, 0, GL_RGBA, 64, 64, 29, 0,
                        GL_BGRA, GL_UNSIGNED_BYTE, NULL);
```

Then we need to load up our other images one at a time. We set up a loop that creates the filename for each file based on the loop index and use the `glTexSubImage3D` function to load the image one slice at a time.

```
for(int i = 0; i < 29; i++) {
    char cFile[32];
    sprintf(cFile, "moon%02d.tga", i);

    GLbyte *pBits;
    int nWidth, nHeight, nComponents;
    GLenum eFormat;

    // Read the texture bits
    pBits = gltReadTGABits(cFile, &nWidth, &nHeight, &nComponents, &eFormat);
    glTexSubImage3D(GL_TEXTURE_2D_ARRAY, 0, 0, 0, i, nWidth, nHeight,
                                         1, GL_BGRA, GL_UNSIGNED_BYTE, pBits);

    free(pBits);
    }
```

Indexing the Texture Array

Now our texture array is loaded and ready to use. We bind to this texture object before rendering the moon, and now we can access the entire array of moon images through a single sampler. Of course, we need a way of communicating with the shader as to which image to use. We set up a timer and cycle through as the seconds tick off. The following code sets the appropriate uniform in our vertex shader before rendering the moon (which is simply a triangle fan).

```
// fTime goes from 0.0 to 28.0 and recycles
float fTime = timer.GetElapsedSeconds();
fTime = fmod(fTime, 28.0f);
glUniform1f(locTimeStamp, fTime);


moonBatch.Draw();
```

In our vertex shader, we already have an attribute that receives the texture coordinates, and we copy just the s and t coordinates to the vec3 variable vMoonCoords. The p texture coordinate comes from the uniform that contains the time that has passed (don't forget, we cycle this from 0 to 28 in actuality). This third texture coordinate dimension value comes into play in the fragment shader. The vertex shader is shown in Listing 7.12.

LISTING 7.12   Vertex Shader for the TextureArray Sample

```
// MoonShader
// Vertex Shader
// Richard S. Wright Jr.
// OpenGL SuperBible
#version 330
in vec4 vTexCoords;

uniform mat4 mvpMatrix;
uniform float fTime;

smooth out vec3 vMoonCoords;

void main(void)
    {
    vMoonCoords.st = vTexCoords.st;
    vMoonCoords.p = fTime;

    gl_Position = mvpMatrix * vVertex;
    }
```

Accessing Texture Arrays

In the fragment shader (shown in Listing 7.13) we have a new type of sampler for a 2D texture array, `sampler2DArray`. To sample this texture we use the function `texture2DArray`, and we pass in a three-component texture coordinate. The first two components of this texture coordinate, the s and t (see the variable `vMoonCoords`), are used as typical two-dimensional texture coordinates. The third component, the p element, is actually an integer index into the texture array. Recall we set this in the vertex program, and it is going to vary from 0 to 28, one integer value every second. The result is an animated image, changing its picture once per second.

LISTING 7.13   The Fragment Shader for the TextureArray Sample

```
// MoonShader
// Fragment Shader
// Richard S. Wright Jr.
// OpenGL SuperBible
#version 330

out vec4 vFragColor;
```

```
uniform sampler2DArray moonImage;

smooth in vec3 vMoonCoords;

void main(void)
    {
    vFragColor = texture2DArray(moonImage, vMoonCoords.stp);
    }
```

The final output of the TextureArray sample program is shown in Figure 7.12.

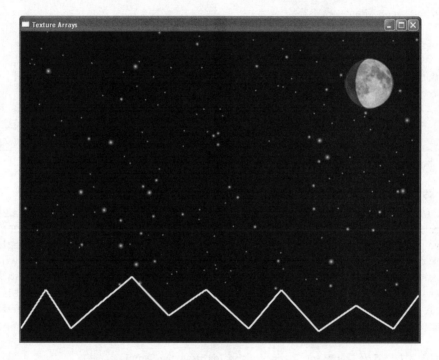

FIGURE 7.12 An animated moon image using texture arrays.

Texture Proxies

Texture memory is an important and limited resource that developers need to pay close attention to. Texture data comes in many different sizes and data types, and at times it's useful to be able to find out more about how textures are managed and stored by a specific implementation, much less if you can even load a particular texture. Often we simply load moderately sized textures, and if they show up on our screen during development, then there is a high degree of confidence that they will also show up on your end user's screen. This is a bit like Russian roulette and a terrible programming practice for high quality commercial software. One of the simplest tests you can do is find out the maximum texture size the current implementation can support.

```
GLint maxSize;
glGetIntegerv(GL_MAX_TEXTURE_SIZE , &maxSize);
```

This gives you the lower bound on the largest width or height for a one- or two-dimensional texture map (you can also use GL_MAX_3D_TEXTURE_SIZE and GL_MAX_CUBE_MAP_TEXTURE_SIZE for those corresponding texture types). If maxSize comes back as 2048, then a 2048 x 2048 2D texture should work. However, a 2048 x 4096 texture size could also be supported, and the 2048 value merely indicates that 4096 x 4096 is not.

To find out whether a particular texture size and format are supported, we use a *texture proxy*. A texture proxy is a "fake" or stand-in texture that takes up no memory (and don't even think about trying to apply it to any geometry!), but otherwise acts like a valid attempt to load a texture. To create a texture proxy, we use the by now familiar glTexImage2D function.

```
glTexImage2D(GL_PROXY_TEXTURE_2D, level, internalFormat,
                       width, height, border, format, type, NULL);
```

Texture proxies also work on the other texture targets GL_PROXY_TEXTURE_1D, GL_PROXY_TEXTURE_3D, and GL_PROXY_TEXTURE_CUBE_MAP. Note that we passed in NULL for the last parameter, which is typically used as the pointer to the texture data. Again, texture proxies do not actually create a real texture. Once you've created the texture proxy, you can query all of the texture values with glGetTexLevelParameter. If OpenGL reformatted the data internally, you can query the GL_TEXTURE_INTERNAL_FORMAT value for example and see what the actual value would be. If the texture could not be loaded at all, the queries from this function come back as zero. For example, to see if a 2048 x 4096 BGRA texture would indeed load, you'd create the proxy like this:

```
glTexImage2D(GL_PROXY_TEXTURE_2D, 0, GL_RGBA, 2048, 4096,
                       0, GL_BGRA, GL_UNSIGNED_BYTE, NULL);
```

Then check to see if the corresponding height of 4096 was supported:

```
void glGetTexLevelParameter(GL_PROXY_TEXTURE_2D, 0,
                       GL_TEXTURE_HEIGHT, &height);
```

You can query all sorts of things about the currently loaded texture, be it a real texture or a texture proxy. The complete list for this function is provided in Appendix C.

Summary

In this chapter, we continued our exploration of OpenGL texture technologies by introducing two new types of texture targets, rectangle textures and cube maps. Rectangle textures are convenient and efficient, especially when you have imaging needs and are not specifically texturing 3D models. Cube maps are a powerful means of creating three-dimensional light maps or image-based reflections. Next we covered multitexture, a bedrock technology for a great many special effects and techniques.

You saw how to apply a texture across the surface of a point and how useful this is for creating dramatic particle systems. You also learned how to load a larger number of textures into a single texture object with a texture array. Finally, we talked about texture proxies and how you can easily query the OpenGL implementation about the internal representation of texture data or even if a texture can be stored internally at all. Texture mapping is a large topic within OpenGL, and at this point you should have a good grasp of the basic principles upon which the even more advanced techniques are based.

PART II

Intermediate to Advanced Ideas

It's time to go a bit deeper. If you've been reading this book in order, you've been getting not only an introduction to OpenGL, but also an introduction to basic 3D graphics programming principles. In fact, Part I, "Basic Concepts," is pretty much everything you *need* to know about how to create real-time interactive 3D graphics. Coordinate systems, vertex transformations, primitive assembly, texture mapping, basic shader operation and programming—these are the bedrock of 3D graphics effects in games, simulation, visualization, and a myriad of consumer and commercial applications.

In this part of the book, we begin to tackle some of the more advanced features of the OpenGL API. Beyond the basics, it's time to discover how much more flexible and powerful OpenGL can be when applied to more complex rendering problems. Not everything to come is concerned with simple rendering effects, however; a number of OpenGL features are specifically geared toward performance. While the API and manner have changed, the principles of Part I have been the same for decades. In this part of the book, we really begin to explore where the state of the art and future of graphics hardware is taking us.

Enjoy the ride!

CHAPTER 8

Buffer Objects: Storage Is Now in Your Hands

by Nicholas Haemel

WHAT YOU'LL LEARN IN THIS CHAPTER:

How To	Functions You'll Use
Create and use buffer objects	glGenBuffers/glBindBuffer/glBufferData
Create, bind, and use framebuffer objects	glGenFramebuffers/glBindFramebuffer
Create, bind, and use renderbuffer objects	glGenRenderbuffers/glBindRenderbuffer
Use texture buffer objects	glTexBuffer
Allocate storage for renderbuffers and attach	glRenderbufferStorage/
to framebuffers	glFramebufferRenderbuffer
Attach textures to framebuffer objects	glFramebufferTexture2D
Set up multiple color outputs	glDrawBuffers

Up until this point you have had a chance to learn about the basics of OpenGL, how to specify geometry, what shaders are, how to use textures, and so on. Now it's time to blow the lid off of your applications and introduce faster and more flexible ways of rendering and moving data around. You also learn about off-screen rendering and how to create and control your own framebuffer.

Buffer objects are a powerful concept that allows your applications to quickly and easily move data from one part of the rendering pipeline to another, from one object binding to another. Your data has finally been freed from strongly typed objects! Not only can you move data around as you see fit, but you can do so without the involvement of the CPU.

Framebuffer objects give you true control over your pixels. You no longer are relegated to the limitations of the OS window your context is tied to. In fact, you can now render off-screen to nearly as many buffers as you'd like. Not only that, but you can use whatever size and format surfaces that best fit your needs. Now your fragment shaders have ultimate control over which pixels go where.

Buffers

Instead of creating a hundred different objects of varying types and making developers keep track of which is which, OpenGL 3.2 generalizes the use of most objects that hold data. Now you can allocate as many buffers as you need and then decide how you want to use them later. Buffers have many different uses. They can hold vertex data, pixel data, texture data, inputs for shader execution, or the output of different shader stages.

Buffers are stored in GPU memory, which provides very fast and efficient access. Before OpenGL had buffer objects, applications had limited options for storing data on the GPU. Additionally, updates to data on the GPU often required reloading the whole object. Moving data back and forth between system memory and GPU memory can be a slow process.

First let's look at the basics of dealing with buffer objects. Later, we cover more advanced ways of accessing your data in buffer objects and how to use them for different purposes.

Creating Your Very Own Buffers

Creating a new buffer is simple. Just call `glGenBuffers` to create names for as many new buffers as you need. The actual buffer object will be created at first use.

```
Gluint    pixBuffObjs[1];
glGenBuffers(1, pixBuffObjs);
```

Once you have the name of your new buffer, you can bind that name to use the buffer. There are many different binding points in OpenGL. Each binding point allows you to use a buffer for a different purpose. You can think of each attachment or binding point as a slot where only one object can be attached at a time. These binding points are listed in Table 8.1. We explore how to use each of these bindings in more detail later on.

TABLE 8.1   Buffer Object Binding Points

Target Name	Description
GL_ARRAY_BUFFER	Array buffers store vertex attributes such as color, position, texture coordinates, or other custom attributes.
GL_COPY_READ_BUFFER	Buffer used as the data source for copies with glCopyBufferSubData.
GL_COPY_WRITE_BUFFER	Buffer used as the target for copies with glCopyBufferSubData.
GL_ELEMENT_ARRAY_BUFFER	Index array buffer used for sourcing indices for glDrawElements, glDrawRangeElements, and glDrawElementsInstanced.
GL_PIXEL_PACK_BUFFER	Target buffer for pixel pack operations such as glReadPixels.
GL_PIXEL_UNPACK_BUFFER	Source buffer for texture update functions such as glTexImage1D, glTexImage2D, glTexImage3D, glTexSubImage1D, glTexSubImage2D, and glTexSubImage3D.

Target Name	Description
GL_TEXTURE_BUFFER	Buffer accessible to shaders through texel fetches.
GL_TRANSFORM_FEEDBACK_BUFFER	Buffer written to by a transform feedback vertex shader.
GL_UNIFORM_BUFFER	Uniform values accessible to shaders.

To bind a buffer for use, you can call glBindBuffer with a target from Table 8.1 and the name of the buffer. Next we bind our new buffer to the pixel pack buffer attachment point so that we can use glReadPixels to copy pixel data into the buffer.

```
glBindBuffer(GL_PIXEL_PACK_BUFFER, pixBuffObjs[0]);
```

To unbind a buffer from an attachment, call glBindBuffer again with the same target and use "0" for the buffer name. You can also just bind another valid buffer to the same target. When you are finished with a buffer, it needs to be cleaned up, just as all other OpenGL objects should be. Delete it by calling glDeleteBuffers. As a general practice, make sure the buffer is not bound to any of the binding points before deleting.

```
glDeleteBuffers(1, pixBuffObjs);
```

Filling Buffers

Creating and deleting buffers is one thing. But how do you get valid data into a buffer to use it? There are many ways to fill a buffer with data; some of the more complex ones are covered in following chapters. To simply upload your data straight into a buffer of any type you can use the glBufferData function.

```
glBindBuffer(GL_PIXEL_PACK_BUFFER, pixBuffObjs[0]);
glBufferData(GL_PIXEL_PACK_BUFFER, pixelDataSize, pixelData, GL_DYNAMIC_COPY);
glBindBuffer(GL_PIXEL_PACK_BUFFER, 0);
```

The buffer you want to use must be bound before calling glBufferData. Use the same target for glBufferData as you used to bind the buffer for the first parameter. The second parameter is the size of the data you are going to upload in bytes, and the third parameter is the data to be uploaded. Note that this pointer can also be NULL if you want to allocate a buffer of a specific size but do not need to fill it right away. The fourth parameter of glBufferData is where you tell OpenGL how you intend to use the buffer.

Picking the right value for usage is a little trickier. The possible usage options are listed in Table 8.2. The value of usage is really just a performance hint to help the OpenGL driver allocate memory in the correct location. For instance, some memory may be easily accessible by the CPU and would be a good choice if your application needs to read from it frequently. Other memory might be inaccessible for direct access by the CPU but can be accessed quickly by the GPU. By telling the OpenGL driver what your plan is ahead of time, your buffer can be allocated in a spot where it can serve you best.

8

TABLE 8.2   Buffer Object Usage Models

Buffer Usage	Description
GL_STREAM_DRAW	Buffer contents will be set once by the application and used infrequently for drawing.
GL_STREAM_READ	Buffer contents will be set once as output from an OpenGL command and used infrequently for drawing.
GL_STREAM_COPY	Buffer contents will be set once as output from an OpenGL command and used infrequently for drawing or copying to other images.
GL_STATIC_DRAW	Buffer contents will be set once by the application and used frequently for drawing or copying to other images.
GL_STATIC_READ	Buffer contents will be set once as output from an OpenGL command and queried many times by the application.
GL_STATIC_COPY	Buffer contents will be set once as output from an OpenGL command and used frequently for drawing or copying to other images.
GL_DYNAMIC_DRAW	Buffer contents will be updated frequently by the application and used frequently for drawing or copying to other images.
GL_DYNAMIC_READ	Buffer contents will be updated frequently as output from OpenGL commands and queried many times by the application.
GL_DYNAMIC_COPY	Buffer contents will be updated frequently as output from OpenGL commands and used frequently for drawing or copying to other images.

Using GL_DYNAMIC_DRAW is a safe value for general buffer usage or situations where you aren't sure what the buffer will be used for. You can always call glBufferData again, refilling the buffer and possibly changing the usage hint. But if you do call glBufferData again, any data originally in the buffer will be deleted. You can use glBufferSubData to update a part of a preexisting buffer without invalidating the contents of the rest of the buffer.

```
void glBufferSubData(GLenum target, intptr offset, sizeiptr size, const void *data);
```

Most of the parameters for glBufferSubData are the same as those for glBufferData. The new offset parameter allows you to start updating the buffer at a location other than the beginning. You also cannot change the usage of the buffer because memory has already been allocated.

Pixel Buffer Objects

Many of the newest and most important advances in graphics involve new ways of doing some of the same old operations but in much faster and more efficient ways. Pixel buffer objects are similar to texture buffer objects in that they hold pixel/texel data. Just like all buffer objects they live in GPU memory. You can access and fill pixel buffer objects, or PBOs, in the same ways you would for any other buffer object type. In fact, the only time a buffer object is really a PBO is when it is attached to a PBO buffer attachment.

The first PBO attachment point is `GL_PIXEL_PACK_BUFFER`. When a PBO is attached to this target, any OpenGL operations that read pixels get their data from the PBO. These operations include `glReadPixels`, `glGetTexImage`, and `glGetCompressedTexImage`. Normally these operations pull data out of a framebuffer or texture and read it back into client memory. When a PBO is attached to the pack buffer, pixel data ends up in the PBO in GPU memory instead of downloaded to the client.

The second PBO attachment point is `GL_PIXEL_UNPACK_BUFFER`. When a PBO is attached to this target, any OpenGL operations that draw pixels put their data into an attached PBO. Some of these operations are `glTexImage*D`, `glTexSubImage*D`, `glCompressedTexImage*D`, and `glCompressedTexSubImage*D`. These operations put data into framebuffers and textures from local CPU memory. But having a PBO bound as the unpack buffer directs the read operations to be the PBO in GPU memory instead of memory on the CPU.

Why bother with these pixel buffer objects anyway? After all, you can get pixels to, from, and around the GPU without them. For starters, any calls that read from or write to PBOs or any buffer object are pipelined. That means the GPU doesn't have to finish doing everything else, initiate the data copy, wait for the copy to complete, and then continue. Because buffer objects don't have the same ordering issues, they can provide a huge advantage when dealing with apps that have to frequently get to, modify, or update pixel data. Some examples are

- Stream texture updates—In some cases, your application might need to update a texture on every frame. Maybe you need to change it based on user input, or maybe you want to stream video. PBOs allow your application to make changes to texture data without necessarily having to download and then re-upload the whole surface.

- Rendering vertex data—Because buffer objects are generic data storage, an application can easily use the same buffer for very different purposes. For instance, an application can write vertex data out to a color buffer and then copy that data into a PBO. Once complete, the buffer can be attached as a vertex buffer and used to draw new geometry. This just shows how flexible OpenGL is; it allows you to "color" new vertex data!

- Asynchronous calls to `glReadPixels`—Often applications want to grab pixels off the screen, perform some manipulation, and then either save them or use them for drawing again. Unfortunately, reading pixel data into CPU memory requires the GPU to wrap up everything else it's doing and then perform the copy before any other work can begin or before the actual call can return. What if future draw calls are dependent on the result of the read or of multiple reads? Using `glReadPixels` can throw a real wrench into the works when trying to keep the GPU busy drawing all of your 3D graphics! PBOs come to the rescue. Because the read operation is pipelined, the call to `glReadPixels` can return immediately. You can even call multiple times with different buffer targets to read different areas.

Pixel buffer objects are a great container for temporarily storing pixel data locally on the GPU, but remember they need to have storage allocated before they can be used. Just like all other buffer objects, calling `glBufferData` allocates storage for a buffer and fills it with your data. But you don't necessarily have to provide data; passing in NULL for the data pointer simply allocates the memory without filling it. If you don't allocate storage for a buffer before trying to fill it, OpenGL throws an error.

```
glBufferData(GL_PIXEL_PACK_BUFFER, pixelDataSize, pixelData, GL_DYNAMIC_COPY);
```

Pixel buffers are often used to hold 2D images coming from a render target, texture, or other source. But buffer objects are one-dimensional by nature; they don't have an intrinsic width or height. When allocating storage space for 2D images, you can just multiply the width by the height by the size of a pixel. There is no additional padding necessary for storing the pixel data, but your buffer can be larger than necessary for a given set of data. In fact, if you plan to use the same PBO for multiple data sizes, you are much better off sizing the PBO for the largest data set right away than resizing it frequently.

All calls to `glBufferData` are pipelined with the rest of your draw calls. That means the OpenGL implementation won't have to wait for all activities to stop before sending the new data to the GPU. There are some times when this can be particularly important. Think about all those times you have to wait a few minutes for your favorite games as a new level loads. Part of that is uploading a whole bunch of new texture data. Or the small hiccups as you enter a new room and texture data is updated. PBOs can help solve some of these problems by providing the texture data when necessary and in a way that doesn't stall all other work.

Reading Pixel Data out of a Buffer

Once your drawing has reached the screen, you may need to get those pixels back again before they're gone forever. One reason might be to check on what was actually rendered to help decide what needs to be rendered in future scenes. Another is to use pixels from previous frames in effects applied to future frames. Whatever the reason, the `glReadPixels` function is there to help. This function takes pixels from the specified location of the currently enabled read buffer and copies them into local CPU memory.

```
void* data = (void*)malloc(pixelDataSize);
glReadBuffer(GL_BACK_LEFT);
glReadPixels(0, 0, GetWidth(), GetHeight(), GL_RGB, GL_UNSIGNED_BYTE, pixelData);
```

When you execute a read of pixel data into client memory, the entire pipeline often has to be emptied to ensure all drawing that would affect the pixels you are about to read has completed. This can have a major impact on your application's performance. But the good news is we can use buffer objects to overcome this performance issue. You can bind a buffer object to the GL_PIXEL_PACK_BUFFER before you call `glReadPixels` and set the data pointer in the `glReadPixels` call to null. This redirects the pixels into a buffer located on the GPU and avoids the performance issues that copying to client memory can cause.

```
glReadBuffer(GL_BACK_LEFT);
glBindBuffer(GL_PIXEL_PACK_BUFFER, pixBuffObjs[0]);
glReadPixels(0, 0, GetWidth(), GetHeight(), GL_RGB, GL_UNSIGNED_BYTE, NULL);
```

We use both of these approaches in our first sample application, pix_bufs.

Using PBOs

Incorporating PBOs into your application can be simple but can have huge positive performance impacts. The first sample program for this chapter does a few things, but most importantly it demonstrates how effective PBOs really are.

Motion blur is an effect that helps to signal which objects in a scene are moving and how fast they are going. You've probably seen these blurring effects in movies, television, or video. When an object moves past the camera at a rate too fast for the shutter speed of a single frame, the image is smeared across pixels of that frame and neighboring frames in the direction of motion. The same effect occurs when the camera is moving quickly relative to an object or the entire scene. Think about taking a picture sideways out a car window as a passenger while driving on the highway.

There are many complex ways to create such an effect in OpenGL. An application can render multiple times to a buffer, slightly offsetting the fast moving objects and blending the results together. Another option is to sample texel data for an object image multiple times in the direction of movement and then blend the sample results together. There are even more involved methods that use depth buffer data to apply a more dramatic blur to objects closer to the camera.

For the pix_buffs sample application we use another simple approach that stores the results of previous frames and blends them together with the current frame. To make a visible motion blur, the program stores the last five frames. The program can use both the old-fashioned way of copying data to the CPU and back as well as the faster PBO path. First, in Listing 8.1 we initialize the textures and the PBOs necessary.

LISTING 8.1 Set Up PBO and Textures for pix_buffs Sample Program

```
// Create blur textures
glGenTextures(6, blurTextures);

// Allocate a pixel buffer to initialize textures and PBOs
pixelDataSize = GetWidth()*GetHeight()*3*sizeof(unsigned byte);
void* data = (void*)malloc(pixelDataSize);
memset(data, 0x00, pixelDataSize);

// Setup 6 texture units for blur effect
// Initialize texture data
for (int i=0; i<6;i++)
```

```
{
    glActiveTexture(GL_TEXTURE1+i);
    glBindTexture(GL_TEXTURE_2D, blurTextures[i]);
    glTexParameteri(GL_TEXTURE_2D, GL_TEXTURE_WRAP_S, GL_CLAMP_TO_EDGE);
    glTexParameteri(GL_TEXTURE_2D, GL_TEXTURE_WRAP_T, GL_CLAMP_TO_EDGE);
    glTexParameteri(GL_TEXTURE_2D, GL_TEXTURE_MIN_FILTER, GL_LINEAR);
    glTexParameteri(GL_TEXTURE_2D, GL_TEXTURE_MAG_FILTER, GL_LINEAR);
    glTexImage2D(GL_TEXTURE_2D, 0, GL_RGB, GetWidth(), GetHeight(), 0, GL_RGB,
                        GL_UNSIGNED_BYTE, data);
}

// Allocate space for copying pixels so we don't call malloc on every draw
glGenBuffers(1, pixBuffObjs);
glBindBuffer(GL_PIXEL_PACK_BUFFER, pixBuffObjs[0]);
glBufferData(GL_PIXEL_PACK_BUFFER, pixelDataSize, pixelData, GL_DYNAMIC_COPY);
glBindBuffer(GL_PIXEL_PACK_BUFFER, 0);
```

When all resources are set up, the scene is rendered into the back buffer as if nothing special was going on. Instead of just calling swap, the result is copied into a texture to be used for the blur effect. For the traditional path, this happens by calling glReadPixels to get the pixel data and then glTexImage2D to move the pixel data into a texture object. The texture target for the data rotates between each of the six blur textures. If texture 3 was used last time, texture 4 will be used next. That means texture 4 will contain data from this frame, texture 3 from the last, texture 2 from two frames ago, and so on. The target for the current frame wraps around again after the last texture has been used. The pixel data for the last six frames is always ordered and available in this "texture ring buffer."

The PBO path is slightly different. Instead of copying the data back to the CPU, the PBO is bound to the GL_PIXEL_PACK_BUFFER, and when we call glReadPixels, the pixels are redirected to the PBO instead of back to the CPU. Then that same buffer is unbound from the GL_PIXEL_PACK_BUFFER attachment and bound to the GL_PIXEL_UNPACK_BUFFER. When glTexImage2D is called next, the pixel data in the buffer is loaded into the texture, all without ever leaving the GPU and remaining pipelined with other OpenGL commands. You can see this process in Listing 8.2. Finally, the ring buffer is updated to point to the next blur texture. You can press the P button while running the program to switch between the two paths.

LISTING 8.2   After Scene Is Rendered, Copy the Result to the Most Recent Texture Object

```
if(bUsePBOPath)
{
    // First bind the PBO as the pack buffer,
    // then read the pixels directly to the PBO
```

```
        glBindBuffer(GL_PIXEL_PACK_BUFFER, pixBuffObjs[0]);
        glReadPixels(0, 0, GetWidth(), GetHeight(), GL_RGB,
                    GL_UNSIGNED_BYTE, NULL);
        glBindBuffer(GL_PIXEL_PACK_BUFFER, 0);

        // Next bind the PBO as the unpack buffer,
        // then push the pixels straight into the texture
        glBindBuffer(GL_PIXEL_UNPACK_BUFFER, pixBuffObjs[0]);

        // Setup texture unit for new blur, this gets imcremented every frame
        glActiveTexture(GL_TEXTURE0+GetBlurTarget0() );
        glTexImage2D(GL_TEXTURE_2D, 0, GL_RGB8, GetWidth(), GetHeight(),
                    0, GL_RGB, GL_UNSIGNED_BYTE, NULL);
        glBindBuffer(GL_PIXEL_UNPACK_BUFFER, 0);
}
else
{
        // Grab the screen pixels and copy into client memory
        glReadPixels(0, 0, GetWidth(), GetHeight(), GL_RGB,
                    GL_UNSIGNED_BYTE, pixelData);

        // Push pixels from client memory into texture
        // Setup texture unit for new blur, this gets incremented every frame
        glActiveTexture(GL_TEXTURE0+GetBlurTarget0() );
        glTexImage2D(GL_TEXTURE_2D, 0, GL_RGB8, GetWidth(), GetHeight(),
                    0, GL_RGB, GL_UNSIGNED_BYTE, pixelData);
}

// Draw full screen quad with blur shader and all blur textures
projectionMatrix.PushMatrix();
    projectionMatrix.LoadIdentity();
    projectionMatrix.LoadMatrix(orthoMatrix);
    modelViewMatrix.PushMatrix();
        modelViewMatrix.LoadIdentity();
        glDisable(GL_DEPTH_TEST);
        SetupBlurProg(); // Program that blurs all textures together
        screenQuad.Draw();
        glEnable(GL_DEPTH_TEST);
    modelViewMatrix.PopMatrix();
projectionMatrix.PopMatrix();

// Move to the next blur texture for the next frame
AdvanceBlurTaget();
```

To do the actual blur, the fragment shader samples from all six textures and averages the results. The fragment shader only needs one set of texture coordinates given that all textures are the same size and need to align with the other textures. Listing 8.3 shows the shader code for performing all six texture samples. This shader is used to shade the screen aligned quad setup by building an orthographic modelview projection matrix based on the window width and height. The orthographic matrix creates a transform that maps coordinates directly to screen space. For every unit you increase the x coordinate of geometry, you move one more pixel to the right on the screen. Going up one unit in the y direction equates to one pixel higher on the screen. The result is 2D rendering where the coordinates of the geometry are also the pixel locations on the screen.

LISTING 8.3   Fragment Shader—blur.fs

```
// blur.fs
// outputs weighted, blended result of four textures
//
#version 150
in vec2 vTexCoord;

uniform sampler2D textureUnit0;
uniform sampler2D textureUnit1;
uniform sampler2D textureUnit2;
uniform sampler2D textureUnit3;
uniform sampler2D textureUnit4;
uniform sampler2D textureUnit5;

void main(void)
{
    // 0 is the newest image and 5 is the oldest
    vec4 blur0 = texture(textureUnit0, vTexCoord);
    vec4 blur1 = texture(textureUnit1, vTexCoord);
    vec4 blur2 = texture(textureUnit2, vTexCoord);
    vec4 blur3 = texture(textureUnit3, vTexCoord);
    vec4 blur4 = texture(textureUnit4, vTexCoord);
    vec4 blur5 = texture(textureUnit5, vTexCoord);

    vec4 summedBlur = blur0 + blur1 + blur2 +blur3 + blur4 + blur5;
    gl_FragColor = summedBlur/6.0;
}
```

When you first start pix_buffs, the program will be using the client-side memory path to load the blur textures. As the object moves from side-to-side, notice how the blur occurs only on the axis of movement. You can see the effect in Figure 8.1, also shown in Color

Plate 11. Pressing P switches the PBO path on and off. The + and - keys on the number pad speed up and slow down the movement of the object. As the speed changes, notice how the amount of motion blur also changes.

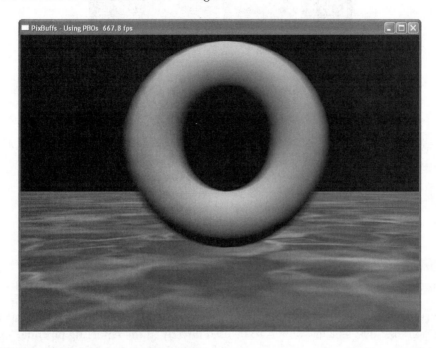

FIGURE 8.1   Motion blur of moving object.

The speed of the program is printed in the title bar. Notice the difference in performance between the client copy and PBO copy speeds—it's *huge*! On slower systems the PBO path is almost six times faster than the client memory path. How would you like your programs to run six times faster? Paying attention to how you move your data around can help do exactly that. These huge performance gains are one reason why buffer objects are now an important part of OpenGL programs.

When you switch to the PBO path, the amount of blur is reduced. That happens because the sample program uses the last five frames to create the blended output no matter how fast the program is running. When using PBOs, the last five frames are visually much closer together (because the faster rendering permits a higher frame rate), creating less blur. Take a look at Figure 8.2. You can try to change the program to create more blur for the PBO path or change the program so the blur is the same regardless of the path chosen. Another good exercise is to try different methods of applying motion blur or use weightings when combining the frame textures.

8

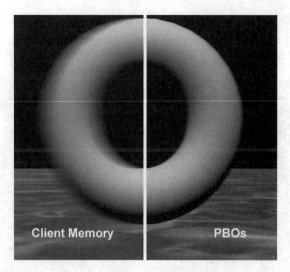

FIGURE 8.2   Blur differences between GPU and client copies.

Texture Buffer Objects

You have seen how some buffer binding targets such as GL_PIXEL_PACK_BUFFER and GL_COPY_READ_BUFFER are used for updating and fetching data from a buffer while it is on the GPU. Other buffer bindings like GL_TEXTURE_BUFFER, GL_TRANSFORM_FEEDBACK_BUFFER, and GL_UNIFORM_BUFFER allow buffers to be used directly in the rendering pipeline. Some of these binding points are explored in the following chapters, but now it's time to see how buffer objects can be used directly with textures.

A texture consists of two main components: texture sampling state and a data buffer containing the texture values. Now you can attach a buffer object to the GL_TEXTURE_BUFFER buffer binding point of a texture as well. You may ask, "Why bother with another texture binding?" That's a fair question! Texture buffers, also known as texBOs or TBOs, allow you to do several things that traditional textures do not. First, texture buffers can be filled directly with data from other rendering results such as transform feedback, pixels read operations, or vertex data. This saves quite a bit of time since your application can turn right around and fetch pixel data from a previous render call directly in a shader.

Another feature of texBOs is relaxed size restrictions. Texture buffers are similar to a traditional one-dimensional texture but can be much larger. The maximum size prescribed by the OpenGL specification for texture buffers is 64 times larger than 1D textures, but on some implementations the size of texture buffers can be tens of thousands of times larger!

So what can you do with these texBOs? Well, for starters all sorts of shader math that was previously difficult if not impossible. TexBOs provide shaders with access to large amounts of data in many different formats and types, allowing shaders to operate on data in ways usually reserved for CPUs. Texture buffers can be used to provide access to vertex arrays in both fragment and vertex shaders. This can be useful when shaders need information about neighboring geometry to make runtime decisions and calculations. But to do this, you often need to also pass the size of your texBO into the shader as a uniform.

Texture buffers are born as normal buffers and become true texture buffers when bound to a texture or to the GL_TEXTURE_BUFFER binding point.

```
glBindBuffer(GL_TEXTURE_BUFFER, texBO[0]);
glBufferData(GL_TEXTURE_BUFFER, sizeof(float)*count, fileData,
            GL_STATIC_DRAW);
```

But texBOs must be bound to a texture unit before they can be truly useful. To bind a texBO to a texture, call glTexBuffer but first make sure the texture you want to use is bound:

```
glActiveTexture(GL_TEXTURE1);
glBindTexture(GL_TEXTURE_BUFFER, texBOTexture);
glTexBuffer(GL_TEXTURE_BUFFER, GL_R32F, texBO[0]);
```

Although texture buffer objects look and operate much like normal textures, there are some important differences. Texture buffers cannot be accessed by normal samplers in shaders—i.e., sampler1D and sampler2D. Instead, you must use a new sampler called samplerBuffer. Because the sampler type is different, the sample function used to get a value from the texture buffer is also different. You can use texelFetch to read from a texture buffer.

```
uniform samplerBuffer lumCurveSampler;
void main(void) {
    . . .
    int offset = int(vColor.r * (1024-1));
    lumFactor.r = texelFetch(lumCurveSampler, offset ).r;
}
```

When your shader looks up values in a texture buffer, it must use a nonnormalized integer-based index. Traditional sample functions like texture accept coordinates from 0.0 to 1.0. But the texBO lookup function, texelFetch, takes an integer index from 0 to the size of the buffer. If your texture lookup coordinates are already normalized, you can convert to an index by multiplying by the size of the texBO minus one and casting the result to an integer.

Framebuffer Objects, Going Beyond the Window

When most people think of 3D rendering, the first thing that comes to mind is the screen output of a 3D game or a computer aided design program. After all, seeing interactive 3D output is what most users are looking for. But OpenGL allows you to do so much more than simply render to a window or to the full screen. The surface of an OpenGL window has long been referred to as "the framebuffer." But now OpenGL encapsulates the state required for drawing to a framebuffer into an object called a framebuffer object.

The default framebuffer object is the one associated with the OpenGL window you created and is bound automatically when a new context is bound. You can create multiple framebuffer objects, also called FBOs, and render directly an FBO instead of the window. Using this method of off-screen rendering allows your application to perform many different sorts of rendering algorithms like shadow mapping, applying radiosity, reflections, post processing, and many other effects. In addition, FBOs are not limited to the size of the window and can contain multiple color buffers. You can even attach texture to an FBO, which means you can directly render into a texture.

Even though framebuffers have the word "buffer" in them, they really are not buffers at all. In fact, there is no real memory storage associated with a framebuffer object. Instead, framebuffer objects are containers that can hold other objects that do have memory storage and can be rendered to, such as textures or renderbuffers. In this way, framebuffer objects tie together the state and surfaces needed to hold the rendering output of the OpenGL pipeline.

How to Use FBOs

Creating and setting up a new FBO is pretty straightforward, but remember that an FBO is just a container for image objects. So before we can render to an FBO, we have to add images. Once an FBO has been created, set up, and bound, most OpenGL operations act the same as if you were rendering to a window, but the output is stored in the images attached to the FBO.

Creating New FBOs

To create FBOs, first generate FBO buffer names. You can generate any number of names all at the same time:

```
GLuint fboName;
glGenFramebuffers(1, &fboName);
```

Then bind a new FBO to modify and use it:

```
glBindFramebuffer(GL_DRAW_FRAMEBUFFER, fboName);
```

Only one FBO can be bound for drawing, and only one FBO can be bound for reading at a time. When binding a framebuffer, the first parameter of glBindFramebuffer can be either

GL_DRAW_FRAMEBUFFER or GL_READ_FRAMEBUFFER. This means you can use one framebuffer for reading and a different one for drawing. We see an example in the first program of this chapter. Binding the name 0 to either FBO target unbinds the current buffer and attaches the default FBO again. Once the default FBO is reattached, reads and writes are tied to the window's framebuffer again.

Destroying FBOs
When finished using FBOs or when cleaning up on exit, delete FBOs:

```
glDeleteFramebuffers(1, &fboName);
```

Renderbuffer Objects
Now that we can interact with FBOs, we need something to put in them! Renderbuffer objects, or RBOs, are an image surface explicitly designed for attaching to FBOs. A renderbuffer object can be a color, depth, stencil, or a combination depth/stencil surface. You can pick whichever combination of RBOs you need for a given FBO. In fact, you can even draw to many color buffers at one time!

Creating RBOs is just like creating FBOs and most other OpenGL objects:

```
glGenRenderbuffers(3, renderBufferNames);
```

Similar to FBOs, RBOs need to be bound before they can be changed. The only valid target for binding a renderbuffer is GL_RENDERBUFFER:

```
glBindRenderbuffer(GL_RENDERBUFFER, renderBufferNames[0]);
```

Now that the RBO is bound, we need to allocate the memory that backs the RBO. RBOs are created with no initial storage. Without storage we won't have anything to render to. First, decide what RBOs your application needs. Then pick appropriate formats that coincide with the buffer usage. Most formats that are valid texture formats are also valid renderbuffer formats. Additionally, you can create renderbuffer storage that contains a stencil format. Textures can have a combined DEPTH_STENCIL format, but not just a stencil format.

```
glBindRenderbuffer(GL_RENDERBUFFER, renderBufferNames[0]);
glRenderbufferStorage(GL_RENDERBUFFER, GL_RGBA8, screenWidth, screenHeight);
glBindRenderbuffer(GL_RENDERBUFFER, depthBufferName);
glRenderbufferStorage(GL_RENDERBUFFER, GL_DEPTH_COMPONENT32, screenWidth,
                      screenHeight);
```

In the preceding example, RBO storage is allocated at the size of the sample program's window. But renderbuffers do not have to be the size of the window. You can find the

maximum dimensions supported by your OpenGL implementation by calling
`glGetIntegerv` with the parameter `GL_MAX_RENDERBUFFER_SIZE`; your width and height
values must be smaller than this maximum. The only valid target for creating storage is
`GL_RENDERBUFFER`.

You can also create multisampled renderbuffer storage using a similar function called
`glRenderbufferStorageMultisample`, which takes an additional sample argument. The
great thing about this is you can do your own off-screen multisampling before any pixels
ever hit the screen!

Attaching RBOs

Once you have created all of the rendering surfaces for your FBO, it's time to hook them
up. A framebuffer object has multiple attachment points for binding: a depth attachment,
a stencil attachment, and numerous color attachments. You can query
`GL_MAX_COLOR_ATTACHMENTS` with `glGetIntegerv` to find out how many color buffers can
be attached at once. In our example application we use a depth buffer and three color
buffers all at one time. Before attempting to attach a renderbuffer make sure the FBO is
bound.

```
glBindFramebuffer(GL_DRAW_FRAMEBUFFER, fboName);
glFramebufferRenderbuffer(GL_DRAW_FRAMEBUFFER, GL_DEPTH_ATTACHMENT,
                          GL_RENDERBUFFER, depthBufferName);
glFramebufferRenderbuffer(GL_DRAW_FRAMEBUFFER, GL_COLOR_ATTACHMENT0,
                          GL_RENDERBUFFER, renderBufferNames[0]);
glFramebufferRenderbuffer(GL_DRAW_FRAMEBUFFER, GL_COLOR_ATTACHMENT1,
                          GL_RENDERBUFFER, renderBufferNames[1]);
glFramebufferRenderbuffer(GL_DRAW_FRAMEBUFFER, GL_COLOR_ATTACHMENT2,
                          GL_RENDERBUFFER, renderBufferNames[2]);
```

The first parameter can be `GL_DRAW_FRAMEBUFFER` or `GL_READ_FRAMEBUFFER` and depends on
where you attached your FBO. Then specify the attachment point. The third parameter is
always `GL_RENDERBUFFER`, and the last parameter is the name of the renderbuffer to be
used.

If you call `glFramebufferRenderbuffer` with a name of 0, whatever buffer is attached to
the current FBO at the specified attachment point will be detached. A special attachment
point called `GL_DEPTH_STENCIL_ATTACHMENT` allows you to attach a single buffer to the
depth and stencil attachment points simultaneously. To use this, you have to create an
RBO with an internal `GL_DEPTH_STENCIL` format.

Before you get any crazy ideas, there is no way to change the attachments of the default
framebuffer. There is also no way to attach one of the surfaces of the default framebuffer
to a user-generated framebuffer.

RBO Sizing

Framebuffer objects are surprisingly flexible in what they let you hook up. You can attach renderbuffers with different color formats to the same framebuffer. In fact, you can even attach RBOs with different sizes to the same framebuffer. If your RBOs do have different sizes, you will only be able to render into a rectangle the size of the smallest buffer. This can be more useful than you might think. For instance, depth buffers can take up quite a bit of space. If you have multiple FBOs or multiple buffers that need to do depth testing, you can create one depth buffer and use it for all FBOs or rendering passes, provided you clear the depth in between uses. All you have to do is make sure you allocate a depth format RBO that is large enough to cover your biggest FBO configuration.

Draw Buffers

Now that you know how to attach a whole bunch of renderbuffers to a framebuffer, we'd better make sure you can use them all at once! There are two important steps to gaining access to your renderbuffers. The first is to make sure the fragment shader is set up properly, and the second is to make sure the output is being directed to the right place.

Shader Output

To get color output to multiple buffers, the shader has to be configured to write multiple color outputs. Even better, the values written to each buffer can be different; otherwise, what's the point? One way of writing color outputs from a shader is to write to the built-in output called gl_FragData[n]. You can't use gl_FragData[n] and gl_FragColor in the same shader though. The value of n is the output index for the shader. The entire listing for the fragment shader of the first sample program is shown in Listing 8.4. Three color outputs are used, and a different shading technique is used on each output.

LISTING 8.4   Fragment Shader for fbo_drawbuffers—multibuffer.fs

```
// multibuffer.fs
// outputs to 3 buffers: normal color, grayscale,
// and luminance adjusted color
#version 150

in vec4 vFragColor;
in vec2 vTexCoord;

uniform sampler2D textureUnit0;
uniform int bUseTexture;
uniform samplerBuffer lumCurveSampler;

void main(void) {
    vec4 vColor;
    vec4 lumFactor;
```

```
    if (bUseTexture != 0)
       vColor = texture(textureUnit0, vTexCoord);
    else
       vColor = vFragColor;

    // Untouched output goes to first buffer
    gl_FragData[0] = vColor;

     // Grayscale to second buffer
    float grey = dot(vColor.rgb, vec3(0.3, 0.59, 0.11));
    gl_FragData[1] = vec4(grey, grey, grey, 1.0f);

    // clamp input color to make sure it is between 0.0 and 1.0
    vColor = clamp(vColor, 0.0f, 1.0f);

    int offset = int(vColor.r * (1024 - 1));
    lumFactor.r = texelFetch(lumCurveSampler, offset ).r;

    offset = int(vColor.g * (1024 - 1));
    lumFactor.g = texelFetch(lumCurveSampler, offset ).r;

    offset = int(vColor.b * (1024 - 1));
    lumFactor.b = texelFetch(lumCurveSampler, offset ).r;

    lumFactor.a = 1.0f;
    gl_FragData[2] = lumFactor;
}
```

Buffer Mappings

Now that we know what outputs our shader will write, we need to tell OpenGL where we want that output to go. We saw how multiple buffers can be bound to an FBO and how shaders can write to different output indexes. OpenGL allows an application to map the shader outputs to different FBO buffers by specifying the color attachment for each buffer. The default behavior is for a single color output to be sent down to color attachment 0. If you do not tell OpenGL what to do with your shader outputs, only the first output will be routed through, even if you have multiple shader outputs and multiple color buffers attached to your framebuffer object.

You can route shader outputs by making a call to glDrawBuffers. This overwrites all previous mappings, even if you specify fewer mappings than last time:

```
GLenum fboBuffs[] = { GL_COLOR_ATTACHMENT0,
                      GL_COLOR_ATTACHMENT1,
                      GL_COLOR_ATTACHMENT2 };
glDrawBuffers(3, fboBuffs);
```

The second parameter is a pointer to an array of GLenums specifying the color attachment to route the shader output index value to. Figure 8.3 shows how shader outputs are mapped to actual buffers. The index of the array passed into glDrawBuffers corresponds to the index of the shader output. Most of the time you probably just want a one-to-one mapping with the index of the shader output being the same as the color attachment offset.

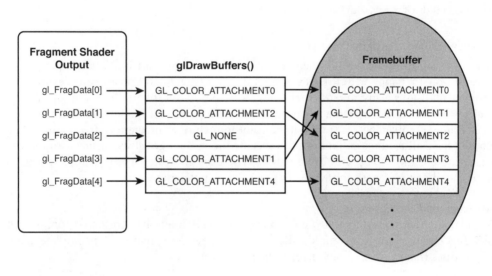

FIGURE 8.3   Mapping shader outputs to actual buffers.

Again, make sure your FBO is bound before calling glDrawBuffers. If you use glDrawBuffers while a user-created FBO is bound, the valid buffer targets are GL_COLOR_ATTACHMENT0 through 1 – the maximum, or GL_NONE. But if the default FBO is bound, you can use color buffer names associated with the window, most popularly GL_BACK_LEFT. Note that regardless of the type of FBO being used, no value besides GL_NONE can be used more than once in the array. If the default framebuffer is bound or your shader program writes to gl_FragColor, all of the buffers you pass into glDrawBuffers get the same color. Remember to set the draw buffers back after you are finished using a FBO, or you'll end up generating GL errors:

```
GLenum windowBuff [] = { GL_FRONT_LEFT };
glDrawBuffers(1, windowBuff);
```

Of course, there's no reason you need to map the color output from `gl_FragData[0]` to `GL_COLOR_ATTACHMENT0`. You can mix it up however you like, or set an entry in the draw buffers list to `GL_NONE` if you don't need one of the outputs from the fragment shader. In the example mapping shown in Figure 8.3, the first shader output is routed to the first FBO color buffer attachment while the second shader output is routed to the third color buffer attachment. The third shader output is not routed to any buffer, and the fourth color buffer receives no shader output. There is a limit to how many mappings can be set with `glDrawBuffers`. You can find the maximum supported mappings by calling `glGetIntegerv` with parameter `GL_MAX_DRAW_BUFFERS`.

Using `glDrawBuffers` to select the buffers your shader writes to has no effect on the read buffer binding. You can set the read buffer by calling `glReadBuffer` with the same values as those used for `glDrawBuffers`.

Framebuffer Completeness

Before we can finish up with framebuffer objects, there is one last important topic. Just because you are happy with the way you set up your FBO doesn't mean your OpenGL implementation is ready to render. The only way to find out if your FBO is set up correctly and in a way that the implementation can use it is to check for framebuffer completeness. Framebuffer completeness is similar in concept to texture completeness. If a texture doesn't have all required mipmap levels specified with the right sizes, formats, and so on, that texture is incomplete and can't be used. There are two categories of completeness: attachment completeness and whole framebuffer completeness.

Attachment Completeness

Each attachment point of an FBO must meet certain criteria to be considered complete. If any attachment point is incomplete, the whole framebuffer will also be incomplete. Some of the cases that cause an attachment to be incomplete are

- No image is associated with the attached object.

- Width or height of zero for attached image.

- A non-color renderable format is attached to a color attachment.

- A non-depth renderable format is attached to a depth attachment.

- A non-stencil renderable format is attached to a stencil attachment.

Whole Framebuffer Completeness

Not only does each attachment point have to be valid and meet certain criteria, but the framebuffer object as a whole must also be complete. The default framebuffer, if one exists, will always be complete. Common cases for the whole framebuffer being incomplete are

- No images are attached to the framebuffer.
- glDrawBuffers is mapped to an FBO attachment where no image is attached.
- The combination of internal formats is not supported.

Checking the Framebuffer

When you think you are finished setting up an FBO, you can check to see whether it is complete by calling

```
GLenum fboStatus = glCheckFramebufferStatus(GL_DRAW_FRAMEBUFFER);
```

If glCheckFramebufferStatus returns GL_FRAMEBUFFER_COMPLETE, all is well, and you may use the FBO. The return value of glCheckFramebufferStatus provides clues to what might be wrong if the framebuffer is not complete. Table 8.3 describes all possible return conditions and what they mean.

TABLE 8.3   Framebuffer Completeness Return Values

Return Value	Description
GL_FRAMEBUFFER_UNDEFINED	The current FBO binding is 0, but no default framebuffer exists.
GL_FRAMEBUFFER_COMPLETE	A user-defined FBO is bound and is complete. OK to render.
GL_FRAMEBUFFER_INCOMPLETE_ATTACHMENT	One of the buffers enabled for rendering is incomplete.
GL_FRAMEBUFFER_INCOMPLETE_MISSING_ATTACHMENT	No buffers are attached to the FBO.
GL_FRAMEBUFFER_INCOMPLETE_DRAW_BUFFER	One of the buffer attachments enabled for rendering does not have a buffer attached.
GL_FRAMEBUFFER_INCOMPLETE_READ_BUFFER	One of the buffer attachments enabled for reading does not have a buffer attached.
GL_FRAMEBUFFER_UNSUPPORTED	The combination of internal buffer formats is not supported.
GL_FRAMEBUFFER_INCOMPLETE_MULTISAMPLE	The number of samples or the value for TEXTURE_FIXED_SAMPLE_LOCATIONS for all buffers does not match.
GL_FRAMEBUFFER_INCOMPLETE_LAYER_TARGETS	Not all color attachments are layered textures or bound to the same target.

Many of these return values are helpful when debugging an application but are less useful after an application has shipped. Nonetheless, the first sample application checks to make sure none of these conditions occurred. It pays to do this check in applications that use FBOs, making sure your use case hasn't hit some implementation dependent limitation. An example of this might look like the following code:

```
GLenum fboStatus = glCheckFramebufferStatus(GL_DRAW_FRAMEBUFFER);
if(fboStatus != GL_FRAMEBUFFER_COMPLETE)
{
    switch (fboStatus)
    {
    case GL_FRAMEBUFFER_UNDEFINED:
        // Oops, no window exists?
        break;
    case GL_FRAMEBUFFER_INCOMPLETE_ATTACHMENT:
        // Check the status of each attachment
        break;
    case GL_FRAMEBUFFER_INCOMPLETE_MISSING_ATTACHMENT:
        // Attach at least one buffer to the FBO
        break;
    case GL_FRAMEBUFFER_INCOMPLETE_DRAW_BUFFER:
        // Check that all attachments enabled via
        // glDrawBuffers exist in FBO
    case GL_FRAMEBUFFER_INCOMPLETE_READ_BUFFER:
        // Check that the buffer specified via
        // glReadBuffer exists in FBO
        break;
    case GL_FRAMEBUFFER_UNSUPPORTED:
        // Reconsider formats used for attached buffers
        break;
    case GL_FRAMEBUFFER_INCOMPLETE_MULTISAMPLE:
        // Make sure the number of samples for each
        // attachment is the same
        break;
    case GL_FRAMEBUFFER_INCOMPLETE_LAYER_TARGETS:
        // Make sure the number of layers for each
        // attachment is the same
        break;
    }
}
```

If you attempt to perform any command that reads from or writes to the framebuffer
while an incomplete FBO is bound, the command simply returns after throwing the error
GL_INVALID_FRAMEBUFFER_OPERATION, retrievable by calling glGetError.

Read Framebuffers Need to Be Complete Too!

In the previous examples, we test the FBO attached to the draw buffer binding point,
GL_DRAW_FRAMEBUFFER. But a framebuffer attached to GL_READ_FRAMEBUFFER also has to be
attachment complete and whole framebuffer complete for reads to work. Because only one

read buffer can be enabled at a time, making sure an FBO is complete for reading is a little easier.

Copying Data in Framebuffers

Rendering to these off-screen framebuffers is fine and dandy, but ultimately you have to do something useful with the result. Traditionally graphics APIs allowed an application to read pixel or buffer data back to system memory and also provided ways to draw it back to the screen. While these methods are functional, they required copying data from the GPU into CPU memory and then turning right around and copying it back. Very inefficient! We now have a way to quickly move pixel data from one spot to another using a blit command. *Blit* is a term that refers to direct, efficient bit-level data/memory copies. There are many theories of the origin of this term, but the most likely candidates are Bit-Level-Image-Transfer or Block-Transfer. Whatever the etymology of blit may be, the action is the same. Performing these copies is simple; the function looks like this:

```
void glBlitFramebuffer(GLint srcX0, Glint srcY0,  Glint srcX1, Glint srcY1,
                       GLint dstX0, Glint dstY0,  Glint dstX1, Glint dstY1,
                       GLbitfield mask, GLenum filter);
```

Even though this function has "blit" in the name, it does much more than a simple bitwise copy. In fact, it's more like an automated texturing operation. The source of the copy is the read buffer specified by calling `glReadBuffer`, and the area copied is region defined by the rectangle with corners at (srcX0, srcY0) and (srcX1, srcY1). Likewise, the target of the copy is the current draw buffer specified by calling `glDrawBuffer`, and the area copied to is region defined by the rectangle with corners at (dstX0, dstY0) and (dstX1, dstY1). Because the rectangles for the source and destination do not have to be of equal size, you can use this function to scale the pixels being copied. If you have set the read and draw buffers to the same FBO and have bound the same FBO to the GL_DRAW_FRAME-BUFFER and GL_READ_FRAMEBUFFER bindings, you can even copy data from one portion of a buffer to another.

The mask argument can be any or all of GL_DEPTH_BUFFER_BIT, GL_STENCIL_BUFFER_BIT, or GL_COLOR_BUFFER_BIT. The filter can be either GL_LINEAR or GL_NEAREST but must be GL_LINEAR if you are copying depth or stencil data. These filters behave the same as they would for texturing. For our example we are only copying color data and can use a linear filter.

```
GLint width  = 800;
GLint height = 600;
GLenum fboBuffs[] = {  GL_COLOR_ATTACHMENT0 };
glBindFramebuffer(GL_DRAW_FRAMEBUFFER, fboName);
glBindFramebuffer(GL_READ_FRAMEBUFFER, fboName);
glDrawBuffers(1, fboBuffs);
glReadBuffer(GL_COLOR_ATTACHMENT0);
```

```
glBlitFramebuffer(0, 0, width, height,
        (width *0.8), (height*0.8), width, height,
        GL_COLOR_BUFFER_BIT, GL_LINEAR );
```

Assume the width and height of the RBOs attached to the FBO bound in the preceding code is 800 and 600. This code creates a copy of the whole buffer scaled down to 20% of the total size and places it in the upper-right corner.

Putting It All Together—Using FBOs

Our second sample application brings together FBOs, RBOs, texBOs, framebuffer blitting, and much more! The model is simple, but all rendering is done in one pass with one fragment shader (refer to Listing 8.4). To capture all of this output, we use an FBO with a depth buffer and three color buffers. These are set up in Listing 8.5.

LISTING 8.5   Creating and Setting Up an FBO with Four Attachments

```
// Create a new FBO
glGenFramebuffers(1,&fboName);

// Create depth renderbuffer
glGenRenderbuffers(1, &depthBufferName);
glBindRenderbuffer(GL_RENDERBUFFER, depthBufferName);
glRenderbufferStorage(GL_RENDERBUFFER, GL_DEPTH_COMPONENT32, screenWidth,
                    screenHeight);

// Create 3 color renderbuffers
glGenRenderbuffers(3, renderBufferNames);
glBindRenderbuffer(GL_RENDERBUFFER, renderBufferNames[0]);
glRenderbufferStorage(GL_RENDERBUFFER, GL_RGBA8, screenWidth, screenHeight);
glBindRenderbuffer(GL_RENDERBUFFER, renderBufferNames[1]);
glRenderbufferStorage(GL_RENDERBUFFER, GL_RGBA8, screenWidth, screenHeight);
glBindRenderbuffer(GL_RENDERBUFFER, renderBufferNames[2]);
glRenderbufferStorage(GL_RENDERBUFFER, GL_RGBA8, screenWidth, screenHeight);

// Attach all 4 renderbuffers to FBO
glBindFramebuffer(GL_DRAW_FRAMEBUFFER, fboName);
glFramebufferRenderbuffer(GL_DRAW_FRAMEBUFFER, GL_DEPTH_ATTACHMENT,
                        GL_RENDERBUFFER, depthBufferName);
glFramebufferRenderbuffer(GL_DRAW_FRAMEBUFFER, GL_COLOR_ATTACHMENT0,
                        GL_RENDERBUFFER, renderBufferNames[0]);
glFramebufferRenderbuffer(GL_DRAW_FRAMEBUFFER, GL_COLOR_ATTACHMENT1,
                        GL_RENDERBUFFER, renderBufferNames[1]);
glFramebufferRenderbuffer(GL_DRAW_FRAMEBUFFER, GL_COLOR_ATTACHMENT2,
                        GL_RENDERBUFFER, renderBufferNames[2]);
```

```
// Setup shader for processing
processProg = gltLoadShaderPairWithAttributes("multibuffer.vs",
                "multibuffer.fs", 3, GLT_ATTRIBUTE_VERTEX,
                "vVertex", GLT_ATTRIBUTE_NORMAL,
                "vNormal", GLT_ATTRIBUTE_TEXTURE0, "vTexCoord0");

// Create 3 new buffer objects
glGenBuffers(3,texBO);
glGenTextures(1, &texBOTexture);

int count = 0;
float* fileData = 0;

// Load first texBO with a tangent-like curve, 1024 values
fileData = LoadFloatData("LumTan.data", &count);
if (count > 0)
{
    glBindBuffer(GL_TEXTURE_BUFFER_ARB, texBO[0]);
    glBufferData(GL_TEXTURE_BUFFER_ARB, sizeof(float)*count,
                fileData, GL_STATIC_DRAW);
    delete fileData;
}


// Load second texBO with a sine-like curve, 1024 values
fileData = LoadFloatData("LumSin.data", &count);
if (count > 0)
{
    glBindBuffer(GL_TEXTURE_BUFFER_ARB, texBO[1]);
    glBufferData(GL_TEXTURE_BUFFER_ARB, sizeof(float)*count,
                fileData, GL_STATIC_DRAW);
    delete fileData;
}

// Load third texBO with a linear curve, 1024 values
fileData = LoadFloatData("LumLinear.data", &count);
if (count > 0)
{
    glBindBuffer(GL_TEXTURE_BUFFER_ARB, texBO[2]);
    glBufferData(GL_TEXTURE_BUFFER_ARB, sizeof(float)*count,
                fileData, GL_STATIC_DRAW);
    delete fileData;
}
```

```
// Load the Tan ramp first
glBindBuffer(GL_TEXTURE_BUFFER_ARB, 0);
glActiveTexture(GL_TEXTURE1);
glBindTexture(GL_TEXTURE_BUFFER_ARB, texBOTexture);
glTexBuffer(GL_TEXTURE_BUFFER_ARB, GL_R32F, texBO[0]);
glActiveTexture(GL_TEXTURE0);

// Reset framebuffer binding
glBindFramebuffer(GL_DRAW_FRAMEBUFFER, 0);
```

The first part of Listing 8.5 sets up and puts together the FBO and RBOs. Next we use the GLTools library to create our shaders and program, all compiled and linked together. Then we create three buffer objects and fill them with floating-point data from off-line files. The data contained in the files are biased ramps. One has a sine bias, one a tangent bias, and one is linear. These ramps are plotted against each other in Figure 8.4 for comparison. After the texture buffers have been created and loaded, the default framebuffer object is rebound again.

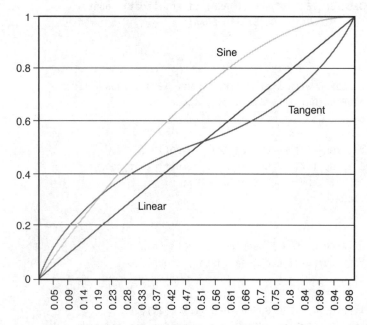

FIGURE 8.4   Comparison of bias curves for fbo_drawbuffers sample program.

The code shown in Listing 8.6 sets up all of the necessary shader state for OpenGL to use the program, which renders to multiple render targets. The texture buffer object is already loaded. But because the texture buffer object uses a texture unit to fetch values, the texture buffer sampler, lumCurveSampler, must be set to the texture unit the texture buffer is loaded on.

LISTING 8.6   Set Up OpenGL State for the Program

```
glUseProgram(processProg);

// Set Matrices for Vertex Program
glUniformMatrix4fv(glGetUniformLocation(processProg, "mvMatrix"),
                  1, GL_FALSE, transformPipeline.GetModelViewMatrix());
glUniformMatrix4fv(glGetUniformLocation(processProg, "pMatrix"),
                  1, GL_FALSE, transformPipeline.GetProjectionMatrix());

// Set the light position
glUniform3fv(glGetUniformLocation(processProg, "vLightPos"), 1, vLightPos);

// Set the vertex color for rendered pixels
glUniform4fv(glGetUniformLocation(processProg, "vColor"), 1, vColor);

// Set the texture unit for the texBO fetch
glUniform1i(glGetUniformLocation(processProg, "lumCurveSampler"), 1);

// If this geometry is textured, set the texture unit
if(textureUnit != -1)
{
    glUniform1i(glGetUniformLocation(processProg, "bUseTexture"), 1);
    glUniform1i(glGetUniformLocation(processProg, "textureUnit0"),
              textureUnit);
}
else
{
    glUniform1i(glGetUniformLocation(processProg, "bUseTexture"), 0);
}
```

The last interesting part of the sample program is to set the FBO, specify which buffers will be drawn to, and then render the scene. In Listing 8.7, the app-created FBO is bound, and the drawbuffers are set to the first three color attachments. Next the buffers are cleared, the processing program is bound, and the scene is rendered. When rendering is complete, the results are presented to the window through three calls to glBlitFramebuffer. The read buffer is set to the appropriate FBO attachment for each. Notice how all three outputs can be viewed simultaneously in Figure 8.5 and also in Color Plate 12.

LISTING 8.7 Perform Rendering to FBO, Copy to Screen

```
GLenum fboBuffs[] = { GL_COLOR_ATTACHMENT0,
                      GL_COLOR_ATTACHMENT1,
                      GL_COLOR_ATTACHMENT2  };

glBindFramebuffer(GL_DRAW_FRAMEBUFFER, fboName);
glDrawBuffers(3, fboBuffs);
glClear(GL_COLOR_BUFFER_BIT | GL_DEPTH_BUFFER_BIT);

UseProcessProgram(vLightTransformed, vFloorColor, 0);

floorBatch.Draw();
DrawWorld(yRot);

// Direct drawing to the window
glBindFramebuffer(GL_DRAW_FRAMEBUFFER, 0);
glDrawBuffers(1, windowBuff);
glViewport(0, 0, GetWidth(), GetHeight());

// Source buffer reads from the framebuffer object
glBindFramebuffer(GL_READ_FRAMEBUFFER, fboName);

// Copy grayscale output to the left half of the screen
glReadBuffer(GL_COLOR_ATTACHMENT1);
glBlitFramebuffer(0, 0, GetWidth()/2, GetHeight(),
                  0, 0, GetWidth()/2, GetHeight(),
                  GL_COLOR_BUFFER_BIT, GL_NEAREST);

// Copy the luminance adjusted color to the right half of the screen
glReadBuffer(GL_COLOR_ATTACHMENT2);
glBlitFramebuffer(GetWidth()/2, 0, GetWidth(), GetHeight(),
                  GetWidth()/2, 0, GetWidth(), GetHeight(),
                  GL_COLOR_BUFFER_BIT, GL_NEAREST);

// Scale the unaltered image to the upper right of the screen
glReadBuffer(GL_COLOR_ATTACHMENT0);
glBlitFramebuffer(0, 0, GetWidth(), GetHeight(),
                  (int)(GetWidth() *(0.8)), (int)(GetHeight()*(0.8)),
                  GetWidth(), GetHeight(),
                  GL_COLOR_BUFFER_BIT, GL_LINEAR );
```

FIGURE 8.5   Multiple buffers drawn simultaneously.

Pressing the F3, F4, and F5 keys switches the luminance ramp applied to the right side of the window. The processing shader takes the final color, scales the color values by the size of the texture buffer objects, and then looks up new R, G, and B values before storing the value in the their color output. You can try changing the data that generates these ramps, adding your own ramps, or applying different factors to each of the color channels. Pressing the F2 key switches between rendering multiple outputs to the FBO or rendering straight to the screen.

Remember that the drawing surface size is dependent on the surfaces bound. In the case of the fbo_drawbuffers sample program, the sizes of the renderbuffers are the same as the window. So no matter where it's rendering, the buffer sizes are the same. Even though it isn't necessary in this case, remember that you must also change the viewport size by calling glViewport to draw into the entire buffer (and not overdraw either!)

Rendering to Textures

Well, we have come a long way from traditional window rendering. FBOs are a flexible tool for off-screen rendering. However, RBOs definitely have their limitations. In fact, they are really only useful when attached directly to an FBO. That means getting data out requires a copy we would like to avoid. Fortunately you aren't limited to using RBOs. Instead, you can bind a texture directly to an FBO attachment. Because textures come in many different flavors, there are three entry points to bind textures to a framebuffer attachment:

```
void glFramebufferTexture1D(GLenum target, GLenum attachment,
                            GLenum textarget, GLuint texture, GLint level);

void glFramebufferTexture2D(GLenum target, GLenum attachment,
                            GLenum textarget, GLuint texture, GLint level);
void glFramebufferTexture3D(GLenum target, GLenum attachment,
                            GLenum textarget, GLuint texture, GLint level,
                            GLint layer);
```

The target can be either GL_DRAW_FRAMEBUFFER or GL_READ_FRAMEBUFFER just as it is for renderbuffers. Also similar to binding renderbuffers, the second argument specifies the FBO attachment point and can be GL_DEPTH_ATTACHMENT, GL_STENCIL_ATTACHMENT, or any of the GL_COLOR_ATTACHMENTn values. For most textures, the third argument is the corresponding texture type, but for cube maps you have to pass in the target of the face. Next, give the name of the texture and then the mipmap level of the texture to bind. For glFramebufferTexture3D, you also must specify the layer of the 3D texture to use. One-dimensional textures can only be bound via glFramebufferTexture1D, and glFramebufferTexture3D can only be used for three-dimensional textures. Use glFramebufferTexture2D for two-dimensional, rectangle, and cube map textures.

In our third sample program, fbo_textures, we use a texture attached to an FBO to create a mirror effect for the scene. First, set up the FBO just as in the first sample program. But this time the program attaches a texture to the FBO as in Listing 8.8.

LISTING 8.8   Set Up an FBO with Texture Attachments

```
// Create and bind an FBO
glGenFramebuffers(1,&fboName);
glBindFramebuffer(GL_DRAW_FRAMEBUFFER, fboName);

// Create depth renderbuffer
glGenRenderbuffers(1, &depthBufferName);
glBindRenderbuffer(GL_RENDERBUFFER, depthBufferName);
glRenderbufferStorage(GL_RENDERBUFFER, GL_DEPTH_COMPONENT32, 800, 800);

// Create the reflection texture
glGenTextures(1, &mirrorTexture);
glBindTexture(GL_TEXTURE_2D, mirrorTexture);
glTexImage2D(GL_TEXTURE_2D, 0, GL_RGBA8, 800, 800, 0, GL_RGBA, GL_FLOAT,
             NULL);
```

```
// Attach texture to first color attachment and the depth RBO
glFramebufferTexture2D(GL_DRAW_FRAMEBUFFER, GL_COLOR_ATTACHMENT0,
                        GL_TEXTURE_2D, mirrorTexture, 0);
glFramebufferRenderbuffer(GL_DRAW_FRAMEBUFFER, GL_DEPTH_ATTACHMENT,
                        GL_RENDERBUFFER, depthBufferName);
```

All rendering to the new FBO is done the same way as with RBO color attachments. However, there are a few things to watch out for. Because the texture now bound to the FBO can also be used for rendering, it's possible to create a rendering loop. A shader could be fetching texels from a texture and then writing the final shaded result back to the same texture, possibly overwriting the same locations. This would cause undefined results and can be a problem that is very hard to track down. As a general rule, it is best to make sure textures that are bound to an FBO and are being written to are also not bound to any texture units.

The state of each texture bound to the FBO also affects FBO completeness. The size and format of a texture image surface can change asynchronously while bound to an FBO through calls such as glTexImage2D. If you make changes to a texture's image surface while it is a render target, you should make sure the framebuffer is still valid for rendering by calling glCheckFramebufferStatus. You can bind any mipmap level of a texture by specifying it when attaching the texture. If you are then planning on using mipmaps for texturing, you want to generate the rest of the mip chain for the texture you just rendered into. This doesn't happen automatically, but you can call glGenerateMipmap with the texture type you want updated. This updates all levels beyond the base level using the contents of the base level.

There is no magic in this mirror effect; check out Figure 8.6 (also shown in Color Plate 13). But FBOs allow you to achieve a realistic reflection that is nearly impossible any other way. You have used alpha blending and image inversion earlier in the book to imitate reflections on marble floors. The alpha-inversion effect works okay when the reflection is always at the same angle. But it breaks down at the edge of the marble floor, when angles change, walking up a steep ramp perhaps. It also doesn't play nice with obstacles that should be blocking the reflection, maybe a box or stool. Additionally, using the alpha-inversion method may also cause depth testing issues.

FIGURE 8.6   Using FBOs and textures to create accurate reflections.

Using an FBO, we first change our perspective to that of the mirror. This means the world and all contents will be rendered from the position of the mirror. But which direction should the mirror "look?" Straight out from the mirror surface? That would mean the reflection wouldn't change as the viewer moved relative to the mirror. How about back at the viewer? Well that would mean you could always see your reflection no matter where you stood, close but not correct. You can draw a vector from the viewer's position to the center of the mirror. The mirror should be looking in the direction of this vector reflected over the perpendicular normal vector of the mirror surface. You can imagine yourself standing behind the mirror looking in the direction of the reflection to see what the mirror should show. Take a look at Figure 8.7 to get an idea of how this works. Remember that the angle of incidence here is not the direction the viewer/camera is looking, but the angle made by drawing a line between the position of the viewer and the center of the mirror.

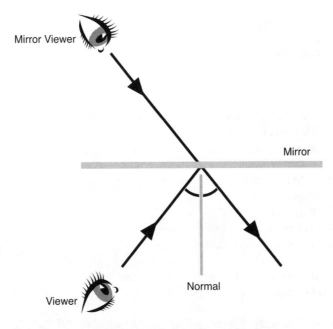

FIGURE 8.7   Finding the mirror viewing angle based on reflection.

Once you have the position of the mirror figured out and the angle of the mirror's view calculated, you can render the scene from the mirror's position and perspective. Listing 8.9 shows how the scene is drawn as the mirror sees it. In the fbo_textures sample program, we use a GLFrame object from the GLTools resources to generate the adjustment to the modelview matrix based on the position, up vector, and view direction. Then, the modelview matrix is inverted in the x direction to simulate the reflection—everything is backward in a mirror. As a bonus the viewer, you, is drawn as a blue cone in the reflected image to help visualize where the camera is.

LISTING 8.9   Drawing from the Mirror's Perspective

```
// Set position of mirror frame (camera)
vMirrorPos[0] = 0.0;
vMirrorPos[1] = 0.1f;
vMirrorPos[2] = -6.0f; // view pos is actually behind mirror
mirrorFrame.SetOrigin(vMirrorPos);

// Calculate direction of mirror frame (camera)
// Because the position of the mirror is known relative to the origin
// find the direction vector by adding the mirror offset to the vector
// of the viewer-origin
vMirrorForward[0] = vCameraPos[0];
```

```
vMirrorForward[1] = vCameraPos[1];
vMirrorForward[2] = (vCameraPos[2] + 5);
m3dNormalizeVector3(vMirrorForward);
mirrorFrame.SetForwardVector(vMirrorForward);

// first render from the mirror's perspective
glBindFramebuffer(GL_DRAW_FRAMEBUFFER, fboName);
glDrawBuffers(1, fboBuffs);
glViewport(0, 0, mirrorTexWidth, mirrorTexHeight);

// Draw scene from the perspective of the mirror camera
modelViewMatrix.PushMatrix();
    M3DMatrix44f mMirrorView;
    mirrorFrame.GetCameraMatrix(mMirrorView);
    modelViewMatrix.MultMatrix(mMirrorView);

    // Flip the mirror camera horizontally for the reflection
    modelViewMatrix.Scale(-1.0f, 1.0f, 1.0f);

    glBindTexture(GL_TEXTURE_2D, textures[0]); // Marble
    glClear(GL_COLOR_BUFFER_BIT | GL_DEPTH_BUFFER_BIT);
    shaderManager.UseStockShader(GLT_SHADER_TEXTURE_MODULATE,
                transformPipeline.GetModelViewProjectionMatrix(),
                vWhite, 0);
    floorBatch.Draw();
    DrawWorld(yRot);

    // Now draw a cylinder representing the viewer
    M3DVector4f vLightTransformed;
    modelViewMatrix.GetMatrix(mMirrorView);
    m3dTransformVector4(vLightTransformed, vLightPos, mMirrorView);
    modelViewMatrix.Translate(vCameraPos[0],vCameraPos[1]-0.8f,
                            vCameraPos[2]-1.0f);
    modelViewMatrix.Rotate(-90.0f, 1.0f, 0.0f, 0.0f);

    shaderManager.UseStockShader(GLT_SHADER_POINT_LIGHT_DIFF,
                                modelViewMatrix.GetMatrix(),
                                transformPipeline.GetProjectionMatrix(),
                                vLightTransformed, vBlue, 0);
    cylinderBatch.Draw();
modelViewMatrix.PopMatrix();
```

Next the scene is drawn in Listing 8.10. The framebuffer, viewport, and drawbuffers are all set back to the default for rendering to the window. Then the scene is drawn again, this time from the perspective of the viewer/camera. Once finished, the mirror itself can finally be drawn. Before applying the texture containing the mirror image, the sample program figures out which side of the mirror the viewer is on. To avoid goofy reflections on the back of the mirror, the program checks to see if the viewer is in front of or behind the mirror. If the viewer is behind, the mirror is just drawn as black.

LISTING 8.10 Drawing the Rest of the Scene, Including the Mirror

```
// Reset FBO. Draw world again from the real cameras perspective
glBindFramebuffer(GL_DRAW_FRAMEBUFFER, 0);
glDrawBuffers(1, windowBuff);
glViewport(0, 0, screenWidth, screenHeight);
modelViewMatrix.PushMatrix();
    M3DMatrix44f mCamera;
    cameraFrame.GetCameraMatrix(mCamera);
    modelViewMatrix.MultMatrix(mCamera);

    glBindTexture(GL_TEXTURE_2D, textures[0]); // Marble
    glClear(GL_COLOR_BUFFER_BIT | GL_DEPTH_BUFFER_BIT);
    shaderManager.UseStockShader(GLT_SHADER_TEXTURE_MODULATE,
                transformPipeline.GetModelViewProjectionMatrix(),
                vWhite, 0);

    floorBatch.Draw();
    DrawWorld(yRot);

    // Now draw the mirror surfaces
    modelViewMatrix.PushMatrix();
        modelViewMatrix.Translate(0.0f, -0.4f, -5.0f);
        if(vCameraPos[2] > -5.0)
        {
            glBindTexture(GL_TEXTURE_2D, mirrorTexture); // Reflection
            shaderManager.UseStockShader(GLT_SHADER_TEXTURE_REPLACE,
                    transformPipeline.GetModelViewProjectionMatrix(), 0);
        }
        else
        {
            // If the camera is behind the mirror, just draw black
            shaderManager.UseStockShader(GLT_SHADER_FLAT,
                    transformPipeline.GetModelViewProjectionMatrix(), vBlack);
        }
```

∞

```
        mirrorBatch.Draw();
        shaderManager.UseStockShader(GLT_SHADER_FLAT,
                transformPipeline.GetModelViewProjectionMatrix(), vGrey);
        mirrorBorderBatch.Draw();
    modelViewMatrix.PopMatrix();
```

There are some limitations to this approach. For one, the entire scene has to be drawn twice, which could be a performance issue if many objects were behind the mirror or out of view. In Chapter 12, "Advanced Geometry Management," you learn about occlusion queries and how to draw only what will be seen. Another issue is that the viewer position of the mirror in the sample program is taken from the center of the mirror to keep the math fairly simple. This isn't very realistic. One way to generate a more accurate reflection might be to use the closest point on the mirror to the camera instead. As an exercise, you can try to modify the application so that the mirror also rotates in the scene. In this case you have to recalculate the angle of incidence based on both the position of the camera relative to the mirror and the angle of the mirror to the camera.

Summary

This chapter brought some major changes in how you can manage memory and buffers in OpenGL. Using pixel buffer objects, you can efficiently move data around the GPU and pipeline data loads for things like texture updates. You can use texture buffer objects to bind arbitrary data to a texture unit and then fetch that data in a shader.

Framebuffer objects teamed up with render buffer objects, and textures open a whole new world of possibilities for off-screen rendering. Now nearly any pixel surface can be attached and rendered to directly without affecting what happens in the window. You also learned how to use shaders to draw to a large number of color surfaces simultaneously.

CHAPTER 9

Advanced Buffers: Beyond the Basics

by Nicholas Haemel

WHAT YOU'LL LEARN IN THIS CHAPTER:

How To	Functions You'll Use
Use custom fragment shader output bindings	`glBindFragDataLocation/`
	`glBindFragDataLocationIndexed`
Update existing buffers	`glMapBuffer/glMapBufferRange/glUnmapBuffer`
Load compressed textures	`glCompressedTexSubImage2D`
Copy data between buffer objects	`glCopyBufferSubData`
Render to multisample textures	`glRenderBufferStorageMultisample`
Get locations of samples in multisample buffers	`glGetMultisamplefv`
Render in full definition using floating-point buffers and textures	

By now framebuffer objects are old hat. We can use the flexibility provided by FBOs, textures, and buffer objects to really push the OpenGL pipeline. So far most of our work has been with traditional 8-bit color textures and renderbuffers. Even depth buffers mapped all values to 24 or 32 bits of physical fixed-point range.

New data formats open a whole new world, allowing your application to store the actual output of the fragment shader without loss of precision. The fun doesn't stop there. OpenGL also provides many ways of accessing and updating buffers on the GPU without bringing rendering to a grinding halt.

Getting at Your Data

Most of this chapter focuses on all the new data formats and ways to use them. But before we get to that, let's build on what we learned in Chapter 8, "Buffer Objects: Storage Is Now in Your Hands," and cover a few important ways of accessing your buffers that will help you to optimize your performance.

Mapping Buffers

In the previous chapter, you uploaded buffer objects using `glBufferData` once to fill the buffer. But what if you have to make changes or update the buffer after it has been loaded on the GPU? Well that's what `glMapBuffer` and `glMapBufferRange` are for. When you call `glMapBufferRange`, OpenGL provides a pointer to memory that you can use to directly read or update the data in a buffer. All you have to do is tell the implementation what you are planning on doing with the data. You can choose to only read from the mapped buffer in cases where the GPU has written to the buffer and you want to bring the results back to the CPU. Or you can map the buffer for writing in which case your changes are reflected on the buffer stored in GPU memory. The type of mapping you choose will have performance implications; try to avoid mapping a buffer for writing when you only need to read from it. Likewise, don't map a buffer for reading if you are only going to write to it. Table 9.1 shows the possible bitfield values for mapping buffers.

TABLE 9.1   Map Buffer Access Types

Access Flags	Usage
`GL_MAP_READ_BIT`	Returned pointer may be used for reading the buffer.
`GL_MAP_WRITE_BIT`	Returned pointer may be used for modifying the buffer.
`GL_MAP_INVALIDATE_RANGE_BIT`	Signals that OpenGL can throw away the previous contents of the mapped range. Data in the range is undefined unless updated by the application.
`GL_MAP_INVALIDATE_BUFFER_BIT`	Signals that OpenGL can throw away the previous contents of the entire buffer. Data in the buffer is undefined unless updated by the application.
`GL_MAP_FLUSH_EXPLICIT_BIT`	Using this bit with `GL_MAP_WRITE_BIT` requires an application to explicitly flush each range updated by calling `glFlushMappedBufferRange`. If this bit is not specified, the entire buffer will be flushed when `glUnmapBuffer` is called.
`GL_MAP_UNSYNCHRONIZED_BIT`	Tells OpenGL to aviod trying to sychronize any pending GPU writes to this buffer before mapping.

When done updating the mapped buffer, call `glUnmapBuffer` to tell OpenGL you are finished.

```
Glint accessFlags =    GL_MAP_WRITE_BIT | GL_MAP_INVALIDATE_RANGE_BIT |
                       GL_MAP_FLUSH_EXPLICIT_BIT;
Glint offset = 32* 100;
Glint length = 32*48;
GLvoid *bufferData = glMapBufferRange(GL_TEXTURE_BUFFER, offset, length, access-
Flags);
// Update buffer here
. . .
glUnmapBuffer(GL_TEXTURE_BUFFER);
```

If you set the GL_MAP_FLUSH_EXPLICIT_FLAG, you have to tell OpenGL which portions of the buffer you want flushed, or which portions you updated by calling glFlushMappedBufferRange before unmapping the buffer. You can call glFlushMappedBufferRange as many times as you need for as many ranges as you updated:

GLvoid glFlushMappedBufferRange(GLenum target, intprt offset, sizeiptr length);

Use the same target the buffer is bound to. The offset and length parameters are used to signal which portion of the buffer was changed.

You can also map an entire buffer by calling glMapBuffer instead of glMapBufferRange.

GLvoid *bufferData = glMapBuffer(GL_TEXTURE_BUFFER, accessFlags);

You use glMapBuffer and glMapBufferRange extensively in the rest of the book to load and update data on the GPU.

Copying Buffers

Once your data has been sent to the GPU, it's entirely possible you may want to share that data between buffers or copy the results from one buffer into another. Thankfully, OpenGL provides an easy to use way of doing that as well. glCopyBufferSubData lets you specify which buffers are involved as well as the size and offsets to use.

glCopyBufferSubData(GL_COPY_READ_BUFFER, GL_COPY_WRITE_BUFFER, readStart, writeStart, size);

The buffers you are copying to and from can be any buffers bound to any of the buffer binding points listed in Table 8.1 back in Chapter 8. But since buffer binding points can only have one buffer bound at a time, you couldn't copy between two buffers both bound to GL_TEXTURE_BUFFER, for example. The creators of OpenGL thought of this too! Remember the GL_COPY_READ_BUFFER and GL_COPY_WRITE_BUFFER you first saw in Chapter 8 but haven't used for anything yet? Well these binding points were added specifically for you to copy data from one buffer to another. You can bind your read and write buffers to these binding points without affecting any other buffer bindings. Then pick the offsets into each buffer and specify the size.

Be sure that the ranges you are reading from and writing to remain within the size of the buffers; otherwise your copy will fail. glCopyBufferSubData can be use for many clever algorithms. One common use is for an application to create a second thread with an OpenGL context used for loading data. In this case glCopyBufferSubData is quite handy for updating geometry data in the primary context without major interruptions rendering.

Controlling the Destiny of Your Pixel Shaders; Mapping Fragment Outputs

In Chapter 8 you learned how to hook up multiple buffer objects to a framebuffer and render many different outputs from the same fragment shader. To do this, your shader could write to the built-in shader outputs called gl_FragData[n] instead of gl_FragColor. Although you can still compile a GLSL 1.50 shader using either of these outputs, both are deprecated. That means future versions of OpenGL will remove them, and we are better off using the "new and improved" way of writing shader color outputs.

Using built-in shader outputs is so 2006! One problem with the old way is that you can write gl_FragData or gl_FragColor, but never both. Also, your fragment shader must contain hard-coded indexes if it renders to multiple outputs. Additionally, how are you supposed to keep track of and make logical sense of what is being written to gl_FragData[7] across multiple shaders?

Instead of setting the value of a built-in color output index, you can define your own shader outputs. For color outputs, declare your output as out vec4 in your fragment shader. The outputs for the Chapter 8 draw buffers sample program have been rewritten to use custom locations:

```
out vec4 oStraightColor;
out vec4 oGreyscale;
out vec4 oLumAdjColor;
```

Then before linking the program, tell OpenGL where you want to map the outputs by using glBindFragDataLocation. Just specify which index each output maps to:

```
glBindFragDataLocation(processProg, 0, "oStraightColor");
glBindFragDataLocation(processProg, 1, "oGreyscale");
glBindFragDataLocation(processProg, 2, "oLumAdjColor");
glLinkProgram(processProg);
```

You can also compile your shaders, link your program together, and then specify the locations of your outputs. Just remember to relink the program again before you use it so that setting the output locations takes effect. Now your shader output is configured. Each color is written to a unique index. Remember that you can't assign an output to more than one index. The entire listing for the fragment shader of the draw buffers sample program from Chapter 8 is shown in Listing 9.1. Three color outputs are declared, and a different shading technique is used for each output.

LISTING 9.1   Fragment Shader for fbo_drawbuffers, multibuffer_frag_location.fs

```
#version 150
// multibuffer_frag_location.fs
// outputs to 3 buffers: normal color, grayscale,
// and luminance adjusted color

in vec4 vFragColor;
in vec2 vTex;
```

```
uniform sampler2D textureUnit0;
uniform int bUseTexture;
uniform samplerBuffer lumCurveSampler;

out vec4 oStraightColor;
out vec4 oGrayscale;
out vec4 oLumAdjColor;

void main(void) {
    vec4 vColor;
    vec4 lumFactor;

    if (bUseTexture != 0)
        vColor =  texture(textureUnit0, vTex);
    else
        vColor = vFragColor;

    // Untouched output goes to first buffer
    oStraightColor = vColor;

    // Grayscale to second buffer
    float grey = dot(vColor.rgb, vec3(0.3, 0.59, 0.11));
    oGrayscale = vec4(gray, gray, gray, 1.0f);

    // clamp input color to make sure it is between 0.0 and 1.0
    vColor = clamp(vColor, 0.0f, 1.0f);

    int offset = int(vColor.r * 1024);
    oLumAdjColor.r = texelFetch(lumCurveSampler, offset ).r;

    offset = int(vColor.g * 1024);
    oLumAdjColor.g = texelFetch(lumCurveSampler, offset ).r;

    offset = int(vColor.b * 1024);
    oLumAdjColor.b = texelFetch(lumCurveSampler, offset ).r;
    oLumAdjColor.a = 1.0f;
}
```

There are many advantages to using `glBindFragDataLocation`. You can use logical names for outputs in shaders that actually have a meaning. You can also use the same name in multiple shaders and map that name to the appropriate logical buffer index at runtime.

We take a deeper look into how your application can use blending in Chapter 10, "Fragment Operations: The End of the Pipeline." Some blending equations in OpenGL 3.3

require a shader to output two different colors per fragment. You can use
glBindFragDataLocationIndexed to do this.

```
glBindFragDataLocationIndexed(program, colorNumber. index, outputName);
```

This function behaves similarly to glBindFragDataLocation. In OpenGL 3.3 there are two
possible index values for the index parameter. If you choose 0, the color will be used as
the first input color, just as if you had used glBindFragDataLocation. If you use 1, the
color will be used as the second input color for blending.

New Formats for a New Hardware Generation

One way OpenGL has progressed in the past few years is to add native support for a slew
of new data formats and data types. The writers of the OpenGL standard continue to bring
flexibility to 3D application development—first with completely customizable sections of
the graphics pipeline, next with flexible buffer usage, and now finally with flexible data
formats.

At first such an idea might seem trivial or unimportant. But anyone who has spent time
trying to express all of their color data in 8 bits can sympathize. Most data that enters the
OpenGL rendering pipeline has come from some other application or tool. Vertex and
texture data for most games come from artistic authoring tools such as Maya or 3DS Max.
CAD programs use complex engines to generate 3D surfaces based on user input and file
formats. Because vertex, texture, and related data can be large and complex, it can be
nearly impossible to convert all of this data from various sources to a small set of formats.
But conversion is usually unnecessary with OpenGL now that the most common and
many uncommon formats are supported natively.

Floats—True Precision at Last!

One of the most useful additions is floating-point formats. Although internally the
OpenGL pipeline usually works with floating-point data, the sources and targets have
often been fixed-point and of significantly less precision. As a result, many portions of the
pipeline used to clamp all values between 0 and 1 so they could be stored in a fixed-point
format in the end. While OpenGL 3.2 still allowed you to clamp the output of fragment
shaders, OpenGL 3.3 has removed clamping altogether.

The data type passed into a vertex shader is up to you but is typically declared as vec4, or
a vector of four floats. Similarly, you decide what outputs your vertex shader should write
when you declare variables as out or varying in a vertex shader. These outputs are then
rasterized across your geometry and passed into your fragment shader. You have complete
control of the type of data you decide to use for color throughout the whole pipeline,
although it's most common to just use floats. You now have complete control over how
and in what format your data is in as it travels from vertex arrays all the way to the final
output.

This is great! Now instead of 256 values, you can color and shade using values from 1.18 * 10^{-38} all the way to 3.4 * 10^{38}! (Negative colors just wouldn't make sense.) But wait, if you are drawing to a window that only has 8 bits per color, what happens? Unfortunately, the output is clamped to the range of 0 to 1 and then mapped to a fixed point value. That's no fun! Until someone invents monitors or displays that can understand and display floating-point data, you are still limited by the final output device.

But that doesn't mean floating-point rendering isn't useful. Quite the contrary! You can still render to both textures and renderbuffers in full floating-point precision. Not only that, but you have complete control over how floating-point data gets mapped to a fixed output format. This can have a huge impact on the final result and is commonly referred to High Dynamic Range, or HDR.

Using Floating-Point Formats

Upgrading your applications to use floating-point buffers is easier than you may think. In fact, you don't even have to call any new functions. Instead, there are two new tokens you can use when creating buffers, GL_RGBA16F and GL_RGBA32F. These can be used when creating storage for RBOs (renderbuffer objects) or when allocating textures:

```
glRenderbufferStorage(GL_RENDERBUFFER, GL_RGBA16F, nWidth, nHeight);
glRenderbufferStorage(GL_RENDERBUFFER, GL_RGBA32F, nWidth, nHeight);


glTexImage2D(GL_TEXTURE_2D, 0, GL_RGBA16F, texWidth, texHeight, 0, GL_RGBA,
             GL_FLOAT, texels);
glTexImage2D(GL_TEXTURE_2D, 0, GL_RGBA32F, texWidth, texHeight, 0, GL_RGBA,
             GL_FLOAT, texels);
```

In addition to the more traditional RGBA formats, Table 9.2 lists other formats allowed for creating floating-point renderbuffers. Textures are more open-minded and can be created with far more formats, but only two of those are float formats. Remember what we said earlier about OpenGL being flexible to allow many different applications to work easily? Having so many floating-point formats available allows applications to often use the format their data is stored in directly without first converting, which can be very time-consuming.

TABLE 9.2   Float Renderbuffer and Texture Formats

Renderbuffers	Textures
GL_RGBA32F	GL_RGBA32F
GL_RGBA16F	GL_RGBA16F
GL_R11_G11_B10F	GL_R11_G11_B10F
GL_RG32F	GL_RG32F
GL_RG16F	GL_RG16F
GL_R32F	GL_R32F
GL_R16F	GL_R16F
	GL_RGB32F
	GL_RGB16F

HDR

Many modern game applications use floating-point rendering to generate all of the great eye candy we now expect. The level of realism possible when generating lighting effects such as light bloom, lens flare, light reflections, light refractions, crepuscular rays, and the effects of participating media such as dust or clouds are often not possible without floating-point buffers. HDR rendering to floating-point buffers can make the bright areas of a scene really bright, keep shadow areas very dark, and still allow you to see detail in both. After all, the human eye has an incredible ability to perceive very high contrast levels well beyond the capabilities of today's displays.

Instead of drawing a complex scene with a lot of geometry and lighting in our sample programs to show how effective HDR can be, we use images already generated in HDR for simplicity. The first sample program, hdr_imaging, loads HDR (floating-point) images using a file format called OpenEXR. Industrial Light and Magic developed OpenEXR as a tool to help store all of the image data necessary for high fidelity image processing. Think of an OpenEXR image as a composite of multiple images captured by a camera at different exposure levels. The low exposures capture detail in the bright areas of the scene while the high exposures capture detail in the dark areas of the scene. Figure 9.1 (also shown in Color Plate 14) shows three views of a scene with a tree in the foreground and a bright field in the background. The left side rendered at a very low exposure and shows all of the detail of the field even though it is very bright. The center image begins to show the foreground, trunk, and the leaves of the closest tree. The right image really brings out the detail of the ground in front of the tree and even lets you see inside the hollow base of the tree! The three images show the incredible amount of detail and range that are stored in a single image. OpenEXR comes with sample images we can use to demonstrate HDR rendering.

FIGURE 9.1   Different views of an OpenEXR HDR image. Lowest exposure on left and highest on right.

The only way possible to store so much detail in a single image is to use floating-point data. Any scene you render in OpenGL, especially if it has very bright or dark areas, can look more realistic when the true color output can be preserved instead of clamped between 0.0 and 1.0, and then divided into only 256 possible values.

Using OpenEXR

Because OpenEXR is a custom data format, we can't use ordinary file access methods for reading and interpreting the data. Thankfully Industrial Light and Magic has provided the libraries necessary to do all the heavy lifting for us. By including a few OpenEXR header files and linking against the OpenEXR lib files, we can use the already built tools to load images. OpenEXR treats all access to EXR files as "windows" or "views" of the data contained in the file. In our application, first we create an `RGBAInputFile` object by passing the constructor the name of the file we want to open. Next, we get the width and height of the OpenEXR image by creating a Box2i object and filling it with the strongly typed data returned from a call to `dataWindow`. Then the width and height are used to create a 2D array of pixels containing RGBA data:

```
Array2D<Rgba> pixels;
Box2i dw = file.dataWindow();
texWidth  = dw.max.x - dw.min.x + 1;
texHeight = dw.max.y - dw.min.y + 1;
pixels.resizeErase (texHeight, texWidth);
```

After the file is opened and we have a place to store the data, we have to tell the `RgbaInputFile` object where we want to put the data by calling `setFrameBuffer` and then read the actual data by calling `readPixels`:

```
file.setFrameBuffer (&pixels[0][0] - dw.min.x - dw.min.y * texWidth, 1, texWidth);
file.readPixels (dw.min.y, dw.max.y);
```

Now that we have the data, it's time to load it into a texture. But first the data needs to be in a layout that OpenGL understands. The data must be copied to an array of floats:

```
GLfloat* texels = (GLfloat*)malloc(texWidth * texHeight * 3 * sizeof(GLfloat));
GLfloat* pTex = texels;
// Copy OpenEXR into local buffer for loading into a texture
for (unsigned int v = 0; v < texHeight; v++)
{
    for (unsigned int u = 0; u < texWidth; u++)
    {
        Imf::Rgba texel = pixels[texHeight - v - 1][u];
        pTex[0] = texel.r;
        pTex[1] = texel.g;
        pTex[2] = texel.b;
        pTex += 3;
    }
}
```

Then, finally load the array of floats into the designated texture object:

```
// Bind texture, load image, set tex state
glBindTexture(GL_TEXTURE_2D, textureName);
glTexImage2D(GL_TEXTURE_2D, 0, GL_RGB16F, texWidth, texHeight, 0, GL_RGB, GL_FLOAT,
texels);
glTexParameteri(GL_TEXTURE_2D, GL_TEXTURE_WRAP_S, GL_CLAMP_TO_EDGE);
glTexParameteri(GL_TEXTURE_2D, GL_TEXTURE_WRAP_T, GL_CLAMP_TO_EDGE);
glTexParameteri(GL_TEXTURE_2D, GL_TEXTURE_MAG_FILTER, GL_LINEAR);
glTexParameteri(GL_TEXTURE_2D, GL_TEXTURE_MIN_FILTER, GL_LINEAR);
free(texels);
```

That's it! Now the HDR image data is loaded into an OpenGL texture image and is ready for use.

Tone Mapping

Now that you've seen some of the benefits of using floating-point rendering, how do you use that data to generate a dynamic image that still has to be displayed using values from 0 to 255? Tone mapping is the action of mapping color data from one set of colors to another or from one color space to another. Because we can't directly display floating-point data, it has to be tone mapped into a color space that can be displayed.

The first sample program, hdr_imaging, uses three approaches to map the high-definition output to the low-definition screen. The first method, enabled by pressing the 1 key, is a simple and naïve direct texturing of the floating-point texture to the screen. The histogram in Figure 9.2 shows that most of the image data is between 0 and 1, but many of the important highlights are well beyond 1.0. In fact, the highest luminance level for this image is 9.16!

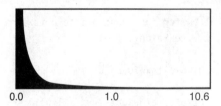

FIGURE 9.2   Histogram of levels for Tree.exr.

The result is that the image is clamped, and all of the bright areas look white. Additionally, because the majority of the data is in the lower one-fourth of the range, or between 0 and 63 when mapped directly to 8 bits, it all blends together to look black. Figure 9.3 shows the result; the bright areas are practically white, and the dark areas are nearly black.

FIGURE 9.3   Naïve approach to tone mapping; clamp between 0.0 and 1.0.

The second approach in the sample program is to vary the "exposure" of the image, similar to how a camera can vary exposure to the environment. Enter this mode by pressing 2. Each exposure level provides a slightly different window into the texture data. Low exposures show the detail in the very bright sections of the scene; high exposures allow you to see detail in the dark areas but wash out the bright parts. This is similar to the images in Figure 9.1 with the low exposure on the left and the high exposure on the right. For our tone mapping pass, the hdr_imaging sample program reads from a floating-point texture and writes to a framebuffer object with an 8-bit texture attached to the first render target. This allows the conversion from HDR to LDR (Low Dynamic Range) to be on a pixel by pixel basis, which reduces artifacts that occur when a texel is interpolated between bright and dark areas. Once the LDR image has been generated, it is drawn directly to the screen as a texture. Listing 9.2 shows the setup of the FBO and textures as well as the rendering pass to do the conversion.

LISTING 9.2   Rendering HDR Content to an FBO and then to the Window

```
// Create and bind an FBO
glGenFramebuffers(1,&fboName);
glBindFramebuffer(GL_DRAW_FRAMEBUFFER, fboName);
```

```
// Create the FBO texture
glGenTextures(1, fboTextures);
glBindTexture(GL_TEXTURE_2D, fboTextures[0]);
glTexImage2D(GL_TEXTURE_2D, 0, GL_RGB8, hdrTexturesWidth[curHDRTex],
             hdrTexturesHeight[curHDRTex], 0, GL_RGBA, GL_FLOAT, NULL);
glFramebufferTexture2D(GL_DRAW_FRAMEBUFFER, GL_COLOR_ATTACHMENT0,
                       GL_TEXTURE_2D, fboTextures[0], 0);

. . .

// Setup HDR texture(s)
glActiveTexture(GL_TEXTURE0);
glGenTextures(1, hdrTextures);
glBindTexture(GL_TEXTURE_2D, hdrTextures[curHDRTex]);

// Load HDR image from EXR file
LoadOpenEXRImage("Tree.exr", hdrTextures[curHDRTex],
hdrTexturesWidth[curHDRTex], hdrTexturesHeight[curHDRTex]);

. . .

// first, draw to FBO at full FBO resolution

// Bind FBO with 8b attachment
glBindFramebuffer(GL_DRAW_FRAMEBUFFER, fboName);
glViewport(0, 0, hdrTexturesWidth[curHDRTex], hdrTexturesHeight[curHDRTex]);
glClear(GL_COLOR_BUFFER_BIT);

// Bind texture with HDR image
glBindTexture(GL_TEXTURE_2D, hdrTextures[curHDRTex]);

// Render pass, down-sample to 8b using selected program
projectionMatrix.LoadMatrix(fboOrthoMatrix);
SetupHDRProg();
fboQuad.Draw();

// Then draw the resulting image to the screen, maintain image proportions
glBindFramebuffer(GL_DRAW_FRAMEBUFFER, 0);
glViewport(0, 0, screenWidth, screenHeight);
glClear(GL_DEPTH_BUFFER_BIT | GL_COLOR_BUFFER_BIT);

// Attach 8b texture with HDR image
glBindTexture(GL_TEXTURE_2D, fboTextures[0]);
```

```
// draw screen sized, proportional quad with 8b texture
projectionMatrix.LoadMatrix(orthoMatrix);
SetupStraightTexProg();
screenQuad.Draw();
```

The code in Listing 9.2 looks similar to other sample programs we have seen before. The magic sauce is in the fragment shader that does the actual conversion. Listing 9.3 contains the source of the fragment shader that performs the conversion based on exposure. You can use the up and down keys to adjust the exposure once the program is in the variable exposure mode. The range of exposures for this program goes from 0.01 to 20.0. Notice how the level of detail in different locations in the image changes with the exposure level.

LISTING 9.3 hdr_exposure.fs Fragment Shader for HDR to LDR Conversion

```
#version 150
// hdr_exposure.fs
// Scale floating point texture to 0.0 - 1.0 based
// on the specified exposure
//

in vec2 vTexCoord;

uniform sampler2D textureUnit0;
uniform float exposure;

out vec4 oColor;

void main(void)
{
    // fetch from HDR texture
    vec4 vColor = texture(textureUnit0, vTexCoord);

    // Apply the exposure to this texel
    oColor = 1.0 - exp2(-vColor * exposure);
    oColor.a = 1.0f;
}
```

The last tone mapping shader used in the first sample program performs dynamic adjustments to the exposure level based on the relative brightness of different portions of the scene. First, the shader needs to know the relative luminance of the area near the current texel being tone mapped. The shader does this by sampling a 5 x 5 matrix with the current texel in the center. All the surrounding samples are then weighted and added together. The final summed color is converted to a luminance value. The sample program uses a lookup table to convert the luminance to an exposure. The exposure is then used to convert the HDR texel to an LDR value. Listing 9.4 shows the adaptive HDR shader.

LISTING 9.4   hdr_adaptive Fragment Shader for Adaptive Exposure Levels in HDR to LDR Conversion

```
#version 150
// hdr_adaptive.fs
//
//

in vec2 vTex;

uniform sampler2D textureUnit0;
uniform sampler1D textureUnit1;
uniform vec2 tc_offset[25];

out vec4 oColor;

void main(void)
{
    vec4 hdrSample[25];
    for (int i = 0; i < 25; i++)
    {
        // Perform 25 lookups around the current texel
        hdrSample[i] = texture(textureUnit0, vTex.st + tc_offset[i]);
    }
    // Calculate weighted color of region
    vec4 vColor = hdrSample[12];
    vec4 kernelcolor = (
        (1.0  * (hdrSample[0] + hdrSample[4] + hdrSample[20] + hdrSample[24])) +
        (4.0  * (hdrSample[1] + hdrSample[3] + hdrSample[5] + hdrSample[9] +
                hdrSample[15] + hdrSample[19] + hdrSample[21] + hdrSample[23])) +
        (7.0  * (hdrSample[2] + hdrSample[10] + hdrSample[14] + hdrSample[22])) +
        (16.0 * (hdrSample[6] + hdrSample[8] + hdrSample[16] + hdrSample[18])) +
        (26.0 * (hdrSample[7] + hdrSample[11] + hdrSample[13] + hdrSample[17])) +
        (41.0 * hdrSample[12])
        ) / 273.0;

    // Calculate the luminance for the whole filter kernel
    float kernelLuminance = dot(kernelcolor.rgb, vec3(0.3, 0.59, 0.11));

    // look up the corresponding exposure
```

```
float exposure = texture(textureUnit1, kernelLuminance/2.0).r;
exposure = clamp(exposure, 0.02f, 20.0f);

// Apply the exposure to this texel
oColor = 1.0 - exp2(-vColor * exposure);
oColor.a = 1.0f;
}
```

When using one exposure for an image, you can adjust for the best results by taking the range for the whole and using an average. Considerable detail is still lost with this approach in the bright and dim areas. The lookup table used with the adaptive fragment shader brings out the detail in both the bright and dim areas of the image; take a look at Figure 9.4. The lookup table uses a logarithmic-like scale to map luminance values to exposure levels. You can change this table to increase or decrease the range of exposures used and the resulting amount of detail in different dynamic ranges.

FIGURE 9.4 Adaptive tone mapping brings out detail in dark and light areas. (Also shown in Color Plate 15.)

The filter kernel and lookup table approach used here is one of many. As an exercise, try modifying the hdr_adaptive.fs fragment shader to calculate exposures programmatically. You can also use lower mipmap levels of an HDR texture to find the luminance of a neighborhood.

Great, so now you know how to image process an OpenEXR file, but what good is that in a typical OpenGL program? Lots! The OpenEXR image is only a stand-in for any lit OpenGL scene. Many OpenGL games and applications now render HDR scenes and other content to floating-point buffers and then display the result to the scene. You can use the same methods you just learned to render in HDR, generating much more realistic lighting environments and showing the dynamic range and detail of each frame.

(e)Making Your Scene Bloom

HDR rendering doesn't stop with floating-point buffers. In fact, that's just the beginning. All sorts of effects are made possible by the additional precision. Now that you've seen the beginnings of what floating-point buffers can do, let's throw in one more effect to add more realism to directly lit scenes. Have you ever noticed how the sun or a bright light can sometimes engulf tree branches or other objects between you and the light source? That's called light bloom. Figure 9.5 (also shown in Color Plate 16) shows how light bloom can affect an indoor scene.

FIGURE 9.5   Left image shows detail in stained glass. Light bloom in the right image brighter exposure obscures the stained glass.

Notice how you can see all the detail in the lower exposure of the left side of Figure 9.5. The right side is a much higher exposure, and the grid in the stained glass is covered by the light bloom. Even the wooden post on the bottom right looks smaller as it gets covered by bloom. By adding bloom to a scene you can enhance the sense of brightness in certain areas. We can simulate this bloom effect caused by bright light sources. Although you could also perform this effect using 8-bit precision buffers, it's much more effective when used with floating-point buffers on an HDR scene.

The first step is to draw your scene in HDR. For the hdr_bloom sample program, an FBO is set up with two float textures bound. The scene is rendered as normal to the first bound texture. But the second bound texture gets only the bright areas of the field. To be efficient, the hdr_bloom sample program fills both textures in one pass from one shader, see Listing 9.5. The bright area data is used to generate the bloom effect. The bloom level used is adjustable via a uniform. To filter for the bright areas, the cutoff is applied first to zero out all fragments below the cutoff. Then the remaining fragments are scaled between 0.0 and 1.0 for brightness levels of 0.0 to 0.5; any values above 0.5 are clamped to one.

LISTING 9.5   tex_replace Fragment Shader; Output Bright Data to a Separate Buffer

```
#version 150
// tex_replace.fs
// outputs 1 color using texture replace
//

varying vec2 vTexCoord;
uniform sampler2D textureUnit0;
uniform vec4 vColor;
out vec4 oColor;
out vec4 oBright;

void main(void)
{
    const float bloomLimit = 1.0;

    oColor =  vColor*texture(textureUnit0, vTexCoord);
    oColor.a = 1.0;

    vec3 brightColor = max(vColor.rgb - vec3(bloomLimit), vec3(0.0));
    float bright = dot(brightColor, vec3(1.0));
    bright = smoothstep(0.0, 0.5, bright);
    oBright.rgb = mix(vec3(0.0), vColor.rgb, bright).rgb;
    oBright.a = 1.0;
}
```

After that, the resulting brightness level, between 0.0 and 0.5, is mixed with the original color. That means the result of the mix operation is a color between (0, 0, 0) and the original color based on the value of the brightness. In the end, the bright pass buffer is filled with values other than 0.0 only in the bright areas of the screen, stored in floating-point format.

Now after the scene has been rendered, there is still some work to do to finish the bright pass. The bright data must be blurred for the bloom effect to work. For this, we create fourfloat textures with the first texture one-third the width and height of the screen and each subsequent texture one-third the size of the previous. We render to the first texture by performing a Gaussian blur of the original image. The second texture is drawn to with a Gaussian blur of the first texture and so on through all four textures. To apply the blur, the sample program uses the shader in Listing 9.6, which applies a 5 x 5 convolution kernel to the incoming texture, combining the results of the 24 closest texels to generate a new value.

LISTING 9.6   Blur Fragment Shader; Apply a 5 x 5 Gaussian Blur Kernel to the Input Texture

```
#version 150
// blur.fs
// outputs 1 color using a gaussian blur of the input texture
//

in vec4 vFragColor;
in vec2 vTexCoords;

uniform sampler2D textureUnit0;
uniform vec2 tc_offset[25];

out vec4 oColor;

void main(void)
{
    vec4 sample[25];
    for (int i = 0; i < 25; i++)
    {
        sample[i] = texture(textureUnit0, vTexCoords.st + tc_offset[i]);
    }

    //   1  4  7  4 1
    //   4 16 26 16 4
    //   7 26 41 26 7 / 273
    //   4 16 26 16 4
    //   1  4  7  4 1

    oColor = (
                (1.0  * (sample[0] + sample[4] + sample[20] + sample[24])) +
                (4.0  * (sample[1] + sample[3] + sample[5] + sample[9] +
                    sample[15] + sample[19] + sample[21] + sample[23])) +
                (7.0  * (sample[2] + sample[10] + sample[14] + sample[22])) +
                (16.0 * (sample[6] + sample[8] + sample[16] + sample[18])) +
                (26.0 * (sample[7] + sample[11] + sample[13] + sample[17])) +
                (41.0 * sample[12])
                ) / 273.0;
}
```

After the blurring passes are complete, the blur results are combined with the full color texture of the scene to produce the final results. In Listing 9.7 you can see how the final shader samples from five textures: the full color texture, the bright pass, and the four progressively blurred versions of the bright pass. The bright pass and the blurred results are added together to form the bloom effect, which is multiplied by a user-controlled uniform. You can scale the bloom effect up with the right key on the keyboard and down with the left cursor key. The final HDR color result is then put through exposure calculations, which you should be familiar with from the last sample program.

LISTING 9.7   hdr_exposure Fragment Shader; Add Bloom Effect to Scene

```
#version 150
// hdr_exposure.fs
// Apply blur effect from float blur textures
// Scale floating point scene texture to 0.0 - 1.0 based
// on the specified exposure
//

in vec2 vTexCoord;

uniform sampler2D origImage;
uniform sampler2D brightImage;
uniform sampler2D blur1;
uniform sampler2D blur2;
uniform sampler2D blur3;
uniform sampler2D blur4;

uniform float exposure;
uniform float bloomLevel;

out vec4 oColor;
out vec4 oBright;

void main(void)
{
    // fetch from HDR & blur textures
    vec4 vBaseImage = texture(origImage, vTexCoord);
    vec4 vBrightPass = texture(brightImage, vTexCoord);
    vec4 vBlurColor1 = texture(blur1, vTexCoord);
    vec4 vBlurColor2 = texture(blur2, vTexCoord);
    vec4 vBlurColor3 = texture(blur3, vTexCoord);
    vec4 vBlurColor4 = texture(blur4, vTexCoord);
```

6

```
    vec4 vBloom = vBrightPass +
                  vBlurColor1 +
                  vBlurColor2 +
                  vBlurColor3 +
                  vBlurColor4;

    vec4 vColor = vBaseImage + bloomLevel * vBloom;

    // Apply the exposure to this texel
    vColor = 1.0 - exp2(-vColor * exposure);
    oColor = vColor;
    oColor.a = 1.0f;
}
```

The exposure shader shown in Listing 9.7 is used to draw a screen-sized textured quad to the window. That's it! Dial up and down the bloom effect to your heart's content. Figure 9.6 shows the hdr_bloom sample program with both low and high bloom levels. Try changing the program to use a single mipmapped texture instead of a series of four blur textures.

FIGURE 9.6   hdr_bloom program. Left side shows no bloom; right side has excessive bloom. (Also shown in Color Plate 17.)

Floating-Point Depth Buffers

Not only can you use float formats for color data to, but you can also use them for depth data as well! Typically depth buffers are 24 bits deep, giving you 16,777,216 possible depth values usually scaled between 0.0 and 1.0. Quite frankly this seems like a lot! But the bigger issue with a fixed data format used as a depth buffer is that each depth increment is the same distance. You may have a bunch of geometry that all falls within the same depth value because you are layering geometry or because you end up only using a small portion of the total depth range. This can result in z-fighting, low differential precision, or other nondeterministic behavior.

Floating-point depth buffers help solve some of these problems. Instead of being tied to fixed increment, nearby geometry written to a floating-point depth buffer has a lot more room to maneuver. Take a look at Figure 9.7 to see how this works out. This added precision can come in handy in many cases, especially when dealing with shadow volumes. But as great as floating-point depth buffers are, it's best not to use them everywhere. Float depth buffers can take up more room than other fixed point formats and also may be slower for the GPU to write to and read from. Fixed precision is usually sufficient for many traditional uses.

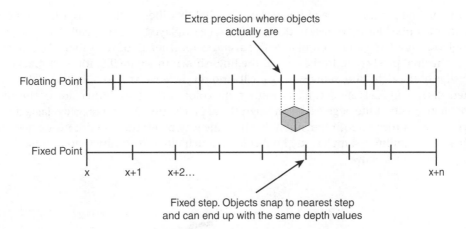

FIGURE 9.7   Fixed depth buffer precision versus float depth buffers.

Even with floating-point depth buffers, it's still possible to see z-fighting issues if your geometry is packed too close together. But since floating-point depth buffers are not limited to the 0.0 to 1.0 range, one way to help avoid z-fighting issues with floating-point depth buffers is to spread your geometry out! Go beyond the typical 0.0-1.0 range and make full use of your floating-point storage.

OpenGL provides a clip volume for rendering into. Geometry that falls outside the clip volume is "clipped off" and not rasterized. For rendering to displayed windows, the clip volume usually consists of the top, right, bottom, and left edges of the window. There is also a near and far plane. If an object is too close or too far, it won't be drawn. The far plane can help prevent you from drawing geometry that might be so far away, it isn't even as big as a single pixel. But there are cases such as shadow volumes in which we are just looking for all the depth data, no matter how close or far. To do this, you can disable depth clamping by calling glDisable(GL_DEPTH_CLAMP), which bypasses any clipping to the near and far clip planes. Depth clamping is disabled by default.

Multisampling

Sometimes one sample just isn't enough! There are a plenty of cases where drawing a line or a polygon at a slight angle to screen-space vertical or horizontal generates a jagged edge as that edge is rasterized across only a handful of pixel rows or columns. Take the top of the window in the hdr_bloom sample program, which can be seen in Figure 9.6. As the top of the window is rasterized, the window starts in pixel row x, but as it continues to extend it eventually snaps to row x+1. This effect known as aliasing is ugly, unrealistic, and undesirable.

Multisampling generates several fragments with slightly different locations, called subpixels, for each pixel location. Before the buffer can be displayed, the subpixels have to be "resolved." Resolving a multisample buffer averages together all of the subpixels to determine the final pixel color. In the case of the lines shown in Figure 9.8, for each pixel on the edge of the right line, some samples will land on the edge and some will not. Then when all the subpixels are averaged together, the color of pixels on either side of the edge show how much of the edge passes through those pixels. Instead of a raggedy, jaggedy edge you get a nice smooth transition. In the same way pixels that are not near edges are enhanced by multiple samples, the final color is much closer to reality than a single sample could ever show.

FIGURE 9.8   Zoomed in view of line segments. Left—an aliased line; right—the same line multisampled.

The subpixel locations are not regularly distributed. Instead, subpixel locations are pseudo-randomly spread throughout the pixel region. This enhances the effect of multisampled antialiasing. Figure 9.9 shows possible subpixel locations for 2x, 4x, and 8x antialiasing. You can get the actual locations for each subpixel by calling glGetMultisamplefv. First, call glGetIntegerv with the GL_SAMPLES enum to find out how many samples the current framebuffer has.

```
// Get the location of each multisample sub-pixel
int sampleCount = 0;
glGetIntegerv(GL_SAMPLES, &sampleCount);

float positions[64]; // Enough for at least 32 samples
for(int i =0; i < sampleCount; i++)
```

```
{
    glGetMultisamplefv(GL_SAMPLE_POSITION, i, &positions[i*2]);
}
```

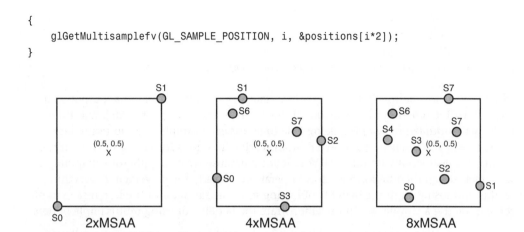

FIGURE 9.9   Possible sample locations for 2x, 4x, and 8x multisample antialiasing.

OpenGL allows you to use several surfaces that support multiple samples. The first is the window surface itself. You learn more about how to create a multisampled window in Chapters 13, 14, and 15 where the details of the OS-specific window management are discussed. Second are render buffers. You can use `glRenderBufferStorageMultisample` to create storage for an RBO that is multisampled. Similarly, you can also create multisample textures by using `glTexImage2DMultisample` and `glTexImage3DMultisample`.

```
glGenTextures(1, hdrTextures);
glBindTexture(GL_TEXTURE_2D_MULTISAMPLE, hdrTextures[0]);
glTexImage2DMultisample(GL_TEXTURE_2D_MULTISAMPLE, 8, GL_RGB16F,
                        screenWidth, screenHeight, GL_FALSE);
```

The important part to notice here is the new texture target for MSAA textures. When you bind an MSAA texture, you have to use `GL_TEXTURE_2D_MULTISAMPLE` instead of `GL_TEXTURE_2D`. For multisample arrays, you can use the `GL_TEXTURE_2D_MULTISAMPLE_ARRAY` target.

Now that you know how to make multisample surfaces, there are a few things you need to know about accessing multisample textures in shaders. The old `sampler2D` won't do the trick. Instead declare a new sampler called `sampler2DMS`. Then in your fragment shader you can use `texelFetch()` to fetch any given sample for a fragment. `texelFetch()` sample functions require that you specify an integer fragment location instead of providing texture coordinates between 0.0 and 1.0. GLSL has provided a function called `textureSize()` to help you figure out the size of a multisampled texture in your shader. With that, you can convert normalized texture coordinates to integer texture coordinates.

```
// fetch from HDR & blur textures
iTmp = textureSize(origImage);
tmp = floor(iTmp * vTex);
vec4 vBaseImage  = texelFetch(origImage, ivec2(tmp), sampleNumber);
```

A resolve of a multisample buffer takes all the samples and creates one final output value. A typical resolve function may just add all the colors of each sample together and then divide by the number of samples. Being able to access each sample of a multisampled texture allows you to create your own custom resolve functions instead of relying on the default. This is especially useful in HDR rendering because we can apply tone mapping to each subpixel and then perform a resolve operation instead of just averaging everything together and losing all of the benefits of having multiple samples. In the hdr_msaa sample program, we use a familiar setup to demonstrate the benefits of using multisample buffers.

First, we create the MSAA texture and bind it to the MSAA texture target. Then in Listing 9.8 we get the locations of each subpixel and use them to calculate the distance from the center. That information is used to create weightings that will be applied to each subpixel when we do our custom shader resolve in the fragment shader.

LISTING 9.8   Calculate Subpixel Distances, Program Texture Buffer Object

```
// Add up the distances to get the total used for calculating weights
for(int i=1; i<8; i++)
{
    float totalWeight = 0.0f;
    for(int j=0; j<=i; j++)
    {
        totalWeight += invertedSampleDistances[j];
    }

    // Invert to get the factor used for each sample,
    // the sum of all sample weights is always 1.0
    float perSampleFactor = 1 / totalWeight;
    for(int j=0; j<=i; j++)
    {
        sampleWeights[i][j] = invertedSampleDistances[j] * perSampleFactor;
    }
}


// Setup a texture buffer object for holding the sample weights
glGenBuffers(1, &sampleWeightBuf);
glBindBuffer(GL_TEXTURE_BUFFER_ARB, sampleWeightBuf);
glBufferData(GL_TEXTURE_BUFFER_ARB, sizeof(float)*8, sampleWeights,
             GL_DYNAMIC_DRAW);
glBindBuffer(GL_TEXTURE_BUFFER_ARB, 0);
```

Then it's time to set up program and object state. We can render the scene to the MSAA FBO as if nothing was different. The GPU automatically generates all of the subpixels and calls the fragment shader on each subpixel. Once the scene is complete in the FBO, the program runs a resolve shader to tone map and resolve the multisample buffer for display on the window. Because part of the scene is rendered in HDR, tone mapping is an important step. In fact, if we didn't do the resolve ourselves in the shader, the HDR values would badly skew the hardware resolve. The result would be an image that looks even more aliased than if you used a buffer with only one sample.

Listing 9.9 shows the resolve shader. Two different kinds of resolves are done. The first is a simple average done by adding all the samples together and dividing by the number of samples. This value is stored in vColor. The other resolve is done by multiplying each sample by a weighting that is dependent on the sample location and is stored in vWeightedColor. The user can decide which resolve will be displayed by pressing W for the weighted resolve or Q for the straight average resolve.

LISTING 9.9   Perform MSAA Resolve and Tone Map Operations in hdr_exposure.fs

```
#version 150
// hdr_exposure.fs
// Scale floating point texture to 0.0 - 1.0 based
// on the specified exposure.
// Resolve multisample buffer based on input sample count
//

in vec2 vTexCoord;

uniform sampler2DMS origImage;
uniform samplerBuffer sampleWeightSampler;
uniform int sampleCount;       // 0-based, 0=1sample, 1=2samples, etc
uniform int useWeightedResolve; // 0-false, 1-true
uniform float exposure;

out vec4 oColor;

// do all tone mapping in a separate function
vec4 toneMap(vec4 vHdrColor)
{
    vec4 vLdrColor;
    vLdrColor = 1.0 - exp2(-vHdrColor * exposure);
    vLdrColor.a = 1.0f;
    return vLdrColor;
}
```

```
void main(void)
{
    // Calculate integer texture coordinates
    vec2 tmp = floor(textureSize(origImage) * vTexCoord);

    // Find both the weighted and unweighted colors
    vec4 vColor = vec4(0.0, 0.0, 0.0, 1.0);
    vec4 vWeightedColor = vec4(0.0, 0.0, 0.0, 1.0);

    for (int i = 0; i <= sampleCount; i++)
    {
        // Get the weight for this sample from the texBo, this changes
        // based on the number of samples
        float weight = texelFetchBuffer(sampleWeightSampler, i).r;

        // tone-map the HDR texel before it is weighted
        vec4 sample = toneMap(texelFetch(origImage, ivec2(tmp), i));

        vWeightedColor += sample * weight;
        vColor += sample;
    }

    // now, decide on the type of resolve to perform
    oColor = vWeightedColor;

    // if the user selected the unweighed resolve, output the
    // equally weighted value
    if (useWeightedResolve != 0)
    {
        oColor = vColor / (sampleCount+1);
    }
    oColor.a = 1.0f;
}
```

The number of samples used to perform the resolve is also configurable by the user. You can use the number keys 1 through 8 to select the number of samples to use in the resolve. Figure 9.10 (also shown in Color Plate 18) shows the difference between a single sample and eight samples. Using multisample buffers can make a big difference in the quality of your scenes.

FIGURE 9.10   Results of multisampling. Left image has one sample, right has eight.

Integers

GLSL once started out with many of its own data types that didn't strictly conform to IEEE standards for floats and other industry standards for other data types commonly used on the CPU. But these days things have become much more standardized. Not only can you use floating-point data in a shader and expect it to behave the same as on the CPU, but other data types such as integer and unsigned integer are also available.

New texture formats also exist to feed your shaders' hungry appetite. You can create textures with a plethora of different integer formats, both signed and unsigned. They range from one channel (R only) through all four channels (RGBA) and can contain precision ranging from 8 bits per channel through 32. There is a format for nearly every integer texture need! In addition to textures, RBOs can also be created with integer formats. To clear an integer-based buffer bound to a FBO, you can call `glClearBufferiv` for integer buffers and `glClearBufferuiv` for unsigned integer buffers.

Why are integer and unsigned integer formats important? First, you can now send integers via textures and uniforms to shaders that can be greater than 255. Shaders also allow you to access the data in integer textures in a bitwise manner, allowing you to pack data any way you want. Integer buffers and textures can be used for indexing or selection when modifying geometry rendered in large quantities, such as a forest of trees. To access individual texels of integer textures, you can use the `texelFetch` command in GLSL shaders. This sample function takes an integer vector for specifying the location in a texture, so you can be sure about which texel you get. You can also bind integer data to texture buffer objects.

The most important reason for adding integer formats is they create a truly flexible and parallel compute environment in shaders. You can load arbitrary texture data in float- or integer-based formats and perform any computations you need such as physics, image processing, modeling, and pretty much anything math related that requires intensive parallel processing. This General Purpose Computing, often called GPGPU, really opens the door to the amount of work that can be done on the GPU in record time.

sRGB

Gone are the days when the RGB color space was enough. Now you can use Super-RGB! Actually, it's called sRGB, but it is much more powerful than the traditional RGB color space we have grown accustomed to over the past 20 years. Even though RGB is the most common color space for computer graphics, there are limitations on just how far it can go. The sensitivity of the human eye is much higher than what can be represented in RGB.

The RGB color space uses values from 0 to 1, but applies a linear gamma ramp to the final result. The sRGB color space also uses values from 0 to 1, but also uses a nonlinear gamma ramp to expand the range of the colors that can be represented. Darker colors of the sRGB spectrum use a gamma value near 2.2 for darker areas, but has an expanded gamma reaching 2.4 for brighter areas. This means sRGB formats have a built-in expanded dynamic range. sRGB was originally created for use in imaging and photo processing to help better map and display colors in the typical viewing environments of offices and dim rooms.

When you use an sRGB texture in OpenGL, the sRGB format is converted to RGB when the texture is sampled. But only the RGB components are converted; alpha is left as-is. Each component is converted individually according to the following rules.

If the texel value is less than or equal to 0.04045, the implementation will convert using

> Sample = Texel / 12.92

If the texel value greater than 0.04045, the sample is converted as

> Sample = ((Texel + 0.055) / 1.055)$^{2.4}$

Renderbuffers also support storage formats that are sRGB; specifically the format `GL_SRGB8_ALPHA8` must be supported. That means you can bind RBOs and textures that have an internal sRGB format to a framebuffer object and then render to it. Because we just talked about how sRGB formats are not linear, you probably don't want your writes to sRGB FBOs to be linear either; that would defeat the whole purpose! The good news is OpenGL can convert the linear color values your shader outputs into sRGB values automatically when you call `glEnable(GL_FRAMEBUFFER_SRGB)`. Remember, this only works for color attachments that contain an sRGB surface. You can call `glGetFramebufferAttachmentParameteriv` with the value `GL_FRAMEBUFFER_ATTACHMENT_COLOR_ENCODING` to find out if the attached surface is sRGB. sRGB surfaces return `GL_SRGB` while other surfaces return `GL_LINEAR`. This conversion follows the equations listed in Table 9.3 for fragment colors (fc).

TABLE 9.3   Conversion Equations for Color Outputs to sRGB

Fragment Values	Conversion Equation
fc <= 0.0	0.0
0.0 < fc < 0.0031308	12.92 * fc
0.0031308 < fc < 1.0	1.055 * fc 0.41666 – 0.055
fc > 1.0	1.0

Texture Compression

Continuing along the line of new formats that help make OpenGL both useful and flexible, texture compression can be helpful even when modern GPUs can have gigabytes of memory available. Textures can take up an incredible amount of space! Some modern games can easily use 1 Gigabyte of texture data in a given level. That's a lot of data! Where do you put it all? Textures are an important part to making rich, realistic, and impressive scenes, but if you can't load all of the data onto the GPU, your rendering will be slow if not impossible. One way to deal with storing and using a large amount of texture data is to compress the data.

OpenGL implementations support at least the compression schemes listed in Table 9.4, one of which is RGTC (Red-Green Texture Compression). The RGTC format breaks a texture image into 4 x 4 texel blocks compressing the individual channels within that block using a series of codes. This compression mode works only for one and two channel signed and unsigned textures. You don't need to worry about the exact compression scheme unless you are planning on writing a compressor. Just note that space savings from using RGTC is 50%.

TABLE 9.4   Native OpenGL Texture Compression Formats

Formats	Type
GL_COMPRESSED_RED	Generic
GL_COMPRESSED_RG	Generic
GL_COMPRESSED_RGB	Generic
GL_COMPRESSED_RGBA	Generic
GL_COMPRESSED_SRGB	Generic
GL_COMPRESSED_SRGB_ALPHA	Generic
GL_COMPRESSED_RED_RGTC1	RGTC
GL_COMPRESSED_SIGNED_RED_RGTC1	RGTC
GL_COMPRESSED_RG_RGTC1	RGTC
GL_COMPRESSED_SIGNED_RG_RGTC1	RGTC

The first six formats listed in Table 9.4 are generic and allow the OpenGL driver to decide what compression mechanism to use. This means your driver can use the format that best meets current conditions. The catch is that it is implementation specific and not portable. Your implementation may also support other compressed formats such as ETC1 and S3TC. You should check for the availability of formats not required by OpenGL before attempting to use them. The best way to do this is to check for support of the related extension; you learn more on this later in Chapters 13, 14, and 15.

Using Compression

You can ask OpenGL to compress a texture when you load it. All you have to do is request that the internal format be one of the compressed formats. OpenGL takes your uncompressed data and converts it as the texture image is loaded. There is no real difference in how you use compressed textures and uncompressed textures. The GPU handles the conversion when it samples from the texture. Many imaging tools used for creating textures and other images allow you to save your data directly in a compressed format.

Once you have loaded a texture using a nongeneric compressed internal format, you can get the compressed image back by calling glGetCompressedTexImage. Just pick the texture target and mipmap level you are interested in. Because you may not know how the image is compressed or what format is used, you should check the image size to make sure you have enough room for the whole surface.

```
Glint imageSize = 0;
glGetTexParameteri(GL_TEXTURE_2D, TEXTURE_COMPRESSED_IMAGE_SIZE, &imageSize);
void *data = malloc(imageSize);
glGetCompressedTexImage(GL_TEXTURE_2D, 0, data);
```

To load compressed texture images, you can use one of the dedicated texture load functions; glCompressedTexImage1D, glCompressedTexImage2D, and glCompressedTexImage3D. Use these functions the same way you would for glTexImage1D, glTexImage2D, and so on. You can also update compressed texture images with glCompressedTexSubImage1D, glCompressedTexSubImage2D, or glCompressedTexSubImage3D.

Shared Exponent

Although shared exponent textures are not technically a compressed format in the truest sense, they do allow you to use floating-point texture data while saving storage space. Instead of storing an exponent for each of the R, G, and B values, shared exponent formats use the same exponent value for the whole texel. The fractional and exponential parts of each value are stored as integers and then assembled when the texture is sampled. For the format GL_RGB9_E5, 9 bits are used to store each color and 5 bits are the common exponent for all channels. This format packs three floating-point values into 32 bits; that's a savings of 67%! To make use of shared exponents, you can get the texture data directly in this format from a content creation tool or write a converter that compresses your float RGB values into a shared exponent format.

Summary

OpenGL goes well beyond basic framebuffer access you first saw in Chapter 8. In this chapter you learned how logical names for your fragment shaders can be used and how those names can be mapped to output indexes. Then you experienced the power of floating-point buffers and how they can dramatically enhance the realism of your scenes. Floating-point depth buffers also came into play providing additional precision, and multisample buffers brought sample level access straight to the fragment shader.

We spent quite a bit of time looking at multisampled antialiasing and how you can use it to improve the quality of your output. You learned how to access each sample of multisample buffers directly in fragment shaders. You also got a taste of how integer textures can be used to provide easy external indexing of what your shaders do and enable general computation in shader units. Finally, we explored new ways of storing texture and buffer data in sRGB, compressed, and shared exponent formats, which provide more realistic color mapping and help save space.

CHAPTER 10

Fragment Operations: The End of the Pipeline

by Nicholas Haemel

WHAT YOU'LL LEARN IN THIS CHAPTER:

How To	Functions You'll Use
Finely tune multisample rendering	`glSampleMask`, `glSampleCoverage`
Create and use stencil patterns	`glStencilFuncSeparate`, `glStencilOpSeparate`, `glClearStencil`
Blend color and alpha outputs together	`glBlendFuncSeparate`, `glBlendOpSeparate`, `glBlendColor`
Use logic ops	`glLogicOp`
Mask the final output	`glColorMask`, `glColorMaski`, `glDepthMask`, `glStencilMask`, `glStencilMaskSeparate`

After reading through the first nine chapters, you should be well-versed in using vertex and fragment shaders to generate output based on your geometry. But what happens when your fragment shader is finished? Where do all the fragments go? It just so happens there are a few more steps these fragments must make before they can retire to a final resting place in a buffer or window.

This chapter walks through the last steps in the OpenGL pipeline, the per-fragment operations. We start with the scissor test, which is the first stop along the way and follow a virtual fragment through multisample operations, stencil testing, depth buffer testing, blending, dithering, and logic ops. Figure 10.1 shows the path a fragment follows when all stages are enabled.

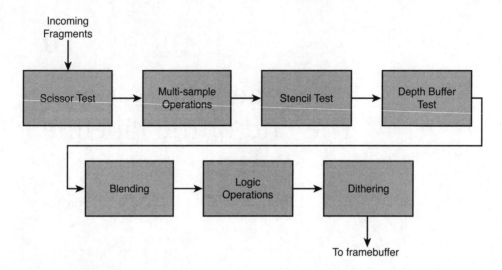

FIGURE 10.1   Per-pixel operations.

Scissoring—Cutting Your Geometry Down To Size

The first step in sending those fragments to their final resting place is to decide whether they lie in a region that has been cut out of the renderable area. Scissoring is performed on window coordinates. That means all incoming fragments have a window coordinate between (0, 0) and (width, height) where width and height are the window dimensions. Applications can define a scissor plane that cuts off portions of geometry. This is done through a maximum and minimum x value as well as a maximum and minimum y value. To set a scissor region, call glScissor:

```
void glScissor(GLint left, Glint bottom, sizei width, sizei height);
```

Scissoring must also be enabled by calling glEnable(GL_SCISSOR_TEST) for the scissor test to work. If the window coordinates of the fragment fall within the region defined by the scissor, the fragment will continue on down the pipeline. Otherwise it will be discarded. Another way to express this operation is through two equations using the values you passed into glScissor. If left <= x_w < (left + width) and bottom <= y_w < (bottom + height), then the test passes. You learned about the scissor test back in Chapter 3, "Basic Rendering." Take a look back there for a refresher if scissor operations are a bit hazy.

Multisampling

After scissoring is performed, the next stop in the pixel pipeline is multisampling. You had your first taste of multisampling back in Chapter 9, "Advanced Buffers: Beyond the Basics." Now let's look into how you can control the specifics of multisampling.

Remember that the multisampling stage generates multiple subsamples for any given pixel. This can be particularly helpful when a pixel happens to fall near the edge of a line or polygon. The number of samples a buffer has is determined at allocation time. For window surfaces, you have to specify the sample count when you choose a pixel format or config. For framebuffers, you can select your sample count when creating the storage of the textures and renderbuffers bound to the framebuffer. Note that the sample count for all attachments of a framebuffer should be the same.

Back in Chapter 9 you also learned how to get each subpixel sample location within the pixel by calling glGetMultisamplefv. Now let's look at how you can control those subpixels. There are two stages you can control that affect how multisampling is handled: modifying coverage values and masking off samples.

Sample Coverage

Coverage refers to how much area a subpixel "covers." You can convert the alpha value of a fragment directly to a coverage value to determine how many samples of the framebuffer will be updated by the fragment. To do this, call glEnable(GL_SAMPLE_ALPHA_TO_COVERAGE). The coverage value for a fragment is used to determine how many subsamples will be written. For instance, a fragment with an alpha of 0.4 would generate a coverage value of 40%. For an 8-sample MSAA buffer, three of that pixel's samples would be written to.

Because the alpha value was already used to decide how many subsamples should be written, it wouldn't make sense to then blend those subsamples with the same alpha value. After all, using alpha-to-coverage is a way of doing blending. To help prevent these subpixels from also being blended when blending is enabled, you can force the alpha values for those samples to 1 by calling glEnable(GL_SAMPLE_ALPHA_TO_ONE).

Using alpha-to-coverage has several advantages over simple blending. When rendering to a multisampled buffer, the alpha blend would normally be applied equally to the entire pixel. With alpha-to-coverage, alpha masked edges are antialiased, producing a much more natural and smooth result. This is particularly useful when drawing bushes, trees, or dense foliage where parts of the brush are alpha transparent.

OpenGL also allows you to set the sample coverage manually by calling glSampleCoverage. Manually applying a coverage value for a pixel occurs after the mask for alpha-to-coverage is applied. For this step to take effect, sample coverage must be enabled by calling glEnable(GL_SAMPLE_COVERAGE).

```
glSampleCoverage(clampf value, Boolean invert)
```

The coverage value passed into the value parameter can be between 0 and 1. The invert parameter signals to OpenGL if the resulting mask should be inverted. For instance, if you were drawing two overlapping trees, one with a coverage of 60% and the other with 40%, you would want to invert one of the coverage values to make sure the same mask was not used for both draw calls.

```
glSampleCoverage(0.5, GL_FALSE);
// Draw first geometry set
. . .
glSampleCoverage(0.5, GL_TRUE);
// Draw second geometry set
. . .
```

Sample Mask

The last configurable option in the multisample stage is the sample mask. This step allows you to mask off specific samples using the `glSampleMaski` function. Unlike the earlier stages, you can specify exactly which samples you want to turn off. Remember that the alpha-to-coverage and sample coverage affect which samples are enabled before we get to this stage. That means setting the sample mask to one in this stage does not guarantee samples will be enabled.

```
glSampleMaski(GLuint maskNumber, GLbitfield mask);
```

The `mask` parameter is essentially a 32-bit bitwise mask of the pixel samples with bit 0 mapping to sample 0, bit 1 mapping to sample 1, and so on. You can use the `maskNumber` to address bits beyond the first 32 bits with each incremental mask value representing another 32 bits. You can query `GL_MAX_SAMPLE_MASK_WORDS` to find out how many masks are supported. As of this writing, implementations only support one word, which makes sense considering no implementations support more than 32 samples per pixel.

There is another way to modify the sample mask. You can write to the built-in output `gl_SampleMask[]` array in a fragment shader to set the mask inside your shaders.

Putting It All Together

The sample program for this chapter, called `oit`, draws several semitransparent objects shaped like a tinted glass wind chime. When several semitransparent surfaces are drawn in OpenGL, simply blending them together produces the wrong result. Think about what happens if you draw an object with alpha of 0.5 and then try to draw another object behind it, also with an alpha of 0.5. If you leave depth testing enabled, the back object is simply discarded as a result of failing the depth test. If depth testing is disabled, the back object just draws over the front one and looks as if it is in front. We dig into blending in more detail later in this chapter.

To overcome this blending shortcoming, we need to use order independent transparency, or OIT. Most algorithms for correctly rendering transparent geometry involve sorting the objects being rendered by depth and then rendering the farthest objects first. This can be very complex and time-consuming. Even worse, in many situations there is no correct sorting.

To deal with this, we store each rendering pass in a separate sample of a multisampled framebuffer using sample masks. After the scene is rendered, the resolve operation combines all samples for each pixel in the correct order. Let's get started.

The first step is to draw all of the geometry to a multisampled framebuffer. Part of the geometry is drawn in Listing 10.1. All nontransparent objects are masked to sample 0. Each semitransparent object is rendered to a unique sample using the sample mask.

LISTING 10.1   Setting Up Sample Mask State

```
    glSampleMaski(0, 0x01);
        glEnable(GL_SAMPLE_MASK);
. . .
        glBindTexture(GL_TEXTURE_2D, textures[1]);
        shaderManager.UseStockShader(GLT_SHADER_TEXTURE_REPLACE,
                    transformPipeline.GetModelViewProjectionMatrix(), 0);
        bckgrndCylBatch.Draw();
. . .

    modelViewMatrix.Translate(0.0f, 0.8f, 0.0f);
    modelViewMatrix.PushMatrix();
        modelViewMatrix.Translate(-0.3f, 0.f, 0.0f);
        modelViewMatrix.Scale(0.40, 0.8, 0.40);
        modelViewMatrix.Rotate(50.0, 0.0, 10.0, 0.0);
        glSampleMaski(0, 0x02);
        shaderManager.UseStockShader(GLT_SHADER_FLAT,
                transformPipeline.GetModelViewProjectionMatrix(), vLtYellow);
        glass1Batch.Draw();
    modelViewMatrix.PopMatrix();

    modelViewMatrix.PushMatrix();
        modelViewMatrix.Translate(0.4f, 0.0f, 0.0f);
        modelViewMatrix.Scale(0.5, 0.8, 1.0);
        modelViewMatrix.Rotate(-20.0, 0.0, 1.0, 0.0);
        glSampleMaski(0, 0x04);
        shaderManager.UseStockShader(GLT_SHADER_FLAT,
                transformPipeline.GetModelViewProjectionMatrix(), vLtGreen);
        glass2Batch.Draw();
    modelViewMatrix.PopMatrix();
. . .
```

Once all surfaces are drawn to unique sample locations, they have to be combined. But using an ordinary multisample resolve just won't do! Instead we use the custom resolve shader shown in Listing 10.2. The color and depth values for each sample are first fetched into an array and then analyzed to determine the color of the fragment.

LISTING 10.2   Resolving Multiple Layers by Depth

```
#version 150

// oitResolve.fs
//

in vec2 vTexCoord;

uniform sampler2DMS origImage;
uniform sampler2DMS origDepth;

out vec4 oColor;

void main(void)
{
    const int sampleCount = 8;

    vec4  vColor[sampleCount];
    float vDepth[sampleCount];
    int   vSurfOrder[sampleCount];
    int   i = 0;

    // Calculate un-normalized texture coordinates
    vec2 tmp = floor(textureSize(origDepth) * vTexCoord);

    // First, get sample data and init the surface order
    for (i = 0; i < sampleCount; i++)
    {
        vSurfOrder[i] = i;
        vColor[i] = texelFetch(origImage, ivec2(tmp), i);
        vDepth[i] = texelFetch(origDepth, ivec2(tmp), i).r;
    }

    // Sort depth values, largest to front and smallest to back
    // Must run through array (size^2-size) times, or early-exit
    // if any pass shows all samples to be in order
    for (int j = 0; j < sampleCount; j++)
    {
        bool bFinished = true;
        for (i = 0; i < (sampleCount-1); i++)
```

```
    {
        float temp1 = vDepth[vSurfOrder[i]];
        float temp2 = vDepth[vSurfOrder[i+1]];

        if (temp2 < temp1)
        {
            // swap values
            int tempIndex   = vSurfOrder[i];
            vSurfOrder[i]   = vSurfOrder[i+1];
            vSurfOrder[i+1] = tempIndex;
            bFinished = false;
        }
    }


    if (bFinished)
        j = 8; // Done. Early out!
}


// Now, sum all colors in order from front to back. Apply alpha.
bool bFoundFirstColor = false;
vec4 summedColor = vec4(0.0, 0.0, 0.0, 0.0);

for (i = (sampleCount-1); i >= 0; i—)
{
    int surfIndex = vSurfOrder[i];
    if(vColor[surfIndex].a > 0.001)
    {
        if (bFoundFirstColor == false)
        {
            // apply 100% of the first color
            summedColor = vColor[surfIndex];
            bFoundFirstColor = true;
        }
        else
        {
            // apply color with alpha
            // same as using glBlendFunc(GL_SRC_ALPHA,
                                    GL_ONE_MINUS_SRC_ALPHA);
            summedColor.rgb =
                (summedColor.rgb * (1 - vColor[surfIndex].a)) +
                (vColor[surfIndex].rgb * vColor[surfIndex].a);
        }
    }
```

10

```
    }

    oColor = summedColor;
    oColor.a = 1.0f;
}
```

For transparency to work correctly, the color of each piece of geometry must be applied from back to front. To do this, we need to figure out what geometry is overlapping other geometry. That means the depth values have to be parsed and sorted. We store the result of the sort in the vSurfOrder array for use in the next step. This array holds indexes that point to the sample arrays. Index 0 points to the closest sample, index 1 to the next closest, and so on. For locations where only one or two layers of geometry were drawn, all other samples contain 0 for color and alpha. Figure 10.2 shows the result of the sort. On the far left are all of the closest samples pointed to by vSurfOrder[0], second are the next closest samples as indicated by vSurfOrder[1], and so on. Notice that sample 0 contains mostly background because nothing is overlapping the background; therefore, the background is the closest, and only one sample in vSurfOrder is relevant. For this app, there are only at most four overlapping pieces of geometry in any given region.

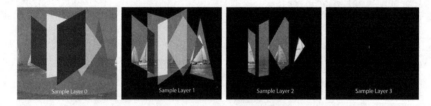

FIGURE 10.2   Samples sorted by depth. Closest samples on the left, farthest on the right.

Now that we know what order each sample is in, and therefore the order for each piece of geometry, we can correctly apply the transparency of each. The whole process can be carried out by running a single resolve shader on the multisample buffer containing the transparency data. To perform the resolve, the shader simply looks up each sample in the color array vColor according to the order specified in vSurfOrder. Each color is then applied to the total color for each pixel. The new top layer color is multiplied by its alpha and added to the existing summed color, which is multiplied by one minus the incoming alpha.

This process, performed completely in hardware, builds up the transparent colors at each pixel. The final result is shown in Figure 10.3 (also in Color Plate 19). It doesn't matter what order the translucent glasslike objects are rendered in; the final result will be blended correctly. You can rotate the scene in the oit program by using the right and left arrow keys on the keyboard. Notice how the objects closest to you always appear on top, even though the order they are rendered in does not change.

FIGURE 10.3   Final result of order-independent depth.

A similar method could be done with separate color buffers attached to an FBO, but many implementations are limited in the number of buffer attachments. Using multisample buffers to do order-independent transparency provides easy buffer access and does not intrude significantly into the normal rendering process. However, there are some limitations to this approach. First, only a limited number of transparent or intersecting pieces of geometry can be rendered. There are only so many samples in a multisample buffer. This means complex transparent geometry that contains hundreds or thousands of possibly overlapping objecs are out of reach for this method. Additionally, you couldn't use a multisample buffer for oit and also do multisampled rendering. But for simple oit situations, this approach works well and does not require geometry to be presorted.

Stencil Operations

The next step in the fragment pipeline is the stencil test. Think about the stencil test as cutting out a shape in cardboard and then using that cutout to spray paint the shape on a mural. The spray paint only hits the wall in places where the cardboard is cut out. If you have a pixel format that supports a stencil buffer, you can similarly mask your draws to the framebuffer. You can enable stenciling by calling glEnable(GL_STENCIL_TEST). Most stencil buffers contain 8 bits, but some configurations may support fewer bits.

Your draw commands can have a direct effect on the stencil buffer, and the value of the stencil buffer can have a direct effect on the pixels you draw. To control interactions with the stencil buffer, OpenGL provides two commands: glStencilFuncSeparate and glStencilOpSeparate. OpenGL lets you set both of these separately for front- and back-facing geometry.

```
void glStencilFuncSeparate(GLenum face, GLenum func, GLint ref, Gluint mask);
void glStencilOpSeparate(GLenum face, GLenum sfail, GLenum dpfail, Glenum dppass);
```

First let's look at glStencilFuncSeparate, which controls the conditions under which the stencil test passes or fails. You can pass GL_FRONT, GL_BACK, or GL_FRONT_AND_BACK for face, signifying which geometry will be affected. The value of func can be any of the values in Table 10.1. These describe under what conditions geometry will pass the stencil test. The ref value is the reference used to compute the pass/fail result, and the mask lets you control which bits of the reference and the buffer are compared.

TABLE 10.1   Stencil Functions

Functions	Pass Condition
GL_NEVER	Never pass test.
GL_ALWAYS	Always pass test.
GL_LESS	Reference value is less than buffer value.
GL_LEQUAL	Reference value is less than or equal to buffer value.
GL_EQUAL	Reference value is equal to buffer value.
GL_GEQUAL	Reference value is greater than or equal to buffer value.
GL_GREATER	Reference value is greater than buffer value.
GL_NOTEQUAL	Reference value is not equal to buffer value.

The next step is to tell OpenGL what to do when the stencil test passes or fails by using glStencilOpSeparate. This function takes four parameters with the first specifying which faces will be affected. The next three parameters control what happens after the stencil test is performed and can be any of the values in Table 10.2. The second parameter, sfail, is the action taken if the stencil test fails. dpfail parameter specifies the action taken if the depth buffer test fails, and the final parameter, dppass, specifies what happens if the depth buffer test passes.

TABLE 10.2   Stencil Operations

Operation	Result
GL_KEEP	Do not modify the stencil buffer.
GL_ZERO	Set stencil buffer value to 0.
GL_REPLACE	Replace stencil value with reference value.
GL_INCR	Increment stencil with saturation.
GL_DECR	Decrement stencil with saturation.
GL_INVERT	Bitwise invert stencil value.
GL_INCR_WRAP	Increment stencil without saturation.
GL_DECR_WRAP	Decrement stencil without saturation.

So how does this actually work out? Let's look at a simple example of typical usage shown in Listing 10.2. The first step is to clear the stencil buffer to 0 by setting the stencil clear value through glClearStencil and then calling clear with the stencil buffer bit. Next a window border is drawn that may contain details such as a player's score and statistics. Set up the stencil test to always pass with the reference value being 1 by calling glStencilFuncSeparate. Then tell OpenGL to replace the value in the stencil buffer only when the depth test passes by calling glStencilOpSeparate followed by rendering the border geometry. This turns the border area pixels to 1 while the rest of the framebuffer remains at 0.

Next, set up the stencil state so that the stencil test will only pass if the stencil buffer value is 0 and then render the rest of the scene. This causes all pixels that would overwrite the border we just drew to fail the stencil test and not be drawn to the framebuffer. Listing 10.3 shows an example of how stencil can be used.

LISTING 10.3   Example Stencil Buffer Usage, Stencil Border Decorations

```
// Clear stencil buffer to 0
glClearStencil(0);
glClear(GL_STENCIL_BUFFER_BIT);

// Setup Stencil state for border rendering
glStencilFuncSeparate(GL_FRONT, GL_ALWAYS, 1, 0xff);
glStencilOpSeparate(GL_FRONT, GL_KEEP, GL_ZERO, GL_REPLACE);

// Render border decorations
. . .

// Now, border decoration pixels have a stencil value of 1
// All other pixels have a stencil value of 0.

// Setup Stencil state for regular rendering,
// fail if pixel would overwrite border
glStencilFuncSeparate(GL_FRONT_AND_BACK, GL_LESS, 1, 0xff);
glStencilOpSeparate(GL_FRONT, GL_KEEP, GL_KEEP, GL_KEEP);

// Reder the rest of the scene, will not render over stenciled
// boarder content
. . .
```

There are also two other stencil functions: glStencilFunc and glStencilOp. These behave the same way as glStencilFuncSeparate and glStencilOpSeparate with the face set to GL_FRONT_AND_BACK.

Depth Testing

After stencil operations are complete, the hardware tests the depth value of a fragment when depth testing is enabled. If depth writes are enabled and the fragment has passed the depth test, the depth buffer is updated with the new depth value of the fragment. If the depth test fails, the fragment is killed and does not pass to the other stages of fragment operations. We have used depth buffers and depth testing throughout the entire book. Their operation should be as familiar as waking up in the morning! As a refresher you can take a peek back at Chapter 3.

Depth Clamp

There is one more useful piece of functionality related to depth testing called *depth clamping*. Depth clamping is disabled by default but can be enabled by calling glEnable(GL_DEPTH_CLAMP). If depth clamping is enabled, the incoming pixel's depth will be clamped to the near and far clip planes before the depth test is performed.

Depth clamping can be useful in preventing geometry from being clipped to the clip volume. One applicable case is shadow volume rendering. When rendering shadow volumes you want to preserve as much of the geometry along the z-axis as possible. To do this you can enable depth clamping, which prevents data that is farther than the far clip plane or nearer than the near clip plane from being cut off.

Blending Everything Together

Once a fragment passes depth testing, it is handed off to the blending stage. Blending allows you to combine the incoming source color with the color already in the color buffer or with other constants using one of the many supported blend equations. Blending can only be done on fixed and floating-point formats. You can't blend with integer formats such as GL_RGB_16I or GL_RGB32I. Also if the buffer you are drawing to is fixed-point, the incoming source colors will be clamped to 0.0-1.0 before any blending operations occur. Blending is controlled on a per-drawbuffer basis and is enabled by calling glEnablei(GL_BLEND, bufferIndex). Just like using glDrawBuffers, the buffer index can be GL_DRAW_BUFFER0, GL_DRAW_BUFFER1, and so on. If the default FBO is bound, blending is performed on all enabled buffers.

Blend Equation

Blending is highly customizable. The first aspect to consider is how you want to combine the pixel value (source) with the framebuffer color (destination). You can choose separate operations for the RGB values and the alpha values if you use glBlendEquationSeperate or use the same equation for both RGB and alpha if you use glBlendEquation. The blend equations available are listed in Table 10.3. Blending is performed as if the source and destination colors were floating-point.

```
glBlendEquation(GLenum mode);
glBlendEquationSeparate(GLenum modeRGB, GLenum modeAlpha);
```

TABLE 10.3   Blend Equations

Blend Equation	RGB	Alpha
GL_FUNC_ADD	$R = R_s * S_r + R_d * D_r$ $G = G_s * S_g + G_d * D_g$ $B = B_s * S_b + B_d * D_b$	$A = A_s * S_a + A_d * D_a$
GL_FUNC_SUBTRACT	$R = R_s * S_r - R_d * D_r$ $G = G_s * S_g - G_d * D_g$ $B = B_s * S_b - B_d * D_b$	$A = A_s * S_a - A_d * D_a$
GL_FUNC_REVERSE_SUBTRACT	$R = R_d * D_r - R_s * S_r$ $G = G_d * D_g - G_s * S_g$ $B = B_d * D_b - B_s * S_b$	$A = A_d * D_a - A_s * S_a$
GL_MIN	$R = min(R_s, R_d)$ $G = min(G_s, G_d)$ $B = min(B_s, B_d)$	$A = min(A_s, A_d)$
GL_MAX	$R = max(R_s, R_d)$ $G = max(G_s, G_d)$ $B = max(B_s, B_d)$	$A = max(A_s, A_d)$

Blend Function

Now that you have chosen an equation to combine the source and destination colors; you have to set the factors used in the blend equation. This can be done by calling glBlendFunc or glBlendFuncSeparate with the factors you intend to use. Just like glBlendEquation, you can either set separate functions for RGB and alpha or use one command to set them both to the same value.

```
glBlendFuncSeparate(GLenum srcRGB, GLenum dstRGB, GLenum srcAlpha, GLenum
                    dstaAlpha);
glBlendFunc(GLenum src, GLenum dst);
```

The possible values for these calls can be found in Table 10.4. Note that functions that require addition or subtraction perform these operations as vectors. Some also require a constant value that can be set by calling glBlendColor:

```
glBlendColor(clampf red, clampf green, clampf blue, clampf alpha);
```

TABLE 10.4   Blend Functions

Blend Function	RGB	Alpha
GL_ZERO	$(0, 0, 0,)$	0
GL_ONE	$(1, 1, 1)$	1
GL_SRC_COLOR	(R_{s0}, G_{s0}, B_{s0})	A_{s0}
GL_ONE_MINUS_SRC_COLOR	$(1, 1, 1) - (R_{s0}, G_{s0}, B_{s0})$	$1 - A_{s0}$
GL_DST_COLOR	(R_d, G_d, B_d)	A_d

TABLE 10.4   Blend Functions

Blend Function	RGB	Alpha
GL_ONE_MINUS_DST_COLOR	$(1, 1, 1) - (R_d, G_d, B_d)$	$1 - A_d$
GL_SRC_ALPHA	(A_{s0}, A_{s0}, A_{s0})	A_{s0}
GL_ONE_MINUS_SRC_ALPHA	$(1, 1, 1) - (A_{s0}, A_{s0}, A_{s0})$	$1 - A_{s0}$
GL_DST_ALPHA	(A_{d0}, A_{d0}, A_{d0})	A_{d0}
GL_ONE_MINUS_DST_ALPHA	$(1, 1, 1) - (A_{d0}, A_{d0}, A_{d0})$	$1 - A_{d0}$
GL_CONSTANT_COLOR	(R_c, G_c, B_c)	A_c
GL_ONE_MINUS_CONSTANT_COLOR	$(1, 1, 1) - (R_c, G_c, B_c)$	$1 - A_c$
GL_CONSTANT_ALPHA	(A_c, A_c, A_c)	A_c
GL_ONE_MINUS_CONSTANT_ALPHA	$(1, 1, 1) - (A_c, A_c, A_c)$	$1 - A_c$
GL_ALPHA_SATURATE	(f, f, f) $f = \min(A_{s0}, 1 - A_d)$	1
GL_SRC1_COLOR	(R_{s1}, G_{s1}, B_{s1})	A_{s1}
GL_ONE_MINUS_SRC1_COLOR	$(1, 1, 1) - (R_{s1}, G_{s1}, B_{s1})$	$1 - A_{s1}$
GL_SRC1_ALPHA	(A_{s1}, A_{s1}, A_{s1})	A_{s1}
GL_ONE_MINUS_SRC1_ALPHA	$(1, 1, 1) - (A_{s1}, A_{s1}, A_{s1})$	$1 - A_{s1}$

You may have noticed that some of the factors in Table 10.4 use source 0 colors, and others use source 1 colors. Your shaders can export more than one final color for a given color attachment by setting up the outputs using glBindFragDataLocationIndexed. The way to make use of two outputs is by blending the colors togther using appropriate blend factors. You can find out how many dual output buffers are supported by querying the value of GL_MAX_DUAL_SOURCE_DRAW_BUFFERS.

Putting It All Together

The oit sample program we looked at earlier is also outfitted to do simple blending as well. Just press the B key on the keyboard to switch to blending mode. Each of the glasslike pieces is drawn separately, blended with the background. You can choose between a few preset blending modes by pressing the keyboard keys 1 through 7 to create several different effects. Check out Figure 10.4 to see the result of using one of the most common blend function sets, GL_SRC_ALPHA and GL_SRC_ONE_MINUS_ALPHA.

FIGURE 10.4 Blended transparent glass shares.

If the blending mode is selected, the program enables blend mode and then sets the appropriate blend parameters (see Listing 10.4). OpenGL takes care of the rest, blending each additional piece of geometry with the framebuffer as it is drawn. The last step is to resolve the multisample FBO to display the final result on the screen.

LISTING 10.4 Example Stencil Buffer Usage, Stencil Border Decorations

```
// Setup blend state
glEnable(GL_BLEND);
switch (blendMode)
{
case 1:
    glBlendFunc(GL_SRC_ALPHA, GL_ONE_MINUS_SRC_ALPHA);
    break;
case 2:
    glBlendFunc(GL_SRC_ALPHA, GL_ONE_MINUS_DST_ALPHA);
    break;
. . .
```

Notice how when using blending the rendering order matters, unlike with the order-independent transparency example we saw earlier. Once you have given the stock program a spin, try modifying the sample modes. You can set different blend functions and different blend equations to see what result they have.

10

Dithering

Great! Your pixel has almost gotten to the end of the pipeline. After blending, pixel data is still represented as a set of floating-point numbers. But unless your framebuffer is a floating-point buffer, the pixel data has to be converted before it can be stored. For instance, most window-renderable formats only support 8 bits of color per channel. That means the GPU has to convert the final color output before it can be stored.

This conversion can happen one of two ways depending on whether dithering is disabled or enabled. First, the result can be simply mapped to the largest positive representable color. For instance, if the R-value of a particular pixel is 0.3222 and the window format is GL_RGB_8, the GPU could map this to either value 82 of 256 or 83 of 256. If dithering is disabled, the GPU automatically chooses 83. You can force this behavior by calling glDisable(GL_DITHER).

The second option is to dither the result. Dithering is enabled by default, but you can also enable it by calling glEnable(GL_DITHER). What is dithering? It's a way for the hardware to blend the transition from one representable color to the next step. Instead of an abrupt switch from one color level to another, a GPU can soften the boarder of the transition by mixing the two colors together in areas where neither neighboring color can truly represent the color at that location. Take a look at Figure 10.5. The top half shows no dithering, while the bottom demonstrates how dithering can blend color transitions. There are several formulas to compute how dithering is done. But basically if the underlying color is between 82 and 83 for an 8-bit color buffer, the percentage of each used is proportional to how close the color is to 82 and 83. It is worth noting that the dithering algorithm is up to each vendor. Some implementations may choose to simply step right to the next shade when certain color buffer formats are used.

FIGURE 10.5   Dithering blends color transitions. Top half not blended. Bottom half noise blended.

Dithering can be very handy. It can eliminate banding issues when your objects are gradually smooth-shaded. The best part is you don't even have to worry about it. Dithering is enabled by default and works to make your rendering more pleasing and natural.

Logic Ops

Once the pixel color is in the same format and bit depth as the framebuffer, there are two more steps that can affect the final result. The first allows you to apply a logical operation to the pixel color before it is passed on. When enabled, the effects of blending are ignored. Logic operations do not affect floating-point buffers. You can enable logic ops by calling

```
glEnable(GL_COLOR_LOGIC_OP);
```

Logic operations use the values of the incoming pixel and the exiting framebuffer to compute a final value. You can pick the operation that computes the final value. The possible options are listed in Table 10.5. Pass your logic op of choice into glLogicOp:

```
glLogicOp(GLenum op);
```

TABLE 10.5   Logic Operations

Operation	Result
GL_CLEAR	Set all values to 0
GL_AND	Source & Destination
GL_AND_REVERSE	Source & ~Destination
GL_COPY	Source
GL_AND_INVERTED	~(Source & Destination)
GL_NOOP	Destination
GL_XOR	Source ^ Destination
GL_OR	Source | Destination
GL_NOR	~ (Source | Destination)
GL_EQUIV	~(Source ^ Destination)
GL_INVERT	~Destination
GL_OR_REVERSE	Source | ~destination
GL_COPY_INVERTED	~Source
GL_OR_INVERTED	~Source | Destination
GL_NAND	~(Source & Destination)
GL_SET	Set all values to 1

Logic ops are applied seperately to each color channel. Operations that combine source and destination are performed bitwise on the color values. Logic ops are not commonly used in today's graphics applications but still remain part of OpenGL because the functionality is still supported on common GPUs.

10

Masking Output

One of the last modifications that can be made to a fragment before it is written is masking. By now you recognize that three different types of data can be written by a fragment shader: color, depth, and stencil data. Likewise, there are separate operations you can use to mask the result of each.

Color

To mask color writes or prevent color writes from happening, you can use glColorMask and glColorMaski. You don't have to mask all color channels at once; you can choose to mask the Red and Green channels while permitting writes to the Blue channel for instance. You can pass in GL_TRUE for a channel to allow writes for that channel to occur, or GL_FALSE to mask these writes off. The first function, glColorMask, allows you to mask all buffers currently enabled for rendering while the second function, glColorMaski, allows you to set the mask for a specific color buffer.

```
glColorMask(writeR, writeG, writeB);
glColorMaski(colorBufIndex, writeR, writeG, writeB);
```

Depth

Writes to the depth buffer can be masked in a similar way. glDepthMask also takes a Boolean value that turns writes on if GL_TRUE and off if GL_FALSE.

```
glDepthMask(GL_FALSE);
```

Stencil

Stencil buffers can be masked too. You guessed it; the function you use for stencil buffers is called glStencilMask. But unlike the other functions, you have more granular control over what gets masked off. Instead of just setting a Boolean value, the stencil mask functions take a bitfield. The least significant portion of this bitfield maps to the same number of bits in the stencil buffer. If a mask bit is set to 1, the corresponding bit in the stencil buffer can be updated. But if the mask bit is 0, the corresponding stencil bit will not be written to.

```
GLuint mask = 0x0007;
glStencilMask(mask);
glStencilMaskSeparate(GL_BACK, mask);
```

In the preceding example, the first call to glStencilMask enables the lower three bits of the stencil buffer for writing while leaving the rest disabled. The second call, glStencilMaskSeparate, allows you to set separate masks for primitives that are front-facing and back-facing.

Usage

Write masks can be useful for many operations. For instance, if you want to fill a shadow volume with depth information, you can mask off all color writes because only the depth information is important. Or if you want to draw a decal directly to screen space, you can disable depth writes to prevent the depth data from being polluted. The key point about masks is you can set them and immediately call your normal rendering paths, which may set up necessary buffer state and output all color, depth, and stencil data you would normally use without needing any knowledge of the mask state. You don't have to alter your shaders to not write some value, detach some set of buffers, or change the enabled draw buffers. The rest of your rendering paths can be completely oblivious and still generate the right results.

Summary

In this chapter you learned about the end of the OpenGL pipeline. The first step is scissoring. Next, you learned about how to fine-control multisampling to adjust sample coverage or apply a sample mask. Then, stencil operations control which fragments are allowed to continue down the pipeline. After that, the depth buffer comes into play, testing to see whether a fragment falls behind already-rendered geometry. Next, the resulting fragment is blended with the framebuffer based on user controlled functions and equations. Then, the result is dithered to smooth color transitions. Last, the result can be masked to prevent depth, stencil, and color operations from being applied where applicable.

You learned how to interact directly with individual samples of a multisample buffer with the oit sample program. You used sample mask interfaces to blend semitransparent objects correctly regardless of the order they were drawn in. The oit sample program also demonstrated how blending works, demonstrating several common blend modes.

10

CHAPTER 11

Advanced Shader Usage

by Graham Sellers

WHAT YOU'LL LEARN IN THIS CHAPTER:

How To	Features You'll Use
Use a transform feedback buffer	glBindBuffer
Store transformed vertices into a buffer	glBeginTransformFeedback, glEndTransformFeedback
Use a geometry shader	glCreateShader(GL_GEOMETRY_SHADER)
Create, bind, and use uniform blocks	glGetUniformBlockIndex, glUniformBlockBinding
Use indexed binding points	glBindBufferBase, glBindBufferRange
Control interpolation and storage	Layout qualifiers

In this chapter, we cover some more advanced shader topics that will allow you to use your programmable graphics hardware for more than simple polygon rendering. We present a detailed example of using the GPU for physical simulation by recirculating data through transform feedback. We introduce an entirely new shader stage—the geometry shader, which can process entire primitives and even generate new primitives on the fly. We also discuss using the fragment shader to perform advanced per-pixel operations, including image processing and generating fractals.

Layout qualifiers are introduced, allowing you to control storage, interpolation, and other parameters affecting inputs and outputs of shaders. We also introduce a method of throwing work away in the fragment shader.

By the end of the chapter, the shaders you'll be capable of writing will be so complex that you might get sick of using shader uniforms! We introduce the uniform buffer object, which allows you to share large blocks of uniforms between different program objects.

Advanced Vertex Shaders

Until now, the vertex shader has been used to transform vertices from object space into world or view space. It has been viewed as a fairly simple one-in, one-out shader stage that simply does geometric transformations. However, the vertex shader is very powerful—on most modern hardware it has access to all of the resources that the fragment shader does. It can be put to work on tasks that are not necessarily geometric in nature. Combined with transform feedback (which is discussed in detail in Chapter 12, "Advanced Geometry Management"), the vertex shader can circulate results around in a loop, iterating and updating them on each pass. The data doesn't need to be positions, and the results of the vertex shader don't necessarily need to be rendered directly. This section covers a few examples of some nonobvious usages for vertex shaders.

Physical Simulation in the Vertex Shader

In this example, we build a physical simulation of a mesh of springs and masses. Each vertex represents a weight, connected to up to four neighbors by elastic tethers. The example iterates over the vertices, processing each one with a vertex shader. A number of advanced features are used in this example. We use a texture buffer object (TBO) to hold vertex position data in addition to a regular attribute array. The same buffer is bound to both the TBO and the VBO associated with the position input to the vertex shader. This allows us to arbitrarily access the current position of other vertices in the system. We also use an integer vertex attribute to hold indices of neighboring vertices. Furthermore, we use transform feedback to store the positions and velocities of each of the masses between each iteration of the algorithm.

For each vertex, we need a position, velocity, and mass. We can pack the positions and masses into one vertex array and pack the velocities into another. Each element of the position array is actually a vec4, with x, y, and z being the three-dimensional coordinate of the vertex, and w containing the weight of the vertex. The velocity array can simply be an array of vec3. Additionally, we use an array of ivec4s to store information about the springs connecting the weights together. There is one ivec4 for each vertex, and each of the four components of the vector contains the index of the vertex that is connected to the other end of the spring. We call this the connection vector. This means that we can connect each mass to up to four other masses. To record that there is no connection, we point the element of the connection back at the same vertex (see Figure 11.1).

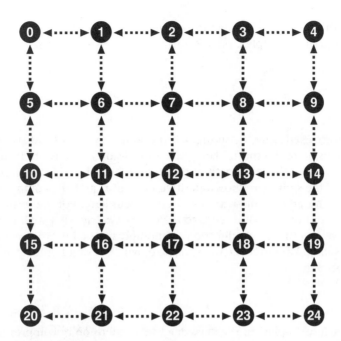

FIGURE 11.1   Connections of vertices in the spring mass system.

Consider vertex 12. It has associated with it an `ivec4` connection vector containing <7, 13, 17, 11>—the indices of the vertices to which it is connected. Likewise, the connection vector for vertex 13 contains <8, 14, 18, 12>. There is a bidirectional connection between vertex 12 and 13. The vertices at the edges of the mesh don't have all of their springs attached. So vertex 14 has a connection vector containing <9, 14, 19, 13>. Notice that the y component of the vector points back at vertex 14, indicating that there is no spring there.

In addition to the indices of the vertices to which it is connected (using a self reference to notate no connection), we define a special values to mean other things. The index -1 is used to mean that the vertex is held in position. No matter what the forces acting on it, its position won't be updated. This allows us to fix the position of some of the vertices. If the x component of the connection vector is -1, then the calculations for updating the position and velocity of the vertex will be skipped.

At each vertex, our vertex shader runs and obtains its own position and connection vector using regular vertex attributes. It then looks up the current positions of the vertices it's connected to by indexing into the TBO using the elements of the connection vector (which is also a regular vertex attribute). For each connected vertex, it can calculate the distance to it and thus the extension of the virtual spring between them. From this, it can calculate the force exerted upon it by the spring, calculate the acceleration this produces given the mass of the vertex, and produce a new position and velocity vector to use in the next iteration. It sounds complex, but it's not—it's just Newtonian physics and Hooke's law.

Hooke's law is

$$F = -kx$$

where F is the force exerted by the spring, k is the spring constant (how stiff the spring is), and x is the extension of the spring. The spring's extension is relative to its resting length. For our system, we keep the rest length of the springs the same and store it in a uniform. Any stretching of the spring produces a positive value of x, and any compression of the spring produces a negative value of x. The instantaneous length of the spring is simply the length of the vector from one of its ends to the other—exactly what we'll calculate in the vertex shader. We give the force a direction by multiplying the linear force F by the direction along the spring. We introduce the variable d, which is simply the normalized direction along the spring:

$$\vec{F} = \vec{d}F$$

This gives us the force applied to the mass due to the extension or compression of the spring. If we were to simply apply this force to the mass, the system would oscillate and, due to numerical imprecision, would eventually become unstable. All real spring. systems have some loss due to friction, and this can be modeled by including damping into the force equation. The force due to damping is determined by the equation

$$\vec{F}_d = -c\vec{v}$$

where c represents the damping coefficient. Ideally, we would calculate the damping force for each spring, but for this simple system, a single force based on the mass's velocity will do. Also we use the initial velocity at each time-step to approximate the continuous differential that would be required by this equation. In our shader, we initialize F by calculating the damping force and then accumulate the force exerted by each spring on the mass.

Finally, we can apply gravity to the system by treating it as simply one more force acting on each mass. Gravity is a constant force that generally acts in a downward direction. We can just add that to the initial force acting on the mass:

$$F_{total} = G - \vec{d}\vec{k}x - c\vec{v}$$

Once we have the total force, we can simply apply Newton's laws. First, Newton's second law allows us to calculate the acceleration of the mass:

$$\vec{F} = m\vec{a}$$

$$\vec{a} = \frac{\vec{F}}{m}$$

Here, F is the force we just calculated using gravity, the damping coefficient, and Hook's law; m is the mass of the vertex (stored in the w component of the position attribute); and a is the resulting acceleration. Given the initial velocity (which we get from our other attribute array), we can plug it into the following equations of motion to find out what our final velocity will be and how far we moved in a fixed time:

$$\vec{v} = \vec{u} + \vec{a}t$$

$$\vec{s} = \vec{u} + \frac{\vec{a}t^2}{2}$$

where u is the initial velocity (read from our velocity attribute array), v is the final velocity, t is our time-step (supplied by the application), and s is the distance we've travelled. Don't forget, a, u, v, and s are all vectors. All that's left to do is write the shaders and hook them up to an application. Listing 11.1 shows what the vertex shader looks like.

LISTING 11.1   Spring Mass System Vertex Shader

```
#version 330
precision highp float;

// This input vector contains the vertex position in xyz, and the mass of
// the vertex in w
in vec4 position_mass;
// This is the current velocity of the vertex
in vec3 velocity;
// This is our connection vector
in ivec4 connection;

// This is a TBO that will be bound to the same buffer as the
// position_mass input attribute
uniform samplerBuffer tex_position_mass;

// The outputs of the vertex shader are the same as the inputs, just
// wrapped in an interface block
```

```glsl
out Vertex
{
    vec4 position_mass;
    vec3 velocity;
} vertex;

// A uniform to hold the timestep. The application can update this.
uniform float t;

// The global spring constant
uniform float k;

// The global damping constant
uniform float c;
// Gravity
const vec3 gravity = vec3(0.0, -0.03, 0.0);

// Resting length of the springs
uniform float rest_length;

// Model-view-projection matrix
uniform mat4 mvp;

void main(void)
{
    vec3 p = position_mass.xyz;    // p can be our position
    float m = position_mass.w;     // m is the mass of our vertex
    vec3 u = velocity;             // u is the initial velocity
    vec3 F;                        // F is the force on the mass
    vec3 v = u;                    // v is the final velocity
    vec3 s = vec3(0.0);            // s is the displacement in this step

    // Check if this is a 'fixed' vertex
    if (connection[0] != -1) {
        // Initialize F using gravity and damping
        F  = gravity - c * u;

        for (int i = 0; i < 4; i++) {
            if (connection[i] != gl_VertexID) {
                // q is the position of the other vertex
                // We don't care about the other vertex's mass
                vec3 q = texture(tex_position_mass, connection[i]).xyz;
                vec3 d = q - p;
```

```
            float x = length(d);
            F += -k * (1.0 - x) * normalize(d);
        }
    }

    // Acceleration due to force
    float a = F / m;
    // Displacement
    s = u * t + 0.5 * a * t * t;
    // Final velocity
    v = u + a * t;
    }

    // Write the outputs
    vertex.position_mass = vec4(p + s, m);
    vertex.velocity = v;

    // Update gl_Position so we can render the points
    gl_Position = mvp * vec4(p + s, 1.0);
}
```

That wasn't so hard, was it? We also need to construct buffers to hold the position, velocity, and connection information. We need to double-buffer the position and velocity information so that we can read from one set of buffers and write to the other on one pass, and then swap the buffers around so that the data moves back and forth from one buffer to the other. The connection information remains the same on each pass, so it's going to be constant. To do this, two pairs of VBOs and a pair of VAOs are used. The first VAO has one set of position and velocity attributes attached to it, referring to the first pair of VBOs, along with the common connection information. The other VAO has the other set of position and velocity attributes attached referring to the second pair of VBOs and the same, common connection information. In total, we need five VBOs—two buffers to hold position, two buffers to hold velocity and one buffer containing the connection vectors.

In addition to the VBOs, we need two TBOs. We use each buffer as a position VBO and as a TBO, *simultaneously*. This seems strange, but is perfectly legal in OpenGL—after all, we're just reading from the same buffer via two different methods. To set this up, we generate two textures, bind them to the GL_BUFFER_TEXTURE binding point, and attach the buffers to them using glTexBuffer, as explained earlier in this book. When we bind VAO A, we also bind texture A. When we bind VAO B, we bind texture B. That way, the same data appears in both the position vertex attribute and in the tex_position samplerBuffer buffer texture.

The code to set this up isn't particularly complex but is repetitive. A complete implementation can be found on this book's Web site. The example application includes the code to create and initialize the buffers, perform double buffering, and visualize the results. The application fixes a couple of the vertices in place so that the whole system doesn't just fall off the bottom of the screen. Once we have all of the buffers hooked up, we can simulate a time-step in the system with a single call to glDrawArrays. Each node in the system is represented by a single GL_POINT primitive. If we initialize the modelviewprojection matrix (stored in the mvp uniform) and let the system run, we see a result that looks like Figure 11.2.

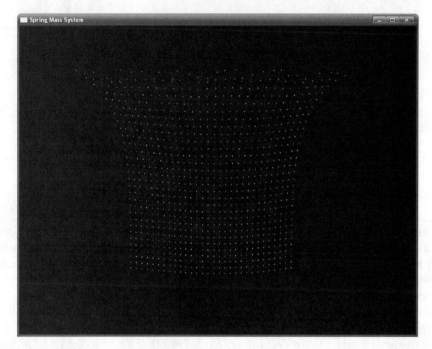

FIGURE 11.2   Simulation of points connected by springs.

The image in Figure 11.2 is not particularly interesting, but it does demonstrate that our simulation is running correctly. To make the visual result more appealing, we can set the point size to a larger value, and we can also issue a second, indexed draw using glDrawElements and GL_LINES primitives to visualize the connections between nodes. Note that the same vertex positions can be used as input to this second pass, but we need to construct another buffer to use with the GL_ELEMENT_ARRAY binding that contains the indices of the vertices at the end of each spring. This additional step is also performed by the example program. Figure 11.3 shows the final result.

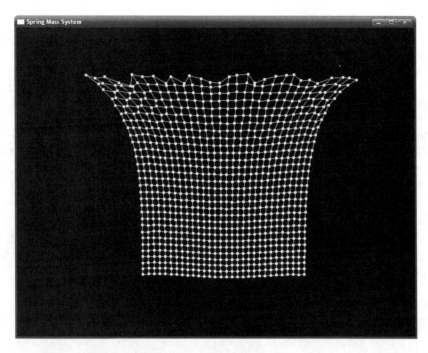

FIGURE 11.3   Visualizing springs in the Spring Mass System.

Of course, the physical simulation (and the vertex data produced by it) can be used for anything. If you don't want to draw the points on the screen, you can enable GL_RASTERIZER_DISCARD as explained in the next chapter.

Geometry Shaders

The geometry shader is a new shader type that was first introduced in the form of an extension to OpenGL and then made part of the OpenGL core specification as of OpenGL 3.2. What makes a geometry shader unique in contrast to the other shader types is that it processes a whole primitive (triangle, line, or point) at once and can actually change the amount of data in the OpenGL pipeline. A vertex shader processes one vertex at a time; it cannot access any other vertex's information and is strictly one-in, one-out. That is, it cannot generate new vertices, and it cannot stop the vertex from being processed further by OpenGL. Likewise, the fragment shader processes a single fragment at a time, cannot access any data owned by another fragment, cannot create new fragments, and can only destroy fragments by discarding them. On the other hand, a geometry shader has access to all of the vertices in a primitive (up to six with the new primitive modes GL_TRIANGLES_ADJACENCY and GL_TRIANGLE_STRIP_ADJACENCY), can change the type of a primitive, and can even create and destroy primitives.

The other difference between geometry shaders and vertex and fragment shaders is that geometry shaders are an optional part of the OpenGL pipeline. It is perfectly legal to have only a vertex and fragment shader linked into a program object, and this is, until now, the only way you've used OpenGL. When no geometry shader is present, the OpenGL pipeline operates as normal; the outputs from the vertex shader are interpolated across the primitive being rendered and are fed directly to the fragment shader. When a geometry shader is present, however, the outputs of the vertex shader become the inputs to the geometry shader, and the outputs of the geometry shader are what are interpolated and fed to the fragment shader. The geometry shader can further process the output of the vertex shader, and if it is generating new primitives (this is called *amplification*) can apply different transformations to each primitive as it creates them.

The Pass-Through Geometry Shader

Geometry shaders are written in GLSL, just like vertex and fragment shaders, and there's nothing magical about them. This will all be explained shortly, but Listing 11.2 shows a simple geometry shader in its entirety.

LISTING 11.2   Source Code for a Simple Geometry Shader

```
#version 330

precision highp float;

layout (triangles) in;
layout (triangle_strip) out;
layout (max_vertices = 3) out;

void main(void)
{
    int i;

    for (i = 0; i < gl_in.length(); i++) {
        gl_Position = gl_in[i].gl_Position;
        EmitVertex();
    }
    EndPrimitive();
}
```

This is a very simple pass-through geometry shader, which sends its input to its output without modifying it. It looks similar to a vertex shader, but there are a few extra differences to cover. Going over the shader a few lines at a time makes everything clear. The first few lines simply set up the version number (330) and the precision of the shader just like in any vertex or fragment shader. The next couple of lines are the first geometry shader-specific parts. They are shown again in Listing 11.3.

LISTING 11.3   Geometry Shader Layout Qualifiers

```
#version 330

precision highp float;

layout (triangles) in;
layout (triangle_strip) out;
layout (max_vertices = 3) out;
```

These set the input and output primitive modes using a `layout` qualifier. In this particular shader we're using `triangles` for the input, and `triangle_strip` for the output. Other primitive types, along with the `layout` qualifier, are covered later. For the geometry shader's output, not only do we specify the primitive type, but the maximum number of vertices expected to be generated by the shader (through the `max_vertices` qualifier). This shader produces individual triangles (generated as very short triangle strips), so we specified three here.

Next is our `main()` function, which is again similar to what might be seen in vertex or fragment shader. The shader contains a loop, and the loop runs a number of times determined by the length of the built-in array, `gl_in`. This is another geometry shader-specific variable. Because the geometry shader has access to all of the vertices of the input primitive, the input has to be declared as an array. All of the built-in variables that are written by the vertex shader (such as `gl_Position`) are placed into a structure, and an array of these structures is presented to the geometry shader in a variable called `gl_in`.

The. length of the `gl_in[]` array is determined by the input primitive mode and because in this particular shader, triangles are the input primitive mode, the size of `gl_in[]` is three. The inner loop is given again in Listing 11.4.

LISTING 11.4   Iterating over the Elements of `gl_in[]`

```
    for (i = 0; i < gl_in.length(); i++) {
        gl_Position = gl_in[i].gl_Position;
        EmitVertex();
    }
```

Inside our loop, we're generating vertices by simply copying the elements of `gl_in[]` to the geometry shader's output. A geometry shader's outputs are similar to the vertex shader's outputs. Here, we're writing to `gl_Position`, just as we would in a vertex shader. When we're done setting up all of the new vertex's attributes, we call `EmitVertex()`. This is a built-in function, specific to geometry shaders that tells the shader that we're done with our work for this vertex and that it should store all that information away and prepare to start setting up the next vertex.

Finally, after the loop has finished executing, there's a call to another special, geometry shader-only function, EndPrimitive(). EndPrimitive() tells the shader that we're done producing vertices for the current primitive and to move on to the next one. We specified triangle_strip as the output for our shader, and so if we continue to call EmitVertex() more than three times, OpenGL continues adding triangles to the triangle strip. If we need our geometry shader to generate separate, individual triangles or multiple, unconnected triangle strips (remember, geometry shaders can create new or amplify geometry), we could call EndPrimitive() between each one to mark their boundaries. If you don't call EndPrimitive() somewhere in your shader, the primitive is automatically ended when the shader ends.

Using Geometry Shaders in an Application

Geometry shaders, like the other shader types, are created by calling the glCreateShader function and using GL_GEOMETRY_SHADER as the shader type, as follows:

```
glCreateShader(GL_GEOMETRY_SHADER);
```

Once the shader has been created, it is used like any other shader object. You give OpenGL your shader source code by calling glShaderSource, compile the shader using the glCompileShader function, and attach it to a program object by calling the glAttachShader function. Then the program is linked as normal using the glLinkProgram function.

Now that you have a program object with a geometry shader linked into it, when you draw geometry using a function like glDrawArrays, the vertex shader will run once per vertex, the geometry shader will run once per primitive (point, line, or triangle), and the fragment will run once per fragment. The primitive mode you use when sending geometry to OpenGL must match the input primitive mode of the geometry shader. For example, if the geometry shader's input primitive mode is points, then you may only use GL_POINTS when you call glDrawArrays. If the geometry shader's input primitive mode is triangles, then you may use GL_TRIANGLES, GL_TRIANGLE_STRIP, or GL_TRIANGLE_FAN in your glDrawArrays call. A complete list of the geometry shader input primitive modes and the allowed geometry types is given in Table 11.1.

TABLE 11.1   Allowed Draw Modes for Geometry Shader Input Modes

Geometry Shader Input Mode	Allowed Draw Modes
points	GL_POINTS
lines	GL_LINES, GL_LINE_LOOP, GL_LINE_STRIP
triangles	GL_TRIANGLES, GL_TRIANGLE_FAN, GL_TRIANGLE_STRIP
lines_adjacency	GL_LINES_ADJACENCY
triangles_adjacency	GL_TRIANGLES_ADJACENCY

The input primitive type is specified in the body of the geometry shader using a layout qualifier. The general form of the input layout qualifier is

```
layout (primitive_type) in;
```

This specifies that primitive_type is the input primitive type that the geometry shader is expected to handle, and primitive_type must be one of the supported primitive modes: points, lines, triangles, lines_adjacency, or triangles_adjacency. The geometry shader runs once per primitive. This means that it'll run once per point for GL_POINTS; once per line for GL_LINES, GL_LINE_STRIP, and GL_LINE_LOOP; and once per triangle for GL_TRIANGLES, GL_TRIANGLE_STRIP, and GL_TRIANGLE_FAN. The inputs to the geometry shader are presented in arrays containing all of the vertices making up the input primitive. The predefined inputs are stored in a built-in array called gl_in[], which is an array of structures and defined as shown in Listing 11.5.

LISTING 11.5   The Definition of gl_in[]

```
in gl_PerVertex
{
    vec4  gl_Position;
    float gl_PointSize;
    float gl_ClipDistance[];
} gl_in[];
```

The members of this structure are the built-in variables that are written in the vertex shader: gl_Position, gl_PointSize, and gl_ClipDistance[]. You should be very familiar with gl_Position and gl_PointSize by now, and gl_ClipDistance is explained in Chapter 12. These variables appear as global variables in the vertex shader, but their values end up in the structure members when they appear in the geometry shader. Other variables written by the vertex shader also become arrays in the geometry shader. In the case of individual varyings, outputs in the vertex shader are declared as normal, and the inputs to the geometry shader have a similar declaration, except that they are arrays. Consider a vertex shader that defines outputs as

```
out vec4 color;
out vec3 normal;
```

The corresponding input to the geometry shader would be

```
in vec4 color[];
in vec3 normal[];
```

Notice that both the color and normal varyings have become arrays in the geometry shader. If you have a large amount of data to pass from the vertex to the geometry shader, it can be convenient to wrap per-vertex information passed from the vertex shader to the geometry shader into an *interface block*. In this case, your vertex shader will have a definition like this:

```
out VertexData
{
    vec4 color;
    vec3 normal;
} vertex;
```

And the corresponding input to the geometry shader would look like this:

```
in VertexData
{
    vec4 color;
    vec3 normal;
    // More per-vertex attributes can be inserted here
} vertex[];
```

With this declaration, you'll be able to access the per-vertex data in the geometry shader using vertex[n].color and so on. The length of the input arrays in the geometry shader depends on the type of primitives that it will process. For example, points are formed from a single vertex, and so the arrays will only contain a single element, whereas triangles are formed from three vertices, and so the arrays will be three elements long. If you're writing a geometry shader that's designed specifically to process a particular primitive type, you can explicitly size your input arrays, which provides a small amount of additional compile-time error checking. Otherwise, you can let your arrays be automatically sized by the input primitive type layout qualifier. A complete mapping of the input primitive modes and the resulting size of the input arrays is shown in Table 11.2.

TABLE 11.2   Sizes of Input Arrays to Geometry Shaders

Input Primitive Type	Size of Input Arrays
points	1
lines	2
triangles	3
lines_adjacency	4
triangles_adjacency	6

You also need to specify the primitive type that will be generated by the geometry shader. Again, this is determined using a layout qualifier, like so:

```
layout (primitive_type) out;
```

This is similar to the input primitive type layout qualifier, the only difference being that you are declaring the output of the shader using the out keyword. The allowable output primitive types from the geometry shader are points, line_strip, and triangle_strip. Notice that geometry shaders only support outputting the strip primitive types (not counting points—obviously, there is no such thing as a point strip).

There is one final layout qualifier that must be used to configure the geometry shader. Because a geometry shader is capable of producing a variable amount of data per vertex, OpenGL must be told how much space to allocate for all that data by specifying the maximum number of vertices that the geometry shader is expected to produce. To do this, use the following layout qualifier:

```
layout (max_vertices = n) out;
```

This sets the maximum number of vertices that the geometry shader may produce to n. Because OpenGL may allocate buffer space to store intermediate results for each vertex, this should be the smallest number possible that still allows your application to run correctly. For example, if you are planning to take points and produce one line at a time, then you can safely set this to two. This gives the shader hardware the best opportunity to run fast. If you are going to heavily tessellate the incoming geometry, you might want to set this to a much higher number, although this may cost you some performance. The upper limit on the number of vertices that a geometry shader can produce depends on your OpenGL implementation. It is guaranteed to be at least 256, but the absolute maximum can be found by calling glGetIntegerv with the GL_MAX_GEOMETRY_OUTPUT_VERTICES parameter.

You can also declare more than one layout qualifier with a single statement by separating them with a comma, like so:

```
layout (triangle_strip, max_vertices = n) out;
```

With these layout qualifiers, a boilerplate #version declaration, and an empty main() function you should be able to produce a geometry shader that compiles and links but does absolutely nothing. In fact, it will discard any geometry you send it, and nothing will be drawn by your application. We need to introduce two important functions: EmitVertex() and EndPrimitive(). If you don't call these, nothing will be drawn.

EmitVertex tells the geometry shader that you've finished filling in all of the information for this vertex. Setting up the vertex works much like the vertex shader. You need to write into the built-in variable gl_Position. This sets the clip space coordinates of the vertex that is produced by the geometry shader, just like in a vertex shader. Any other attributes that you want to pass from the geometry shader to the fragment shader can be declared in an interface block or as global variables in the geometry shader. Whenever you call EmitVertex, the geometry shader stores the values currently in all of its output variables and uses them to generate a new vertex. You can call EmitVertex as many times as you like in a geometry shader, until you reach the limit you specified in your max_vertices layout qualifier. Each time, you put new values into your output variables to generate a new vertex.

An important thing to note about `EmitVertex` is that it makes the values of any of your output variables (such as gl_Position) undefined. So, for example, if you want to emit a triangle with a single color, you need to write that color with every one of your vertices; otherwise, you could end up with undefined results.

`EmitPrimitive` indicates that you have finished appending vertices to the end of the primitive. Don't forget, geometry shaders only support the strip primitive types (`line_strip` and `triangle_strip`). If your output primitive type is `triangle_strip` and you call `EmitVertex` more than three times, the geometry shader will produce multiple triangles in a strip. Likewise, if your output primitive type is `line_strip` and you call `EmitVertex` more than twice, you'll get multiple lines. In the geometry shader, `EndPrimitive` refers to the strip. This means that if you want to draw individual lines or triangles, you have to call `EndPrimitive` after every two or three vertices. You can also draw multiple strips by calling `EmitVertex` many times between multiple calls to `EndPrimitive`.

One final thing to note about calling `EmitVertex` and `EndPrimitive` in the geometry shader is that if you haven't produced enough vertices to produce a single primitive (for example, you're generating `triangle_strips` and you call `EndPrimitive` after two vertices), nothing is produced for that primitive, and the vertices you've already produced are simply thrown away.

Discarding Geometry in the Geometry Shader

The geometry shader in your program runs once per primitive. What you do with that primitive is entirely up to you. The two functions `EmitVertex` and `EndPrimitive` allow you to programmatically append new vertices to your triangle or line strip and to start new strips. You can call them as many times as you want (until you reach the maximum defined by your implementation). You're also allowed to not call them at all. This allows you to clip geometry away and discard primitives. If your geometry shader runs and you never call `EmitVertex` for that particular primitive, nothing will be drawn. To illustrate this, we can implement a custom backface culling routine that culls geometry as if it were viewed from an arbitrary point in space.

First, we set up our shader version and precision and declare our geometry shader to accept triangles and to produce triangle strips. Backface culling doesn't really make a lot of sense for lines or points. We also define a uniform that will hold our custom viewpoint in world space. This is shown in Listing 11.6.

LISTING 11.6   Configuring the Custom Culling Geometry Shader

```
#version 330
precision highp float;
```

```
// Input is triangles, output is triangle strip. Because we're going to do a
// 1 in 1 out shader producing a single triangle output for each one input,
// max_vertices can be 3 here.
layout (triangles) in;
layout (triangle_strip, max_vertices=3) out;

// Uniform variable that will hold our custom viewpoint
uniform vec3 viewpoint;
```

Now inside our `main()` function, we need to find the face normal for the triangle. This is simply the cross products of any two vectors in the plane of the triangle—we can use the triangle edges for this. Listing 11.7 shows how this is done.

LISTING 11.7   Finding a Face Normal in a Geometry Shader

```
// Calculate two vectors in the plane of the input triangle
vec3 ab = gl_in[1].gl_Position.xyz - gl_in[0].gl_Position.xyz;
vec3 ac = gl_in[2].gl_Position.xyz - gl_in[0].gl_Position.xyz;
vec3 normal = normalize(cross(ab, ac));
```

Now that we have the normal, we can determine whether it faces toward or away from our user-defined viewpoint. To do this, we need to transform the normal into the same coordinate space as the viewpoint, which is world space. Assuming we have the modelview matrix in a uniform, simply multiply the normal by this matrix. To be more accurate, we should multiply the vector by the inverse of the transpose of the upper left three-by-three submatrix of the modelview matrix. This is known as the *normal matrix*, and you're free to implement this and put it in its own uniform if you like. However, if your modelview matrix only contains translation, uniform scale (no shear), and rotation, you can use it directly. Don't forget, the normal is a three-element vector, and the modelview matrix is a four-by-four matrix. We need to extend the normal to a four-element vector before we can multiply the two. We can then take the dot product of the resulting vector with the vector from the viewpoint to any point on the triangle.

If the sign of the dot product is negative, that means that the normal is facing away from the viewer and the triangle should be culled. If it is positive, the triangle's normal is pointing toward the viewer, and we should pass the triangle on. The code to transform the face normal, perform the dot product, and test the sign of the result is shown in Listing 11.8.

LISTING 11.8   Conditionally Emitting Geometry in a Geometry Shader

```
// Calculate the transformed face normal and the view direction vector
vec3 transformed_normal = (vec4(normal, 0.0) * modelview_matrix).xyz;
vec3 vt = normalize(gl_in[0].gl_Position.xyz - viewpoint);
```

```
// Take the dot product of the normal with the view direction
float d = dot(vt, normal);

// Emit a primitive only if the sign of the dot product is positive
if (d > 0.0) {
    for (int i = 0; i < 3; i++) {
        gl_Position = gl_in[i].gl_Position;
        EmitVertex();
    }
    EndPrimitive();
}
```

In Listing 11.8, if the dot product is positive, we copy the input vertices to the output of the geometry shader and call `EmitVertex` for each one. If the dot product is negative, we simply don't do anything at all. This results in the incoming triangle being discarded altogether and nothing being drawn.

In this particular example, we are generating at most one triangle output for each triangle input to the geometry shader. Although the output of the geometry shader is a triangle strip, our strips only contain a single triangle. Therefore, there doesn't strictly need be a call to `EndPrimitive`. We just leave it there for completeness.

Figure 11.4 shows a selection of screenshots of a program including this shader.

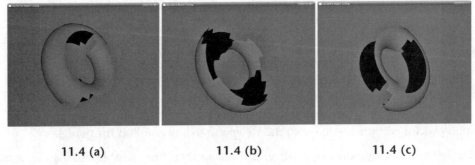

11.4 (a)   **11.4 (b)**   **11.4 (c)**

FIGURE 11.4   Geometry culled from different viewpoints.

In each screenshot of Figure 11.4 (a, b, c), the virtual viewer has been moved to different positions. As you can see, different parts of the model have been culled away by the geometry shader. It's not expected that this example is particularly useful, but it does demonstrate the ability for a geometry shader to perform geometry culling based on application-defined criteria.

Modifying Geometry in the Geometry Shader

The previous example either discarded geometry or passed it through unmodified. It is also possible to modify vertices as they pass through the geometry shader to create new, derived shapes. Even though your geometry shader is passing vertices on one-to-one (that is, no amplification or culling is taking place), this still allows you to do things that would otherwise not be possible with a vertex shader alone. If the input geometry is in the form of triangle strips or fans, for example, the resulting geometry will have shared vertices and shared edges. Using the vertex shader to move shared vertices will move all of the triangles that share that vertex. It is not possible, then, to separate two triangles that share an edge in the original geometry using the vertex shader alone. However, this is trivial using the geometry shader.

Consider a geometry shader that accepts triangles and produces `triangle_strips`. The input to a geometry shader that accepts triangles is individual triangles, regardless of whether they originated from a `glDrawArrays` or a `glDrawElements` function call, or whether the primitive type was `GL_TRIANGLES`, `GL_TRIANGLE_STRIP`, or `GL_TRIANGLE_FAN`. Unless the geometry shader outputs more than three vertices, the result is independent, unconnected triangles.

In this next example, we "explode" a model by pushing all of the triangles out along their face normals. It doesn't matter whether the original model is drawn with individual triangles or with triangle strips or fans. As with the previous example, the input is triangles, the output is `triangle_strip`, and the maximum number of vertices produced by the geometry shader is three because we're not amplifying or decimating geometry. The setup code for this is shown in Listing 11.9.

LISTING 11.9   Setting Up the "Explode" Geometry Shader

```
#version 330
precision highp float;

// Input is triangles, output is triangle strip. Because we're going to do a
// 1 in 1 out shader producing a single triangle output for each one input,
// max_vertices can be 3 here.
layout (triangles) in;
layout (triangle_strip, max_vertices=3) out;
```

To project the triangle outward, we need to calculate the face normal of each triangle. Again, to do this we can take the cross product of two vectors in the plane of the triangle—two edges of the triangle. For this, we can reuse the code from Listing 11.7.

Now that we have the triangle's face normal, we can project vertices along that normal by an application controlled amount. That amount can be stored in a uniform (we call it `explode_factor`) and updated by the application. This simple code is shown in Listing 11.10.

LISTING 11.10   Pushing a Face Out Along Its Normal

```
for (int i = 0; i < 3; i++) {
    gl_Position = gl_in[i].gl_Position + vec4(explode_factor * normal, 0.0);
}
```

The result of running this geometry shader on a model is shown in Figure 11.5. The model has been deconstructed, and the individual triangles have become visible.

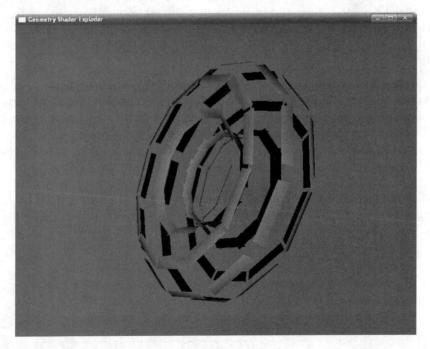

FIGURE 11.5   Exploding a model using the geometry shader.

Generating Geometry in the Geometry Shader

Just as you are not required to call `EmitVertex` or `EndPrimitive` at all if you don't want to produce any output from the geometry shader, it is also possible to call `EmitVertex` and `EndPrimitive` as many times as you need to produce new geometry. That is, until you reach the maximum number of output vertices that you declared at the start of your geometry shader. This functionality can be used for things like making multiple copies of the input or breaking the input into smaller pieces. This is the subject of the next example. The input to our shader is a cube centered around the origin. Each face of the cube is made from a pair of triangles, with a shared edge along the diagonal of the cube face. We tessellate incoming triangles by producing new vertices half way along the diagonal and then moving all of the resulting vertices so that they are equidistant from the origin. This transforms our cube into a rough sphere.

Because the geometry shader operates in object space (remember, the cube's vertices are centered around the origin), we need to do no coordinate transforms in the vertex shader and instead, do the transforms in the geometry shader after we've generated the new vertices. To do this, we need a simple, pass-through vertex shader. The code in Listing 11.11 shows a very simple pass-through vertex shader.

LISTING 11.11   A Simple Pass-Through Vertex Shader

```
#version 330
precision highp float;

in vec4 position;

void main(void)
{
    gl_Position = position;
}
```

This shader only passes the vertex position to the geometry shader. If you have other attributes associated with the vertices such as texture coordinates or normals, you need to pass them through the vertex shader to the geometry shader as well.

As in the previous example, we accept triangles as input to the geometry shader and produce a triangle strip. We break the strip after every triangle so that we can produce separate, independent triangles. In this example, we produce two output triangles for every input triangle. We need to declare our maximum output vertex count as six—two triangles times three vertices. We also need to declare a uniform matrix to store the modelview transformation matrix in the geometry shader because we do that transform after generating vertices. Listing 11.12 shows this code.

LISTING 11.12   Setting Up the "Tessellator" Geometry Shader

```
#version 330
precision highp float;
```

```
layout (triangles) in;
layout (triangle_strip, max_vertices=6) out;

// A uniform to store the model-view-projection matrix
uniform mat4 mvp;
```

To ensure we know which edge is the diagonal, we use indices in our program and `glDrawElements` to draw the cube. This allows us to always make the first vertex the apex of the triangle and the edge between the second and third triangles the diagonal of the cube face. For each generated triangle, we can use the same first vertex as the incoming triangle. Then for the two triangles that we produce, we can use the generated vertex and one of the other incoming vertices.

First, let's normalize the incoming vertex coordinates, which makes them all equidistant from the origin because the length of the vector from the origin to any vertex will be one. This isn't necessary if the original cube's vertex coordinates are already normalized, but this allows the cube to have unit side length—something that is common for stock geometry. We also multiply the resulting vertex coordinates by the modelviewprojection matrix here. This is shown in Listing 11.13.

LISTING 11.13   Setting Up the "Tessellator" Geometry Shader

```
// Push the incoming vertices onto the surface of a sphere of radius 1
vec3 a = normalize(gl_in[0].gl_Position.xyz);
vec3 b = normalize(gl_in[1].gl_Position.xyz);
vec3 c = normalize(gl_in[2].gl_Position.xyz);

// Generate the new vertex midway between b and c. Note that normalizing the
// the vertex means that we don't need to divide by two to get the mean.
vec3 d = normalize(b + c);

// Now transform the generated vertices into world space
a = a * mvp;
b = b * mvp;
c = c * mvp;
d = d * mvp;
```

Now, a is the apex of the triangle, and d is the generated vertex. The edge bc is the diagonal of the cube's face and the edge that we will break in half. The two triangles that we will output will be abd and adc. To produce the two output triangles, we need to set up the vertices, call `EmitVertex` for each one, and then call `EndPrimitive` between each triangle to restart the triangle strips. Listing 11.14 shows this.

LISTING 11.14   Emitting the Tessellated Vertices

```
// Produce first triangle abd
gl_Position = a;
EmitVertex();
gl_Position = b;
EmitVertex();
gl_Position = d;
EmitVertex();
EndPrimitive();

// Produce second triangle adc
gl_Position = a;
EmitVertex();
gl_Position = d;
EmitVertex();
gl_Position = c;
EmitVertex();
EndPrimitive();
```

In this example, we produce two independent triangles for each of the incoming triangles. However, the triangles actually share the edge ad, and by outputting the vertices in the right order, they can be represented by a triangle strip, which is exactly what the geometry shader is designed to output. Our new triangle generation code looks like Listing 11.15.

LISTING 11.15   Tessellating Using a Triangle Strip

```
gl_Position = b;
EmitVertex();
gl_Position = d;
EmitVertex();
gl_Position = a;
EmitVertex();
gl_Position = c;
EmitVertex();
EndPrimitive();
```

Notice that we only call EmitVertex four times instead of six, and we eliminated a call to EndPrimitive. We can reduce our max_vertices for this geometry shader to four, and this may make the program run faster. Even though we doubled the number of *triangles* that the program renders, by using a short strip, we only increase the number of *vertices* to process by one-third.

Figure 11.6 shows a screenshot of our simple geometry shader-based tessellation program.

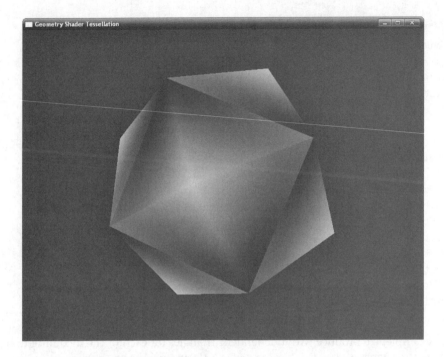

FIGURE 11.6   Basic tessellation using the geometry shader.

It should be noted that using the geometry shader for heavy tessellation may not produce the most optimal performance. If something more complex than that shown in this example is desired, it's best to use one of the OpenGL extensions that expose hardware tessellation. A full explanation of those extensions is beyond the scope of this book.

Changing the Primitive Type in the Geometry Shader

So far, all of the geometry shader examples we've gone through have taken triangles as input and produced triangle strips as output. This doesn't change the geometry type. However, geometry shaders can input and output different types of geometry. For example, you can transform points into triangles or triangles into points. In this next example, we're going to change the geometry type from triangles to lines. For each vertex input to the shader, we take the vertex normal and represent it as a line. We also take the face normal and represent that as another line. This allows us to visualize the model's normals—both at each vertex and for each face. Note, though, that if you want to draw the normals over top of the original model, you need to draw everything twice—once with the geometry shader to visualize the normals and once without the geometry shader to show the model. You can't output a mix of two different primitives from a single geometry shader.

For our geometry shader, in addition to the members of the gl_in structure, we need the per-vertex normal, and that will have to be passed through the vertex shader. An updated version of the pass-through vertex shader from Listing 11.11 is given in Listing 11.16.

LISTING 11.16 A Pass-Through Vertex Shader That Includes Normals

```
#version 330
precision highp float;

in vec4 position;
in vec3 normal;

out Vertex
{
    vec3 normal;
} vertex;

void main(void)
{
    gl_Position = position;
    vertex.normal = normal;
}
```

This passes the position attribute straight through to the gl_Position built-in variable and places the normal into an output block.

The setup code for the geometry shader is shown in Listing 11.17. In this example we accept triangles and produce line strips, each of a single line. Because we output a separate line for each normal we visualize, we produce two vertices for each vertex consumed, plus two more for the face normal. Therefore, the maximum number of vertices that we output per input triangle is eight. To match the Vertex output block that we declared in the vertex shader, we also need to declare a corresponding input interface block in the geometry shader. As we're going to do the object space to world space transformation in the geometry shader, we declare a mat4 uniform called mvp to represent the modelviewprojection matrix. This is necessary so that we can keep the vertex's position in the same coordinate system as its normal until we produce the new vertices representing the line.

LISTING 11.17 Setting Up the "Normal Visualizer" Geometry Shader

```
#version 330
precision highp float;

layout (triangles) in;
layout (line_strip) out;
```

```
layout (max_vertices = 8) out;

in Vertex
{
    vec3 normal;
} vertex[];

// Uniform to hold the model-view-projection matrix
uniform mat4 mvp;

// Uniform to store the length of the visualized normals
uniform float normal_length;
```

Each input vertex is transformed into its final position and emitted from the geometry shader, and then a second vertex is produced by displacing the input vertex along its normal and transforming that into its final position as well. This makes the length of all of our normals one but allows any scaling encoded in our modelviewprojection matrix to be applied to them along with the model. We multiply the normals by the application supplied uniform normal_length, allowing them to be scaled to match the model. Our inner loop is shown in Listing 11.18.

LISTING 11.18   Producing Lines from Normals in the Geometry Shader

```
for (int i = 0; i < gl_in.length(); i++) {
    gl_Position = mvp * gl_in[i].gl_Position;
    EmitVertex();
    gl_Position = mvp * vec4(gl_in[i].gl_Position.xyz +
                             vertex[i].normal * normal_length, 1.0);
    EmitVertex();
    EndPrimitive();
}
```

This generates a short line segment at each vertex pointing in the direction of the normal. Now, we need to produce the face normal. To do this, we need to pick a suitable place from which to draw the normal, and we need to calculate the face normal itself in the geometry shader along which to draw the line.

As in the earlier example given in Listing 11.7, we use a cross product of two of the triangle's edges to find the face normal. To pick a starting point for the line, we choose the centroid of the triangle, which is simply the average of the coordinates of the input vertices. Listing 11.19 shows the shader code.

LISTING 11.19   Drawing a Face Normal in the Geometry Shader

```
vec4 centroid = (gl_in[0].gl_Position +
                 gl_in[1].gl_Position +
                 gl_in[2].gl_Position) / 3.0;
vec3 face_normal = normalize(cross(gl_in[1].gl_Position.xyz -
                                   gl_in[0].gl_Position.xyz,
                                   gl_in[2].gl_Position.xyz -
                                   gl_in[0].gl_Position.xyz));
gl_Position = centroid * mvp;
EmitVertex();
gl_Position = (centroid + vec4(face_normal * normal_length, 0.0)) * mvp;
EmitVertex();
EndPrimitive();
```

Now when we render a model, we get the image shown in Figure 11.7.

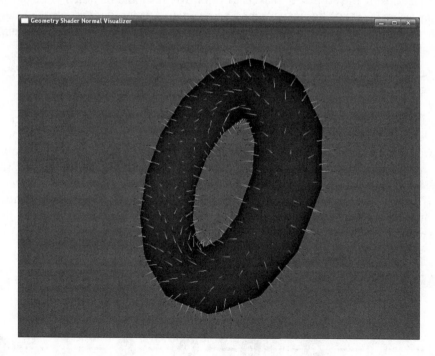

FIGURE 11.7   Displaying the normals of a model using a geometry shader.

New Primitive Types Introduced by the Geometry Shader

Four new primitive types were introduced with geometry shaders, GL_LINES_ADJACENCY, GL_LINE_STRIP_ADJACENCY, GL_TRIANGLES_ADJACENCY, and GL_TRIANGLE_STRIP_ADJACENCY. These primitive types are really only useful when rendering with a geometry shader active. When the new adjacency primitive types are used, for each line or triangle passed into the geometry shader, it not only has access to the vertices defining that primitive, but it also has access to the vertices of the primitive that is next to the one it's processing.

When you render using GL_LINES_ADJACENCY, each line segment consumes four vertices from the enabled attribute arrays. The two center vertices make up the line; the first and last vertices are considered the adjacent vertices. The inputs to the geometry shader are therefore four-element arrays. In fact, because the input and output types of the geometry shader do not have to be related, GL_LINES_ADJACENCY can be seen as a way of sending generalized four-vertex primitives to the geometry shader. The geometry shader is free to transform them into whatever it pleases. For example, your geometry shader could convert each set of four vertices into a triangle strip made up of two triangles. This allows you to render quads using the GL_LINES_ADJACENCY primitive. It should be noted, though, that if you draw using GL_LINES_ADJACENCY when no geometry shader is active, regular lines will be drawn using the two innermost vertices of each set of four vertices. The two outermost vertices will be discarded, and the vertex shader will not run on them at all.

Using GL_LINE_STRIP_ADJACENCY produces a similar effect. The difference is that the entire strip is considered to be a primitive, with one additional vertex on each end. If you send eight vertices to OpenGL using GL_LINES_ADJACENCY, the geometry shader will run twice, whereas if you send the same vertices using GL_LINE_STRIP_ADJACENCY, the geometry shader will run five times. Figure 11.8 should make things clear. The eight vertices in the top row are sent to OpenGL with the GL_LINES_ADJACENCY primitive mode. The geometry shader runs twice on four vertices each time—ABCD and EFGH. In the second row, the same eight vertices are sent to OpenGL using the GL_LINESTRIP_ADJACENCY primitive mode. This time, the geometry shader runs five times—ABCD, BCDE, and so on until EFGH. In each case, the solid arrows are the lines that would be rendered if no geometry shader were present.

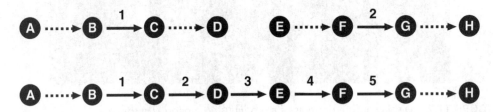

FIGURE 11.8   Lines produced using GL_LINES_ADJACENCY and GL_LINE_STRIP_ADJACENCY.

The GL_TRIANGLES_ADJACENCY primitive mode works similarly to the GL_LINES_ADJACENCY mode. A triangle is sent to the geometry shader for each set of six vertices in the enabled attribute arrays. The first, third, and fifth vertices are considered to make up the real triangle, and the second, fourth, and sixth vertices are considered to be in-between the triangle's vertices. This means that the inputs to the geometry shader are six element arrays. As before, because the you can do anything you want to the vertices using the geometry shader; GL_TRIANGLES_ADJACENCY is a good way to get arbitrary six-vertex primitives into the geometry shader. Figure 11.9 shows this.

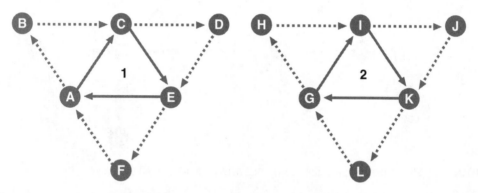

FIGURE 11.9   Triangles produced using GL_TRIANGLES_ADJACENCY.

The final, and perhaps most complex (or alternatively the most difficult to understand), of these primitive types is GL_TRIANGLE_STRIP_ADJACENCY. This primitive represents a triangle strip with every other vertex (the first, third, fifth, seventh, ninth, and so on) forming the strip. The vertices in-between are the adjacent vertices. Figure 11.10 demonstrates the principle. In the figure, the vertices A through P represent 16 vertices sent to OpenGL. A triangle strip is generated from every other vertex (A, C, E, G, I, and so on), and the vertices that come between them (B, D, F, H, J, and so on) are the adjacent vertices.

There are special cases for the triangles that come at the start and end of the strip, but once the strip is started, the vertices fall into a regular pattern that is more clearly seen in Figure 11.11.

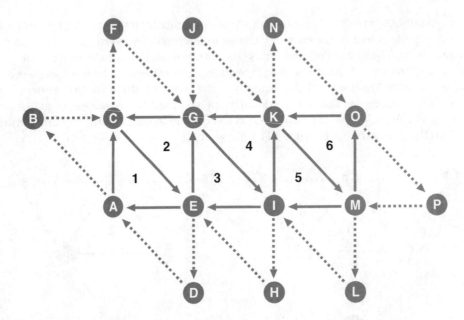

FIGURE 11.10   Triangles produced using GL_TRIANGLE_STRIP_ADJACENCY.

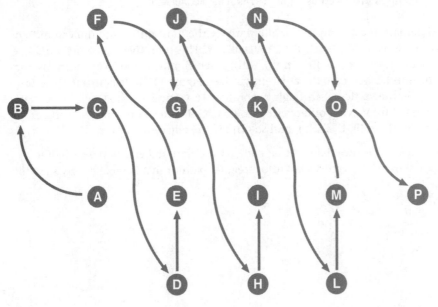

FIGURE 11.11   Ordering of vertices for GL_TRIANGLE_STRIP_ADJACENCY.

The rules for the ordering of GL_TRIANGLE_STRIP_ADJACENCY are spelled out clearly in the OpenGL Specification—in particular, the special cases are noted there. You are encouraged to read that section of the specification if you want to work with this primitive type.

Advanced Fragment Shaders

The fragment shader is a powerful stage in the OpenGL pipeline. Graphics hardware typically has the greatest memory bandwidth when reading from textures and writing to the framebuffer. However, you're not limited to processing visual data in the fragment shader. If you have a data-intensive operation, the fragment shader is probably the best place to perform it. So far, you have used the fragment shader to simulate materials and surfaces using techniques such as texturing, normal mapping, and so on. The fragment shader runs on every fragment generated by a primitive. However, it is possible to use the fragment shader to do more than just simulate the surface of the objects you are rendering.

In this section, we cover some more advanced uses of the fragment shader. For most of these examples, we use a single pair of triangles covering the whole screen as the input geometry. This is often called a full-screen quad because it is a quadrangle that covers the entire screen. First, we go over using the fragment shader to apply post-processing effects such as blur and color correction and enhancement. Later, we show that entire scenes can be generated using only the fragment shader.

For the next few examples, we use the same, simple pass-through vertex shader. All this does is pass the input coordinate to the output position and also copy it into a texture coordinate so that the fragment shader can have access to it. The code is given in Listing 11.20.

LISTING 11.20   Full-Screen Quad Pass-Through Vertex Shader

```
#version 330
precision highp float;

in vec2 position;

out Fragment
{
    vec2 tex_coord;
} fragment;

void main(void)
{
    gl_Position = vec4(position, 0.5, 1.0);
    // This produces a texture coordinate that ranges from
    // (-1.0, -1.0) to (1.0, 1.0)
    fragment.tex_coord = position;
```

```
    // Alternatively, we can make our texture coordinate range from
    // (0.0, 0.0) to (1.0, 1.0) by using this line of code:
    // fragment.tex_coord = position * 0.5 + vec2(0.5, 0.5);
}
```

The input to the shader is a single vec2 attribute, position, which is fed from the coordinates representing the corners of our quad, as shown in Listing 11.21.

LISTING 11.21   Full-Screen Quad Geometry

```
const GLfloat quad_coords[] =
{
    -1.0f, -1.0f,
     1.0f, -1.0f,
    -1.0f,  1.0f,
     1.0f,  1.0f
};
```

Using these coordinates and drawing them as a GL_TRIANGLE_STRIP, a quad can be rendered covering the entire viewport with a single call to glDrawArrays. The fragment.tex_coord output from the vertex shader can range either from (-1.0, -1.0) to (1.0, 1.0) or from (0.0, 0.0) to (1.0, 1.0) depending on which lines are uncommented, as explained in the shader's comments. Some of these examples require the -1.0 to 1.0 variant, and some require the 0.0 to 1.0 variant.

Post-Processing in the Fragment Shader—Color Correction

For this example, we assume that you have an input image in a texture. This can be a pregenerated image, or it can be the result of rendering your scene into a texture attached to a Frame Buffer Object (FBO). To learn more about FBOs and rendering to textures, refer to Chapter 8, "Buffer Objects: Storage Is Now in Your Hands." In this example, we read a single texel from the texture, apply a transformation to the color stored in it, and output that from the fragment shader for display to the user. When we sample from the input texture, we need the texture coordinate to range from (0.0, 0.0) to (1.0, 1.0), so we need to enable that variant of the pass-through vertex shader.

To apply color correction, we transform each fragment using a matrix. By placing this matrix in a uniform, the application can update the matrix at runtime to produce different effects. The code to set up our fragment shader is given in Listing 11.22.

LISTING 11.22   Setting Up the Color Correction Fragment Shader

```
#version 330
precision highp float;

// This is the interface block that is used to pass the texture coordinates
// from the dummy vertex shader.
in Fragment
{
    vec2 texcoord;
} fragment;

// This uniform contains the matrix used to do the color correction
uniform mat4 color_matrix;

// The sampler that represents our input image
uniform sampler2D tex_input_image;

// The final color
out vec4 final_color;
```

Now that we have the inputs to the fragment shader set up, we can go on with the color correction shader. Each output fragment is generated directly from one texel in the source image. We can apply a generalized projective transformation in the input color by using a transformation matrix. The color stored in the input texture is in RGB format. We need to expand this to a homogeneous vector, just like OpenGL positions, by setting the alpha channel 1.0. Then we can multiply it by our transformation matrix and divide through by the w coordinate. The body of our shader is really very simple—only the few lines of code in Listing 11.23.

LISTING 11.23   The Main Body of the Color Correction Fragment Shader

```
void main(void)
{
    // Read the input color from the texture and convert it to a
    // homogeneous vector
    vec4 input_color = vec4(texture(tex_input_image,
                                    fragment.tex_coord).rgb, 1.0);
    // Transform it using our color conversion matrix
    vec4 transformed_color = color_matrix * input_color;
    // This allows us to produce a 'perspective' transform on
    // the final color.
    final_color = transformed_color / transformed_color.a;
}
```

Using this shader, we can take an image and transform it to another color space, modify the brightness, or adjust the color balance of the image. Figure 11.12 gives a few examples of matrices that you can use to apply interesting effects to images.

$$
\begin{pmatrix} 0.5 & 0.4 & 0.2 & 0.0 \\ 0.4 & 0.3 & 0.2 & 0.0 \\ 0.3 & 0.3 & 0.2 & 0.0 \\ 0.0 & 0.0 & 0.0 & 1.0 \end{pmatrix}
\qquad
\begin{pmatrix} 0.3 & 0.6 & 0.1 & 0.0 \\ 0.3 & 0.6 & 0.1 & 0.0 \\ 0.3 & 0.6 & 0.1 & 0.0 \\ 0.0 & 0.0 & 0.0 & 1.0 \end{pmatrix}
\qquad
\begin{pmatrix} 0.0 & 1.0 & 0.0 & 0.0 \\ 1.0 & 0.0 & 0.0 & 0.0 \\ 0.0 & 0.0 & 1.0 & 0.0 \\ 0.0 & 0.0 & 0.0 & 1.0 \end{pmatrix}
$$

Sepia Tone   Grayscale   Swap Red and Green

FIGURE 11.12   Example color processing matrices.

These are fairly simple matrices, and so it is easy to see how they work. The sepia tone matrix essentially averages all of the color channels together, applying a slight bias toward the red channel to give the resulting image the brownish color typical of sepia images. The grayscale matrix takes a weighted average of the input colors—because each of the rows in the matrix is the same, each color channel in the output image is equal to each other. However, the input green channel is weighted slightly higher than the others because the human eye is slightly more sensitive to green than other colors. The matrix mimics our visual system. The red-green swap matrix is simply made of ones and zeros. The result is that the weight of the green channel for the red output is zero, and the weight of the red input for the green output is zero.

Post-Processing in the Fragment Shader—Convolution

In the color correction example, each output fragment was produced from a single input texel. In this example, we can expand the input to the shader to multiple input texels. This allows us to combine the data from multiple texels and implement filtering operations. We can implement convolution with a separable kernel using two passes over the image. A separable kernel is one that can be split into horizontal and vertical vector components that, when their outer product is taken, produce a two-dimensional kernel matrix. An example of this is a Gaussian filter, which can be used to produce smooth blurring effects.

Again, this example uses a full-screen quad as the input geometry and uses the variant of the pass-through vertex shader that produces texture coordinates between (0.0, 0.0) and (1.0, 1.0). To store the filter coefficients, we use a TBO. TBOs were introduced in Chapter 8. To step through the input image, we supply a uniform, tc_scale, which specifies how far to displace the input texture coordinates for each coefficient. This essentially allows us to scale our filter kernel relative to the input image. By setting either its x or y component to zero, we can step through the image vertically or horizontally, respectively.

We can also step in an arbitrary direction through the input image by setting both x and y coordinates to nonzero terms. As long as the vectors used in each pass are orthogonal, the filter will still be separable. The input declarations to the convolution fragment shader are given in Listing 11.24.

LISTING 11.24   Inputs to the Convolution Fragment Shader

```
#version 330
precision highp float;

// Input interface block from vertex shader
in Fragment
{
    vec2 tex_coord;
} fragment;

// The sampler that represents our input image
uniform sampler2D tex_input_image;

// The TBO that holds our filter coefficients
uniform samplerBuffer tbo_coefficient;

// Uniform to scale integers to texture coordinates
uniform vec2 tc_scale;

// The final output color
out vec4 output_color;
```

The size of the filter can be determined from the size of the TBO, which can be found by calling the textureSize function on it. This means that we don't need to explicitly tell the shader how big the filter is, and we can even use a non-square filter by using different sized TBOs on the horizontal and vertical passes. The filter is centered around the output fragment. If we do not center the filter around the output fragment, each pass will shift the image horizontally or vertically. To perform the filtering, we loop over the texels in the input image, weighting each one by a sample from the TBO.

The body of the shader ends up being pretty simple and is shown in Listing 11.25.

LISTING 11.25   Separable Convolution Fragment Shader

```
int filter_size = textureSize(tbo_coefficient);
vec2 color = vec4(0.0);
vec2 tc_offset;
float coefficient;
```

```
for (int i = 0; i < filter_size; i++) {
    coefficient = texelFetch(tbo_vertical_coefficient, i).r;
    tc_offset = float(i - filter_size / 2) * tc_scale;
    color += coefficient * texture(tex_input_image,
                                    fragment.tex_coord + tc_offset);
}

output_color = color;
```

The host application for this shader is also fairly simple. The whole implementation is included in the source code available from the book's Web site. The application performs two passes over the image. The first uses the input image as a texture and renders to a texture attached to an FBO. The second pass uses the texture previously written in the first pass as an input and renders to the framebuffer.

Given the input image of Figure 11.13, the result of convolution with a Gaussian filter is shown in Figure 11.14.

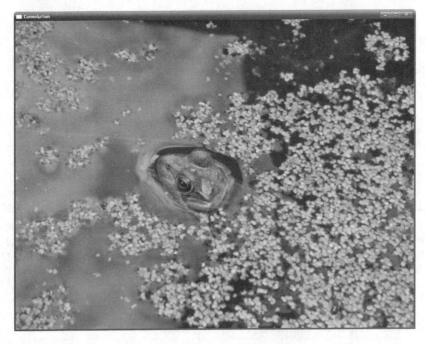

FIGURE 11.13   Input to the convolution example.

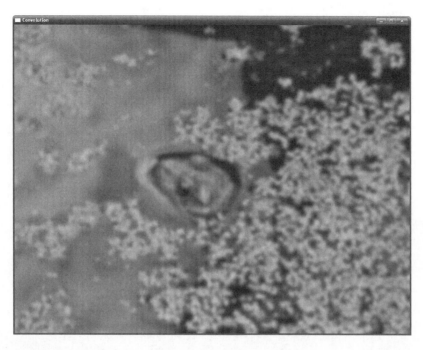

FIGURE 11.14   Result of applying Gaussian blur to an image.

This image has been produced by using the filter kernel in Table 11.3. Note that the kernel weights all add up to one. If they did not, it would cause the output image to become brighter or darker than the input image. Also this kernel is symmetric (a property of the Gaussian kernel). If it were not, then the output image would be shifted horizontally or vertically relative to the input.

TABLE 11.3   Filter Weights for Gaussian Blur Example

0.015625	0.09375	0.234375	0.3125	0.234375	0.09375	0.015625

Another example of a separable filter is the Sobel edge detector. Figure 11.15 shows what Figure 11.13 looks like after the Sobel edge detector has been applied to it.

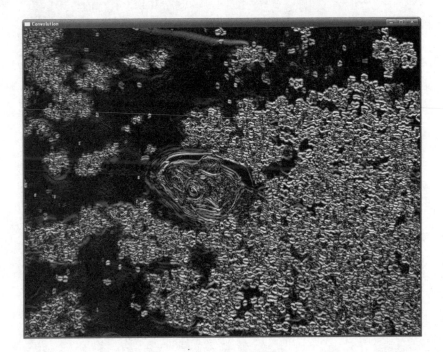

FIGURE 11.15   Result of applying a Sobel edge detector to an image.

The weights for the Sobel operator are given in Table 11.4. Note that the Sobel filter is separated into two different kernels, one for each pass. Also each pass of the Sobel operator detects edges running either horizontally or vertically, and it detects image gradient, which means that we need to take the magnitude of the result to visualize the result. The example application does this.

TABLE 11.4   Separated Filter Weights for Sobel Edge Detection

Pass 1	1.0	2.0	1.0
Pass 2	1.0	0.0	-1.0

Generating Image Data in the Fragment Shader

In the first two examples of using a fragment shader to perform post-processing, we started with a prerendered image that was either a texture supplied by the application or the result of rendering with OpenGL into a texture. In this next example, we render a Julia set, creating image data from nothing but the texture coordinates. Julia sets are related to

COLOR PLATE 1 Shaders allow for unprecedented real-time realism (image courtesy of Software Bisque, Inc.). (For Figure 1.16 in Chapter 1.)

COLOR PLATE 2 A true bitmap, grayscale, and RGB representation of the same image. (For Figures 5.2 and 5.3 in Chapter 5.)

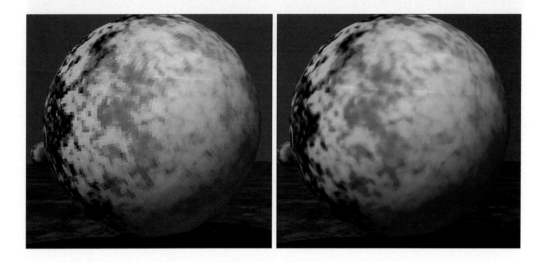

COLOR PLATE 3 Nearest and linear filtering up close. (For Figure 5.9 in Chapter 5.)

COLOR PLATE 4 Trilinear versus anisotropic filtering. (For Figures 5.12 and 5.14 in Chapter 5.)

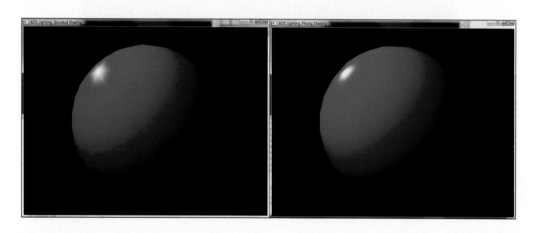

COLOR PLATE 5 Gouraud versus Phong shading with the ADS lighting model. (For Figures 6.7 and 6.8 in Chapter 6.)

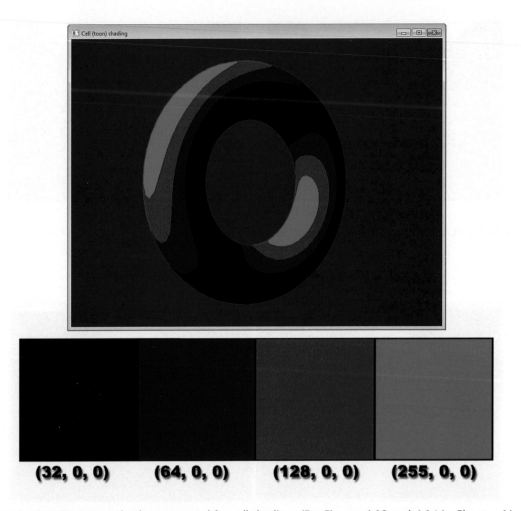

(32, 0, 0)   (64, 0, 0)   (128, 0, 0)   (255, 0, 0)

COLOR PLATE 6   A red color ramp used for cell shading. (For Figures 6.13 and 6.14 in Chapter 6.)

COLOR PLATE 7 Output from the TextureRect sample. (For Figure 7.2 in Chapter 7.)

COLOR PLATE 8 Output from the Cubemap sample program. (For Figure 7.4 in Chapter 7.)

COLOR PLATE 9 Output from the Multitexture sample program. (For Figure 7.6 in Chapter 7.)

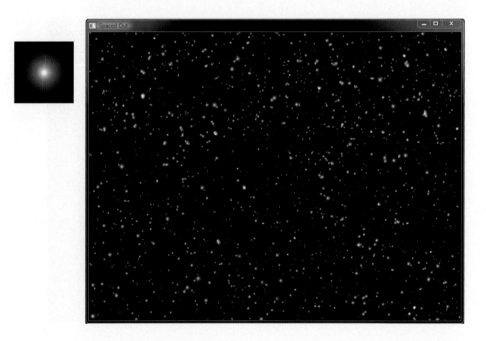

COLOR PLATE 10 Using texture mapped points (point sprites) for a particle effect. (For Figures 7.8 and 7.9 in Chapter 7.)

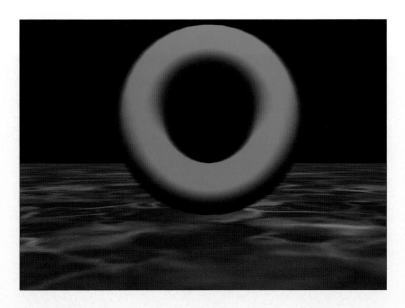

COLOR PLATE 11 A blur effect created using multiple PBOs. (For Figure 8.1 in Chapter 8.)

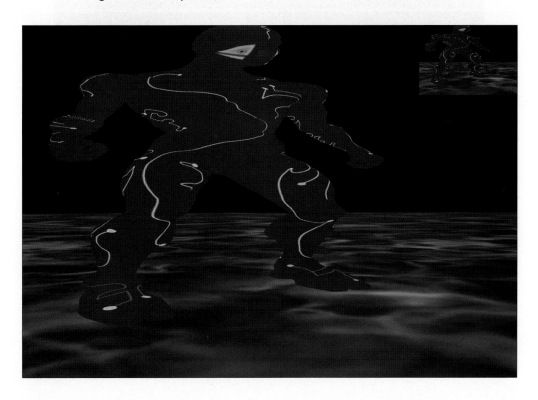

COLOR PLATE 12 Multiple buffers drawn simultaneously using FBOs. (For Figure 8.5 in Chapter 8.)

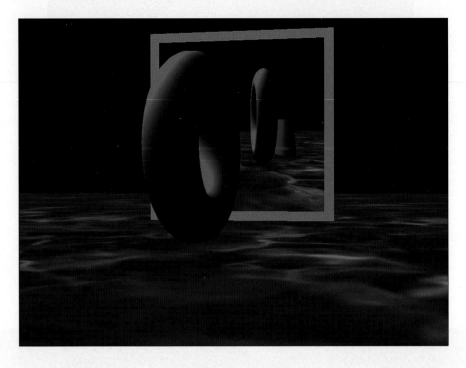

COLOR PLATE 13 Mirror effect using a texture bound to an FBO. (For Figure 8.6 in Chapter 8.)

COLOR PLATE 14 Different views of an HDR image. Low exposure on the left; high exposure on the right. (For Figure 9.1 in Chapter 9.)

COLOR PLATE 15 Adaptive tone mapping of an HDR image. (For Figure 9.4 in Chapter 9.)

COLOR PLATE 16 Brighter exposure on the right showing light bloom. (For Figure 9.5 in Chapter 9.)

COLOR PLATE 17 Adding bloom to a scene. (For Figure 9.6 in Chapter 9.)

COLOR PLATE 18 Multisample helps soften edges for a more natural look. (For Figure 9.10 in Chapter 9.)

COLOR PLATE 19   Order independent transparency used to render glasslike objects.
(For Figure 10.3 in Chapter 10.)

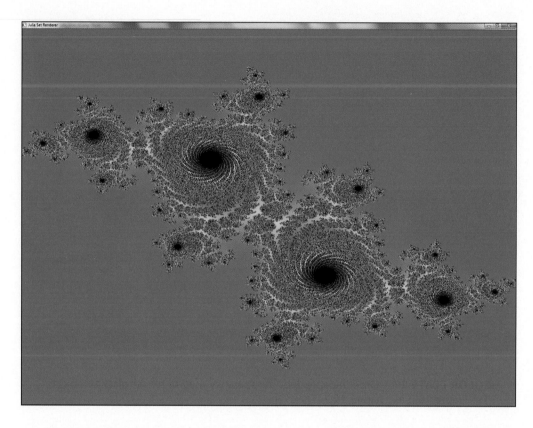

COLOR PLATE 20 A Julia fractal rendered by the program described in Chapter 11.

COLOR PLATE 21 The final field of grass produced by the instanced rendering example described in Chapter 12. (For Figure 12.6 in Chapter 12.)

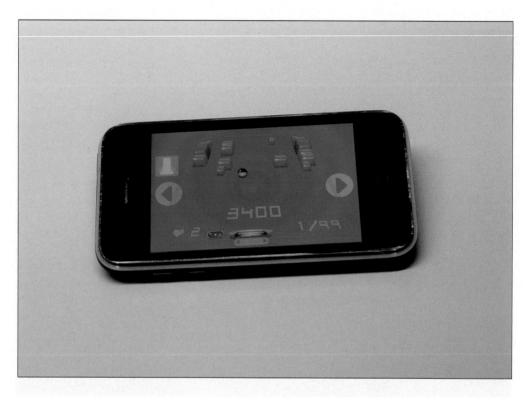

COLOR PLATE 22 OpenGL ES game rendering on a cellphone. (For Figure 16.1 in Chapter 16.)

COLOR PLATE 23   The effects of tearing when the buffer swaps occur before the vertical retrace. (For Figure 14.15 in Chapter 14.)

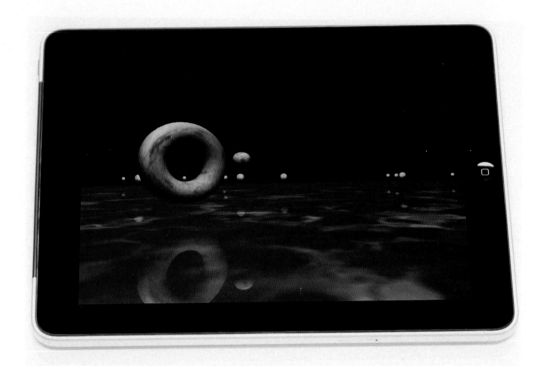

COLOR PLATE 24 The SphereWorld example program using OpenGL ES on another handheld platform. (Not associated with any figure in Chapter 16.)

the Mandelbrot set—the iconic bulblike fractal. The Mandelbrot image is generated by iterating the formula

$$z_n = z_{n-1}^2 + c$$

until the magnitude of z exceeds a threshold and calculating the number of iterations. If the magnitude of z never exceeds the threshold within the allowed number of iterations, that point is determined to be inside the Mandelbrot set and is colored with some default color. If the magnitude of z exceeds the threshold within the allowed number of iterations, then the point is outside the set. A common visualization of the Mandelbrot set colors the point using a function of the iteration count at the time the point was determined to be outside the set. The primary difference between the Mandelbrot set and the Julia set is the initial conditions for z and c.

When rendering the Mandelbrot set, z is set to 0+0i, and c set to the coordinate of the point at which the iterations are to be performed. When rendering the Julia set, z is set to the coordinate of the point at which iterations are performed, and c is set to an application-specified constant. Thus, while there is only one Mandelbrot set, there are infinitely many Julia sets—one for every possible value of c. Because of this, the Julia set can be controlled parametrically and even animated. Just as in the previous examples, we invoke this shader at every fragment by drawing a full-screen quad.

Let's set up the fragment shader with an input block containing just the texture coordinates. We also need a uniform to hold the value of c. To apply interesting colors to the resulting Julia image, we use a one-dimensional texture with a color gradient in it. When we've iterated a point that escapes from the set, we color the output fragment by indexing into this texture using the iteration count. Finally, we also define a uniform containing the maximum number of iterations we want to perform. This allows the application to balance performance against the level of detail in the resulting image. Listing 11.26 shows the setup for our Julia renderer's fragment shader.

LISTING 11.26 Setting Up the Julia Set Renderer

```
#version 330
precision highp float;

in Fragment
{
    vec2 tex_coord;
} fragment;

// Here's our value of c
uniform vec2 c;
```

```
// This is the color gradient texture
uniform sampler1D tex_gradient;

// This is the maximum iterations we'll perform before we consider
// the point to be outside the set
uniform int max_iterations;

// The output color for this fragment
out vec4 output_color;
```

Now that we have the inputs to our shader, we are ready to start rendering the Julia set. The value of c is taken from the uniform supplied by the application. The initial value of z is taken from the incoming texture coordinates supplied by the vertex shader. Our iteration loop is shown in Listing 11.27.

LISTING 11.27   Inner Loop of the Julia Renderer

```
int iterations = 0;
vec2 z = fragment.tex_coords;
const float threshold_squared = 4.0;

while (iterations < max_iterations && dot(z, z) < threshold_squared)
{
    vec2 z_squared;
    z_squared.x = z.x * z.x - z.y * z.y;
    z_squared.y = 2.0 * z.x * z.y;
    z = z_squared + c;
    iterations++;
}
```

The loop terminates under one of two conditions—either we reach the maximum number of iterations allowed (iterations = max_iterations) or the magnitude of z passes our threshold. Note that in this shader, we compare the squared magnitude of z (found using the dot function) to the square of the threshold (the threshold_squared uniform). The two operations are equivalent, but this way avoids a square root in the shader, improving performance. If, at the end of the loop, iterations is equal to max_iterations, we know we ran out of iterations and the point is inside the set—we color it black. Otherwise, our point left the set before we ran out of iterations, and we can color the point accordingly. To do this, we can just figure out what fraction of the total allowed iterations we used up and use that to look up into the gradient texture. Listing 11.28 shows what the code looks like.

LISTING 11.28   Using a Gradient Texture to Color the Julia Set

```
if (iterations == max_iterations) {
    output_color = vec4(0.0, 0.0, 0.0, 0.0);
} else {
    output_color = texture(tex_gradient,
                           float(iterations) / float(max_iterations));
}
```

Now all that's left is to supply the gradient texture and set an appropriate value of c. For our application, we update c on each frame. By keeping track of the number of frames we've rendered, this allows us to animate the fractal. Figure 11.16 shows a few frames of the Julia animation produced by the program. (See Color Plate 20 in the color insert for another example.)

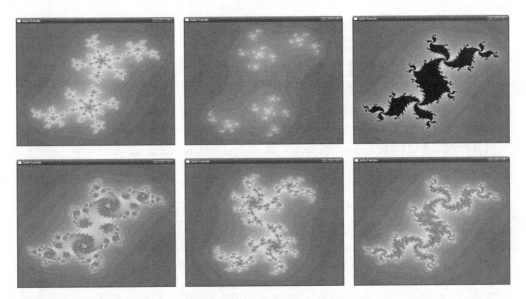

FIGURE 11.16   A few frames from the Julia set animation.

Discarding Work in the Fragment Shader

The fragment shader is a powerful tool to help you calculate the color of the pixels that are rendered. The shapes that you're rendering are determined by the geometry that's rendered. If you want to draw something with a detailed shape, you need to send more geometry to OpenGL. You can use alpha blending to make geometry that's partially transparent, but so far, you haven't been able to control *shapes* with the fragment shader. If your fragment shader determines that something is fully transparent, OpenGL still writes to the depth and stencil buffers, even if it optimizes away writes to the color buffer.

It is possible for the fragment shader to tell OpenGL to throw away the pixel that's being rendered all together. This is accomplished using the `discard` keyword. If the fragment shader executes the `discard` keyword, the results of the shader are thrown away, and no output buffers are written, including the depth, stencil, or color buffer attachments. The example in Listing 11.29 shows how to implement alpha testing in the fragment shader, which allows it to cut holes in the output geometry.

LISTING 11.29   Simple Alpha-Testing Fragment Shader

```
#version 330
precision highp float;
uniform sampler2D my_texture;

in Fragment
{
    vec2 texture_coord;
} fragment;

out vec4 color_out;

void main(void)
{
    vec4 color = texture(my_texture, fragment.texture_coord);
    if (color.a < 0.1)
        discard;
    color_out = color;
}
```

In this example, if the alpha value stored in a texture is less than a certain threshold (0.1 in this case), the `discard` keyword is executed, and the result of the fragment shader is not written to any of the attached buffers. If the alpha value is greater or equal to the threshold, the shader continues as normal, and the resulting color is written. Don't forget, alpha blending is performed by an additional stage after the fragment shader. All the shader has to do is write the color (including its alpha component) to an output variable, and the fixed-function blending stage takes care of the calculations required to mix it into the framebuffer.

The fragment shader can execute the `discard` keyword for any reason it chooses. In addition to basing this on a property of a texture, it could generate the condition analytically from some input varyings. If you use a texture as the determining factor, the level of detail in the resulting image is dependent on the resolution of the texture. If the decision is made analytically, the detail in the resulting image is dependent only on the precision of the fragment shader. For example, we could modify our Julia set renderer here to execute the discard keyword if the fragment is determined to be inside the set, as shown by the code fragment in Listing 11.30.

LISTING 11.30   Modifying the Julia Renderer with the discard Keyword

```
if (iterations == max_iterations)
    discard;

output_color = texture(tex_gradient,
                       float(iterations) / float(max_iterations));
```

Now, when we render the fractal, it will have a hole in it where the pixels are inside the set and only be colored when the pixels have left the set. As we zoom in to the Julia set (or increase the resolution of the display), the edge of the hole becomes more and more detailed—a classic property of fractals. We can draw the Julia set over top of some previously rendered geometry, and that will be seen through the hole.

Controlling Depth Per Fragment

In addition to the output variables you define for your fragment shader, the special built-in variable gl_FragDepth is available for writing an updated depth value to. If the fragment shader doesn't write to this variable, the interpolated depth generated by OpenGL is used as the fragment's depth value. Your fragment shader can either calculate an entirely new value for gl_FragDepth, or it can use the value gl_FragCoord.z to control the depth value. This new value is subsequently used by OpenGL both for the depth test and as the value written to the depth buffer.

You can use this functionality to slightly perturb the values in the depth buffer and create physically bumpy surfaces. When additional geometry is rendered and subsequently depth tested, it will be tested against these perturbed values. Some care should be taken when using this feature, though. If the fragment shader does not write to the gl_FragDepth variable, OpenGL knows, *before the fragment shader runs*, what the final value of depth will be. Therefore, one very common optimization that most modern graphics hardware makes is to perform the depth test before running the fragment shader. If the fragment fails the depth test, OpenGL will not run the fragment shader at all. However, if the shader does write to gl_FragDepth, OpenGL cannot know whether the fragment will pass the depth test or not until after the fragment shader has run. Therefore, it must always run the fragment shader and perform the depth test after the shader runs. This can drastically reduce performance. For best performance, only write gl_FragDepth in your fragment shader if it is absolutely necessary for the correct functioning of the algorithm you're trying to implement.

More Advanced Shader Functions

You've now learned about a number of interesting things that can be done with shaders in OpenGL. There are some further advanced features that require cooperation between shader stages or don't fit into any specific shader stage. We cover a number of those here.

Interpolation and Storage Qualifiers

You already read about storage qualifiers in earlier chapters. You saw how to use the `flat` storage qualifier to turn off interpolation and ask OpenGL to perform flat shading across your primitive. There are a couple more storage qualifiers that control interpolation that you can use for advanced rendering. They are the `centroid` and `noperspective` qualifiers, and we quickly go over each here.

Centroid Sampling

The `centroid` storage qualifier controls where in a pixel OpenGL interpolates the inputs to the fragment shader to. It only applies to situations where you're rendering to a multisampled surface, which has been introduced earlier. You specify the `centroid` storage qualifier just like any other storage qualifier. To create a varying that has the `centroid` storage qualifier, first, in the vertex (or geometry) shader, declare the output varying with the `centroid` keyword:

```
centroid out vec2 tex_coord;
```

And then in the fragment shader, declare the same input varying with the `centroid` keyword:

```
centroid in vec2 tex_coord;
```

Now the `tex_coord` varying is defined to use the `centroid` storage qualifier. If you have a single-sampled draw buffer, this makes no difference, and the varyings that reach the fragment shader are interpolated to the pixel's center. Where centroid sampling becomes useful is when you are rendering to a multisampled draw buffer. According to the OpenGL specification, when centroid sampling is not specified (the default), fragment shader varyings will be interpolated to *"the pixel's center, or anywhere within the pixel, or to one of the pixel's samples"*—which basically means anywhere within the pixel. When you're in the middle of a large triangle, this doesn't really matter. Where it becomes important is when you're shading a pixel that lies right on the edge of the triangle—where an edge of the triangle cuts through the pixel. Figure 11.17 shows an example of how OpenGL might sample from a triangle.

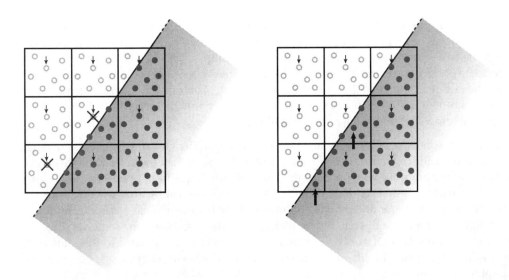

11.17 (a)   **11.17 (b)**

FIGURE 11.17   Partially covered multisampled pixels.

Take a look at Figure 11.17 (a). It shows the edge of a triangle passing through several pixels. The solid dots represent samples that are covered by the triangle, and the clear dots represent those that are not. OpenGL has chosen to interpolate the varyings to the sample closest to the pixel's center. Those samples are indicated by an arrow.

For the pixels in the upper left, this is fine—they are entirely uncovered and the fragment shader will not run for those pixels. Likewise, the pixels in the lower right are fully covered. The fragment shader will run, but it doesn't really matter which sample it runs for. The pixels along the edge of the triangle, however, present a problem. Because OpenGL has chosen the sample closest to the pixel center as its interpolation point, your varyings could actually be interpolated to a point that lies *outside* the triangle! Those samples are marked with an X. Imagine what would happen if you used the varying, say, to sample from a texture. If the texture was aligned such that its edge was supposed to match the edge of the triangle, the texture coordinates would lie outside the texture. At best, you would get a slightly incorrect image. At worst, it would produce noticeable artifacts.

If we declare our varyings with the centroid storage qualifier, the OpenGL specification says that, *"the value must be interpolated to a point that lies in both the pixel and in the primitive being rendered, or to one of the pixel's samples that falls within the primitive."* That means that OpenGL chooses, for each pixel, a sample that is certainly within the triangle to which to interpolate all varyings. You are safe to use the varyings in the fragment shader for any purpose, and you know that they are valid and do not refer to a point outside the triangle.

Now look at Figure 11.17 (b). OpenGL has still chosen to interpolate varyings to the samples closest to the pixel centers for fully covered pixels. However, for those pixels that are partially covered, it has instead chosen another sample that lies within the triangle (marked with larger arrows). This means that the inputs presented to the fragment shader are valid and refer to points that are inside the triangle. You can use them for sampling from a texture or use them in a function whose result is only defined within a certain range and know that you will get meaningful results.

You may be wondering if using the `centroid` storage qualifier guarantees that you're going to get valid results in your fragment shader and not using it may mean that the varyings are outside the primitive why not turn on centroid sampling all the time? Well, there are some drawbacks to using centroid sampling. The most significant is that OpenGL can provide the gradients (or differentials) of inputs to the fragment shader. Implementations may differ, but most use discrete differentials, taking deltas between the same varyings from adjacent pixels. This works well when the varyings are interpolated to the same position within each pixel. In this case, it doesn't matter which sample position is chosen; the samples will always be exactly one pixel apart. However, when centroid sampling is enabled for an input, the values for adjacent pixels may actually be interpolated to different positions within those pixels. That means that the samples are not exactly one pixel apart, and the discrete differentials presented to the fragment shader could be inaccurate. If accurate gradients are required in the fragment shader, it is probably best not to use centroid sampling.

Using Centroid Sampling to Perform Edge Detection

An interesting use case for centroid sampling is hardware accelerated edge detection. You just learned that using the `centroid` storage qualifier ensures that your varyings are interpolated to a point that definitely lies within the primitive being rendered. To do this, OpenGL chooses a sample that it knows lies inside the triangle at which to evaluate those varyings, and that sample may be different from the one that it would have chosen if the pixel was fully covered or the one that it would choose if the `centroid` storage qualifier was not used. You can use this knowledge to your advantage.

To extract edge information from this, declare two varyings, one with and one without the `centroid` storage qualifier, and assign the same value to each of them in the vertex shader. It doesn't matter what the values are, so long as they are different for each vertex. The x and y components of the transformed vertex position are probably a good choice because you know that it will be different for each vertex of any triangle that is actually visible.

```
out vec2 maybe_outside;
```

gives us our noncentroid varying that may be interpolated to a point outside the triangle, and

```
centroid out vec2 certainly_inside;
```

gives us our centroid sampled varying that we know is inside the triangle.

Inside the fragment shader, we can compare the values of the two varyings. If the pixel is entirely covered by the triangle, OpenGL uses the same value for both varyings. However, if the pixel is only partially covered by the triangle, OpenGL uses its normal choice of sample for maybe_outside and picks a sample that is certain to be inside the triangle for certainly_inside. This could be a different sample than was chosen for maybe_outside, and that means that the two varyings may have different values. Now you can compare them to determine that you are on the edge of a primitive:

```
bool may_be_on_edge = any(maybe_outside != certainly_inside);
```

This method is not foolproof. Even if a pixel is on the edge of a triangle, it is possible that it covers OpenGL's original sample of choice, and therefore you still get the same values for maybe_outside and certainly_inside. However, this marks most edge pixels.

To use this information, you can write the value to a texture attached to the framebuffer and subsequently use that texture for further processing later. Another option is to draw only to the stencil buffer. Set your stencil reference to one, disable stencil testing, and set your stencil operation to GL_REPLACE. When you encounter an edge, let the fragment shader continue running. When you encounter a pixel that's not on an edge, use the discard keyword in your shader to prevent the pixel from being written to the stencil buffer. The result is that your stencil buffer contains ones wherever there was an edge in the scene and a zero wherever there was no edge. Later, you can render a full-screen quad with an expensive fragment shader that only runs for pixels that represent the edges of geometry by enabling the stencil test, setting the stencil function to GL_EQUAL, and leaving the reference value at one. The shader can implement one of the image processing operations described earlier. For example, applying Gaussian blur using a convolution operation (as demonstrated earlier in this chapter) can smooth the edges of polygons in the scene, allowing the application to perform its own antialiasing.

Interpolating without Perspective Correction

As you have learned, OpenGL interpolates the values of varyings across the face of primitives, such as triangles, and presents a new value to each invocation of the fragment shader. By default, the interpolation is linear in the space of the triangle. That means that if you were to look at the triangle flat on, the steps that the varyings take across its surface would be equal. However, OpenGL performs interpolation in screen space as it steps from pixel to pixel. Very rarely is a triangle seen directly face on, and so perspective foreshortening means that the step in each varying from pixel to pixel is not constant—that is, they are not linear in screen space. OpenGL corrects for this by using *perspective-correct* interpolation. To do this, it interpolates values that *are* linear in screen space and uses those to derive the actual values of the varyings at each pixel.

Consider a texture coordinate, uv, that is to be interpolated across a triangle. Neither u nor v is linear in screen space. However (due to some math that is beyond the scope of this section), u / w and v / w are linear in screen space, as is 1 / w (the fourth component of the fragment's coordinate). So, what OpenGL actually interpolates is

$$\frac{u}{w}, \frac{v}{w}, \text{ and } \frac{1}{w}$$

At each pixel, it reciprocates 1 / w to find w and then multiplies u / w and v / w by w to find u and v. This provides perspective-correct values of the interpolants to each instance of the fragment shader.

Normally, this is what you want. However, there may be times when you don't want this. If you actually want interpolation to be carried out in screen space regardless of the orientation of the primitive, you can use the noperspective storage qualifier, like this:

```
noperspective out vec2 texcoord;
```

in the vertex shader, and

```
noperspective in vec2 texcoord;
```

in the fragment shader, for example. The results of using perspective correct and screen-space linear (noperspective) rendering are shown in Figure 11.18 (a) and (b), respectively.

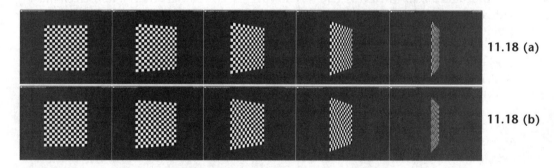

11.18 (a)

11.18 (b)

FIGURE 11.18   Contrasting perspective-correct and linear interpolation.

Figure 11.18 (a) shows perspective-correct interpolation applied to a pair of triangles as its angle to the viewer changes. Meanwhile, Figure 11.18 (b) shows how the noperspective storage qualifier has affected the interpolation of texture coordinates. As the pair of triangles moves to a more and more oblique angle relative to the viewer, the texture becomes more and more skewed.

Other Advanced Built-In Functions

The GL Shading Language (GLSL) is closely modeled on the C language. Language constructs such as for, while, and do loops are virtually identical in definition to C, as are conditional constructs such as if-else statements, switch statements, and the ? operator. Many of the standard math functions that are in the C standard library are also available in GLSL, including trigonometric functions such as sin, cos, and tan; other math functions such as abs, floor, and ceil; exponentials such as pow, exp, and log; and built-in operators such as +, -, and ==. If you have experience with C or other C-like languages, many of these functions will be familiar to you. However, as GLSL is designed to operate on graphics primitives, there are several built-in functions that operate on vector and matrix types that often have optimal implementations in hardware. For the most part, these functions are available to any shader stage.

In addition to the standard math functions, GLSL provides utility functions such as clamp (which clamps a value to a range between two further values), mix (which performs linear interpolation), and step and smoothstep (which create transitions between two values based on their input). Also, bit-casting between floating-point and integer values can be performed using the intBitsToFloat and floatBitsToInt functions and their unsigned variants.

GLSL vector functions include dot and cross, which, as their names suggest, perform a dot product and a cross product, respectively. Additionally, the outerProduct function is available to retrieve the outer product of two vectors. The distance and length functions produce the distance between two points, and the length, or magnitude, of a vector, respectively. A vector can be normalized using the normalize function. Pushing complexity further, the reflect and refract functions provide built-in, potentially optimized implementations of reflection and reflection equations commonly used in lighting and path tracing algorithms.

The more advanced matrix-related functions include transpose, determinant, and inverse, which operate as their names suggest. Furthermore, the function matrixCompMult performs a componentwise multiplication between two matrices. This function is necessary because the behavior of the default multiplication operator (*) when applied to matrices is to perform a matrix-matrix multiply.

Because the relational operators (for example, >, !=, and <=) are defined to produce a single, scalar Boolean result, vector versions of these comparison operators are provided as built-in functions that return Boolean vectors. These include lessThan, notEqual, and lessThanEqual, for example. To perform set operations on the resulting Boolean vectors, the functions any (which returns true if any element of its argument is true) and all (which returns true if all of the elements of its argument are true) are provided. Boolean vectors are not accepted as the expression of an if statement, so you need to use either any or all to convert the vector to a scalar before you can use it in a conditional statement.

Uniform Buffer Objects

By now, the shaders you're writing have become complex. Some of them require a lot of constant data, and the way you've passed this to the shader is to use uniforms. If you have a lot of shaders in an application, you need to set up the uniforms for every one of those shaders, which means a lot of calls to the various glUniform functions. You also need to keep track of which uniforms change. Some change for every object, some change once per frame, while others may only require initializing once for the whole application. This means that you either need to update different sets of uniforms in different places in your application, making it more complex to maintain, or update all the uniforms all the time, costing performance.

To alleviate the cost of all the glUniform calls, to make updating a large set of uniforms simpler, and to be able to easily share a set of uniforms between different programs, OpenGL allows you to combine a group of uniforms into a *uniform block* and store the whole block in a buffer object. The buffer object is just like any other that you may have used before. You can quickly set the whole group of uniforms by either changing your buffer binding or overwriting the content of a bound buffer. You can also leave the buffer bound while you change programs, and the new program will see the current set of uniform values. This functionality is called the *uniform buffer object*, or UBO. In fact, the uniforms you've used up until now live in the *default block*. Any uniform declared at the global scope in a shader ends up in the default uniform block. You can't keep the default block in a uniform buffer object; you need to create one or more named uniform blocks.

To declare a set of uniforms to be stored in a buffer object, you need to use a *named uniform block* in your shader. This looks a lot like an interface block, but it uses the uniform keyword instead. Listing 11.31 shows what the code looks like in a shader.

LISTING 11.31   Example Uniform Block Declaration

```
uniform TransformBlock
{
    float scale;            // Global scale to apply to everything
    vec3  translation;      // Translation in X, Y and Z
    float rotation[3];      // Rotation around X, Y and Z axes
    mat4 projection_matrix; // A generalized projection matrix to apply
                            // after scale and rotate
} transform;
```

This code declares a uniform block whose name is TransformBlock. It also declares a single instance of the block called transform. Inside the shader, you can refer to the members of the block using its instance name, transform. However, to set up the data in the buffer object that you'll use to back the block, you need to know the location of a member of the block, and for that, you need the block name, TransformBlock. If you wanted to have multiple instances of block, each with its own buffer, you could make transform an array.

The members of the block will have the same locations within each block, but there will now be several instances of the block that you can refer to in the shader. Querying the location of members within a block is important when you want to fill the block with data, which is explained in the following section.

Building Uniform Blocks

Data accessed in the shader via named uniform blocks can be stored in buffer objects. In general, it is the application's job to fill the buffer objects with data using functions like `glBufferData` or `glMapBuffer`. The question is, then, what is the data in the buffer supposed to look like? There are actually two possibilities here, and whichever one you choose is a trade-off. The first is to let OpenGL decide where it would like the data. This produces the most efficient shaders, but it means that your application needs to figure out where to put the data so that OpenGL can read it. This can be pretty inconvenient, so the second method is to use a standard, agreed upon layout for the data. This means that your application can just copy data into the buffers and assume specific locations for members within the block—you can even store the data on disk ahead of time and simply read it straight into a buffer that's been mapped using `glMapBuffer`. While this layout is standard across all graphics hardware and drivers, it is unlikely to be optimal for any of them. This is because some empty space is left between the various members of the block, making the buffer larger than it needs to be. You probably trade some performance for this convenience. We cover both methods here and leave it to you to decide what's best for your application.

The first layout for data stored in uniform buffers is the *shared* layout. This is the default layout and is what you get if you don't explicitly ask OpenGL for something else. With the shared layout, the data in the buffer is laid out however OpenGL decides is best for runtime performance and access from the shader. This often allows greater performance to be achieved by the shaders, but requires more work from the application. The reason this is called the shared layout is that while OpenGL has arranged the data within the buffer, that arrangement will be the same between multiple programs and shaders sharing the same declaration of the uniform block. For example, the shader compiler still reserves space for members of the uniform block, even if they are not used by the shader. This allows you to use the same buffer object with any program. To use the shared layout, the application must determine the locations within the buffer object of the members of the uniform block.

Each member of a uniform block has an index that is used to refer to it to find its size and location within the block. To get the index of a member of a uniform block, call

```
void glGetUniformIndices(GLuint program, GLsizei uniformCount, const GLchar **
uniformNames, GLuint * uniformIndices);
```

This seems fairly complex, but it's really not. This function allows you to get the indices of a large set of uniforms—perhaps even all of the uniforms in a program with a single call to

OpenGL, even if they're members of different blocks. It takes a count of the number of uniforms you'd like the indices for (uniformCount) and an array of uniform names (uniformNames) and puts their indices in an array for you (uniformIndices). Listing 11.32 contains an example of how you would retrieve the indices of the members of TransformBlock, which we declared earlier.

LISTING 11.32   Retrieving the Indices of Uniform Block Members

```
const GLchar * uniformNames[4] =
{
    "TransformBlock.scale",
    "TransformBlock.translation",
    "TransformBlock.rotation",
    "TransformBlock.projection_matrix"
};
GLuint uniformIndices[4];

glGetUniformIndices(program, 4, uniformNames, uniformIndices);
```

After this code has run, you have the indices of the three members of the uniform block in the uniformIndices array. Now that you have the indices, you can use them to find the locations of the block members within the buffer. To do this, call

```
void glGetActiveUniformsiv(GLuint program, GLsizei uniformCount, const GLuint *
uniformIndices, GLenum pname, GLint * params);
```

This function can give you a lot of information about specific uniform block members. The information that we're interested in is the offset of the member within the buffer, the array stride (for TransformBlock.rotation), and the matrix stride (for TransformBlock.projection_matrix). These values tell us where to put data within the buffer so that it can be seen in the shader. We can retrieve these from OpenGL by setting pname to GL_UNIFORM_OFFSET, GL_UNIFORM_ARRAY_STRIDE, and GL_UNIFORM_MATRIX_STRIDE, respectively. Listing 11.33 shows what the code looks like.

LISTING 11.33   Retrieving the Information about Uniform Block Members

```
GLint uniformOffsets[4];
GLint arrayStrides[4];
GLint matrixStrides[4];
glGetActiveUniformsiv(program, 4, uniformIndices,
                      GL_UNIFORM_OFFSET, uniformOffsets);
glGetActiveUniformsiv(program, 4, uniformIndices,
                      GL_UNIFORM_ARRAY_STRIDE, arrayStrides);
glGetActiveUniformsiv(program, 4, uniformIndices,
                      GL_UNIFORM_MATRIX_STRIDE, matrixStrides);
```

Once the code in Listing 11.33 has run, uniformOffsets contains the offsets of the members of the TransformBlock block, arrayStrides contains the strides of the array members (only rotation, for now), and matrixStrides contains the strides of the matrix members (only projection_matrix).

The other information that you can find out about uniform block members includes the data type of the uniform, the size in bytes that it consumes in memory, and layout information related to arrays and matrices within the block. You need some of that information to initialize a buffer object with more complex types, although the size and types of the members should be known to you already if you wrote the shaders. The other accepted values for pname and what you get back are listed in Table 11.5.

TABLE 11.5   Uniform Parameter Queries via glGetActiveUniformsiv

Value of pname	What You Get Back
GL_UNIFORM_TYPE	The data type of the uniform as a GLenum.
GL_UNIFORM_SIZE	The size of arrays, in units of whatever GL_UNIFORM_TYPE gives you. If the uniform is not an array, this will always be one.
GL_UNIFORM_NAME_LENGTH	The length, in characters of the names of the uniforms.
GL_UNIFORM_BLOCK_INDEX	The index of the block that the uniform is a member of.
GL_UNIFORM_OFFSET	The offset of the uniform within the block (or more accurately, the buffer that backs the block).
GL_UNIFORM_ARRAY_STRIDE	The number of bytes between consecutive elements of an array. If the uniform is not an array, this will be zero.
GL_UNIFORM_MATRIX_STRIDE	The number of bytes between the first element of each column of a column-major matrix or row of a row-major matrix. If the uniform is not a matrix, this will be zero.
GL_UNIFORM_IS_ROW_MAJOR	Each element of the output array will either be one if the uniform is a row major matrix, or zero if it is a column major matrix or not a matrix at all.

If the type of the uniform you're interested in is a simple type such as int, float, bool, or even vectors of these types (vec4 and so on), all you need is its offset. Once you know the location of the uniform within the buffer, you can either pass the offset to glBufferSubData to load the data at the appropriate location, or you can use the offset directly in your code to assemble the buffer in memory. We demonstrate the latter option here because it reinforces the idea that the uniforms are stored in memory, just like textures or vertex information. It also means fewer calls to OpenGL, which can sometimes lead to higher performance. For these examples, we assemble the data in the application's memory and then load it into a buffer using glBufferData. You could alternatively use glMapBuffer to get a pointer to the buffer's memory and assemble the data directly into that.

Let's start by setting the simplest uniform in the TransformBlock block, scale. This uniform is a single float whose location is stored in the first element of our uniformIndices array. Listing 11.34 shows how to set the value of the single float.

LISTING 11.34   Setting a Single `float` in a Uniform Block

```
// Allocate some memory for our buffer (don't forget to free it later)
unsigned char * buffer = (unsigned char *)malloc(4096);

// We know that TransformBlock.scale is at uniformOffsets[0] bytes into the
// block, so we can offset our buffer pointer by that store the scale there.
*((float *)(buffer + uniformOffsets[0])) = 3.0f;
```

Next, we can initialize data for `TransformBlock.translation`. This is a `vec3`, which means it consists of three floating-point values packed tightly together in memory. To update this, all we need to do is find the location of the first element of the vector and store three consecutive floats in memory starting there. This is shown in Listing 11.35.

LISTING 11.35   Retrieving the Indices of Uniform Block Members

```
// Put three consecutive GLfloat values in memory to update a vec3
*((float *)(buffer + uniformOffsets[1])) = 1.0f;
*((float *)(buffer + uniformOffsets[1] + sizeof(GLfloat))) = 2.0f;
*((float *)(buffer + uniformOffsets[1] + 2 * sizeof(GLfloat))) = 3.0f;
```

Now, we tackle the array `rotation`. We could have also used a `vec3` here, but for the purposes of this example, we use a three-element array to demonstrate the use of the `GL_UNIFORM_ARRAY_STRIDE` parameter. When the shared layout is used, arrays are defined as a sequence of elements separated by an implementation-defined stride in bytes. This means that we have to place the data at locations in the buffer defined both by `GL_UNIFORM_OFFSET` and `GL_UNIFORM_ARRAY_STRIDE`, as in the code snippet of Listing 11.36.

LISTING 11.36   Specifying the Data for an Array in a Uniform Block

```
// TransformBlock.rotations[0] is at uniformOffsets[1] bytes into the buffer.
// Each element of the array is at a multiple of arrayStrides[1] bytes
// past that
const GLfloat rotations[] = { 30.0f, 40.0f, 60.0f };
unsigned int offset = uniformOffsets[2];

for (int n = 0; n < 3; n++) {
    *((float *)(buffer + offset)) = rotations[n];
    offset += arrayStrides[2];
}
```

Finally, we set up the data for `TransformBlock.projection_matrix`. Matrices in uniform blocks behave much like arrays of vectors. For column major matrices (which is the default), each column of the matrix is treated like a vector, the length of which is the height of the matrix. Likewise, row major matrices are treated like an array of vectors where each row is an element in that array. Just like normal arrays, the starting offset for each column (or row) in the matrix is determined by an implementation defined quantity. This can be queried through the GL_UNIFORM_MATRIX_STRIDE parameter to glGetActiveUniformsiv. Each column of the matrix can be initialized using similar code to that which was used to initialize the vec3 TransformBlock.translation. This setup code is given in Listing 11.37.

LISTING 11.37   Setting Up a Matrix in a Uniform Block

```
// The first column of TransformBlock.projection_matrix is at
// uniformOffsets[2] bytes into the buffer. The columns are
// spaced matrixStride[2] bytes apart and are essentially vec4s
// This is the source matrix - remember, it's column major so
const GLfloat matrix[] =
{
    1.0f, 2.0f, 3.0f, 4.0f,
    9.0f, 8.0f, 7.0f, 6.0f,
    2.0f, 4.0f, 6.0f, 8.0f,
    1.0f, 3.0f, 5.0f, 7.0f
};

for (int i = 0; i < 4; i++)
{
    GLuint offset = uniformOffsets[2] + matrixStride[2] * i;
    for (j = 0; j < 4; j++) {
        *((float *)(buffer + offset)) = matrix[i * 4 + j];
        offset += sizeof(GLfloat);
    }
}
```

This method of querying offsets and strides works for any of the layouts. With the shared layout, it is the only option. However, it's somewhat inconvenient, and as you can see, you need quite a lot of code to lay out your data in the buffer in the correct way. As an alternative, you can use the *standard* layout. This allows you to determine where in the buffer data should be placed based on a set of rules that specify the size and alignments for the various data types supported by OpenGL. These rules are common across all OpenGL implementations, and so you don't need to query anything to use it (although, should you query offsets and strides, the results will be correct).

To tell OpenGL that you want to use the standard layout, you need to declare the uniform block with a layout qualifier. A redeclaration of our TransformBlock with the standard layout qualifier, std140, is shown in Listing 11.38.

LISTING 11.38   Retrieving the Indices of Uniform Block Members

```
layout(std140) uniform TransformBlock
{
    float scale;            // Global scale to apply to everything
    vec3  translation;      // Translation in X, Y and Z
    float rotation[3];      // Rotation around X, Y and Z axes
    mat4 projection_matrix; // A generalized projection matrix to
                            // apply after scale and rotate
} transform;
```

Once a uniform block has been declared to use the standard, or std140, layout, each member of the block consumes a predefined amount of space in the buffer and begins at an offset that is predictable by following a set of rules. A summary of the rules is as follows:

Any type consuming N bytes in a buffer begins on an N byte boundary within that buffer. That means that standard GLSL types such as int, float, and bool (which are all defined to be 32-bit or four-byte quantities) begin on multiples of four bytes. A vector of these types of length two always begins on a 2N byte boundary. For example, that means a vec2, which is eight bytes long in memory, always starts on an eight-byte boundary. Three- and four-element vectors always start on a 4N byte boundary; so vec3 and vec4 types start on 16-byte boundaries. Each member of an array of scalar or vector types (ints or vec3s, for example) always start boundaries defined by these same rules, but rounded up to the alignment of a vec4. In particular, this means that arrays of anything but vec4 (and Nx4 matrices) won't be tightly packed, but instead there will be a gap between each of the elements. Matrices are essentially treated like short arrays of vectors, and arrays of matrices are treated like very long arrays of vectors. Finally, structures and arrays of structures have additional packing requirements; the whole structure starts on the boundary required by its largest member, rounded up to the size of a vec4.

Particular attention must be paid to the difference between the std140 layout and the packing rules that are often followed by your compiler of choice. In particular, an array in a uniform block is not necessarily tightly packed. This means that you can't create, for example, an array of floats in a uniform block and simply copy data from a C array of floats into it because the data from the C array will be packed, and the data in the uniform block won't be.

This all sounds complex, but it is logical and well-defined, and allows a large range of graphics hardware to implement uniform buffer objects efficiently. Returning to our TransformBlock example, we can figure out the offsets of the members of the block within the buffer using these rules. Listing 11.39 shows an example of a uniform block declaration along with the offsets of its members.

LISTING 11.39   Example Uniform Block with Offsets

```
layout(std140) uniform TransformBlock
{
//  Member                   base alignment  offset  aligned offset
    float scale;           // 4               0       0
    vec3  translation;     // 16              4       16
    float rotation[3];     // 16              28      32 (rotation[0])
                           //                         48 (rotation[1])
                           //                         64 (rotation[2])
    mat4 projection_matrix; // 16             80      80 (column 0)
                           //                         96 (column 1)
                           //                         112 (column 2)
                           //                         128 (column 3)
} transform;
```

There is a complete example of the alignments of various types in the original ARB_uniform_buffer_object extension specification.

Now that you have filled your buffer, you can bind it to a uniform block in your program. Before you can do this, you need to retrieve the index of the uniform block. Each uniform block in a program has a compiler-assigned index. There is fixed maximum number of uniform blocks that can be used by a single program, and a maximum number that can be used in any given shader stage. You can find these limits by calling glGetIntegerv with the GL_MAX_UNIFORM_BUFFERS parameter (for the total per program) and either GL_MAX_VERTEX_UNIFORM_BUFFERS, GL_MAX_GEOMETRY_UNIFORM_BUFFERS, or GL_MAX_FRAGMENT_UNIFORM_BUFFERS for the vertex, geometry, and fragment shader limits, respectively. To find the index of a uniform block in a program, call

```
GLuint glGetUniformBlockIndex(GLuint program, const GLchar * uniformBlockName);
```

This returns the index of the named uniform block. In our example uniform block declaration here, uniformBlockName would be "TransformBlock". There is a set of buffer binding points to which you can bind a buffer to provide data for the uniform blocks. It is essentially a two-step process to bind a buffer to a uniform block. Uniform blocks are assigned binding points, and then buffers can be bound to those binding points, matching buffers with uniform blocks. This way, different programs can be switched in and out without changing buffer bindings, and the fixed set of uniforms will automatically be seen by the new program. Contrast this to the values of the uniforms in the default block, which are per-program state. Even if two programs contain uniforms with the same names, their values must be set for each program and will change when the active program is changed.

To assign a binding point to a uniform buffer, call

```
void glUniformBlockBinding(GLuint program, GLuint uniformBlockIndex, GLuint
uniformBlockBinding);
```

where `program` is the program where the uniform block you're changing lives. `uniformBlockIndex` is the index of the uniform block you're assigning a binding point to. You just retrieved that by calling `glGetUniformBlockIndex`. `uniformBlockBinding` is the index of the uniform block binding point. An implementation of OpenGL supports a fixed maximum number of binding points, and you can find out what that limit is by calling `glGetIntegerv` with the `GL_MAX_UNIFORM_BUFFER_BINDINGS` parameter.

Once you've assigned binding points to the uniform blocks in your program, you can bind buffers to those same binding points to make the data in the buffers appear in the uniform blocks. To do this, call

```
glBindBufferBase(GL_UNIFORM_BUFFER, index, buffer);
```

Here, `GL_UNIFORM_BUFFER` tells OpenGL that we're binding a buffer to one of the uniform buffer binding points, `index` is the index of the binding point and should match what you specified in `uniformBlockBinding` in your call to `glUniformBlockBinding`. `buffer` is the buffer object that you want to attach. It's important to note that `index` is not the index of the uniform block (`uniformBlockIndex` in `glUniformBlockBinding`), but the index of the uniform buffer binding point. This is a common mistake to make and is easy to miss.

This mixing and matching of binding points with uniform block indices is illustrated in Figure 11.19.

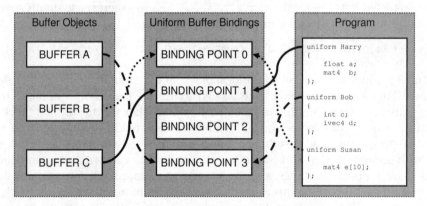

FIGURE 11.19   Binding buffers and uniform blocks to binding points.

In Figure 11.19, there is a program with three uniform blocks (Harry, Bob, and Susan) and three buffer objects (A, B, and C). Harry is assigned to binding point 1, and buffer C is bound to binding point 1, so Harry's data comes from buffer C. Likewise, Bob is assigned to binding point 3, to which buffer A is bound, and so Bob's data comes from buffer A. Finally, Susan is assigned to binding point 0 and buffer B is bound to binding point 0, so Susan's data comes from buffer B. Notice that binding point 2 is not used. That doesn't matter. There could be a buffer bound there, but the program doesn't use it.

The code to set this up is simple and is given in Listing 11.40.

LISTING 11.40   Specifying Bindings for Uniform Blocks

```
// Get the indices of the uniform blocks using glGetUniformBlockIndex
GLuint harry_index = glGetUniformBlockIndex(program, "Harry");
GLuint bob_index = glGetUniformBlockIndex(program, "Bob");
GLuint susan_index = glGetUniformBlockIndex(program, "Susan");

// Assign buffer bindings to uniform blocks, using their indices
glUniformBlockBinding(program, harry_index, 1);
glUniformBlockBinding(program, bob_index, 3);
glUniformBlockBinding(program, susan_index, 0);

// Bind buffers to the binding points
// Binding 0, buffer B, Susan's data
glBindBufferBase(GL_UNIFORM_BUFFER, 0, buffer_b);
// Binding 1, buffer C, Harry's data
glBindBufferBase(GL_UNIFORM_BUFFER, 1, buffer_c);
// Note that we skipped binding 2
// Binding 3, buffer A, Bob's data
glBindBufferBase(GL_UNIFORM_BUFFER, 3, buffer_a);
```

A common use for uniform blocks is to separate steady state from transient state. By setting up the bindings for all your programs using a standard convention, you can leave buffers bound when you change the program. For example, if you have some relatively fixed state—say the projection matrix, the size of the viewport, and a few other things that change once a frame or less often—you can leave that information in a buffer bound to binding point zero. Then, if you set the binding for the fixed state to zero for all programs, whenever you switch program objects using glUseProgram, the uniforms will be sitting there in the buffer, ready to use.

Now let's say that you have a fragment shader that simulates some material (cloth or metal, for example); you could put the parameters for the material into another buffer. In your program that shades that material, bind the uniform block containing the material parameters to binding point 1. Each object would maintain a buffer object containing the parameters of its surface. As you render each object, it uses the common material shader and simply binds its parameter buffer to buffer binding point 1.

Summary

In this chapter you learned some more advanced shader techniques to use in your OpenGL programs. Many of the topics covered here allow you to write more efficient applications, produce shorter shaders, or implement advanced rendering techniques. You saw that it is possible to use the vertex shader to do more than simply transform vertices into their final positions. A whole new shader stage—the geometry shader—was introduced and you learned how to use it to create, destroy, and modify geometric primitives. You even saw that is possible to change the type of the geometry as it passes through the OpenGL pipeline. The fragment shader can be used for more than simply shading pixels on the surface of a model. You can use it to apply post-processing effects to a prerendered image or even produce the entire picture in a the fragment shader.

A number of the more advanced features of the GLSL language were introduced, which you can use to implement interesting effects and algorithms in your shaders. You learned that it is possible to store the values of your uniforms in buffer objects and to leave those buffer objects bound while you switch programs. This greatly reduces the amount of work you need to do to keep often-used uniform values up to date between programs.

CHAPTER **12**

Advanced Geometry Management

by Graham Sellers

WHAT YOU'LL LEARN IN THIS CHAPTER:

How To	Features You'll Use
Manage data in your own vertex buffers	glVertexAttribPointer
Draw lots of geometry	glMultiDrawArrays, glPrimitiveRestartIndex, glDrawArraysInstanced, glVertexAttribDivisor
Store the results of vertex and geometry shaders	glBeginTransformFeedback, glEndTransformFeedback
Get information about the work OpenGL does	glGenQueries, glBeginQuery, glEndQuery, glGetQueryiv
Synchronize two or more OpenGL contexts	glFenceSync, glWaitSync, glClientWaitSync
Control how OpenGL clips geometry	gl_ClipDistance[], GL_DEPTH_CLAMP

In this chapter, we go over some of the more advanced features of OpenGL related to geometry management. This includes figuring out what got rendered and getting information back from OpenGL about the amount of geometry it processed. A way of storing the intermediate results of rendering for later is covered, and we talk about how to synchronize two OpenGL contexts so that one context can consume data produced by the other. We see how to manage our own geometry data in the graphics card's memory and how to control the way that OpenGL processes batch primitives like triangle fans and line strips. We also see how to make an OpenGL application that offloads rendering large amounts of geometry to the graphics card.

Many of these techniques are designed to improve performance and maximize the amount of work that gets done by your GPU. Some, however, enable you to use the GPU for new and interesting techniques that otherwise wouldn't be possible.

Gathering Information about the OpenGL Pipeline— Queries

You'd like to ask OpenGL if it drew anything as a result of the functions you called. This seems like a strange question. You just called a long sequence of OpenGL functions; you sent a lot of geometry to the OpenGL pipeline, so surely something was drawn. Well remember, even geometry that would lie within the bounds of the screen may not actually change any pixels. There are a number of reasons for this, including triangles being discarded due to back-face culling or fragments failing the depth test or being discarded by the fragment shader. It can be useful to know if any pixels made it to the screen or even to know exactly how many made it. As an example, consider a game where there are many characters or objects on the screen. Your game engine may need to know if your player can see some other object, such as an enemy, bonus item, or another player. It is certainly possible to construct a complex line of sight test based on the games geometry assets. But, it's much simpler just to ask the GPU if it actually drew any part of the object in question.

The way to ask the GPU this question is through the occlusion query. The name is somewhat misleading as it's really more of a visibility query. The answer is zero, or false, if there are no pixels drawn and nonzero, or true, if there are some pixels drawn. So the question is really "is this visible?" rather than "is this occluded?" Perhaps it should have been called a visibility query. In any case, a query is an OpenGL object representing a question. There are several types of query objects representing all kinds of different questions, and an occlusion query represents the question, "Did you draw anything?"

Preparing a Query

Remember way back to your early days in school. The teacher wanted you to raise your hand before asking a question. This was almost like reserving your place in line for asking the question—the teacher didn't know yet what your question was going to be, but she knew that you had something to ask. OpenGL is similar. Before we can ask a question, we have to reserve a spot so that OpenGL knows that the question is coming. Questions in OpenGL are represented by *query objects*, and much like any other object in OpenGL, query objects must be reserved, or generated. To do this, call glGenQueries, passing it the number of queries you want to reserve and the address of a variable (or array) where you would like the names of the query objects to be placed:

```
void glGenQueries(GLsizei n, GLuint *ids);
```

The function reserves some query objects for you and gives you their names so that you can refer to them later. You can generate as many query objects you need in one go:

```
GLuint one_query;
GLuint ten_queries[10];
glGenQueries(1, &one_query);
glGenQueries(10, ten_queries);
```

In this example, the first call to glGenQueries generates a single query object and returns its name in the variable one_query. The second call to glGenQueries generates ten query objects and returns ten names in the array ten_queries. In total, 11 query objects have been created, and OpenGL has reserved 11 unique names to represent them. It is very unlikely, but still possible that OpenGL will not be able to create a query for you, and in this case it returns zero as the name of the query. A well-written application always checks that glGenQueries returns a nonzero value for the name of each requested query object. If there is a failure, OpenGL keeps track of the reason, and you can find that out by calling glGetError.

Each query object reserves a small but measurable amount of resources from OpenGL. These resources must be returned to OpenGL because if they are not, OpenGL may run out of space for queries and fail to generate more for the application later. To return the resources to OpenGL, call glDeleteQueries:

```
void glDeleteQueries(GLsizei n, const GLuint *ids);
```

This works similarly to glGenQueries—it takes the number of query objects to delete and the address of a variable or array holding their names:

```
glDeleteQueries(10, ten_queries);
glDeleteQueries(1, &one_query);
```

After the queries are deleted, they are essentially gone for good. The names of the queries can't be used again unless they are given back to you by another call to glGenQueries.

Issuing a Query

Once you've reserved your spot using glGenQueries, you can ask a question. OpenGL doesn't automatically keep track of the number of pixels it has drawn. It has to count, and it must be told when to start counting. To do this, use glBeginQuery. The glBeginQuery function takes two parameters: The first is the question you'd like to ask, and the second is the name of the query object that you reserved earlier:

```
glBeginQuery(GL_SAMPLES_PASSED, one_query);
```

GL_SAMPLES_PASSED represents the question you're asking, "How many samples passed the depth test?" Here, OpenGL counts samples because you might be rendering to a multisampled display format, and in that case, there could be more than one sample per pixel. In the case of a normal, single-sampled format, there is one sample per pixel and therefore a one-to-one mapping of samples to pixels. Every time a sample makes it past the depth test (meaning that hadn't previously been discarded by the fragment shader), OpenGL counts one. It adds up all the samples from all the rendering it is doing and stores the answer in part of the space reserved for the query object.

Now OpenGL is counting samples (or pixels); you can render as normal, and OpenGL keeps track of all the pixels generated as a result. Anything that you render is counted toward the total. When you want OpenGL to add up everything rendered since you told it to start counting, you tell it to stop by calling `glEndQuery`:

```
glEndQuery(GL_SAMPLES_PASSED);
```

This tells OpenGL to stop counting samples that have passed the depth test and made it through the fragment shader without being discarded. All the pixels generated by all the drawing commands between the call to `glBeginQuery` and `glEndQuery` are added up.

Retrieving Query Results

Now that the pixels produced by your drawing commands have been counted, you need to retrieve them from OpenGL. This is accomplished by calling

```
glGetQueryObjectuiv(the_query, GL_QUERY_RESULT, &result);
```

This instructs OpenGL to place the count associated with the query object into your variable. If no pixels were produced as a result of the drawing commands between the last call to `glBeginQuery` and `glEndQuery` for the query object, `result` will be zero. If anything actually made it to the screen, `result` will contain the number of pixels written. By rendering an object between a call to `glBeginQuery` and `glEndQuery` and then checking if `result` is zero or not, you can determine whether the object is visible.

Because OpenGL operates as a pipeline, it may have many drawing commands queued up back-to-back waiting to be processed. It could be the case that not all of the drawing commands issued before the last call to `glEndQuery` have finished producing pixels. In fact, some may not have even started to be executed. In that case, `glGetQueryObjectuiv` causes OpenGL to wait until everything between `glBeginQuery` and `glEndQuery` has been rendered, and it is ready to return an accurate count. If you're planning to use a query object as a performance optimization, this is certainly not what you want. All these short delays could add up and eventually slow down your application! The good news is that it's possible to ask OpenGL if it's finished rendering anything that might affect the result of the query and therefore has a result available for you. To do this, call

```
glGetQueryObjectuiv(the_query, GL_QUERY_RESULT_AVAILABLE, &result);
```

If the result of the query object is not immediately available and trying to retrieve it would cause your application to have to wait for OpenGL to finish what it is working on, `result` becomes `GL_FALSE`. If OpenGL is ready and has your answer, `result` becomes `GL_TRUE`. This means that retrieving the result from OpenGL will not cause any delays. Now you can do useful work while you wait for OpenGL to be ready to give you your pixel count, or you can make decisions based on whether the result is available to you. For example, if you would have skipped rendering something had `result` been zero, you could choose to just go ahead and render it anyway rather than waiting for the result of the query.

Using the Results of a Query

Now that you have this information, what will you do with it? A very common use for occlusion queries is to optimize an application's performance by avoiding unnecessary work. Consider an object that has a very detailed appearance. The object has many triangles and possibly a complex fragment shader with a lot of texture lookups and intensive math operations. Perhaps there are many vertex attributes and textures, and there's a lot of work for the application to do just to get ready to draw the object. The object is very expensive to render. It's also possible that the object may never end up being visible in the scene. Perhaps it's covered by something else. Perhaps it's off the screen altogether. It would be good to know this up front and just not draw it at all if it's never going to be seen by the user anyway.

Occlusion queries are a good way to do this. Take your complex, expensive object and produce a much lower fidelity version of it. Usually, a simple bounding box will do. Start an occlusion query, render the bounding box, and then end the occlusion query and retrieve the result. If no part of the object's bounding box produces any pixels, then the more detailed version of the object will not be visible, and it doesn't need to be sent to OpenGL.

Of course, you probably don't actually want the bounding box to be visible in the final scene. There are a number of ways you can make sure that OpenGL doesn't actually draw the bounding box. The easiest way is probably to use `glColorMask` to turn off writes to the color buffer by passing `GL_FALSE` for all parameters.

Listing 12.1 shows a simple example of how to use `glGetQueryObjectuiv` to get retrieve the result from a query object.

LISTING 12.1   Getting the Result from a Query Object

```
glBeginQuery(GL_SAMPLES_PASSED, the_query);
RenderSimplifiedObject(object);
glEndQuery(GL_SAMPLES_PASSED);
glGetQueryObjectuiv(the_query, GL_QUERY_RESULT, &the_result);
if (the_result != 0)
    RenderRealObject(object);
```

`RenderSimplifiedObject` is a function that renders the low-fidelity version of the object and `RenderRealObject` renders the object with all of its detail. Now, `RenderRealObject` only gets called if at least one pixel is produced by `RenderSimplifiedObject`. Remember that the call to `glGetQueryObjectuiv` causes your application to have to wait if the result of the query is not ready yet. This is likely if the rendering done by `RenderSimplifiedObject` is simple—which is the point of this example. If all you want to know is whether it's safe to skip rendering something, you can find out if the query result is available and render the more complex object if the result is either unavailable (i.e., the object may be visible or hidden), or if the object result is available and nonzero (i.e., the object is certainly visible). Listing 12.2 demonstrates how you might determine whether a query object result is ready before you ask for the actual count, allowing you to make decisions based on both the availability and the value of a query result.

LISTING 12.2   Figuring Out If Occlusion Query Results Are Ready

```
glBeginQuery(GL_SAMPLES_PASSED, the_query);
RenderSimplifiedObject(object);
glEndQuery(GL_SAMPLES_PASSED);
glGetQueryObjectuiv(the_query, GL_QUERY_RESULT_AVAILABLE, &the_result);
if (the_result != 0)
    glGetQueryObjectuiv(the_query, GL_QUERY_RESULT, &the_result);
else
    the_result = 1;
if (the_result != 0)
    RenderRealObject(object);
```

In this new example, we determine whether the result is available and if so, retrieve it from OpenGL. If it's not available, we put a count of one into the result so that the complex version of the object will be rendered.

It is possible to have multiple occlusion queries active at the same time. Using multiple query objects is another way for the application to avoid having to wait for OpenGL. OpenGL can only count and add up results into one query object at a time, but it can manage several query objects and perform many queries back-to-back. We can expand our example to render multiple objects with multiple occlusion queries. If we had an array of ten objects to render, each with a simplified representation, we might rewrite the example provided as follows in Listing 12.3.

LISTING 12.3   Simple, Application Side Conditional Rendering

```
int n;
for (n = 0; n < 10; n++) {
    glBeginQuery(GL_SAMPLES_PASSSED, ten_queries[n]);
    RenderSimplifiedObject(&object[n]);
    glEndQuery(GL_SAMPLES_PASSED);
}
for (n = 0; n < 10; n++) {
    glGetQueryObjectuiv(ten_queries[n], GL_QUERY_RESULT, &the_result);
    if (the_result != 0)
        RenderRealObject(&object[n]);
}
```

As discussed earlier, OpenGL is modeled as a pipeline and can have many things going on at the same time. If you draw something simple, like a bounding box, it's likely that it hasn't reached the end of the pipeline and been rendered by the time you need the result of your query. This means that when you call glGetQueryObjectuiv, your application may have to wait a while for OpenGL to finish working on your bounding box before it can give you the answer and you can act on it.

In our next example, we render ten bounding boxes before we ask for the result of the first query. This means that OpenGL's pipeline can be filled, and it can have a lot of work to do and is therefore much more likely to have finished working on the first bounding box before we ask for the result of the first query. In short, the more time we give OpenGL to finish working on what we've asked it for, the more likely it is that it'll have the result of your query and the less likely it is that your application will have to wait for results. Some complex applications take this to the extreme and use the results of queries from the previous frame to make decisions about the new frame.

Finally, putting both techniques together into a single example, we have the code in Listing 12.4.

LISTING 12.4   Rendering When Query Results Aren't Available

```
int n;
for (n = 0; n < 10; n++) {
    glBeginQuery(GL_SAMPLES_PASSSED, ten_queries[n]);
    RenderSimplifiedObject(&object[n]);
    glEndQuery(GL_SAMPLES_PASSED);
}
for (n = 0; n < 10; n++) {
    glGetQueryObjectuiv(ten_queries[n],
                        GL_QUERY_RESULT_AVAILABLE,
                        &the_result);
    if (the_result != 0)
        glGetQueryObjectuiv(ten_queries[n],
                            GL_QUERY_RESULT,
                            &the_result);
    else
        the_result = 1;
    if (the_result != 0)
        RenderRealObject(&object[n]);
}
```

Because the amount of work sent to OpenGL by RenderRealObject is much greater than by RenderSimplifiedObject, by the time we ask for the result of the second, third, fourth, and additional query objects, more and more work has been sent into the OpenGL pipeline, and it becomes more likely that our query results are ready. Within reason, the more complex our scene, and the more query objects we use, the more likely we are to see positive a performance impact.

If you don't care about the actual value of the query result, as in the preceding example where we just care whether it's zero or not, there is an additional query type that you can use that may produce answers more quickly for you, depending on the graphics hardware and drivers that you're using. Instead of using the `GL_SAMPLES_PASSED` query, you can use the special `GL_ANY_SAMPLES_PASSED` query. The result of this query is strictly Boolean. That is, it's either true or false, zero or nonzero. The reason that this may go faster on some hardware is that as soon as the first pixel is rendered, OpenGL knows that the result of the query is true. Therefore, it can stop counting pixels. It can also return the answer to you as soon as it figures this out, even if it isn't done rendering the geometry sent inside the occlusion query. If your OpenGL implementation supports it, you can directly substitute `GL_ANY_SAMPLES_PASSED` for `GL_SAMPLES_PASSED` in algorithms like the one here, and you may see a performance increase in your application.

Getting OpenGL to Make Decisions for You

The preceding examples show how to ask OpenGL to count pixels and how to get the result back from OpenGL into your application so that it can make decisions about what to do next. However, the application doesn't really care about the actual value of the result. It's only using it to decide whether to send more work to OpenGL or to make other changes to the way it might render things. The results have to be sent back from OpenGL to the application, perhaps over a CPU bus or even a network connection when you're using a remote rendering system, just so the application can decide whether to send more commands to OpenGL. This causes latency and can hurt performance, sometimes outweighing any potential benefits to using the queries in the first place.

What would be much better is if we could send all the rendering commands to OpenGL and tell it to obey them only if the result of a query object says it should. This is called *predication*, and fortunately, it is possible through a technique called *conditional rendering*. Conditional rendering allows you to wrap up a sequence of OpenGL function calls and send them to OpenGL with a query object and a message that says "ignore all of this if the result stored in the query object is zero." To mark the start of this sequence of calls, use

```
glBeginConditionalRender(the_query, GL_QUERY_WAIT);
```

and to mark the end of the sequence, use

```
glEndConditionalRender();
```

Everything that is called between `glBeginConditionalRender` and `glEndConditionalRender` is ignored if the result of the query object (the same value that you could have retrieved using `glGetQueryObjectuiv`) is zero. This means that the actual result of the query doesn't have to be sent back to your application. The graphics hardware can make the decision as to whether to render for you. To modify the previous example to use conditional rendering, we could use the code in Listing 12.5.

LISTING 12.5   Basic Conditional Rendering Example

```
// Ask OpenGL to count the samples rendered between the start and end of
// the occlusion query
glBeginQuery(GL_SAMPLES_PASSED, the_query);
RenderSimplifiedObject(object);
glEndQuery(GL_SAMPLES_PASSED);
// Only obey the next few commands if the occlusion query says something
// was rendered
glBeginConditionalRender(the_query, GL_QUERY_WAIT);
RenderRealObject(object);
glEndConditionalRender();
```

The two functions, `RenderSimplifiedObject` and `RenderRealObject`, are functions within our hypothetical example application that render simplified (perhaps just the bounding box, for example) and more complex versions of the object, respectively.

Notice now that we never call `glGetQueryResultuiv`, and we never read any information (such as the result of the query object) back from OpenGL. This can be especially advantageous for remote rendering where the results would have to make a trip across a network before reaching your application.

The astute reader will have noticed the `GL_QUERY_WAIT` parameter passed to `glBeginConditionalRender`. You may be wondering what that's for if the application doesn't have to wait for results to be ready any more. As mentioned earlier, OpenGL operates as a pipeline and may not have finished dealing with `RenderSimplifiedObject` before `glBeginConditionalRender` is called or before the first drawing function is called from `RenderRealObject`. In this case, OpenGL can either wait for everything called from `RenderSimplifiedObject` to reach the end of the pipeline before deciding whether to obey the commands sent by the application, or it can go ahead and start working on `RenderRealObject` if the results aren't ready in time. To tell OpenGL not to wait and to just go ahead and start rendering if the results aren't available, call

```
glBeginConditionalRender(the_query, GL_QUERY_NO_WAIT);
```

This tells OpenGL, "If the results of the query aren't available yet, don't wait for them; just go ahead and render anyway." This is of greatest use when occlusion queries are being used to improve performance. Waiting for the results of occlusion queries can use up any time gained by using them in the first place. Thus, using the `GL_QUERY_NO_WAIT` flag essentially allows the occlusion query to be used as an optimization if the results are ready in time and to behave as if they aren't used at all if the results aren't ready. The use of

GL_QUERY_NO_WAIT is similar to using GL_QUERY_RESULT_AVAILABLE in the preceding examples. Don't forget, though, if you use GL_QUERY_NO_WAIT, the actual geometry rendered is going to depend on whether the commands contributing to the query object have finished executing. This could depend on the performance of the machine your application is running on and can therefore vary from run to run. You should be sure that the result of your program is not dependent on the second set of geometry being rendered (unless this is what you want). If it is, your program might end up producing different output on a faster system than on a slower system.

Of course, it is also possible to use multiple query objects with conditional rendering, and so a final, combined example using all of the techniques in this section is given in Listing 12.6.

LISTING 12.6   A More Complete Conditional Rendering Example

```
// Render simplified versions of 10 objects, each with its own occlusion
// query
int n;
for (n = 0; n < 10; n++) {
    glBeginQuery(GL_SAMPLES_PASSSED, ten_queries[n]);
    RenderSimplifiedObject(&object[n]);
    glEndQuery(GL_SAMPLES_PASSED);
}
// Render the more complex versions of the objects, skipping them
// if the occlusion query results are available and zero
for (n = 0; n < 10; n++) {
    glBeginConditionalRender(ten_queries[n], GL_QUERY_NO_WAIT);
    RenderRealObject(&object[n]);
    glEndConditionalRender();
}
```

In this example, simplified versions of ten objects are rendered first, each with its own occlusion query. Once the simplified versions of the objects have been rendered, the more complex versions of the objects are conditionally rendered based on the results of those occlusion queries. If the simplified versions of the objects are not visible, the more complex versions are skipped, potentially improving performance.

Measuring Time Taken to Execute Commands

One further query type that you can use to judge how long rendering is taking is the timer query. Timer queries are used by passing the GL_TIME_ELAPSED query type as the target parameter of glBeginQuery and glEndQuery. When you call glGetQueryObjectuiv to get the result from the query object, the value is the number of nanoseconds that elapsed between the call to glBeginQuery and glEndQuery. This is actually the amount of time it took OpenGL to process all the commands between the glBeginQuery and glEndQuery commands. You can use this, for example, to figure out what the most expensive part of your scene is. Consider the code shown in Listing 12.7.

LISTING 12.7   Timing Operations Using Timer Queries

```
// Declare our variables
GLuint queries[3];        // Three query objects that we'll use
GLuint world_time;        // Time taken to draw the world
GLuint objects_time;      // Time taken to draw objects in the world
GLuint HUD_time;          // Time to draw the HUD and other UI elements

// Create three query objects
glGenQueries(3, queries);
// Start the first query
glBeginQuery(GL_TIME_ELAPSED, queries[0]);
// Render the world
RenderWorld();
// Stop the first query and start the second...
// Note, we're not reading the value from the query yet
glEndQuery(GL_TIME_ELAPSED);
glBeginQuery(GL_TIME_ELAPSED, queries[1]);
// Render the objects in the world
RenderObjects();
// Stop the second query and start the third
glEndQuery(GL_TIME_ELAPSED);
glBeginQuery(GL_TIME_ELAPSED, queries[2]);
// Render the HUD
RenderHUD();
// Stop the last query
glEndQuery(GL_TIME_ELAPSED);
// Now, we can retrieve the results from the three queries. By the
// time we get here, hopefully RenderWorld() has made it through the
// OpenGL pipeline and the result is ready.
glGetQueryObjectuiv(queries[0], GL_QUERY_RESULT, &world_time);
glGetQueryObjectuiv(queries[1], GL_QUERY_RESULT, &objects_time);
glGetQueryObjectuiv(queries[2], GL_QUERY_RESULT, &HUD_time);
// Done. world_time, objects_time and hud_time contain the values we want.
// Clean up after ourselves.
glDeleteQueries(3, queries);
```

After this code is executed, world_time, objects_time, and HUD_time will contain the number of nanoseconds it took to render the world, all the objects in the world, and the heads-up display (HUD), respectively. You can use this to determine what fraction of the graphics hardware's time is taken up rendering each of the elements of your scene. This is useful for profiling your code during development—you can figure out what the most expensive parts of your application are, and so know from this where to spend optimization effort. You can also use it during runtime to alter the behavior of your application to try to get the best possible performance out of the graphics subsystem. For example, you could increase or reduce the number of objects in the scene depending on the relative value of objects_time. You could also dynamically switch between more or less complex shaders for elements of the scene based on the power of the graphics hardware.

If you just want to know how much time passes, according to OpenGL, between two actions that your program takes, you can use glQueryCounter, whose prototype is

```
void glQueryCounter(GLuint id, GLenum target);
```

You need to set id to GL_TIMESTAMP and target to the name of a query object that you've created earlier. This function puts the query straight into the OpenGL pipeline, and when that query reaches the end of the pipeline, OpenGL records its view of the current time into the query object. The time zero is not really defined—it just indicates some unspecified time in the past. To use this effectively, your application needs to take deltas between multiple time stamps. To implement the previous example using glQueryCounter, we could write code as shown in Listing 12.8.

LISTING 12.8   Timing Operations Using glQueryCounter

```
// Declare our variables
GLuint queries[4];      // Now we need four query objects
GLuint start_time;      // The start time of the application
GLuint world_time;      // Time taken to draw the world
GLuint objects_time;    // Time taken to draw objects in the world
GLuint HUD_time;        // Time to draw the HUD and other UI elements

// Create four query objects
glGenQueries(4, queries);
// Get the start time
glQueryCounter(GL_TIMESTAMP, queries[0]);
// Render the world
RenderWorld();
// Get the time after RenderWorld is done
glQueryCounter(GL_TIMESTAMP, queries[1]);
// Render the objects in the world
RenderObjects();
// Get the time after RenderObjects is done
glQueryCounter(GL_TIMESTAMP, queries[2]);
```

```
// Render the HUD
RenderHUD();
// Get the time after everything is done
glQueryCounter(GL_TIMESTAMP, queries[3]);
// Get the result from the three queries, and subtract them to find deltas
glGetQueryObjectuiv(queries[0], GL_QUERY_RESULT, &start_time);
glGetQueryObjectuiv(queries[1], GL_QUERY_RESULT, &world_time);
glGetQueryObjectuiv(queries[2], GL_QUERY_RESULT, &objects_time);
glGetQueryObjectuiv(queries[3], GL_QUERY_RESULT, &HUD_time);
HUD_time -= objects_time;
objects_time -= world_time;
world_time -= start_time;
// Done. world_time, objects_time and hud_time contain the values we want.
// Clean up after ourselves.
glDeleteQueries(4, queries);
```

As you can see, the code in this example is not that much different from that in Listing 12.7 shown earlier. You need to create four query objects instead of three, and you need to subtract out the results at the end to find time deltas. However, you don't need to call glBeginQuery and glEndQuery in pairs, which means that there are less calls to OpenGL, in total.

Storing Data in GPU Memory

So far, all geometry you've been using (vertices, colors, normals, and other vertex attribute data) has been managed by the GLTools library. When you've called functions like GLBatch::CopyVertexData or GLBatch::CopyNormalData, the pointer you've specified is a real pointer to an area of memory containing vertex coordinates, colors, normals, and other data you'd like to render. If each time you called glDrawArrays, glDrawElements, or some other OpenGL function that required vertex data, the information was taken from the application's memory, on a high performance system with a local GPU, this would mean that the data would be transferred from the application's memory (attached to the CPU) across the bus connecting the CPU to the GPU (usually PCI-Express) to the GPU's local memory so that it can work it. This would take so much time that it would slow down the application significantly. On a remote system, the data might be transferred across a network connection to the server for rendering. This can be devastating for performance.

When the GPU accesses memory that is local to it (physically attached to the video card, for example), it is often several times, perhaps even orders of magnitude faster than accessing the same data stored in system memory. In the case of a remote rendering system, accessing local GPU memory can literally be tens of thousands of times faster than sending the data across a network connection. If the data to be rendered is more or less the same every frame, or if many copies of the same data will be rendered in a single frame, it is advantageous to copy the data to the GPU's local memory once and then reuse that copy over and over again.

To allow this to happen, the various classes in GLTools manage buffers in the GPU's local memory and hide the complexities of this from you. In fact, though, it's not particularly difficult to manage these buffers yourself. You will need to do this eventually as you start to write more complex applications that require data other than simple position, color, and normal vectors.

In this section, you learn how to ensure that vertex data and other information required by the GPU is available and is stored in its memory. To do this, you use buffer objects containing the data that is supplied by your application. You learn how to manage these objects, how to tell OpenGL what you intend to use them for, and how to best keep your data in GPU memory.

Using Buffers to Store Vertex Data

In OpenGL, it is possible to store vertex attribute data such as positions, colors, or anything else needed by the vertex shader in a buffer object. Buffer objects are OpenGL objects that represent storage for data and have already been introduced earlier in this book. Here, we use an OpenGL buffer as a *vertex buffer object* (VBO). A VBO is a buffer object that represents storage for vertex data. Data can be placed in these buffers with hints that tell OpenGL how you plan to use it, and OpenGL can then use those hints to decide what it will do with that data. If the data is to be used more than once or twice, OpenGL will more than likely copy it into the fast memory attached to the graphics card.

Because a nontrivial application may require several VBOs and many vertex attributes, a special container object called a *vertex array object* (VAO) is available to OpenGL to manage all of this state. VAOs are discussed in more detail in the next section. However, because there is no default VAO, you need to create and bind one before you can use any of the code in this section. Some code like the following should be sufficient:

```
glGenVertexArrays(1, &vao);
glBindVertexArray(vao);
```

This creates and binds a single VAO. This can stay bound for the duration of your application, and you'll be in a position to use and manipulate vertex buffers. To create one or more buffer objects, call

```
glGenBuffers(1, &one_buffer);
```

or

```
glGenBuffers(10, ten_buffers);
```

To store vertex data into or retrieve vertex data from a buffer, it must be bound to the GL_ARRAY_BUFFER binding. To do this, call

```
glBindBuffer(GL_ARRAY_BUFFER, one_buffer);
```

Once bound, you can use many of the functions requiring a buffer binding as a parameter to manipulate the buffer object. Examples of these functions are glBufferData, glBufferSubData, glMapBuffer, and glCopyBuffer.

When glVertexAttribPointer is called, the value of the attribute pointer is not interpreted as a real, physical pointer to data in memory. The pointer is actually interpreted as an offset into the buffer object that is bound to the GL_ARRAY_BUFFER binding at the time of the call. Also, a record of the currently bound buffer is made in the current VAO and used for that attribute. That is, not only does glVertexAttribPointer tell OpenGL the offset into the buffer that a vertex attribute's data can be found, but it also tells OpenGL *which* buffer contains the data.

It is therefore possible to use multiple buffers—one for each attribute—simultaneously by calling glBindBuffer followed by glVertexAttribPointer for each attribute. It is also possible to store several different attributes in a single buffer by interleaving them. To do this, call glVertexArrayPointer with the stride parameter set to the distance (in bytes) between attributes of the same type. Finally, because each vertex attribute has its own set of parameters, including offset, stride, and buffer binding, it is possible to use a combination of interleaved and separate buffers. For example, a single model could have positions and normals interleaved in one buffer and texture coordinates in a second separate buffer. This would allow different textures to be used with different texture coordinates on the same model by changing only the buffer binding for the texture coordinate vertex attribute.

The following example, shown in Listing 12.9 creates a single buffer, binds it to the GL_ARRAY_BUFFER binding, places some data in it, and then sets a vertex attribute pointer to refer to that buffer. There is one large chunk of data placed into the buffer (the data array), and it occupies the whole buffer.

LISTING 12.9 Allocating and Initializing a Single VBO

```
// This variable will hold the name of our buffer.
GLuint my_buffer;
// This array contains the data that we'll initialize the buffer with.
// Often, the data is actually stored in a file rather than a raw C
// array.
static const GLfloat data[] = { 1.0f, 2.0f, 3.0f, 4.0f, ... };
// Create a buffer.
glGenBuffers(1, &my_buffer);
// A well behaved application would check that buffer creation
```

```
// succeeded here. We're just going to bind it and hope for the best.
glBindBuffer(GL_ARRAY_BUFFER, my_buffer);
// There is no storage space allocated for the buffer until we put
// some data into it. This copies the contents of the 'data' array
// into the buffer.
glBufferData(GL_ARRAY_BUFFER, sizeof(data), data, GL_STATIC_DRAW);
// Now, we set the vertex attribute pointer. The location is zero (we
// somehow know this), the size is 4 (the attribute in the vertex
// shader is declared as vec4), we have floating point data that is
// not normalized. Stride is zero because the data in this case is
// tightly packed. Finally, notice that we're passing zero as the
// pointer to the data. This is legal because it will be interpreted as
// an offset into 'my_buffer',
// and the data really does start at offset zero.
glVertexAttribPointer(0, 4, GL_FLOAT, GL_FALSE, 0, (const GLvoid *)0);
```

The next example in Listing 12.10 creates a single buffer, places data at different locations within it, and then sets several vertex attribute pointers to the offsets of that data. This is a demonstration of using one buffer to hold several separate attributes, but keeping all of the data for each attribute together.

LISTING 12.10   Using a Single VBO to Hold Multiple Vertex Attributes

```
// This is the new data we're going to use:
static const GLfloat positions[] = { /* many floating point vec4s */ };
static const GLfloat colors[] = { /* more floating point vec4s */ };
static const GLfloat normals[] = { /* a bunch of floating point vec3s */ };
// Assume we've created and bound a buffer as in the previous example
// Now, we're going to allocate space for data by specifying a size,
// but NULL as a pointer to the data.
glBufferData(GL_ARRAY_BUFFER,
             sizeof(positions) + sizeof(colors) + sizeof(normals),
             NULL, GL_STATIC_DRAW);
// We can now copy the individual arrays into this one big buffer:
glBufferSubData(GL_ARRAY_BUFFER, 0,
                sizeof(positions), positions);
glBufferSubData(GL_ARRAY_BUFFER, sizeof(positions),
                sizeof(colors), colors);
glBufferSubData(GL_ARRAY_BUFFER, sizeof(positions) + sizeof(colors),
                sizeof(normals), normals);
// Now the buffer contains the data for three attributes in three big
// chunks, one after another we can set the vertex attribute pointers to
// the offsets of that data within the buffer.
```

```
// Positions first:
glVertexAttribPointer(0, 4, GL_FLOAT, GL_FALSE, 0,
                      (const GLvoid *)0);
// Then colors:
glVertexAttribPointer(1, 4, GL_FLOAT, GL_FALSE, 0,
                      (const GLvoid *)sizeof(positions));
// Then normals:
glVertexAttribPointer(2, 3, GL_FLOAT, GL_FALSE, 0,
                      (const GLvoid *)(sizeof(positions) + sizeof(colors)));
```

In the final example given in Listing 12.11, a single buffer is used to hold interleaved attribute data. The data is declared as a C structure and copied directly into the buffer. The stride parameter of glVertexAttribPointer is used to tell OpenGL how many bytes apart the attributes are in memory. This is an example of *interleaved attributes*. All of the attributes for a single vertex end up right next to each other in the buffer.

LISTING 12.11   Using a Single VBO to Hold Interleaved Attributes

```
// The VERTEX structure contains the position, color and normal for a
// single vertex packed together in memory
struct VERTEX_t
{
    vec4 position;
    vec4 color;
    vec3 normal;
};
typedef struct VERTEX_t VERTEX;
// Assume there is some external array of vertex data
extern VERTEX vertices[];

// Now, we can upload all of the vertex data into one, large buffer
glBufferData(GL_ARRAY_BUFFER, vertex_count * sizeof(VERTEX),
             vertices, GL_STATIC_DRAW);
// Each vertex attribute is now sourced from the same buffer. The
// stride parameter is the distance, in bytes, between one vertex and the
// next - i.e. sizeof(VERTEX) and the location of the data within the
// buffer is simply the offset of the element within the structure.
glVertexAttribPointer(0, 4, GL_FLOAT, GL_FALSE, sizeof(VERTEX),
                      (const GLvoid *)OFFSETOF(VERTEX, position));
glVertexAttribPointer(1, 4, GL_FLOAT, GL_FALSE, sizeof(VERTEX),
                      (const GLvoid *)OFFSETOF(VERTEX, color));
glVertexAttribPointer(2, 3, GL_FLOAT, GL_FALSE, sizeof(VERTEX),
                      (const GLvoid *)OFFSETOF(VERTEX, normal));
```

The resulting layouts of the data in the buffers are shown in Figure 12.1. In (a), the data is simply copied into the buffer and appears in the GPU's memory as it would have in the application's memory. In (b), several arrays of attributes are placed into the buffer back to back. Finally, in (c), the individual attributes for each vertex are interleaved together.

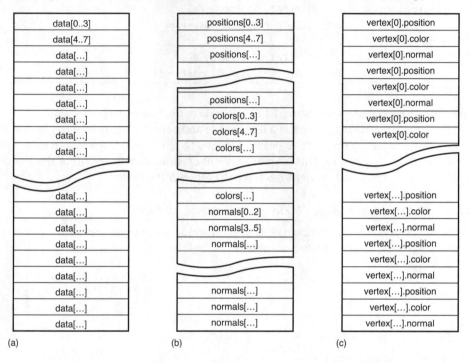

FIGURE 12.1   Layout of data in buffers using packed, multiple, and interleaved buffers.

Unlike some other OpenGL objects, there is no *default* buffer object. This means that before you can call glVertexAttribPointer, you must create a vertex buffer object and bind it. The buffer object named zero is reserved by OpenGL to mean "no buffer." Thus, to unbind a buffer without specifying a new buffer to use in its place, simply bind the name zero to the GL_ARRAY_BUFFER binding:

```
glBindBuffer(GL_ARRAY_BUFFER, 0);
```

If the data is changed regularly by the application, it may seem useful to keep data in the application's memory space. However, it is still necessary to use a VBO for this because OpenGL does not support reading data directly from system memory. If you specify the GL_STREAM_DRAW usage mode when calling glBufferData, OpenGL knows that the data is likely to be used only once and the behavior, and performance of the application should be the same as if you had kept data in the application's memory. In any case, even if you were able to keep data in the application's memory, it is very likely that your OpenGL drivers would perform a similar operation internally and end up copying the data to a staging area in the GPU's memory before using it.

Storing Vertex Indices in Buffers

So far we have discussed only the GL_ARRAY_BUFFER binding. Another related buffer binding is the GL_ELEMENT_ARRAY_BUFFER binding. The element array buffer is a buffer that stores the indices of vertices and is used by functions such as glDrawElements and glDrawRangeElements. There is no equivalent to glVertexAttribPointer for the GL_ELEMENT_ARRAY_BUFFER binding. That is, there is no glElementPointer function, for example. You can use the GL_ELEMENT_ARRAY_BUFFER binding just like any other binding for the purposes of allocating it or putting data into it (using glBufferData or glBufferSubData, for example). Let's take a look at the function prototype of glDrawElements:

```
void glDrawElements(GLenum mode, GLsizei count, GLenum type, const GLvoid *
indices);
```

The last parameter, indices, is the offset of the first index within the element array buffer. Remember that when glVertexAttribPointer is called, the last parameter, pointer, is interpreted as an offset into the buffer that is bound to the GL_ARRAY_BUFFER binding. The same is true with the indices parameter of glDrawElements and the buffer bound to the GL_ELEMENT_ARRAY_BUFFER binding. If a nonzero buffer is bound to the GL_ELEMENT_ARRAY_BUFFER binding when glDrawElements is called, indices is interpreted as an offset into that buffer, and the indices of the vertices to be drawn are fetched from that buffer.

If no buffer is bound to the GL_ELEMENT_ARRAY_BUFFER binding, glDrawElements won't do anything. Without an element buffer, there is no storage for the indices of the vertices to be drawn. Just as OpenGL does not support reading vertex attribute data from the application's memory, it cannot read vertex indices either. Thus, you must have a buffer bound to the GL_ELEMENT_ARRAY_BUFFER binding point in order to use the glDrawElements function.

There is also a more advanced version of glDrawElements that allows you to use the same indices but different vertex data for each call. The glDrawElementsBaseVertex function allows you to specify an offset that will be added to every vertex index before it is used to read data from the vertex buffers. Its prototype is

```
void glDrawElementsBaseVertex(GLenum mode, GLsizei count, GLenum type, GLvoid
*indices, GLint basevertex);
```

Consider a complex model that uses several vertex buffers—say, one for position data, one for normals, two or three for texture coordinates, and maybe a few more for other data that might be needed to render it. If the model is animated, you'll need several frames, each with its own complete set of this data. In each frame, the positions move, the normals change, but the indices of the vertices would stay the same. You have a few options here. You could use a separate set of VBOs for each frame. This would require quite a bit of setup, but would be an acceptable solution. You could use a separate VAO (which is discussed in more detail in the following section) for each frame of the object, which would store all the bindings. Another alternative is to store all of the data in a single, large buffer, with each frame packed one after another. That would require you to call glVertexAttribPointer a bunch of times for each frame. Again, you could store that information in a separate VAO for each frame.

The glDrawElementsBaseVertex function is an alternative that allows you to simply specify the offset into the buffers that the indices in the element buffer are relative to. Thus, if you have a model with 1000 vertices, say, then the first frame starts at offset 0, the second frame starts at offset 1000, the third at 2000, and so on. Passing the offset to the glDrawElementsBaseVertex command is a much simpler operation (from OpenGL's point of view) than rebinding VBOs or VAOs, or processing several calls to glVertexAttribPointer. In fact, for every variant of glDrawElements, there is an equivalent version that takes a basevertex parameter: glDrawElementsBaseVertex, glDrawRangeElementsBaseVertex, glDrawElementsInstancedBaseVertex, and glMultiDrawElementsBaseVertex. They are explained in some detail in the OpenGL specification.

Using Vertex Array Objects to Organize Your Buffers

You just read about vertex buffer objects. Each vertex attribute has an offset within a buffer and a set of other state such as data type and stride. Each one also has an associated buffer, which can be different for each attribute. Calling glVertexAttribPointer sets all of this state, including the buffer binding for the attribute. If you have a fairly complex scene with several objects in it and each object keeps its vertex data in its own VBO, then that is a reasonable amount of state per object. If the application is well-written, drawing one of these object may end up as simple as a single call to a function like glDrawElements or glDrawArrays.

Even if the layout of data is the same between objects (it probably will be for many applications) and the offsets of the data are the same (maybe all data starts at offset zero, for example), it is still necessary to call glVertexAttribPointer for every vertex attribute. For an object that has, say, eight vertex attributes, this means at least one call to glBindBuffer (possibly up to eight if all the vertex attributes are in separate buffer objects), and eight calls to glVertexAttribPointer. If you're using indexed vertices, you also need to bind your GL_ELEMENT_ARRAY_BUFFER. All this to prepare for a single call to glDrawElements. This is a lot of state to set, a lot of error checking that the driver has to do, and a lot of information that the application has to look after.

To help organize all this information, OpenGL provides an object called a vertex array object (VAO). A VAO is a container that packages together all of the state that can be set by glVertexAttribPointer and a few other functions. When using a VAO, all state specified through a call to glVertexAttribPointer is stored in the current VAO. There is no default VAO in OpenGL. This means that before you can even specify your vertex point-ers, you need to create and bind a VAO. For simple applications, it may be sufficient to create a single VAO, bind it, and leave it bound for the lifetime of the application (as we did when we introduced VBOs earlier). However, an application can create as many VAOs as it needs and use them to manage all of the array state. When it's time to draw using a particular set of vertex attributes, simply bind the VAO containing that set of state and start drawing. This allows each object in a scene to manage its own vertex buffers by creat-ing a VAO to maintain its state and binding it before drawing. That way, the object won't upset the vertex array state of any other object in the scene.

To create one or more VAOs, call

```
void glGenVertexArrays(GLsizei n, GLuint *arrays);
```

Like most other OpenGL objects, VAOs are referred to by name represented as unsigned integers. The glGenVertexArrays function creates n vertex arrays and places their names in the array arrays. If glGenVertexArrays fails to allocate a VAO for some reason, it returns zero for its name. A well-written application should always check for this condition before trying to use the result. Like buffer objects, the VAO name zero is reserved by OpenGL to mean "no VAO." Again, when no VAO is bound, glVertexAttribPointer will not work and will generate an error if you call it. To delete VAOs, call

```
void glDeleteVertexArrays(GLsizei n, GLuint *arrays);
```

This function deletes the n VAOs whose names are in arrays. It is important for your application to clean up after itself. If arrays has an element containing the name zero, that will be ignored. This means that you can safely pass an array previously written to by glGenVertexArrays to glDeleteVertexArrays without worrying whether some of the names might be zero (due to an error during the execution of glGenVertexArrays, for example). To start using a VAO, call

```
void glBindVertexArray(GLuint array);
```

This makes array the current VAO. When a new VAO is bound for the first time, it contains all of the default state that would be present in a freshly created context. From now on, any time you call a function that accesses the vertex array state, it will access the state contained in the currently bound VAO. This includes functions that set state, such as glVertexAttribPointer; functions that implicitly use that state, such as glDrawArrays or glDrawElements; and functions that explicitly read vertex array state, such as glGetIntegerv.

Now that we have a VAO, we can set as much state on it as we like. We can call glVertexAttribPointer as many times as we need and the state will be stored in the VAO. If we call glBindBuffer followed by glVertexAttribPointer, the buffer binding will also be stored in the VAO. Note, though, that while the buffer binding associated with the vertex attribute is stored in the VAO, binding a new VAO does not change the current buffer bindings. That is, the actual state of the currently bound buffers is not stored in the VAO. To return to the example at the start of this section—the object with many vertex attributes, each with different state and buffer bindings—we can improve the performance of this greatly using VAOs.

Instead of calling `glBindBuffer` and `glVertexAttribPointer` many times right before drawing the object, we can do it at initialization time. When it is created, the object can generate a VAO, bind it using `glBindVertexArray`, and set all of its vertex array state as if it were about to render itself. After initialization, return OpenGL to having no VAO bound by calling

```
glBindVertexArray(0);
```

Now, when the object is about to be rendered, call `glBindVertexArray` again with the object's VAO, and then call the rendering functions such as `glDrawArrays`. Thus, rendering a complete object that has many vertex attributes, all stored in a collection of VBOs with different parameters, can be as simple as two function calls—`glBindVertexArray` and `glDrawElements`, for example. This is also beneficial for layered libraries, scene graph managers, and middleware that might want to render without disturbing the current OpenGL state. If the normal behavior of the environment is to have no VAO bound, then each object binds its own VAO, renders itself, and then binds VAO zero, resetting everything.

Drawing a lot of Geometry Efficiently

So far, you have seen how to send blocks of data to OpenGL to render using functions such as `glDrawArrays`. It's possible to send huge numbers of vertices—millions if necessary—to OpenGL using a single call to this function. However, this is only of any use when the geometry is nicely arranged in a large contiguous block. In any nontrivial application, there will be many different, unrelated objects. There is likely to be a world or some kind of background, and each of these may require several calls to one of the drawing functions. It is not unusual to see a complex application making thousands or even hundreds of thousands of calls to the various drawing functions that OpenGL provides in every frame. In this section, we go over a number of methods that you can use to draw a lot of independent pieces of geometry with very few calls to OpenGL.

Combining Drawing Functions

If you have a lot of geometry to send to OpenGL in a single application, it's likely that you will have one preferred method of drawing. This might be to use `glDrawArrays` or `glDrawElements`, for example. If you were to pack all of the vertex data for all of your objects into a single buffer, it would be reasonable to have a loop in your code that looks something like this:

```
for (int i = 0; i < num_objects; i++) {
    glDrawArrays(GL_TRIANGLES,
                    object[n]->first_vertex,
                    object[n]->vertex_count);
}
```

This might produce a lot of calls into OpenGL, and each one carries some overhead. If you have a large number of objects in your scene, and each has a relatively small number of triangles, the cost of each of these calls to glDrawArrays will start to add up and could negatively affect the performance of your application. A couple of functions that might help in this case are

void glMultiDrawArrays(GLenum mode, GLint *first, GLsizei *count, GLsizei primcount);

and

void glMultiDrawElements(GLenum mode, GLsizei *count, GLenum type, GLvoid **indices, GLsizei primcount);

These two functions operate similarly to the previous code. Each behaves as if its non-Multi versions had been called primcount times. For glMultiDrawArrays, first and count are arrays. Also, for glMultiDrawElements, count and indices are arrays. This allows OpenGL to perform all of its setup once, check that all the parameters are correct once, and if the driver supports it, send a single command to the graphics hardware. This can allow a lot of the overhead associated with calling OpenGL functions to be amortized across the number of function calls the glMultiDraw function replaces.

By rewriting this example, we can see that only one function call to glMultiDrawArrays can be used to replace the many (potentially thousands) calls to glDrawArrays. This new version is shown in Listing 12.12. Although there is more code, there are fewer calls to OpenGL, which often translates to better performance.

LISTING 12.12 Simple Example of glMultiDrawArrays

```
// These arrays are assumed to be sized large enough to hold enough data to
// represent all of the objects in the scene
GLint first[];
GLsizei count[];

// Build our lists of first vertex and vertex count
for (int i = 0; i < num_objects; i++) {
    first[i] = object[n]->first_vertex;
    count[i] = object[n]->vertex_count;
```

```
}

// Now make a single call to glDrawArrays
glMultiDrawArrays(GL_TRIANGLES, first, count, num_objects);
```

If the list of objects doesn't change (or doesn't change very often), you can build the first and count arrays up front, removing the for-loop from the example entirely. For example, if you have a simple game with enemies and bonus items in a level, you may only need to update the first and count arrays when one of the enemies dies or a bonus item is collected by the player.

Combining Geometry Using Primitive Restart

There are many tools out there that "stripify" geometry. The idea of these tools is that by taking "triangle soup," which means a large collection of unconnected triangles, and attempting to merge it into a set of triangle strips, performance can be improved. This works because individual triangles each take three vertices to represent, but a triangle strip reduces this to a single vertex per triangle (not counting the first triangle in the strip). By converting the geometry from triangle soup to triangle strips, there is less geometry data to process, and the system should run faster. If the tool does a good job and produces a small number of long strips containing many triangles each, this generally works well. There has been a lot of research into this type of algorithm, and a new method's success is measured by passing some well-known models through the new "stripifier" and comparing the number and average length of the strips generated by the tool to that produced by current cutting-edge stripifiers.

Despite all of this research, the reality is that a soup can be rendered with a single call to glDrawArrays or glDrawElements, but unless the functionality that is about to be introduced is used, a set of strips needs to be rendered with separate calls to OpenGL. This means that there is likely to be a lot more function calls in a program that uses stripified geometry, and if the stripping application hasn't done a decent job or if the model just doesn't lend well to stripification, this can eat any performance gains seen by using strips in the first place. Even functions like glMultiDrawArrays and glMultiDrawElements don't always help because the graphics hardware may not implement these functions directly, and so OpenGL essentially has to convert them to multiple calls to glDrawArrays internally anyway.

A feature that is almost universally supported by recent graphics hardware and is part of OpenGL is *primitive restart*. Primitive restart applies to the GL_TRIANGLE_STRIP, GL_TRIANGLE_FAN, GL_LINE_STRIP, and GL_LINE_LOOP geometry types. It is a method of informing OpenGL when one strip (or fan or loop) has ended and that another should be started. To indicate the position in the geometry where one strip ends and the next starts, a special marker is placed as a reserved value in the element array. As OpenGL either fetches vertex indices from the element array or generates them internally, in the case of nonindexed draw commands like glDrawArrays, it checks for this special index value and whenever it comes across it, it ends the current strip and starts a new one with the next vertex. This mode is disabled by default but can be enabled by calling

```
glEnable(GL_PRIMITIVE_RESTART);
```

and disabled again by calling

```
glDisable(GL_PRIMITIVE_RESTART);
```

When primitive restart mode is enabled, OpenGL watches for the special index value as it fetches or generates them and when it comes across it, stops the current strip and starts a new one. To set the index that OpenGL should watch for, call

```
glPrimitiveRestartIndex(index);
```

OpenGL watches for the value specified by index and uses that as the primitive restart marker. Because the marker is a vertex index, primitive restart is best used with indexed drawing functions such as glDrawElements. You can still use primitive restart with glDrawArrays, for example. In this case, OpenGL may eventually generate the restart index internally, and when it does, it restarts the primitive. For example, if you set the restart index to ten and then draw 20 vertices using the GL_TRIANGLE_STRIP mode, you get two separate strips.

The default value of the primitive restart index is zero. Because that's almost certainly the index of a real vertex that will be contained in the model, it's a good idea to set the restart index to a new value whenever you're using primitive restart mode. A good value to use is 0xFFFFFFFF because you can be almost certain that it will not be used as a valid index of a vertex. Many stripping tools have an option to either create separate strips or to create a single strip with the restart index in it. The stripping tool may use a predefined index or output the index it used when creating the stripped version of the model (for example, one greater than the number of vertices in the model). You need to know this and set it using the glPrimitiveRestartIndex function to use the output of the tool in your application.

The primitive restart feature is illustrated in Figure 12.2.

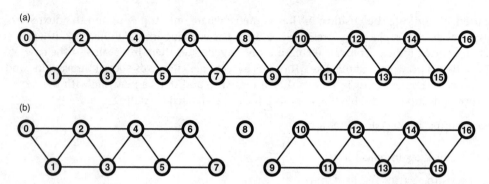

FIGURE 12.2   Triangle strips generated with primitive restart disabled and enabled.

In Figure 12.2, a triangle strip is pictured with the vertices marked with their indices. In (a), the strip is made up of 17 vertices, which produces a total of 15 triangles in a single, connected strip. By enabling primitive restart mode and setting the primitive restart index to 8, vertex 8 is recognized by OpenGL as the special restart marker, and the triangle strip is terminated at vertex 7. This is shown in (b). The actual position of vertex 8 is ignored because this is not seen by OpenGL as the index of a real vertex. The next vertex processed (vertex 9) becomes the start of a new triangle strip. So while 17 vertices are still sent to OpenGL, the result is that two separate triangle strips of 8 vertices and 6 triangles each are drawn.

Instanced Rendering

There will probably be times when you want to draw the same object many times. Imagine a fleet of starships, or a field of grass. There could be thousands of copies of what are essentially identical sets of geometry, modified only slightly from instance to instance. A simple application might just loop over all of the individual blades of grass in a field and render them separately, calling glDrawArrays once for each blade and perhaps updating a set of shader uniforms on each iteration. Supposing each blade of grass were made up of a strip of four triangles, the code might look something like Listing 12.13.

LISTING 12.13   Drawing the Same Geometry Many Times

```
glBindVertexArray(grass_vao);
for (int n = 0; n < number_of_blades_of_grass; n++) {
    SetupGrassBladeParameters();
    glDrawArrays(GL_TRIANGLE_STRIP, 0, 6);
}
```

How many blades of grass are there in a field? What is the value of number_of_blades_of_grass? It could be thousands, maybe millions. Each blade of grass is likely to take up a very small area on the screen, and the number of vertices representing the blade is also very small. Your graphics card doesn't really have a lot of work to do to render a single blade of grass, and the system is likely to spend most of its time sending commands to OpenGL rather than actually drawing anything. OpenGL addresses this through *instanced rendering*, which is a way to ask it to draw many copies of the same geometry.

Instanced rendering is a method provided by OpenGL to specify that you want to draw many copies of the same geometry with a single function call. This functionality is accessed through *instanced* rendering functions, such as

```
void glDrawArraysInstanced(GLenum mode, GLint first, GLsizei count, GLsizei
primcount);
```

and

```
void glDrawElementsInstanced(GLenum mode, GLsizei count, GLenum type, const void *
indices, GLsizei primcount);
```

These two functions behave much like `glDrawArrays` and `glDrawElements`, except that they tell OpenGL to render `primcount` copies of the geometry. The first parameters of each (`mode`, `first`, and `count` for `glDrawArraysInstanced`, and `mode`, `count`, `type`, and `indices` for `glDrawElementsInstanced`) take the same meaning as in the regular, noninstanced versions of the functions. When you call one of these functions, OpenGL makes any preparations it needs to draw your geometry (such as copying vertex data to the graphics card's memory, for example) only once and then renders the same vertices many times.

If all that these functions did were send many copies of the same vertices to OpenGL as if `glDrawArrays` or `glDrawElements` had been called in a tight loop, they wouldn't be very useful. One of the things that makes instanced rendering usable and very powerful is a special, built-in variable in GLSL named `gl_InstanceID`. The `gl_InstanceID` variable appears in GLSL as if it were an integer uniform. When the first copy of the vertices is sent to OpenGL, `gl_InstanceID` will be zero. It will then be incremented once for each copy of the geometry and will eventually reach `primcount` - 1. Because `gl_InstanceID` is an integer, there is a practical upper limit of a couple of billion instances that you can render in one call to `glDrawArraysInstanced` or `glDrawElementsInstanced`, but that should be enough for the vast majority of applications. If you need to render more than two billion copies of your geometry, your application will probably run very slowly anyway, and you won't see a significant performance penalty for breaking your rendering into blocks of, say one billion vertices.

The `glDrawArraysInstanced` function essentially operates as if the code in Listing 12.14 were executed.

LISTING 12.14   Pseudo-code Illustrating the Behavior of `glDrawArraysInstanced`

```
// Loop over all of the instances (i.e. primcount)
for (int n = 0; n < primcount; n++) {
    // Set the gl_InstanceID uniform - here gl_InstanceID is a C variable
    // holding the location of the 'virtual' gl_InstanceID uniform.
    glUniform1i(gl_InstanceID, n);
    // Now, when we call glDrawArrays, the gl_InstanceID variable in the
    // shader will contain the index of the instance that's being rendered.
    glDrawArrays(mode, first, count);
}
```

Likewise, the `glDrawElementsInstanced` function operates similarly to the code in Listing 12.15.

LISTING 12.15   Pseudo-code Illustrating the Behavior of `glDrawElementsInstanced`

```
for (int n = 0; n < primcount; n++) {
    // Set the value of gl_InstanceID
    glUniform1i(gl_InstanceID, n);
    // Make a normal call to glDrawElements
    glDrawElements(mode, count, type, indices);
}
```

Of course, `gl_InstanceID` is not a real uniform, and you can't get a location for it by calling `glGetUniformLocation`. The value of `gl_InstanceID` is managed by OpenGL and is very likely generated in hardware, meaning that it's essentially free to use in terms of performance. The power of instanced rendering comes from imaginative use of this variable, along with *instanced arrays*, which are explained in a moment.

The value of `gl_InstanceID` can be used directly as a parameter to a shader function or to index into data such as textures or uniform arrays. To return to our example of the field of grass, let's figure out what we're going to do with `gl_InstanceID` to make our field not just be thousands of identical blades of grass growing out of a single point. Each of our grass blades is made out of a little triangle strip with four triangles in it, a total of just six vertices. It could be tricky to get them to all look different. However, with some shader magic, we can make each blade of grass look sufficiently different so as to produce an interesting output. We won't go over the shader code here (there's plenty of advanced shader examples in the last chapter), but we walk through a few ideas of how you can use `gl_InstanceID` to add variation to your scenes.

First, we need each blade of grass to have a different position; otherwise, they'll all be drawn on top of each other. Let's arrange the blades of grass more or less evenly. If the number of blades of grass we're going to render is a power of two, we can use half the bits of `gl_InstanceID` to represent the x coordinate of the a blade, and the y coordinate to represent the z coordinate (our ground lies in the x-z plane, with y being altitude). For this example, we render 2^20, or a little over a million blades of grass (actually 1,048,576 blades, but who's counting?). By using the ten least significant bits (bits 9 through 0) as the x coordinate and the ten most significant bits (19 through 10) as the z coordinate, we have a uniform grid of grass blades. Let's take a look at Figure 12.3 to see what we have so far.

FIGURE 12.3   First attempt at an instanced field of grass.

Our uniform grid of grass probably looks a little plain, as if a particularly attentive groundskeeper hand-planted each blade. What we really need to do is displace each blade of grass by some random amount within its grid square. That'll make the field look a little less uniform. A simple way of generating random numbers is to multiply a seed value by a large number and take a subset bits of the resulting product and use it as the input to a function. We're not aiming for a perfect distribution here, so this simple generator should do. Usually, with this type of algorithm, you'd reuse the seed value as input to the next iteration of the random number generator. In this case, though, we can just use `gl_InstanceID` directly as we're really generating the next few numbers after `gl_InstanceID` in a pseudo-random sequence. By iterating over our pseudo-random function only a couple of times, we can get a reasonably random distribution. Because we need to displace in both x and z, we generate two successive random numbers from `gl_InstanceID` and use them to displace the blade of grass within the plane. Look at Figure 12.4 to see what we get now.

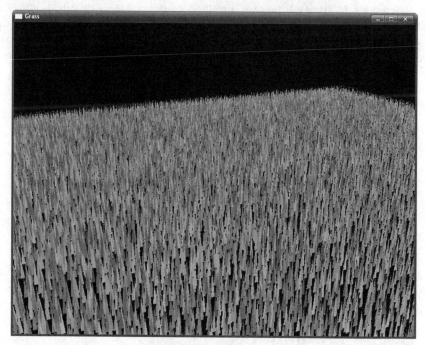

FIGURE 12.4   Slightly perturbed blades of grass.

At this point, our field of grass is distributed evenly with random perturbations in position for each blade of grass. All the grass blades look the same, though. (Actually, we used the same random number generator to assign a slightly different color to each blade of grass just so that they'd show up in the figures.) We can apply some variation over the field to make each blade look slightly different. This is something that we'd probably want to have control over, so we use a texture to hold information about blades of grass.

You have an x and a z coordinate for each blade of grass that was calculated by generating a grid coordinate directly from `gl_InstanceID` and then generating a random number and displacing the blade within the x-z plane. That coordinate pair can be used as a coordinate to look up a texel within a 2D texture, and you can put whatever you want in it. Let's control the length of the grass using the texture. We can put a length parameter in the texture (let's use the red channel) and multiply the y coordinate of each vertex of the grass geometry by that to make longer or shorter grass. A value of zero in the texture would produce very short (or nonexistent) grass, and a value of one would produce grass of some maximum length. Now you can design a texture where each texel represents the length of the grass in a region of your field. Why not draw a few crop circles? The texture can be sampled with `GL_LINEAR` sampling, and you can even use mipmapping.

Now, the grass is evenly distributed over the field, and you have control of the length of the grass in different areas. However, the grass blades are still just scaled copies of each other. Perhaps we can introduce some more variation. Next, we rotate each blade of grass around its axis according to another parameter from the texture. We use the green channel of the texture to store the angle through which the grass blade should be rotated around the y-axis, with zero representing no rotation and one representing a full 360 degrees. We've still only done one texture fetch in our vertex shader, and still the only input to the shader is `gl_InstanceID`. Things are starting to come together. Take a look at Figure 12.5.

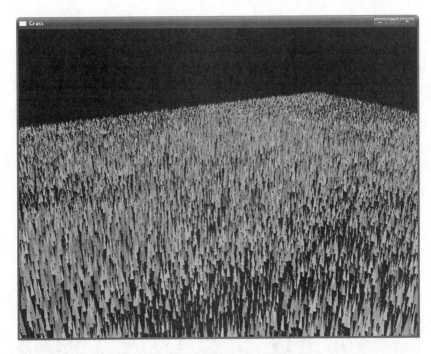

Figure 12.5   Control over the length and orientation of our grass.

Our field is still looking a little bland. The grass just sticks straight up and doesn't move. Real grass sways in the wind and gets flattened when things roll over it. We need the grass to bend, and we'd like to have control over that. Why not use another channel from the parameter texture (the blue channel) to control a bend factor? We can use that as another angle and rotate the grass around the x-axis before we apply the rotation in the green channel. This allows us to make the grass bend over based on the parameter in the texture. Use zero to represent no bending (the grass stands straight up) and one to represent fully flattened grass. Normally, the grass will sway gently, and so the parameter will have a low value. When the grass gets flattened, the value can be much higher.

Finally, we can control the color of the grass. It seems logical to just store the color of the grass in a large texture. This might be a good idea if you want to draw a sports field with lines, markings, or advertising on it for example, but it's fairly wasteful if the grass is all varying shades of green. Instead, let's make a palette for our grass in a 1D texture and use the final channel within our parameter texture (the alpha channel) to store the index into that palette. The palette can start with an anemic looking dead-grass yellow at one end and a lush, deep green at the other end. Now we read the alpha channel from the parameter texture along with all the other parameters and use it to index into the 1D texture—a dependent texture fetch. Our final field is shown in Figure 12.6. (See also Color Plate 21 in the color insert.)

FIGURE 12.6   The final field of grass.

Now, our final field has a million blades of grass, evenly distributed, with application control over length, "flatness," direction of bend, or sway and color. Remember, the only input to the shader that differentiates one blade of grass from another is `gl_InstanceID`, the total amount of geometry sent to OpenGL is six vertices, and the total amount of code required to draw all the grass in the field is a single call to `glDrawArraysInstanced`.

The parameter texture can be read using linear texturing to provide smooth transitions between regions of grass and can be a fairly low resolution. If you want to make your grass wave in the wind or get trampled as hoards of armies march across it, you can animate the texture by updating it every frame or two and uploading a new version of it before you render the grass. Also because the gl_InstanceID is used to generate random numbers, adding an offset to it before passing it to the random number generator allows a different but predetermined chunk of "random" grass to be generated with the same shader.

Getting Your Data Automatically

When you call glDrawArraysInstanced or glDrawElementsInstanced, the built-in variable gl_InstanceID will be available in your shaders to tell you which instance you're working on, and it will increment by one for each new instance of the geometry that you're rendering. It's actually available even when you're not using one of the instanced drawing functions—it'll just be zero in those cases. This means that you can use the same shaders for instanced and noninstanced rendering.

You can use gl_InstanceID to index into arrays that are the same length as the number of instances that you're rendering. For example, you can use it to look up texels in a texture or to index into a uniform array. Really, what you'd be doing though is treating the array as if it were an "instanced attribute." That is, a new value of the attribute is read for each instance you're rendering. OpenGL can feed this data to your shader automatically using a feature called *instanced arrays*. To use instanced arrays, declare an input to your shader as normal. The input attribute will have an index that you would use in calls to functions like glVertexAttribPointer. Normally, the vertex attributes would be read per vertex and a new value would be fed to the shader. However, to make OpenGL read attributes from the arrays once per instance, you can call

```
void glVertexAttribDivisor(GLuint index, GLuint divisor);
```

Pass the index of the attribute to the function in index and set divisor to the number of instances you'd like to pass between each new value being read from the array. If divisor is zero, then the array becomes a regular vertex attribute array with a new value read per vertex. If divisor is nonzero, however, then new data is read from the array once every few instances. For example, if you set divisor to one, you'll get a new value from the array for each instance. If you set divisor to two, you'll get a new value for every second instance, and so on. You can mix and match the divisors, setting different values for each attribute.

An example of using this functionality would be when you want to draw a set of objects with different colors. Consider the simple vertex shader in Listing 12.16.

LISTING 12.16   Simple Vertex Shader with Per-Vertex Color

```
#version 150

precision highp float;

in vec4 position;
```

```
in vec4 color;

out Fragment
{
    vec4 color;
} fragment;

uniform mat4 mvp;

void main(void)
{
    gl_Position = mvp * position;
    fragment.color = color;
}
```

Normally, the attribute `color` would be read once per vertex, and so every vertex would end up having a different color. The application would have to supply an array of colors with as many elements as there were vertices in the model. Also it wouldn't be possible for every instance of the object to have a different color because the shader doesn't know anything about instancing. We can make `color` an instanced array if we call

```
glVertexAttribDivisor(index_of_color, 1);
```

where `index_of_color` is the index of the slot to which the `color` attribute has been bound.

Now, a new value of `color` will be fetched from the vertex array *once per instance*. Every vertex within any particular instance will receive the same value for color, and the result will be that each instance of the object will be rendered in a different color. The size of the vertex array holding the data for `color` only needs to be as long as the number of indices we want to render. If we increase the value of the divisor, new data will be read from the array with less and less frequency. If the divisor is two, a new value of color will be presented every second instance; if the divisor is three, color will be updated every third instance; and so on.

If we render geometry using this simple shader, each instance will be drawn on top of the others. We need to modify the position of each instance so that we can see each one. We can use another instanced array for this. Listing 12.17 shows a simple modification to the vertex shader in Listing 12.16.

LISTING 12.17   Simple Instanced Vertex Shader

```
#version 150

precision highp float;

in vec4 position;
in vec4 instance_color;
in vec4 instance_position;

out Fragment
{
    vec4 color;
} fragment;

uniform mat4 mvp;

void main(void)
{
    gl_Position = mvp * (position + instance_position);
    fragment.color = instance_color;
}
```

Now, we have a per-instance position as well as a per-vertex position. We can add these together in the vertex shader before multiplying with the model-view-projection matrix. We can set the `instance_position` input attribute to an instanced array by calling

```
glVertexAttribDivisor(index_of_instance_position, 1);
```

Again, `index_of_instance_position` is the index of the location to which the `instance_position` attribute has been bound. Any type of input attribute can be made instanced using `glVertexAttribDivisor`. This example is simple and only uses a translation (the value held in `instance_position`). A more advanced application could use matrix vertex attributes or pack some transformation matrices into uniforms and pass matrix weights in instanced arrays. The application can use this to render an army of soldiers, each with a different pose, or a fleet of spaceships all flying in different directions.

Now let's hook this simple shader up to a real program. First, we load our shaders and set the attribute positions like normal before linking the program as shown in Listing 12.18.

LISTING 12.18 Setting Up Instanced Attributes

```
instancingProg = gltLoadShaderPair("instancing.vs", "instancing.fs");
glBindAttribLocation(instancingProg, 0, "position");
glBindAttribLocation(instancingProg, 1, "instance_color");
glBindAttribLocation(instancingProg, 2, "instance_position");
glLinkProgram(instancingProg);
```

In Listing 12.19, we declare some data and load it into a vertex buffer (attached to a vertex array object).

LISTING 12.19 Getting Ready for Instanced Rendering

```
static const GLfloat square_vertices[] =
{
    -1.0f, -1.0f, 0.0f, 1.0f,
     1.0f, -1.0f, 0.0f, 1.0f,
     1.0f,  1.0f, 0.0f, 1.0f,
    -1.0f,  1.0f, 0.0f, 1.0f
};

static const GLfloat instance_colors[] =
{
    1.0f, 0.0f, 0.0f, 1.0f,
    0.0f, 1.0f, 0.0f, 1.0f,
    0.0f, 0.0f, 1.0f, 1.0f,
    1.0f, 1.0f, 0.0f, 1.0f
};

static const GLfloat instance_positions[] =
{
    -2.0f, -2.0f, 0.0f, 0.0f,
     2.0f, -2.0f, 0.0f, 0.0f,
     2.0f,  2.0f, 0.0f, 0.0f,
    -2.0f,  2.0f, 0.0f, 0.0f
};

GLuint offset = 0;

glGenVertexArrays(1, &square_vao);
glGenBuffers(1, &square_vbo);
glBindVertexArray(square_vao);
glBindBuffer(GL_ARRAY_BUFFER, square_vbo);
glBufferData(GL_ARRAY_BUFFER,
```

```
                    sizeof(square_vertices) +
                    sizeof(instance_colors) +
                    sizeof(instance_positions), NULL, GL_STATIC_DRAW);
glBufferSubData(GL_ARRAY_BUFFER, offset,
                  sizeof(square_vertices),
                  square_vertices);
offset += sizeof(square_vertices);
glBufferSubData(GL_ARRAY_BUFFER, offset,
                  sizeof(instance_colors), instance_colors);
offset += sizeof(instance_colors);
glBufferSubData(GL_ARRAY_BUFFER, offset,
                  sizeof(instance_positions), instance_positions);
offset += sizeof(instance_positions);

glVertexAttribPointer(0, 4, GL_FLOAT, GL_FALSE, 0, 0);
glVertexAttribPointer(1, 4, GL_FLOAT, GL_FALSE, 0,
                        (GLvoid *)sizeof(square_vertices));
glVertexAttribPointer(2, 4, GL_FLOAT, GL_FALSE, 0,
                        (GLvoid *)(sizeof(square_vertices) +
                                    sizeof(instance_colors)));

glEnableVertexAttribArray(0);
glEnableVertexAttribArray(1);
glEnableVertexAttribArray(2);
```

Now all that remains is to set the vertex attrib divisors for the instance_color and
instance_position attribute arrays:

```
glVertexAttribDivisor(1, 1);
glVertexAttribDivisor(2, 1);
```

Now we draw four instances of the geometry we put into our vertex buffer. Each instance
consists of four vertices, each with its own position. The same vertex in each instance has
the same position. However, all of the vertices in a single instance see the same value of
instance_color and instance_position, and a new value of each is presented at each
instance. Our rendering loop looks like this:

```
glClearColor(0.0f, 0.0f, 0.0f, 0.0f);
glClear(GL_COLOR_BUFFER_BIT);

glUseProgram(instancingProg);
glBindVertexArray(square_vao);
glDrawArraysInstanced(GL_TRIANGLE_FAN, 0, 4, 4);
```

What we get is shown in Figure 12.7.

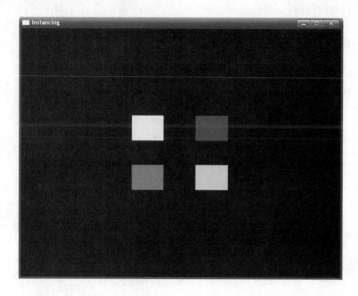

FIGURE 12.7   Result of instanced rendering.

In Figure 12.7, you can see that four squares have been rendered. Each is at a different position, and each has a different color. This can be extended to thousands or even millions of instances, and modern graphics hardware should be able to handle this without any issue.

Storing Transformed Vertices—Transform Feedback

In OpenGL, it is possible to save the results of the vertex or geometry shader into a buffer object. This is a feature known as *transform feedback*. When transform feedback is used, a specified set of attributes output from the vertex shader or geometry shader are written into a buffer. When no geometry shader is present (remember, geometry shaders are optional), the data comes from the vertex shader. When a geometry shader is present, the vertices generated by the geometry shader are recorded. The buffers used for capturing the output of vertex and geometry shaders are known as *transform feedback buffers*. Once data has been placed into a buffer using transform feedback, it can be read back using a function like `glGetBufferSubData` or by mapping it into the application's address space using `glMapBuffer` and reading from it directly. It can also be used as the source of data for subsequent drawing commands.

Transform Feedback

Transform feedback is a special mode of OpenGL that allows the results of a vertex or geometry shader to be saved into a buffer. Once the information is present in the buffer, it can be used as a source of vertex data for more drawing commands. Any attribute output from the vertex or geometry shader can be stored into the buffers. However, you can't simultaneously record the output of the vertex shader and the geometry shader. If a geometry shader is active, only the output of the geometry shader is accessible. If you need the raw data from the vertex shader, you need to pass it through the geometry shader unmodified. The position of transform feedback is illustrated in Figure 12.8.

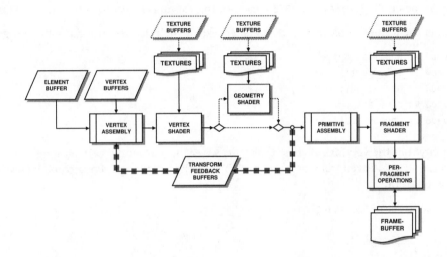

FIGURE 12.8   Schematic of the OpenGL pipeline, including transform feedback.

As you can see, transform feedback buffers sit between the output of the geometry shading and vertex assembly stages. As the geometry shader is an optional stage, if it is not present, the data actually comes from the vertex shader—this is denoted by dotted lines. Although the diagram shows transform feedback buffers feeding the vertex assembly stage, this is only to illustrate the feedback loop that is created (hence the term, transform *feedback*). While OpenGL will allow you to bind the same buffer as a transform feedback buffer and as a vertex buffer simultaneously, the results will not be defined if you do this, and you almost certainly won't get what you wanted.

The set of vertex attributes, or varyings, to be recorded during transform feedback mode is specified using

```
void glTransformFeedbackVaryings(GLuint program, GLsizei count, const GLchar **
varyings, GLenum bufferMode);
```

The first parameter to `glTransformFeedbackVaryings` is the name of a program object. The transform feedback varying state is maintained per program object. This means that different programs can record different sets of vertex attributes, even if the same vertex or geometry shaders are used in them. The second parameter is the number of varyings to record and is also the length of the array whose address is given in the third parameter. This third parameter is simply an array of C-style strings giving the names of the varyings to record. These are the names of the out variables in the vertex or geometry shader. Finally, the last parameter specifies the mode in which the varyings are to be recorded. This must be either `GL_SEPARATE_ATTRIBS` or `GL_INTERLEAVED_ATTRIBS`. If bufferMode is `GL_INTERLEAVED_ATTRIBS`, the varyings are recorded into a single buffer, one after another. If bufferMode is `GL_SEPARATE_ATTRIBS`, each of the varyings is recorded into its own buffer.

Consider the following piece of vertex shader code, which declares the output varyings:

```
out vec4 vs_position_out;
out vec4 vs_color_out;
out vec3 vs_normal_out;
out vec3 vs_binormal_out;
out vec3 vs_tangent_out;
```

To specify that the varyings vs_position_out, vs_color_out, and so on should be written into a single interleaved transform feedback buffer, the following C code could be used in your application:

```
static const char * varying_names[] =
{
    "vs_position_out",
    "vs_color_out",
    "vs_normal_out",
    "vs_binormal_out",
    "vs_tangent_out"
};
glTransformFeedbackVaryings(program, 5, varying_names,
                            GL_INTERLEAVED_ATTRIBS);
```

Not all of the outputs from your vertex (or geometry) shader need to be stored into the transform feedback buffer. It is possible to save a subset of the vertex shader outputs to the transform feedback buffer and send more to the fragment shader for interpolation. Likewise, it is also possible to save some outputs from the vertex shader into a transform feedback buffer that are not used by the fragment shader. Because of this, outputs from the vertex shader that may have been considered inactive (because they're not used by the fragment shader) may become active due to their being stored in a transform feedback buffer. Therefore, after specifying a new set of transform feedback varyings by calling `glTransformFeedbackVaryings`, it is necessary to link the program object using

```
glLinkProgram(program);
```

Once the transform feedback varyings have been specified and the program has been linked, it may be used as normal. Before actually capturing anything, you need to bind a buffer object as the transform feedback buffer. When you have specified the transform feedback mode as `GL_INTERLEAVED_ATTRIBS`, all of the stored vertex attributes are written one after another into a single buffer. To specify this buffer, call

```
glBindBuffer(GL_TRANSFORM_FEEDBACK_BUFFER, buffer);
```

Here, `GL_TRANSFORM_FEEDBACK_BUFFER` tells OpenGL that we want to bind a buffer to be used to store the results of the vertex or geometry shader to the `GL_TRANSFORM_FEEDBACK_BUFFER` binding point. The second parameter is the name of the buffer object that we previously created with a call to `glGenBuffers`.

Before any data can be written to a buffer, space must be allocated in the buffer for it. To allocate space without specifying data, call

```
glBufferData(GL_TRANSFORM_FEEDBACK_BUFFER, size, NULL, GL_DYNAMIC_COPY);
```

The first parameter is the buffer to allocate space for. You can use any buffer binding you like just for the purpose of binding a buffer and allocating space for it. However, OpenGL might make assumptions about what the buffer is going to be used for based on the first binding point it is bound to, and so, especially if this is a new buffer, the `GL_TRANSFORM_FEEDBACK_BUFFER` binding point is a good choice. The `size` parameter specifies how much space you want to allocate in bytes. This is up to your application's needs, but if, during transform feedback, too much data is generated to fit into the buffer, the excess will be thrown away. `NULL` tells OpenGL that no data is being given that you only want to allocate space for later. The last parameter, `usage`, gives OpenGL a hint as to what you plan to do with the buffer.

There are many possible values for `usage`, but `GL_DYNAMIC_COPY` is probably a good choice for a transform feedback buffer. The `DYNAMIC` part tells OpenGL that the data is likely to change often but will likely be used a few times between each update. The `COPY` part says that you plan to update the data in the buffer through OpenGL functionality (such as transform feedback) and then hand that data back to OpenGL for use in another operation (such as drawing). More information about buffer usage is available in Chapter 8, "Buffer Objects: Storage Is Now in Your Hands."

To specify which buffer the transform feedback data will be written to, you need to bind a buffer to one of the indexed transform feedback binding points. There are actually multiple `GL_TRANSFORM_FEEDBACK_BUFFER` binding points for this purpose, which are conceptually separate, but related to the general binding `GL_TRANSFORM_FEEDBACK_BUFFER` binding point. A schematic of this is shown in Figure 12.9.

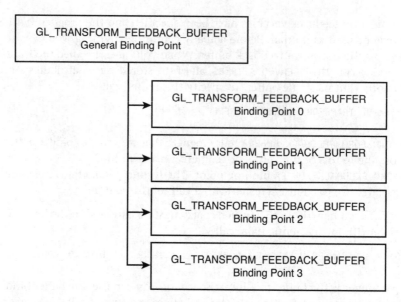

FIGURE 12.9   Relationship of transform feedback binding points.

To bind a buffer to any of the indexed binding points, call

```
glBindBufferBase(GL_TRANSFORM_FEEDBACK_BUFFER, index, buffer);
```

As before, `GL_TRANSFORM_FEEDBACK_BUFFER` tells OpenGL that we're binding a buffer object to store the results of transform feedback, and the last parameter, `buffer`, is the name of the buffer object we want to bind. The extra parameter, `index`, is the index of the `GL_TRANSFORM_FEEDBACK_BUFFER` binding point. An important thing to note is that there is no way to directly address any of the extra binding points provided by `glBindBufferBase` through functions like `glBufferData` or `glCopyBuffer`. However, when you call `glBindBufferBase`, it actually binds the buffer to the indexed binding point *and* to the generic binding point. Therefore, you can use the extra binding points to allocate space in the buffer if you access the general binding point right after calling `glBindBufferBase`.

A slightly more advanced version of `glBindBufferBase` is `glBindBufferRange`, whose prototype is

```
void glBindBufferRange(GLenum target, GLuint index, GLuint buffer, GLintptr offset,
GLsizeiptr size);
```

The `glBindBufferRange` function allows you to bind a *section* of a buffer to an indexed binding point, whereas `glBindBuffer` and `glBindBufferBase` can only bind the whole buffer at once. The first three parameters (`target`, `index`, and `buffer`) have the same meanings as in `glBindBufferBase`. The `offset` and `size` parameters are used to specify the start and length of the section of the buffer that you'd like to bind, respectively. You can bind different sections of the same buffer to several different indexed binding points simultaneously. This enables you to use transform feedback in GL_SEPARATE_ATTRIBS mode to write each attribute of the output vertices into separate sections of a single buffer. If your application packs all attributes into a single vertex buffer and uses glVertexAttribPointer to specify nonzero offsets into the buffer, this allows you to make the output of transform feedback match the input of your vertex shader.

If you specified that all of the attributes should be recorded into a single transform feed-back buffer by using the GL_INTERLEAVED_ATTRIBS parameter to glTransformFeedbackVaryings, the data will be written into the buffer bound to the first GL_TRANSFORM_FEEDBACK_BUFFER binding point (that with index zero). However, if you specified that the mode for transform feedback is GL_SEPARATE_ATTRIBS, each output from the vertex shader will be recorded into its own separate buffer (or section of a buffer, if you used glBindBufferRange). In this case, you need to bind multiple buffers or buffer sections as transform feedback buffers. The index parameter must be between zero and one less than the maximum number of varyings that can be recorded into separate buffers using transform feedback mode. This limit depends on your graphics hardware and drivers and can be found by calling glGetIntegerv with the GL_MAX_TRANSFORM_FEEDBACK_ SEPARATE_ATTRIBS parameter. This limit is also applied to the count parameter to glTransformFeedbackVaryings.

There is no upper limit on the number of separate varyings that can be written to trans-form feedback buffers in GL_INTERLEAVED_ATTRIBS mode, but there is a maximum number of *components* that can be written into a buffer. For example, it is possible to write more vec3s than vec4s into a buffer using transform feedback. Again, this limit depends on your graphics hardware and can be found using glGetIntegerv with the GL_MAX_ TRANSFORM_FEEDBACK_INTERLEAVED_COMPONENTS parameter.

It is not possible to write one set of output varyings interleaved into one buffer while writing another set of attributes into another buffer. When transform feedback is active, the output varyings are either all stored, interleaved into one buffer, or stored packed into several different buffers or sections of buffers. Therefore, if you plan to use transform feed-back to generate vertex data for subsequent passes, you need to consider this when you plan your input vertex layout. The vertex shader is generally a little more flexible in the way that it is able to read vertex data than in the way data can be written through trans-form feedback.

Once the buffers that are to receive the results of the transform feedback have been bound, transform feedback mode is activated by calling

```
void glBeginTransformFeedback(GLenum primitiveMode);
```

Now whenever vertices pass through a vertex or geometry shader, output varyings from the later shader will be written to the transform feedback buffers. The parameter to the function, primitiveMode, tells OpenGL what types of geometry to expect. The acceptable parameters are GL_POINTS, GL_LINES, or GL_TRIANGLES. When you call glDrawArrays or another OpenGL drawing function, the basic geometric type must match what you have specified as the transform feedback primitive mode, or you must have a geometry shader that outputs the appropriate primitive type. For example, if `primitiveMode` is `GL_TRIANGLES`, you must call `glDrawArrays` with `GL_TRIANGLES`, `GL_TRIANGLE_STRIP`, or `GL_TRIANGLE_FAN`, or you must have a geometry shader that produces `GL_TRIANGLE_STRIP` primitives. The mapping of transform feedback primitive mode to draw types is shown in Table 12.1.

TABLE 12.1   Values for primitiveMode

Value of PrimitiveMode	Allowed Draw Types
GL_POINTS	GL_POINTS
GL_LINES	GL_LINES, GL_LINE_STRIP, GL_LINE_LOOP
GL_TRIANGLES	GL_TRIANGLES, GL_TRIANGLE_STRIP, GL_TRIANGLE_FAN

Vertices are recorded into the transform feedback buffers until transform feedback mode is exited or until the space allocated for the transform feedback buffers is exhausted. To exit transform feedback mode, call

```
glEndTransformFeedback();
```

All rendering that occurs between a call to `glBeginTransformFeedback` and `glEndTransformFeedback` results in data being written into the currently bound transform feedback buffers. Each time `glBeginTransformFeedback` is called, OpenGL starts writing data at the beginning of the buffers bound for transform feedback, overwriting what might be there already. Some care should be taken while transform feedback is active as changing transform feedback state between calls to `glBeginTransformFeedback` and `glEndTransformFeedback` is not allowed. For example, it's not possible to change the transform feedback buffer bindings or to resize or reallocate any of the transform feedback buffers while transform feedback mode is active.

Turning Off Rasterization

So far, you have seen that transform feedback is a mechanism to save the intermediate results of vertex or geometry shaders *while* OpenGL is rendering. But, what if you don't want to actually draw anything? What if you only want to use transform feedback on its own without changing the contents of the screen? This is the kind of thing you may want to do if you're using the vertex shader for computation other than geometry processing (physical simulation, for example). It is possible to use transform feedback for this purpose by turning off rasterization. This means that the vertex and geometry shaders will still run so that transform feedback will work, but the OpenGL pipeline will be chopped off after that and the fragment shader will not run at all. This is therefore more efficient than simply making a fragment shader that discards everything, or turning off color writes with `glColorMask`, for example. To turn off rasterization, you actually need tell to OpenGL that it should discard all rasterization by calling

```
glEnable(GL_RASTERIZER_DISCARD);
```

To turn rasterization back on, simply call

```
glDisable(GL_RASTERIZER_DISCARD);
```

When GL_RASTERIZER_DISCARD is enabled, anything produced by the vertex or geometry shader (if present) does not create any fragments, and the fragment shader never runs. If you turn off rasterization and do not use transform feedback mode, the OpenGL pipeline is essentially turned off.

Counting Vertices Using Primitive Queries

When a vertex shader but no geometry shader is present, the output from the vertex shader is recorded, and the number of vertices stored into the transform feedback is the same as the number of vertices sent to OpenGL unless the available space in any of the transform feedback buffers is exhausted. If a geometry shader is present, that shader may create or discard vertices and so the number of vertices written to the transform feedback buffer may be different than the number of vertices sent to OpenGL. OpenGL can keep track of the number of vertices written to the transform feedback buffers through query objects. The application can then use this information to draw the resulting data or to know how much to read back from the transform feedback buffer, should it want to keep the data.

Query objects were introduced earlier in this chapter in the context of occlusion queries. It was stated that there are many questions that can be asked of OpenGL. Both the number of primitives generated and the number of primitives actually written to the transform feedback buffers are available as queries.

As before, to generate a query object, call

```
glGenQueries(1, &one_query);
```

or to generate a number of query objects, call

```
glGenQueries(10, ten_queries);
```

Now that you have created your query objects, you can ask OpenGL to start counting primitives as it produces them by beginning a GL_PRIMITIVES_GENERATED or GL_TRANSFORM_FEEDBACK_PRIMITIVES_WRITTEN query by beginning the query of the appropriate type. To start either query, call

```
glBeginQuery(GL_PRIMITIVES_GENERATED, one_query);
```

or

```
glBeginQuery(GL_TRANSFORM_FEEDBACK_PRIMITIVES_WRITTEN, one_query);
```

After a call to glBeginQuery with either GL_PRIMITIVES_GENERATED or GL_TRANSFORM_FEEDBACK_PRIMTIVES_WRITTEN, OpenGL keeps track of how many primitives were produced by the vertex or geometry shader, or how many were actually written into the transform feedback buffers until the query is ended using

```
glEndQuery(GL_PRIMITIVES_GENERATED);
```

or

```
glEndQuery(GL_TRANSFORM_FEEDBACK_PRIMITIVES_WRITTEN);
```

The results of the query can be read by calling glGetQueryObjectuiv with the GL_QUERY_RESULT parameter and the name of the query object. As with other OpenGL queries, the result might not be available immediately because of the pipelined nature of OpenGL. To find out if the results are available, call glGetQueryObjectuiv with the GL_QUERY_RESULT_AVAILABLE parameter. See the "Gathering Information about the OpenGL Pipeline—Queries" section earlier in this chapter for more information about query objects.

There are a couple of subtle differences between the GL_PRIMITIVES_GENERATED and GL_TRANSFORM_FEEDBACK_PRIMITIVES_WRITTEN queries. The first is that the GL_PRIMITIVES_GENERATED query counts the number of primitives emitted by the geometry shader, but the GL_TRANSFORM_FEEDBACK_PRIMITIVES_WRITTEN query only counts primitives that were successfully written into the transform feedback buffers. The primitive count generated by the geometry shader may be more or less than the number of primitives sent to OpenGL, depending on what it does. Normally, the results of these two queries would be the same, but if not enough space is available in the transform feedback buffers, GL_PRIMITIVES_GENERATED will keep counting, but GL_TRANSFORM_FEEDBACK_PRIMITIVES_WRITTEN will stop.

You can check whether all of the primitives produced by your application were captured into the transform feedback buffer by running one of each query simultaneously and comparing the results. If they are equal, then all the primitives were successfully written. If they differ, the buffers you used for transform feedback were probably too small.

The second difference is that GL_TRANSFORM_FEEDBACK_PRIMITIVES_WRITTEN is only meaningful when transform feedback is active. That is why it has TRANSFORM_FEEDBACK in its name but GL_PRIMITIVES_GENERATED does not. If you run a GL_TRANSFORM_FEEDBACK_PRIMITIVES_WRITTEN query when transform feedback is not active, the result will be zero. However, the GL_PRIMITIVES_GENERATED query can be used at any time and will produce a meaningful count of the number of primitives produced by OpenGL. You can use this to find out how many vertices your geometry shader produced or discarded.

Using the Results of a Primitive Query

Now you have the results of your vertex or geometry shader stored in a buffer. You also know how much data is in that buffer by using a query object. Now it's time to use those results in further rendering. Remember that the results of the vertex or geometry shader are placed into a buffer using transform feedback. The only thing making the buffer a transform feedback buffer is that it's bound to one of the GL_TRANSFORM_FEEDBACK_BUFFER binding points. However, buffers in OpenGL are generic chunks of data and can be used for other purposes.

Generally, after running a rendering pass that produces data into a transform feedback buffer, you bind the buffer object to the GL_ARRAY_BUFFER binding point so that it can be used as a vertex buffer. If you are using a geometry shader that might produce an unknown amount of data, you need to use a GL_TRANSFORM_FEEDBACK_PRIMITIVES_WRITTEN query to figure out how many vertices to render on the second pass. Listing 12.20 shows an example of what such code might look like.

LISTING 12.20   Drawing Data Written to a Transform Feedback Buffer

```
// We have two buffers, buffer1 and buffer2. First, we'll bind buffer1 as the
// source of data for the draw operation (GL_ARRAY_BUFFER), and buffer2 as
// the destination for transform feedback (GL_TRANSFORM_FEEDBACK_BUFFER).
glBindBuffer(GL_ARRAY_BUFFER, buffer1);
glBindBuffer(GL_TRANSFORM_FEEDBACK_BUFFFER, buffer2);
// Now, we need to start a query to count how many vertices get written to
// the transform feedback buffer
glBeginQuery(GL_TRANSFORM_FEEDBACK_PRIMITIVES_WRITTEN, q);
// Ok, start transform feedback...
glBeginTransformFeedback(GL_POINTS);
// Draw something to get data into the transform feedback buffer
DrawSomePoints();
// Done with transform feedback
glEndTransformFeedback();
// End the query and get the result back
glEndQuery(GL_TRANSFORM_FEEDBACK_PRIMITIVES_WRITTEN);
glGetQueryObjectuiv(q, GL_QUERY_RESULT, &vertices_to_render);
// Now we bind buffer2 (which has just been used as a transform
// feedback buffer) as a vertex buffer and render some more points
// from it.
glBindBuffer(GL_ARRAY_BUFFER, buffer2);
glDrawArrays(GL_POINTS, 0, vertices_to_render);
```

Example Uses for Transform Feedback

Here are a couple of examples of how you might use data stored in a transform feedback buffer. Remember, though, OpenGL is very flexible, and there are a myriad of other potential applications for transform feedback.

Storing Intermediate Results

The first example usage for transform feedback is the storage of intermediate results. You already read about instanced rendering. Consider an algorithm that performs a set of operations per instance and then requires the results of those operations per vertex. Now imagine that you want to render many copies of the object using instanced rendering. You could set up a vertex shader that uses as its input a few instanced arrays and a few regular, per-vertex attributes. All of those per-instance calculations would have to be performed for every copy of the object, even though they produce identical results each time.

Instead of writing one, large vertex shader that does all of the calculations in a single pass, it is possible to break this kind of algorithm into two passes. Write a first vertex shader that calculates the common per-instance results and writes them as a set of output varyings into a transform feedback buffer. This shader can now be run once, per instance. Next, write a second vertex shader that performs the rest of the calculations (those that will be different for each copy of the object) and combines them with the intermediate results from the first vertex shader by reading the per-instance attributes using an instanced array.

Now that you have your pair of shaders, you can run the first shader once for each instance (using a regular `glDrawArrays` command) and then use the second to actually render each copy of the object. The first shader (the per-instance one) should be run with rasterization off (using the `GL_RASTERIZER_DISCARD` enable discussed earlier). This produces the intermediate results in the transform feedback buffer without actually rendering anything. Now, turn rasterization back on and render all of the individual copies of the object using the second shader and a call to one of the instanced rendering functions such as `glDrawArarysInstanced`.

Iterative or Recursive Algorithms

Many algorithms are recursive, recirculating results from one step to another. Physical simulations are a prime example of this type of algorithm, and transform feedback is an ideal way to produce data that is reused in subsequent passes. Because transform feedback writes data into buffers in a format that allows those buffers to be subsequently bound as vertex buffers, no conversion or copying is required between passes over the data. All that is required is a simple double-buffering scheme.

A good example of a recirculating algorithm is a particle system simulation. At each step in the simulation, each particle has a position and a velocity that must be updated. It may also have some fixed parameters such as mass, color, or any number of other attributes. To produce a simple particle system using transform feedback, each particle can be represented as a vertex and its attributes stored in vertex buffers. A vertex shader can be constructed that calculates an updated position and velocity for the particles in the system. The particle parameters that don't change between iterations of the particle system can be stored in one vertex buffer, best allocated using the `GL_STATIC_DRAW` usage mode. The parameters that change between allocations should be double-buffered. One buffer is used as a vertex buffer and the source of parameters for rendering the particle system. The second buffer is bound as a transform feedback buffer and updated parameters written into it by the vertex shader. Between each iteration, the two buffers are swapped.

When the particle system is rendered, a time-step is passed to the vertex shader to indicate how much time has passed since the last update. The vertex shader calculates the approximate force on the particle due to its mass (gravity), input velocity (wind resistance), and any other factors important to the application; integrates the particle's velocity over the appropriate time-step; and produces a new position and velocity.

To simply render the particles as points, send the particles to OpenGL using a command such as `glDrawArrays` with `GL_POINTS` as the primitive type. You may want to only update the particle positions using transform feedback but draw something more complex at each particle (a ball, or spaceship, for example). You can do this by enabling `GL_RASTERIZER_DISCARD` to turn off rasterization during the update phase and then use the position data as an input to a second pass that turns the points into more complex sets of geometry for rendering on the screen.

An In-Depth Example of Transform Feedback—Flocking

Let's combine these two examples into one and create an implementation of a flocking algorithm. Flocking algorithms show emergent behavior within a large group by updating the properties of individual members independently of all others. This kind of behavior is regularly seen in nature, and examples are swarms of bees, flocks of birds, and schools of fish apparently moving in unison even though the members of the group don't communicate directly. The decisions made by an individual are based solely on its perception of the other members of the group. However, no collaboration is made between members over the outcome of any particular decision. This means that each group member's new properties can be calculated in parallel—ideal for a GPU implementation.

To demonstrate both of the ideas outlined previously (storing intermediate results and iterative algorithms), we implement the flocking algorithm with a pair of vertex shaders. We represent each member of the flock as a single vertex. Each vertex has a position and a velocity updated by the first vertex shader. The result is written to a buffer using transform feedback. That buffer is then bound as a vertex buffer and used as an instanced input to the second shader. Each member of the flock is an instance in the second draw. The second vertex shader is responsible for transforming a mesh (perhaps a model of a bird) into the position and orientation calculated in the first vertex shader. The algorithm then iterates, starting again with the first vertex shader, reusing the positions and velocities calculated in the previous pass. No data leaves the graphics card's memory, and the CPU is not involved in any calculations.

The data structures we need in this example are a set of VAOs to represent the vertex array state for each pass and a set of VBOs to hold the positions and velocities of the members within the flock and the vertex data for the model we use to represent them. The flock positions and velocities need to be double-buffered because we can't read and write the same buffer at the same time using transform feedback. Also because each member of the flock (vertex) needs to have access to the current position and velocity of all the other members of the flock, we bind the position and velocity buffers to a pair of texture buffer objects (TBOs) *simultaneously*. That way, the vertex shader can read arbitrarily from the TBO to access the properties of other vertices. TBOs were introduced in Chapter 8.

Figure 12.10 illustrates the passes that the algorithm makes.

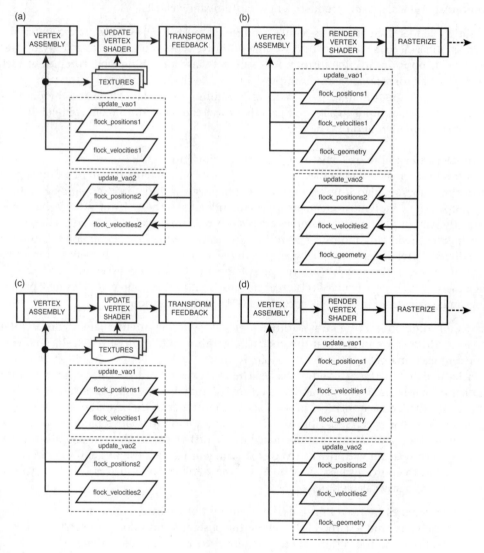

FIGURE 12.10   Stages in the iterative flocking algorithm.

In (a), we perform the update for an even frame. The first position and velocity buffers are bound as input to the vertex shader, and the second position and velocity buffers are bound as transform feedback buffers. Notice that we also use the first set of position and velocity buffers as backing for textures (actually TBOs) that are used by the vertex shader. Next we render, in (b), using the same set of buffers as inputs as in the update pass. We use the same buffers as input in both the update and render passes so that the render pass has no dependency on the update pass. That means that OpenGL may be able to start working on the render pass before the update pass has finished. The position and velocity buffers are now instanced, and the additional geometry buffer is used to provide vertex position data.

In (c), we move to the next frame. The buffers have been exchanged—the second set of buffers is now the input to the vertex shader, and the first set is written using transform feedback. Finally, in (d), we render the odd frames. The second set of buffers is used as input to the vertex shader. Notice, though, that the flock_geometry buffer is a member of both render_vao1 and render_vao2 because the same data is used in both passes, and so we don't need two copies of it.

The code to set all that up is shown in Listing 12.21. It isn't particularly complex, but there is a fair amount of repetition, making it long. The listing contains the bulk of the initialization, with some parts omitted for brevity (those parts are indicated by *** in the comments).

LISTING 12.21   Initializing Data Structures for the Flocking Example

```
// Create the four VAOs - update_vao1, update_vao2, render_vao1 and render
// vao2. Yes, we could use an array, but for the purposes of this example,
// this is more explicit
glGenVertexArrays(1, &update_vao1);
// *** Create update_vao2, render_vao1 and render_vao2 the same way

// Create the buffer objects. We'll bind and initialize them in a moment
glGenBuffers(1, &flock_positions1);
// *** Create flock_positions2, flock_velocities1, flock_velocities2 and
// flock_geometry the same way

// Set up the VAOs and buffers - first update_vao1
glBindVertexArray(update_vao1);
glBindBuffer(GL_ARRAY_BUFFER, flock_positions1);
// *** Put some initial positions in flock_positions1 here
glVertexAttribPointer(0, 3, GL_FLOAT, GL_FALSE, 0, NULL);
glEnableVertexAttribArray(0);
glBindBuffer(GL_ARRAY_BUFFER, flock_velocities1);
// *** Initialize flock_velocities1 with zeroes
```

```
//     (glBufferData(... NULL), glMapBuffer, memset, for example))
glVertexAttribPointer(1, 3, GL_FLOAT, GL_FALSE, 0, NULL);
glEnableVertexAttribArray(1);

// Next, update_vao2
// *** This is pretty much the same as update_vao1, except we don't need
// *** initial data for flock_positions2 or flock_velocities2 because
// *** they'll be written on the first pass. We do need to allocate them
// *** using glBufferData(... NULL), though

// Now the render VAOs - render_vao1 first
// We bind the same flock_positions1 and flock_positions2 buffers to this
// VAO, but this time they're instanced arrays. We also bind flock_geometry
// as a regular vertex array
glBindVertexArray(render_vao1);
glBindBuffer(GL_ARRAY_BUFFER, flock_positions1);
glVertexAttribPointer(0, 3, GL_FLOAT, GL_FALSE, 0, NULL);
glEnableVertexAttribArray(0);
glVertexAttribDivisor(0, 1);
glBindBuffer(GL_ARRAY_BUFFER, flock_velocities1);
glVertexAttribPointer(1, 3, GL_FLOAT, GL_FALSE, 0, NULL);
glEnableVertexAttribArray(1);
glVertexAttribDivisor(1, 1);
glBindBuffer(GL_ARRAY_BUFFER, flock_geometry);
glVertexAttribPointer(2, 3, GL_FLOAT, GL_FALSE, 0, NULL);
glEnableVertexAttribArray(2);

// Set up render_vao2
// *** This looks just like the setup for render_vao1, except we're using
// *** flock_positions2, and flock_velocities2. Note, though, that we'd
// *** still bind flock_geometry because that doesn't change from iteration
// *** to iteration.

// Finally, set up the TBOs
glGenTextures(1, &position_texture1);
glBindTexture(GL_TEXTURE_BUFFER, position_texture1);
glBindBuffer(GL_TEXTURE_BUFFER, flock_positions1);
// *** Create a buffer texture for each of flock_velocities1, flock_position2,
// *** and flock_velocities2 in the same way
```

Once we have our buffers set up, we need to compile our shaders and link them together in a program. Before the program is linked, we need to bind the attributes in the vertex shader to the appropriate locations so that they match the vertex arrays that we set up.

We also need to tell OpenGL which varyings we're planning on writing to the transform feedback buffers. Listing 12.22 shows how the vertex attributes and transform feedback varyings are initialized.

LISTING 12.22 Initializing Attributes and Transform Feedback for the Flocking Example

```
// *** Assume we've created our vertex and fragment shaders, compiled them
// *** and attached them to our program object.
// First, we'll set up the attributes in the update program
glBindAttribLocation(update_program, 0, "position");
glBindAttribLocation(update_program, 1, "velocity");
// Now the rendering program. The first two attributes are actually the
// same as those written by the update_program. The third is the position
// of the vertices in the geometry
glBindAttribLocation(render_program, 0, "instance_position");
glBindAttribLocation(render_program, 1, "instance_velocity");
glBindAttribLocation(render_program, 2, "geometry_position");
// Now we set up the transform feedback varyings:
static const char * tf_varyings[] = { "position_out", "velocity_out" };
glTransformFeedbackVaryings(update_program, 2, tf_varyings,
                            GL_SEPARATE_ATTRIBS);
// Now, everything's set up so we can go ahead and link our program objects
glLinkProgram(update_program);
glLinkProgram(render_program);
```

Now we need a rendering loop to update our flock positions and draw the members of the flock. It's actually pretty simple, now that we have our data encapsulated in VAOs. The rendering loop is shown in Listing 12.23.

LISTING 12.23 The Rendering Loop for the Flocking Example

```
// Make the update program current
glUseProgram(update_program);
// We use one set of buffers as shader inputs, and another as transform
// feedback buffers to hold the shader outputs. On alternating frames,
// we'll swap the two around
if (frame_index & 1)  {
    glBindBufferBase(GL_TRANSFORM_FEEDBACK_BUFFER, 0, position_buffer1);
    glBindBufferBase(GL_TRANSFORM_FEEDBACK_BUFFER, 1, velocity_buffer1);
    glBindVertexArray(update_vao2);
    glActiveTexture(GL_TEXTURE0);
    glBindTexture(GL_TEXTURE_BUFFER, position_texture2);
    glActiveTexture(GL_TEXTURE1);
    glBindTexture(GL_TEXTURE_BUFFER, velocity_texture2);
```

```
    } else {
        // *** This is the same again, only using position_buffer2, and velocity
        // *** buffer2 as transform feedback buffers, and update_vao1, position
        // *** texture1 and velocity_texture1 as shader inputs
    }
    // Turn off rasterization (enable rasterizer discard)
    glEnable(GL_RASTERIZER_DISCARD);
    // Start transform feedback - record updated positions
    glBeginTransformFeedback(GL_POINTS);
    // Draw arrays - one point for each member of the flock
    glDrawArrays(GL_POINTS, 0, flock_size);
    // Done with transform feedback
    glEndTransformFeedback(GL_POINTS);
    // Ok, now we'll draw everything. Need to turn rasterization back on.
    glDisable(GL_RASTERIZER_DISCARD);
    // Use the rendering program
    glUseProgram(render_program);
    if (frame_index & 1) {
        glBindVertexArray(render_vao2);
    } else {
        glBindVertexArray(render_vao1);
    }
    // Do an instanced draw - each member is an instance. The data updated
    // by the 'update_program' on the last frame is now an instanced array
    // in the render_program
    glDrawArraysInstanced(GL_TRIANGLES, 0, 50, flock_size);
    frame_index++;
```

That's pretty much the interesting part of the program side. Let's take a look at the shader side of things. The flocking algorithm works by applying a set of rules for each member of the flock to decide which direction to travel in. Each rule considers the current properties of the flock member and the properties of the other members of the flock as perceived by the individual being updated. Most of the rules require access to the other member's position and velocity data, so update_program uses a pair of TBOs to read from the buffers containing that information. Listing 12.24 shows the start of the update vertex shader.

LISTING 12.24   Initializing Attributes and Transform Feedback for the Flocking Example

```
#version 150

precision highp float;

// These are the input attributes
```

```
in vec3 position;
in vec3 velocity;

// These get written to transform feedback buffers
out vec3 position_out;
out vec3 velocity_out;

// These are the TBOs that are mapped to the same buffers as position
// and velocity
uniform samplerBuffer tex_position;
uniform samplerBuffer tex_velocity;

// The number of members in the flock
uniform int flock_size;

// Parameters for the simulation
uniform Parameters
{
    // *** Put all the simulation parameters here
};
```

The main body of the program is simple. We simply read the position and velocity of the other members of the flock, apply each rule in turn, sum up the resulting vector, and output an updated position and velocity. Code to do this is given in Listing 12.25.

LISTING 12.25   Main Body of the Flocking Update Vertex Shader

```
void main(void)
{
    vec3 other_position;
    vec3 other_velocity;
    vec3 accelleration = vec3(0.0);
    int i;

    for (i = 0; i < flock_size; i++) {
        other_position = texelFetch(tex_position, i).xyz;
        other_velocity = texelFetch(tex_velocity, i).xyz;
        accelleraton += rule1(position, velocity,
                              other_position, other_velocity);
        accelleraton += rule2(position, velocity,
                              other_position, other_velocity);
        // *** And so on... we can apply as many rules as we want.
        // *** Three or four is is enough to produce a convincing
```

```
    // *** simulation
  }

  position_out = position + velocity;
  velocity_out = velocity + acceleration / float(flock_size);
}
```

Now we have to define our rules. The rules we use are as follows:

- Members try not to hit each other. They need to stay at least a short distance from each other.

- Members try to fly in the same direction as those around them.

- Members try to keep with the rest of the flock. They will fly toward the center of the flock.

Listing 12.26 contains the shader code for the first rule. If we're closer to another member than we're supposed to be, we simply move away from that member:

LISTING 12.26   The First Rule of Flocking

```
vec3 rule1(vec3 my_position, vec3 my_velocity,
        vec3 their_position, vec3 their_velocity)
{
    vec3 d = my_position - their_position;
    if (dot(d, d) < parameters.closest_allowed_position)
        return d * parameters.rule1_weight;
    return vec3(0.0);
}
```

Here's the shader code for the second rule (see Listing 12.27). It returns a change in velocity weighted by the inverse square of the distance from to other member.

LISTING 12.27   The Second Rule of Flocking

```
vec3 rule2(vec3 my_position, vec3 my_velocity,
        vec3 their_position, vec3 their_velocity)
{
    vec3 dv = (their_velocity - my_velocity);
    return parameters.rule2_weight *
        dv / (dot(my_position, their_position) + 1.0);
}
```

Putting all this together along with any other rules we want to implement completes the update part of the program. Now we need to produce the second vertex shader—the one responsible for rendering the flock. This uses the position and velocity data as instanced arrays and transforms a fixed set of vertices into position based on the position and velocity of the individual member. Listing 12.28 shows the inputs to the shader.

LISTING 12.28   Declarations of Inputs to the Flocking Rendering Vertex Shader

```
#version 150

precision highp float;

// These are the instanced arrays
in vec3 instance_position;
in vec3 instance_velocity;

// The regular geometry array
in vec3 position;
```

The body of our shader (given in Listing 12.29) simply transforms the mesh represented by position into the correct orientation and location for the particular instance.

LISTING 12.29   Flocking Vertex Shader Body

```
void main(void)
{
    // rotate_to_match is a function that rotates a point
    // (position) around the origin to match a direction vector
    // (instance_velocity)
    vec3 local_position = rotate_to_match(position, instance_velocity);
    gl_Position = mvp * vec4(instance_position + local_position, 1.0);
}
```

That's it! We're not going to cover rotate_to_match here; it's beyond the scope of this example. You can find a complete implementation, along with the rest of the code for this example on the book's Web site. Of course, the final rendering vertex shader may need to be more complex if you want to render something more interesting than plain, white blobs. It also needs to include some additional logic to try to keep the flock members upright (and to stop them from spinning around their axes). Also, we're not covering the fragment shader here because it's not related to either instancing or transform feedback.

Clipping and Determining What Should Be Drawn

When you send geometry to OpenGL, it is transformed by your vertex and geometry shaders from the incoming (object) coordinate space into the clip coordinate space. This is where OpenGL performs clipping to determine which vertices lie within the viewport and which lie outside the viewport.

To do this, OpenGL divides 3D space into six half spaces defined by the bounds of the clipping volume. The half spaces are defined by what are known as the left, right, top, bottom, near, and far clip planes. As each vertex passes through the clipping stage, OpenGL calculates a signed distance of that vertex to each of the planes. The absolute value of the distance is not important—only its sign. If the signed distance to the plane is positive, the vertex lies on the inside of the plane (the side that would be visible if you were to stand in the middle of the view volume and look toward the plane). If the distance is negative, the vertex lies on the outside of the plane. If the distance value is exactly zero, then the vertex lies exactly on the plane. Now, OpenGL can tell very quickly whether a vertex lies inside or outside the view volume by simply examining the signs of the six distances to the six planes and by combining the results from several vertices can determine whether larger chunks of geometry are visible.

If all of the vertices of a single triangle lie on the outside of any single plane—that is, the distance from all of the triangle's vertices to the same plane are negative—then that triangle is known to be entirely outside the view volume and can be trivially discarded. Similarly, if none of the distances from any of a triangle's vertices to any plane is negative, then the triangle is entirely contained within the view volume and is therefore visible. Only when a triangle straddles one of the planes does further work need to be done. This case means that the triangle will be partially visible. Different implementations of OpenGL handle these cases in different ways. Some may break the triangle down into several smaller triangles using a clipping algorithm such as Sutherland-Hodgman. Others may simply rasterize the whole triangle and use brute force to discard fragments that end up outside the viewport.

These six planes make up an oblong shape in clip space, which appears as a box in the greater 3D space. When this is transformed to window coordinates, it may undergo a perspective transformation and become a frustum. This is what is referred to as the *view frustum*.

Clip Distances—Defining Your Own Custom Clip Space

In addition to the six distances to the six standard clip planes making up the view frustum, a set of additional distances is available to the application that can be written inside the vertex or geometry shader. The clip distances are available for writing in the vertex shader through the built-in variable `gl_ClipDistance[]`, which is an array of floating-point values. The number of clip distances supported depends on your implementation of OpenGL. These distances are interpreted exactly as the built-in clip distances. If a shader writer wants to use user-defined clip distances, they should be enabled by the application by calling

```
glEnable(GL_CLIP_DISTANCE0 + n);
```

Here, n is the index of the clip distance to enable. The tokens `GL_CLIP_DISTANCES1`, `GL_CLIP_DISTANCES2`, and so on up to `GL_CLIP_DISTANCES5` are usually defined in standard OpenGL header files. However, the maximum value of n is implementation defined and can be found by calling `glGetIntegerv` with the token `GL_MAX_CLIP_DISTANCES`. You can disable the user-defined clip distance by calling `glDisable` with the same token. If the user-defined clip distance at a particular index is not enabled, the value written to `gl_Clip_Distance[]` at that index is ignored.

As with the built-in clipping planes, the sign of the distance written into the `gl_Clip_Distance[]` array is used to determine whether a vertex is inside or outside the user-defined clipping volume. If the signs of all the distances for every vertex of a single triangle are negative, the triangle is clipped. If it is determined that the triangle may be partially visible, then the clip distances are linearly interpolated across the triangle and the visibility determination is made at each pixel. Thus, the rendered result will be a linear approximation to the per-vertex distance function evaluated by the vertex shader. This allows a vertex shader to clip geometry against an arbitrary set of planes (the distance of a point to a plane can be found with a simple dot product).

The `gl_Clip_Distance[]` array is also available as an input to the fragment shader. Fragments that would have a negative value in any element of `gl_Clip_Distance[]` are clipped away and never reach the fragment shader. However, any fragment that only has positive values in `gl_Clip_Distance[]` passes through the fragment shader, and this value can then be read and used by the shader for any purpose. One example use of this functionality is to fade the fragment by reducing its alpha value based as its clip distance approaches zero. This allows a large primitive clipped against a plane by the vertex shader to fade smoothly or be antialiased by the fragment shader, rather than generating a hard clipped edge.

It is important to note that if all of the vertices making up a single primitive (point, line, or triangle) are clipped against the same plane, then the whole primitive is eliminated. This seems to make sense and behaves as expected for regular polygon meshes. However, when using points and lines, you need to be careful. With points, you can render a point with a single vertex that covers multiple pixels by setting the `gl_PointSize` parameter to a value greater than 1.0. When `gl_PointSize` is large, a big point is rendered around the vertex. This means that if you have a large point that is moving slowly toward and eventually off the edge of the screen, it will suddenly disappear when the center of the point exits the view volume and the vertex representing that point is clipped. Likewise, OpenGL can render wide lines. If a line is drawn whose vertices are both outside one of the clipping planes but would otherwise be visible, nothing will be drawn. This can produce strange popping artifacts if you're not careful.

The left, right, top, and bottom planes all correspond to real-world things—the limits of your field of view. In reality, your field of view isn't a perfect rectangle. It's more of an oval shape with fuzzy edges. In practice, though, a hard limit is defined by the bounds of the viewport—the edges of your monitor, for example. Likewise, the near plane roughly corresponds to your own eye plane. Anything behind the near plane is really behind you, and thus you shouldn't be able to see it, but there isn't really anything directly equivalent to it in the real world. What about the far plane? There just is no real-world equivalent to the far plane at all. Light travels an infinite distance unless it hits something. You can see the stars in the sky just as clearly as this book. So why do we need a far plane at all?

OpenGL represents the depth of each fragment as a finite number, scaled between zero and one. A fragment with a depth of zero is intersecting the near plane (and would be jabbing you in the eye if it were real), and a fragment with a depth of one is at the farthest representable depth but not infinitely far away. To eliminate the far plane and draw things at any arbitrary distance, we would need to store arbitrarily large numbers in the depth buffer—something that's not really possible. To get around this, OpenGL has the option to turn off clipping against the near and far planes and instead clamp the generated depth values to the range zero to one. This means that any geometry that protrudes behind the near plane or past the far plane will essentially be projected onto that plane.

To enable depth clamping (and simultaneously turn off clipping against the near and far planes), call

```
glEnable(GL_DEPTH_CLAMP);
```

and to disable depth clamping, call

```
glDisable(GL_DEPTH_CLAMP);
```

Of course, this only affects OpenGL's built-in near and far plane clipping calculations. You can still use a user-defined clip distance in your vertex shader to simulate a depth plane that would actually have a depth value greater than one if you need to.

Figure 12.11 illustrates the effect of enabling depth clamping and drawing a primitive that intersects the near plane.

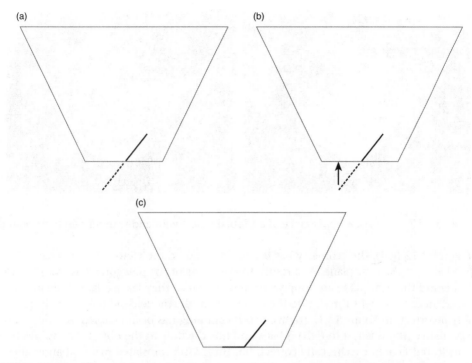

FIGURE 12.11   Effect of depth clamping on a primitive that intersects the near plane.

It is simpler to demonstrate this in two dimensions, so in Figure 12.11 (a), a the view frustum is displayed as if we are looking straight down on it. The dark line represents the primitive that would have been clipped against the near plane, and the dotted line represents the portion of the primitive that was clipped away. When depth clamping is enabled, rather than clipping the primitive, the depth values that would have been generated outside the range zero to one are clamped into that range, effectively projecting the primitive onto the near plane (or the far plane, if the primitive would have clipped that). Figure 12.11 (b) shows this projection. What actually gets rendered is shown in Figure 12.11 (c). The dark line represents the values that eventually get written into the depth buffer. Figure 12.12 shows how this translates to a real application.

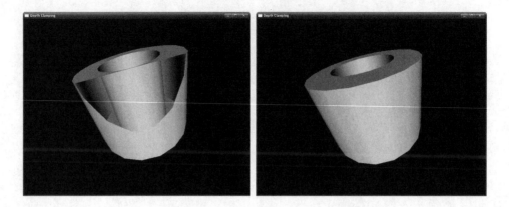

FIGURE 12.12   The visual appearance of a clipped object with and without depth clamping.

In Figure 12.12 (left), the geometry has become so close to the viewer that it is partially clipped against the near plane. As a result, the portions of the polygons that would have been behind the near plane are simply not drawn, and so they leave a large hole in the model. You can see right through to the other side of the model, and the image is quite visibly incorrect. In Figure 12.12 (right), depth clamping has been enabled. As you can see, the geometry that was lost in (left) is back and fills the hole in the object. The values in the depth buffer aren't technically correct, but this hasn't translated to visual anomalies, and the produced picture looks better than that in (left).

Synchronizing When OpenGL Begins to Draw

In an advanced application, OpenGL's order of operation and the pipeline nature of the system may be important. Examples of such applications are those with multiple contexts and multiple threads, or those sharing data between OpenGL and other APIs such as OpenCL. In some cases, it may be necessary to determine whether commands sent to OpenGL have finished yet and whether the results of those commands are ready. OpenGL includes two commands to force it to start working on commands or to finish working on commands that have been issued so far. These are

```
glFlush();
```

and

```
glFinish();
```

There are subtle differences between the two. The first, `glFlush`, ensures that any commands issued so far are at least placed into the start of the OpenGL pipeline and that they will eventually be executed. `glFinish`, on the other hand actually ensures that all commands issued have been fully executed and that the OpenGL pipeline is empty. The problem is that `glFlush` doesn't tell you anything about the execution status of the commands issued—only that they will eventually be executed, and while `glFinish` does ensure that all of your OpenGL commands have been processed, it will empty the OpenGL pipeline, causing a *bubble* and reducing performance, sometimes drastically.

Sometimes it may be necessary to know whether OpenGL has finished executing commands *up to some point*. This is especially useful when you are sharing data between two contexts or between OpenGL and OpenCL, for example. This type of synchronization is managed by what are known as *sync objects*. Like any other OpenGL object, they must be created before they are used and destroyed when they are no longer needed. Sync objects have two possible states: *signaled* and *unsignaled*. They start out in the unsignaled state, and when some particular event occurs, they move to the signaled state. The event that triggers their transition from unsignaled to signaled depends on their type. The type of sync object we are interested in is called a fence sync, and one can be created by calling

```
GLsync glFenceSync(GL_SYNC_GPU_COMMANDS_COMPLETE, 0);
```

The first parameter is a token specifying the event we're going to wait for. In this case, `GL_SYNC_GPU_COMMANDS_COMPLETE` says that we want the GPU to have processed all commands in the pipeline before setting the state of the sync object to signaled. The second parameter is a flags field and is zero here because no flags are relevant for this type of sync object. The `glFenceSync` function returns a new `GLsync` object. As soon as the fence sync is created, it enters (in the unsignaled state) the OpenGL pipeline and is processed along with all the other commands without stalling OpenGL or consuming significant resources. When it reaches the end of the pipeline, it is "executed" like any other command, and this sets its state to signaled. Because of the in-order nature of OpenGL, this tells us that any OpenGL commands issued before the call to `glFenceSync` have completed, even though commands issued after the `glFenceSync` may not have reached the end of the pipeline yet.

Once the sync object has been created (and has therefore entered the OpenGL pipeline), we can query its state to find out if it's reached the end of the pipeline yet, and we can ask OpenGL to wait for it to become signaled before returning to the application.

To determine whether the sync object has become signaled yet, call

```
glGetSynciv(sync, GL_SYNC_STATUS, sizeof(GLint), NULL, &result);
```

When `glGetSynciv` returns, `result` (which is a `GLint`) will contain `GL_SIGNALED` if the sync object was in the signaled state and `GL_UNSIGNALED` otherwise. This allows the application to poll the state of the sync object and use this information to potentially do some useful work while the GPU is busy with previous commands. For example, consider the code in Listing 12.30.

LISTING 12.30   Working While Waiting for a Sync Object

```
GLint result = GL_UNSIGNALED;
glGetSynciv(sync, GL_SYNC_STATUS, sizeof(GLint), NULL, &result);
while (result != GL_SIGNALED) {
    DoSomeUsefulWork();
    glGetSynciv(sync, GL_SYNC_STATUS, sizeof(GLint), NULL, &result);
}
```

This code loops, doing a small amount of useful work on each iteration until the sync object becomes signaled. If the application were to create a sync object at the start of each frame, the application could wait for the sync object from two frames ago and do a variable amount of work depending on how long it takes the GPU to process the commands for that frame. This allows an application to balance the amount of work done by the CPU (such as the number of sound effects to mix together or the number of iterations of a physics simulation to run, for example) with the speed of the GPU.

To actually cause OpenGL to wait for a sync object to become signaled (and therefore, for the commands in the pipeline before the sync to complete), there are two functions that you can use:

```
glClientWaitSync(sync, GL_SYNC_FLUSH_COMMANDS_BIT, timeout);
```

or

```
glWaitSync(sync, 0, GL_TIMEOUT_IGNORED);
```

The first parameter to both functions is the name of the sync object that was returned by glFenceSync. The second and third parameters to the two functions have the same names but must be set differently.

For glClientWaitSync, the second parameter is a bitfield specifying additional behavior of the function. The GL_SYNC_FLUSH_COMMANDS_BIT tells glClientWaitSync to ensure that the sync object has entered the OpenGL pipeline before beginning to wait for it to become signaled. Without this bit, there is a possibility that OpenGL could watch for a sync object that hasn't been sent down the pipeline yet, and the application could end up waiting forever and hang. It's a good idea to set this bit unless you have a really good reason not to. The third parameter is a timeout value in nanoseconds to wait. If the sync object doesn't become signaled within this time, glClientWaitSync returns a status code to indicate so. glClientWaitSync won't return until either the sync object becomes signaled or a timeout occurs.

There are four possible status codes that might be returned by glClientWaitSync. They are summarized in Table 12.2.

TABLE 12.2   Possible Return Values for glClientWaitSync

Status Returned by glClientWaitSync	Meaning
GL_ALREADY_SIGNALED	The sync object was already signaled when `glClientWaitSync` was called and so the function returned immediately.
GL_TIMEOUT_EXPIRED	The timeout specified in the timeout parameter expired, meaning that the sync object never became signaled in the allowed time.
GL_CONDITION_SATISFIED	The sync object became signaled within the allowed timeout period (but was not already signaled when `glClientWaitSync` was called).
GL_WAIT_FAILED	An error occurred (such as sync not being a valid sync object), and the user should check the result of `glGetError()` to get more information.

There are a couple of things to note about the timeout value. First, while the unit of measurement is nanoseconds, there is no accuracy requirement in OpenGL. If you specify that you want to wait for one nanosecond, OpenGL could round this up to the next millisecond or more. Second, if you specify a timeout value of zero, `glClientWaitSync` will return GL_ALREADY_SIGNALED if the sync object was in a signaled state at the time of the call and GL_TIMEOUT_EXPIRED otherwise. It will never return GL_CONDITION_SATISFIED.

For `glWaitSync`, the behavior is slightly different. The application won't actually wait for the sync object to become signaled, only the GPU will. Therefore, `glWaitSync` will return to the application immediately. This makes the second and third parameters somewhat irrelevant. Because the application doesn't wait for the function to return, there is no danger of hanging, and so the GL_SYNC_FLUSH_COMMANDS_BIT is not needed and would actually cause an error if specified. Also, the timeout will actually be implementation dependent and so the special timeout value GL_TIMEOUT_IGNORED is specified to make this clear. If you're interested, you can find out what the timeout value used by your implementation is by calling `glGetInteger64v` with the GL_MAX_SERVER_WAIT_TIMEOUT parameter.

You might be wondering, "What is the point of asking the GPU to wait for a sync object to reach the end of the pipeline?" After all, the sync object will become signaled when it reaches the end of the pipeline, and so if you wait for it to reach the end of the pipeline, it will of course be signaled. Therefore, won't `glWaitSync` just do nothing? This would be true if we only considered simple applications that only use a single OpenGL context and that don't use other APIs. However, the power of sync objects is harnessed when using multiple OpenGL contexts. Sync objects can be shared between OpenGL contexts and between compatible APIs such as OpenCL. That is, a sync object created by a call to `glFenceSync` on one context can be waited for by a call to `glWaitSync` (or `glClientWaitSync`) on another context.

Consider this. You can ask one OpenGL context to hold off rendering something until another context has finished doing something. This allows synchronization between two contexts. You can have an application with two threads and two contexts (or more, if you want). If you create a sync object in each context, and then in each context you wait for the sync objects from the other contexts using either `glClientWaitSync`, you know that when all of the functions have returned, all of those contexts are synchronized with each other. Together with thread synchronization primitives provided by your OS (such as semaphores), you can keep rendering to multiple windows in sync.

An example of this type of usage is when a buffer is shared between two contexts. The first context is writing to the buffer using transform feedback, while the second context wants to draw the results of the transform feedback. The first context would draw using transform feedback mode. After calling `glEndTransformFeedback`, it immediately calls `glFenceSync`. Now, the application makes the second context current and calls `glWaitSync` to wait for the sync object to become signaled. It can then issue more commands to OpenGL (on the new context), and those are queued up by the drivers, ready to execute. Only when the GPU has finished recording data into the transform feedback buffers with the first context does it start to work on the commands using that data in the second context.

There are also extensions and other functionality in APIs like OpenCL that allow asynchronous writes to buffers. You can use `glWaitSync` to ask a GPU to wait until the data in a buffer is valid by creating a sync object on the context that generates the data and then waiting for that sync object to become signaled on the context that's going to consume the data.

Sync objects only ever go from the unsignaled to the signaled state. There is no mechanism to put a sync object back into the unsignaled state, even manually. This is because a manual flip of a sync object can cause race conditions and possibly hang the application. Consider the situation where a sync object is created, reaches the end of the pipeline and becomes signaled, and then the application set it back to unsignaled. If another thread tried to wait for that sync object but didn't start waiting until after the application had already set the sync object back to the unsignaled state, it would wait forever. Each sync object therefore represents a one-shot event, and every time a synchronization is required, a new sync object must be created by calling `glFenceSync`. Although it is always important to clean up after yourself by deleting objects when you're done with them, this is particularly important with sync objects because you might be creating many new ones every frame. To delete a sync object, call

```
glDeleteSync(sync);
```

This deletes the sync object. This may not occur immediately; any thread that is watching for the sync object to become signaled will still wait for its respective timeouts, and the object will actually be deleted once nobody's watching it any more. Thus, it is perfectly legal to call `glWaitSync` followed by `glDeleteSync` even though the sync object is still in the OpenGL pipeline.

Summary

In this chapter, you learned how to manage large amounts of vertex and other data, control how OpenGL accesses that data, and get information about what OpenGL did with it. You saw how to store the data produced by one pass of your algorithm and reuse it in another pass. You have the tools to synchronize multiple contexts so that data produced by one can be consumed by another. You read about methods of drawing many copies of a single set of geometry, and you learned how to provide data to OpenGL to use on each of those copies. You also know how to time the operation of the OpenGL pipeline, allowing you to make informed decisions about the rendering your application does to improve performance.

PART III
Platform-Specific Notes

Now, about that word "portable." Although OpenGL itself remains purely a platform-independent abstraction of graphics hardware, there is always the need to interface OpenGL with native operating systems and windowing systems. On each platform, there are families of nonportable binding functions that glue OpenGL to the native window or display system. In addition, there are always platform-specific notes and characteristics that these implementations have. This part of the book is about those interfaces and characteristics.

The four most popular platforms for OpenGL today are undoubtedly Windows, Mac OS X, UNIX, and the myriad of handheld systems utilizing a subset of OpenGL called OpenGL ES. In this part you find specific chapters that take you through the peculiarities and strengths of using OpenGL on these platforms. OpenGL is by far the most popular 3D graphics API today, used in nearly every application category, on nearly every platform where 3D hardware can be found.

OpenGL. It's everywhere. Do the math.

CHAPTER 13

OpenGL on Windows

by Nicholas Haemel

WHAT YOU'LL LEARN IN THIS CHAPTER

How To	Functions You'll Use
Request and select an OpenGL pixel format	`wglChoosePixelFormatARB/` `SetPixelFormat`
Create and use OpenGL rendering contexts	`wglCreateContextAttribsARB/` `wglDeleteContext/` `wglMakeCurrent`
Use double buffering in Windows	`SwapBuffers`

As you have seen, OpenGL is a powerful API. Its low-level nature leaves all of the control in the hands of application developers. Additionally, the core OpenGL code is portable across many different platforms and operating systems. Because every operating system has a different means of window management, each operating system has a different layer to help applications interface with OpenGL. This helps the driver implementation understand what types of buffers, color formats, and other characteristics should be used for any specific instance.

On Microsoft Windows desktop operating systems (netbooks, laptops, desktops, servers, and so on) a set of functions specifically tied to the Windows API is used, called WGL (Windows-GL). WGL functions have the prefix wgl in front of functions symbolizing that these functions are for interfaces between Windows and OpenGL. They are also sometimes referred to as *wiggle* functions because of their prefix. From here on in we use real wgl functions to directly interface with Windows and the OpenGL drivers instead of using the GLUT library. GLUT is great for getting simple apps up and running but comes at the cost of reduced control and flexibility.

In this chapter you learn how to use wgl to probe a system's capabilities, create and manage windows, as well as handle applicable system messages. The concepts of this chapter are introduced gradually, as we build a model OpenGL program that provides a framework for Windows-specific OpenGL support. Up until now this book has not required prior knowledge or experience with 3D graphics or OpenGL. But for this chapter we assume you have at least an entry-level knowledge of Windows programming. Otherwise, we would have wound up writing a book twice the size of this one. We would have spent more time on the details of writing programs for Windows and less on OpenGL programming. Many good books and resources exist that explain the details of writing Windows applications.

OpenGL Implementations on Windows

OpenGL first became natively available for the Win32 platform with the release of Windows NT version 3.5. Later, it was released as an add-on for Windows 95 and then began shipping as part of the Windows 95 operating system with the OSR2 release. OpenGL is now a native API on any full Windows platform (Windows XP, Vista, Win 7, Server 2003, Server 2008, and so on), with its functions exported through the opengl32.dll library. Many different levels of OpenGL hardware are available for Windows platforms, from chipsets with part of OpenGL done in software, to entry level video cards, to screaming fast workstation class cards. You should be aware that your application may be running on any one of these platforms.

Microsoft's OpenGL

Microsoft currently ships a generic software implementation of OpenGL as the default version with its operating systems. If no 3D hardware exists on a system or if the appropriate hardware drivers have not been installed, the Microsoft version of the OpenGL implementation is the one you will get. Microsoft has not contributed to OpenGL in many years. The version of OpenGL supported on most Microsoft operating systems is 1.0 or 1.1. This is not sufficient for most modern 3D applications. In addition, a software implementation is often not fast enough to support any meaningful graphics. For this reason, many OpenGL applications will check the supported version of OpenGL and decide to not run if a newer version of the OpenGL specification is not supported.

Modern Graphics Drivers

The Installable Client Driver (ICD) was the original hardware driver interface provided for Windows NT. The ICD must implement the entire OpenGL pipeline using a combination of software and the specific hardware for which it was written. Creating an ICD from scratch is a considerable amount of work for a vendor to undertake.

ICDs drop in and work with Microsoft's OpenGL implementation. Applications linked to opengl32.dll are automatically passed through by Microsoft to an installed ICD driver for OpenGL calls. Because a common interface exists, drivers and applications do not have to be recompiled to take advantage of OpenGL hardware on a system, even if it changes. The ICD is actually a part of the display driver and does not affect the existing `opengl32.dll` system DLL. This driver model provides the vendor with the most opportunities to optimize its driver and hardware combination.

All major hardware vendors currently use the ICD model. If a given piece of hardware does not support some part of OpenGL natively, the ICD must implement the missing functionality. In this way, all ICD drivers should support the entire feature set for the version(s) of OpenGL exported by that driver.

Because the `opengl32.dll` portion of the OpenGL call stack belongs to the operating system, applications and drivers have to use the library that ships with a given operating system. Because the Microsoft software implementation only supports either OpenGL 1.0 or 1.1, the entrypoints for the `opengl32.dll` also only support the same versions of OpenGL. This has created a dilemma as OpenGL has grown, evolved, and added new functionality. We have come a long way in the last 18 years since OpenGL 1.1 was released.

Because a display driver cannot modify the `opengl32.dll` to add new features for the current version, OpenGL needed a way to allow applications to access parts that were not exposed by the `opengl32.dll`. This is done through the extension mechanism and an interface that allows applications to get the entrypoint address for any supported interfaces. Not only does this work for the newer versions of OpenGL, but this mechanism can be used by hardware vendors to extend the feature set of OpenGL as we see in a few pages.

OpenGL on Vista and Windows 7
OpenGL on Vista and Windows 7 works in much the same way as on earlier operating systems. The operating system still has a version of the `opengl32.dll`, and applications call OpenGL functions much the same way. But on these newer operating systems, desktop compositing is used to create the final image a user sees. On previous operating systems each window rendered into the desktop pixels it owned. But on Vista and Win7, each window renders into a surface that is handed off a new component of the operating system called the Desktop Window Manager, or DWM.

Each window surface is "presented" to the DWM, which directly interfaces with the graphics kernel driver. DWM takes all the windows from each running 2D and 3D application and uses the GPU to combine them together with desktop components to create a final image that the user sees. This new mechanism separates the render surfaces for each window and allows the operating system to take advantage of advanced GPU capabilities to provide cool blending and 3D effects.

The version of `opengl32.dll` on Vista and Win7 still only supports OpenGL 1.1. However, Microsoft has implemented an OpenGL to D3D emulator that supports OpenGL version 1.4. This implementation looks like an ICD, but only shows up if a real ICD is not installed. As of the initial release of Vista, there is no way to turn this implementation on manually. Only a few games (selected by Microsoft) are "tricked" into seeing this implementation. Vista, like XP, does not ship with ICD drivers on the distribution media. Once a user downloads a new display driver from a vendor's Web site, however, she will get a true ICD-based driver and full OpenGL support in both windowed and full-screen games.

Extended OpenGL

Before we get into the intricacies of using wgl, let's look at how to extend the core functionality of OpenGL and wgl. Because the core opengl32.dll only exposes a minimum set of entrypoints, you need to know how to get at the newer functions to really make use of wgl and OpenGL. You learn two ways of dealing with extensions: using the interfaces directly and letting the GLEW library do some of the lifting for you.

An extension is any addition to a core version of OpenGL. Extensions are listed in the OpenGL extension registry on the OpenGL Web site. These extensions are written as difference specifications. That means the text of the extensions describes how the core OpenGL specification must be changed if the extension is supported.

There are three major classifications of extensions: vendor, EXT, and ARB. Vendor extensions are written and implemented on one vendor's hardware. Initials representing the specific vendor are usually part of the extension name—"AMD" for Advanced Micro Devices or "NV" for NVIDIA. It is possible that more than one vendor might support a specific vendor extension, especially if it becomes widely accepted. EXT extensions are written together by two or more vendors. They often start their lives as a vendor-specific extensions. ARB extensions are an official part of OpenGL because they are approved by the OpenGL governing body, the Architecture Review Board (ARB). These extensions are often supported by all major hardware vendors and also start as vendor or EXT extensions.

This extension process may sound confusing at first. Hundreds of extensions currently are available! But new versions of OpenGL are often constructed from extensions programmers have found useful. In this way each extension gets its time in the sun. The ones that shine can be promoted to core; the ones that are less useful are not considered. This "natural selection" process helps to ensure only the most useful and important new features make it into a core version of OpenGL.

Using Extensions

Back in Chapter 2, "Getting Started," you learned how to find out about what extensions are available on a given system. Extensions can have many different effects on OpenGL functionality. They can simply remove some restrictions currently in place. They can introduce new enumerants that can be used for things such as setting state. They can also add entirely new functions to the API. The only cases that require special attention are those where your application has to use new entrypoints.

On the Windows platform, you do not have direct access to the OpenGL driver. The OpenGL function calls in OpenGL 3.2 that were part of OpenGL 1.1 are routed through the `opengl32.dll` library. Because this DLL understands only OpenGL 1.1 entrypoints (function names), OpenGL drivers provide a way for you to get pointers to all of the newer OpenGL functions supported directly by the driver. The Windows OpenGL implementation has a function named `wglGetProcAddress` that allows you to retrieve a pointer to an OpenGL function supported by the driver:

```
PROC wglGetProcAddress(LPSTR lpszProc);
```

This function takes the name of an OpenGL function or extension function and returns a function pointer that you can use to call that function directly. For this to work, you must know the full function prototype for the function so you can create a pointer to it and subsequently call the function.

The number of extensions is large, especially when you add in the newer OpenGL core functionality and vendor-specific extensions. Complete coverage of all OpenGL extensions would require an entire book in itself (if not an encyclopedia!). When you have some time, take a look at the extension registry; a link is provided in Appendix A, "Further Reading."

Fortunately, the following two header files give you programmatic access to most OpenGL extensions:

```
#include <wglext.h>
#include <glext.h>
```

These files can be found at the OpenGL extension registry Web site, but they are also maintained by most graphics card vendors (see their developer support Web sites). For the samples shown in this book, we use the GLEW versions, which are included in `\src\GLTools\include\GL\`. The `wglext.h` header contains a number of extensions that are Windows-specific, and the `glext.h` header contains both standard OpenGL extensions and many vendor-specific OpenGL extensions.

WGL Extensions

Several Windows-specific WGL extensions are also available. You access the WGL extension entrypoints in the same manner as the OpenGL extensions—using the `wglGetProcAddress` function. There is, however, an important exception. Typically, among the many WGL extensions, only two are advertised by using `glGetString(GL_EXTENSIONS)`. One is the swap interval extension (which allows you to synchronize buffer swaps with the vertical retrace), and the other is the `WGL_ARB_extensions_string` extension. This extension provides yet another entrypoint that is used exclusively to query for the WGL extensions. The ARB extensions string function is prototyped as follows:

```
const char *wglGetExtensionsStringARB(HDC hdc);
```

This function retrieves the list of WGL extensions in the same manner you previously would have used `glGetString`. Using the `wglext.h` header file, you can retrieve a pointer to this function like this:

```
PFNWGLGETEXTENSIONSSTRINGARBPROC *wglGetExtensionsStringARB;
wglGetExtensionsStringARB = (PFNWGLGETEXTENSIONSSTRINGARBPROC)
                        wglGetProcAddress("wglGetExtensionsStringARB");
```

`glGetString` returns the `WGL_ARB_extensions_string` identifier, but often developers skip this check and simply look for the entrypoint, as shown in the preceding code fragment. This approach usually works with most OpenGL extensions, but you should realize that this is, strictly speaking, "coloring outside the lines." Some vendors export extensions on an "experimental" basis, and these extensions may not be officially supported, or the functions may not function properly if you skip the extension string check. Also, more than one extension may use the same function or functions. Testing only for function availability provides no information on the availability or the reliability of the specific extension or extensions that are supported.

GLEW It All Together!

Most normal developers would grow weary fairly quickly of always having to query for new function pointers at the beginning of the program. There is a faster way, and in fact, we used this shortcut for all the samples in this book so far. The GLEW (GL Extension Wrangler) library is included in the `\GLTools` directory with the source distribution for the book. Automatically gaining access to all the function pointers supported by the driver is a simple matter of adding `glew.c` to your project and `glew.h` to the top of your header list. Then call `glewInit()` when your application starts up before any OpenGL calls are made. All the function pointers for extensions and core features beyond OpenGL 1.1 will be set up automatically. If the function fails, it returns an error, and the extension pointers may not be initialized.

```
GLenum err = glewInit();
if (GLEW_OK != err)
{
    /* Problem: glewInit failed, something is seriously wrong. */
    fprintf(stderr, "Error: %s\n", glewGetErrorString(err));
}
```

Using GLEW removes the need to perform any specialized initialization to gain access to all the OpenGL functionality available by a particular driver on Windows. This does not, however, remove the need to check for which version of OpenGL is currently supported by the driver. If an entrypoint does not exist in the driver, then the function pointer for that entrypoint will be NULL, and calling the function will crash your program. This may not be a big deal on your local system, but you wouldn't want to ship your program to a friend or customer and have it crash because their system used older hardware. Although we are using GLEW for this book and the related sample programs, other tools provide similar extension loading support.

Basic Windows Rendering

Now it's time to get back to setting up your application using wgl. The commonly used GLUT library provides only one window, and OpenGL function calls always produced output in that window. (Where else would they go?) Your own real-world Windows applications, however, will often have more than one window. In fact, dialog boxes, controls, and even menus are actually all windows at a fundamental level; having a useful program that contains only one window is nearly impossible (well, okay, maybe games are an important exception!). Also GLUT requires the use of the control function glutMainLoop(). This works fine for simple applications but doesn't work with libraries or any time your code doesn't control the main event loop. Let's look at more flexible ways of managing windows and contexts.

GDI Device Contexts

There are many methods for drawing into a window on a Microsoft operating system. The oldest and most widely supported is the Windows GDI (Graphics Device Interface). GDI has since been updated with the release of GDI+. GDI is strictly a 2D drawing interface and was widely hardware accelerated before Windows Vista. While GDI is still available on Vista and Win7, it is no longer hardware accelerated in the same way. The preferred high-level drawing technology is based on the .NET framework and is called the Windows Presentation Foundation (WPF). WPF is also available via a download for Windows XP. Over the years some minor 2D API variations have come and gone, as well as many incarnations of Direct3D. On Vista, the new low-level rendering interface is called Windows Graphics Foundation (WGF) and is essentially just Direct3D 10.

The one native rendering API common to all versions of Windows (even Windows Mobile) is GDI. This is fortunate because GDI is how we initialize OpenGL and interact with OpenGL on all versions of Windows (except Windows Mobile, where OpenGL is not natively supported by Microsoft). On Vista and Win7, GDI is no longer hardware accelerated, but this is irrelevant because we will never (at least when using OpenGL) actually use GDI for any drawing operations anyway.

When using GDI, each window has a device context that actually receives the graphics output, and each GDI function takes a device context as an argument to indicate which window you want the function to affect. You can have multiple device contexts, but only one for each window.

Before you jump to the conclusion that OpenGL should work in a similar way, remember that GDI is Windows-specific. OpenGL was designed to be completely portable across environments and hardware platforms (and it didn't start on Windows anyway!). Adding a device context parameter to OpenGL functions would render your OpenGL code useless in any environment other than Windows.

OpenGL does have a context identifier, however, and it is called the *rendering context*. The OpenGL rendering context has many similarities to the GDI device context because it is the rendering context that remembers current colors, state settings, and so on, much like the device context holds onto the current brush or pen color for Windows.

Pixel Formats

The Windows concept of the device context is limited for 3D graphics because it was designed for 2D graphics applications. In Windows, you request a device context identifier for a given window. The nature of the device context depends on the nature of the device. If your desktop is set to 16-bit color, the device context Windows gives you knows about and understands 16-bit color only. You cannot tell Windows, for example, that one window is to be a 16-bit color window and another is to be a 32-bit color window. You, the programmer, have no control over the intrinsic characteristics of a windows device context.

Any window or device that will be rendering 3D graphics has far more characteristics to it than simply color depth. Up until now, GLUT has taken care of these details for you. When you initialized GLUT, you told it what buffers you needed (double or single color buffer, depth buffer, stencil, and alpha).

Before OpenGL can render into a window, you must first configure that window according to your rendering needs. Will the rendering be single or double buffered? Do you need a depth buffer? How about stencil or destination alpha? What version of OpenGL do you need? After you set these parameters for a window, you cannot change them later. To switch from a window with only a depth and color buffer to a window with only a stencil and color buffer, you have to destroy the first window and re-create a new window with the characteristics you need.

OpenGL on Windows uses pixel formats to encapsulate all of this information into grouped capabilities. You need to find a pixel format that has the characteristics and capabilities that match the needs of your application. This pixel format is then used to create an OpenGL rendering context. There are two ways to go about looking for a pixel format. The first method is the more preferred and capable mechanism exposed by OpenGL directly. The second method uses the original Windows interfaces, which have been around for as long as OpenGL has been supported on Windows.

Finding a Pixel Format the New Way

The pixel format for a window is identified by a one-based integer index number. An implementation exports a number of pixel formats from which to choose. The Windows interfaces for OpenGL have not grown along with OpenGL. As a result, features were added to OpenGL that could not be accessed using traditional Windows functions. Thankfully, OpenGL added a way to get at these new features. The new mechanisms also provide advanced search capabilities to save you time in finding the right pixel format for your application.

Now it's time to use our first and maybe the most important wgl extension. The WGL_ARB_pixel_format extension provides a mechanism that allows you to check for and select pixel format features that go beyond what Windows provides access to. For example, you can use this extension to find a pixel format that supports multisampled rendering.

This extension defines a long list of attributes that can be associated with a context, listed in Table 13.1. The function wglChoosePixelFormatARB is used to find pixel formats that match your requirements:

```
BOOL wglChoosePixelFormatARB(HDC hdc, const int *piAttribIList,
                             const float *pfAttribFList, UINT nMaxFormats,
                             const int *piFormats, UINT *nNumFormats);
```

It's important to notice the "ARB" suffix on this function. wglChoosePixelFormatARB is not the same as wglChoosePixelFormat. You should always use wglChoosePixelFormatARB. Also note that an OpenGL context must be created before you can set up this extension and call wglChoosePixelFormatARB. To do this, you can create a dummy context that gets deleted as soon as you find the pixel format you need.

There are a lot of attributes to handle here. The first argument, hdc, is the device context of the window that the pixel format will be used for. The second and third arguments are used to specify the attributes you are searching for. Both arguments are lists of attribute and value pairs. piAttribIList is a list of integer values, and pfAttribIList is a list of float values. Some attributes are better defined as floats than integers. Both are null terminated. To use these attributes, create an array of one type and then set the first index to the value of the first attribute you'd like to specify. Set the second index to the minimum value you require. Repeat for the second attribute in the third index and so on. Once you have added all attributes, add a null to the end of the array. Some attributes require an exact match such as WGL_DRAW_TO_WINDOW_ARB and WGL_SWAP_METHOD. Some attributes you specify are only a minimum such as WGL_COLOR_BITS_ARB and WGL_ALPHA_BITS_ARB.

You have to allocate a second array to hold the results of the search. Then pass the size of the results array into nMaxFormats and pass a pointer to the integer array into piFormats. The actual number of formats that were written into the results array is passed back in the nNumFormats argument. Normally this is also the number of formats found, but if your array is too small and nNumFormats is the same as nMaxFormats, the driver found more matching formats than fit into your results array. If you don't specify an attribute in piAttribIList or pfAttribIList, the function ignores it when looking for matches; no default is used. If you pass in null for piAttribIList and pfAttribIList, you get all supported formats back.

The results returned by wglChoosePixelFormatARB in the piFormats attribute are sorted with the "best" matching formats at the start of the list. The "best" match is defined by the implementation and is device-dependent. It is usually advantageous to pick formats that the implementation thinks are the best match as long as they meet the requirements of your application.

Some attributes are required on most queries for the resulting pixel formats to be useful. Most programs should request the WGL_SUPPORT_OPENGL_ARB, WGL_DRAW_TO_WINDOW_ARB, and WGL_ACCELERATION_ARB attributes. These attributes are described in more detail in the next section. All this information may seem confusing, but finding a pixel format is easier than it may seem. Listing 13.1 gives an example of how to choose a pixel format.

LISTING 13.1   Finding a Pixel Format to Match Your Needs

```
int nPixCount = 0;

// Specify the important attributes we care about
int pixAttribs[] = {
            WGL_SUPPORT_OPENGL_ARB, 1, // Must support OGL rendering
            WGL_DRAW_TO_WINDOW_ARB, 1, // pf that can run a window
            WGL_RED_BITS_ARB,       8, // 8 bits of red precision in window
            WGL_GREEN_BITS_ARB,     8, // 8 bits of green precision in window
            WGL_BLUE_BITS_ARB,      8, // 8 bits of blue precision in window
            WGL_DEPTH_BITS_ARB,    16, // 16 bits of depth precision for window
            WGL_ACCELERATION_ARB,
            WGL_FULL_ACCELERATION_ARB, // must be HW accelerated
            WGL_PIXEL_TYPE_ARB,
            WGL_TYPE_RGBA_ARB, // pf should be RGBA type
            0}; // NULL termination

// Ask OpenGL to find the most relevant format matching our attribs
// Only get one format back.
wglChoosePixelFormatARB(g_hDC, &pixAttribs[0], NULL, 1, &nPixelFormat,
(UINT*)&nPixCount);

if(nPixelFormat == -1)
{
    // Couldn't find a format, perhaps no 3D HW or drivers are installed
    g_hDC = 0;
    g_hDC = 0;
    bRetVal = false;
    printf("!!! An error occurred trying to find a pixel format with the requested
attribs.\n");
}
```

Pixel Format Attributes

Once your application has chosen a pixel format, or while walking through the entire list yourself, you can get information on any particular attribute of a pixel format by using the wglGetPixelFormatAttribivARB and wglGetPixelFormatAttribfvARB functions:

```
BOOL wglGetPixelFormatAttribivARB(HDC hdc, int iPixelFormat,
                              int iLayerPlane, UINT nAttributes,
                              const int *piAttributes, int *piValues);
BOOL wglGetPixelFormatAttribfvARB(HDC hdc, int iPixelFormat,
                              int iLayerPlane, UINT nAttributes,
                              const int *piAttributes, float *pfValues);
```

These two variations of the same function allow you to query the properties of a particular pixel format index and retrieve an array containing the attribute data for that pixel format. The first argument, hdc, is the device context of the window that the pixel format will be used for, followed by the pixel format index. The iLayerPlane argument specifies which layer plane to query (0 on Vista, Win7, and implementations that do not support layer planes). Next, nAttributes specifies how many attributes you are querying for this pixel format, and the array piAttributes contains the list of attribute names to be queried. The attributes that can be specified are listed in Table 13.1. The final argument is an array that will be filled with the corresponding pixel format attributes.

TABLE 13.1   Pixel Format Attributes

Constant	Description
WGL_NUMBER_PIXEL_FORMATS_ARB	The number of pixel formats for this device.
WGL_DRAW_TO_WINDOW_ARB	Nonzero if the pixel format can be used with a window.
WGL_DRAW_TO_BITMAP_ARB	Nonzero if the pixel format can be used with a memory Device Independent Bitmap (DIB).
WGL_DEPTH_BITS_ARB	The number of bits in the depth buffer.
WGL_STENCIL_BITS_ARB	The number of bits in the stencil buffer.
WGL_ACCELERATION_ARB	One of the values in Table 13.2 that specifies which, if any, hardware driver is used.
WGL_NEED_PALETTE_ARB	Nonzero if a palette is required.
WGL_NEED_SYSTEM_PALETTE_ARB	Nonzero if the hardware supports one palette only in 256-color mode.
WGL_SWAP_LAYER_BUFFERS_ARB	Nonzero if the hardware supports swapping layer planes.
WGL_SWAP_METHOD_ARB	The method by which the buffer swap is accomplished for double-buffered pixel formats. It is one of the values listed in Table 13.3.
WGL_NUMBER_OVERLAYS_ARB	The number of overlay planes.
WGL_NUMBER_UNDERLAYS_ARB	The number of underlay planes.
WGL_SAMPLES_ARB	The number of multisample samples per pixel. Default is 1.
WGL_TRANSPARENT_ARB	Nonzero if transparency is supported.
WGL_TRANSPARENT_RED_VALUE_ARB	Transparent red color.

13

TABLE 13.1   Pixel Format Attributes *continued*

Constant	Description
WGL_TRANSPARENT_GREEN_VALUE_ARB	Transparent green color.
WGL_TRANSPARENT_BLUE_VALUE_ARB	Transparent blue color.
WGL_TRANSPARENT_ALPHA_VALUE_ARB	Transparent alpha color.
WGL_SHARE_DEPTH_ARB	Nonzero if layer planes share a depth buffer with the main plane.
WGL_SHARE_STENCIL_ARB	Nonzero if layer planes share a stencil buffer with the main plane.
WGL_SHARE_ACCUM_ARB	Nonzero if layer planes share an accumulation buffer with the main plane.
WGL_SUPPORT_GDI_ARB	Nonzero if GDI rendering is supported (front buffer only).
WGL_SUPPORT_OPENGL_ARB	Nonzero if OpenGL is supported.
WGL_DOUBLE_BUFFER_ARB	Nonzero if double buffered.
WGL_STEREO_ARB	Nonzero if left and right buffers are supported.
WGL_PIXEL_TYPE_ARB	WGL_TYPE_RGBA_ARB for RGBA color modes; WGL_TYPE_COLORINDEX_ARB for color index mode.
WGL_COLOR_BITS_ARB	Number of bit planes in the color buffer.
WGL_RED_BITS_ARB	Number of red bit planes in the color buffer.
WGL_RED_SHIFT_ARB	Shift count for red bit planes.
WGL_GREEN_BITS_ARB	Number of green bit planes in the color buffer.
WGL_GREEN_SHIFT_ARB	Shift count for green bit planes.
WGL_BLUE_BITS_ARB	Number of blue bit planes in the color buffer.
WGL_BLUE_SHIFT_ARB	Shift count for blue bit planes.
WGL_ALPHA_BITS_ARB	Number of alpha bit planes in the color buffer.
WGL_ALPHA_SHIFT_ARB	Shift count for alpha bit planes.

TABLE 13.2   Acceleration Flags for WGL_ACCELERATION_ARB

Constant	Description
WGL_NO_ACCELERATION_ARB	Software rendering, no acceleration.
WGL_GENERIC_ACCELERATION_ARB	Acceleration via an MCD driver.
WGL_FULL_ACCELERATION_ARB	Acceleration via an ICD driver.

TABLE 13.3   Buffer Swap Values for WGL_SWAP_METHOD_ARB

Constant	Description
WGL_SWAP_EXCHANGE_ARB	Swapping exchanges the front and back buffers.
WGL_SWAP_COPY_ARB	The back buffer is copied to the front buffer.
WGL_SWAP_UNDEFINED_ARB	The back buffer is copied to the front buffer, but the back buffer contents remain undefined after the buffer swap.

There is, however, a catch-22 to these and all other OpenGL extensions. You must have a valid OpenGL rendering context before you can call either glGetString or wglGetProcAddress of most OpenGL functions. This means that you must first create a temporary window, set a pixel format (we can actually cheat and just specify pixel format 1, which will be the first hardware accelerated format), and then obtain a pointer to one of the wglGetPixelFormatAttribARB functions. A convenient place to do this might be the splash screen or perhaps an initial options dialog box that is presented to the user. You should not, however, try to use the Windows desktop because your application does not own it!

The following simple example queries for a single attribute—the number of pixel formats supported—so that you know how many you may need to look at:

```
int attrib[] = { WGL_NUMBER_PIXEL_FORMATS_ARB };
int nResults[1] = {0};
int pixFmt = 1;
wglGetPixelFormatAttribivARB (hDC, pixFmt, 0, 1, attrib, nResults);
// nResults[0] now contains the number of exported pixelformats
```

For a more detailed example showing how to look for a specific pixel format (including a multisampled pixel format), see the sphere_world_redux sample program coming up next.

It's also important to understand that all entrypoints you get for OpenGL are only valid for the current OpenGL context. If you delete a context and create another, you should fill in the entrypoints again. It is possible that the entrypoints are different between contexts, especially if you create contexts that support different versions of OpenGL or might be on different monitors driven by multiple graphics cards.

Finding a Pixel Format the Old Way

Windows also exposes several functions that can be used for finding an OpenGL pixel format. But these methods are limited and do not expose all formats or all attributes. We show you how to use these for completeness. If you are writing a new OpenGL app, you are better off using the method we just described. Many newer OpenGL features such as multisample buffers are not accessible through the old pixel format selection methods.

The 3D characteristics of the window are set one time, usually just after window creation. The collective name for these settings is the pixel format. Windows provides a structure named PIXELFORMATDESCRIPTOR that describes the pixel format. This structure is defined as follows:

```
typedef struct tagPIXELFORMATDESCRIPTOR {
WORD  nSize;          // Size of this structure
WORD  nVersion;       // Version of structure (should be 1)
DWORD dwFlags;        // Pixel buffer properties
```

```
BYTE  iPixelType;        // Type of pixel data (RGBA or Color Index)
BYTE  cColorBits;        // Number of color bit planes in color buffer
BYTE  cRedBits;          // How many bits for red
BYTE  cRedShift;         // Shift count for red bits
BYTE  cGreenBits;        // How many bits for green
BYTE  cGreenShift;       // Shift count for green bits
BYTE  cBlueBits;         // How many bits for blue
BYTE  cBlueShift;        // Shift count for blue
BYTE  cAlphaBits;        // How many bits for destination alpha
BYTE  cAlphaShift;       // Shift count for destination alpha
BYTE  cAccumBits;        // How many bits for accumulation buffer
BYTE  cAccumRedBits;     // How many red bits for accumulation buffer
BYTE  cAccumGreenBits;   // How many green bits for accumulation buffer
BYTE  cAccumBlueBits;    // How many blue bits for accumulation buffer
BYTE  cAccumAlphaBits;   // How many alpha bits for accumulation buffer
BYTE  cDepthBits;        // How many bits for depth buffer
BYTE  cStencilBits;      // How many bits for stencil buffer
BYTE  cAuxBuffers;       // How many auxiliary buffers
BYTE  iLayerType;        // Obsolete - ignored
BYTE  bReserved;         // Number of overlay and underlay planes
DWORD dwLayerMask;       // Obsolete - ignored
DWORD dwVisibleMask;     // Transparent color of underlay plane
DWORD dwDamageMask;      // Obsolete - ignored
} PIXELFORMATDESCRIPTOR;
```

For a given OpenGL device (hardware or software), the values of these members are not arbitrary. Only a limited number of pixel formats is available for a specific window. Pixel formats are said to be exported by the OpenGL driver or software renderer. On old software implementations, applications used to use ChoosePixelFormat to get a pixel format from Microsoft. This was done by filling in a PIXELFORMATDESCRIPTOR and calling ChoosePixelFormat. Although this call still works, you are much better off using wglChoosePixelFormatARB, which is implemented by the OpenGL driver itself. wglChoosePixelFormatARB can return formats that the Microsoft interface cannot. But ChoosePixelFormat is shown here in case you run across it in older apps.

```
PIXELFORMATDESCRIPTOR pfd;
// Fill in pfd here
int nPf = ChoosePixelFormat(g_hdc, &pfd);
```

Enumerating Pixel Formats

You many have noticed in Table 13.1 that one of the possible values that can be queried by wglGetPixelFormatAttribivARB and wglGetPixelFormatAttribfvARB is WGL_NUMBER_PIXEL_FORMATS_ARB. You can make an initial call to `wglGetPixelFormatAttribivARB` to get the total number of formats and then use that information to step throught the entire list and query the information you care about for each pixel format available:

```
    GLint pfAttribCount[]= { WGL_NUMBER_PIXEL_FORMATS_ARB
};
    GLint pfAttribList[] = { WGL_DRAW_TO_WINDOW_ARB,
                             WGL_ACCELERATION_ARB,
                             WGL_SUPPORT_OPENGL_ARB,
                             WGL_DOUBLE_BUFFER_ARB,
                             WGL_DEPTH_BITS_ARB,
                             WGL_STENCIL_BITS_ARB,
                             WGL_RED_BITS_ARB,
                             WGL_GREEN_BITS_ARB,
                             WGL_BLUE_BITS_ARB,
                             WGL_ALPHA_BITS_ARB
                             };

    int nPixelFormatCount = 0;
    wglGetPixelFormatAttribivARB(g_hDC, 1, 0, 1, pfAttribCount,
                                &nPixelFormatCount);
    for (int i=0; i<nPixelFormatCount; i++)
    {
        GLint results[10];
        printf("Pixel format %d details:\n", nPixelFormatCount);
        wglGetPixelFormatAttribivARB(g_hDC, i, 0, 10, pfAttribList, results);
        printf("    Draw to Window  = %d:\n", results[0]);
        printf("    HW Accelerated  = %d:\n", results[1]);
        printf("    Supports OpenGL = %d:\n", results[2]);
        printf("    Double Buffered = %d:\n", results[3]);
        printf("    Depth Bits   = %d:\n", results[4]);
        printf("    Stencil Bits = %d:\n", results[5]);
        printf("    Red Bits     = %d:\n", results[6]);
        printf("    Green Bits   = %d:\n", results[7]);
        printf("    Blue Bits    = %d:\n", results[8]);
        printf("    Alpha Bits   = %d:\n", results[9]);
    }
```

This code prints a list of pixel formats, but you could use the same method to choose your own pixel format if you didn't want to use the more automated method provided by `wglChoosePixelFormatARB`.

Selecting and Setting a Pixel Format

After you have found a pixel format with `wglChoosePixelFormatARB` and `wglGetPixelFormatAttribARB`, it's time to tell the Windows and the OpenGL driver which format you want to use. To do that, you use the `SetPixelFormat` function:

```
int nPixelFormat;
. . .
static PIXELFORMATDESCRIPTOR pfd;
// Set the pixel format for the device context
SetPixelFormat(hDC, nPixelFormat, &pfd);
```

The original contents of the `PIXELFORMATDESCRIPTOR` do not affect the functioning of the `SetPixelFormat` function. Pass in the window device context handle in the `hDC` parameter and your chosen pixel format in the `nPixelFormat` parameter. `SetPixelFormat` can only be called once. To change the pixel format, your window will have to be destroyed and re-created.

The OpenGL Rendering Context

A typical Windows application can consist of many windows. You can even set a pixel format for each one (using that windows device context) if you want! When you call an OpenGL command, how does the driver know which window to send its output to? In the previous chapters, we used the GLUT framework, which provided a single window to display OpenGL output. Recall that with normal Windows GDI-based drawing, each window has its own device context.

To accomplish the portability of the core OpenGL functions, each environment must implement some means of specifying a current rendering window before executing any OpenGL commands. Just as the Windows GDI functions use the window's device contexts, the OpenGL environment is embodied in what is known as the *rendering context*. The rendering context remembers OpenGL settings and state.

Many different versions of OpenGL have been released in the last 15 years. Some are not backward-compatible with others. For this reason you can pick the specific version of OpenGL your application will use. If OpenGL did not allow you to do this, your application could stop working when a new version of OpenGL was released that was not compatible with the one you designed your application for. You create an OpenGL rendering context by calling the `wglCreateContextAttribsARB` function, another extension:

```
HGLRC wglCreateContextAttribsARB(HDC hDC, HGLRC hShareContext, const int *attribList);
```

The data type of an OpenGL rendering context is `HGLRC`. If everything succeeds, the new context handle is returned. OpenGL can share objects (textures, FBOs, vertex arrays, and so on) between contexts. If you want to share objects between two or more contexts, pass in the context handle of an already created context in the hShareContext parameter. If you pass NULL to the new context, no other existing contexts will share data with the new context.

The attribList parameter is a value-pair list of attributes you can request in a new context. First specify the attribute name in the array followed by the value for the attribute. The attributes WGL_CONTEXT_MAJOR_VERSION_ARB and WGL_CONTEXT_MINOR_VERSION_ARB are used to explicitly ask for a specific context version of OpenGL. If your application was written for OpenGL 3.3, you would pass in 3 as the major version and 3 as the minor version. Similarly, if your application was older and you needed an OpenGL 3.0 context, you could ask for that. However, OpenGL drivers are allowed to return any version that is 100% backward-compatible with the version you requested. If you do not specify a version of OpenGL or if you ask for version 1.0, the driver will probably create an OpenGL 3.1 context. The exact behavior differs between vendors. The best idea is to ask for a specific OpenGL version. For new applications you create, request OpenGL 3.3 or later.

You can only create a context up to the version supported by your OpenGL driver. You can find out what the newest supported version is by calling glGetString with the GL_VERSION enum:

```
ubyte *verString = glGetString(GL_VERSION);
```

Or the version can also be queried through the glGetIntegerv command, which returns the version as integer components:

```
int majorVer, minorVer;
glGetIntegerv(GL_MAJOR_VERSION, &majorVer);
glGetIntegerv(GL_MINOR_VERSION, &minorVer);
```

There are several other types of attributes you can request through the attrib_list. The attribute WGL_CONTEXT_PROFILE_MASK_ARB is followed by a bitfield containing either WGL_CONTEXT_CORE_PROFILE_BIT_ARB or WGL_CONTEXT_COMPATIBILITY_PROFILE_BIT_ARB. Only one bit can be used at a time. Setting the WGL_CONTEXT_CORE_PROFILE_BIT_ARB bit causes the driver to return a context containing only core functionality, no deprecated OpenGL functionality. Using this bit is a good way to prepare an application for the next revision of OpenGL where deprecated functionality may be removed. Setting the WGL_CONTEXT_COMPATIBILITY_PROFILE_BIT_ARB bit asks the driver to create a context that is backward-compatible with all older versions of OpenGL. In other words, no deprecated functionality will be removed. A context created with this bit may run slower than a core profile context because of the additional state and functionality that needs to be tracked.

The WGL_CONTEXT_FLAGS_ARB attribute can be used to set other flags for context creation. The only supported flag is WGL_CONTEXT_DEBUG_BIT. Specifying this bit creates a context with additional debugging information available for applications under development. What information and how it can be accessed is vendor-specific.

If any of the attributes you have specified are not supported by the OpenGL driver on your system, `wglCreateContextAttribsARB` returns null, and an error is generated. The error `WGL_ERROR_INVALID_VERSION_ARB` is thrown if the combination of minor and major version attributes with the forward-compatible context bit is not a valid OpenGL version. If any of the bits specified for `WGL_CONTEXT_PROFILE_MASK_ARB` are not supported, the error `WGL_ERROR_INVALID_PROFILE_ARB` is thrown.

Debug Contexts

Using a debug context can be helpful in determining where your application is coming off its rails. At the time of this writing, the only vendor supporting debug contexts is AMD through an extension called `GL_AMD_debug_context`, which defines how the additional debug information can be accessed by developers.

A callback function is provided that allows an application to set an interrupt or breakpoint and find out immediately when an error has occurred. The extension also allows an application to select specific error types to be monitored and supports multiple severity levels.

For more information on how to use the `GL_AMD_debug_context` extension, you can check out the extension specification, which is also in the OpenGL extension registry.

Using Contexts

A rendering context is created that is compatible with the window for which it was created. You can have more than one rendering context in your application—for instance, two windows that are using different drawing modes, perspectives, and so on. However, for OpenGL commands to know which window they are operating on, only one rendering context can be active at any one time per thread. When a rendering context is made active, it is said to be *current*.

When made current, a rendering context is also associated with a device context and thus with a particular window. Now, OpenGL knows which window to direct rendering into. You can even move an OpenGL rendering context from window to window, but each window must have the same pixel format. To make a rendering context current and associate it with a particular window, you call the `wglMakeCurrent` function. This function takes two parameters, the device context of the window and the OpenGL rendering context:

```
void wglMakeCurrent(g_hDC, g_hRC);
```

To detach a rendering context, you can call `wglMakeCurrent` again with the `hDC` and null as the `hRC`. If you are finished rendering or are exiting your application, you should delete the OpenGL context to free any remaining resources. Once a context is no longer current, you can use the `wglDeleteContext` to destroy the OpenGL context:

```
bool wglDeleteContext(g_hRC);
```

One important thing to remember is that you can only have one context current in a thread at a time. You can, however, have two different contexts current at the same time in different threads. You can even share objects between multiple contexts. When you create your second context, pass in the handle of the first context in the second call to wglCreateContextAttribsARB.

```
GLint attribs[] = {WGL_CONTEXT_MAJOR_VERSION_ARB,  3,
                   WGL_CONTEXT_MINOR_VERSION_ARB,  3,
                   0 };
HGLRC  oglRC1 = wglCreateContextAttribsARB(g_hDC, 0, attribs);
HGLRC  oglRC2 = wglCreateContextAttribsARB(g_hDC, oglRC1, attribs);
```

Contexts—The Way It Used To Be

An application can also create OpenGL contexts using wglCreateContext. This older function does not allow you to specify exactly what parameters you want. In fact, it is hard to know what OpenGL version you'll get back. For this reason it is much better for your applications to use wglCreateContextAttribsARB. However, many older applications may still use the older version:

```
HGLRC wglCreateContext(g_hDC);
```

Putting It All Together

We covered a lot of ground over the past several pages. We described each piece of the puzzle individually, but now let's look at all the pieces put together. In addition to seeing all the OpenGL-related code, we should examine some of the minimum requirements for any Windows program to support OpenGL. Our sample programs for this section are block_redux and sphere_world_redux. Block_redux should look somewhat familiar because it is also the first GLUT-based sample program from Chapter 1, "Introduction to 3D Graphics and OpenGL," while sphere_world_redux showed up in Chapter 5, "Basic Texturing." Now these programs are full-fledged Windows programs written with nothing but C++ and the Win32 API. Figure 13.1 shows the output of the sphere_world_redux, which now uses a multisampled window.

FIGURE 13.1   Output from the sphere_world_redux, this time multisampled.

Creating the Window

The starting place for any low-level Windows-based GUI program is the main function. We do all the window setup in a second function called SetupWindow. Listing 13.2 shows excerpts from the SetupWindow and main functions for the first sample.

LISTING 13.2   The WinMain Function of the GLRECT Sample Program

```
///////////////////////////////////////////////////////////////////
//////////////////
// Setup the actual window and related state.
// Create the window, find a pixel format, create the OpenGL context
bool SetupWindow(int nWidth, int nHeight)
{
// Initialize

...

    TCHAR szWindowName[50] =  TEXT("GLRECT Redux");
    TCHAR szClassName[50]  =  TEXT("OGL_CLASS");
```

```
// setup window class
g_windClass.lpszClassName = szClassName;      // Set the name of the Class
g_windClass.lpfnWndProc   = (WNDPROC)WndProc;
g_windClass.hInstance     = g_hInstance; // Use this for the module handle

// Pick the default mouse cursor
g_windClass.hCursor       = LoadCursor(NULL, IDC_ARROW);

// Pick the default windows icons
g_windClass.hIcon         = LoadIcon(NULL, IDI_WINLOGO);
g_windClass.hbrBackground = NULL; // No Background
g_windClass.lpszMenuName  = NULL; // No menu for this window

// set styles for this class, specifically to catch
// window redraws, unique DC, and resize
g_windClass.style         = CS_HREDRAW ¦ CS_OWNDC ¦ CS_VREDRAW;
g_windClass.cbClsExtra    = 0; // Extra class memory
g_windClass.cbWndExtra    = 0; // Extra window memory

// Register the newly defined class
if(!RegisterClass( &g_windClass ))
    bRetVal = false;


dwExtStyle  = WS_EX_APPWINDOW ¦ WS_EX_WINDOWEDGE;
dwWindStyle = WS_OVERLAPPEDWINDOW;
ShowCursor(TRUE);

// Setup window width and height
g_windowRect.left   = nWindowX;
g_windowRect.right  = nWindowX + nWidth;
g_windowRect.top    = nWindowY;
g_windowRect.bottom = nWindowY + nHeight;
AdjustWindowRectEx(&g_windowRect, dwWindStyle, FALSE, dwExtStyle);
int nWindowWidth  = g_windowRect.right  - g_windowRect.left;
int nWindowHeight = g_windowRect.bottom - g_windowRect.top;

// Create window
g_hWnd = CreateWindowEx(dwExtStyle,      // Extended style
                        szClassName,     // class name
                        szWindowName,    // window name
                        dwWindStyle ¦
                        WS_CLIPSIBLINGS ¦
                        WS_CLIPCHILDREN,// window stlye
```

13

```
                            nWindowX,          // window position, x
                            nWindowY,          // window position, y
                            nWindowWidth,      // height
                            nWindowHeight,     // width
                            NULL,              // Parent window
                            NULL,              // menu
                            g_hInstance,       // instance
                            NULL);             // pass this to WM_CREATE

// now that we have a window, setup the pixel format descriptor
g_hDC = GetDC(g_hWnd);

// Set a dummy pixel format so that we can get access to wgl functions
SetPixelFormat( g_hDC, 1,&pfd);
// Create OGL context and make it current
g_hRC = wglCreateContext( g_hDC );
wglMakeCurrent( g_hDC, g_hRC );

if (g_hDC == 0 ||
    g_hRC == 0)
{
    bRetVal = false;
    printf("!!! An error occured creating an OpenGL window.\n");
}

// Setup GLEW which loads OGL function pointers
GLenum err = glewInit();
if (GLEW_OK != err)
{
/* Problem: glewInit failed, something is seriously wrong. */
    bRetVal = false;
printf("Error: %s\n", glewGetErrorString(err));
}
const GLubyte *oglVersion = glGetString(GL_VERSION);
printf("This system supports OpenGL Version %s.\n", oglVersion);

// Now that extensions are setup,
// delete window and start over picking a real format.
wglMakeCurrent(NULL, NULL);
wglDeleteContext(g_hRC);
ReleaseDC(g_hWnd, g_hDC);
DestroyWindow(g_hWnd);
```

```
// Create the window again
...

int nPixCount = 0;

// Specify the important attributes we care about
int pixAttribs[] = {
    WGL_SUPPORT_OPENGL_ARB,   1, // Must support OGL rendering
    WGL_DRAW_TO_WINDOW_ARB,    1, // pf that can run a window
    WGL_ACCELERATION_ARB,      1, // must be HW accelerated
    WGL_COLOR_BITS_ARB,       24, // 8 bits of each R, G and B
    WGL_DEPTH_BITS_ARB,       16, // 16 bits of depth precision for window
    WGL_DOUBLE_BUFFER_ARB,   GL_TRUE, // Double buffered context
    WGL_SAMPLE_BUFFERS_ARB, GL_TRUE, // MSAA on
    WGL_SAMPLES_ARB,          8, // 8x MSAA
    WGL_PIXEL_TYPE_ARB,       WGL_TYPE_RGBA_ARB, // pf should be RGBA type
    0 }; // NULL termination

// Ask OpenGL to find the most relevant format matching our attribs
// Only get one format back.
wglChoosePixelFormatARB(g_hDC, &pixAttribs[0], NULL, 1,
                        &nPixelFormat, (UINT*)&nPixCount);

if(nPixelFormat != -1)
{
    // Got a format, now set it as the current one
    SetPixelFormat( g_hDC, nPixelFormat, &pfd );
    GLint attribs[] = {WGL_CONTEXT_MAJOR_VERSION_ARB,  3,
                       WGL_CONTEXT_MINOR_VERSION_ARB,  3,
                       0 };
    g_hRC = wglCreateContextAttribsARB(g_hDC, 0, attribs);
    if (g_hRC == NULL)
    {
        // Handle Error . . .
    }
    wglMakeCurrent( g_hDC, g_hRC );
}
ShowWindow( g_hWnd, SW_SHOW );
SetForegroundWindow( g_hWnd );
SetFocus( g_hWnd );
g_ContinueRendering = true;
return bRetVal;
}
```

```
/////////////////////////////////////////////////////////////////////////////
// Main program function, called on startup
// First setup the window and OGL state, then enter rendering loop
int main(int argc, char* argv[])
{
    gltSetWorkingDirectory(argv[0]);
    if(SetupWindow(800, 600))
    {
        SetupRC();
        ChangeSize(800, 600);
        while (g_ContinueRendering)
        {
            mainLoop();
            Sleep(0);
        }
    }
    KillWindow();
    return 0;
}
```

This listing pretty much contains your standard window setup code. Note that we include CS_OWNDC for the window style. Specifying this flag causes Windows to allocate a DC (device context) specifically for your window. You need a device context for both GDI rendering and for OpenGL double-buffered page flipping. The device context is what you can use to refer to your specific window.

First, You Need a Device Context

Before you can draw anything in a window with GDI, you first need a Windows device context. You need it whether you're doing OpenGL, GDI, or even DirectX programming. Any drawing or painting operation in Windows (even if you're drawing on a bitmap in memory) requires a device context that identifies the specific object being drawn on. You retrieve the device context to a window with a simple function call:

```
HDC hDC = GetDC(hWnd);
```

The hDC variable is your handle to the device context of the window identified by the window handle hWnd. You use the device context for all GDI functions that draw in the window. You also need the device context for creating an OpenGL rendering context, making it current, and performing the buffer swap. You tell Windows that you don't need the device context for the window any longer with another simple function call, using the same two values:

```
ReleaseDC(hWnd ,hDC);
```

Initializing the Rendering Context

The first thing you do when the window is being created is retrieve the device context (remember, you hang on to it) and set the pixel format:

```
// Store the device context
g_hDC = GetDC(g_hWnd);

// Dummy pfd
PIXELFORMATDESCRIPTOR pfd;

// Set the pixel format
SetPixelFormat(g_hDC, nPixelFormat, &pfd);
```

Then you create the OpenGL rendering context and make it current:

```
// Create the rendering context and make it current
GLint attribs[] = { WGL_CONTEXT_MAJOR_VERSION_ARB,  3,
                    WGL_CONTEXT_MINOR_VERSION_ARB,  3, 0 };
g_hRC = wglCreateContextAttribsARB(g_hDC, 0, attribs);
wglMakeCurrent(hDC, hRC);
```

Shutting Down the Rendering Context

When the window procedure receives the WM_DESTROY message or once you decide you are done, the OpenGL rendering context must be deleted. Before you delete the rendering context with the wglDeleteContext function, you must first call wglMakeCurrent again, but this time with NULL as the parameter for the OpenGL rendering context:

```
// Deselect the current rendering context and delete it
wglMakeCurrent(g_hDC, NULL);
wglDeleteContext(g_hRC);
```

Before deleting the rendering context, you should delete any display lists, texture objects, or other OpenGL-allocated memory. Well-written programs are careful to clean up all objects and memory they allocate. Failure to clean up objects tied to a context may result in memory leaks or other side effects.

Full-Screen Rendering

Windowed OpenGL apps are great, but it's hard to create an immersive game if your app isn't in full-screen! One of the most common developer questions is "How do I do full-screen rendering with OpenGL?" The truth is, if you've read this chapter, you already know how to do full-screen rendering with OpenGL—it's just like rendering into any other window! The real question is "How do I create a window that takes up the entire screen and has no borders?" Once you do this, rendering into this window is no different from rendering into any other window in any other sample in this book.

Even though this issue isn't strictly related to OpenGL, it is of enough interest to a wide number of our readers that we give this topic some coverage here. Creating a full-screen window is almost as simple as creating a regular window the size of the screen and starting at (0,0). We also use a different window style because we have no need for a title bar or border because none of that is visible. The code in Listing 13.3 does just that.

LISTING 13.3   Setting Up a Full-Screen Window

```
if(bUseFS)
{
    // Prepare for a mode set to the requested resolution
    DEVMODE dm;
    memset(&dm,0,sizeof(dm));
    dm.dmSize=sizeof(dm);
    dm.dmPelsWidth    = nWidth;
    dm.dmPelsHeight   = nHeight;
    dm.dmBitsPerPel   = 32;
    dm.dmFields=DM_BITSPERPEL¦DM_PELSWIDTH¦DM_PELSHEIGHT;

    long error = ChangeDisplaySettings(&dm, CDS_FULLSCREEN);

    if (error != DISP_CHANGE_SUCCESSFUL)
    {
        // Oops, something went wrong, let the user know.
        if (MessageBox(NULL, "Could not set fullscreen mode.\n"
            "Your video card may not support the requested mode.\n"
            "Use windowed mode instead?", g_szAppName,
             MB_YESNO¦MB_ICONEXCLAMATION)==IDYES)
        {
            g_InFullScreen = false;
            dwExtStyle  = WS_EX_APPWINDOW ¦ WS_EX_WINDOWEDGE;
            dwWindStyle = WS_OVERLAPPEDWINDOW;
        }
        else
        {
            MessageBox(NULL, "Program will exit.",
                        "ERROR", MB_OK¦MB_ICONSTOP);
            return false;
        }
    }
    else
    {
        // Mode set passed, setup the styles for fullscreen
```

```
        g_InFullScreen = true;
        dwExtStyle  = WS_EX_APPWINDOW;
        dwWindStyle = WS_POPUP;
        ShowCursor(FALSE);
    }
}

AdjustWindowRectEx(&g_windowRect, dwWindStyle, FALSE, dwExtStyle);

// Create the window again
    . . .
```

Double Buffering

The sphere_world_redux sample program requests a double buffered pixel format by specifying WGL_DOUBLE_BUFFER_ARB the in the list of attributes when searching for a pixel format using wglChoosePixelFormatARB. By this time you have seen many sample programs that are double buffered. But let's revisit briefly given that this is relevant to how we allocate the pixel format and how the program is controlled. When a double buffered pixel format is used, two surfaces the size of the window are allocated. One acts as the front buffer and the other as the back buffer. You can draw to them by calling glDrawBuffers with GL_FRONT or GL_BACK as you saw in Chapter 8, "Buffer Objects: Storage Is Now in Your Hands," and Chapter 9, "Advanced Buffers: Beyond the Basics."

Why would you want to do that? Double buffering allows OpenGL to draw your entire scene to the back buffer without any intermediate results showing up on the screen. This can provide a smoother and more visually pleasing experience for your users.

But how do users see anything if you are always rendering to a buffer that is not visible? Easy, just tell OpenGL when you are done drawing and the buffers need to be swapped. This is done simply by calling SwapBuffers with the device handle of the window. Once this call is made, the back buffer will be displayed, and our program will have a new back buffer to work with.

```
// Do the buffer swap
SwapBuffers(g_hDC);
```

Eliminating Visual Tearing

If your application is able to draw quickly and call SwapBuffers at a faster rate than the refresh rate of the monitor, an ugly effect called *tearing* can occur. If your application calls SawBuffers before the previous frame is finished being scanned out, someone using your application will see part of one frame and part of the next.

The widely supported extension WGL_EXT_swap_control comes to the rescue! You can tell OpenGL how many video frames, or V-Syncs, are allowed to happen at minimum between swap calls. Just use the following function to set the interval:

```
Bool wglSwapIntervalEXT(GLint interval);
```

If you pass in 0 for interval, the calls to SwapBuffers are unrestricted just as they are without this extension. But if you pass 1 for interval, only one SwapBuffers call is allowed to return for every vertical refresh of the monitor (every video frame). This is exactly what you want to eliminate tearing! All of the additional CPU time can be used for other things while your app waits for the swap to complete.

You can also pass larger intervals to wglSwapIntervalEXT to wait more frames between swaps, but this can cause considerable stutter in your applications. Also many drivers may not support larger intervals than one and will quietly clamp the interval back to 1.

Summary

This chapter introduced you to using OpenGL on the Windows platform. You read about the different driver models and implementations available for Windows and what to watch. You also learned how to search for, enumerate, and select a pixel format to get the kind of hardware-accelerated or software rendering support you want. You've now seen the basic framework for a Win32 program that replaces the GLUT framework, so you can write true native Win32 and Win64 application code. We also showed you how to create a full-screen window for games or simulation-type applications.

Finally, we offered in the source code a program to help you get started with Windows in the form of block_redux, and a further extended full-screen and multisampled version of SphereWorld in the sphere_world_redux program. These programs demonstrate how to use a number of Windows-specific features and WGL extensions if they are available.

CHAPTER 14

OpenGL on OS X

by Richard S. Wright, Jr.

WHAT YOU'LL LEARN IN THIS CHAPTER:

- Use Cocoa and Interface Builder to make an OpenGL view

- Create an optimized full-screen OpenGL window

- Eliminate onscreen visual tearing

- Optimize fill performance

- Enable the multicore version of OpenGL

OpenGL is the native and preferred 3D rendering API on the Mac OS X platform. In fact, OpenGL is used at the lowest levels of the operating system for the desktop, GUI, and Mac OS X's own 2D graphics APIs and compositing engine (Quartz). The importance of OpenGL on the Mac platform cannot be overstated. With its favored status in the eyes of Apple (somewhat analogous to Direct3D's status with Microsoft), it enjoys significant support and investment by Apple in continual tuning and extension to the API.

Remember, this chapter is not about OS X programming, but about using OpenGL on OS X. The sections following assume some prior Mac programming experience. You can probably still get things up and going, but the material offers less insight into how to develop on OS X than it does on how to use OpenGL in that environment.

The Four Faces of OpenGL on the Mac

There are four supported programming interfaces to OpenGL on the Mac, each with its own personality, history, and uses. Which one you use will vary greatly depending on how you prefer to create applications on the Mac and your specific rendering needs. You encounter all four of these technologies as you traverse the OS X programming landscape, but not all of them are still relevant today. Table 14.1 lists these four interfaces.

TABLE 14.1   OpenGL Interface Technologies in OS X

Name	Description
GLUT	Provides a complete framework for simple rendering-based applications. This interface is layered on top of NSOpenGL.
AGL	Provides the OpenGL interface to developers using Carbon as their framework.
NSOpenGL	Provides the OpenGL interface for developers using the Cocoa object-oriented framework for their applications.
CGL	The lowest-level OpenGL interface, available to all application technologies. Both the AGL and NSOpenGL interfaces are layered on top of CGL.

We use these interfaces to do the setup for OpenGL in a window or on a display device. After that is out of the way, OpenGL is just OpenGL! We covered how to set up a GLUT-based program with Xcode in Chapter 2, "Getting Started," and all of the sample programs from the preceding chapters have been GLUT-based, thus no further discussion of how to use GLUT is warranted here. GLUT is a good choice for quick and easy demonstration programs or even very simplistic apps that have little to no user interface needs. The AGL interface is still supported (and by supported, we really only mean "it still works"), even on the newest incarnation of OS X, version 10.6 (Snow Leopard). However AGL is a Carbon only API, and AGL along with Carbon have been deprecated and are considered legacy APIs. Carbon has not been carried forward to the 64-bit era of OS X's evolution either, and thus we do not cover AGL in this edition. CGL is the lowest-level OpenGL interface available on the Mac and can be called directly from any OpenGL program. However, the use of CGL with Snow Leopard has become less of a necessity for full-screen high-performance rendering due to advancements in the OS architecture, which we see later this chapter. Our primary focus then for this chapter is Cocoa-based OpenGL programming because this is by and large the primary means by which you will structure your application framework and OpenGL initialization.

OpenGL with Cocoa

Many programming languages are available to developers on Mac OS X. One very popular language on the Mac (but not quite so popular elsewhere) is Objective-C. To the uninitiated, Objective-C may appear as a strange blend of C and C++ with some completely new syntax thrown in. But Objective-C is also the foundation of a very popular application development technology called Cocoa.

Cocoa is best described as both a collection of application framework classes and a visual programming paradigm. Developers do quite a bit of work in Interface Builder, designing user interfaces, assigning properties, and even making connections between events. Objective-C classes are subclassed from controls or are created from scratch to add application functionality. Fortunately, OpenGL is a first-class citizen in this development environment.

Creating a Cocoa Program

A Cocoa-based program can be created using the New Project Assistant in Xcode. We did this in Chapter 2, when we created our first GLUT-based OpenGL program using Xcode. This time, however, we do not replace the generated project with GLUT-based code. Figure 14.1 shows our newly created CocoaGL project after we added the OpenGL framework (do not add the GLUT framework this time either!).

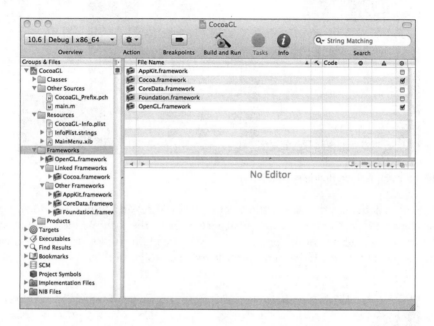

FIGURE 14.1   The initial CocoaGL project.

Adding an OpenGL View

Cocoa applications store resources and GUI layouts in a XIB file (a compiled version of the old NIB, which for historic reasons stands for NEXTSTEP Interface Builder). Double-click the MainMenu.xib file under the Resources folder. This starts Interface Builder and opens the main XIB for editing. You should see a screen similar to that shown in Figure 14.2, with the main window already open.

FIGURE 14.2 Interface Builder—ready to go!

In the library palette, use the tabs at the top to select Classes and then scroll down until you see NSOpenGLView. Click and drag an NSOpenGLView to the main window and resize it to fill most of the main window. You can also resize the main window to taste. You can see in Figure 14.3 that we now have an NSOpenGLView ready to go in the center of the window.

FIGURE 14.3 A very basic interface window.

Creating a Custom OpenGL Class

The next task is to create a custom class derived from NSOpenGLView and associate it with the OpenGL view in the window. Click the Classes tab in the library window, scroll down to the NSOpenGLView entry, and right-click it as shown in Figure 14.4. Then select New Subclass.

FIGURE 14.4   Subclassing the NSOpenGLView class.

In the pop-up window that is presented, name your subclass. In this case, we can go with the default MyOpenGLView. It is very important that you check the Generate Source Files box, as shown in Figure 14.5.

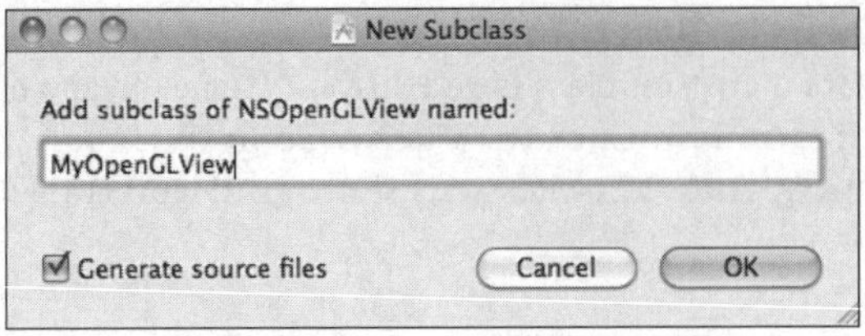

FIGURE 14.5   Generating the derived class.

The next pop-up asks for the name of the file to put your derived class in. This is shown in Figure 14.6. Make sure you check the Create '.h' File box, if it isn't already.

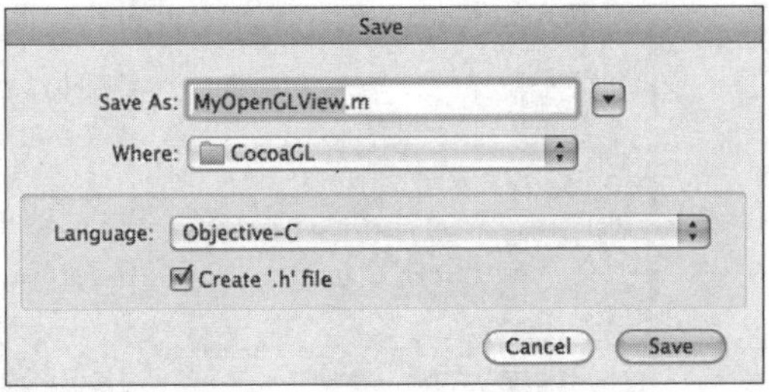

FIGURE 14.6   Actually adding the file to the project.

Finally, Interface Builder asks whether you want to add this class to your project as shown in Figure 14.7. Check the box next to the project name and then click the Add button. Now that you have a real Cocoa OpenGL view class, it's time to start putting things together.

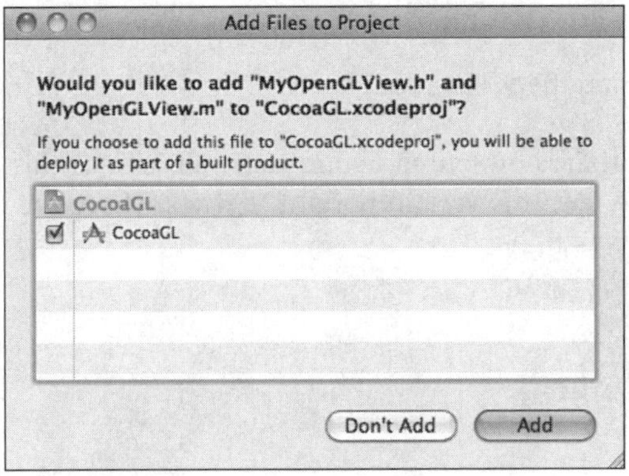

FIGURE 14.7   Actually adding the file to the project.

Wiring It Together

There are still two more things we need to do in Interface Builder before we can start writing code. The first is we need to set our NSOpenGLView window to be connected to our custom MyOpenGLView class. Select the NSOpenGLView window in Interface Builder and from the Tools menu, select Inspector. The Inspector window is shown in Figure 14.8 with the Identity tab selected. In the class combo box, change NSOpenGLView to MyOpenGLView.

FIGURE 14.8   Connecting the custom MyOpenGLView class.

The second is to change the parent window so that it does not use One Shot memory. This flag is on by default, and it tells the parent window that it is okay to delete the subwindow objects when it is minimized to the dock or hidden. With an OpenGL window, this would have the unfortunate side effect of breaking the link between the view and the OpenGL context, which would prevent further rendering operations from being displayed. Figure 14.9 shows the One Shot box unchecked in the Attributes tab. Click the caption of the main window to get to it.

FIGURE 14.9   Turn off the One Shot memory attribute.

Setting OpenGL View Properties

Interface Builder also gives you access to all the framebuffers' properties in an NSOpenGLView control. Click the control itself and then select the Attributes tab of the inspector window. You see a myriad of options shown in Figure 14.10.

FIGURE 14.10   The OpenGL View Attributes window.

Here you can select things like the bit depth and format of the color, depth, and stencil buffer. You can also configure an accumulation buffer, but this feature is deprecated in the core profile, and its use is discouraged (and for good reason no longer covered in this book). You can also select a multisampled color buffer, stereo (left and right buffers), and even force a fallback software renderer instead of using OpenGL hardware.

Wiring It All Together

Back in the Xcode project window, you see the MyOpenGLView header and implementation files. These contain the stubbed definition of the MyOpenGLView class, derived from NSOpenGLView. Interface Builder has already wired this class to our OpenGL view in the main window, and we now only need to add the class framework and OpenGL rendering code.

The edited header file for the new class is trivial and simply contains a member pointer to an NSTimer that will be used for animation:

```
#import <Cocoa/Cocoa.h>

@interface MyOpenGLView : NSOpenGLView {
    NSTimer *pTimer;
}

@end
```

In the implementation file, we add an idle function and implement four essential top-level OpenGL tasks that every OpenGL program needs: prepareGL for OpenGL initialization, clearGLContext for OpenGL cleanup, reshape for calculating the viewport and window bounds, and finally drawRect where we perform our rendering tasks. The entire source for our minimal OpenGL framework is given in Listing 14.1.

LISTING 14.1   A Skeleton OpenGL View Class

```
#import "MyOpenGLView.h"

@implementation MyOpenGLView

- (void)idle:(NSTimer *)pTimer
    {
    [self drawRect:[self bounds]];
    }


- (void) prepareOpenGL
    {
    pTimer = [NSTimer timerWithTimeInterval:(1.0/60.0) target:self
            selector:@selector(idle:) userInfo:nil repeats:YES];
    [[NSRunLoop currentRunLoop]addTimer:pTimer forMode:
                                    NSDefaultRunLoopMode];

    glClearColor(0.0f, 0.0f, 1.0f, 1.0f);
```

```
    }

- (void) clearGLContext
    {
    // Do any OpenGL Cleanup
    }

- (void) reshape
    {
    NSRect rect = [self bounds];
    glViewport(0, 0, rect.size.width, rect.size.height);
    }

- (void) drawRect:(NSRect)dirtyRect
    {
    glClear(GL_COLOR_BUFFER_BIT);

    glFlush();
    }

@end
```

14

The output for CocoaGL is shown in Figure 14.11. As you can see it's nothing but an empty blue window, but now we have a complete framework to build on for our next example.

FIGURE 14.11   OpenGL in a Cocoa view.

Double or Single Buffered?

At this point, the astute reader may be imagining the sound of screeching tires on pavement. Was that a `glFlush` you saw in Listing 14.1 instead of some sort of buffer swap call? Indeed it was, and this brings us to an interesting subtlety of OpenGL on Mac OS X (as well as a nice segue into the next section).

On Mac OS X, the entire desktop is actually OpenGL accelerated. Anytime you are rendering with OpenGL, you are always rendering to an off-screen buffer. A buffer swap does nothing but signal the OS that your rendering is ready to be composited with the rest of the desktop. You can think of the desktop compositing engine as your front buffer. Thus, in windowed OpenGL applications (this applies to both Cocoa and the now deprecated Carbon), all OpenGL windows are really single buffered. Depending on how you look at it, it would also be okay to say that all OpenGL windows are really double buffered, with the desktop composite being the front buffer. Pick whichever one helps you sleep best at night! In fact, if you were to execute a `glDrawBuffer(GL_FRONT)`, the drivers on the Mac actually would fall into a triple-buffered mode! In reality, all OpenGL windows on the Mac should be treated as single buffered. The buffer swap calls are really just doing a `glFlush`, unless you are working with a full-screen context. For this reason (and many others—the least of which is that you are bypassing the driver's own good sense as to when to flush) you should avoid `glFlush` in Cocoa views until you have completed all of your OpenGL rendering.

SphereWorld

To fill out our previous example, we port the SphereWorld example from Chapter 5, "Basic Texturing," from the GLUT framework to the Cocoa framework we just constructed. We begin by creating a new Xcode project and following all of the same steps as we did for CocoaGL, with the exception that we call the custom view class SphereWorldView. Next, we copy the SphereWorld.cpp file and the three texture files to the folder with our new project. Add SphereWorld.cpp to the project and add the three texture files to the /Resources folder in Xcode.

GLTools and Objective-C++

For this example we use our C++ library GLTools again. We can add GLTools the same way we did for our previous GLUT-based examples, and this was covered step-by-step in Chapter 2, so we do not rehash that here. However, what we do need to do here that is new is allow our C++ code to work with Objective-C. As it turns out...you can't. The solution is surprisingly simple: We change our project to use Objective-C++ instead! All you have to do is rename the .m files to .mm, and they become Objective-C++ files, and you can use your C++ classes within them just as if they were C++ files themselves. As a bonus, all the Cocoa Objective-C classes work just the same as well. Figure 14.12 shows our Xcode project with these changes so far. Now it's time to clean up the SphereWorld.cpp file and place the appropriate functions calls in the Cocoa class.

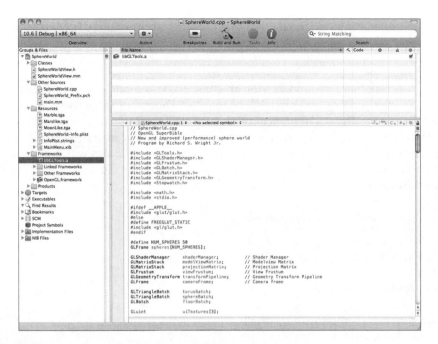

FIGURE 14.12   Our Objective-C++ and GLTools-based project.

Pruning SphereWorld

If we remove the GLUT framework code from SphereWorld.cpp, we are left with four functions that need to be called from our Cocoa framework: SetupRC, ShutdownRC, ChangeSize, and RenderScene. You can probably guess where they go. Removing GLUT turns out to be trivial. First, remove the GLUT headers from the top of the source file.

```
#ifdef __APPLE__
#include <glut/glut.h>
#else
#define FREEGLUT_STATIC
#include <gl/glut.h>
#endif
```

Next, at the end of the RenderScene function, we perform a buffer swap and trigger a refresh. We don't need the buffer swap any longer as the Cocoa framework takes care of that and has a timer that takes care of periodic refreshes. Removing these two lines nearly completes the job.

```
// Do the buffer Swap
glutSwapBuffers();

// Do it again
glutPostRedisplay();
```

The final bit of pruning is to remove the main function in its entirety and delete the SpecialKeys callback, as we no longer are receiving keyboard input through GLUT.

Wiring It In

Calling a function in a C++ module from an Objective-C++ module is no different than normal C++ cross module programming. Listing 14.2 shows our SphereWorldView implementation with the appropriate functions from SphereWorld declared and called where needed in the framework. We have also added the Cocoa message keyDown to catch keystrokes and the acceptFirstResponder method so that keystrokes will be handled by the OpenGL window. This allows us to move the camera in the same manner as we did in the GLUT-based version.

LISTING 14.2   The Cocoa-Based SphereWorld

```
#include <GLTools.h>
#include <GLFrame.h>

#import "SphereWorldView.h"

void ChangeSize(int nWidth, int nHeight);
void RenderScene(void);
void ShutdownRC(void);
void SetupRC(void);

extern GLFrame       cameraFrame;      // Camera frame

@implementation SphereWorldView
- (void)idle:(NSTimer *)pTimer
{
    [self drawRect:[self bounds]];
}


- (BOOL)acceptsFirstResponder
{
    [[self window] makeFirstResponder:self];
    return YES;
}

- (void)keyDown:(NSEvent*)event
{
    float linear = 0.1f;
    float angular = float(m3dDegToRad(5.0f));

    int key = (int)[[event characters] characterAtIndex:0];
```

```
    switch(key)
        {
        case NSUpArrowFunctionKey:
            cameraFrame.MoveForward(linear);
            break;
        case NSDownArrowFunctionKey:
            cameraFrame.MoveForward(-linear);
            break;
        case NSLeftArrowFunctionKey:
            cameraFrame.RotateWorld(angular, 0.0f, 1.0f, 0.0f);
            break;
        case NSRightArrowFunctionKey:
            cameraFrame.RotateWorld(-angular, 0.0f, 1.0f, 0.0f);
            break;
        }
}


- (void) prepareOpenGL
{
    pTimer = [NSTimer timerWithTimeInterval:(1.0/60.0) target:self
                                   selector:@selector(idle:) userInfo:nil
                                   repeats:YES];

[[NSRunLoop currentRunLoop]addTimer:pTimer forMode: NSDefaultRunLoopMode];

    SetupRC();
}


- (void) clearGLContext
{
    ShutdownRC();
}


- (void) reshape
{
    NSRect rect = [self bounds];
    ChangeSize(rect.size.width, rect.size.height);
}


- (void) drawRect:(NSRect)dirtyRect
{
    RenderScene();
```

```
    glFlush();
}

@end
```

Finding the Texture Files

Like in our GLUT-based samples, we put the texture files for SphereWorld in the Resources group in Xcode. Again, we must reset the current working directory so that our file functions can find them. In our GLUT samples, we put this in the main function. For Cocoa, we also put this in the main function. The entire main.mm file is shown here:

```
#include <GLTools.h>
#import <Cocoa/Cocoa.h>

int main(int argc, char *argv[])
    {
    gltSetWorkingDirectory(argv[0]);
    return NSApplicationMain(argc,  (const char **) argv);
    }
```

We needed to add the `GLTools.h` header file at the top of the file, and then the call to the by now familiar `gltSetWorkingDirectory` function takes care of the rest.

GLEW Versus Cocoa

There is one last thing we need to take care of. SphereWorld makes use of GLTools, but GLTools makes use of the GLEW library, which brings in additional OpenGL functions and extensions. There is a funny requirement about using GLEW, which is that the GLEW header files must be included before the actual system OpenGL header, gl.h. With our GLUT-based programs, this was never an issue, as GLTools brought in all the headers as needed. When we added SphereWorld.cpp to this project, again we had no problem. But as soon as we add GLTools to an .mm file…we get compiler errors. If you trace the errors down into the headers, you'll find that they are caused because glew.h was included after gl.h. Search as you may, you will not find out where this is occurring by inspection of the source code of the project.

As it turns out, Cocoa itself is including the OpenGL headers. Remember, OpenGL is used everywhere on the Mac. There is a file in the Xcode project called SphereWorld_Prefix.pch that is the "prefix header." It's a precompiled header that automatically gets added to all the Objective-C/C++ modules. What we need to do is sneak our glew.h header file into that file. Not hard to do—it's only four lines long, and that's with our change!

```
#ifdef __OBJC__
    #include <gl/glew.h>
    #import <Cocoa/Cocoa.h>
#endif
```

Finally, we can get a clean build, and we have a real full- (well, mostly full) featured Cocoa-based OpenGL program. Figure 14.13 shows our final masterpiece.

FIGURE 14.13   SphereWorld in a Cocoa-based application.

Full-Screen Rendering

Many OpenGL applications need to render to the entire screen, rather than live within the confines of a window. This would include many games, media players, kiosk-hosted applications, and other specialized types of applications. One way to accomplish this is to simply make a large window that is the size of the entire display. Prior to OS X 10.6 (Snow Leopard), this was not the most optimal approach, and it was necessary to use the CGL functions to "capture" the display for full-screen rendering to get the best results.

With Snow Leopard, these APIs are still supported but are no longer necessary, and in fact the screen capturing technique is discouraged by Apple. When rendering to a full-screen window, you set a special context flag, and OS X automatically tries to optimize the rendering output in the manner that the old screen capturing technique did. However, by not capturing the display, critical UI messages or other windows are also allowed to pop up over the full-screen window. Capturing the display by modern standards is a bit heavy handed. There is even a simple way now to render into a smaller back buffer to improve fill performance without having to change the display resolution. Let's start by creating a full-screen version of SphereWorld, SphereWorldFS.

Going Full-Screen with Cocoa

To begin our new version of SphereWorld, we again start with a brand new Xcode Cocoa project, which we call SphereWorldFS. Like in the previous example, we add the OpenGL framework, add the GLTools library, rename our .m files to .mm, and copy over the SphereWorldView Cocoa class and the SphereWorld.cpp rendering code along with the texture files that we add to the /Resources folder of the project. This time, however, we are not going to touch Interface Builder. Instead we are going to create and manage our window manually. The application delegate in a Cocoa-based program has a method called `applicationDidFinishLaunching` that is called as soon as your application has successfully launched. In our new project, this is located in the file SphereWorldFSAppDelegate.mm.

Selecting a Pixel Format

Before OpenGL can be initialized for a window, you must first select an appropriate pixel format. A pixel format describes the hardware buffer configuration for 3D rendering— things like the depth of the color buffer, the size of the stencil buffer, and whether the buffer is on-screen (the default) or off-screen. The pixel format is described by the Cocoa data type `NSOpenGLPixelFormat`.

To select an appropriate pixel format for your needs, you first construct an array of integer attributes. For example, the following array requests a double-buffered pixel format with red, green, blue, and alpha components in the destination buffer, a 16-bit depth buffer, and you want an accelerated pixel format, not the software OpenGL renderer. You may get other attributes as well, but you are essentially saying these are all you really care about:

```
NSOpenGLPixelFormatAttribute attrs[] = {

        // Set up our other criteria
        NSOpenGLPFAColorSize, 32,
        NSOpenGLPFADepthSize, 16,
        NSOpenGLPFADoubleBuffer,
        NSOpenGLPFAAccelerated,
        0
    };
```

Note that you must terminate the array with 0 or `nil`. Next, you allocate the pixel format using this array of attributes. If the pixel format cannot be created, the allocation routine returns `nil`, and you should do something appropriate because as far as your OpenGL rendering is concerned, it's game over.

```
NSOpenGLPixelFormat* pixelFormat = [[NSOpenGLPixelFormat alloc]
                                    initWithAttributes:attrs];
   if(pixelFormat == nil)
      NSLog(@"No valid matching OpenGL Pixel Format found");
```

Most attributes are either a Boolean flag or contain an integer value. The Boolean flags set the attribute by simply being present, for example, NSOpenGLPFADoubleBuffer in the preceding example. An integer flag on the other hand, such as NSOpenGLPFADepthSize, is expected to be followed by an integer value that specifies the number of bits desired for the depth buffer. The available attributes and their meanings are listed in Table 14.2.

TABLE 14.2   Cocoa Pixel Format Attributes

Attribute	Meaning
NSOpenGLPFAAllRenderers	Boolean: Allow all available renderers.
NSOpenGLPFADoubleBuffer	Boolean: Must be double buffered.
NSOpenGLPFAStereo	Boolean: Must be stereo.
NSOpenGLPFAAuxBuffers	Integer: Number of auxiliary buffers.
NSOpenGLPFAColorSize	Integer: Depth in bits of the color buffer (default matches the screen).
NSOpenGLPFAAlphaSize	Integer: Depth in bits for alpha in the color buffer.
NSOpenGLPFADepthSize	Integer: Depth in bits for the depth buffer.
NSOpenGLPFAStencilSize	Integer: Depth in bits for the stencil buffer.
NSOpenGLPFAAccumSize	Integer: Depth in bits for the accumulation buffer (deprecated in OpenGL 3.x).
NSOpenGLPFAMinimumPolicy	Boolean: Only buffers greater than or equal to the depths specified are considered.
NSOpenGLPFAMaximumPolicy	Boolean: Use the largest depth values available of any buffers requested.
NSOpenGLPFAOffScreen	Boolean: Use only renderers that can render off-screen.
NSOpenGLPFAFullScreen	Boolean: Use only renderers that can render to a full-screen context. This flag implies the NSOpenGLPFASingleRenderer flag.
NSOpenGLPFASampleBuffers	Integer: Number of multisample buffers.
NSOpenGLPFASamples	Integer: Number of samples per multisample buffer.
NSOpenGLPFAAuxDepthStencil	Standalone: Each auxiliary buffer has its own depth stencil.
NSOpenGLPFAColorFloat	Boolean: Select a floating-point color buffer.
NSOpenGLPFAMultisample	Boolean: Prefer multisampling.
NSOpenGLPFASupersample	Boolean: Prefer supersampling.
NSOpenGLPFASampleAlpha	Boolean: Update multisample alpha values.
NSOpenGLPFARendererID	Integer: Use a specific renderer identified by the integer specified.
NSOpenGLPFASingleRenderer	Boolean: Force a single renderer on a single monitor.

14

TABLE 14.2   Cocoa Pixel Format Attributes *continued*

Attribute	Meaning
NSOpenGLPFANoRecovery	Boolean: Forces continued rendering on a single context when resources have run out. Not generally useful.
NSOpenGLPFAAccelerated	Boolean: Only select a hardware accelerated renderer.
NSOpenGLPFAClosestPolicy	Boolean: Select the color buffer closest to the one specified.
NSOpenGLPFARobust	Boolean: Select only renderers that do not have failure modes due to lack of resources. Not generally useful.
NSOpenGLPFABackingStore	Boolean: Select only a renderer with a back buffer equal in size to the front buffer. Additionally, guarantees the back buffer's contents remain intact after the flushBuffer call.
NSOpenGLPFAMPSafe	Boolean: Select a multiprocessor safe renderer.
NSOpenGLPFAWindow	Boolean: Select only a renderer that can render to a window.
NSOpenGLPFAMultiScreen	Boolean: Select only a renderer capable of driving multiple screens.
NSOpenGLPFACompliant	Boolean: Use only OpenGL-compliant renderers.
NSOpenGLPFAScreenMask	Integer: A bit mask of supported physical screens.
NSOpenGLPFAPixelBuffer	Boolean: Allow rendering to a pixel buffer.
NSOpenGLPFARemotePixelBuffer	Boolean: Allow rendering to an offline pixel buffer.
NSOpenGLPFAAllowOffLineRenderers	Boolean: Allow offline renderers.
NSOpenGLPFAAcceleratedCompute	Boolean: Select only renderers that also support OpenGL.
NSOpenGLPFAVirtualScreenCount	Integer: The number of virtual screens required.

The Full-Screen App Core

Now let's take a look at what is essentially the main program body for the full-screen version of SphereWorld. Listing 14.3 shows the entire applicationDidFinishLaunching implementation.

LISTING 14.3   Creating and Managing Our Full-Screen Window

```
- (void)applicationDidFinishLaunching:(NSNotification *)aNotification {

    NSOpenGLPixelFormatAttribute attrs[] = {

        NSOpenGLPFAFullScreen,  1,// Full Screen context flag

        // Which screen do we want to appear on (you must do this for
        // full screen contexts)
        NSOpenGLPFAScreenMask,
            CGDisplayIDToOpenGLDisplayMask(kCGDirectMainDisplay),
```

```
    // Set up our other criteria
    NSOpenGLPFAColorSize, 24,
    NSOpenGLPFADepthSize, 16,
    NSOpenGLPFADoubleBuffer,
    NSOpenGLPFAAccelerated,
    0
};


NSOpenGLPixelFormat* pixelFormat =
            [[NSOpenGLPixelFormat alloc] initWithAttributes:attrs];
if(pixelFormat == nil)
    NSLog(@"No valid matching OpenGL Pixel Format found");


NSRect mainDisplayRect = [[NSScreen mainScreen] frame];
NSWindow *pMainWindow =
    [[NSWindow alloc] initWithContentRect: mainDisplayRect
    styleMask:NSBorderlessWindowMask
    backing:NSBackingStoreBuffered defer:YES];

[pMainWindow setLevel:NSMainMenuWindowLevel+1];
[pMainWindow setOpaque:YES];
[pMainWindow setHidesOnDeactivate:YES];


NSRect viewRect = NSMakeRect(0.0, 0.0,
    mainDisplayRect.size.width, mainDisplayRect.size.height);
SphereWorldView *fullScreenView =
    [[SphereWorldView alloc] initWithFrame:viewRect
    pixelFormat: [ pixelFormat autorelease] ];
[pMainWindow setContentView: fullScreenView];
[pMainWindow makeKeyAndOrderFront:self];

// Hide the cursor
CGDisplayHideCursor (kCGDirectMainDisplay);

bool bQuit = false;
while(!bQuit) {
    // Check for and process input events.
    NSEvent *event;
    event = [NSApp nextEventMatchingMask:NSAnyEventMask
        untilDate:[NSDate distantPast]
```

14

```
                    inMode:NSDefaultRunLoopMode dequeue:YES];
            if(event != nil)
               switch ([event type]) {
                   case NSKeyDown:
                       [fullScreenView keyDown:event];

                       if((int)[[event characters]
                          characterAtIndex:0] == 27) // ESC Exits
                          bQuit = true;
                       break;

                   case NSKeyUp:
                       [fullScreenView keyUp:event];
                   break;

                   default:
                       break;
               }

          [fullScreenView drawRect:viewRect];
      }

      // Show the cursor again
      CGDisplayShowCursor(kCGDirectMainDisplay);

      // Terminate the application
      [NSApp terminate:self];
      }
```

The first order of business is to create a full-screen pixel format. Note the use of the flag NSOpenGLPFAFullScreen and the accompanying NSOpenGLPFAScreenMask. You must use these two flags together to get a valid pixel format for a full-screen context and get the full benefit of Snow Leopard's ability to optimize the rendering for full-screen windows.

Second, we create a main window that is the size of the current desktop. Here we use the NSBorderlessWindowMask to eliminate the caption, minimize buttons, and so on.

```
NSRect mainDisplayRect = [[NSScreen mainScreen] frame];
    NSWindow *pMainWindow =
        [[NSWindow alloc] initWithContentRect: mainDisplayRect
        styleMask:NSBorderlessWindowMask
        backing:NSBackingStoreBuffered defer:YES];
```

A couple of other settings also come in useful for a true full-screen experience. We set the window level to be above the menu bar, make sure the window is not transparent, and set the setHideOnDeactivate flag. This hides the window whenever you switch away from the window and then automatically restores the full-screen status when you reactivate the application.

```
[pMainWindow setLevel:NSMainMenuWindowLevel+1];
[pMainWindow setOpaque:YES];
[pMainWindow setHidesOnDeactivate:YES];
```

Next we create the actual OpenGL-based view based on our previously constructed SphereWorldView class. This view is assigned to the main window, which is then activated and displayed. Although Interface Builder gives us some control over the pixel format, the option to create your NSOpenGLView classes with the initWithFrame method gives you the ultimate control and flexibility.

```
NSRect viewRect = NSMakeRect(0.0, 0.0,
        mainDisplayRect.size.width, mainDisplayRect.size.height);
    SphereWorldView *fullScreenView =
        [[SphereWorldView alloc] initWithFrame:viewRect
        pixelFormat: [ pixelFormat autorelease] ];
    [pMainWindow setContentView: fullScreenView];
    [pMainWindow makeKeyAndOrderFront:self];
```

Once we have created the full-screen window, we usually do not need to display the mouse cursor. The Core GL (CGL) method CGDisplayHideCursor hides the cursor for us until either the application terminates or we call the corresponding CGDisplayShowCursor.

```
CGDisplayHideCursor(kCGDirectMainDisplay);
```

For a full-screen window, we need to process the Cocoa event loop ourselves. The NSApp method nextEventMatchingMask retrieves the latest event and removes it from the event queue. In the case of an NSKeyDown event, we forward it to the SphereWorldView class, which checks for arrow keys to facilitate camera movement. We also check here for the escape key, which if pressed changes the value of bQuit to true, terminating the event loop and finally terminating the application.

```
[NSApp terminate:self];
```

View Class Changes
There is one additional change we need to make to the SphereWorldView class when using our own pixel format in full-screen mode. At the end of the drawRect method, we replace glFlush with a call to flushBuffer on the OpenGL context:

```
[[self openGLContext ]flushBuffer];
```

This performs the equivalent of a buffer swap for our double-buffered renderer. Because we are no longer in "windowed" mode, just flushing the command buffer is not enough; we also need the buffer swap, which now is actually taking place.

Given that we have gone full-screen, we've also thrown in a few other goodies. For one, we ported the GLString class from one of the Apple OpenGL demos (Apple's own CocoGL demo) to use only the new OpenGL core profile and the stock shaders in GLTools. We use this in the SphereWorldView class to calculate and display the frame rate of our new full-screen SphereWorld, which is running unrestrained as fast as it can. Figure 14.14 shows our SphereWorld running at 199 frames per second.

FIGURE 14.14   SphereWorld with fps display.

Finally, we also modified our keyboard handling of movement to smooth things out. Instead of moving the camera when a key is pressed, we set a flag for each movement key to true when the key is pressed and to false when the key is released. In the render function, we then move based on the state of those flags. This keeps movement smooth and less jerky as a result of the latency inherent in keyboard messages. Compare the navigation between SphereWorldFS and the original SphereWorld in a window yourself!

CGL

As we have already stated, Core GL, or CGL as it is usually referred to, is the lowest-level support for OpenGL on Mac OS X. It can be used with any of the other OpenGL technologies listed in Table 14.1, and we can use a few interesting functions for our SphereWorldFS example as well. We cover here just a few quick and easy but useful recipes for using CGL in our Cocoa-based application. There may be Cocoa equivalents to some of these, but the CGL version will also work with your GLUT-based OpenGL programs or even a higher level third-party C++ framework you might choose to use. You can also use CGL exclusively to create a full-screen context and render to it as needed, but as we've just shown, this is no longer necessary with Snow Leopard.

All CGL functions we are interested in require the current CGL context as one of the parameters. In any OpenGL application, you can retrieve the current CGL context by calling CGLGetCurrentContext.

```
CGLContextObj CGLGetCurrentContext(void);
```

Sync Frame Rate

In our previous example program SphereWorldFS, our event loop ran and rendered at full speed as many frames per second as possible. This is useful when doing performance testing of your rendering or processing code, as the frames per second is a simple metric of just how fast your code can execute. In a shipping application, there are two drawbacks to this, however. First, in addition to excessive use of the GPU, you are also taking up all the cycles on one of your CPU cores (at least!). If you consider that your display refreshes typically 60 times per second, there is no real need or purpose to displaying more than 60 frames per second. That excess GPU power could be used to generate more sophisticated rendering effects, or the CPU power could be used to improve other application processing performance or perhaps add more detail or features to the application or game.

Second, because the display only refreshes so many times per second, rendering more frames per second than the display can show causes *tearing*. Tearing occurs when the buffer swap occurs at any point other than the vertical retrace of the screen. Essentially, you get two different frames displayed on-screen at the same time. The old frame occupies the area of the display above the current display refresh position, and the bottom of the screen is then filled with the new buffer contents. This is especially jarring when the view is moving horizontally in the scene. Figure 14.15 shows a typical tearing example, where the display briefly shows two different frames.

FIGURE 14.15   Tearing caused by an unsynced buffer swap. (This figure also appears as Color Plate 23.)

In a double-buffered application, such as our previous full-screen example, the swap interval sets the number of vertical retraces that should occur before the buffer swap occurs. Setting this value to one forces no more than one frame per vertical retrace, while setting it to two allows two vertical retraces between buffer swaps. For example, if the swap interval was set to one, and the display refresh rate was 60 (about typical), you would get no more than 60 fps. For a swap interval of two, you'd get a maximum of 30 fps, and so on. You set the swap interval with the CGL function CGLSetParameter.

```
GLint sync = 1;
CGLSetParameter (CGLGetCurrentContext(), kCGLCPSwapInterval, &sync);
```

Note, this does not "fix" the frame rate to equal the refresh of the monitor. If your rendering, or CPU code for that matter, takes an excessive amount of time, you may get less than the full refresh rate of your monitor. What you still gain, however, is that the buffer swaps only occur between refreshes, thus eliminating the tearing issue.

Increasing Fill Performance

Fill performance refers to the performance overhead in rendering that specifically relates to the time spent writing data to pixels in the frame buffer. One easy way to improve fill performance is to simply render to a smaller window, or in the case of the full-screen application such as a game, to change the screen resolution to a smaller value. Before Snow Leopard, it was not uncommon for a full-screen OpenGL game, for example, to change the screen resolution before running, capture the display, and so on. Now that we no longer need the display capturing solution, we can make use of CGL's ability to change the size of the back buffer instead of changing the screen resolution. Changing the back buffer to be smaller than the front buffer has the added fill performance benefit, without the need for a display mode change. The contents of the back buffer are then automatically stretched to fill the entire display when the buffer swap occurs.

To set the back surface size, we set the CGL parameter `kCGLCPSurfaceBackingSize` to the integer dimensions that we want. In addition, we must enable the `kCGLCESurfaceBackingSize` feature with `CGLEnable`. The following code shows how you would do this for a desired new size of `newWidth` x `newHeight`.

```
GLint dim[2] = {newWidth, newHeight};
CGLSetParameter(CGLGetCurrentContext(), kCGLCPSurfaceBackingSize, dim);
CGLEnable(CGLGetCurrentContext(), kCGLCESurfaceBackingSize);
```

Multithreaded OpenGL

The OpenGL driver does a significant amount of processing of your rendering data before it eventually shows up on the hardware for rendering. On OS X 10.5 or later, you can enable a multithreaded OpenGL core that offloads some of these tasks to another thread. On a multicore system, this can have a positive performance impact. You can enable this feature by calling `CGLEnable` on the `kCGLCEMPEngine` flag.

```
CGLEnable(CGLGetCurrentContext(), kCGLCEMPEngine);
```

This does not always improve performance, and in fact sometimes can reduce performance! If your OpenGL code is not hampered by CPU processing, this may have little to no effect on your rendering performance, for example. For another, if your rendering code calls a lot of functions that produce pipeline stalls (`glGetFloatv`, `glGetIntegerv`, `glReadPixels`, etc.), these too can interfere with this potential optimization.

Summary

In this chapter we covered how to build native OS X applications that use OpenGL with Interface Builder and Cocoa. While GLUT has its uses, here we covered how to create an OpenGL-capable Mac application using the native application frameworks in Objective-C. We also showed how new technology in the latest version of OS X, 10.6 (Snow Leopard), makes high-performance full-screen applications easier to build than ever. Finally we took a look at some simple tricks we can pull with the Mac's lowest-level OpenGL interface, CGL.

OpenGL is a core foundational technology for the Macintosh. A basic understanding of OpenGL and how applications can natively interact with it is an essential skill for any Mac OS X developer. This chapter only scratched the surface of a potentially deep and complex topic. We purposely stayed in the shallow end of the pool, as it were, so that you can get going quickly and experiment as much as possible with OpenGL on this wonderful platform. In Appendix A, "Further Reading," you find some additional great coverage of this exciting topic.

CHAPTER 15

OpenGL on Linux

by Nicholas Haemel

WHAT YOU'LL LEARN IN THIS CHAPTER:

How To	Functions You'll Use
Manage Visuals	`glXChooseVisual, glXChooseFBConfig`
Create GLX windows	`glXCreateWindow`
Manage OpenGL drawing contexts	`glXCreateContextAttribsARB,`
	`glXDestroyContext,`
	`glXMakeCurrent`
Create OpenGL windows	`glXCreateWindow`
Do double-buffered drawing	`glXSwapBuffers`

One great thing about OpenGL is that it's supported on so many different platforms. We looked at how to use OpenGL on Windows and on Macs. Now let's dig into 3D rendering on one of the most popular open source platforms—Linux.

In this chapter we look at how Linux supports OpenGL, how to pick a specific version of OpenGL, what interfaces are available for developers, and how to set up an application. We also touch on GLUT, context management, and how to allocate, render to, and deal with windows on X Windows.

The Basics

OpenGL has been the go-to API for 3D rendering on various versions of Linux, UNIX, and similar platforms for nearly as long as 3D rendering has been possible. Linux offers several ways to do OpenGL. Most major graphics hardware provides some form of acceleration. Mesa3D, a software implementation that does not depend on hardware, can also be installed on most X Server configurations.

Brief History

In the late 1980s Silicon Graphics (SGI) introduced a proprietary API for 2D and 3D graphics on its workstations called IRIS GL (Integrated Raster Imaging System Graphics Language). In 1992 SGI revised the specification and published it as an open industry standard called OpenGL. In 1993 Brian Paul started a project to create a software-only implementation of OpenGL called Mesa3D, opening the door to wider support of 3D rendering not tied to a specific hardware vendor.

Most computer systems available today contain some sort of 3D acceleration. Modern 3D hardware vendors provide support for the latest versions of OpenGL. Currently both ATI/AMD and NVIDIA provide OpenGL drivers that support OpenGL 3.3. The most recent version of Mesa at the time of publication (7.7) supports OpenGL 2.1.

What Is X?

The X Window System is a graphical user interface that provides a more intuitive environment for users than a command prompt, similar to Microsoft Windows and Mac OS. X Window sessions are not restricted to use on local systems. For instance, you can start an X Server session from your computer that accesses a supercomputer halfway across the country. This allows you to use the remote computer as if you were sitting right in front of it. In X Window terminology, the computer providing the user display services is called the X Window Server, and the computer running the actual application is referred to as the client. This may be counter to the common roles known as server and client.

We run our Linux OpenGL applications inside X Windows. Most Linux distributions use the XFree86 implementation of the X Windows System. Many different desktop managers are available, such as KDE and Gnome, which run atop the basic X Window software and provide user interaction for moving and resizing windows, launching programs, and other basic operations.

Getting Started

You need several components set up for your OpenGL applications to compile and run. First and most obviously you need a Linux system. Different Linux distributions such as OpenSUSE, Fedora, and Ubuntu are available for free download.

Next, it is highly recommended you have a modern graphics card or system with a graphics chip that supports current versions of OpenGL. It is also important that recent drivers be available and installed. Although it is possible to run a software implementation of OpenGL, these software implementations may not support all features of OpenGL and are considerably slower.

You also need the header files and libraries for OpenGL and GLX. These are necessary for compiling your own applications.

Checking for OpenGL

Let's take a quick look at how you can make sure OpenGL is supported on your system. Without that, the rest of this chapter is pretty meaningless. Try running the `glxinfo` command as shown here:

```
glxinfo ¦grep rendering
```

You should get one of two responses:

```
direct rendering: Yes
```

```
direct rendering: No
```

If the answer is yes, good news! You have hardware support for 3D rendering. If no, then you may not have hardware that supports OpenGL, or you may not have drivers installed for OpenGL. If hardware support is not available, try running the following:

```
glxinfo ¦grep "OpenGL vendor"
glxinfo ¦grep "OpenGL version"
```

This prints out the currently installed OpenGL driver information. Remember to be careful about capitalization! If you do not have hardware drivers but do have Mesa installed, the information for the Mesa driver will be displayed. You will also get the current version of OpenGL your Mesa implementation supports.

If the `glxinfo` command fails or no vendor/version information is available, your Linux distribution is not set up for rendering with OpenGL. You have several options. First, you can install Mesa. Or you could install a video card that supports 3D rendering and has driver support for Linux.

Most Linux distributions use one of several package managers (based on RPM or deb files) to manage installed software. If your Linux system does not have OpenGL itself, OpenGL hardware drivers, or the OpenGL development headers/libraries installed, you may need to utilize your package manager to obtain and install them. Additional components like Mesa3D, GLUT, and GLEW may also be available as packages in your distribution permitting easy installation. However, package-distributed versions of these tools may be outdated compared to those available by direct download from the project's Web site.

Setting Up Mesa

The latest version of Mesa can be downloaded from the Mesa3D Web site; a link is provided in Appendix A, "Further Reading." From there you can get the download link for SourceForge. Once downloaded, unpack the files (example shown for Mesa 7.7):

```
gunzip MesaLib-7.7.tar.gz
tar xf MesaLib-7.7.tar
```

15

Next, you need to compile the source that you just unpacked. Go to the directory that was just created from the tar package and run the following:

```
make linux-x86
```

It takes a while to build the Mesa software for your system. After the build has finished, a number of libraries will have been created. Now you need to install the libraries and headers to allow the operating system and build environment to find them when necessary. To do the install, run the following command:

```
make install
```

The library and include locations are usually located in the following directories:

```
Libraries: /usr/X11R6/lib
Includes: /usr/include/
```

You have now finished the Mesa install. If you have more questions about the Mesa setup or install, visit the Mesa3D Web site.

Setting Up Hardware Drivers

If you have modern graphics hardware, you want to make sure you have drivers installed and that they are up to date. Driver support for Linux differs by hardware vendor. Both AMD and NVIDIA provide a proprietary driver package that can be downloaded from their Web sites. The install process is usually simple, just a matter of running the downloaded package and following the prompts. Specific installation instructions can be found on manufacturer Web sites.

Some hardware vendors may also provide an open source version of their display drivers. Although it is often nice to have the source for the driver build, these drivers are often slower, updated less frequently, and have fewer features or more limitations than their proprietary counterparts. It's worth noting that some distros may have drivers prepackaged. These can be outdated, and it is often easiest to simply not install the packaged versions and install the newest vendor drivers instead.

Setting Up GLUT and GLEW

GLUT was covered earlier in this book. It is basically a useful set of functions that help make interfacing with OpenGL and the system much more user-friendly, taking care of many of the unsightly details. OpenGL code written with GLUT is also platform-agnostic, making the code very portable. The version used with this book is freeglut, which is more up to date than the original version of GLUT.

GLUT and freeglut are available for download and install on Linux as well as other operating systems. This helps to make any applications that use GLUT very portable given that the code can be compiled on Windows, Mac, and Linux. It is also a good way to get applications up and running quickly because no window management is required. GLUT does not allow for direct interface with the X Server. This means some things that can be done directly communicating with the OS or the X Server are more difficult or impossible when using GLUT.

The GLEW (GL extension wrangler) library has also been used earlier in the book. GLEW provides a set of tools that help load extensions in OpenGL. Like GLUT, GLEW is available for many different operating systems and platforms. By using GLEW, applications can focus on 3D rendering and worry less about making applications work across different platforms.

Installing GLUT

GLUT may not be already installed on your system. If that's the case, it can be easily downloaded. Then go to the GLUT directory and perform the following commands:

```
./mkmkfiles.imake
make
make install
```

The first command creates the make files you use to compile the code. The make files are custom made for each system because different resources may be located in different places on each system. The second command actually compiles the code. And the third installs the result.

To use GLUT in your applications you need to add the GLUT library to your link command:

```
-lglut
```

Mesa3D also supplies a version of GLUT that can be downloaded and installed.

Installing GLEW

GLEW is pretty straightforward and is contained in two headers and a single source file. These are included in the \GLTools_directory with the source distribution for the book. Automatically gaining access to all the function pointers supported by the driver is a simple matter of adding glew.c to your project, and glew.h to the top of your header list. Then call glewInit() when your application starts up before any OpenGL calls are made. All the function pointers for extensions and core features beyond OpenGL 1.1 will be set up automatically. If the glewInit function fails, it returns an error, and the extension pointers may not be initialized.

Building OpenGL Apps

Now that we've gone through all that setup and our system is prepped for running and compiling OpenGL programs, let's take a look at how to build these programs. If you have spent time working with Linux, you are probably already familiar with creating makefiles. If so, skip ahead.

15

Makefiles are used on Linux systems to compile and link source code, creating an executable file. Makefiles hold instructions for the compiler and linker, telling them where to find files and what to do with them. A sample makefile follows. It can be modified and expanded to accommodate your own projects.

```
LIBDIRS = -L/usr/X11R6/lib -L/usr/X11R6/lib64 -L/usr/local/lib
INCDIRS = -I/usr/include -L/usr/local/include

CC = gcc
CFLAGS = $(COMPILERFLAGS) -g $(INCDIRS)
LIBS = -lX11 -lXi -lXmu -lglut -lGL -lGLU -lm

example : example.o
    $(CC) $(CFLAGS) -o example $(LIBDIRS) example.c $(LIBS)
clean:
    rm -f *.o
```

The first line creates a variable that contains the link parameters for libraries to be included. The one used here looks in both the standard lib directory for X11 as well as the version for 64-bit specific libraries.

The second line lists the include paths the compiler should use when trying to find header files. `CC = gcc` selects the compiler to use. The next line specifies the compile flags to use with this instance. Then `LIBS =` selects all the libraries that need to be linked into our program.

Finally we compile and link the single source file specified for this example, called `example.c`. The last line cleans up intermediate objects that were created during the process. This example can be used while substituting your file in the script. Other files can also be compiled together as well. Many resources and tutorials are on the Web; two good makefile primers are listed in Appendix A to help you get started.

GLX—Interfacing with X Windows

On X Windows a common interface called GLX exists for allowing applications that use OpenGL to communicate with X Windows. This interface is similar to WGL on Windows and AGL on Mac. There are many different versions of GLX; version 1.4 is the most recent. GLX 1.4 is similar to GLX version 1.3 but includes a few minor changes. GLX 1.2 is much older and is missing much of the functionality of the newer versions. For this reason, GLX 1.4 is used for our applications.

To find out more information about your installation of GLX, you can use the `glxinfo` command again. Try the following:

```
glxinfo ¦grep "glx vendor"
glxinfo ¦grep "glx version"
```

This displays the GLX information for both server and client components of X Windows. The effective version you can use is the older of the server and client versions. So if your client reports 1.4 and your server reports 1.3, then you can only use version GLX 1.3. If your client or server driver does not support GLX 1.4, you can try updating your display driver as described earlier.

From inside a program you can also call glXQueryVersion to get the GLX version:

```
Bool glXQueryVersion(Display * dpy, int *major, int *minor);
```

This call would look like

```
int majorVer, minorVer;
glXQueryVersion(dpy, majorVer, minorVer);
```

Displays and X Windows

Before we get too far into using GLX, there are a few prerequisites for understanding how GLX works on Linux. An OpenGL application runs inside a window on the X Server. I mentioned earlier that X Windows supports client and server components running on separate systems, essentially allowing you to run your desktop from somewhere else. Additionally, an X Server can have multiple displays active or even multiple graphics cards.

Before we can create a window, we need to find out what display the OpenGL application will be executing on. The display helps the X Server understand where we are rendering. Use the XOpenDisplay() function to get the current display.

```
Display *dpy = XOpenDisplay(getenv("DISPLAY"));
```

This gives us a pointer to the display object for the default display. We can use this later to tell the X Server where we are. After our application is done, it also needs to close the display using the XCloseDisplay() function. This tells the X Server that we are finished, and it can close the connection.

```
XCloseDisplay(Display * display);
```

Config Management and Visuals

Before we can create a window or an OpenGL rendering context, we need to know what sort of traits are required. Configs on Linux are similar to configs on OpenGL ES or pixel formats on Windows. A config is an enumerated set of attributes supported by X Windows or the OpenGL/GLX driver. An implementation often supports many combinations of window and rendering attributes, and therefore a large number of configs. Because there are so many factors all tied into configs, they can be tricky to handle.

For starters, you can use the glXGetFBConfigs interface to get information on all of the configs supported.

```
GLXFBConfig *glXGetFBConfigs(Display * dpy, int screen, int *nelements);
```

Use the display handle that you got from calling XOpenDisplay. For our purposes we can use the default screen for the screen parameter. When the call returns, nelements tells you how many configs were returned.

There's more to each config than its index. Each config has a unique set of attributes that represent the functionality of that config. These attributes and their descriptions are listed in Table 15.1.

TABLE 15.1   GLX Config Attribute List

Attribute	Description
GLX_BUFFER SIZE	Total number of bits of the color buffer.
GLX_RED_SIZE	Number of bits in red channel of color buffer.
GLX_GREEN_SIZE	Number of bits in green channel of color buffer.
GLX_BLUE_SIZE	Number of bits in blue channel of color buffer.
GLX_ALPHA_SIZE	Number of bits in alpha channel of color buffer.
GLX_DEPTH_SIZE	Number of bits in depth buffer.
GLX_STENCIL_SIZE	Number of bits in stencil buffer.
GLX_CONFIG_CAVEAT	Set to one of the following caveats: GLX_NONE, GLX_SLOW_CONFIG, or GLX_NON_CONFORMANT_CONFIG. These can warn of potential issues for this config. A slow config may be software emulated because it exceeds HW limits. A nonconformant config will not pass the conformance test.
GLX_X_RENDERABLE	Is set to GLX_TRUE if the X Server can render to this surface.
GLX_VISUAL_ID	The XID of the related Visual.
GLX_X_VISUAL_TYPE	Type of a X visual if config supports window rendering (associated visual exists).
GLX_DRAWABLE_TYPE	Valid surface targets supported. May be any or all of GLX_WINDOW_BIT, GLX_PIXMAP_BIT, or GLX_PBUFFER_BIT.
GLX_RENDER_TYPE	Bitfield indicating the types of contexts that can be bound. May be GLX_RGBA_BIT or GLX_COLOR_INDEX_BIT.
GLX_FBCONFIG_ID	The XID for the GLXFBConfig.
GLX_LEVEL	The frame buffer level.
GLX_DOUBLEBUFFER	Is GLX_TRUE if color buffers are double buffered.

Attribute	Description
GLX_STEREO	Is GLX_TRUE if color buffers support stereo rendering.
GLX_SAMPLE_BUFFERS	Number of multisample buffers. Must be 0 or 1.
GLX_SAMPLES	Number of samples per pixel for multisample buffers. Will be 0 if GLX_SAMPLE_BUFFERS is 0.
GLX_TRANSPARENT_TYPE	Indicates support of transparency. Value may be GLX_NONE, GLX_TRANSPARENT_RGB, or GLX_TRANSPARENT_INDEX. If transparency is supported, a transparent pixel is drawn when the pixel's components are all equal to the respective transparent RGB values.
GLX_TRANSPARENT_RED_VALUE	Red value a framebuffer pixel must have to be transparent.
GLX_TRANSPARENT_GREEN_VALUE	Green value a framebuffer pixel must have to be transparent.
GLX_TRANSPARENT_BLUE_VALUE	Blue value a framebuffer pixel must have to be transparent.
GLX_TRANSPARENT_ALPHA_VALUE	Alpha value a framebuffer pixel must have to be transparent.
GLX_TRANSPARENT_INDEX_VALUE	Index value a framebuffer pixel must have to be transparent. For color index configs only.
GLX_AUX_BUFFERS	The number of supported auxiliary buffers.
GLX_ACCUM_RED_SIZE	Number of bits in red channel of the auxiliary buffer.
GLX_ACCUM_GREEN_SIZE	Number of bits in green channel of the auxiliary buffer.
GLX_ACCUM_BLUE_SIZE	Number of bits in blue channel of the auxiliary buffer.
GLX_ACCUM_ALPHA_SIZE	Number of bits in alpha channel of the auxiliary buffer.

You can query any configs to find the value of each of these attributes by using the glXGetFBConfigAttrib command.

```
int glXGetFBConfigAttrib(Display * dpy, GLXFBConfig config,
                         int attribute, int *value);
```

Set the config parameter to the config number you are interested in querying and the attribute parameter to the attribute you would like to query. The result is returned in the value parameter. If the glXGetFBConfigAttrib call fails, it may return the error GLX_BAD_ATTRIBUTE if the attribute you are requesting doesn't exist.

GLX also provides a method for getting a subset of configs that meet a set of criteria. This can help narrow down the total set to just those that you care about, making it much easier to find a config that works for your application. For instance, if you have an application for rendering into a window, the config you select needs to support rendering to a window.

```
GLXFBConfig *glXChooseFBConfig(Display * dpy, int screen,
                const int *attrib_list, int *nelements);
```

Pass in the screen that you are interested in as the screen parameter and specify the elements that are required for a config match. This is done with a NULL terminated list of parameter and value pairs. These attributes are the same config attributes listed in Table 15.1.

```
attrib_list = {attribute1, attribute_value1,
               attribute2, attribute_value2,
               attribute3, attribute_value3,
               0};
```

Similar to glXGetFBConfigs, the number of configs that match the attribute list is returned in nelements. A pointer to a list of matching configs is returned by the function. Remember to use XFree to clean up the memory that was returned by the glXChooseFBConfig call. All configs returned will match the minimum criteria you set in the attrib list.

There are a few key attributes that you may want to pay attention to when creating a config. For instance GLX_X_RENDERABLE should be GLX_TRUE so that you can use OpenGL to perform rendering, GLX_DRAWABLE_TYPE needs to include GLX_WINDOW_BIT if you are rendering to a window, GLX_RENDER_TYPE should be GLX_RGBA_BIT, and GLX_CONFIG_CAVEAT should be set to GLX_NONE or at the very least not have the GLX_SLOW_CONFIG bit set. After that you may also want to make sure the color, depth, and stencil channels meet minimum requirements. The pBuffer, accumulation, and transparency values are less commonly used.

For attributes you don't specify, the glXChooseFBConfigs command uses default values implicitly. These are listed in the GLX specification. The sort mechanism automatically sorts the list of returned configs using an attribute priority. The order for the highest priority attributes is GLX_CONFIG_CAVEAT, the color buffer bit depths, GLX_BUFFER_SIZE, and then GLX_DOUBLEBUFFER.

If a config has the GLX_WINDOW_BIT set for the GLX_DRAWABLE_TYPE attribute, the config will have an associated X visual. The visual can be queried using the following command:

```
XVisualInfo *glXGetVisualFromFBConfig(Display * dpy, GLXFBConfig config);
```

NULL is returned if there isn't an associated X visual. Don't forget to free the returned memory with XFree.

PBuffers are not discussed because this functionality is deprecated and may not be supported by hardware vendors. There are much more flexible ways to achieve off-screen rendering, or rendering without a window. Pixmaps fall into the same category. Instead, framebuffer objects replace this functionality. Also color index mode is not covered here. It also has been deprecated and is not supported on most PC-based implementations.

Windows and Render Surfaces

Now that we're through the messy stuff, let's create a window. We can do this by calling the X Server function XCreateWindow. The result is a handle for the new X Window. The function needs a parent window, but you can also use the main X Window for this, and you should already be familiar with the Display parameter here. You also need to tell X how big of a window you would like and where to put it using the x,y position and the width/height parameters.

Also tell the X Server what kind of a window you want with the window class. This can be one of three values: InputOnly, InputOutput, or CopyFromParent. An InputOnly window cannot be used as a source or destination for graphics requests, and the CopyFromParent value inherits the value that the parent window was created with, so InputOutput is most useful. The attributes and valuemask fields let you tell X what types of characteristics the window should have. The attributes field holds the values, and the valuemask tells X which values it should pay attention to. To get more information on attributes refer to the X Server documentation. The full function declaration looks like this:

```
Window XCreateWindow(Display * dpy, Window parent, int x, int y,
                     unsigned int width, unsigned int height,
                     unsigned int border_width, int depth,
                     unsigned int class, Visual *visual,
                     unsigned_long valuemask,
                     XSetWindowAttributes *attributes);
```

After choosing good values for creating your window and calling XCreateWindow, the handle to the new window is returned. This window handle can then be used to create a corresponding GLX window. When creating the GLX window, the configs you use must be compatible with the visual you created the X Window with. Use the glXCreateWindow command to create a new on-screen OpenGL rendering area associated with your newly created X Window.

```
GLXWindow glXCreateWindow(Display * dpy, GLXFBConfig config,
                          Window win, const int *attrib_list);
```

15

By now you are already familiar with the Display parameter. You can use the config you selected in the section using glXGetFBConfigs or glXChooseFBConfig. The Window handle is the same handle returned from XCreateWindow. The attrib_list currently does not support any parameters and is for future expansion, so you should pass in NULL.

glXCreateWindow throws an error and fails if the config is not compatible with the window visual, if the config doesn't support window rendering, if the window parameter is invalid, if a GLXFBConfig has already been associated with the window, if the GLXFBConfig is invalid, or if there was a general failure creating the GLX window. Also remember that glXCreateWindow is only supported in GLX 1.3 or later. It does not work on older versions. Remember we checked the GLX versions earlier by running glxinfo ¦grep "glx version" in a terminal.

Once you are done rendering, you also have to clean up the windows you created. To destroy the GLX window, call glXDestroyWindow with the GLX window handle returned when you called glXCreateWindow.

```
glXDestroyWindow(Display * dpy, GLXWindow window);
```

Finally, destroy the X Window you originally created. You can use the similarly named XDestroyWindow command and pass back the X Window handle.

```
XDestroyWindow(Display * dpy, Window win);
```

GLX Strings

You can query various GLX strings to get more information on what your system can do. One of the most important strings is the extension string. This is a list of all the extensions the current implementation of GLX supports. To get the extension string, use

```
const char *glXQueryExtensionsString(Display *dpy, int screen);
```

The returned string, or character array, is a list of extension names separated by spaces. The array is terminated by the value 0.

You can also call glXGetClientString or glXQueryServerString to find out information about the client library or the server, respectively. Pass one of the following enums for the name argument: GLX_VENDOR, GLX_VERSION, or GLX_EXTENSIONS.

```
const char *glXGetClientString(Display *dpy,  int name);
const char *glXQueryServerString(Display *dpy, int screen, int name);
```

Extending OpenGL and GLX

Before going any further, let's look at how GLX can be extended without creating a whole new version of GLX. Vendors can write new extensions for GLX and OpenGL to add new functionality for applications to use. This allows applications to use features that are either vendor-specific or are available before they can become part of the core specification. You just learned how to get the list of GLX extensions by calling glXQueryExtensionString. In Chapter 2, "Getting Started," you also learned how to get a list of all OpenGL extensions. The descriptions of new extensions can be found in the OpenGL extension repository on the Web. Once you know what extensions are available and what they do, you may have to get new entrypoints to use them. GLX provides the glXGetProcAddress to look up function addresses for extensions.

```
void (*glXGetProcAddress(const ubyte *procname))();
```

Context Management

A context is a set of OpenGL state that is associated with a handle. A context must be bound to a drawable (such as a window) for state to be set or for rendering to occur. Multiple contexts can be created, but only one can be bound to a drawable at a time. At least one context must be created for your app to be able to render.

Creating Contexts

One way you can create a new context is with the glXCreateNewContext command.

```
GLXContext glXCreateNewContext(Display * dpy, GLXFBConfig config,
             int render_type, GLXContext share_list, bool direct);
```

When successful, this function returns a context handle that you can use when telling GLX which context you want to use when rendering. The config that you use to create this context needs to be compatible with the render surface you intend to draw on. For common cases it is easiest to use the same config that was used to create the GLX window.

The render_type parameter accepts GLX_RGBA_TYPE or GLX_COLOR_INDEX_TYPE. GLX_RGBA_TYPE should be used because we are not using color index mode. Most implementations no longer support color index mode. Normally you should also pass NULL in the share_list parameter. However, if you have multiple contexts for an app and want to share GL objects such as textures, VBOs, FBOs, and so on, you can pass the first context handle in when creating the second. This causes both contexts to use the same namespace. Specifying TRUE for the direct parameter requests a direct hardware context for a local X Server connection; FALSE may create a context that renders through the X Server.

If creation fails, the function returns NULL; otherwise, it initializes the context to default OpenGL state. The function throws an error if you pass an invalid handle as the share_list parameter, if the config is invalid, or if the system is out of resources.

The OpenGL version of the context created will be up to OpenGL 3.1 if your implementation supports that version or any newer context version if it is 100% backward-compatible with OpenGL 3.1. Because you can't be sure what version of the OpenGL context you are going to get when calling glXCreateNewContext, this is not the preferred method. Instead use the newer version, glXCreateContextAttribsARB.

15

Before using glXCreateContextAttribsARB, you should check that the extension string
GLX_ARB_create_context_profile is in the list of GLX extensions. Then, you need to get
the function pointer for this extension. After that, you are all set to use the preferred way
of creating contexts.

```
GLint attribs[] = {
      GLX_CONTEXT_MAJOR_VERSION_ARB, 3,
      GLX_CONTEXT_MINOR_VERSION_ARB, 3,
      0 };
rcx->ctx = glXCreateContextAttribsARB(rcx->dpy, fbConfigs[0], 0,
                                      True, attribs);
glXMakeCurrent(rcx->dpy, rcx->win, rcx->ctx);
```

The new method, glXCreateContextAttribsARB, takes an additional parameter and allows
you to select exactly the context you want.

```
GLXContext glXCreateContextAttribsARB(Display * dpy, GLXFBConfig config,
                      int render_type, GLXContext share_list, bool direct,
                      const int *attrib_list);
```

The attrib_list parameter is a value-pair list of attributes you can request in a new
context. First specify the attribute name in the array followed by the value for the
attribute. The attributes GLX_CONTEXT_MAJOR_VERSION_ARB and
GLX_CONTEXT_MINOR_VERSION_ARB are used to explicitly ask for a specific context version of
OpenGL. If your application was written for OpenGL 3.3, you would pass in 3 as the
major version and 3 as the minor version. Similarly, if your application was older and you
needed an OpenGL 3.0 context, you could ask for that. However, OpenGL drivers are
allowed to return any version that is 100% backward-compatible with the version you
requested. If you do not specify a version of OpenGL or if you ask for version 1.0, the
driver will probably create an OpenGL 3.1 context. The exact behavior differs between
vendors. The best idea is to ask for a specific OpenGL version.

You can only create a context up to the version supported by your OpenGL driver. You
can find out what the newest supported version is by calling glGetString with the
GL_VERSION enum:

```
ubyte *verString = glGetString(GL_VERSION);
```

Or the version can also be queried through the glGetIntegerv command, which returns
the version as integer components:

```
int majorVer, minorVer;
glGetIntegerv(GL_MAJOR_VERSION, &majorVer);
glGetIntegerv(GL_MINOR_VERSION, &minorVer);
```

There are several other types of attributes you can request through the `attrib_list`. The attribute `GLX_CONTEXT_PROFILE_MASK_ARB` is followed by a bitfield containing either `GLX_CONTEXT_CORE_PROFILE_BIT_ARB` or `GLX_CONTEXT_COMPATIBILITY_PROFILE_BIT_ARB`. Only one can be used at a time. Setting the `GLX_CONTEXT_CORE_PROFILE_BIT_ARB` bit causes the driver to return a context containing only core functionality, no deprecated OpenGL functionality. Using this bit is a good way to prepare an application for the next revision of OpenGL where deprecated functionality may be removed. Setting the `GLX_CONTEXT_COMPATIBILITY_PROFILE_BIT_ARB` bit asks the driver to create a context that is backward compatible with all older versions of OpenGL. In other words, no deprecated functionality is removed. A context created with this bit may run slower than a core profile context because of the additional state and functionality that needs to be tracked.

The `GLX_CONTEXT_FLAGS_ARB` attribute can be used to set other flags for context creation. The only supported flag is `GLX_CONTEXT_DEBUG_BIT`. Specifying this bit creates a context with additional debugging information available for applications under development. What information and how it can be accessed is vendor-specific.

If any of the attributes you have specified are not supported by the OpenGL driver on your system, errors will be generated. The error `GLXBadMatch` is thrown if the combination of minor and major version attributes with the forward-compatible context bit is not a valid OpenGL version. If any of the bits specified for `GLX_CONTEXT_PROFILE_MASK_ARB` are not supported, the error `GLXBadProfileARB` is thrown.

When finished with a context, it is important to destroy the context so the implementation can free all related resources. Use the `glXDestroyContext` command to destroy contexts.

```
glXDestroyContext(Display * dpy, GLXContext ctx);
```

If the context is currently bound to any thread, the context will not be destroyed until it is no longer current. The function throws an error if you pass an invalid context handle.

One other handy feature provided by GLX is the ability to copy data from one context to another with `glXCopyContext`. Pass in the source and destination context handles as well as a mask to specify the pieces of OpenGL state that you would like to copy. These are the same enums that may be passed into `glPushAttrib`/`glPopAttrib`. To copy everything you can pass `GL_ALL_ATTRIB_BITS`. Client-side state will not be copied.

```
glXCopyContext(Display * dpy, GLXContext source, GLXContext dest, unsigned long
mask);
```

In GLX, a direct context is one that supports direct rendering to a local X Server. To find out if an existing context is a direct context you can call `glXIsDirect`. This returns true if the context is a direct rendering context.

```
glXIsDirect(Display * dpy, GLXContext ctx);
```

Debug Contexts

Using a debug context can be helpful in determining where your application is coming off its rails. At the time of this writing, the only vendor supporting debug contexts is AMD through an extension called `GL_AMD_debug_context`, which defines how the additional debug information can be accessed by developers.

A callback function is provided that allows an application to set an interrupt or breakpoint and find out immediately when an error has occurred. The extension also allows an application to select specific error types to be monitored and supports multiple severity levels.

For more information on how to use the `GL_AMD_debug_context` extension, you can check out the extension specification, which is also in the OpenGL extension registry.

Using Contexts

To use a context you have created, you can call `glXMakeContextCurrent`.

```
glXMakeContextCurrent(Display * dpy, GLXDrawable draw, GLXDrawable read,
                      GLXContext ctx);
```

For most cases you should specify the same drawable for `read` and `draw` for a context. This means that the same context will be used for both read and draw operations. If a different context was bound before you made this call, it will be flushed and marked as no longer current. If the context you pass is not valid or either drawable is not valid, the function throws an error. It also throws an error if the context's config is not compatible with the config used to create the drawables. Contexts can be released from a thread by passing `None` in the `read` and `draw` drawable parameters and NULL as the context. Without passing `None` for the drawables, GLX throws an error.

Synchronization

GLX has several synchronization commands that are similar to those on other OSes.

```
void glXWaitGL(void);
```

Making a call to `glXWaitGL` guarantees that all GL rendering will finish for a window before other native rendering occurring after the call to `glXWaitGL` is allowed to proceed. This allows an app to ensure that all rendering happens in the correct order and that rendering is not incorrectly overlapped or overwritten.

On some implementations, a call to `glXWaitGL` may return immediately with no rendering visible. An implementation may wait for other rendering to be initiated before completing earlier rendering.

```
void glXWaitX(void);
```

Likewise, a call to glXWaitX ensures that all native rendering made before the call to glXWaitX completes before any OpenGL rendering after the call is allowed to happen.

```
void glXSwapBuffers(Display *dpy, GLXDrawable draw);
```

When using a double buffered config, a call to glXSwapBuffers presents the contents of the back buffer to the window. The call also performs an implicit glFlush before the swap occurs. In addition, the contents of the new back buffer are undefined. You should not assume after a call to glXSwapBuffers the new back buffer will have the same contents as the old back buffer, the old contents of the front buffer, or any other defined content to maintain portability between vendors. GLX throws an error if the drawable or display are invalid, or if the window is no longer valid.

GLX Queries

GLX allows you to query certain attributes of a context as well. Use the glXQueryContext command to query GLX_FBCONFIG_ID, GLX_RENDER_TYPE, or GLX_SCREEN attributes associated with the context.

```
int glXQueryContext(Display * dpy, GLXContext ctx, int attribute, int *value);
```

There are a few other context-related commands in GLX; these are mostly self-descriptive. glXGetCurrentReadDrawable returns the current read drawable handle:

```
GLXDrawable glXGetCurrentReadDrawable(void);
```

In addition, the current context, drawable, and display can be queried with the following functions:

```
GLXContext glXGetCurrentContext(void);
GLXDrawable glXGetCurrentDrawable(void);
GLXDrawable glXGetCurrentReadDrawable(void);
Display glXGetCurrentDisplay(void);
```

There are a few less-common components of GLX we haven't covered yet. For completeness, let's take a quick look at them. You can query certain state from the current drawable with the function glXQueryDrawable. Pass the drawable that you are interested in as well as the attribute you are interested in: GLX_WIDTH, GLX_HEIGHT, GLX_PRESERVED_CONTENTS, GLX_LARGEST_PBUFFER, or GLX_FBCONFIG_ID. The result is returned in the value field.

```
void glXQueryDrawable(Display *dpy, GLXDrawable draw, int attribute, unsigned int *value);
```

There also is a set of functions for creating, dealing with, and deleting pixmaps and pBuffers. These are not covered here because we are not using and do not recommend you use pixmaps or pBuffers.

Putting It All Together

Now, for the fun part! Let's put all this GLX stuff together and create applications that use GLX for window creation and maintenance instead of GLUT. GLUT is great for creating quick, simple apps but does not allow for very granular control over the GLX environment. This chapter has two sample programs. Block is the same program you saw from Chapter 1, "Introduction to 3D Graphics and OpenGL," but this time uses GLX instead of GLUT. GLXBasics is an app written from scratch that uses GLX and also demonstrates handling of GLX callbacks, including how to interpret the mouse position. The first step is to open a connection to the X Server.

```
rcx->dpy = XOpenDisplay(NULL);
```

Then, let's check the supported GLX version to make sure that the functionality we use later is supported.

```
glXQueryVersion(rcx->dpy, &nMajorVer, &nMinorVer);
printf("Supported GLX version - %d.%d\n", nMajorVer, nMinorVer);

if(nMajorVer == 1 && nMinorVer < 3)
{
    printf("ERROR: GLX 1.3 or greater is necessary\n");
    XCloseDisplay(rcx->dpy);
    exit(0);
}
```

Now that we know we are good to go, look for a config that meets our requirements. We aren't very picky here considering this app doesn't have any complex interactions with the framebuffer.

```
GLXFBConfig *fbConfigs;
int numConfigs = 0;
static int fbAttribs[] = {
    GLX_RENDER_TYPE,    GLX_RGBA_BIT,
    GLX_X_RENDERABLE,   True,
    GLX_DRAWABLE_TYPE,  GLX_WINDOW_BIT,
    GLX_DOUBLEBUFFER,   True,
    GLX_RED_SIZE,       8,
    GLX_BLUE_SIZE,      8,
    GLX_GREEN_SIZE,     8,
    0 };
// Get a new fb config that meets our attrib requirements
fbConfigs = glXChooseFBConfig(rcx->dpy, DefaultScreen(rcx->dpy),
                        fbAttribs, &numConfigs);
```

We also need a visual to create the X Window. Once we have a config, we can get the corresponding visual from it:

```
XVisualInfo *visualInfo;
visualInfo = glXGetVisualFromFBConfig(rcx->dpy, fbConfigs[0]);
```

After we have a visual, we can use it to create a new X Window. Before calling into XCreateWindow, we have to figure out what things we want the window to do. Pick the events that are of interest and add them to the event mask. Do the same with the window mask. Set the border size and gravity we want. We also have to create a color map for the window to use. While we are at it, map the window to the display.

```
winAttribs.event_mask = ExposureMask | VisibilityChangeMask |
                         KeyPressMask | PointerMotionMask    |
                         StructureNotifyMask ;

winAttribs.border_pixel = 0;
winAttribs.bit_gravity = StaticGravity;
winAttribs.colormap = XCreateColormap(rcx->dpy,
                        RootWindow(rcx->dpy, visualInfo->screen),
                        visualInfo->visual, AllocNone);
winmask = CWBorderPixel | CWBitGravity | CWEventMask| CWColormap;

rcx->win = XCreateWindow(rcx->dpy, DefaultRootWindow(rcx->dpy), 20, 20,
                        rcx->nWinWidth, rcx->nWinHeight, 0,
                        visualInfo->depth, InputOutput,
                        visualInfo->visual, winmask, &winAttribs);

XMapWindow(rcx->dpy, rcx->win);
```

Great! We have a window! A few steps still need to be completed before we can render. First let's create a context and make it the current context. Remember, to create the context we need the config that corresponds with the visual used to create the window.

```
// Also create a new GL context for rendering
GLint attribs[] = {
    GLX_CONTEXT_MAJOR_VERSION_ARB, 3,
    GLX_CONTEXT_MINOR_VERSION_ARB, 3,
    0 };
rcx->ctx = glXCreateContextAttribsARB(rcx->dpy, fbConfigs[0], 0,
                                      True, attribs);
glXMakeCurrent(rcx->dpy, rcx->win, rcx->ctx);
```

Once a context is bound, we can make GL calls. First set the viewport:

```
glViewport(0, 0, rcx->nWinWidth, rcx->nWinHeight);
```

Next, clear the color buffer and prepare to render:

```
glClearColor(0.0f, 1.0f, 1.0f, 1.0f);
glClear(GL_COLOR_BUFFER_BIT);
```

This little demo application shown in Figure 15.1 just draws two eyeballs that do their best to follow your mouse pointer around the window. Some math is done to figure out where to put the eyeballs, where the mouse pointer is, and where the eyeballs should be looking. You can take a look at the rest of the GLXBasics sample program to see how all this works together. Only the important GLX snippets are listed here because this chapter is not introducing new OpenGL functionality.

FIGURE 15.1   Here's looking at you!

Now OpenGL setup is complete, and we can concentrate on rendering something. When the window changes or user input such as the pointer position moves are received, the contents of the window are redrawn. Afterward glXSwapBuffers is called.

```
// Flush drawing commands
glXSwapBuffers(rcx->dpy, rcx->win);
```

Before the app closes, some cleanup needs to be done. Remember when we started the application, a connection to the X Server was opened, an X Window was created, and a context was created and bound. Now before we quit, all of the resources we allocated have to be cleaned up. Note that the context should be unbound before it is destroyed.

```
glXMakeCurrent(rcx->dpy, None, NULL);

glXDestroyContext(rcx->dpy, rcx->ctx);
rcx->ctx = NULL;

XDestroyWindow(rcx->dpy, rcx->win);
```

```
rcx->win = (Window)NULL;

XCloseDisplay(rcx->dpy);
rcx->dpy = 0;
```

Summary

OpenGL is an important part of Linux because it is the only commonly supported hardware 3D API available. Although we have seen how GLUT can be used with Linux, direct use of GLX is necessary for defining buffer resources, window management, and other Linux-specific interfaces with OpenGL.

Even though GLUT can be used to handle window management on Linux, GLX 1.4 and related extensions allow greater control for an application to choose a specific version of OpenGL when creating new contexts. GLX provides methods to synchronize rendering with the OS, similar to WGL and AGL interfaces. You learned how to search for configs that meet your rendering needs. You also learned how to create a context supporting a specific version of OpenGL. Finally, you saw how to clean up GLX state after your application is finished.

CHAPTER 16

OpenGL ES on Mobile Devices

by Nicholas Haemel and Richard S. Wright, Jr.

WHAT YOU'LL LEARN IN THIS CHAPTER:

How To	Functions You'll Use
Choose configs	eglGetConfig/eglChooseConfig/eglGetConfigAttrib
Create EGL windows	eglCreateWindowSurface
Manage EGL contexts	eglCreateContext/eglDestroyContext/eglMakeCurrent
Post buffers to the window and synchronize	eglSwapBuffers/eglSwapInterval/eglWaitGL

This chapter is a peek into the world of OpenGL ES rendering. This set of APIs is intended for use in embedded environments where traditionally resources are much more limited. OpenGL ES dares to go where other rendering APIs can only dream of.

There is a lot of ground to cover, but we go over many of the basics. There are several versions of OpenGL ES in existence, but we focus on the newest and most relevant, OpenGL ES 2.0. We also cover the windowing interfaces designed for use with OpenGL ES and touch on some issues specific to dealing with embedded environments. Last, but not least, we learn how to develop applications using OpenGL ES 2.0 for the iPhone and iPad.

OpenGL on a Diet

You will find that OpenGL ES is similar to regular OpenGL. This isn't accidental; the OpenGL ES specifications were developed from different versions of OpenGL. As you have seen up until now, OpenGL provides a great interface for 3D rendering. It is very flexible and can be used in many applications, from gaming to full-blown CAD workstations to medical imaging.

What's the ES For?

Over time, the OpenGL API has been expanded to support new features. This has caused older versions of the OpenGL application programming interface to become bloated, providing many different methods of doing the same thing. Take, for instance, drawing a single point. In older versions of OpenGL this could be accomplished through immediate mode, which used `glBegin`/`glEnd` with the vertex information defined in between or through display lists that captured and replayed immediate mode commands. You could also use `glDrawArrays` with points prespecified in arrays or through vertex buffer objects.

The simple action of drawing a point can be done four different ways, each having different advantages. Although it is nice to have many choices when implementing your own application, all of this flexibility has produced a very large API. This in turn requires a very large and complex driver to support it. In addition, special hardware is often required to make each path efficient and fast. At the time that the OpenGL ES 2.0 specification was written, the current OpenGL APIs were just too big. OpenGL ES 2.0 fixed that by only including a subset of the most common and useful portions of OpenGL 2.1. Recent versions of OpenGL have drastically reduced the functionality overlap, but these revisions include features and functionality that most OpenGL ES hardware can only dream about! OpenGL ES 2.0 provides the perfect balance between flexibility and usability for embedded environments.

A Brief History

As hardware costs have come down and more functionality fits into smaller areas on semiconductors, user interfaces have become more and more complex for embedded devices. A common example is the automobile. In the 1980s the first visual feedback from car computers was provided in the form of single- and multiline text. These interfaces provided warnings about seatbelt usage, current gas mileage, and so on. After that, two-dimensional displays became prevalent. These often used bitmap-like rendering to present 2D graphics. Most recently, 3D-capable systems have been integrated to help support GPS navigation and other graphics-intensive features. A similar technological history exists for aeronautical instrumentation and cell phones.

Early embedded 3D interfaces were often proprietary and tied closely to the specific hardware features. This was often the case because the supported feature set was small and varied greatly from device to device. But as each vendor's 3D engine increased in complexity it became time-consuming and challenging to port applications between devices and vendors. The only solution was a standard interface. With this in mind, a consortium was formed to help define an interface that would be flexible and portable, yet tailored to embedded environments and conscious of their limitations. This standards body would be called the Khronos Group.

Khronos

The Khronos Group was originally founded in 2000 by members of the OpenGL ARB, the OpenGL governing body. Many capable graphics APIs existed for the PC space, but the goal of Khronos was to help define interfaces that were more applicable to devices beyond the personal computer. The first embedded API it developed was OpenGL ES.

Khronos consists of many industry leaders in both hardware and software. Some of the current members are AMD, Texas Instruments, ARM, Intel, NVIDIA, Nokia, and Qualcomm. The complete list is long and distinguished. You can visit the Khronos Web site for more information (www.khronos.org).

Version Development

The first version of OpenGL ES released, cleverly called ES 1.0, was an attempt to drastically reduce the API footprint of a full-featured PC API. This release used the OpenGL 1.3 specification as a basis. Although very capable, OpenGL ES 1.0 removed many of the less frequently used or very complex portions of the full OpenGL specification. Just like its big brother, OpenGL ES 1.0 defines a fixed functionality pipe for vertex transform and fragment processing.

OpenGL ES SC 1.0 is a separate specification based on OpenGL ES 1.0 and was designed for execution environments with extreme reliability requirements. These applications are considered "Safety Critical," hence the SC designator. Typical applications are in avionics, automobile, and military environments. In these areas 3D applications are often used for instrumentation, mapping, and representing terrain.

ES 1.1 was completed soon after the first specification was released. Although similar to OpenGL ES 1.0, the 1.1 specification is written from the OpenGL 1.5 specification. In addition, a more advanced texture path, buffer objects, and a draw texture interface were added. All in all, the ES 1.1 release was similar to ES 1.0 but added a few new interesting features.

ES 2.0 was a complete break from the pack. It is not backward-compatible with the ES 1.x versions. The biggest difference is that the fixed functionality portions of the pipeline have been removed. Instead, programmable shaders are used to perform the vertex and fragment processing steps. The ES 2.0 specification is based on the OpenGL 2.0 specification.

To fully support programmable shaders, ES 2.0 employs the OpenGL ES Shading Language. This is a high-level shading language that is similar to the OpenGL Shading Language that is paired with OpenGL 2.0+. The reason ES 2.0 is such a large improvement is that all the fixed functionality no longer encumbers the API. This means applications can implement and use only the methods they need in their own shaders.

So, to recap, the OpenGL ES versions currently defined and the OpenGL version they were based on are listed in Table 16.1.

16

TABLE 16.1   Base OpenGL versions for ES

OpenGL ES	OpenGL
ES 1.0	GL 1.3
ES 1.1	GL 1.5
ES 2.0	GL 2.0
ES SC 1.0	GL 1.3

Which Version Is Right for You?

Often hardware is created with a specific API in mind. These platforms usually support only a single accelerated version of ES. It is sometimes helpful to think of the different versions of ES as profiles that represent the functionality of the underlying hardware.

For traditional GL, typically new hardware is designed to support the latest version available. ES is a little different. The type of features targeted for new hardware are chosen based on several factors; targeted production cost, typical uses, and system support are a few. That said, semiconductor technology has come a long way in the last five years; it's now feasible to make a very small, cost effective, and efficient chips. Many common smartphones such as the Apple iPhone use OpenGL ES. Rather than introduce you to the old versions of ES, which are on their way out, this chapter focuses on OpenGL ES 2.0.

To get the most out of this chapter, you should be comfortable with most of the OpenGL feature set. This chapter is more about showing you what the major differences are between regular OpenGL and OpenGL ES and less about describing each feature again in detail.

ES 2.0

OpenGL ES 2.0 and OpenGL 3.3 are surprisingly similar. Both have slimmed-down interfaces that have removed old cruft. However, OpenGL 3.3 has added many new features not yet available on embedded hardware. Transform feedback, multisampling, geometry shaders, float buffers, and many other newer additions to OpenGL were not even around when ES 2.0 was born. In fact, a big step for OpenGL ES 2.0 when it was first defined was to support floating-point data types in commands. Previously, floating-point data needed to be emulated using fixed-point types. Floats can take up a lot of space!

Vertex Processing and Coloring

Vertex buffer objects, or the client-side vertex arrays, must be used for vertex specification. Vertex buffer objects can be mapped just as OpenGL 3.3 allows. Specify vertex attributes by using `glVertexAttribPointer`.

```
glVertexAttribPointer(GLuint index, GLuint size, GLenum type,
        GLboolean normalized, sizei stride, const void *ptr);
```

To draw geometry, you can use glDrawArrays and glDrawElements. However, the more specialized commands in OpenGL 3.3, glMultiDrawElements, glDrawRangeElements, and so on, are not available in OpenGL ES 2.0.

Shaders

OpenGL ES 2.0 uses programmable shaders in much the same way as OpenGL 3.3. However, the only two supported shader stages are vertex and fragment processing. OpenGL ES 2.0 uses a shading language similar to the GLSL language specification, called the OpenGL ES Shading Language. This version has changes that are specific to embedded environments and the hardware they contain.

Although a built-in compiler is convenient for applications, including the compiler in the OpenGL driver can be large (several megabytes), and the compile process can be very CPU-intensive. These requirements do not work well with smaller handheld embedded systems, which have much more stringent limitations for both memory and processing power. While OpenGL ES has kept the mechanisms that allow you to compile shaders at runtime, it has also added the ability to compile shaders offline and then load the compiled result at runtime. Neither method individually is required, but an OpenGL ES 2.0 implementation must support at least one.

Many of the original OpenGL 2.0 shader and program functions are still part of ES. The same semantics of program and shader management are still in play. The first step in using the programmable pipeline is to create the necessary shader and program objects. This is done with the following commands:

```
GLuint glCreateShader(GLenum type);
GLuint glCreateProgram(void);
```

After that, shader objects can be attached to program objects:

```
glAttachShader(GLuint program, GLuint shader);
```

If your implementation supports OES_shader_source, you can pass your shader strings in directly and then compile them at runtime using the familiar functions we already saw with OpenGL 3.3:

```
glShaderSource(GLuint shader, sizei count, const char **string,
               const int *length);
glCompileShader(GLuint shader);
```

Likewise, if your implementation supports OES_shader_binary, your shader source can be compiled offline using implementation-specific methods. Refer to your device's SDK for more info on these. Then instead of passing source code in at runtime, you can just give OpenGL ES the shader binary you got from the offline compile. A single binary can be loaded for a fragment-vertex pair if they were compiled together offline.

16

```
glShaderBinaryOES(GLint n, GLuint *shaders, GLenum binaryformat,
                  const void *binary, GLint length);
```

One or both of these methods must be supported. Check your device documentation to see which option works best for your embedded device. Once your shaders are loaded and compiled, bind the attribute channels to the attribute names used in your shaders:

```
glBindAttribLocation(GLuint program, GLuint index, const char *name);
```

The program can then be linked. If the shader binary interface is supported, the shader binaries for the compiled shaders need to be loaded before the link method is called.

```
glLinkProgram(GLuint program);
```

After the program has been successfully linked, you can set it as the currently executing program by calling glUseProgram. Also, at this point uniforms can be set as needed. Most of the normal OpenGL 3.3 attribute and uniform interfaces are supported. However, the transpose bit for setting uniform matrices must be GL_FALSE. This feature is not essential to the functioning of the programmable pipeline. Trying to draw without a valid program bound generates undefined results. Also uniform blocks are not part of OpenGL ES 2.0, so you have to use individual uniforms.

```
glUseProgram(GLuint program);
glUniform{1234}{if}(GLint location, T values);
glUniform{1234}{if}v(GLint location, sizei count, T value);
glUniformMatrix{234}fv(GLint location, sizei count,
                       GLboolean transpose, T value);
```

The shader language paired with OpenGL ES 2.0 is pretty similar to OpenGL 3.3 (GLSL 1.50). In fact you can often get started with your ES shaders by developing them on a PC or Mac and then transferring them over to ES once things work as you expect.

Rasterization

Handling of points is slightly different in OpenGL ES 2.0. Only aliased points are supported. Vertex shaders are responsible for outputting point size; there is no other way for point size to be specified through the API. GL_COORD_REPLACE can be used to generate point texture coordinates from 0 to 1 for s and t coordinates. Also the point coordinate origin is set to GL_UPPER_LEFT and cannot be changed. Point parameters are also not available.

Antialiased lines are not supported. OpenGL ES 2.0 does not have polygon smooth, polygon antialiasing, or multiple polygon modes.

Texturing

With OpenGL ES 2.0, 2D textures and cubemaps are supported. Depth textures, rectangle textures, and array textures are not supported, and 3D textures remain optional. Non-power-of-two textures are valid only for 2D textures when mipmapping is not in use and the texture wrap mode is set to clamp to edge. Textures do not have to be a power of two. OpenGL ES 2.0 also does not have sampler objects.

Framebuffers

Similar to full OpenGL 3.3, OpenGL ES 2.0 also supports framebuffer and renderbuffer objects. Applications can create and bind their own framebuffer objects. There are some limitations. Only one color buffer can be attached at a time, but you can still use depth and stencil buffers. You are also allowed to bind textures to framebuffer attachments.

Fragment Operations

There are also a few changes to the per-fragment operations allowed in ES 2.0. It is required that there be at least one config available that supports both a depth buffer and a stencil buffer. This guarantees that an application depending on the use of depth information and stencil compares will function on any implementation that supports OpenGL ES 2.0.

A few things have also been removed relative to the OpenGL 3.3 spec. First, the alpha test stage has been removed given that an application can implement this stage in a fragment shader. The glLogicOp interface is no longer supported. Occlusion queries are also not part of OpenGL ES.

Blending works as it does in OpenGL 3.3, but the scope is more limited. Blending cannot be set differently for each render target, and dual source blending is not supported.

State

OpenGL ES 2.0 state can be queried in the same way as OpenGL 3.3 state. You can use glGetBooleanv, glGetIntegerv, and glGetFloatv to query most state. Other specific queries such as glGetBufferParameteriv and glIsTexture are also available.

Core Additions

OpenGL ES supports extensions similar to how OpenGL 3.3 does. Although these extensions are not required and may not be supported on all implementations, they may be useful on platforms where they are supported.

- **Half-float vertex format**—OES_vertex_half_float—With this optional extension it is possible to specify vertex data with 16-bit floating-point values. When this is done, the required storage for vertex data can be significantly reduced from the size of larger data types. Also, the smaller data type can have a positive effect on the efficiency of the vertex transform portions of the pipeline. Use of half-floats for data like colors often does not have any adverse effects, especially for limited display color depth.

16

- **Floating-point textures**—Two new optional extensions, OES_texture_half_float and OES_texture_float, define new texture formats using floating-point components. The OES_texture_float uses a 32-bit floating format, whereas OES_texture_half_float uses a 16-bit format. Both extensions support GL_NEAREST magnification as well as GL_NEAREST and GL_NEAREST_MIPMAP_NEAREST minification filters. To use the other minification and magnification filters defined in OpenGL ES, the support of OES_texture_half_float_linear and OES_texture_float_linear extension is required.

- **Unsigned integer element indices**—OES_element_index_uint—Element index use in OpenGL ES is inherently limited by the maximum size of the index data types. The use of unsigned bytes and unsigned shorts allows for only 256 or 65,536 elements to be used. This optional extension allows for the use of element indexing with unsigned integers, extending the maximum reference index to beyond what current hardware could store.

- **Mapping buffers**—OES_mapbuffer—For vertex buffer object support in previous OpenGL ES versions, the capability to specify and use anything other than a static buffer was removed. When this optional extension is available, use of the tokens GL_STREAM_DRAW, GL_STREAM_COPY, GL_STREAM_READ, GL_STATIC_READ, GL_DYNAMIC_COPY, and GL_DYNAMIC_READ are valid, as well as the glMapBuffer and glUnmapBuffer entrypoints. This permits applications to map and edit existing VBOs.

- **3D textures**—OES_texture_3D—Generally, most ES applications do not require support for 3D textures. This extension was kept as optional to allow implementations to decide whether support could be accelerated and would be useful on an individual basis. Also texture wrap modes and mipmapping are supported for 3D textures that have power-of-two dimensions. Non-power-of-two 3D textures only support GL_CLAMP_TO_EDGE for mipmapping and texture wrap.

- **High-precision floats and integers in fragment shaders**—OES_fragment_precision_high—This optional extension allows for support of the high-precision qualifier for integers and floats defined in fragment shaders.

- **Ericsson compressed texture format**—OES_compressed_ETC1_RGB8_texture—The need for compressed texture support in OpenGL ES has long been understood, but format specification and implementation have been left to each individual implementer. This optional extension formalizes one of these formats for use on multiple platforms.

To load a compressed texture using the ETC_RGB8 format, call glCompressedTexImage2D with an internal format of GL_ETC1_RGB8_OES. This format defines a scheme by which each 4x4 texel block is grouped. A base color is then derived, and modifiers for each texel are selected from a table. The modifiers are then added to the base color and clamped to 0–255 to determine the final texel color. The full OES_compressed_ETC1_RGB8_texture description has more details on this process.

The ES Environment

Now that we have seen what the spec allows applications to do, we are almost ready to take a peek at an example. Figure 16.1 shows an example of OpenGL ES running in a game on a cell phone. This figure is also shown in Color Plate 22. But before that, there are a few issues unique to embedded systems that you should keep in mind while working with OpenGL ES and targeting embedded environments.

FIGURE 16.1   OpenGL ES rendering on a cell phone.

Application Design Considerations

For first-timers to the embedded world, things are a bit different here than when working on a PC. The ES world spans a wide variety of hardware profiles. The most capable of these might be multicore systems with extensive dedicated graphics resources, such as the Sony PlayStation 3. Alternatively, and probably more often, you may be developing for or porting to an entry-level cell phone with a 50MHz processor and 16MB of storage.

On limited systems, special attention must be paid to instruction count because every cycle counts if you are looking to maintain reasonable performance. Certain operations can be very slow. An example might be finding the sine of an angle. Instead of calling sin() in a math library, it would be much faster to do a lookup in a precalculated table if a close approximation would do the job. In general, the types of calculations and algorithms that might be part of a PC application should be updated for use in an embedded system. One example might be physics calculations, which are often very expensive. These can usually be simplified and approximated for use on embedded systems like cell phones.

On older systems it's also important to be aware of native floating-point support. Many of these systems do not have the capability to perform floating-point operations directly. This means all floating-point operations will be emulated in software. These operations are generally very slow and should be avoided at all costs.

Dealing with a Limited Environment

Not only can the environment be limiting when working on embedded systems, but the graphics processing power itself is unlikely to be on par with the bleeding edge of PC graphics. These restrictions force you to pay special attention to resources when you're looking to optimize the performance of your app, or just to get it to load and run at all!

It may be helpful to create a budget for storage space. In this way you can break up into pieces the maximum graphics/system memory available for each memory-intensive category. This helps to provide a perspective on how much data each unique piece of your app can use and when you are starting to run low.

One of the most obvious areas is texturing. Large detailed textures can help make for rich and detailed environments on PC-targeted applications. This is great for user experience, but textures can be a huge resource hog in most embedded systems. Many of the older platforms may not have full hardware support for texturing. These situations can cause large performance drops when many fragments are textured, especially if each piece of overlapping geometry is textured and drawn in the wrong order.

In addition to core hardware texturing performance, texture sizes can also be a major limitation. Both 3D and cube map textures can quickly add up to a large memory footprint, which is why 3D textures are optional for ES 2.0. Usually when the amount of graphics and system memory is limited, the screen size is also small. This means that a much smaller texture can be used with similar visual results. Also it may be worth avoiding multitexture because it requires multiple texture passes as well as more texture memory.

Vertex storage can also impact memory, similar to textures. In addition to setting a cap for the total memory used for vertices, it may also be helpful to decide which parts of a scene are important and divide up the vertex allotment along those lines.

One trick to keeping rendering smooth while many objects are on the screen is to change the vertex counts for objects relative to their distance from the viewer. This is a level-of-detail approach to geometry management. For instance, if you want to generate a forest scene, three different models of trees could be used. One level would have a very small vertex count and would be used to render the farthest of the trees. A medium vertex count could be used for trees of intermediate distance, and a larger count would be used on the closest. This would allow many trees to be rendered much quicker than if they were all at a high detail level. Because the least detailed trees are the farthest away, and may also be partially occluded, it is unlikely the lower detail would be noticed. But there may be significant savings in vertex processing as a result.

Fixed-Point Math

You may ask yourself, "What is fixed-point math and why should I care?" The truth is that you may not care if your hardware supports floating-point numbers and the version of OpenGL ES you are using does as well. But many platforms do not natively support floating point. Floating-point calculations in CPU emulation are very slow and should be avoided. In those instances, a representation of a floating-point number can be used to communicate nonwhole numbers. We are definitely not going to turn this into a math class! But instead a few basic things about fixed-point math are covered to give you an idea of what's involved. If you need to know more, many great resources are available that go to great lengths in discussing fixed-point math.

First, let's review how floating-point numbers work. There are basically two components to a floating-point number: The mantissa describes the fractional value, and the exponent is the scale or power. In this way large numbers are represented with the same number of significant digits as small numbers. They are related by $m * 2^e$ where m is the mantissa and e is the exponent.

Fixed-point representation is different. It looks more like a normal integer. The bits are divided into two parts, with one part being the integer portion and the other part being the fractional. The position between the integer and fractional components is the "imaginary point." There also may be a sign bit. Putting these pieces together, a fixed-point format of s15.16 means that there is 1 sign bit, 15 bits represent the integer, and 16 bits represent the fraction. This is the format used natively by OpenGL ES to represent fixed-point numbers.

Addition of two fixed-point numbers is simple. Because a fixed-point number is basically an integer with an arbitrary "point," the two numbers can be added together with a common scalar addition operation. The same is true for subtraction. There is one requirement for performing these operations. The fixed-point numbers must be in the same format. If they are not, one must be converted to the format of the other first. So to add or subtract a number with format s23.8 and one with s15.16, one format must be chosen and both numbers converted to that format.

Multiplication and division are a bit more complex. When two fixed-point numbers are multiplied together, the imaginary point of the result is the sum of that in the two operands. For instance, if you were multiplying two numbers with formats of s23.8 together, the result would be in the format of s15.16. So it is often helpful to first convert the operands into a format that allows for a reasonably accurate result format. You probably don't want to multiply two s15.16 formats together if they are greater than 1.0—the result format would have no integer portion! Division is similar, except the size of the fractional component of the second number is subtracted from the first.

When using fixed-point numbers, you have to be especially careful about overflow issues. With normal floating point, when the fractional component would overflow, the exponent portion is modified to preserve accuracy and prevent the overflow. This is not the case for fixed-point. To avoid overflowing fixed-point numbers when performing operations that might cause problems, the format can be altered. The numbers can be converted to a format that has a larger integer component and then converted back before calling into OpenGL ES. With multiplication, similar issues result in precision loss of the fractional component when the result is converted back to one of the operand formats. There are also math packages available to help you convert to and from fixed-point formats, as well as perform math functions. This is probably the easiest way to handle fixed-point math if you need to use it for an entire application.

That's it! Now you have an idea how to do basic math operations using fixed-point formats. This will help get you started if you find yourself stuck having to use fixed-point values when working with embedded systems. There are many great references for learning more about fixed-point math. One is *Essential Mathematics for Games and Interactive Applications* by James Van Verth and Lars Bishop (Elsevier, Inc., 2004).

EGL: A New Windowing Environment

You have already heard about GLX, AGL, and WGL. These are the OpenGL-related system interfaces for OSes like Linux, Apple's Mac OS, and Microsoft Windows. These interfaces are necessary to do the setup and management for system-side resources that OpenGL uses. The EGL implementation often is also provided by the graphics hardware vendor. Unlike the other windowing interfaces, EGL is not OS-specific. It's an interface that's designed to run under Windows, Linux, or embedded OSes such as Brew and Symbian. A block diagram of how EGL and OpenGL ES fit into an embedded system is shown in Figure 16.2.

EGL has its own native types just like OpenGL does. EGLBoolean has two values that are named similarly to their OpenGL counterparts: EGL_TRUE and EGL_FALSE. EGL also defines the type EGLint. This is an integer that is sized the same as the native platform integer type. The most current version of EGL as of this writing is EGL 1.4.

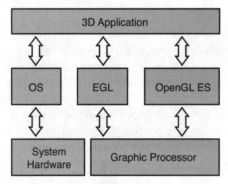

FIGURE 16.2   A typical embedded system diagram.

EGL Displays

Most EGL entrypoints take a parameter called `EGLDisplay`. This is a reference to the rendering target where drawing can take place. It might be easiest to think of this as corresponding to a physical monitor. The first step in setting up EGL is to get the default display. This can be done through the following function:

```
EGLDisplay eglGetDisplay(NativeDisplayType display_id);
```

The native display ID that is taken as a parameter is dependent on the system. For instance, if you were working with an EGL implementation on Windows, the `display_id` parameter you pass would be the device context. You can also pass `EGL_DEFAULT_DISPLAY` if you don't have the display ID and just want to render on the default device. If `EGL_NO_DISPLAY` is returned, an error occurred.

Now that you have a display handle, you can use it to initialize EGL. If you try to use other EGL interfaces without initializing EGL first, you get an `EGL_NOT_INITIALIZED` error.

```
EGLBoolean eglInitialize(EGLDisplay dpy, EGLint *major, EGLint *minor);
```

The other two parameters returned are the major and minor EGL version numbers. By calling the initialize command, you tell EGL you are getting ready to do rendering, which allows it to allocate and set up any necessary resources.

EGL also exposes an interface called `eglBindAPI`. This allows an application to select from different rendering APIs, such as OpenGL ES and OpenVG. Only one context can be current for each API per thread. Use this interface to tell EGL which interface it should use for subsequent calls to `eglMakeCurrent` in a thread. Pass in one of `EGL_OPENGL_ES_API`, `EGL_OPENVG_API`, or `EGL_OPENGL_API` to signify the correct API. The call fails if an invalid enum is passed in. Open VG is a different open API supporting vector graphics commonly found in embedded systems.

```
EGLBoolean eglBindAPI(EGLenum api);
```

EGL also provides a method to query the current API, `eglQueryAPI`. This interface returns one of the three EGLenums previously listed: `EGL_OPENGL_ES_API`, `EGL_OPENVG_API`, or `EGL_OPENGL_API`.

```
EGLenum eglQueryAPI(void);
```

On exit of your application, or after you are done rendering, a call must be made to EGL again to clean up all allocated resources. After this call is made, further references to EGL resources with the current display will be invalid until `eglInitialize` is called on it again.

```
EGLBoolean eglTerminate(EGLDisplay dpy);
```

16

Also on exit and when finished rendering from a thread, call `eglReleaseThread`. This allows EGL to release any resources it has allocated in that thread. If a context is still bound, `eglReleaseThread` releases it as well. It is still valid to make EGL calls after calling `eglReleaseThread`, but that causes EGL to reallocate any state it just released.

```
EGLBoolean eglReleaseThread(EGLDisplay dpy);
```

Creating a Window

As on most platforms, creating a window to render in can be a complex task. Windows are created in the native operating system. Later we look at how to tell EGL about native windows. Thankfully the process is similar enough to that for Windows and Linux.

Display Configs

An EGL config is analogous to a pixel format on Windows or visuals on Linux. Each config represents a group of attributes or properties for a set of render surfaces. In this case the render surface is a window on a display. It is typical for an implementation to support multiple configs. Each config is identified by a unique number. Different constants are defined that correlate to attributes of a config. They are defined in Table 16.2.

TABLE 16.2   EGL Config Attribute List

Attribute	Description
EGL_BUFFER SIZE	Total depth in bits of color buffer.
EGL_RED_SIZE	Number of bits in red channel of color buffer.
EGL_GREEN_SIZE	Number of bits in green channel of color buffer.
EGL_BLUE_SIZE	Number of bits in blue channel of color buffer.
EGL_ALPHA_SIZE	Number of bits in alpha channel of color buffer.
EGL_DEPTH_SIZE	Number of bits in depth buffer.
EGL_LUMINANCE_SIZE	Number of bits of luminance in the color buffer
EGL_STENCIL_SIZE	Number of bits in stencil buffer.
EGL_BIND_TO_TEXTURE_RGB	True if config is bindable to RGB textures.
EGL_BIND_TO_TEXTURE_RGBA	True if config is bindable to RGBA textures.
EGL_CONFIG_CAVEAT	Set to one of the following caveats: EGL_NONE, EGL_SLOW_CONFIG, or EGL_NON_CONFORMANT_CONFIG. These can warn of potential issues for this config. A slow config may be software emulated because it exceeds hardware limits. A nonconformant config will not pass the conformance test.
EGL_CONFIG_ID	Unique identifier for this config.
EGL_LEVEL	Framebuffer level.
EGL_NATIVE_RENDERABLE	Is set to EGL_TRUE if native APIs can render to this surface.
EGL_NATIVE_VISUAL_ID	May represent the ID of the native visual if the config supports a window; otherwise, is 0.

Attribute	Description
EGL_NATIVE_VISUAL_TYPE	Type of a native visual if config supports window rendering.
EGL_RENDERABLE_TYPE	Native type of visual. May be EGL_OPENGL_ES_BIT or EGL_OPENVG_BIT
EGL_SURFACE_TYPE	Valid surface targets supported. May be any or all of EGL_WINDOW_BIT, EGL_PIXMAP_BIT, or EGL_PBUFFER_BIT.
EGL_COLOR_BUFFER_TYPE	Type of color buffer. May be EGL_RGB_BUFFER or EGL_LUMINANCE_BUFFER.
EGL_MIN_SWAP_INTERVAL	Smallest value that can be accepted by eglSwapInterval. Smaller values will be clamped to this minimum.
EGL_MAX_SWAP_INTERVAL	Largest value that can be accepted by eglSwapInterval. Larger values will be clamped to this maximum.
EGL_SAMPLE_BUFFERS	Number of multisample buffers supported. Must be 0 or 1.
EGL_SAMPLES	Number of samples per pixel for multisample buffers. Will be 0 if EGL_SAMPLE_BUFFERS is 0.
EGL_ALPHA_MASK_SIZE	Number of bits of alpha mask.
EGL_TRANSPARENT_TYPE	Indicates support of transparency. Value may be EGL_NONE or EGL_TRANSPARENT_RGB. If transparency is supported, a transparent pixel is drawn when the pixel's components are all equal to the respective transparent RGB values.
EGL_TRANSPARENT_RED_VALUE	Red value a framebuffer pixel must have to be transparent.
EGL_TRANSPARENT_GREEN_VALUE	Green value a framebuffer pixel must have to be transparent.
EGL_TRANSPARENT_BLUE_VALUE	Blue value a framebuffer pixel must have to be transparent.

It is necessary to choose a config before creating a render surface. But with all the possible combinations of attributes, the process may seem difficult. EGL provides several tools to help you decide which config best supports your needs. If you have an idea of the kind of options you need for a window, you can use the eglChooseConfig interface to let EGL choose the best config for your requirements.

```
EGLBoolean eglChooseConfig(EGLDisplay dpy, const EGLint *attrib_list,
                    EGLConfig *configs,EGLint config_size,
                    EGLint *num_configs);
```

First decide how many matches you are willing to look through. Then allocate memory to hold the returned config handles. The matching config handles will be returned through the configs pointer. The number of configs will be returned through the num_config pointer. Next comes the tricky part. You have to decide which parameters are important to you in a functional config. Then, you create a list of each attribute followed by the corresponding value. For simple applications, some important attributes might be the bit depths of the color and depth buffers, and the surface type. The list must be terminated with EGL_NONE. An example of an attribute list is shown here:

```
EGLint attributes[] = {EGL_BUFFER_SIZE,      24,
                       EGL_RED_SIZE,          6,
                       EGL_GREEN_SIZE,        6,
                       EGL_BLUE_SIZE,         6,
                       EGL_DEPTH_SIZE,        12,
                       EGL_SURFACE_TYPE,      EGL_WINDOW_BIT,
                       EGL_NONE};
```

For attributes that are not specified in the array, the default values are used. During the search for a matching config, some of the attributes you list are required to make an exact match, whereas others are not. Table 16.3 lists the default values and the compare method for each attribute.

TABLE 16.3   EGL Config Attribute List

Attribute	Compare Operator	Default
EGL_BUFFER_SIZE	Minimum	0
EGL_RED_SIZE	Minimum	0
EGL_GREEN_SIZE	Minimum	0
EGL_BLUE_SIZE	Minimum	0
EGL_ALPHA_SIZE	Minimum	0
EGL_DEPTH_SIZE	Minimum	0
EGL_LUMINANCE_SIZE	Minimum	0
EGL_STENCIL_SIZE	Minimum	0
EGL_BIND_TO_TEXTURE_RGB	Equal	EGL_DONT_CARE
EGL_BIND_TO_TEXTURE_RGBA	Equal	EGL_DONT_CARE
EGL_CONFIG_CAVEAT	Equal	EGL_DONT_CARE
EGL_CONFIG_ID	Equal	EGL_DONT_CARE
EGL_LEVEL	Equal	0
EGL_NATIVE_RENDERABLE	Equal	EGL_DONT_CARE
EGL_NATIVE_VISUAL_TYPE	Equal	EGL_DONT_CARE
EGL_RENDERABLE_TYPE	Mask	EGL_OPENGL_ES_BIT
EGL_SURFACE_TYPE	Equal	EGL_WINDOW_BIT
EGL_COLOR_BUFFER_TYPE	Equal	EGL_RGB_BUFFER
EGL_MIN_SWAP_INTERVAL	Equal	EGL_DONT_CARE
EGL_MAX_SWAP_INTERVAL	Equal	EGL_DONT_CARE
EGL_SAMPLE_BUFFERS	Minimum	0
EGL_SAMPLES	Minimum	0
EGL_ALPHA_MASK_SIZE	Minimum	0
EGL_TRANSPARENT_TYPE	Equal	EGL_NONE
EGL_TRANSPARENT_RED_VALUE	Equal	EGL_DONT_CARE
EGL_TRANSPARENT_GREEN_VALUE	Equal	EGL_DONT_CARE
EGL_TRANSPARENT_BLUE_VALUE	Equal	EGL_DONT_CARE

EGL uses a set of rules to sort the matching results before they are returned to you. Basically, the caveat field is matched first, followed by the color buffer channel depths, then the total buffer size, and next the sample buffer information. So the config that is the best match should be first. After you receive the matching configs, you can peruse the results to find the best option for you. The first one will often be sufficient.

To analyze the attributes for each config, you can use `eglGetConfigAttrib`. This allows you to query the attributes for a config, one at a time:

```
EGLBoolean eglGetConfigAttrib(EGLDisplay dpy, EGLConfig config,
                          EGLint attribute, EGLint *value);
```

If you prefer a more "hands-on" approach to choosing a config, a more direct method for accessing supported configs is also provided. You can use `eglGetConfigs` to get all the configs supported by EGL:

```
EGLBoolean eglGetConfigs(EGLDisplay dpy, EGLConfig *configs,
                     EGLint config_size, EGLint *num_configs);
```

This function is very similar to `eglChooseConfig` except that it returns a list that is not dependent on some search criteria. The number of configs returned is either the maximum available or the number passed in by `config_size`, whichever is smaller. Here also a buffer needs to be preallocated based on the expected number of formats. After you have the list, it is up to you to pick the best option, examining each with `eglGetConfigAttrib`. It is unlikely that multiple different platforms will have the same configs or list configs in the same order. So it is important to properly select a config instead of blindly using the config handle.

Creating Rendering Surfaces

Now that we know how to pick a config that will support our needs, it's time to look at creating an actual render surface. The focus will be window surfaces, although it is also possible to create nondisplayable surfaces such as pBuffers and pixmaps. The first step is to create a native window that has the same attributes as those in the config you chose. Then you can use the window handle to create a window surface. The window handle type is related to the platform or OS you are using. In this way the same interface supports many different OSes without having to define a new method for each.

```
EGLSurface eglCreateWindowSurface(EGLDisplay dpy, EGLConfig config,
                          NativeWindowType win, EGLint *attrib_list);
```

The handle for the on-screen surface is returned if the call succeeds. The `attrib_list` parameter is intended to specify window attributes, but currently none is defined. After you are done rendering, you have to destroy your surface using the `eglDestroySurface` function:

```
EGLBoolean eglDestroySurface(EGLDisplay dpy, EGLSurface surface);
```

After a window render surface has been created and the hardware resources have been configured, you are almost ready to go!

Context Management

The last step is to create a render context to use. The rendering context is a set of state used for rendering. Creation of at least one context must be supported on all hardware.

```
EGLContext eglCreateContext(EGLDisplay dpy, EGLConfig config,
            EGLContext share_context, const EGLint *attrib_list);
```

To create a context, call the `eglCreateContext` function with the display handle you have been using all along. Also pass in the config used to create the render surface. The config used to create the context must be compatible with the config used to create the window. The `share_context` parameter is used to share objects like textures and shaders between contexts. Pass in the context you want to share with. Normally you pass `EGL_NO_CONTEXT` here given that sharing is not necessary. The context handle is passed back if the context was successfully created; otherwise, `EGL_NO_CONTEXT` is returned.

Now that you have a rendering surface and a context, you're ready to go! The last thing to do is to tell EGL which context you want to consider since it can use multiple contexts for rendering. Use `eglMakeCurrent` to set a context as current. You can use the surface you just created as both the read and the draw surfaces.

```
EGLBoolean eglMakeCurrent(EGLDisplay dpy, EGLSurface draw,
                    EGLSurface read, EGLContext ctx);
```

You get an error if the draw or read surfaces are invalid or if they are not compatible with the context. To release a bound context, you can call `eglMakeCurrent` with `EGL_NO_CONTEXT` as the context. You must use `EGL_NO_SURFACE` as the read and write surfaces when releasing a context. To delete a context you are finished with, call `eglDestroyContext`:

```
EGLBoolean eglDestroyContex(EGLDisplay dpy, EGLContext ctx);
```

Presenting Buffers and Rendering Synchronization

For rendering, there are certain EGL functions you may need to help keep things running smoothly. The first is `eglSwapBuffers`. This interface allows you to present a color buffer to a window. Just pass in the window surface you would like to post to:

```
EGLBoolean eglSwapBuffers(EGLDisplay dpy, EGLSurface surface);
```

Just because `eglSwapBuffers` is called doesn't mean it's the best time to actually post the buffer to the monitor. It's possible that the display is in the middle of displaying a frame when `eglSwapBuffers` is called. This case causes an artifact called tearing that looks like the frame is slightly skewed on a horizontal line. EGL provides a way to decide if it should wait until the current display update is complete before posting the swapped buffer to the display:

```
EGLBoolean eglSwapInterval(EGLDisplay dpy, EGLint interval);
```

By setting the swap interval to 0, you are telling EGL to not synchronize swaps and that an `eglSwapBuffers` call should be posted immediately. The default value is 1, which means each swap is synchronized with the next post to the display. The interval is clamped to the values of `EGL_MIN_SWAP_INTERVAL` and `EGL_MAX_SWAP_INTERVAL`.

If you plan to render to your window using other APIs besides OpenGL ES/EGL, there are some things you can do to ensure that rendering is posted in the right order:

```
EGLBoolean eglWaitGL(void);
EGLBoolean eglWaitNative(EGLint engine);
```

Use `eglWaitGL` to prevent other API rendering from operating on a window surface before OpenGL ES rendering completes. Use `eglWaitNative` to prevent OpenGL ES from executing before native API rendering completes. The engine parameter can be defined in EGL extensions specific to an implementation, but `EGL_CORE_NATIVE_ENGINE` can also be used and will refer to the most common native rendering engine besides OpenGL ES. This is implementation/system specific.

More EGL Stuff

We have covered the most important and commonly used EGL interfaces. There are a few more EGL functions left to talk about that are more peripheral to the common execution path.

EGL Errors

EGL provides a method for getting EGL-specific errors that may be thrown during EGL execution. Most functions return `EGL_TRUE` or `EGL_FALSE` to indicate whether they were successful, but in the event of a failure, a Boolean provides very little information on what went wrong. In this case, `eglGetError` may be called to get more information:

```
EGLint eglGetError();
```

The last thrown error is returned. This will be one of the following self-explanatory errors: `EGL_SUCCESS`, `EGL_NOT_INITIALIZED`, `EGL_BAD_ACCESS`, `EGL_BAD_ALLOC`, `EGL_BAD_ATTRIBUTE`, `EGL_BAD_CONTEXT`, `EGL_BAD_CONFIG`, `EGL_BAD_CURRENT_SURFACE`, `EGL_BAD_DISPLAY`, `EGL_BAD_SURFACE`, `EGL_BAD_MATCH`, `EGL_BAD_PARAMETER`, `EGL_BAD_NATIVE_PIXMAP`, `EGL_BAD_NATIVE_WINDOW`, or `EGL_CONTEXT_LOST`.

Getting EGL Strings

A few EGL state strings may be of interest. These include the EGL version string and extension string. To get these, use the `eglQueryString` interface with the `EGL_VERSION` and `EGL_EXTENSIONS` enums:

```
const char *eglQueryString(EGLDisplay dpy, EGLint name);
```

Extending EGL

Like OpenGL, EGL provides support for various extensions. These are often extensions specific to the current platform and can provide for extended functionality beyond that of the core specification. To find out what extensions are available on your system, you can use the `eglQueryString` function previously discussed. To get more information on specific extensions, you can visit the Khronos Web site listed in the reference section. Some of these extensions may require additional entrypoints. To get the entrypoint address for these extensions, pass the name of the new entrypoint into the following function:

```
void (*eglGetProcAddress(const char *procname))();
```

Use of this entrypoint is similar to `wglGetProcAddress`. A NULL return means the entrypoint does not exist. But just because a non-NULL address is returned does not mean the function is actually supported. The related extensions must exist in the EGL extension string or the OpenGL ES extension string. It is important to ensure that you have a valid function pointer (non-NULL) returned from calling `eglGetProcAddress`.

Negotiating Embedded Environments

After examining how OpenGL ES and EGL work on an embedded system, it's time to look closer at the environment of an embedded system and how it affects an OpenGL ES application. The environment plays an important role in how you approach creating ES applications.

Popular Operating Systems

Because OpenGL ES is not limited to certain platforms as many 3D APIs are, a wide variety of OSes can be used. This decision is often already made for you because most embedded systems are designed for use with certain OSes and certain OSes are intended for use on specific hardware.

Brew and Symbian are common cell phone operating systems. But one of the fastest growing environments is the iPhone OS, running on the iPhone, iPod Touch, and the iPad. In fact, just about anyone with a Mac can create an app for the iPhone OS and submit to the Apple App Store. We take a look at how to go about creating an app for the iPhone in a few short pages.

Vendor-Specific Extensions

Each OpenGL ES vendor often has a set of extensions that are specific to its hardware and implementation. These often extend the number and types of formats available. Because these extensions are useful only for limited sets of hardware, they are not discussed here.

For the Home Gamer

For those of us not lucky enough to be working on a hardware emulator or hardware itself, there are other options if you still want to try your hand at OpenGL ES. Several OpenGL ES implementations are available that execute on a full-scale operating system. These are also great for doing initial development.

AMD provides an emulator that allows you to do just that. A link to the emulator is provided in the reference section at the end of the book. You can use this emulator to get started writing OpenGL ES 2.0 applications right on your desktop computer. The emulator includes a sample program you can start with. You can use the simple sample program as a basis for building your own OpenGL ES 2.0 applications. The emulator even has a control panel that allows you to replicate the constraints for an embedded environment.

If you have an Intel-based Mac, Apple's iPhone SDK is also available for free. Apple's iPhone, iPod Touch, and new iPad are all OpenGL ES-based devices. Even without a device, the SDK and Xcode tools work with a software emulator that allows you to do development without a hardware device.

Apple Handheld Platforms

Apple has not one, but three handheld platforms that use OpenGL ES 2.0: the iPhone, the iPod Touch, and most recently the iPad. The iPhone is one of the most popular smartphones ever made and has a 320 x 480 touch screen interface. The first two generations of the iPhone supported OpenGL ES 1.1, while the third and later generations allow either OpenGL ES 1.1 or 2.0 applications. Because we are only concerned with the latest and most relevant edition, we restrict our discussion to OpenGL ES 2.0 on the iPhone. What about the iPod Touch? I'm sure Apple's marketing czar would object, but essentially as far as OpenGL programming goes, iPod Touch is simply an iPhone without the phone part. The iPad on the other hand, could be thought of as the "Large Print Edition" of the iPod Touch: more real estate. It does have a different graphics processor under the hood too, but thankfully OpenGL hides that sort of thing from us. To make things simple, we are not going to bother saying iPhone/iPod Touch/iPad all over the place. We'll just say iPhone, and you should know that the other devices are essentially the same as far as OpenGL ES programming is concerned.

So, let's go through an example, shall we?

Setting Up An iPhone Project

The very first thing you need to do is acquire the iPhone SDK from Apple's developer relations Web site, http://developer.apple.com. Launching Xcode presents the familiar welcome screen shown in Figure 16.3.

If you've been working on other projects recently, you'll see them listed to the right under Recent Projects. Click the Create a New Xcode Project button to open the project wizard screen. On the New Project screen, shown in Figure 16.4, select Application under the iPhoneOS group (see, there is no iPod Touch or iPad OS group; they are all the same thing). You see various application templates in the upper pane, one of which is the OpenGL ES Application. Click to highlight this and click Choose in the lower right-hand corner of the window.

The next screen asks you to choose a location and to name your new project. Select SphereWorld—yes, we are going to bring SphereWorld back from Chapter 5 and port it to the iPhone. Once your project is created, you should see a screen similar to that shown in Figure 16.5.

FIGURE 16.3   Xcode welcome screen.

FIGURE 16.4 The Xcode New Project screen.

16

Here we expanded all the groups so you can see all the files and frameworks that make up your project. Also make sure you've selected or changed the combo box in the upper left to be one of the Simulator options and not one of the Device options. Getting your app on the device and configuring your hardware certificate is well beyond the scope of this book! In Appendix A, "Further Reading," we list a couple of our favorite iPhone programming books. As is typical for Xcode, just press Command-R to compile, link, and launch your program in the simulator. The default OpenGL ES application is just a bouncing shaded triangle strip. The simulator is shown with Xcode running on the desktop in Figure 16.6.

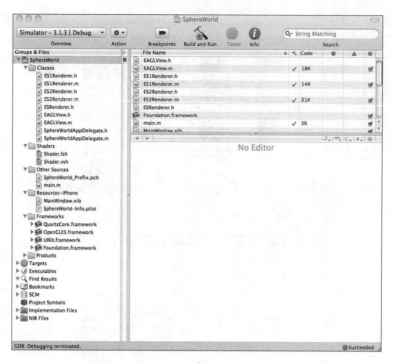

FIGURE 16.5   The freshly created SphereWorld project.

FIGURE 16.6   Your iPhone OpenGL ES development environment.

Using C++ on the iPhone

The native iPhone programming environment uses the Objective C programming language. There is a good bit of passion and sometimes vitriol about this, as the majority of non-Mac programmers in the world would much rather use C++. In fact, a good number of Mac programmers would rather use C++ as it turns out. Other than making use of Apple's frameworks, however, there is no reason why anyone cannot use C++ for other portions of their code, and in fact, we are going to make use of Objective C as little as possible in moving our SphereWorld example to the iPhone.

Objective C is essentially C with objects. These objects, however, do not act like C++ objects, and incorporating C++ into Objective C does not work as well as incorporating C code into Objective C. There is a simple and almost trivial solution to this: Rename all the Objective C files from *.m to *.mm. Now, you are essentially using "Objective C++," and you can incorporate C++ code with ease in the project, create and use C++ classes in Objective C code, and call C++ methods from Objective C modules.

The next step then is to rename all the .m source files in your project to .mm. Why? Because GLTools is a C++ library, and it works just fine on the iPhone. Right-click each file in the Groups & Files pane and select Rename. This turns the filename into an edit control, and you can add an extra "m" to the filename and press Enter. Repeat this for all the .m files in your project. You can rebuild the project after you've done this for a sanity check.

Using GLTools on the iPhone

The GLTools library works on the iPhone and has some #defines here and there to account for platform differences. Most notably, the shaders are tweaked slightly to account for some differences in the shading language, but they function identically. From the API level, GLTools looks and works exactly the same on the iPhone as it does on the desktop. You can use it in C++ modules that you call from the Objective C framework of the iPhone, or you can code it right in place in an Objective C file.

Instead of having multiple versions of the GLTools library for the different iPhone SDK versions, simulator, device, and so on we simply add the GLTools source code to our project. Right-click the project name under Groups & Files and select Add, New Group from the pop-up menu. Name the group GLTools. Next, right-click the newly formed GLTools group and select Add, Existing Files. Using the file dialog sheet that is presented, navigate to the GLTools source code directory (Src/GLTools/src) and select all the source code files except glew.c. We will not use GLEW on the iPhone; this is only for desktop development, and the OpenGL ES 2.0 code in GLTools does not need it. Once you've added the GLTools files, your Xcode project should appear similar to Figure 16.7.

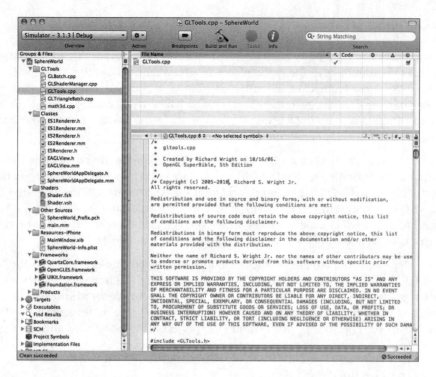

FIGURE 16.7   Your project with the GLTools source code added.

Before you can compile your code, however, you still need to tell Xcode where the GLTools headers are. This procedure is identical to that shown in Chapter 2, "Getting Started," when setting up Xcode projects for the desktop OS X, and we won't repeat it here. At this time, you should do a build just for a sanity check. If all is well, you have a functioning OpenGL ES framework running on the iPhone simulator (or device if you have a hardware certificate), with the GLTools library already wired in. You are about to see how easy it is to move your desktop OpenGL code to the iPhone.

Moving to the iPhone

Moving our GLUT-based example from Chapter 5, "Basic Texturing," is going to be fairly straightforward. In fact, we start by copying the SphereWorld.cpp file from Chapter 5 directly to our project directory and adding it to our project. Also copy the three texture files, Marble.tga, Moonlike.tga, and Marslike.tga. Add the three texture files to the project's Resources-iPhone folder and the SphereWorld.cpp file to the project in the group Other Sources.

Now, SphereWorld.cpp is our entire GLUT-based program, and we do not need or want GLUT in our iPhone program. Essentially, we just need to tweak the headers at the top of the source file and prune out any GLUT-specific code. Near the top right, after most of the headers, you see the GLUT include files:

```
#ifdef __APPLE__
#include <glut/glut.h>
#else
#define FREEGLUT_STATIC
#include <gl/glut.h>
#endif
```

Just delete this entire block. No GLUT. All of the module variables declared here will simply be global to this module, and we are going to call the same functions that we registered with GLUT as callback functions in the Objective C framework. The next offending line is in the SetupRC function where we initialize GLEW. We don't need GLEW either, so you can delete this line of code as well:

```
// Make sure OpenGL entry points are set
glewInit();
```

At the bottom of RenderScene, we call GLUT functions to perform the buffer swap and trigger a refresh. Neither of these is necessary, as the Objective C framework takes care of presenting our rendering and sets up an animation timer by default that triggers screen refreshes at a maximum of 60fps. Next, remove these lines:

```
// Do the buffer Swap
glutSwapBuffers();

// Do it again
glutPostRedisplay();
```

The next bit of pruning is even easier; just completely delete the SpecialKeys and main functions. The main function serves no purpose now that this source file just contains functions and data accessed by the real main program. SpecialKeys, however, did serve a useful purpose that we still want for our iPhone version of SphereWorld. It allowed us to use the arrow keys to move around in SphereWorld, and we have to replace this functionality using the Cocoa Touch API.

At this point, your project should compile and run without problem. Unfortunately, it is still the bouncing shaded rectangle shown in Figure 16.6.

Wiring It In

Your very first C or C++ class or book should have taught you how to call a function declared in another module. You simply declare the functions or classes that are in another module in the module from which you want to call them. This is most typically done with a header file. In the case of SphereWorld, there are just four functions we need to call from SphereWorld.cpp, and their declarations are as follows:

```
void ChangeSize(int nWidth, int nHeight);
void SetupRC(void);
void ShutdownRC(void);
void RenderScene(void);
```

We just place this code at the top of the ES2Renderer.mm file. Objective C as we've said before will have no problem calling these functions declared in the .cpp file. Now the question is, where to place these four functions, and how do we get rid of that bouncing square.

The iPhone SDK supports using OpenGL ES 1.1 or OpenGL ES 2.0. By default, the sample programs use OpenGL ES 2.0, which is what we want anyway. You can even decide at runtime, which may be useful if you want to target a much wider audience, but of course it requires that you have two complete sets of rendering code. For the OpenGL ES 2.0 path, all the action happens in ES2Renderer.mm, and so this is where we hook in our OpenGL code.

On the iPhone, all OpenGL ES rendering is done to a framebuffer object. The `init` method in this module performs the initialization of the framebuffer object, and we put our call to `SetupRC` here, right after the framebuffer object initialization.

```
. . .
. . .
    glBindRenderbuffer(GL_RENDERBUFFER, colorRenderbuffer);
    glFramebufferRenderbuffer(GL_FRAMEBUFFER, GL_COLOR_ATTACHMENT0,
                        GL_RENDERBUFFER, colorRenderbuffer);
    }

    // Call into our SphereWorld to do its initialization
    SetupRC();

    return self;
}
```

The next method you encounter is `render`. Render contains an assortment of OpenGL ES rendering calls and some framebuffer management calls that we need to not mess with. Listing 16.1 provides the function in its entirety.

LISTING 16.1   Our Newly Slimmed-Down Render Method

```
- (void)render
    {
```

```
    // Replace the implementation of this method to do your own custom drawing
    // Okay, thanks I will!

    // This application only creates a single context which is already
    // set current at this point.
    // This call is redundant, but needed if dealing with multiple contexts.
    [EAGLContext setCurrentContext:context];

    // This application only creates a single default framebuffer
    // which is already bound at this point.
    // This call is redundant, but needed if dealing with multiple framebuffers.
    glBindFramebuffer(GL_FRAMEBUFFER, defaultFramebuffer);

    // Draw — Call our SphereWorld rendering routine!
    RenderScene();

    // This application only creates a single color renderbuffer
    /// which is already bound at this point.
    // This call is redundant, but needed if dealing with multiple renderbuffers.
    glBindRenderbuffer(GL_RENDERBUFFER, colorRenderbuffer);
    [context presentRenderbuffer:GL_RENDERBUFFER];
    }
```

Almost done! The `resizeFromLayer` method is called at least once with the size of the framebuffer. We make use of the class variables `backingWidth` and `backingHeight` and call our `ChangeSize` function from SphereWorld.cpp here.

```
ChangeSize(backingWidth, backingHeight);
```

Finally, our forth callback function `ShutdownRC` is placed at the beginning of the `dealloc` method.

```
- (void)dealloc
    {
    ShutdownRC();

    // Tear down GL
    . . .
```

At last, we should see SphereWorld on the iPhone, right? Not quite. If you run the program now you see a blank screen. There is one last thing we have to do, which is to tell our application where to look for its texture files.

Texture Considerations

There are two things we need to do to get our texture code from Chapter 5 to work on the iPhone. The first is we need to set the working directory to be the same location as the application bundle. When we added the texture files to the Resources-iPhone group in Xcode, we told Xcode to bundle these files unmodified and place them on the iPhone in the same directory as the application bundle. When we try to load the textures, we pass in the filename of the texture, but we need to make sure the current working folder (this applies because we are using the standard C runtime function fopen to access the file) is the same as the application bundle's. We had the same problem on the desktop Mac OS X too, and we called the function gltSetWorkingDirectory in the main function of our GLUT program. We simply need to do the same thing but this time in the module main.mm. Listing 16.2 shows the entire main.mm module. It's pretty sparse; we only added the GLTools header and the call to gltSetWorkingDirectory.

LISTING 16.2   The Modified Main Function

```
#import <UIKit/UIKit.h>
#include <GLTools.h>

int main(int argc, char *argv[]) {

    gltSetWorkingDirectory(*argv);

    NSAutoreleasePool * pool = [[NSAutoreleasePool alloc] init];
    int retVal = UIApplicationMain(argc, argv, nil, nil);
    [pool release];
    return retVal;
}
```

The second thing is already done for you but bears mentioning. OpenGL ES does not support the GL_BGR texture image format, which .TGA files use. GLTools takes this into account and swaps the colors around for you when you load a .TGA on the iPhone. Otherwise, your reddish textures in this sample would look blue. OpenGL ES also does not support the generic texture compression attribute, so in the LoadTGA function, we need to use the nComponents value returned from gltReadTGABits.

```
glTexImage2D(GL_TEXTURE_2D, 0, nComponents, nWidth, nHeight, 0,
                        eFormat, GL_UNSIGNED_BYTE, pBits);
```

We are nearly there. Figure 16.8 shows both our progress and our last remaining hurdle. The artifact you see on the torus is due to the fact that we do not have a depth buffer...yet.

FIGURE 16.8   Almost there, lacking only a depth buffer.

Adding a Depth Buffer

The iPhone SDK does not give you a depth buffer by default when you create an OpenGL ES project. There used to be a #define you could turn on that could trigger the code to give you a depth buffer, but for some reason Apple removed that from newer SDKs. Creating and attaching your own depth buffer is simple enough, however (see Chapter 9, "Advanced Buffers: Beyond the Basics," for details on how this works). Listing 16.3 shows our complete resizeFromLayer function, which is where we create our complete framebuffer object.

LISTING 16.3   Attaching a Depth Buffer to Our Framebuffer Object

```
- (BOOL)resizeFromLayer:(CAEAGLLayer *)layer
{
    // Allocate color buffer backing based on the current layer size
    glBindRenderbuffer(GL_RENDERBUFFER, colorRenderbuffer);
    [context renderbufferStorage:GL_RENDERBUFFER fromDrawable:layer];
    glGetRenderbufferParameteriv(GL_RENDERBUFFER, GL_RENDERBUFFER_WIDTH,
                                                &backingWidth);
```

```
    glGetRenderbufferParameteriv(GL_RENDERBUFFER, GL_RENDERBUFFER_HEIGHT,
                                                  &backingHeight);

    glGenRenderbuffers(1, &depthRenderbuffer);
    glBindRenderbuffer(GL_RENDERBUFFER, depthRenderbuffer);
    glRenderbufferStorage(GL_RENDERBUFFER, GL_DEPTH_COMPONENT16,
                                  backingWidth, backingHeight);
    glFramebufferRenderbuffer(GL_FRAMEBUFFER, GL_DEPTH_ATTACHMENT,
                                  GL_RENDERBUFFER, depthRenderbuffer);

    if (glCheckFramebufferStatus(GL_FRAMEBUFFER) != GL_FRAMEBUFFER_COMPLETE)
        {
        NSLog(@"Failed to make complete framebuffer object %x",
                              glCheckFramebufferStatus(GL_FRAMEBUFFER));
        return NO;
        }

    ChangeSize(backingWidth, backingHeight);

    return YES;
}
```

Success at last!

Landscape Mode

Many iPhone apps can detect when your phone turns on its side. We are not going to
discuss this because it requires a lot more non-OpenGL plumbing than we have any business getting into, and it's not trivial to add to the stock OpenGL ES template. Again, we
refer you to Appendix A to fulfill your curiosity. We are not trying to be an iPhone tutorial
here as much as just show how OpenGL works on this platform. That said, how exactly
would we render in landscape mode? In fact, a good many OpenGL ES games work in
landscape mode only, and we could just simply force SphereWorld to run in Landscape
mode and be happy with it couldn't we? Indeed, have a look at Listing 16.4, which
contains a simple change in the ChangeSize function that does exactly this.

LISTING 16.4   Rotating Our Point of View

```
void ChangeSize(int nWidth, int nHeight)
    {
    glViewport(0, 0, nWidth, nHeight);
    transformPipeline.SetMatrixStacks(modelViewMatrix, projectionMatrix);

    viewFrustum.SetPerspective(60.0f, float(nWidth)/float(nHeight), 1.0f, 100.0f);
```

```
projectionMatrix.LoadMatrix(viewFrustum.GetProjectionMatrix());
projectionMatrix.Rotate(-90.0f, 0.0f, 0.0f, 1.0f);
modelViewMatrix.LoadIdentity();
}
```

All we really need to do is rotate the projection matrix by 90 degrees. One other tweak was to increase the field of view to 60 degrees so that we can see more of the world at once. This gives a pretty pleasing landscape view of SphereWorld that can be seen in Figure 16.9.

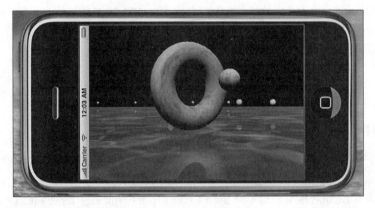

FIGURE 16.9   SphereWorld in landscape mode on the iPhone.

Touch Me!

Finally we come to our last missing feature of SphereWorld—the ability to move around. There are a number of ways to do this, and some games use the accelerometer for a visceral feel to game navigation. A simpler interface is the Touch API. The Touch API is very simple to use and is something akin to detecting mouse movements on the screen. The touch messages are routed to the view (a descendent of UIView), so we have to step outside the OpenGL ES-specific framework to the EAGLView.mm file where the EAGLView class is defined. Listing 16.5 shows the message added to this class to receive touch movement notifications. The message contains both the new touch location, as well as the last touch location, making detecting movement in the x and y direction trivial.

LISTING 16.5   Using the Touch Messages for Camera Movement

```
- (void) touchesMoved:(NSSet *)touches withEvent:(UIEvent *)event {
    CGPoint ptNow = [[touches anyObject] locationInView:self];
    CGPoint ptLast = [[touches anyObject] previousLocationInView:self];

    float deltaX = ptNow.x - ptLast.x;
```

```
    float deltaY = ptNow.y - ptLast.y;


    cameraFrame.MoveForward(deltaX * 0.05f);
    cameraFrame.RotateLocalY(m3dDegToRad(deltaY * 0.25f));
    }
```

Here we simply moved the camera forward with up and down swipes and rotate the camera left and right with side-to-side swipes. The amount to scale the movement was chosen purely on aesthetic considerations. Of course, the camera frame is declared in SphereWorld.cpp, so we must share it with EAGLView.mm by declaring it at the top of the file.

```
#include <GLFrame.h>
extern GLFrame        cameraFrame;    // Camera frame
```

Summary

We covered a lot of ground in this chapter. OpenGL ES 2.0, loosely based on OpenGL 2.0, is a much simpler and slimmed-down version of OpenGL for use in embedded environments. The types of hardware that run OpenGL ES 2.0 are very diverse. We also were introduced to EGL and how it can be used to do window management with OpenGL ES. In addition, we went over some of the differences in working with an embedded environment and where to find emulators to develop for OpenGL ES 2.0. Finally, we demonstrated how easily modern desktop OpenGL code can be adapted to an OpenGL ES environment, such as the iPhone. OpenGL truly is the ultimate cross platform 3D API.

Further Reading

Real-time 3D graphics and OpenGL are popular topics. More information is available and more techniques are in practice than can ever be published in a single book. You might find the following resources helpful as you further your knowledge and experience.

Other Good OpenGL Books

Advanced Graphics Programming Using OpenGL. Tom McReynolds and David Blythe. The Morgan Kaufmann Series in Computer Graphics, 2005.

Interactive Computer Graphics: A Top-Down Approach with OpenGL, 4th Edition. Edward Angel. Addison-Wesley, 2005.

More OpenGL Game Programming. Dave Astle, Editor. Thomson Course Technology, 2006.

OpenGL ES 2.0 Programming Guide. Aaftab Munshi, Dan Ginsburg, and Dave Shreiner. Addison-Wesley, 2008.

OpenGL Programming Guide, 7th Edition: The Official Guide to Learning OpenGL, Version 3.0 and 3.1. Dave Shreiner, The Khronos OpenGL ARB Working Group. Addison-Wesley, 2009.

OpenGL Shading Language, 3rd Edition. Randi J. Rost and Bill Licea-Kane. Addison-Wesley, 2009.

OpenGL Programming on Mac OS X: Architecture, Performance, and Integration. Robert P. Kuehne and J. D. Sullivan. Addison-Wesley, 2007.

OpenGL Programming for the X Window System. Mark J. Kilgard. Addison-Wesley, 1996.

3D Graphics Books

3D Computer Graphics, 3rd Edition. Alan Watt. Addison-Wesley, 1999.

3D Math Primer for Graphics and Game Development. Fletcher Dunn and Ian Parbery. Wordware Publishing, 2002.

Advanced Animation and Rendering Techniques: Theory and Practice. Alan Watt and Mark Watt (contributor). Addison-Wesley, 1992.

Essential Mathematics for Games and Interactive Applications. James Van Verth and Lars Bishop. The Morgan Kaufmann Series in Interactive 3d Technology, 2004.

Introduction to Computer Graphics. James D. Foley, Andries van Dam, Steven K. Feiner, John F. Hughes, and Richard L. Phillips. Addison-Wesley, 1993.

Mathematics for 3D Game Programming & Computer Graphics, 2nd Edition. Eric Lengyel. Charles River Media, 2003.

Open Geometry: OpenGL + Advanced Geometry. Georg Glaeser and Hellmuth Stachel. Springer-Verlag, 1999.

Shader X 4: Advanced Rendering Techniques. Wolfgang Engel, Editor. Charles River Media, 2006.

Texturing & Modeling: A Procedural Approach, 3rd Edition. David S. Ebert, F. Kenton Musgrave, Darwyn Peachey, Ken Perlin, and Steven Worley. The Morgan Kaufmann Series in Computer Graphics, 2003.

Web Sites

- The OpenGL SuperBible Web site: www.starstonesoftware.com/opengl

- The official OpenGL Web site: www.opengl.org

- The OpenGL SDK (lots of tutorials and tools): www.opengl.org/sdk/

The preceding three Web sites are the gateways to OpenGL information on the Web, and of course, the official source of information for all things OpenGL and SuperBible related. The following sites also pertain to information covered in this book and offer vendor-specific OpenGL support, tutorials, demos, and news.

- The Khronos Group OpenGL ES home page: www.khronos.org/opengles/

- The OpenGL Extension Registry: www.opengl.org/registry/

- AMD/ATI's developer home page: www.ati.amd.com/developer/

- NVIDIA's developer home page: developer.nvidia.com/

- The Mesa 3D OpenGL "work-a-like": www.mesa3d.org

- GLView OpenGL Extension Viewer: www.realtech-vr.com/glview

Glossary

Aliasing   Technically, the loss of signal information in an image reproduced at some finite resolution. It is most often characterized by the appearance of sharp jagged edges along points, lines, or polygons due to the nature of having a limited number of fixed-sized pixels.

Alpha   A fourth color value added to provide a degree of transparency to the color of an object. An alpha value of 0.0 means complete transparency; 1.0 denotes no transparency (opaque).

Ambient light   Light in a scene that doesn't come from any specific point source or direction. Ambient light illuminates all surfaces evenly and on all sides.

Antialiasing   A rendering method used to smooth lines and curves and polygon edges. This technique averages the color of pixels adjacent to the line. It has the visual effect of softening the transition from the pixels on the line and those adjacent to the line, thus providing a smoother appearance.

ARB   The Architecture Review Board. The committee body consisting of 3D graphics hardware vendors, previously charged with maintaining the OpenGL Specification. This function has since been assumed by the Khronos Group.

Aspect ratio   The ratio of the width of a window to the height of the window. Specifically, the width of the window in pixels divided by the height of the window in pixels.

Bézier curve   A curve whose shape is defined by control points near the curve rather than by the precise set of points that define the curve itself.

Bitplane   An array of bits mapped directly to screen pixels.

Buffer   An area of memory used to store image information. This can be color, depth, or blending information. The red, green, blue, and alpha buffers are often collectively referred to as the color buffers.

Cartesian   A coordinate system based on three directional axes placed at a 90° orientation to one another. These coordinates are labeled x, y, and z.

Clip coordinates   The 2D geometric coordinates that result from the modelview and projection transformation.

Clipping   The elimination of a portion of a single primitive or group of primitives. The points that would be rendered outside the clipping region or volume are not drawn. The clipping volume is generally specified by the projection matrix. Clipped primitives are reconstructed such that the edges of the primitive do not lay outside the clipping region.

Convex   A reference to the shape of a polygon. A convex polygon has no indentations, and no straight line can be drawn through the polygon that intersects it more than twice (once entering, once leaving).

Culling   The elimination of graphics primitives that would not be seen if rendered. Backface culling eliminates the front or back face of a primitive so that the face isn't drawn. Frustum culling eliminates whole objects that would fall outside the viewing frustum.

Destination color   The stored color at a particular location in the color buffer. This terminology is usually used when describing blending operations to distinguish between the color already present in the color buffer and the color coming into the color buffer (source color).

Dithering   A method used to simulate a wider range of color depth by placing different-colored pixels together in patterns that give the illusion of shading between the two colors.

Double buffered   A drawing technique used by OpenGL. The image to be displayed is assembled in memory and then placed on the screen in a single update operation, rather than built primitive by primitive on the screen. Double buffering is a much faster and smoother update operation and can produce animations.

Extruded   The process of taking a 2D image or shape and adding a third dimension uniformly across the surface. This process can transform 2D fonts into 3D lettering.

Eye coordinates   The coordinate system based on the position of the viewer. The viewer's position is placed along the positive z-axis, looking down the negative z-axis.

Frustum   A pyramid-shaped viewing volume that creates a perspective view. (Near objects are large; far objects are small.)

GLSL   Acronym for the OpenGL Shading Language, a high-level C-Like shading language.

GLUT library   The OpenGL utility library. A window system independent utility library useful for creating sample programs and simple 3D rendering programs that are independent of the operating system and windowing system. Typically used to provide portability between Windows, X-Window, Linux, and so on.

Immediate mode   A graphics rendering mode in which commands and functions are sent individually and have an immediate effect on the state of the rendering engine.

Implementation   A software or hardware based device that performs OpenGL rendering operations.

Khronos Group   An industry consortium that now manages the maintenance and promotion of the OpenGL specification.

Literal   A value, not a variable name. A specific string or numeric constant embedded directly in source code.

Matrix   A 2D array of numbers. Matrices can be operated on mathematically and are used to perform coordinate transformations.

Mipmapping   A technique that uses multiple levels of detail for a texture. This technique selects from among the different sizes of an image available, or possibly combines the two nearest sized matches to produce the final fragments used for texturing.

Modelview matrix   The OpenGL matrix that transforms primitives to eye coordinates from object coordinates.

Normal   A directional vector that points perpendicularly to a plane or surface. When used, normals must be specified for each vertex in a primitive.

Normalize   The reduction of a normal to a unit normal. A unit normal is a vector that has a length of exactly 1.0.

Orthographic   A drawing mode in which no perspective or foreshortening takes place. Also called parallel projection. The lengths and dimensions of all primitives are undistorted regardless of orientation or distance from the viewer.

Perspective   A drawing mode in which objects farther from the viewer appear smaller than nearby objects.

Pixel   Condensed from the words *picture element*. This is the smallest visual division available on the computer screen. Pixels are arranged in rows and columns and are individually set to the appropriate color to render any given image.

Pixmap   A two-dimensional array of color values that comprise a color image. Pixmaps are so called because each picture element corresponds to a pixel on the screen.

Polygon   A 2D shape drawn with any number of sides (must be at least three sides).

Primitive   A 2D polygonal shape defined by OpenGL. All objects and scenes are composed of various combinations of primitives.

Projection   The transformation of lines, points, and polygons from eye coordinates to clipping coordinates on the screen.

Quadrilateral   A polygon with exactly four sides.

B

Rasterize   The process of converting projected primitives and bitmaps into pixel fragments in the framebuffer.

Retained Mode   A style of 3D programming where an object's representation is held in memory by the programming library.

Render   The conversion of primitives in object coordinates to an image in the framebuffer. The rendering pipeline is the process by which OpenGL commands and statements become pixels on the screen.

Scintillation   A sparkling or flashing effect produced on objects when a nonmipmapped texture map is applied to a polygon that is significantly smaller than the size of the texture being applied.

Shader   A small program that is executed by the graphics hardware, often in parallel, to operate on individual vertices or pixels.

Source color   The color of the incoming fragment, as opposed to the color already present in the color buffer (destination color). This terminology is usually used when describing how the source and destination colors are combined during a blending operation.

Specification   The design document that specifies OpenGL operation and fully describes how an implementation must work.

Spline   A general term used to describe any curve created by placing control points near the curve, which have a pulling effect on the curve's shape. This is similar to the reaction of a piece of flexible material when pressure is applied at various points along its length.

Stipple   A binary bit pattern used to mask out pixel generation in the framebuffer. This is similar to a monochrome bitmap, but one-dimensional patterns are used for lines and two-dimensional patterns are used for polygons.

Tessellation   The process of breaking down a complex polygon or analytic surface into a mesh of convex polygons. This process can also be applied to separate a complex curve into a series of less complex lines.

Texel   Similar to pixel (picture element), a texel is a *texture element*. A texel represents a color from a texture that is applied to a pixel fragment in the framebuffer.

Texture   An image pattern of colors applied to the surface of a primitive.

Texture mapping   The process of applying a texture image to a surface. The surface does not have to be planar (flat). Texture mapping is often used to wrap an image around a curved object or to produce patterned surfaces such as wood or marble.

Transformation   The manipulation of a coordinate system. This can include rotation, translation, scaling (both uniform and nonuniform), and perspective division.

Translucence   A degree of transparency of an object. In OpenGL, this is represented by an alpha value ranging from 1.0 (opaque) to 0.0 (transparent).

Vector   A directional quantity usually represented by X, Y, and Z components.

Vertex   A single point in space. Except when used for point and line primitives, it also defines the point at which two edges of a polygon meet.

Viewing volume   The area in 3D space that can be viewed in the window. Objects and points outside the viewing volume are clipped (cannot be seen).

Viewport   The area within a window that is used to display an OpenGL image. Usually, this encompasses the entire client area. Stretched viewports can produce enlarged or shrunken output within the physical window.

Wireframe   The representation of a solid object by a mesh of lines rather than solid shaded polygons. Wireframe models are usually rendered faster and can be used to view both the front and back of an object at the same time.

B

OpenGL Man Pages for (Core) OpenGL 3.3

glActiveTexture

select active texture unit

C Specification

```
void glActiveTexture(GLenum texture);
```

Parameters

texture

Specifies which texture unit to make active. The number of texture units is implementation dependent, but must be at least two. *texture* must be one of GL_TEXTURE*i*, where *i* ranges from 0 (GL_MAX_COMBINED_TEXTURE_IMAGE_UNITS - 1). The initial value is GL_TEXTURE0.

Description

`glActiveTexture` selects which texture unit subsequent texture state calls will affect. The number of texture units an implementation supports is implementation dependent, but must be at least 48.

Errors

GL_INVALID_ENUM is generated if *texture* is not one of GL_TEXTURE*i*, where *i* ranges from 0 to (GL_MAX_COMBINED_TEXTURE_IMAGE_UNITS - 1).

Associated Gets

glGet with argument GL_ACTIVE_TEXTURE, or GL_MAX_COMBINED_TEXTURE_IMAGE_UNITS.

See Also

```
glGenTextures, glBindTexture, glCompressedTexImage1D,
glCompressedTexImage2D, glCompressedTexImage3D, glCompressedTexSubImage1D,
glCompressedTexSubImage2D, glCompressedTexSubImage3D, glCopyTexImage1D,
glCopyTexImage2D, glCopyTexSubImage1D, glCopyTexSubImage2D,
glCopyTexSubImage3D, glDeleteTextures glIsTexture, glTexImage1D, glTexImage2D,
glTexImage2DMultisample, glTexImage3D, glTexImage3DMultisample,
glTexSubImage1D, glTexSubImage2D, glTexSubImage3D, glTexParameter.
```

Copyright

glAttachShader

Attaches a shader object to a program object

C Specification

```
void glAttachShader(GLuint program,
                    GLuint shader);
```

Parameters

program

Specifies the program object to which a shader object will be attached.

shader

Specifies the shader object that is to be attached.

Description

In order to create a complete shader program, there must be a way to specify the list of things that will be linked together. Program objects provide this mechanism. Shaders that are to be linked together in a program object must first be attached to that program object. glAttachShader attaches the shader object specified by *shader* to the program object specified by *program*. This indicates that *shader* will be included in link operations that will be performed on *program*.

All operations that can be performed on a shader object are valid whether or not the shader object is attached to a program object. It is permissible to attach a shader object to a program object before source code has been loaded into the shader object or before the shader object has been compiled. It is permissible to attach multiple shader objects of the same type because each may contain a portion of the complete shader. It is also permissible to attach a shader object to more than one program object. If a shader object is deleted while it is attached to a program object, it will be flagged for deletion, and deletion will not occur until glDetachShader is called to detach it from all program objects to which it is attached.

Errors

GL_INVALID_VALUE is generated if either *program* or *shader* is not a value generated by OpenGL.

GL_INVALID_OPERATION is generated if *program* is not a program object.

GL_INVALID_OPERATION is generated if *shader* is not a shader object.

GL_INVALID_OPERATION is generated if *shader* is already attached to *program*.

Associated Gets

glGetAttachedShaders with the handle of a valid program object

glGetShaderInfoLog

glGetShaderSource

glIsProgram

glIsShader

See Also

glCompileShader, glCreateShader, glDeleteShader, glDetachShader, glLinkProgram, glShaderSource

Copyright

glBeginConditionalRender

start conditional rendering

C Specification

```
void glBeginConditionalRender(GLuint id,
                              GLenum mode);
```

Parameters

id

Specifies the name of an occlusion query object whose results are used to determine if the rendering commands are discarded.

mode

Specifies how `glBeginConditionalRender` interprets the results of the occlusion query.

C Specification

```
void glEndConditionalRender(void);
```

Description

Conditional rendering is started using `glBeginConditionalRender` and ended using `glEndConditionalRender`. During conditional rendering, all vertex array commands, as well as glClear and glClearBuffer have no effect if the (GL_SAMPLES_PASSED) result of the query object *id* is zero, or if the (GL_ANY_SAMPLES_PASSED) result is GL_FALSE. The results of commands setting the current vertex state, such as glVertexAttrib are undefined. If the (GL_SAMPLES_PASSED) result is non-zero or if the (GL_ANY_SAMPLES_PASSED) result is GL_TRUE, such commands are not discarded. The *id* parameter to `glBeginConditionalRender` must be the name of a query object previously returned from a call to glGenQueries. *mode* specifies how the results of the query object are to be interpreted. If *mode* is GL_QUERY_WAIT, the GL waits for the results of the query to be available and then uses the results to determine if subsequent rendering commands are discarded. If *mode* is GL_QUERY_NO_WAIT, the GL may choose to unconditionally execute the subsequent rendering commands without waiting for the query to complete.

If *mode* is GL_QUERY_BY_REGION_WAIT, the GL will also wait for occlusion query results and discard rendering commands if the result of the occlusion query is zero. If the query result is non-zero, subsequent rendering commands are executed, but the GL may discard the results of the commands for any region of the framebuffer that did not contribute to the sample count in the specified occlusion query. Any such discarding is done in an implementation-dependent manner, but the rendering command results may not be discarded for any samples that contributed to the occlusion query sample count. If *mode* is GL_QUERY_BY_REGION_NO_WAIT, the GL operates as in GL_QUERY_BY_REGION_WAIT, but may choose to unconditionally execute the subsequent rendering commands without waiting for the query to complete.

Notes

`glBeginConditionalRender` and `glEndConditionalRender` are available only if the GL version is 3.0 or greater.

The GL_ANY_SAMPLES_PASSED query result is available only if the GL version is 3.3 or greater.

Errors

GL_INVALID_VALUE is generated if *id* is not the name of an existing query object.

GL_INVALID_ENUM is generated if *mode* is not one of the accepted tokens.

GL_INVALID_OPERATION is generated if `glBeginConditionalRender` is called while conditional rendering is active, or if `glEndConditionalRender` is called while conditional rendering is inactive.

GL_INVALID_OPERATION is generated if *id* is the name of a query object with a target other than GL_SAMPLES_PASSED or GL_ANY_SAMPLES_PASSED.

GL_INVALID_OPERATION is generated if *id* is the name of a query currently in progress.

See Also

`glGenQueries`, `glDeleteQueries`, `glBeginQuery`

Copyright

glBeginQuery

delimit the boundaries of a query object

C Specification

```
void glBeginQuery(GLenum target,
                  GLuint id);
```

Parameters

target

Specifies the target type of query object established between `glBeginQuery` and the subsequent glEndQuery. The symbolic constant must be one of GL_SAMPLES_PASSED, GL_ANY_SAMPLES_PASSED, GL_PRIMITIVES_GENERATED, GL_TRANSFORM_FEEDBACK_PRIMITIVES_WRITTEN, or GL_TIME_ELAPSED.

id

Specifies the name of a query object.

C Specification

```
void glEndQuery(GLenum target);
```

Parameters

target

Specifies the target type of query object to be concluded. The symbolic constant must be one of GL_SAMPLES_PASSED, GL_ANY_SAMPLES_PASSED, GL_PRIMITIVES_GENERATED, GL_TRANSFORM_FEEDBACK_PRIMITIVES_WRITTEN, or GL_TIME_ELAPSED.

Description

glBeginQuery and glEndQuery delimit the boundaries of a query object. *query* must be a name previously returned from a call to glGenQueries. If a query object with name *id* does not yet exist it is created with the type determined by *target*. *target* must be one of GL_SAMPLES_PASSED, GL_ANY_SAMPLES_PASSED, GL_PRIMITIVES_GENERATED, GL_TRANSFORM_FEEDBACK_PRIMITIVES_WRITTEN, or GL_TIME_ELAPSED. The behavior of the query object depends on its type and is as follows.

If *target* is GL_SAMPLES_PASSED, *target* must be an unused name, or the name of an existing occlusion query object. When glBeginQuery is executed, the query object's samples-passed counter is reset to 0. Subsequent rendering will increment the counter for every sample that passes the depth test. If the value of GL_SAMPLE_BUFFERS is 0, then the samples-passed count is incremented by 1 for each fragment. If the value of GL_SAMPLE_BUFFERS is 1, then the samples-passed count is incremented by the number of samples whose coverage bit is set. However, implementations, at their discretion may instead increase the samples-passed count by the value of GL_SAMPLES if any sample in the fragment is covered. When glEndQuery is executed, the samples-passed counter is assigned to the query object's result value. This value can be queried by calling glGetQueryObject with *pname* GL_QUERY_RESULT.

If *target* is GL_ANY_SAMPLES_PASSED, *target* must be an unused name, or the name of an existing boolean occlusion query object. When glBeginQuery is executed, the query object's samples-passed flag is reset to GL_FALSE. Subsequent rendering causes the flag to be set to GL_TRUE if any sample passes the depth test. When glEndQuery is executed, the samples-passed flag is assigned to the query object's result value. This value can be queried by calling glGetQueryObject with *pname* GL_QUERY_RESULT.

If *target* is GL_PRIMITIVES_GENERATED, *target* must be an unused name, or the name of an existing primitive query object previously bound to the GL_PRIMITIVES_GENERATED query binding. When glBeginQuery is executed, the query object's primitives-generated counter is reset to 0. Subsequent rendering will increment the counter once for every vertex that is emitted from the geometry shader, or from the vertex shader if no geometry shader is present. When glEndQuery is executed, the primitives-generated counter is assigned to the query object's result value. This value can be queried by calling glGetQueryObject with *pname* GL_QUERY_RESULT.

If *target* is GL_TRANSFORM_FEEDBACK_PRIMITIVES_WRITTEN, *target* must be an unused name, or the name of an existing primitive query object previously bound to the GL_TRANSFORM_FEEDBACK_PRIMITIVES_WRITTEN query binding. When glBeginQuery is executed, the query object's primitives-written counter is reset to 0. Subsequent rendering will increment the counter once for every vertex that is written into the bound transform feedback buffer(s). If transform feedback mode is not activated between the call to glBeginQuery and glEndQuery, the counter will not be incremented. When glEndQuery is executed, the primitives-written counter is assigned to the query object's result value. This value can be queried by calling glGetQueryObject with *pname* GL_QUERY_RESULT.

If *target* is GL_TIME_ELAPSED, *target* must be an unused name, or the name of an existing timer query object previously bound to the GL_TIME_ELAPSED query binding. When glBeginQuery is executed, the query object's time counter is reset to 0. When glEndQuery is executed, the elapsed server time that has passed since the call to glBeginQuery is written into the query object's time counter. This value can be queried by calling glGetQueryObject with *pname* GL_QUERY_RESULT.

Querying the GL_QUERY_RESULT implicitly flushes the GL pipeline until the rendering delimited by the query object has completed and the result is available. GL_QUERY_RESULT_AVAILABLE can be queried to determine if the result is immediately available or if the rendering is not yet complete.

Notes

If the query target's count exceeds the maximum value representable in the number of available bits, as reported by glGetQueryiv with *target* set to the appropriate query target and *pname* GL_QUERY_COUNTER_BITS, the count becomes undefined.

An implementation may support 0 bits in its counter, in which case query results are always undefined and essentially useless.

When GL_SAMPLE_BUFFERS is 0, the samples-passed counter of an occlusion query will increment once for each fragment that passes the depth test. When GL_SAMPLE_BUFFERS is 1, an implementation may either increment the samples-passed counter individually for each sample of a fragment that passes the depth test, or it may choose to increment the counter for all samples of a fragment if any one of them passes the depth test.

The query targets GL_ANY_SAMPLES_PASSED, and GL_TIME_ELAPSED are availale only if the GL version is 3.3 or higher.

Errors

GL_INVALID_ENUM is generated if *target* is not one of the accepted tokens.

GL_INVALID_OPERATION is generated if `glBeginQuery` is executed while a query object of the same *target* is already active.

GL_INVALID_OPERATION is generated if glEndQuery is executed when a query object of the same *target* is not active.

GL_INVALID_OPERATION is generated if *id* is 0.

GL_INVALID_OPERATION is generated if *id* is the name of an already active query object.

GL_INVALID_OPERATION is generated if *id* refers to an existing query object whose type does not does not match *target*.

See Also

`glDeleteQueries`, `glGenQueries`, `glGetQueryiv`, `glGetQueryObject`, `glIsQuery`

Copyright

glBeginTransformFeedback

start transform feedback operation

C Specification

```
void glBeginTransformFeedback(GLenum primitiveMode);
```

Parameters

primitiveMode
    Specify the output type of the primitives that will be recorded into the buffer objects that are bound for transform feedback.

C Specification

```
void glEndTransformFeedback(void);
```

Description

Transform feedback mode captures the values of varying variables written by the vertex shader (or, if active, the geometry shader). Transform feedback is said to be active after a call to `glBeginTransformFeedback` until a subsequent call to glEndTransformFeedback. Transform feedback commands must be paired.

If no geometry shader is present, while transform feedback is active the *mode* parameter to glDrawArrays must match those specified in the following table:

If a geometry shader is present, the output primitive type from the geometry shader must match those provided in the following table:

Transform Feedback *primitiveMode*	Allowed Geometry Shader Output Primitive Type
GL_POINTS	points
GL_LINES	line_strip
GL_TRIANGLES	triangle_strip

Transform Feedback *primitiveMode*	Allowed Render Primitive *modes*
GL_POINTS	GL_POINTS
GL_LINES	GL_LINES, GL_LINE_LOOP, GL_LINE_STRIP, GL_LINES_ADJACENCY, GL_LINE_STRIP_ADJACENCY
GL_TRIANGLES	GL_TRIANGLES, GL_TRIANGLE_STRIP, GL_TRIANGLE_FAN, GL_TRIANGLES_ADJACENCY, GL_TRIANGLE_STRIP_ADJACENCY

Notes

Geometry shaders, and the GL_TRIANGLES_ADJACENCY, GL_TRIANGLE_STRIP_ADJACENCY, GL_LINES_ADJACENCY and GL_LINE_STRIP_ADJACENCY primtive modes are available only if the GL version is 3.2 or greater.

Errors

GL_INVALID_OPERATION is generated if glBeginTransformFeedback is executed while transform feedback is active.

GL_INVALID_OPERATION is generated if glEndTransformFeedback is executed while transform feedback is not active.

GL_INVALID_OPERATION is generated by glDrawArrays if no geometry shader is present, transform feedback is active and *mode* is not one of the allowed modes.

GL_INVALID_OPERATION is generated by glDrawArrays if a geometry shader is present, transform feedback is active and the output primitive type of the geometry shader does not match the transform feedback *primitiveMode*.

GL_INVALID_OPERATION is generated by glEndTransformFeedback if any binding point used in transform feedback mode does not have a buffer object bound.

GL_INVALID_OPERATION is generated by glEndTransformFeedback if no binding points would be used, either because no program object is active or because the active program object has specified no varying variables to record.

Copyright

glBindAttribLocation

Associates a generic vertex attribute index with a named attribute variable

C Specification

```
void glBindAttribLocation(GLuint program,
                          GLuint index,
                          const GLchar *name);
```

Parameters

program
> Specifies the handle of the program object in which the association is to be made.

index
> Specifies the index of the generic vertex attribute to be bound.

name
> Specifies a null terminated string containing the name of the vertex shader attribute variable to which *index* is to be bound.

Description

glBindAttribLocation is used to associate a user-defined attribute variable in the program object specified by *program* with a generic vertex attribute index. The name of the user-defined attribute variable is passed as a null terminated string in *name*. The generic vertex attribute index to be bound to this variable is specified by *index*. When *program* is made part of current state, values provided via the generic vertex attribute *index* will modify the value of the user-defined attribute variable specified by *name*.

If *name* refers to a matrix attribute variable, *index* refers to the first column of the matrix. Other matrix columns are then automatically bound to locations *index+1* for a matrix of type mat2; *index+1* and *index+2* for a matrix of type mat3; and *index+1*, *index+2*, and *index+3* for a matrix of type mat4.

This command makes it possible for vertex shaders to use descriptive names for attribute variables rather than generic variables that are numbered from 0 to GL_MAX_VERTEX_ATTRIBS -1. The values sent to each generic attribute index are part of current state. If a different program object is made current by calling glUseProgram, the generic vertex attributes are tracked in such a way that the same values will be observed by attributes in the new program object that are also bound to *index*.

Attribute variable name-to-generic attribute index bindings for a program object can be explicitly assigned at any time by calling glBindAttribLocation. Attribute bindings do not go into effect until glLinkProgram is called. After a program object has been linked successfully, the index values for generic attributes remain fixed (and their values can be queried) until the next link command occurs.

Any attribute binding that occurs after the program object has been linked will not take effect until the next time the program object is linked.

Notes

glBindAttribLocation can be called before any vertex shader objects are bound to the specified program object. It is also permissible to bind a generic attribute index to an attribute variable name that is never used in a vertex shader.

If *name* was bound previously, that information is lost. Thus you cannot bind one user-defined attribute variable to multiple indices, but you can bind multiple user-defined attribute variables to the same index.

Applications are allowed to bind more than one user-defined attribute variable to the same generic vertex attribute index. This is called *aliasing*, and it is allowed only if just one of the aliased attributes is active in the executable program, or if no path through the shader consumes more than one attribute of a set of attributes aliased to the same location. The compiler and linker are allowed to assume that no aliasing is done and are free to employ optimizations that work only in the absence of aliasing. OpenGL implementations are not required to do error checking to detect aliasing.

Active attributes that are not explicitly bound will be bound by the linker when glLinkProgram is called. The locations assigned can be queried by calling glGetAttribLocation.

OpenGL copies the *name* string when `glBindAttribLocation` is called, so an application may free its copy of the *name* string immediately after the function returns.

Generic attribute locations may be specified in the shader source text using a `location` layout qualifier. In this case, the location of the attribute specified in the shader's source takes precedence and may be queried by calling glGetAttribLocation.

Errors

GL_INVALID_VALUE is generated if *index* is greater than or equal to GL_MAX_VERTEX_ATTRIBS.
GL_INVALID_OPERATION is generated if *name* starts with the reserved prefix "gl_".
GL_INVALID_VALUE is generated if *program* is not a value generated by OpenGL.
GL_INVALID_OPERATION is generated if *program* is not a program object.

Associated Gets

glGet with argument GL_MAX_VERTEX_ATTRIBS
glGetActiveAttrib with argument *program*
glGetAttribLocation with arguments *program* and *name*
glIsProgram

See Also

`glDisableVertexAttribArray`, `glEnableVertexAttribArray`, `glUseProgram`, `glVertexAttrib`, `glVertexAttribPointer`

Copyright

Copyright © 2003-2005 3Dlabs Inc. Ltd. This material may be distributed subject to the terms and conditions set forth in the Open Publication License, v 1.0, 8 June 1999. http://opencontent.org/openpub/.

glBindBuffer

bind a named buffer object

C Specification

```
void glBindBuffer(GLenum target,
                  GLuint buffer);
```

Parameters

target

Specifies the target to which the buffer object is bound. The symbolic constant must be GL_ARRAY_BUFFER, GL_COPY_READ_BUFFER, GL_COPY_WRITE_BUFFER, GL_ELEMENT_ARRAY_BUFFER, GL_PIXEL_PACK_BUFFER, GL_PIXEL_UNPACK_BUFFER, GL_TEXTURE_BUFFER, GL_TRANSFORM_FEEDBACK_BUFFER, or GL_UNIFORM_BUFFER.

buffer

Specifies the name of a buffer object.

Description

glBindBuffer binds a buffer object to the specified buffer binding point. Calling glBindBuffer with *target* set to one of the accepted symbolic constants and *buffer* set to the name of a buffer object binds that buffer object name to the target. If no buffer object with name *buffer* exists, one is created with that name. When a buffer object is bound to a target, the previous binding for that target is automatically broken.

Buffer object names are unsigned integers. The value zero is reserved, but there is no default buffer object for each buffer object target. Instead, *buffer* set to zero effectively unbinds any buffer object previously bound, and restores client memory usage for that buffer object target (if supported for that target). Buffer object names and the corresponding buffer object contents are local to the shared object space of the current GL rendering context; two rendering contexts share buffer object names only if they explicitly enable sharing between contexts through the appropriate GL windows interfaces functions.

glGenBuffers must be used to generate a set of unused buffer object names.

The state of a buffer object immediately after it is first bound is an unmapped zero-sized memory buffer with GL_READ_WRITE access and GL_STATIC_DRAW usage.

While a non-zero buffer object name is bound, GL operations on the target to which it is bound affect the bound buffer object, and queries of the target to which it is bound return state from the bound buffer object. While a buffer object name zero is bound, as in the initial state, attempts to modify or query state on the target to which it is bound generates an GL_INVALID_OPERATION error.

When a non-zero buffer object is bound to the GL_ARRAY_BUFFER target, the vertex array pointer parameter is interpreted as an offset within the buffer object measured in basic machine units.

While a non-zero buffer object is bound to the GL_ELEMENT_ARRAY_BUFFER target, the indices parameter of glDrawElements, glDrawElementsInstanced, glDrawElementsBaseVertex, glDrawRangeElements, glDrawRangeElementsBaseVertex, glMultiDrawElements, or glMultiDrawElementsBaseVertex is interpreted as an offset within the buffer object measured in basic machine units.

While a non-zero buffer object is bound to the GL_PIXEL_PACK_BUFFER target, the following commands are affected: glGetCompressedTexImage, glGetTexImage, and glReadPixels. The pointer parameter is interpreted as an offset within the buffer object measured in basic machine units.

While a non-zero buffer object is bound to the GL_PIXEL_UNPACK_BUFFER target, the following commands are affected: glCompressedTexImage1D, glCompressedTexImage2D, glCompressedTexImage3D, glCompressedTexSubImage1D, glCompressedTexSubImage2D, glCompressedTexSubImage3D, glTexImage1D, glTexImage2D, glTexImage3D, glTexSubImage1D, glTexSubImage2D, and glTexSubImage3D. The pointer parameter is interpreted as an offset within the buffer object measured in basic machine units.

The buffer targets GL_COPY_READ_BUFFER and GL_COPY_WRITE_BUFFER are provided to allow glCopyBufferSubData to be used without disturbing the state of other bindings. However, glCopyBufferSubData may be used with any pair of buffer binding points.

The GL_TRANSFORM_FEEDBACK_BUFFER buffer binding point may be passed to glBindBuffer, but will not directly affect transform feedback state. Instead, the indexed GL_TRANSFORM_FEEDBACK_BUFFER bindings must be used through a call to glBindBufferBase or glBindBufferRange. This will affect the generic GL_TRANSFORM_FEEDABCK_BUFFER binding.

Likewise, the GL_UNIFORM_BUFFER buffer binding point may be used, but does not directly affect uniform buffer state. glBindBufferBase or glBindBufferRange must be used to bind a buffer to an indexed uniform buffer binding point.

A buffer object binding created with glBindBuffer remains active until a different buffer object name is bound to the same target, or until the bound buffer object is deleted with glDeleteBuffers.

Once created, a named buffer object may be re-bound to any target as often as needed. However, the GL implementation may make choices about how to optimize the storage of a buffer object based on its initial binding target.

Notes

The GL_COPY_READ_BUFFER, GL_UNIFORM_BUFFER and GL_TEXTURE_BUFFER targets are available only if the GL version is 3.1 or greater.

Errors

GL_INVALID_ENUM is generated if *target* is not one of the allowable values.

GL_INVALID_VALUE is generated if *buffer* is not a name previously returned from a call to glGenBuffers.

Associated Gets

glGet with argument GL_ARRAY_BUFFER_BINDING
glGet with argument GL_COPY_READ_BUFFER_BINDING
glGet with argument GL_COPY_WRITE_BUFFER_BINDING
glGet with argument GL_ELEMENT_ARRAY_BUFFER_BINDING
glGet with argument GL_PIXEL_PACK_BUFFER_BINDING
glGet with argument GL_PIXEL_UNPACK_BUFFER_BINDING
glGet with argument GL_TRANSFORM_FEEDBACK_BUFFER_BINDING
glGet with argument GL_UNIFORM_BUFFER_BINDING

See Also

glGenBuffers, glBindBufferBase, glBindBufferRange, glMapBuffer, glUnmapBuffer, glDeleteBuffers, glGet, glIsBuffer

Copyright

glBindBufferBase

bind a buffer object to an indexed buffer target

C Specification

```
void glBindBufferBase(GLenum target,
                      GLuint index,
                      GLuint buffer);
```

Parameters

target
> Specify the target of the bind operation. *target* must be either GL_TRANSFORM_FEEDBACK_BUFFER or GL_UNIFORM_BUFFER.

index
> Specify the index of the binding point within the array specified by *target*.

buffer
> The name of a buffer object to bind to the specified binding point.

Description

glBindBufferBase binds the buffer object *buffer* to the binding point at index *index* of the array of targets specified by *target*. Each *target* represents an indexed array of buffer binding points, as well as a single general binding point that can be used by other buffer manipulation functions such as glBindBuffer or glMapBuffer. In addition to binding *buffer* to the indexed buffer binding target, glBindBufferBase also binds *buffer* to the generic buffer binding point specified by *target*.

Notes

glBindBufferBase is available only if the GL version is 3.0 or greater.

Calling glBindBufferBase is equivalent to calling glBindBufferRange with *offset* zero and *size* equal to the size of the buffer.

Errors

GL_INVALID_ENUM is generated if *target* is not GL_TRANSFORM_FEEDBACK_BUFFER or GL_UNIFORM_BUFFER.

GL_INVALID_VALUE is generated if *index* is greater than or equal to the number of *target*-specific indexed binding points.

See Also

glGenBuffers, glDeleteBuffers, glBindBuffer, glBindBufferRange, glMapBuffer, glUnmapBuffer.

Copyright

Copyright © 2010 Khronos Group. This material may be distributed subject to the terms and conditions set forth in the Open Publication License, v 1.0, 8 June 1999. http://opencontent.org/openpub/.

glBindBufferRange

bind a range within a buffer object to an indexed buffer target

C Specification

```
void glBindBufferRange(GLenum     target,
                       GLuint     index,
                       GLuint     buffer,
                       GLintptr   offset,
                       GLsizeiptr size);
```

Parameters

target

Specify the target of the bind operation. *target* must be either GL_TRANSFORM_FEEDBACK_BUFFER or GL_UNIFORM_BUFFER.

index

Specify the index of the binding point within the array specified by *target*.

buffer

The name of a buffer object to bind to the specified binding point.

offset

The starting offset in basic machine units into the buffer object *buffer*.

size

The amount of data in machine units that can be read from the buffet object while used as an indexed target.

Description

glBindBufferRange binds a range the buffer object *buffer* represented by *offset* and *size* to the binding point at index *index* of the array of targets specified by *target*. Each *target* represents an indexed array of buffer binding points, as well as a single general binding point that can be used by other buffer manipulation functions such as glBindBuffer or glMapBuffer. In addition to binding a range of *buffer* to the indexed buffer binding target, **glBindBufferBase** also binds the range to the generic buffer binding point specified by *target*.

offset specifies the offset in basic machine units into the buffer object *buffer* and *size* specifies the amount of data that can be read from the buffer object while used as an indexed target.

Errors

GL_INVALID_ENUM is generated if *target* is not GL_TRANSFORM_FEEDBACK_BUFFER or GL_UNIFORM_BUFFER.

GL_INVALID_VALUE is generated if *index* is greater than or equal to the number of *target*-specific indexed binding points.

GL_INVALID_VALUE is generated if *size* is less than or equal to zero, or if *offset* + *size* is greater than the value of GL_BUFFER_SIZE.

Additional errors may be generated if *offset* violates any *target*-specific alignmemt restrictions.

See Also

`glGenBuffers`, `glDeleteBuffers`, `glBindBuffer`, `glBindBufferBase`, `glMapBuffer`, `glUnmapBuffer`.

Copyright

Copyright © 2010 Khronos Group. This material may be distributed subject to the terms and conditions set forth in the Open Publication License, v 1.0, 8 June 1999. http://opencontent.org/openpub/.

glBindFragDataLocation

bind a user-defined varying out variable to a fragment shader color number

C Specification

```
void glBindFragDataLocation(GLuint program,
                            GLuint colorNumber,
                            const char * name);
```

Parameters

program
    The name of the program containing varying out variable whose binding to modify
colorNumber
    The color number to bind the user-defined varying out variable to
name
    The name of the user-defined varying out variable whose binding to modify

Description

glBindFragDataLocation explicitly specifies the binding of the user-defined varying out variable *name* to fragment shader color number *colorNumber* for program *program*. If *name* was bound previously, its assigned binding is replaced with *colorNumber*. *name* must be a null-terminated string. *colorNumber* must be less than GL_MAX_DRAW_BUFFERS.

The bindings specified by glBindFragDataLocation have no effect until *program* is next linked. Bindings may be specified at any time after *program* has been created. Specifically, they may be specified before shader objects are attached to the program. Therefore, any name may be specified in *name*, including a name that is never used as a varying out variable in any fragment shader object. Names beginning with gl_ are reserved by the GL.

In addition to the errors generated by glBindFragDataLocation, the program *program* will fail to link if:

> The number of active outputs is greater than the value GL_MAX_DRAW_BUFFERS.
> More than one varying out variable is bound to the same color number.

Notes

Varying out variables may have indexed locations assigned explicitly in the shader text using a `location` layout qualifier. If a shader statically assigns a location to a varying out variable in the shader text, that location is used and any location assigned with glBindFragDataLocation is ignored.

Errors

GL_INVALID_VALUE is generated if *colorNumber* is greater than or equal to GL_MAX_DRAW_BUFFERS.

GL_INVALID_OPERATION is generated if *name* starts with the reserved gl_ prefix.

GL_INVALID_OPERATION is generated if program is not the name of a program object.

Associated Gets

glGetFragDataLocation with a valid program object and the the name of a user-defined varying out variable

See Also

glCreateProgram, glGetFragDataLocation

Copyright

Copyright © 2010 Khronos Group. This material may be distributed subject to the terms and conditions set forth in the Open Publication License, v 1.0, 8 June 1999. http://opencontent.org/openpub/.

glBindFragDataLocationIndexed

bind a user-defined varying out variable to a fragment shader color number and index

C Specification

```
void glBindFragDataLocationIndexed(GLuint program,
                                   GLuint colorNumber,
                                   GLuint index,
                                   const char * name);
```

Parameters

program
> The name of the program containing varying out variable whose binding to modify

colorNumber
> The color number to bind the user-defined varying out variable to

index
> The index of the color input to bind the user-defined varying out variable to

name
> The name of the user-defined varying out variable whose binding to modify

Description

glBindFragDataLocationIndexed specifies that the varying out variable *name* in *program* should be bound to fragment color *colorNumber* when the program is next linked. *index* may be zero or one to specify that the color be used as either the first or second color input to the blend equation, respectively.

The bindings specified by glBindFragDataLocationIndexed have no effect until *program* is next linked. Bindings may be specified at any time after *program* has been created. Specifically, they may be specified before shader objects are attached to the program. Therefore, any name may be specified in *name*, including a name that is never used as a varying out variable in any fragment shader object. Names beginning with gl_ are reserved by the GL.

If *name* was bound previously, its assigned binding is replaced with *colorNumber* and *index*. *name* must be a null-terminated string. *index* must be less than or equal to one, and *colorNumber* must be less than the value of GL_MAX_DRAW_BUFFERS if *index* is zero, and less than the value of GL_MAX_DUAL_SOURCE_DRAW_BUFFERS if index is greater than or equal to one.

In addition to the errors generated by glBindFragDataLocationIndexed, the program *program* will fail to link if:

      The number of active outputs is greater than the value GL_MAX_DRAW_BUFFERS.

      More than one varying out variable is bound to the same color number.

Notes

Varying out variables may have locations assigned explicitly in the shader text using a location layout qualifier. If a shader statically assigns a location to a varying out variable in the shader text, that location is used and any location assigned with glBindFragDataLocation is ignored.

Errors

GL_INVALID_VALUE is generated if *colorNumber* is greater than or equal to GL_MAX_DRAW_BUFFERS.

GL_INVALID_VALUE is generated if *colorNumber* is greater than or equal to GL_MAX_DUAL_SOURCE_DRAW_BUFERS and *index* is greater than or equal to one.

GL_INVALID_VALUE is generated if *index* is greater than one.

GL_INVALID_OPERATION is generated if *name* starts with the reserved gl_ prefix.

GL_INVALID_OPERATION is generated if program is not the name of a program object.

Associated Gets

glGetFragDataLocation with a valid program object and the the name of a user-defined varying out variable

glGetFragDataIndex with a valid program object and the the name of a user-defined varying out variable

See Also

glCreateProgram, glLinkProgram glGetFragDataLocation, glGetFragDataIndex glBindFragDataLocation

Copyright

glBindFramebuffer

bind a framebuffer to a framebuffer target

C Specification

```
void glBindFramebuffer(GLenum target,
                       GLuint framebuffer);
```

Parameters

target
> Specifies the framebuffer target of the binding operation.

framebuffer
> Specifies the name of the framebuffer object to bind.

Description

glBindFramebuffer binds the framebuffer object with name *framebuffer* to the framebuffer target specified by *target*. *target* must be either GL_DRAW_FRAMEBUFFER, GL_READ_FRAMEBUFFER or GL_FRAMEBUFFER. If a framebuffer object is bound to GL_DRAW_FRAMEBUFFER or GL_READ_FRAMEBUFFER, it becomes the target for rendering or readback operations, respectively, until it is deleted or another framebuffer is bound to the corresponding bind point. Calling glBindFramebuffer with *target* set to GL_FRAMEBUFFER binds *framebuffer* to both the read and draw framebuffer targets. *framebuffer* is the name of a framebuffer object previously returned from a call to glGenFramebuffers, or zero to break the existing binding of a framebuffer object to *target*.

Errors

GL_INVALID_ENUM is generated if *target* is not GL_DRAW_FRAMEBUFFER, GL_READ_FRAME-BUFFER or GL_FRAMEBUFFER.

GL_INVALID_OPERATION is generated if *framebuffer* is not zero or the name of a framebuffer previously returned from a call to glGenFramebuffers.

See Also

glGenFramebuffers, glDeleteFramebuffers, glFramebufferRenderbuffer, glFramebufferTexture, glFramebufferTexture1D, glFramebufferTexture2D, glFramebufferTexture3D, glFramebufferTextureFace, glFramebufferTextureLayer, glIsFramebuffer

Copyright

glBindRenderbuffer

bind a renderbuffer to a renderbuffer target

C Specification

```
void glBindRenderbuffer(GLenum target,
                        GLuint renderbuffer);
```

Parameters

target

> Specifies the renderbuffer target of the binding operation. *target* must be GL_RENDERBUFFER.

renderbuffer

> Specifies the name of the renderbuffer object to bind.

Description

glBindRenderbuffer binds the renderbuffer object with name *renderbuffer* to the renderbuffer target specified by *target*. *target* must be GL_RENDERBUFFER. *renderbuffer* is the name of a renderbuffer object previously returned from a call to glGenRenderbuffers, or zero to break the existing binding of a renderbuffer object to *target*.

Errors

GL_INVALID_ENUM is generated if *target* is not GL_RENDERBUFFER.

GL_INVALID_OPERATION is generated if *renderbuffer* is not zero or the name of a renderbuffer previously returned from a call to glGenRenderbuffers.

See Also

glGenRenderbuffers, glDeleteRenderbuffers, glRenderbufferStorage, glRenderbufferStorageMultisample, glIsRenderbuffer

Copyright

glBindSampler

bind a named sampler to a texturing target

C Specification

```
void glBindSampler(GLuint unit,
                   GLuint texture);
```

Parameters

unit

> Specifies the index of the texture unit to which the sampler is bound.

sampler

> Specifies the name of a sampler.

Description

glBindSampler binds *sampler* to the texture unit at index *unit*. *sampler* must be zero or the name of a sampler object previously returned from a call to glGenSamplers. *unit* must be less than the value of GL_MAX_COMBINED_TEXTURE_IMAGE_UNITS.

When a sampler object is bound to a texture unit, its state supersedes that of the texture object bound to that texture unit. If the sampler name zero is bound to a texture unit, the currently bound texture's sampler state becomes active. A single sampler object may be bound to multiple texture units simultaneously.

Notes

glBindSampler is available only if the GL version is 3.3 or higher.

Errors

GL_INVALID_VALUE is generated if *unit* is greater than or equal to the value of GL_MAX_COMBINED_TEXTURE_IMAGE_UNITS.

GL_INVALID_OPERATION is generated if *sampler* is not zero or a name previously returned from a call to glGenSamplers, or if such a name has been deleted by a call to glDeleteSamplers.

Associated Gets

glGet with argument GL_SAMPLER_BINDING

See Also

glGenSamplers, glDeleteSamplers, glGet, glSamplerParameter, glGetSamplerParameter, glGenTextures, glBindTexture, glDeleteTextures

Copyright

glBindTexture

bind a named texture to a texturing target

C Specification

```
void glBindTexture(GLenum target,
                   GLuint texture);
```

Parameters

target

Specifies the target to which the texture is bound. Must be either GL_TEXTURE_1D, GL_TEXTURE_2D, GL_TEXTURE_3D, or GL_TEXTURE_1D_ARRAY, GL_TEXTURE_2D_ARRAY, GL_TEXTURE_RECTANGLE, GL_TEXTURE_CUBE_MAP, GL_TEXTURE_2D_MULTISAMPLE or GL_TEXTURE_2D_MULTISAMPLE_ARRAY.

texture

Specifies the name of a texture.

Description

glBindTexture lets you create or use a named texture. Calling glBindTexture with *target* set to GL_TEXTURE_1D, GL_TEXTURE_2D, GL_TEXTURE_3D, or GL_TEXTURE_1D_ARRAY, GL_TEXTURE_2D_ARRAY, GL_TEXTURE_RECTANGLE, GL_TEXTURE_CUBE_MAP, GL_TEXTURE_2D_MULTISAMPLE or GL_TEXTURE_2D_MULTISAMPLE_ARRAY and *texture* set to the name of the new texture binds the texture name to the target. When a texture is bound to a target, the previous binding for that target is automatically broken.

Texture names are unsigned integers. The value zero is reserved to represent the default texture for each texture target. Texture names and the corresponding texture contents are local to the shared object space of the current GL rendering context; two rendering contexts share texture names only if they explicitly enable sharing between contexts through the appropriate GL windows interfaces functions.

You must use glGenTextures to generate a set of new texture names.

When a texture is first bound, it assumes the specified target: A texture first bound to GL_TEXTURE_1D becomes one-dimensional texture, a texture first bound to GL_TEXTURE_2D becomes two-dimensional texture, a texture first bound to GL_TEXTURE_3D becomes three-dimensional texture, a texture first bound to GL_TEXTURE_1D_ARRAY becomes one-dimensional array texture, a texture first bound to GL_TEXTURE_2D_ARRAY becomes two-dimensional arary texture, a texture first bound to GL_TEXTURE_RECTANGLE becomes rectangle texture, a, texture first bound to GL_TEXTURE_CUBE_MAP becomes a cube-mapped texture, a texture first bound to GL_TEXTURE_2D_MULTISAMPLE becomes a two-dimensional multisampled texture, and a texture first bound to GL_TEXTURE_2D_MULTISAMPLE_ARRAY becomes a two-dimensional multisampled array texture. The state of a one-dimensional texture immediately after it is first bound is equivalent to the state of the default GL_TEXTURE_1D at GL initialization, and similarly for the other texture types.

While a texture is bound, GL operations on the target to which it is bound affect the bound texture, and queries of the target to which it is bound return state from the bound texture. In effect, the texture targets become aliases for the textures currently bound to them, and the texture name zero refers to the default textures that were bound to them at initialization.

A texture binding created with **glBindTexture** remains active until a different texture is bound to the same target, or until the bound texture is deleted with glDeleteTextures.

Once created, a named texture may be re-bound to its same original target as often as needed. It is usually much faster to use **glBindTexture** to bind an existing named texture to one of the texture targets than it is to reload the texture image using glTexImage1D, glTexImage2D, glTexImage3D or another similar function.

Notes

The GL_TEXTURE_2D_MULTISAMPLE and GL_TEXTURE_2D_MULTISAMPLE_ARRAY targets are available only if the GL version is 3.2 or higher.

Errors

GL_INVALID_ENUM is generated if *target* is not one of the allowable values.

GL_INVALID_VALUE is generated if *target* is not a name returned from a previous call to glGenTextures.

GL_INVALID_OPERATION is generated if *texture* was previously created with a target that doesn't match that of *target*.

Associated Gets

glGet with argument GL_TEXTURE_BINDING_1D, GL_TEXTURE_BINDING_2D, GL_TEXTURE_BINDING_3D, GL_TEXTURE_BINDING_1D_ARRAY, GL_TEXTURE_BINDING_2D_ARRAY, GL_TEXTURE_BINDING_RECTANGLE, GL_TEXTURE_BINDING_2D_MULTISAMPLE, or GL_TEXTURE_BINDING_2D_MULTISAMPLE_ARRAY.

See Also

glDeleteTextures, glGenTextures, glGet, glGetTexParameter, glIsTexture, glTexImage1D, glTexImage2D, glTexImage2DMultisample, glTexImage3D, glTexImage3DMultisample, glTexParameter

Copyright

Copyright © 1991-2006 Silicon Graphics, Inc. This document is licensed under the SGI Free Software B License. For details, see http://oss.sgi.com/projects/FreeB/.

glBindVertexArray

bind a vertex array object

C Specification

```
void glBindVertexArray(GLuint array);
```

Parameters

array
> Specifies the name of the vertex array to bind.

Description

glBindVertexArray binds the vertex array object with name *array*. *array* is the name of a vertex array object previously returned from a call to glGenVertexArrays, or zero to break the existing vertex array object binding.

If no vertex array object with name *array* exists, one is created when *array* is first bound. If the bind is successful no change is made to the state of the vertex array object, and any previous vertex array object binding is broken.

Errors

GL_INVALID_OPERATION is generated if *array* is not zero or the name of a vertex array object previously returned from a call to glGenVertexArrays.

See Also

glGenVertexArrays, glDeleteVertexArrays glVertexAttribPointer glEnableVertexAttribArray

Copyright

Copyright © 2010 Khronos Group. This material may be distributed subject to the terms and conditions set forth in the Open Publication License, v 1.0, 8 June 1999. http://opencontent.org/openpub/.

glBlendColor

set the blend color

C Specification

```
void glBlendColor(GLclampf red,
                  GLclampf green,
                  GLclampf blue,
                  GLclampf alpha);
```

Parameters

red
green
blue
alpha
> specify the components of GL_BLEND_COLOR

Description

The GL_BLEND_COLOR may be used to calculate the source and destination blending factors. The color components are clamped to the range [0,1] before being stored. See glBlendFunc for a complete description of the blending operations. Initially the GL_BLEND_COLOR is set to (0, 0, 0, 0).

Associated Gets

glGet with an argument of GL_BLEND_COLOR

See Also

glBlendEquation, glBlendFunc, glGetString

Copyright

Copyright © 1991-2006 Silicon Graphics, Inc. This document is licensed under the SGI Free Software B License. For details, see http://oss.sgi.com/projects/FreeB/.

glBlendEquation

specify the equation used for both the RGB blend equation and the Alpha blend equation

C Specification

void glBlendEquation(GLenum *mode*);

Parameters

mode

> specifies how source and destination colors are combined. It must be GL_FUNC_ADD, GL_FUNC_SUBTRACT, GL_FUNC_REVERSE_SUBTRACT, GL_MIN, GL_MAX.

Description

The blend equations determine how a new pixel (the "source" color) is combined with a pixel already in the framebuffer (the "destination" color). This function sets both the RGB blend equation and the alpha blend equation to a single equation.

These equations use the source and destination blend factors specified by either glBlendFunc or glBlendFuncSeparate. See glBlendFunc or glBlendFuncSeparate for a description of the various blend factors.

Mode	RGB Components	Alpha Component
GL_FUNC_ADD	$Rr = R_s s_R + R_d d_R$ $\quad$ $Gr = G_s s_G + G_d d_G$ $\quad$ $Br = B_s s_B + B_d d_B$	$Ar = A_s s_A + A_d d_A$
GL_FUNC_SUBTRACT	$Rr = R_s s_R - R_d d_R$ $\quad$ $Gr = G_s s_G - G_d d_G$ $\quad$ $Br = B_s s_B - B_d d_B$	$Ar = A_s s_A - A_d d_A$
GL_FUNC_REVERSE_SUBTRACT	$Rr = R_d d_R - R_s s_R$ $\quad$ $Gr = G_d d_G - G_s s_G$ $\quad$ $Br = B_d d_B - B_s s_B$	$Ar = A_d d_A - A_s s_A$

Mode	RGB Components	Alpha Component
GL_MIN	$Rr = min(R_s, R_d)$ $Gr = min(G_s, G_d)$ $Br = min(B_s, B_d)$	$Ar = min(A_s, A_d)$
GL_MAX	$Rr = max(R_s, R_d)$ $Gr = max(G_s, G_d)$ $Br = max(B_s, B_d)$	$Ar = max(A_s, A_d)$

In the equations that follow, source and destination color components are referred to as (R_s, G_s, B_s, A_s) and (R_d, G_d, B_d, A_d), respectively. The resulting color is referred to as (R_r, G_r, B_r, A_r). The source and destination blend factors are denoted (s_R, s_G, s_B, s_A) and (d_R, d_G, d_B, d_A), respectively. For these equations all color components are understood to have values in the range $[0,1]$.

The results of these equations are clamped to the range $[0,1]$.

The GL_MIN and GL_MAX equations are useful for applications that analyze image data (image thresholding against a constant color, for example). The GL_FUNC_ADD equation is useful for antialiasing and transparency, among other things.

Initially, both the RGB blend equation and the alpha blend equation are set to GL_FUNC_ADD.

Notes

The GL_MIN, and GL_MAX equations do not use the source or destination factors, only the source and destination colors.

Errors

GL_INVALID_ENUM is generated if *mode* is not one of GL_FUNC_ADD, GL_FUNC_SUBTRACT, GL_FUNC_REVERSE_SUBTRACT, GL_MAX, or GL_MIN.

Associated Gets

glGet with an argument of GL_BLEND_EQUATION_RGB
glGet with an argument of GL_BLEND_EQUATION_ALPHA

See Also

`glBlendColor, glBlendFunc glBlendFuncSeparate`

Copyright

Copyright © 1991-2006 Silicon Graphics, Inc. This document is licensed under the SGI Free Software B License. For details, see http://oss.sgi.com/projects/FreeB/.

glBlendEquationSeparate

set the RGB blend equation and the alpha blend equation separately

C Specification

```
void glBlendEquationSeparate(GLenum modeRGB,
                             GLenum modeAlpha);
```

Parameters

modeRGB

specifies the RGB blend equation, how the red, green, and blue components of the source and destination colors are combined. It must be GL_FUNC_ADD, GL_FUNC_SUBTRACT, GL_FUNC_REVERSE_SUBTRACT, GL_MIN, GL_MAX.

modeAlpha

specifies the alpha blend equation, how the alpha component of the source and destination colors are combined. It must be GL_FUNC_ADD, GL_FUNC_SUBTRACT, GL_FUNC_REVERSE_SUBTRACT, GL_MIN, GL_MAX.

Description

The blend equations determines how a new pixel (the "source" color) is combined with a pixel already in the framebuffer (the "destination" color). This function specifies one blend equation for the RGB-color components and one blend equation for the alpha component.

The blend equations use the source and destination blend factors specified by either glBlendFunc or glBlendFuncSeparate. See glBlendFunc or glBlendFuncSeparate for a description of the various blend factors.

Mode	RGB Components	Alpha Component
GL_FUNC_ADD	$Rr = R_s s_R + R_d d_R$ $Gr = G_s s_G + G_d d_G$ $Br = B_s s_B + B_d d_B$	$Ar = A_s s_A + A_d d_A$
GL_FUNC_SUBTRACT	$Rr = R_s s_R - R_d d_R$ $Gr = G_s s_G - G_d d_G$ $Br = B_s s_B - B_d d_B$	$Ar = A_s s_A - A_d d_A$
GL_FUNC_REVERSE_SUBTRACT	$Rr = R_d d_R - R_s s_R$ $Gr = G_d d_G - G_s s_G$ $Br = B_d d_B - B_s s_B$	$Ar = A_d d_A - A_s s_A$
GL_MIN	$Rr = \min(R_s, R_d)$ $Gr = \min(G_s, G_d)$ $Br = \min(B_s, B_d)$	$Ar = \min(A_s, A_d)$
GL_MAX	$Rr = \max(R_s, R_d)$ $Gr = \max(G_s, G_d)$ $Br = \max(B_s, B_d)$	$Ar = \max(A_s, A_d)$

In the equations that follow, source and destination color components are referred to as (R_s, G_s, B_s, A_s) and (R_d, G_d, B_d, A_d), respectively. The resulting color is referred to as (R_r, G_r, B_r, A_r). The source and destination blend factors are denoted (s_R, s_G, s_B, s_A) and (d_R, d_G, d_B, d_A), respectively. For these equations all color components are understood to have values in the range $[0,1]$.

The results of these equations are clamped to the range $[0,1]$.

The GL_MIN and GL_MAX equations are useful for applications that analyze image data (image thresholding against a constant color, for example). The GL_FUNC_ADD equation is useful for antialiasing and transparency, among other things.

Initially, both the RGB blend equation and the alpha blend equation are set to GL_FUNC_ADD.

Notes

The GL_MIN, and GL_MAX equations do not use the source or destination factors, only the source and destination colors.

Errors

GL_INVALID_ENUM is generated if either *modeRGB* or *modeAlpha* is not one of GL_FUNC_ADD, GL_FUNC_SUBTRACT, GL_FUNC_REVERSE_SUBTRACT, GL_MAX, or GL_MIN.

Associated Gets

glGet with an argument of GL_BLEND_EQUATION_RGB
glGet with an argument of GL_BLEND_EQUATION_ALPHA

See Also

glGetString, glBlendColor, glBlendFunc, glBlendFuncSeparate

Copyright

Copyright © 2006 Khronos Group. This material may be distributed subject to the terms and conditions set forth in the Open Publication License, v 1.0, 8 June 1999. http://opencontent.org/openpub/.

glBlendFunc

specify pixel arithmetic

C Specification

```
void glBlendFunc(GLenum  sfactor,
                 GLenum dfactor);
```

Parameters

sfactor

Specifies how the red, green, blue, and alpha source blending factors are computed. The initial value is GL_ONE.

dfactor

Specifies how the red, green, blue, and alpha destination blending factors are computed. The following symbolic constants are accepted: GL_ZERO, GL_ONE, GL_SRC_COLOR, GL_ONE_MINUS_SRC_COLOR, GL_DST_COLOR, GL_ONE_MINUS_DST_COLOR, GL_SRC_ALPHA, GL_ONE_MINUS_SRC_ALPHA, GL_DST_ALPHA, GL_ONE_MINUS_DST_ALPHA. GL_CONSTANT_COLOR, GL_ONE_MINUS_CONSTANT_COLOR, GL_CONSTANT_ALPHA, and GL_ONE_MINUS_CONSTANT_ALPHA. The initial value is GL_ZERO.

Description

Pixels can be drawn using a function that blends the incoming (source) RGBA values with the RGBA values that are already in the frame buffer (the destination values). Blending is initially disabled. Use glEnable and glDisable with argument GL_BLEND to enable and disable blending.

glBlendFunc defines the operation of blending when it is enabled. *sfactor* specifies which method is used to scale the source color components. *dfactor* specifies which method is used to scale the destination color components. Both parameters must be one of the following symbolic constants: GL_ZERO, GL_ONE, GL_SRC_COLOR, GL_ONE_MINUS_SRC_COLOR, GL_DST_COLOR, GL_ONE_MINUS_DST_COLOR, GL_SRC_ALPHA, GL_ONE_MINUS_SRC_ALPHA, GL_DST_ALPHA, GL_ONE_MINUS_DST_ALPHA, GL_CONSTANT_COLOR, GL_ONE_MINUS_CONSTANT_COLOR, GL_CONSTANT_ALPHA, GL_ONE_MINUS_CONSTANT_ALPHA, GL_SRC_ALPHA_SATURATE, GL_SRC1_COLOR, GL_ONE_MINUS_SRC1_COLOR, GL_SRC1_ALPHA, and GL_ONE_MINUS_SRC1_ALPHA. The possible methods are described in the following table. Each method defines four scale factors, one each for red, green, blue, and alpha. In the table and in subsequent equations, first source, second source and destination color components are referred to as $(R_{s0}, G_{s0}, B_{s0}, A_{s0})$, $(R_{s1}, G_{s1}, B_{s1}, A_{s1})$ and (R_d, G_d, B_d, A_d), respectively. The color specified by glBlendColor is referred to as (R_c, G_c, B_c, A_c). They are understood to have integer values between 0 and (k_R, k_G, k_B, k_A), where

Parameter	(f_R, f_G, f_B, f_A)
GL_ZERO	$(0,0,0,0)$
GL_ONE	$(1,1,1,1)$
GL_SRC_COLOR	$\left(\dfrac{R_{s0}}{k_R}, \dfrac{G_{s0}}{k_G}, \dfrac{B_{s0}}{k_B}, \dfrac{A_{s0}}{k_A} \right)$
GL_ONE_MINUS_SRC_COLOR	$(1,1,1,1) - \left(\dfrac{R_{s0}}{k_R}, \dfrac{G_{s0}}{k_G}, \dfrac{B_{s0}}{k_B}, \dfrac{A_{s0}}{k_A} \right)$
GL_DST_COLOR	$\left(\dfrac{R_d}{k_R}, \dfrac{G_d}{k_G}, \dfrac{B_d}{k_B}, \dfrac{A_d}{k_A} \right)$
GL_ONE_MINUS_DST_COLOR	$(1,1,1,1) - \left(\dfrac{R_d}{k_R}, \dfrac{G_d}{k_G}, \dfrac{B_d}{k_B}, \dfrac{A_d}{k_A} \right)$
GL_SRC_ALPHA	$\left(\dfrac{A_{s0}}{k_A}, \dfrac{A_{s0}}{k_A}, \dfrac{A_{s0}}{k_A}, \dfrac{A_{s0}}{k_A} \right)$
GL_ONE_MINUS_SRC_ALPHA	$(1,1,1,1) - \left(\dfrac{A_{s0}}{k_A}, \dfrac{A_{s0}}{k_A}, \dfrac{A_{s0}}{k_A}, \dfrac{A_{s0}}{k_A} \right)$
GL_DST_ALPHA	$\left(\dfrac{A_d}{k_A}, \dfrac{A_d}{k_A}, \dfrac{A_d}{k_A}, \dfrac{A_d}{k_A} \right)$
GL_ONE_MINUS_DST_ALPHA	$(1,1,1,1) - \left(\dfrac{A_d}{k_A}, \dfrac{A_d}{k_A}, \dfrac{A_d}{k_A}, \dfrac{A_d}{k_A} \right)$
GL_CONSTANT_COLOR	(R_c, G_c, B_c, A_c)

Parameter	(f_R, f_G, f_B, f_A)
GL_ONE_MINUS_CONSTANT_COLOR	$(1,1,1,1) - (R_c, G_c, B_c, A_c)$
GL_CONSTANT_ALPHA	(A_c, A_c, A_c, A_c)
GL_ONE_MINUS_CONSTANT_ALPHA	$(1,1,1,1) - (A_c, A_c, A_c, A_c)$
GL_SRC_ALPHA_SATURATE	$(i, i, i, 1)$
GL_SRC1_COLOR	$a\dfrac{R_{s1}}{k_R}, \dfrac{G_{s1}}{k_G}, \dfrac{B_{s1}}{k_B}, \dfrac{A_{s1}}{k_A}b$
GL_ONE_MINUS_SRC1_COLOR	$(1,1,1,1) - a\dfrac{R_{s1}}{k_R}, \dfrac{G_{s1}}{k_G}, \dfrac{B_{s1}}{k_B}, \dfrac{A_{s1}}{k_A}b$
GL_SRC1_ALPHA	$a\dfrac{A_{s1}}{k_A}, \dfrac{A_{s1}}{k_A}, \dfrac{A_{s1}}{k_A}, \dfrac{A_{s1}}{k_A}b$
GL_ONE_MINUS_SRC1_ALPHA	$(1,1,1,1) - a\dfrac{A_{s1}}{k_A}, \dfrac{A_{s1}}{k_A}, \dfrac{A_{s1}}{k_A}, \dfrac{A_{s1}}{k_A}b$

$$k_c = 2^{m_c} - 1$$

and (m_R, m_G, m_B, m_A) is the number of red, green, blue, and alpha bitplanes.

Source and destination scale factors are referred to as (s_R, s_G, s_B, s_A) and (d_R, d_G, d_B, d_A). The scale factors described in the table, denoted (f_R, f_G, f_B, f_A), represent either source or destination factors. All scale factors have range $[0,1]$.

In the table,

$$i = \frac{min(A_s, k_A - A_d)}{k_A}$$

To determine the blended RGBA values of a pixel, the system uses the following equations:

$$R_d = min(k_R, R_s s_R + R_d d_R) \quad G_d = min(k_G, G_s s_G + G_d d_G) \quad B_d = min(k_B, B_s s_B + B_d d_B)$$

$$A_d = min(k_A, A_s s_A + A_d d_A)$$

Despite the apparent precision of the above equations, blending arithmetic is not exactly specified, because blending operates with imprecise integer color values. However, a blend factor that should be equal to 1 is guaranteed not to modify its multiplicand, and a blend factor equal to 0 reduces its multiplicand to 0. For example, when *sfactor* is GL_SRC_ALPHA, *dfactor* is GL_ONE_MINUS_SRC_ALPHA, and A_s is equal to k_A, the equations reduce to simple replacement:

$$R_d = R_s \quad G_d = G_s \quad B_d = B_s \quad A_d = A_s$$

Examples

Transparency is best implemented using blend function (GL_SRC_ALPHA, GL_ONE_MINUS_SRC_ALPHA) with primitives sorted from farthest to nearest. Note that this transparency calculation does not require the presence of alpha bitplanes in the frame buffer.

Blend function (GL_SRC_ALPHA, GL_ONE_MINUS_SRC_ALPHA) is also useful for rendering antialiased points and lines in arbitrary order.

Polygon antialiasing is optimized using blend function (GL_SRC_ALPHA_SATURATE, GL_ONE) with polygons sorted from nearest to farthest. (See the glEnable, glDisable reference page and the GL_POLYGON_SMOOTH argument for information on polygon antialiasing.) Destination alpha bitplanes, which must be present for this blend function to operate correctly, store the accumulated coverage.

Notes

Incoming (source) alpha is correctly thought of as a material opacity, ranging from 1.0 (κ_A), representing complete opacity, to 0.0 (0), representing complete transparency.

When more than one color buffer is enabled for drawing, the GL performs blending separately for each enabled buffer, using the contents of that buffer for destination color. (See glDrawBuffer.)

When dual source blending is enabled (i.e., one of the blend factors requiring the second color input is used), the maximum number of enabled draw buffers is given by GL_MAX_DUAL_SOURCE_DRAW_BUFFERS, which may be lower than GL_MAX_DRAW_BUFFERS.

Errors

GL_INVALID_ENUM is generated if either *sfactor* or *dfactor* is not an accepted value.

Associated Gets

glGet with argument GL_BLEND_SRC
glGet with argument GL_BLEND_DST
glIsEnabled with argument GL_BLEND

See Also

glBlendColor, glBlendEquation, glBlendFuncSeparate, glClear, glDrawBuffer, glEnable, glLogicOp, glStencilFunc

Copyright

glBlendFuncSeparate

specify pixel arithmetic for RGB and alpha components separately

C Specification

```
void glBlendFuncSeparate(GLenum srcRGB,
                         GLenum dstRGB,
                         GLenum srcAlpha,
                         GLenum dstAlpha);
```

Parameters

srcRGB
> Specifies how the red, green, and blue blending factors are computed. The initial value is GL_ONE.

dstRGB
> Specifies how the red, green, and blue destination blending factors are computed. The initial value is GL_ZERO.

srcAlpha
> Specified how the alpha source blending factor is computed. The initial value is GL_ONE.

dstAlpha
> Specified how the alpha destination blending factor is computed. The initial value is GL_ZERO.

Description

Pixels can be drawn using a function that blends the incoming (source) RGBA values with the RGBA values that are already in the frame buffer (the destination values). Blending is initially disabled. Use glEnable and glDisable with argument GL_BLEND to enable and disable blending.

glBlendFuncSeparate defines the operation of blending when it is enabled. *srcRGB* specifies which method is used to scale the source RGB-color components. *dstRGB* specifies which method is used to scale the destination RGB-color components. Likewise, *srcAlpha* specifies which method is used to scale the source alpha color component, and *dstAlpha* specifies which method is used to scale the destination alpha component. The possible methods are described in the following table. Each method defines four scale factors, one each for red, green, blue, and alpha.

In the table and in subsequent equations, first source, second source and destination color components are referred to as $(R_{s0}, G_{s0}, B_{s0}, A_{s0})$, $(R_{s1}, G_{s1}, B_{s1}, A_{s1})$, and (R_d, G_d, B_d, A_d), respectively. The color specified by glBlendColor is referred to as (R_c, G_c, B_c, A_c). They are understood to have integer

Parameter	RGB Factor	Alpha Factor
GL_ZERO	$(0, 0, 0)$	0
GL_ONE	$(1, 1, 1)$	1
GL_SRC_COLOR	$\left(\dfrac{R_{s0}}{k_R}, \dfrac{G_{s0}}{k_G}, \dfrac{B_{s0}}{k_B}\right)$	$\dfrac{A_{s0}}{k_A}$
GL_ONE_MINUS_SRC_COLOR	$(1,1,1,1) - \left(\dfrac{R_{s0}}{k_R}, \dfrac{G_{s0}}{k_G}, \dfrac{B_{s0}}{k_B}\right)$	$1 - \dfrac{A_{s0}}{k_A}$
GL_DST_COLOR	$\left(\dfrac{R_d}{k_R}, \dfrac{G_d}{k_G}, \dfrac{B_d}{k_B}\right)$	$\dfrac{A_d}{k_A}$
GL_ONE_MINUS_DST_COLOR	$(1,1,1) - \left(\dfrac{R_d}{k_R}, \dfrac{G_d}{k_G}, \dfrac{B_d}{k_B}\right)$	$1 - \dfrac{A_d}{k_A}$
GL_SRC_ALPHA	$\left(\dfrac{A_{s0}}{k_A}, \dfrac{A_{s0}}{k_A}, \dfrac{A_{s0}}{k_A}\right)$	$\dfrac{A_{s0}}{k_A}$
GL_ONE_MINUS_SRC_ALPHA	$(1,1,1) - \left(\dfrac{A_{s0}}{k_A}, \dfrac{A_{s0}}{k_A}, \dfrac{A_{s0}}{k_A}\right)$	$1 - \dfrac{A_{s0}}{k_A}$
GL_DST_ALPHA	$\left(\dfrac{A_d}{k_A}, \dfrac{A_d}{k_A}, \dfrac{A_d}{k_A}\right)$	$\dfrac{A_d}{k_A}$
GL_ONE_MINUS_DST_ALPHA	$(1,1,1) - \left(\dfrac{A_d}{k_A}, \dfrac{A_d}{k_A}, \dfrac{A_d}{k_A}\right)$	$1 - \dfrac{A_d}{k_A}$
GL_CONSTANT_COLOR	(R_c, G_c, B_c)	A_c
GL_ONE_MINUS_CONSTANT_COLOR	$(1,1,1) - (R_c, G_c, B_c)$	$1 - A_c$
GL_CONSTANT_ALPHA	(A_c, A_c, A_c)	A_c

Parameter	RGB Factor	Alpha Factor
GL_ONE_MINUS_CONSTANT_ALPHA	$(1,1,1) - (A_c, A_c, A_c)$	$1 - A_c$
GL_SRC_ALPHA_SATURATE	(i, i, i)	1
GL_SRC1_COLOR	$\left(\dfrac{R_{s1}}{k_R}, \dfrac{G_{s1}}{k_G}, \dfrac{B_{s1}}{k_B}\right)$	$\dfrac{A_{s1}}{k_A}$
GL_ONE_MINUS_SRC_COLOR	$(1,1,1,1) - \left(\dfrac{R_{s1}}{k_R}, \dfrac{G_{s1}}{k_G}, \dfrac{B_{s1}}{k_B}\right)$	$1 - \dfrac{A_{s1}}{k_A}$
GL_SRC1_ALPHA	$\left(\dfrac{A_{s1}}{k_A}, \dfrac{A_{s1}}{k_A}, \dfrac{A_{s1}}{k_A}\right)$	$\dfrac{A_{s1}}{k_A}$
GL_ONE_MINUS_SRC_ALPHA	$(1,1,1) - \left(\dfrac{A_{s1}}{k_A}, \dfrac{A_{s1}}{k_A}, \dfrac{A_{s1}}{k_A}\right)$	$1 - \dfrac{A_{s1}}{k_A}$

values between 0 and (k_R, k_G, k_B, k_A), where

$k_c = 2^{m_c} - 1$

and (m_R, m_G, m_B, m_A) is the number of red, green, blue, and alpha bitplanes.

Source and destination scale factors are referred to as (s_R, s_G, s_B, s_A) and (d_R, d_G, d_B, d_A). All scale factors have range $[0,1]$.

In the table,

$i = \min(A_s, 1 - A_d)$

To determine the blended RGBA values of a pixel, the system uses the following equations:

$R_d = \min(k_R, R_s s_R + R_d d_R)\quad G_d = \min(k_G, G_s s_G + G_d d_G)\quad B_d = \min(k_B, B_s s_B + B_d d_B)$
$A_d = \min(k_A, A_s s_A + A_d d_A)$

Despite the apparent precision of the above equations, blending arithmetic is not exactly specified, because blending operates with imprecise integer color values. However, a blend factor that should be equal to 1 is guaranteed not to modify its multiplicand, and a blend factor equal to 0 reduces its multiplicand to 0. For example, when *srcRGB* is GL_SRC_ALPHA, *dstRGB* is GL_ONE_MINUS_SRC_ALPHA, and A_s is equal to k_A, the equations reduce to simple replacement:

$R_d = R_s\quad G_d = G_s\quad B_d = B_s\quad A_d = A_s$

Notes

Incoming (source) alpha is correctly thought of as a material opacity, ranging from 1.0 (K_A), representing complete opacity, to 0.0 (0), representing complete transparency.

When more than one color buffer is enabled for drawing, the GL performs blending separately for each enabled buffer, using the contents of that buffer for destination color. (See glDrawBuffer.)

When dual source blending is enabled (i.e., one of the blend factors requiring the second color input is used), the maximum number of enabled draw buffers is given by GL_MAX_DUAL_SOURCE_DRAW_BUFFERS, which may be lower than GL_MAX_DRAW_BUFFERS.

Errors

GL_INVALID_ENUM is generated if either *srcRGB* or *dstRGB* is not an accepted value.

Associated Gets

glGet with argument GL_BLEND_SRC_RGB
glGet with argument GL_BLEND_SRC_ALPHA

glGet with argument GL_BLEND_DST_RGB
glGet with argument GL_BLEND_DST_ALPHA
glIsEnabled with argument GL_BLEND

See Also

glBlendColor, glBlendFunc, glBlendEquation, glClear, glDrawBuffer, glEnable, glLogicOp, glStencilFunc

Copyright

Copyright © 1991-2006 Silicon Graphics, Inc. This document is licensed under the SGI Free Software B License. For details, see http://oss.sgi.com/projects/FreeB/.

glBlitFramebuffer

bind a vertex array object

C Specification

```
void glBlitFramebuffer(GLint srcX0,
                       GLint srcY0,
                       GLint srcX1,
                       GLint srcY1,
                       GLint dstX0,
                       GLint dstY0,
                       GLint dstX1,
                       GLint dstY1,
                       GLbitfield mask,
                       GLenum filter);
```

Parameters

srcX0
srcY0
srcX1
srcY1
    Specify the bounds of the source rectangle within the read buffer of the read framebuffer.

dstX0
dstY0
dstX1
dstY1
    Specify the bounds of the destination rectangle within the write buffer of the write framebuffer.

mask
    The bitwise OR of the flags indicating which buffers are to be copied. The allowed flags are GL_COLOR_BUFFER_BIT, GL_DEPTH_BUFFER_BIT and GL_STENCIL_BUFFER_BIT.

filter
    Specifies the interpolation to be applied if the image is stretched. Must be GL_NEAREST or GL_LINEAR.

Description

glBlitFramebuffer transfers a rectangle of pixel values from one region of the read framebuffer to another region in the draw framebuffer. *mask* is the bitwise OR of a number of values indicating which buffers are to be copied. The values are GL_COLOR_BUFFER_BIT, GL_DEPTH_BUFFER_BIT, and

GL_STENCIL_BUFFER_BIT. The pixels corresponding to these buffers are copied from the source rectangle bounded by the locations (*srcX0*; *srcY0*) and (*srcX1*; *srcY1*) to the destination rectangle bounded by the locations (*dstX0*; *dstY0*) and (*dstX1*; *dstY1*). The lower bounds of the rectangle are inclusive, while the upper bounds are exclusive.

The actual region taken from the read framebuffer is limited to the intersection of the source buffers being transferred, which may include the color buffer selected by the read buffer, the depth buffer, and/or the stencil buffer depending on mask. The actual region written to the draw framebuffer is limited to the intersection of the destination buffers being written, which may include multiple draw buffers, the depth buffer, and/or the stencil buffer depending on mask. Whether or not the source or destination regions are altered due to these limits, the scaling and offset applied to pixels being transferred is performed as though no such limits were present.

If the sizes of the source and destination rectangles are not equal, *filter* specifies the interpolation method that will be applied to resize the source image, and must be GL_NEAREST or GL_LINEAR. GL_LINEAR is only a valid interpolation method for the color buffer. If *filter* is not GL_NEAREST and *mask* includes GL_DEPTH_BUFFER_BIT or GL_STENCIL_BUFFER_BIT, no data is transferred and a GL_INVALID_OPERATION error is generated.

If *filter* is GL_LINEAR and the source rectangle would require sampling outside the bounds of the source framebuffer, values are read as if the GL_CLAMP_TO_EDGE texture wrapping mode were applied.

When the color buffer is transferred, values are taken from the read buffer of the read framebuffer and written to each of the draw buffers of the draw framebuffer.

If the source and destination rectangles overlap or are the same, and the read and draw buffers are the same, the result of the operation is undefined.

Notes

glBindVertexArray is available only if the GL version is 3.0 or greater.

Errors

GL_INVALID_OPERATION is generated if *mask* contains any of the GL_DEPTH_BUFFER_BIT or GL_STENCIL_BUFFER_BIT and *filter* is not GL_NEAREST.

GL_INVALID_OPERATION is generated if *mask* contains GL_COLOR_BUFFER_BIT and any of the following conditions hold:

> The read buffer contains fixed-point or floating-point values and any draw buffer contains neither fixed-point nor floating-point values.
> The read buffer contains unsigned integer values and any draw buffer does not contain unsigned integer values.
> The read buffer contains signed integer values and any draw buffer does not contain signed integer values.

GL_INVALID_OPERATION is generated if *mask* contains GL_DEPTH_BUFFER_BIT or GL_DEPTH_BUFFER_BIT and the source and destination depth and stencil formats do not match.

GL_INVALID_OPERATION is generated if *filter* is GL_LINEAR and the read buffer contains integer data.

GL_INVALID_OPERATION is generated if the value of *GL_SAMPLES* for the read and draw buffers is not identical.

GL_INVALID_OPERATION is generated if *GL_SAMPLE_BUFFERS* for both read and draw buffers greater than zero and the dimensions of the source and destination rectangles is not identical.

GL_INVALID_FRAMEBUFFER_OPERATION is generated if the objects bound to GL_DRAW_FRAMEBUFFER_BINDING or GL_READ_FRAMEBUFFER_BINDING are not framebuffer complete.

See Also

glReadPixels glCheckFramebufferStatus, glGenFramebuffers glBindFramebuffer glDeleteFramebuffers

Copyright

glBufferData

creates and initializes a buffer object's data store

C Specification

```
void glBufferData(GLenum target,
                  GLsizeiptr size,
                  const GLvoid * data,
                  GLenum usage);
```

Parameters

target

Specifies the target buffer object. The symbolic constant must be GL_ARRAY_BUFFER, GL_COPY_READ_BUFFER, GL_COPY_WRITE_BUFFER, GL_ELEMENT_ARRAY_BUFFER, GL_PIXEL_PACK_BUFFER, GL_PIXEL_UNPACK_BUFFER, GL_TEXTURE_BUFFER, GL_TRANSFORM_FEEDBACK_BUFFER, or GL_UNIFORM_BUFFER.

size

Specifies the size in bytes of the buffer object's new data store.

data

Specifies a pointer to data that will be copied into the data store for initialization, or NULL if no data is to be copied.

usage

Specifies the expected usage pattern of the data store. The symbolic constant must be GL_STREAM_DRAW, GL_STREAM_READ, GL_STREAM_COPY, GL_STATIC_DRAW, GL_STATIC_READ, GL_STATIC_COPY, GL_DYNAMIC_DRAW, GL_DYNAMIC_READ, or GL_DYNAMIC_COPY.

Description

glBufferData creates a new data store for the buffer object currently bound to *target*. Any preexisting data store is deleted. The new data store is created with the specified *size* in bytes and *usage*. If *data* is not NULL, the data store is initialized with data from this pointer. In its initial state, the new data store is not mapped, it has a NULL mapped pointer, and its mapped access is GL_READ_WRITE.

usage is a hint to the GL implementation as to how a buffer object's data store will be accessed. This enables the GL implementation to make more intelligent decisions that may significantly impact buffer object performance. It does not, however, constrain the actual usage of the data store. *usage* can be broken down into two parts: first, the frequency of access (modification and usage), and second, the nature of that access. The frequency of access may be one of these:

STREAM

The data store contents will be modified once and used at most a few times.

STATIC

The data store contents will be modified once and used many times.

DYNAMIC

The data store contents will be modified repeatedly and used many times.

The nature of access may be one of these:

DRAW

The data store contents are modified by the application, and used as the source for GL drawing and image specification commands.

READ

The data store contents are modified by reading data from the GL, and used to return that data when queried by the application.

COPY

The data store contents are modified by reading data from the GL, and used as the source for GL drawing and image specification commands.

Notes

If *data* is NULL, a data store of the specified size is still created, but its contents remain uninitialized and thus undefined.

Clients must align data elements consistent with the requirements of the client platform, with an additional base-level requirement that an offset within a buffer to a datum comprising NN.

Errors

GL_INVALID_ENUM is generated if *target* is not one of the accepted buffer targets.

GL_INVALID_ENUM is generated if *usage* is not GL_STREAM_DRAW, GL_STREAM_READ, GL_STREAM_COPY, GL_STATIC_DRAW, GL_STATIC_READ, GL_STATIC_COPY, GL_DYNAMIC_DRAW, GL_DYNAMIC_READ, or GL_DYNAMIC_COPY.

GL_INVALID_VALUE is generated if *size* is negative.

GL_INVALID_OPERATION is generated if the reserved buffer object name 0 is bound to *target*.

GL_OUT_OF_MEMORY is generated if the GL is unable to create a data store with the specified *size*.

Associated Gets

glGetBufferSubData

glGetBufferParameter with argument GL_BUFFER_SIZE or GL_BUFFER_USAGE

See Also

glBindBuffer, glBufferSubData, glMapBuffer, glUnmapBuffer

Copyright

glBufferSubData

updates a subset of a buffer object's data store

C Specification

```
void glBufferSubData(GLenum target,
                     GLintptr offset,
                     GLsizeiptr size,
                     const GLvoid * data);
```

Parameters

target

Specifies the target buffer object. The symbolic constant must be GL_ARRAY_BUFFER, GL_COPY_READ_BUFFER, GL_COPY_WRITE_BUFFER, GL_ELEMENT_ARRAY_BUFFER, GL_PIXEL_PACK_BUFFER, GL_PIXEL_UNPACK_BUFFER, GL_TEXTURE_BUFFER, GL_TRANSFORM_FEEDBACK_BUFFER, or GL_UNIFORM_BUFFER.

offset

Specifies the offset into the buffer object's data store where data replacement will begin, measured in bytes.

size

Specifies the size in bytes of the data store region being replaced.

data

Specifies a pointer to the new data that will be copied into the data store.

Description

glBufferSubData redefines some or all of the data store for the buffer object currently bound to *target*. Data starting at byte offset *offset* and extending for *size* bytes is copied to the data store from the memory pointed to by *data*. An error is thrown if *offset* and *size* together define a range beyond the bounds of the buffer object's data store.

Notes

When replacing the entire data store, consider using glBufferSubData rather than completely recreating the data store with glBufferData. This avoids the cost of reallocating the data store.

Consider using multiple buffer objects to avoid stalling the rendering pipeline during data store updates. If any rendering in the pipeline makes reference to data in the buffer object being updated by glBufferSubData, especially from the specific region being updated, that rendering must drain from the pipeline before the data store can be updated.

Clients must align data elements consistent with the requirements of the client platform, with an additional base-level requirement that an offset within a buffer to a datum comprising NN.

Errors

GL_INVALID_ENUM is generated if *target* is not one of the accepted buffer targets.

GL_INVALID_VALUE is generated if *offset* or *size* is negative, or if together they define a region of memory that extends beyond the buffer object's allocated data store.

GL_INVALID_OPERATION is generated if the reserved buffer object name 0 is bound to *target*.

GL_INVALID_OPERATION is generated if the buffer object being updated is mapped.

Associated Gets

glGetBufferSubData

See Also

glBindBuffer, glBufferData, glMapBuffer, glUnmapBuffer

Copyright

glCheckFramebufferStatus

check the completeness status of a framebuffer

C Specification

```
GLenum glCheckFramebufferStatus(GLenum target);
```

Parameters

target

Specify the target of the framebuffer completeness check.

Description

glCheckFramebufferStatus queries the completeness status of the framebuffer object currently bound to *target*. *target* must be GL_DRAW_FRAMEBUFFER, GL_READ_FRAMEBUFFER or GL_FRAMEBUFFER. GL_FRAMEBUFFER is equivalent to GL_DRAW_FRAMEBUFFER.

The return value is GL_FRAMEBUFFER_COMPLETE if the framebuffer bound to *target* is complete. Otherwise, the return value is determined as follows:

GL_FRAMEBUFFER_UNDEFINED is returned if *target* is the default framebuffer, but the default framebuffer does not exist.

GL_FRAMEBUFFER_INCOMPLETE_ATTACHMENT is returned if any of the framebuffer attachment points are framebuffer incomplete.

GL_FRAMEBUFFER_INCOMPLETE_MISSING_ATTACHMENT is returned if the framebuffer does not have at least one image attached to it.

GL_FRAMEBUFFER_INCOMPLETE_DRAW_BUFFER is returned if the value of GL_FRAMEBUFFER_ATTACHMENT_OBJECT_TYPE is GL_NONE for any color attachment point(s) named by GL_DRAWBUFFERi.

GL_FRAMEBUFFER_INCOMPLETE_READ_BUFFER is returned if GL_READ_BUFFER is not GL_NONE and the value of GL_FRAMEBUFFER_ATTACHMENT_OBJECT_TYPE is GL_NONE for the color attachment point named by GL_READ_BUFFER.

GL_FRAMEBUFFER_UNSUPPORTED is returned if the combination of internal formats of the attached images violates an implementation-dependent set of restrictions.

GL_FRAMEBUFFER_INCOMPLETE_MULTISAMPLE is returned if the value of GL_RENDERBUFFER_SAMPLES is not the same for all attached renderbuffers; if the value of GL_TEXTURE_SAMPLES is the not same for all attached textures; or, if the attached images are a mix of renderbuffers and textures, the value of GL_RENDERBUFFER_SAMPLES does not match the value of GL_TEXTURE_SAMPLES. GL_FRAMEBUFFER_INCOMPLETE_MULTISAMPLE is also returned if the value of GL_TEXTURE_FIXED_SAMPLE_LOCATIONS is not the same for all attached textures; or, if the attached images are a mix of renderbuffers and textures, the value of GL_TEXTURE_FIXED_SAMPLE_LOCATIONS is not GL_TRUE for all attached textures.

GL_FRAMEBUFFER_INCOMPLETE_LAYER_TARGETS is returned if any framebuffer attachment is layered, and any populated attachment is not layered, or if all populated color attachments are not from textures of the same target.

Additionally, if an error occurs, zero is returned.

Errors

GL_INVALID_ENUM is generated if *target* is not GL_DRAW_FRAMEBUFFER, GL_READ_FRAMEBUFFER or GL_FRAMEBUFFER.

See Also

glGenFramebuffers, glDeleteFramebuffers glBindFramebuffer

Copyright

glClampColor

specify whether data read via glReadPixels should be clamped

C Specification

```
void glClampColor(GLenum target,
                  GLenum clamp);
```

Parameters

target

Target for color clamping. *target* must be GL_CLAMP_READ_COLOR.

clamp

Specifies whether to apply color clamping. *clamp* must be GL_TRUE or GL_FALSE.

Description

`glClampColor` controls color clamping that is performed during glReadPixels. *target* must be GL_CLAMP_READ_COLOR. If *clamp* is GL_TRUE, read color clamping is enabled; if *clamp* is GL_FALSE, read color clamping is disabled. If *clamp* is GL_FIXED_ONLY, read color clamping is enabled only if the selected read buffer has fixed point components and disabled otherwise.

Errors

GL_INVALID_ENUM is generated if *target* is not GL_CLAMP_READ_COLOR.
GL_INVALID_ENUM is generated if *clamp* is not GL_TRUE or GL_FALSE.

Associated Gets

glGet with argument GL_CLAMP_READ_COLOR.

Copyright

Copyright © 2010 Khronos Group. This material may be distributed subject to the terms and conditions set forth in the Open Publication License, v 1.0, 8 June 1999. http://opencontent.org/openpub/.

glClear

clear buffers to preset values

C Specification

```
void glClear(GLbitfield mask);
```

Parameters

mask

Bitwise OR of masks that indicate the buffers to be cleared. The three masks are GL_COLOR_BUFFER_BIT, GL_DEPTH_BUFFER_BIT, and GL_STENCIL_BUFFER_BIT.

Description

`glClear` sets the bitplane area of the window to values previously selected by `glClearColor`, `glClearDepth`, and `glClearStencil`. Multiple color buffers can be cleared simultaneously by selecting more than one buffer at a time using glDrawBuffer.

The pixel ownership test, the scissor test, dithering, and the buffer writemasks affect the operation of glClear. The scissor box bounds the cleared region. Alpha function, blend function, logical operation, stenciling, texture mapping, and depth-buffering are ignored by glClear.

glClear takes a single argument that is the bitwise OR of several values indicating which buffer is to be cleared.

The values are as follows:

GL_COLOR_BUFFER_BIT

   Indicates the buffers currently enabled for color writing.

GL_DEPTH_BUFFER_BIT

   Indicates the depth buffer.

GL_STENCIL_BUFFER_BIT

   Indicates the stencil buffer.

The value to which each buffer is cleared depends on the setting of the clear value for that buffer.

Notes

If a buffer is not present, then a glClear directed at that buffer has no effect.

Errors

GL_INVALID_VALUE is generated if any bit other than the three defined bits is set in *mask*.

Associated Gets

glGet with argument GL_DEPTH_CLEAR_VALUE

glGet with argument GL_COLOR_CLEAR_VALUE

glGet with argument GL_STENCIL_CLEAR_VALUE

See Also

glClearColor, glClearDepth, glClearStencil, glColorMask, glDepthMask, glDrawBuffer, glScissor, glStencilMask

Copyright

Copyright © 1991-2006 Silicon Graphics, Inc. This document is licensed under the SGI Free Software B License. For details, see http://oss.sgi.com/projects/FreeB/.

glClearBuffer

clear individual buffers of the currently bound draw framebuffer

C Specification

```
void glClearBufferiv(GLenum buffer,
                     GLint drawBuffer,
                     const GLint * value);
void glClearBufferuiv(GLenum buffer,
                      GLint drawBuffer,
                      const GLuint * value);
void glClearBufferfv(GLenum buffer,
                     GLint drawBuffer,
                     const GLfloat * value);
void glClearBufferfi(GLenum buffer,
                     GLint drawBuffer,
                     GLfloat depth,
                     GLint stencil);
```

Parameters

buffer

   Specify the buffer to clear.

drawBuffer

   Specify a particular draw buffer to clear.

value

   For color buffers, a pointer to a four-element vector specifying R, G, B and A values to clear the buffer to. For depth buffers, a pointer to a single depth value to clear the buffer to. For stencil buffers, a pointer to a single stencil value to clear the buffer to.

depth

   The value to clear a depth render buffer to.

stencil

   The value to clear a stencil render buffer to.

Description

`glClearBuffer*` clears the specified buffer to the specified value(s). If *buffer* is GL_COLOR, a particular draw buffer GL_DRAWBUFFER*i* is specified by passing *i* as *drawBuffer*. In this case, *value* points to a four-element vector specifying the R, G, B and A color to clear that draw buffer to. If *buffer* is one of GL_FRONT, GL_BACK, GL_LEFT, GL_RIGHT, or GL_FRONT_AND_BACK, identifying multiple buffers, each selected buffer is cleared to the same value. Clamping and conversion for fixed-point color buffers are performed in the same fashion as glClearColor.

If *buffer* is GL_DEPTH, *drawBuffer* must be zero, and *value* points to a single value to clear the depth buffer to. Only `glClearBufferfv` should be used to clear depth buffers. Clamping and conversion for fixed-point depth buffers are performed in the same fashion as glClearDepth.

If *buffer* is GL_STENCIL, *drawBuffer* must be zero, and *value* points to a single value to clear the stencil buffer to. Only `glClearBufferiv` should be used to clear stencil buffers. Masing and type conversion are performed in the same fashion as glClearStencil.

`glClearBufferfi` may be used to clear the depth and stencil buffers. *buffer* must be GL_DEPTH_STENCIL and *drawBuffer* must be zero. *depth* and *stencil* are the depth and stencil values, respectively.

The result of `glClearBuffer` is undefined if no conversion between the type of *value* and the buffer being cleared is defined. However, this is not an error.

Errors

GL_INVALID_ENUM is generated by `glClearBufferif`, `glClearBufferfv` and `glClearBufferuiv` if *buffer* is not GL_COLOR, GL_FRONT, GL_BACK, GL_LEFT, GL_RIGHT, GL_FRONT_AND_BACK, GL_DEPTH or GL_STENCIL.

GL_INVALID_ENUM is generated by `glClearBufferfi` if *buffer* is not GL_DEPTH_STENCIL.

GL_INVALID_VALUE is generated if *buffer* is GL_COLOR, GL_FRONT, GL_BACK, GL_LEFT, GL_RIGHT, or GL_FRONT_AND_BACK and *drawBuffer* is greater than or equal to GL_MAX_DRAW_BUFFERS.

GL_INVALID_VALUE is generated if *buffer* is GL_DEPTH, GL_STENCIL or GL_DEPTH_STENCIL and *drawBuffer* is not zero.

See Also

`glClearColor`, `glClearDepth`, `glClearStencil`, `glClear`

Copyright

glClearColor

specify clear values for the color buffers

C Specification

```
void glClearColor(GLclampf red,
                  GLclampf green,
                  GLclampf blue,
                  GLclampf alpha);
```

Parameters

red
green
blue
alpha

> Specify the red, green, blue, and alpha values used when the color buffers are cleared. The initial values are all 0.

Description

glClearColor specifies the red, green, blue, and alpha values used by glClear to clear the color buffers. Values specified by glClearColor are clamped to the range [0,1].

Associated Gets

glGet with argument GL_COLOR_CLEAR_VALUE

See Also

glClear

Copyright

Copyright © 1991-2006 Silicon Graphics, Inc. This document is licensed under the SGI Free Software B License. For details, see http://oss.sgi.com/projects/FreeB/.

glClearDepth

specify the clear value for the depth buffer

C Specification

```
void glClearDepth(GLclampd depth);
```

Parameters

depth

> Specifies the depth value used when the depth buffer is cleared. The initial value is 1.

Description

glClearDepth specifies the depth value used by glClear to clear the depth buffer. Values specified by glClearDepth are clamped to the range [0,1].

Associated Gets

glGet with argument GL_DEPTH_CLEAR_VALUE

See Also

glClear

Copyright

Copyright © 1991-2006 Silicon Graphics, Inc. This document is licensed under the SGI Free Software B License. For details, see http://oss.sgi.com/projects/FreeB/.

glClearStencil

specify the clear value for the stencil buffer

C Specification

void glClearStencil(GLint *s*);

Parameters

s

Specifies the index used when the stencil buffer is cleared. The initial value is 0.

Description

glClearStencil specifies the index used by glClear to clear the stencil buffer. *s* is masked with $2^m - 1$, where m is the number of bits in the stencil buffer.

Associated Gets

glGet with argument GL_STENCIL_CLEAR_VALUE
glGet with argument GL_STENCIL_BITS

See Also

glClear, glStencilFunc, glStencilFuncSeparate, glStencilMask, glStencilMaskSeparate, glStencilOp, glStencilOpSeparate

Copyright

Copyright © 1991-2006 Silicon Graphics, Inc. This document is licensed under the SGI Free Software B License. For details, see http://oss.sgi.com/projects/FreeB/.

glClientWaitSync

block and wait for a sync object to become signaled

C Specification

GLenum glClientWaitSync(GLsync *sync*,
                        GLbitfield *flags*,
                        GLuint64 *timeout*);

Parameters

sync

The sync object whose status to wait on.

flags

A bitfield controlling the command flushing behavior. *flags* may be GL_SYNC_FLUSH_COMMANDS_BIT.

timeout

The timeout, specified in nanoseconds, for which the implementation should wait for *sync* to become signaled.

Description

glClientWaitSync causes the client to block and wait for the sync object specified by *sync* to become signaled. If *sync* is signaled when glClientWaitSync is called, glClientWaitSync returns immediately, otherwise it will block and wait for up to *timeout* nanoseconds for *sync* to become signaled.

The return value is one of four status values:

GL_ALREADY_SIGNALED indicates that *sync* was signaled at the time that glClientWaitSync was called.

GL_TIMEOUT_EXPIRED indicates that at least *timeout* nanoseconds passed and *sync* did not become signaled.

GL_CONDITION_SATISFIED indicates that *sync* was signaled before the *timeout* expired.

GL_WAIT_FAILED indicates that an *error* occurred. Additionally, an OpenGL *error* will be generated.

Notes

glClientWaitSync is available only if the GL version is 3.2 or greater.

Errors

GL_INVALID_VALUE is generated if *sync* is not the name of an existing sync object.
GL_INVALID_VALUE is generated if *flags* contains any unsupported flag.

See Also

glFenceSync, glIsSync glWaitSync

Copyright

Copyright © 2010 Khronos Group. This material may be distributed subject to the terms and conditions set forth in the Open Publication License, v 1.0, 8 June 1999. http://opencontent.org/openpub/.

glColorMask

enable and disable writing of frame buffer color components

C Specification

```
void glColorMask(GLboolean red,
                 GLboolean green,
                 GLboolean blue,
                 GLboolean alpha);
```

Parameters

red
green
blue
alpha

Specify whether red, green, blue, and alpha can or cannot be written into the frame buffer. The initial values are all GL_TRUE, indicating that the color components can be written.

Description

glColorMask specifies whether the individual color components in the frame buffer can or cannot be written. If *red* is GL_FALSE, for example, no change is made to the red component of any pixel in any of the color buffers, regardless of the drawing operation attempted.

Changes to individual bits of components cannot be controlled. Rather, changes are either enabled or disabled for entire color components.

Associated Gets

glGet with argument GL_COLOR_WRITEMASK

See Also

glClear, glDepthMask, glStencilMask

Copyright

Copyright © 1991-2006 Silicon Graphics, Inc. This document is licensed under the SGI Free Software B License. For details, see http://oss.sgi.com/projects/FreeB/.

glCompileShader

Compiles a shader object

C Specification

void glCompileShader(GLuint *shader*);

Parameters

shader
        Specifies the shader object to be compiled.

Description

glCompileShader compiles the source code strings that have been stored in the shader object specified by *shader*.

The compilation status will be stored as part of the shader object's state. This value will be set to GL_TRUE if the shader was compiled without errors and is ready for use, and GL_FALSE otherwise. It can be queried by calling glGetShader with arguments *shader* and GL_COMPILE_STATUS.

Compilation of a shader can fail for a number of reasons as specified by the OpenGL Shading Language Specification. Whether or not the compilation was successful, information about the compilation can be obtained from the shader object's information log by calling glGetShaderInfoLog.

Errors

GL_INVALID_VALUE is generated if *shader* is not a value generated by OpenGL.
GL_INVALID_OPERATION is generated if *shader* is not a shader object.

Associated Gets

glGetShaderInfoLog with argument *shader*
glGetShader with arguments *shader* and GL_COMPILE_STATUS
glIsShader

See Also

`glCreateShader, glLinkProgram, glShaderSource`

Copyright

Copyright © 2003-2005 3Dlabs Inc. Ltd. This material may be distributed subject to the terms and conditions set forth in the Open Publication License, v 1.0, 8 June 1999. http://opencontent.org/openpub/.

glCompressedTexImage1D

specify a one-dimensional texture image in a compressed format

C Specification

```
void glCompressedTexImage1D(GLenum target,
                            GLint level,
                            GLenum internalformat,
                            GLsizei width,
                            GLint border,
                            GLsizei imageSize,
                            const GLvoid * data);
```

Parameters

target

Specifies the target texture. Must be GL_TEXTURE_1D or GL_PROXY_TEXTURE_1D.

level

Specifies the level-of-detail number. Level 0 is the base image level. Level *n* is the *n*th mipmap reduction image.

internalformat

Specifies the format of the compressed image data stored at address *data*.

width

Specifies the width of the texture image. All implementations support texture images that are at least 64 texels wide. The height of the 1D texture image is 1.

border

This value must be 0.

imageSize

Specifies the number of unsigned bytes of image data starting at the address specified by *data*.

data

Specifies a pointer to the compressed image data in memory.

Description

Texturing allows elements of an image array to be read by shaders.

`glCompressedTexImage1D` loads a previously defined, and retrieved, compressed one-dimensional texture image if *target* is GL_TEXTURE_1D (see glTexImage1D).

If *target* is GL_PROXY_TEXTURE_1D, no data is read from *data*, but all of the texture image state is recalculated, checked for consistency, and checked against the implementation's capabilities. If the implementation cannot handle a texture of the requested texture size, it sets all of the image state to 0, but does not generate an error (see glGetError). To query for an entire mipmap array, use an image array level greater than or equal to 1.

internalformat must be an extension-specified compressed-texture format. When a texture is loaded with glTexImage1D using a generic compressed texture format (e.g., GL_COMPRESSED_RGB) the GL selects from one of its extensions supporting compressed textures. In order to load the compressed texture image using `glCompressedTexImage1D`, query the compressed texture image's size and format using glGetTexLevelParameter.

If a non-zero named buffer object is bound to the GL_PIXEL_UNPACK_BUFFER target (see glBindBuffer) while a texture image is specified, *data* is treated as a byte offset into the buffer object's data store.

Errors

GL_INVALID_ENUM is generated if *internalformat* is not a supported specific compressed internal formats, or is one of the generic compressed internal formats: GL_COMPRESSED_RED, GL_COMPRESSED_RG, GL_COMPRESSED_RGB, GL_COMPRESSED_RGBA. GL_COMPRESSED_SRGB, or GL_COMPRESSED_SRGB_ALPHA.

GL_INVALID_VALUE is generated if *imageSize* is not consistent with the format, dimensions, and contents of the specified compressed image data.

GL_INVALID_VALUE is generated if *border* is not 0.

GL_INVALID_OPERATION is generated if parameter combinations are not supported by the specific compressed internal format as specified in the specific texture compression extension.

GL_INVALID_OPERATION is generated if a non-zero buffer object name is bound to the GL_PIXEL_UNPACK_BUFFER target and the buffer object's data store is currently mapped.

GL_INVALID_OPERATION is generated if a non-zero buffer object name is bound to the GL_PIXEL_UNPACK_BUFFER target and the data would be unpacked from the buffer object such that the memory reads required would exceed the data store size.

Undefined results, including abnormal program termination, are generated if *data* is not encoded in a manner consistent with the extension specification defining the internal compression format.

Associated Gets

glGetCompressedTexImage
glGet with argument GL_TEXTURE_COMPRESSED
glGet with argument GL_NUM_COMPRESSED_TEXTURE_FORMATS
glGet with argument GL_COMPRESSED_TEXTURE_FORMATS
glGet with argument GL_PIXEL_UNPACK_BUFFER_BINDING
glGetTexLevelParameter with arguments GL_TEXTURE_INTERNAL_FORMAT and GL_TEXTURE_COMPRESSED_IMAGE_SIZE

See Also

glActiveTexture, glCompressedTexImage2D, glCompressedTexImage3D, glCompressedTexSubImage1D, glCompressedTexSubImage2D, glCompressedTexSubImage3D, glCopyTexImage1D, glCopyTexImage2D, glCopyTexSubImage1D, glCopyTexSubImage2D, glCopyTexSubImage3D, glPixelStore, glTexImage2D, glTexImage3D, glTexSubImage1D, glTexSubImage2D, glTexSubImage3D, glTexParameter

Copyright

Copyright © 1991-2006 Silicon Graphics, Inc. This document is licensed under the SGI Free Software B License. For details, see http://oss.sgi.com/projects/FreeB/.

glCompressedTexImage2D

specify a two-dimensional texture image in a compressed format

C Specification

```
void glCompressedTexImage2D(GLenum   target,
                            GLint    level,
                            GLenum   internalformat,
                            GLsizei  width,
                            GLsizei  height,
                            GLint    border
                            GLsizei  imageSize,
                            const GLvoid * data);
```

Parameters

target

Specifies the target texture. Must be GL_TEXTURE_2D, GL_PROXY_TEXTURE_2D, GL_TEXTURE_1D_ARRAY, GL_PROXY_TEXTURE_1D_ARRAY, GL_TEXTURE_CUBE_MAP_POSITIVE_X, GL_TEXTURE_CUBE_MAP_NEGATIVE_X, GL_TEXTURE_CUBE_MAP_POSITIVE_Y, GL_TEXTURE_CUBE_MAP_NEGATIVE_Y, GL_TEXTURE_CUBE_MAP_POSITIVE_Z, GL_TEXTURE_CUBE_MAP_NEGATIVE_Z, or GL_PROXY_TEXTURE_CUBE_MAP.

level

Specifies the level-of-detail number. Level 0 is the base image level. Level n is the nth mipmap reduction image.

internalformat

Specifies the format of the compressed image data stored at address *data*.

width

Specifies the width of the texture image. All implementations support 2D texture images that are at least 64 texels wide and cube-mapped texture images that are at least 16 texels wide.

height

Specifies the height of the texture image. All implementations support 2D texture images that are at least 64 texels high and cube-mapped texture images that are at least 16 texels high.

border

This value must be 0.

imageSize

Specifies the number of unsigned bytes of image data starting at the address specified by *data*.

data

Specifies a pointer to the compressed image data in memory.

Description

Texturing allows elements of an image array to be read by shaders.

glCompressedTexImage2D loads a previously defined, and retrieved, compressed two-dimensional texture image if *target* is GL_TEXTURE_2D, or one of the cube map faces such as GL_TEXTURE_CUBE_MAP_POSITIVE_X. (see glTexImage2D).

If *target* is GL_TEXTURE_1D_ARRAY, *data* is treated as an array of compressed 1D textures.

If *target* is GL_PROXY_TEXTURE_2D, GL_PROXY_TEXTURE_1D_ARRAY or GL_PROXY_CUBE_MAP, no data is read from *data*, but all of the texture image state is recalculated, checked for consistency, and checked against the implementation's capabilities. If the implementation cannot handle a texture of the requested texture size, it sets all of the image state to 0, but does not generate an error (see glGetError). To query for an entire mipmap array, use an image array level greater than or equal to 1.

internalformat must be a known compressed image format (such as GL_RGTC) or an extension-specified compressed-texture format. When a texture is loaded with glTexImage2D using a generic compressed texture format (e.g., GL_COMPRESSED_RGB), the GL selects from one of its extensions supporting compressed textures. In order to load the compressed texture image using glCompressedTexImage2D, query the compressed texture image's size and format using glGetTexLevelParameter.

If a non-zero named buffer object is bound to the GL_PIXEL_UNPACK_BUFFER target (see glBindBuffer) while a texture image is specified, *data* is treated as a byte offset into the buffer object's data store.

Errors

GL_INVALID_ENUM is generated if *internalformat* is not one of the generic compressed internal formats: GL_COMPRESSED_RED, GL_COMPRESSED_RG, GL_COMPRESSED_RGB, GL_COMPRESSED_RGBA, GL_COMPRESSED_SRGB, or GL_COMPRESSED_SRGB_ALPHA.

GL_INVALID_VALUE is generated if *imageSize* is not consistent with the format, dimensions, and contents of the specified compressed image data.

GL_INVALID_VALUE is generated if *border* is not 0.

GL_INVALID_OPERATION is generated if parameter combinations are not supported by the specific compressed internal format as specified in the specific texture compression extension.

GL_INVALID_OPERATION is generated if a non-zero buffer object name is bound to the GL_PIXEL_UNPACK_BUFFER target and the buffer object's data store is currently mapped.

GL_INVALID_OPERATION is generated if a non-zero buffer object name is bound to the GL_PIXEL_UNPACK_BUFFER target and the data would be unpacked from the buffer object such that the memory reads required would exceed the data store size.

Undefined results, including abnormal program termination, are generated if *data* is not encoded in a manner consistent with the extension specification defining the internal compression format.

Associated Gets

glGetCompressedTexImage
glGet with argument GL_TEXTURE_COMPRESSED
glGet with argument GL_PIXEL_UNPACK_BUFFER_BINDING
glGetTexLevelParameter with arguments GL_TEXTURE_INTERNAL_FORMAT and GL_TEXTURE_COMPRESSED_IMAGE_SIZE

See Also

glActiveTexture, glCompressedTexImage1D, glCompressedTexImage3D, glCompressedTexSubImage1D, glCompressedTexSubImage2D, glCompressedTexSubImage3D, glCopyTexImage1D, glCopyTexSubImage1D, glCopyTexSubImage2D, glCopyTexSubImage3D, glPixelStore, glTexImage2D, glTexImage3D, glTexSubImage1D, glTexSubImage2D, glTexSubImage3D, glTexParameter

Copyright

glCompressedTexImage3D

specify a three-dimensional texture image in a compressed format

C Specification

```
void glCompressedTexImage3D(GLenum target,
                            GLint level,
                            GLenum internalformat,
                            GLsizei width,
                            GLsizei height,
                            GLsizei depth,
                            GLint border,
                            GLsizei imageSize,
                            const GLvoid * data);
```

Parameters

target

Specifies the target texture. Must be GL_TEXTURE_3D, GL_PROXY_TEXTURE_3D, GL_TEXTURE_2D_ARRAY or GL_PROXY_TEXTURE_2D_ARRAY.

level

Specifies the level-of-detail number. Level 0 is the base image level. Level *n* is the *n*th mipmap reduction image.

internalformat

Specifies the format of the compressed image data stored at address *data*.

width

Specifies the width of the texture image. All implementations support 3D texture images that are at least 16 texels wide.

height

Specifies the height of the texture image. All implementations support 3D texture images that are at least 16 texels high.

depth

Specifies the depth of the texture image. All implementations support 3D texture images that are at least 16 texels deep.

border

This value must be 0.

imageSize

Specifies the number of unsigned bytes of image data starting at the address specified by *data*.

data

Specifies a pointer to the compressed image data in memory.

Description

Texturing allows elements of an image array to be read by shaders.

glCompressedTexImage3D loads a previously defined, and retrieved, compressed three-dimensional texture image if *target* is GL_TEXTURE_3D (see glTexImage3D).

If *target* is GL_TEXTURE_2D_ARRAY, *data* is treated as an array of compressed 2D textures.

If *target* is GL_PROXY_TEXTURE_3D or GL_PROXY_TEXTURE_2D_ARRAY, no data is read from *data*, but all of the texture image state is recalculated, checked for consistency, and checked against the implementation's capabilities. If the implementation cannot handle a texture of the requested texture size, it sets all of the image state to 0, but does not generate an error (see glGetError). To query for an entire mipmap array, use an image array level greater than or equal to 1.

internalformat must be a known compressed image format (such as GL_RGTC) or an extension-specified compressed-texture format. When a texture is loaded with glTexImage2D using a generic compressed texture format (e.g., GL_COMPRESSED_RGB), the GL selects from one of its extensions supporting compressed textures. In order to load the compressed texture image using glCompressedTexImage3D, query the compressed texture image's size and format using glGetTexLevelParameter.

If a non-zero named buffer object is bound to the GL_PIXEL_UNPACK_BUFFER target (see glBindBuffer) while a texture image is specified, *data* is treated as a byte offset into the buffer object's data store.

Errors

GL_INVALID_ENUM is generated if *internalformat* is not one of the generic compressed internal formats: GL_COMPRESSED_RED, GL_COMPRESSED_RG, GL_COMPRESSED_RGB, GL_COMPRESSED_RGBA, GL_COMPRESSED_SRGB, or GL_COMPRESSED_SRGB_ALPHA.

GL_INVALID_VALUE is generated if *imageSize* is not consistent with the format, dimensions, and contents of the specified compressed image data.

GL_INVALID_VALUE is generated if *border* is not 0.

GL_INVALID_OPERATION is generated if parameter combinations are not supported by the specific compressed internal format as specified in the specific texture compression extension.

GL_INVALID_OPERATION is generated if a non-zero buffer object name is bound to the GL_PIXEL_UNPACK_BUFFER target and the buffer object's data store is currently mapped.

GL_INVALID_OPERATION is generated if a non-zero buffer object name is bound to the GL_PIXEL_UNPACK_BUFFER target and the data would be unpacked from the buffer object such that the memory reads required would exceed the data store size.

Undefined results, including abnormal program termination, are generated if *data* is not encoded in a manner consistent with the extension specification defining the internal compression format.

Associated Gets

glGetCompressedTexImage
glGet with argument GL_TEXTURE_COMPRESSED
glGet with argument GL_PIXEL_UNPACK_BUFFER_BINDING
glGetTexLevelParameter with arguments GL_TEXTURE_INTERNAL_FORMAT and GL_TEXTURE_COMPRESSED_IMAGE_SIZE

See Also

glActiveTexture, glCompressedTexImage1D, glCompressedTexImage2D, glCompressedTexSubImage1D, glCompressedTexSubImage2D, glCompressedTexSubImage3D, glCopyTexImage1D, glCopyTexSubImage1D, glCopyTexSubImage2D, glCopyTexSubImage3D, glPixelStore, glTexImage1D, glTexImage2D, glTexSubImage1D, glTexSubImage2D, glTexSubImage3D, glTexParameter

Copyright

glCompressedTexSubImage1D

specify a one-dimensional texture subimage in a compressed format

C Specification

```
void glCompressedTexSubImage1D(GLenum target,
                               GLint level,
                               GLint xoffset,
                               GLsizei width,
                               GLenum format,
                               GLsizei imageSize,
                               const GLvoid * data);
```

Parameters

target
> Specifies the target texture. Must be GL_TEXTURE_1D.

level
> Specifies the level-of-detail number. Level 0 is the base image level. Level *n* is the *n*th mipmap reduction image.

xoffset
> Specifies a texel offset in the x direction within the texture array.

width
> Specifies the width of the texture subimage.

format
> Specifies the format of the compressed image data stored at address *data*.

imageSize
> Specifies the number of unsigned bytes of image data starting at the address specified by *data*.

data
> Specifies a pointer to the compressed image data in memory.

Description

Texturing allows elements of an image array to be read by shaders.

glCompressedTexSubImage1D redefines a contiguous subregion of an existing one-dimensional texture image. The texels referenced by *data* replace the portion of the existing texture array with x indices *xoffset* and xoffset + width − 1, inclusive. This region may not include any texels outside the range of the texture array as it was originally specified. It is not an error to specify a subtexture with width of 0, but such a specification has no effect.

internalformat must be a known compressed image format (such as GL_RGTC) or an extension-specified compressed-texture format. The *format* of the compressed texture image is selected by the GL implementation that compressed it (see glTexImage1D), and should be queried at the time the texture was compressed with glGetTexLevelParameter.

If a non-zero named buffer object is bound to the GL_PIXEL_UNPACK_BUFFER target (see glBindBuffer) while a texture image is specified, *data* is treated as a byte offset into the buffer object's data store.

Errors

GL_INVALID_ENUM is generated if *internalformat* is not one of the generic compressed internal formats: GL_COMPRESSED_RED, GL_COMPRESSED_RG, GL_COMPRESSED_RGB, GL_COMPRESSED_RGBA. GL_COMPRESSED_SRGB, or GL_COMPRESSED_SRGB_ALPHA.

GL_INVALID_VALUE is generated if *imageSize* is not consistent with the format, dimensions, and contents of the specified compressed image data.

GL_INVALID_OPERATION is generated if parameter combinations are not supported by the specific compressed internal format as specified in the specific texture compression extension.

GL_INVALID_OPERATION is generated if a non-zero buffer object name is bound to the GL_PIXEL_UNPACK_BUFFER target and the buffer object's data store is currently mapped.

GL_INVALID_OPERATION is generated if a non-zero buffer object name is bound to the GL_PIXEL_UNPACK_BUFFER target and the data would be unpacked from the buffer object such that the memory reads required would exceed the data store size.

Undefined results, including abnormal program termination, are generated if *data* is not encoded in a manner consistent with the extension specification defining the internal compression format.

Associated Gets

glGetCompressedTexImage
glGet with argument GL_TEXTURE_COMPRESSED
glGet with argument GL_PIXEL_UNPACK_BUFFER_BINDING
glGetTexLevelParameter with arguments GL_TEXTURE_INTERNAL_FORMAT and
GL_TEXTURE_COMPRESSED_IMAGE_SIZE

See Also

glActiveTexture, glCompressedTexImage1D, glCompressedTexImage2D,
glCompressedTexImage3D, glCompressedTexSubImage2D, glCompressedTexSubImage3D,
glCopyTexImage1D, glCopyTexImage2D, glCopyTexSubImage1D, glCopyTexSubImage2D,
glCopyTexSubImage3D, glPixelStore, glTexImage2D, glTexImage3D, glTexSubImage1D,
glTexSubImage2D, glTexSubImage3D, glTexParameter

Copyright

glCompressedTexSubImage2D

specify a two-dimensional texture subimage in a compressed format

C Specification

```
void glCompressedTexSubImage2D(GLenum target,
                               GLint level,
                               GLint xoffset,
                               GLint yoffset,
                               GLsizei width,
                               GLsizei height,
                               GLenum format,
                               GLsizei imageSize,
                               const GLvoid * data);
```

Parameters

target

Specifies the target texture. Must be GL_TEXTURE_2D, GL_TEXTURE_CUBE_MAP_POSITIVE_X, GL_TEXTURE_CUBE_MAP_NEGATIVE_X, GL_TEXTURE_CUBE_MAP_POSITIVE_Y, GL_TEXTURE_CUBE_MAP_NEGATIVE_Y, GL_TEXTURE_CUBE_MAP_POSITIVE_Z, or GL_TEXTURE_CUBE_MAP_NEGATIVE_Z.

level

Specifies the level-of-detail number. Level 0 is the base image level. Level *n* is the *n*th mipmap reduction image.

xoffset
    Specifies a texel offset in the x direction within the texture array.
yoffset
    Specifies a texel offset in the y direction within the texture array.
width
    Specifies the width of the texture subimage.
height
    Specifies the height of the texture subimage.
format
    Specifies the format of the compressed image data stored at address *data*.
imageSize
    Specifies the number of unsigned bytes of image data starting at the address specified
    by *data*.
data
    Specifies a pointer to the compressed image data in memory.

Description

Texturing allows elements of an image array to be read by shaders.

glCompressedTexSubImage2D redefines a contiguous subregion of an existing two-dimensional
texture image. The texels referenced by *data* replace the portion of the existing texture array with x
indices *xoffset* and xoffset + width − 1, and the y indices *yoffset* and yoffset + height − 1, inclusive. This region may not include any texels outside the range of the texture array as it was originally
specified. It is not an error to specify a subtexture with width of 0, but such a specification has no
effect.

internalformat must be a known compressed image format (such as GL_RGTC) or an extension-specified compressed-texture format. The *format* of the compressed texture image is selected by
the GL implementation that compressed it (see glTexImage2D) and should be queried at the time the
texture was compressed with glGetTexLevelParameter.

If a non-zero named buffer object is bound to the GL_PIXEL_UNPACK_BUFFER target (see
glBindBuffer) while a texture image is specified, *data* is treated as a byte offset into the buffer object's
data store.

Errors

GL_INVALID_ENUM is generated if *internalformat* is of the generic compressed internal
formats: GL_COMPRESSED_RED, GL_COMPRESSED_RG, GL_COMPRESSED_RGB,
GL_COMPRESSED_RGBA, GL_COMPRESSED_SRGB, or GL_COMPRESSED_SRGB_ALPHA.

GL_INVALID_VALUE is generated if *imageSize* is not consistent with the format, dimensions,
and contents of the specified compressed image data.

GL_INVALID_OPERATION is generated if parameter combinations are not supported by the
specific compressed internal format as specified in the specific texture compression extension.

GL_INVALID_OPERATION is generated if a non-zero buffer object name is bound to the
GL_PIXEL_UNPACK_BUFFER target and the buffer object's data store is currently mapped.

GL_INVALID_OPERATION is generated if a non-zero buffer object name is bound to the
GL_PIXEL_UNPACK_BUFFER target and the data would be unpacked from the buffer object such that
the memory reads required would exceed the data store size.

Undefined results, including abnormal program termination, are generated if *data* is not encoded
in a manner consistent with the extension specification defining the internal compression format.

Associated Gets

glGetCompressedTexImage
glGet with argument GL_TEXTURE_COMPRESSED
glGet with argument GL_PIXEL_UNPACK_BUFFER_BINDING
glGetTexLevelParameter with arguments GL_TEXTURE_INTERNAL_FORMAT and
GL_TEXTURE_COMPRESSED_IMAGE_SIZE

See Also

glActiveTexture, glCompressedTexImage1D, glCompressedTexImage2D, glCompressedTexImage3D, glCompressedTexSubImage1D, glCompressedTexSubImage3D, glCopyTexImage1D, glCopyTexImage2D, glCopyTexSubImage1D, glCopyTexSubImage2D, glCopyTexSubImage3D, glPixelStore, glTexImage2D, glTexImage3D, glTexSubImage1D, glTexSubImage2D, glTexSubImage3D, glTexParameter

Copyright

glCompressedTexSubImage3D

specify a three-dimensional texture subimage in a compressed format

C Specification

```
void glCompressedTexSubImage3D(GLenum target,
                               GLint level,
                               GLint xoffset,
                               GLint yoffset,
                               GLint zoffset,
                               GLsizei width,
                               GLsizei height,
                               GLsizei depth,
                               GLenum format,
                               GLsizei imageSize,
                               const GLvoid * data);
```

Parameters

target
> Specifies the target texture. Must be GL_TEXTURE_3D.

level
> Specifies the level-of-detail number. Level 0 is the base image level. Level *n* is the *n*th mipmap reduction image.

xoffset
> Specifies a texel offset in the x direction within the texture array.

yoffset
> Specifies a texel offset in the y direction within the texture array.

width
> Specifies the width of the texture subimage.

height
> Specifies the height of the texture subimage.

depth
> Specifies the depth of the texture subimage.

format
> Specifies the format of the compressed image data stored at address *data*.

imageSize
> Specifies the number of unsigned bytes of image data starting at the address specified by *data*.

data
> Specifies a pointer to the compressed image data in memory.

Description

Texturing allows elements of an image array to be read by shaders.

`glCompressedTexSubImage3D` redefines a contiguous subregion of an existing three-dimensional texture image. The texels referenced by *data* replace the portion of the existing texture array with x indices *xoffset* and xoffset + weight – 1, and the y indices *yoffset* and yoffset + height – 1, and the z indices *zoffset* and zoffset + depth – 1, inclusive. This region may not include any texels outside the range of the texture array as it was originally specified. It is not an error to specify a subtexture with width of 0, but such a specification has no effect.

internalformat must be a known compressed image format (such as GL_RGTC) or an extension-specified compressed-texture format. The *format* of the compressed texture image is selected by the GL implementation that compressed it (see glTexImage3D) and should be queried at the time the texture was compressed with glGetTexLevelParameter.

If a non-zero named buffer object is bound to the GL_PIXEL_UNPACK_BUFFER target (see glBindBuffer) while a texture image is specified, *data* is treated as a byte offset into the buffer object's data store.

Errors

GL_INVALID_ENUM is generated if *internalformat* is one of the generic compressed internal formats: GL_COMPRESSED_RED, GL_COMPRESSED_RG, GL_COMPRESSED_RGB, GL_COMPRESSED_RGBA, GL_COMPRESSED_SRGB, or GL_COMPRESSED_SRGB_ALPHA.

GL_INVALID_VALUE is generated if *imageSize* is not consistent with the format, dimensions, and contents of the specified compressed image data.

GL_INVALID_OPERATION is generated if parameter combinations are not supported by the specific compressed internal format as specified in the specific texture compression extension.

GL_INVALID_OPERATION is generated if a non-zero buffer object name is bound to the GL_PIXEL_UNPACK_BUFFER target and the buffer object's data store is currently mapped.

GL_INVALID_OPERATION is generated if a non-zero buffer object name is bound to the GL_PIXEL_UNPACK_BUFFER target and the data would be unpacked from the buffer object such that the memory reads required would exceed the data store size.

Undefined results, including abnormal program termination, are generated if *data* is not encoded in a manner consistent with the extension specification defining the internal compression format.

Associated Gets

glGetCompressedTexImage

glGet with argument GL_TEXTURE_COMPRESSED

glGet with argument GL_PIXEL_UNPACK_BUFFER_BINDING

glGetTexLevelParameter with arguments GL_TEXTURE_INTERNAL_FORMAT and GL_TEXTURE_COMPRESSED_IMAGE_SIZE

See Also

glActiveTexture, glCompressedTexImage1D, glCompressedTexImage2D, glCompressedTexImage3D, glCompressedTexSubImage1D, glCompressedTexSubImage2D, glCopyTexImage1D, glCopyTexImage2D, glCopyTexSubImage1D, glCopyTexSubImage2D, glCopyTexSubImage3D, glPixelStore, glTexImage2D, glTexImage3D, glTexSubImage1D, glTexSubImage2D, glTexSubImage3D, glTexParameter

Copyright

glCopyBufferSubData

copy part of the data store of a buffer object to the data store of another buffer object

C Specification

```
void glCopyBufferSubData(GLenum readtarget,
                         GLenum writetarget,
                         GLintptr readoffset,
                         GLintptr writeoffset,
                         GLsizeiptr size);
```

Parameters

readtarget
> Specifies the target from whose data store data should be read.

writetarget
> Specifies the target to whose data store data should be written.

readoffset
> Specifies the offset, in basic machine units, within the data store of *readtarget* from which data should be read.

writeoffset
> Specifies the offset, in basic machine units, within the data store of *writetarget* to which data should be written.

size
> Specifies the size, in basic machine units, of the data to be copied from *readtarget* to *writetarget*.

Description

glCopyBufferSubData copies part of the data store attached to *readtarget* to the data store attached to *writetarget*. The number of basic machine units indicated by *size* is copied from the source, at offset *readoffset* to the destination at *writeoffset*, also in basic machine units.

readtarget and *writetarget* must be GL_ARRAY_BUFFER, GL_COPY_READ_BUFFER, GL_COPY_WRITE_BUFFER, GL_ELEMENT_ARRAY_BUFFER, GL_PIXEL_PACK_BUFFER, GL_PIXEL_UNPACK_BUFFER, GL_TEXTURE_BUFFER, GL_TRANSFORM_FEEDBACK_BUFFER or GL_UNIFORM_BUFFER. Any of these targets may be used, although the targets GL_COPY_READ_BUFFER and GL_COPY_WRITE_BUFFER are provided specifically to allow copies between buffers without disturbing other GL state.

readoffset, *writeoffset* and *size* must all be greater than or equal to zero. Furthermore, *readoffset* + *size* must not exceeed the size of the buffer object bound to *readtarget*, and *readoffset* + *size* must not exceeed the size of the buffer bound to *writetarget*. If the same buffer object is bound to both *readtarget* and *writetarget*, then the ranges specified by *readoffset*, *writeoffset* and *size* must not overlap.

Notes

glCopyBufferSubData is available only if the GL version is 3.1 or greater.

Errors

GL_INVALID_VALUE is generated if any of *readoffset*, *writeoffset* or *size* is negative, if *readoffset* + *size* exceeds the size of the buffer object bound to *readtarget* or if *writeoffset* + *size* exceeds the size of the buffer object bound to *writetarget*.

GL_INVALID_VALUE is generated if the same buffer object is bound to both *readtarget* and *writetarget* and the ranges [*readoffset*, *readoffset* + *size*) and [*writeoffset*, *writeoffset* + *size*) overlap.

GL_INVALID_OPERATION is generated if zero is bound to *readtarget* or *writetarget*.
GL_INVALID_OPERATION is generated if the buffer object bound to either *readtarget* or *writetarget* is mapped.

See Also

glGenBuffers, glBindBuffer, glBufferData, glBufferSubData, glGetBufferSubData

Copyright

Copyright © 2010 Khronos Group. This material may be distributed subject to the terms and conditions set forth in the Open Publication License, v 1.0, 8 June 1999. http://opencontent.org/openpub/.

glCopyTexImage1D

copy pixels into a 1D texture image

C Specification

```
void glCopyTexImage1D(GLenum target,
                      GLint level,
                      GLenum internalformat,
                      GLint x,
                      GLint y,
                      GLsizei width,
                      GLint border);
```

Parameters

target
> Specifies the target texture. Must be GL_TEXTURE_1D.

level
> Specifies the level-of-detail number. Level 0 is the base image level. Level n is the nth mipmap reduction image.

internalformat
> Specifies the internal format of the texture. Must be one of the following symbolic constants: GL_COMPRESSED_RED, GL_COMPRESSED_RG, GL_COMPRESSED_RGB, GL_COMPRESSED_RGBA. GL_COMPRESSED_SRGB, GL_COMPRESSED_SRGB_ALPHA. GL_DEPTH_COMPONENT, GL_DEPTH_COMPONENT16, GL_DEPTH_COMPONENT24, GL_DEPTH_COMPONENT32, GL_RED, GL_RG, GL_RGB, GL_R3_G3_B2, GL_RGB4, GL_RGB5, GL_RGB8, GL_RGB10, GL_RGB12, GL_RGB16, GL_RGBA, GL_RGBA2, GL_RGBA4, GL_RGB5_A1, GL_RGBA8, GL_RGB10_A2, GL_RGBA12, GL_RGBA16, GL_SRGB, GL_SRGB8, GL_SRGB_ALPHA, or GL_SRGB8_ALPHA8.

x
y
> Specify the window coordinates of the left corner of the row of pixels to be copied.

width
> Specifies the width of the texture image. Must be 0 or $2^n + 2$ (border) for some integer n. The height of the texture image is 1.

border
> Specifies the width of the border. Must be either 0 or 1.

Description

glCopyTexImage1D defines a one-dimensional texture image with pixels from the current GL_READ_BUFFER.

The screen-aligned pixel row with left corner at (x, y) and with a length of $width + 2(border)$ defines the texture array at the mipmap level specified by *level*. *internalformat* specifies the internal format of the texture array.

The pixels in the row are processed exactly as if glReadPixels had been called, but the process stops just before final conversion. At this point all pixel component values are clamped to the range $[0, 1]$ and then converted to the texture's internal format for storage in the texel array.

Pixel ordering is such that lower x screen coordinates correspond to lower texture coordinates.

If any of the pixels within the specified row of the current GL_READ_BUFFER are outside the window associated with the current rendering context, then the values obtained for those pixels are undefined.

glCopyTexImage1D defines a one-dimensional texture image with pixels from the current GL_READ_BUFFER.

When *internalformat* is one of the sRGB types, the GL does not automatically convert the source pixels to the sRGB color space. In this case, the glPixelMap function can be used to accomplish the conversion.

Notes

1, 2, 3, and 4 are not accepted values for *internalformat*.

An image with 0 width indicates a NULL texture.

Errors

GL_INVALID_ENUM is generated if *target* is not one of the allowable values.

GL_INVALID_VALUE is generated if *level* is less than 0.

GL_INVALID_VALUE may be generated if *level* is greater than $\log_2 max$, where max is the returned value of GL_MAX_TEXTURE_SIZE.

GL_INVALID_VALUE is generated if *internalformat* is not an allowable value.

GL_INVALID_VALUE is generated if *width* is less than 0 or greater than 2 + GL_MAX_TEXTURE_SIZE.

GL_INVALID_VALUE is generated if non-power-of-two textures are not supported and the *width* cannot be represented as $2^n + 2(border)$ for some integer value of *n*.

GL_INVALID_VALUE is generated if *border* is not 0 or 1.

GL_INVALID_OPERATION is generated if *internalformat* is GL_DEPTH_COMPONENT, GL_DEPTH_COMPONENT16, GL_DEPTH_COMPONENT24, or GL_DEPTH_COMPONENT32 and there is no depth buffer.

Associated Gets

glGetTexImage

glIsEnabled with argument GL_TEXTURE_1D

See Also

glCopyTexImage2D, glCopyTexSubImage1D, glCopyTexSubImage2D, glPixelStore, glTexImage1D, glTexImage2D, glTexSubImage1D, glTexSubImage2D, glTexParameter

Copyright

glCopyTexImage2D

copy pixels into a 2D texture image

C Specification

```
void glCopyTexImage2D(GLenum target,
                      GLint level,
                      GLenum internalformat,
                      GLint x,
                      GLint y,
                      GLsizei width,
                      GLsizei height,
                      GLint border);
```

Parameters

target

Specifies the target texture. Must be GL_TEXTURE_2D, GL_TEXTURE_CUBE_MAP_ POSITIVE_X, GL_TEXTURE_CUBE_MAP_NEGATIVE_X, GL_TEXTURE_CUBE_MAP_ POSITIVE_Y, GL_TEXTURE_CUBE_MAP_NEGATIVE_Y, GL_TEXTURE_CUBE_MAP_ POSITIVE_Z, or GL_TEXTURE_CUBE_MAP_NEGATIVE_Z.

level

Specifies the level-of-detail number. Level 0 is the base image level. Level *n* is the *n*th mipmap reduction image.

internalformat

Specifies the internal format of the texture. Must be one of the following symbolic constants: GL_COMPRESSED_RED, GL_COMPRESSED_RG, GL_COMPRESSED_RGB, GL_COMPRESSED_RGBA. GL_COMPRESSED_SRGB, GL_COMPRESSED_SRGB_ALPHA. GL_DEPTH_COMPONENT, GL_DEPTH_COMPONENT16, GL_DEPTH_COMPONENT24, GL_DEPTH_COMPONENT32, GL_RED, GL_RG, GL_RGB, GL_R3_G3_B2, GL_RGB4, GL_RGB5, GL_RGB8, GL_RGB10, GL_RGB12, GL_RGB16, GL_RGBA, GL_RGBA2, GL_RGBA4, GL_RGB5_A1, GL_RGBA8, GL_RGB10_A2, GL_RGBA12, GL_RGBA16, GL_SRGB, GL_SRGB8, GL_SRGB_ALPHA, or GL_SRGB8_ALPHA8.

x
y

Specify the window coordinates of the lower left corner of the rectangular region of pixels to be copied.

width

Specifies the width of the texture image. Must be 0 or $2^n + 2$ (border) for some integer n.

height

Specifies the height of the texture image. Must be 0 or $2^m + 2$ (border) for some integer m.

border

Specifies the width of the border. Must be either 0 or 1.

Description

glCopyTexImage2D defines a two-dimensional texture image, or cube-map texture image with pixels from the current GL_READ_BUFFER.

The screen-aligned pixel rectangle with lower left corner at (*x*, *y*) and with a width of width + 2 (border) and a height of height + 2 (border) defines the texture array at the mipmap level specified by *level*. *internalformat* specifies the internal format of the texture array.

The pixels in the rectangle are processed exactly as if glReadPixels had been called, but the process stops just before final conversion. At this point all pixel component values are clamped to the range [0,1] and then converted to the texture's internal format for storage in the texel array.

Pixel ordering is such that lower x and y screen coordinates correspond to lower s and t texture coordinates.

If any of the pixels within the specified rectangle of the current GL_READ_BUFFER are outside the window associated with the current rendering context, then the values obtained for those pixels are undefined.

When *internalformat* is one of the sRGB types, the GL does not automatically convert the source pixels to the sRGB color space. In this case, the `glPixelMap` function can be used to accomplish the conversion.

Notes

1, 2, 3, and 4 are not accepted values for *internalformat*.
An image with height or width of 0 indicates a NULL texture.

Errors

GL_INVALID_ENUM is generated if *target* is not GL_TEXTURE_2D, GL_TEXTURE_CUBE_MAP_POSITIVE_X, GL_TEXTURE_CUBE_MAP_NEGATIVE_X, GL_TEXTURE_CUBE_MAP_POSITIVE_Y, GL_TEXTURE_CUBE_MAP_NEGATIVE_Y, GL_TEXTURE_CUBE_MAP_POSITIVE_Z, or GL_TEXTURE_CUBE_MAP_NEGATIVE_Z.

GL_INVALID_VALUE is generated if *level* is less than 0.

GL_INVALID_VALUE may be generated if *level* is greater than $\log_2 max$, where max is the returned value of GL_MAX_TEXTURE_SIZE.

GL_INVALID_VALUE is generated if *width* is less than 0 or greater than 2 + GL_MAX_TEXTURE_SIZE.

GL_INVALID_VALUE is generated if non-power-of-two textures are not supported and the *width* or *depth* cannot be represented as $2^k + 2(border)$ for some integer k.

GL_INVALID_VALUE is generated if *border* is not 0 or 1.

GL_INVALID_VALUE is generated if *internalformat* is not an accepted format.

GL_INVALID_OPERATION is generated if *internalformat* is GL_DEPTH_COMPONENT, GL_DEPTH_COMPONENT16, GL_DEPTH_COMPONENT24, or GL_DEPTH_COMPONENT32 and there is no depth buffer.

Associated Gets

glGetTexImage
glIsEnabled with argument GL_TEXTURE_2D or GL_TEXTURE_CUBE_MAP

See Also

glCopyTexImage1D, glCopyTexSubImage1D, glCopyTexSubImage2D, glPixelStore, glTexImage1D, glTexImage2D, glTexSubImage1D, glTexSubImage2D, glTexParameter

Copyright

glCopyTexSubImage1D

copy a one-dimensional texture subimage

C Specification

```
void glCopyTexSubImage1D(GLenum target,
                         GLint level,
                         GLint xoffset,
                         GLint x,
                         GLint y,
                         GLsizei width);
```

Parameters

target

Specifies the target texture. Must be GL_TEXTURE_1D.

level

Specifies the level-of-detail number. Level 0 is the base image level. Level *n* is the *n*th mipmap reduction image.

xoffset

Specifies the texel offset within the texture array.

x

y

Specify the window coordinates of the left corner of the row of pixels to be copied.

width

Specifies the width of the texture subimage.

Description

glCopyTexSubImage1D replaces a portion of a one-dimensional texture image with pixels from the current GL_READ_BUFFER (rather than from main memory, as is the case for glTexSubImage1D).

The screen-aligned pixel row with left corner at $(x, \backslash y)$, and with length *width* replaces the portion of the texture array with x indices *xoffset* through xoffset + width − 1, inclusive. The destination in the texture array may not include any texels outside the texture array as it was originally specified.

The pixels in the row are processed exactly as if glReadPixels had been called, but the process stops just before final conversion. At this point, all pixel component values are clamped to the range [0,1] and then converted to the texture's internal format for storage in the texel array.

It is not an error to specify a subtexture with zero width, but such a specification has no effect. If any of the pixels within the specified row of the current GL_READ_BUFFER are outside the read window associated with the current rendering context, then the values obtained for those pixels are undefined.

No change is made to the *internalformat*, *width*, or *border* parameters of the specified texture array or to texel values outside the specified subregion.

Notes

The glPixelStore mode affects texture images.

Errors

GL_INVALID_ENUM is generated if /*target* is not GL_TEXTURE_1D.

GL_INVALID_OPERATION is generated if the texture array has not been defined by a previous glTexImage1D or glCopyTexImage1D operation.

GL_INVALID_VALUE is generated if *level* is less than 0.

GL_INVALID_VALUE may be generated if level 7 $\log_2$(max), where *max* is the returned value of GL_MAX_TEXTURE_SIZE.

GL_INVALID_VALUE is generated if xoffset 6 −b, or (xoffset + width) 7 (w − b), where w is the GL_TEXTURE_WIDTH and b is the GL_TEXTURE_BORDER of the texture image being modified. Note that w includes twice the border width.

Associated Gets

glGetTexImage

glIsEnabled with argument GL_TEXTURE_1D

See Also

glCopyTexImage1D, glCopyTexImage2D, glCopyTexSubImage2D, glCopyTexSubImage3D, glPixelStore, glReadBuffer, glTexImage1D, glTexImage2D, glTexImage3D, glTexParameter, glTexSubImage1D, glTexSubImage2D, glTexSubImage3D

Copyright

glCopyTexSubImage2D

copy a two-dimensional texture subimage

C Specification

```
void glCopyTexSubImage2D(GLenum target,
                         GLint level,
                         GLint xoffset,
                         GLint yoffset,
                         GLint x,
                         GLint y,
                         GLsizei width,
                         GLsizei height);
```

Parameters

target

Specifies the target texture. Must be GL_TEXTURE_2D, GL_TEXTURE_CUBE_MAP_ POSITIVE_X, GL_TEXTURE_CUBE_MAP_NEGATIVE_X, GL_TEXTURE_CUBE_MAP_ POSITIVE_Y, GL_TEXTURE_CUBE_MAP_NEGATIVE_Y, GL_TEXTURE_CUBE_MAP_ POSITIVE_Z, or GL_TEXTURE_CUBE_MAP_NEGATIVE_Z.

level

Specifies the level-of-detail number. Level 0 is the base image level. Level *n* is the *n*th mipmap reduction image.

xoffset

Specifies a texel offset in the x direction within the texture array.

yoffset

Specifies a texel offset in the y direction within the texture array.

x
y

Specify the window coordinates of the lower left corner of the rectangular region of pixels to be copied.

width

Specifies the width of the texture subimage.

height

Specifies the height of the texture subimage.

Description

glCopyTexSubImage2D replaces a rectangular portion of a two-dimensional texture image or cube-map texture image with pixels from the current GL_READ_BUFFER (rather than from main memory, as is the case for glTexSubImage2D).

The screen-aligned pixel rectangle with lower left corner at (x, y) and with width *width* and height *height* replaces the portion of the texture array with x indices *xoffset* through xoffset + width – 1, inclusive, and y indices *yoffset* through yoffset + height – 1, inclusive, at the mipmap level specified by *level*.

The pixels in the rectangle are processed exactly as if glReadPixels had been called, but the process stops just before final conversion. At this point, all pixel component values are clamped to the range [0,1] and then converted to the texture's internal format for storage in the texel array.

The destination rectangle in the texture array may not include any texels outside the texture array as it was originally specified. It is not an error to specify a subtexture with zero width or height, but such a specification has no effect.

If any of the pixels within the specified rectangle of the current GL_READ_BUFFER are outside the read window associated with the current rendering context, then the values obtained for those pixels are undefined.

No change is made to the *internalformat*, *width*, *height*, or *border* parameters of the specified texture array or to texel values outside the specified subregion.

Notes

glPixelStore modes affect texture images.

Errors

GL_INVALID_ENUM is generated if *target* is not GL_TEXTURE_2D, GL_TEXTURE_CUBE_MAP_POSITIVE_X, GL_TEXTURE_CUBE_MAP_NEGATIVE_X, GL_TEXTURE_CUBE_MAP_POSITIVE_Y, GL_TEXTURE_CUBE_MAP_NEGATIVE_Y, GL_TEXTURE_CUBE_MAP_POSITIVE_Z, or GL_TEXTURE_CUBE_MAP_NEGATIVE_Z.

GL_INVALID_OPERATION is generated if the texture array has not been defined by a previous glTexImage2D or glCopyTexImage2D operation.

GL_INVALID_VALUE is generated if *level* is less than 0.

GL_INVALID_VALUE may be generated if $level > \log_2(max)$, where max is the returned value of GL_MAX_TEXTURE_SIZE.

GL_INVALID_VALUE is generated if $xoffset < -b$, $(xoffset + width) > (w - b)$, $yoffset < -b$, or $(yoffset + height) > (h - b)$, where w is the GL_TEXTURE_WIDTH, h is the GL_TEXTURE_HEIGHT, and b is the GL_TEXTURE_BORDER of the texture image being modified. Note that w and h include twice the border width.

Associated Gets

glGetTexImage
glIsEnabled with argument GL_TEXTURE_2D

See Also

glCopyTexImage1D, glCopyTexImage2D, glCopyTexSubImage1D, glCopyTexSubImage3D, glPixelStore, glReadBuffer, glTexImage1D, glTexImage2D, glTexImage3D, glTexParameter, glTexSubImage1D, glTexSubImage2D, glTexSubImage3D

Copyright

glCopyTexSubImage3D

copy a three-dimensional texture subimage

C Specification

```
void glCopyTexSubImage3D(GLenum target,
                         GLint level,
                         GLint xoffset,
                         GLint yoffset,
                         GLint zoffset,
                         GLint x,
                         GLint y,
                         GLsizei width,
                         GLsizei height);
```

Parameters

target
>Specifies the target texture. Must be GL_TEXTURE_3D

level
>Specifies the level-of-detail number. Level 0 is the base image level. Level *n* is the *n*th mipmap reduction image.

xoffset
>Specifies a texel offset in the x direction within the texture array.

yoffset
>Specifies a texel offset in the y direction within the texture array.

zoffset
>Specifies a texel offset in the z direction within the texture array.

x
y
>Specify the window coordinates of the lower left corner of the rectangular region of pixels to be copied.

width
>Specifies the width of the texture subimage.

height
>Specifies the height of the texture subimage.

Description

glCopyTexSubImage3D replaces a rectangular portion of a three-dimensional texture image with pixels from the current GL_READ_BUFFER (rather than from main memory, as is the case for glTexSubImage3D).

The screen-aligned pixel rectangle with lower left corner at (*x*, *y*) and with width *width* and height *height* replaces the portion of the texture array with x indices *xoffset* through xoffset + width − 1, inclusive, and y indices *yoffset* through yoffset + height − 1, inclusive, at z index *zoffset* and at the mipmap level specified by *level*.

The pixels in the rectangle are processed exactly as if glReadPixels had been called, but the process stops just before final conversion. At this point, all pixel component values are clamped to the range [0,1] and then converted to the texture's internal format for storage in the texel array.

The destination rectangle in the texture array may not include any texels outside the texture array as it was originally specified. It is not an error to specify a subtexture with zero width or height, but such a specification has no effect.

If any of the pixels within the specified rectangle of the current GL_READ_BUFFER are outside the read window associated with the current rendering context, then the values obtained for those pixels are undefined.

No change is made to the *internalformat*, *width*, *height*, *depth*, or *border* parameters of the specified texture array or to texel values outside the specified subregion.

Notes

glPixelStore modes affect texture images.

Errors

GL_INVALID_ENUM is generated if /*target* is not GL_TEXTURE_3D.

GL_INVALID_OPERATION is generated if the texture array has not been defined by a previous glTexImage3D operation.

GL_INVALID_VALUE is generated if *level* is less than 0.

GL_INVALID_VALUE may be generated if level 7 log$_2$(m ax), where m ax is the returned value of GL_MAX_3D_TEXTURE_SIZE.

GL_INVALID_VALUE is generated if xoffset 6 −b, (xoffset + width) 7 (w − b), yoffset 6 −b, (yoffset + height) 7 (h − b), zoffset 6 −b, or (zoffset + 1) 7 (d − b), where w is the GL_TEXTURE_WIDTH, h is the GL_TEXTURE_HEIGHT, d is the GL_TEXTURE_DEPTH, and b is the GL_TEXTURE_BORDER of the texture image being modified. Note that w, h, and d include twice the border width.

Associated Gets

glGetTexImage
glIsEnabled with argument GL_TEXTURE_3D

See Also

glCopyTexImage1D, glCopyTexImage2D, glCopyTexSubImage1D, glCopyTexSubImage2D, glPixelStore, glReadBuffer, glTexImage1D, glTexImage2D, glTexImage3D, glTexParameter, glTexSubImage1D, glTexSubImage2D, glTexSubImage3D

Copyright

glCreateProgram

Creates a program object

C Specification

GLuint glCreateProgram(*void*);

Description

glCreateProgram creates an empty program object and returns a non-zero value by which it can be referenced. A program object is an object to which shader objects can be attached. This provides a mechanism to specify the shader objects that will be linked to create a program. It also provides a means for checking the compatibility of the shaders that will be used to create a program (for instance, checking the compatibility between a vertex shader and a fragment shader). When no longer needed as part of a program object, shader objects can be detached.

One or more executables are created in a program object by successfully attaching shader objects to it with glAttachShader, successfully compiling the shader objects with glCompileShader, and successfully linking the program object with glLinkProgram. These executables are made part of current state when glUseProgram is called. Program objects can be deleted by calling glDeleteProgram. The memory associated with the program object will be deleted when it is no longer part of current rendering state for any context.

Notes

Like buffer and texture objects, the name space for program objects may be shared across a set of contexts, as long as the server sides of the contexts share the same address space. If the name space is shared across contexts, any attached objects and the data associated with those attached objects are shared as well.

Applications are responsible for providing the synchronization across API calls when objects are accessed from different execution threads.

Errors

This function returns 0 if an error occurs creating the program object.

Associated Gets

glGet with the argument GL_CURRENT_PROGRAM

glGetActiveAttrib with a valid program object and the index of an active attribute variable

glGetActiveUniform with a valid program object and the index of an active uniform variable

glGetAttachedShaders with a valid program object

glGetAttribLocation with a valid program object and the name of an attribute variable

glGetProgram with a valid program object and the parameter to be queried

glGetProgramInfoLog with a valid program object

glGetUniform with a valid program object and the location of a uniform variable

glGetUniformLocation with a valid program object and the name of a uniform variable

glIsProgram

See Also

`glAttachShader`, `glBindAttribLocation`, `glCreateShader`, `glDeleteProgram`, `glDetachShader`, `glLinkProgram`, `glUniform`, `glUseProgram`, `glValidateProgram`

Copyright

glCreateShader

Creates a shader object

C Specification

```
GLuint glCreateShader(GLenum shaderType);
```

Parameters

shaderType

Specifies the type of shader to be created. Must be one of GL_VERTEX_SHADER, GL_GEOMETRY_SHADER or GL_FRAGMENT_SHADER.

Description

`glCreateShader` creates an empty shader object and returns a non-zero value by which it can be referenced. A shader object is used to maintain the source code strings that define a shader. *shaderType* indicates the type of shader to be created. Three types of shaders are supported. A shader of type GL_VERTEX_SHADER is a shader that is intended to run on the programmable vertex processor. A shader of type GL_GEOMETRY_SHADER is a shader that is intended to run on the programmable geometry processor. A shader of type GL_FRAGMENT_SHADER is a shader that is intended to run on the programmable fragment processor.

When created, a shader object's GL_SHADER_TYPE parameter is set to either GL_VERTEX_SHADER, GL_GEOMETRY_SHADER or GL_FRAGMENT_SHADER, depending on the value of *shaderType*.

Notes

Like buffer and texture objects, the name space for shader objects may be shared across a set of contexts, as long as the server sides of the contexts share the same address space. If the name space is shared across contexts, any attached objects and the data associated with those attached objects are shared as well.

Applications are responsible for providing the synchronization across API calls when objects are accessed from different execution threads.

Errors

This function returns 0 if an error occurs creating the shader object.
GL_INVALID_ENUM is generated if *shaderType* is not an accepted value.

Associated Gets

glGetShader with a valid shader object and the parameter to be queried
glGetShaderInfoLog with a valid shader object
glGetShaderSource with a valid shader object
glIsShader

See Also

`glAttachShader`, `glCompileShader`, `glDeleteShader`, `glDetachShader`,
`glShaderSource`

Copyright

Copyright © 2003-2005 3Dlabs Inc. Ltd. This material may be distributed subject to the terms and
conditions set forth in the Open Publication License, v 1.0, 8 June 1999. http://opencontent.org/openpub/.

glCullFace

specify whether front- or back-facing facets can be culled

C Specification

```
void glCullFace(GLenum mode);
```

Parameters

mode
> Specifies whether front- or back-facing facets are candidates for culling. Symbolic
> constants GL_FRONT, GL_BACK, and GL_FRONT_AND_BACK are accepted. The initial
> value is GL_BACK.

Description

`glCullFace` specifies whether front- or back-facing facets are culled (as specified by *mode*) when
facet culling is enabled. Facet culling is initially disabled. To enable and disable facet culling, call the
glEnable and glDisable commands with the argument GL_CULL_FACE. Facets include triangles,
quadrilaterals, polygons, and rectangles.

glFrontFace specifies which of the clockwise and counterclockwise facets are front-facing and
back-facing. See glFrontFace.

Notes

If *mode* is GL_FRONT_AND_BACK, no facets are drawn, but other primitives such as points and
lines are drawn.

Errors

GL_INVALID_ENUM is generated if *mode* is not an accepted value.

Associated Gets

glIsEnabled with argument GL_CULL_FACE
glGet with argument GL_CULL_FACE_MODE

726

See Also

glEnable, glFrontFace

Copyright

Copyright © 1991-2006 Silicon Graphics, Inc. This document is licensed under the SGI Free Software B License. For details, see http://oss.sgi.com/projects/FreeB/.

glDeleteBuffers

delete named buffer objects

C Specification

```
void glDeleteBuffers(GLsizei n,
                     const GLuint * buffers);
```

Parameters

n
Specifies the number of buffer objects to be deleted.
buffers
Specifies an array of buffer objects to be deleted.

Description

glDeleteBuffers deletes *n* buffer objects named by the elements of the array *buffers*. After a buffer object is deleted, it has no contents, and its name is free for reuse (for example by glGenBuffers). If a buffer object that is currently bound is deleted, the binding reverts to 0 (the absence of any buffer object).

glDeleteBuffers silently ignores 0's and names that do not correspond to existing buffer objects.

Errors

GL_INVALID_VALUE is generated if *n* is negative.

Associated Gets

glIsBuffer

See Also

glBindBuffer, glGenBuffers, glGet

Copyright

Copyright © 2005 Addison-Wesley. This material may be distributed subject to the terms and conditions set forth in the Open Publication License, v 1.0, 8 June 1999. http://opencontent.org/openpub/.

glDeleteFramebuffers

delete framebuffer objects

C Specification

```
void glDeleteFramebuffers(GLsizei n,
                          GLuint *framebuffers);
```

Parameters

n
> Specifies the number of framebuffer objects to be deleted.

framebuffers
> A pointer to an array containing *n* framebuffer objects to be deleted.

Description

glDeleteFramebuffers deletes the *n* framebuffer objects whose names are stored in the array addressed by *framebuffers*. The name zero is reserved by the GL and is silently ignored, should it occur in *framebuffers*, as are other unused names. Once a framebuffer object is deleted, its name is again unused and it has no attachments. If a framebuffer that is currently bound to one or more of the targets GL_DRAW_FRAMEBUFFER or GL_READ_FRAMEBUFFER is deleted, it is as though glBindFramebuffer had been executed with the corresponding *target* and *framebuffer* zero.

Errors

GL_INVALID_VALUE is generated if *n* is negative.

See Also

glGenFramebuffers, glBindFramebuffer, glCheckFramebufferStatus

Copyright

Copyright © 2010 Khronos Group. This material may be distributed subject to the terms and conditions set forth in the Open Publication License, v 1.0, 8 June 1999. http://opencontent.org/openpub/.

glDeleteProgram

Deletes a program object

C Specification

```
void glDeleteProgram(GLuint program);
```

Parameters

program
> Specifies the program object to be deleted.

Description

glDeleteProgram frees the memory and invalidates the name associated with the program object specified by *program.* This command effectively undoes the effects of a call to glCreateProgram.

If a program object is in use as part of current rendering state, it will be flagged for deletion, but it will not be deleted until it is no longer part of current state for any rendering context. If a program object to be deleted has shader objects attached to it, those shader objects will be automatically detached but not deleted unless they have already been flagged for deletion by a previous call to glDeleteShader. A value of 0 for *program* will be silently ignored.

To determine whether a program object has been flagged for deletion, call glGetProgram with arguments *program* and GL_DELETE_STATUS.

Errors

GL_INVALID_VALUE is generated if *program* is not a value generated by OpenGL.

Associated Gets

glGet with argument GL_CURRENT_PROGRAM
glGetProgram with arguments *program* and GL_DELETE_STATUS
glIsProgram

See Also

`glCreateShader`, `glDetachShader`, `glUseProgram`

Copyright

Copyright © 2003-2005 3Dlabs Inc. Ltd. This material may be distributed subject to the terms and conditions set forth in the Open Publication License, v 1.0, 8 June 1999. http://opencontent.org/openpub/.

glDeleteQueries

delete named query objects

C Specification

```
void glDeleteQueries(GLsizei n,
                     const GLuint * ids);
```

Parameters

n
> Specifies the number of query objects to be deleted.

ids
> Specifies an array of query objects to be deleted.

Description

`glDeleteQueries` deletes *n* query objects named by the elements of the array *ids*. After a query object is deleted, it has no contents, and its name is free for reuse (for example by glGenQueries).

`glDeleteQueries` silently ignores 0's and names that do not correspond to existing query objects.

Errors

GL_INVALID_VALUE is generated if *n* is negative.

GL_INVALID_OPERATION is generated if `glDeleteQueries` is executed between the execution of glBeginQuery and the corresponding execution of glEndQuery.

Associated Gets

glIsQuery

See Also

`glBeginQuery`, `glEndQuery`, `glGenQueries`, `glGetQueryiv`, `glGetQueryObject`

Copyright

glDeleteRenderbuffers

delete renderbuffer objects

C Specification

```
void glDeleteRenderbuffers(GLsizei n,
                            GLuint *renderbuffers);
```

Parameters

n
> Specifies the number of renderbuffer objects to be deleted.

renderbuffers
> A pointer to an array containing *n* renderbuffer objects to be deleted.

Description

`glDeleteRenderbuffers` deletes the *n* renderbuffer objects whose names are stored in the array addressed by *renderbuffers*. The name zero is reserved by the GL and is silently ignored, should it occur in *renderbuffers*, as are other unused names. Once a renderbuffer object is deleted, its name is again unused and it has no contents. If a renderbuffer that is currently bound to the target GL_RENDERBUFFER is deleted, it is as though glBindRenderbuffer had been executed with a *target* of GL_RENDERBUFFER and a *name* of zero.

If a renderbuffer object is attached to one or more attachment points in the currently bound framebuffer, then it as if glFramebufferRenderbuffer had been called, with a *renderbuffer* of zero for each attachment point to which this image was attached in the currently bound framebuffer. In other words, this renderbuffer object is first detached from all attachment points in the currently bound framebuffer. Note that the renderbuffer image is specifically *not* detached from any non-bound framebuffers.

Errors

GL_INVALID_VALUE is generated if *n* is negative.

See Also

glGenRenderbuffers, glFramebufferRenderbuffer, glRenderbufferStorage, glRenderbufferStorageMultisample

Copyright

glDeleteSamplers

delete named sampler objects

C Specification

```
void glDeleteSamplers(GLsizei n,
                       const GLuint * ids);
```

Parameters

n
> Specifies the number of sampler objects to be deleted.

ids
> Specifies an array of sampler objects to be deleted.

Description

glDeleteSamplers deletes *n* sampler objects named by the elements of the array *ids*. After a sampler object is deleted, its name is again unused. If a sampler object that is currently bound to a sampler unit is deleted, it is as though glBindSampler is called with unit set to the unit the sampler is bound to and sampler zero. Unused names in samplers are silently ignored, as is the reserved name zero.

Notes

glDeleteSamplers is available only if the GL version is 3.3 or higher.

Errors

GL_INVALID_VALUE is generated if *n* is negative.

Associated Gets

glIsSampler

See Also

glGenSamplers, glBindSampler, glDeleteSamplers, glIsSampler

Copyright

Copyright © 2010 Khronos Group. This material may be distributed subject to the terms and conditions set forth in the Open Publication License, v 1.0, 8 June 1999. http://opencontent.org/openpub/.

glDeleteShader

Deletes a shader object

C Specification

void glDeleteShader(GLuint *shader*);

Parameters

shader
> Specifies the shader object to be deleted.

Description

glDeleteShader frees the memory and invalidates the name associated with the shader object specified by *shader*. This command effectively undoes the effects of a call to glCreateShader.

If a shader object to be deleted is attached to a program object, it will be flagged for deletion, but it will not be deleted until it is no longer attached to any program object, for any rendering context (i.e., it must be detached from wherever it was attached before it will be deleted). A value of 0 for *shader* will be silently ignored.

To determine whether an object has been flagged for deletion, call glGetShader with arguments *shader* and GL_DELETE_STATUS.

Errors

GL_INVALID_VALUE is generated if *shader* is not a value generated by OpenGL.

Associated Gets

glGetAttachedShaders with the program object to be queried
glGetShader with arguments *shader* and GL_DELETE_STATUS
glIsShader

See Also

`glCreateProgram`, `glCreateShader`, `glDetachShader`, `glUseProgram`

Copyright

Copyright © 2003-2005 3Dlabs Inc. Ltd. This material may be distributed subject to the terms and conditions set forth in the Open Publication License, v 1.0, 8 June 1999. http://opencontent.org/openpub/.

glDeleteSync

delete a sync object

C Specification

`void glDeleteSync(GLsync sync);`

Parameters

sync
    The sync object to be deleted.

Description

`glDeleteSync` deletes the sync object specified by *sync*. If the fence command corresponding to the specified sync object has completed, or if no glWaitSync or glClientWaitSync commands are blocking on *sync*, the object is deleted immediately. Otherwise, *sync* is flagged for deletion and will be deleted when it is no longer associated with any fence command and is no longer blocking any glWaitSync or glClientWaitSync command. In either case, after `glDeleteSync` returns, the name *sync* is invalid and can no longer be used to refer to the sync object.

`glDeleteSync` will silently ignore a *sync* value of zero.

Notes

`glSync` is only supported if the GL version is 3.2 or greater, or if the `ARB_sync` extension is supported.

Errors

GL_INVALID_VALUE is generated if *sync* is neither zero or the name of a sync object.

See Also

glFenceSync, glWaitSync, glClientWaitSync

Copyright

glDeleteTextures

delete named textures

C Specification

```
void glDeleteTextures(GLsizei n,
                      const GLuint * textures);
```

Parameters

n
> Specifies the number of textures to be deleted.

textures
> Specifies an array of textures to be deleted.

Description

glDeleteTextures deletes *n* textures named by the elements of the array *textures*. After a texture is deleted, it has no contents or dimensionality, and its name is free for reuse (for example by glGenTextures). If a texture that is currently bound is deleted, the binding reverts to 0 (the default texture).

glDeleteTextures silently ignores 0's and names that do not correspond to existing textures.

Errors

GL_INVALID_VALUE is generated if *n* is negative.

Associated Gets

glIsTexture

See Also

glBindTexture, glCopyTexImage1D, glCopyTexImage2D, glGenTextures, glGet, glGetTexParameter, glTexImage1D, glTexImage2D, glTexParameter

Copyright

glDeleteVertexArrays

delete vertex array objects

C Specification

```
void glDeleteVertexArrays(GLsizei n,
                          const GLuint * arrays);
```

Parameters

n
> Specifies the number of vertex array objects to be deleted.

arrays
> Specifies the address of an array containing the *n* names of the objects to be deleted.

Description

glDeleteVertexArrays deletes *n* vertex array objects whose names are stored in the array addressed by *arrays*. Once a vertex array object is deleted it has no contents and its name is again unused. If a vertex array object that is currently bound is deleted, the binding for that object reverts to zero and the default vertex array becomes current. Unused names in *arrays* are silently ignored, as is the value zero.

Errors

GL_INVALID_VALUE is generated if *n* is negative.

See Also

glGenVertexArrays, glIsVertexArray, glBindVertexArray

Copyright

glDepthFunc

specify the value used for depth buffer comparisons

C Specification

```
void glDepthFunc(GLenum func);
```

Parameters

func
> Specifies the depth comparison function. Symbolic constants GL_NEVER, GL_LESS, GL_EQUAL, GL_LEQUAL, GL_GREATER, GL_NOTEQUAL, GL_GEQUAL, and GL_ALWAYS are accepted. The initial value is GL_LESS.

Description

glDepthFunc specifies the function used to compare each incoming pixel depth value with the depth value present in the depth buffer. The comparison is performed only if depth testing is enabled. (See glEnable and glDisable of GL_DEPTH_TEST.)

func specifies the conditions under which the pixel will be drawn. The comparison functions are as follows:

GL_NEVER
> Never passes.

GL_LESS
> Passes if the incoming depth value is less than the stored depth value.

GL_EQUAL
> Passes if the incoming depth value is equal to the stored depth value.

GL_LEQUAL

    Passes if the incoming depth value is less than or equal to the stored depth value.

GL_GREATER

    Passes if the incoming depth value is greater than the stored depth value.

GL_NOTEQUAL

    Passes if the incoming depth value is not equal to the stored depth value.

GL_GEQUAL

    Passes if the incoming depth value is greater than or equal to the stored depth value.

GL_ALWAYS

    Always passes.

The initial value of *func* is GL_LESS. Initially, depth testing is disabled. If depth testing is disabled or if no depth buffer exists, it is as if the depth test always passes.

Notes

Even if the depth buffer exists and the depth mask is non-zero, the depth buffer is not updated if the depth test is disabled. In order to unconditionally write to the depth buffer, the depth test should be enabled and set to GL_ALWAYS.

Errors

GL_INVALID_ENUM is generated if *func* is not an accepted value.

Associated Gets

glGet with argument GL_DEPTH_FUNC
glIsEnabled with argument GL_DEPTH_TEST

See Also

`glDepthRange`, `glEnable`, `glPolygonOffset`

Copyright

Copyright © 1991-2006 Silicon Graphics, Inc. This document is licensed under the SGI Free Software B License. For details, see http://oss.sgi.com/projects/FreeB/.

glDepthMask

enable or disable writing into the depth buffer

C Specification

`void glDepthMask(GLboolean flag);`

Parameters

flag

    Specifies whether the depth buffer is enabled for writing. If *flag* is GL_FALSE, depth buffer writing is disabled. Otherwise, it is enabled. Initially, depth buffer writing is enabled.

Description

`glDepthMask` specifies whether the depth buffer is enabled for writing. If *flag* is GL_FALSE, depth buffer writing is disabled. Otherwise, it is enabled. Initially, depth buffer writing is enabled.

Associated Gets

glGet with argument GL_DEPTH_WRITEMASK

See Also

glColorMask, glDepthFunc, glDepthRange, glStencilMask

Copyright

glDepthRange

specify mapping of depth values from normalized device coordinates to window coordinates

C Specification

```
void glDepthRange(GLclampd nearVal,
                  GLclampd farVal);
```

Parameters

nearVal

Specifies the mapping of the near clipping plane to window coordinates. The initial value is 0.

farVal

Specifies the mapping of the far clipping plane to window coordinates. The initial value is 1.

Description

After clipping and division by *w*, depth coordinates range from -1 to 1, corresponding to the near and far clipping planes. glDepthRange specifies a linear mapping of the normalized depth coordinates in this range to window depth coordinates. Regardless of the actual depth buffer implementation, window coordinate depth values are treated as though they range from 0 through 1 (like color components). Thus, the values accepted by glDepthRange are both clamped to this range before they are accepted.

The setting of (0,1) maps the near plane to 0 and the far plane to 1. With this mapping, the depth buffer range is fully utilized.

Notes

It is not necessary that *nearVal* be less than *farVal*. Reverse mappings such as nearVal = 1, and farVal = 0 are acceptable.

Associated Gets

glGet with argument GL_DEPTH_RANGE

See Also

glDepthFunc, glPolygonOffset, glViewport

Copyright

glDetachShader

Detaches a shader object from a program object to which it is attached

C Specification

```
void glDetachShader(GLuint program,
                    GLuint shader);
```

Parameters

program

Specifies the program object from which to detach the shader object.

shader

Specifies the shader object to be detached.

Description

glDetachShader detaches the shader object specified by *shader* from the program object specified by *program*. This command can be used to undo the effect of the command glAttachShader.

If *shader* has already been flagged for deletion by a call to glDeleteShader and it is not attached to any other program object, it will be deleted after it has been detached.

Errors

GL_INVALID_VALUE is generated if either *program* or *shader* is a value that was not generated by OpenGL.

GL_INVALID_OPERATION is generated if *program* is not a program object.

GL_INVALID_OPERATION is generated if *shader* is not a shader object.

GL_INVALID_OPERATION is generated if *shader* is not attached to *program*.

Associated Gets

glGetAttachedShaders with the handle of a valid program object

glGetShader with arguments *shader* and GL_DELETE_STATUS

glIsProgram

glIsShader

See Also

glAttachShader

Copyright

glDrawArrays

render primitives from array data

C Specification

```
void glDrawArrays(GLenum mode,
                  GLint first,
                  GLsizei count);
```

Parameters

mode

Specifies what kind of primitives to render. Symbolic constants GL_POINTS, GL_LINE_STRIP, GL_LINE_LOOP, GL_LINES, GL_LINE_STRIP_ADJACENCY, GL_LINES_ADJACENCY, GL_TRIANGLE_STRIP, GL_TRIANGLE_FAN, GL_TRIANGLES, GL_TRIANGLE_STRIP_ADJACENCY and GL_TRIANGLES_ADJACENCY are accepted.

first

Specifies the starting index in the enabled arrays.

count

Specifies the number of indices to be rendered.

Description

`glDrawArrays` specifies multiple geometric primitives with very few subroutine calls. Instead of calling a GL procedure to pass each individual vertex, normal, texture coordinate, edge flag, or color, you can prespecify separate arrays of vertices, normals, and colors and use them to construct a sequence of primitives with a single call to `glDrawArrays`.

When `glDrawArrays` is called, it uses *count* sequential elements from each enabled array to construct a sequence of geometric primitives, beginning with element *first*. *mode* specifies what kind of primitives are constructed and how the array elements construct those primitives.

Vertex attributes that are modified by `glDrawArrays` have an unspecified value after `glDrawArrays` returns. Attributes that aren't modified remain well defined.

Notes

GL_LINE_STRIP_ADJACENCY, GL_LINES_ADJACENCY, GL_TRIANGLE_STRIP_ADJACENCY and GL_TRIANGLES_ADJACENCY are available only if the GL version is 3.2 or greater.

Errors

GL_INVALID_ENUM is generated if *mode* is not an accepted value.

GL_INVALID_VALUE is generated if *count* is negative.

GL_INVALID_OPERATION is generated if a non-zero buffer object name is bound to an enabled array and the buffer object's data store is currently mapped.

GL_INVALID_OPERATION is generated if a geometry shader is active and *mode* is incompatible with the input primitive type of the geometry shader in the currently installed program object.

See Also

`glDrawArraysInstanced`, `glDrawElements`, `glDrawRangeElements`.

Copyright

glDrawArraysInstanced

draw multiple instances of a range of elements

C Specification

```
void glDrawArraysInstanced(GLenum mode,
                           GLint first,
                           GLsizei count,
                           GLsizei primcount);
```

Parameters

mode

Specifies what kind of primitives to render. Symbolic constants GL_POINTS, GL_LINE_STRIP, GL_LINE_LOOP, GL_LINES, GL_TRIANGLE_STRIP, GL_TRIANGLE_FAN, GL_TRIANGLES, GL_LINES_ADJACENCY, GL_LINE_STRIP_ADJACENCY, GL_TRIANGLES_ADJACENCY andGL_TRIANGLE_STRIP_ADJACENCY are accepted.

first

Specifies the starting index in the enabled arrays.

count

Specifies the number of indices to be rendered.

primcount

Specifies the number of instances of the specified range of indices to be rendered.

Description

glDrawArraysInstanced behaves identically to glDrawArrays except that *primcount* instances of the range of elements are executed and the value of the internal counter *instanceID* advances for each iteration. *instanceID* is an internal 32-bit integer counter that may be read by a vertex shader as gl_InstanceID.

glDrawArraysInstanced has the same effect as:

```
<![CDATA[ if ( mode or count is invalid )
generate appropriate error
else {
for (int i = 0; i < primcount ; i++) {
instanceID = i;
glDrawArrays(mode, first, count);
}
instanceID = 0;
}]]>
```

Notes

glDrawArraysInstanced is available only if the GL version is 3.1 or greater.
GL_LINE_STRIP_ADJACENCY, GL_LINES_ADJACENCY, GL_TRIANGLE_STRIP_ADJACENCY and GL_TRIANGLES_ADJACENCY are available only if the GL version is 3.2 or greater.

Errors

GL_INVALID_ENUM is generated if *mode* is not one of the accepted values.

GL_INVALID_OPERATION is generated if a geometry shader is active and *mode* is incompatible with the input primitive type of the geometry shader in the currently installed program object.

GL_INVALID_VALUE is generated if *count* or *primcount* are negative.

GL_INVALID_OPERATION is generated if a non-zero buffer object name is bound to an enabled array and the buffer object's data store is currently mapped.

See Also

glDrawArrays, glDrawElementsInstanced

Copyright

Copyright © 2010 Khronos Group. This material may be distributed subject to the terms and conditions set forth in the Open Publication License, v 1.0, 8 June 1999. http://opencontent.org/openpub/.

glDrawBuffer

specify which color buffers are to be drawn into

C Specification

void glDrawBuffer(GLenum *mode*);

Parameters

mode

Specifies up to four color buffers to be drawn into. Symbolic constants GL_NONE, GL_FRONT_LEFT, GL_FRONT_RIGHT, GL_BACK_LEFT, GL_BACK_RIGHT, GL_FRONT, GL_BACK, GL_LEFT, GL_RIGHT, and GL_FRONT_AND_BACK are accepted. The initial value is GL_FRONT for single-buffered contexts, and GL_BACK for double-buffered contexts.

Description

When colors are written to the frame buffer, they are written into the color buffers specified by glDrawBuffer. The specifications are as follows:

GL_NONE

No color buffers are written.

GL_FRONT_LEFT

Only the front left color buffer is written.

GL_FRONT_RIGHT

Only the front right color buffer is written.

GL_BACK_LEFT

Only the back left color buffer is written.

GL_BACK_RIGHT

Only the back right color buffer is written.

GL_FRONT

Only the front left and front right color buffers are written. If there is no front right color buffer, only the front left color buffer is written.

GL_BACK

Only the back left and back right color buffers are written. If there is no back right color buffer, only the back left color buffer is written.

GL_LEFT

Only the front left and back left color buffers are written. If there is no back left color buffer, only the front left color buffer is written.

GL_RIGHT

Only the front right and back right color buffers are written. If there is no back right color buffer, only the front right color buffer is written.

GL_FRONT_AND_BACK

All the front and back color buffers (front left, front right, back left, back right) are written. If there are no back color buffers, only the front left and front right color buffers are written. If there are no right color buffers, only the front left and back left color buffers are written. If there are no right or back color buffers, only the front left color buffer is written.

If more than one color buffer is selected for drawing, then blending or logical operations are computed and applied independently for each color buffer and can produce different results in each buffer.

Monoscopic contexts include only *left* buffers, and stereoscopic contexts include both *left* and *right* buffers. Likewise, single-buffered contexts include only *front* buffers, and double-buffered contexts include both *front* and *back* buffers. The context is selected at GL initialization.

Errors

GL_INVALID_ENUM is generated if *mode* is not an accepted value.
GL_INVALID_OPERATION is generated if none of the buffers indicated by *mode* exists.

Associated Gets

glGet with argument GL_DRAW_BUFFER

See Also

glBlendFunc, glColorMask, glDrawBuffers, glLogicOp, glReadBuffer

Copyright

Copyright © 1991-2006 Silicon Graphics, Inc. This document is licensed under the SGI Free Software B License. For details, see http://oss.sgi.com/projects/FreeB/.

glDrawBuffers

Specifies a list of color buffers to be drawn into

C Specification

```
void glDrawBuffers(GLsizei n,
                   const GLenum * bufs);
```

Parameters

n

Specifies the number of buffers in *bufs*.

bufs

Points to an array of symbolic constants specifying the buffers into which fragment colors or data values will be written.

Description

glDrawBuffers defines an array of buffers into which outputs from the fragment shader data will be written. If a fragment shader writes a value to one or more user defined output variables, then the value of each variable will be written into the buffer specified at a location within *bufs* corresponding to the location assigned to that user defined output. The draw buffer used for user defined outputs assigned to locations greater than or equal to *n* is implicitly set to GL_NONE and any data written to such an output is discarded.

The symbolic constants contained in *bufs* may be any of the following:
GL_NONE

The fragment shader output value is not written into any color buffer.
GL_FRONT_LEFT

The fragment shader output value is written into the front left color buffer.
GL_FRONT_RIGHT

The fragment shader output value is written into the front right color buffer.

GL_BACK_LEFT
>The fragment shader output value is written into the back left color buffer.

GL_BACK_RIGHT
>The fragment shader output value is written into the back right color buffer.

GL_COLOR_ATTACHMENT*n*
>The fragment shader output value is written into the *n*th color attachment of the current framebuffer. *n* may range from 0 to the value of GL_MAX_COLOR_ATTACHMENTS.

Except for GL_NONE, the preceding symbolic constants may not appear more than once in *bufs*. The maximum number of draw buffers supported is implementation dependent and can be queried by calling glGet with the argument GL_MAX_DRAW_BUFFERS.

Notes

The symbolic constants GL_FRONT, GL_BACK, GL_LEFT, GL_RIGHT, and GL_FRONT_AND_BACK are not allowed in the *bufs* array since they may refer to multiple buffers.

If a fragment shader does not write to a user defined output variable, the values of the fragment colors following shader execution are undefined. For each fragment generated in this situation, a different value may be written into each of the buffers specified by *bufs*.

Errors

GL_INVALID_ENUM is generated if one of the values in *bufs* is not an accepted value.

GL_INVALID_ENUM is generated if the GL is bound to the default framebuffer and one or more of the values in *bufs* is one of the GL_COLOR_ATTACHMENT*n* tokens.

GL_INVALID_ENUM is generated if the GL is bound to a framebuffer object and one or more of the values in *bufs* is anything other than GL_NONE or one of the GL_COLOR_ATTACHMENTS*n* tokens.

GL_INVALID_ENUM is generated if *n* is less than 0.

GL_INVALID_OPERATION is generated if a symbolic constant other than GL_NONE appears more than once in *bufs*.

GL_INVALID_OPERATION is generated if any of the entries in *bufs* (other than GL_NONE) indicates a color buffer that does not exist in the current GL context.

GL_INVALID_VALUE is generated if *n* is greater than GL_MAX_DRAW_BUFFERS.

Associated Gets

glGet with argument GL_MAX_DRAW_BUFFERS

glGet with argument GL_DRAW_BUFFER*i* where i indicates the number of the draw buffer whose value is to be queried

See Also

glBlendFunc, glColorMask, glDrawBuffers, glLogicOp, glReadBuffer

Copyright

glDrawElements

render primitives from array data

C Specification

```
void glDrawElements(GLenum mode,
                    GLsizei count,
                    GLenum type,
                    const GLvoid * indices);
```

Parameters

mode

Specifies what kind of primitives to render. Symbolic constants GL_POINTS, GL_LINE_STRIP, GL_LINE_LOOP, GL_LINES, GL_LINE_STRIP_ADJACENCY, GL_LINES_ADJACENCY, GL_TRIANGLE_STRIP, GL_TRIANGLE_FAN, GL_TRIANGLES, GL_TRIANGLE_STRIP_ADJACENCY and GL_TRIANGLES_ADJACENCY are accepted.

count

Specifies the number of elements to be rendered.

type

Specifies the type of the values in *indices*. Must be one of GL_UNSIGNED_BYTE, GL_UNSIGNED_SHORT, or GL_UNSIGNED_INT.

indices

Specifies a pointer to the location where the indices are stored.

Description

glDrawElements specifies multiple geometric primitives with very few subroutine calls. Instead of calling a GL function to pass each individual vertex, normal, texture coordinate, edge flag, or color, you can prespecify separate arrays of vertices, normals, and so on, and use them to construct a sequence of primitives with a single call to glDrawElements.

When glDrawElements is called, it uses *count* sequential elements from an enabled array, starting at *indices* to construct a sequence of geometric primitives. *mode* specifies what kind of primitives are constructed and how the array elements construct these primitives. If more than one array is enabled, each is used.

Vertex attributes that are modified by glDrawElements have an unspecified value after glDrawElements returns. Attributes that aren't modified maintain their previous values.

Notes

GL_LINE_STRIP_ADJACENCY, GL_LINES_ADJACENCY, GL_TRIANGLE_STRIP_ADJACENCY and GL_TRIANGLES_ADJACENCY are available only if the GL version is 3.2 or greater.

Errors

GL_INVALID_ENUM is generated if *mode* is not an accepted value.

GL_INVALID_VALUE is generated if *count* is negative.

GL_INVALID_OPERATION is generated if a geometry shader is active and *mode* is incompatible with the input primitive type of the geometry shader in the currently installed program object.

GL_INVALID_OPERATION is generated if a non-zero buffer object name is bound to an enabled array or the element array and the buffer object's data store is currently mapped.

See Also

glDrawArrays, glDrawElementsInstanced, glDrawElementsBaseVertex, glDrawRangeElements

Copyright

Copyright © 1991-2006 Silicon Graphics, Inc. This document is licensed under the SGI Free Software B License. For details, see http://oss.sgi.com/projects/FreeB/.

glDrawElementsBaseVertex

render primitives from array data with a per-element offset

C Specification

```
void glDrawElementsBaseVertex(GLenum mode,
                             GLsizei count,
                             GLenum type,
                             GLvoid * indices,
                             GLint basevertex);
```

Parameters

mode

Specifies what kind of primitives to render. Symbolic constants GL_POINTS, GL_LINE_STRIP, GL_LINE_LOOP, GL_LINES, GL_TRIANGLE_STRIP, GL_TRIANGLE_FAN, and GL_TRIANGLES are accepted.

count

Specifies the number of elements to be rendered.

type

Specifies the type of the values in indices. Must be one of GL_UNSIGNED_BYTE, GL_UNSIGNED_SHORT, or GL_UNSIGNED_INT.

indices

Specifies a pointer to the location where the indices are stored.

basevertex

Specifies a constant that should be added to each element of *indices* when choosing elements from the enabled vertex arrays.

Description

glDrawElementsBaseVertex behaves identically to glDrawElements except that the *i*th element transferred by the corresponding draw call will be taken from element *indices*[i] + *basevertex* of each enabled array. If the resulting value is larger than the maximum value representable by *type*, it is as if the calculation were upconverted to 32-bit unsigned integers (with wrapping on overflow conditions). The operation is undefined if the sum would be negative.

Notes

glDrawElementsBaseVertex is only supported if the GL version is 3.2 or greater, or if the ARB_draw_elements_base_vertex extension is supported.

Errors

GL_INVALID_ENUM is generated if *mode* is not an accepted value.

GL_INVALID_VALUE is generated if *count* is negative.

GL_INVALID_OPERATION is generated if a geometry shader is active and *mode* is incompatible with the input primitive type of the geometry shader in the currently installed program object.

GL_INVALID_OPERATION is generated if a non-zero buffer object name is bound to an enabled array or the element array and the buffer object's data store is currently mapped.

glDrawElementsInstanced

draw multiple instances of a set of elements

C Specification

```
void glDrawElementsInstanced(GLenum mode,
                             GLsizei count,
                             GLenum type,
                             const void * indices,
                             GLsizei primcount);
```

Parameters

mode

Specifies what kind of primitives to render. Symbolic constants GL_POINTS, GL_LINE_STRIP, GL_LINE_LOOP, GL_LINES, GL_LINE_STRIP_ADJACENCY, GL_LINES_ADJACENCY, GL_TRIANGLE_STRIP, GL_TRIANGLE_FAN, GL_TRIANGLES, GL_TRIANGLE_STRIP_ADJACENCY and GL_TRIANGLES_ADJACENCY are accepted.

count

Specifies the number of elements to be rendered.

type

Specifies the type of the values in *indices*. Must be one of GL_UNSIGNED_BYTE, GL_UNSIGNED_SHORT, or GL_UNSIGNED_INT.

indices

Specifies a pointer to the location where the indices are stored.

primcount

Specifies the number of instances of the specified range of indices to be rendered.

Description

glDrawElementsInstanced behaves identically to glDrawElements except that *primcount* instances of the set of elements are executed and the value of the internal counter *instanceID* advances for each iteration. *instanceID* is an internal 32-bit integer counter that may be read by a vertex shader as gl_InstanceID.

glDrawElementsInstanced has the same effect as:

```
<![CDATA[ if (mode, count, or type is invalid )
generate appropriate error
else {
for (int i = 0; i < primcount ; i++) {
instanceID = i;
glDrawElements(mode, count, type, indices);
}
instanceID = 0;
}]]>
```

Notes

glDrawElementsInstanced is available only if the GL version is 3.1 or greater.
GL_LINE_STRIP_ADJACENCY, GL_LINES_ADJACENCY, GL_TRIANGLE_STRIP_ADJACENCY and GL_TRIANGLES_ADJACENCY are available only if the GL version is 3.2 or greater.

Errors

GL_INVALID_ENUM is generated if *mode* is not one of GL_POINTS, GL_LINE_STRIP, GL_LINE_LOOP, GL_LINES, GL_TRIANGLE_STRIP, GL_TRIANGLE_FAN, or GL_TRIANGLES.

GL_INVALID_VALUE is generated if *count* or *primcount* are negative.

GL_INVALID_OPERATION is generated if a geometry shader is active and *mode* is incompatible with the input primitive type of the geometry shader in the currently installed program object.

GL_INVALID_OPERATION is generated if a non-zero buffer object name is bound to an enabled array and the buffer object's data store is currently mapped.

See Also

glDrawElements, glDrawArraysInstanced

Copyright

Copyright © 2010 Khronos Group. This material may be distributed subject to the terms and conditions set forth in the Open Publication License, v 1.0, 8 June 1999. http://opencontent.org/openpub/.

glDrawElementsInstancedBaseVertex

render multiple instances of a set of primitives from array data with a per-element offset

C Specification

```
void glDrawElementsInstancedBaseVertex(GLenum mode,
                                       GLsizei count,
                                       GLenum type,
                                       GLvoid * indices,
                                       GLsizei primcount,
                                       GLint basevertex);
```

Parameters

mode
> Specifies what kind of primitives to render. Symbolic constants GL_POINTS, GL_LINE_STRIP, GL_LINE_LOOP, GL_LINES, GL_TRIANGLE_STRIP, GL_TRIANGLE_FAN, and GL_TRIANGLES are accepted.

count
> Specifies the number of elements to be rendered.

type
> Specifies the type of the values in indices. Must be one of GL_UNSIGNED_BYTE, GL_UNSIGNED_SHORT, or GL_UNSIGNED_INT.

indices
> Specifies a pointer to the location where the indices are stored.

primcount
> Specifies the number of instances of the indexed geometry that should be drawn.

basevertex
> Specifies a constant that should be added to each element of *indices* when choosing elements from the enabled vertex arrays.

Description

glDrawElementsInstancedBaseVertex behaves identically to glDrawElementsInstanced except that the *i*th element transferred by the corresponding draw call will be taken from element *indices*[i] + *basevertex* of each enabled array. If the resulting value is larger than the maximum value representable by *type*, it is as if the calculation were upconverted to 32-bit unsigned integers (with wrapping on overflow conditions). The operation is undefined if the sum would be negative.

Notes

glDrawElementsInstancedBaseVertex is only supported if the GL version is 3.2 or greater.

Errors

GL_INVALID_ENUM is generated if *mode* is not an accepted value.

GL_INVALID_VALUE is generated if *count* or *primcount* is negative.

GL_INVALID_OPERATION is generated if a geometry shader is active and *mode* is incompatible with the input primitive type of the geometry shader in the currently installed program object.

GL_INVALID_OPERATION is generated if a non-zero buffer object name is bound to an enabled array or the element array and the buffer object's data store is currently mapped.

See Also

glDrawElements, glDrawRangeElements, glDrawRangeElementsBaseVertex, glDrawElementsInstanced, glDrawElementsInstancedBaseVertex

Copyright

glDrawRangeElements

render primitives from array data

C Specification

```
void glDrawRangeElements(GLenum mode,
                         GLuint start,
                         GLuint end,
                         GLsizei count,
                         GLenum type,
                         const GLvoid * indices);
```

Parameters

mode

Specifies what kind of primitives to render. Symbolic constants GL_POINTS, GL_LINE_STRIP, GL_LINE_LOOP, GL_LINES, GL_LINE_STRIP_ADJACENCY, GL_LINES_ADJACENCY, GL_TRIANGLE_STRIP, GL_TRIANGLE_FAN, GL_TRIANGLES, GL_TRIANGLE_STRIP_ADJACENCY and GL_TRIANGLES_ADJACENCY are accepted.

start

Specifies the minimum array index contained in *indices*.

end

Specifies the maximum array index contained in *indices*.

count

Specifies the number of elements to be rendered.

type

Specifies the type of the values in *indices*. Must be one of GL_UNSIGNED_BYTE, GL_UNSIGNED_SHORT, or GL_UNSIGNED_INT.

indices
Specifies a pointer to the location where the indices are stored.

Description

glDrawRangeElements is a restricted form of glDrawElements. *mode*, *start*, *end*, and *count* match the corresponding arguments to glDrawElements, with the additional constraint that all values in the arrays *count* must lie between *start* and *end*, inclusive.

Implementations denote recommended maximum amounts of vertex and index data, which may be queried by calling glGet with argument GL_MAX_ELEMENTS_VERTICES and GL_MAX_ELEMENTS_INDICES. If *end* – *start* + 1 is greater than the value of GL_MAX_ELEMENTS_VERTICES, or if *count* is greater than the value of GL_MAX_ELEMENTS_INDICES, then the call may operate at reduced performance. There is no requirement that all vertices in the range [start, end] be referenced. However, the implementation may partially process unused vertices, reducing performance from what could be achieved with an optimal index set.

When glDrawRangeElements is called, it uses *count* sequential elements from an enabled array, starting at *start* to construct a sequence of geometric primitives. *mode* specifies what kind of primitives are constructed, and how the array elements construct these primitives. If more than one array is enabled, each is used.

Vertex attributes that are modified by glDrawRangeElements have an unspecified value after glDrawRangeElements returns. Attributes that aren't modified maintain their previous values.

Notes

GL_LINE_STRIP_ADJACENCY, GL_LINES_ADJACENCY, GL_TRIANGLE_STRIP_ADJACENCY and GL_TRIANGLES_ADJACENCY are available only if the GL version is 3.2 or greater.

Errors

It is an error for indices to lie outside the range [start, end], but implementations may not check for this situation. Such indices cause implementation-dependent behavior.

GL_INVALID_ENUM is generated if *mode* is not an accepted value.

GL_INVALID_VALUE is generated if *count* is negative.

GL_INVALID_VALUE is generated if *end* 6 *start*.

GL_INVALID_OPERATION is generated if a geometry shader is active and *mode* is incompatible with the input primitive type of the geometry shader in the currently installed program object.

GL_INVALID_OPERATION is generated if a non-zero buffer object name is bound to an enabled array or the element array and the buffer object's data store is currently mapped.

Associated Gets

glGet with argument GL_MAX_ELEMENTS_VERTICES
glGet with argument GL_MAX_ELEMENTS_INDICES

See Also

glDrawArrays, glDrawElements, glDrawElementsBaseVertex

Copyright

glDrawRangeElementsBaseVertex

render primitives from array data with a per-element offset

C Specification

```
void glDrawRangeElementsBaseVertex(GLenum mode,
                                   GLuint start,
                                   GLuint end,
                                   GLsizei count,
                                   GLenum type,
                                   GLvoid * indices,
                                   GLint basevertex);
```

Parameters

mode

Specifies what kind of primitives to render. Symbolic constants GL_POINTS, GL_LINE_STRIP, GL_LINE_LOOP, GL_LINES, GL_TRIANGLE_STRIP, GL_TRIANGLE_FAN, and GL_TRIANGLES are accepted.

start

Specifies the minimum array index contained in *indices*.

end

Specifies the maximum array index contained in *indices*.

count

Specifies the number of elements to be rendered.

type

Specifies the type of the values in indices. Must be one of GL_UNSIGNED_BYTE, GL_UNSIGNED_SHORT, or GL_UNSIGNED_INT.

indices

Specifies a pointer to the location where the indices are stored.

basevertex

Specifies a constant that should be added to each element of *indices* when choosing elements from the enabled vertex arrays.

Description

glDrawRangeElementsBaseVertex is a restricted form of glDrawElementsBaseVertex. *mode*, *start*, *end*, *count* and *basevertex* match the corresponding arguments to glDrawElementsBaseVertex, with the additional constraint that all values in the array *indices* must lie between *start* and *end*, inclusive, prior to adding *basevertex*. Index values lying outside the range [*start*, *end*] are treated in the same way as glDrawElementsBaseVertex. The *i*th element transferred by the corresponding draw call will be taken from element *indices*[i] + *basevertex* of each enabled array. If the resulting value is larger than the maximum value representable by *type*, it is as if the calculation were upconverted to 32-bit unsigned integers (with wrapping on overflow conditions). The operation is undefined if the sum would be negative.

Notes

glDrawRangeElementsBaseVertex is only supported if the GL version is 3.2 or greater, or if the ARB_draw_elements_base_vertex extension is supported.

Errors

GL_INVALID_ENUM is generated if *mode* is not an accepted value.
GL_INVALID_VALUE is generated if *count* is negative.

GL_INVALID_VALUE is generated if *end* < *start*.

GL_INVALID_OPERATION is generated if a geometry shader is active and *mode* is incompatible with the input primitive type of the geometry shader in the currently installed program object.

GL_INVALID_OPERATION is generated if a non-zero buffer object name is bound to an enabled array or the element array and the buffer object's data store is currently mapped.

See Also

glDrawElements, glDrawElementsBaseVertex, glDrawRangeElements, glDrawElementsInstanced, glDrawElementsInstancedBaseVertex

Copyright

Copyright © 2010 Khronos Group. This material may be distributed subject to the terms and conditions set forth in the Open Publication License, v 1.0, 8 June 1999. http://opencontent.org/openpub/.

glEnable

enable or disable server-side GL capabilities

C Specification

```
void glEnable(GLenum cap);
```

Parameters

cap
> Specifies a symbolic constant indicating a GL capability.

C Specification

```
void glDisable(GLenum cap);
```

Parameters

cap
> Specifies a symbolic constant indicating a GL capability.

C Specification

```
void glEnablei(GLenum cap,
               GLuint index);
```

Parameters

cap
> Specifies a symbolic constant indicating a GL capability.

index
> Specifies the index of the swtich to enable.

C Specification

```
void glDisablei(GLenum cap,
                GLuint index);
```

Parameters

cap
> Specifies a symbolic constant indicating a GL capability.

index
> Specifies the index of the swtich to disable.

Description

glEnable and glDisable enable and disable various capabilities. Use glIsEnabled or glGet to determine the current setting of any capability. The initial value for each capability with the exception of GL_DITHER and GL_MULTISAMPLE is GL_FALSE. The initial value for GL_DITHER and GL_MULTISAMPLE is GL_TRUE.

Both glEnable and glDisable take a single argument, *cap*, which can assume one of the following values:

Some of the GL's capabilities are indicated. glEnablei and glDisablei enable and disable indexed capabilities.

GL_BLEND

If enabled, blend the computed fragment color values with the values in the color buffers. See glBlendFunc.

GL_CLIP_DISTANCE*i*

If enabled, clip geometry against user-defined half space *i*.

GL_COLOR_LOGIC_OP

If enabled, apply the currently selected logical operation to the computed fragment color and color buffer values. See glLogicOp.

GL_CULL_FACE

If enabled, cull polygons based on their winding in window coordinates. See glCullFace.

GL_DEPTH_TEST

If enabled, do depth comparisons and update the depth buffer. Note that even if the depth buffer exists and the depth mask is non-zero, the depth buffer is not updated if the depth test is disabled. See glDepthFunc and glDepthRange.

GL_DITHER

If enabled, dither color components or indices before they are written to the color buffer.

GL_LINE_SMOOTH

If enabled, draw lines with correct filtering. Otherwise, draw aliased lines. See glLineWidth.

GL_MULTISAMPLE

If enabled, use multiple fragment samples in computing the final color of a pixel. See glSampleCoverage.

GL_POLYGON_OFFSET_FILL

If enabled, and if the polygon is rendered in GL_FILL mode, an offset is added to depth values of a polygon's fragments before the depth comparison is performed. See glPolygonOffset.

GL_POLYGON_OFFSET_LINE

If enabled, and if the polygon is rendered in GL_LINE mode, an offset is added to depth values of a polygon's fragments before the depth comparison is performed. See glPolygonOffset.

GL_POLYGON_OFFSET_POINT

If enabled, an offset is added to depth values of a polygon's fragments before the depth comparison is performed, if the polygon is rendered in GL_POINT mode. See glPolygonOffset.

GL_POLYGON_SMOOTH

If enabled, draw polygons with proper filtering. Otherwise, draw aliased polygons. For correct antialiased polygons, an alpha buffer is needed and the polygons must be sorted front to back.

GL_PRIMITIVE_RESTART

Enables primitive restarting. If enabled, any one of the draw commands which transfers a set of generic attribute array elements to the GL will restart the primitive when the index of the vertex is equal to the primitive restart index. See glPrimitiveRestartIndex.

GL_SAMPLE_ALPHA_TO_COVERAGE

> If enabled, compute a temporary coverage value where each bit is determined by the alpha value at the corresponding sample location. The temporary coverage value is then ANDed with the fragment coverage value.

GL_SAMPLE_ALPHA_TO_ONE

> If enabled, each sample alpha value is replaced by the maximum representable alpha value.

GL_SAMPLE_COVERAGE

> If enabled, the fragment's coverage is ANDed with the temporary coverage value. If GL_SAMPLE_COVERAGE_INVERT is set to GL_TRUE, invert the coverage value. See glSampleCoverage.

GL_SCISSOR_TEST

> If enabled, discard fragments that are outside the scissor rectangle. See glScissor.

GL_STENCIL_TEST

> If enabled, do stencil testing and update the stencil buffer. See glStencilFunc and glStencilOp.

GL_TEXTURE_CUBE_MAP_SEAMLESS

> If enabled, modifies the way sampling is performed on cube map textures. See the spec for more information.

GL_PROGRAM_POINT_SIZE

> If enabled and a vertex or geometry shader is active, then the derived point size is taken from the (potentially clipped) shader built in gl_PointSize and clamped to the implementation-dependent point size range.

Errors

GL_INVALID_ENUM is generated if *cap* is not one of the values listed previously.

GL_INVALID_VALUE is generated by `glEnablei` and `glDisablei` if *index* is greater than or equal to the number of indexed capabilities for *cap*.

Notes

GL_PRIMITIVE_RESTART is available only if the GL version is 3.1 or greater.

GL_TEXTURE_CUBE_MAP_SEAMLESS is available only if the GL version is 3.2 or greater.

Any token accepted by `glEnable` or `glDisable` is also accepted by `glEnablei` and `glDisablei`, but if the capability is not indexed, the maximum value that *index* may take is zero.

In general, passing an indexed capability to `glEnable` or `glDisable` will enable or disable that capability for all indices, resepectively.

Associated Gets

glIsEnabled
glGet

See Also

`glActiveTexture`, `glBlendFunc`, `glCullFace`, `glDepthFunc`, `glDepthRange`, `glGet`, `glIsEnabled`, `glLineWidth`, `glLogicOp`, `glPointSize`, `glPolygonMode`, `glPolygonOffset`, `glSampleCoverage`, `glScissor`, `glStencilFunc`, `glStencilOp`, `glTexImage1D`, `glTexImage2D`, `glTexImage3D`

Copyright

glEnableVertexAttribArray

Enable or disable a generic vertex attribute array

C Specification

```
void glEnableVertexAttribArray(GLuint index);
void glDisableVertexAttribArray(GLuint index);
```

Parameters

index

Specifies the index of the generic vertex attribute to be enabled or disabled.

Description

glEnableVertexAttribArray enables the generic vertex attribute array specified by *index*. glDisableVertexAttribArray disables the generic vertex attribute array specified by *index*. By default, all client-side capabilities are disabled, including all generic vertex attribute arrays. If enabled, the values in the generic vertex attribute array will be accessed and used for rendering when calls are made to vertex array commands such as glDrawArrays, glDrawElements, glDrawRangeElements, glMultiDrawElements, or glMultiDrawArrays.

Errors

GL_INVALID_VALUE is generated if *index* is greater than or equal to GL_MAX_VERTEX_ATTRIBS.

Associated Gets

glGet with argument GL_MAX_VERTEX_ATTRIBS
glGetVertexAttrib with arguments *index* and GL_VERTEX_ATTRIB_ARRAY_ENABLED
glGetVertexAttribPointerv with arguments *index* and GL_VERTEX_ATTRIB_ARRAY_POINTER

See Also

glBindAttribLocation, glDrawArrays, glDrawElements, glDrawRangeElements, glMultiDrawElements, glVertexAttrib, glVertexAttribPointer

Copyright

Copyright © 2003-2005 3Dlabs Inc. Ltd. This material may be distributed subject to the terms and conditions set forth in the Open Publication License, v 1.0, 8 June 1999. http://opencontent.org/openpub/.

glFenceSync

create a new sync object and insert it into the GL command stream

C Specification

```
GLsync glFenceSync(GLenum condition,
                   GLbitfield flags);
```

Parameters

condition

Specifies the condition that must be met to set the sync object's state to signaled. *condition* must be GL_SYNC_GPU_COMMANDS_COMPLETE.

flags

Specifies a bitwise combination of flags controlling the behavior of the sync object. No flags are presently defined for this operation and *flags* must be zero.˙

Description

glFenceSync creates a new fence sync object, inserts a fence command into the GL command stream and associates it with that sync object, and returns a non-zero name corresponding to the sync object.

When the specified *condition* of the sync object is satisfied by the fence command, the sync object is signaled by the GL, causing any glWaitSync, glClientWaitSync commands blocking in *sync* to *unblock*. No other state is affected by glFenceSync or by the execution of the associated fence command.

condition must be GL_SYNC_GPU_COMMANDS_COMPLETE. This condition is satisfied by completion of the fence command corresponding to the sync object and all preceding commands in the same command stream. The sync object will not be signaled until all effects from these commands on GL client and server state and the framebuffer are fully realized. Note that completion of the fence command occurs once the state of the corresponding sync object has been changed, but commands waiting on that sync object may not be unblocked until after the fence command completes.

Notes

glFenceSync is only supported if the GL version is 3.2 or greater, or if the ARB_sync extension is supported.

Errors

GL_INVALID_ENUM is generated if *condition* is not GL_SYNC_GPU_COMMANDS_COMPLETE.
GL_INVALID_VALUE is generated if *flags* is not zero.
Additionally, if glFenceSync fails, it will return zero.

See Also

glDeleteSync, glGetSync, glWaitSync, glClientWaitSync

Copyright

glFinish

block until all GL execution is complete

C Specification

void glFinish(*void*);

Description

glFinish does not return until the effects of all previously called GL commands are complete. Such effects include all changes to GL state, all changes to connection state, and all changes to the frame buffer contents.

˙ *flags is a placeholder for anticipated future extensions of fence sync object capabilities.*

754

Notes

glFinish requires a round trip to the server.

See Also

glFlush

Copyright

Copyright © 1991-2006 Silicon Graphics, Inc. This document is licensed under the SGI Free Software B License. For details, see http://oss.sgi.com/projects/FreeB/.

glFlush

force execution of GL commands in finite time

C Specification

void glFlush(*void*);

Description

Different GL implementations buffer commands in several different locations, including network buffers and the graphics accelerator itself. glFlush empties all of these buffers, causing all issued commands to be executed as quickly as they are accepted by the actual rendering engine. Though this execution may not be completed in any particular time period, it does complete in finite time.

Because any GL program might be executed over a network, or on an accelerator that buffers commands, all programs should call glFlush whenever they count on having all of their previously issued commands completed. For example, call glFlush before waiting for user input that depends on the generated image.

Notes

glFlush can return at any time. It does not wait until the execution of all previously issued GL commands is complete.

See Also

glFinish

Copyright

Copyright © 1991-2006 Silicon Graphics, Inc. This document is licensed under the SGI Free Software B License. For details, see http://oss.sgi.com/projects/FreeB/.

glFlushMappedBufferRange

indicate modifications to a range of a mapped buffer

C Specification

GLsync glFlushMappedBufferRange(GLenum *target*,
                                GLintptr *offset*,
                                GLsizeiptr *length*);

Parameters

target

> Specifies the target of the flush operation. *target* must be GL_ARRAY_BUFFER, GL_COPY_READ_BUFFER, GL_COPY_WRITE_BUFFER, GL_ELEMENT_ARRAY_BUFFER, GL_PIXEL_PACK_BUFFER, GL_PIXEL_UNPACK_BUFFER, GL_TEXTURE_BUFFER, GL_TRANSFORM_FEEDBACK_BUFFER, or GL_UNIFORM_BUFFER.

offset

> Specifies the start of the buffer subrange, in basic machine units.

length

> Specifies the length of the buffer subrange, in basic machine units.

Description

glFlushMappedBufferRange indicates that modifications have been made to a range of a mapped buffer. The buffer must previously have been mapped with the GL_MAP_FLUSH_EXPLICIT flag. *offset* and *length* indicate the modified subrange of the mapping, in basic units. The specified subrange to flush is relative to the start of the currently mapped range of the buffer. glFlushMappedBufferRange may be called multiple times to indicate distinct subranges of the mapping which require flushing.

Errors

GL_INVALID_VALUE is generated if *offset* or *length* is negative, or if *offset* + *length* exceeds the size of the mapping.

GL_INVALID_OPERATION is generated if zero is bound to *target*.

GL_INVALID_OPERATION is generated if the buffer bound to *target* is not mapped, or is mapped without the GL_MAP_FLUSH_EXPLICIT flag.

See Also

glMapBufferRange, glMapBuffer, glUnmapBuffer

Copyright

Copyright © 2010 Khronos Group. This material may be distributed subject to the terms and conditions set forth in the Open Publication License, v 1.0, 8 June 1999. http://opencontent.org/openpub/.

glFramebufferRenderbuffer

attach a renderbuffer as a logical buffer to the currently bound framebuffer object

C Specification

```
GLsync glFramebufferRenderbuffer(GLenum target,
                                 GLenum attachment,
                                 GLenum renderbuffertarget,
                                 GLuint renderbuffer);
```

Parameters

target

> Specifies the framebuffer target. *target* must be GL_DRAW_FRAMEBUFFER, GL_READ_FRAMEBUFFER, or GL_FRAMEBUFFER. GL_FRAMEBUFFER is equivalent to GL_DRAW_FRAMEBUFFER.

attachment

> Specifies the attachment point of the framebuffer.

renderbuffertarget
>   Specifies the renderbuffer target and must be GL_RENDERBUFFER.

renderbuffer
>   Specifies the name of an existing renderbuffer object of type *renderbuffertarget* to attach.

Description

>   glFramebufferRenderbuffer attaches a renderbuffer as one of the logical buffers of the currently bound framebuffer object. *renderbuffer* is the name of the renderbuffer object to attach and must be either zero, or the name of an existing renderbuffer object of type *renderbuffertarget*. If *renderbuffer* is not zero and if glFramebufferRenderbuffer is successful, then the renderbuffer name *renderbuffer* will be used as the logical buffer identified by *attachment* of the framebuffer currently bound to *target*.

>   The value of GL_FRAMEBUFFER_ATTACHMENT_OBJECT_TYPE for the specified attachment point is set to GL_RENDERBUFFER and the value of GL_FRAMEBUFFER_ATTACHMENT_OBJECT_NAME is set to *renderbuffer*. All other state values of the attachment point specified by *attachment* are set to their default values. No change is made to the state of the renderbuuffer object and any previous attachment to the *attachment* logical buffer of the framebuffer *target* is broken.

>   Calling glFramebufferRenderbuffer with the renderbuffer name zero will detach the image, if any, identified by *attachment*, in the framebuffer currently bound to *target*. All state values of the attachment point specified by attachment in the object bound to target are set to their default values.

>   Setting *attachment* to the value GL_DEPTH_STENCIL_ATTACHMENT is a special case causing both the depth and stencil attachments of the framebuffer object to be set to *renderbuffer*, which should have the base internal format GL_DEPTH_STENCIL.

Errors

>   GL_INVALID_ENUM is generated if *target* is not one of the accepted tokens.
>   GL_INVALID_ENUM is generated if *renderbuffertarget* is not GL_RENDERBUFFER.
>   GL_INVALID_OPERATION is generated if zero is bound to *target*.

See Also

>   glGenFramebuffers, glBindFramebuffer, glGenRenderbuffers, glFramebufferTexture, glFramebufferTexture1D, glFramebufferTexture2D, glFramebufferTexture3D

Copyright

glFramebufferTexture

>   attach a level of a texture object as a logical buffer to the currently bound framebuffer object

C Specification

```
void glFramebufferTexture(GLenum target,
                          GLenum attachment,
                          GLuint texture,
                          GLint level);
void glFramebufferTexture1D(GLenum target,
                            GLenum attachment,
                            GLuint texture,
                            GLint level);
```

```
void glFramebufferTexture2D(GLenum target,
                            GLenum attachment,
                            GLuint texture,
                            GLint level);
void glFramebufferTexture3D(GLenum target,
                            GLenum attachment,
                            GLuint texture,
                            GLint level,
                            GLint layer);
```

Parameters

target

> Specifies the framebuffer target. *target* must be GL_DRAW_FRAMEBUFFER, GL_READ_FRAMEBUFFER, or GL_FRAMEBUFFER. GL_FRAMEBUFFER is equivalent to GL_DRAW_FRAMEBUFFER.

attachment

> Specifies the attachment point of the framebuffer. *attachment* must be GL_COLOR_ATTACHMENT*i*, GL_DEPTH_ATTACHMENT, GL_STENCIL_ATTACHMENT or GL_DEPTH_STENCIL_ATTACHMMENT.

texture

> Specifies the texture object to attach to the framebuffer attachment point named by *attachment*.

level

> Specifies the mipmap level of *texture* to attach.

Description

glFramebufferTexture, glFramebufferTexture1D, glFramebufferTexture2D, and glFramebufferTexture attach a selected mipmap level or image of a texture object as one of the logical buffers of the framebuffer object currently bound to *target*. *target* must be GL_DRAW_FRAMEBUFFER, GL_READ_FRAMEBUFFER, or GL_FRAMEBUFFER. GL_FRAMEBUFFER is equivalent to GL_DRAW_FRAMEBUFFER.

attachment specifies the logical attachment of the framebuffer and must be GL_COLOR_ATTACHMENT*i*, GL_DEPTH_ATTACHMENT, GL_STENCIL_ATTACHMENT or GL_DEPTH_STENCIL_ATTACHMMENT. *i* in GL_COLOR_ATTACHMENT*i* may range from zero to the value of GL_MAX_COLOR_ATTACHMENTS - 1. Attaching a level of a texture to GL_DEPTH_STENCIL_ATTACHMENT is equivalent to attaching that level to both the GL_DEPTH_ATTACHMENT *and* the GL_STENCIL_ATTACHMENT attachment points simultaneously.

If *texture* is non-zero, the specified *level* of the texture object named *texture* is attached to the framebfufer attachment point named by *attachment*. For glFramebufferTexture1D, glFramebufferTexture2D, and glFramebufferTexture3D, *texture* must be zero or the name of an existing texture with a target of *textarget*, or *texture* must be the name of an existing cube-map texture and *textarget* must be one of GL_TEXTURE_CUBE_MAP_POSITIVE_X, GL_TEXTURE_CUBE_MAP_POSITIVE_Y, GL_TEXTURE_CUBE_MAP_POSITIVE_Z, GL_TEXTURE_CUBE_MAP_NEGATIVE_X, GL_TEXTURE_CUBE_MAP_NEGATIVE_Y, or GL_TEXTURE_CUBE_MAP_NEGATIVE_Z.

If *textarget* is GL_TEXTURE_RECTANGLE, GL_TEXTURE_2D_MULTISAMPLE, or GL_TEXTURE_2D_MULTISAMPLE_ARRAY, then *level* must be zero. If *textarget* is GL_TEXTURE_3D, then level must be greater than or equal to zero and less than or equal to $\log_2$ of the value of GL_MAX_3D_TEXTURE_SIZE. If *textarget* is one of GL_TEXTURE_CUBE_MAP_POSITIVE_X, GL_TEXTURE_CUBE_MAP_POSITIVE_Y, GL_TEXTURE_CUBE_MAP_POSITIVE_Z, GL_TEXTURE_CUBE_MAP_NEGATIVE_X, GL_TEXTURE_CUBE_MAP_NEGATIVE_Y, or GL_TEXTURE_CUBE_MAP_NEGATIVE_Z, then *level* must be greater than or equal to zero and less than or equal to $\log_2$ of the value of GL_MAX_CUBE_MAP_TEXTURE_SIZE. For all other values of *textarget*, *level* must be greater than or equal to zero and no larger than log₂ of the value of GL_MAX_TEXTURE_SIZE.

layer specifies the layer of a 2-dimensional image within a 3-dimensional texture.

For glFramebufferTexture1D, if *texture* is not zero, then *textarget* must be GL_TEXTURE_1D. For glFramebufferTexture2D, if *texture* is not zero, *textarget* must be one of GL_TEXTURE_2D, GL_TEXTURE_RECTANGLE, GL_TEXTURE_CUBE_MAP_POSITIVE_X, GL_TEXTURE_CUBE_MAP_POSITIVE_Y, GL_TEXTURE_CUBE_MAP_POSITIVE_Z, GL_TEXTURE_CUBE_MAP_NEGATIVE_X, GL_TEXTURE_CUBE_MAP_NEGATIVE_Y, GL_TEXTURE_CUBE_MAP_NEGATIVE_Z, or GL_TEXTURE_2D_MULTISAMPLE. For glFramebufferTexture3D, if *texture* is not zero, then *textarget* must be GL_TEXTURE_3D.

Notes

glFramebufferTexture is available only if the GL version is 3.2 or greater.

Errors

GL_INVALID_ENUM is generated if *target* is not one of the accepted tokens.
GL_INVALID_ENUM is generated if *renderbuffertarget* is not GL_RENDERBUFFER.
GL_INVALID_OPERATION is generated if zero is bound to *target*.

See Also

glGenFramebuffers, glBindFramebuffer, glGenRenderbuffers, glFramebufferTexture, glFramebufferTexture1D, glFramebufferTexture2D, glFramebufferTexture3D

Copyright

Copyright © 2010 Khronos Group. This material may be distributed subject to the terms and conditions set forth in the Open Publication License, v 1.0, 8 June 1999. http://opencontent.org/openpub/.

glFramebufferTextureFace

attach a face of a cube map texture as a logical buffer to the currently bound framebuffer

C Specification

```
void glFramebufferTextureFace(GLenum target,
                              GLenum attachment,
                              GLuint texture,
                              GLint level,
                              GLenum face);
```

Parameters

target
>Specifies the framebuffer target. *target* must be GL_DRAW_FRAMEBUFFER, GL_READ_FRAMEBUFFER, or GL_FRAMEBUFFER. GL_FRAMEBUFFER is equivalent to GL_DRAW_FRAMEBUFFER.

attachment
>Specifies the attachment point of the framebuffer. *attachment* must be GL_COLOR_ATTACHMENT*i*, GL_DEPTH_ATTACHMENT, GL_STENCIL_ATTACHMENT or GL_DEPTH_STENCIL_ATTACHMMENT.

texture
>Specifies the texture object to attach to the framebuffer attachment point named by *attachment*. *texture* must be the name of an existing cube-map texture.

level

    Specifies the mipmap level of *texture* to attach.

face

    Specifies the face of *texture* to attach.

Description

glFramebufferTextureFace operates like glFramebufferTexture, except that only a single face of a cube map texture, given by *face*, is attached to the attachment point. *face* must be GL_TEXTURE_CUBE_MAP_POSITIVE_X, GL_TEXTURE_CUBE_MAP_POSITIVE_Y, GL_TEXTURE_CUBE_MAP_POSITIVE_Z, GL_TEXTURE_CUBE_MAP_NEGATIVE_X, GL_TEXTURE_CUBE_MAP_NEGATIVE_Y, or GL_TEXTURE_CUBE_MAP_NEGATIVE_Z. *texture* must either be zero, or the name of an existing cube map texture.

Errors

GL_INVALID_ENUM is generated if *target* is not one of the accepted tokens.

GL_INVALID_ENUM is generated if *attachment* is not one of the accepted tokens.

GL_INVALID_ENUM is generated if *face* is not one of the accepted tokens.

GL_INVALID_OPERATION is generated if zero is bound to *target*.

GL_INVALID_OPERATION is generated if *texture* is not zero or the name of an existing cube map texture.

See Also

glGenFramebuffers, glBindFramebuffer, glGenRenderbuffers, glFramebufferTexture, glFramebufferTextureLayer

Copyright

Copyright © 2010 Khronos Group. This material may be distributed subject to the terms and conditions set forth in the Open Publication License, v 1.0, 8 June 1999. http://opencontent.org/openpub/.

glFramebufferTextureLayer

attach a face of a cube map texture as a logical buffer to the currently bound framebuffer

C Specification

```
void glFramebufferTextureLayer(GLenum target,
                               GLenum attachment,
                               GLuint texture,
                               GLint level,
                               GLint layer);
```

Parameters

target

    Specifies the framebuffer target. *target* must be GL_DRAW_FRAMEBUFFER, GL_READ_FRAMEBUFFER, or GL_FRAMEBUFFER. GL_FRAMEBUFFER is equivalent to GL_DRAW_FRAMEBUFFER.

attachment

    Specifies the attachment point of the framebuffer. *attachment* must be GL_COLOR_ATTACHMENT*i*, GL_DEPTH_ATTACHMENT, GL_STENCIL_ATTACHMENT or GL_DEPTH_STENCIL_ATTACHMMENT.

texture

    Specifies the texture object to attach to the framebuffer attachment point named by *attachment*.

level

Specifies the mipmap level of *texture* to attach.

layer

Specifies the level of *texture* to attach.

Description

glFramebufferTextureLevel operates like glFramebufferTexture, except that only a single layer of the texture level, given by *layer*, is attached to the attachment point. If *texture* is not zero, *layer* must be greater than or equal to zero. *texture* must either be zero or the name of an existing three-dimensional two-dimensional array texture.

Notes

glFramebufferTextureLayer is available only if the GL version is 3.2 or greater.

Errors

GL_INVALID_ENUM is generated if *target* is not one of the accepted tokens.

GL_INVALID_ENUM is generated if *attachment* is not one of the accepted tokens.

GL_INVALID_VALUE is generated if *texture* is not zero or the name of an existing texture object.

GL_INVALID_VALUE is generated if *texture* is not zero and *layer* is negative.

GL_INVALID_OPERATION is generated if zero is bound to *target*.

GL_INVALID_OPERATION is generated if *texture* is not zero or the name of an existing cube map texture.

See Also

glGenFramebuffers, glBindFramebuffer, glGenRenderbuffers, glFramebufferTexture, glFramebufferTextureFace

Copyright

Copyright © 2010 Khronos Group. This material may be distributed subject to the terms and conditions set forth in the Open Publication License, v 1.0, 8 June 1999. http://opencontent.org/openpub/.

glFrontFace

define front- and back-facing polygons

C Specification

void glFrontFace(GLenum *mode*);

Parameters

mode

Specifies the orientation of front-facing polygons. GL_CW and GL_CCW are accepted. The initial value is GL_CCW.

Description

In a scene composed entirely of opaque closed surfaces, back-facing polygons are never visible. Eliminating these invisible polygons has the obvious benefit of speeding up the rendering of the image. To enable and disable elimination of back-facing polygons, call glEnable and glDisable with argument GL_CULL_FACE.

The projection of a polygon to window coordinates is said to have clockwise winding if an imaginary object following the path from its first vertex, its second vertex, and so on, to its last vertex, and finally back to its first vertex, moves in a clockwise direction about the interior of the polygon. The polygon's winding is said to be counterclockwise if the imaginary object following the same path moves in a counterclockwise direction about the interior of the polygon. glFrontFace specifies whether polygons with clockwise winding in window coordinates, or counterclockwise winding in window coordinates, are taken to be front-facing. Passing GL_CCW to *mode* selects counterclockwise polygons as front-facing; GL_CW selects clockwise polygons as front-facing. By default, counterclockwise polygons are taken to be front-facing.

Errors

GL_INVALID_ENUM is generated if *mode* is not an accepted value.

Associated Gets

glGet with argument GL_FRONT_FACE

See Also

glCullFace.

Copyright

Copyright © 1991-2006 Silicon Graphics, Inc. This document is licensed under the SGI Free Software B License. For details, see http://oss.sgi.com/projects/FreeB/.

glGenBuffers

generate buffer object names

C Specification

```
void glGenBuffers(GLsizei n,
                  GLuint * buffers);
```

Parameters

n
> Specifies the number of buffer object names to be generated.

buffers
> Specifies an array in which the generated buffer object names are stored.

Description

glGenBuffers returns *n* buffer object names in *buffers*. There is no guarantee that the names form a contiguous set of integers; however, it is guaranteed that none of the returned names was in use immediately before the call to glGenBuffers.

Buffer object names returned by a call to glGenBuffers are not returned by subsequent calls, unless they are first deleted with glDeleteBuffers.

No buffer objects are associated with the returned buffer object names until they are first bound by calling glBindBuffer.

Errors

GL_INVALID_VALUE is generated if *n* is negative.

Associated Gets

glIsBuffer

    glBindBuffer, glDeleteBuffers, glGet

Copyright

Copyright © 2005 Addison-Wesley. This material may be distributed subject to the terms and conditions set forth in the Open Publication License, v 1.0, 8 June 1999. http://opencontent.org/openpub/.

glGenerateMipmap

generate mipmaps for a specified texture target

C Specification

    void glGenerateMipmap(GLenum target);

Parameters

target

> Specifies the target to which the texture whose mimaps to generate is bound. *target* must be GL_TEXTURE_1D, GL_TEXTURE_2D, GL_TEXTURE_3D, GL_TEXTURE_1D_ARRAY, GL_TEXTURE_2D_ARRAY or GL_TEXTURE_CUBE_MAP.

Description

glGenerateMipmap generates mipmaps for the texture attached to *target* of the active texture unit. For cube map textures, a GL_INVALID_OPERATION error is generated if the texture attached to *target* is not cube complete.

Mipmap generation replaces texel array levels $level_{base}$ + 1 through q with arrays derived from the $level_{base}$ array, regardless of their previous contents. All other mipmap arrays, including the $level_{base}$ array, are left unchanged by this computation.

The internal formats of the derived mipmap arrays all match those of the $level_{base}$ array. The contents of the derived arrays are computed by repeated, filtered reduction of the $level_{base}$ array. For one- and two-dimensional texture arrays, each layer is filtered independently.

Errors

GL_INVALID_ENUM is generated if *target* is not one of the accepted texture targets.

GL_INVALID_OPERATION is generated if *target* is GL_TEXTURE_CUBE_MAP and the texture bound to the GL_TEXTURE_CUBE_MAP target of the active texture unit is not cube complete.

See Also

    glTexImage2D, glBindTexture, glGenTextures

Copyright

Copyright © 2010 Khronos Group. This material may be distributed subject to the terms and conditions set forth in the Open Publication License, v 1.0, 8 June 1999. http://opencontent.org/openpub/.

glGenFramebuffers

generate framebuffer object names

C Specification

    void glGenFramebuffers(GLsizei *n*,
                           GLuint *ids*);

Parameters

n

Specifies the number of framebuffer object names to generate.

ids

Specifies an array in which the generated framebuffer object names are stored.

Description

`glGenFramebuffers` returns *n* framebuffer object names in *ids*. There is no guarantee that the names form a contiguous set of integers; however, it is guaranteed that none of the returned names was in use immediately before the call to `glGenFramebuffers`.

Framebuffer object names returned by a call to `glGenFramebuffers` are not returned by subsequent calls, unless they are first deleted with glDeleteFramebuffers.

The names returned in *ids* are marked as used, for the purposes of `glGenFramebuffers` only, but they acquire state and type only when they are first bound.

Errors

GL_INVALID_VALUE is generated if *n* is negative.

See Also

`glBindFramebuffer, glDeleteFramebuffers`

Copyright

Copyright © 2010 Khronos Group. This material may be distributed subject to the terms and conditions set forth in the Open Publication License, v 1.0, 8 June 1999. http://opencontent.org/openpub/.

glGenQueries

generate query object names

C Specification

```
void glGenQueries(GLsizei n,
                  GLuint * ids);
```

Parameters

n

Specifies the number of query object names to be generated.

ids

Specifies an array in which the generated query object names are stored.

Description

`glGenQueries` returns *n* query object names in *ids*. There is no guarantee that the names form a contiguous set of integers; however, it is guaranteed that none of the returned names was in use immediately before the call to `glGenQueries`.

Query object names returned by a call to `glGenQueries` are not returned by subsequent calls, unless they are first deleted with glDeleteQueries.

No query objects are associated with the returned query object names until they are first used by calling glBeginQuery.

Errors

GL_INVALID_VALUE is generated if *n* is negative.

GL_INVALID_OPERATION is generated if `glGenQueries` is executed between the execution of glBeginQuery and the corresponding execution of glEndQuery.

Associated Gets

glIsQuery

See Also

`glBeginQuery, glDeleteQueries, glEndQuery`

Copyright

Copyright © 2005 Addison-Wesley. This material may be distributed subject to the terms and conditions set forth in the Open Publication License, v 1.0, 8 June 1999. http://opencontent.org/openpub/.

glGenRenderbuffers

generate renderbuffer object names

C Specification

```
void glGenRenderbuffers(GLsizei n,
                        GLuint *renderbuffers);
```

Parameters

n
Specifies the number of renderbuffer object names to generate.
renderbuffers
Specifies an array in which the generated renderbuffer object names are stored.

Description

`glGenRenderbuffers` returns *n* renderbuffer object names in *renderbuffers*. There is no guarantee that the names form a contiguous set of integers; however, it is guaranteed that none of the returned names was in use immediately before the call to `glGenRenderbuffers`.

Renderbuffer object names returned by a call to `glGenRenderbuffers` are not returned by subsequent calls, unless they are first deleted with glDeleteRenderbuffers.

The names returned in *renderbuffers* are marked as used, for the purposes of `glGenRenderbuffers` only, but they acquire state and type only when they are first bound.

Errors

GL_INVALID_VALUE is generated if *n* is negative.

See Also

`glFramebufferRenderbuffer, glDeleteRenderbuffers`

Copyright

Copyright © 2010 Khronos Group. This material may be distributed subject to the terms and conditions set forth in the Open Publication License, v 1.0, 8 June 1999. http://opencontent.org/openpub/.

glGenSamplers

generate sampler object names

C Specification

```
void glGenSamplers(GLsizei n,
                   GLuint *samplers);
```

Parameters

n

        Specifies the number of sampler object names to generate.

samplers

        Specifies an array in which the generated sampler object names are stored.

Description

glGenSamplers returns *n* sampler object names in *samplers*. There is no guarantee that the names form a contiguous set of integers; however, it is guaranteed that none of the returned names was in use immediately before the call to glGenSamplers.

Sampler object names returned by a call to glGenSamplers are not returned by subsequent calls, unless they are first deleted with glDeleteSamplers.

The names returned in *samplers* are marked as used, for the purposes of glGenSamplers only, but they acquire state and type only when they are first bound.

Notes

glGenSamplers is available only if the GL version is 3.3 or higher.

Errors

GL_INVALID_VALUE is generated if *n* is negative.

See Also

glBindSampler, glIsSampler, glDeleteSamplers

Copyright

glGenTextures

generate texture names

C Specification

```
void glGenTextures(GLsizei n,
                   GLuint * textures);
```

Parameters

n

        Specifies the number of texture names to be generated.

textures

        Specifies an array in which the generated texture names are stored.

Description

glGenTextures returns *n* texture names in *textures*. There is no guarantee that the names form a contiguous set of integers; however, it is guaranteed that none of the returned names was in use immediately before the call to glGenTextures.

The generated textures have no dimensionality; they assume the dimensionality of the texture target to which they are first bound (see glBindTexture).

Texture names returned by a call to glGenTextures are not returned by subsequent calls, unless they are first deleted with glDeleteTextures.

Errors

GL_INVALID_VALUE is generated if *n* is negative.

Associated Gets

glIsTexture

See Also

glBindTexture, glCopyTexImage1D, glCopyTexImage2D, glDeleteTextures, glGet, glGetTexParameter, glTexImage1D, glTexImage2D, glTexImage3D, glTexParameter

Copyright

glGenVertexArrays

generate vertex array object names

C Specification

```
void glGenVertexArrays(GLsizei n,
                       GLuint *arrays);
```

Parameters

n

Specifies the number of vertex array object names to generate.

arrays

Specifies an array in which the generated vertex array object names are stored.

Description

glGenVertexArrays returns *n* vertex array object names in *arrays*. There is no guarantee that the names form a contiguous set of integers; however, it is guaranteed that none of the returned names was in use immediately before the call to glGenVertexArrays.

Vertex array object names returned by a call to glGenVertexArrays are not returned by subsequent calls, unless they are first deleted with glDeleteVertexArrays.

The names returned in *arrays* are marked as used, for the purposes of glGenVertexArrays only, but they acquire state and type only when they are first bound.

Errors

GL_INVALID_VALUE is generated if *n* is negative.

See Also

glBindVertexArray, glDeleteVertexArrays

Copyright

glGet

return the value or values of a selected parameter

C Specification

```
void glGetBooleanv(GLenum pname,
                   GLboolean * params);
```

C Specification

```
void glGetDoublev(GLenum pname,
                  GLdouble * params);
```

C Specification

```
void glGetFloatv(GLenum pname,
                 GLfloat * params);
```

C Specification

```
void glGetIntegerv(GLenum pname,
                   GLint * params);
```

C Specification

```
void glGetInteger64v(GLenum pname,
                     GLint64 * params);
```

Parameters

pname

Specifies the parameter value to be returned. The symbolic constants in the list below are accepted.

params

Returns the value or values of the specified parameter.

C Specification

```
void glGetBooleani_v(GLenum pname,
                     GLuint index,
                     GLboolean * data);
```

C Specification

```
void glGetIntegeri_v(GLenum pname,
                     GLuint index,
                     GLint * data);
```

C Specification

```
void glGetInteger64i_v(GLenum pname,
                       GLuint index,
                       GLint64 * data);
```

Parameters

pname

Specifies the parameter value to be returned. The symbolic constants in the list below are accepted.

index

Specifies the index of the particular element being queried.

data

Returns the value or values of the specified parameter.

Description

These four commands return values for simple state variables in GL. *pname* is a symbolic constant indicating the state variable to be returned, and *params* is a pointer to an array of the indicated type in which to place the returned data.

Type conversion is performed if *params* has a different type than the state variable value being requested. If glGetBooleanv is called, a floating-point (or integer) value is converted to GL_FALSE if and only if it is 0.0 (or 0). Otherwise, it is converted to GL_TRUE. If glGetIntegerv is called, boolean values are returned as GL_TRUE or GL_FALSE, and most floating-point values are rounded to the nearest integer value. Floating-point colors and normals, however, are returned with a linear mapping that maps 1.0 to the most positive representable integer value and -1.0 to the most negative representable integer value. If glGetFloatv or glGetDoublev is called, boolean values are returned as GL_TRUE or GL_FALSE, and integer values are converted to floating-point values.

The following symbolic constants are accepted by *pname*:

GL_ACTIVE_TEXTURE

params returns a single value indicating the active multitexture unit. The initial value is GL_TEXTURE0. See glActiveTexture.

GL_ALIASED_LINE_WIDTH_RANGE

params returns a pair of values indicating the range of widths supported for aliased lines. See glLineWidth.

GL_SMOOTH_LINE_WIDTH_RANGE

params returns a pair of values indicating the range of widths supported for smooth (antialiased) lines. See glLineWidth.

GL_SMOOTH_LINE_WIDTH_GRANULARITY

params returns a single value indicating the level of quantization applied to smooth line width parameters.

GL_ARRAY_BUFFER_BINDING

params returns a single value, the name of the buffer object currently bound to the target GL_ARRAY_BUFFER. If no buffer object is bound to this target, 0 is returned. The initial value is 0. See glBindBuffer.

GL_BLEND

params returns a single boolean value indicating whether blending is enabled. The initial value is GL_FALSE. See glBlendFunc.

GL_BLEND_COLOR

params returns four values—the red, green, blue, and alpha values—which are the components of the blend color. See glBlendColor.

GL_BLEND_DST_ALPHA

params returns one value, the symbolic constant identifying the alpha destination blend function. The initial value is GL_ZERO. See glBlendFunc and glBlendFuncSeparate.

GL_BLEND_DST_RGB

params returns one value, the symbolic constant identifying the RGB destination blend function. The initial value is GL_ZERO. See glBlendFunc and glBlendFuncSeparate.

GL_BLEND_EQUATION_RGB

>*params* returns one value, a symbolic constant indicating whether the RGB blend equa-
tion is GL_FUNC_ADD, GL_FUNC_SUBTRACT, GL_FUNC_REVERSE_SUBTRACT, GL_MIN
or GL_MAX. See glBlendEquationSeparate.

GL_BLEND_EQUATION_ALPHA

>*params* returns one value, a symbolic constant indicating whether the Alpha blend equa-
tion is GL_FUNC_ADD, GL_FUNC_SUBTRACT, GL_FUNC_REVERSE_SUBTRACT, GL_MIN
or GL_MAX. See glBlendEquationSeparate.

GL_BLEND_SRC_ALPHA

>*params* returns one value, the symbolic constant identifying the alpha source blend
function. The initial value is GL_ONE. See glBlendFunc and glBlendFuncSeparate.

GL_BLEND_SRC_RGB

>*params* returns one value, the symbolic constant identifying the RGB source blend func-
tion. The initial value is GL_ONE. See glBlendFunc and glBlendFuncSeparate.

GL_COLOR_CLEAR_VALUE

>*params* returns four values: the red, green, blue, and alpha values used to clear the color
buffers. Integer values, if requested, are linearly mapped from the internal floating-point
representation such that 1.0 returns the most positive representable integer value, and
-1.0 returns the most negative representable integer value. The initial value is (0, 0, 0,
0). See glClearColor.

GL_COLOR_LOGIC_OP

>*params* returns a single boolean value indicating whether a fragment's RGBA color values
are merged into the framebuffer using a logical operation. The initial value is GL_FALSE.
See glLogicOp.

GL_COLOR_WRITEMASK

>*params* returns four boolean values: the red, green, blue, and alpha write enables for the
color buffers. The initial value is (GL_TRUE, GL_TRUE, GL_TRUE, GL_TRUE). See
glColorMask.

GL_COMPRESSED_TEXTURE_FORMATS

>*params* returns a list of symbolic constants of length
GL_NUM_COMPRESSED_TEXTURE_FORMATS indicating which compressed texture
formats are available. See glCompressedTexImage2D.

GL_CULL_FACE

>*params* returns a single boolean value indicating whether polygon culling is enabled.
The initial value is GL_FALSE. See glCullFace.

GL_CURRENT_PROGRAM

>*params* returns one value, the name of the program object that is currently active, or 0 if
no program object is active. See glUseProgram.

GL_DEPTH_CLEAR_VALUE

>*params* returns one value, the value that is used to clear the depth buffer. Integer values,
if requested, are linearly mapped from the internal floating-point representation such
that 1.0 returns the most positive representable integer value, and -1.0 returns the most
negative representable integer value. The initial value is 1. See glClearDepth.

GL_DEPTH_FUNC

>*params* returns one value, the symbolic constant that indicates the depth comparison
function. The initial value is GL_LESS. See glDepthFunc.

GL_DEPTH_RANGE

>*params* returns two values: the near and far mapping limits for the depth buffer. Integer
values, if requested, are linearly mapped from the internal floating-point representation
such that 1.0 returns the most positive representable integer value, and -1.0 returns the
most negative representable integer value. The initial value is (0, 1). See glDepthRange.

GL_DEPTH_TEST

>*params* returns a single boolean value indicating whether depth testing of fragments is
enabled. The initial value is GL_FALSE. See glDepthFunc and glDepthRange.

GL_DEPTH_WRITEMASK
> *params* returns a single boolean value indicating if the depth buffer is enabled for writing. The initial value is GL_TRUE. See glDepthMask.

GL_DITHER
> *params* returns a single boolean value indicating whether dithering of fragment colors and indices is enabled. The initial value is GL_TRUE.

GL_DOUBLEBUFFER
> *params* returns a single boolean value indicating whether double buffering is supported.

GL_DRAW_BUFFER
> *params* returns one value, a symbolic constant indicating which buffers are being drawn to. See glDrawBuffer. The initial value is GL_BACK if there are back buffers, otherwise it is GL_FRONT.

GL_DRAW_BUFFER*i*
> *params* returns one value, a symbolic constant indicating which buffers are being drawn to by the corresponding output color. See glDrawBuffers. The initial value of GL_DRAW_BUFFER0 is GL_BACK if there are back buffers, otherwise it is GL_FRONT. The initial values of draw buffers for all other output colors is GL_NONE.

GL_DRAW_FRAMEBUFFER_BINDING
> *params* returns one value, the name of the framebuffer object currently bound to the GL_DRAW_FRAMEBUFFER target. If the default framebuffer is bound, this value will be zero. The initial value is zero. See glBindFramebuffer.

GL_READ_FRAMEBUFFER_BINDING
> *params* returns one value, the name of the framebuffer object currently bound to the GL_READ_FRAMEBUFFER target. If the default framebuffer is bound, this value will be zero. The initial value is zero. See glBindFramebuffer.

GL_ELEMENT_ARRAY_BUFFER_BINDING
> *params* returns a single value, the name of the buffer object currently bound to the target GL_ELEMENT_ARRAY_BUFFER. If no buffer object is bound to this target, 0 is returned. The initial value is 0. See glBindBuffer.

GL_RENDERBUFFER_BINDING
> *params* returns a single value, the name of the renderbuffer object currently bound to the target GL_RENDERBUFFER. If no renderbuffer object is bound to this target, 0 is returned. The initial value is 0. See glBindRenderbuffer.

GL_FRAGMENT_SHADER_DERIVATIVE_HINT
> *params* returns one value, a symbolic constant indicating the mode of the derivative accuracy hint for fragment shaders. The initial value is GL_DONT_CARE. See glHint.

GL_LINE_SMOOTH
> *params* returns a single boolean value indicating whether antialiasing of lines is enabled. The initial value is GL_FALSE. See glLineWidth.

GL_LINE_SMOOTH_HINT
> *params* returns one value, a symbolic constant indicating the mode of the line antialiasing hint. The initial value is GL_DONT_CARE. See glHint.

GL_LINE_WIDTH
> *params* returns one value, the line width as specified with glLineWidth. The initial value is 1.

GL_LINE_WIDTH_GRANULARITY
> *params* returns one value, the width difference between adjacent supported widths for antialiased lines. See glLineWidth.

GL_LINE_WIDTH_RANGE
> *params* returns two values: the smallest and largest supported widths for antialiased lines. See glLineWidth.

GL_LOGIC_OP_MODE
> *params* returns one value, a symbolic constant indicating the selected logic operation mode. The initial value is GL_COPY. See glLogicOp.

GL_MAX_3D_TEXTURE_SIZE
> *params* returns one value, a rough estimate of the largest 3D texture that the GL can handle. The value must be at least 64. Use GL_PROXY_TEXTURE_3D to determine if a texture is too large. See glTexImage3D.

GL_MAX_CLIP_DISTANCES
> *params* returns one value, the maximum number of application-defined clipping distances. The value must be at least 8.

GL_MAX_COMBINED_FRAGMENT_UNIFORM_COMPONENTS
> *params* returns one value, the number of words for fragment shader uniform variables in all uniform blocks (including default). The value must be at least 1. See glUniform.

GL_MAX_COMBINED_TEXTURE_IMAGE_UNITS
> *params* returns one value, the maximum supported texture image units that can be used to access texture maps from the vertex shader and the fragment processor combined. If both the vertex shader and the fragment processing stage access the same texture image unit, then that counts as using two texture image units against this limit. The value must be at least 48. See glActiveTexture.

GL_MAX_COMBINED_VERTEX_UNIFORM_COMPONENTS
> *params* returns one value, the number of words for vertex shader uniform variables in all uniform blocks (including default). The value must be at least 1. See glUniform.

GL_MAX_COMBINED_GEOMETRY_UNIFORM_COMPONENTS
> *params* returns one value, the number of words for geometry shader uniform variables in all uniform blocks (including default). The value must be at least 1. See glUniform.

GL_MAX_VARYING_COMPONENTS
> *params* returns one value, the number components for varying variables, which must be at least 60.

GL_MAX_COMBINED_UNIFORM_BLOCKS
> *params* returns one value, the maximum number of uniform blocks per program. The value must be at least 36. See glUniformBlockBinding.

GL_MAX_CUBE_MAP_TEXTURE_SIZE
> *params* returns one value. The value gives a rough estimate of the largest cube-map texture that the GL can handle. The value must be at least 1024. Use GL_PROXY_TEXTURE_CUBE_MAP to determine if a texture is too large. See glTexImage2D.

GL_MAX_DRAW_BUFFERS
> *params* returns one value, the maximum number of simultaneous outputs that may be written in a fragment shader. The value must be at least 8. See glDrawBuffers.

GL_MAX_DUALSOURCE_DRAW_BUFFERS
> *params* returns one value, the maximum number of active draw buffers when using dual-source blending. The value must be at least 1. See glBlendFunc and glBlendFuncSeparate.

GL_MAX_ELEMENTS_INDICES
> *params* returns one value, the recommended maximum number of vertex array indices. See glDrawRangeElements.

GL_MAX_ELEMENTS_VERTICES
> *params* returns one value, the recommended maximum number of vertex array vertices. See glDrawRangeElements.

GL_MAX_FRAGMENT_UNIFORM_COMPONENTS

params returns one value, the maximum number of individual floating-point, integer, or boolean values that can be held in uniform variable storage for a fragment shader. The value must be at least 1024. See glUniform.

GL_MAX_FRAGMENT_UNIFORM_BLOCKS

params returns one value, the maximum number of uniform blocks per fragment shader. The value must be at least 12. See glUniformBlockBinding.

GL_MAX_FRAGMENT_INPUT_COMPONENTS

params returns one value, the maximum number of components of the inputs read by the fragment shader, which must be at least 128.

GL_MIN_PROGRAM_TEXEL_OFFSET

params returns one value, the minimum texel offset allowed in a texture lookup, which must be at most -8.

GL_MAX_PROGRAM_TEXEL_OFFSET

params returns one value, the maximum texel offset allowed in a texture lookup, which must be at least 7.

GL_MAX_RECTANGLE_TEXTURE_SIZE

params returns one value. The value gives a rough estimate of the largest rectangular texture that the GL can handle. The value must be at least 1024. Use GL_PROXY_RECTANGLE_TEXTURE to determine if a texture is too large. See glTexImage2D.

GL_MAX_TEXTURE_IMAGE_UNITS

params returns one value, the maximum supported texture image units that can be used to access texture maps from the fragment shader. The value must be at least 16. See glActiveTexture.

GL_MAX_TEXTURE_LOD_BIAS

params returns one value, the maximum, absolute value of the texture level-of-detail bias. The value must be at least 2.0.

GL_MAX_TEXTURE_SIZE

params returns one value. The value gives a rough estimate of the largest texture that the GL can handle. The value must be at least 1024. Use a proxy texture target such as GL_PROXY_TEXTURE_1D or GL_PROXY_TEXTURE_2D to determine if a texture is too large. See glTexImage1D and glTexImage2D.

GL_MAX_RENDERBUFFER_SIZE

params returns one value. The value indicates the maximum supported size for render-buffers. See glFramebufferRenderbuffer.

GL_MAX_ARRAY_TEXTURE_LAYERS

params returns one value. The value indicates the maximum number of layers allowed in an array texture, and must be at least 256. See glTexImage2D.

GL_MAX_TEXTURE_BUFFER_SIZE

params returns one value. The value gives the maximum number of texels allowed in the texel array of a texture buffer object. Value must be at least 65536.

GL_MAX_UNIFORM_BLOCK_SIZE

params returns one value, the maximum size in basic machine units of a uniform block. The value must be at least 16384. See glUniformBlockBinding.

GL_MAX_VARYING_FLOATS

params returns one value, the maximum number of interpolators available for processing varying variables used by vertex and fragment shaders. This value represents the number of individual floating-point values that can be interpolated; varying variables declared as vectors, matrices, and arrays will all consume multiple interpolators. The value must be at least 32.

GL_MAX_VERTEX_ATTRIBS

>*params* returns one value, the maximum number of 4-component generic vertex attributes accessible to a vertex shader. The value must be at least 16. See glVertexAttrib.

GL_MAX_VERTEX_TEXTURE_IMAGE_UNITS

>*params* returns one value, the maximum supported texture image units that can be used to access texture maps from the vertex shader. The value may be at least 16. See glActiveTexture.

GL_MAX_GEOMETRY_TEXTURE_IMAGE_UNITS

>*params* returns one value, the maximum supported texture image units that can be used to access texture maps from the geometry shader. The value must be at least 16. See glActiveTexture.

GL_MAX_VERTEX_UNIFORM_COMPONENTS

>*params* returns one value, the maximum number of individual floating-point, integer, or boolean values that can be held in uniform variable storage for a vertex shader. The value must be at least 1024. See glUniform.

GL_MAX_VERTEX_OUTPUT_COMPONENTS

>*params* returns one value, the maximum number of components of output written by a vertex shader, which must be at least 64.

GL_MAX_GEOMETRY_UNIFORM_COMPONENTS

>*params* returns one value, the maximum number of individual floating-point, integer, or boolean values that can be held in uniform variable storage for a geometry shader. The value must be at least 1024. See glUniform.

GL_MAX_SAMPLE_MASK_WORDS

>*params* returns one value, the maximum number of sample mask words.

GL_MAX_COLOR_TEXTURE_SAMPLES

>*params* returns one value, the maximum number of samples in a color multisample texture.

GL_MAX_DEPTH_TEXTURE_SAMPLES

>*params* returns one value, the maximum number of samples in a multisample depth or depth-stencil texture.

GL_MAX_DEPTH_TEXTURE_SAMPLES

>*params* returns one value, the maximum number of samples in a multisample depth or depth-stencil texture.

GL_MAX_INTEGER_SAMPLES

>*params* returns one value, the maximum number of samples supported in integer format multisample buffers.

GL_MAX_SERVER_WAIT_TIMEOUT

>*params* returns one value, the maximum glWaitSync timeout interval.

GL_MAX_UNIFORM_BUFFER_BINDINGS

>*params* returns one value, the maximum number of uniform buffer binding points on the context, which must be at least 36.

GL_MAX_UNIFORM_BLOCK_SIZE

>*params* returns one value, the maximum size in basic machine units of a uniform block, which must be at least 16384.

GL_UNIFORM_BUFFER_OFFSET_ALIGNMENT

>*params* returns one value, the minimum required alignment for uniform buffer sizes and offsets.

GL_MAX_VERTEX_UNIFORM_BLOCKS

>*params* returns one value, the maximum number of uniform blocks per vertex shader. The value must be at least 12. See glUniformBlockBinding.

GL_MAX_GEOMETRY_UNIFORM_BLOCKS

    params returns one value, the maximum number of uniform blocks per geometry shader. The value must be at least 12. See glUniformBlockBinding.

GL_MAX_GEOMETRY_INPUT_COMPONENTS

    params returns one value, the maximum number of components of inputs read by a geometry shader, which must be at least 64.

GL_MAX_GEOMETRY_OUTPUT_COMPONENTS

    params returns one value, the maximum number of components of outputs written by a geometry shader, which must be at least 128.

GL_MAX_VIEWPORT_DIMS

    params returns two values: the maximum supported width and height of the viewport. These must be at least as large as the visible dimensions of the display being rendered to. See glViewport.

GL_NUM_COMPRESSED_TEXTURE_FORMATS

    params returns a single integer value indicating the number of available compressed texture formats. The minimum value is 4. See glCompressedTexImage2D.

GL_PACK_ALIGNMENT

    params returns one value, the byte alignment used for writing pixel data to memory. The initial value is 4. See glPixelStore.

GL_PACK_IMAGE_HEIGHT

    params returns one value, the image height used for writing pixel data to memory. The initial value is 0. See glPixelStore.

GL_PACK_LSB_FIRST

    params returns a single boolean value indicating whether single-bit pixels being written to memory are written first to the least significant bit of each unsigned byte. The initial value is GL_FALSE. See glPixelStore.

GL_PACK_ROW_LENGTH

    params returns one value, the row length used for writing pixel data to memory. The initial value is 0. See glPixelStore.

GL_PACK_SKIP_IMAGES

    params returns one value, the number of pixel images skipped before the first pixel is written into memory. The initial value is 0. See glPixelStore.

GL_PACK_SKIP_PIXELS

    params returns one value, the number of pixel locations skipped before the first pixel is written into memory. The initial value is 0. See glPixelStore.

GL_PACK_SKIP_ROWS

    params returns one value, the number of rows of pixel locations skipped before the first pixel is written into memory. The initial value is 0. See glPixelStore.

GL_PACK_SWAP_BYTES

    params returns a single boolean value indicating whether the bytes of two-byte and four-byte pixel indices and components are swapped before being written to memory. The initial value is GL_FALSE. See glPixelStore.

GL_PIXEL_PACK_BUFFER_BINDING

    params returns a single value, the name of the buffer object currently bound to the target GL_PIXEL_PACK_BUFFER. If no buffer object is bound to this target, 0 is returned. The initial value is 0. See glBindBuffer.

GL_PIXEL_UNPACK_BUFFER_BINDING

    params returns a single value, the name of the buffer object currently bound to the target GL_PIXEL_UNPACK_BUFFER. If no buffer object is bound to this target, 0 is returned. The initial value is 0. See glBindBuffer.

GL_POINT_FADE_THRESHOLD_SIZE

params returns one value, the point size threshold for determining the point size. See glPointParameter.

GL_PRIMITIVE_RESTART_INDEX

params returns one value, the current primitive restart index. The initial value is 0. See glPrimitiveRestartIndex.

GL_PROVOKING_VERTEX

params returns one value, the currently selected provoking vertex convention. The initial value is GL_LAST_VERTEX_CONVENTION. See glProvokingVertex.

GL_POINT_SIZE

params returns one value, the point size as specified by glPointSize. The initial value is 1.

GL_POINT_SIZE_GRANULARITY

params returns one value, the size difference between adjacent supported sizes for antialiased points. See glPointSize.

GL_POINT_SIZE_RANGE

params returns two values: the smallest and largest supported sizes for antialiased points. The smallest size must be at most 1, and the largest size must be at least 1. See glPointSize.

GL_POLYGON_OFFSET_FACTOR

params returns one value, the scaling factor used to determine the variable offset that is added to the depth value of each fragment generated when a polygon is rasterized. The initial value is 0. See glPolygonOffset.

GL_POLYGON_OFFSET_UNITS

params returns one value. This value is multiplied by an implementation-specific value and then added to the depth value of each fragment generated when a polygon is rasterized. The initial value is 0. See glPolygonOffset.

GL_POLYGON_OFFSET_FILL

params returns a single boolean value indicating whether polygon offset is enabled for polygons in fill mode. The initial value is GL_FALSE. See glPolygonOffset.

GL_POLYGON_OFFSET_LINE

params returns a single boolean value indicating whether polygon offset is enabled for polygons in line mode. The initial value is GL_FALSE. See glPolygonOffset.

GL_POLYGON_OFFSET_POINT

params returns a single boolean value indicating whether polygon offset is enabled for polygons in point mode. The initial value is GL_FALSE. See glPolygonOffset.

GL_POLYGON_SMOOTH

params returns a single boolean value indicating whether antialiasing of polygons is enabled. The initial value is GL_FALSE. See glPolygonMode.

GL_POLYGON_SMOOTH_HINT

params returns one value, a symbolic constant indicating the mode of the polygon antialiasing hint. The initial value is GL_DONT_CARE. See glHint.

GL_READ_BUFFER

params returns one value, a symbolic constant indicating which color buffer is selected for reading. The initial value is GL_BACK if there is a back buffer, otherwise it is GL_FRONT. See glReadPixels.

GL_SAMPLE_BUFFERS

params returns a single integer value indicating the number of sample buffers associated with the framebuffer. See glSampleCoverage.

GL_SAMPLE_COVERAGE_VALUE

params returns a single positive floating-point value indicating the current sample coverage value. See glSampleCoverage.

GL_SAMPLE_COVERAGE_INVERT

params returns a single boolean value indicating if the temporary coverage value should be inverted. See glSampleCoverage.

GL_SAMPLER_BINDING

params returns a single value, the name of the sampler object currently bound to the active texture unit. The initial value is 0. See glBindSampler.

GL_SAMPLES

params returns a single integer value indicating the coverage mask size. See glSampleCoverage.

GL_SCISSOR_BOX

params returns four values: the x and y window coordinates of the scissor box, followed by its width and height. Initially the x and y window coordinates are both 0 and the width and height are set to the size of the window. See glScissor.

GL_SCISSOR_TEST

params returns a single boolean value indicating whether scissoring is enabled. The initial value is GL_FALSE. See glScissor.

GL_STENCIL_BACK_FAIL

params returns one value, a symbolic constant indicating what action is taken for back-facing polygons when the stencil test fails. The initial value is GL_KEEP. See glStencilOpSeparate.

GL_STENCIL_BACK_FUNC

params returns one value, a symbolic constant indicating what function is used for back-facing polygons to compare the stencil reference value with the stencil buffer value. The initial value is GL_ALWAYS. See glStencilFuncSeparate.

GL_STENCIL_BACK_PASS_DEPTH_FAIL

params returns one value, a symbolic constant indicating what action is taken for back-facing polygons when the stencil test passes, but the depth test fails. The initial value is GL_KEEP. See glStencilOpSeparate.

GL_STENCIL_BACK_PASS_DEPTH_PASS

params returns one value, a symbolic constant indicating what action is taken for back-facing polygons when the stencil test passes and the depth test passes. The initial value is GL_KEEP. See glStencilOpSeparate.

GL_STENCIL_BACK_REF

params returns one value, the reference value that is compared with the contents of the stencil buffer for back-facing polygons. The initial value is 0. See glStencilFuncSeparate.

GL_STENCIL_BACK_VALUE_MASK

params returns one value, the mask that is used for back-facing polygons to mask both the stencil reference value and the stencil buffer value before they are compared. The initial value is all 1's. See glStencilFuncSeparate.

GL_STENCIL_BACK_WRITEMASK

params returns one value, the mask that controls writing of the stencil bitplanes for back-facing polygons. The initial value is all 1's. See glStencilMaskSeparate.

GL_STENCIL_CLEAR_VALUE

params returns one value, the index to which the stencil bitplanes are cleared. The initial value is 0. See glClearStencil.

GL_STENCIL_FAIL

params returns one value, a symbolic constant indicating what action is taken when the stencil test fails. The initial value is GL_KEEP. See glStencilOp. This stencil state only affects non-polygons and front-facing polygons. Back-facing polygons use separate stencil state. See glStencilOpSeparate.

GL_STENCIL_FUNC

> *params* returns one value, a symbolic constant indicating what function is used to compare the stencil reference value with the stencil buffer value. The initial value is GL_ALWAYS. See glStencilFunc. This stencil state only affects non-polygons and front-facing polygons. Back-facing polygons use separate stencil state. See glStencilFuncSeparate.

GL_STENCIL_PASS_DEPTH_FAIL

> *params* returns one value, a symbolic constant indicating what action is taken when the stencil test passes, but the depth test fails. The initial value is GL_KEEP. See glStencilOp. This stencil state only affects non-polygons and front-facing polygons. Back-facing polygons use separate stencil state. See glStencilOpSeparate.

GL_STENCIL_PASS_DEPTH_PASS

> *params* returns one value, a symbolic constant indicating what action is taken when the stencil test passes and the depth test passes. The initial value is GL_KEEP. See glStencilOp. This stencil state only affects non-polygons and front-facing polygons. Back-facing polygons use separate stencil state. See glStencilOpSeparate.

GL_STENCIL_REF

> *params* returns one value, the reference value that is compared with the contents of the stencil buffer. The initial value is 0. See glStencilFunc. This stencil state only affects non-polygons and front-facing polygons. Back-facing polygons use separate stencil state. See glStencilFuncSeparate.

GL_STENCIL_TEST

> *params* returns a single boolean value indicating whether stencil testing of fragments is enabled. The initial value is GL_FALSE. See glStencilFunc and glStencilOp.

GL_STENCIL_VALUE_MASK

> *params* returns one value, the mask that is used to mask both the stencil reference value and the stencil buffer value before they are compared. The initial value is all 1's. See glStencilFunc. This stencil state only affects non-polygons and front-facing polygons. Back-facing polygons use separate stencil state. See glStencilFuncSeparate.

GL_STENCIL_WRITEMASK

> *params* returns one value, the mask that controls writing of the stencil bitplanes. The initial value is all 1's. See glStencilMask. This stencil state only affects non-polygons and front-facing polygons. Back-facing polygons use separate stencil state. See glStencilMaskSeparate.

GL_STEREO

> *params* returns a single boolean value indicating whether stereo buffers (left and right) are supported.

GL_SUBPIXEL_BITS

> *params* returns one value, an estimate of the number of bits of subpixel resolution that are used to position rasterized geometry in window coordinates. The value must be at least 4.

GL_TEXTURE_BINDING_1D

> *params* returns a single value, the name of the texture currently bound to the target GL_TEXTURE_1D. The initial value is 0. See glBindTexture.

GL_TEXTURE_BINDING_1D_ARRAY

> *params* returns a single value, the name of the texture currently bound to the target GL_TEXTURE_1D_ARRAY. The initial value is 0. See glBindTexture.

GL_TEXTURE_BINDING_2D

> *params* returns a single value, the name of the texture currently bound to the target GL_TEXTURE_2D. The initial value is 0. See glBindTexture.

GL_TEXTURE_BINDING_2D_ARRAY

> *params* returns a single value, the name of the texture currently bound to the target GL_TEXTURE_2D_ARRAY. The initial value is 0. See glBindTexture.

GL_TEXTURE_BINDING_2D_MULTISAMPLE

> *params* returns a single value, the name of the texture currently bound to the target GL_TEXTURE_2D_MULTISAMPLE. The initial value is 0. See glBindTexture.

GL_TEXTURE_BINDING_2D_MULTISAMPLE_ARRAY

> *params* returns a single value, the name of the texture currently bound to the target GL_TEXTURE_2D_MULTISAMPLE_ARRAY. The initial value is 0. See glBindTexture.

GL_TEXTURE_BINDING_3D

> *params* returns a single value, the name of the texture currently bound to the target GL_TEXTURE_3D. The initial value is 0. See glBindTexture.

GL_TEXTURE_BINDING_BUFFER

> *params* returns a single value, the name of the texture currently bound to the target GL_TEXTURE_BUFFER. The initial value is 0. See glBindTexture.

GL_TEXTURE_BINDING_CUBE_MAP

> *params* returns a single value, the name of the texture currently bound to the target GL_TEXTURE_CUBE_MAP. The initial value is 0. See glBindTexture.

GL_TEXTURE_BINDING_RECTANGLE

> *params* returns a single value, the name of the texture currently bound to the target GL_TEXTURE_RECTANGLE. The initial value is 0. See glBindTexture.

GL_TEXTURE_COMPRESSION_HINT

> *params* returns a single value indicating the mode of the texture compression hint. The initial value is GL_DONT_CARE.

GL_TEXTURE_BUFFER_BINDING

> *params* returns a single value, the name of the texture buffer object currently bound. The initial value is 0. See glBindBuffer.

GL_TIMESTAMP

> *params* returns a single value, the 64-bit value of the current GL time. See glQueryCounter.

GL_TRANSFORM_FEEDBACK_BUFFER_BINDING

> When used with non-indexed variants of `glGet` (such as `glGetIntegerv`), *params* returns a single value, the name of the buffer object currently bound to the target GL_TRANSFORM_FEEDBACK_BUFFER. If no buffer object is bound to this target, 0 is returned. When used with indexed variants of `glGet` (such as `glGetIntegeri_v`), *params* returns a single value, the name of the buffer object bound to the indexed transform feedback attribute stream. The initial value is 0 for all targets. See glBindBuffer, glBindBufferBase, and glBindBufferRange.

GL_TRANSFORM_FEEDBACK_BUFFER_START

> When used with indexed variants of `glGet` (such as `glGetInteger64i_v`), *params* returns a single value, the start offset of the binding range for each transform feedback attribute stream. The initial value is 0 for all streams. See glBindBufferRange.

GL_TRANSFORM_FEEDBACK_BUFFER_SIZE

> When used with indexed variants of `glGet` (such as `glGetInteger64i_v`), *params* returns a single value, the size of the binding range for each transform feedback attribute stream. The initial value is 0 for all streams. See glBindBufferRange.

GL_UNIFORM_BUFFER_BINDING

> When used with non-indexed variants of `glGet` (such as `glGetIntegerv`), *params* returns a single value, the name of the buffer object currently bound to the target GL_UNIFORM_BUFFER. If no buffer object is bound to this target, 0 is returned. When used with indexed variants of `glGet` (such as `glGetIntegeri_v`), *params* returns a single value, the name of the buffer object bound to the indexed uniform buffer binding point. The initial value is 0 for all targets. See glBindBuffer, glBindBufferBase, and glBindBufferRange.

GL_UNIFORM_BUFFER_START

>When used with indexed variants of glGet (such as glGetInteger64i_v), *params* returns a single value, the start offset of the binding range for each indexed uniform buffer binding. The initial value is 0 for all bindings. See glBindBufferRange.

GL_UNIFORM_BUFFER_SIZE

>When used with indexed variants of glGet (such as glGetInteger64i_v), *params* returns a single value, the size of the binding range for each indexed uniform buffer binding. The initial value is 0 for all bindings. See glBindBufferRange.

GL_UNIFORM_BUFFER_OFFSET_ALIGNMENT

>*params* returns a single value, the minimum required alignment for uniform buffer sizes and offset. The initial value is 1. See glUniformBlockBinding.

GL_UNPACK_ALIGNMENT

>*params* returns one value, the byte alignment used for reading pixel data from memory. The initial value is 4. See glPixelStore.

GL_UNPACK_IMAGE_HEIGHT

>*params* returns one value, the image height used for reading pixel data from memory. The initial is 0. See glPixelStore.

GL_UNPACK_LSB_FIRST

>*params* returns a single boolean value indicating whether single-bit pixels being read from memory are read first from the least significant bit of each unsigned byte. The initial value is GL_FALSE. See glPixelStore.

GL_UNPACK_ROW_LENGTH

>*params* returns one value, the row length used for reading pixel data from memory. The initial value is 0. See glPixelStore.

GL_UNPACK_SKIP_IMAGES

>*params* returns one value, the number of pixel images skipped before the first pixel is read from memory. The initial value is 0. See glPixelStore.

GL_UNPACK_SKIP_PIXELS

>*params* returns one value, the number of pixel locations skipped before the first pixel is read from memory. The initial value is 0. See glPixelStore.

GL_UNPACK_SKIP_ROWS

>*params* returns one value, the number of rows of pixel locations skipped before the first pixel is read from memory. The initial value is 0. See glPixelStore.

GL_UNPACK_SWAP_BYTES

>*params* returns a single boolean value indicating whether the bytes of two-byte and four-byte pixel indices and components are swapped after being read from memory. The initial value is GL_FALSE. See glPixelStore.

GL_NUM_EXTENSIONS

>*params* returns one value, the number of extensions supported by the GL implementation for the current context. See glGetString.

GL_MAJOR_VERSION

>*params* returns one value, the major version number of the OpenGL API supported by the current context.

GL_MINOR_VERSION

>*params* returns one value, the minor version number of the OpenGL API supported by the current context.

GL_CONTEXT_FLAGS

>*params* returns one value, the flags with which the context was created (such as debugging functionality).

GL_VERTEX_PROGRAM_POINT_SIZE

>*params* returns a single boolean value indicating whether vertex program point size mode is enabled. If enabled, and a vertex shader is active, then the point size is taken from the shader built-in gl_PointSize. If disabled, and a vertex shader is active, then the point size is taken from the point state as specified by glPointSize. The initial value is GL_FALSE.

GL_VIEWPORT

> *params* returns four values: the x and y window coordinates of the viewport, followed by its width and height. Initially the x and y window coordinates are both set to 0, and the width and height are set to the width and height of the window into which the GL will do its rendering. See glViewport.

Many of the boolean parameters can also be queried more easily using glIsEnabled.

Notes

The following parameters return the associated value for the active texture unit: GL_TEXTURE_1D, GL_TEXTURE_BINDING_1D, GL_TEXTURE_2D, GL_TEXTURE_BINDING_2D, GL_TEXTURE_3D and GL_TEXTURE_BINDING_3D.

GL_MAX_RECTANGLE_TEXTURE_SIZE, GL_MAX_TEXTURE_BUFFER_SIZE, GL_UNIFORM_BUFFER_BINDING, GL_TEXTURE_BUFFER_BINDING, GL_MAX_VERTEX_UNIFORM_BLOCKS, GL_MAX_FRAGMENT_UNIFORM_BLOCKS, GL_MAX_COMBINED_FRAGMENT_UNIFORM_COMPONENTS, GL_MAX_COMBINED_VERTEX_UNIFORM_COMPONENTS GL_MAX_COMBINED_UNIFORM_BLOCKS, GL_MAX_UNIFORM_BLOCK_SIZE, and GL_UNIFORM_BUFFER_OFFSET_ALIGNMENT are available only if the GL version is 3.1 or greater.

GL_MAX_COMBINED_GEOMETRY_UNIFORM_COMPONENTS, GL_MAX_GEOMETRY_UNIFORM_BLOCKS, GL_MAX_GEOMETRY_INPUT_COMPONENTS, GL_MAX_GEOMETRY_OUTPUT_COMPONENTS, GL_MAX_GEOMETRY_OUTPUT_VERTICES, GL_MAX_GEOMETRY_TOTAL_OUTPUT_COMPONENTS and GL_MAX_GEOMETRY_TEXTURE_IMAGE_UNITS are available only if the GL version is 3.2 or greater.

glGetInteger64v and glGetInteger64i_v are available only if the GL version is 3.2 or greater.

GL_MAX_DUALSOURCE_DRAW_BUFFERS, GL_SAMPLER_BINDING, and GL_TIMESTAMP are available only if the GL version is 3.3 or greater.

Errors

GL_INVALID_ENUM is generated if *pname* is not an accepted value.

GL_INVALID_VALUE is generated on any of glGetBooleani_v, glGetIntegeri_v, or glGetInteger64i_v if *index* is outside of the valid range for the indexed state *target*.

See Also

glGetActiveUniform, glGetAttachedShaders, glGetAttribLocation, glGetBufferParameter, glGetBufferPointerv, glGetBufferSubData, glGetCompressedTexImage, glGetError, glGetProgram, glGetProgramInfoLog, glGetQueryiv, glGetQueryObject, glGetShader, glGetShaderInfoLog, glGetShaderSource, glGetString, glGetTexImage, glGetTexLevelParameter, glGetTexParameter, glGetUniform, glGetUniformLocation, glGetVertexAttrib, glGetVertexAttribPointerv, glIsEnabled

Copyright

glGetActiveAttrib

Returns information about an active attribute variable for the specified program object

C Specification

```
void glGetActiveAttrib(GLuint program,
                       GLuint index,
                       GLsizei bufSize,
```

```
GLsizei * length,
GLint * size,
GLenum * type,
GLchar * name);
```

Parameters

program

Specifies the program object to be queried.

index

Specifies the index of the attribute variable to be queried.

bufSize

Specifies the maximum number of characters OpenGL is allowed to write in the character buffer indicated by *name*.

length

Returns the number of characters actually written by OpenGL in the string indicated by *name* (excluding the null terminator) if a value other than NULL is passed.

size

Returns the size of the attribute variable.

type

Returns the data type of the attribute variable.

name

Returns a null terminated string containing the name of the attribute variable.

Description

`glGetActiveAttrib` returns information about an active attribute variable in the program object specified by *program*. The number of active attributes can be obtained by calling glGetProgram with the value GL_ACTIVE_ATTRIBUTES. A value of 0 for *index* selects the first active attribute variable. Permissible values for *index* range from 0 to the number of active attribute variables minus 1.

A vertex shader may use either built-in attribute variables, user-defined attribute variables, or both. Built-in attribute variables have a prefix of "gl_" and reference conventional OpenGL vertex attributes (e.g., *gl_Vertex*, *gl_Normal*, etc., see the OpenGL Shading Language specification for a complete list.) User-defined attribute variables have arbitrary names and obtain their values through numbered generic vertex attributes. An attribute variable (either built-in or user-defined) is considered active if it is determined during the link operation that it may be accessed during program execution. Therefore, *program* should have previously been the target of a call to glLinkProgram, but it is not necessary for it to have been linked successfully.

The size of the character buffer required to store the longest attribute variable name in *program* can be obtained by calling glGetProgram with the value GL_ACTIVE_ATTRIBUTE_MAX_LENGTH. This value should be used to allocate a buffer of sufficient size to store the returned attribute name. The size of this character buffer is passed in *bufSize*, and a pointer to this character buffer is passed in *name*.

`glGetActiveAttrib` returns the name of the attribute variable indicated by *index*, storing it in the character buffer specified by *name*. The string returned will be null terminated. The actual number of characters written into this buffer is returned in *length*, and this count does not include the null termination character. If the length of the returned string is not required, a value of NULL can be passed in the *length* argument.

The *type* argument will return a pointer to the attribute variable's data type. The symbolic constants GL_FLOAT, GL_FLOAT_VEC2, GL_FLOAT_VEC3, GL_FLOAT_VEC4, GL_FLOAT_MAT2, GL_FLOAT_MAT3, GL_FLOAT_MAT4, GL_FLOAT_MAT2x3, GL_FLOAT_MAT2x4, GL_FLOAT_MAT3x2, GL_FLOAT_MAT3x4, GL_FLOAT_MAT4x2, GL_FLOAT_MAT4x3, GL_INT, GL_INT_VEC2, GL_INT_VEC3, GL_INT_VEC4, GL_UNSIGNED_INT_VEC, GL_UNSIGNED_INT_VEC2, GL_UNSIGNED_INT_VEC3, or GL_UNSIGNED_INT_VEC4 may be returned. The *size* argument will return the size of the attribute, in units of the type returned in *type*.

The list of active attribute variables may include both built-in attribute variables (which begin with the prefix "gl_") as well as user-defined attribute variable names.

This function will return as much information as it can about the specified active attribute variable. If no information is available, *length* will be 0, and *name* will be an empty string. This situation could occur if this function is called after a link operation that failed. If an error occurs, the return values *length*, *size*, *type*, and *name* will be unmodified.

Errors

GL_INVALID_VALUE is generated if *program* is not a value generated by OpenGL.

GL_INVALID_OPERATION is generated if *program* is not a program object.

GL_INVALID_VALUE is generated if *index* is greater than or equal to the number of active attribute variables in *program*.

GL_INVALID_VALUE is generated if *bufSize* is less than 0.

Associated Gets

glGet with argument GL_MAX_VERTEX_ATTRIBS.

glGetProgram with argument GL_ACTIVE_ATTRIBUTES or GL_ACTIVE_ATTRIBUTE_MAX_LENGTH.

glIsProgram

See Also

glBindAttribLocation, glLinkProgram, glVertexAttrib, glVertexAttribPointer

Copyright

Copyright © 2003-2005 3Dlabs Inc. Ltd. Copyright © 2010 Khronos Group. This material may be distributed subject to the terms and conditions set forth in the Open Publication License, v 1.0, 8 June 1999. http://opencontent.org/openpub/.

glGetActiveUniform

Returns information about an active uniform variable for the specified program object

C Specification

```
void glGetActiveUniform(GLuint program,
                        GLuint index,
                        GLsizei bufSize,
                        GLsizei *length,
                        GLint *size,
                        GLenum *type,
                        GLchar *name);
```

Parameters

program

        Specifies the program object to be queried.

index

        Specifies the index of the uniform variable to be queried.

bufSize

        Specifies the maximum number of characters OpenGL is allowed to write in the character buffer indicated by *name*.

length
  Returns the number of characters actually written by OpenGL in the string indicated by *name* (excluding the null terminator) if a value other than NULL is passed.

size
  Returns the size of the uniform variable.

type
  Returns the data type of the uniform variable.

name
  Returns a null terminated string containing the name of the uniform variable.

Description

glGetActiveUniform returns information about an active uniform variable in the program object specified by *program*. The number of active uniform variables can be obtained by calling glGetProgram with the value GL_ACTIVE_UNIFORMS. A value of 0 for *index* selects the first active uniform variable. Permissible values for *index* range from 0 to the number of active uniform variables minus 1.

Shaders may use either built-in uniform variables, user-defined uniform variables, or both. Built-in uniform variables have a prefix of "gl_" and reference existing OpenGL state or values derived from such state (e.g., *gl_DepthRangeParameters*, see the OpenGL Shading Language specification for a complete list.) User-defined uniform variables have arbitrary names and obtain their values from the application through calls to glUniform. A uniform variable (either built-in or user-defined) is considered active if it is determined during the link operation that it may be accessed during program execution. Therefore, *program* should have previously been the target of a call to glLinkProgram, but it is not necessary for it to have been linked successfully.

The size of the character buffer required to store the longest uniform variable name in *program* can be obtained by calling glGetProgram with the value GL_ACTIVE_UNIFORM_MAX_LENGTH. This value should be used to allocate a buffer of sufficient size to store the returned uniform variable name. The size of this character buffer is passed in *bufSize*, and a pointer to this character buffer is passed in *name.*

glGetActiveUniform returns the name of the uniform variable indicated by *index*, storing it in the character buffer specified by *name*. The string returned will be null terminated. The actual number of characters written into this buffer is returned in *length*, and this count does not include the null termination character. If the length of the returned string is not required, a value of NULL can be passed in the *length* argument.

The *type* argument will return a pointer to the uniform variable's data type. The symbolic constants returned for uniform types are shown in the table below.

If one or more elements of an array are active, the name of the array is returned in *name*, the type is returned in *type*, and the *size* parameter returns the highest array element index used, plus one, as determined by the compiler and/or linker. Only one active uniform variable will be reported for a uniform array.

Uniform variables that are declared as structures or arrays of structures will not be returned directly by this function. Instead, each of these uniform variables will be reduced to its fundamental components containing the "." and "[]" operators such that each of the names is valid as an argument to glGetUniformLocation. Each of these reduced uniform variables is counted as one active uniform variable and is assigned an index. A valid name cannot be a structure, an array of structures, or a subcomponent of a vector or matrix.

Returned Symbolic Contant	Shader Uniform Type
GL_FLOAT	float
GL_FLOAT_VEC2	vec2

Returned Symbolic Contant	Shader Uniform Type
GL_FLOAT_VEC3	vec3
GL_FLOAT_VEC4	vec4
GL_INT	int
GL_INT_VEC2	ivec2
GL_INT_VEC3	ivec3
GL_INT_VEC4	ivec4
GL_UNSIGNED_INT	unsigned int
GL_UNSIGNED_INT_VEC2	uvec2
GL_UNSIGNED_INT_VEC3	uvec3
GL_UNSIGNED_INT_VEC4	uvec4
GL_BOOL	bool
GL_BOOL_VEC2	bvec2
GL_BOOL_VEC3	bvec3
GL_BOOL_VEC4	bvec4
GL_FLOAT_MAT2	mat2
GL_FLOAT_MAT3	mat3
GL_FLOAT_MAT4	mat4
GL_FLOAT_MAT2x3	mat2x3
GL_FLOAT_MAT2x4	mat2x4
GL_FLOAT_MAT3x2	mat3x2
GL_FLOAT_MAT3x4	mat3x4
GL_FLOAT_MAT4x2	mat4x2
GL_FLOAT_MAT4x3	mat4x3
GL_SAMPLER_1D	sampler1D
GL_SAMPLER_2D	sampler2D
GL_SAMPLER_3D	sampler3D
GL_SAMPLER_CUBE	samplerCube
GL_SAMPLER_1D_SHADOW	sampler1DShadow
GL_SAMPLER_2D_SHADOW	sampler2DShadow

Returned Symbolic Contant	Shader Uniform Type
GL_SAMPLER_1D_ARRAY	sampler1DArray
GL_SAMPLER_2D_ARRAY	sampler2DArray
GL_SAMPLER_1D_ARRAY_SHADOW	sampler1DArrayShadow
GL_SAMPLER_2D_ARRAY_SHADOW	sampler2DArrayShadow
GL_SAMPLER_2D_MULTISAMPLE	sampler2DMS
GL_SAMPLER_2D_MULTISAMPLE_ARRAY	sampler2DMSArray
GL_SAMPLER_CUBE_SHADOW	samplerCubeShadow
GL_SAMPLER_BUFFER	samplerBuffer
GL_SAMPLER_2D_RECT	sampler2DRect
GL_SAMPLER_2D_RECT_SHADOW	sampler2DRectShadow
GL_INT_SAMPLER_1D	isampler1D
GL_INT_SAMPLER_2D	isampler2D
GL_INT_SAMPLER_3D	isampler3D
GL_INT_SAMPLER_CUBE	isamplerCube
GL_INT_SAMPLER_1D_ARRAY	isampler1DArray
GL_INT_SAMPLER_2D_ARRAY	isampler2DArray
GL_INT_SAMPLER_2D_MULTISAMPLE	isampler2DMS
GL_INT_SAMPLER_2D_MULTISAMPLE_ARRAY	isampler2DMSArray
GL_INT_SAMPLER_BUFFER	isamplerBuffer
GL_INT_SAMPLER_2D_RECT	isampler2DRect
GL_UNSIGNED_INT_SAMPLER_1D	usampler1D
GL_UNSIGNED_INT_SAMPLER_2D	usampler2D
GL_UNSIGNED_INT_SAMPLER_3D	usampler3D
GL_UNSIGNED_INT_SAMPLER_CUBE	usamplerCube
GL_UNSIGNED_INT_SAMPLER_1D_ARRAY	usampler2DArray
GL_UNSIGNED_INT_SAMPLER_2D_ARRAY	usampler2DArray
GL_UNSIGNED_INT_SAMPLER_2D_MULTISAMPLE	usampler2DMS
GL_UNSIGNED_INT_SAMPLER_2D_MULTISAMPLE_ARRAY	usampler2DMSArray

Returned Symbolic Contant	Shader Uniform Type
GL_UNSIGNED_INT_SAMPLER_BUFFER	usamplerBuffer
GL_UNSIGNED_INT_SAMPLER_2D_RECT	usampler2DRect

The size of the uniform variable will be returned in *size*. Uniform variables other than arrays will have a size of 1. Structures and arrays of structures will be reduced as described earlier, such that each of the names returned will be a data type in the earlier list. If this reduction results in an array, the size returned will be as described for uniform arrays; otherwise, the size returned will be 1.

The list of active uniform variables may include both built-in uniform variables (which begin with the prefix "gl_") as well as user-defined uniform variable names.

This function will return as much information as it can about the specified active uniform variable. If no information is available, *length* will be 0, and *name* will be an empty string. This situation could occur if this function is called after a link operation that failed. If an error occurs, the return values *length*, *size*, *type*, and *name* will be unmodified.

Errors

GL_INVALID_VALUE is generated if *program* is not a value generated by OpenGL.
GL_INVALID_OPERATION is generated if *program* is not a program object.
GL_INVALID_VALUE is generated if *index* is greater than or equal to the number of active uniform variables in *program*.
GL_INVALID_VALUE is generated if *bufSize* is less than 0.

Associated Gets

glGet with argument GL_MAX_VERTEX_UNIFORM_COMPONENTS, GL_MAX_GEOMETRY_UNIFORM_COMPONENTS, GL_MAX_FRAGMENT_UNIFORM_COMPONENTS, or GL_MAX_COMBINED_UNIFORM_COMPONENTS.
glGetProgram with argument GL_ACTIVE_UNIFORMS or GL_ACTIVE_UNIFORM_MAX_LENGTH.
glIsProgram

See Also

glGetUniform, glGetUniformLocation, glLinkProgram, glUniform, glUseProgram

Copyright

glGetActiveUniformBlock

query information about an active uniform block

C Specification

```
void glGetActiveUniformBlockiv(GLuint program,
                               GLuint uniformBlockIndex,
                               GLenum pname,
                               GLint params);
```

Parameters

program

Specifies the name of a program containing the uniform block.

uniformBlockIndex

Specifies the index of the uniform block within *program*.

pname

Specifies the name of the parameter to query.

params

Specifies the address of a variable to receive the result of the query.

Description

glGetActiveUniformBlockiv retrieves information about an active uniform block within *program*.

program must be the name of a program object for which the command glLinkProgram must have been called in the past, although it is not required that glLinkProgram must have succeeded. The link could have failed because the number of active uniforms exceeded the limit.

uniformBlockIndex is an active uniform block index of *program*, and must be less than the value of GL_ACTIVE_UNIFORM_BLOCKS.

Upon success, the uniform block parameter(s) specified by *pname* are returned in *params*. If an error occurs, nothing will be written to *params*.

If *pname* is GL_UNIFORM_BLOCK_BINDING, then the index of the uniform buffer binding point last selected by the uniform block specified by *uniformBlockIndex* for *program* is returned. If no uniform block has been previously specified, zero is returned.

If *pname* is GL_UNIFORM_BLOCK_DATA_SIZE, then the implementation-dependent minimum total buffer object size, in basic machine units, required to hold all active uniforms in the uniform block identified by *uniformBlockIndex* is returned. It is neither guaranteed nor expected that a given implementation will arrange uniform values as tightly packed in a buffer object. The exception to this is the *std140 uniform block layout*, which guarantees specific packing behavior and does not require the application to query for offsets and strides. In this case the minimum size may still be queried, even though it is determined in advance based only on the uniform block declaration.

If *pname* is GL_UNIFORM_BLOCK_NAME_LENGTH, then the total length (including the nul terminator) of the name of the uniform block identified by *uniformBlockIndex* is returned.

If *pname* is GL_UNIFORM_BLOCK_ACTIVE_UNIFORMS, then the number of active uniforms in the uniform block identified by *uniformBlockIndex* is returned.

If *pname* is GL_UNIFORM_BLOCK_ACTIVE_UNIFORM_INDICES, then a list of the active uniform indices for the uniform block identified by *uniformBlockIndex* is returned. The number of elements that will be written to *params* is the value of GL_UNIFORM_BLOCK_ACTIVE_UNIFORMS for *uniformBlockIndex*.

If *pname* is GL_UNIFORM_BLOCK_REFERENCED_BY_VERTEX_SHADER, GL_UNIFORM_BLOCK_REFERENCED_BY_GEOMETRY_SHADER, or GL_UNIFORM_BLOCK_REFERENCED_BY_FRAGMENT_SHADER, then a boolean value indicating whether the uniform block identified by *uniformBlockIndex* is referenced by the vertex, geometry, or fragment programming stages of program, respectively, is returned.

Errors

GL_INVALID_VALUE is generated if *uniformBlockIndex* is greater than or equal to the value of GL_ACTIVE_UNIFORM_BLOCKS or is not the index of an active uniform block in *program*.

GL_INVALID_ENUM is generated if *pname* is not one of the accepted tokens.

GL_INVALID_OPERATION is generated if *program* is not the name of a program object for which glLinkProgram has been called in the past.

Notes

glGetActiveUniformBlockiv is available only if the GL version is 3.1 or greater.

See Also

glGetActiveUniformBlockName, glGetUniformBlockIndex, glLinkProgram

Copyright

Copyright © 2010 Khronos Group. This material may be distributed subject to the terms and conditions set forth in the Open Publication License, v 1.0, 8 June 1999. http://opencontent.org/openpub/.

glGetActiveUniformBlockName

retrieve the name of an active uniform block

C Specification

```
void glGetActiveUniformBlockName(GLuint program,
                                 GLuint uniformBlockIndex,
                                 GLsizei bufSize,
                                 GLsizei *length,
                                 GLchar *uniformBlockName);
```

Parameters

program
> Specifies the name of a program containing the uniform block.

uniformBlockIndex
> Specifies the index of the uniform block within *program*.

bufSize
> Specifies the size of the buffer addressed by *uniformBlockName*.

length
> Specifies the address of a variable to receive the number of characters that were written to *uniformBlockName*.

uniformBlockName
> Specifies the address of an array of characters to receive the name of the uniform block at *uniformBlockIndex*.

Description

glGetActiveUniformBlockName retrieves the name of the active uniform block at *uniformBlockIndex* within *program*.

program must be the name of a program object for which the command glLinkProgram must have been called in the past, although it is not required that glLinkProgram must have succeeded. The link could have failed because the number of active uniforms exceeded the limit.

uniformBlockIndex is an active uniform block index of *program*, and must be less than the value of GL_ACTIVE_UNIFORM_BLOCKS.

Upon success, the name of the uniform block identified by *unifomBlockIndex* is returned into *uniformBlockName*. The name is nul-terminated. The actual number of characters written into *uniformBlockName*, excluding the nul terminator, is returned in *length*. If *length* is NULL, no length is returned.

bufSize contains the maximum number of characters (including the nul terminator) that will be written into *uniformBlockName*.

If an error occurs, nothing will be written to *uniformBlockName* or *length*.

Errors

GL_INVALID_OPERATION is generated if *program* is not the name of a program object for which glLinkProgram has been called in the past.

GL_INVALID_VALUE is generated if *uniformBlockIndex* is greater than or equal to the value of GL_ACTIVE_UNIFORM_BLOCKS or is not the index of an active uniform block in *program*.

Notes

glGetActiveUniformBlockName is available only if the GL version is 3.1 or greater.

See Also

glGetActiveUniformBlock, glGetUniformBlockIndex

Copyright

Copyright © 2010 Khronos Group. This material may be distributed subject to the terms and conditions set forth in the Open Publication License, v 1.0, 8 June 1999. http://opencontent.org/openpub/.

glGetActiveUniformName

query the name of an active uniform

C Specification

```
void glGetActiveUniformName(GLuint program,
                            GLuint uniformIndex,
                            GLsizei bufSize,
                            GLsizei *length,
                            GLchar *uniformName);
```

Parameters

program
> Specifies the program containing the active uniform index *uniformIndex*.

uniformIndex
> Specifies the index of the active uniform whose name to query.

bufSize
> Specifies the size of the buffer, in units of GLchar, of the buffer whose address is specified in *uniformName*.

length
> Specifies the address of a variable that will receive the number of characters that were or would have been written to the buffer addressed by *uniformName*.

uniformName
> Specifies the address of a buffer into which the GL will place the name of the active uniform at *uniformIndex* within *program*.

Description

glGetActiveUniformName returns the name of the active uniform at *uniformIndex* within *program*. If *uniformName* is not NULL, up to *bufSize* characters (including a nul-terminator) will be written into the array whose address is specified by *uniformName*. If *length* is not NULL, the number of characters that were (or would have been) written into *uniformName* (not including the nul-terminator) will be placed in the variable whose address is specified in *length*. If *length* is NULL, no length is returned. The length of the longest uniform name in *program* is given by the value of GL_ACTIVE_UNIFORM_MAX_LENGTH, which can be queried with glGetProgram.

If glGetActiveUniformName is not successful, nothing is written to *length* or *uniformName*.

program must be the name of a program for which the command glLinkProgram has been issued in the past. It is not necessary for *program* to have been linked successfully. The link could have failed because the number of active uniforms exceeded the limit.

uniformIndex must be an active uniform index of the program *program*, in the range zero to GL_ACTIVE_UNIFORMS - 1. The value of GL_ACTIVE_UNIFORMS can be queried with glGetProgram.

Errors

GL_INVALID_VALUE is generated if *uniformIndex* is greater than or equal to the value of GL_ACTIVE_UNIFORMS.

GL_INVALID_VALUE is generated if *bufSize* is negative.

GL_INVALID_VALUE is generated if *program* is not the name of a program object for which glLinkProgram has been issued.

See Also

glGetActiveUniform, glGetUniformIndices, glGetProgram, glLinkProgram

Copyright

glGetAttachedShaders

Returns the handles of the shader objects attached to a program object

C Specification

```
void glGetAttachedShaders(GLuint program,
                          GLsizei maxCount,
                          GLsizei * count,
                          GLuint * shaders);
```

Parameters

program
> Specifies the program object to be queried.

maxCount
> Specifies the size of the array for storing the returned object names.

count
> Returns the number of names actually returned in *objects*.

shaders
> Specifies an array that is used to return the names of attached shader objects.

Description

glGetAttachedShaders returns the names of the shader objects attached to *program*. The names of shader objects that are attached to *program* will be returned in *shaders.* The actual number of shader names written into *shaders* is returned in *count.* If no shader objects are attached to *program*, *count* is set to 0. The maximum number of shader names that may be returned in *shaders* is specified by *maxCount*.

If the number of names actually returned is not required (for instance, if it has just been obtained by calling glGetProgram), a value of NULL may be passed for count. If no shader objects are attached to *program*, a value of 0 will be returned in *count*. The actual number of attached shaders can be obtained by calling glGetProgram with the value GL_ATTACHED_SHADERS.

Errors

GL_INVALID_VALUE is generated if *program* is not a value generated by OpenGL.
GL_INVALID_OPERATION is generated if *program* is not a program object.
GL_INVALID_VALUE is generated if *maxCount* is less than 0.

Associated Gets

glGetProgram with argument GL_ATTACHED_SHADERS
glIsProgram

See Also

glAttachShader, glDetachShader.

Copyright

glGetAttribLocation

Returns the location of an attribute variable

C Specification

```
GLint glGetAttribLocation(GLuint program,
                          const GLchar * name);
```

Parameters

program
  Specifies the program object to be queried.
name
  Points to a null terminated string containing the name of the attribute variable whose location is to be queried.

Description

glGetAttribLocation queries the previously linked program object specified by *program* for the attribute variable specified by *name* and returns the index of the generic vertex attribute that is bound to that attribute variable. If *name* is a matrix attribute variable, the index of the first column of the matrix is returned. If the named attribute variable is not an active attribute in the specified program object or if *name* starts with the reserved prefix "gl_", a value of -1 is returned.

The association between an attribute variable name and a generic attribute index can be specified at any time by calling glBindAttribLocation. Attribute bindings do not go into effect until glLinkProgram is called. After a program object has been linked successfully, the index values for attribute variables remain fixed until the next link command occurs. The attribute values can only be queried after a link if the link was successful. glGetAttribLocation returns the binding that actually went into effect the last time glLinkProgram was called for the specified program object. Attribute bindings that have been specified since the last link operation are not returned by glGetAttribLocation.

792

Errors

GL_INVALID_OPERATION is generated if *program* is not a value generated by OpenGL.
GL_INVALID_OPERATION is generated if *program* is not a program object.
GL_INVALID_OPERATION is generated if *program* has not been successfully linked.

Associated Gets

glGetActiveAttrib with argument *program* and the index of an active attribute
glIsProgram

See Also

`glBindAttribLocation, glLinkProgram, glVertexAttrib, glVertexAttribPointer`

Copyright

Copyright © 2003-2005 3Dlabs Inc. Ltd. This material may be distributed subject to the terms and conditions set forth in the Open Publication License, v 1.0, 8 June 1999. http://opencontent.org/openpub/.

glGetBufferParameteriv

return parameters of a buffer object

C Specification

```
void glGetBufferParameteriv(GLenum target,
                            GLenum value,
                            GLint * data);
```

Parameters

target
> Specifies the target buffer object. The symbolic constant must be GL_ARRAY_BUFFER, GL_COPY_READ_BUFFER, GL_COPY_WRITE_BUFFER, GL_ELEMENT_ARRAY_BUFFER, GL_PIXEL_PACK_BUFFER, GL_PIXEL_UNPACK_BUFFER, GL_TEXTURE_BUFFER, GL_TRANSFORM_FEEDBACK_BUFFER, or GL_UNIFORM_BUFFER.

value
> Specifies the symbolic name of a buffer object parameter. Accepted values are GL_BUFFER_ACCESS, GL_BUFFER_MAPPED, GL_BUFFER_SIZE, or GL_BUFFER_USAGE.

data
> Returns the requested parameter.

Description

glGetBufferParameteriv returns in *data* a selected parameter of the buffer object specified by *target*.

value names a specific buffer object parameter, as follows:

GL_BUFFER_ACCESS
> *params* returns the access policy set while mapping the buffer object. The initial value is GL_READ_WRITE.

GL_BUFFER_MAPPED
> *params* returns a flag indicating whether the buffer object is currently mapped. The initial value is GL_FALSE.

GL_BUFFER_SIZE
> *params* returns the size of the buffer object, measured in bytes. The initial value is 0.

GL_BUFFER_USAGE

> *params* returns the buffer object's usage pattern. The initial value is GL_STATIC_DRAW.

Notes

If an error is generated, no change is made to the contents of *data*.

Errors

GL_INVALID_ENUM is generated if *target* or *value* is not an accepted value.

GL_INVALID_OPERATION is generated if the reserved buffer object name 0 is bound to *target*.

See Also

`glBindBuffer`, `glBufferData`, `glMapBuffer`, `glUnmapBuffer`

Copyright

glGetBufferPointerv

return the pointer to a mapped buffer object's data store

C Specification

```
void glGetBufferPointerv(GLenum target,
                         GLenum pname,
                         GLvoid ** params);
```

Parameters

target

> Specifies the target buffer object. The symbolic constant must be GL_ARRAY_BUFFER, GL_COPY_READ_BUFFER, GL_COPY_WRITE_BUFFER, GL_ELEMENT_ARRAY_BUFFER, GL_PIXEL_PACK_BUFFER, GL_PIXEL_UNPACK_BUFFER, GL_TEXTURE_BUFFER, GL_TRANSFORM_FEEDBACK_BUFFER, or GL_UNIFORM_BUFFER.

pname

> Specifies the pointer to be returned. The symbolic constant must be GL_BUFFER_MAP_POINTER.

params

> Returns the pointer value specified by *pname*.

Description

`glGetBufferPointerv` returns pointer information. *pname* is a symbolic constant indicating the pointer to be returned, which must be GL_BUFFER_MAP_POINTER, the pointer to which the buffer object's data store is mapped. If the data store is not currently mapped, NULL is returned. *params* is a pointer to a location in which to place the returned pointer value.

Notes

If an error is generated, no change is made to the contents of *params*.

The initial value for the pointer is NULL.

Errors

GL_INVALID_ENUM is generated if *target* or *pname* is not an accepted value.
GL_INVALID_OPERATION is generated if the reserved buffer object name 0 is bound to *target*.

See Also

`glBindBuffer`, `glMapBuffer`

Copyright

glGetBufferSubData

returns a subset of a buffer object's data store

C Specification

```
void glGetBufferSubData(GLenum target,
                        GLintptr offset,
                        GLsizeiptr size,
                        GLvoid * data);
```

Parameters

target

Specifies the target buffer object. The symbolic constant must be GL_ARRAY_BUFFER, GL_COPY_READ_BUFFER, GL_COPY_WRITE_BUFFER, GL_ELEMENT_ARRAY_BUFFER, GL_PIXEL_PACK_BUFFER, GL_PIXEL_UNPACK_BUFFER, GL_TEXTURE_BUFFER, GL_TRANSFORM_FEEDBACK_BUFFER, or GL_UNIFORM_BUFFER.

offset

Specifies the offset into the buffer object's data store from which data will be returned, measured in bytes.

size

Specifies the size in bytes of the data store region being returned.

data

Specifies a pointer to the location where buffer object data is returned.

Description

`glGetBufferSubData` returns some or all of the data from the buffer object currently bound to *target*. Data starting at byte offset *offset* and extending for *size* bytes is copied from the data store to the memory pointed to by *data*. An error is thrown if the buffer object is currently mapped, or if *offset* and *size* together define a range beyond the bounds of the buffer object's data store.

Notes

If an error is generated, no change is made to the contents of *data*.

Errors

GL_INVALID_ENUM is generated if *target* is not GL_ARRAY_BUFFER, GL_ELEMENT_ARRAY_BUFFER, GL_PIXEL_PACK_BUFFER, or GL_PIXEL_UNPACK_BUFFER.

GL_INVALID_VALUE is generated if *offset* or *size* is negative, or if together they define a region of memory that extends beyond the buffer object's allocated data store.

GL_INVALID_OPERATION is generated if the reserved buffer object name 0 is bound to *target*.

GL_INVALID_OPERATION is generated if the buffer object being queried is mapped.

See Also

`glBindBuffer`, `glBufferData`, `glBufferSubData`, `glMapBuffer`, `glUnmapBuffer`

Copyright

glGetCompressedTexImage

return a compressed texture image

C Specification

```
void glGetCompressedTexImage(GLenum target,
                             GLint lod,
                             GLvoid * img);
```

Parameters

target

Specifies which texture is to be obtained. GL_TEXTURE_1D, GL_TEXTURE_2D, GL_TEXTURE_3D, GL_TEXTURE_CUBE_MAP_POSITIVE_X, GL_TEXTURE_CUBE_MAP_NEGATIVE_X, GL_TEXTURE_CUBE_MAP_POSITIVE_Y, GL_TEXTURE_CUBE_MAP_NEGATIVE_Y, GL_TEXTURE_CUBE_MAP_POSITIVE_Z, and GL_TEXTURE_CUBE_MAP_NEGATIVE_Z are accepted.

lod

Specifies the level-of-detail number of the desired image. Level 0 is the base image level. Level n is the nth mipmap reduction image.

img

Returns the compressed texture image.

Description

`glGetCompressedTexImage` returns the compressed texture image associated with *target* and *lod* into *img*. *img* should be an array of GL_TEXTURE_COMPRESSED_IMAGE_SIZE bytes. *target* specifies whether the desired texture image was one specified by glTexImage1D (GL_TEXTURE_1D), glTexImage2D (GL_TEXTURE_2D or any of GL_TEXTURE_CUBE_MAP_*), or glTexImage3D (GL_TEXTURE_3D). *lod* specifies the level-of-detail number of the desired image.

If a non-zero named buffer object is bound to the GL_PIXEL_PACK_BUFFER target (see glBindBuffer) while a texture image is requested, *img* is treated as a byte offset into the buffer object's data store.

To minimize errors, first verify that the texture is compressed by calling glGetTexLevelParameter with argument GL_TEXTURE_COMPRESSED. If the texture is compressed, then determine the amount of memory required to store the compressed texture by calling glGetTexLevelParameter with argument GL_TEXTURE_COMPRESSED_IMAGE_SIZE. Finally, retrieve the internal format of the texture by calling glGetTexLevelParameter with argument GL_TEXTURE_INTERNAL_FORMAT. To store the texture for later use, associate the internal format and size with the retrieved texture image. These data can be used by the respective texture or subtexture loading routine used for loading *target* textures.

Errors

GL_INVALID_VALUE is generated if *lod* is less than zero or greater than the maximum number of LODs permitted by the implementation.

GL_INVALID_OPERATION is generated if `glGetCompressedTexImage` is used to retrieve a texture that is in an uncompressed internal format.

GL_INVALID_OPERATION is generated if a non-zero buffer object name is bound to the GL_PIXEL_PACK_BUFFER target and the buffer object's data store is currently mapped.

GL_INVALID_OPERATION is generated if a non-zero buffer object name is bound to the GL_PIXEL_PACK_BUFFER target and the data would be packed to the buffer object such that the memory writes required would exceed the data store size.

Associated Gets

glGetTexLevelParameter with argument GL_TEXTURE_COMPRESSED
glGetTexLevelParameter with argument GL_TEXTURE_COMPRESSED_IMAGE_SIZE
glGetTexLevelParameter with argument GL_TEXTURE_INTERNAL_FORMAT
glGet with argument GL_PIXEL_PACK_BUFFER_BINDING

See Also

`glActiveTexture`, `glCompressedTexImage1D`, `glCompressedTexImage2D`, `glCompressedTexImage3D`, `glCompressedTexSubImage1D`, `glCompressedTexSubImage2D`, `glCompressedTexSubImage3D`, `glReadPixels`, `glTexImage1D`, `glTexImage2D`, `glTexImage3D`, `glTexParameter`, `glTexSubImage1D`, `glTexSubImage2D`, `glTexSubImage3D`

Copyright

glGetError

return error information

C Specification

```
GLenum glGetError(void);
```

Description

glGetError returns the value of the error flag. Each detectable error is assigned a numeric code and symbolic name. When an error occurs, the error flag is set to the appropriate error code value. No other errors are recorded until glGetError is called, the error code is returned, and the flag is reset to GL_NO_ERROR. If a call to glGetError returns GL_NO_ERROR, there has been no detectable error since the last call to glGetError, or since the GL was initialized.

To allow for distributed implementations, there may be several error flags. If any single error flag has recorded an error, the value of that flag is returned and that flag is reset to GL_NO_ERROR when glGetError is called. If more than one flag has recorded an error, glGetError returns and clears an arbitrary error flag value. Thus, glGetError should always be called in a loop, until it returns GL_NO_ERROR, if all error flags are to be reset.

Initially, all error flags are set to GL_NO_ERROR.

The following errors are currently defined:

GL_NO_ERROR
> No error has been recorded. The value of this symbolic constant is guaranteed to be 0.

GL_INVALID_ENUM
> An unacceptable value is specified for an enumerated argument. The offending command is ignored and has no other side effect than to set the error flag.

GL_INVALID_VALUE
> A numeric argument is out of range. The offending command is ignored and has no other side effect than to set the error flag.

GL_INVALID_OPERATION
> The specified operation is not allowed in the current state. The offending command is ignored and has no other side effect than to set the error flag.

GL_INVALID_FRAMEBUFFER_OPERATION
> The framebuffer object is not complete. The offending command is ignored and has no other side effect than to set the error flag.

GL_OUT_OF_MEMORY
> There is not enough memory left to execute the command. The state of the GL is undefined, except for the state of the error flags, after this error is recorded.

When an error flag is set, results of a GL operation are undefined only if GL_OUT_OF_MEMORY has occurred. In all other cases, the command generating the error is ignored and has no effect on the GL state or frame buffer contents. If the generating command returns a value, it returns 0. If glGetError itself generates an error, it returns 0.

Copyright

Copyright © 1991-2006 Silicon Graphics, Inc. This document is licensed under the SGI Free Software B License. For details, see http://oss.sgi.com/projects/FreeB/.

glGetFragDataIndex

query the bindings of color indices to user-defined varying out variables

C Specification

```
GLint glGetFragDataIndex(GLuint program,
                         const char * name);
```

Parameters

program

> The name of the program containing varying out variable whose binding to query

name

> The name of the user-defined varying out variable whose index to query

Description

`glGetFragDataIndex` returns the index of the fragment color to which the variable *name* was bound when the program object *program* was last linked. If *name* is not a varying out variable of *program*, or if an error occurs, -1 will be returned.

Notes

`glGetFragDataIndex` is available only if the GL version is 3.3 or greater.

Errors

GL_INVALID_OPERATION is generated if *program* is not the name of a program object.

See Also

`glCreateProgram`, `glBindFragDataLocation`, `glBindFragDataLocationIndexed`, `glGetFragDataLocation`

Copyright

Copyright © 2010 Khronos Group. This material may be distributed subject to the terms and conditions set forth in the Open Publication License, v 1.0, 8 June 1999. http://opencontent.org/openpub/.

glGetFragDataLocation

query the bindings of color numbers to user-defined varying out variables

C Specification

```
GLint glGetFragDataLocation(GLuint program,
                            const char * name);
```

Parameters

program

> The name of the program containing varying out variable whose binding to query

name

> The name of the user-defined varying out variable whose binding to query

Description

`glGetFragDataLocation` retrieves the assigned color number binding for the user-defined varying out variable *name* for program *program*. *program* must have previously been linked. *name* must be a null-terminated string. If *name* is not the name of an active user-defined varying out fragment shader variable within *program*, -1 will be returned.

Errors

GL_INVALID_OPERATION is generated if *program* is not the name of a program object.

See Also

glCreateProgram, glBindFragDataLocation

Copyright

Copyright © 2010 Khronos Group. This material may be distributed subject to the terms and conditions set forth in the Open Publication License, v 1.0, 8 June 1999. http://opencontent.org/openpub/.

glGetFramebufferAttachmentParameteriv

retrieve information about attachments of a bound framebuffer object

C Specification

```
void glGetFramebufferAttachmentParameter(GLenum target,
                                         GLenum attachment,
                                         GLenum pname,
                                         GLint *params);
```

Parameters

target
    Specifies the target of the query operation.
attachment
    Specifies the attachment within *target*
pname
    Specifies the parameter of *attachment* to query.
params
    Specifies the address of a variable receive the value of *pname* for *attachment*.

Description

glGetFramebufferAttachmentParameter returns information about attachments of a bound framebuffer object. *target* specifies the framebuffer binding point and must be GL_DRAW_FRAMEBUFFER, GL_READ_FRAMEBUFFER or GL_FRAMEBUFFER. GL_FRAMEBUFFER is equivalent to GL_DRAW_FRAMEBUFFER.

If the default framebuffer is bound to *target* then *attachment* must be one of GL_FRONT_LEFT, GL_FRONT_RIGHT, GL_BACK_LEFT, or GL_BACK_RIGHT, identifying a color buffer, GL_DEPTH, identifying the depth buffer, or GL_STENCIL, identifying the stencil buffer.

If a framebuffer object is bound, then *attachment* must be one of GL_COLOR_ATTACHMENTi, GL_DEPTH_ATTACHMENT, GL_STENCIL_ATTACHMENT, or GL_DEPTH_STENCIL_ATTACHMENT. i in GL_COLOR_ATTACHMENTi must be in the range zero to the value of GL_MAX_COLOR_ATTACHMENTS - 1.

If *attachment* is GL_DEPTH_STENCIL_ATTACHMENT and different objects are bound to the depth and stencil attachment points of *target* the query will fail. If the same object is bound to both attachment points, information about that object will be returned.

Upon successful return from glGetFramebufferAttachmentParameteriv, if *pname* is GL_FRAMEBUFFER_ATTACHMENT_OBJECT_TYPE, then *params* will contain one of GL_NONE, GL_FRAMEBUFFER_DEFAULT, GL_TEXTURE, or GL_RENDERBUFFER, identifying the type of object which contains the attached image. Other values accepted for *pname* depend on the type of object, as described below.

If the value of GL_FRAMEBUFFER_ATTACHMENT_OBJECT_TYPE is GL_NONE, no framebuffer is bound to *target*. In this case querying *pname* GL_FRAMEBUFFER_ATTACHMENT_OBJECT_NAME will return zero, and all other queries will generate an error.

If the value of GL_FRAMEBUFFER_ATTACHMENT_OBJECT_TYPE is not GL_NONE, these queries apply to all other framebuffer types:

> If *pname* is GL_FRAMEBUFFER_ATTACHMENT_RED_SIZE, GL_FRAMEBUFFER_ATTACHMENT_ GREEN_SIZE, GL_FRAMEBUFFER_ATTACHMENT_BLUE_SIZE, GL_FRAMEBUFFER_ ATTACHMENT_ALPHA_SIZE, GL_FRAMEBUFFER_ATTACHMENT_DEPTH_SIZE, or GL_FRAMEBUFFER_ATTACHMENT_STENCIL_SIZE, then *params* will contain the number of bits in the corresponding red, green, blue, alpha, depth, or stencil component of the specified attachment. Zero is returned if the requested component is not present in *attachment*.

> If *pname* is GL_FRAMEBUFFER_ATTACHMENT_COMPONENT_TYPE, *params* will contain the format of components of the specified attachment, one of GL_FLOAT, *GL_INT*, *GL_UNSIGNED_INT*, *GL_SIGNED_NORMALIZED*, or *GL_UNSIGNED_NORMALIZED* for float-ing-point, signed integer, unsigned integer, signed normalized fixed-point, or unsigned normalized fixed-point components respectively. Only color buffers may have integer components.

> If *pname* is GL_FRAMEBUFFER_ATTACHMENT_COLOR_ENCODING, *param* will contain the encoding of components of the specified attachment, one of GL_LINEAR or GL_SRGB for linear or sRGB-encoded components, respectively. Only color buffer components may be sRGB-encoded; such components are treated as described in sections 4.1.7 and 4.1.8. For the default framebuffer, color encoding is determined by the implementation. For framebuffer objects, components are sRGB-encoded if the internal format of a color attachment is one of the color-renderable SRGB formats.

If the value of GL_FRAMEBUFFER_ATTACHMENT_OBJECT_TYPE is GL_RENDERBUFFER, then:

> If *pname* is GL_FRAMEBUFFER_ATTACHMENT_OBJECT_NAME, *params* will contain the name of the renderbuffer object which contains the attached image.

If the value of GL_FRAMEBUFFER_ATTACHMENT_OBJECT_TYPE is GL_TEXTURE, then:

> If *pname* is GL_FRAMEBUFFER_ATTACHMENT_OBJECT_NAME, then *params* will contain the name of the texture object which contains the attached image.

> If *pname* is GL_FRAMEBUFFER_ATTACHMENT_TEXTURE_LEVEL, then *params* will contain the mipmap level of the texture object which contains the attached image.

> If *pname* is GL_FRAMEBUFFER_ATTACHMENT_TEXTURE_CUBE_MAP_FACE and the texture object named GL_FRAMEBUFFER_ATTACHMENT_OBJECT_NAME is a cube map texture, then *params* will contain the cube map face of the cubemap texture object which contains the attached image. Otherwise *params* will contain the value zero.

> If *pname* is GL_FRAMEBUFFER_ATTACHMENT_TEXTURE_LAYER and the texture object named GL_FRAMEBUFFER_ATTACHMENT_OBJECT_NAME is a layer of a three-dimen-sional texture or a one-or two-dimensional array texture, then *params* will contain the number of the texture layer which contains the attached image. Otherwise *params* will contain the value zero.

If *pname* is GL_FRAMEBUFFER_ATTACHMENT_LAYERED, then *params* will contain GL_TRUE if an entire level of a three-dimesional texture, cube map texture, or one-or two-dimensional array texture is attached. Otherwise, *params* will contain GL_FALSE. Any combinations of framebuffer type and *pname* not described above will generate an error.

Errors

GL_INVALID_ENUM is generated if *target* is not one of the accepted tokens.

GL_INVALID_ENUM is generated if *pname* is not valid for the value of GL_FRAMEBUFFER_ATTACHMENT_OBJECT_TYPE.

GL_INVALID_OPERATION is generated if *attachment* is not the accepted values for *target*.

GL_INVALID_OPERATION is generated if *attachment* is GL_DEPTH_STENCIL_ATTACHMENT and different objects are bound to the depth and stencil attachment points of *target*.

GL_INVALID_OPERATION is generated if the value of GL_FRAMEBUFFER_ATTACHMENT_OBJECT_TYPE is GL_NONE and *pname* is not GL_FRAMEBUFFER_ATTACHMENT_OBJECT_NAME.

See Also

glGenFramebuffers, glBindFramebuffer

Copyright

glGetMultisamplefv

retrieve the location of a sample

C Specification

```
void glGetMultisamplefv(GLenum pname,
                        GLuint index,
                        GLfloat *val);
```

Parameters

pname
> Specifies the sample parameter name. *pname* must be GL_SAMPLE_POSITION.

index
> Specifies the index of the sample whose position to query.

val
> Specifies the address of an array to receive the position of the sample.

Description

glGetMultisamplefv queries the location of a given sample. *pname* specifies the sample parameter to retrieve and must be GL_SAMPLE_POSITION. *index* corresponds to the sample for which the location should be returned. The sample location is returned as two floating-point values in *val[0]* and *val[1]*, each between 0 and 1, corresponding to the *x* and *y* locations respectively in the GL pixel space of that sample. (0.5, 0.5) this corresponds to the pixel center. *index* must be between zero and the value of GL_SAMPLES - 1.

If the multisample mode does not have fixed sample locations, the returned values may only reflect the locations of samples within some pixels.

Errors

GL_INVALID_ENUM is generated if *pname* is not one GL_SAMPLE_POSITION.
GL_INVALID_VALUE is generated if *index* is greater than or equal to the value of GL_SAMPLES.

See Also

`glGenFramebuffers, glBindFramebuffer`

Copyright

Copyright © 2010 Khronos Group. This material may be distributed subject to the terms and conditions set forth in the Open Publication License, v 1.0, 8 June 1999. http://opencontent.org/openpub/.

glGetProgramiv

Returns a parameter from a program object

C Specification

```
void glGetProgramiv(GLuint program,
                    GLenum pname,
                    GLint *params);
```

Parameters

program

Specifies the program object to be queried.

pname

Specifies the object parameter. Accepted symbolic names are GL_DELETE_STATUS, GL_LINK_STATUS, GL_VALIDATE_STATUS, GL_INFO_LOG_LENGTH, GL_ATTACHED_SHADERS, GL_ACTIVE_ATTRIBUTES, GL_ACTIVE_ATTRIBUTE_MAX_LENGTH, GL_ACTIVE_UNIFORMS, GL_ACTIVE_UNIFORM_BLOCKS, GL_ACTIVE_UNIFORM_BLOCK_MAX_NAME_LENGTH, GL_ACTIVE_UNIFORM_MAX_LENGTH, GL_TRANSFORM_FEEDBACK_BUFFER_MODE, GL_TRANSFORM_FEEDBACK_VARYINGS, GL_TRANSFORM_FEEDBACK_VARYING_MAX_LENGTH, GL_GEOMETRY_VERTICES_OUT, GL_GEOMETRY_INPUT_TYPE, and GL_GEOMETRY_OUTPUT_TYPE.

params

Returns the requested object parameter.

Description

`glGetProgram` returns in *params* the value of a parameter for a specific program object. The following parameters are defined:

GL_DELETE_STATUS

params returns GL_TRUE if *program* is currently flagged for deletion, and GL_FALSE otherwise.

GL_LINK_STATUS

params returns GL_TRUE if the last link operation on *program* was successful, and GL_FALSE otherwise.

GL_VALIDATE_STATUS

> *params* returns GL_TRUE or if the last validation operation on *program* was successful, and GL_FALSE otherwise.

GL_INFO_LOG_LENGTH

> *params* returns the number of characters in the information log for *program* including the null termination character (i.e., the size of the character buffer required to store the information log). If *program* has no information log, a value of 0 is returned.

GL_ATTACHED_SHADERS

> *params* returns the number of shader objects attached to *program*.

GL_ACTIVE_ATTRIBUTES

> *params* returns the number of active attribute variables for *program*.

GL_ACTIVE_ATTRIBUTE_MAX_LENGTH

> *params* returns the length of the longest active attribute name for *program*, including the null termination character (i.e., the size of the character buffer required to store the longest attribute name). If no active attributes exist, 0 is returned.

GL_ACTIVE_UNIFORMS

> *params* returns the number of active uniform variables for *program*.

GL_ACTIVE_UNIFORM_MAX_LENGTH

> *params* returns the length of the longest active uniform variable name for *program*, including the null termination character (i.e., the size of the character buffer required to store the longest uniform variable name). If no active uniform variables exist, 0 is returned.

GL_TRANSFORM_FEEDBACK_BUFFER_MODE

> *params* returns a symbolic constant indicating the buffer mode used when transform feedback is active. This may be GL_SEPARATE_ATTRIBS or GL_INTERLEAVED_ATTRIBS.

GL_TRANSFORM_FEEDBACK_VARYINGS

> *params* returns the number of varying variables to capture in transform feedback mode for the program.

GL_TRANSFORM_FEEDBACK_VARYING_MAX_LENGTH

> *params* returns the length of the longest variable name to be used for transform feedback, including the null-terminator.

GL_GEOMETRY_VERTICES_OUT

> *params* returns the maximum number of vertices that the geometry shader in *program* will output.

GL_GEOMETRY_INPUT_TYPE

> *params* returns a symbolic constant indicating the primitive type accepted as input to the geometry shader contained in *program*.

GL_GEOMETRY_OUTPUT_TYPE

> *params* returns a symbolic constant indicating the primitive type that will be output by the geometry shader contained in *program*.

Notes

GL_ACTIVE_UNIFORM_BLOCKS and GL_ACTIVE_UNIFORM_BLOCK_MAX_NAME_LENGTH are available only if the GL version 3.1 or greater.

GL_GEOMETRY_VERTICES_OUT, GL_GEOMETRY_INPUT_TYPE and GL_GEOMETRY_OUTPUT_TYPE are accepted only if the GL version is 3.2 or greater.

If an error is generated, no change is made to the contents of *params*.

Errors

GL_INVALID_VALUE is generated if *program* is not a value generated by OpenGL.

GL_INVALID_OPERATION is generated if *program* does not refer to a program object.

GL_INVALID_OPERATION is generated if *pname* is GL_GEOMETRY_VERTICES_OUT, GL_GEOMETRY_INPUT_TYPE, or GL_GEOMETRY_OUTPUT_TYPE, and *program* does not contain a geometry shader.

GL_INVALID_ENUM is generated if *pname* is not an accepted value.

Associated Gets

glGetActiveAttrib with argument *program*
glGetActiveUniform with argument *program*
glGetAttachedShaders with argument *program*
glGetProgramInfoLog with argument *program*
glIsProgram

See Also

glAttachShader, glCreateProgram, glDeleteProgram, glGetShader, glLinkProgram, glValidateProgram

Copyright

glGetProgramInfoLog

Returns the information log for a program object

C Specification

```
void glGetProgramInfoLog(GLuint program,
                         GLsizei maxLength,
                         GLsizei *length,
                         GLchar *infoLog)
```

Parameters

program
    Specifies the program object whose information log is to be queried.
maxLength
    Specifies the size of the character buffer for storing the returned information log.
length
    Returns the length of the string returned in *infoLog* (excluding the null terminator).
infoLog
    Specifies an array of characters that is used to return the information log.

Description

glGetProgramInfoLog returns the information log for the specified program object. The information log for a program object is modified when the program object is linked or validated. The string that is returned will be null terminated.

glGetProgramInfoLog returns in *infoLog* as much of the information log as it can, up to a maximum of *maxLength* characters. The number of characters actually returned, excluding the null termination character, is specified by *length*. If the length of the returned string is not required, a value of NULL can be passed in the *length* argument. The size of the buffer required to store the returned information log can be obtained by calling glGetProgram with the value GL_INFO_LOG_LENGTH.

The information log for a program object is either an empty string, or a string containing information about the last link operation, or a string containing information about the last validation operation. It may contain diagnostic messages, warning messages, and other information. When a program object is created, its information log will be a string of length 0.

Notes

The information log for a program object is the OpenGL implementer's primary mechanism for conveying information about linking and validating. Therefore, the information log can be helpful to application developers during the development process, even when these operations are successful. Application developers should not expect different OpenGL implementations to produce identical information logs.

Errors

GL_INVALID_VALUE is generated if *program* is not a value generated by OpenGL.
GL_INVALID_OPERATION is generated if *program* is not a program object.
GL_INVALID_VALUE is generated if *maxLength* is less than 0.

Associated Gets

glGetProgram with argument GL_INFO_LOG_LENGTH
glIsProgram

See Also

glCompileShader, glGetShaderInfoLog, glLinkProgram, glValidateProgram

Copyright

glGetQueryiv

return parameters of a query object target

C Specification

```
void glGetQueryiv(GLenum target,
                  GLenum pname,
                  GLint * params);
```

Parameters

target

Specifies a query object target. Must be GL_SAMPLES_PASSED, GL_ANY_SAMPLES_PASSED, GL_PRIMITIVES_GENERATED, GL_TRANSFORM_FEEDBACK_PRIMITIVES_WRITTEN, GL_TIME_ELAPSED, or GL_TIMESTAMP.

pname

Specifies the symbolic name of a query object target parameter. Accepted values are GL_CURRENT_QUERY or GL_QUERY_COUNTER_BITS.

params

Returns the requested data.

Description

glGetQueryiv returns in *params* a selected parameter of the query object target specified by *target*.

pname names a specific query object target parameter. When *pname* is GL_CURRENT_QUERY, the name of the currently active query for *target*, or zero if no query is active, will be placed in *params*. If *pname* is GL_QUERY_COUNTER_BITS, the implementation-dependent number of bits used to hold the result of queries for *target* is returned in *params*.

Notes

If an error is generated, no change is made to the contents of *params*.

Errors

GL_INVALID_ENUM is generated if *target* or *pname* is not an accepted value.

See Also

glGetQueryObject, glIsQuery

Copyright

glGetQueryObject

return parameters of a query object

C Specification

```
void glGetQueryObjectiv(GLuint id,
                        GLenum pname,
                        GLint * params);
void glGetQueryObjectuiv(GLuint id,
                         GLenum pname,
                         GLuint * params);
void glGetQueryObjecti64v(GLuint id,
                          GLenum pname,
                          GLint64 * params);
void glGetQueryObjectui64v(GLuint id,
                           GLenum pname,
                           GLuint64 * params);
```

Parameters

id

Specifies the name of a query object.

pname

Specifies the symbolic name of a query object parameter. Accepted values are GL_QUERY_RESULT or GL_QUERY_RESULT_AVAILABLE.

params

Returns the requested data.

Description

glGetQueryObject returns in *params* a selected parameter of the query object specified by *id*. *pname* names a specific query object parameter. *pname* can be as follows:

GL_QUERY_RESULT

> *params* returns the value of the query object's passed samples counter. The initial value is 0.

GL_QUERY_RESULT_AVAILABLE

> *params* returns whether the passed samples counter is immediately available. If a delay would occur waiting for the query result, GL_FALSE is returned. Otherwise, GL_TRUE is returned, which also indicates that the results of all previous queries are available as well.

Notes

If an error is generated, no change is made to the contents of *params*.

glGetQueryObject implicitly flushes the GL pipeline so that any incomplete rendering delimited by the occlusion query completes in finite time.

If multiple queries are issued using the same query object *id* before calling glGetQueryObject, the results of the most recent query will be returned. In this case, when issuing a new query, the results of the previous query are discarded.

glGetQueryObjecti64v and glGetQueryObjectui64v are available only if the GL version is 3.3 or greater.

Errors

GL_INVALID_ENUM is generated if *pname* is not an accepted value.

GL_INVALID_OPERATION is generated if *id* is not the name of a query object.

GL_INVALID_OPERATION is generated if *id* is the name of a currently active query object.

See Also

glBeginQuery, glEndQuery, glGetQueryiv, glIsQuery, glQueryCounter

Copyright

glGetRenderbufferParameteriv

retrieve information about a bound renderbuffer object

C Specification

```
void glGetRenderbufferParameteriv(GLenum target,
                                  GLenum pname,
                                  GLint *params);
```

Parameters

target

> Specifies the target of the query operation. *target* must be GL_RENDERBUFFER.

pname

> Specifies the parameter whose value to retrieve from the renderbuffer bound to *target*.

params

> Specifies the address of an array to receive the value of the queried parameter.

Description

glGetRenderbufferParameteriv retrieves information about a bound renderbuffer object. *target* specifies the target of the query operation and must be GL_RENDERBUFFER. *pname* specifies the parameter whose value to query and must be one of GL_RENDERBUFFER_WIDTH, GL_RENDERBUFFER_HEIGHT, GL_RENDERBUFFER_INTERNAL_FORMAT, GL_RENDERBUFFER_RED_SIZE, GL_RENDERBUFFER_GREEN_SIZE, GL_RENDERBUFFER_BLUE_SIZE, GL_RENDERBUFFER_ALPHA_SIZE, GL_RENDERBUFFER_DEPTH_SIZE, GL_RENDERBUFFER_DEPTH_SIZE, GL_RENDERBUFFER_STENCIL_SIZE, or GL_RENDERBUFFER_SAMPLES.

Upon a successful return from glGetRenderbufferParameteriv, if *pname* is GL_RENDERBUFFER_WIDTH, GL_RENDERBUFFER_HEIGHT, GL_RENDERBUFFER_INTERNAL_FORMAT, or GL_RENDERBUFFER_SAMPLES, then *params* will contain the width in pixels, the height in pixels, the internal format, or the number of samples, respectively, of the image of the renderbuffer currently bound to *target*.

If *pname* is GL_RENDERBUFFER_RED_SIZE, GL_RENDERBUFFER_GREEN_SIZE, GL_RENDERBUFFER_BLUE_SIZE, GL_RENDERBUFFER_ALPHA_SIZE, GL_RENDERBUFFER_DEPTH_SIZE, or GL_RENDERBUFFER_STENCIL_SIZE, then *params* will contain the actual resolutions (not the resolutions specified when the image array was defined) for the red, green, blue, alpha depth, or stencil components, respectively, of the image of the renderbuffer currently bound to *target*.

Errors

GL_INVALID_ENUM is generated if *pname* is not one of the accepted tokens.

See Also

glGenRenderbuffers, glFramebufferRenderbuffer, glBindRenderbuffer, glRenderbufferStorage, glRenderbufferStorageMultisample

Copyright

glGetSamplerParameter

return sampler parameter values

C Specification

```
void glGetSamplerParameterfv(GLuint sampler,
                             GLenum pname,
                             GLfloat * params);
void glGetSamplerParameteriv(GLuint sampler,
                             GLenum pname,
                             GLint * params);
```

Parameters

sampler

Specifies name of the sampler object from which to retrieve parameters.

pname

Specifies the symbolic name of a sampler parameter. GL_TEXTURE_MAG_FILTER, GL_TEXTURE_MIN_FILTER, GL_TEXTURE_MIN_LOD, GL_TEXTURE_MAX_LOD, GL_TEXTURE_LOD_BIAS, GL_TEXTURE_WRAP_S, GL_TEXTURE_WRAP_T,

GL_TEXTURE_WRAP_R, GL_TEXTURE_BORDER_COLOR,
GL_TEXTURE_COMPARE_MODE, and GL_TEXTURE_COMPARE_FUNC are accepted.

params

Returns the sampler parameters.

Description

glGetSamplerParameter returns in *params* the value or values of the sampler parameter speci-fied as *pname*. *sampler* defines the target sampler, and must be the name of an existing sampler object, returned from a previous call to glGenSamplers. *pname* accepts the same symbols as glSamplerParameter, with the same interpretations:

GL_TEXTURE_MAG_FILTER

Returns the single-valued texture magnification filter, a symbolic constant. The initial value is GL_LINEAR.

GL_TEXTURE_MIN_FILTER

Returns the single-valued texture minification filter, a symbolic constant. The initial value is GL_NEAREST_MIPMAP_LINEAR.

GL_TEXTURE_MIN_LOD

Returns the single-valued texture minimum level-of-detail value. The initial value is -1000.

GL_TEXTURE_MAX_LOD

Returns the single-valued texture maximum level-of-detail value. The initial value is 1000.

GL_TEXTURE_WRAP_S

Returns the single-valued wrapping function for texture coordinate s, a symbolic constant. The initial value is GL_REPEAT.

GL_TEXTURE_WRAP_T

Returns the single-valued wrapping function for texture coordinate t, a symbolic constant. The initial value is GL_REPEAT.

GL_TEXTURE_WRAP_R

Returns the single-valued wrapping function for texture coordinate r, a symbolic constant. The initial value is GL_REPEAT.

GL_TEXTURE_BORDER_COLOR

Returns four integer or floating-point numbers that comprise the RGBA color of the texture border. Floating-point values are returned in the range [0,1]. Integer values are returned as a linear mapping of the internal floating-point representation such that 1.0 maps to the most positive representable integer and -1.0 maps to the most negative representable integer. The initial value is (0, 0, 0, 0).

GL_TEXTURE_COMPARE_MODE

Returns a single-valued texture comparison mode, a symbolic constant. The initial value is GL_NONE. See glSamplerParameter.

GL_TEXTURE_COMPARE_FUNC

Returns a single-valued texture comparison function, a symbolic constant. The initial value is GL_LEQUAL. See glSamplerParameter.

Notes

If an error is generated, no change is made to the contents of *params*.
glGetSamplerParameter is available only if the GL version is 3.3 or higher.

Errors

GL_INVALID_VALUE is generated if *sampler* is not the name of a sampler object returned from a previous call to glGenSamplers.
GL_INVALID_ENUM is generated if *pname* is not an accepted value.

See Also

glSamplerParameter, glGenSamplers, glDeleteSamplers, glSamplerParameter

Copyright

glGetShaderiv

Returns a parameter from a shader object

C Specification

```
void glGetShaderiv(GLuint shader,
                   GLenum pname,
                   GLint *params);
```

Parameters

shader

Specifies the shader object to be queried.

pname

Specifies the object parameter. Accepted symbolic names are GL_SHADER_TYPE, GL_DELETE_STATUS, GL_COMPILE_STATUS, GL_INFO_LOG_LENGTH, GL_SHADER_SOURCE_LENGTH.

params

Returns the requested object parameter.

Description

glGetShader returns in *params* the value of a parameter for a specific shader object. The following parameters are defined:

GL_SHADER_TYPE

params returns GL_VERTEX_SHADER if *shader* is a vertex shader object, GL_GEOMETRY_SHADER if *shader* is a geometry shader object, and GL_FRAGMENT_SHADER if *shader* is a fragment shader object.

GL_DELETE_STATUS

params returns GL_TRUE if *shader* is currently flagged for deletion, and GL_FALSE otherwise.

GL_COMPILE_STATUS

params returns GL_TRUE if the last compile operation on *shader* was successful, and GL_FALSE otherwise.

GL_INFO_LOG_LENGTH

params returns the number of characters in the information log for *shader* including the null termination character (i.e., the size of the character buffer required to store the information log). If *shader* has no information log, a value of 0 is returned.

GL_SHADER_SOURCE_LENGTH

params returns the length of the concatenation of the source strings that make up the shader source for the *shader*, including the null termination character. (i.e., the size of the character buffer required to store the shader source). If no source code exists, 0 is returned.

Notes

If an error is generated, no change is made to the contents of *params*.

Errors

GL_INVALID_VALUE is generated if *shader* is not a value generated by OpenGL.
GL_INVALID_OPERATION is generated if *shader* does not refer to a shader object.
GL_INVALID_ENUM is generated if *pname* is not an accepted value.

Associated Gets

glGetShaderInfoLog with argument *shader*
glGetShaderSource with argument *shader*
glIsShader

See Also

`glCompileShader`, `glCreateShader`, `glDeleteShader`, `glGetProgram`,
`glShaderSource`

Copyright

glGetShaderInfoLog

Returns the information log for a shader object

C Specification

```
void glGetShaderInfoLog(GLuint shader,
                        GLsizei maxLength,
                        GLsizei *length,
                        GLchar *infoLog);
```

Parameters

shader
Specifies the shader object whose information log is to be queried.
maxLength
Specifies the size of the character buffer for storing the returned information log.
length
Returns the length of the string returned in *infoLog* (excluding the null terminator).
infoLog
Specifies an array of characters that is used to return the information log.

Description

glGetShaderInfoLog returns the information log for the specified shader object. The information log for a shader object is modified when the shader is compiled. The string that is returned will be null terminated.

glGetShaderInfoLog returns in *infoLog* as much of the information log as it can, up to a maximum of *maxLength* characters. The number of characters actually returned, excluding the null termination character, is specified by *length*. If the length of the returned string is not required, a value of NULL can be passed in the *length* argument. The size of the buffer required to store the returned information log can be obtained by calling glGetShader with the value GL_INFO_LOG_LENGTH.

The information log for a shader object is a string that may contain diagnostic messages, warning messages, and other information about the last compile operation. When a shader object is created, its information log will be a string of length 0.

Notes

The information log for a shader object is the OpenGL implementer's primary mechanism for conveying information about the compilation process. Therefore, the information log can be helpful to application developers during the development process, even when compilation is successful. Application developers should not expect different OpenGL implementations to produce identical information logs.

Errors

GL_INVALID_VALUE is generated if *shader* is not a value generated by OpenGL.
GL_INVALID_OPERATION is generated if *shader* is not a shader object.
GL_INVALID_VALUE is generated if *maxLength* is less than 0.

Associated Gets

glGetShader with argument GL_INFO_LOG_LENGTH
glIsShader

See Also

`glCompileShader`, `glGetProgramInfoLog`, `glLinkProgram`, `glValidateProgram`

Copyright

glGetShaderSource

Returns the source code string from a shader object

C Specification

```
void glGetShaderSource(GLuint shader,
                       GLsizei bufSize,
                       GLsizei * length,
                       GLchar * source);
```

Parameters

shader
> Specifies the shader object to be queried.

bufSize
> Specifies the size of the character buffer for storing the returned source code string.

length
> Returns the length of the string returned in *source* (excluding the null terminator).

source
> Specifies an array of characters that is used to return the source code string.

Description

`glGetShaderSource` returns the concatenation of the source code strings from the shader object specified by *shader*. The source code strings for a shader object are the result of a previous call to glShaderSource. The string returned by the function will be null terminated.

`glGetShaderSource` returns in *source* as much of the source code string as it can, up to a maximum of *bufSize* characters. The number of characters actually returned, excluding the null termination character, is specified by *length*. If the length of the returned string is not required, a value of NULL can be passed in the *length* argument. The size of the buffer required to store the returned source code string can be obtained by calling glGetShader with the value GL_SHADER_SOURCE_LENGTH.

Errors

GL_INVALID_VALUE is generated if *shader* is not a value generated by OpenGL.
GL_INVALID_OPERATION is generated if *shader* is not a shader object.
GL_INVALID_VALUE is generated if *bufSize* is less than 0.

Associated Gets

glGetShader with argument GL_SHADER_SOURCE_LENGTH
glIsShader

See Also

`glCreateShader`, `glShaderSource`

Copyright

glGetString

return a string describing the current GL connection

C Specification

```
const GLubyte* glGetString (GLenum name);
```

C Specification

```
const GLubyte* glGetStringi (GLenum name,
                             GLuint index);
```

Parameters

name

Specifies a symbolic constant, one of GL_VENDOR, GL_RENDERER, GL_VERSION, or GL_SHADING_LANGUAGE_VERSION. Additionally, `glGetStringi` accepts the GL_EXTENSIONS token.

index

For `glGetStringi`, specifies the index of the string to return.

Description

`glGetString` returns a pointer to a static string describing some aspect of the current GL connection. *name* can be one of the following:

GL_VENDOR

Returns the company responsible for this GL implementation. This name does not change from release to release.

GL_RENDERER

Returns the name of the renderer. This name is typically specific to a particular configuration of a hardware platform. It does not change from release to release.

GL_VERSION

       Returns a version or release number.

GL_SHADING_LANGUAGE_VERSION

       Returns a version or release number for the shading language.

`glGetStringi` returns a pointer to a static string indexed by *index*. *name* can be one of the following:

GL_EXTENSIONS

       For `glGetStringi` only, returns the extension string supported by the implementation at *index*.

Strings GL_VENDOR and GL_RENDERER together uniquely specify a platform. They do not change from release to release and should be used by platform-recognition algorithms.

The GL_VERSION and GL_SHADING_LANGUAGE_VERSION strings begin with a version number. The version number uses one of these forms:

major_number.minor_number major_number.minor_number.release_number

Vendor-specific information may follow the version number. Its format depends on the implementation, but a space always separates the version number and the vendor-specific information.

All strings are null-terminated.

Notes

If an error is generated, `glGetString` returns 0.

The client and server may support different versions. `glGetString` always returns a compatible version number. The release number always describes the server.

Errors

GL_INVALID_ENUM is generated if *name* is not an accepted value.

GL_INVALID_VALUE is generated by `glGetStringi` if *index* is outside the valid range for indexed state *name*.

Copyright

Copyright © 1991-2006 Silicon Graphics, Inc. Copyright © 2010 Khronos Group. This document is licensed under the SGI Free Software B License. For details, see http://oss.sgi.com/projects/FreeB/.

glGetSynciv

query the properties of a sync object

C Specification

```
void glGetSynciv(GLsync sync,
                 GLenum pname,
                 GLsizei bufSize,
                 GLsizei *length,
                 GLint *values);
```

Parameters

sync

       Specifies the sync object whose properties to query.

pname

       Specifies the parameter whose value to retrieve from the sync object specified in *sync*.

bufSize

       Specifies the size of the buffer whose address is given in *values*.

length

       Specifies the address of a variable to receive the number of integers placed in *values*.

values

       Specifies the address of an array to receive the values of the queried parameter.

Description

glGetSynciv retrieves properties of a sync object. *sync* specifies the name of the sync object whose properties to retrieve.

On success, glGetSynciv replaces up to *bufSize* integers in *values* with the corresponding property values of the object being queried. The actual number of integers replaced is returned in the variable whose address is specified in *length*. If *length* is NULL, no length is returned.

If *pname* is GL_OBJECT_TYPE, a single value representing the specific type of the sync object is placed in *values*. The only type supported is GL_SYNC_FENCE.

If *pname* is GL_SYNC_STATUS, a single value representing the status of the sync object (GL_SIGNALED or GL_UNSIGNALED) is placed in *values*.

If *pname* is GL_SYNC_CONDITION, a single value representing the condition of the sync object is placed in *values*. The only condition supported is GL_SYNC_GPU_COMMANDS_COMPLETE.

If *pname* is GL_SYNC_FLAGS, a single value representing the flags with which the sync object was created is placed in *values*. No flags are currently supported˙.

If an error occurs, nothing will be written to *values* or *length*.

Errors

GL_INVALID_VALUE is generated if *sync* is not the name of a sync object.
GL_INVALID_ENUM is generated if *pname* is not one of the accepted tokens.

See Also

glFenceSync, glWaitSync, glClientWaitSync

Copyright

glGetTexImage

return a texture image

C Specification

```
void glGetTexImage(GLenum target,
                   GLint level,
                   GLenum format,
                   GLenum type,
                   GLvoid * img);
```

Parameters

target

Specifies which texture is to be obtained. GL_TEXTURE_1D, GL_TEXTURE_2D, GL_TEXTURE_3D, GL_TEXTURE_1D_ARRAY, GL_TEXTURE_2D_ARRAY, GL_TEXTURE_RECTANGLE, GL_TEXTURE_CUBE_MAP_POSITIVE_X, GL_TEXTURE_CUBE_MAP_NEGATIVE_X, GL_TEXTURE_CUBE_MAP_POSITIVE_Y, GL_TEXTURE_CUBE_MAP_NEGATIVE_Y, GL_TEXTURE_CUBE_MAP_POSITIVE_Z, and GL_TEXTURE_CUBE_MAP_NEGATIVE_Z are accepted.

˙ *flags is expected to be used in future extensions to the sync objects.*

level

Specifies the level-of-detail number of the desired image. Level 0 is the base image level. Level n is the nth mipmap reduction image.

format

Specifies a pixel format for the returned data. The supported formats are GL_STENCIL_INDEX, GL_DEPTH_COMPONENT, GL_DEPTH_STENCIL, GL_RED, GL_GREEN, GL_BLUE, GL_RG, GL_RGB, GL_RGBA, GL_BGR, GL_BGRA, GL_RED_INTEGER, GL_GREEN_INTEGER, GL_BLUE_INTEGER, GL_RG_INTEGER, GL_RGB_INTEGER, GL_RGBA_INTEGER, GL_BGR_INTEGER, GL_BGRA_INTEGER.

type

Specifies a pixel type for the returned data. The supported types are GL_UNSIGNED_BYTE, GL_BYTE, GL_UNSIGNED_SHORT, GL_SHORT, GL_UNSIGNED_INT, GL_INT, GL_HALF_FLOAT, GL_FLOAT, GL_UNSIGNED_BYTE_3_3_2, GL_UNSIGNED_BYTE_2_3_3_REV, GL_UNSIGNED_SHORT_5_6_5, GL_UNSIGNED_SHORT_5_6_5_REV, GL_UNSIGNED_SHORT_4_4_4_4, GL_UNSIGNED_SHORT_4_4_4_4_REV, GL_UNSIGNED_SHORT_5_5_5_1, GL_UNSIGNED_SHORT_1_5_5_5_REV, GL_UNSIGNED_INT_8_8_8_8, GL_UNSIGNED_INT_8_8_8_8_REV, GL_UNSIGNED_INT_10_10_10_2, GL_UNSIGNED_INT_2_10_10_10_REV, GL_UNSIGNED_INT_24_8, GL_UNSIGNED_INT_10F_11F_11F_REV, GL_UNSIGNED_INT_5_9_9_9_REV, and GL_FLOAT_32_UNSIGNED_INT_24_8_REV.

img

Returns the texture image. Should be a pointer to an array of the type specified by *type*.

Description

glGetTexImage returns a texture image into *img*. *target* specifies whether the desired texture image is one specified by glTexImage1D (GL_TEXTURE_1D), glTexImage2D (GL_TEXTURE_1D_ARRAY, GL_TEXTURE_RECTANGLE, GL_TEXTURE_2D or any of GL_TEXTURE_CUBE_MAP_*), or glTexImage3D (GL_TEXTURE_2D_ARRAY, GL_TEXTURE_3D). *level* specifies the level-of-detail number of the desired image. *format* and *type* specify the format and type of the desired image array. See the reference page for glTexImage1D for a description of the acceptable values for the *format* and *type* parameters, respectively.

If a non-zero named buffer object is bound to the GL_PIXEL_PACK_BUFFER target (see glBindBuffer) while a texture image is requested, *img* is treated as a byte offset into the buffer object's data store.

To understand the operation of glGetTexImage, consider the selected internal four-component texture image to be an RGBA color buffer the size of the image. The semantics of glGetTexImage are then identical to those of glReadPixels, with the exception that no pixel transfer operations are performed, when called with the same *format* and *type*, with x and y set to 0, *width* set to the width of the texture image and *height* set to 1 for 1D images, or to the height of the texture image for 2D images.

If the selected texture image does not contain four components, the following mappings are applied. Single-component textures are treated as RGBA buffers with red set to the single-component value, green set to 0, blue set to 0, and alpha set to 1. Two-component textures are treated as RGBA buffers with red set to the value of component zero, alpha set to the value of component one, and green and blue set to 0. Finally, three-component textures are treated as RGBA buffers with red set to component zero, green set to component one, blue set to component two, and alpha set to 1.

To determine the required size of *img*, use glGetTexLevelParameter to determine the dimensions of the internal texture image, then scale the required number of pixels by the storage required for each pixel, based on *format* and *type*. Be sure to take the pixel storage parameters into account, especially GL_PACK_ALIGNMENT.

Notes

If an error is generated, no change is made to the contents of *img*.
glGetTexImage returns the texture image for the active texture unit.

Errors

GL_INVALID_ENUM is generated if *target*, *format*, or *type* is not an accepted value.

GL_INVALID_VALUE is generated if *level* is less than 0.

GL_INVALID_VALUE may be generated if *level* is greater than $\log_2(max)$, where max is the returned value of GL_MAX_TEXTURE_SIZE.

GL_INVALID_OPERATION is returned if *type* is one of GL_UNSIGNED_BYTE_3_3_2, GL_UNSIGNED_BYTE_2_3_3_REV, GL_UNSIGNED_SHORT_5_6_5, GL_UNSIGNED_SHORT_5_6_5_REV, or GL_UNSIGNED_INT_10F_11F_11F_REV and *format* is not GL_RGB.

GL_INVALID_OPERATION is returned if *type* is one of GL_UNSIGNED_SHORT_4_4_4_4, GL_UNSIGNED_SHORT_4_4_4_4_REV, GL_UNSIGNED_SHORT_5_5_5_1, GL_UNSIGNED_SHORT_1_5_5_5_REV, GL_UNSIGNED_INT_8_8_8_8, GL_UNSIGNED_INT_8_8_8_8_REV, GL_UNSIGNED_INT_10_10_10_2, GL_UNSIGNED_INT_2_10_10_10_REV, or GL_UNSIGNED_INT_5_9_9_9_REV and *format* is neither GL_RGBA or GL_BGRA.

GL_INVALID_OPERATION is generated if a non-zero buffer object name is bound to the GL_PIXEL_PACK_BUFFER target and the buffer object's data store is currently mapped.

GL_INVALID_OPERATION is generated if a non-zero buffer object name is bound to the GL_PIXEL_PACK_BUFFER target and the data would be packed to the buffer object such that the memory writes required would exceed the data store size.

GL_INVALID_OPERATION is generated if a non-zero buffer object name is bound to the GL_PIXEL_PACK_BUFFER target and *img* is not evenly divisible into the number of bytes needed to store in memory a datum indicated by *type*.

Associated Gets

glGetTexLevelParameter with argument GL_TEXTURE_WIDTH
glGetTexLevelParameter with argument GL_TEXTURE_HEIGHT
glGetTexLevelParameter with argument GL_TEXTURE_INTERNAL_FORMAT
glGet with arguments GL_PACK_ALIGNMENT and others
glGet with argument GL_PIXEL_PACK_BUFFER_BINDING

See Also

glActiveTexture, glReadPixels, glTexImage1D, glTexImage2D, glTexImage3D, glTexSubImage1D, glTexSubImage2D, glTexSubImage3D, glTexParameter

Copyright

glGetTexLevelParameter

return texture parameter values for a specific level of detail

C Specification

```
void glGetTexLevelParameterfv(GLenum target,
                              GLint level,
                              GLenum pname,
                              GLfloat * params);
```

```
void glGetTexLevelParameteriv(GLenum target,
                              GLint level,
                              GLenum pname,
                              GLint * params);
```

Parameters

target

Specifies the symbolic name of the target texture, one of GL_TEXTURE_1D, GL_TEXTURE_2D, GL_TEXTURE_3D, GL_TEXTURE_1D_ARRAY, GL_TEXTURE_2D_ARRAY, GL_TEXTURE_RECTANGLE, GL_TEXTURE_2D_MULTISAMPLE, GL_TEXTURE_2D_MULTISAMPLE_ARRAY, GL_TEXTURE_CUBE_MAP_POSITIVE_X, GL_TEXTURE_CUBE_MAP_NEGATIVE_X, GL_TEXTURE_CUBE_MAP_POSITIVE_Y, GL_TEXTURE_CUBE_MAP_NEGATIVE_Y, GL_TEXTURE_CUBE_MAP_POSITIVE_Z, GL_TEXTURE_CUBE_MAP_NEGATIVE_Z, GL_PROXY_TEXTURE_1D, GL_PROXY_TEXTURE_2D, GL_PROXY_TEXTURE_3D, GL_PROXY_TEXTURE_1D_ARRAY, GL_PROXY_TEXTURE_2D_ARRAY, GL_PROXY_TEXTURE_RECTANGLE, GL_PROXY_TEXTURE_2D_MULTISAMPLE, GL_PROXY_TEXTURE_2D_MULTISAMPLE_ARRAY, GL_PROXY_TEXTURE_CUBE_MAP, or GL_TEXTURE_BUFFER.

level

Specifies the level-of-detail number of the desired image. Level 0 is the base image level. Level n is the nth mipmap reduction image.

pname

Specifies the symbolic name of a texture parameter. GL_TEXTURE_WIDTH, GL_TEXTURE_HEIGHT, GL_TEXTURE_DEPTH, GL_TEXTURE_INTERNAL_FORMAT, GL_TEXTURE_BORDER, GL_TEXTURE_RED_SIZE, GL_TEXTURE_GREEN_SIZE, GL_TEXTURE_BLUE_SIZE, GL_TEXTURE_ALPHA_SIZE, GL_TEXTURE_DEPTH_SIZE, GL_TEXTURE_COMPRESSED, and GL_TEXTURE_COMPRESSED_IMAGE_SIZE are accepted.

params

Returns the requested data.

Description

glGetTexLevelParameter returns in *params* texture parameter values for a specific level-of-detail value, specified as *level*. *target* defines the target texture, either GL_TEXTURE_1D, GL_TEXTURE_2D, GL_TEXTURE_3D, GL_PROXY_TEXTURE_1D, GL_PROXY_TEXTURE_2D, GL_PROXY_TEXTURE_3D, GL_TEXTURE_CUBE_MAP_POSITIVE_X, GL_TEXTURE_CUBE_MAP_NEGATIVE_X, GL_TEXTURE_CUBE_MAP_POSITIVE_Y, GL_TEXTURE_CUBE_MAP_NEGATIVE_Y, GL_TEXTURE_CUBE_MAP_POSITIVE_Z, GL_TEXTURE_CUBE_MAP_NEGATIVE_Z, or GL_PROXY_TEXTURE_CUBE_MAP.

GL_MAX_TEXTURE_SIZE, and GL_MAX_3D_TEXTURE_SIZE are not really descriptive enough. It has to report the largest square texture image that can be accommodated with mipmaps and borders, but a long skinny texture, or a texture without mipmaps and borders, may easily fit in texture memory. The proxy targets allow the user to more accurately query whether the GL can accommodate a texture of a given configuration. If the texture cannot be accommodated, the texture state variables, which may be queried with glGetTexLevelParameter, are set to 0. If the texture can be accommodated, the texture state values will be set as they would be set for a non-proxy target.

pname specifies the texture parameter whose value or values will be returned.

The accepted parameter names are as follows:

GL_TEXTURE_WIDTH

params returns a single value, the width of the texture image. This value includes the border of the texture image. The initial value is 0.

GL_TEXTURE_HEIGHT

    params returns a single value, the height of the texture image. This value includes the border of the texture image. The initial value is 0.

GL_TEXTURE_DEPTH

    params returns a single value, the depth of the texture image. This value includes the border of the texture image. The initial value is 0.

GL_TEXTURE_INTERNAL_FORMAT

    params returns a single value, the internal format of the texture image.

GL_TEXTURE_RED_TYPE,
GL_TEXTURE_GREEN_TYPE,
GL_TEXTURE_BLUE_TYPE,
GL_TEXTURE_ALPHA_TYPE,
GL_TEXTURE_DEPTH_TYPE

    The data type used to store the component. The types GL_NONE, GL_SIGNED_ NORMALIZED, GL_UNSIGNED_NORMALIZED, GL_FLOAT, GL_INT, and GL_UNSIGNED_INT may be returned to indicate signed normalized fixed-point, unsigned normalized fixed-point, floating-point, integer unnormalized, and unsigned integer unnormalized components, respectively.

GL_TEXTURE_RED_SIZE,
GL_TEXTURE_GREEN_SIZE,
GL_TEXTURE_BLUE_SIZE,
GL_TEXTURE_ALPHA_SIZE,
GL_TEXTURE_DEPTH_SIZE

    The internal storage resolution of an individual component. The resolution chosen by the GL will be a close match for the resolution requested by the user with the component argument of glTexImage1D, glTexImage2D, glTexImage3D, glCopyTexImage1D, and glCopyTexImage2D. The initial value is 0.

GL_TEXTURE_COMPRESSED

    params returns a single boolean value indicating if the texture image is stored in a compressed internal format. The initial value is GL_FALSE.

GL_TEXTURE_COMPRESSED_IMAGE_SIZE

    params returns a single integer value, the number of unsigned bytes of the compressed texture image that would be returned from glGetCompressedTexImage.

Notes

If an error is generated, no change is made to the contents of *params*.

`glGetTexLevelParameter` returns the texture level parameters for the active texture unit.

Errors

GL_INVALID_ENUM is generated if *target* or *pname* is not an accepted value.

GL_INVALID_VALUE is generated if *level* is less than 0.

GL_INVALID_VALUE may be generated if *level* is greater than $\log_2 max$, where *max* is the returned value of GL_MAX_TEXTURE_SIZE.

GL_INVALID_VALUE is generated if *target* is GL_TEXTURE_BUFFER and *level* is not zero.

GL_INVALID_OPERATION is generated if GL_TEXTURE_COMPRESSED_IMAGE_SIZE is queried on texture images with an uncompressed internal format or on proxy targets.

See Also

glActiveTexture, glGetTexParameter, glCopyTexImage1D, glCopyTexImage2D, glCopyTexSubImage1D, glCopyTexSubImage2D, glCopyTexSubImage3D, glTexImage1D, glTexImage2D, glTexImage3D, glTexSubImage1D, glTexSubImage2D, glTexSubImage3D, glTexParameter

Copyright

glGetTexParameter

return texture parameter values

C Specification

```
void glGetTexParameterfv(GLenum target,
                         GLenum pname,
                         GLfloat * params);
void glGetTexParameteriv(GLenum target,
                         GLenum pname,
                         GLint * params);
```

Parameters

target

Specifies the symbolic name of the target texture. GL_TEXTURE_1D, GL_TEXTURE_2D, GL_TEXTURE_1D_ARRAY, GL_TEXTURE_2D_ARRAY, GL_TEXTURE_3D, GL_TEXTURE_RECTANGLE, and GL_TEXTURE_CUBE_MAP are accepted.

pname

Specifies the symbolic name of a texture parameter. GL_TEXTURE_BASE_LEVEL, GL_TEXTURE_BORDER_COLOR, GL_TEXTURE_COMPARE_MODE, GL_TEXTURE_COMPARE_FUNC, GL_TEXTURE_LOD_BIAS, GL_TEXTURE_MAG_FILTER, GL_TEXTURE_MAX_LEVEL, GL_TEXTURE_MAX_LOD, GL_TEXTURE_MIN_FILTER, GL_TEXTURE_MIN_LOD, GL_TEXTURE_SWIZZLE_R, GL_TEXTURE_SWIZZLE_G, GL_TEXTURE_SWIZZLE_B, GL_TEXTURE_SWIZZLE_A, GL_TEXTURE_SWIZZLE_RGBA, GL_TEXTURE_WRAP_S, GL_TEXTURE_WRAP_T, and GL_TEXTURE_WRAP_R are accepted.

params

Returns the texture parameters.

Description

glGetTexParameter returns in *params* the value or values of the texture parameter specified as *pname*. *target* defines the target texture. GL_TEXTURE_1D, GL_TEXTURE_2D, GL_TEXTURE_3D, GL_TEXTURE_1D_ARRAY, GL_TEXTURE_2D_ARRAY, GL_TEXTURE_RECTANGLE, and GL_TEXTURE_CUBE_MAP specify one-, two-, or three-dimensional, one-dimensional array, two-dimensional array, rectangle or cube-mapped texturing, respectively. *pname* accepts the same symbols as glTexParameter, with the same interpretations:

GL_TEXTURE_MAG_FILTER

Returns the single-valued texture magnification filter, a symbolic constant. The initial value is GL_LINEAR.

GL_TEXTURE_MIN_FILTER

Returns the single-valued texture minification filter, a symbolic constant. The initial value is GL_NEAREST_MIPMAP_LINEAR.

GL_TEXTURE_MIN_LOD

Returns the single-valued texture minimum level-of-detail value. The initial value is -1000.

GL_TEXTURE_MAX_LOD

Returns the single-valued texture maximum level-of-detail value. The initial value is 1000.

GL_TEXTURE_BASE_LEVEL
> Returns the single-valued base texture mipmap level. The initial value is 0.

GL_TEXTURE_MAX_LEVEL
> Returns the single-valued maximum texture mipmap array level. The initial value is 1000.

GL_TEXTURE_SWIZZLE_R
> Returns the red component swizzle. The initial value is GL_RED.

GL_TEXTURE_SWIZZLE_G
> Returns the green component swizzle. The initial value is GL_GREEN.

GL_TEXTURE_SWIZZLE_B
> Returns the blue component swizzle. The initial value is GL_BLUE.

GL_TEXTURE_SWIZZLE_A
> Returns the alpha component swizzle. The initial value is GL_ALPHA.

GL_TEXTURE_SWIZZLE_RGBA
> Returns the component swizzle for all channels in a single query.

GL_TEXTURE_WRAP_S
> Returns the single-valued wrapping function for texture coordinate s, a symbolic constant. The initial value is GL_REPEAT.

GL_TEXTURE_WRAP_T
> Returns the single-valued wrapping function for texture coordinate t, a symbolic constant. The initial value is GL_REPEAT.

GL_TEXTURE_WRAP_R
> Returns the single-valued wrapping function for texture coordinate r, a symbolic constant. The initial value is GL_REPEAT.

GL_TEXTURE_BORDER_COLOR
> Returns four integer or floating-point numbers that comprise the RGBA color of the texture border. Floating-point values are returned in the range $[0,1]$. Integer values are returned as a linear mapping of the internal floating-point representation such that 1.0 maps to the most positive representable integer and -1.0 maps to the most negative representable integer. The initial value is (0, 0, 0, 0).

GL_TEXTURE_COMPARE_MODE
> Returns a single-valued texture comparison mode, a symbolic constant. The initial value is GL_NONE. See glTexParameter.

GL_TEXTURE_COMPARE_FUNC
> Returns a single-valued texture comparison function, a symbolic constant. The initial value is GL_LEQUAL. See glTexParameter.

Notes

If an error is generated, no change is made to the contents of *params*.

Errors

GL_INVALID_ENUM is generated if *target* or *pname* is not an accepted value.

See Also

`glTexParameter`

Copyright

glGetTransformFeedbackVarying

retrieve information about varying variables selected for transform feedback

C Specification

```
void glGetTransformFeedbackVarying(GLuint program,
                                   GLuint index,
                                   GLsizei bufSize,
                                   GLsizei * length,
                                   GLsizei size,
                                   GLenum * type, char * name);
```

Parameters

program
> The name of the target program object.

index
> The index of the varying variable whose information to retrieve.

bufSize
> The maximum number of characters, including the null terminator, that may be written into *name*.

length
> The address of a variable which will receive the number of characters written into *name*, excluding the null-terminator. If *length* is NULL no length is returned.

size
> The address of a variable that will receive the size of the varying.

type
> The address of a variable that will recieve the type of the varying.

name
> The address of a buffer into which will be written the name of the varying.

Description

Information about the set of varying variables in a linked program that will be captured during transform feedback may be retrieved by calling glGetTransformFeedbackVarying. glGetTransformFeedbackVarying provides information about the varying variable selected by *index*. An *index* of 0 selects the first varying variable specified in the *varyings* array passed to glTransformFeedbackVaryings, and an *index* of GL_TRANSFORM_FEEDBACK_VARYINGS-1 selects the last such variable.

The name of the selected varying is returned as a null-terminated string in *name*. The actual number of characters written into *name*, excluding the null terminator, is returned in *length*. If *length* is NULL, no length is returned. The maximum number of characters that may be written into *name*, including the null terminator, is specified by *bufSize*.

The length of the longest varying name in program is given by GL_TRANSFORM_FEEDBACK_VARYING_MAX_LENGTH, which can be queried with glGetProgram.

For the selected varying variable, its type is returned into *type*. The size of the varying is returned into *size*. The value in *size* is in units of the type returned in *type*. The type returned can be any of the scalar, vector, or matrix attribute types returned by glGetActiveAttrib. If an error occurred, the return parameters *length*, *size*, *type* and *name* will be unmodified. This command will return as much information about the varying variables as possible. If no information is available, *length* will be set to zero and *name* will be an empty string. This situation could arise if glGetTransformFeedbackVarying is called after a failed link.

Errors

GL_INVALID_VALUE is generated if *program* is not the name of a program object.
GL_INVALID_VALUE is generated if *index* is greater or equal to the value of
GL_TRANSFORM_FEEDBACK_VARYINGS.
GL_INVALID_OPERATION is generated *program* has not been linked.

Associated Gets

glGetProgram with argument GL_TRANSFORM_FEEDBACK_VARYING_MAX_LENGTH.

See Also

glBeginTransformFeedback, glEndTransformFeedback,
glTransformFeedbackVaryings, glGetProgram

Copyright

Copyright © 2010 Khronos Group. This material may be distributed subject to the terms and conditions set forth in the Open Publication License, v 1.0, 8 June 1999. http://opencontent.org/openpub/.

glGetUniform

Returns the value of a uniform variable

C Specification

```
void glGetUniformfv(GLuint program,
                    GLint location,
                    GLfloat * params);
void glGetUniformiv(GLuint program,
                    GLint location,
                    GLint * params);
```

Parameters

program
> Specifies the program object to be queried.

location
> Specifies the location of the uniform variable to be queried.

params
> Returns the value of the specified uniform variable.

Description

glGetUniform returns in *params* the value(s) of the specified uniform variable. The type of the uniform variable specified by *location* determines the number of values returned. If the uniform variable is defined in the shader as a boolean, int, or float, a single value will be returned. If it is defined as a vec2, ivec2, or bvec2, two values will be returned. If it is defined as a vec3, ivec3, or bvec3, three values will be returned, and so on. To query values stored in uniform variables declared as arrays, call glGetUniform for each element of the array. To query values stored in uniform variables declared as structures, call glGetUniform for each field in the structure. The values for uniform variables declared as a matrix will be returned in column major order.

The locations assigned to uniform variables are not known until the program object is linked. After linking has occurred, the command glGetUniformLocation can be used to obtain the location of a uniform variable. This location value can then be passed to glGetUniform in order to query the current value of the uniform variable. After a program object has been linked successfully, the index values for uniform variables remain fixed until the next link command occurs. The uniform variable values can only be queried after a link if the link was successful.

Notes

If an error is generated, no change is made to the contents of *params*.

Errors

GL_INVALID_VALUE is generated if *program* is not a value generated by OpenGL.
GL_INVALID_OPERATION is generated if *program* is not a program object.
GL_INVALID_OPERATION is generated if *program* has not been successfully linked.
GL_INVALID_OPERATION is generated if *location* does not correspond to a valid uniform variable location for the specified program object.

Associated Gets

glGetActiveUniform with arguments *program* and the index of an active uniform variable
glGetProgram with arguments *program* and GL_ACTIVE_UNIFORMS or
GL_ACTIVE_UNIFORM_MAX_LENGTH
glGetUniformLocation with arguments *program* and the name of a uniform variable
glIsProgram

See Also

`glCreateProgram`, `glLinkProgram`, `glUniform`

Copyright

Copyright © 2003-2005 3Dlabs Inc. Ltd. This material may be distributed subject to the terms and conditions set forth in the Open Publication License, v 1.0, 8 June 1999. http://opencontent.org/openpub/.

glGetUniformBlockIndex

retrieve the index of a named uniform block

C Specification

```
GLuint glGetUniformBlockIndex(GLuint program,
                              const GLchar *uniformBlockName);
```

Parameters

program
> Specifies the name of a program containing the uniform block.

uniformBlockName
> Specifies the address an array of characters to containing the name of the uniform block whose index to retrieve.

Description

`glGetUniformBlockIndex` retrieves the index of a uniform block within *program*.

program must be the name of a program object for which the command glLinkProgram must have been called in the past, although it is not required that glLinkProgram must have succeeded. The link could have failed because the number of active uniforms exceeded the limit.

uniformBlockName must contain a nul-terminated string specifying the name of the uniform block.

`glGetUniformBlockIndex` returns the uniform block index for the uniform block named *uniformBlockName* of *program*. If *uniformBlockName* does not identify an active uniform block of *program*, `glGetUniformBlockIndex` returns the special identifier, GL_INVALID_INDEX. Indices of the active uniform blocks of a program are assigned in consecutive order, beginning with zero.

Errors

GL_INVALID_OPERATION is generated if *program* is not the name of a program object for which glLinkProgram has been called in the past.

Notes

glGetUniformBlockIndex is available only if the GL version is 3.1 or greater.

See Also

glGetActiveUniformBlockName, glGetActiveUniformBlock, glLinkProgram

Copyright

glGetUniformIndices

retrieve the index of a named uniform block

C Specification

```
GLuint glGetUniformIndices(GLuint program,
                           GLsizei uniformCount,
                           const GLchar **uniformNames,
                           GLuint *uniformIndices);
```

Parameters

program
> Specifies the name of a program containing uniforms whose indices to query.

uniformCount
> Specifies the number of uniforms whose indices to query.

uniformNames
> Specifies the address of an array of pointers to buffers containing the names of the queried uniforms.

uniformIndices
> Specifies the address of an array that will receive the indices of the uniforms.

Description

glGetUniformIndices retrieves the indices of a number of uniforms within *program*.

program must be the name of a program object for which the command glLinkProgram must have been called in the past, although it is not required that glLinkProgram must have succeeded. The link could have failed because the number of active uniforms exceeded the limit.

uniformCount indicates both the number of elements in the array of names *uniformNames* and the number of indices that may be written to *uniformIndices*.

uniformNames contains a list of *uniformCount* name strings identifying the uniform names to be queried for indices. For each name string in *uniformNames*, the index assigned to the active uniform of that name will be written to the corresponding element of *uniformIndices*. If a string in *uniformNames* is not the name of an active uniform, the special value GL_INVALID_INDEX will be written to the corresponding element of *uniformIndices*.

If an error occurs, nothing is written to *uniformIndices*.

Errors

GL_INVALID_OPERATION is generated if *program* is not the name of a program object for which glLinkProgram has been called in the past.

Notes

`glGetUniformIndices` is available only if the GL version is 3.1 or greater.

See Also

`glGetActiveUniform, glGetActiveUniformName, glLinkProgram`

Copyright

glGetUniformLocation

Returns the location of a uniform variable

C Specification

```
GLint glGetUniformLocation(GLuint program,
                           const GLchar * name);
```

Parameters

program
> Specifies the program object to be queried.

name
> Points to a null terminated string containing the name of the uniform variable whose location is to be queried.

Description

`glGetUniformLocation` returns an integer that represents the location of a specific uniform variable within a program object. *name* must be a null terminated string that contains no white space. *name* must be an active uniform variable name in *program* that is not a structure, an array of structures, or a subcomponent of a vector or a matrix. This function returns -1 if *name* does not correspond to an active uniform variable in *program* or if *name* starts with the reserved prefix "gl_".

Uniform variables that are structures or arrays of structures may be queried by calling `glGetUniformLocation` for each field within the structure. The array element operator "[]" and the structure field operator "." may be used in *name* in order to select elements within an array or fields within a structure. The result of using these operators is not allowed to be another structure, an array of structures, or a subcomponent of a vector or a matrix. Except if the last part of *name* indicates a uniform variable array, the location of the first element of an array can be retrieved by using the name of the array, or by using the name appended by "[0]".

The actual locations assigned to uniform variables are not known until the program object is linked successfully. After linking has occurred, the command `glGetUniformLocation` can be used to obtain the location of a uniform variable. This location value can then be passed to glUniform to set the value of the uniform variable or to glGetUniform in order to query the current value of the uniform variable. After a program object has been linked successfully, the index values for uniform variables remain fixed until the next link command occurs. Uniform variable locations and values can only be queried after a link if the link was successful.

Errors

GL_INVALID_VALUE is generated if *program* is not a value generated by OpenGL.
GL_INVALID_OPERATION is generated if *program* is not a program object.
GL_INVALID_OPERATION is generated if *program* has not been successfully linked.

Associated Gets

glGetActiveUniform with arguments *program* and the index of an active uniform variable
glGetProgram with arguments *program* and GL_ACTIVE_UNIFORMS or
GL_ACTIVE_UNIFORM_MAX_LENGTH
glGetUniform with arguments *program* and the name of a uniform variable
glIsProgram

See Also

glLinkProgram, glUniform

Copyright

Copyright © 2003-2005 3Dlabs Inc. Ltd. This material may be distributed subject to the terms and conditions set forth in the Open Publication License, v 1.0, 8 June 1999. http://opencontent.org/openpub/.

glGetVertexAttrib

Return a generic vertex attribute parameter

C Specification

```
void glGetVertexAttribdv(GLuint index,
                         GLenum pname,
                         GLdouble * params);
void glGetVertexAttribfv(GLuint index,
                         GLenum  pname,
                         GLfloat * params);
void glGetVertexAttribiv(GLuint index,
                         GLenum pname,
                         GLint * params);
void glGetVertexAttribIiv(GLuint index,
                          GLenum pname,
                          GLint * params);
void glGetVertexAttribIuiv(GLuint index,
                           GLenum pname,
                           GLuint * params);
```

Parameters

index

Specifies the generic vertex attribute parameter to be queried.

pname

Specifies the symbolic name of the vertex attribute parameter to be queried. Accepted values are GL_VERTEX_ATTRIB_ARRAY_BUFFER_BINDING, GL_VERTEX_ATTRIB_ARRAY_ENABLED, GL_VERTEX_ATTRIB_ARRAY_SIZE, GL_VERTEX_ATTRIB_ARRAY_STRIDE, GL_VERTEX_ATTRIB_ARRAY_TYPE, GL_VERTEX_ATTRIB_ARRAY_NORMALIZED, GL_VERTEX_ATTRIB_ARRAY_INTEGER, GL_VERTEX_ATTRIB_ARRAY_DIVISOR, or GL_CURRENT_VERTEX_ATTRIB.

params

Returns the requested data.

Description

glGetVertexAttrib returns in *params* the value of a generic vertex attribute parameter. The generic vertex attribute to be queried is specified by *index*, and the parameter to be queried is specified by *pname*.

The accepted parameter names are as follows:

GL_VERTEX_ATTRIB_ARRAY_BUFFER_BINDING

params returns a single value, the name of the buffer object currently bound to the binding point corresponding to generic vertex attribute array *index*. If no buffer object is bound, 0 is returned. The initial value is 0.

GL_VERTEX_ATTRIB_ARRAY_ENABLED

params returns a single value that is non-zero (true) if the vertex attribute array for *index* is enabled and 0 (false) if it is disabled. The initial value is GL_FALSE.

GL_VERTEX_ATTRIB_ARRAY_SIZE

params returns a single value, the size of the vertex attribute array for *index*. The size is the number of values for each element of the vertex attribute array, and it will be 1, 2, 3, or 4. The initial value is 4.

GL_VERTEX_ATTRIB_ARRAY_STRIDE

params returns a single value, the array stride for (number of bytes between successive elements in) the vertex attribute array for *index*. A value of 0 indicates that the array elements are stored sequentially in memory. The initial value is 0.

GL_VERTEX_ATTRIB_ARRAY_TYPE

params returns a single value, a symbolic constant indicating the array type for the vertex attribute array for *index*. Possible values are GL_BYTE, GL_UNSIGNED_BYTE, GL_SHORT, GL_UNSIGNED_SHORT, GL_INT, GL_UNSIGNED_INT, GL_FLOAT, and GL_DOUBLE. The initial value is GL_FLOAT.

GL_VERTEX_ATTRIB_ARRAY_NORMALIZED

params returns a single value that is non-zero (true) if fixed-point data types for the vertex attribute array indicated by *index* are normalized when they are converted to floating point, and 0 (false) otherwise. The initial value is GL_FALSE.

GL_VERTEX_ATTRIB_ARRAY_INTEGER

params returns a single value that is non-zero (true) if fixed-point data types for the vertex attribute array indicated by *index* have integer data types, and 0 (false) otherwise. The initial value is 0 (GL_FALSE).

GL_VERTEX_ATTRIB_ARRAY_DIVISOR

params returns a single value that is the frequency divisor used for instanced rendering. See glVertexAttribDivisor. The initial value is 0.

GL_CURRENT_VERTEX_ATTRIB

params returns four values that represent the current value for the generic vertex attribute specified by index. Generic vertex attribute 0 is unique in that it has no current state, so an error will be generated if *index* is 0. The initial value for all other generic vertex attributes is (0,0,0,1).

All of the parameters except GL_CURRENT_VERTEX_ATTRIB represent state stored in the currently bound vertex array object.

Notes

If an error is generated, no change is made to the contents of *params*.

Errors

GL_INVALID_OPERATION is generated if *pname* is not GL_CURRENT_VERTEX_ATTRIB and there is no currently bound vertex array object.

GL_INVALID_VALUE is generated if *index* is greater than or equal to GL_MAX_VERTEX_ATTRIBS.

GL_INVALID_ENUM is generated if *pname* is not an accepted value.

GL_INVALID_OPERATION is generated if *index* is 0 and *pname* is

GL_CURRENT_VERTEX_ATTRIB.

Associated Gets

glGet with argument GL_MAX_VERTEX_ATTRIBS

glGetVertexAttribPointerv with arguments *index* and GL_VERTEX_ATTRIB_ARRAY_POINTER

See Also

`glBindAttribLocation`, `glBindBuffer`, `glDisableVertexAttribArray`, `glEnableVertexAttribArray`, `glVertexAttrib`, `glVertexAttribDivisor`, `glVertexAttribPointer`

Copyright

glGetVertexAttribPointerv

return the address of the specified generic vertex attribute pointer

C Specification

```
void glGetVertexAttribPointerv(GLuint index,
                               GLenum pname,
                               GLvoid ** pointer);
```

Parameters

index

> Specifies the generic vertex attribute parameter to be returned.

pname

> Specifies the symbolic name of the generic vertex attribute parameter to be returned. Must be GL_VERTEX_ATTRIB_ARRAY_POINTER.

pointer

> Returns the pointer value.

Description

`glGetVertexAttribPointerv` returns pointer information. *index* is the generic vertex attribute to be queried, *pname* is a symbolic constant indicating the pointer to be returned, and *params* is a pointer to a location in which to place the returned data.

The *pointer* returned is a byte offset into the data store of the buffer object that was bound to the GL_ARRAY_BUFFER target (see glBindBuffer) when the desired pointer was previously specified.

Notes

The state returned is retrieved from the currently bound vertex array object.

The initial value for each pointer is 0.

Errors

GL_INVALID_OPERATION is generated if no vertex array object is currently bound.

GL_INVALID_VALUE is generated if *index* is greater than or equal to GL_MAX_VERTEX_ATTRIBS.

GL_INVALID_ENUM is generated if *pname* is not an accepted value.

Associated Gets

glGet with argument GL_MAX_VERTEX_ATTRIBS

See Also

`glGetVertexAttrib`, `glVertexAttribPointer`

Copyright

glHint

specify implementation-specific hints

C Specification

```
void glHint(GLenum target,
            GLenum mode);
```

Parameters

target

Specifies a symbolic constant indicating the behavior to be controlled. GL_LINE_SMOOTH_HINT, GL_POLYGON_SMOOTH_HINT, GL_TEXTURE_COMPRESSION_ HINT, and GL_FRAGMENT_SHADER_DERIVATIVE_HINT are accepted.

mode

Specifies a symbolic constant indicating the desired behavior. GL_FASTEST, GL_NICEST, and GL_DONT_CARE are accepted.

Description

Certain aspects of GL behavior, when there is room for interpretation, can be controlled with hints. A hint is specified with two arguments. *target* is a symbolic constant indicating the behavior to be controlled, and *mode* is another symbolic constant indicating the desired behavior. The initial value for each *target* is GL_DONT_CARE. *mode* can be one of the following:

GL_FASTEST

The most efficient option should be chosen.

GL_NICEST

The most correct, or highest quality, option should be chosen.

GL_DONT_CARE

No preference.

Though the implementation aspects that can be hinted are well defined, the interpretation of the hints depends on the implementation. The hint aspects that can be specified with *target*, along with suggested semantics, are as follows:

GL_FRAGMENT_SHADER_DERIVATIVE_HINT

Indicates the accuracy of the derivative calculation for the GL shading language fragment processing built-in functions: dFdx, dFdy, and fwidth.

GL_LINE_SMOOTH_HINT

Indicates the sampling quality of antialiased lines. If a larger filter function is applied, hinting GL_NICEST can result in more pixel fragments being generated during rasterization.

GL_POLYGON_SMOOTH_HINT

> Indicates the sampling quality of antialiased polygons. Hinting GL_NICEST can result in more pixel fragments being generated during rasterization, if a larger filter function is applied.

GL_TEXTURE_COMPRESSION_HINT

> Indicates the quality and performance of the compressing texture images. Hinting GL_FASTEST indicates that texture images should be compressed as quickly as possible, while GL_NICEST indicates that texture images should be compressed with as little image quality loss as possible. GL_NICEST should be selected if the texture is to be retrieved by glGetCompressedTexImage for reuse.

Notes

The interpretation of hints depends on the implementation. Some implementations ignore glHint settings.

Errors

GL_INVALID_ENUM is generated if either *target* or *mode* is not an accepted value.

Copyright

gIIsBuffer

determine if a name corresponds to a buffer object

C Specification

```
GLboolean glIsBuffer(GLuint buffer);
```

Parameters

buffer
> Specifies a value that may be the name of a buffer object.

Description

glIsBuffer returns GL_TRUE if *buffer* is currently the name of a buffer object. If *buffer* is zero, or is a non-zero value that is not currently the name of a buffer object, or if an error occurs, glIsBuffer returns GL_FALSE.

A name returned by glGenBuffers, but not yet associated with a buffer object by calling glBindBuffer, is not the name of a buffer object.

See Also

glBindBuffer, glDeleteBuffers, glGenBuffers, glGet

Copyright

glIsEnabled

test whether a capability is enabled

C Specification

```
GLboolean glIsEnabled(GLenum cap);
```

Parameters

cap

Specifies a symbolic constant indicating a GL capability.

Description

glIsEnabled returns GL_TRUE if *cap* is an enabled capability and returns GL_FALSE otherwise. Initially all capabilities except GL_DITHER are disabled; GL_DITHER is initially enabled.

The following capabilities are accepted for *cap*:

Notes

If an error is generated, glIsEnabled returns GL_FALSE.

Errors

GL_INVALID_ENUM is generated if *cap* is not an accepted value.

See Also

glEnable, glGet

Copyright

Copyright © 1991-2006 Silicon Graphics, Inc. This document is licensed under the SGI Free Software B License. For details, see http://oss.sgi.com/projects/FreeB/.

Constant	See
GL_BLEND	glBlendFunc, glLogicOp
GL_CLIP_DISTANCE*i*	glEnable
GL_COLOR_LOGIC_OP	glLogicOp
GL_CULL_FACE	glCullFace
GL_DEPTH_CLAMP	glEnable
GL_DEPTH_TEST	glDepthFunc, glDepthRange
GL_DITHER	glEnable
GL_FRAMEBUFFER_SRGB	glEnable
GL_LINE_SMOOTH	glLineWidth
GL_MULTISAMPLE	glSampleCoverage

Constant	See
GL_POLYGON_SMOOTH	glPolygonMode
GL_POLYGON_OFFSET_FILL	glPolygonOffset
GL_POLYGON_OFFSET_LINE	glPolygonOffset
GL_POLYGON_OFFSET_POINT	glPolygonOffset
GL_PROGRAM_POINT_SIZE	glEnable
GL_PRIMITIVE_RESTART	glEnable, glPrimitiveRestartIndex
GL_SAMPLE_ALPHA_TO_COVERAGE	glSampleCoverage
GL_SAMPLE_ALPHA_TO_ONE	glSampleCoverage
GL_SAMPLE_COVERAGE	glSampleCoverage
GL_SAMPLE_MASK	glEnable
GL_SCISSOR_TEST	glScissor
GL_STENCIL_TEST	glStencilFunc, glStencilOp
GL_TEXTURE_CUBEMAP_SEAMLESS	glEnable

gIIsFramebuffer

determine if a name corresponds to a framebuffer object

C Specification

```
GLboolean glIsFramebuffer(GLuint framebuffer);
```

Parameters

framebuffer
Specifies a value that may be the name of a framebuffer object.

Description

glIsFramebuffer returns GL_TRUE if *framebuffer* is currently the name of a framebuffer object. If *framebuffer* is zero, or if framebuffer is not the name of a framebuffer object, or if an error occurs, glIsFramebuffer returns GL_FALSE. If *framebuffer* is a name returned by glGenFramebuffers, by that has not yet been bound through a call to glBindFramebuffer, then the name is not a framebuffer object and glIsFramebuffer returns GL_FALSE.

See Also

glGenFramebuffers, glBindFramebuffer, glDeleteFramebuffers

Copyright

glIsProgram

Determines if a name corresponds to a program object

C Specification

```
GLboolean glIsProgram(GLuint program);
```

Parameters

program

Specifies a potential program object.

Description

glIsProgram returns GL_TRUE if *program* is the name of a program object previously created with glCreateProgram and not yet deleted with glDeleteProgram. If *program* is zero or a non-zero value that is not the name of a program object, or if an error occurs, glIsProgram returns GL_FALSE.

Notes

No error is generated if *program* is not a valid program object name.

A program object marked for deletion with glDeleteProgram but still in use as part of current rendering state is still considered a program object and glIsProgram will return GL_TRUE.

Associated Gets

glGet with the argument GL_CURRENT_PROGRAM

glGetActiveAttrib with arguments *program* and the index of an active attribute variable

glGetActiveUniform with arguments *program* and the index of an active uniform variable

glGetAttachedShaders with argument *program*

glGetAttribLocation with arguments *program* and the name of an attribute variable

glGetProgram with arguments *program* and the parameter to be queried

glGetProgramInfoLog with argument *program*

glGetUniform with arguments *program* and the location of a uniform variable

glGetUniformLocation with arguments *program* and the name of a uniform variable

See Also

glAttachShader, glBindAttribLocation, glCreateProgram, glDeleteProgram, glDetachShader, glLinkProgram, glUniform, glUseProgram, glValidateProgram

Copyright

glIsQuery

determine if a name corresponds to a query object

C Specification

```
GLboolean glIsQuery(GLuint id);
```

Parameters

id

       Specifies a value that may be the name of a query object.

Description

glIsQuery returns GL_TRUE if *id* is currently the name of a query object. If *id* is zero, or is a non-zero value that is not currently the name of a query object, or if an error occurs, glIsQuery returns GL_FALSE.

A name returned by glGenQueries, but not yet associated with a query object by calling glBeginQuery, is not the name of a query object.

See Also

glBeginQuery, glDeleteQueries, glEndQuery, glGenQueries

Copyright

glIsRenderbuffer

determine if a name corresponds to a renderbuffer object

C Specification

GLboolean glIsRenderbuffer(GLuint *renderbuffer*);

Parameters

renderbuffer

       Specifies a value that may be the name of a renderbuffer object.

Description

glIsRenderbuffer returns GL_TRUE if *renderbuffer* is currently the name of a renderbuffer object. If *renderbuffer* is zero, or if *renderbuffer* is not the name of a renderbuffer object, or if an error occurs, glIsRenderbuffer returns GL_FALSE. If *renderbuffer* is a name returned by glGenRenderbuffers, but that has not yet been bound through a call to glBindRenderbuffer or glFramebufferRenderbuffer, then the name is not a renderbuffer object and glIsRenderbuffer returns GL_FALSE.

See Also

glGenRenderbuffers, glBindRenderbuffer, glFramebufferRenderbuffer, glDeleteRenderbuffers

Copyright

glIsSampler

determine if a name corresponds to a sampler object

C Specification

```
GLboolean glIsSampler(GLuint id);
```

Parameters

id
Specifies a value that may be the name of a sampler object.

Description

glIsSampler returns GL_TRUE if *id* is currently the name of a sampler object. If *id* is zero, or is a non-zero value that is not currently the name of a sampler object, or if an error occurs, glIsSampler returns GL_FALSE.

A name returned by glGenSamplers, is the name of a sampler object.

Notes

glIsSampler is available only if the GL version is 3.3 or higher.

See Also

glGenSamplers, glBindSampler, glDeleteSamplers

Copyright

glIsShader

Determines if a name corresponds to a shader object

C Specification

```
GLboolean glIsShader(GLuint shader);
```

Parameters

shader
Specifies a potential shader object.

Description

glIsShader returns GL_TRUE if *shader* is the name of a shader object previously created with glCreateShader and not yet deleted with glDeleteShader. If *shader* is zero or a non-zero value that is not the name of a shader object, or if an error occurs, glIsShader returns GL_FALSE.

Notes

No error is generated if *shader* is not a valid shader object name.

A shader object marked for deletion with glDeleteShader but still attached to a program object is still considered a shader object and glIsShader will return GL_TRUE.

Associated Gets

glGetAttachedShaders with a valid program object
glGetShader with arguments *shader* and a parameter to be queried
glGetShaderInfoLog with argument *object*
glGetShaderSource with argument *object*

See Also

`glAttachShader`, `glCompileShader`, `glCreateShader`, `glDeleteShader`, `glDetachShader`, `glLinkProgram`, `glShaderSource`

Copyright

Copyright © 2003-2005 3Dlabs Inc. Ltd. This material may be distributed subject to the terms and conditions set forth in the Open Publication License, v 1.0, 8 June 1999. http://opencontent.org/openpub/.

gIIsSync

determine if a name corresponds to a sync object

C Specification

```
GLboolean glIsSync(GLsync sync);
```

Parameters

sync
Specifies a value that may be the name of a sync object.

Description

`glIsSync` returns GL_TRUE if *sync* is currently the name of a sync object. If *sync* is not the name of a sync object, or if an error occurs, `glIsSync` returns GL_FALSE. Note that zero is not the name of a sync object.

Notes

`glIsSync` is available only if the GL version is 3.2 or greater.

See Also

`glFenceSync`, `glWaitSync`, `glClientWaitSync`, `glDeleteSync`

Copyright

Copyright © 2010 Khronos Group. This material may be distributed subject to the terms and conditions set forth in the Open Publication License, v 1.0, 8 June 1999. http://opencontent.org/openpub/.

gIIsTexture

determine if a name corresponds to a texture

C Specification

```
GLboolean glIsTexture(GLuint texture);
```

Parameters

texture
> Specifies a value that may be the name of a texture.

Description

glIsTexture returns GL_TRUE if *texture* is currently the name of a texture. If *texture* is zero, or is a non-zero value that is not currently the name of a texture, or if an error occurs, glIsTexture returns GL_FALSE.

A name returned by glGenTextures, but not yet associated with a texture by calling glBindTexture, is not the name of a texture.

See Also

glBindTexture, glCopyTexImage1D, glCopyTexImage2D, glDeleteTextures, glGenTextures, glGet, glGetTexParameter, glTexImage1D, glTexImage2D, glTexImage3D, glTexParameter

Copyright

glIsVertexArray

determine if a name corresponds to a vertex array object

C Specification

GLboolean glIsVertexArray(GLuint *array*);

Parameters

array
> Specifies a value that may be the name of a vertex array object.

Description

glIsVertexArray returns GL_TRUE if *array* is currently the name of a renderbuffer object. If *renderbuffer* is zero, or if *array* is not the name of a renderbuffer object, or if an error occurs, glIsVertexArray returns GL_FALSE. If *array* is a name returned by glGenVertexArrays, but that has not yet been bound through a call to glBindVertexArray, then the name is not a vertex array object and glIsVertexArray returns GL_FALSE.

See Also

glGenVertexArrays, glBindVertexArray, glDeleteVertexArrays

Copyright

glLineWidth

specify the width of rasterized lines

C Specification

```
void glLineWidth(GLfloat width);
```

Parameters

width
> Specifies the width of rasterized lines. The initial value is 1.

Description

glLineWidth specifies the rasterized width of both aliased and antialiased lines. Using a line width other than 1 has different effects, depending on whether line antialiasing is enabled. To enable and disable line antialiasing, call glEnable and glDisable with argument GL_LINE_SMOOTH. Line antialiasing is initially disabled.

If line antialiasing is disabled, the actual width is determined by rounding the supplied width to the nearest integer. (If the rounding results in the value 0, it is as if the line width were 1.) If $|\Delta x| \geq |\Delta y|$, i pixels are filled in each column that is rasterized, where i is the rounded value of *width*. Otherwise, i pixels are filled in each row that is rasterized.

If antialiasing is enabled, line rasterization produces a fragment for each pixel square that intersects the region lying within the rectangle having width equal to the current line width, length equal to the actual length of the line, and centered on the mathematical line segment. The coverage value for each fragment is the window coordinate area of the intersection of the rectangular region with the corresponding pixel square. This value is saved and used in the final rasterization step.

Not all widths can be supported when line antialiasing is enabled. If an unsupported width is requested, the nearest supported width is used. Only width 1 is guaranteed to be supported; others depend on the implementation. Likewise, there is a range for aliased line widths as well. To query the range of supported widths and the size difference between supported widths within the range, call glGet with arguments GL_ALIASED_LINE_WIDTH_RANGE, GL_SMOOTH_LINE_WIDTH_RANGE, and GL_SMOOTH_LINE_WIDTH_GRANULARITY.

Notes

The line width specified by glLineWidth is always returned when GL_LINE_WIDTH is queried. Clamping and rounding for aliased and antialiased lines have no effect on the specified value.

Nonantialiased line width may be clamped to an implementation-dependent maximum. Call glGet with GL_ALIASED_LINE_WIDTH_RANGE to determine the maximum width.

In OpenGL 1.2, the tokens GL_LINE_WIDTH_RANGE and GL_LINE_WIDTH_GRANULARITY were replaced by GL_ALIASED_LINE_WIDTH_RANGE, GL_SMOOTH_LINE_WIDTH_RANGE, and GL_SMOOTH_LINE_WIDTH_GRANULARITY. The old names are retained for backward compatibility, but should not be used in new code.

Errors

GL_INVALID_VALUE is generated if *width* is less than or equal to 0.

Associated Gets

glGet with argument GL_LINE_WIDTH
glGet with argument GL_ALIASED_LINE_WIDTH_RANGE
glGet with argument GL_SMOOTH_LINE_WIDTH_RANGE
glGet with argument GL_SMOOTH_LINE_WIDTH_GRANULARITY
glIsEnabled with argument GL_LINE_SMOOTH

See Also

glEnable

Copyright

Copyright © 1991-2006 Silicon Graphics, Inc. This document is licensed under the SGI Free Software B License. For details, see http://oss.sgi.com/projects/FreeB/.

glLinkProgram

Links a program object

C Specification

void glLinkProgram(GLuint *program*);

Parameters

program
Specifies the handle of the program object to be linked.

Description

glLinkProgram links the program object specified by *program*. If any shader objects of type GL_VERTEX_SHADER are attached to *program*, they will be used to create an executable that will run on the programmable vertex processor. If any shader objects of type GL_GEOMETRY_SHADER are attached to *program*, they will be used to create an executable that will run on the programmable geometry processor. If any shader objects of type GL_FRAGMENT_SHADER are attached to *program*, they will be used to create an executable that will run on the programmable fragment processor.

The status of the link operation will be stored as part of the program object's state. This value will be set to GL_TRUE if the program object was linked without errors and is ready for use, and GL_FALSE otherwise. It can be queried by calling glGetProgram with arguments *program* and GL_LINK_STATUS.

As a result of a successful link operation, all active user-defined uniform variables belonging to *program* will be initialized to 0, and each of the program object's active uniform variables will be assigned a location that can be queried by calling glGetUniformLocation. Also, any active user-defined attribute variables that have not been bound to a generic vertex attribute index will be bound to one at this time.

Linking of a program object can fail for a number of reasons as specified in the *OpenGL Shading Language Specification*. The following lists some of the conditions that will cause a link error.

The number of active attribute variables supported by the implementation has been exceeded.
The storage limit for uniform variables has been exceeded.
The number of active uniform variables supported by the implementation has been exceeded.
The main function is missing for the vertex, geometry or fragment shader.

A varying variable actually used in the fragment shader is not declared in the same way (or is not declared at all) in the vertex shader, or geometry shader present.

A reference to a function or variable name is unresolved.

A shared global is declared with two different types or two different initial values.

One or more of the attached shader objects has not been successfully compiled.

Binding a generic attribute matrix caused some rows of the matrix to fall outside the allowed maximum of GL_MAX_VERTEX_ATTRIBS.

Not enough contiguous vertex attribute slots could be found to bind attribute matrices.

The program object contains objects to form a fragment shader but does not contain objects to form a vertex shader.

The program object contains objects to form a geometry shader but does not contain objects to form a vertex shader.

The program object contains objects to form a geometry shader and the input primitive type, output primitive type, or maximum output vertex count is not specified in any compiled geometry shader object.

The program object contains objects to form a geometry shader and the input primitive type, output primitive type, or maximum output vertex count is specified differently in multiple geometry shader objects.

The number of active outputs in the fragment shader is greater than the value of GL_MAX_DRAW_BUFFERS.

The program has an active output assigned to a location greater than or equal to the value of GL_MAX_DUAL_SOURCE_DRAW_BUFFERS and has an active output assigned an index greater than or equal to one.

More than one varying out variable is bound to the same number and index.

The explicit binding assigments do not leave enough space for the linker to automatically assign a location for a varying out array, which requires multiple contiguous locations.

The *count* specified by glTransformFeedbackVaryings is non-zero, but the program object has no vertex or geometry shader.

Any variable name specified to glTransformFeedbackVaryings in the *varyings* array is not declared as an output in the vertex shader (or the geometry shader, if active).

Any two entries in the *varyings* array given glTransformFeedbackVaryings specify the same varying variable.

The total number of components to capture in any transform feedback varying variable is greater than the constant GL_MAX_TRANSFORM_FEEDBACK_SEPARATE_COMPONENTS and the buffer mode is SEPARATE_ATTRIBS.

When a program object has been successfully linked, the program object can be made part of current state by calling glUseProgram. Whether or not the link operation was successful, the program object's information log will be overwritten. The information log can be retrieved by calling glGetProgramInfoLog.

glLinkProgram will also install the generated executables as part of the current rendering state if the link operation was successful and the specified program object is already currently in use as a result of a previous call to glUseProgram. If the program object currently in use is relinked unsuccessfully, its link status will be set to GL_FALSE, but the executables and associated state will remain part of the current state until a subsequent call to glUseProgram removes it from use. After it is removed from use, it cannot be made part of current state until it has been successfully relinked.

If *program* contains shader objects of type GL_VERTEX_SHADER, and optionally of type GL_GEOMETRY_SHADER, but does not contain shader objects of type GL_FRAGMENT_SHADER, the vertex shader executable will be installed on the programmable vertex processor, the geometry shader executable, if present, will be installed on the programmable geometry processor, but no executable will be installed on the fragment processor. The results of rasterizing primitives with such a program will be undefined.

The program object's information log is updated and the program is generated at the time of the link operation. After the link operation, applications are free to modify attached shader objects, compile attached shader objects, detach shader objects, delete shader objects, and attach additional shader objects. None of these operations affects the information log or the program that is part of the program object.

Notes

If the link operation is unsuccessful, any information about a previous link operation on *program* is lost (i.e., a failed link does not restore the old state of *program*). Certain information can still be retrieved from *program* even after an unsuccessful link operation. See for instance glGetActiveAttrib and glGetActiveUniform.

Errors

GL_INVALID_VALUE is generated if *program* is not a value generated by OpenGL.
GL_INVALID_OPERATION is generated if *program* is not a program object.
GL_INVALID_OPERATION is generated if *program* is the currently active program object and transform feedback mode is active.

Associated Gets

glGet with the argument GL_CURRENT_PROGRAM
glGetActiveAttrib with argument *program* and the index of an active attribute variable
glGetActiveUniform with argument *program* and the index of an active uniform variable
glGetAttachedShaders with argument *program*
glGetAttribLocation with argument *program* and an attribute variable name
glGetProgram with arguments *program* and GL_LINK_STATUS
glGetProgramInfoLog with argument *program*
glGetUniform with argument *program* and a uniform variable location
glGetUniformLocation with argument *program* and a uniform variable name
glIsProgram

See Also

glAttachShader, glBindAttribLocation, glCompileShader, glCreateProgram, glDeleteProgram, glDetachShader, glUniform, glUseProgram, glValidateProgram

Copyright

Copyright © 2003-2005 3Dlabs Inc. Ltd. Copyright © 2010 Khronos Group. This material may be distributed subject to the terms and conditions set forth in the Open Publication License, v 1.0, 8 June 1999. http://opencontent.org/openpub/.

glLogicOp

specify a logical pixel operation for rendering

C Specification

```
void glLogicOp(GLenum opcode);
```

Parameters

opcode

Specifies a symbolic constant that selects a logical operation. The following symbols are accepted: GL_CLEAR, GL_SET, GL_COPY, GL_COPY_INVERTED, GL_NOOP, GL_INVERT, GL_AND, GL_NAND, GL_OR, GL_NOR, GL_XOR, GL_EQUIV, GL_AND_REVERSE, GL_AND_INVERTED, GL_OR_REVERSE, and GL_OR_INVERTED. The initial value is GL_COPY.

Description

glLogicOp specifies a logical operation that, when enabled, is applied between the incoming RGBA color and the RGBA color at the corresponding location in the frame buffer. To enable or disable the logical operation, call glEnable and glDisable using the symbolic constant GL_COLOR_LOGIC_OP. The initial value is disabled.

opcode is a symbolic constant chosen from the list above. In the explanation of the logical operations, *s* represents the incoming color and *d* represents the color in the frame buffer. Standard C-language operators are used. As these bitwise operators suggest, the logical operation is applied independently to each bit pair of the source and destination colors.

Notes

When more than one RGBA color buffer is enabled for drawing, logical operations are performed separately for each enabled buffer, using for the destination value the contents of that buffer (see glDrawBuffer).

Logic operations have no effect on floating point draw buffers. However, if GL_COLOR_LOGIC_OP is enabled, blending is still disabled in this case.

Opcode	Resulting Operation
GL_CLEAR	0
GL_SET	1
GL_COPY	s
GL_COPY_INVERTED	~s
GL_NOOP	d
GL_INVERT	~d
GL_AND	s & d
GL_NAND	~(s & d)
GL_OR	s | d
GL_NOR	~(s | d)
GL_XOR	s ^ d
GL_EQUIV	~(s ^ d)
GL_AND_REVERSE	s & ~d

844

Opcode	Resulting Operation
GL_AND_INVERTED	~s & d
GL_OR_REVERSE	s	~d
GL_OR_INVERTED	~s	d

Errors

GL_INVALID_ENUM is generated if *opcode* is not an accepted value.

Associated Gets

glGet with argument GL_LOGIC_OP_MODE.
glIsEnabled with argument GL_COLOR_LOGIC_OP.

See Also

glBlendFunc, glDrawBuffer, glEnable, glStencilOp

Copyright

Copyright © 1991-2006 Silicon Graphics, Inc. This document is licensed under the SGI Free Software B License. For details, see http://oss.sgi.com/projects/FreeB/.

glMapBuffer

map a buffer object's data store

C Specification

```
void * glMapBuffer(GLenum target,
                   GLenum access);
```

Parameters

target
Specifies the target buffer object being mapped. The symbolic constant must be GL_ARRAY_BUFFER, GL_COPY_READ_BUFFER, GL_COPY_WRITE_BUFFER, GL_ELEMENT_ARRAY_BUFFER, GL_PIXEL_PACK_BUFFER, GL_PIXEL_UNPACK_BUFFER, GL_TEXTURE_BUFFER, GL_TRANSFORM_FEEDBACK_BUFFER, or GL_UNIFORM_BUFFER.

access
Specifies the access policy, indicating whether it will be possible to read from, write to, or both read from and write to the buffer object's mapped data store. The symbolic constant must be GL_READ_ONLY, GL_WRITE_ONLY, or GL_READ_WRITE.

C Specification

GLboolean glUnmapBuffer GLenum *target*

Parameters

target
Specifies the target buffer object being unmapped. The symbolic constant must be GL_ARRAY_BUFFER, GL_COPY_READ_BUFFER, GL_COPY_WRITE_BUFFER, GL_ELEMENT_ARRAY_BUFFER, GL_PIXEL_PACK_BUFFER, GL_PIXEL_UNPACK_BUFFER, GL_TEXTURE_BUFFER, GL_TRANSFORM_FEEDBACK_BUFFER, or GL_UNIFORM_BUFFER.

Description

glMapBuffer maps to the client's address space the entire data store of the buffer object currently bound to *target*. The data can then be directly read and/or written relative to the returned pointer, depending on the specified *access* policy. If the GL is unable to map the buffer object's data store, glMapBuffer generates an error and returns NULL. This may occur for system-specific reasons, such as low virtual memory availability.

If a mapped data store is accessed in a way inconsistent with the specified *access* policy, no error is generated, but performance may be negatively impacted and system errors, including program termination, may result. Unlike the *usage* parameter of glBufferData, *access* is not a hint, and does in fact constrain the usage of the mapped data store on some GL implementations. In order to achieve the highest performance available, a buffer object's data store should be used in ways consistent with both its specified *usage* and *access* parameters.

A mapped data store must be unmapped with glUnmapBuffer before its buffer object is used. Otherwise an error will be generated by any GL command that attempts to dereference the buffer object's data store. When a data store is unmapped, the pointer to its data store becomes invalid. glUnmapBuffer returns GL_TRUE unless the data store contents have become corrupt during the time the data store was mapped. This can occur for system-specific reasons that affect the availability of graphics memory, such as screen mode changes. In such situations, GL_FALSE is returned and the data store contents are undefined. An application must detect this rare condition and reinitialize the data store.

A buffer object's mapped data store is automatically unmapped when the buffer object is deleted or its data store is recreated with glBufferData.

Notes

If an error is generated, glMapBuffer returns NULL, and glUnmapBuffer returns GL_FALSE.

Parameter values passed to GL commands may not be sourced from the returned pointer. No error will be generated, but results will be undefined and will likely vary across GL implementations.

Errors

GL_INVALID_ENUM is generated if *target* is not GL_ARRAY_BUFFER, GL_COPY_READ_BUFFER, GL_COPY_WRITE_BUFFER, GL_ELEMENT_ARRAY_BUFFER, GL_PIXEL_PACK_BUFFER, GL_PIXEL_UNPACK_BUFFER, GL_TEXTURE_BUFFER, GL_TRANSFORM_FEEDBACK_BUFFER, or GL_UNIFORM_BUFFER.

GL_INVALID_ENUM is generated if *access* is not GL_READ_ONLY, GL_WRITE_ONLY, or GL_READ_WRITE.

GL_OUT_OF_MEMORY is generated when glMapBuffer is executed if the GL is unable to map the buffer object's data store. This may occur for a variety of system-specific reasons, such as the absence of sufficient remaining virtual memory.

GL_INVALID_OPERATION is generated if the reserved buffer object name 0 is bound to *target*.

GL_INVALID_OPERATION is generated if glMapBuffer is executed for a buffer object whose data store is already mapped.

GL_INVALID_OPERATION is generated if glUnmapBuffer is executed for a buffer object whose data store is not currently mapped.

Associated Gets

glGetBufferPointerv with argument GL_BUFFER_MAP_POINTER

glGetBufferParameter with argument GL_BUFFER_MAPPED, GL_BUFFER_ACCESS, or GL_BUFFER_USAGE

See Also

glBindBuffer, glBindBufferBase, glBindBufferRange, glBufferData, glBufferSubData, glDeleteBuffers

glMapBufferRange

map a section of a buffer object's data store

C Specification

```
void *glMapBufferRange(GLenum target,
                       GLintptr offset,
                       GLsizeiptr length,
                       GLbitfield access);
```

Parameters

target
Specifies a binding to which the target buffer is bound.

offset
Specifies a the starting offset within the buffer of the range to be mapped.

length
Specifies a length of the range to be mapped.

access
Specifies a combination of access flags indicating the desired access to the range.

Description

`glMapBufferRange` maps all or part of the data store of a buffer object into the client's address space. *target* specifies the target to which the buffer is bound and must be one of GL_ARRAY_BUFFER, GL_COPY_READ_BUFFER, GL_COPY_WRITE_BUFFER, GL_ELEMENT_ARRAY_BUFFER, GL_PIXEL_PACK_BUFFER, GL_PIXEL_UNPACK_BUFFER, GL_TEXTURE_BUFFER, GL_TRANSFORM_FEEDBACK_BUFFER, or GL_UNIFORM_BUFFER. *offset* and *length* indicate the range of data in the buffer object htat is to be mapped, in terms of basic machine units. *access* is a bitfield containing flags which describe the requested mapping. These flags are described below.

If no error occurs, a pointer to the beginning of the mapped range is returned once all pending operations on that buffer have completed, and may be used to modify and/or query the corresponding range of the buffer, according to the following flag bits set in *access*:

GL_MAP_READ_BIT indicates that the returned pointer may be used to read buffer object data. No GL error is generated if the pointer is used to query a mapping which excludes this flag, but the result is undefined and system errors (possibly including program termination) may occur.

GL_MAP_WRITE_BIT indicates that the returned pointer may be used to modify buffer object data. No GL error is generated if the pointer is used to modify a mapping which excludes this flag, but the result is undefined and system errors (possibly including program termination) may occur.

Furthermore, the following *optional* flag bits in *access* may be used to modify the mapping:

GL_MAP_INVALIDATE_RANGE_BIT indicates that the previous contents of the specified range may be discarded. Data within this range are undefined with the exception of subsequently written data. No GL error is generated if sub- sequent GL operations access unwritten data, but the result is undefined and system errors (possibly including program termination) may occur. This flag may not be used in combination with GL_MAP_READ_BIT.

GL_MAP_INVALIDATE_BUFFER_BIT indicates that the previous contents of the entire buffer may be discarded. Data within the entire buffer are undefined with the exception of subsequently written data. No GL error is generated if subsequent GL operations access unwritten data, but the result is undefined and system errors (possibly including program termination) may occur. This flag may not be used in combination with GL_MAP_READ_BIT.

GL_MAP_FLUSH_EXPLICIT_BIT indicates that one or more discrete subranges of the mapping may be modified. When this flag is set, modifications to each subrange must be explicitly flushed by calling glFlushMappedBufferRange. No GL error is set if a subrange of the mapping is modified and not flushed, but data within the corresponding subrange of the buffer are undefined. This flag may only be used in conjunction with GL_MAP_WRITE_BIT. When this option is selected, flushing is strictly limited to regions that are explicitly indicated with calls to glFlushMappedBufferRange prior to unmap; if this option is not selected glUnmapBuffer will automatically flush the entire mapped range when called.

GL_MAP_UNSYNCHRONIZED_BIT indicates that the GL should not attempt to synchronize pending operations on the buffer prior to returning from `glMapBufferRange`. No GL error is generated if pending operations which source or modify the buffer overlap the mapped region, but the result of such previous and any subsequent operations is undefined.

If an error occurs, `glMapBufferRange` returns a NULL pointer.

Errors

GL_INVALID_VALUE is generated if either of *offset* or *length* is negative, or if *offset* + *length* is greater than the value of GL_BUFFER_SIZE.

GL_INVALID_VALUE is generated if *access* has any bits set other than those defined above.

GL_INVALID_OPERATION is generated for any of the following conditions:

The buffer is already in a mapped state.

Neither GL_MAP_READ_BIT or GL_MAP_WRITE_BIT is set.

GL_MAP_READ_BIT is set and any of GL_MAP_INVALIDATE_RANGE_BIT, GL_MAP_INVALIDATE_BUFFER_BIT, or GL_MAP_UNSYNCHRONIZED_BIT is set.

GL_MAP_FLUSH_EXPLICIT_BIT is set and GL_MAP_WRITE_BIT is not set.

GL_OUT_OF_MEMORY is generated if `glMapBufferRange` fails because memory for the mapping could not be obtained.

See Also

glMapBuffer, glFlushMappedBufferRange, glBindBuffer

Copyright

glMultiDrawArrays

render multiple sets of primitives from array data

C Specification

```
void glMultiDrawArrays(GLenum mode,
                       GLint * first,
                       GLsizei * count,
                       GLsizei primcount);
```

848

Parameters

mode

Specifies what kind of primitives to render. Symbolic constants GL_POINTS, GL_LINE_STRIP, GL_LINE_LOOP, GL_LINES, GL_LINE_STRIP_ADJACENCY, GL_LINES_ADJACENCY, GL_TRIANGLE_STRIP, GL_TRIANGLE_FAN, GL_TRIANGLES, GL_TRIANGLE_STRIP_ADJACENCY, and GL_TRIANGLES_ADJACENCY are accepted.

first

Points to an array of starting indices in the enabled arrays.

count

Points to an array of the number of indices to be rendered.

primcount

Specifies the size of the first and count

Description

glMultiDrawArrays specifies multiple sets of geometric primitives with very few subroutine calls. Instead of calling a GL procedure to pass each individual vertex, normal, texture coordinate, edge flag, or color, you can prespecify separate arrays of vertices, normals, and colors and use them to construct a sequence of primitives with a single call to glMultiDrawArrays.

glMultiDrawArrays behaves identically to glDrawArrays except that *primcount* separate ranges of elements are specified instead.

When glMultiDrawArrays is called, it uses *count* sequential elements from each enabled array to construct a sequence of geometric primitives, beginning with element *first. mode* specifies what kind of primitives are constructed, and how the array elements construct those primitives.

Vertex attributes that are modified by glMultiDrawArrays have an unspecified value after glMultiDrawArrays returns. Attributes that aren't modified remain well defined.

Notes

GL_LINE_STRIP_ADJACENCY, GL_LINES_ADJACENCY, GL_TRIANGLE_STRIP_ADJACENCY, and GL_TRIANGLES_ADJACENCY are available only if the GL version is 3.2 or greater.

Errors

GL_INVALID_ENUM is generated if *mode* is not an accepted value.

GL_INVALID_VALUE is generated if *primcount* is negative.

GL_INVALID_OPERATION is generated if a non-zero buffer object name is bound to an enabled array and the buffer object's data store is currently mapped.

See Also

glDrawElements, glDrawRangeElements

Copyright

glMultiDrawElements

render multiple sets of primitives by specifying indices of array data elements

C Specification

```
void glMultiDrawElements(GLenum mode,
                         const GLsizei * count,
                         GLenum type, const
                         GLvoid ** indices,
                         GLsizei primcount);
```

Parameters

mode

Specifies what kind of primitives to render. Symbolic constants GL_POINTS, GL_LINE_STRIP, GL_LINE_LOOP, GL_LINES, GL_LINE_STRIP_ADJACENCY, GL_LINES_ADJACENCY, GL_TRIANGLE_STRIP, GL_TRIANGLE_FAN, GL_TRIANGLES, GL_TRIANGLE_STRIP_ADJACENCY, and GL_TRIANGLES_ADJACENCY are accepted.

count

Points to an array of the elements counts.

type

Specifies the type of the values in *indices*. Must be one of GL_UNSIGNED_BYTE, GL_UNSIGNED_SHORT, or GL_UNSIGNED_INT.

indices

Specifies a pointer to the location where the indices are stored.

primcount

Specifies the size of the *count* array.

Description

glMultiDrawElements specifies multiple sets of geometric primitives with very few subroutine calls. Instead of calling a GL function to pass each individual vertex, normal, texture coordinate, edge flag, or color, you can prespecify separate arrays of vertices, normals, and so on, and use them to construct a sequence of primitives with a single call to glMultiDrawElements.

glMultiDrawElements is identical in operation to glDrawElements except that *primcount* separate lists of elements are specified.

Vertex attributes that are modified by glMultiDrawElements have an unspecified value after glMultiDrawElements returns. Attributes that aren't modified maintain their previous values.

Notes

GL_LINE_STRIP_ADJACENCY, GL_LINES_ADJACENCY, GL_TRIANGLE_STRIP_ADJACENCY, and GL_TRIANGLES_ADJACENCY are available only if the GL version is 3.2 or greater.

Errors

GL_INVALID_ENUM is generated if *mode* is not an accepted value.

GL_INVALID_VALUE is generated if *primcount* is negative.

GL_INVALID_OPERATION is generated if a non-zero buffer object name is bound to an enabled array or the element array and the buffer object's data store is currently mapped.

See Also

glDrawArrays, glDrawRangeElements

Copyright

glMultiDrawElementsBaseVertex

render multiple sets of primitives by specifying indices of array data elements and an index to apply to each index

C Specification

```
void glMultiDrawElementsBaseVertex(GLenum mode,
                                   const GLsizei *count,
                                   GLenum type,
                                   const GLvoid **indices,
                                   GLsizei primcount,
                                   GLint *basevertex);
```

Parameters

mode

Specifies what kind of primitives to render. Symbolic constants GL_POINTS, GL_LINE_STRIP, GL_LINE_LOOP, GL_LINES, GL_LINE_STRIP_ADJACENCY, GL_LINES_ADJACENCY, GL_TRIANGLE_STRIP, GL_TRIANGLE_FAN, GL_TRIANGLES, GL_TRIANGLE_STRIP_ADJACENCY, and GL_TRIANGLES_ADJACENCY are accepted.

count

Points to an array of the elements counts.

type

Specifies the type of the values in *indices*. Must be one of GL_UNSIGNED_BYTE, GL_UNSIGNED_SHORT, or GL_UNSIGNED_INT.

indices

Specifies a pointer to the location where the indices are stored.

primcount

Specifies the size of the *count* array.

basevertex

Specifies a pointer to the location where the base vertices are stored.

Description

glMultiDrawElementsBaseVertex behaves identically to glDrawElementsBaseVertex, except that *primcount* separate lists of elements are specifried instead.

It has the same effect as:

```
for (int i = 0; i < primcount; i++)
if (count[i] > 0)
glDrawElementsBaseVertex(mode,
count[i],
type,
indices[i],
basevertex[i]);
```

Notes

glMultiDrawElementsBaseVertex is available only if the GL version is 3.1 or greater.
GL_LINE_STRIP_ADJACENCY, GL_LINES_ADJACENCY, GL_TRIANGLE_STRIP_ADJACENCY, and GL_TRIANGLES_ADJACENCY are available only if the GL version is 3.2 or greater.

Errors

GL_INVALID_ENUM is generated if *mode* is not an accepted value.

GL_INVALID_VALUE is generated if *primcount* is negative.

GL_INVALID_OPERATION is generated if a non-zero buffer object name is bound to an enabled array or the element array and the buffer object's data store is currently mapped.

See Also

glMultiDrawElements, glDrawElementsBaseVertex, glDrawArrays, glVertexAttribPointer

Copyright

glMultiTexCoord

set the current texture coordinates

C Specification

```
void glMultiTexCoord1s GLenum target GLshort s
void glMultiTexCoord1i GLenum target GLint s
void glMultiTexCoord1f GLenum target GLfloat s
void glMultiTexCoord1d GLenum target GLdouble s
void glMultiTexCoord2s GLenum target GLshort s GLshort t
void glMultiTexCoord2i GLenum target GLint s GLint t
void glMultiTexCoord2f GLenum target GLfloat s GLfloat t
void glMultiTexCoord2d GLenum target GLdouble s GLdouble t
void glMultiTexCoord3s GLenum target GLshort s GLshort t GLshort r
void glMultiTexCoord3i GLenum target GLint s GLint t GLint r
void glMultiTexCoord3f GLenum target GLfloat s GLfloat t GLfloat r
void glMultiTexCoord3d GLenum target GLdouble s GLdouble t GLdouble r
void glMultiTexCoord4s GLenum target GLshort s GLshort t GLshort r GLshort q
void glMultiTexCoord4i GLenum target GLint s GLint t GLint r GLint q
void glMultiTexCoord4f GLenum target GLfloat s GLfloat t GLfloat r GLfloat q
void glMultiTexCoord4d GLenum target GLdouble s GLdouble t GLdouble r GLdouble q
```

Parameters

target

Specifies the texture unit whose coordinates should be modified. The number of texture units is implementation dependent, but must be at least two. Symbolic constant must be one of GL_TEXTUREi, where i ranges from 0 to GL_MAX_TEXTURE_COORDS - 1, which is an implementation-dependent value.

s
t
r
q

Specify *s*, *t*, *r*, and *q* texture coordinates for *target* texture unit. Not all parameters are present in all forms of the command.

C Specification

```
void glMultiTexCoord1sv GLenum target const GLshort * v
void glMultiTexCoord1iv GLenum target const GLint * v
void glMultiTexCoord1fv GLenum target const GLfloat * v
void glMultiTexCoord1dv GLenum target const GLdouble * v
void glMultiTexCoord2sv GLenum target const GLshort * v
void glMultiTexCoord2iv GLenum target const GLint * v
void glMultiTexCoord2fv GLenum target const GLfloat * v
void glMultiTexCoord2dv GLenum target const GLdouble * v
void glMultiTexCoord3sv GLenum target const GLshort * v
void glMultiTexCoord3iv GLenum target const GLint * v
void glMultiTexCoord3fv GLenum target const GLfloat * v
void glMultiTexCoord3dv GLenum target const GLdouble * v
void glMultiTexCoord4sv GLenum target const GLshort * v
void glMultiTexCoord4iv GLenum target const GLint * v
void glMultiTexCoord4fv GLenum target const GLfloat * v
void glMultiTexCoord4dv GLenum target const GLdouble * v
```

Parameters

target

Specifies the texture unit whose coordinates should be modified. The number of texture units is implementation dependent, but must be at least two. Symbolic constant must be one of GL_TEXTURE*i*, where i ranges from 0 to GL_MAX_TEXTURE_COORDS - 1, which is an implementation-dependent value.

v

Specifies a pointer to an array of one, two, three, or four elements, which in turn specify the s, t, r, and q texture coordinates.

Description

glMultiTexCoord specifies texture coordinates in one, two, three, or four dimensions. glMultiTexCoord1 sets the current texture coordinates to $(s,0,0,1)$; a call to glMultiTexCoord2 sets them to $(s,t,0,1)$. Similarly, glMultiTexCoord3 specifies the texture coordinates as $(s,t,r,1)$, and glMultiTexCoord4 defines all four components explicitly as (s,t,r,q).

The current texture coordinates are part of the data that is associated with each vertex and with the current raster position. Initially, the values for (s,t,r,q) are $(0,0,0,1)$.

Notes

The current texture coordinates can be updated at any time.
It is always the case that GL_TEXTURE i = GL_TEXTURE0 + i.

Associated Gets

glGet with argument GL_CURRENT_TEXTURE_COORDS with appropriate texture unit selected.
glGet with argument GL_MAX_TEXTURE_COORDS

See Also

glActiveTexture, glTexCoord, glVertex

Copyright

glPixelStore

set pixel storage modes

C Specification

```
void glPixelStoref(GLenum pname,
                   GLfloat param);
void glPixelStorei(GLenum pname,
                   GLint param);
```

Parameters

pname

Specifies the symbolic name of the parameter to be set. Six values affect the packing of pixel data into memory: GL_PACK_SWAP_BYTES, GL_PACK_LSB_FIRST, GL_PACK_ROW_LENGTH, GL_PACK_IMAGE_HEIGHT, GL_PACK_SKIP_PIXELS, GL_PACK_SKIP_ROWS, GL_PACK_SKIP_IMAGES, and GL_PACK_ALIGNMENT. Six more affect the unpacking of pixel data *from* memory: GL_UNPACK_SWAP_BYTES, GL_UNPACK_LSB_FIRST, GL_UNPACK_ROW_LENGTH, GL_UNPACK_IMAGE_HEIGHT, GL_UNPACK_SKIP_PIXELS, GL_UNPACK_SKIP_ROWS, GL_UNPACK_SKIP_IMAGES, and GL_UNPACK_ALIGNMENT.

param

Specifies the value that *pname* is set to.

Description

glPixelStore sets pixel storage modes that affect the operation of subsequent glReadPixels as well as the unpacking of texture patterns (see glTexImage1D, glTexImage2D, glTexImage3D, glTexSubImage1D, glTexSubImage2D, glTexSubImage3D).

pname is a symbolic constant indicating the parameter to be set, and *param* is the new value. Six of the twelve storage parameters affect how pixel data is returned to client memory. They are as follows:

GL_PACK_SWAP_BYTES

If true, byte ordering for multibyte color components, depth components, or stencil indices is reversed. That is, if a four-byte component consists of bytes b_0, b_1, b_2, b_3, it is stored in memory as b_3, b_2, b_1, b_0 if GL_PACK_SWAP_BYTES is true. GL_PACK_SWAP_BYTES has no effect on the memory order of components within a pixel, only on the order of bytes within components or indices. For example, the three components of a GL_RGB format pixel are always stored with red first, green second, and blue third, regardless of the value of GL_PACK_SWAP_BYTES.

GL_PACK_LSB_FIRST

If true, bits are ordered within a byte from least significant to most significant; otherwise, the first bit in each byte is the most significant one.

GL_PACK_ROW_LENGTH

If greater than 0, GL_PACK_ROW_LENGTH defines the number of pixels in a row. If the first pixel of a row is placed at location p in memory, then the location of the first pixel of the next row is obtained by skipping

$$k = d \quad \frac{nl}{\frac{a}{s} 2\frac{snl}{a} 2} \quad \begin{matrix} s7=a \\ s6a \end{matrix}$$

components or indices, where n is the number of components or indices in a pixel, l is the number of pixels in a row (GL_PACK_ROW_LENGTH if it is greater than 0, the width argument to the pixel routine otherwise), a is the value of GL_PACK_ALIGNMENT, and s is the size, in bytes, of a single component (if a 6 s, then it is as if a = s). In the case of 1-bit values, the location of the next row is obtained by skipping

$$k = 8a \left\lceil \frac{nl}{8a} \right\rceil$$

components or indices.

The word *component* in this description refers to the nonindex values red, green, blue, alpha, and depth. Storage format GL_RGB, for example, has three components per pixel: first red, then green, and finally blue.

GL_PACK_IMAGE_HEIGHT

If greater than 0, GL_PACK_IMAGE_HEIGHT defines the number of pixels in an image three-dimensional texture volume, where ``image'' is defined by all pixels sharing the same third dimension index. If the first pixel of a row is placed at location p in memory, then the location of the first pixel of the next row is obtained by skipping

$$k = \begin{cases} nlh & s \geq a \\ \dfrac{a}{s}\left\lceil \dfrac{snlh}{a} \right\rceil & s < a \end{cases}$$

components or indices, where n is the number of components or indices in a pixel, l is the number of pixels in a row (GL_PACK_ROW_LENGTH if it is greater than 0, the width argument to glTexImage3D otherwise), h is the number of rows in a pixel image (GL_PACK_IMAGE_HEIGHT if it is greater than 0, the height argument to the glTexImage3D routine otherwise), a is the value of GL_PACK_ALIGNMENT, and s is the size, in bytes, of a single component (if a 6 s, then it is as if a = s).

The word *component* in this description refers to the nonindex values red, green, blue, alpha, and depth. Storage format GL_RGB, for example, has three components per pixel: first red, then green, and finally blue.

GL_PACK_SKIP_PIXELS, GL_PACK_SKIP_ROWS, and GL_PACK_SKIP_IMAGES

These values are provided as a convenience to the programmer; they provide no functionality that cannot be duplicated simply by incrementing the pointer passed to glReadPixels. Setting GL_PACK_SKIP_PIXELS to i is equivalent to incrementing the pointer by in components or indices, where n is the number of components or indices in each pixel. Setting GL_PACK_SKIP_ROWS to j is equivalent to incrementing the pointer by jm components or indices, where m is the number of components or indices per row, as just computed in the GL_PACK_ROW_LENGTH section. Setting GL_PACK_SKIP_IMAGES to k is equivalent to incrementing the pointer by kp, where p is the number of components or indices per image, as computed in the GL_PACK_IMAGE_HEIGHT section.

GL_PACK_ALIGNMENT

Specifies the alignment requirements for the start of each pixel row in memory. The allowable values are 1 (byte-alignment), 2 (rows aligned to even-numbered bytes), 4 (word-alignment), and 8 (rows start on double-word boundaries).

The other six of the twelve storage parameters affect how pixel data is read from client memory. These values are significant for glTexImage1D, glTexImage2D, glTexImage3D, glTexSubImage1D, glTexSubImage2D, and glTexSubImage3D

They are as follows:

GL_UNPACK_SWAP_BYTES

If true, byte ordering for multibyte color components, depth components, or stencil indices is reversed. That is, if a four-byte component consists of bytes b_0, b_1, b_2, b_3, it is taken from memory as b_3, b_2, b_1, b_0 if GL_UNPACK_SWAP_BYTES is true. GL_UNPACK_SWAP_BYTES has no effect on the memory order of components within a pixel, only on the order of bytes within components or indices. For example, the three components of a GL_RGB format pixel are always stored with red first, green second, and blue third, regardless of the value of GL_UNPACK_SWAP_BYTES.

GL_UNPACK_LSB_FIRST

If true, bits are ordered within a byte from least significant to most significant; otherwise, the first bit in each byte is the most significant one.

GL_UNPACK_ROW_LENGTH

If greater than 0, GL_UNPACK_ROW_LENGTH defines the number of pixels in a row. If the first pixel of a row is placed at location p in memory, then the location of the first pixel of the next row is obtained by skipping

$$k = \begin{cases} nl & s \geq a \\ \dfrac{a}{s} \left\lceil \dfrac{snl}{a} \right\rceil & s < a \end{cases}$$

components or indices, where n is the number of components or indices in a pixel, l is the number of pixels in a row (GL_UNPACK_ROW_LENGTH if it is greater than 0, the width argument to the pixel routine otherwise), a is the value of GL_UNPACK_ALIGNMENT, and s is the size, in bytes, of a single component (if a < s, then it is as if a = s). In the case of 1-bit values, the location of the next row is obtained by skipping

$$k = 8a \left\lceil \dfrac{nl}{8a} \right\rceil$$

components or indices.

The word *component* in this description refers to the nonindex values red, green, blue, alpha, and depth. Storage format GL_RGB, for example, has three components per pixel: first red, then green, and finally blue.

GL_UNPACK_IMAGE_HEIGHT

If greater than 0, GL_UNPACK_IMAGE_HEIGHT defines the number of pixels in an image of a three-dimensional texture volume. Where ``image'' is defined by all pixel sharing the same third dimension index. If the first pixel of a row is placed at location p in memory, then the location of the first pixel of the next row is obtained by skipping

$$k = \begin{cases} nlh & s \geq a \\ \dfrac{a}{s} \left\lceil \dfrac{snlh}{a} \right\rceil & s < a \end{cases}$$

components or indices, where n is the number of components or indices in a pixel, l is the number of pixels in a row (GL_UNPACK_ROW_LENGTH if it is greater than 0, the width argument to glTexImage3D otherwise), h is the number of rows in an image (GL_UNPACK_IMAGE_HEIGHT if it is greater than 0, the height argument to glTexImage3D otherwise), a is the value of GL_UNPACK_ALIGNMENT, and s is the size, in bytes, of a single component (if a < s, then it is as if a = s).

The word *component* in this description refers to the nonindex values red, green, blue, alpha, and depth. Storage format GL_RGB, for example, has three components per pixel: first red, then green, and finally blue.

GL_UNPACK_SKIP_PIXELS and GL_UNPACK_SKIP_ROWS

These values are provided as a convenience to the programmer; they provide no functionality that cannot be duplicated by incrementing the pointer passed to glTexImage1D, glTexImage2D, glTexSubImage1D or glTexSubImage2D. Setting GL_UNPACK_SKIP_PIXELS to i is equivalent to incrementing the pointer by in components or indices, where n is the number of components or indices in each pixel. Setting GL_UNPACK_SKIP_ROWS to j is equivalent to incrementing the pointer by jk components or indices, where k is the number of components or indices per row, as just computed in the GL_UNPACK_ROW_LENGTH section.

GL_UNPACK_ALIGNMENT

Specifies the alignment requirements for the start of each pixel row in memory. The allowable values are 1 (byte-alignment), 2 (rows aligned to even-numbered bytes), 4 (word-alignment), and 8 (rows start on double-word boundaries).

The following table gives the type, initial value, and range of valid values for each storage parameter that can be set with glPixelStore.

glPixelStoref can be used to set any pixel store parameter. If the parameter type is boolean, then if *param* is 0, the parameter is false; otherwise it is set to true. If *pname* is a integer type parameter, *param* is rounded to the nearest integer.

Likewise, glPixelStorei can also be used to set any of the pixel store parameters. Boolean parameters are set to false if *param* is 0 and true otherwise.

Errors

GL_INVALID_ENUM is generated if *pname* is not an accepted value.

GL_INVALID_VALUE is generated if a negative row length, pixel skip, or row skip value is specified, or if alignment is specified as other than 1, 2, 4, or 8.

Associated Gets

glGet with argument GL_PACK_SWAP_BYTES

pname	Type	Initial Value	Valid Range
GL_PACK_SWAP_BYTES	boolean	false	true or false
GL_PACK_LSB_FIRST	boolean	false	true or false
GL_PACK_ROW_LENGTH	integer	0	[0, q)
GL_PACK_IMAGE_HEIGHT	integer	0	[0, q)
GL_PACK_SKIP_ROWS	integer	0	[0, q)
GL_PACK_SKIP_PIXELS	integer	0	[0, q)
GL_PACK_SKIP_IMAGES	integer	0	[0, q)
GL_PACK_ALIGNMENT	integer	4	1, 2, 4, or 8
GL_UNPACK_SWAP_BYTES	boolean	false	true or false
GL_UNPACK_LSB_FIRST	boolean	false	true or false
GL_UNPACK_ROW_LENGTH	integer	0	[0, q)

pname	Type	Initial Value	Valid Range
GL_UNPACK_IMAGE_HEIGHT	integer	0	[0, q)
GL_UNPACK_SKIP_ROWS	integer	0	[0, q)
GL_UNPACK_SKIP_PIXELS	integer	0	[0, q)
GL_UNPACK_SKIP_IMAGES	integer	0	[0, q)
GL_UNPACK_ALIGNMENT	integer	4	1, 2, 4, or 8

glGet with argument GL_PACK_LSB_FIRST
glGet with argument GL_PACK_ROW_LENGTH
glGet with argument GL_PACK_IMAGE_HEIGHT
glGet with argument GL_PACK_SKIP_ROWS
glGet with argument GL_PACK_SKIP_PIXELS
glGet with argument GL_PACK_SKIP_IMAGES
glGet with argument GL_PACK_ALIGNMENT
glGet with argument GL_UNPACK_SWAP_BYTES
glGet with argument GL_UNPACK_LSB_FIRST
glGet with argument GL_UNPACK_ROW_LENGTH
glGet with argument GL_UNPACK_IMAGE_HEIGHT
glGet with argument GL_UNPACK_SKIP_ROWS
glGet with argument GL_UNPACK_SKIP_PIXELS
glGet with argument GL_UNPACK_SKIP_IMAGES
glGet with argument GL_UNPACK_ALIGNMENT

See Also

glReadPixels, glTexImage1D, glTexImage2D, glTexImage3D, glTexSubImage1D, glTexSubImage2D, glTexSubImage3D

Copyright

glPointParameter

specify point parameters

C Specification

```
void glPointParameterf(GLenum pname,
                       GLfloat param);
void glPointParameteri(GLenum pname,
                       GLint param);
```

Parameters

pname

Specifies a single-valued point parameter. GL_POINT_FADE_THRESHOLD_SIZE and GL_POINT_SPRITE_COORD_ORIGIN are accepted.

param

Specifies the value that *pname* will be set to.

C Specification

```
void glPointParameterfv(GLenum pname,
                        const GLfloat * params);
void glPointParameteriv(GLenum pname,
                        const GLint * params);
```

Parameters

pname

Specifies a point parameter. GL_POINT_FADE_THRESHOLD_SIZE and GL_POINT_SPRITE_COORD_ORIGIN are accepted.

params

Specifies the value to be assigned to *pname*.

Description

The following values are accepted for *pname*:

GL_POINT_FADE_THRESHOLD_SIZE

params is a single floating-point value that specifies the threshold value to which point sizes are clamped if they exceed the specified value. The default value is 1.0.

GL_POINT_SPRITE_COORD_ORIGIN

params is a single enum specifying the point sprite texture coordinate origin, either GL_LOWER_LEFT or GL_UPPER_LEFT. The default value is GL_UPPER_LEFT.

Errors

GL_INVALID_VALUE is generated if the value specified for GL_POINT_FADE_THRESHOLD_SIZE is less than zero.

GL_INVALID_ENUM is generated If the value specified for GL_POINT_SPRITE_COORD_ORIGIN is not GL_LOWER_LEFT or GL_UPPER_LEFT.

Associated Gets

glGet with argument GL_POINT_FADE_THRESHOLD_SIZE
glGet with argument GL_POINT_SPRITE_COORD_ORIGIN

See Also

glPointSize

Copyright

glPointSize

specify the diameter of rasterized points

C Specification

```
void glPointSize(GLfloat size);
```

Parameters

size
Specifies the diameter of rasterized points. The initial value is 1.

Description

glPointSize specifies the rasterized diameter of points. If point size mode is disabled (see glEnable with parameter GL_PROGRAM_POINT_SIZE), this value will be used to rasterize points. Otherwise, the value written to the shading language built-in variable gl_PointSize will be used.

Notes

The point size specified by glPointSize is always returned when GL_POINT_SIZE is queried. Clamping and rounding for points have no effect on the specified value.

Errors

GL_INVALID_VALUE is generated if *size* is less than or equal to 0.

Associated Gets

glGet with argument GL_POINT_SIZE_RANGE
glGet with argument GL_POINT_SIZE_GRANULARITY
glGet with argument GL_POINT_SIZE
glGet with argument GL_POINT_SIZE_MIN
glGet with argument GL_POINT_SIZE_MAX
glGet with argument GL_POINT_FADE_THRESHOLD_SIZE
glIsEnabled with argument GL_PROGRAM_POINT_SIZE

See Also

glEnable, glPointParameter

Copyright

glPolygonMode

select a polygon rasterization mode

C Specification

```
void glPolygonMode(GLenum face,
                   GLenum mode);
```

Parameters

face

Specifies the polygons that *mode* applies to. Must be GL_FRONT_AND_BACK for front- and back-facing polygons.

mode

Specifies how polygons will be rasterized. Accepted values are GL_POINT, GL_LINE, and GL_FILL. The initial value is GL_FILL for both front- and back-facing polygons.

Description

`glPolygonMode` controls the interpretation of polygons for rasterization. *face* describes which polygons *mode* applies to: both front- and back-facing polygons (GL_FRONT_AND_BACK). The polygon mode affects only the final rasterization of polygons. In particular, a polygon's vertices are lit and the polygon is clipped and possibly culled before these modes are applied.

Three modes are defined and can be specified in *mode*:

GL_POINT

Polygon vertices that are marked as the start of a boundary edge are drawn as points. Point attributes such as GL_POINT_SIZE and GL_POINT_SMOOTH control the rasterization of the points. Polygon rasterization attributes other than GL_POLYGON_MODE have no effect.

GL_LINE

Boundary edges of the polygon are drawn as line segments. Line attributes such as GL_LINE_WIDTH and GL_LINE_SMOOTH control the rasterization of the lines. Polygon rasterization attributes other than GL_POLYGON_MODE have no effect.

GL_FILL

The interior of the polygon is filled. Polygon attributes such as GL_POLYGON_SMOOTH control the rasterization of the polygon.

Examples

To draw a surface with outlined polygons, call

```
glPolygonMode(GL_FRONT_AND_BACK, GL_LINE);
```

Notes

Vertices are marked as boundary or nonboundary with an edge flag. Edge flags are generated internally by the GL when it decomposes triangle stips and fans.

Errors

GL_INVALID_ENUM is generated if either *face* or *mode* is not an accepted value.

Associated Gets

glGet with argument GL_POLYGON_MODE

See Also

`glLineWidth`, `glPointSize`

Copyright

glPolygonOffset

set the scale and units used to calculate depth values

C Specification

```
void glPolygonOffset(GLfloat factor,
                     GLfloat units);
```

Parameters

factor

Specifies a scale factor that is used to create a variable depth offset for each polygon. The initial value is 0.

units

Is multiplied by an implementation-specific value to create a constant depth offset. The initial value is 0.

Description

When GL_POLYGON_OFFSET_FILL, GL_POLYGON_OFFSET_LINE, or GL_POLYGON_OFFSET_POINT is enabled, each fragment's *depth* value will be offset after it is interpolated from the *depth* values of the appropriate vertices. The value of the offset is factor * D Z + r * units, where D Z is a measurement of the change in depth relative to the screen area of the polygon, and r is the smallest value that is guaranteed to produce a resolvable offset for a given implementation. The offset is added before the depth test is performed and before the value is written into the depth buffer.

glPolygonOffset is useful for rendering hidden-line images, for applying decals to surfaces, and for rendering solids with highlighted edges.

Notes

glPolygonOffset has no effect on depth coordinates placed in the feedback buffer.
glPolygonOffset has no effect on selection.

Errors

Associated Gets

glIsEnabled with argument GL_POLYGON_OFFSET_FILL, GL_POLYGON_OFFSET_LINE, or GL_POLYGON_OFFSET_POINT.
glGet with argument GL_POLYGON_OFFSET_FACTOR or GL_POLYGON_OFFSET_UNITS.

See Also

glDepthFunc, glEnable, glGet, glIsEnabled

Copyright

glPrimitiveRestartIndex

specify the primitive restart index

C Specification

```
void glPrimitiveRestartIndex(GLuint index);
```

Parameters

index
> Specifies the value to be interpreted as the primitive restart index.

Description

`glPrimitiveRestartIndex` specifies a vertex array element that is treated specially when primitive restarting is enabled. This is known as the primitive restart index.

When one of the `Draw*` commands transfers a set of generic attribute array elements to the GL, if the index within the vertex arrays corresponding to that set is equal to the primitive restart index, then the GL does not process those elements as a vertex. Instead, it is as if the drawing command ended with the immediately preceding transfer, and another drawing command is immediately started with the same parameters, but only transferring the immediately following element through the end of the originally specified elements.

When either glDrawElementsBaseVertex, glDrawElementsInstancedBaseVertex or glMultiDrawElementsBaseVertex is used, the primitive restart comparison occurs before the basevertex offset is added to the array index.

Notes

`glPrimitiveRestartIndex` is available only if the GL version is 3.1 or greater.

See Also

`glDrawArrays`, `glDrawElements`, `glDrawElementsBaseVertex`, `glDrawElementsInstancedBaseVertex`

Copyright

glProvokingVertex

specifiy the vertex to be used as the source of data for flat shaded varyings

C Specification

```
void glProvokingVertex(GLenum provokeMode);
```

Parameters

provokeMode
> Specifies the vertex to be used as the source of data for flat shaded varyings.

Description

Flatshading a vertex shader varying output means to assign all vetices of the primitive the same value for that output. The vertex from which these values is derived is known as the *provoking vertex* and glProvokingVertex specifies which vertex is to be used as the source of data for flat shaded varyings.

provokeMode must be either GL_FIRST_VERTEX_CONVENTION or GL_LAST_VERTEX_CONVENTION, and controls the selection of the vertex whose values are assigned to flatshaded varying outputs. The interpretation of these values for the supported primitive types is:

If a vertex or geometry shader is active, user-defined varying outputs may be flatshaded by using the flat qualifier when declaring the output.

Notes

glProvokingVertex is available only if the GL version is 3.2 or greater.

Errors

GL_INVALID_ENUM is generated if *provokeMode* is not an accepted value.

Copyright

Copyright © 2010 Khronos Group. This material may be distributed subject to the terms and conditions set forth in the Open Publication License, v 1.0, 8 June 1999. http://opencontent.org/openpub/.

Primitive Type of Polygon i	First Vertex Convention	Last Vertex Convention
point	i	i
independent line	$2i - 1$	$2i$
line loop	i	$i + 1$, if $i < n$ 1, if $i = n$
line strip	i	$i + 1$
independent triangle	$3i - 2$	$3i$
triangle strip	i	$i + 2$
triangle fan	$i + 1$	$i + 2$
line adjacency	$4i - 2$	$4i - 1$
line strip adjacency	$i + 1$	$i + 2$
triangle adjacency	$6i - 5$	$6i - 1$
triangle strip adjacency	$2i - 1$	$2i + 3$

glQueryCounter

record the GL time into a query object after all previous commands have reached the GL server but have not yet necessarily executed.

C Specification

```
void glQueryCounter(GLuint id,
                    GLenum target);
```

Parameters

id
> Specify the name of a query object into which to record the GL time.

target
> Specify the counter to query. *target* must be GL_TIMESTAMP.

Description

glQueryCounter causes the GL to record the current time into the query object named *id*. *target* must be GL_TIMESTAMP. The time is recorded after all previous commands on the GL client and server state and the framebuffer have been fully realized. When the time is recorded, the query result for that object is marked available. glQueryCounter timer queries can be used within a glBeginQuery / glEndQuery block where the target is GL_TIME_ELAPSED and it does not affect the result of that query object.

Notes

glQueryCounter is available only if the GL version is 3.3 or higher.

Errors

GL_INVALID_OPERATION is generated if *id* is the name of a query object that is already in use within a glBeginQuery / glEndQuery block.

GL_INVALID_VALUE is generated if *id* is not the name of a query object returned from a previous call to glGenQueries.

GL_INVALID_ENUM is generated if *target* is not GL_TIMESTAMP.

See Also

glGenQueries, glBeginQuery, glEndQuery, glDeleteQueries, glGetQueryObject, glGetQueryiv, glGet

Copyright

Copyright © 2010 Khronos Group. This material may be distributed subject to the terms and conditions set forth in the Open Publication License, v 1.0, 8 June 1999. http://opencontent.org/openpub/.

glReadBuffer

select a color buffer source for pixels

C Specification

```
void glReadBuffer(GLenum mode);
```

Parameters

mode

Specifies a color buffer. Accepted values are GL_FRONT_LEFT, GL_FRONT_RIGHT, GL_BACK_LEFT, GL_BACK_RIGHT, GL_FRONT, GL_BACK, GL_LEFT, and GL_RIGHT.

Description

glReadBuffer specifies a color buffer as the source for subsequent glReadPixels, glCopyTexImage1D, glCopyTexImage2D, glCopyTexSubImage1D, glCopyTexSubImage2D, and glCopyTexSubImage3D commands. *mode* accepts one of twelve or more predefined values. In a fully configured system, GL_FRONT, GL_LEFT, and GL_FRONT_LEFT all name the front left buffer, GL_FRONT_RIGHT and GL_RIGHT name the front right buffer, and GL_BACK_LEFT and GL_BACK name the back left buffer.

Nonstereo double-buffered configurations have only a front left and a back left buffer. Single-buffered configurations have a front left and a front right buffer if stereo, and only a front left buffer if nonstereo. It is an error to specify a nonexistent buffer to glReadBuffer.

mode is initially GL_FRONT in single-buffered configurations and GL_BACK in double-buffered configurations.

Errors

GL_INVALID_ENUM is generated if *mode* is not one of the twelve (or more) accepted values. GL_INVALID_OPERATION is generated if *mode* specifies a buffer that does not exist.

Associated Gets

glGet with argument GL_READ_BUFFER

See Also

glCopyTexImage1D, glCopyTexImage2D, glCopyTexSubImage1D, glCopyTexSubImage2D, glCopyTexSubImage3D, glDrawBuffer, glReadPixels

Copyright

Copyright © 1991-2006 Silicon Graphics, Inc. This document is licensed under the SGI Free Software B License. For details, see http://oss.sgi.com/projects/FreeB/.

glReadPixels

read a block of pixels from the frame buffer

C Specification

```
void glReadPixels(GLint x,
                  GLint y,
                  GLsizei width,
                  GLsizei height,
                  GLenum format,
                  GLenum type,
                  GLvoid * data);
```

Parameters

x
y

Specify the window coordinates of the first pixel that is read from the frame buffer. This location is the lower left corner of a rectangular block of pixels.

width
height

Specify the dimensions of the pixel rectangle. *width* and *height* of one correspond to a single pixel.

format

Specifies the format of the pixel data. The following symbolic values are accepted: GL_STENCIL_INDEX, GL_DEPTH_COMPONENT, GL_DEPTH_STENCIL, GL_RED, GL_GREEN, GL_BLUE, GL_RGB, GL_BGR, GL_RGBA, and GL_BGRA.

type

Specifies the data type of the pixel data. Must be one of GL_UNSIGNED_BYTE, GL_BYTE, GL_UNSIGNED_SHORT, GL_SHORT, GL_UNSIGNED_INT, GL_INT, GL_HALF_FLOAT, GL_FLOAT, GL_UNSIGNED_BYTE_3_3_2, GL_UNSIGNED_BYTE_2_3_3_REV, GL_UNSIGNED_SHORT_5_6_5, GL_UNSIGNED_SHORT_5_6_5_REV, GL_UNSIGNED_SHORT_4_4_4_4, GL_UNSIGNED_SHORT_4_4_4_4_REV, GL_UNSIGNED_SHORT_5_5_5_1, GL_UNSIGNED_SHORT_1_5_5_5_REV, GL_UNSIGNED_INT_8_8_8_8, GL_UNSIGNED_INT_8_8_8_8_REV, GL_UNSIGNED_INT_10_10_10_2, GL_UNSIGNED_INT_2_10_10_10_REV, GL_UNSIGNED_INT_24_8, GL_UNSIGNED_INT_10F_11F_11F_REV, GL_UNSIGNED_INT_5_9_9_9_REV, or GL_FLOAT_32_UNSIGNED_INT_24_8_REV.

data

Returns the pixel data.

Description

glReadPixels returns pixel data from the frame buffer, starting with the pixel whose lower left corner is at location (x, y), into client memory starting at location *data*. Several parameters control the processing of the pixel data before it is placed into client memory. These parameters are set with glPixelStore. This reference page describes the effects on glReadPixels of most, but not all of the parameters specified by these three commands.

If a non-zero named buffer object is bound to the GL_PIXEL_PACK_BUFFER target (see glBindBuffer) while a block of pixels is requested, *data* is treated as a byte offset into the buffer object's data store rather than a pointer to client memory.

glReadPixels returns values from each pixel with lower left corner at $(x + i, y + j)$ for $0 <= i < width$ and $0 <= j < height$. This pixel is said to be the ith pixel in the jth row. Pixels are returned in row order from the lowest to the highest row, left to right in each row.

format specifies the format for the returned pixel values; accepted values are:

GL_STENCIL_INDEX

Stencil values are read from the stencil buffer. Each index is converted to fixed point, shifted left or right depending on the value and sign of GL_INDEX_SHIFT, and added to GL_INDEX_OFFSET. If GL_MAP_STENCIL is GL_TRUE, indices are replaced by their mappings in the table GL_PIXEL_MAP_S_TO_S.

GL_DEPTH_COMPONENT

Depth values are read from the depth buffer. Each component is converted to floating point such that the minimum depth value maps to 0 and the maximum value maps to 1. Each component is then multiplied by GL_DEPTH_SCALE, added to GL_DEPTH_BIAS, and finally clamped to the range $[0,1]$.

GL_DEPTH_STENCIL

Values are taken from both the depth and stencil buffers. The *type* parameter must be GL_UNSIGNED_INT_24_8 or GL_FLOAT_32_UNSIGNED_INT_24_8_REV.

GL_RED
GL_GREEN
GL_BLUE

GL_RGB
GL_BGR
GL_RGBA
GL_BGRA

Finally, the indices or components are converted to the proper format, as specified by *type*. If *format* is GL_STENCIL_INDEX and *type* is not GL_FLOAT, each index is masked with the mask value given in the following table. If *type* is GL_FLOAT, then each integer index is converted to single-precision floating-point format.

If *format* is GL_RED, GL_GREEN, GL_BLUE, GL_RGB, GL_BGR, GL_RGBA, or GL_BGRA and *type* is not GL_FLOAT, each component is multiplied by the multiplier shown in the following table. If type is GL_FLOAT, then each component is passed as is (or converted to the client's single-precision floating-point format if it is different from the one used by the GL).

Return values are placed in memory as follows. If *format* is GL_STENCIL_INDEX, GL_DEPTH_COMPONENT, GL_RED, GL_GREEN, or GL_BLUE, a single value is returned and the data for the ith pixel in the jth row is placed in location ($j$width + i GL_RGB and GL_BGR return three

type	Index Mask	Component Conversion
GL_UNSIGNED_BYTE	$2^8 - 1$	$(2^8 - 1)c$
GL_BYTE	$2^7 - 1$	$\dfrac{(2^8 - 1)c - 1}{2}$
GL_UNSIGNED_SHORT	$2^{16} - 1$	$(2^{16} - 1)c$
GL_SHORT	$2^{15} - 1$	$\dfrac{(2^{16} - 1)c - 1}{2}$
GL_UNSIGNED_INT	$2^{32} - 1$	$(2^{32} - 1)c$
GL_INT	$2^{31} - 1$	$\dfrac{(2^{32} - 1)c - 1}{2}$
GL_HALF_FLOAT	none	c
GL_FLOAT	none	c
GL_UNSIGNED_BYTE_3_3_2	$2^N - 1$	$(2^N - 1)c$
GL_UNSIGNED_BYTE_2_3_3_REV	$2^N - 1$	$(2^N - 1)c$
GL_UNSIGNED_SHORT_5_6_5	$2^N - 1$	$(2^N - 1)c$
GL_UNSIGNED_SHORT_5_6_5_REV	$2^N - 1$	$(2^N - 1)c$
GL_UNSIGNED_SHORT_4_4_4_4	$2^N - 1$	$(2^N - 1)c$
GL_UNSIGNED_SHORT_4_4_4_4_REV	$2^N - 1$	$(2^N - 1)c$

type	Index Mask	Component Conversion
GL_UNSIGNED_SHORT_5_5_5_1	$2^N - 1$	$\lfloor 2^N - 1 \rfloor c$
GL_UNSIGNED_SHORT_1_5_5_5_REV	$2^N - 1$	$\lfloor 2^N - 1 \rfloor c$
GL_UNSIGNED_INT_8_8_8_8	$2^N - 1$	$\lfloor 2^N - 1 \rfloor c$
GL_UNSIGNED_INT_8_8_8_8_REV	$2^N - 1$	$\lfloor 2^N - 1 \rfloor c$
GL_UNSIGNED_INT_10_10_10_2	$2^N - 1$	$\lfloor 2^N - 1 \rfloor c$
GL_UNSIGNED_INT_2_10_10_10_REV	$2^N - 1$	$\lfloor 2^N - 1 \rfloor c$
GL_UNSIGNED_INT_24_8	$2^N - 1$	$\lfloor 2^N - 1 \rfloor c$
GL_UNSIGNED_INT_10F_11F_11F_REV	—	Special
GL_UNSIGNED_INT_5_9_9_9_REV	—	Special
GL_FLOAT_32_UNSIGNED_INT_24_8_REV	none	c (Depth Only)

values, GL_RGBA and GL_BGRA return four values for each pixel, with all values corresponding to a single pixel occupying contiguous space in *data*. Storage parameters set by glPixelStore, such as GL_PACK_LSB_FIRST and GL_PACK_SWAP_BYTES, affect the way that data is written into memory. See glPixelStore for a description.

Notes

Values for pixels that lie outside the window connected to the current GL context are undefined. If an error is generated, no change is made to the contents of *data*.

Errors

GL_INVALID_ENUM is generated if *format* or *type* is not an accepted value.

GL_INVALID_VALUE is generated if either *width* or *height* is negative.

GL_INVALID_OPERATION is generated if *format* is GL_STENCIL_INDEX and there is no stencil buffer.

GL_INVALID_OPERATION is generated if *format* is GL_DEPTH_COMPONENT and there is no depth buffer.

GL_INVALID_OPERATION is generated if *format* is GL_DEPTH_STENCIL and there is no depth buffer or if there is no stencil buffer.

GL_INVALID_ENUM is generated if *format* is GL_DEPTH_STENCIL and *type* is not GL_UNSIGNED_INT_24_8 or GL_FLOAT_32_UNSIGNED_INT_24_8_REV.

GL_INVALID_OPERATION is generated if *type* is one of GL_UNSIGNED_BYTE_3_3_2, GL_UNSIGNED_BYTE_2_3_3_REV, GL_UNSIGNED_SHORT_5_6_5, or GL_UNSIGNED_SHORT_5_6_5_REV and *format* is not GL_RGB.

GL_INVALID_OPERATION is generated if *type* is one of GL_UNSIGNED_SHORT_4_4_4_4, GL_UNSIGNED_SHORT_4_4_4_4_REV, GL_UNSIGNED_SHORT_5_5_5_1, GL_UNSIGNED_SHORT_1_5_5_5_REV, GL_UNSIGNED_INT_8_8_8_8, GL_UNSIGNED_INT_8_8_8_8_REV, GL_UNSIGNED_INT_10_10_10_2, or GL_UNSIGNED_INT_2_10_10_10_REV and *format* is neither GL_RGBA nor GL_BGRA.

GL_INVALID_OPERATION is generated if a non-zero buffer object name is bound to the GL_PIXEL_PACK_BUFFER target and the buffer object's data store is currently mapped.

GL_INVALID_OPERATION is generated if a non-zero buffer object name is bound to the GL_PIXEL_PACK_BUFFER target and the data would be packed to the buffer object such that the memory writes required would exceed the data store size.

GL_INVALID_OPERATION is generated if a non-zero buffer object name is bound to the GL_PIXEL_PACK_BUFFER target and *data* is not evenly divisible into the number of bytes needed to store in memory a datum indicated by *type*.

GL_INVALID_OPERATION is generated if GL_READ_FRAMEBUFFER_BINDING is non-zero, the read framebuffer is complete, and the value of GL_SAMPLE_BUFFERS for the read framebuffer is greater than zero.

Associated Gets

glGet with argument GL_INDEX_MODE
glGet with argument GL_PIXEL_PACK_BUFFER_BINDING

See Also

glPixelStore, glReadBuffer

Copyright

Copyright © 1991-2006 Silicon Graphics, Inc. This document is licensed under the SGI Free Software B License. For details, see http://oss.sgi.com/projects/FreeB/.

glRenderbufferStorage

establish data storage, format and dimensions of a renderbuffer object's image

C Specification

```
void glRenderbufferStorage(GLenum target,
                           GLenum internalformat,
                           GLsizei width,
                           GLsizei height);
```

Parameters

target
    Specifies a binding to which the target of the allocation and must be GL_RENDERBUFFER.
internalformat
    Specifies the internal format to use for the renderbuffer object's image.
width
    Specifies the width of the renderbuffer, in pixels.
height
    Specifies the height of the renderbuffer, in pixels.

Description

glRenderbufferStorage is equivalent to calling glRenderbufferStorageMultisample with the *samples* set to zero.

The target of the operation, specified by *target* must be GL_RENDERBUFFER. *internalformat* specifies the internal format to be used for the renderbuffer object's storage and must be a color-renderable, depth-renderable, or stencil-renderable format. *width* and *height* are the dimensions, in pixels, of the renderbuffer. Both *width* and *height* must be less than or equal to the value of GL_MAX_RENDERBUFFER_SIZE.

Upon success, glRenderbufferStorage deletes any existing data store for the renderbuffer image and the contents of the data store after calling glRenderbufferStorage are undefined.

Errors

GL_INVALID_ENUM is generated if *target* is not GL_RENDERBUFFER.

GL_INVALID_VALUE is generated if either of *width* or *height* is negative, or greater than the value of GL_MAX_RENDERBUFFER_SIZE.

GL_INVALID_ENUM is generated if *internalformat* is not a color-renderable, depth-renderable, or stencil-renderable format.

GL_OUT_OF_MEMORY is generated if the GL is unable to create a data store of the requested size.

See Also

glGenRenderbuffers, glBindRenderbuffer, glRenderbufferStorageMultisample, glFramebufferRenderbuffer, glDeleteRenderbuffers

Copyright

glRenderbufferStorageMultisample

establish data storage, format, dimensions and sample count of a renderbuffer object's image

C Specification

```
void glRenderbufferStorageMultisample(GLenum target,
                                      GLsizei samples,
                                      GLenum internalformat,
                                      GLsizei width,
                                      GLsizei height);
```

Parameters

target
Specifies a binding to which the target of the allocation and must be GL_RENDERBUFFER.
samples
Specifies the number of samples to be used for the renderbuffer object's storage.
internalformat
Specifies the internal format to use for the renderbuffer object's image.
width
Specifies the width of the renderbuffer, in pixels.
height
Specifies the height of the renderbuffer, in pixels.

Description

glRenderbufferStorageMultisample establishes the data storage, format, dimensions and number of samples of a renderbuffer object's image.

The target of the operation, specified by *target* must be GL_RENDERBUFFER. *internalformat* specifies the internal format to be used for the renderbuffer object's storage and must be a color-renderable, depth-renderable, or stencil-renderable format. *width* and *height* are the dimensions, in pixels, of the renderbuffer. Both *width* and *height* must be less than or equal to the value of GL_MAX_RENDERBUFFER_SIZE. *samples* specifies the number of samples to be used for the render-buffer object's image, and must be less than or equal to the value of GL_MAX_SAMPLES. If *internalformat* is a signed or unsigned integer format then *samples* must be less than or equal to the value of GL_MAX_INTEGER_SAMPLES.

Upon success, `glRenderbufferStorageMultisample` deletes any existing data store for the renderbuffer image and the contents of the data store after calling `glRenderbufferStorageMultisample` are undefined.

Errors

GL_INVALID_ENUM is generated if *target* is not GL_RENDERBUFFER.

GL_INVALID_VALUE is generated if *samples* is greater than GL_MAX_SAMPLES.

GL_INVALID_ENUM is generated if *internalformat* is not a color-renderable, depth-renderable, or stencil-renderable format.

GL_INVALID_OPERATION is generated if *internalformat* is a signed or unsigned integer format and *samples* is greater than the value of GL_MAX_INTEGER_SAMPLES

GL_INVALID_VALUE is generated if either of *width* or *height* is negative, or greater than the value of GL_MAX_RENDERBUFFER_SIZE.

GL_OUT_OF_MEMORY is generated if the GL is unable to create a data store of the requested size.

See Also

`glGenRenderbuffers`, `glBindRenderbuffer`, `glRenderbufferStorage`, `glFramebufferRenderbuffer`, `glDeleteRenderbuffers`

Copyright

glSampleCoverage

specify multisample coverage parameters

C Specification

```
void glSampleCoverage(GLclampf value,
                      GLboolean invert);
```

Parameters

value

Specify a single floating-point sample coverage value. The value is clamped to the range [0,1]. The initial value is 1.0.

invert

Specify a single boolean value representing if the coverage masks should be inverted. GL_TRUE and GL_FALSE are accepted. The initial value is GL_FALSE.

Description

Multisampling samples a pixel multiple times at various implementation-dependent subpixel locations to generate antialiasing effects. Multisampling transparently antialiases points, lines, polygons, and images if it is enabled.

value is used in constructing a temporary mask used in determining which samples will be used in resolving the final fragment color. This mask is bitwise-anded with the coverage mask generated from the multisampling computation. If the *invert* flag is set, the temporary mask is inverted (all bits flipped) and then the bitwise-and is computed.

If an implementation does not have any multisample buffers available, or multisampling is disabled, rasterization occurs with only a single sample computing a pixel's final RGB color.

Provided an implementation supports multisample buffers, and multisampling is enabled, then a pixel's final color is generated by combining several samples per pixel. Each sample contains color, depth, and stencil information, allowing those operations to be performed on each sample.

Associated Gets

glGet with argument GL_SAMPLE_COVERAGE_VALUE
glGet with argument GL_SAMPLE_COVERAGE_INVERT
glIsEnabled with argument GL_MULTISAMPLE
glIsEnabled with argument GL_SAMPLE_ALPHA_TO_COVERAGE
glIsEnabled with argument GL_SAMPLE_ALPHA_TO_ONE
glIsEnabled with argument GL_SAMPLE_COVERAGE

See Also

glEnable

Copyright

glSampleMaski

set the value of a sub-word of the sample mask

C Specification

```
void glSampleMaski(GLuint maskNumber,
                   GLbitfield mask);
```

Parameters

maskNumber
Specifies which 32-bit sub-word of the sample mask to update.
mask
Specifies the new value of the mask sub-word.

Description

glSampleMaski sets one 32-bit sub-word of the multi-word sample mask, GL_SAMPLE_MASK_VALUE.

maskIndex specifies which 32-bit sub-word of the sample mask to update, and *mask* specifies the new value to use for that sub-word. *maskIndex* must be less than the value of GL_MAX_SAMPLE_MASK_WORDS. Bit B of mask word M corresponds to sample $32 \times M + B$.

Notes

glSampleMaski is available only if the GL version is 3.2 or greater, or if the ARB_texture_multisample extension is supported.

Errors

GL_INVALID_VALUE is generated if *maskIndex* is greater than or equal to the value of GL_MAX_SAMPLE_MASK_WORDS.

See Also

glGenRenderbuffers, glBindRenderbuffer, glRenderbufferStorageMultisample, glFramebufferRenderbuffer, glDeleteRenderbuffers

Copyright

Copyright © 2010 Khronos Group. This material may be distributed subject to the terms and conditions set forth in the Open Publication License, v 1.0, 8 June 1999. http://opencontent.org/openpub/.

glSamplerParameter

set sampler parameters

C Specification

```
void glSamplerParameterf(GLuint sampler,
                         GLenum pname,
                         GLfloat param);
void glSamplerParameteri(GLuint sampler,
                         GLenum pname,
                         GLint param);
```

Parameters

sampler
> Specifies the sampler object whose parameter to modify.

pname
> Specifies the symbolic name of a single-valued texture parameter. *pname* can be one of the following: GL_TEXTURE_WRAP_S, GL_TEXTURE_WRAP_T, GL_TEXTURE_WRAP_R, GL_TEXTURE_MIN_FILTER, GL_TEXTURE_MAG_FILTER, GL_TEXTURE_MIN_LOD, GL_TEXTURE_MAX_LOD, GL_TEXTURE_LOD_BIAS GL_TEXTURE_COMPARE_MODE, or GL_TEXTURE_COMPARE_FUNC.

param
> Specifies the value of *pname*.

C Specification

```
void glSamplerParameterfv GLuint sampler GLenum pname const GLfloat * params
void glSamplerParameteriv GLuint sampler GLenum pname const GLint * params
```

Parameters

sampler
> Specifies the sampler object whose parameter to modify.

pname
> Specifies the symbolic name of a texture parameter. *pname* can be one of the following: GL_TEXTURE_WRAP_S, GL_TEXTURE_WRAP_T, GL_TEXTURE_WRAP_R, GL_TEXTURE_MIN_FILTER, GL_TEXTURE_MAG_FILTER, GL_TEXTURE_BORDER_COLOR, GL_TEXTURE_MIN_LOD, GL_TEXTURE_MAX_LOD, GL_TEXTURE_LOD_BIAS GL_TEXTURE_COMPARE_MODE, or GL_TEXTURE_COMPARE_FUNC.

params
> Specifies a pointer to an array where the value or values of *pname* are stored.

Description

glSamplerParameter assigns the value or values in *params* to the sampler parameter specified as *pname*. *sampler* specifies the sampler object to be modified, and must be the name of a sampler object previously returned from a call to glGenSamplers. The following symbols are accepted in *pname*:

GL_TEXTURE_MIN_FILTER

The texture minifying function is used whenever the pixel being textured maps to an area greater than one texture element. There are six defined minifying functions. Two of them use the nearest one or nearest four texture elements to compute the texture value. The other four use mipmaps.

A mipmap is an ordered set of arrays representing the same image at progressively lower resolutions. If the texture has dimensions $2^n * 2^m$, there are $\max (n,m) + 1$ mipmaps. The first mipmap is the original texture, with dimensions $2^n * 2^m$. Each subsequent mipmap has dimensions $2^{k-1} * 2^{l-1}$, where $2^k * 2^l$ are the dimensions of the previous mipmap, until either $k = 0$ or $l = 0$. At that point, subsequent mipmaps have dimension $1 * 2^{l-1}$ or $2^{k-1} * 1$ until the final mipmap, which has dimension $1 * 1$. To define the mipmaps, call glTexImage1D, glTexImage2D, glTexImage3D, glCopyTexImage1D, or glCopyTexImage2D with the *level* argument indicating the order of the mipmaps. Level 0 is the original texture; level $\max(n,m)$ is the final $1 * 1$ mipmap.

params supplies a function for minifying the texture as one of the following:

GL_NEAREST

Returns the value of the texture element that is nearest (in Manhattan distance) to the center of the pixel being textured.

GL_LINEAR

Returns the weighted average of the four texture elements that are closest to the center of the pixel being textured. These can include border texture elements, depending on the values of GL_TEXTURE_WRAP_S and GL_TEXTURE_WRAP_T, and on the exact mapping.

GL_NEAREST_MIPMAP_NEAREST

Chooses the mipmap that most closely matches the size of the pixel being textured and uses the GL_NEAREST criterion (the texture element nearest to the center of the pixel) to produce a texture value.

GL_LINEAR_MIPMAP_NEAREST

Chooses the mipmap that most closely matches the size of the pixel being textured and uses the GL_LINEAR criterion (a weighted average of the four texture elements that are closest to the center of the pixel) to produce a texture value.

GL_NEAREST_MIPMAP_LINEAR

Chooses the two mipmaps that most closely match the size of the pixel being textured and uses the GL_NEAREST criterion (the texture element nearest to the center of the pixel) to produce a texture value from each mipmap. The final texture value is a weighted average of those two values.

GL_LINEAR_MIPMAP_LINEAR

Chooses the two mipmaps that most closely match the size of the pixel being textured and uses the GL_LINEAR criterion (a weighted average of the four texture elements that are closest to the center of the pixel) to produce a texture value from each mipmap. The final texture value is a weighted average of those two values.

As more texture elements are sampled in the minification process, fewer aliasing artifacts will be apparent. While the GL_NEAREST and GL_LINEAR minification functions can be faster than the other four, they sample only one of four texture elements to determine the texture value of the pixel being rendered and can produce moire patterns or ragged transitions. The initial value of GL_TEXTURE_MIN_FILTER is GL_NEAREST_MIPMAP_LINEAR.

GL_TEXTURE_MAG_FILTER

    The texture magnification function is used when the pixel being textured maps to an area less than or equal to one texture element. It sets the texture magnification function to either GL_NEAREST or GL_LINEAR (see below). GL_NEAREST is generally faster than GL_LINEAR, but it can produce textured images with sharper edges because the transition between texture elements is not as smooth. The initial value of GL_TEXTURE_MAG_FILTER is GL_LINEAR.

GL_NEAREST

    Returns the value of the texture element that is nearest (in Manhattan distance) to the center of the pixel being textured.

GL_LINEAR

    Returns the weighted average of the four texture elements that are closest to the center of the pixel being textured. These can include border texture elements, depending on the values of GL_TEXTURE_WRAP_S and GL_TEXTURE_WRAP_T, and on the exact mapping.

GL_TEXTURE_MIN_LOD

    Sets the minimum level-of-detail parameter. This floating-point value limits the selection of highest resolution mipmap (lowest mipmap level). The initial value is -1000.

GL_TEXTURE_MAX_LOD

    Sets the maximum level-of-detail parameter. This floating-point value limits the selection of the lowest resolution mipmap (highest mipmap level). The initial value is 1000.

GL_TEXTURE_WRAP_S

    Sets the wrap parameter for texture coordinate s to either GL_CLAMP_TO_EDGE, GL_MIRRORED_REPEAT, or GL_REPEAT. GL_CLAMP_TO_BORDER causes the s coordinate to be clamped to the range $\left[\frac{-1}{2}, +\frac{1}{2}\right]$, where N is the size of the texture in the direction of clamping. GL_CLAMP_TO_EDGE causes s coordinates to be clamped to the range $\left[\frac{1}{2}, 1-\frac{1}{2}\right]$, where N is the size of the texture in the direction of clamping. GL_REPEAT causes the integer part of the s coordinate to be ignored; the GL uses only the fractional part, thereby creating a repeating pattern. GL_MIRRORED_REPEAT causes the s coordinate to be set to the fractional part of the texture coordinate if the integer part of s is even; if the integer part of s is odd, then the s texture coordinate is set to 1 − frac(s), where frac(s) represents the fractional part of s. Initially, GL_TEXTURE_WRAP_S is set to GL_REPEAT.

GL_TEXTURE_WRAP_T

    Sets the wrap parameter for texture coordinate t to either GL_CLAMP_TO_EDGE, GL_MIRRORED_REPEAT, or GL_REPEAT. See the discussion under GL_TEXTURE_WRAP_S. Initially, GL_TEXTURE_WRAP_T is set to GL_REPEAT.

GL_TEXTURE_WRAP_R

    Sets the wrap parameter for texture coordinate r to either GL_CLAMP_TO_EDGE, GL_MIRRORED_REPEAT, or GL_REPEAT. See the discussion under GL_TEXTURE_WRAP_S. Initially, GL_TEXTURE_WRAP_R is set to GL_REPEAT.

GL_TEXTURE_BORDER_COLOR

    Sets a border color. *params* contains four values that comprise the RGBA color of the texture border. Integer color components are interpreted linearly such that the most positive integer maps to 1.0, and the most negative integer maps to -1.0. The values are clamped to the range [0,1] when they are specified. Initially, the border color is (0, 0, 0, 0).

GL_TEXTURE_COMPARE_MODE

Specifies the texture comparison mode for currently bound textures. That is, a texture whose internal format is GL_DEPTH_COMPONENT_*; see glTexImage2D) Permissible values are:

GL_COMPARE_REF_TO_TEXTURE

Specifies that the interpolated and clamped r texture coordinate should be compared to the value in the currently bound texture. See the discussion of GL_TEXTURE_COMPARE_FUNC for details of how the comparison is evaluated. The result of the comparison is assigned to the red channel.

GL_NONE

Specifies that the red channel should be assigned the appropriate value from the currently bound texture.

GL_TEXTURE_COMPARE_FUNC

Specifies the comparison operator used when GL_TEXTURE_COMPARE_MODE is set to GL_COMPARE_REF_TO_TEXTURE. Permissible values are:

where r is the current interpolated texture coordinate, and D_t is the texture value sampled from the currently bound texture. $result$ is assigned to R_t

Notes

glSamplerParameter is available only if the GL version is 3.3 or higher.

Errors

GL_INVALID_VALUE is generated if *sampler* is not the name of a sampler object previously returned from a call to glGenSamplers.

GL_INVALID_ENUM is generated if *params* should have a defined constant value (based on the value of *pname*) and does not.

Texture Comparison Function	Computed result
GL_LEQUAL	$$result = c \begin{cases} 1.0 & r \le D_t \\ 0.0 & r > D_t \end{cases}$$
GL_GEQUAL	$$result = c \begin{cases} 1.0 & r \ge D_t \\ 0.0 & r < D_t \end{cases}$$
GL_LESS	$$result = c \begin{cases} 1.0 & r < D_t \\ 0.0 & r \ge D_t \end{cases}$$
GL_GREATER	$$result = c \begin{cases} 1.0 & r > D_t \\ 0.0 & r \le D_t \end{cases}$$

Texture Comparison Function	Computed result
GL_EQUAL	$$result = \begin{matrix} 1.0 & r = D_t \\ 0.0 & r \ne D_t \end{matrix}$$
GL_NOTEQUAL	$$result = \begin{matrix} 1.0 & r \ne D_t \\ 0.0 & r = D_t \end{matrix}$$
GL_ALWAYS	$result = 1.0$
GL_NEVER	$result = 0.0$

Associated Gets

glGetSamplerParameter

See Also

glGenSamplers, glBindSampler, glDeleteSamplers, glIsSampler, glBindTexture

Copyright

glScissor

define the scissor box

C Specification

```
void glScissor(GLint x,
               GLint y,
               GLsizei width,
               GLsizei height);
```

Parameters

x
y
> Specify the lower left corner of the scissor box. Initially (0, 0).

width
height
> Specify the width and height of the scissor box. When a GL context is first attached to a window, *width* and *height* are set to the dimensions of that window.

Description

glScissor defines a rectangle, called the scissor box, in window coordinates. The first two arguments, *x* and *y*, specify the lower left corner of the box. *width* and *height* specify the width and height of the box.

To enable and disable the scissor test, call glEnable and glDisable with argument GL_SCISSOR_TEST. The test is initially disabled. While the test is enabled, only pixels that lie within the scissor box can be modified by drawing commands. Window coordinates have integer values at the shared corners of frame buffer pixels. glScissor(0,0,1,1) allows modification of only the lower left pixel in the window, and glScissor(0,0,0,0) doesn't allow modification of any pixels in the window.

When the scissor test is disabled, it is as though the scissor box includes the entire window.

Errors

GL_INVALID_VALUE is generated if either *width* or *height* is negative.

Associated Gets

glGet with argument GL_SCISSOR_BOX
glIsEnabled with argument GL_SCISSOR_TEST

See Also

glEnable, glViewport

Copyright

Copyright © 1991-2006 Silicon Graphics, Inc. This document is licensed under the SGI Free Software B License. For details, see http://oss.sgi.com/projects/FreeB/.

glShaderSource

Replaces the source code in a shader object

C Specification

```
void glShaderSource(GLuint shader,
                    GLsizei count,
                    const GLchar **string,
                    const GLint *length);
```

Parameters

shader
Specifies the handle of the shader object whose source code is to be replaced.

count
Specifies the number of elements in the *string* and *length* arrays.

string
Specifies an array of pointers to strings containing the source code to be loaded into the shader.

length
Specifies an array of string lengths.

Description

glShaderSource sets the source code in *shader* to the source code in the array of strings specified by *string*. Any source code previously stored in the shader object is completely replaced. The number of strings in the array is specified by *count*. If *length* is NULL, each string is assumed to be null terminated. If *length* is a value other than NULL, it points to an array containing a string length for each of the corresponding elements of *string*. Each element in the *length* array may contain the length of the corresponding string (the null character is not counted as part of the string length) or a value less than 0 to indicate that the string is null terminated. The source code strings are not scanned or parsed at this time; they are simply copied into the specified shader object.

Notes

OpenGL copies the shader source code strings when glShaderSource is called, so an application may free its copy of the source code strings immediately after the function returns.

Errors

GL_INVALID_VALUE is generated if *shader* is not a value generated by OpenGL.
GL_INVALID_OPERATION is generated if *shader* is not a shader object.
GL_INVALID_VALUE is generated if *count* is less than 0.

Associated Gets

glGetShader with arguments *shader* and GL_SHADER_SOURCE_LENGTH
glGetShaderSource with argument *shader*
glIsShader

See Also

glCompileShader, glCreateShader, glDeleteShader

Copyright

Copyright © 2003-2005 3Dlabs Inc. Ltd. This material may be distributed subject to the terms and conditions set forth in the Open Publication License, v 1.0, 8 June 1999. http://opencontent.org/openpub/.

glStencilFunc

set front and back function and reference value for stencil testing

C Specification

```
void glStencilFunc(GLenum func,
                   GLint ref,
                   GLuint mask);
```

Parameters

func

Specifies the test function. Eight symbolic constants are valid: GL_NEVER, GL_LESS, GL_LEQUAL, GL_GREATER, GL_GEQUAL, GL_EQUAL, GL_NOTEQUAL, and GL_ALWAYS. The initial value is GL_ALWAYS.

ref

Specifies the reference value for the stencil test. *ref* is clamped to the range $[0, 2^n - 1]$ where n is the number of bitplanes in the stencil buffer. The initial value is 0.

mask

Specifies a mask that is ANDed with both the reference value and the stored stencil value when the test is done. The initial value is all 1's.

Description

Stenciling, like depth-buffering, enables and disables drawing on a per-pixel basis. Stencil planes are first drawn into using GL drawing primitives, then geometry and images are rendered using the stencil planes to mask out portions of the screen. Stenciling is typically used in multipass rendering algorithms to achieve special effects, such as decals, outlining, and constructive solid geometry rendering.

The stencil test conditionally eliminates a pixel based on the outcome of a comparison between the reference value and the value in the stencil buffer. To enable and disable the test, call glEnable and glDisable with argument GL_STENCIL_TEST. To specify actions based on the outcome of the stencil test, call glStencilOp or glStencilOpSeparate.

There can be two separate sets of *func*, *ref*, and *mask* parameters; one affects back-facing polygons, and the other affects front-facing polygons as well as other non-polygon primitives. glStencilFunc sets both front and back stencil state to the same values. Use glStencilFuncSeparate to set front and back stencil state to different values.

func is a symbolic constant that determines the stencil comparison function. It accepts one of eight values, shown in the following list. *ref* is an integer reference value that is used in the stencil comparison. It is clamped to the range $[0, 2^n - 1]$, where n is the number of bitplanes in the stencil buffer. *mask* is bitwise ANDed with both the reference value and the stored stencil value, with the ANDed values participating in the comparison.

If *stencil* represents the value stored in the corresponding stencil buffer location, the following list shows the effect of each comparison function that can be specified by *func*. Only if the comparison succeeds is the pixel passed through to the next stage in the rasterization process (see glStencilOp). All tests treat *stencil* values as unsigned integers in the range $[0, 2^n - 1]$, where n is the number of bitplanes in the stencil buffer.

The following values are accepted by *func*:

GL_NEVER

Always fails.

GL_LESS

Passes if (*ref* & *mask*) < (*stencil* & *mask*).

GL_LEQUAL

Passes if (*ref* & *mask*) <= (*stencil* & *mask*).

GL_GREATER

Passes if (*ref* & *mask*) > (*stencil* & *mask*).

GL_GEQUAL

Passes if (*ref* & *mask*) >= (*stencil* & *mask*).

GL_EQUAL

Passes if (*ref* & *mask*) = (*stencil* & *mask*).

GL_NOTEQUAL

Passes if (*ref* & *mask*) != (*stencil* & *mask*).

GL_ALWAYS

Always passes.

Notes

Initially, the stencil test is disabled. If there is no stencil buffer, no stencil modification can occur and it is as if the stencil test always passes.

glStencilFunc is the same as calling glStencilFuncSeparate with *face* set to GL_FRONT_AND_BACK.

Errors

GL_INVALID_ENUM is generated if *func* is not one of the eight accepted values.

Associated Gets

glGet with argument GL_STENCIL_FUNC, GL_STENCIL_VALUE_MASK, GL_STENCIL_REF, GL_STENCIL_BACK_FUNC, GL_STENCIL_BACK_VALUE_MASK, GL_STENCIL_BACK_REF, or GL_STENCIL_BITS

glIsEnabled with argument GL_STENCIL_TEST

See Also

glBlendFunc, glDepthFunc, glEnable, glLogicOp, glStencilFuncSeparate, glStencilMask, glStencilMaskSeparate, glStencilOp, glStencilOpSeparate

Copyright

glStencilFuncSeparate

set front and/or back function and reference value for stencil testing

C Specification

```
void glStencilFuncSeparate(GLenum face,
                           GLenum func,
                           GLint ref,
                           GLuint mask);
```

Parameters

face

Specifies whether front and/or back stencil state is updated. Three symbolic constants are valid: GL_FRONT, GL_BACK, and GL_FRONT_AND_BACK.

func

Specifies the test function. Eight symbolic constants are valid: GL_NEVER, GL_LESS, GL_LEQUAL, GL_GREATER, GL_GEQUAL, GL_EQUAL, GL_NOTEQUAL, and GL_ALWAYS. The initial value is GL_ALWAYS.

ref

Specifies the reference value for the stencil test. *ref* is clamped to the range $[0, 2^n - 1]$, where n is the number of bitplanes in the stencil buffer. The initial value is 0.

mask

Specifies a mask that is ANDed with both the reference value and the stored stencil value when the test is done. The initial value is all 1's.

Description

Stenciling, like depth-buffering, enables and disables drawing on a per-pixel basis. You draw into the stencil planes using GL drawing primitives, then render geometry and images, using the stencil planes to mask out portions of the screen. Stenciling is typically used in multipass rendering algorithms to achieve special effects, such as decals, outlining, and constructive solid geometry rendering.

The stencil test conditionally eliminates a pixel based on the outcome of a comparison between the reference value and the value in the stencil buffer. To enable and disable the test, call glEnable and glDisable with argument GL_STENCIL_TEST. To specify actions based on the outcome of the stencil test, call glStencilOp or glStencilOpSeparate.

There can be two separate sets of *func*, *ref*, and *mask* parameters; one affects back-facing polygons, and the other affects front-facing polygons as well as other non-polygon primitives. glStencilFunc sets both front and back stencil state to the same values, as if glStencilFuncSeparate were called with *face* set to GL_FRONT_AND_BACK.

func is a symbolic constant that determines the stencil comparison function. It accepts one of eight values, shown in the following list. *ref* is an integer reference value that is used in the stencil comparison. It is clamped to the range $[0, 2^n - 1]$, where n is the number of bitplanes in the stencil buffer. *mask* is bitwise ANDed with both the reference value and the stored stencil value, with the ANDed values participating in the comparison.

If *stencil* represents the value stored in the corresponding stencil buffer location, the following list shows the effect of each comparison function that can be specified by *func*. Only if the comparison succeeds is the pixel passed through to the next stage in the rasterization process (see glStencilOp). All tests treat *stencil* values as unsigned integers in the range $[0, 2^n - 1]$ where n is the number of bitplanes in the stencil buffer.

The following values are accepted by *func*:

GL_NEVER

    Always fails.

GL_LESS

    Passes if (*ref* & *mask*) < (*stencil* & *mask*).

GL_LEQUAL

    Passes if (*ref* & *mask*) <= (*stencil* & *mask*).

GL_GREATER

    Passes if (*ref* & *mask*) > (*stencil* & *mask*).

GL_GEQUAL

    Passes if (*ref* & *mask*) >= (*stencil* & *mask*).

GL_EQUAL

    Passes if (*ref* & *mask*) = (*stencil* & *mask*).

GL_NOTEQUAL

    Passes if (*ref* & *mask*) != (*stencil* & *mask*).

GL_ALWAYS

    Always passes.

Notes

Initially, the stencil test is disabled. If there is no stencil buffer, no stencil modification can occur and it is as if the stencil test always passes.

Errors

GL_INVALID_ENUM is generated if *func* is not one of the eight accepted values.

Associated Gets

glGet with argument GL_STENCIL_FUNC, GL_STENCIL_VALUE_MASK, GL_STENCIL_REF, GL_STENCIL_BACK_FUNC, GL_STENCIL_BACK_VALUE_MASK, GL_STENCIL_BACK_REF, or GL_STENCIL_BITS

glIsEnabled with argument GL_STENCIL_TEST

See Also

glBlendFunc, glDepthFunc, glEnable, glLogicOp, glStencilFunc, glStencilMask, glStencilMaskSeparate, glStencilOp, glStencilOpSeparate

Copyright

Copyright © 2006 Khronos Group. This material may be distributed subject to the terms and conditions set forth in the Open Publication License, v 1.0, 8 June 1999. http://opencontent.org/openpub/.

glStencilMask

control the front and back writing of individual bits in the stencil planes

C Specification

```
void glStencilMask(GLuint mask);
```

Parameters

mask

Specifies a bit mask to enable and disable writing of individual bits in the stencil planes. Initially, the mask is all 1's.

Description

glStencilMask controls the writing of individual bits in the stencil planes. The least significant n bits of *mask*, where n is the number of bits in the stencil buffer, specify a mask. Where a 1 appears in the mask, it's possible to write to the corresponding bit in the stencil buffer. Where a 0 appears, the corresponding bit is write-protected. Initially, all bits are enabled for writing.

There can be two separate *mask* writemasks; one affects back-facing polygons, and the other affects front-facing polygons as well as other non-polygon primitives. glStencilMask sets both front and back stencil writemasks to the same values. Use glStencilMaskSeparate to set front and back stencil writemasks to different values.

Notes

glStencilMask is the same as calling glStencilMaskSeparate with *face* set to GL_FRONT_AND_BACK.

Associated Gets

glGet with argument GL_STENCIL_WRITEMASK, GL_STENCIL_BACK_WRITEMASK, or GL_STENCIL_BITS

See Also

glColorMask, glDepthMask, glStencilFunc, glStencilFuncSeparate, glStencilMaskSeparate, glStencilOp, glStencilOpSeparate

Copyright

Copyright © 1991-2006 Silicon Graphics, Inc. This document is licensed under the SGI Free Software B License. For details, see http://oss.sgi.com/projects/FreeB/.

glStencilMaskSeparate

control the front and/or back writing of individual bits in the stencil planes

C Specification

```
void glStencilMaskSeparate(GLenum face,
                           GLuint mask);
```

Parameters

face

Specifies whether the front and/or back stencil writemask is updated. Three symbolic constants are valid: GL_FRONT, GL_BACK, and GL_FRONT_AND_BACK.

mask

Specifies a bit mask to enable and disable writing of individual bits in the stencil planes. Initially, the mask is all 1's.

Description

`glStencilMaskSeparate` controls the writing of individual bits in the stencil planes. The least significant n bits of *mask*, where n is the number of bits in the stencil buffer, specify a mask. Where a 1 appears in the mask, it's possible to write to the corresponding bit in the stencil buffer. Where a 0 appears, the corresponding bit is write-protected. Initially, all bits are enabled for writing.

There can be two separate *mask* writemasks; one affects back-facing polygons, and the other affects front-facing polygons as well as other non-polygon primitives. glStencilMask sets both front and back stencil writemasks to the same values, as if glStencilMaskSeparate were called with *face* set to GL_FRONT_AND_BACK.

Errors

GL_INVALID_ENUM is generated if *face* is not one of the accepted tokens.

Associated Gets

glGet with argument GL_STENCIL_WRITEMASK, GL_STENCIL_BACK_WRITEMASK, or GL_STENCIL_BITS

See Also

`glColorMask`, `glDepthMask`, `glStencilFunc`, `glStencilFuncSeparate`, `glStencilMask`, `glStencilOp`, `glStencilOpSeparate`

Copyright

Copyright © 2006 Khronos Group. This material may be distributed subject to the terms and conditions set forth in the Open Publication License, v 1.0, 8 June 1999. http://opencontent.org/openpub/.

glStencilOp

set front and back stencil test actions

C Specification

```
void glStencilOp(GLenum sfail,
                 GLenum dpfail,
                 GLenum dppass);
```

Parameters

sfail

Specifies the action to take when the stencil test fails. Eight symbolic constants are accepted: GL_KEEP, GL_ZERO, GL_REPLACE, GL_INCR, GL_INCR_WRAP, GL_DECR, GL_DECR_WRAP, and GL_INVERT. The initial value is GL_KEEP.

dpfail

Specifies the stencil action when the stencil test passes, but the depth test fails. *dpfail* accepts the same symbolic constants as *sfail*. The initial value is GL_KEEP.

dppass

> Specifies the stencil action when both the stencil test and the depth test pass, or when the stencil test passes and either there is no depth buffer or depth testing is not enabled. *dppass* accepts the same symbolic constants as *sfail*. The initial value is GL_KEEP.

Description

Stenciling, like depth-buffering, enables and disables drawing on a per-pixel basis. You draw into the stencil planes using GL drawing primitives, then render geometry and images, using the stencil planes to mask out portions of the screen. Stenciling is typically used in multipass rendering algorithms to achieve special effects, such as decals, outlining, and constructive solid geometry rendering.

The stencil test conditionally eliminates a pixel based on the outcome of a comparison between the value in the stencil buffer and a reference value. To enable and disable the test, call glEnable and glDisable with argument GL_STENCIL_TEST; to control it, call glStencilFunc or glStencilFuncSeparate.

There can be two separate sets of *sfail*, *dpfail*, and *dppass* parameters; one affects back-facing polygons, and the other affects front-facing polygons as well as other non-polygon primitives. glStencilOp sets both front and back stencil state to the same values. Use glStencilOpSeparate to set front and back stencil state to different values.

glStencilOp takes three arguments that indicate what happens to the stored stencil value while stenciling is enabled. If the stencil test fails, no change is made to the pixel's color or depth buffers, and *sfail* specifies what happens to the stencil buffer contents. The following eight actions are possible.

GL_KEEP

> Keeps the current value.

GL_ZERO

> Sets the stencil buffer value to 0.

GL_REPLACE

> Sets the stencil buffer value to *ref*, as specified by glStencilFunc.

GL_INCR

> Increments the current stencil buffer value. Clamps to the maximum representable unsigned value.

GL_INCR_WRAP

> Increments the current stencil buffer value. Wraps stencil buffer value to zero when incrementing the maximum representable unsigned value.

GL_DECR

> Decrements the current stencil buffer value. Clamps to 0.

GL_DECR_WRAP

> Decrements the current stencil buffer value. Wraps stencil buffer value to the maximum representable unsigned value when decrementing a stencil buffer value of zero.

GL_INVERT

> Bitwise inverts the current stencil buffer value.

Stencil buffer values are treated as unsigned integers. When incremented and decremented, values are clamped to 0 and $2^n - 1$, where $2^n - 1$ is the value returned by querying GL_STENCIL_BITS.

The other two arguments to glStencilOp specify stencil buffer actions that depend on whether subsequent depth buffer tests succeed (*dppass*) or fail (*dpfail*) (see glDepthFunc). The actions are specified using the same eight symbolic constants as *sfail*. Note that *dpfail* is ignored when there is no depth buffer, or when the depth buffer is not enabled. In these cases, *sfail* and *dppass* specify stencil action when the stencil test fails and passes, respectively.

Notes

Initially the stencil test is disabled. If there is no stencil buffer, no stencil modification can occur and it is as if the stencil tests always pass, regardless of any call to `glStencilOp`.

glStencilOp is the same as calling glStencilOpSeparate with *face* set to GL_FRONT_AND_BACK.

Errors

GL_INVALID_ENUM is generated if *sfail*, *dpfail*, or *dppass* is any value other than the defined constant values.

Associated Gets

glGet with argument GL_STENCIL_FAIL, GL_STENCIL_PASS_DEPTH_PASS, GL_STENCIL_PASS_DEPTH_FAIL, GL_STENCIL_BACK_FAIL, GL_STENCIL_BACK_PASS_DEPTH_PASS, GL_STENCIL_BACK_PASS_DEPTH_FAIL, or GL_STENCIL_BITS

glIsEnabled with argument GL_STENCIL_TEST

See Also

`glBlendFunc`, `glDepthFunc`, `glEnable`, `glLogicOp`, `glStencilFunc`, `glStencilFuncSeparate`, `glStencilMask`, `glStencilMaskSeparate`, `glStencilOpSeparate`

Copyright

glStencilOpSeparate

set front and/or back stencil test actions

C Specification

```
void glStencilOpSeparate(GLenum face,
                         GLenum sfail,
                         GLenum dpfail,
                         GLenum dppass);
```

Parameters

face

Specifies whether front and/or back stencil state is updated. Three symbolic constants are valid: GL_FRONT, GL_BACK, and GL_FRONT_AND_BACK.

sfail

Specifies the action to take when the stencil test fails. Eight symbolic constants are accepted: GL_KEEP, GL_ZERO, GL_REPLACE, GL_INCR, GL_INCR_WRAP, GL_DECR, GL_DECR_WRAP, and GL_INVERT. The initial value is GL_KEEP.

dpfail

Specifies the stencil action when the stencil test passes, but the depth test fails. *dpfail* accepts the same symbolic constants as *sfail*. The initial value is GL_KEEP.

dppass

Specifies the stencil action when both the stencil test and the depth test pass, or when the stencil test passes and either there is no depth buffer or depth testing is not enabled. *dppass* accepts the same symbolic constants as *sfail*. The initial value is GL_KEEP.

Description

Stenciling, like depth-buffering, enables and disables drawing on a per-pixel basis. You draw into the stencil planes using GL drawing primitives, then render geometry and images, using the stencil planes to mask out portions of the screen. Stenciling is typically used in multipass rendering algorithms to achieve special effects, such as decals, outlining, and constructive solid geometry rendering.

The stencil test conditionally eliminates a pixel based on the outcome of a comparison between the value in the stencil buffer and a reference value. To enable and disable the test, call glEnable and glDisable with argument GL_STENCIL_TEST; to control it, call glStencilFunc or glStencilFuncSeparate.

There can be two separate sets of *sfail*, *dpfail*, and *dppass* parameters; one affects back-facing polygons, and the other affects front-facing polygons as well as other non-polygon primitives. glStencilOp sets both front and back stencil state to the same values, as if glStencilOpSeparate were called with *face* set to GL_FRONT_AND_BACK.

`glStencilOpSeparate` takes three arguments that indicate what happens to the stored stencil value while stenciling is enabled. If the stencil test fails, no change is made to the pixel's color or depth buffers, and *sfail* specifies what happens to the stencil buffer contents. The following eight actions are possible.

GL_KEEP
>   Keeps the current value.

GL_ZERO
>   Sets the stencil buffer value to 0.

GL_REPLACE
>   Sets the stencil buffer value to *ref*, as specified by glStencilFunc.

GL_INCR
>   Increments the current stencil buffer value. Clamps to the maximum representable unsigned value.

GL_INCR_WRAP
>   Increments the current stencil buffer value. Wraps stencil buffer value to zero when incrementing the maximum representable unsigned value.

GL_DECR
>   Decrements the current stencil buffer value. Clamps to 0.

GL_DECR_WRAP
>   Decrements the current stencil buffer value. Wraps stencil buffer value to the maximum representable unsigned value when decrementing a stencil buffer value of zero.

GL_INVERT
>   Bitwise inverts the current stencil buffer value.

Stencil buffer values are treated as unsigned integers. When incremented and decremented, values are clamped to 0 and $2^n - 1$, where n is the value returned by querying GL_STENCIL_BITS.

The other two arguments to `glStencilOpSeparate` specify stencil buffer actions that depend on whether subsequent depth buffer tests succeed (*dppass*) or fail (*dpfail*) (see glDepthFunc). The actions are specified using the same eight symbolic constants as *sfail*. Note that *dpfail* is ignored when there is no depth buffer, or when the depth buffer is not enabled. In these cases, *sfail* and *dppass* specify stencil action when the stencil test fails and passes, respectively.

Notes

Initially the stencil test is disabled. If there is no stencil buffer, no stencil modification can occur and it is as if the stencil test always passes.

Errors

GL_INVALID_ENUM is generated if *face* is any value other than GL_FRONT, GL_BACK, or GL_FRONT_AND_BACK.

GL_INVALID_ENUM is generated if *sfail*, *dpfail*, or *dppass* is any value other than the eight defined constant values.

Associated Gets

glGet with argument GL_STENCIL_FAIL, GL_STENCIL_PASS_DEPTH_PASS, GL_STENCIL_PASS_DEPTH_FAIL, GL_STENCIL_BACK_FAIL, GL_STENCIL_BACK_PASS_DEPTH_PASS, GL_STENCIL_BACK_PASS_DEPTH_FAIL, or GL_STENCIL_BITS

glIsEnabled with argument GL_STENCIL_TEST

See Also

glBlendFunc, glDepthFunc, glEnable, glLogicOp, glStencilFunc, glStencilFuncSeparate, glStencilMask, glStencilMaskSeparate, glStencilOp

Copyright

glTexBuffer

attach the storage for a buffer object to the active buffer texture

C Specification

```
void glTexBuffer(GLenum target,
                 GLenum internalFormat,
                 Gluint buffer);
```

Parameters

target
> Specifies the target of the operation and must be GL_TEXTURE_BUFFER.

internalFormat
> Specifies the internal format of the data in the store belonging to *buffer*.

buffer
> Specifies the name of the buffer object whose storage to attach to the active buffer texture.

Description

glTexBuffer attaches the storage for the buffer object named *buffer* to the active buffer texture, and specifies the internal format for the texel array found in the attached buffer object. If *buffer* is zero, any buffer object attached to the buffer texture is detached and no new buffer object is attached. If *buffer* is non-zero, it must be the name of an existing buffer object. *target* must be GL_TEXTURE_BUFFER. *internalformat* specifies the storage format, and must be one of the following sized internal formats:

When a buffer object is attached to a buffer texture, the buffer object's data store is taken as the texture's texel array. The number of texels in the buffer texture's texel array is given by

$$\frac{buffer\ size}{components\ A\ -\ size\ of\ (base\_type)}$$

where *buffer_size* is the size of the buffer object, in basic machine units and components and base type are the element count and base data type for elements, as specified in the table above. The number of texels in the texel array is then clamped to the implementation-dependent limit GL_MAX_TEXTURE_BUFFER_SIZE. When a buffer texture is accessed in a shader, the results of a texel fetch are undefined if the specified texel coordinate is negative, or greater than or equal to the clamped number of texels in the texel array.

Sized Internal Format	Base Type	Components	Norm	Component 0	Component 1	Component 2	Component 3
GL_R8	ubyte	1	YES	R	0	0	1
GL_R16	ushort	1	YES	R	0	0	1
GL_R16F	half	1	NO	R	0	0	1
GL_R32F	float	1	NO	R	0	0	1
GL_R8I	byte	1	NO	R	0	0	1
GL_R16I	short	1	NO	R	0	0	1
GL_R32I	int	1	NO	R	0	0	1
GL_R8UI	ubyte	1	NO	R	0	0	1
GL_R16UI	ushort	1	NO	R	0	0	1
GL_R32UI	uint	1	NO	R	0	0	1
GL_RG8	ubyte	2	YES	R	G	0	1
GL_RG16	ushort	2	YES	R	G	0	1
GL_RG16F	half	2	NO	R	G	0	1
GL_RG32F	float	2	YES	R	G	0	1
GL_RG8I	byte	2	NO	R	G	0	1
GL_RG16I	short	2	NO	R	G	0	1
GL_RG32I	int	2	NO	R	G	0	1
GL_RG8UI	ubyte	2	NO	R	G	0	1
GL_RG16UI	ushort	2	NO	R	G	0	1
GL_RG32UI	uint	2	NO	R	G	0	1
GL_RGBA8	uint	4	YES	R	G	B	A
GL_RGBA16	short	4	YES	R	G	B	A

				Component			
GL_RGBA16F	half	4	NO	R	G	B	A
GL_RGBA32F	float	4	NO	R	G	B	A
GL_RGBA8I	byte	4	NO	R	G	B	A
GL_RGBA16I	short	4	NO	R	G	B	A
GL_RGBA32I	int	4	NO	R	G	B	A
GL_RGBA8UI	ubyte	4	NO	R	G	B	A
GL_RGBA16UI	ushort	4	NO	R	G	B	A
GL_RGBA32UI	uint	4	NO	R	G	B	A

Errors

GL_INVALID_ENUM is generated if *target* is not GL_TEXTURE_BUFFER.
GL_INVALID_ENUM is generated if *internalFormat* is not one of the accepted tokens.
GL_INVALID_OPERATION is generated if *buffer* is not zero or the name of an existing buffer object.

Notes

glTexBuffer is available only if the GL version is 3.1 or greater.

Associated Gets

glGet with argument GL_MAX_TEXTURE_BUFFER_SIZE
glGet with argument GL_TEXTURE_BINDING_BUFFER
glGetTexLevelParameter with argument GL_TEXTURE_BUFFER_DATA_STORE_BINDING

See Also

glGenBuffers, glBindBuffer, glBufferData, glDeleteBuffers, glGenTextures, glBindTexture, glDeleteTextures

Copyright

glTexImage1D

specify a one-dimensional texture image

C Specification

```
void glTexImage1D(GLenum target,
                  GLint level,
                  GLint internalFormat,
                  GLsizei width,
                  GLint border,
                  GLenum format,
                  GLenum type,
                  const GLvoid * data);
```

Parameters

target

Specifies the target texture. Must be GL_TEXTURE_1D or GL_PROXY_TEXTURE_1D.

level

Specifies the level-of-detail number. Level 0 is the base image level. Level *n* is the *n*th mipmap reduction image.

internalFormat

Specifies the number of color components in the texture. Must be one of the following symbolic constants: GL_COMPRESSED_RED, GL_COMPRESSED_RG, GL_COMPRESSED_RGB, GL_COMPRESSED_RGBA, GL_COMPRESSED_SRGB, GL_COMPRESSED_SRGB_ALPHA, GL_DEPTH_COMPONENT, GL_DEPTH_COMPO-NENT16, GL_DEPTH_COMPONENT24, GL_DEPTH_COMPONENT32, GL_R3_G3_B2, GL_RED, GL_RG, GL_RGB, GL_RGB4, GL_RGB5, GL_RGB8, GL_RGB10, GL_RGB12, GL_RGB16, GL_RGBA, GL_RGBA2, GL_RGBA4, GL_RGB5_A1, GL_RGBA8, GL_RGB10_A2, GL_RGBA12, GL_RGBA16, GL_SRGB, GL_SRGB8, GL_SRGB_ALPHA, or GL_SRGB8_ALPHA8.

width

Specifies the width of the texture image. All implementations support texture images that are at least 1024 texels wide. The height of the 1D texture image is 1.

border

This value must be 0.

format

Specifies the format of the pixel data. The following symbolic values are accepted: GL_RED, GL_RG, GL_RGB, GL_BGR, GL_RGBA, and GL_BGRA.

type

Specifies the data type of the pixel data. The following symbolic values are accepted: GL_UNSIGNED_BYTE, GL_BYTE, GL_UNSIGNED_SHORT, GL_SHORT, GL_UNSIGNED_INT, GL_INT, GL_FLOAT, GL_UNSIGNED_BYTE_3_3_2, GL_UNSIGNED_BYTE_2_3_3_REV, GL_UNSIGNED_SHORT_5_6_5, GL_UNSIGNED_SHORT_5_6_5_REV, GL_UNSIGNED_SHORT_4_4_4_4, GL_UNSIGNED_SHORT_4_4_4_4_REV, GL_UNSIGNED_SHORT_5_5_5_1, GL_UNSIGNED_SHORT_1_5_5_5_REV, GL_UNSIGNED_INT_8_8_8_8, GL_UNSIGNED_INT_8_8_8_8_REV, GL_UNSIGNED_INT_10_10_10_2, and GL_UNSIGNED_INT_2_10_10_10_REV.

data

Specifies a pointer to the image data in memory.

Description

Texturing maps a portion of a specified texture image onto each graphical primitive for which texturing is enabled. To enable and disable one-dimensional texturing, call glEnable and glDisable with argument GL_TEXTURE_1D.

Texture images are defined with `glTexImage1D`. The arguments describe the parameters of the texture image, such as width, width of the border, level-of-detail number (see glTexParameter), and the internal resolution and format used to store the image. The last three arguments describe how the image is represented in memory.

If *target* is GL_PROXY_TEXTURE_1D, no data is read from *data*, but all of the texture image state is recalculated, checked for consistency, and checked against the implementation's capabilities. If the implementation cannot handle a texture of the requested texture size, it sets all of the image state to 0, but does not generate an error (see glGetError). To query for an entire mipmap array, use an image array level greater than or equal to 1.

If *target* is GL_TEXTURE_1D, data is read from *data* as a sequence of signed or unsigned bytes, shorts, or longs, or single-precision floating-point values, depending on *type*. These values are grouped into sets of one, two, three, or four values, depending on *format*, to form elements. Each data byte is treated as eight 1-bit elements, with bit ordering determined by GL_UNPACK_LSB_FIRST (see glPixelStore).

If a non-zero named buffer object is bound to the GL_PIXEL_UNPACK_BUFFER target (see glBindBuffer) while a texture image is specified, *data* is treated as a byte offset into the buffer object's data store.

The first element corresponds to the left end of the texture array. Subsequent elements progress left-to-right through the remaining texels in the texture array. The final element corresponds to the right end of the texture array.

format determines the composition of each element in *data*. It can assume one of these symbolic values:

GL_RED

    Each element is a single red component. The GL converts it to floating point and assembles it into an RGBA element by attaching 0 for green and blue, and 1 for alpha. Each component is then multiplied by the signed scale factor GL_c_SCALE, added to the signed bias GL_c_BIAS, and clamped to the range [0,1].

GL_RG

    Each element is a single red/green double The GL converts it to floating point and assembles it into an RGBA element by attaching 0 for blue, and 1 for alpha. Each component is then multiplied by the signed scale factor GL_c_SCALE, added to the signed bias GL_c_BIAS, and clamped to the range [0,1].

GL_RGB
GL_BGR

    Each element is an RGB triple. The GL converts it to floating point and assembles it into an RGBA element by attaching 1 for alpha. Each component is then multiplied by the signed scale factor GL_c_SCALE, added to the signed bias GL_c_BIAS, and clamped to the range [0,1].

GL_RGBA
GL_BGRA

    Each element contains all four components. Each component is multiplied by the signed scale factor GL_c_SCALE, added to the signed bias GL_c_BIAS, and clamped to the range [0,1].

GL_DEPTH_COMPONENT

    Each element is a single depth value. The GL converts it to floating point, multiplies by the signed scale factor GL_DEPTH_SCALE, adds the signed bias GL_DEPTH_BIAS, and clamps to the range [0,1].

If an application wants to store the texture at a certain resolution or in a certain format, it can request the resolution and format with *internalFormat*. The GL will choose an internal representation that closely approximates that requested by *internalFormat*, but it may not match exactly. (The representations specified by GL_RED, GL_RG, GL_RGB and GL_RGBA must match exactly.)

If the *internalFormat* parameter is one of the generic compressed formats, GL_COMPRESSED_RED, GL_COMPRESSED_RG, GL_COMPRESSED_RGB, or GL_COMPRESSED_RGBA, the GL will replace the internal format with the symbolic constant for a specific internal format and compress the texture before storage. If no corresponding internal format is available, or the GL cannot compress that image for any reason, the internal format is instead replaced with a corresponding base internal format.

If the *internalFormat* parameter is GL_SRGB, GL_SRGB8, GL_SRGB_ALPHA, or GL_SRGB8_ALPHA8, the texture is treated as if the red, green, or blue components are encoded in the sRGB color space. Any alpha component is left unchanged. The conversion from the sRGB encoded component c_s to a linear component c_l is:

$$c_l = \begin{cases} \dfrac{c_s}{12.92} & \text{if } c_s \leq 0.04045 \\ \left(\dfrac{c_s + 0.055}{1.055}\right)^{2.4} & \text{if } c_s > 0.04045 \end{cases}$$

Assume c_s is the sRGB component in the range [0,1].

Use the GL_PROXY_TEXTURE_1D target to try out a resolution and format. The implementation will update and recompute its best match for the requested storage resolution and format. To then query this state, call glGetTexLevelParameter. If the texture cannot be accommodated, texture state is set to 0.

A one-component texture image uses only the red component of the RGBA color from *data*. A two-component image uses the R and A values. A three-component image uses the R, G, and B values. A four-component image uses all of the RGBA components.

Image-based shadowing can be enabled by comparing texture r coordinates to depth texture values to generate a boolean result. See glTexParameter for details on texture comparison.

Notes

glPixelStore modes affect texture images.

data may be a null pointer. In this case texture memory is allocated to accommodate a texture of width *width*. You can then download subtextures to initialize the texture memory. The image is undefined if the program tries to apply an uninitialized portion of the texture image to a primitive.

glTexImage1D specifies the one-dimensional texture for the current texture unit, specified with glActiveTexture.

Errors

GL_INVALID_ENUM is generated if *target* is not GL_TEXTURE_1D or GL_PROXY_TEXTURE_1D.

GL_INVALID_ENUM is generated if *format* is not an accepted format constant. Format constants other than GL_STENCIL_INDEX are accepted.

GL_INVALID_ENUM is generated if *type* is not a type constant.

GL_INVALID_VALUE is generated if *level* is less than 0.

GL_INVALID_VALUE may be generated if *level* is greater than $\log_2(max)$, where *max* is the returned value of GL_MAX_TEXTURE_SIZE.

GL_INVALID_VALUE is generated if *internalFormat* is not one of the accepted resolution and format symbolic constants.

GL_INVALID_VALUE is generated if *width* is less than 0 or greater than GL_MAX_TEXTURE_SIZE.

GL_INVALID_VALUE is generated if non-power-of-two textures are not supported and the *width* cannot be represented as $2^n + 2(border)$ for some integer value of *n*.

GL_INVALID_VALUE is generated if *border* is not 0 or 1.

GL_INVALID_OPERATION is generated if *type* is one of GL_UNSIGNED_BYTE_3_3_2, GL_UNSIGNED_BYTE_2_3_3_REV, GL_UNSIGNED_SHORT_5_6_5, or GL_UNSIGNED_SHORT_5_6_5_REV and *format* is not GL_RGB.

GL_INVALID_OPERATION is generated if *type* is one of GL_UNSIGNED_SHORT_4_4_4_4, GL_UNSIGNED_SHORT_4_4_4_4_REV, GL_UNSIGNED_SHORT_5_5_5_1, GL_UNSIGNED_SHORT_1_5_5_5_REV, GL_UNSIGNED_INT_8_8_8_8, GL_UNSIGNED_INT_8_8_8_8_REV, GL_UNSIGNED_INT_10_10_10_2, or GL_UNSIGNED_INT_2_10_10_10_REV and *format* is neither GL_RGBA nor GL_BGRA.

GL_INVALID_OPERATION is generated if *format* is GL_DEPTH_COMPONENT and *internalFormat* is not GL_DEPTH_COMPONENT, GL_DEPTH_COMPONENT16, GL_DEPTH_COMPONENT24, or GL_DEPTH_COMPONENT32.

GL_INVALID_OPERATION is generated if *internalFormat* is GL_DEPTH_COMPONENT, GL_DEPTH_COMPONENT16, GL_DEPTH_COMPONENT24, or GL_DEPTH_COMPONENT32, and *format* is not GL_DEPTH_COMPONENT.

GL_INVALID_OPERATION is generated if a non-zero buffer object name is bound to the GL_PIXEL_UNPACK_BUFFER target and the buffer object's data store is currently mapped.

GL_INVALID_OPERATION is generated if a non-zero buffer object name is bound to the GL_PIXEL_UNPACK_BUFFER target and the data would be unpacked from the buffer object such that the memory reads required would exceed the data store size.

GL_INVALID_OPERATION is generated if a non-zero buffer object name is bound to the GL_PIXEL_UNPACK_BUFFER target and *data* is not evenly divisible into the number of bytes needed to store in memory a datum indicated by *type*.

Associated Gets

glGetTexImage
glGet with argument GL_PIXEL_UNPACK_BUFFER_BINDING

See Also

glActiveTexture, glCompressedTexImage1D, glCompressedTexSubImage1D, glCopyTexImage1D, glCopyTexSubImage1D, glGetCompressedTexImage, glPixelStore, glTexImage2D, glTexImage3D, glTexSubImage1D, glTexSubImage2D, glTexSubImage3D, glTexParameter

Copyright

glTexImage2D

specify a two-dimensional texture image

C Specification

```
void glTexImage2D(GLenum target,
                  GLint level,
                  GLint internalFormat,
                  GLsizei width,
                  GLsizei height,
                  GLint border,
                  GLenum format,
                  GLenum type,
                  const GLvoid * data);
```

Parameters

target

Specifies the target texture. Must be GL_TEXTURE_2D, GL_PROXY_TEXTURE_2D, GL_TEXTURE_1D_ARRAY, GL_PROXY_TEXTURE_1D_ARRAY, GL_TEXTURE_RECTANGLE, GL_PROXY_TEXTURE_RECTANGLE, GL_TEXTURE_CUBE_MAP_POSITIVE_X, GL_TEXTURE_CUBE_MAP_NEGATIVE_X, GL_TEXTURE_CUBE_MAP_POSITIVE_Y, GL_TEXTURE_CUBE_MAP_NEGATIVE_Y, GL_TEXTURE_CUBE_MAP_POSITIVE_Z, GL_TEXTURE_CUBE_MAP_NEGATIVE_Z, or GL_PROXY_TEXTURE_CUBE_MAP.

level

Specifies the level-of-detail number. Level 0 is the base image level. Level *n* is the *n*th mipmap reduction image. If *target* is GL_TEXTURE_RECTANGLE or GL_PROXY_TEXTURE_RECTANGLE, *level* must be 0.

internalFormat

Specifies the number of color components in the texture. Must be one of the following symbolic constants: GL_COMPRESSED_RED, GL_COMPRESSED_RG, GL_COMPRESSED_RGB, GL_COMPRESSED_RGBA, GL_COMPRESSED_SRGB, GL_COMPRESSED_SRGB_ALPHA, GL_DEPTH_COMPONENT, GL_DEPTH_COMPONENT16, GL_DEPTH_COMPONENT24, GL_DEPTH_COMPONENT32, GL_R3_G3_B2, GL_RED, GL_RG, GL_RGB, GL_RGB4, GL_RGB5, GL_RGB8, GL_RGB10, GL_RGB12, GL_RGB16, GL_RGBA, GL_RGBA2, GL_RGBA4, GL_RGB5_A1, GL_RGBA8, GL_RGB10_A2, GL_RGBA12, GL_RGBA16, GL_SRGB, GL_SRGB8, GL_SRGB_ALPHA, or GL_SRGB8_ALPHA8.

width

Specifies the width of the texture image. All implementations support texture images that are at least 1024 texels wide.

height

Specifies the height of the texture image, or the number of layers in a texture array, in the case of the GL_TEXTURE_1D_ARRAY and GL_PROXY_TEXTURE_1D_ARRAY targets. All implementations support 2D texture images that are at least 1024 texels high, and texture arrays that are at least 256 layers deep.

border

This value must be 0.

format

Specifies the format of the pixel data. The following symbolic values are accepted: GL_RED, GL_RG, GL_RGB, GL_BGR, GL_RGBA, and GL_BGRA.

type

Specifies the data type of the pixel data. The following symbolic values are accepted: GL_UNSIGNED_BYTE, GL_BYTE, GL_UNSIGNED_SHORT, GL_SHORT, GL_UNSIGNED_INT, GL_INT, GL_FLOAT, GL_UNSIGNED_BYTE_3_3_2, GL_UNSIGNED_BYTE_2_3_3_REV, GL_UNSIGNED_SHORT_5_6_5, GL_UNSIGNED_SHORT_5_6_5_REV, GL_UNSIGNED_SHORT_4_4_4_4, GL_UNSIGNED_SHORT_4_4_4_4_REV, GL_UNSIGNED_SHORT_5_5_5_1, GL_UNSIGNED_SHORT_1_5_5_5_REV, GL_UNSIGNED_INT_8_8_8_8, GL_UNSIGNED_INT_8_8_8_8_REV, GL_UNSIGNED_INT_10_10_10_2, and GL_UNSIGNED_INT_2_10_10_10_REV.

data

Specifies a pointer to the image data in memory.

Description

Texturing allows elements of an image array to be read by shaders.

To define texture images, call glTexImage2D. The arguments describe the parameters of the texture image, such as height, width, width of the border, level-of-detail number (see glTexParameter), and number of color components provided. The last three arguments describe how the image is represented in memory.

If *target* is GL_PROXY_TEXTURE_2D, GL_PROXY_TEXTURE_1D_ARRAY, GL_PROXY_TEXTURE_CUBE_MAP, or GL_PROXY_TEXTURE_RECTANGLE, no data is read from *data*, but all of the texture image state is recalculated, checked for consistency, and checked against the implementation's capabilities. If the implementation cannot handle a texture of the requested texture size, it sets all of the image state to 0, but does not generate an error (see glGetError). To query for an entire mipmap array, use an image array level greater than or equal to 1.

If *target* is GL_TEXTURE_2D, GL_TEXTURE_RECTANGLE or one of the GL_TEXTURE_CUBE_MAP targets, data is read from *data* as a sequence of signed or unsigned bytes, shorts, or longs, or single-precision floating-point values, depending on *type*. These values are grouped into sets of one, two, three, or four values, depending on *format*, to form elements. Each data byte is treated as eight 1-bit elements, with bit ordering determined by GL_UNPACK_LSB_FIRST (see glPixelStore).

If *target* is GL_TEXTURE_1D_ARRAY, data is interpreted as an array of one-dimensional images.

If a non-zero named buffer object is bound to the GL_PIXEL_UNPACK_BUFFER target (see glBindBuffer) while a texture image is specified, *data* is treated as a byte offset into the buffer object's data store.

The first element corresponds to the lower left corner of the texture image. Subsequent elements progress left-to-right through the remaining texels in the lowest row of the texture image, and then in successively higher rows of the texture image. The final element corresponds to the upper right corner of the texture image.

format determines the composition of each element in *data*. It can assume one of these symbolic values:

GL_RED

        Each element is a single red component. The GL converts it to floating point and assembles it into an RGBA element by attaching 0 for green and blue, and 1 for alpha. Each component is then multiplied by the signed scale factor GL_c_SCALE, added to the signed bias GL_c_BIAS, and clamped to the range [0,1].

GL_RG

        Each element is a red/green double. The GL converts it to floating point and assembles it into an RGBA element by attaching 0 for blue, and 1 for alpha. Each component is then multiplied by the signed scale factor GL_c_SCALE, added to the signed bias GL_c_BIAS, and clamped to the range [0,1].

GL_RGB
GL_BGR

        Each element is an RGB triple. The GL converts it to floating point and assembles it into an RGBA element by attaching 1 for alpha. Each component is then multiplied by the signed scale factor GL_c_SCALE, added to the signed bias GL_c_BIAS, and clamped to the range [0,1].

GL_RGBA
GL_BGRA

        Each element contains all four components. Each component is multiplied by the signed scale factor GL_c_SCALE, added to the signed bias GL_c_BIAS, and clamped to the range [0,1].

GL_DEPTH_COMPONENT

        Each element is a single depth value. The GL converts it to floating point, multiplies by the signed scale factor GL_DEPTH_SCALE, adds the signed bias GL_DEPTH_BIAS, and clamps to the range [0,1].

GL_DEPTH_STENCIL

        Each element is a pair of depth and stencil values. The depth component of the pair is interpreted as in GL_DEPTH_COMPONENT. The stencil component is interpreted based on specified the depth + stencil internal format.

If an application wants to store the texture at a certain resolution or in a certain format, it can request the resolution and format with *internalFormat*. The GL will choose an internal representation that closely approximates that requested by *internalFormat*, but it may not match exactly. (The representations specified by GL_RED, GL_RG, GL_RGB, and GL_RGBA must match exactly.)

If the *internalFormat* parameter is one of the generic compressed formats, GL_COMPRESSED_RED, GL_COMPRESSED_RG, GL_COMPRESSED_RGB, or GL_COMPRESSED_RGBA, the GL will replace the internal format with the symbolic constant for a specific internal format and compress the texture before storage. If no corresponding internal format is available, or the GL can not compress that image for any reason, the internal format is instead replaced with a corresponding base internal format.

If the *internalFormat* parameter is GL_SRGB, GL_SRGB8, GL_SRGB_ALPHA, or GL_SRGB8_ALPHA8, the texture is treated as if the red, green, or blue components are encoded in the sRGB color space. Any alpha component is left unchanged. The conversion from the sRGB encoded component c_s to a linear component c_l is:

$$c_l = d \begin{cases} \dfrac{c_s}{12.92} & \text{if } c_s \ldots 0.04045 \\[2ex] a\dfrac{c_s + 0.055}{1.055}^{2.4} b & \text{if } c_s\ 7\ 0.04045 \end{cases}$$

Assume c_s is the sRGB component in the range [0,1].

Use the GL_PROXY_TEXTURE_2D, GL_PROXY_TEXTURE_1D_ARRAY, GL_PROXY_TEXTURE_RECTANGLE, or GL_PROXY_TEXTURE_CUBE_MAP target to try out a resolution and format. The implementation will update and recompute its best match for the requested storage resolution and format. To then query this state, call glGetTexLevelParameter. If the texture cannot be accommodated, texture state is set to 0.

A one-component texture image uses only the red component of the RGBA color extracted from *data*. A two-component image uses the R and G values. A three-component image uses the R, G, and B values. A four-component image uses all of the RGBA components.

Image-based shadowing can be enabled by comparing texture r coordinates to depth texture values to generate a boolean result. See glTexParameter for details on texture comparison.

Notes

The glPixelStore mode affects texture images.

data may be a null pointer. In this case, texture memory is allocated to accommodate a texture of width *width* and height *height*. You can then download subtextures to initialize this texture memory. The image is undefined if the user tries to apply an uninitialized portion of the texture image to a primitive.

`glTexImage2D` specifies the two-dimensional texture for the current texture unit, specified with glActiveTexture.

Errors

GL_INVALID_ENUM is generated if *target* is not GL_TEXTURE_2D, GL_TEXTURE_1D_ARRAY, GL_TEXTURE_RECTANGLE, GL_PROXY_TEXTURE_2D, GL_PROXY_TEXTURE_1D_ARRAY, GL_PROXY_TEXTURE_RECTANGLE, GL_PROXY_TEXTURE_CUBE_MAP, GL_TEXTURE_CUBE_MAP_POSITIVE_X, GL_TEXTURE_CUBE_MAP_NEGATIVE_X, GL_TEXTURE_CUBE_MAP_POSITIVE_Y, GL_TEXTURE_CUBE_MAP_NEGATIVE_Y, GL_TEXTURE_CUBE_MAP_POSITIVE_Z, or GL_TEXTURE_CUBE_MAP_NEGATIVE_Z.

GL_INVALID_ENUM is generated if *target* is one of the six cube map 2D image targets and the width and height parameters are not equal.

GL_INVALID_ENUM is generated if *type* is not a type constant.

GL_INVALID_VALUE is generated if *width* is less than 0 or greater than GL_MAX_TEXTURE_SIZE.

GL_INVALID_VALUE is generated if *target* is not GL_TEXTURE_1D_ARRAY or GL_PROXY_TEXTURE_1D_ARRAY and *height* is less than 0 or greater than GL_MAX_TEXTURE_SIZE.

GL_INVALID_VALUE is generated if *target* is GL_TEXTURE_1D_ARRAY or GL_PROXY_TEXTURE_1D_ARRAY and *height* is less than 0 or greater than GL_MAX_ARRAY_TEXTURE_LAYERS.

GL_INVALID_VALUE is generated if *level* is less than 0.

GL_INVALID_VALUE may be generated if *level* is greater than $\log_2(\max)$, where *max* is the returned value of GL_MAX_TEXTURE_SIZE.

GL_INVALID_VALUE is generated if *internalFormat* is not one of the accepted resolution and format symbolic constants.

GL_INVALID_VALUE is generated if *width* or *height* is less than 0 or greater than GL_MAX_TEXTURE_SIZE.

GL_INVALID_VALUE is generated if non-power-of-two textures are not supported and the *width* or *height* cannot be represented as $2^k + 2(border)$ for some integer value of *k*.

GL_INVALID_VALUE is generated if *border* is not 0.

GL_INVALID_OPERATION is generated if *type* is one of GL_UNSIGNED_BYTE_3_3_2, GL_UNSIGNED_BYTE_2_3_3_REV, GL_UNSIGNED_SHORT_5_6_5, GL_UNSIGNED_SHORT_5_6_5_REV, or GL_UNSIGNED_INT_10F_11F_11F_REV, and *format* is not GL_RGB.

GL_INVALID_OPERATION is generated if *type* is one of GL_UNSIGNED_SHORT_4_4_4_4, GL_UNSIGNED_SHORT_4_4_4_4_REV, GL_UNSIGNED_SHORT_5_5_5_1, GL_UNSIGNED_SHORT_1_5_5_5_REV, GL_UNSIGNED_INT_8_8_8_8, GL_UNSIGNED_INT_8_8_8_8_REV, GL_UNSIGNED_INT_10_10_10_2, GL_UNSIGNED_INT_2_10_10_10_REV, or GL_UNSIGNED_INT_5_9_9_9_REV, and *format* is neither GL_RGBA nor GL_BGRA.

GL_INVALID_OPERATION is generated if *target* is not GL_TEXTURE_2D, GL_PROXY_TEXTURE_2D, GL_TEXTURE_RECTANGLE, or GL_PROXY_TEXTURE_RECTANGLE, and *internalFormat* is GL_DEPTH_COMPONENT, GL_DEPTH_COMPONENT16, GL_DEPTH_COMPONENT24, or GL_DEPTH_COMPONENT32F.

GL_INVALID_OPERATION is generated if *format* is GL_DEPTH_COMPONENT and *internalFormat* is not GL_DEPTH_COMPONENT, GL_DEPTH_COMPONENT16, GL_DEPTH_COMPONENT24, or GL_DEPTH_COMPONENT32F.

GL_INVALID_OPERATION is generated if *internalFormat* is GL_DEPTH_COMPONENT, GL_DEPTH_COMPONENT16, GL_DEPTH_COMPONENT24, or GL_DEPTH_COMPONENT32F, and *format* is not GL_DEPTH_COMPONENT.

GL_INVALID_OPERATION is generated if a non-zero buffer object name is bound to the GL_PIXEL_UNPACK_BUFFER target and the buffer object's data store is currently mapped.

GL_INVALID_OPERATION is generated if a non-zero buffer object name is bound to the GL_PIXEL_UNPACK_BUFFER target and the data would be unpacked from the buffer object such that the memory reads required would exceed the data store size.

GL_INVALID_OPERATION is generated if a non-zero buffer object name is bound to the GL_PIXEL_UNPACK_BUFFER target and *data* is not evenly divisible into the number of bytes needed to store in memory a datum indicated by *type*.

GL_INVALID_VALUE is generated if *target* is GL_TEXTURE_RECTANGLE or GL_PROXY_TEXTURE_RECTANGLE and *level* is not 0.

Associated Gets

glGetTexImage
glGet with argument GL_PIXEL_UNPACK_BUFFER_BINDING

See Also

glActiveTexture, glCopyTexImage1D, glCopyTexImage2D, glCopyTexSubImage1D, glCopyTexSubImage2D, glCopyTexSubImage3D, glPixelStore, glTexImage1D, glTexImage3D, glTexSubImage1D, glTexSubImage2D, glTexSubImage3D, glTexParameter

Copyright

glTexImage2DMultisample

establish the data storage, format, dimensions, and number of samples of a multisample texture's image

C Specification

```
void glTexImage2DMultisample(GLenum target,
                             GLsizei samples,
                             GLint internalformat,
                             GLsizei width,
                             GLsizei height,
                             GLboolean fixedsamplelocations);
```

Parameters

target

Specifies the target of the operation. *target* must be GL_TEXTURE_2D_ MULTISAMPLE_ARRAY or GL_PROXY_TEXTURE_2D_MULTISAMPLE_ARRAY.

samples

The number of samples in the multisample texture's image.

internalformat

The internal format to be used to store the multisample texture's image. *internalformat* must specify a color-renderable, depth-renderable, or stencil-renderable format.

width

The width of the multisample texture's image, in texels.

height

The height of the multisample texture's image, in texels.

fixedsamplelocations

Specifies whether the image will use identical sample locations and the same number of samples for all texels in the image, and the sample locations will not depend on the internal format or size of the image.

Description

glTexImage2DMultisample establishes the data storage, format, dimensions and number of samples of a multisample texture's image.

target must be GL_TEXTURE_2D_MULTISAMPLE or GL_PROXY_TEXTURE_2D_MULTISAMPLE. *width* and *height* are the dimensions in texels of the texture, and must be in the range zero to GL_MAX_TEXTURE_SIZE - 1. *samples* specifies the number of samples in the image and must be in the range zero to GL_MAX_SAMPLES - 1.

internalformat must be a color-renderable, depth-renderable, or stencil-renderable format.

If *fixedsamplelocations* is GL_TRUE, the image will use identical sample locations and the same number of samples for all texels in the image, and the sample locations will not depend on internal format or size of the image.

When a multisample texture is accessed in a shader, the access takes one vector of integers describing which texel to fetch and an integer corresponding to the sample numbers describing which sample within the texel to fetch. No standard sampling instructions are allowed on the multisample texture targets.

Notes

glTexImage2DMultisample is available only if the GL version is 3.2 or greater.

Errors

GL_INVALID_OPERATION is generated if *internalformat* is a depth- or stencil-renderable format and *samples* is greater than the value of GL_MAX_DEPTH_TEXTURE_SAMPLES.

GL_INVALID_OPERATION is generated if *internalformat* is a color-renderable format and *samples* is greater than the value of GL_MAX_COLOR_TEXTURE_SAMPLES.

GL_INVALID_OPERATION is generated if *internalformat* is a signed or unsigned integer format and *samples* is greater than the value of GL_MAX_INTEGER_SAMPLES.

GL_INVALID_VALUE is generated if either *width* or *height* negative or is greater than GL_MAX_TEXTURE_SIZE.

GL_INVALID_VALUE is generated if *samples* is greater than GL_MAX_SAMPLES.

See Also

glTexImage3D, glTexImage2DMultisample

Copyright

glTexImage3D

specify a three-dimensional texture image

C Specification

```
void glTexImage3D(GLenum target,
                  GLint level,
                  GLint internalFormat,
                  GLsizei width,
                  GLsizei height,
                  GLsizei depth,
                  GLint border,
                  GLenum format,
                  GLenum type,
                  const GLvoid * data);
```

Parameters

target

Specifies the target texture. Must be one of GL_TEXTURE_3D, GL_PROXY_TEXTURE_3D, GL_TEXTURE_2D_ARRAY or GL_PROXY_TEXTURE_2D_ARRAY.

level

Specifies the level-of-detail number. Level 0 is the base image level. Level n is the nth mipmap reduction image.

internalFormat

Specifies the number of color components in the texture. Must be one of the following symbolic constants: GL_RGBA32F, GL_RGBA32I, GL_RGBA32UI, GL_RGBA16, GL_RGBA16F, GL_RGBA16I, GL_RGBA16UI, GL_RGBA8, GL_RGBA8UI, GL_SRGB8_ALPHA8, GL_RGB10_A2, GL_RGBA10_A2UI, GL_R11_G11_B10F, GL_RG32F, GL_RG32I, GL_RG32UI, GL_RG16, GL_RG16F, GL_RGB16I, GL_RGB16UI, GL_RG8, GL_RG8I, GL_RG8UI, GL_R23F, GL_R32I, GL_R32UI, GL_R16F, GL_R16I, GL_R16UI, GL_R8, GL_R8I, GL_R8UI, GL_RGBA16_UNORM, GL_RGBA8_SNORM, GL_RGB32F, GL_RGB32I, GL_RGB32UI, GL_RGB16_SNORM, GL_RGB16F, GL_RGB16I, GL_RGB16UI, GL_RGB16, GL_RGB8_SNORM, GL_RGB8, GL_RGB8I, GL_RGB8UI, GL_SRGB8, GL_RGB9_E5, GL_RG16_SNORM, GL_RG8_SNORM, GL_COMPRESSED_RG_RGTC2,

GL_COMPRESSED_SIGNED_RG_RGTC2, GL_R16_SNORM, GL_R8_SNORM,
GL_COMPRESSED_RED_RGTC1, GL_COMPRESSED_SIGNED_RED_RGTC1,
GL_DEPTH_COMPONENT32F, GL_DEPTH_COMPONENT24, GL_DEPTH_
COMPONENT16, GL_DEPTH32F_STENCIL8, GL_DEPTH24_STENCIL8.

width

Specifies the width of the texture image. All implementations support 3D texture images that are at least 16 texels wide.

height

Specifies the height of the texture image. All implementations support 3D texture images that are at least 256 texels high.

depth

Specifies the depth of the texture image, or the number of layers in a texture array. All implementations support 3D texture images that are at least 256 texels deep, and texture arrays that are at least 256 layers deep.

border

This value must be 0.

format

Specifies the format of the pixel data. The following symbolic values are accepted: GL_RED, GL_RG, GL_RGB, GL_BGR, GL_RGBA, and GL_BGRA.

type

Specifies the data type of the pixel data. The following symbolic values are accepted: GL_UNSIGNED_BYTE, GL_BYTE, GL_UNSIGNED_SHORT, GL_SHORT, GL_UNSIGNED_INT, GL_INT, GL_FLOAT, GL_UNSIGNED_BYTE_3_3_2, GL_UNSIGNED_BYTE_2_3_3_REV, GL_UNSIGNED_SHORT_5_6_5, GL_UNSIGNED_SHORT_5_6_5_REV, GL_UNSIGNED_SHORT_4_4_4_4, GL_UNSIGNED_SHORT_4_4_4_4_REV, GL_UNSIGNED_SHORT_5_5_5_1, GL_UNSIGNED_SHORT_1_5_5_5_REV, GL_UNSIGNED_INT_8_8_8_8, GL_UNSIGNED_INT_8_8_8_8_REV, GL_UNSIGNED_INT_10_10_10_2, and GL_UNSIGNED_INT_2_10_10_10_REV.

data

Specifies a pointer to the image data in memory.

Description

Texturing maps a portion of a specified texture image onto each graphical primitive for which texturing is enabled. To enable and disable three-dimensional texturing, call glEnable and glDisable with argument GL_TEXTURE_3D.

To define texture images, call `glTexImage3D`. The arguments describe the parameters of the texture image, such as height, width, depth, width of the border, level-of-detail number (see glTexParameter), and number of color components provided. The last three arguments describe how the image is represented in memory.

If *target* is GL_PROXY_TEXTURE_3D, no data is read from *data*, but all of the texture image state is recalculated, checked for consistency, and checked against the implementation's capabilities. If the implementation cannot handle a texture of the requested texture size, it sets all of the image state to 0, but does not generate an error (see glGetError). To query for an entire mipmap array, use an image array level greater than or equal to 1.

If *target* is GL_TEXTURE_3D, data is read from *data* as a sequence of signed or unsigned bytes, shorts, or longs, or single-precision floating-point values, depending on *type*. These values are grouped into sets of one, two, three, or four values, depending on *format*, to form elements. Each data byte is treated as eight 1-bit elements, with bit ordering determined by GL_UNPACK_LSB_FIRST (see glPixelStore).

If a non-zero named buffer object is bound to the GL_PIXEL_UNPACK_BUFFER target (see glBindBuffer) while a texture image is specified, *data* is treated as a byte offset into the buffer object's data store.

The first element corresponds to the lower left corner of the texture image. Subsequent elements progress left-to-right through the remaining texels in the lowest row of the texture image, and then in successively higher rows of the texture image. The final element corresponds to the upper right corner of the texture image.

format determines the composition of each element in *data*. It can assume one of these symbolic values:

GL_RED

> Each element is a single red component. The GL converts it to floating point and assembles it into an RGBA element by attaching 0 for green and blue, and 1 for alpha. Each component is then multiplied by the signed scale factor GL_c_SCALE, added to the signed bias GL_c_BIAS, and clamped to the range [0,1].

GL_RG

> Each element is a red and green pair. The GL converts each to floating point and assembles it into an RGBA element by attaching 0 for blue, and 1 for alpha. Each component is then multiplied by the signed scale factor GL_c_SCALE, added to the signed bias GL_c_BIAS, and clamped to the range [0,1].

GL_RGB
GL_BGR

> Each element is an RGB triple. The GL converts it to floating point and assembles it into an RGBA element by attaching 1 for alpha. Each component is then multiplied by the signed scale factor GL_c_SCALE, added to the signed bias GL_c_BIAS, and clamped to the range [0,1].

GL_RGBA
GL_BGRA

> Each element contains all four components. Each component is multiplied by the signed scale factor GL_c_SCALE, added to the signed bias GL_c_BIAS, and clamped to the range [0,1].

If an application wants to store the texture at a certain resolution or in a certain format, it can request the resolution and format with *internalFormat*. The GL will choose an internal representation that closely approximates that requested by *internalFormat*, but it may not match exactly. (The representations specified by GL_RED, GL_RG, GL_RGB, and GL_RGBA must match exactly.)

If the *internalFormat* parameter is one of the generic compressed formats, GL_COMPRESSED_RED, GL_COMPRESSED_RG, GL_COMPRESSED_RGB, or GL_COMPRESSED_RGBA, the GL will replace the internal format with the symbolic constant for a specific internal format and compress the texture before storage. If no corresponding internal format is available, or the GL can not compress that image for any reason, the internal format is instead replaced with a corresponding base internal format.

If the *internalFormat* parameter is GL_SRGB, GL_SRGB8, GL_SRGB_ALPHA, or GL_SRGB8_ALPHA8, the texture is treated as if the red, green, blue, or luminance components are encoded in the sRGB color space. Any alpha component is left unchanged. The conversion from the sRGB encoded component c_s to a linear component c_l is:

$$c_l = \begin{cases} \dfrac{c_s}{12.92} & \text{if } c_s \leq 0.04045 \\ \left(\dfrac{c_s + 0.055}{1.055}\right)^{2.4} & \text{if } c_s > 0.04045 \end{cases}$$

Assume c_s is the sRGB component in the range [0,1].

Use the GL_PROXY_TEXTURE_3D target to try out a resolution and format. The implementation will update and recompute its best match for the requested storage resolution and format. To then query this state, call glGetTexLevelParameter. If the texture cannot be accommodated, texture state is set to 0.

A one-component texture image uses only the red component of the RGBA color extracted from *data*. A two-component image uses the R and A values. A three-component image uses the R, G, and B values. A four-component image uses all of the RGBA components.

Notes

The glPixelStore mode affects texture images.

data may be a null pointer. In this case texture memory is allocated to accommodate a texture of width *width*, height *height*, and depth *depth*. You can then download subtextures to initialize this texture memory. The image is undefined if the user tries to apply an uninitialized portion of the texture image to a primitive.

glTexImage3D specifies the three-dimensional texture for the current texture unit, specified with glActiveTexture.

Errors

GL_INVALID_ENUM is generated if *target* is not GL_TEXTURE_3D or GL_PROXY_TEXTURE_3D.

GL_INVALID_ENUM is generated if *format* is not an accepted format constant. Format constants other than GL_STENCIL_INDEX and GL_DEPTH_COMPONENT are accepted.

GL_INVALID_ENUM is generated if *type* is not a type constant.

GL_INVALID_VALUE is generated if *level* is less than 0.

GL_INVALID_VALUE may be generated if *level* is greater than $\log_2(max)$, where *max* is the returned value of GL_MAX_TEXTURE_SIZE.

GL_INVALID_VALUE is generated if *internalFormat* is not one of the accepted resolution and format symbolic constants.

GL_INVALID_VALUE is generated if *width*, *height*, or *depth* is less than 0 or greater than GL_MAX_TEXTURE_SIZE.

GL_INVALID_VALUE is generated if non-power-of-two textures are not supported and the *width*, *height*, or *depth* cannot be represented as $2^k + 2(border)$ for some integer value of *k*.

GL_INVALID_VALUE is generated if *border* is not 0 or 1.

GL_INVALID_OPERATION is generated if *type* is one of GL_UNSIGNED_BYTE_3_3_2, GL_UNSIGNED_BYTE_2_3_3_REV, GL_UNSIGNED_SHORT_5_6_5, or GL_UNSIGNED_SHORT_5_6_5_REV and *format* is not GL_RGB.

GL_INVALID_OPERATION is generated if *type* is one of GL_UNSIGNED_SHORT_4_4_4_4, GL_UNSIGNED_SHORT_4_4_4_4_REV, GL_UNSIGNED_SHORT_5_5_5_1, GL_UNSIGNED_SHORT_1_5_5_5_REV, GL_UNSIGNED_INT_8_8_8_8, GL_UNSIGNED_INT_8_8_8_8_REV, GL_UNSIGNED_INT_10_10_10_2, or GL_UNSIGNED_INT_2_10_10_10_REV and *format* is neither GL_RGBA nor GL_BGRA.

GL_INVALID_OPERATION is generated if *format* or *internalFormat* is GL_DEPTH_COMPONENT, GL_DEPTH_COMPONENT16, GL_DEPTH_COMPONENT24, or GL_DEPTH_COMPONENT32.

GL_INVALID_OPERATION is generated if a non-zero buffer object name is bound to the GL_PIXEL_UNPACK_BUFFER target and the buffer object's data store is currently mapped.

GL_INVALID_OPERATION is generated if a non-zero buffer object name is bound to the GL_PIXEL_UNPACK_BUFFER target and the data would be unpacked from the buffer object such that the memory reads required would exceed the data store size.

GL_INVALID_OPERATION is generated if a non-zero buffer object name is bound to the GL_PIXEL_UNPACK_BUFFER target and *data* is not evenly divisible into the number of bytes needed to store in memory a datum indicated by *type*.

Associated Gets

glGetTexImage
glGet with argument GL_PIXEL_UNPACK_BUFFER_BINDING

See Also

glActiveTexture, glCompressedTexImage1D, glCompressedTexImage2D, glCompressedTexImage3D, glCompressedTexSubImage1D, glCompressedTexSubImage2D, glCompressedTexSubImage3D, glCopyTexImage1D, glCopyTexImage2D, glCopyTexSubImage1D, glCopyTexSubImage2D, glCopyTexSubImage3D, glGetCompressedTexImage, glPixelStore, glTexImage1D, glTexImage2D, glTexSubImage1D, glTexSubImage2D, glTexSubImage3D, glTexParameter

Copyright

glTexImage3DMultisample

establish the data storage, format, dimensions, and number of samples of a multisample texture's image

C Specification

```
void glTexImage3DMultisample(GLenum target,
                             GLsizei samples,
                             GLint internalformat,
                             GLsizei width,
                             GLsizei height,
                             GLsizei depth,
                             GLboolean fixedsamplelocations);
```

Parameters

target

Specifies the target of the operation. *target* must be GL_TEXTURE_2D_MULTISAMPLE_ARRAY or GL_PROXY_TEXTURE_2D_MULTISAMPLE_ARRAY.

samples

The number of samples in the multisample texture's image.

internalformat

The internal format to be used to store the multisample texture's image. *internalformat* must specify a color-renderable, depth-renderable, or stencil-renderable format.

width

The width of the multisample texture's image, in texels.

height

The height of the multisample texture's image, in texels.

fixedsamplelocations

Specifies whether the image will use identical sample locations and the same number of samples for all texels in the image, and the sample locations will not depend on the internal format or size of the image.

Description

glTexImage3DMultisample establishes the data storage, format, dimensions and number of samples of a multisample texture's image.

target must be GL_TEXTURE_2D_MULTISAMPLE_ARRAY or GL_PROXY_TEXTURE_2D_MULTI-SAMPLE_ARRAY. *width* and *height* are the dimensions in texels of the texture, and must be in the range zero to GL_MAX_TEXTURE_SIZE - 1. *depth* is the number of array slices in the array texture's image. *samples* specifies the number of samples in the image and must be in the range zero to GL_MAX_SAMPLES - 1.

internalformat must be a color-renderable, depth-renderable, or stencil-renderable format.

If *fixedsamplelocations* is GL_TRUE, the image will use identical sample locations and the same number of samples for all texels in the image, and the sample locations will not depend on the internal format or size of the image.

When a multisample texture is accessed in a shader, the access takes one vector of integers describing which texel to fetch and an integer corresponding to the sample numbers describing which sample within the texel to fetch. No standard sampling instructions are allowed on the multisample texture targets.

Notes

glTexImage2DMultisample is available only if the GL version is 3.2 or greater.

Errors

GL_INVALID_OPERATION is generated if *internalformat* is a depth- or stencil-renderable format and *samples* is greater than the value of GL_MAX_DEPTH_TEXTURE_SAMPLES.

GL_INVALID_OPERATION is generated if *internalformat* is a color-renderable format and *samples* is greater than the value of GL_MAX_COLOR_TEXTURE_SAMPLES.

GL_INVALID_OPERATION is generated if *internalformat* is a signed or unsigned integer format and *samples* is greater than the value of GL_MAX_INTEGER_SAMPLES.

GL_INVALID_VALUE is generated if either *width* or *height* negative or is greater than GL_MAX_TEXTURE_SIZE.

GL_INVALID_VALUE is generated if *depth* is negative or is greater than GL_MAX_ARRAY_TEXTURE_LAYERS.

GL_INVALID_VALUE is generated if *samples* is greater than GL_MAX_SAMPLES.

See Also

glTexImage3D, glTexImage2DMultisample

Copyright

glTexParameter

set texture parameters

C Specification

```
void glTexParameterf(GLenum target,
                     GLenum pname,
                     GLfloat param);
void glTexParameteri(GLenum target,
                     GLenum pname,
                     GLint param);
```

Parameters

target

Specifies the target texture, which must be either GL_TEXTURE_1D, GL_TEXTURE_2D, GL_TEXTURE_3D, GL_TEXTURE_1D_ARRAY, GL_TEXTURE_2D_ARRAY, GL_TEXTURE_RECTANGLE, or GL_TEXTURE_CUBE_MAP.

pname

>Specifies the symbolic name of a single-valued texture parameter. *pname* can be one of the following: GL_TEXTURE_BASE_LEVEL, GL_TEXTURE_COMPARE_FUNC, GL_TEXTURE_COMPARE_MODE, GL_TEXTURE_LOD_BIAS, GL_TEXTURE_MIN_FILTER, GL_TEXTURE_MAG_FILTER, GL_TEXTURE_MIN_LOD, GL_TEXTURE_MAX_LOD, GL_TEXTURE_MAX_LEVEL, GL_TEXTURE_SWIZZLE_R, GL_TEXTURE_SWIZZLE_G, GL_TEXTURE_SWIZZLE_B, GL_TEXTURE_SWIZZLE_A, GL_TEXTURE_WRAP_S, GL_TEXTURE_WRAP_T, or GL_TEXTURE_WRAP_R.

param

>Specifies the value of *pname*.

C Specification

```
void glTexParameterfv GLenum target GLenum pname const  GLfloat * params
void glTexParameteriv GLenum target GLenum pname const  GLint * params
void glTexParameterIiv GLenum target GLenum pname const  GLint * params
void glTexParameterIuiv GLenum target GLenum pname const  GLuint * params
```

Parameters

target

>Specifies the target texture, which must be either GL_TEXTURE_1D, GL_TEXTURE_2D, GL_TEXTURE_3D, GL_TEXTURE_1D_ARRAY, GL_TEXTURE_2D_ARRAY, GL_TEXTURE_RECTANGLE, or GL_TEXTURE_CUBE_MAP.

pname

>Specifies the symbolic name of a texture parameter. *pname* can be one of the following: GL_TEXTURE_BASE_LEVEL, GL_TEXTURE_BORDER_COLOR, GL_TEXTURE_COMPARE_FUNC, GL_TEXTURE_COMPARE_MODE, GL_TEXTURE_LOD_BIAS, GL_TEXTURE_MIN_FILTER, GL_TEXTURE_MAG_FILTER, GL_TEXTURE_MIN_LOD, GL_TEXTURE_MAX_LOD, GL_TEXTURE_MAX_LEVEL, GL_TEXTURE_SWIZZLE_R, GL_TEXTURE_SWIZZLE_G, GL_TEXTURE_SWIZZLE_B, GL_TEXTURE_SWIZZLE_A, GL_TEXTURE_SWIZZLE_RGBA, GL_TEXTURE_WRAP_S, GL_TEXTURE_WRAP_T, or GL_TEXTURE_WRAP_R.

params

>Specifies a pointer to an array where the value or values of *pname* are stored.

Description

glTexParameter assigns the value or values in *params* to the texture parameter specified as *pname*. *target* defines the target texture, either GL_TEXTURE_1D, GL_TEXTURE_2D, GL_TEXTURE_1D_ARRAY, GL_TEXTURE_2D_ARRAY, GL_TEXTURE_RECTANGLE, or GL_TEXTURE_3D. The following symbols are accepted in *pname*:

GL_TEXTURE_BASE_LEVEL

>Specifies the index of the lowest defined mipmap level. This is an integer value. The initial value is 0.

GL_TEXTURE_BORDER_COLOR

>The data in *params* specifies four values that define the border values that should be used for border texels. If a texel is sampled from the border of the texture, the values of GL_TEXTURE_BORDER_COLOR are interpreted as an RGBA color to match the texture's internal format and substituted for the non-existent texel data. If the texture contains depth components, the first component of GL_TEXTURE_BORDER_COLOR is interpreted as a depth value. The initial value is ().

If the values for GL_TEXTURE_BORDER_COLOR are specified with $\texttt{glTexParameterIiv}$ or $\texttt{glTexParameterIuiv}$, the values are stored unmodified with an internal data type of integer. If specified with $\texttt{glTexParameteriv}$, they are converted to floating point with the following equation: $f = \dfrac{2_c + 1}{2^b - 1}$. If specified with $\texttt{glTexParameterfv}$, they are stored unmodified as floating-point values.

GL_TEXTURE_COMPARE_FUNC

Specifies the comparison operator used when GL_TEXTURE_COMPARE_MODE is set to GL_COMPARE_REF_TO_TEXTURE. Permissible values are:

where r is the current interpolated texture coordinate, and D_t is the depth texture value sampled from the currently bound depth texture. result is assigned to the the red channel.

GL_TEXTURE_COMPARE_MODE

Specifies the texture comparison mode for currently bound depth textures. That is, a texture whose internal format is GL_DEPTH_COMPONENT_*; see glTexImage2D) Permissible values are:

GL_COMPARE_REF_TO_TEXTURE

Specifies that the interpolated and clamped r texture coordinate should be compared to the value in the currently bound depth texture. See the discussion of GL_TEXTURE_COMPARE_FUNC for details of how the comparison is evaluated. The result of the comparison is assigned to the red channel.

GL_NONE

Specifies that the red channel should be assigned the appropriate value from the currently bound depth texture.

Texture Comparison Function	Computed result
GL_LEQUAL	$\text{result} = \begin{cases} 1.0 & r \le D_t \\ 0.0 & r > D_t \end{cases}$
GL_GEQUAL	$\text{result} = \begin{cases} 1.0 & r \ge D_t \\ 0.0 & r < D_t \end{cases}$
GL_LESS	$\text{result} = \begin{cases} 1.0 & r < D_t \\ 0.0 & r \ge D_t \end{cases}$
GL_GREATER	$\text{result} = \begin{cases} 1.0 & r > D_t \\ 0.0 & r \le D_t \end{cases}$

Texture Comparison Function	Computed result
GL_EQUAL	$\text{result} = c \begin{cases} 1.0 & r = D_t \\ 0.0 & r \not= D_t \end{cases}$
GL_NOTEQUAL	$\text{result} = c \begin{cases} 1.0 & r \not= D_t \\ 0.0 & r = D_t \end{cases}$
GL_ALWAYS	$\text{result} = 1.0$
GL_NEVER	$\text{result} = 0.0$

GL_TEXTURE_LOD_BIAS

params specifies a fixed bias value that is to be added to the level-of-detail parameter for the texture before texture sampling. The specified value is added to the shader-supplied bias value (if any) and subsequently clamped into the implementation-defined range $[-bias_{max}, bias_{max}]$, where $bias_{max}$ is the value of the implementation defined constant GL_MAX_TEXTURE_LOD_BIAS. The initial value is 0.0.

GL_TEXTURE_MIN_FILTER

The texture minifying function is used whenever the level-of-detail function used when sampling from the texture determines that the texture should be minified. There are six defined minifying functions. Two of them use either the nearest texture elements or a weighted average of multiple texture elements to compute the texture value. The other four use mipmaps.

A mipmap is an ordered set of arrays representing the same image at progressively lower resolutions. If the texture has dimensions $2^n \ast 2^m$, there are $\max(n,m) + 1$ mipmaps. The first mipmap is the original texture, with dimensions $2^n \ast 2^m$. Each subsequent mipmap has dimensions $2^{k-1} \ast 2^{l-1}$, where $2^k \ast 2^l$ are the dimensions of the previous mipmap, until either $k = 0$ or $l = 0$. At that point, subsequent mipmaps have dimension $1 \ast 2^{l-1}$ or $2^{k-1} \ast 1$ until the final mipmap, which has dimension $1 \ast 1$. To define the mipmaps, call glTexImage1D, glTexImage2D, glTexImage3D, glCopyTexImage1D, or glCopyTexImage2D with the *level* argument indicating the order of the mipmaps. Level 0 is the original texture; level $\max(n,m)$ is the final $1 \ast 1$ mipmap.

params supplies a function for minifying the texture as one of the following:

GL_NEAREST

Returns the value of the texture element that is nearest (in Manhattan distance) to the specified texture coordinates.

GL_LINEAR

Returns the weighted average of the four texture elements that are closest to the specified texture coordinates. These can include items wrapped or repeated from other parts of a texture, depending on the values of GL_TEXTURE_WRAP_S and GL_TEXTURE_WRAP_T, and on the exact mapping.

GL_NEAREST_MIPMAP_NEAREST

Chooses the mipmap that most closely matches the size of the pixel being textured and uses the GL_NEAREST criterion (the texture element closest to the specified texture coordinates) to produce a texture value.

GL_LINEAR_MIPMAP_NEAREST

> Chooses the mipmap that most closely matches the size of the pixel being textured and uses the GL_LINEAR criterion (a weighted average of the four texture elements that are closest to the specified texture coordinates) to produce a texture value.

GL_NEAREST_MIPMAP_LINEAR

> Chooses the two mipmaps that most closely match the size of the pixel being textured and uses the GL_NEAREST criterion (the texture element closest to the specified texture coordinates) to produce a texture value from each mipmap. The final texture value is a weighted average of those two values.

GL_LINEAR_MIPMAP_LINEAR

> Chooses the two mipmaps that most closely match the size of the pixel being textured and uses the GL_LINEAR criterion (a weighted average of the texture elements that are closest to the specified texture coordinates) to produce a texture value from each mipmap. The final texture value is a weighted average of those two values.

As more texture elements are sampled in the minification process, fewer aliasing artifacts will be apparent. While the GL_NEAREST and GL_LINEAR minification functions can be faster than the other four, they sample only one or multiple texture elements to determine the texture value of the pixel being rendered and can produce more patterns or ragged transitions. The initial value of GL_TEXTURE_MIN_FILTER is GL_NEAREST_MIPMAP_LINEAR.

GL_TEXTURE_MAG_FILTER

> The texture magnification function is used whenever the level-of-detail function used when sampling from the texture determines that the texture should be magified. It sets the texture magnification function to either GL_NEAREST or GL_LINEAR (see below). GL_NEAREST is generally faster than GL_LINEAR, but it can produce textured images with sharper edges because the transition between texture elements is not as smooth. The initial value of GL_TEXTURE_MAG_FILTER is GL_LINEAR.

GL_NEAREST

> Returns the value of the texture element that is nearest (in Manhattan distance) to the specified texture coordinates.

GL_LINEAR

> Returns the weighted average of the texture elements that are closest to the specified texture coordinates. These can include items wrapped or repeated from other parts of a texture, depending on the values of GL_TEXTURE_WRAP_S and GL_TEXTURE_WRAP_T, and on the exact mapping.

GL_TEXTURE_MIN_LOD

> Sets the minimum level-of-detail parameter. This floating-point value limits the selection of highest resolution mipmap (lowest mipmap level). The initial value is -1000.

GL_TEXTURE_MAX_LOD

> Sets the maximum level-of-detail parameter. This floating-point value limits the selection of the lowest resolution mipmap (highest mipmap level). The initial value is 1000.

GL_TEXTURE_MAX_LEVEL

> Sets the index of the highest defined mipmap level. This is an integer value. The initial value is 1000.

GL_TEXTURE_SWIZZLE_R

> Sets the swizzle that will be applied to the r component of a texel before it is returned to the shader. Valid values for *param* are GL_RED, GL_GREEN, GL_BLUE, GL_ALPHA, GL_ZERO and GL_ONE. If GL_TEXTURE_SWIZZLE_R is GL_RED, the value for r will be taken from the first channel of the fetched texel. If GL_TEXTURE_SWIZZLE_R is GL_GREEN, the value for r will be taken from the second channel of the fetched texel. If

GL_TEXTURE_SWIZZLE_R is GL_BLUE, the value for r will be taken from the third channel of the fetched texel. If GL_TEXTURE_SWIZZLE_R is GL_ALPHA, the value for r will be taken from the fourth channel of the fetched texel. If GL_TEXTURE_SWIZZLE_R is GL_ZERO, the value for r will be subtituted with 0.0. If GL_TEXTURE_SWIZZLE_R is GL_ONE, the value for r will be subtituted with 1.0. The initial value is GL_RED.

GL_TEXTURE_SWIZZLE_G

Sets the swizzle that will be applied to the g component of a texel before it is returned to the shader. Valid values for *param* and their effects are similar to those of GL_TEXTURE_SWIZZLE_R. The initial value is GL_GREEN.

GL_TEXTURE_SWIZZLE_B

Sets the swizzle that will be applied to the b component of a texel before it is returned to the shader. Valid values for *param* and their effects are similar to those of GL_TEXTURE_SWIZZLE_R. The initial value is GL_BLUE.

GL_TEXTURE_SWIZZLE_A

Sets the swizzle that will be applied to the a component of a texel before it is returned to the shader. Valid values for *param* and their effects are similar to those of GL_TEXTURE_SWIZZLE_R. The initial value is GL_ALPHA.

GL_TEXTURE_SWIZZLE_RGBA

Sets the swizzles that will be applied to the r, g, b, and a components of a texel before they are returned to the shader. Valid values for *params* and their effects are similar to those of GL_TEXTURE_SWIZZLE_R, except that all channels are specified simultaneously. Setting the value of GL_TEXTURE_SWIZZLE_RGBA is equivalent (assuming no errors are generated) to setting the parameters of each of GL_TEXTURE_SWIZZLE_R, GL_TEXTURE_SWIZZLE_G, GL_TEXTURE_SWIZZLE_B, and GL_TEXTURE_SWIZZLE_A successively.

GL_TEXTURE_WRAP_S

Sets the wrap parameter for texture coordinate s to either GL_CLAMP_TO_EDGE, GL_CLAMP_TO_BORDER, GL_MIRRORED_REPEAT, or GL_REPEAT.

GL_CLAMP_TO_EDGE causes s coordinates to be clamped to the range $\left[\frac{1}{2}, 1 - \frac{1}{2}\right]$, where N is the size of the texture in the direction of clamping. GL_CLAMP_TO_BORDER evaluates s coordinates in a similar manner to GL_CLAMP_TO_EDGE. However, in cases where clamping would have occurred in GL_CLAMP_TO_EDGE mode, the fetched texel data is substituted with the values specified by GL_TEXTURE_BORDER_COLOR. GL_REPEAT causes the integer part of the s coordinate to be ignored; the GL uses only the fractional part, thereby creating a repeating pattern. GL_MIRRORED_REPEAT causes the s coordinate to be set to the fractional part of the texture coordinate if the integer part of s is even; if the integer part of s is odd, then the s texture coordinate is set to $1 - \mathrm{frac}(s)$, where frac(s) represents the fractional part of s. Initially, GL_TEXTURE_WRAP_S is set to GL_REPEAT.

GL_TEXTURE_WRAP_T

Sets the wrap parameter for texture coordinate t to either GL_CLAMP_TO_EDGE, GL_CLAMP_TO_BORDER, GL_MIRRORED_REPEAT, or GL_REPEAT. See the discussion under GL_TEXTURE_WRAP_S. Initially, GL_TEXTURE_WRAP_T is set to GL_REPEAT.

GL_TEXTURE_WRAP_R

Sets the wrap parameter for texture coordinate r to either GL_CLAMP_TO_EDGE, GL_CLAMP_TO_BORDER, GL_MIRRORED_REPEAT, or GL_REPEAT. See the discussion under GL_TEXTURE_WRAP_S. Initially, GL_TEXTURE_WRAP_R is set to GL_REPEAT.

Notes

Suppose that a program attempts to sample from a texture and has set GL_TEXTURE_MIN_FILTER to one of the functions that requires a mipmap. If either the dimensions of the texture images currently defined (with previous calls to glTexImage1D, glTexImage2D, glTexImage3D, glCopyTexImage1D, or glCopyTexImage2D) do not follow the proper sequence for mipmaps (described above), or there are fewer texture images defined than are needed, or the set of texture images have differing numbers of texture components, then the texture is considered *incomplete*.

Linear filtering accesses the four nearest texture elements only in 2D textures. In 1D textures, linear filtering accesses the two nearest texture elements. In 3D textures, linear filtering accesses the eight nearest texture elements.

glTexParameter specifies the texture parameters for the active texture unit, specified by calling glActiveTexture.

Errors

GL_INVALID_ENUM is generated if *target* or *pname* is not one of the accepted defined values.
GL_INVALID_ENUM is generated if *params* should have a defined constant value (based on the value of *pname*) and does not.

Associated Gets

glGetTexParameter
glGetTexLevelParameter

See Also

glActiveTexture, glBindTexture, glCopyTexImage1D, glCopyTexImage2D, glCopyTexSubImage1D, glCopyTexSubImage2D, glCopyTexSubImage3D, glPixelStore, glSamplerParameter, glTexImage1D, glTexImage2D, glTexImage3D, glTexSubImage1D, glTexSubImage2D, glTexSubImage3D

Copyright

Copyright © 1991-2006 Silicon Graphics, Inc. This document is licensed under the SGI Free Software B License. For details, see http://oss.sgi.com/projects/FreeB/.

glTexSubImage1D

specify a one-dimensional texture subimage

C Specification

```
void glTexSubImage1D(GLenum target,
                     GLint level,
                     GLint xoffset,
                     GLsizei width,
                     GLenum format,
                     GLenum type,
                     const GLvoid * data);
```

Parameters

target

Specifies the target texture. Must be GL_TEXTURE_1D.

level

Specifies the level-of-detail number. Level 0 is the base image level. Level *n* is the *n*th mipmap reduction image.

xoffset
> Specifies a texel offset in the x direction within the texture array.

width
> Specifies the width of the texture subimage.

format
> Specifies the format of the pixel data. The following symbolic values are accepted: GL_RED, GL_RG, GL_RGB, GL_BGR, GL_RGBA, and GL_BGRA.

type
> Specifies the data type of the pixel data. The following symbolic values are accepted: GL_UNSIGNED_BYTE, GL_BYTE, GL_UNSIGNED_SHORT, GL_SHORT, GL_UNSIGNED_INT, GL_INT, GL_FLOAT, GL_UNSIGNED_BYTE_3_3_2, GL_UNSIGNED_BYTE_2_3_3_REV, GL_UNSIGNED_SHORT_5_6_5, GL_UNSIGNED_SHORT_5_6_5_REV, GL_UNSIGNED_SHORT_4_4_4_4, GL_UNSIGNED_SHORT_4_4_4_4_REV, GL_UNSIGNED_SHORT_5_5_5_1, GL_UNSIGNED_SHORT_1_5_5_5_REV, GL_UNSIGNED_INT_8_8_8_8, GL_UNSIGNED_INT_8_8_8_8_REV, GL_UNSIGNED_INT_10_10_10_2, and GL_UNSIGNED_INT_2_10_10_10_REV.

data
> Specifies a pointer to the image data in memory.

Description

Texturing maps a portion of a specified texture image onto each graphical primitive for which texturing is enabled. To enable or disable one-dimensional texturing, call glEnable and glDisable with argument GL_TEXTURE_1D.

glTexSubImage1D redefines a contiguous subregion of an existing one-dimensional texture image. The texels referenced by *data* replace the portion of the existing texture array with x indices *xoffset* and xoffset + width − 1, inclusive. This region may not include any texels outside the range of the texture array as it was originally specified. It is not an error to specify a subtexture with width of 0, but such a specification has no effect.

If a non-zero named buffer object is bound to the GL_PIXEL_UNPACK_BUFFER target (see glBindBuffer) while a texture image is specified, *data* is treated as a byte offset into the buffer object's data store.

Notes

glPixelStore modes affect texture images.

glTexSubImage1D specifies a one-dimensional subtexture for the current texture unit, specified with glActiveTexture.

Errors

GL_INVALID_ENUM is generated if *target* is not one of the allowable values.

GL_INVALID_ENUM is generated if *format* is not an accepted format constant.

GL_INVALID_ENUM is generated if *type* is not a type constant.

GL_INVALID_VALUE is generated if *level* is less than 0.

GL_INVALID_VALUE may be generated if *level* is greater than $\log_2$ *max*, where *max* is the returned value of GL_MAX_TEXTURE_SIZE.

GL_INVALID_VALUE is generated if xoffset 6 −b, or if (xoffset + width) 7 (w − b), where w is the GL_TEXTURE_WIDTH, and b is the width of the GL_TEXTURE_BORDER of the texture image being modified. Note that w includes twice the border width.

GL_INVALID_VALUE is generated if *width* is less than 0.

GL_INVALID_OPERATION is generated if the texture array has not been defined by a previous glTexImage1D operation.

GL_INVALID_OPERATION is generated if *type* is one of GL_UNSIGNED_BYTE_3_3_2, GL_UNSIGNED_BYTE_2_3_3_REV, GL_UNSIGNED_SHORT_5_6_5, or GL_UNSIGNED_SHORT_5_6_5_REV and *format* is not GL_RGB.

GL_INVALID_OPERATION is generated if *type* is one of GL_UNSIGNED_SHORT_4_4_4_4, GL_UNSIGNED_SHORT_4_4_4_4_REV, GL_UNSIGNED_SHORT_5_5_5_1, GL_UNSIGNED_SHORT_1_5_5_5_REV, GL_UNSIGNED_INT_8_8_8_8, GL_UNSIGNED_INT_8_8_8_8_REV, GL_UNSIGNED_INT_10_10_10_2, or GL_UNSIGNED_INT_2_10_10_10_REV and *format* is neither GL_RGBA nor GL_BGRA.

GL_INVALID_OPERATION is generated if a non-zero buffer object name is bound to the GL_PIXEL_UNPACK_BUFFER target and the buffer object's data store is currently mapped.

GL_INVALID_OPERATION is generated if a non-zero buffer object name is bound to the GL_PIXEL_UNPACK_BUFFER target and the data would be unpacked from the buffer object such that the memory reads required would exceed the data store size.

GL_INVALID_OPERATION is generated if a non-zero buffer object name is bound to the GL_PIXEL_UNPACK_BUFFER target and *data* is not evenly divisible into the number of bytes needed to store in memory a datum indicated by *type*.

Associated Gets

glGetTexImage
glGet with argument GL_PIXEL_UNPACK_BUFFER_BINDING

See Also

glActiveTexture, glCopyTexImage1D, glCopyTexImage2D, glCopyTexSubImage1D, glCopyTexSubImage2D, glCopyTexSubImage3D, glPixelStore, glTexImage1D, glTexImage2D, glTexImage3D, glTexParameter, glTexSubImage2D, glTexSubImage3D

Copyright

Copyright © 1991-2006 Silicon Graphics, Inc. This document is licensed under the SGI Free Software B License. For details, see http://oss.sgi.com/projects/FreeB/.

glTexSubImage2D

specify a two-dimensional texture subimage

C Specification

```
void glTexSubImage2D(GLenum target,
                     GLint level,
                     GLint xoffset,
                     GLint yoffset,
                     GLsizei width,
                     GLsizei height,
                     GLenum format,
                     GLenum type,
                     const GLvoid * data);
```

Parameters

target

Specifies the target texture. Must be GL_TEXTURE_2D, GL_TEXTURE_CUBE_MAP_POSITIVE_X, GL_TEXTURE_CUBE_MAP_NEGATIVE_X, GL_TEXTURE_CUBE_MAP_POSITIVE_Y, GL_TEXTURE_CUBE_MAP_NEGATIVE_Y, GL_TEXTURE_CUBE_MAP_POSITIVE_Z, or GL_TEXTURE_CUBE_MAP_NEGATIVE_Z.

level

Specifies the level-of-detail number. Level 0 is the base image level. Level *n* is the *n*th mipmap reduction image.

xoffset
    Specifies a texel offset in the x direction within the texture array.

yoffset
    Specifies a texel offset in the y direction within the texture array.

width
    Specifies the width of the texture subimage.

height
    Specifies the height of the texture subimage.

format
    Specifies the format of the pixel data. The following symbolic values are accepted: GL_RED, GL_RG, GL_RGB, GL_BGR, GL_RGBA, and GL_BGRA.

type
    Specifies the data type of the pixel data. The following symbolic values are accepted: GL_UNSIGNED_BYTE, GL_BYTE, GL_UNSIGNED_SHORT, GL_SHORT, GL_UNSIGNED_INT, GL_INT, GL_FLOAT, GL_UNSIGNED_BYTE_3_3_2, GL_UNSIGNED_BYTE_2_3_3_REV, GL_UNSIGNED_SHORT_5_6_5, GL_UNSIGNED_SHORT_5_6_5_REV, GL_UNSIGNED_SHORT_4_4_4_4, GL_UNSIGNED_SHORT_4_4_4_4_REV, GL_UNSIGNED_SHORT_5_5_5_1, GL_UNSIGNED_SHORT_1_5_5_5_REV, GL_UNSIGNED_INT_8_8_8_8, GL_UNSIGNED_INT_8_8_8_8_REV, GL_UNSIGNED_INT_10_10_10_2, and GL_UNSIGNED_INT_2_10_10_10_REV.

data
    Specifies a pointer to the image data in memory.

Description

Texturing maps a portion of a specified texture image onto each graphical primitive for which texturing is enabled. To enable and disable two-dimensional texturing, call glEnable and glDisable with argument GL_TEXTURE_2D.

glTexSubImage2D redefines a contiguous subregion of an existing two-dimensional texture image. The texels referenced by *data* replace the portion of the existing texture array with x indices *xoffset* and xoffset + width − 1, inclusive, and y indices *yoffset* and yoffset + height − 1, inclusive. This region may not include any texels outside the range of the texture array as it was originally specified. It is not an error to specify a subtexture with zero width or height, but such a specification has no effect.

If a non-zero named buffer object is bound to the GL_PIXEL_UNPACK_BUFFER target (see glBindBuffer) while a texture image is specified, *data* is treated as a byte offset into the buffer object's data store.

Notes

glPixelStore modes affect texture images.

glTexSubImage2D specifies a two-dimensional subtexture for the current texture unit, specified with glActiveTexture.

Errors

GL_INVALID_ENUM is generated if *target* is not GL_TEXTURE_2D, GL_TEXTURE_CUBE_MAP_POSITIVE_X, GL_TEXTURE_CUBE_MAP_NEGATIVE_X, GL_TEXTURE_CUBE_MAP_POSITIVE_Y, GL_TEXTURE_CUBE_MAP_NEGATIVE_Y, GL_TEXTURE_CUBE_MAP_POSITIVE_Z, or GL_TEXTURE_CUBE_MAP_NEGATIVE_Z.

GL_INVALID_ENUM is generated if *format* is not an accepted format constant.

GL_INVALID_ENUM is generated if *type* is not a type constant.

GL_INVALID_VALUE is generated if *level* is less than 0.

GL_INVALID_VALUE may be generated if *level* is greater than $\log_2$ *max*, where *max* is the returned value of GL_MAX_TEXTURE_SIZE.

GL_INVALID_VALUE is generated if xoffset 6 −b, (xoffset + width) 7 (w − b), yoffset 6 −b, or (yoffset + height) 7 (h − b), where w is the GL_TEXTURE_WIDTH, h is the GL_TEXTURE_HEIGHT, and b is the border width of the texture image being modified. Note that w and h include twice the border width.

GL_INVALID_VALUE is generated if *width* or *height* is less than 0.

GL_INVALID_OPERATION is generated if the texture array has not been defined by a previous glTexImage2D operation.

GL_INVALID_OPERATION is generated if *type* is one of GL_UNSIGNED_BYTE_3_3_2, GL_UNSIGNED_BYTE_2_3_3_REV, GL_UNSIGNED_SHORT_5_6_5, or GL_UNSIGNED_SHORT_5_6_5_REV and *format* is not GL_RGB.

GL_INVALID_OPERATION is generated if *type* is one of GL_UNSIGNED_SHORT_4_4_4_4, GL_UNSIGNED_SHORT_4_4_4_4_REV, GL_UNSIGNED_SHORT_5_5_5_1, GL_UNSIGNED_SHORT_1_5_5_5_REV, GL_UNSIGNED_INT_8_8_8_8, GL_UNSIGNED_INT_8_8_8_8_REV, GL_UNSIGNED_INT_10_10_10_2, or GL_UNSIGNED_INT_2_10_10_10_REV and *format* is neither GL_RGBA nor GL_BGRA.

GL_INVALID_OPERATION is generated if a non-zero buffer object name is bound to the GL_PIXEL_UNPACK_BUFFER target and the buffer object's data store is currently mapped.

GL_INVALID_OPERATION is generated if a non-zero buffer object name is bound to the GL_PIXEL_UNPACK_BUFFER target and the data would be unpacked from the buffer object such that the memory reads required would exceed the data store size.

GL_INVALID_OPERATION is generated if a non-zero buffer object name is bound to the GL_PIXEL_UNPACK_BUFFER target and *data* is not evenly divisible into the number of bytes needed to store in memory a datum indicated by *type*.

Associated Gets

glGetTexImage
glGet with argument GL_PIXEL_UNPACK_BUFFER_BINDING

See Also

glActiveTexture, glCopyTexImage1D, glCopyTexImage2D, glCopyTexSubImage1D, glCopyTexSubImage2D, glCopyTexSubImage3D, glPixelStore, glTexImage1D, glTexImage2D, glTexImage3D, glTexSubImage1D, glTexSubImage3D, glTexParameter

Copyright

Copyright © 1991-2006 Silicon Graphics, Inc. This document is licensed under the SGI Free Software B License. For details, see http://oss.sgi.com/projects/FreeB/.

glTexSubImage3D

specify a three-dimensional texture subimage

C Specification

```
void glTexSubImage3D(GLenum target,
                     GLint level,
                     GLint xoffset,
                     GLint yoffset,
                     GLint zoffset,
                     GLsizei width,
                     GLsizei height,
                     GLsizei depth,
                     GLenum format,
                     GLenum type,
                     const GLvoid * data);
```

Parameters

target
> Specifies the target texture. Must be GL_TEXTURE_3D.

level
> Specifies the level-of-detail number. Level 0 is the base image level. Level n is the nth mipmap reduction image.

xoffset
> Specifies a texel offset in the x direction within the texture array.

yoffset
> Specifies a texel offset in the y direction within the texture array.

zoffset
> Specifies a texel offset in the z direction within the texture array.

width
> Specifies the width of the texture subimage.

height
> Specifies the height of the texture subimage.

depth
> Specifies the depth of the texture subimage.

format
> Specifies the format of the pixel data. The following symbolic values are accepted: GL_RED, GL_RG, GL_RGB, GL_BGR, GL_RGBA, and GL_BGRA.

type
> Specifies the data type of the pixel data. The following symbolic values are accepted: GL_UNSIGNED_BYTE, GL_BYTE, GL_UNSIGNED_SHORT, GL_SHORT, GL_UNSIGNED_INT, GL_INT, GL_FLOAT, GL_UNSIGNED_BYTE_3_3_2, GL_UNSIGNED_BYTE_2_3_3_REV, GL_UNSIGNED_SHORT_5_6_5, GL_UNSIGNED_SHORT_5_6_5_REV, GL_UNSIGNED_SHORT_4_4_4_4, GL_UNSIGNED_SHORT_4_4_4_4_REV, GL_UNSIGNED_SHORT_5_5_5_1, GL_UNSIGNED_SHORT_1_5_5_5_REV, GL_UNSIGNED_INT_8_8_8_8, GL_UNSIGNED_INT_8_8_8_8_REV, GL_UNSIGNED_INT_10_10_10_2, and GL_UNSIGNED_INT_2_10_10_10_REV.

data
> Specifies a pointer to the image data in memory.

Description

Texturing maps a portion of a specified texture image onto each graphical primitive for which texturing is enabled. To enable and disable three-dimensional texturing, call glEnable and glDisable with argument GL_TEXTURE_3D.

glTexSubImage3D redefines a contiguous subregion of an existing three-dimensional texture image. The texels referenced by *data* replace the portion of the existing texture array with x indices *xoffset* and xoffset + width − 1, inclusive, y indices *yoffset* and yoffset + height − 1, inclusive, and z indices *zoffset* and zoffset + depth − 1, inclusive. This region may not include any texels outside the range of the texture array as it was originally specified. It is not an error to specify a subtexture with zero width, height, or depth but such a specification has no effect.

If a non-zero named buffer object is bound to the GL_PIXEL_UNPACK_BUFFER target (see glBindBuffer) while a texture image is specified, *data* is treated as a byte offset into the buffer object's data store.

Notes

The glPixelStore modes affect texture images.

glTexSubImage3D specifies a three-dimensional subtexture for the current texture unit, specified with glActiveTexture.

Errors

GL_INVALID_ENUM is generated if /*target* is not GL_TEXTURE_3D.

GL_INVALID_ENUM is generated if *format* is not an accepted format constant.

GL_INVALID_ENUM is generated if *type* is not a type constant.

GL_INVALID_VALUE is generated if *level* is less than 0.

GL_INVALID_VALUE may be generated if *level* is greater than $\log_2 max$, where *max* is the returned value of GL_MAX_TEXTURE_SIZE.

GL_INVALID_VALUE is generated if xoffset 6 −b, (xoffset + width) 7 (w − b), yoffset 6 −b, or (yoffset + height) 7 (h − b), or zoffset 6 −b, or (zoffset + depth) 7 (d − b), where w is the GL_TEXTURE_WIDTH, h is the GL_TEXTURE_HEIGHT, d is the GL_TEXTURE_DEPTH and b is the border width of the texture image being modified. Note that w, h, and d include twice the border width.

GL_INVALID_VALUE is generated if *width*, *height*, or *depth* is less than 0.

GL_INVALID_OPERATION is generated if the texture array has not been defined by a previous glTexImage3D operation.

GL_INVALID_OPERATION is generated if *type* is one of GL_UNSIGNED_BYTE_3_3_2, GL_UNSIGNED_BYTE_2_3_3_REV, GL_UNSIGNED_SHORT_5_6_5, or GL_UNSIGNED_SHORT_5_6_5_REV and *format* is not GL_RGB.

GL_INVALID_OPERATION is generated if *type* is one of GL_UNSIGNED_SHORT_4_4_4_4, GL_UNSIGNED_SHORT_4_4_4_4_REV, GL_UNSIGNED_SHORT_5_5_5_1, GL_UNSIGNED_SHORT_1_5_5_5_REV, GL_UNSIGNED_INT_8_8_8_8, GL_UNSIGNED_INT_8_8_8_8_REV, GL_UNSIGNED_INT_10_10_10_2, or GL_UNSIGNED_INT_2_10_10_10_REV and *format* is neither GL_RGBA nor GL_BGRA.

GL_INVALID_OPERATION is generated if a non-zero buffer object name is bound to the GL_PIXEL_UNPACK_BUFFER target and the buffer object's data store is currently mapped.

GL_INVALID_OPERATION is generated if a non-zero buffer object name is bound to the GL_PIXEL_UNPACK_BUFFER target and the data would be unpacked from the buffer object such that the memory reads required would exceed the data store size.

GL_INVALID_OPERATION is generated if a non-zero buffer object name is bound to the GL_PIXEL_UNPACK_BUFFER target and *data* is not evenly divisible into the number of bytes needed to store in memory a datum indicated by *type*.

Associated Gets

glGetTexImage
glGet with argument GL_PIXEL_UNPACK_BUFFER_BINDING

See Also

glActiveTexture, glCopyTexImage1D, glCopyTexImage2D, glCopyTexSubImage1D, glCopyTexSubImage2D, glCopyTexSubImage3D, glPixelStore, glTexImage1D, glTexImage2D, glTexImage3D, glTexSubImage1D, glTexSubImage2D, glTexParameter

Copyright

Copyright © 1991-2006 Silicon Graphics, Inc. This document is licensed under the SGI Free Software B License. For details, see http://oss.sgi.com/projects/FreeB/.

glTransformFeedbackVaryings

specify values to record in transform feedback buffers

C Specification

```
void glTransformFeedbackVaryings(GLuint program,
                                 GLsizei count,
                                 const char **varyings,
                                 GLenum bufferMode);
```

Parameters

program
> The name of the target program object.

count
> The number of varying variables used for transform feedback.

varyings
> An array of *count* zero-terminated strings specifying the names of the varying variables to use for transform feedback.

bufferMode
> Identifies the mode used to capture the varying variables when transform feedback is active. *bufferMode* must be GL_INTERLEAVED_ATTRIBS or GL_SEPARATE_ATTRIBS.

Description

The names of the vertex or geometry shader outputs to be recorded in transform feedback mode are specified using glTransformFeedbackVaryings. When a geometry shader is active, transform feedback records the values of selected geometry shader output variables from the emitted vertices. Otherwise, the values of the selected vertex shader outputs are recorded.

The state set by glTranformFeedbackVaryings is stored and takes effect next time glLinkProgram is called on *program*. When glLinkProgram is called, *program* is linked so that the values of the specified varying variables for the vertices of each primitive generated by the GL are written to a single buffer object if *bufferMode* is GL_INTERLEAVED_ATTRIBS or multiple buffer objects if *bufferMode* is GL_SEPARATE_ATTRIBS.

In addition to the errors generated by glTransformFeedbackVaryings, the program *program* will fail to link if:

> The count specified by glTransformFeedbackVaryings is non-zero, but the program object has no vertex or geometry shader.

> Any variable name specified in the *varyings* array is not declared as an output in the vertex shader (or the geometry shader, if active).

> Any two entries in the *varyings* array specify the same varying variable.

> The total number of components to capture in any varying variable in *varyings* is greater than the constant GL_MAX_TRANSFORM_FEEDBACK_SEPARATE_COMPONENTS and the buffer mode is GL_SEPARATE_ATTRIBS.

> The total number of components to capture is greater than the constant GL_MAX_TRANSFORM_FEEDBACK_INTERLEAVED_COMPONENTS and the buffer mode is GL_INTERLEAVED_ATTRIBS.

Notes

glGetTransformFeedbackVarying is available only if the GL version is 3.0 or greater.

Errors

GL_INVALID_VALUE is generated if *program* is not the name of a program object.

GL_INVALID_VALUE is generated if *bufferMode* is GL_SEPARATE_ATTRIBS and *count* is greater than the implementation-dependent limit GL_MAX_TRANSFORM_FEEDBACK_SEPARATE_ATTRIBS.

Associated Gets

glGetTransformFeedbackVarying

See Also

glBeginTransformFeedback, glEndTransformFeedback,
glGetTransformFeedbackVarying

Copyright

Copyright © 2010 Khronos Group. This material may be distributed subject to the terms and conditions set forth in the Open Publication License, v 1.0, 8 June 1999. http://opencontent.org/openpub/.

glUniform

Specify the value of a uniform variable for the current program object

C Specification

```
void glUniform1f(GLint location,
                 GLfloat v0);
void glUniform2f(GLint location,
                 GLfloat v0,
                 GLfloat v1);
void glUniform3f(GLint location,
                 GLfloat v0,
                 GLfloat v1,
                 GLfloat v2);
void glUniform4f(GLint location,
                 GLfloat v0,
                 GLfloat v1,
                 GLfloat v2,
                 GLfloat v3);
void glUniform1i(GLint location,
                 GLint v0);
void glUniform2i(GLint location,
                 GLint v0,
                 GLint v1);
void glUniform3i(GLint location,
                 GLint v0,
                 GLint v1,
                 GLint v2);
void glUniform4i(GLint location,
                 GLint v0,
                 GLint v1,
                 GLint v2,
                 GLint v3);
```

```
void glUniform1ui(GLint location,
                  GLuint v0);
void glUniform2ui(GLint location,
                  GLint v0,
                  GLuint v1);
void glUniform3ui(GLint location,
                  GLint v0,
                  GLint v1,
                  GLuint v2);
void glUniform4ui(GLint location,
                  GLint v0,
                  GLint v1,
                  GLint v2,
                  GLuint v3);
```

Parameters

location
>   Specifies the location of the uniform variable to be modified.

v0, v1, v2, v3
>   Specifies the new values to be used for the specified uniform variable.

C Specification

```
void glUniform1fv(GLint location,
                  GLsizei count,
                  const GLfloat * value);
void glUniform2fv(GLint location,
                  GLsizei count,
                  const GLfloat * value);
void glUniform3fv(GLint location,
                  GLsizei count,
                  const GLfloat * value);
void glUniform4fv(GLint location,
                  GLsizei count,
                  const GLfloat * value);
void glUniform1iv(GLint location,
                  GLsizei count,
                  const GLint * value);
void glUniform2iv(GLint location,
                  GLsizei count,
                  const GLint * value);
void glUniform3iv(GLint location,
                  GLsizei count,
                  const GLint * value);
void glUniform4iv(GLint location,
                  GLsizei count,
                  const GLint * value);
void glUniform1uiv(GLint location,
                   GLsizei count,
                   const GLuint * value);
void glUniform2uiv(GLint location,
                   GLsizei count,
                   const GLuint * value);
```

```
void glUniform3uiv(GLint location,
                   GLsizei count,
                   const GLuint * value);
void glUniform4uiv(GLint location,
                   GLsizei count,
                   const GLuint * value);
```

Parameters

location

Specifies the location of the uniform value to be modified.

count

Specifies the number of elements that are to be modified. This should be 1 if the targeted uniform variable is not an array, and 1 or more if it is an array.

value

Specifies a pointer to an array of *count* values that will be used to update the specified uniform variable.

C Specification

```
void glUniformMatrix2fv(GLint location,
                        GLsizei count,
                        GLboolean transpose,
                        const GLfloat * value);
void glUniformMatrix3fv(GLint location,
                        GLsizei count,
                        GLboolean transpose,
                        const GLfloat * value);
void glUniformMatrix4fv(GLint location,
                        GLsizei count,
                        GLboolean transpose,
                        const GLfloat * value);
void glUniformMatrix2x3fv(GLint location,
                          GLsizei count,
                          GLboolean transpose,
                          const GLfloat * value);
void glUniformMatrix3x2fv(GLint location,
                          GLsizei count,
                          GLboolean transpose,
                          const GLfloat * value);
void glUniformMatrix2x4fv(GLint location,
                          GLsizei count,
                          GLboolean transpose,
                          const GLfloat * value);
void glUniformMatrix4x2fv(GLint location,
                          GLsizei count,
                          GLboolean transpose,
                          const GLfloat * value);
void glUniformMatrix3x4fv(GLint location,
                          GLsizei count,
                          GLboolean transpose,
                          const GLfloat * value);
void glUniformMatrix4x3fv(GLint location,
                          GLsizei count,
                          GLboolean transpose,
                          const GLfloat * value);
```

Parameters

location
> Specifies the location of the uniform value to be modified.

count
> Specifies the number of matrices that are to be modified. This should be 1 if the targeted uniform variable is not an array of matrices, and 1 or more if it is an array of matrices.

transpose
> Specifies whether to transpose the matrix as the values are loaded into the uniform variable.

value
> Specifies a pointer to an array of *count* values that will be used to update the specified uniform variable.

Description

glUniform modifies the value of a uniform variable or a uniform variable array. The location of the uniform variable to be modified is specified by *location*, which should be a value returned by glGetUniformLocation. glUniform operates on the program object that was made part of current state by calling glUseProgram.

The commands glUniform{1¦2¦3¦4}{f¦i¦ui} are used to change the value of the uniform variable specified by *location* using the values passed as arguments. The number specified in the command should match the number of components in the data type of the specified uniform variable (e.g., 1 for float, int, unsigned int, bool; 2 for vec2, ivec2, uvec2, bvec2, etc.). The suffix f indicates that floating-point values are being passed; the suffix i indicates that integer values are being passed; the suffix ui indicates that unsigned integer values are being passed, and this type should also match the data type of the specified uniform variable. The i variants of this function should be used to provide values for uniform variables defined as int, ivec2, ivec3, ivec4, or arrays of these. The ui variants of this function should be used to provide values for uniform variables defined as unsigned int, uvec2, uvec3, uvec4, or arrays of these. The f variants should be used to provide values for uniform variables of type float, vec2, vec3, vec4, or arrays of these. Either the i, ui or f variants may be used to provide values for uniform variables of type bool, bvec2, bvec3, bvec4, or arrays of these. The uniform variable will be set to false if the input value is 0 or 0.0f, and it will be set to true otherwise.

All active uniform variables defined in a program object are initialized to 0 when the program object is linked successfully. They retain the values assigned to them by a call to glUniform until the next successful link operation occurs on the program object, when they are once again initialized to 0.

The commands glUniform{1¦2¦3¦4}{f¦i¦ui}v can be used to modify a single uniform variable or a uniform variable array. These commands pass a count and a pointer to the values to be loaded into a uniform variable or a uniform variable array. A count of 1 should be used if modifying the value of a single uniform variable, and a count of 1 or greater can be used to modify an entire array or part of an array. When loading n elements starting at an arbitrary position m in a uniform variable array, elements $m + n - 1$ in the array will be replaced with the new values. If $m + n - 1$ is larger than the size of the uniform variable array, values for all array elements beyond the end of the array will be ignored. The number specified in the name of the command indicates the number of components for each element in *value*, and it should match the number of components in the data type of the specified uniform variable (e.g., 1 for float, int, bool; 2 for vec2, ivec2, bvec2, etc.). The data type specified in the name of the command must match the data type for the specified uniform variable as described previously for glUniform{1¦2¦3¦4}{f¦i¦ui}.

For uniform variable arrays, each element of the array is considered to be of the type indicated in the name of the command (e.g., glUniform3f or glUniform3fv can be used to load a uniform variable array of type vec3). The number of elements of the uniform variable array to be modified is specified by *count*

The commands glUniformMatrix{2¦3¦4¦2x3¦3x2¦2x4¦4x2¦3x4¦4x3}fv are used to modify a matrix or an array of matrices. The numbers in the command name are interpreted as the dimensionality of the matrix. The number 2 indicates a 2×2 matrix (i.e., 4 values), the number 3 indicates a 3×3 matrix (i.e., 9 values), and the number 4 indicates a 4×4 matrix (i.e., 16 values). Non-square matrix dimensionality is explicit, with the first number representing the number of columns and the second number representing the number of rows. For example, 2x4 indicates a 2×4 matrix with 2 columns and 4 rows (i.e., 8 values). If *transpose* is GL_FALSE, each matrix is assumed to be supplied in column major order. If *transpose* is GL_TRUE, each matrix is assumed to be supplied in row major order. The *count* argument indicates the number of matrices to be passed. A count of 1 should be used if modifying the value of a single matrix, and a count greater than 1 can be used to modify an array of matrices.

Notes

glUniform1i and glUniform1iv are the only two functions that may be used to load uniform variables defined as sampler types. Loading samplers with any other function will result in a GL_INVALID_OPERATION error.

If *count* is greater than 1 and the indicated uniform variable is not an array, a GL_INVALID_OPERATION error is generated and the specified uniform variable will remain unchanged.

Other than the preceding exceptions, if the type and size of the uniform variable as defined in the shader do not match the type and size specified in the name of the command used to load its value, a GL_INVALID_OPERATION error will be generated and the specified uniform variable will remain unchanged.

If *location* is a value other than -1 and it does not represent a valid uniform variable location in the current program object, an error will be generated, and no changes will be made to the uniform variable storage of the current program object. If *location* is equal to -1, the data passed in will be silently ignored and the specified uniform variable will not be changed.

Errors

GL_INVALID_OPERATION is generated if there is no current program object.

GL_INVALID_OPERATION is generated if the size of the uniform variable declared in the shader does not match the size indicated by the glUniform command.

GL_INVALID_OPERATION is generated if one of the signed or unsigned integer variants of this function is used to load a uniform variable of type float, vec2, vec3, vec4, or an array of these, or if one of the floating-point variants of this function is used to load a uniform variable of type int, ivec2, ivec3, ivec4, unsigned int, uvec2, uvec3, uvec4, or an array of these.

GL_INVALID_OPERATION is generated if one of the signed integer variants of this function is used to load a uniform variable of type unsigned int, uvec2, uvec3, uvec4, or an array of these.

GL_INVALID_OPERATION is generated if one of the unsigned integer variants of this function is used to load a uniform variable of type int, ivec2, ivec3, ivec4, or an array of these.

GL_INVALID_OPERATION is generated if *location* is an invalid uniform location for the current program object and *location* is not equal to -1.

GL_INVALID_VALUE is generated if *count* is less than 0.

GL_INVALID_OPERATION is generated if *count* is greater than 1 and the indicated uniform variable is not an array variable.

GL_INVALID_OPERATION is generated if a sampler is loaded using a command other than glUniform1i and glUniform1iv.

Associated Gets

glGet with the argument GL_CURRENT_PROGRAM

glGetActiveUniform with the handle of a program object and the index of an active uniform variable

glGetUniform with the handle of a program object and the location of a uniform variable
glGetUniformLocation with the handle of a program object and the name of a uniform variable

See Also

glLinkProgram, glUseProgram

Copyright

Copyright © 2003-2005 3Dlabs Inc. Ltd. Copyright © 2010 Khronos Group. This material may be distributed subject to the terms and conditions set forth in the Open Publication License, v 1.0, 8 June 1999. http://opencontent.org/openpub/.

glUniformBlockBinding

assign a binding point to an active uniform block

C Specification

```
void glUniformBlockBinding(GLuint program,
                           GLuint uniformBlockIndex,
                           GLuint uniformBlockBinding);
```

Parameters

program
> The name of a program object containing the active uniform block whose binding to assign.

uniformBlockIndex
> The index of the active uniform block within *program* whose binding to assign.

uniformBlockBinding
> Specifies the binding point to which to bind the uniform block with index *uniformBlockIndex* within *program*.

Description

Binding points for active uniform blocks are assigned using glUniformBlockBinding. Each of a program's active uniform blocks has a corresponding uniform buffer binding point. *program* is the name of a program object for which the command glLinkProgram has been issued in the past.

If successful, glUniformBlockBinding specifies that *program* will use the data store of the buffer object bound to the binding point *uniformBlockBinding* to extract the values of the uniforms in the uniform block identified by *uniformBlockIndex*.

When a program object is linked or re-linked, the uniform buffer object binding point assigned to each of its active uniform blocks is reset to zero.

Errors

GL_INVALID_VALUE is generated if *uniformBlockIndex* is not an active uniform block index of *program*.

GL_INVALID_VALUE is generated if *uniformBlockBinding* is greater than or equal to the value of GL_MAX_UNIFORM_BUFFER_BINDINGS.

GL_INVALID_VALUE is generated *program* is not the name of a program object generated by the GL.

Notes

glUniformBlockBinding is available only if the GL version is 3.1 or greater.

Associated Gets

glGetActiveUniformBlock with argument GL_UNIFORM_BLOCK_BINDING

See Also

`glLinkProgram`, `glBindBufferBase`, `glBindBufferRange`, `glGetActiveUniformBlock`

Copyright

glUseProgram

Installs a program object as part of current rendering state

C Specification

```
void glUseProgram(GLuint program);
```

Parameters

program
> Specifies the handle of the program object whose executables are to be used as part of current rendering state.

Description

`glUseProgram` installs the program object specified by *program* as part of current rendering state. One or more executables are created in a program object by successfully attaching shader objects to it with glAttachShader, successfully compiling the shader objects with glCompileShader, and successfully linking the program object with glLinkProgram.

A program object will contain an executable that will run on the vertex processor if it contains one or more shader objects of type GL_VERTEX_SHADER that have been successfully compiled and linked. A program object will contain an executable that will run on the geometry processor if it contains one or more shader objects of type GL_GEOMETRY_SHADER that have been successfully compiled and linked. Similarly, a program object will contain an executable that will run on the fragment processor if it contains one or more shader objects of type GL_FRAGMENT_SHADER that have been successfully compiled and linked.

While a program object is in use, applications are free to modify attached shader objects, compile attached shader objects, attach additional shader objects, and detach or delete shader objects. None of these operations will affect the executables that are part of the current state. However, relinking the program object that is currently in use will install the program object as part of the current rendering state if the link operation was successful (see glLinkProgram). If the program object currently in use is relinked unsuccessfully, its link status will be set to GL_FALSE, but the executables and associated state will remain part of the current state until a subsequent call to `glUseProgram` removes it from use. After it is removed from use, it cannot be made part of current state until it has been successfully relinked.

If *program* is zero, then the current rendering state refers to an *invalid* program object and the results of shader execution are undefined. However, this is not an error.

If *program* does not contain shader objects of type GL_FRAGMENT_SHADER, an executable will be installed on the vertex, and possibly geometry processors, but the results of fragment shader execution will be undefined.

926

Notes

Like buffer and texture objects, the name space for program objects may be shared across a set of contexts, as long as the server sides of the contexts share the same address space. If the name space is shared across contexts, any attached objects and the data associated with those attached objects are shared as well.

Applications are responsible for providing the synchronization across API calls when objects are accessed from different execution threads.

Errors

GL_INVALID_VALUE is generated if *program* is neither 0 nor a value generated by OpenGL.
GL_INVALID_OPERATION is generated if *program* is not a program object.
GL_INVALID_OPERATION is generated if *program* could not be made part of current state.
GL_INVALID_OPERATION is generated if transform feedback mode is active.

Associated Gets

glGet with the argument GL_CURRENT_PROGRAM
glGetActiveAttrib with a valid program object and the index of an active attribute variable
glGetActiveUniform with a valid program object and the index of an active uniform variable
glGetAttachedShaders with a valid program object
glGetAttribLocation with a valid program object and the name of an attribute variable
glGetProgram with a valid program object and the parameter to be queried
glGetProgramInfoLog with a valid program object
glGetUniform with a valid program object and the location of a uniform variable
glGetUniformLocation with a valid program object and the name of a uniform variable
glIsProgram

See Also

glAttachShader, glBindAttribLocation, glCompileShader, glCreateProgram, glDeleteProgram, glDetachShader, glLinkProgram, glUniform, glValidateProgram, glVertexAttrib

Copyright

glValidateProgram

Validates a program object

C Specification

void glValidateProgram(GLuint *program*);

Parameters

program
Specifies the handle of the program object to be validated.

Description

glValidateProgram checks to see whether the executables contained in *program* can execute given the current OpenGL state. The information generated by the validation process will be stored in *program*'s information log. The validation information may consist of an empty string, or it may be a string containing information about how the current program object interacts with the rest of current OpenGL state. This provides a way for OpenGL implementers to convey more information about why the current program is inefficient, suboptimal, failing to execute, and so on.

The status of the validation operation will be stored as part of the program object's state. This value will be set to GL_TRUE if the validation succeeded, and GL_FALSE otherwise. It can be queried by calling glGetProgram with arguments *program* and GL_VALIDATE_STATUS. If validation is successful, *program* is guaranteed to execute given the current state. Otherwise, *program* is guaranteed to not execute.

This function is typically useful only during application development. The informational string stored in the information log is completely implementation dependent; therefore, an application should not expect different OpenGL implementations to produce identical information strings.

Notes

This function mimics the validation operation that OpenGL implementations must perform when rendering commands are issued while programmable shaders are part of current state. The error GL_INVALID_OPERATION will be generated by any command that triggers the rendering of geometry if:

>   any two active samplers in the current program object are of different types, but refer to the same texture image unit.

>   the number of active samplers in the program exceeds the maximum number of texture image units allowed.

It may be difficult or cause a performance degradation for applications to catch these errors when rendering commands are issued. Therefore, applications are advised to make calls to `glValidateProgram` to detect these issues during application development.

Errors

GL_INVALID_VALUE is generated if *program* is not a value generate by OpenGL.
GL_INVALID_OPERATION is generated if *program* is not a program object.

Associated Gets

glGetProgram with arguments *program* and GL_VALIDATE_STATUS
glGetProgramInfoLog with argument *program*
glIsProgram

See Also

`glLinkProgram, glUseProgram`

Copyright

glVertexAttrib

Specifies the value of a generic vertex attribute

C Specification

```
void glVertexAttrib1f(GLuint index,
                      GLfloat v0);
void glVertexAttrib1s(GLuint index,
                      GLshort v0);
void glVertexAttrib1d(GLuint index,
                      GLdouble v0);
void glVertexAttribI1i(GLuint index,
                       GLint v0);
void glVertexAttribI1ui(GLuint index,
                        GLuint v0);
void glVertexAttrib2f(GLuint index,
                      GLfloat v0,
                      GLfloat v1);
void glVertexAttrib2s(GLuint index,
                      GLshort v0,
                      GLshort v1);
void glVertexAttrib2d(GLuint index,
                      GLdouble v0,
                      GLdouble v1);
void glVertexAttribI2i(GLuint index,
                       GLint v0,
                       GLint v1);
void glVertexAttribI2ui(GLuint index,
                        GLuint v0,
                        GLuint v1);
void glVertexAttrib3f(GLuint index,
                      GLfloat v0,
                      GLfloat v1,
                      GLfloat v2);
void glVertexAttrib3s(GLuint index,
                      GLshort v0,
                      GLshort v1,
                      GLshort v2);
void glVertexAttrib3d(GLuint index,
                      GLdouble v0,
                      GLdouble v1,
                      GLdouble v2);
void glVertexAttribI3i(GLuint index,
                       GLint v0,
                       GLint v1,
                       GLint v2);
void glVertexAttribI3ui(GLuint index,
                        GLoint v0,
                        GLoint v1,
                        GLoint v2);
void glVertexAttrib4f(GLuint index,
                      GLfloat v0,
                      GLfloat v1,
                      GLfloat v2,
                      GLfloat v3);
```

```
void glVertexAttrib4s(GLuint index,
                      GLshort v0,
                      GLshort v1,
                      GLshort v2,
                      GLshort v3);
void glVertexAttrib4d(GLuint index,
                      GLdouble v0,
                      GLdouble v1,
                      GLdouble v2,
                      GLdouble v3);
void glVertexAttrib4Nub(GLuint index,
                        GLubyte v0,
                        GLubyte v1,
                        GLubyte v2,
                        GLubyte v3);
void glVertexAttribI4i(GLuint index,
                       GLint v0,
                       GLint v1,
                       GLint v2,
                       GLint v3);
void glVertexAttribI4ui(GLuint index,
                        GLuint v0,
                        GLuint v1,
                        GLuint v2,
                        GLuint v3);
```

Parameters

index
> Specifies the index of the generic vertex attribute to be modified.

v0, v1, v2, v3
> Specifies the new values to be used for the specified vertex attribute.

C Specification

```
void glVertexAttrib1fv(GLuint index,
                       const GLfloat * v);
void glVertexAttrib1sv(GLuint index,
                       const GLshort * v);
void glVertexAttrib1dv(GLuint index,
                       const GLdouble * v);
void glVertexAttribI1iv(GLuint index,
                        const GLint * v);
void glVertexAttribI1uiv(GLuint index,
                         const GLuint * v);
void glVertexAttrib2fv(GLuint index,
                       const GLfloat * v);
void glVertexAttrib2sv(GLuint index,
                       const GLshort * v);
void glVertexAttrib2dv(GLuint index,
                       const GLdouble * v);
void glVertexAttribI2iv(GLuint index,
                        const GLint * v);
```

```
    void glVertexAttribI2uiv(GLuint index,
                             const GLuint * v);
  void glVertexAttrib3fv(GLuint index,
                         const GLfloat * v);
  void glVertexAttrib3sv(GLuint index,
                         const GLshort * v);
  void glVertexAttrib3dv(GLuint index,
                         const GLdouble * v);
  void glVertexAttribI3iv(GLuint index,
                          const GLint * v);
  void glVertexAttribI3uiv(GLuint index,
                           const GLuint * v);
  void glVertexAttrib4fv(GLuint index,
                         const GLfloat * v);
  void glVertexAttrib4sv(GLuint index,
                         const GLshort * v);
  void glVertexAttrib4dv(GLuint index,
                         const GLdouble * v);
  void glVertexAttrib4iv(GLuint index,
                         const GLint * v);
  void glVertexAttrib4bv(GLuint index,
                         const GLbyte * v);
  void glVertexAttrib4ubv(GLuint index,
                          const GLubyte * v);
  void glVertexAttrib4usv(GLuint index,
                          const GLushort * v);
  void glVertexAttrib4uiv(GLuint index,
                          const GLuint * v);
  void glVertexAttrib4Nbv(GLuint index,
                          const GLbyte * v);
  void glVertexAttrib4Nsv(GLuint index,
                          const GLshort * v);
  void glVertexAttrib4Niv(GLuint index,
                          const GLint * v);
  void glVertexAttrib4Nubv(GLuint index,
                           const GLubyte * v);
  void glVertexAttrib4Nusv(GLuint index,
                           const GLushort * v);
  void glVertexAttrib4Nuiv(GLuint index,
                           const GLuint * v);
  void glVertexAttribI4bv(GLuint index,
                          const GLbyte * v);
  void glVertexAttribI4ubv(GLuint index,
                           const GLubyte * v);
  void glVertexAttribI4sv(GLuint index,
                          const GLshort * v);
  void glVertexAttribI4usv(GLuint index,
                           const GLushort * v);
  void glVertexAttribI4iv(GLuint index,
                          const GLint * v);
  void glVertexAttribI4uiv(GLuint index,
                           const GLuint * v);
```

Parameters

index

> Specifies the index of the generic vertex attribute to be modified.

v

> Specifies a pointer to an array of values to be used for the generic vertex attribute.

C Specification

```
void glVertexAttribP1ui(GLuint index,
                        GLenum type,
                        GLboolean normalized,
                        GLuint value);
void glVertexAttribP2ui(GLuint index,
                        GLenum type,
                        GLboolean normalized,
                        GLuint value);
void glVertexAttribP3ui(GLuint index,
                        GLenum type,
                        GLboolean normalized,
                        GLuint value);
void glVertexAttribP4ui(GLuint index,
                        GLenum type,
                        GLboolean normalized,
                        GLuint value);
```

Parameters

index

> Specifies the index of the generic vertex attribute to be modified.

type

> Type of packing used on the data. This parameter must be GL_INT_10_10_10_2 or GL_UNSIGNED_INT_10_10_10_2 to specify signed or unsigned data, respectively.

normalized

> If GL_TRUE, then the values are to be converted to floating point values by normalizing. Otherwise, they are converted directly to floating point values.

value

> Specifies the new packed value to be used for the specified vertex attribute.

Description

OpenGL defines a number of standard vertex attributes that applications can modify with standard API entry points (color, normal, texture coordinates, etc.). The glVertexAttrib family of entry points allows an application to pass generic vertex attributes in numbered locations.

Generic attributes are defined as four-component values that are organized into an array. The first entry of this array is numbered 0, and the size of the array is specified by the implementation-dependent constant GL_MAX_VERTEX_ATTRIBS. Individual elements of this array can be modified with a glVertexAttrib call that specifies the index of the element to be modified and a value for that element.

These commands can be used to specify one, two, three, or all four components of the generic vertex attribute specified by *index*. A 1 in the name of the command indicates that only one value is passed, and it will be used to modify the first component of the generic vertex attribute. The second and third components will be set to 0, and the fourth component will be set to 1. Similarly, a 2 in the name of the command indicates that values are provided for the first two components, the third component will be set to 0, and the fourth component will be set to 1. A 3 in the name of the command indicates that values are provided for the first three components and the fourth component will be set to 1, whereas a 4 in the name indicates that values are provided for all four components.

The letters s, f, i, d, ub, us, and ui indicate whether the arguments are of type short, float, int, double, unsigned byte, unsigned short, or unsigned int. When v is appended to the name, the commands can take a pointer to an array of such values.

Additional capitalized letters can indicate further alterations to the default behavior of the glVertexAttrib function:

The commands containing N indicate that the arguments will be passed as fixed-point values that are scaled to a normalized range according to the component conversion rules defined by the OpenGL specification. Signed values are understood to represent fixed-point values in the range [-1,1], and unsigned values are understood to represent fixed-point values in the range [0,1].

The commands containing I indicate that the arguments are extended to full signed or unsigned integers.

The commands containing P indicate that the arguments are stored as packed components within a larger natural type.

OpenGL Shading Language attribute variables are allowed to be of type mat2, mat3, or mat4. Attributes of these types may be loaded using the glVertexAttrib entry points. Matrices must be loaded into successive generic attribute slots in column major order, with one column of the matrix in each generic attribute slot.

A user-defined attribute variable declared in a vertex shader can be bound to a generic attribute index by calling glBindAttribLocation. This allows an application to use more descriptive variable names in a vertex shader. A subsequent change to the specified generic vertex attribute will be immediately reflected as a change to the corresponding attribute variable in the vertex shader.

The binding between a generic vertex attribute index and a user-defined attribute variable in a vertex shader is part of the state of a program object, but the current value of the generic vertex attribute is not. The value of each generic vertex attribute is part of current state, just like standard vertex attributes, and it is maintained even if a different program object is used.

An application may freely modify generic vertex attributes that are not bound to a named vertex shader attribute variable. These values are simply maintained as part of current state and will not be accessed by the vertex shader. If a generic vertex attribute bound to an attribute variable in a vertex shader is not updated while the vertex shader is executing, the vertex shader will repeatedly use the current value for the generic vertex attribute.

Notes

Generic vertex attributes can be updated at any time.

It is possible for an application to bind more than one attribute name to the same generic vertex attribute index. This is referred to as aliasing, and it is allowed only if just one of the aliased attribute variables is active in the vertex shader, or if no path through the vertex shader consumes more than one of the attributes aliased to the same location. OpenGL implementations are not required to do error checking to detect aliasing, they are allowed to assume that aliasing will not occur, and they are allowed to employ optimizations that work only in the absence of aliasing.

There is no provision for binding standard vertex attributes; therefore, it is not possible to alias generic attributes with standard attributes.

glVertexAttrib4bv, glVertexAttrib4sv, glVertexAttrib4iv, glVertexAttrib4ubv, glVertexAttrib4usv, glVertexAttrib4uiv, and glVertexAttrib4N versions are available only if the GL version is 3.1 or higher.

glVertexAttribP versions are available only if the GL version is 3.3 or higher.

Errors

GL_INVALID_VALUE is generated if *index* is greater than or equal to GL_MAX_VERTEX_ATTRIBS.

GL_INVALID_ENUM is generated if glVertexAttribP is used with a *type* other than GL_INT_10_10_10_2 or GL_UNSIGNED_INT_10_10_10_2.

Associated Gets

glGet with the argument GL_CURRENT_PROGRAM
glGetActiveAttrib with argument *program* and the index of an active attribute variable
glGetAttribLocation with argument *program* and an attribute variable name
glGetVertexAttrib with arguments GL_CURRENT_VERTEX_ATTRIB and *index*

See Also

glBindAttribLocation, glVertexAttribPointer

Copyright

glVertexAttribDivisor

modify the rate at which generic vertex attributes advance during instanced rendering

C Specification

```
void glVertexAttribDivisor(GLuint index,
                           GLuint divisor);
```

Parameters

index
    Specify the index of the generic vertex attribute.
divisor
    Specify the number of instances that will pass between updates of the generic attribute at slot *index*.

Description

glVertexAttribDivisor modifies the rate at which generic vertex attributes advance when rendering multiple instances of primitives in a single draw call. If *divisor* is zero, the attribute at slot *index* advances once per vertex. If *divisor* is non-zero, the attribute advances once per *divisor* instances of the set(s) of vertices being rendered. An attribute is referred to as instanced if its GL_VERTEX_ATTRIB_ARRAY_DIVISOR value is non-zero.
    index must be less than the value of GL_MAX_VERTEX_ATTRIBUTES.

Notes

glVertexAttribDivisor is available only if the GL version is 3.3 or higher.

Errors

GL_INVALID_VALUE is generated if *index* is greater than or equal to the value of GL_MAX_VERTEX_ATTRIBUTES.

See Also

glVertexAttribPointer, glEnableVertexAttribArray, glDisableVertexAttribArray

Copyright

glVertexAttribPointer

define an array of generic vertex attribute data

C Specification

```
void glVertexAttribPointer(GLuint index,
                           GLint size,
                           GLenum type,
                           GLboolean normalized,
                           GLsizei stride,
                           const GLvoid * pointer);
void glVertexAttribIPointer(GLuint index,
                            GLint size,
                            GLenum type,
                            GLsizei stride,
                            const GLvoid * pointer);
```

Parameters

index

Specifies the index of the generic vertex attribute to be modified.

size

Specifies the number of components per generic vertex attribute. Must be 1, 2, 3, 4. Additionally, the symbolic constant GL_BGRA is accepted by `glVertexAttribPointer`. The initial value is 4.

type

Specifies the data type of each component in the array. The symbolic constants GL_BYTE, GL_UNSIGNED_BYTE, GL_SHORT, GL_UNSIGNED_SHORT, GL_INT, and GL_UNSIGNED_INT are accepted by both functions. Additionally GL_HALF_FLOAT, GL_FLOAT, GL_DOUBLE, GL_INT_2_10_10_10_REV, and GL_UNSIGNED_INT_2_10_10_10_REV are accepted by `glVertexAttribPointer`. The initial value is GL_FLOAT.

normalized

For `glVertexAttribPointer`, specifies whether fixed-point data values should be normalized (GL_TRUE) or converted directly as fixed-point values (GL_FALSE) when they are accessed.

stride

Specifies the byte offset between consecutive generic vertex attributes. If *stride* is 0, the generic vertex attributes are understood to be tightly packed in the array. The initial value is 0.

pointer

Specifies a offset of the first component of the first generic vertex attribute in the array in the data store of the buffer currently bound to the GL_ARRAY_BUFFER target. The initial value is 0.

Description

`glVertexAttribPointer` and `glVertexAttribIPointer` specify the location and data format of the array of generic vertex attributes at index *index* to use when rendering. *size* specifies the number of components per attribute and must be 1, 2, 3, 4, or GL_BGRA. *type* specifies the data type of each component, and *stride* specifies the byte stride from one attribute to the next, allowing vertices and attributes to be packed into a single array or stored in separate arrays.

For `glVertexAttribPointer`, if *normalized* is set to GL_TRUE, it indicates that values stored in an integer format are to be mapped to the range [-1,1] (for signed values) or [0,1] (for unsigned values) when they are accessed and converted to floating point. Otherwise, values will be converted to floats directly without normalization.

For `glVertexAttribIPointer`, only the integer types GL_BYTE, GL_UNSIGNED_BYTE, GL_SHORT, GL_UNSIGNED_SHORT, GL_INT, and GL_UNSIGNED_INT are accepted. Values are always left as integer values.

If *pointer* is not NULL, a non-zero named buffer object must be bound to the GL_ARRAY_BUFFER target (see glBindBuffer), otherwise an error is generated. *pointer* is treated as a byte offset into the buffer object's data store. The buffer object binding (GL_ARRAY_BUFFER_BINDING) is saved as generic vertex attribute array state (GL_VERTEX_ATTRIB_ARRAY_BUFFER_BINDING) for index *index*.

When a generic vertex attribute array is specified, *size*, *type*, *normalized*, *stride*, and *pointer* are saved as vertex array state, in addition to the current vertex array buffer object binding.

To enable and disable a generic vertex attribute array, call glEnableVertexAttribArray and glDisableVertexAttribArray with *index*. If enabled, the generic vertex attribute array is used when glDrawArrays, glMultiDrawArrays, glDrawElements, glMultiDrawElements, or glDrawRangeElements is called.

Notes

Each generic vertex attribute array is initially disabled and isn't accessed when glDrawElements, glDrawRangeElements, glDrawArrays, glMultiDrawArrays, or glMultiDrawElements is called.

`glVertexAttribIPointer` is available only if the GL version is 3.0 or higher.

Errors

GL_INVALID_VALUE is generated if *index* is greater than or equal to GL_MAX_VERTEX_ATTRIBS.

GL_INVALID_VALUE is generated if *size* is not 1, 2, 3, 4 or (for `glVertexAttribPointer`), GL_BGRA.

GL_INVALID_ENUM is generated if *type* is not an accepted value.

GL_INVALID_VALUE is generated if *stride* is negative.

GL_INVALID_OPERATION is generated if *size* is GL_BGRA and *type* is not GL_INT_2_10_10_10_REV or GL_UNSIGNED_INT_2_10_10_10_REV.

GL_INVALID_OPERATION is generated if *type* is GL_INT_2_10_10_10_REV or GL_UNSIGNED_INT_2_10_10_10_REV and *size* is not 4 or GL_BGRA.

GL_INVALID_OPERATION is generated by `glVertexAttribPointer` if *size* is GL_BGRA and *noramlized* is GL_FALSE.

GL_INVALID_OPERATION is generated if zero is bound to the GL_ARRAY_BUFFER buffer object binding point and the *pointer* argument is not NULL.

Associated Gets

glGet with argument GL_MAX_VERTEX_ATTRIBS
glGetVertexAttrib with arguments *index* and GL_VERTEX_ATTRIB_ARRAY_ENABLED
glGetVertexAttrib with arguments *index* and GL_VERTEX_ATTRIB_ARRAY_SIZE
glGetVertexAttrib with arguments *index* and GL_VERTEX_ATTRIB_ARRAY_TYPE
glGetVertexAttrib with arguments *index* and GL_VERTEX_ATTRIB_ARRAY_NORMALIZED
glGetVertexAttrib with arguments *index* and GL_VERTEX_ATTRIB_ARRAY_STRIDE
glGetVertexAttrib with arguments *index* and GL_VERTEX_ATTRIB_ARRAY_BUFFER_BINDING
glGet with argument GL_ARRAY_BUFFER_BINDING
glGetVertexAttribPointerv with arguments *index* and GL_VERTEX_ATTRIB_ARRAY_POINTER

See Also

glBindAttribLocation, glBindBuffer, glDisableVertexAttribArray, glDrawArrays, glDrawElements, glDrawRangeElements, glEnableVertexAttribArray, glMultiDrawArrays, glMultiDrawElements, glVertexAttrib

Copyright

glViewport

set the viewport

C Specification

```
void glViewport(GLint x,
                GLint y,
                GLsizei width,
                GLsizei height);
```

Parameters

x
y

Specify the lower left corner of the viewport rectangle, in pixels. The initial value is (0,0).

width
height

Specify the width and height of the viewport. When a GL context is first attached to a window, *width* and *height* are set to the dimensions of that window.

Description

glViewport specifies the affine transformation of x and y from normalized device coordinates to window coordinates. Let (x_{nd}, y_{nd}) be normalized device coordinates. Then the window coordinates (x_w, y_w) are computed as follows:

$$x_w = (x_{nd} + 1)a\frac{width}{2}b + x$$

$$y_w = (y_{nd} + 1)a\frac{height}{2}b + y$$

Viewport width and height are silently clamped to a range that depends on the implementation. To query this range, call glGet with argument GL_MAX_VIEWPORT_DIMS.

Errors

GL_INVALID_VALUE is generated if either *width* or *height* is negative.

Associated Gets

glGet with argument GL_VIEWPORT
glGet with argument GL_MAX_VIEWPORT_DIMS

See Also

glDepthRange

Copyright

Copyright © 1991-2006 Silicon Graphics, Inc. This document is licensed under the SGI Free Software B License. For details, see http://oss.sgi.com/projects/FreeB/.

glWaitSync

instruct the GL server to block until the specified sync object becomes signaled

C Specification

```
void glWaitSync(GLsync sync,
                GLbitfield flags,
                GLuint64 timeout);
```

Parameters

sync

Specifies the sync object whose status to wait on.

flags

A bitfield controlling the command flushing behavior. *flags* may be zero.

timeout

Specifies the timeout that the server should wait before continuing. *timeout* must be GL_TIMEOUT_IGNORED.

Description

glWaitSync causes the GL server to block and wait until *sync* becomes signaled. *sync* is the name of an existing sync object upon which to wait. *flags* and *timeout* are currently not used and must be set to zero and the special value GL_TIMEOUT_IGNORED, respectively˙. glWaitSync will always wait no longer than an implementation-dependent timeout. The duration of this timeout in nanoseconds may be queried by calling glGet with the parameter GL_MAX_SERVER_WAIT_TIMEOUT. There is currently no way to determine whether glWaitSync unblocked because the timeout expired or because the sync object being waited on was signaled.

If an error occurs, glWaitSync does not cause the GL server to block.

Notes

glWaitSync is available only if the GL version is 3.2 or higher.

Errors

GL_INVALID_OPERATION is generated if *sync* is not the name of a sync object.
GL_INVALID_VALUE is generated if *flags* is not zero.
GL_INVALID_VALUE is generated if *timeout* is not GL_TIMEOUT_IGNORED.

˙ *flags* and *timeout* are placeholders for anticipated future extensions of sync object capabilities. They must have these reserved values in order that existing code calling glWaitSync operate properly in the presence of such extensions.

See Also

glFenceSync, glClientWaitSync

Copyright

Index

Numbers

A

How can we make this index more useful? Email us at indexes@samspublishing.com

More Titles in the OpenGL Series

OpenGL® Programming Guide, Seventh Edition

The Official Guide to Learning OpenGL® Versions 3.0 and 3.1

Dave Shreiner and The Khronos OpenGL ARB Working Group

0-321-55262-8

Provides definitive and comprehensive information on OpenGL and the OpenGL Utility Library. This seventh edition of the best-selling "red book" describes the latest features of OpenGL Versions 3.0 and 3.1.

OpenGL® Shading Language, Third Edition

Randi Rost, Bill Licea-Kane, et al.

0-321-63763-1

Extensively updated for OpenGL 3.1, this is the experienced application programmer's guide to writing shaders. Part reference, part tutorial, this book thoroughly explains the shift from fixed-functionality graphics hardware to the new era of programmable graphics hardware and the additions to the OpenGL API that support this programmability.

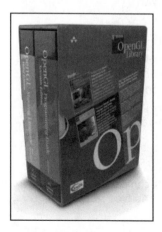

OpenGL® Library, Fifth Edition

0-321-63764-X

This special boxed set contains both *OpenGL® Programming Guide, Seventh Edition,* and *OpenGL® Shading Language, Third Edition.*

OpenGL® ES 2.0 Programming Guide
Aaftab Munshi, Dan Ginsburg, and Dave Shreiner
0-321-50279-5

In the *OpenGL® ES 2.0 Programming Guide*, three leading authorities on the OpenGL ES 2.0 interface—including the specification's editor—provide start-to-finish guidance for maximizing the interface's value in a wide range of high-performance applications.

OpenGL® Distilled
Paul Martz
0-321-33679-8

OpenGL® Distilled provides the fundamental information you need to start programming 3D graphics, from setting up an OpenGL development environment to creating realistic textures and shadows. Written in an engaging, easy-to-follow style, you'll quickly learn the essential and most-often-used features of OpenGL, along with the best coding practices and troubleshooting tips.

OpenGL® Programming on Mac® OS X
Architecture, Performance, and Integration
Robert P. Kuehne and J. D. Sullivan
0-321-35652-7

Apple's highly efficient, modern OpenGL implementation makes Mac OS X one of today's best platforms for OpenGL development. *OpenGL® Programming on Mac OS® X* is the first comprehensive resource for every graphics programmer who wants to create, port, or optimize OpenGL applications for this high-volume platform.

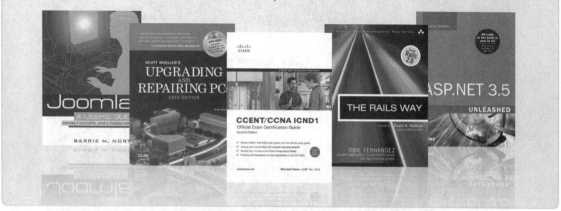